1 MONTH OF
FREE
READING

at

www.ForgottenBooks.com

By purchasing this book you are eligible for one month membership to ForgottenBooks.com, giving you unlimited access to our entire collection of over 700,000 titles via our web site and mobile apps.

To claim your free month visit:

www.forgottenbooks.com/free172877

ISBN 978-0-483-00244-9
PIBN 10172877

This book is a reproduction of an important historical work. Forgotten Books uses
state-of-the-art technology to digitally reconstruct the work, preserving the original format
whilst repairing imperfections present in the aged copy. In rare cases, an imperfection in
the original, such as a blemish or missing page, may be replicated in our edition. We do,
however, repair the vast majority of imperfections successfully; any imperfections that
remain are intentionally left to preserve the state of such historical works.

For support please visit www.forgottenbooks.com

ANNUAL REPORT

OF THE

United States Indian Inspector for the Indian Territory,

TOGETHER WITH

THE REPORTS OF THE SUPERINTENDENT OF SCHOOLS IN
THAT TERRITORY, AND OF THE INDIAN AGENT
IN CHARGE OF THE UNION AGENCY,

TO THE

SECRETARY OF THE INTERIOR

FOR THE

FISCAL YEAR ENDED JUNE 30, 1899.

WASHINGTON:
GOVERNMENT PRINTING OFFICE.
1899.

ANNUAL REPORT

OF THE

United States Indian Inspector for the Indian Territory,

TOGETHER WITH

THE REPORTS OF THE SUPERINTENDENT OF SCHOOLS IN THAT TERRITORY, AND OF THE INDIAN AGENT IN CHARGE OF THE UNION AGENCY,

TO THE

SECRETARY OF THE INTERIOR

FOR THE

FISCAL YEAR ENDED JUNE 30, 1899.

————◆•◆•►————

WASHINGTON:
GOVERNMENT PRINTING OFFICE.
1899.

verax (handwritten)

ANNUAL REPORT

OF THE

UNITED STATES INDIAN INSPECTOR FOR THE INDIAN TERRITORY.

OFFICE OF U. S. INDIAN INSPECTOR
FOR INDIAN TERRITORY,
Muscogee, Ind. T., August 19, 1899.

SIR: In compliance with Department instructions, directing me to submit a report of the work of this office during the year ended June 30, 1899, under provisions of an act of Congress approved June 28, 1898, together with a statement concerning the legislation which I consider necessary to properly execute the provisions of said act as appears from the existing conditions in the Five Civilized Tribes, I have the honor to report as follows:

The act of Congress referred to provides:

The Secretary of the Interior is authorized to locate one Indian inspector in the Indian Territory, who may, under his authority and direction, perform any duties required of the Secretary of the Interior by law relating to affairs therein.

The Five Civilized Tribes comprise the Seminoles, aggregating some 2,825 people; the Choctaws, 19,406; the Chickasaws, 9,048; the Creeks, 14,771, and the Cherokees, 34,461 in population.

These various tribes have heretofore controlled their own affairs, conducting their governments, having their respective governors or principal chiefs, and other national or state officers, their legislatures or councils, enacting such laws governing their country, schools, and affairs generally as they deemed proper, acting independent of the United States Government. By their respective laws and treaties their lands have been owned in common, citizens being authorized to use and rent to noncitizens as their laws permitted, in many instances comprising large areas.

Numerous thriving towns throughout the Territory have been built upon the common property of the respective tribes, all noncitizens located therein being assessed for the privilege of residing therein or conducting business within the limits of the nation, and others also for introducing cattle, mining coal, cutting timber, etc., citizens being also required to remit a tax for each noncitizen to whom farms are rented.

These various taxes are supposed to have amounted to considerable, but owing to the loose manner in which affairs have been conducted and records kept, it has been impossible to ascertain the aggregate amounts collected or accounted for. In many instances, however, it has been found that amounts due have not all been paid, but "compromised" with collectors and others. In many instances, of amounts so

3

collected by officers, but a small percentage has reached the treasury of the nation to which it belongs.

The act of Congress referred to included the ratification of an agreement entered into between the commission to the Five Civilized Tribes and the commission on behalf of the Choctaw and Chickasaw nations, which was in August, 1898, adopted by a majority vote of the citizens of said nations, which, with certain modifications, provided for the continuation of their government for a period of eight years. It also provided for the ratification of a similar agreement with the Creek Nation, which, however, was subsequently defeated when submitted to a vote of their people. Therefore the affairs of the Creek and Cherokee nations are under the general provisions of the act referred to, which provide for equal distribution of lands per capita, abolishment of their tribal courts, requiring that all payments of money by the United States to either of said tribes should not be made to any tribal officer for disbursement as heretofore, but should be made under direction of the Secretary of the Interior by an officer appointed by him; also directing that all royalties, rents, etc., due such tribes should be collected by the United States officers under direction of the Secretary of the Interior for credit of said tribes respectively.

The Seminoles, on December 16, 1897, entered into an agreement with the United States, which was subsequently ratified by Congress, under the terms of which their lands were to be appraised and distributed equally among all and their form of government to continue as at present.

As provided by law, all acts of the various councils of these nations, with the exception of the Seminoles, are required to be submitted to the President of the United States for his approval before being effective.

Under date of August 17, 1898, I was directed to proceed to Indian Territory, with headquarters at Muscogee, to perform any duties required of the Secretary of the Interior by law; to advise the Indian agent of Union Agency as to his duties under the new legislation; to generally inspect and supervise his office; to see that the law was efficiently enforced, that all revenues were collected and properly accounted for, all disbursements of money correctly made, and to keep the Department fully informed by special report of all matters which ought to be brought to its attention, with such recommendations as might be thought advisable; also to refer all communications regarding citizenship and renting of lands to the commission to the Five Civilized Tribes. Under these instructions I first visited various parts of the Territory inspecting schools and familiarizing myself with condition of affairs generally, procuring statistics in regard to revenues and indebtedness of the various nations, and submitting reports and recommendations in detail to the Department.

Subsequently rules and regulations have been issued by the Department governing the various matters under supervision and direction of the Secretary of the Interior.

On February 23, 1899, the offices of the inspector and Indian agent at Muscogee, together with a considerable portion of the business part of the town, were burned, at which time all records of both offices were completely destroyed, causing considerable embarrassment for some time by reason of the loss of all data, decisions, and rulings of the honorable Secretary of the Interior on matters pertaining to the Territory under new legislation.

A general superintendent of schools for the Indian Territory was appointed in February last, who has general supervision of Indian schools, under direction of the Secretary of the Interior, in the Choctaw Nation, and, so far as practicable under existing conditions, in other tribes, with a supervisor in each of the four nations (Choctaw, Chickasaw, Cherokee, and Creek), who act under his instructions.

The present status of work performed under existing laws in each nation is briefly as follows:

SEMINOLE NATION.

There are, according to a census completed by the commission to the Five Civilized Tribes, 2,825 Seminole Indians, who have 366,000 acres within the limits of their territory.

By provision of recent agreement this land is to be divided equally among all, after appraisal, excepting lands reserved for schools, churches, and other purposes; also one acre in each township, which may be purchased by the United States for schools for noncitizens. Their tribal government continues as heretofore, acts of their council not requiring Executive action, and the United States courts are given jurisdiction in certain matters.

As no duties are required of the Secretary of the Interior in said nation at this time demanding attention of the inspector, no examination or investigation of affairs of that nation has been made or schools inspected.

Under Department instructions an investigation of damages sustained by the burning to death of two Seminole boys and maltreatment of others at the hands of a mob of white men was made in December last, and subsequently, under direction of the Secretary of the Interior, an aggregate payment of $2,470.75 was made certain Seminole Indians for damages sustained, and, in addition, the sum of $5,000 each was paid to the proper relatives of the two Seminole Indian boys who were burned, the various amounts of damages paid ranging from $25 to $300.

The action of this mob was inspired by an outrage alleged to have been committed on a white woman by these Seminole boys.

Arrests of those participating in this lynching have since been made, several tried in the United States court, and three men convicted and sentenced to the penitentiary for a term of years, one acquitted, and a number of others indicted and awaiting trial.

CHOCTAWS AND CHICKASAWS.

The census of the citizens of these nations has not yet been completed by the Commission to the Five Tribes, but the estimated population is 19,406 Choctaws and 9,048 Chickasaws, their country all together comprising about 11,338,935 acres.

Under provisions of an agreement ratified by Congress and adopted by these people in August, 1898, their lands are to be appraised and allotted equally among all, with certain reservation for schools, town sites, and other purposes.

All coal and asphalt is also reserved from allotment to remain and be the common property of the tribe, mines to be under supervision and control of two trustees who are Indians by blood and who shall act under instructions from the Secretary of the Interior, all mines to be operated and royalties to be paid into the Treasury of the United States and used, under rules and regulations of the Secretary of the Interior, for education of children of Indian blood.

Town-site commissioners are provided for to lay out and plat the towns; also to appraise and dispose of lots for the benefit of the respective nations under rules and regulations of the Department, which also require that all money arising from sale of lots shall be deposited with the Indian agent of Union Agency for credit of the tribe.

The United States courts are given jurisdiction in certain matters and as so modified the government and tribal officers of these nations are continued for a period of eight years, though acts passed by their council are submitted through this office to the Secretary of the Interior for Executive action.

Town-site commissioners have been appointed by the Secretary and are now engaged in their duties.

Under supervision of the Commission to the Five Tribes appraisers are also at work classifying the land to be allotted, and the commission is also completing a census of the citizens.

Two mineral trustees have been appointed for the Choctaw and Chickasaw nations, who have been engaged to the present time in receiving applications for and in examining tracts of land in those nations to be leased, acting under instructions issued by the Department, and where controversies have arisen between parties claiming prior right to a lease investigations have been made and decided by the inspector, and where appeals have been filed reports have been submitted to the Department.

As provided in the agreement each mining lease covers 960 acres, and the royalty is fixed at 15 cents per ton on all coal mined, which rate, however, is subject to change by the Secretary of the Interior, and by him has been reduced to 10 cents per ton on all coal after being screened, which rate took effect from January 1, 1899. To June 30, 1899, 38 leases of 960 acres each have been made and approved by the Department. In addition to these, several mines have been operated under former tribal leases with the national authorities, which under provisions of agreement are continued or to be renewed. All royalties are remitted to the Indian agent, accompanied by sworn statements of operators, whose books are also open to inspection at all times. During the fiscal year ending June 30, 1899, there has been paid to the Indian agent, in royalties on coal and asphalt, $110,145.25 for the credit of said tribes, and of which $7,367.30 has been used up to this date in the settlement of the indebtedness incurred since July 1, 1898, at Choctaw neighborhood or day schools, and $41,033.43 in claims for the support of boarding schools since that date, which have been submitted to the Department for settlement.

The royalties on coal have been materially reduced, owing to a strike of miners which occurred in February last and which has been the subject of a recent investigation by Special Inspector Zevely, detailed by the Department, with reference to the request of the principal chief for removal from the Territory of certain striking miners for interfering with operations of mines and thereby reducing revenues of the same, the United States statutes providing that noncitizens may, under certain conditions, be removed from the Indian country by order of the Secretary of the Interior.

The agreement provides that leases shall include coal and asphalt or other minerals and shall be for a period of thirty years, while another provision states the allottee shall receive, after the completion of allotments, a patent conveying to him all the right, title, and interest in and to the land which has been allotted to him, excepting coal and asphalt.

The agreement also provides that money arising from coal and asphalt mineral shall be used only for education of children of Indian blood, thereby excluding children of colored freedmen, though no mention is made of the use of funds arising from other minerals. There are also a large number of noncitizens within the Choctaw Nation who are not provided with schools, and while a few of their children have attended by paying teachers, the majority of children of noncitizens are growing up in ignorance, and some provision for them should, if possible, be made. In many incorporated towns, however, in the different nations, schools have been provided for and maintained by said town governments.

Indian schools in the Choctaw Nation were closed in January last by reason of there not being sufficient funds to continue them, and also because the authorities found many teachers incompetent and unsatisfactory, as shown by previous detailed reports of my inspection of many of the schools. Although liberal appropriations have been made in the past for these schools, many were found to be improperly conducted and funds not judiciously used. As these schools are now under supervision of the Secretary of the Interior, a supervisor has been appointed for the Choctaw Nation, acting under direction of the general superintendent of schools for the Indian Territory, and a material improvement in conducting the same will hereafter be made.

A supervisor has also been provided for the Chickasaw Nation, but as their schools are being conducted with their own tribal funds, other than coal royalties, it is not considered that the Department has the same control, except over schools conducted with funds arising from such royalties. However, it is hoped that the presence and assistance of the supervisor will result in an improvement in the management of these various schools.

From July, 1898, to December 31, 1898, under the provisions of the act of Congress referred to and regulations of the honorable Secretary of Interior, various revenues and taxes in the Choctaw and Chickasaw nations, in addition to mineral royalties, were paid to the United States Indian agent and amounted to $2,985.97, which was deposited in the United States Treasury to the credit of said tribes; but upon the ratification of their agreement their government was reestablished, and since that time their own officials have made collections of all revenues other than mineral royalties.

At the request of their council Congress, at its last session, appropriated $75,000 from Choctaw invested funds to pay their outstanding indebtedness after investigation of such claims by the Secretary of the Interior. Such investigation has recently been completed by Special Inspector J. W. Zevely, and his report submitted to the Department. No further action concerning payment of this indebtedness has yet been made.

By the provisions of the recent agreement $558,520.54 was placed to the credit of the Chickasaw Nation, and by act of their council, approved by the President, $200,000 was appropriated to pay their outstanding indebtedness, which has been done, but it was not required to be supervised by a United States officer.

Their council also provided for the balance due to be paid out per capita by a United States officer, but has not been approved by the President owing to a claim of heirs of so-called "Incompetents" to part of said sum, which is now being investigated.

The tribal laws of the Choctaw Nation are continued for eight years, and impose taxes on noncitizens as follows:

Citizens are taxed 50 cents per head upon all cattle introduced or purchased from noncitizens who have introduced them into the nation and 25 cents per head per year.

Merchants, both citizen and noncitizen, are required to pay a tax of one-fourth of 1 per cent on all bills of purchase.

A tax of 20 cents per ton is levied upon all prairie hay cut for sale or shipment.

Peddlers are taxed 5 per cent on the amount of goods sold.

Under the treaty of 1866 noncitizen merchants in the Canadian district (being that part of the Cherokee Nation lying south of the Arkansas River) are not required to pay a tax. In my opinion this condition should be changed by appropriate action of Congress, so that the revenue laws of the Cherokee Nation shall apply uniformly in all portions of the Nation.

Itinerant venders of drugs, nostrums, etc., are taxed at the rate of $50 per month.

The laws of the Creek Nation assess the following taxes:

On merchants 1 per cent of first cost of goods or merchandise offered for sale,

On physicians, $25 per annum.

On lawyers, $25 per annum.

The various other professionals and tradesmen are taxed amounts per annum ranging from $6 to $150.

These tribal laws are considered still in force, and the regulations of the honorable Secretary of the Interior require that all revenues due tribes shall be collected and deposited to the credit of the tribe to which it belongs.

These taxes are paid to the United States Indian agent, Union Agency, and have aggregated to June 30, 1899, $2,911.16 for Cherokees, and $4,913.63 for Creeks. If all due were paid, these amounts would be materially increased, but until recently there has been no method whereby payments could be enforced. Revenue inspectors have, since July last, been appointed to visit different towns and localities, ascertain and report delinquents, and the Secretary of the Interior has authorized and directed that noncitizens refusing should be removed from the Territory, under the provisions of section 2149 of the Revised Statutes, which provides that—

The Commissioner of Indian Affairs is authorized and required, with the approval of the Secretary of the Interior, to remove from any tribal reservation any person being therein without authority of law, or whose presence within the limits of the reservation may, in the judgment of the Commissioner, be detrimental to the peace and welfare of the Indians; and may employ for the purpose such force as may be necessary to enable the agent to effect the removal of such person.

A town-site commission has been appointed for the town of Muscogee in the Creek Nation, and at present are engaged in platting and surveying the town, but as yet no lots have been appraised or disposed of.

A payment of $113,441.55 was made by the Indian agent in April and May last, being interest due from the United States on Cherokee invested funds, and which was applied to their outstanding indebtedness by paying the interest on their warrants now in circulation, together with the principal of as many others as funds would permit. Another payment of about $95,000, being Cherokee interest due to July 1, 1899, will also soon be made. A similar payment is now being made of interest due the Creek Nation, an examination of warrants in circulation having just been completed, which will amount to about $185,000.

Smallpox appeared among the Creek Indians in February last, which spread rapidly and as the tribal authorities took no measures to check same, under direction of the Department this office assumed charge of the matter, except at the extreme western part of the country, where the Indian agent in charge of Sac and Fox Agency, Okla., assumed charge of certain territory which was most accessible from his agency, and where the disease was most prevalent. The Indian agent above referred to reports that within the territory under his supervision there were 140 cases, with 76 deaths; also, that a total of about 1,000 were vaccinated, and that the total cost of attending to same, including services of guards stationed at places quarantined, nurses, physicians, traveling expenses, clothing, medicines, care of sick, etc., amounted to $6,652.55. In addition there has been incurred by this office a similar indebtedness amounting to $4,609.93. The physicians report having attended 27 cases, with 5 deaths, and that 2,259 persons were vaccinated. This will make an aggregate of $11,262.48 expended for this purpose, which has been approved by the Department. Arrangements were also made whereby any suspicious cases appearing in towns surrounding the Creek Nation would be properly reported and necessary action taken to prevent further spread.

The annual report of the United States Indian agent for Union Agency is submitted herewith.

The agent recommends a reduction of the present force of Indian police and increasing the pay of those retained for the reasons set forth in his report.

While it would be impracticable to increase the pay of these police without Congressional legislation—which there is some doubt whether Congress would assent to—yet it would be desirable to do so, as it is frequently necessary under existing conditions to enforce tribal laws, to detail policemen on extensive and expensive trips requiring their entire time, and for which they should receive a rate of compensation commensurate with the character of the service performed. At present officers receive $15 and privates $10 per month.

Statistics showing in detail the amount of revenues collected are shown by the agent's report, to which attention is respectfully invited.

GENERAL.

The present complicated condition of affairs in the various nations, as above briefly enumerated, renders it extremely difficult for this office to supervise and see that all laws are complied with as directed.

The offices of inspector and Indian agent are also constantly flooded with communications from interested parties—both citizens and noncitizens—located in all parts of the Territory, as well as from others outside, requesting information in reference to the construction of the law and of their rights in the premises.

Although there are many who criticise the Department for decisions averse to their interests, the majority are desirous of complying with the law as construed; and in view of the condition of affairs which has existed in this country for years—the influx of outsiders, nonenforcement of some tribal laws, and improper collection and uses of revenue—it is surprising that all concerned should submit to so radical a change with such good grace. The rights of the full-blood Indian appear to have been rarely considered or recognized in the past.

Where cases of unlawful cutting of timber have been reported they have been investigated and referred to the proper United States attorney for appropriate action.

TAXES OR PERMITS OF NONCITIZES.

It is estimated there are about 400,000 white people who are non-citizens within the Indian Territory, many of whom feel they have acquired rights and are not subject to tribal laws or required to pay any permits or other tax.

All tribal permit laws are considered by the Department as still in force, not having been repealed by their own council or by Congress. In the Choctaw and Chickasaw nations their government continues about eight years, together with their tribal laws.

There have been no recent permit laws enacted in the Cherokee Nation or Creek Nation, and under instructions from the Department all existing permit and other taxes from noncitizens are being collected. In the Cherokee Nation, however, taxes are all due from citizens, some of whom have paid, but many others have not remitted. Their tribal laws provide a penalty for nonpayment, but as their tribal courts have been abolished there has been no method yet adopted to enforce payment of these taxes from citizens as provided by their own laws.

Resident noncitizen lawyers of the Creek Nation protested against the payment of $25 per annum, but were advised by the Department that such payment should be made, otherwise they would be subject to removal under section 2149, Revised Statutes, above referred to, which this office was instructed to enforce throughout the Indian Territory.

Section 2134 also provides that all foreigners who shall go into an Indian country without passport from the Department of the Interior or other officer of the United States, or who shall remain therein after the expiration of such passport, shall be liable to a penalty of $1,000.

These lawyers appeared before the Hon. J. R. Thomas, judge of the United States court at this place, for an injunction against the enforcement of this payment or removal from the Territory, but application was refused and they were considered by the court as intruders unless they complied with the tribal laws or the regulations of the Interior Department.

Many also feel that where living within the limits of an incorporated town, subject to its laws, they should not be required to also pay a tax or permit to the nation. So long, however, as this is considered an Indian country and the affairs under the supervision of the Secretary of the Interior it would seem that they are subject to such laws and regulations, or suffer removal therefrom.

Section 26 of the Curtis bill provides—

That on and after the passage of this act the laws of the various tribes or nations shall not be enforced at law or in equity by the courts of the United States in the Indian Territory.

It will be noticed, however, that no provision is made that such laws are not to be otherwise enforced, thereby leaving it to the Interior Department as guardians of the Indians to require, by rules and regulations, enforcement of tribal laws, as provided by the United States statutes.

It has repeatedly been considered and so held by the courts that discretion being given the Department for removal, as provided in section 2149, such discretion could not be controlled by any court.

It is claimed, however, that the necessity for collection of this revenue has now ceased to exist and therefore should not be enforced. This, however, does not appear to justify noncitizens from remaining within the limits of the Indian country without the permission of such Indians or of the Government.

The condition of the finances of these nations, as shown under the head of "Finances," also demonstrates that these revenues are at the present time much needed by the respective nations.

It is also claimed by noncitizens that, by the payment of these taxes for permission to remain in the Territory to trade, practice professions, or engage in other business for which a revenue is provided, they receive no benefits therefrom—evidently not considering the fact that by the payment of such taxes or revenues they are given permission to transact their business in the Indian Territory, and are not subject to such taxes as would be levied elsewhere by counties or States.

I would, however, suggest the advisability of recommending to Congress or to the authorities of the different nations that all taxes or revenues of whatever character throughout the nations be uniform, and that Congress direct all such to be collected by the Department and the proceeds used as a general school fund for all noncitizens and others, as much of the crime in this Territory may be traced to the illiteracy of persons within the Territory outside of the various towns.

PENITENTIARY.

From the records of the United States courts in the Indian Territory, as reported to me, it appears there have been sent to the various penitentiaries in the States for the fiscal year ending June 30, 1898, the following number of persons convicted of crimes:

From the southern district, 108, at a cost to the Government for transportation of $4,347.13.

From the central district, 183 prisoners, costing the Government for transportation, $3,374.08.

From the northern district, 403 prisoners, but the cost to the Government for their transportation could not be obtained.

In view of this cost of transportation, and the advisability of establishing a Government penitentiary in the Indian Territory, the various United States judges, in reply to inquiries upon the subject, report as follows:

Hon. W. H. H. Clayton, judge of central district, states:

If the three jails be built, as now provided by law, I do not see the necessity for establishing a penitentiary here, provided the Attorney-General has power under the law to designate them as places of imprisonment for persons who may be sentenced for more than one year. Otherwise, I believe that the building of a penitentiary here, where all of our criminals may be sentenced, will be greatly to the interest of the Government, and in my opinion ought to be done.

Hon. William M. Springer, judge for the northern district, states:

My own opinion is that a penitentiary in the Indian Territory would result in a great economy to the Government. This is only an opinion, which can only be verified by a practical test.

Hon. Hosea Townsend, judge for the southern district, states:

So far as my opinion would go as to the advisability of establishing a penitentiary, my judgment would be that the sooner these Indian governments could be wound up, the lands allotted, and the country put into a Territorial form of government, and finally a State, would be the best and most correct solution of this Indian business.

The agreement with the Cherokees in January last, which, however, was not ratified by Congress, provided for a reservation for an army post and a penitentiary on the site of the old military reservation at Fort Gibson.

In view of the unsettled condition of affairs which now exists, and must exist in this section of the country for some years, it would appear desirable to establish a military post, as suggested, as the presence of troops in this country would have a beneficial effect in assisting preserving law and order. The large annual expense for transporting prisoners would also seem to suggest the advisability of locating a Government penitentiary within the Territory.

FINANCE AND TRIBAL GOVERNMENTS.

No information has been requested concerning the condition of finances of the Seminole Indians, as, according to a recent agreement, they still act independently of the United States Government in the management of their affairs.

No information has been received of amount of revenue collected or received by the authorities of the Choctaw or Chickasaw nations.

The Choctaw Nation receives from the United States Government $59,570.95 annually, being interest on invested funds. As mentioned above, Congress, at the request of the nation, recently appropriated $75,000 of their funds to pay outstanding indebtedness, and an investigation by Inspector J. W. Zevely developed the fact that it could not be ascertained from the meager records kept, or information of officials, the amount of such indebtedness. Therefore public notice was given requesting holders of warrants to forward them to him for inspection. The warrants submitted aggregated about $112,000, but it was impossible to ascertain if such included all outstanding indebtedness or were valid claims against the nation, there being no records to show by what authority many warrants had been issued. It was also found that many warrants in the executive office claimed by the authorities to have been paid had not been canceled or showed any evidence upon their face that they were not lawful warrants still outstanding. The Choctaw law requires all warrants to be marked " Paid " across same when taken up, which, however, in many instances has not been done. Therefore it may be questioned if many warrants now outstanding have not once been paid, and it is surprising that their indebtedness is not now much greater. Several appropriations have been made during the past year by their council which were not submitted for the President's approval, providing for issue of duplicate warrants claimed to have been lost. There appears to be no information, however, that the original warrant issued is not still in circulation and by the issue of which the nation discharged whatever obligation existed and should not now issue a duplicate warrant and thereby possibly, at some later day, pay both.

According to the record of their laws passed at the regular session of October, 1898, and March, 1899 (pamphlet edition 1899), the Choctaw national council appropriated during the past year large sums of money to defray the expenses of their tribal government, among which are appropriations of $11,111.90 to pay the salaries of members and other expenses of the national council of the sessions named, and of $34,977.22 for expenses of the tribal courts for the current year.

The Chickasaw Nation has also made large appropriations for similar purposes, and recently used $200,000 with which to liquidate their outstanding indebtedness.

In the Creek and Cherokee nations the tribal courts have been abolished, and the necessity for their reestablishment has not been demonstrated. Therefore the expenses incident to maintaining such have been saved the nation, as they might be by the abolishment of the courts in the others mentioned.

In the Creek Nation it has been impracticable to obtain any information whatever concerning their outstanding indebtedness or amounts of revenues due and from what sources, by reason of the fact that they have kept no records at all.

Section 19 of the Curtis bill provides—

That no payment of any moneys on any account whatever shall hereafter be made by the United States to any of the tribal governments or to any officer thereof for disbursement, but payment of all sums to members of said tribes shall be made under direction of the Secretary of the Interior by an officer appointed by him; and per capita payments shall be made direct to each individual in lawful money of the United States, and the same shall not be liable to the payment of any previously contracted obligation.

Under this provision, regulations have been issued by the Department requiring that all disbursements should be made by the Indian agent of the Union Agency, under the supervision of the inspector.

The Creeks have an annual allowance from the Government of $123,646.54, being interest on invested funds, while the Cherokees have $136,890.88 due them annually. The payment of about $185,000 outstanding indebtedness of the Creek Nation is now being made by the Indian agent. A payment of $113,441.55 was recently, in April and May last, made by the Indian agent to holders of Cherokee warrants, of which $12,662.37 was paid for interest on some still outstanding (all warrants bearing 6 per cent interest), and the balance, $100,779.18, on both interest and principal, thereby taking up and canceling as many warrants as possible. An examination of these warrants demonstrated that they were legal and proper claims against the nation, according to their records.

A payment of all Creek warrants is now in progress. There being no records whatever of their indebtedness, public notice was given requiring holders of all warrants to present them for examination. So far, warrants to the amount of about $185,000 have been presented, but it is impossible to state how many more are outstanding. Many of those presented were improperly issued, being signed in the chief's name, though not by him, as required by law. Many others were issued for which there appears to have been no appropriation, and consequently can not be paid, while others represent amounts due for tribal court officials for services rendered after October 1, at which time their courts were abolished by the Curtis bill and the chief so notified. It has, therefore, required a large amount of time and labor to examine and ascertain the correctness of each warrant presented for payment.

The total amount of warrants presented which can not be paid aggregate $2,800, approximately.

I recommend that no more warrants be allowed to be issued and circulated by tribal authorities until submitted to and approved by the Indian agent or superintendent of schools.

The present condition of the finances of these various nations demonstrates the necessity for their obtaining all revenue possible.

As the Cherokee warrants draw 6 per cent, while the nation only receives 5 per cent interest from the United States for interest on their invested funds, it would appear desirable that they be permitted to withdraw sufficient funds with which to pay all outstanding indebtedness.

The Cherokee and Creek nations appropriated considerable amounts to pay members and expenses of their council meetings, besides large sums for other purposes which, while not necessary, must continue so long as their governments are permitted to remain in existence.

The fact that these various nations appropriate large amounts annually without rendering any practical benefit to the people, except for schools, should be sufficient argument for the advisability of discontinuing their national governments, especially if Congress should make provisions for supervision of schools in the Cherokee and Creek nations.

The coal royalty supplies funds for schools in the Choctaw Nation, and undoubtedly will also furnish sufficient revenue for schools in the Chickasaw Nation hereafter.

SCHOOLS.

The superintendent of schools for the Indian Territory recently submitted a report to the honorable Commissioner of Indian Affairs recommending certain changes in management of schools in the Indian Territory, particularly in the Creek and Cherokee nations, in which I fully concur. His annual report is also submitted herewith.

It is absolutely essential that all schools in the Territory be placed under the supervision of the Department. The various nations are liberal in making appropriations for education, but funds so appropriated have not always been properly or judiciously expended. There is also an entire absence of industrial training at any school, both boys and girls being instructed in schoolroom work and music only.

RECOMMENDATIONS, AND NEW LEGISLATION DESIRABLE.

Being directed to state what legislation I consider necessary to properly execute the provisions of the act of Congress approved June 28, 1898, as appears from the existing condition in the Territory, I have the honor to submit the following:

It appears by agreement that all mineral land, other than coal and asphalt, is not reserved from allotment in the Chickasaw and Choctaw nations; therefore, to avoid complications later, it would appear desirable that further legislation be enacted reserving all minerals from allotment, or only to lease coal and asphalt, as the agreement provides at present that leases shall include all minerals.

That steps be taken to secure a uniform system of taxes or permits from noncitizens and all others, including citizens, to trade, introduce stock, etc., and noncitizens to reside within the limits of the Five Tribes, to be collected by the Department and applied as a common school fund for all, which is much needed, and for which some provision for noncitizens is essential, and which plan would meet with little opposition.

Also, that all tribal governments be abolished, as they are of no practical benefit to any community other than providing appropriations for the maintenance of schools, which should be under the supervision of the Department, and uniform rules and regulations adopted to apply to the various tribes.

In consideration of that clause of the agreement between the Choctaw and Chickasaw nations and the United States which provides for the continuance of the tribal governments of those nations for a period of eight years from March 4, 1898, and that this provision shall not be construed to be in any respect an abdication by Congress of power at any time to make needful rules and regulations respecting said tribes, it is suggested that an international council of representatives from each of the Five Civilized Tribes meet together annually and enact uniform laws covering the various nations, to be approved by the President of the United States before becoming effective, until further Congressional legislative action is had regarding affairs in this Territory.

The office of principal chief of each of the five tribes should, however, be continued, to transfer title to lands allotted or town lots sold and represent the Nation in other matters, but the other machinery of their government, including councils, do not appear necessary and are of no benefit to their people generally.

·That the advisability of establishing a military post and Government penitentiary within the limits of the Indian Territory be considered.

Also, the establishment of an insane asylum. Reports from different officials of the Five Tribes show there are a considerable number of insane persons (19 citizens and 2 noncitizens being reported as within the limits of the Cherokee Nation) for which no provision is made in any other nation, except the Cherokee Nation, where a national asylum is maintained.

Some legislation is desired concerning the laying out and working of public roads. Under the present system of allotting there appears to be no provision made for such, and much complaint has been and is repeatedly being made to this office that citizens selecting allotments fence up existing roads, thereby seriously inconveniencing the traveling public and the carrying of the mail.

It is also desirable that Congress be asked to apply the "estray" laws of Arkansas, as set forth in Chapter LVIII, entitled "Estrays," of Mansfield's Digest of the Statutes of the State of Arkansas, to the Indian Territory, and that the poll tax of said State also be made to apply to incorporated towns in the Indian Territory, together with a law as to qualifications of legal voters and prohibiting persons convicted of felonies from voting.

Very respectfully, your obedient servant,

J. GEO. WRIGHT,
United States Indian Inspector for Indian Territory.

The SECRETARY OF THE INTERIOR.

REPORT OF SUPERINTENDENT OF SCHOOLS FOR INDIAN TERRITORY.

OFFICE OF SUPERINTENDENT OF SCHOOLS FOR INDIAN TERRITORY,
Muscogee, Ind. T., August 19, 1899.

DEAR SIR: I beg leave to submit my first annual report as superintendent of schools in Indian Territory, together with the report of the supervisors of the Cherokee, Creek, and Chickasaw nations.

Supervisor McArthur, of the Choctaw Nation, has been so exceedingly busy that he has not yet found time to complete his report.

Respectfully submitted.

JOHN D. BENEDICT,
Superintendent of Schools in Indian Territory.

The COMMISSIONER OF INDIAN AFFAIRS,
· *Washington, D. C.*

OFFICE OF SUPERINTENDENT OF SCHOOLS FOR INDIAN TERRITORY,
Muscogee, Ind. T., August 19, 1899.

DEAR SIR: I have the honor to submit to you my first annual report as superintendent of schools in the Indian Territory. This report must necessarily be incomplete, for the reason that we have had charge of these schools but a few months, our jurisdiction over them has been limited, and no records are available from which we can gather any reliable statistics.

5553——2

The Indian Territory is about as large as all of New England, omitting Maine. This vast tract of land, comprising more than 20,000,000 acres, was ceded by the United States Government about sixty years ago to what are known as the Five Civilized Tribes, to wit, the Cherokees, Choctaws, Chickasaws, Creeks, and Seminoles, in exchange for lands held by them in the States east of the Mississippi River. Soon after the Indians located here they were visited by numerous missionaries, who established little schools and churches in various parts of the Territory. It proved to be a fruitful field for mission work, and it was not long until the Presbyterians, Baptists, and Methodists had established substantial boarding schools in all the nations. These schools were at first maintained entirely by the various church boards of home missions, but as the years advanced, the patient, untiring, self-sacrificing efforts of these mission teachers resulted in gaining for them the confidence and support of the Indian authorities, until finally the various Indian councils were induced to make annual appropriations for the support of these schools. So long as these mission boards remained in charge of these schools the educational affairs of the Territory progressed fairly well, but there came a time, not many years ago, when the Indian authorities thought themselves wise enough to control these schools and appoint the teachers and superintendents therein. Many an honest old Indian looks back to that time with regret, and it is very generally conceded that the schools of the Territory have not made any material advancement since that change was made. Too much can not be said in praise of the earnest efforts of these various mission boards to civilize, educate, and Christianize the Indians. Their influence is yet everywhere visible; a few of their schools are still continued under their own management, and these schools are among the best in the Territory. As soon as the Indian authorities assumed control of these schools many of their school officials began the practice of such extreme favoritism and partisanship in their management as to render educational progress an absolute impossibility. Here and there has occasionally been found an educated Indian school official who seemed to appreciate the necessity and the value of thorough educational work. but in most cases his efforts to build up the schools have been thwarted by his more ignorant colleagues, who seemed to regard it their first duty to secure positions for their own relatives and political friends regardless of their qualifications.

For several years past each nation has had its own school laws and school officials, the Cherokee Nation having had control of its own educational affairs for a longer period than any other nation or tribe. The laws and rules of management have varied somewhat in the several nations, but the defects, the weak points, in each have been very much alike. In each nation there are two classes of schools, viz: boarding schools or academies and neighborhood schools.

While in some instances attempts have been made to convert the boarding schools into higher institutions of learning, yet, on account of the favoritism manifested in the selection of pupils to attend them, scarcely any of them have risen above the grade of the average common school, and in nearly every instance the primary pupils now outnumber the advanced students in each academy.

It is not unusual to find four or five children of one family in a boarding school, while some citizens who have reared large families of children have never been able to get any of them assigned to the academies. In every nation these boarding schools have been regarded as favored institutions by the various boards of education. Money has been lavishly spent in the erection of buildings, the purchase of supplies, and the employment of teachers and other employes, while the neighborhood schools have suffered from neglect. The Indian authorities have built no neighborhood school buildings at all, it being a general requirement that every neighborhood desiring a school must furnish its own schoolhouse. As a natural result of this plan the country and village schoolhouses are cheaply built, poorly furnished, and illy adapted to the purposes of a school.

The following is an estimate of the total population of the Indian Territory, compiled from the records of the Dawes Commission:

Cherokee Indians	30,000	
Cherokee freedmen	4,000	
Total number of Cherokees		34,000
Choctaw Indians	14,500	
Choctaw freedmen	4,500	
Total number of Choctaws		19,000
Creek Indians	10,000	
Creek freedmen	4,500	
Total number of Creeks		14,500

```
Chickasaw Indians......................................................  6,000
Chickasaw freedmen ....................................................  4,500
                                                                        _____
    Total number of Chickasaws.........................................        10,500
Seminole Indians ......................................................  2,000
Seminole freedmen .....................................................  1,000
                                                                        _____
    Total number of Seminoles..........................................         3,000
                                                                                ======
Total number of Indians in Territory...................................        62,500
Total number of freedmen in Territory .................................        18,500
Total white population in Territory....................................       200,000
                                                                               _____
    Total population of Territory ......................................       281,000
```

ENROLLMENT AND ANNUAL COST OF BOARDING SCHOOLS.

The following table shows the enrollment and annual cost of each boarding school in the Territory. It has not been possible to secure exact data from every school, but the figures given below are approximately correct:

Name of school.	Enroll-ment.	Aver-age at-tend-ance.	Months of school.	Annual cost of mainte-nance.	Average annual cost per pupil.	Number of em-ployes.
Choctaw Nation:						
Jones Academy (male)....................	85	75	10	$15,000	$200.00	12
Spencer Academy (male).................	84	70	10	15,000	214.00	12
Tushkahoma Female Institute	90	75	10	15,000	200.00	10
Armstrong Orphan Academy (male)......	65	62	10	9,000	145.00	8
Wheelock Orphan Academy (female)	60	50	10	8,000	160.00	8
Cherokee Nation:						
Male Seminary	90	78	9	11,625	149.00	13
Female Seminary	125	105	9	18,500	176.00	15
Orphan Home.............................	129	110	9	15,000	136.00	15
Colored High School......................	25	20	9	3,500	175.00	7
Chickasaw Nation:						
Chickasaw Orphan Home.................	60	....	10	9,000	150.00	9
Wahpanucka Institute (male).............	60	....	10	9,600	160.00	8
Collins Institute (female).................	40	....	10	6,000	150.00	6
Harley Institute (male)...................	60	....	10	10,000	166.00	8
Bloomfield Seminary (female).............	80	....	10	12,500	156.25	10
Seminole Nation:						
Mekusukey Male Academy................	100	65	8	10,500	160.00	10
Emahaka Female Academy................	100	80	8	10,500	131.00	10
Creek Nation:						
Eufaula.............................	100	71	9	9,600	135.00	10
Creek Orphan Home......................	62	52	9	7,266	140.00	8
Euchie...................................	70	65	9	7,700	118.00	8
Wetumka.................................	100	85	9	9,600	110.00	12
Coweta	50	37	9	5,000	135.00	9
Wealaka..................................	50	45	9	5,000	118.00	8
Tallahassee	80	66	9	9,600	144.00	10
Colored Orphan Home	35	24	9	3,833	138.00	6
Pecan Creek	60	52	9	5,000	100.00	7
Nuyaka..................................	100	89	9	10,500	100.00	15
Total	1,958	1,231	....	251,824	....	254

Neighborhood schools.

Nation.	No. of schools.	Annual cost.	Enroll-ment.
Cherokee..	124	$30,780	4,258
Choctaw..	160	35,000	....
Creek	65	17,100	....
Chickasaw	13	26,000	355
Seminole...	2	500	....
Total...	365	113,880	....

DEFECTS IN INDIAN TERRITORY SCHOOLS.

Some of the most serious defects in the schools of the Territory may be enumerated as follows:

1. *Incompetent supervision.*—Nearly every nation has had a law upon its statute books to the effect that none but citizens of the nation were eligible to the position of superintendent of a boarding school. These important, responsible positions have been regarded as political perquisites, and no educational standard or requirement is demanded of the men who fill these positions.

There are at present 26 boarding schools in the Territory, and the superintendents of not more than four of these schools are competent to teach any of the common school branches; yet these superintendents usually select all of their own teachers and have unquestioned authority in the supervision and management of their schools. Some of these superintendents are well-meaning men, who do the best they can for the children; but others are unfit, morally and educationally, for the positions which they have held.

The work in every one of these schools bears the impress and reflects in a marked degree the character of its superintendent. The truth of the old saying, that "a stream can not rise above its source," may be fully demonstrated here. In those few schools where the superintendents have manifested a commendable degree of interest in the welfare of the children, and have been fortunate enough to secure good teachers, the task of educating the children has been fairly well performed; but where the superintendent has insisted upon giving the best positions to his relatives or political friends, regardless of their qualifications, and then, notwithstanding his ignorance of educational methods and management, has persisted in personally supervising and directing the educational work of the school, the results have not been satisfactory. Teachers are not stimulated to exert their best efforts in behalf of the children, oftentimes saying that their employers do not appreciate thorough drill and training.

So long as teachers are thus led to believe that the permanency of their positions depends upon their ability to "get along easily" with their pupils, rather than upon their ability to do successful work, but little real progress will be made toward thorough educational training.

2. *Irregular attendance.*—The parents of most Indian children do not appreciate the importance of keeping their children in school regularly. It is not unusual for parents to visit the boarding schools and upon returning home to take their children with them, keeping the latter out of school several weeks at a time, with no excuse therefor further than wanting the children to visit at home a while. The reports received from neighborhood schools show very irregular attendance also. Parents often refuse to send their children to school because the teacher does not belong to the church of their choice. Pupils are often kept at home to pick cotton, gather crops, or to take care of the babies. Parents do not seem to understand that it is necessary that they should send their children to school regularly. Some plan of compulsory attendance is needed.

3. *Financial mismanagement.*—For a boarding school containing 100 pupils it has been customary for the Indian authorities to annually appropriate about $10,000 for board, clothing, medical attendance, and books. One-fourth of this amount is paid to each superintendent in warrants, in advance, at the beginning of each quarter. The superintendent has been allowed to dispose of these warrants about as he pleased, often discounting them for cash or trading them to merchants for provisions. This plan of paying the boarding-school superintendents in advance has encouraged extravagance on their part, and as a result nearly every school has closed its year's work in debt. To cover these deficits special appropriations would be made, and as a result the expenditures for school purposes have for several years past exceeded the amount of money available for school purposes. In many instances teachers have been compelled to wait a year or more for their salaries, and superintendents have discounted their warrants or have been compelled to buy provisions on time, agreeing to pay exorbitant prices therefor. Merchants, not knowing when they would be paid, have in many instances refused to sell provisions to these schools at any price. The fiscal year with nearly all the Indian nations begins and ends in December, yet several boarding schools have already expended the full amount of their present year's appropriations, and, as usual, will be compelled to buy provisions for the next three months on credit, wherever they can obtain such credit, leaving the merchants with whom they deal to run the risk of securing special appropriations from the Indian councils and often being compelled to wait a year or more for their money. A merchant of limited means can not afford to sell goods at any price, under such circumstances, and those who are able to assume the risk must charge more than ordinary prices therefor. Under these circumstances, these boarding schools, instead of being able to buy goods below the regular retail prices, as they should, are compelled to pay more than current market prices.

Instead of allowing these boarding-school superintendents to buy goods wherever and at whatever prices they choose, it would be better to advertise and let contracts to the lowest responsible bidders for furnishing such supplies as are needed, upon estimates carefully made in advance, for each school.

4. *Neglect of the English language.*—In view of the many changes that will probably take place in the Territory within the next few years, it is very important that the Indian children acquire a thorough knowledge of the English language. So long as the superintendents of the boarding schools persist in conversing with their pupils in the language of their nation or tribe, as many of them have done and still continue to do, it will be impossible for these Indian children to acquire that practical knowledge of the English language which they so sadly need. Learning to speak the English language correctly is perhaps the greatest task ever imposed upon the Indian, and his children should be assisted and encouraged in this difficult work by hearing and speaking it as much as possible.

NEEDED IMPROVEMENTS.

Aside from the needed changes and improvements that may be inferred from the "defects" above described, there are other improvements necessary before the schools of the Indian Territory will rank with the public schools of the States, some of which may be enumerated as follows:

1. *Competent teachers.*—Many of the teachers are natives of the Territory; some are whites who have spent the greater part of their lives among the Indians. But very few of them have had any normal or special training for their work. Fewer still have read any books on teaching or any educational journals. Many of them evince a desire now, however, to better prepare themselves for their work, and attribute their want of thorough preparation to the fact that they have had no encouragement, no intelligent supervision, no incentive to work.

Summer normals or review terms have heretofore been practically unheard of, but during the summer just past at least three successful summer normals were held in different parts of the Territory.

Already the teachers of the Territory are asking that they be given an opportunity to review the school branches next summer under the direction of competent instructors.

2. *Better sanitary conditions.*—Nearly all the boarding schools of the Territory are located in the country, remote from towns and railroads. The natural surroundings are conducive to health, but sanitary conditions have been neglected. Large pools of stagnant water have been found in the basements of some of these buildings. In some instances it has been customary to throw slops out the windows of the school buildings. Dirt and filth have been allowed to accumulate in and around the buildings. Pupils have not been properly trained in habits of cleanliness and neatness. In some instances the food has been of poor quality and poorly cooked. Fat bacon and badly baked bread have constituted too large a portion of the daily diet of pupils. As a result of such unsanitary conditions, sickness has been too prevalent, and contagious diseases too frequently attack these schools.

The stalwart, robust, agile Indian, so well known in history and fiction, did not, as a rule, receive his training in one of these schools.

3. *Manual training.*—In the very nature of things these Indians must continue to be an agricultural people. Changes now going on will soon result in placing every Indian man, woman, and child in the Territory in possession and ownership of a farm. In the preparation and enforcement of courses of study in the past it has seemed to be the aim of those in charge to prepare the pupils for college rather than to prepare them for the life which, in all human probability, the vast majority of them will be compelled to live. The girls, who must become housewives, have been taught Latin (too often neglecting the common-school branches), but have been studiously encouraged to neglect sewing, cooking, and all other branches of domestic economy. Almost every boarding school has a farm surrounding it; yet the boys have not been encouraged to study the various kinds of soils, crops, or plants. But little attention has been given to stock raising, although the facilities for training of this kind have been excellent. It is a deplorable fact that some of these schools, owning 640 acres of fine agricultural land each, have been compelled to import condensed milk and do without eggs and butter.

The climate of the Territory is well adapted to fruit raising; yet one seldom finds a fruit tree or a berry bush growing upon an academy farm. No attention is given to the use of tools or to shopwork of any kind in these schools, and no tools other than a dull ax and rusty hatchet are usually found on the premises.

The very things which are most needed to improve the home life and surroundings of these Indians have apparently been wholly neglected in these schools. Schools have been conducted upon the hypothesis that the children were to become professional men and women rather than breadwinners. An eminent French educational writer has said concerning this subject:

"Now it seems to us necessary, in order that this practical instruction may bear all its fruits, that the child should learn to handle the principal tools by the aid of which man is made the master of the materials which are furnished him by nature and the fundamental industries—wood, the metals, leather, etc. In this innovation we think we see a triple advantage—a physical advantage, for in learning to use the plane, the saw, the hammer, the child will complete his gymnastic education, and will acquire a manual dexterity which will always be useful to him, whatever he may afterwards do, and will hold him in readiness, now and always, for all apprenticeships; an intellectual advantage, for the thousand little difficulties which he will meet with will accustom him to observation and reflection; a social advantage, it may be said, for after having appreciated by his own experience the qualities necessary for success in professional duties and for becoming a skillful workman there is not the least fear that if fortune favors him, to whatever position he may afterwards come, he will despise those of his companions who always work with their hands."

A change in the direction of intelligent work along the lines of industrial and manual training is badly needed in these schools, yet owing to the natives' dislike for work, this change should be inaugurated gradually.

CHEROKEE SCHOOLS.

The schools of the Cherokee Nation have been under the control of a board of education consisting of three members, all of whom are appointed by the principal chief. This board appoints all teachers, fixes their salaries, and has general supervision over all schools in the nation.

This nation has 4 boarding schools, viz: the National Male Seminary, the National Female Seminary, the National Orphan Asylum, and the Colored High School.

The male seminary is a substantial two-story brick structure, located near Tahlequah, the capital of the nation. It is probably the oldest school building in the Territory and has accommodations for 175 pupils.

The female seminary is a three-story brick building standing in a beautiful grove in the suburbs of Tahlequah. It is capable of accommodating 250 pupils, and is the finest school building in the Territory.

CHOCTAW SCHOOLS.

The schools of the Choctaw Nation have heretofore been controlled by a board of education consisting of five members, viz, the principal chief, a superintendent of education, and three district trustees. This nation has recently surrendered the entire control and management of its schools to the United States Government, and the principal chief, who is a progressive Indian, interested in the welfare of his people, seems glad to be relieved of the responsibility of directing the educational affairs of his nation. The three district trustees, who have each heretofore controlled one-third of the schools of the nation, are intelligent Indians, and are loyally supporting our efforts to improve the educational work of that nation.

CREEK SCHOOLS.

The schools of the Creek Nation have been under the entire control of their superintendent of education, who is appointed by the principal chief. The superintendent appoints all the boarding-school superintendents and all the teachers in the 65 neighborhood schools. His power to remove any superintendent or teacher at will has heretofore been unquestioned. Large sums of money have been spent by the Creeks for education, but in all their schools not more than a dozen pupils could be found who would be classed as high-school students. The superintendent is not an educated man and does not attempt to conduct his own examinations. "Too much politics" has kept the Creek schools from making any material advancement, and the citizens of that nation who are interested in thorough education welcome the dawn of a brighter day.

CHICKASAW SCHOOLS.

The Chickasaw schools have been under the control of a superintendent of public instruction, appointed by their legislature. Their boarding schools are let by contract on five year terms. This nation maintains but about 16 neighborhood schools and the pupils in these are usually boarded at the nation's expense. Instead of spending so large a sum of money upon these few schools, it would be advisable to establish schools in every part of the nation, and reduce the expense of each. The common school and the influence of a refined, intelligent, sympathetic teacher should be brought as near as possible to the home of the Indian. Unfortunately, this nation has a law upon its statute books which reads as follows:

"*Be it further enacted*, That hereafter all citizens, school teachers who may wish to teach school in this nation, shall not be required to undergo an examination as to his or her qualifications, as a teacher, before being permitted to teach said school."

So long as such a law is in force, the schools of that nation can not effect much material progress.

CHOCTAW AND CHICKASAW FREEDMEN.

By the provisions of the Atoka agreement the Freedmen of the Choctaw and Chickasaw nations are prohibited from sharing in the school funds of these nations which are derived from royalties on coal and asphalt.

These colored citizens, as a rule, are poor. They are anxious, however, to secure educational privileges for their children, and some provision should be made for them. The ancestors of these colored people were brought here prior to the war as slaves of the Indians, and after the war many of them were adopted as citizens of the various Indian nations. They are not "intruders," but have certain rights here as citizens, and some provision should be made for educating their children.

CONDITION OF WHITE SETTLERS.

It is estimated that there are 200,000 white people in the Indian Territory, which, according to the usual rules for computing statistics of population, places the number of white children of scholastic age at from 40,000 to 50,000. This vast army of boys and girls have been practically debarred from school privileges; none of them are allowed to attend the Indian academies. In a few instances, they have been permitted to attend the crude neighborhood schools, upon paying tuition.

The white man came to the Territory with the consent of the Indian. He has done much toward building up the towns of the Territory. He has been compelled to pay into the various Indian treasuries vast sums of money in the form of "permit" taxes. These taxes have been levied upon almost every kind of business, upon the professions, and in some instances a poll-tax has been imposed upon every white man entering the Territory.

Oftentimes as much as 1 per cent is levied upon the full value of all goods sold by merchants.

No part of this fund is used for public schools, building bridges or improving roads, and none of it reaches the treasury of the city in which the man who pays it transacts his business.

It would seem that this money, or a portion of it, at least, might well be converted into a common school fund, for the benefit of all the people residing in the Territory. At present a few of the incorporated towns and cities of the Territory are struggling heroically in an effort to establish and maintain free public schools for all the children, but they are embarrassed by the fact that they are dependent solely upon funds derived from taxes on personal property, the title to all the real estate in the Territory being vested in the Indians and is nontaxable.

Congress ought to be induced to give this matter serious consideration, for conditions here are serious and anomalous. It can not be claimed that Congress would be establishing a dangerous precedent by affording relief to the residents of the Territory, for no other portion of the United States presents circumstances and conditions similar to those existing here. The jails of the Territory are filled to overflowing and the Government is being urged to build more jails and penitentiaries. Let Congress make it possible to establish free schools in every town and township in the Territory, and crime and criminals will become less expensive to the Government.

THE TERRITORIAL PRESS.

I can not close this report without a word of thanks to the daily and weekly newspapers of the Territory. So far as heard from, every newspaper in the Territory has heartily commended every effort toward improving educational conditions. Their columns are always open to us, and their editorials tend to create a livelier interest among the nations in educational matters. They are doing much toward enlightening the nations upon the many vexatious questions which constantly arise, as a result of the important changes now going on in Territorial affairs, and their influence tends toward a higher and better civilization.

Respectfully submitted.

JOHN D. BENEDICT,
Superintendent of Schools in Indian Territory.

The COMMISSIONER OF INDIAN AFFAIRS,
Washington, D. C.

ARDMORE, IND. T., *July 22, 1899.*

SIR: In reply to your letter of July 10, 1899, and in compliance with the inclosed request of the 5th instant from the honorable Commissioner of Indian Affairs, I submit herewith a few statistics, such as the limited time and impassable roads permitted me to gather, regarding the educational conditions in the Chickasaw Nation.

Owing to recent heavy rains and an entire absence of bridges, it has been impossible to interview the superintendent of public instruction and many other persons from whom I could obtain the most accurate data relative to schools and population in this nation.

I submit a conservative estimate of the noncitizen population of the Chickasaw Nation after consulting a number of persons who have traveled over this country extensively and figuring carefully the population of the towns through which I have traveled myself.

The Chickasaw country is about 100 miles long and about 90 miles wide, is situated between 33° 30′ and 34° 45′ north latitude, and is one of the richest agricultural countries in the United States, being composed largely of rolling, calcareous, prairie lands, with stretches of gravelly timber lands interspersed. It is well watered and thickly populated, containing probably, at a low estimate, 150,000 people, divided as follows:

Chickasaws and intermarried whites	6,000
Citizen freedmen, negroes	4,500
Noncitizen negroes, estimated	12,000
Noncitizen whites, estimated	127,500
Total	150,000

Estimated population of school age between 6 and 18 years, 37,500, obtained by counting one-fourth the population as of school age.

The 6,000 Chickasaws are the only people out of this vast population who have any school privileges for their children. This nation has set apart the interest on their trust fund, amounting to over $78,000 annually for the support of their national schools, consisting of 5 academies or boarding schools and 13 primary or neighborhood schools, with a total enrollment of 655 pupils for the last school year, divided as follows:

Name.	Enroll-ment.	Cost.
Bloomfield Seminary	80	$12,375.00
Orphans' Home	60	8,500.00
Collins Institute	40	6,400.00
Harley Institute	60	9,900.00
Wappanucka Institute	60	9,600.00
Thirteen neighborhool schools	355	26,000.00
Superintendent's salary		750.00
Special State scholars (act repealed Jan. 1, 1899) and repairs to buildings, with other expenses, etc		4,669.05
Total appropriation	655	78,194.05

These schools are exclusive to children of Chickasaw blood only, and are limited by law to an enrollment of 685 pupils, while there are probably about 1,500 children of school age and of Chickasaw blood in this nation. More schools and a larger expenditure of money are necessary for the accommodation of these children.

I inclose a letter herewith from Judge H. C. Potterf, president of the board of school directors of the city of Ardmore, setting forth very clearly the conditions and difficulties encountered by them in establishing free schools here, which may be of value to you in compiling your report to the Commissioner of Indian Affairs.

Regretting that I have not been able to obtain some items which you suggest,

I am, very truly, yours,

JOHN M. SIMPSON,
Supervisor of Schools, Chickasaw Nation.

Hon. JOHN D. BENEDICT,
Superintendent of Schools, Muscogee, Ind. T.

Hon. JOHN D. BENEDICT,
Superintendent of Schools, Muscogee, Ind. T.

SIR: I submit my report on the condition of educational matters in the Cherokee Nation at the close of fiscal year 1899. As my services began only May 1 and my duties are new in this nation, report must be fragmentary. Through the courtesy of the officials of the Cherokee Nation I have access to their records.

The Cherokees early welcomed religious teachers and mission schools. Their great genius, Sequoyah, invented their alphabet of 85 characters, each representing a syllable. After memorizing these characters any one who could talk the language could at once read it. The Bible and select books were soon in nearly every family. A weekly paper printed in Cherokee characters was published at the expense of the nation and a whole people were at once put in touch with current news almost without schools. But the ability to read their own language gave the desire to read the English, and with it the demand for schools came, and early in the century schools were encouraged.

In 1817 a written constitution was adopted and an elective form of government was established, in which intelligence and statesmanship found a demand, while heroes in battle and hereditary chiefs took a second place. Progress was rapid, and in 1827 an elaborate constitution was adopted and a modern form of government was made effective. An article of this constitution reads, "Religion, morality, and knowledge being necessary to good government, the preservation of liberty, and the happiness of mankind, schools and the means of education shall forever be encouraged in this nation." This article is in force in the present constitution. Schools were established and a school fund provided. Seminaries were opened for secondary instruction and thoroughly competent teachers were secured.

In the early sixties the hostile forces engaged in the civil war passed and repassed through the nation. The male seminary is the only building that is left to testify of former school facilities.

In the past thirty years much has been done by school authorities to rebuild and recover. The present female seminary building is a commodious structure, of pleasing appearance, with accommodations for 250 girls.

The male seminary has been enlarged to afford boarding and school facilities for 175 boys.

The orphan asylum accommodates 150 and the colored high school 60 pupils. There are at present 124 primary or day schools scattered throughout the nation.

These four high schools and 124 primary schools are maintained the current year at a cost, from Cherokee funds, of $80,505.90, viz: Male seminary, $10,625; female seminary, $17,403.27; orphan asylum, $14,125; colored high school, $3,013.03; 124 primary schools, $30,380; school board. books, insurance, etc., $4,559.60. In addition to above, pupils at the high schools pay for their board $7.50 per month at the seminaries and $5 per month at the colored high school.

The schools are supported by an interest-bearing fund, held by the United States Government, amounting to $797,756.01, an orphan fund of $352,456.05, and an asylum fund of $64,147.17.

Schools are in session sixteen weeks in the fall and twenty weeks in the spring, or nine months a year.

The 124 primary school teachers receive $35 per month of twenty days. The principals of the seminaries receive $100 and their assistants $50 to $75.

The enrollment the last term was at the male seminary 90, the female seminary 125, the orphan asylum 129, colored high school 25.

The enrollment of the 124 primary schools was 4,258; the average attendance, 2,368; males enrolled, 2,089; females, 2,169. Of these schools 14 are for colored pupils, and had an aggregate attendance of 790, or 365 males and 425 females. The 14 colored schools had an average enrollment of 56.4; an average attendance of 30.8. The 110 Cherokee schools had an average enrollment of 31.5 and an average attendance of 17.6.

The following statistics of general and scholastic population are the most reliable obtainable:

School children (ages 6 to 18 years):

Cherokees, by blood	9,253
Shawnees, by blood	305
Delawares, by blood	306
Freedmen	1,223
Orphans at asylum	135
Total	11,222
Cherokees, by blood	26,500
Delawares, by blood	871
Shawnees, by blood	790
Intermarried whites, by blood	2,300
Freedmen	4,000
Total of Cherokee citizens	34,461

The most general estimate of noncitizen resident population is that it equals or slightly exceeds the citizen population.

Under law of Congress approved June 28, 1898, there have been incorporated 26 towns in the limits of the Cherokee Nation. When duly elected and organized the school boards of these towns may buy, own, or lease school property, organize, equip, and conduct schools, and for these purposes the town authorities may assess and collect taxes to the amount of one-half cent on the dollar of all taxable property within said towns. Vinita and Fairland have already fulfilled the requirements of law and will conduct public schools of their own from this on.

There are several mission schools in the nation. At Tahlequah the Presbyterians maintain Tahlequah Institute, with an attendance of 150, and Park Hill Mission, 4 miles south, with 65 pupils, and also the Elm Spring Mission School.

The Cherokee Baptist Academy at Tahlequah, with 125 pupils, is supported by the Baptist Church, and the Friends maintain a school at Skiatook. These schools have been of value in the educational work of the Cherokees.

It was my privilege to attend the commencement exercises of the seminaries. Five young men and 11 young ladies graduated. Their addresses were every way creditable, reflecting ability and culture. These schools are the especial pride of the nation.

In several localities the noncitizen people maintain subscription schools for their children. A goodly representation of Cherokee youths attend schools in the States for advanced instruction and professional training.

Very respectfully,

BENJAMIN S. COPPOCK,
School Supervisor, Cherokee Nation.

MUSCOGEE, IND. T., *August 16, 1899.*

DEAR SIR: I herewith submit to you my general report as school supervisor of the Creek Nation, Indian Territory.

Early in May, shortly after I entered upon my duties as supervisor, the schools of the nation closed; hence I did not get to visit any of them while in session, and can not report fully as to the work of the schools or the efficiency of the teachers. However, from the most reliable information obtainable I am convinced that the schools are very elementary.

There are 10 boarding schools and about 65 neighborhood schools in the nation.

BOARDING SCHOOLS.

The following is a list of the boarding schools, with a brief description of each:

1. Eufaula High School.
2. Creek Orphan Home.
3. Euchie High School.
4. Wetumka.
5. Coweta.
6. Wealaka.
7. Tallahassee.
8. Colored Orphan Home.
9. Pecan Creek.
10. Nuyaka.

Eufaula High School.—This school is located about 1 mile west of Eufaula, a town situated about 35 miles south of Muscogee, on the Missouri, Kansas and Texas Railroad.

The main building at this school is a three-story brick structure about 50 by 80 feet. The first floor is used for teachers' rooms, dining room, and kitchen. The second floor contains the chapel, recitation rooms, and employees' rooms. The third floor contains the sleeping apartments of 100 pupils—50 boys and 50 girls. There are four large rooms on this floor, and 25 pupils are supposed to sleep comfortably in each.

A new dormitory is needed badly at this school.

There are several small frame buildings here; small cottage used by superintendent and his family, washhouse, storeroom, etc.

There are five teachers, including a music teacher.

The man who has had charge of this school is a Creek citizen, who wields quite an influence over his people, thereby holding his position, but whose moral character is bad. He has repeatedly been before his pupils in a drunken state; however, two weeks ago, when he was attending our Creek institute and teachers' examination in a beastly drunken condition, he was soon thereafter forced to send his resignation to Superintendent Benedict.

Creek Orphan Home.—This school is situated 40 miles west of Muscogee, near the old town of Okmulgee, the capital of the Creek Nation. The main building at this school is a two-story brick structure, where 60 full-blood Creek orphans receive instructions.

The building is in a fairly good condition, yet there are several minor improvements necessary that can not be made for want of appropriation. There is a fine young orchard here and 60 acres of land cultivated. The boys are required to work on the farm regularly one hour each day.

There are three teachers, the principal one of whom is a young Creek Indian, exceptionally intelligent.

The superintendent of this school is a Creek citizen of good character, but who is somewhat careless and does not keep the building and surroundings in good condition. Everything, including clothing, is furnished free to the pupils.

Euchie High School.—This school is situated near Sapulpa, a small town on the St. Louis and San Francisco Railroad, about 60 miles northwest of Muscogee. This school was established by the Creek government about six years ago for the instruction of the full-blood Euchie Indians, who, while of the Creek tribe, rarely mix with, or allow their children to mix with, the Creeks, making it necessary to establish a separate school. This school accommodates 80 children.

The buildings at this institution are all of frame structure. There are three main buildings—the girls' dormitory, the boys' dormitory, and the chapel or school building.

The dormitories are duplicate buildings, except the dining room and kitchen are annexed to the girls' dormitory. The main part of each building is 22 by 44 feet, two stories high, with a one-story addition 24 by 28 feet. The size of the chapel is 34 by 48 feet.

Wetumka School.—This school is situated about 60 miles southwest of Muscogee near the small village of Wetumka. This school is known as the Wetumka National Labor School. There are 100 children accommodated here—50 boys and 50 girls. The boys are required to work about three hours every day. There are two fine orchards at this place.

All the buildings are frame. The large building known as the girls' dormitory has the dining room attached; also apartments for the superintendent and his family. The boys' dormitory is a two-story building, situated about 200 yards south of the girls' building. There are five teachers here, including the music teacher.

The superintendent is a Creek citizen, a fatherly man of 66 years, who has the reputation of being one of the best superintendents in the nation.

Coweta.—This school is situated about 30 miles northwest of Muscogee, and is managed by a young, intelligent Creek Indian. The buildings at this school are duplicates of the buildings at the Euchie School, described above. There are 50 Creek Indian children here, who receive instruction from three teachers.

Wealaka.—This school is situated about 40 miles northwest of Muscogee, on the Arkansas River. The buildings here are the same size and constructed on the same general plan as the buildings at the Euchie School, above described. There are 50 children here, who are instructed by two teachers.

The superintendent is a Creek citizen, who shows but very little interest in the management of his school. An excellent orchard is at this place.

Tallahassee.—This is the largest of the three colored schools of the nation, situated about 8 miles northwest of Muscogee near the Arkansas River.

There are 100 children instructed here by five teachers. There are three large buildings, in a fairly good condition, of frame structure. There is a very fine orchard at this school.

The superintendent is a good, lively negro, who seems to take quite an active interest in the management of his school.

The Colored Orphan Home.—This school is situated about 3 miles west of Muscogee, on a high hill. Thirty-five orphans are cared for here and are instructed by two teachers. The main building is a large two-story stone structure, used for the superintendent and his family, dining room and kitchen, and sleeping apartments for the girls. There is a small 1½-story frame building used for the boys' and teachers' sleeping rooms.

The superintendent is a Creek citizen, who does not show a very great interest in the welfare of his school.

The Pecan School.—This is a colored school situated about 6 miles west of Muscogee, and is attended by 50 children, who receive instruction from two teachers. The buildings are not in very good condition, but for want of appropriation no improvements will be made this year.

This superintendent is a Creek citizen, who shows quite a decided interest in educational affairs.

Nuyaka.—The Nuyaka school is situated about 60 miles west of Muscogee. It was established several years ago for full-blood Creek children, and has been under the management of the Presbyterian Board of Home Missions. The Creek Nation pays the Presbyterian Board $5,600 a year for boarding 80 children.

The teachers (all white) are employed by the church board and are all very competent. The instruction is thorough and the discipline is excellent. It has the name of being decidedly the best school in the nation.

The buildings are all in good repair, and cleanliness is a very noticeable feature.

GENERAL STATEMENTS WHICH APPLY TO ALL THE BOARDING SCHOOLS.

1. *Condition of buildings.*—All of the buildings need some repairing. The plaster-
ing, in many places, has been broken off; the walls are badly marked up by careless
pupils, and there needs to be a general cleaning up. (This statement does not apply
to the Nuyaka school.)

The Creek council made appropriations for the repairing of the buildings at six
of the schools, and these repairs and improvements are now being made under the
supervision of the Creek superintendent of schools, the superintendent of the respective schools, and myself.

We hope to have these buildings in excellent condition at the opening of the
schools in September, and I shall insist upon the superintendents keeping the buildings and surroundings in good repair.

2. *Age of pupils.*—The age of the pupil ranges from 6 to 20 years. The greater
number of the pupils are primary, which, in my judgment, should not be the case
If the pupils admitted to these schools were of the intermediate and advanced
grades it would put the schools upon a higher standard, and would also strengthen
the neighborhood schools by supplying them with a greater number of primary
pupils.

3. *Boarding and medical attendance.*—Boarding is furnished free to all pupils and
employees, and medical attendance is free to pupils only. Clothing is also furnished
to the pupils of the two orphan homes.

4. *Stock and farming.*—There is not much stock at any of these schools—occasionally
a few hogs, a few chickens—not many cattle. In a country like the Indian Territory, where there is an abundance of grazing land, I am of the opinion that it would
be wise for each school to be furnished with a sufficient number of cows to provide
the school with milk.

The farming at these schools is very limited. There is plenty of land near the
schools that could be profitably tilled, but even most of tillable land belonging to
the schools is rented to some one not connected with the schools. There is very
little inclination on the part of the superintendents to work, themselves, or even to
have the boys work.

NEIGHBORHOOD SCHOOLS.

There are about 65 neighborhood schools in the Creek Nation. These schools
have been sadly neglected. From the most reliable information I can obtain the
parents are very indifferent about sending their children to school; the teachers
have not shown very much interest in trying to secure a full and regular attendance,
and in many instances the buildings are in bad, unattractive condition. The buildings are usually small, 10 by 14 foot box buildings, poorly ventilated and badly furnished—most of the seats being old fashion long benches, all of one height, and, of
course, very uncomfortable to the children. There are no maps, charts, and other
necessary apparatus found in these schools—occasionally may be found an old worn-
out map or chart.

When the schools open in September I shall give special attention to the building
up of the neighborhood schools.

Following is a tabulated report of the schools:

EUFAULA HIGH SCHOOL.

Employees.	Position.	Salary.	Date of employment.	Race.	Age.	Single or married.	Birthplace.	By whom appointed.
William McCombs	Superintendent	$600.00	Jan. —1897	Indian	55	Married	Creek Nation	School superintendent, Creek Nation.
R. K. Cornelius	Principal teacher	540.00	Sept. —1897	White	26	do	Mississippi	Superintendent McCombs.
J. E. Emery	First assistant	360.00	Sept. —1898	do	25	do	Arkansas	Do.
P. R. Ewing	Second assistant	315.00	do	Indian	35	Single	Creek Nation	Do.
Susie Grimes	Third assistant	315.00	do	do	26	do	do	Do.
Ada Windsor	Music teacher	315.00	do	White	28	Single	Missouri	Do.
Mrs. William McCombs	Matron	270.00	do	Indian	50	Married	Creek Nation	Do.
Mrs. P. R. Ewing	Second matron	270.00	do	do	25	do	do	Do.
Robert Johnson	Cook	270.00	Sept. —1892	Negro	50	do	do	Do.
Thomas McCombs	Workhand	240.00	Sept. —1898	Indian	20	Single	Creek Nation	Do.

Yearly enrollment ... 100
Average daily attendance ... 71
Per cent of attendance ... 71
Appropriation ... $9,600.00

Amount paid employees ... $3,495.00
Maintenance ... 6,105.00
Average cost of pupil per month ... 15.02

CREEK ORPHAN HOME.

Employees.	Position.	Salary.	Date of employment.	Race.	Age.	Single or married.	Birthplace.	By whom appointed.
Geo. W. Tiger	Superintendent	$600.00	Dec. 4,1897	Indian	33	Married	Creek Nation	School superintendent, Creek Nation.
J. E. Tiger	Principal teacher	540.00	Sept. —1897	do	24	Single	do	Superintendent Posey.
Anna M. Peterson	First assistant teacher	360.00	Sept. —1898	White	23	do	Pennsylvania	Superintendent Tiger.
Anna B. Wright	Second assistant	360.00	Sept. —1897	do	26	do	Virginia	Do.
Mrs. Simpson	Matron	180.00	Apr. —1899	do	40	Widow	Kentucky	Do.
Hepsey E. Jimboy	Assistant matron	180.00	Sept. —1897	Indian	25	Single	Creek Nation	Do.
J. Porter	Cook	225.00	Jan. —1899	Negro	57	Married	Indian Territory	Do.
Moses Bird	Workhand	180.00	Jan. —1899	Indian	28	do	Creek Nation	Do.

Yearly enrollment ... 60
Average daily attendance ... 52
Per cent of attendance ... 87
Appropriation ... $6,666.67

Amount paid employees ... $2,625.00
Maintenance ... 4,041.67
Average cost of pupil per month ... 15.53

EUCHEE BOARDING SCHOOL.

Employees.	Position.	Date of employment.	Salary.	Race.	Age.	Single or married.	Birthplace.	By whom appointed.
J. H. Land	Superintendent	Sept. —, 1897	$500.00	Indian	45	Married	Creek Nation	School superintendent, Creek Nation.
Lalrie Hawkins	Principal teacher	Sept. —, 1896	360.00	White	32	Single	Illinois	Superintendent Land.
Mattie Maitin	Assistant teacher	do	405.00	do	20	do	Creek Nation	Do.
Kate Hawkins	Matron	do	180.00	do	40	do	Illinois	Do.
Anna Milligan	Assistant matron	do	162.00	do	35	do	do	Do.
Ester Votaw	Dining matron	do	108.00	do	19	do	Kansas	Do.
Alice Votaw	Cook	do	225.00	do	24	do	do	Do.
T. E. Wilson	Industrial teacher	do	162.00	do	22	do	Illinois	Do.

Enrollment 70
Average daily attendance 65
Per cent of attendance 92.8
Appropriation $7,200.00

Amount paid employees $2,102.00
Maintenance 5,598.00
Average cost of pupil per month 13.16

WETUMKA BOARDING SCHOOL.

Employees.	Position.	Date of employment.	Salary.	Race.	Age.	Single or married.	Birthplace.	By whom appointed.
Wm. Robinson	Superintendent	Dec. 5, 1897	$600.00	Indian	66	Married	Creek Nation	School superintendent, Creek Nation.
J. M. Reilly	Principal teacher	Sept. —, 1896	450.00	do	20	Single	Cherokee Nation	Superintendent Robinson.
Frances M. Scott	First assistant	do	315.00	White	22	do	Indian Territory	Do.
Lina E. Benson	Second assistant	do	315.00	Indian	24	do	Creek Nation	Do.
Joe Robinson	Third assistant	do	360.00	do	46	Married	do	Do.
Mrs. Wm. Robinson	Dining-room matron	do	315.00	do	51	do	do	Do.
Mattie Alexander	Matron	do	225.00	do	24	Single	do	Do.
Mrs. J. A. Rock	Music	do	315.00	White	27	Married	Missouri	Do.
Dr. J. A. Rock	Physician	do	600.00	do	31	do	do	Do.
Oscar Ogeltree	Cook	do	225.00	German	20	Single	do	Do.
W. K. Ditzer	Workhand	do	225.00	do	45	Married	do	Do.
Miss Harper	Laundress	do	90.00	do	20	Single	do	Do.

Yearly enrollment 100
Average daily attendance 85
Per cent of attendance 85
Appropriation $9,000.00

Amount paid employees $4,020.00
Maintenance 4,980.00
Average cost of pupil per month 12.55

Employees.	Position.	Salary.	Date of employment.	Race.	Age.	Single or married.	Birthplace.	By whom appointed.
O. A. Morton	Superintendent	$500.00	Dec. 5, 1898	Indian	28	Married	Creek Nation	School superintendent, Creek Nation.
N. A. Webb	Principal teacher	450.00	Sept. 1897	White	26	do	Alabama	Superintendent Hays.
Mrs. O. A. Morton	Assistant teacher	495.00	Dec. 1898	do	26	do	Kansas	Superintendent Morton.
Ollie Terry	Matron and music	180.00	Feb. 1899	do	20	Single	Arkansas	Do.
Emma Lynch	Boys' matron	180.00	do	do	28	Widow	Creek Nation	Do.
Susie Biggs	Dining matron	112.50	do	Indian	28	Single	do	Do.
Mrs. Haynie	Laundress	162.00	Dec. 1898	White	32	Married	Washington, D. C.	Do.
Anna Cox	Cook	225.00	Nov. 1898	Indian	40	do	Creek Nation	Do.
Chas. Shoab	Workhand	180.00	Jan. 1899	White	40	Widower	Illinois	Do.

Yearly enrollment 50
Average daily attendance 37
Per cent of attendance 74
Appropriation $5,000.00

Amount paid employees $2,484.50
Maintenance 2,515.50
Average cost of pupil per month ... 15.01

WEALAKA BOARDING SCHOOL.

Employees.	Position.	Salary.	Date of employment.	Race.	Age.	Single or married.	Birthplace.	By whom appointed.
E. R. Hardridge	Superintendent	$500.00	Nov. 1, 1894	Indian	35	Married	Creek Nation	School superintendent Creek Nation.
G. C. Kindley	Principal teacher	405.00	Sept. 1893	White	33	Widower	Arkansas	Board of education.
Mabel Hall	Assistant teacher	315.00	Nov. 1898	do	26	Single	Iowa	Superintendent Hardridge.
Mrs. E. R. Hardridge	Girls' matron	180.00	Nov. 1896	Indian	30	Married	Creek Nation	Do.
Mrs. J. D. Pittman	Boys' matron	180.00	Sept. 1896	do	28	do	do	Do.
Lizzie Moore	Dining matron	180.00	Sept. 1897	do	28	Single	do	Do.
Mrs. J. M. Mundy	Laundress	180.00	Sept. 1898	do	22	Married	do	Do.
J. M. Mundy	Workhand	240.00	Nov. 1896	do	24	do	do	Do.

Yearly enrollment 50
Average daily attendance 45
Per cent of attendance 90
Appropriation $4,500.00

Amount paid employees $2,160.00
Maintenance 2,840.00
Average cost of pupil per month ... 12.59

TALLAHASSEE BOARDING SCHOOL.

Employees.	Position.	Salary.	Date of employment.	Race.	Age.	Single or married.	Birthplace.	By whom appointed.
B. H. Richards	Superintendent	$600.00	Mar. 17, 1898	Negro	38	Married	Creek Nation	School superintendent Creek Nation.
L. E. Willis	Principal teacher	450.00	Sept. —, 1898	do	28	do	Arkansas	Superintendent Richards.
Laura A. Jackson	First assistant teacher	390.00	do	do	26	Single	Kansas	Do.
A. H. Mike	Second assistant teacher	360.00	do	do	23	do	Creek Nation	Do.
Nancy Corbrey	Third assistant teacher	315.00	do	do	23	Married	do	Do.
Celia Roberts	Music teacher	225.00	do	do	26	Single	Missouri	Do.
Mrs. B. H. Richards	Matron	315.00	do	do	33	Married	Texas	Do.
Lou E. Smith	Cook	180.00	Feb. —, 1898	do	35	Widow	Kentucky	Do.
A. J. Jones	Workhand	102.00	Nov. —, 1898	do	26	Single	Creek Nation	Do.
George Rowe	do	113.00	Jan. —, 1899	do	24	do	do	Do.

Yearly enrollment 80
Average daily attendance 66
Per cent of attendance 82.5
Appropriation $9,600.00

Amount paid employees $3,020.00
Maintenance 6,580.00
Average cost of pupil per month 16.10

COLORED ORPHAN HOME.

Employees.	Position.	Salary.	Date of employment.	Race.	Age.	Single or married.	Birthplace.	By whom appointed.
N. W. Perryman	Superintendent	$500.00	May 9, 1898	Negro	31	Married	Creek Nation	School superintendent Creek Nation.
G. L. Trigg	Principal teacher	450.00	Sept. —, 1897	do	40	do	Missouri	Superintendent Perryman.
Jennie McIntosh	Music	270.00	Sept. —, 1898	do	24	Single	Creek Nation	do.
Mrs. N. W. Perryman	Matron	180.00	do	do	24	Married	do	do.
Nettie Thompson	Cook	108.00	do	do	21	Single	do	do.
Crum Island	Workhand	90.00	do	do	18	do	do	do.

Yearly enrollment 23
Average daily attendance 19.6
Per cent of attendance 82.6
Appropriation $3,333.33

Amount paid employees $1,598.00
Maintenance 1,785.33
Average cost of pupil per month 19.47

Employees.	Position.	Salary.	Date of employment.	Race.	Age.	Single or married.	Birthplace.	By whom appointed.
E. S. Jacobs	Superintendent	$500.00	Apr. —, 1898	Negro	44	Married	Creek Nation	School superintendent Creek Nation.
S. E. McIntosh	Principal teacher	405.00	Sept. —, 1898	do	27	Single	do	Superintendent Jacobs.
Mrs. Geo. Trigg	Assistant teacher	360.00	...do	do	40	Married	Washington, D. C.	Do.
Hager Myers	Matron	270.00	...do	do	38	do	Creek Nation	Do.
Julia Douglas	Cook	180.00	...do	do	38	do	do	Do.
Louis Myers	Workhand	135.00	...do	do	25	do	do	Do.
Wm. Lacy	do	50.00	Mar. to July	do	19	Single	do	Do.

Yearly enrollment 61   Amount paid employees $1,900.00
Average daily attendance 52   Maintenance 3,100.00
Per cent of attendance .... 85.2 Average cost of pupil per month 10.68
Appropriation $5,000.00

NUYAKA BOARDING SCHOOL.

Employees.	Position.	Salary.	Date of employment.	Race.	Single or married.	Birthplace.	By whom appointed.
J. M. Robe	Superintendent	$700.00	July 8, 1898	White	Married	Kansas	Presbyterian Board of Home Missions.
Mrs. J. M. Robe	General matron	350.00	Sept. 1, 1898	do	do	Ohio	Do.
H. G. Brown	Principal teacher	500.00	Sept. 15, 1898	do	do	Virginia	Do.
Mrs. H. G. Brown	Intermediate teacher	350.00	...do	do	do	Illinois	Do.
Miss L. A. Robe	Primary teacher	350.00	...do	do	Single	Pennsylvania	Do.
Miss L. A. McCracken	Assistant matron	350.00	...do	do	do	Missouri	Do.
Miss M. F. Robe	do	350.00	Sept. 12, 1898	do	do	Missouri	Do.
Miss M. C. Laughlin	Music	250.00	Sept. 21, 1898	do	do	Ohio	Superintendent J. M. Robe.
Miss M. R. Forsythe	Dining matron	250.00	Aug. 1, 1898	do	do	Missouri	Do.
A. M. Hughes	Farmer	240.00	...do	do	Married	Ohio	Do.
Mrs. A. M. Hughes	Cook	240.00	...do	do	do	Ohio	Do.
Miss E. A. Park	do	240.00	June 1, 1898	do	Single	Arkansas	Do.
Miss M. E. Babb	do	240.00	Sept. 21, 1898	do	do	Missouri	Do.
Miss A. P. Park	Laundress	240.00	July 1, 1898	do	do	Missouri	Do.
Louis E. Miller	Assistant farmer	216.00	Oct. 4, 1898	do	do	Creek Nation	Do.

Enrollment 89
Average attendance 89
Appropriation $5,600.00
Average cost of pupil per month $10.17

SUMMARY.

Schools.	Appropriation.	Maintenance.	Amount paid employees.	Pupils and attendance.						Employees.			
				Males.	Females.	Total.	Average daily attendance.	Per cent of attendance.	Cost per month.	Indian.	Colored.	White.	Total.
Eufaula	$9,000.00	$6,105.00	$3,495.00	50	50	100	71	71	$15.02	6	1	3	10
Creek Orphan Home	6,666.66	4,041.67	2,625.00	30	30	60	52	87	15.53	4	1	3	8
Euchie	7,200.00	5,598.00	2,102.00	35	35	70	65	92	13.00	1		7	8
Wetumka	9,000.00	4,990.00	4,020.00	50	50	100	85	85	12.55	6		6	12
Coweta	4,500.00	2,515.50	2,484.50	25	25	50	37	74	15.01	3		6	9
Wealaka	4,500.00	2,840.00	2,160.00	25	25	50	45	90	12.59	6		2	8
Tallahassee	9,000.00	6,580.00	3,020.00	40	40	80	66	82	16.16		10		10
Colored Orphan Home	3,333.33	1,735.00	1,598.00	18	17	35	24	70	15.40		6		6
Pecan Creek	4,500.00	2,600.00	1,900.00	31	30	61	52	85	10.68		7		7
Nuyaka	5,600.00	5,600.00		50	50	100	89	89	10.17			14	14
Neighborhood schools	17,100.00									24	23	18	64
Total	80,400.00	42,595.17	23,400.50	354	352	706	586	82.6	13.61	50	47	59	156

conclusion, I will say that, besides the work I have done, from which the fore-
; report is made, I have investigated the financial accounts of all the super-
dents of the boarding schools, and have examined, and, when found correct,
approved, the Creek school warrants issued against the within named appro-
ions.
spectfully submitted.

CALVIN BALLARD,
School Supervisor Creek Nation.

n. JOHN D. BENEDICT,
Superintendent of Schools for Indian Territory.

REPORT OF AGENT IN CHARGE OF UNION AGENCY.

UNION AGENCY, *Muscogee, Ind. T., August 10, 1899.*

:: In compliance with your request, I have the honor to submit herewith my
annual report of affairs at this agency, together with statistical information
npanying the same for the fiscal year ending June 30, 1899. In this connection,
ire to state that I assumed charge of this agency June 1, 1899, and my brief
rience does not qualify me to report upon existing conditions as fully and in as
se a manner as I should like.
egret to state that on the night of the 23d day of February last, the building in
h the offices of the agency were located was destroyed by fire, and all the
ds which had accumulated and been carefully preserved for many years,
ther with the furniture, safe, and office fixtures, were entirely destroyed.
nd the work of the agent vastly different from what I had expected, largely on
nt of recent legislation by Congress relating to the Five Civilized Tribes,
h has in a great measure changed the status of affairs at this agency, and is
ing an event of far-reaching importance, as it does away in a large measure
treaties which have been in vogue for many years, and will ultimately result
anging their form of government, and bring them under the laws of the United
28.
ny of the more progressive Indians of the Five Tribes are gradually coming to
ze that they must of necessity accept the conditions imposed upon them by the
enacted by Congress, providing for the final allotting of the tribal lands now
in common, and that they will be required to finally select a tract of land, and
settle down and establish for themselves and their families permanent homes.
hand of improvement is everywhere visible in this Territory. Almost the entire
on is dotted with villages and towns, the homes of many of the Indians and
en freedmen indicating a degree of thrift and enterprise rarely found in an
an country, many of their houses being built in modern style, tastefully painted,
led amidst lawns and gardens neatly inclosed, flanked with orchards of fruit
, giving abundant evidence of ease, plenty, and in many instances of no small
ee of luxury.

AGRICULTURE.

le richness of the soil with the favorable climatic conditions prevailing in the
itory offers great agricultural possibilities. The culture of cotton is largely
nded and profitably pursued. All the cereals are cultivated in their highest
ection. Bunch and other varieties of grasses grow luxuriantly.

INTRUDERS.

le remarkable development in all branches of industry, with corresponding
ease in the volume of business, together with the varied and ever-widening con-
ns favorable to the avocation of the farmer, stockman, fruit grower, lumber-
. and miners, have all combined to make this an inviting field for the intruder
ient from the border States, many of whom enter the Territory with the avowed
ntion of beating the Indian, and wholly disregard and defy the laws of the dif-
nt nations, and refuse to take out permits until they are either forced to comply
the law or threatened with removal from the Territory by the agent, and in
e instances it becomes necessary for the agent to execute the order of removal
the aid of the police force, and where it is necessary to resort to the removal of
nders, the officer executing the order is cautioned to do so with as little friction
ossible, treating the party to be removed with all humanity consistent with the
execution of the order.

POPULATION.

The total estimated population of the various nations, including intermarried whites and freedmen, is 77,686 as shown by the table herewith revised by my predecessor, Agent Wisdom, for the year 1898, since which time very few changes have taken place to materially change these figures.

Choctaw citizens by blood, intermarried whites, and freedmen	19,406
Chickasaw citizens by blood, intermarried whites, and freedmen	9,048
Creek Indians by blood and freedmen	14,771
Cherokees by blood, intermarried whites, freedmen, Delawares, and Shawnees	34,461

The full-blood Indians are to a certain degree civilized, and have to a large extent adopted the habits and customs of the white man. Many of them speak both English and their native tongue; they are peaceful and law abiding, but are slow to accumulate property and are rarely industrious.

The negro population is composed of slaves and their descendants, owned by the more progressive element of the Indians of the Five Tribes before the civil war. Since the emancipation of the race, the different nations composing the Five Tribes, sustained by a just and humane public sentiment, have done everything consistent to efface all the badges of former slavery by granting them the rights of citizenship, and in the Creek and Cherokee nations they are permitted to participate in the allotment of tribal lands; they are required to serve as jurors when called upon, and are given ample freedom in the exercise of their religious belief.

INDIAN POLICE.

The allowance at this agency is 1 captain, 2 lieutenants, 3 sergeants, and 22 privates, making a total of 28, and are stationed as follows:

In the Cherokee Nation	7
In the Choctaw Nation	9
In the Creek Nation	8
In the Chickasaw Nation	3
In the Seminole Nation	1

They are, as a rule, faithful and obedient, prompt and energetic in suppressing crime, and keep this office informed against persons committing unlawful acts within their respective districts, and each member of the force is required to render prompt obedience to superiors, conform strictly to prescribed rules and regulations, be orderly and respectful in deportment and refrain from profane, insolent, or vulgar language, and are absolutely required to abstain from the use of intoxicating liquors, and are held to a strict account for a proper observance of the rules and regulations.

The compensation received by the police at this agency, in my opinion, is not commensurate with the duties required of them. They are called upon to furnish conveyances and pay their own traveling expenses all out of the sum of $10 per month for privates, and $15 per month for the captain and two lieutenants.

The police department, as I understand it, was created for the benefit and protection of Indian reservations and the Indians thereon in the early days when Federal courts and municipal governments did not exist, and it was necessary that unlimited jurisdiction be conferred upon them in order that they might be better enabled to quell disturbances, remove intruders, and assist in training and educating the Indians in the ways of civilization, but as to the Five Civilized Tribes, Federal courts have been provided together with a form of municipal government giving ample protection to all the citizens of the Indian Territory. The Indian half breeds who compose a large majority of the citizens of the Indian Territory are competent and good citizens, and are able to take care of themselves under the laws of the United States Government, but the full-blood Indians are entirely helpless on account of being unable to understand the laws or defend themselves in the courts, and it seems to me that it will naturally take the strong arm of the Interior Department to give them the protection that they now require. The half breed realizes the benefit that will come to him under the new order of things and is willing to accept the conditions. The full blood does not see it, and is therefore discontented; but if it were possible that the existing laws and treaties should be administered speedily and give the Indians the desired and intended results, this feeling and the need for this particular protection to the full blood would be eliminated. I would therefore advise taking into consideration the changes and new conditions in the tribal governments, that the police force be reduced and be distributed as follows:

For the Cherokee Nation 2, for the Creek Nation 3, for the Choctaw Nation 3, for the Chickasaw Nation 3, and for the Seminole Nation 1, and that this number be selected from the best citizens and those most competent; that they be paid a salary of $50 each per month and expenses when traveling, and that the captain be allowed a salary of $100 per month and like expenses. This would reduce the force in this Territory to 13, and the compensation would be sufficient to enable them to devote their entire time to the service, and the change would greatly simplify the work, as it will be readily understood that competent men can not be induced to undertake to discharge the duties devolving upon a policeman in the Indian Territory for $10 per month and pay his own traveling expenses. It might be well to state in this connection that the agreement entered into by the Choctaws and Chickasaws with the commission to the Five Civilized Tribes provides that when allotments of lands are made the Government pledges the nations to put each Indian in possession of his allotment, and, in my opinion, it will naturally fall to the policeman to carry out this provision of the agreement, through the Department of the Interior, under the direction of the United States Indian agent, and as there are a great many intruders both in the Choctaw and Chickasaw Nations I anticipate that it will be necessary to remove a great many noncitizens in order to place the Indians in possession of their allotments.

SMALLPOX IN THE CREEK NATION.

During the months of February, March, and a part of April, 1899, smallpox broke out among the Creek Indians residing adjacent to the Sac and Fox Agency, Okla., and one or two cases were reported at Okmulgee, the capital of the nation. Prompt and diligent efforts were at once made by your office and Agent Wisdom to suppress this outbreak. Doctors, nurses, and guards were hired and a strict quarantine was maintained throughout the northern portion of the Indian Territory. As most of the cases were adjacent to the Sac and Fox Agency, Agent Patrick was directed by the Indian Office to care for them, which he did in a most effectual manner. The outbreak in this immediate section, while never serious, caused considerable alarm, and I am satisfied had not vigorous efforts been taken by the Government an epidemic of considerable magnitude would have prevailed.

CHOCTAW AND CHICKASAW NATIONS.

The Secretary of the Interior has prescribed under the provisions of the act of Congress of June 28, 1898 (30 Stat., 495), rules and regulations governing mineral leases and other matters in the Choctaw and Chickasaw nations, Indian Territory. Section 13 of said regulations prescribes that—

"All royalties, including advance royalties, as provided for in said agreement and in these regulations, shall be payable in lawful money of the United States to the United States Indian agent at the Union Agency in the Indian Territory. All other royalty in accordance with the schedule provided in these regulations, unless modified in any particular case by the Secretary of the Interior, as herein provided, shall be payable to said United States Indian agent monthly, and shall be paid on or before the 25th day of the month succeeding the date when such monthly royalties shall have accrued. All monthly royalties shall be accompanied by a sworn statement, in duplicate, by the person, corporation, or company making the same as to the output of the mine of such person, corporation, or company for the month for which royalties may be tendered. One part of said sworn statement shall be filed with the United States Indian agent, to be transmitted to the Commissioner of Indian Affairs, and the other part thereof shall be filed with the United States Indian inspector for the Indian Territory."

Section 14 of said regulations further provides as follows:

"The said United States Indian agent shall receive and receipt for all royalties paid into his hands when accompanied by a sworn statement as above provided, but not otherwise; and all royalties received by him shall be, as soon as practicable, deposited with the United States subtreasurer at St. Louis, in like manner as are deposited moneys known in the regulations of the Indian Office as Miscellaneous Receipts, Class III, with a statement showing the proportionate shares of each of the Choctaw and Chickasaw nations."

Moneys so collected and deposited by the United States Indian agent, as above set forth, shall be held to the credit of the Choctaw and Chickasaw nations in their respective proportions, and shall be subject to disbursement by the Secretary of the Interior for the support of the schools of the Choctaw and Chickasaw nations, in accordance with the agreement of April 23, 1897, between the commission to the Five Civilized Tribes and the Choctaw and Chickasaw nations, as ratified by the act of June 28, supra.

These regulations were promulgated by the Secretary of the Interior October 7, 1898, but prior to that time, July 21, 1898, the Department promulgated provisional instructions under the provisions of the act of Congress referred to above, in which the Indian agent at this agency was directed to give immediate notice to contractors, lessees, or other persons having permits from the tribal authorities, that all royalties, lease moneys, rents, etc., that have accrued since their last payment to those authorities or since the 28th day of June last and are unpaid, or that may hereafter accrue under their several grants, shall be paid through him into the Treasury of the United States to the credit of the tribe to which they belong.

These provisional instructions were intended to apply to all the tribes of this agency, viz, the Cherokees, Creeks, Choctaws, and Chickasaws, except the Seminoles, who by their agreement with the United States were not subject to the provisions of the act of June 28, 1898.

These instructions were printed and mailed to parties interested in the Indian Territory and at other points, and the Indian agent at once commenced to receive and receipt for all moneys paid into his hands under these regulations.

During the quarter ending September 30, 1898, the following amounts were collected for the Choctaw and Chickasaw nations:

Choctaw Nation.

Tax on circuses and theaters	$33.88
Permit taxes	425.25
Licensed trader taxes	347.44
Royalty on timber	1,224.65
Asphalt, coal, rock, and stone royalty	2,402.18

Chickasaw Nation.

Timber royalty	408.20
Asphalt, coal, rock, and stone royalty	800.72

These amounts were subsequently deposited to the credit of the Treasurer of the United States for the tribes named.

It was afterwards decided by the Department that under the provisions of the agreement made with the Choctaw and Chickasaw Indians by the Dawes Commission that the United States, through its officials, was only to collect coal, asphalt, and other mineral royalties, and that the collection of all other taxes in the Choctaw and Chickasaw nations, such as timber royalty, permit taxes, etc., were to be collected by the Indian officials as heretofore.

Prior to receipt of the amended instructions there was collected by my predecessor, Agent Wisdom, during the quarter ending December 31, 1898, royalties for the Choctaw Nation as follows:

Choctaw Nation.

Royalty on timber	$212.50
Miners' permits	238.21
Tax on circus	25.00

Chickasaw Nation.

Timber royalty	70.84
Total	546.55

And which was subsequently by him deposited to the credit of the Choctaw and Chickasaw nations.

My predecessor, Agent Wisdom, and myself have collected and deposited with the Treasurer of the United States for the Choctaw and Chickasaw nations since the passage of the Curtis act, June 28, 1898, to the close of the fiscal year ending June 30, 1899, the following amounts of royalty:

Choctaw and Chickasaw nations.

Coal royalty	$107,766.03
Asphalt royalty	1,295.32
Rock royalty	1,083.90
Miscellaneous receipts	2,985.97
Total	113,131.22

Coal, asphalt, and rock royalty is divided in the proportion of three-fourths to the Choctaws and one-fourth to the Chickasaws. Miscellaneous receipts are divided as shown above.

Since June 30, 1899, I have received on account of coal, asphalt, and rock royalty for the Choctaw and Chickasaw nations the sum of $10,376.55, which, while having been paid in July, was earned and accrued to the nations during the month of June, hence it is given in this report in order to show total amount earned by the nations from June 28, 1898, to June 30, 1899.

In the Choctaw and Chickasaw nations there are 22 coal mines, 4 asphalt mines, and 1 rock quarry. The principal mine operators in these nations are the Choctaw, Oklahoma and Gulf Railroad Company, with headquarters at South McAlester, Ind. T., and mines at Alderson, Hartshorne, Gowen, and Wilburton; the Osage Coal and Mining Company, with mines at Krebs, Ind. T.; the Osage and Atoka Coal and Mining Company, with mines at Lehigh and Coalgate, Ind. T.; the Kansas and Texas Coal Company, headquarters at St. Louis, Mo., having mines at Krebs, Cherryvale, Carbon, and near Jenson, Ark.; the Southwestern Coal and Improvement Company, with mines at Lehigh and Coalgate, Ind. T. The asphalt mines, with one exception, are located near Dougherty, Chickasaw Nation, Ind. T. The names of the operators are the Gilsonite Roofing and Paving Company, with general offices at St. Louis, Mo.; Mastic and Paving Company, St. Louis, Mo.; the Rock Creek Natural Asphalt Company, Topeka, Kans.; the Moulton Asphalt Company, with mines near Coalgate, Choctaw Nation, Ind. T.

I think it proper to add that the mine operators in the two nations named remit their royalties promptly and accompany the same with the required sworn statements. My relations with the officers of the several companies have been pleasant, and no friction between them and this office has ever occurred.

I am satisfied that the coal royalties for the past year would have been much larger had not the strike, which is now on and which commenced in February, 1899, been prevailing. This strike has very materially reduced the output of the mines for the past five months, and, I regret to add, the trouble between the operators and strikers has not been satisfactorily adjusted.

The Department has recently instructed Special Inspector J. W. Zevely to investigate and report upon this matter, but I have not seen his report and can not therefore, being myself new to this country, give the reason for the strike.

All mineral leases in the Choctaw and Chickasaw nations are entered into by the mineral trustees of said nations, who are appointed by the President of the United States upon the recommendation of the executives of said nations, each of whom is an Indian by blood of the respective nation from which he was appointed. It is the duty of the trustees to receive applications from parties desiring to make leases of lands within the Choctaw and Chickasaw nations for the purpose of engaging in the mining of coal, asphalt, or other minerals; to examine said applications and transmit the same with report of facts to the United States Indian inspector in the Indian Territory, and on receipt of authority from him for that purpose to enter jointly into leases with all parties whom the privilege of leasing lands in said nation for mining purposes shall be approved by him in such form as prescribed by the Secretary.

The rate of royalty prescribed by the Secretary on coal prior to January 1, 1899, was 15 cents per ton for each and every ton of coal produced weighing 2,000 pounds. This regulation was afterwards modified upon the application of the coal companies in the Indian Territory, so as to be 10 cents per ton for each and every ton of screened coal produced weighing 2,000 pounds.

There is also located in the Indian Territory a mine inspector, who is under the direction of the Secretary of the Interior, and who makes his report direct to him. This officer has no connection with this office. His duty is to report on the sanitary condition of the mines and to see that all needful and proper care is taken to prevent explosions or other accidents.

As stated above, all funds arising from mineral royalties are to be used in educating the Choctaw and Chickasaw Indians. They are disbursed by the United States Indian agent under the direction of the United States Indian inspector for the Indian Territory.

CHEROKEE AND CREEK NATIONS.

The Secretary of the Interior, under the general provisions of the act of Congress approved June 28, 1898 (30 Stat., 495), also promulgated certain rules and regulations governing mineral leases, the collection and disbursement of revenues, etc., in the Cherokee and Creek nations. Under these regulations the United States Indian agent is required to receive and receipt for all royalties paid into his hands, when accompanied by sworn statements, and it is also his duty to collect, under the supervision and direction of the United States Indian inspector for the Indian Territory, all rents, permits, revenues, and taxes of whatsoever kind or nature that may be due and payable to either of said nations. These revenues, after having been collected by the Indian agent, are deposited to the credit of the Treasurer of the United States for the tribes named, accompanied by a statement showing the sources from which the royalties, rents, etc., arose.

The principal source of revenue for the Creek and Cherokee nations is the tax imposed by the said nations upon merchants and others doing business within the limits of their territories. There are a few small coal mines in each nation—the output and royalty thereon amounts to but little.

There are in the Creek Nation 33 towns and 520 traders; in the Cherokee Nation there are 89 towns and 612 traders. The tax imposed by the Cherokee Nation upon traders is one-fourth of 1 per cent on all merchandise introduced and exposed for sale in said nation.

It also places an occupation tax upon all persons residing in said nation and making a livelihood by either a trade or a profession. This tax is badly proportioned and should be more uniform.

In the Cherokee Nation no white man is permitted to engage in trade save in the Canadian district thereof. This I think to be a poor plan and not conductive to the welfare of the Indians.

The total amount of revenue collected from all sources by the United States Indian agent at this agency from June 28, 1898, to June 30, 1899, for the Cherokee and Creek nations, is as follows:

Creek Nation $4,913.63
Cherokee Nation 3,150.87

SEMINOLE NATION.

In December, 1897, the Seminole Nation and the commission to the Five Civilized Tribes, otherwise known as the Dawes Commission, entered into an agreement which provides for the allotment of their lands and the establishment of a United States court at Wewoka in said nation, and gives to the United States courts exclusive jurisdiction of all controversies growing out of the title, ownership, occupation, or use of real estate owned by the Seminoles, and to try persons charged with homicide, embezzlement, bribery, and embracery committed in the Seminole country without reference to the citizenship of the person charged with such crime.

The Seminole Indian courts are allowed to retain the jurisdiction that they now have except such as is transferred to the United States courts.

This agreement also provides for the gradual extinction of the tribal government. Ample provision is also made for schools and churches.

By reason of this treaty, which was afterwards ratified by Congress, the Seminoles are not under the provisions of the Curtis act, and the Indian agent does not receive or disburse any of their moneys, it being done by the tribal officers.

The Seminoles are peaceable and law-abiding citizens, and by reason of their conducting their own affairs this office has but little business with them save to enforce intercourse laws.

In conclusion, I desire to express my appreciation for the many courtesies extended and assistance rendered me by yourself and the employees of your office. I am indebted to my clerks, Mr. J. Fentress Wisdom and Miss Blanche Openheimer, for the faithful discharge of their duties. They are competent and reliable. Thanks are also due to the Department for the kind and liberal support given me since taking up the arduous duties devolving upon the agent at this agency.

I have the honor to remain, very respectfully, your obedient servant,

J. BLAIR SHOENFELT,
United States Indian Agent.

J. GEO. WRIGHT,
United States Indian Inspector for the Indian Territory.

T M Buffington, Chief Cherokee Nation.

P Porter Chief Creek Nation.

John Brown. Governor Seminole Nation

Green McCurtain, Governor Choctaw Nation

D H Johnson Governor Chickasaw Nation.

ANNUAL REPORT

OF THE

United States Indian Inspector for the Indian Territory,

TOGETHER WITH

THE REPORTS OF THE INDIAN AGENT IN CHARGE OF THE UNION
AGENCY, THE SUPERINTENDENT AND SUPERVISORS
OF SCHOOLS, AND REVENUE INSPECTORS
IN THAT TERRITORY,

TO THE

SECRETARY OF THE INTERIOR

FOR THE

FISCAL YEAR ENDED JUNE 30, 1900.

————◆•◆•◆————

WASHINGTON:
GOVERNMENT PRINTING OFFICE.
1900.

CONTENTS.

3

ANNUAL REPORT

OF THE

UNITED STATES INDIAN INSPECTOR FOR THE INDIAN TERRITORY.

MUSCOGEE, IND. T., *September 3, 1900.*

SIR: In compliance with instructions, I have the honor to submit this my second annual report, covering the work of the office of the United States Indian inspector for the Indian Territory for the fiscal year ended June 30, 1900, together with recommendations for such additional legislation by Congress as appears to me advisable from existing conditions among the Five Civilized Tribes.

The first important legislation looking to the ending of the tribal form of governments in the Indian Territory, and the common ownership of the lands of the five tribes, was embodied in the act of Congress approved June 28, 1898 (30 Stat., 495), commonly known as the "Curtis act," which provided for radical and important changes in the administration of affairs among the five tribes from those previously existing for many years.

For general information, and in order that the conditions heretofore existing in the Territory and the changes brought about by the legislation of the Curtis act may be understood, the following brief description is necessary.

The five nations or tribes of the Indian Territory comprise the Choctaw, Chickasaw, Creek, Cherokee, and Seminole. The approximate area of the lands embraced in the Indian Territory and controlled by these five tribes is 19,776,286 acres, with an estimated aggregate population of 84,750 Indians, including freedmen, as shown by the last annual report of the commission to the Five Civilized Tribes, as follows:

Tribe.	Population.	Total.	Acres.
Choctaw	16,000		
Choctaw Freedmen	4,250		
		20,250	
Chickasaw	6,000		a 11,338,935
Chickasaw Freedmen	4,500		
		10,500	
Creek	10,000		
Creek Freedmen	6,000		
		16,000	a 3,040,000
Cherokee	31,000		
Cherokee Freedmen	4,000		
		35,000	a 5,031,351
Seminole		3,000	a 366,000
Total		84,750	19,776,286

a About

These lands have heretofore been held in common by the respective tribes, who have a conveyance for same from the United States, and the citizens of the respective nations, under treaties and tribal laws, have used and rented same to noncitizens, as their laws permitted.

These various nations have, for many years past, controlled their own affairs and governments, which provided for their respective governors, or principal chiefs, and other national or State officers, including legislatures or councils, enacting such laws pertaining to their lands, schools, and affairs generally, as they deemed proper, independent of the laws of the United States, and, in each of the nations, noncitizens located or residing therein for the purpose of trading or conducting other business within the limits of the nation, and for introducing cattle, mining coal, or renting lands from Indians, or for any other purpose, were required to pay to the authorities of such nations taxes for such privileges as prescribed by their various laws. It is estimated at the present time that there are approximately between 350,000 and 400,000 white people or noncitizens within the limits of the five nations.

As above stated, the Curtis act provided for radical changes in the administration of affairs among these nations, and included the ratification of an agreement entered into between a commission on behalf of the Government and the Choctaw and Chickasaw nations, which, with certain modifications, provided for the continuance of their government for a period of eight years from March 4, 1898.

It also provided for the abolishment of the tribal courts in the Creek and Cherokee nations, for the allotment of the surface of the lands by the Government to the individual members of said tribes, they having failed to enter into an agreement with the Government for the allotment of their lands in severalty. The agreements subsequently entered into with these two tribes having failed of ratification by Congress, the legislation embodied in the Curtis act still remains in force.

The Curtis act also provided that the Secretary of the Interior was authorized to locate an Indian inspector in the Indian Territory, with authority to supervise the management of the affairs of the different tribes, as required of the Secretary of the Interior, and, under date of August 17, 1898, I was assigned to such duty, and subsequently given detailed instructions fully defining my authority, and directing me to assume supervising control of all the affairs of the Indian Agency and other matters with which the Secretary was charged by law to exercise authority, except matters under control of the commission to the Five Civilized Tribes. Since my assignment to such duty I have been fully occupied in dealing with the many perplexing questions with which it has been necessary for me to cope, and in submitting reports and recommendations to the Department in reference to carrying out the provisions of this legislation.

Under the supervision and general direction of the Indian inspector located in the Indian Territory are the following offices or departments.

The United States Indian agent for the Union Agency, who is charged with the collection of all revenues to be handled by the United States Government, in accordance with existing law, and the disbursement of the funds belonging to the various tribes in the payment of their regularly incurred indebtedness, as evidenced by warrants, which are taken up and canceled, in addition to the general duties of the Indian agent as provided by the statutes of the United States, all of which will be covered by the report of the United States Indian agent accompanying this report.

The superintendent of schools in the Indian Territory and the supervisors for each nation under his immediate direction.

The revenue inspectors for the Creek and Cherokee nations, there being one supervising inspector for each nation with district inspectors under the direct supervision of each.

The mining trustees of the Choctaw and Chickasaw nations, and, more recently, the general supervision and direction of the townsite commissions and townsite work in the various nations.

In my last annual report the details of the work for the fiscal year ended June 30, 1899, were submitted, and this report covers the work for the past year, from July 1, 1899, to June 30, 1900.

As the conditions and laws are different in each of the nations, it will be necessary to report the situation of affairs and the work performed in each of the respective nations separately.

The Seminole Nation effected an agreement with the United States which was duly ratified by both parties, and such agreement is still in force in said nation and a copy of the same is attached hereto. (Appendix No. 1, p. 111.)

The Choctaws and Chickasaws have an agreement, which was ratified by Congress in the act approved June 28, 1898, supra, and matters pertaining thereto are divided for convenience into the following subjects: Mining, education, tribal taxes, townsites, smallpox, Chickasaw incompetent fund, and Chickasaw western boundary.

The Creeks and Cherokees are under the general provisions of said act of June 28, 1898, and as such law does not apply to the Choctaw and Chickasaw nations, the affairs pertaining to the two nations first named are reported separately under the following heads: Mining, tribal taxes, education, townsites, smallpox, and constitutionality of Curtis act.

SEMINOLE NATION.

It appears by a census of the Seminole Indians recently completed by the commission to the Five Civilized Tribes, that they have a population of about 3,000 people, with 366,000 acres of land within the limits of their territory.

A recent agreement with these people provides that the lands shall be divided equally among all after appraisal, excepting such reserved for churches, schools, and other purposes, also 1 acre in each township, which may be purchased by the United States Government for schools for noncitizens. Their tribal government continues as heretofore, and consists of a principal chief, second chief, forty-two band officers, treasurer, school superintendent, two school trustees, superintendent of blacksmith shops, and police or light-horse officers and privates. The chiefs are elected by popular vote and their term of office is four years. The chief is vested with the veto power. The band officers are representatives of fourteen bands, one band chief and two lawmakers from each band, with the same term of office as the chief. These band officers constitute the national council of the Seminole Nation, which body has power to consider all matters under the jurisdiction of the nation. The other officers are elected by the council.

The agreement also provides that noncitizens can lease the allotment of any member of the tribe for a period not exceeding six years, the same to be approved by the principal chiefs, or governor, of the nation before becoming effective.

There have been no matters in the Seminole Nation during the past year requiring the attention of the inspector, except in a few instances where white persons have gone within the limits of said nation without a lease from citizens or without other authority, for the purpose of grazing cattle or cutting hay, and in compliance with a request from the principal chief such persons have been removed by the United States Indian agent through the Indian police without friction or further trouble.

There is no Government school official in said nation, they having complete control of their educational interests.

CHOCTAW AND CHICKASAW.

Before taking up for discussion the general subjects, in the order given heretofore, I would state that the population of these two nations approximates 30,750, and that they have 11,338,935 acres of land within their territory, the Choctaws numbering about 20,250 and the Chickasaws about 10,500 people.

The agreement with these two nations provides that their lands shall be appraised and allotted by the Government, to be valued "according to the location and fertility of the soil," and allotted equally among all, after certain reservations have been made for schools, townsites, cemeteries, and other purposes.

The commission to the Five Civilized Tribes is now engaged in the work of appraising the lands of these nations preparatory to allotment.

Coal and asphalt is also reserved from allotment, and is to remain the common property of the tribes, although the surface of such land is to be allotted.

The per capita allotment of lands in these nations can not be given with any degree of accuracy until the reservations above mentioned are made, but it is estimated that the same will average about 500 acres each.

The agreement further provides that their governments shall continue for a period of 8 years from March 4, 1898, though acts of their councils and legislatures are submitted to this office and forwarded to the Secretary of the Interior for executive action by the President of the United States before becoming effective.

The act of Congress heretofore referred to, approved June 28, 1898, which embodies the agreement with the Choctaws and Chickasaws as set out in section 29 of the act, is submitted for ready reference. (Appendix No. 2, p. 113.)

MINING.

The main coal fields of the Territory are located in the Choctaw Nation and the asphaltum in the Chickasaw Nation.

The agreement provides that coal and asphalt in these nations is to be reserved and remain the common property of the members of the tribes; that leases heretofore made by the nations where mines were in actual operation on April 23, 1897 (the date of the agreement) shall be ratified and confirmed, and that other leases shall be made under rules and regulations of the Secretary of the Interior each to cover not exceeding 960 acres, and to be for a period of 30 years.

Two mining trustees, Mr. N. B. Ainsworth, a Choctaw by blood, and Mr. L. C. Burris, a Chickasaw by blood, have been selected by their respective governments and appointed by the President of the United States to supervise the mines in operation, acting under rules and regulations of the Secretary of the Interior and the direction of this office, and performing such other duties as may be assigned to them in connection with mines leased.

Mr. Luke W. Bryan, located at South McAlester, Ind. T., is the United States mine inspector for the Territory, and has direct supervision of the operation of the mines. His annual report shows in detail the location and workings of all coal mines.

Prior to June 30, 1899, the following coal leases were entered into and approved by the Secretary of the Interior:

The Choctaw, Oklahoma and Gulf Railroad Company, 30 leases of 960 acres each, approved on March 1, 1899.

This company formerly operated under national contracts with the tribal authorities, and under the provisions of the agreement such contracts were ratified and confirmed. They have at the present time mines in operation on 14 of their leases.

John F. McMurray, of South McAlester, Ind. T., 8 leases of 960 acres each, approved on April 27, 1899.

Since July 1, 1899, other coal leases have been approved, as follows:

D. Edwards & Son, 3 leases, approved August 22, 1899.
McKenna, Amos & Amos, 1 lease, approved October 24, 1899.
McAlester Coal Mining Company, 2 leases, approved February 19, 1900.
Choctaw Coal and Mining Company, 3 leases, approved May 4, 1900.
Sans Bois Coal Company, 6 leases, approved on June 25, 1900.

Messrs. McKenna, Amos & Amos, however, after several attempts to develop the coal under their lease, ascertained it was too dirty and unprofitable to work, and have requested authority to relinquish their lease.

The following-named coal companies have operated during the past year on the leases of the Choctaw, Oklahoma and Gulf Railroad Company, and subleases with such companies have been submitted but have not yet been approved by the Department:

Wilburton Coal and Mining Company, 2 leases.
Mexican Gulf Coal and Transportation Company, 5 leases.
Milby & Dow Coal and Mining Company, 2 leases.
Ola Coal and Mining Company, 2 leases.

In addition, the following-named companies have operated under national contracts:

Osage Coal and Mining Company.
Atoka Coal and Mining Company.
Kansas and Texas Coal Company.
Southwestern Coal and Improvement Company.
McAlester Coal and Mineral Company.
Ozark Coal and Railway Company.
Devlin-Wear Coal Company, successors to the Indianola Coal and Railway Company.
Hailey Coal and Mining Company.
Samples Coal and Mining Company.
Crescent Coal Company.
Archibald Coal and Mining Company, now William Busby.

St. Louis-Galveston Coal and Mining Company.
Eastern Coal and Mining Company.
Turkey Creek Coal Company.
J. B. McDougall.
M. Perona.
R. Sarlls.

A few other small operators have also taken out limited quantities of coal. A report from the mine inspector for the Indian Territory shows the total output of these operators as being 1,900,127 tons during the year, as against 1,404,442 tons for the year previous.

The agreement further provides that the Secretary of the Interior may reduce or advance the rate of royalty on coal and asphaltum when he deems it for the best interests of the Choctaws and Chickasaws to do so.

The rate of royalty on coal mined, commencing January 1, 1899, was 10 cents per ton on all coal after being screened. In February, 1900, however, the coal operators petitioned the Secretary of the Interior to reduce the rate of royalty to 6⅔ cents per ton mine run, and after due consideration of the whole subject, the rate was fixed at 8 cents per ton mine run, to take effect March 1, 1900.

The asphalt mines are located in the Chickasaw Nation, and, though covering a large area, have not yet been developed extensively, owing largely to the fact that most of this material is located some distance from railroads. The royalty has been fixed at the rate of 60 cents per ton on refined and 10 cents per ton on crude asphalt.

The following leases, of 960 acres each, for the purpose of mining asphaltum, as provided by the agreement, have been entered into and approved by the Secretary of the Interior:

Brunswick Asphalt Company, 1 lease, approved on March 20, 1900.
Caddo Asphalt Mining Company, 1 lease, approved on April 21, 1900.
Elk Asphalt Company, 1 lease, approved May 3, 1900.

In addition to these companies, the Rock Creek Natural Asphalt Company and the Moulton Asphalt Company have operated to a limited extent under tribal charters and contracts.

Besides the approved coal and asphalt leases as heretofore listed the following leases are now pending before the Department awaiting approval:

Coal.

St. Louis-Galveston Coal and Mining Company................................... 2
Degnan and McConnell.. 3
Ozark Coal and Railway Company 1
Crescent Coal Company 1
Samples Coal and Mining Company 1
Central Coal and Coke Company... 1
William Busby... 1

The first five named were held awaiting certain certificates required of the bond company, and the latter two have only recently been forwarded.

Under the amended regulations of the Department, as approved by the honorable Secretary on May 22, 1900, applications for all mining leases in the Choctaw and Chickasaw nations, which were formerly made to the mining trustees, are now made direct to the inspector, and there are now several applications pending, action upon which is being taken as rapidly as possible. A copy of the regulations above referred to, and blank application, form of "additional information," and leases

for coal and asphalt, and bond are attached.   (Appendix No. 3, p. 132;
No. 4, p. 135; No. 5, p. 136; No. 6, p. 137; No. 7, p. 139; No. 8, p. 142.)

All royalties are remitted to the United States Indian agent, Union
Agency, monthly, accompanied by sworn statements of operators,
whose books are subject to inspection at all times.   During the year
ending June 30, 1900, the royalties on all minerals in these two nations
have amounted to $139,589.50, against $110,145.25 for the previous
year.   Of this amount $137,377.82 has been for coal, $1,108.58 for
asphalt, and $1,103.10 for other minerals.

A detailed statement of all royalties paid during the past twelve
months will be found in the Indian agent's report.

The agreement provides for the leasing of coal, asphalt, and other
minerals, while another part of the agreement provides that only coal
and asphalt shall be reserved from allotment, and under directions of
the Department, until May, 1900, applications for all kinds of mineral,
including gold, silver, copper, lead, zinc, and stone, were received and
considered.

In an opinion dated May 11, 1900, approved by the Secretary of
the Interior on the same date, the Assistant Attorney-General for the
Department of the Interior held:

After a careful consideration of this matter, I am of the opinion, and advise you,
that there is no authority, under the provisions of said agreement, for giving leases
for the purpose of mining any substance other than coal and asphalt, except as an
assurance of rights under a lease of oil or other mineral, assented to by act of
Congress.

The full text of this opinion is shown by Appendix No. 9, page 142.

In view of this holding, therefore, no applications for mineral leases
other than coal and asphalt in these two nations are now considered.

The Acme Cement Plaster Company, of St. Louis, Mo., recently
desired to secure a lease of cement lands in the Chickasaw Nation for
the purpose of manufacturing cement plaster, and submitted the
question as to whether they could lease lands from individual Indians
claiming such as their prospective allotments.   The Department, however, concluded that there was no statute which would authorize an
individual Indian to enter into such a lease at this time, the lands not
having been allotted, and I was advised to notify this company that
the Department was unable to aid them in securing the lease as
desired.

Concerning the several contests with reference to the rights of different parties to lease the same tract of land for mining purposes, they
have been taken up and investigated as required by the regulations,
the most important being one covering a coal claim between the Sans
Bois Coal Company and the Kansas and Indian Territory Coal Mining
Company.   Much testimony was taken in this case, and full reports
submitted to the Department.   The matter was finally submitted to
the Assistant Attorney-General, who held that as it was not shown
that either party was operating the mine under a valid existing
national contract with the tribal governments, therefore neither company was, as a matter of law, entitled to a preference right to a lease
of the lands in controversy, but that in instances of such rival applications the Secretary of the Interior must, in the exercise of a sound
discretion, determine to which applicant a lease will be given.

The Sans Bois Coal Company was subsequently granted six leases
and the Kansas and Indian Territory company was advised that they

could submit an application for one lease, but as yet no lease with said company has been made.

Another controversy arose in the Chickasaw Nation, in which the Davis Mining Company originally was granted a charter from the Chickasaw Nation to mine asphalt in a certain tract of country. A lease was made by this company to parties who, in turn, leased it to the Rock Creek Natural Asphalt Company, which company made a lease to other parties, from whom the Gilsonite Roofing and Paving Company obtained certain rights within the tract now operated. The Rock Creek company is engaged in operating mines on a different tract, but embraced within the charter limits of the Davis company. The Gilsonite company made application for a lease under the agreement for lands embracing improvements made by their company to which they claim rights partially under the agreement with the Rock Creek company, and it was over this application that the controversy arose as between the Rock Creek and Gilsonite companies, and the rights of both were contested by the Davis company. The Davis company claimed by reason of its tribal charter, and the other two companies by reason of certain agreements between the several contestants and by virtue of certain improvements erected by the Gilsonite company on lands which they desired to lease. This matter was also finally submitted to the Assistant Attorney-General for the Interior Department, who, in an opinion dated March 10, 1900, and approved by the Secretary of the Interior on the same date, held:

The Choctaw and Chickasaw nations are joint owners of the lands occupied by them respectively, the Choctaws holding a three-fourths interest in the lands occupied by the Chickasaws and the Chickasaws holding a one-fourth interest in those occupied by the Choctaws. Because of this joint interest it was held that both nations should join in the agreement ratified by the act of June 28, 1898, by which a change in the tenure of their lands was to be effected. The leases or contracts ratified and confirmed by said agreement were those made by the "National agents of the Choctaw and Chickasaw nations" and not those made by the representative of one nation alone. It was not intended by that agreement to recognize any contract or lease made by one of these nations alone through its representatives. As said by the Commissioner of Indian Affairs, it is not shown or claimed that the Choctaw nation ever gave its assent to the Chickasaw act under which the Davis Mining Company claims existence. I am of the opinion that no claim based upon that act is entitled to recognition under the agreement. * * * The Davis Mining Company not having a lease that comes within the confirmatory provisions of said agreement has no preference right to a lease for the land in question.

Neither of the other applicants claims to hold under a contract made directly with the national agents of the Choctaw and Chickasaw nations or either of them, and hence neither has any claim falling within the confirmatory provisions of the agreement ratified in 1898. They, in each instance, went upon the land in pursuance of and under the authority of the license to the Davis Mining Company. * * * Even if it be admitted that parties who are in possession of lands under such license or contract as those presented here, may have a right that should be recognized, the fact still remains that neither of these parties is entitled under those instruments to exclusive possession of the lands in question. * * * If these instruments are to be consulted to determine the rights of these applicants the conclusion would be that neither is entitled to a preference right as against the other to a lease by reason of possession, because neither has a right to exclusive possession of the tract in controversy between them.

In view of this opinion the whole matter was referred back to me with instructions to make an investigation and report of the facts as to possession and improvements, to determine the equities of the parties to the end that each might be given a lease to cover, if possible, the ground upon which he has in good faith made improvements.

As the opinion above referred to is important, covering many questions raised by others, a copy is submitted herewith as Appendix No. 10, page 144.

A date was recently set by me for an investigation of the facts in this case, and all parties notified, but in reply the representatives of both the Gilsonite and Rock Creek companies advised me that their clients desired the hearing to be postponed indefinitely because they could not present their matters at that time, therefore the case is still pending.

EDUCATION.

The agreement referred to with the Choctaw and Chickasaw nations provides:

It is agreed that all the coal and asphalt within the limits of the Choctaw and Chickasaw nations shall remain and be the common property of the members of the Choctaw and Chickasaw tribes (freedmen excepted), so that each and every member shall have an equal and undivided interest in the whole. * * * The revenues from coal and asphalt, or so much as may be necessary, shall be used for the education of the children of Indian blood of the members of said tribes.

All coal and asphalt mines in the two nations, whether now developed or to be hereafter developed, shall be operated and the royalties therefrom paid into the Treasury of the United States, and shall be drawn therefrom under such instructions and regulations as shall be prescribed by the Secretary of the Interior.

Under these provisions a superintendent of schools was appointed, together with a supervisor for each of the Choctaw and Chickasaw nations, whose duties are to visit and inspect the schools and orphan asylums of each nation, acting under the direction of the general superintendent, who reports to the Commissioner of Indian Affairs through this office.

Previous to the agreement the Choctaw Nation had its own school laws, and a board of education consisting of five members had entire control of educational matters.

As stated in my last annual report, while liberal appropriations had previously been made for the schools, many were found to be improperly conducted and funds not judiciously used. Politics and favoritism on the part of the tribal board of education had almost entirely governed the appointment of superintendents and teachers, without reference to their qualifications as instructors, and for that reason all schools were of a low standard of efficiency as compared with Government schools, and although these schools had been maintained for many years, no industrial training of any kind had been taught.

After promulgation of rules and regulations of the Department with reference to the management of these schools, the general superintendent, at their request, attended a meeting of the Choctaw board of education, explaining fully the rules of the Department and the policy proposed to pursue. No protest or objections were made to such plan, and until October last the Choctaw board of education did not attempt to interfere or question the authority of the Department to make appointments, and the work and plans of the Government officials received their full indorsement. Although this tribal board continued to exist, it was the purpose of the Department to act in harmony with them, without reserving the right to them to make application for teachers and appointments, notifying the board to suggest any person they desired appointed for examination.

The principal chief had expressed his opinion that the agreement authorized the Secretary of the Interior to assume control of the schools of the nation, and that such was agreeable to him, but in October last, when the Choctaw council was convened, the right of the Secretary to control the schools was denied, and the council passed an act directing their board to cease cooperating with the Government, and to conduct their schools according to their own laws. At that time, in company with the superintendent, I visited their council and explained matters fully, assuring them that the Government desired to have their cooperation, that the only object was to improve their schools and benefit their children. Full report of the matter was submitted to the Department, and I understand new regulations were prepared, modifying the previous rules, and submitted to the officials of the nation for their approval. Such rules, however, have not yet been adopted, and the schools have continued under former regulations. The superintendent reports that satisfactory progress has been made, a material improvement noticed both in better teachers, larger attendance, that the cost of maintaining academies has been materially reduced, and that pupils have been instructed in manual training and domestic science, never previously taught in any of these schools, and which is considered one of the most important factors in Government Indian schools.

There are in the Choctaw Nation 6 boarding schools or academies, including 2 orphan academies.

During the past year these schools have been maintained nine months. There has been an enrollment of 549 pupils, an average attendance of 471, with a total cost of $63,011.04, or $140.66 per capita. One of these schools—Spencer Academy—was recently destroyed by fire, caused by sparks being blown through an open window from an engine being used for operating a steam pump. The building was erected in 1898, and cost about $7,000, but was a cheaply constructed frame building, not plastered.

There has also been maintained during the nine months of the past year 120 neighborhood or day schools in the Choctaw Nation, with an average enrollment of 2,170 pupils and an average attendance of 1,812, at a cost of $27,570.91, or $12.70 per capita, making a total of all children attending of 2,719, with an average attendance of 2,283, at a cost of $90,581.91. For general repairs, irregular labor, etc., during the year, in addition to this amount, there was expended $2,300.

The Chickasaw boarding schools, 5 in number, are maintained by contract made several years ago with the tribal authorities for a term of five years, and as they are maintained from their own funds and not those arising from royalty on coal and asphalt, the Government has as yet exercised no authority over them.

As they have not sufficient funds to meet the current expenses, these schools are being now financially embarrassed.

The reports as furnished by the superintendent show 5 boarding schools have been maintained, with an enrollment of 348 and an average attendance of 306, at a cost of $56,840, or $151 per capita; also 17 neighborhood or day schools, with an enrollment of 489 and an average attendance of 386, costing $36,115, or $93 per capita, making a total attendance of all children in the Chickasaw Nation of 837 and an average attendance of 692, at a cost aggregating $92,595.

The Chickasaw authorities thus far decline to entertain the proposition to permit the Government to exercise supervision over any of their schools, and in the meantime their proportionate share of the royalties arising from coal and asphalt (about one-fourth) remains to their credit.

A supervisor, however, has been located in the Chickasaw Nation, but as yet, under the above circumstances, has been unable to make much improvement in these schools.

The day or neighborhood schools in both of these nations and throughout the Territory have received practically no attention or encouragement from the tribal authorities. No suitable buildings have been built and none found except where built by private subscription or donation, consequently nearly all are poorly built, with no furniture other than old benches.

The various Indian nations have expended large amounts of money in erecting and maintaining a few boarding academies, at which children of "influential citizens" have been educated, and in consequence little has heretofore been accomplished at these small schools, but it is hoped that their efficiency may be greatly increased.

TRIBAL TAXES.

Under the tribal laws noncitizens are required to pay to these nations, collectible by the proper tribal officers, certain taxes for residing or transacting various kinds of business therein, merchants in the Choctaw Nation being assessed 1¼ per cent on the value of goods introduced for sale, and in the Chickasaw Nation 1 per cent of the capital employed.

In the Choctaw Nation an act of their legislature, passed March 25, 1899, and approved by the President on June 8, 1899, levies a tax of $5 against each citizen for every farmer or renter employed and $2.50 for each "hireland" employed, such permits expiring December 31, regardless of date of issue.

While this permit tax is larger than that prescribed by the Chickasaw law and the same as previous Choctaw laws, the penalty of nonpayment by a citizen is that he shall be fined not less than $25 nor more than $50, while the previous law provided as a penalty that the noncitizen farmer or renter should be reported to the principal chief as an intruder and that the citizen, for nonpayment of fine, should receive not less than 15 nor more than 39 lashes on his bare back.

There is no introduction or annual cattle tax in the Choctaw Nation, but their laws prohibit the introduction of cattle except during the months of November and December, and then only to be kept within feed pens and legal inclosures. A citizen is to be fined $5 per head for violation of this law and noncitizens to be reported to the United States authorities for prosecution under section 2117 of the Revised Statutes, or removal from the Territory.

In the Chickasaw Nation their legislature passed an act in December, 1898, approved by the President on January 19, 1899, providing for a permit and occupation tax, requiring a payment by noncitizens of $1 residence tax; live-stock tax of 5 cents per head on sheep and goats and 25 cents per head on other stock, such tax applying to noncitizens and to all stock over a specified number exempted by said act, and which is a material reduction from former requirements.

This act also provides that noncitizens refusing or neglecting to pay such tax shall be deemed intruders and reported to the United States

Indian agent (or inspector) to the Five Civilized Tribes for removal beyond the limits of the Chickasaw Nation.

As the tribal authorities of these nations handle their revenues and finances, making their own collections and disbursements without supervision of this office, I am unable to furnish any information concerning the condition of their finances or the amount of taxes due and collected. Many noncitizens, however, in both nations have recently refused to comply with such laws, claiming that they are exempt by reason of living in incorporated towns, and others that the recent agreement which provides that residents of towns can purchase lots upon which their improvements are located at 50 per cent of their appraised value recognizes their right to reside within the limits of the Indian Territory.

Much correspondence has been had with the Department on this subject, and I was advised on March 4, 1899, that the tribal laws were still in force and that noncitizens were subject to such laws so long as the governments of those nations continued, regardless of the fact that such parties lived in incorporated towns and owned lots therein.

This holding was sustained in an opinion rendered on July 13, 1900, by the Assistant Attorney-General for the Interior Department, wherein he held that noncitizens are subject to these laws after purchasing lots so long as the tribal government exists, it being a permit to do business within the limits of their nations, and that—

The question is not directly as to the right of these people, not citizens, to occupy the property they have bought, but is as to their right to carry on a business in one of those nations without first obtaining a permit therefor, as required by the laws of the nation. The right of these nations or tribes to prescribe regulations requiring those not citizens engaging in business within the nation to pay a permit tax or license fee has been recognized by this Department and sustained by the courts. In the case of Maxey v. Wright, decided January 6, 1900 (54 S. W. Rep., 807), the court of appeals of Indian Territory upheld the right of the Creek Nation to require the payment of such a tax or fee and the power of this Department to take charge of the matter, collect the money and turn it over to the Indians, or, in case of refusal of anyone to pay the same, to enforce the penalty of removal, prescribed by laws of said nation. * * *

The purchase of a town lot does not make the purchaser a citizen of the nation within whose boundaries such town may be located, nor does it necessarily operate to confer upon him a license to follow a pursuit in disregard of the laws of the nation requiring a noncitizen to secure a permit before engaging in such business. * * *

The contention that the purchase of a town lot in one of these nations exonerates a noncitizen wishing to engage in trade or business from compliance with the laws of such nation and gives him a license to engage in business therein in defiance of such laws can not be sustained. A noncitizen has, in this respect, the same status after such purchase as he had before, and must afterwards, as before, meet the requirements of law if he desires to engage in business there. He is also subject to the same penalty for refusal to comply with the law after such purchase as he was before. If there is any hardship in the matter it does not grow out of conditions arising subsequently to his purchase, as there has been no change in the laws of any of said nations in this respect since provision was made for the sale of town lots. He voluntarily placed himself in the position he occupies and must bear the incident responsibilities. * * *

As said before, the question is not as to the right of the noncitizen to reside in these towns, but is as to their right to carry on a business in the nation in violation of the laws thereof. The provisions of said section 14 do not, in my opinion, operate to relieve the inhabitants of cities or towns in these nations from the payment of the permit tax or fee prescribed by the laws of the nation in which such city or town may be located.

A complete copy of said opinion is attached hereto. (Appendix No. 11, p. 148.)

The principal chief of the Choctaw Nation has recently submitted several communications representing that noncitizens are refusing to pay taxes as required, and has submitted the names of 86 persons or firms so refusing, requesting that they be removed from the limits of the nation.

The governor of the Chickasaw Nation has also reported the names of 654 noncitizens who refuse to pay the taxes as prescribed by their laws, and requesting their removal.   These communications have been forwarded to the Secretary of the Interior for consideration, but no instructions in reference to the same have yet been received.

Section 2149 of the Revised Statutes of the United States provides:

The Commissioner of Indian Affairs is authorized and required, with the approval of the Secretary of the Interior, to remove from any tribal reservation any person being therein without authority of law, or whose presence within the limits of the reservation may, in the judgment of the Commissioner, be detrimental to the peace and welfare of the Indians, and may employ for the purpose such force as may be necessary to enable the agent to effect the removal of such person.

During the past year 12 noncitizens have been removed from the Choctaw Nation and one from the limits of the Chickasaw Nation, under the above provisions and orders from the Department, for non-compliance with these tribal laws.

In addition to these about 60 physicians, who had either failed or refused to take the required examination in the Choctaw Nation, and about 20 cattlemen, within the limits of the nation in violation of the tribal laws, voluntarily removed from the nation when given a specified time to comply with the tribal laws or remove.

Mr. E. C. Baker, a noncitizen, removed on June 16, 1900, from the Chickasaw Nation for refusal to pay tax, subsequently returned, and I am advised that, acting under orders from the Attorney-General, the United States attorney for the southern judicial district of the Indian Territory has instituted criminal proceedings against him under section 2148 of the Revised Statutes, which provides:

If any person who has been removed from the Indian country shall thereafter at any time return or be found within the Indian country, he shall be liable to a penalty of one thousand dollars.

In view of the combined refusal of noncitizens to comply with these laws, as represented by the tribal authorities, and that the only remedy at present is to remove them, as above indicated, I respectfully recommend that this subject be brought to the attention of Congress and that a penalty be prescribed, the same as in the States, for seizure and sale of property sufficient to pay taxes due, or some other method be adopted to compel payment other than removal from the Territory, provided these tribal tax laws are to be in force for six years hence, during the time the governments of these nations are to continue as provided in the agreement.

TOWN SITES.

The agreement with the Choctaw and Chickasaw nations provides for the appointment of a commission for each of the two nations, consisting of two persons for each nation, one member to be appointed by the executive of each tribe and one to be appointed by the President of the United States; that each commission shall lay out and plat town sites, to be restricted as far as possible to their present limits where towns are now located, and that lands on which improvements have been made shall be valued by the commission, exclusive of improvements, at the price a fee-simple title to the same would bring in the market at the time the valuation is made; that the owners of improvements on such lots can purchase one residence and one business lot at 50 per cent of the appraised value and the remainder of such improved property at 62½ per cent of said value, all vacant lots to be sold at public auction. The agreement also provides that after full payment for lots owners of same shall receive a patent for such lots, to be signed by the two executives of the tribes, a form of which has been prepared by the Department, a copy of which will be found accompanying the Indian agent's report. (See Exhibit N, p. 175.)

Under these provisions a commission was appointed for the Choctaw Nation, consisting of Dr. J. A. Sterrett, of Ohio, and the principal chief appointing Mr. B. S. Smiser. A commission was also appointed for the Chickasaw Nation, consisting of Mr. S. N. Johnson, of Kansas, and the governor of said nation appointing Mr. Wesley B. Burney.

About June 1, 1899, these commissions, after procuring necessary information and rules from the Department, began their work.

The Choctaw commission commenced work at the town of Sterrett May 31, 1899, completing the same August 18 of the same year. The population of this town is about 800, with an acreage of 480. The total expense of surveying, platting, and selling the property in this town was $3,235.35. The surveying force at this place was limited, and it being the first town to be taken up, occasioned some considerable delay.

At Sterrett there were 191 improved lots, which were appraised by the commission. Holders of 115 of these improved lots were permitted by law to purchase them at 50 per cent of their appraised value, making $1,593.40 to be paid, and holders of 76 were permitted to purchase at 62½ per cent, making $1,296.96 to be paid, the 191 lots aggregating $2,890.36. There were also 700 unimproved lots sold for an aggregate sum of $14,890, thereby netting the nation for this town $17,780.36. A partial payment on all lots has been made, as required by law, and full payments have been made on 42 improved and 16 unimproved lots, but as yet no patents have been issued.

The commission next visited the town of Atoka, which has a population of about 1,200 and an acreage of 273, commencing the work September 1 and completing it November 6, 1899, with a total expense of $1,768.94.

In Atoka there were 321 improved lots, which were appraised by the commission, at a total value of $42,326. Holders of 162 of these lots were permitted to purchase them at 50 per cent of their appraised value, making $10,850 to be paid, and holders of 159 lots were permitted to purchase same at 62½ per cent, making $13,011.03 to be paid, the 321 lots bringing the nation $23,861.03. Payment on 75 of these lots was defaulted, and the commission has advertised same to be sold. The unimproved lots have been advertised for sale, but not yet sold.

About the time the work was completed at Atoka, and after the plat had been approved by the Secretary of the Interior, and the appraisements had been made, and the commission had given notice of the date of the sale of unimproved property, certain residents of the town applied to Hon. William H. H. Clayton, United States judge for the central judicial district of the Indian Territory, for an injunction restraining the commission from selling the lots as advertised and against the recognition of the plat approved. After duly considering the matter the court denied the injunction, holding that the matter of appraisement rests solely with the commission, who therefore proceeded to carry out their instructions.

Numerous complaints and petitions were made against the appraisements of improved property in this town, the residents claiming they were excessive. A committee of such residents called upon me and presented their grievances, requesting permission to file a brief of their case, which was granted, but as they failed to file such brief, and inasmuch as the law, as set forth in the agreement, provides that the townsite commissions shall appraise the property, and as there is no provision for any appeal from their appraisement when they agree, and as the first payments were being made by some, I was advised by the Department to take no further steps in connection with the matter.

Since the completion of the survey of Atoka, work was commenced at South McAlester on November 8, 1899, the largest town within the limits of the Choctaw Nation, which work is not yet completed. The population of this town is about 5,000, with an acreage of 3,200. The total expense of the commission at this town up to August 1, 1900, was $9,979.82.

The commission estimates that it will require two months to complete the survey and appraisal of the town of South McAlester, and in making report of the work at this town the commission calls attention to the character and size of the town site being surveyed, and states that it is being built on rough, rocky land embracing 3,200 acres, the larger part of which is covered with a heavy growth of timber, necessitating slow progress on account of the great amount of clearing necessary. In addition to the delays occasioned as above, the commission has encountered innumerable complications in adjusting conflicting interests of many individuals holding property rights that interfere with the proper location of streets.

Commencing March 15, 1900, while supervising the work at South McAlester, the commission took steps to establish the exterior limits of towns in the Choctaw Nation with a view to their taking advantage of the ruling allowing them to survey, at their own expense, and the boundaries of the towns of Calvin, 250 people, 160 acres; Allen, 300 people; McAlester, 1,200 people, 754 acres; Guertie, 225 people, 160 acres; Poteau, 800 people, 640 acres; Grant, 250 people, 160 acres; Howe, 1,000 people, and Kiowa, with 250 people and an acreage of 360, were established, and instructions given to the citizens of the towns relative to the manner of procedure in their surveys.

The towns of Calvin, Guertie, McAlester, Grant, Poteau, and Kiowa have taken advantage of the ruling allowing them to survey themselves, and have either completed, or have in process of completion, the plats of their towns. Three of these towns—Calvin, Guertie, and Grant—have already submitted their plats to the commission for approval.

The Chickasaw commission reached Colbert, Ind. T., on May 23, 1899, and remained there looking over the ground, consulting the wishes of the people, and procuring certain instruments, etc., until June 9, when the surveyor started the work of surveying and platting the same. The plat was approved on August 16, and from that time until August 29 the improved lots were being appraised and the vacant lots sold and records of same made. This town has a population of something over 200 and an acreage of 129.74. The total expense of surveying, platting, and selling the property at Colbert was $4,029.38. There was naturally some delay in the work at Colbert, for the reason that it was the first town to be surveyed and platted under the supervision of this commission.

In Colbert there were 70 improved lots which were appraised by the commission. Holders of 34 of these lots were permitted by law to purchase them at 50 per cent of their appraised value, making $910 to be paid, and holders of 36 lots were permitted to purchase same at 62½ per cent, making $1,137.50 to be paid, the 70 lots aggregating $2,047.50. There were 173 unimproved lots sold for an aggregate sum of $3,128.25, making a total of $5,175.75 for the town site. Of the improved lots appraised by the commission there were four defaults.

The commission next visited Ardmore, the largest town in the Chickasaw Nation, which claims a population of between 7,500 and 8,000, commencing the work there on September 1, 1899, and the commission has ever since been engaged in the work at this place. The acreage of this town is 2,260.06. The total amount expended in the surveying and platting of Ardmore up to the present time is $11,454.65.

The work of surveying and platting Ardmore is now practically completed, and the plat will be submitted to the Department within a few days.

No work was done by this commission looking to the establishment of the exterior limits of any towns in the Chickasaw Nation under instructions given prior to the passage of the Indian appropriation bill, May 31, 1900.

These commissions formerly reported direct to the Commissioner of Indian Affairs. In order to expedite matters requiring investigation and further report, directions were issued by the Department, under date of March 26, 1900, that such commissions should be under the direction and supervision of this office.

Prior to the time these commissions were placed under the supervision of this office the question was submitted as to whether the "present limits" of towns were intended to mean incorporated limits.

The incorporated limits of the town of South McAlester had just been established by the court and embraced more territory than the townsite commission considered necessary. After conferring with Hon. William H. H. Clayton, United States judge, the incorporate limits were reestablished, and the commission proceeded to plat the town to the compromise lines.

At Ardmore the same question arose, the town having been incorporated some time and embracing considerable unimproved land which the commission did not feel warranted in including in the townsite limits.

Full report was submitted to the Department and the matter was subsequently settled by Congress in the Indian appropriation act approved May 31, 1900 (Public, 131), as follows:

It shall not be required that the town-site limits established in the course of the platting and disposing of town lots and the corporate limits of the towns, if incorporated, shall be identical or coextensive, but such town-site limits and corporate limits shall be so established as to best subserve the then present needs and the reasonable prospective growth of the town as the same shall appear at the times when such limits are respectively established.

An extract copy of those portions of the said Indian appropriation act which affect the Indian Territory is submitted with this report. (See Appendix No. 12, p. 150.)

The same act provides that exterior limits of all towns shall be designated and fixed at the earliest practicable date, under rules and regulations to be prescribed by the Secretary of the Interior. It provides a further modification from the agreement with the Choctaw and Chickasaw nations of the manner in which towns should be surveyed and platted, to the extent that instead of such work being done by a commission, that all towns having a population of 200 or more inhabitants should be surveyed and platted by competent surveyors under rules and regulations to be prescribed by the Secretary of the Interior, and that the work of townsite commissions should begin as to any town immediately after the approval of the survey by the Secretary of the Interior, and not before. It also authorizes the Secretary to appoint a separate townsite commission for any town where, in his judgment, the public interests will be thereby subserved; and he may also permit the authorities of any town, at the expense of the town, to survey and plat the same.

Under date of June 4, 1900, a supervising engineer, in connection with townsite surveys in the Indian Territory, was appointed by the Secretary of the Interior, to act under the directions of this office, in supervising the detail work of surveyors of the various towns and to make any necessary investigations and reports concerning any matters connected therewith, in order that the work might be expedited and all performed in a uniform manner.

Reports received from postmasters show about 44 towns in the Choctaw Nation and 57 in the Chickasaw Nation having a present population of 200 and over, while there are numerous small villages having less than that number, for which there is no provision.

As the authorities of these nations consider that this legislation by Congress is in violation of their agreement, it was proposed to detach from each of the present commissions, temporarily, the representative of the nation to accompany surveyors for the purpose of establishing the exterior limits, returning to his duties as commissioner when his services were so needed. In a conference with the governor of the Chickasaw Nation and its representative it was fully explained that such procedure was only for the purpose of expediting the work, and that the commission, as provided by the agreement, would make appraisals of the property; therefore the nations would lose nothing and the results would be the same.

Governor Johnston, of the Chickasaw Nation, however, declined to consent to such move without conference with the principal chief of the Choctaw Nation on the subject, nor would the representatives of the nations on the commissions so act until authorized by their respective governors.

Acting, therefore, under directions from the Department, I have proceeded with this work of establishing the exterior limits of towns having 200 inhabitants, and have at present several corps of engineers in the field for that purpose, acting under the direct supervision of the supervising engineer, who has received the following instructions:

Immediately upon receipt of this communication you will proceed to the Choctaw and Chickasaw nations for the purpose of establishing exterior limits of all towns having a population of 200 or more.

Under the provisions of the act of Congress approved May 31, 1900, all towns having a population of 200 or more are to be surveyed and platted in such manner as will best subserve the then present needs and reasonable prospective growth.

The act of Congress approved June 28, 1898, also provides that the town sites shall be restricted as far as possible to their present limits.

In the establishment of exterior limits of town sites in each nation the "present needs and reasonable prospective growth of such towns" should be considered. Such limits should be carefully marked, and diagrams containing each legal subdivision forwarded to this office as soon as the town is completed.

All exterior boundaries should follow the lines of Government township survey of legal subdivisions.

It is further provided in said act of Congress approved May 31, 1900, that "It shall not be required that the town-site limits established in the course of platting and disposing of town lots, and the corporate limits of the town, if incorporated, shall be identical or coextensive, but such town-site limits and corporate limits shall be so established as to best subserve the then present needs and reasonable prospective growth of the town, as the same shall appear at the time when such limits are respectively established."

In performing this work it is desired that it be done in such manner as to accurately locate all necessary subdivision points, putting up proper markers and notices to the public, and also observe that all houses belonging to the town proper are within such limits, if practicable.

Should the town authorities or other persons object to such limits, you will carefully consider such objections, at the same time complying strictly with instructions as above set forth, accompanying the diagram with full report in each instance, and advise the parties that they can submit any further objections to this office for consideration. Five diagrams of each town containing the legal subdivisions should be forwarded to this office immediately after establishing the limits of each town.

You will also have posted in the post-office and in other conspicuous places notices of limits of the town as established.

You will not take any Government employee with you from one town to another, except a surveyor, and you are authorized to employ such irregular assistance as may be necessary to properly aid in the establishment of the limits of each town, not exceeding, however, three irregular employees for each town site. Residents of the town of which the limits are being established should, if possible, be employed, and no irregular employee should be paid exceeding $2 per day.

When submitting your report of each town, the location of same and distance from the railroad, the number of acres contained therein, the population of the town (approximately), and the estimate of the length of time it should require the surveyor to properly survey the same into necessary streets and alleys and platting same, together with any other information which can be used in proceeding in the surveying and platting of the town at a later date, should be fully set forth.

Included in said report you will also state whether the authorities of said town desire to proceed to have the same surveyed and platted at their own expense, as the act of Congress approved May 31, 1900, provides that "the Secretary of the Interior, where in his judgment the public interests will be thereby subserved, may permit the authorities of any town in any of said nations, at the expense of the town, to survey, lay out, and plat the site thereof, subject to his supervision and approval, as in other instances."

Where such work is to be done under supervision of this office, you will also ascertain and report whether the plat of the town incorporated can be used. In other words, it is desired that the work of each town be completed at the earliest practicable date and at the least expense possible.

You will also be guided by verbal instructions given you in connection with these matters, making report each week as to the progress of your work, and submitting for advice before proceeding any questions in connection with this work not heretofore covered.

All expenses incurred in each nation should be properly presented to the town site commission in that nation for payment, including pay of town-site surveyors and irregular employees.

These boundaries are being established to confine each town to its present limits as far as possible, irrespective of the incorporate limits.

The following communication was also addressed to the mayor of each town in reference to the surveying and platting of the same at their own expense. Thus far fourteen towns have indicated a desire to proceed as soon as the exterior limits are established.

I have to advise you that an act of Congress approved May 31, 1900, provides that the Secretary of the Interior is authorized, under rules and regulations to be prescribed by him, to survey, lay out, and plat into town lots, streets, alleys, and parks, the sites of such towns and villages in the Choctaw and Chickasaw nations, Indian Territory, as may at that time have a population of 200 or more, in such manner as will best subserve the then present needs and reasonable prospective growth of such towns.

It also provides that the Secretary of the Interior, when in his judgment the public interests will be thereby subserved, may permit the authorities of any town in any of said nations, at the expense of the town, to survey, lay out, and plat the site thereof, subject to his supervision and approval, as in other instances.

It further provides that the exterior limits of all town sites shall be designated and fixed at the earliest practicable date, under rules and regulations to be prescribed by the Secretary of the Interior.

Under these provisions of the law arrangements are now being made and surveying corps sent to the various towns in the Choctaw and Chickasaw nations having a population of 200 or more to establish the exterior limits of such towns. I am unable, however, at this time to state when your town will be reached for the purpose of establishing such limits, or when the same can subsequently be surveyed and platted.

If, however, the authorities of your town or the citizens thereof desire to lay out and plat same at their own expense, and will so advise me, I will endeavor to have the exterior limits established at an early date.

The act of Congress above referred to provides that as soon as the survey and plat of any town is completed and approved by the Secretary of the Interior a commission will be appointed for the purpose of appraising and disposing of the lots in said town.

Please advise me the population of your town and whether or not it is desired to take any action in reference to surveying and platting the same, as above indicated.

The governors of these nations have recently submitted a joint communication to the Department, protesting against the manner of surveying and platting towns as provided by the legislation contained in the appropriation act approved May 31, 1900, claiming same is in violation of their agreement, and concluding with the remarks that if, after considering the matter in the light of their argument and suggestions, the Department believes it to be its duty to proceed under the provisions of the Indian appropriation act, they will feel it their duty in the interest of their people to make a protest, and so far as they may be able, with the means available, to protect themselves against what they conceive to be an unwarranted innovation, regretting the necessity which impels them to such a course.

The agreement does not provide for the setting aside of any lands in the towns of the Choctaw and Chickasaw nations for park purposes, but after the passage of the Indian appropriation bill of May 31, 1900, the matter of setting aside parks under the provisions of the act of June 28, 1898, and said appropriation act was referred to the Department, and on July 10, 1900, the Department considered the question and advised me that while it is true that the town-site commissions are not expressly authorized to set aside parks under the terms of said agreement, yet it is not believed that it would be a violation of the agreement if the provisions of said section 15 of the act of Congress approved June 28, 1898, as amended by said Indian appropriation act, relative to the reservation of parks, be extended to the Choctaw and Chickasaw nations, and attention was invited to the provisions of said appropriation act authorizing the Secretary of the Interior to survey and plat towns in the Choctaw, Chickasaw, Creek, and Cherokee nations into town lots, streets, alleys, and parks.

The townsite commissions were therefore instructed, in cases where the towns desired and it is deemed for the interest of the town, to plat a suitable park, payment therefor to be made at the rate of $10 per acre, as provided by the act of June 28, 1898, and the Department has since held that where parks are deemed necessary 10 acres should be deemed sufficient.

Choctaw Nation.—During the entire winter of 1899 and 1900 there was a very serious epidemic of smallpox in the Indian Territory, and especially in the Choctaw Nation. This nation being the seat of mining operations, and the disease breaking out among the miners, taking into consideration the class of people who, as a general rule, work in mines—being negroes, foreigners, etc.—it was a difficult matter to control the disease.

The attention of the Department being called to this disease, I was directed to take the necessary steps to stamp out and prevent the spread of the same. Both the United States Indian agent and myself immediately took the matter up with the authorities of the Choctaw Nation, and as a result the work of suppressing the epidemic was taken charge of by the board of health of the Choctaw Nation, under the direction of the principal chief and the supervision of the United States Indian agent and this office, and about twenty-nine pest camps were established at different localities in the nation. Owing to the winter weather it was necessary to fit these camps out in such condition that the patients could be well cared for, providing necessary medical attention and employing the necessary nurses, guards, etc., which necessitated large expenditures. The majority of the cases reported were among miners, and it was frequently necessary to quarantine whole mining camps or towns to prevent exposed parties from spreading the disease.

Nearly 1,000 cases were treated in this nation, nearly 80 per cent being United States citizens. The board vaccinated nearly 8,000 Choctaw citizens, being able to compel such vaccination under their laws, and thus keeping the disease down to a certain extent among the Indians.

The general council of the Choctaw Nation made an appropriation of $10,000 to defray the expenses of this board in the suppression of this disease among its own citizens, and an appropriation of $50,000 was made by Congress in the Indian appropration bill, approved May 31, 1900, for the suppression of the disease among United States citizens, which appropriation applies to the disease throughout the Indian Territory.

Relative to the outbreak of the disease in the other nations I would refer to my report, as it pertains to those nations.

The accounts submitted of indebtedness incurred in the several nations have been before this office, and are now undergoing investigation preparatory to being transmitted to the Department for approval, and there is no question but what the entire appropriation has been exhausted.

For a more complete report as to the details of the work relative to this smallpox outbreak, I would refer to the report of the Indian agent.

Chickasaw Nation.—The epidemic in the Chickasaw Nation was confined largely to two points, one at Colbert and vicinity, on the Missouri, Kansas and Texas Railway, at the southeastern corner of the nation, and the other at Chickasha, in the western portion, on the Chicago, Rock Island and Pacific Railway. The citizens of both these places took charge of the suppression of the disease and paid the expenses by popular subscription, neither place being incorporated or having municipal government at the time.

An investigation into the manner that the cases were being cared for and steps taken to prevent its spread was made by this office through Dr. Fite, who was then in charge of the work in the Creek Nation. The Indian agent furnished his policemen, where necessary, to assist in quarantining infected districts.

The disease was soon stamped out at the places where it appeared, and thereafter the entire matter of looking after the same was left to the Chickasaw tribal authorities, it not being serious enough to require any particular attention or the assistance of the United States Government.

Incorporated towns assumed the expense of fighting the epidemic within their own town limits.

CHICKASAW INCOMPETENT FUND.

Under the provisions of the agreement $558,520.54 were placed to the credit of the Chickasaw Nation, of which $200,000 was appropriated by their legislature and used in the payment of their outstanding indebtedness. Their legislature also passed an act providing for the payment of the remainder of this sum, to be paid out per capita by a United States official. This act was disapproved by the President of the United States, owing to a claim of the heirs of the so-called "incompetents" to a portion of this fund. The Department held that it would have no authority under the then existing law to disburse this fund per capita to the members of the Chickasaw tribe, owing to the claim of these incompetents, but Congress, in the Indian appropriation act, approved May 31, 1900, made provisions for its disbursement as follows:

That the Secretary of the Interior be, and he is hereby, authorized and directed to pay out and distribute in the following manner the sum of two hundred and sixteen thousand six hundred and seventy-nine dollars and forty-eight cents, which amount was appropriated by the act of June twenty-eighth, eighteen hundred and ninety-eight, and credited to the "incompetent" fund of the Chickasaw Indian Nation on the books of the United States Treasury, namely: First, there shall be paid to such survivors of the original beneficiaries of said fund and to such heirs of deceased beneficiaries as shall, within six months from the passage of this act, satisfactorily establish their identity in such manner as the Secretary of the Interior may prescribe, and also the amount of such fund to which they are severally entitled, their respective shares; and, second, so much of said fund as is not paid out upon claims satisfactorily established as aforesaid shall be distributed per capita among the members of said Chickasaw Nation, and all claims of beneficiaries and their respective heirs for participation in said incompetent fund not presented within the period aforesaid shall be, and the same are hereby, barred.

Under instructions from the Department claims under this provision are to be submitted to the United States Indian agent at this place, and in compliance with such instructions the following notice was issued, under date of July 23, 1900:

Notice to Chickasaw citizens.

The Indian appropriation act, approved May 31, 1900, contains the following provision:

[Here followed the quotation of the law as given heretofore on this page.]

It will be observed that it is made the duty of the claimants to satisfactorily establish their identity in such manner as the Secretary of the Interior may prescribe and that the Secretary of the Interior is authorized and directed to pay to each person who shall establish his identity the portion of the fund to which he is entitled.

Notice is therefore hereby given that evidence tending to establish the identity of claims of Chickasaw incompetents, or descendants of those incompetents who are dead, will be received at the Union Agency up to and including October 31, 1900, and all such evidence shall be addressed to the United States Indian agent, Union Agency, Muscogee, Ind. T.

The Chickasaw Nation has a right to file evidence rebutting that filed by any particular claimant, and for that purpose shall be allowed to examine any evidence which may be submitted pertaining to any claimant.

Parties forwarding any claims should set forth in detail treaty, laws, and relationship upon which claims are based and the amount claimed. Before such claims can be considered it will be necessary for parties to satisfactorily establish their claims to such amounts independent of any payments heretorore made by the Chickasaw authorities in 1889 or at any other time.

After October 31 parties having submitted claims will be duly notified of the time when they can personally appear before the United States Indian agent for the purpose of furnishing any additional desired information or proof.

J. BLAIR SHOENFELT,
United States Indian Agent.

These notices were sent to all parties making inquiry and given due publicity, and claims are now being filed.

CHICKASAW WESTERN BOUNDARY.

The agreement with the Choctaw and Chickasaw nations provides the following:

That the United States shall survey and definitely mark and locate the ninety-eighth (98th) meridian of west longitude between Red and Canadian rivers before allotment of the lands herein provided for shall begin.

This meridian is the western boundary of the Chickasaw Nation and separates the Kiowa, Comanche, and Apache and Wichita Indian reservations from the Chickasaw Nation, and under the provisions of the legislation above quoted the Geological Survey, during the past year, reestablished said meridian, and its new location changed the boundary of the Chickasaw Nation very materially, throwing a small portion of the southwest corner of the Chickasaw Nation into the Kiowa and Comanche country, and a strip commencing at a point some 25 miles north of the southwest corner and growing in width to about 2 or 3 miles at the northwest corner of the nation was taken from the reservations named and thrown into the Chickasaw Nation.

Under date of May 23, 1900, the Department directed me to give public notice of the reestablishment of the said meridian and that the recent location of the same was the true dividing line between the said Indian reservations and the Chickasaw Nation, and allowing parties whose improvements were affected by said resurvey to make private disposal of the same to citizens of the tribe within whose reservation or nation the land so occupied was thrown. This notice was issued by me under date of June 6, 1900, and given due publicity, and I understand numerous Chickasaw citizens have made private purchases of improvements of Indians of the Kiowa, Comanche, and Wichita Agency and taken possession of their lands. A certain portion of the lands thrown into the Chickasaw Nation from the Kiowa and Comanche Reservation was covered by grazing leases made by the Department, and all parties were advised that they could not take possession of these lands so leased until the expiration of the time to which pasturage had been paid by such lessees.

CREEKS AND CHEROKEES.

The population of the Creeks aggregates about 16,000 citizens, who have 3,040,000 acres within their territory, while the Cherokees number about 35,000 persons, and the area of their domain is about

5,031,351 acres, although the census of their people has not yet been completed by the commission to the Five Civilized Tribes.

Both of these nations are under the general provisions of the act of Congress approved June 28, 1898, commonly known as the "Curtis act."

The Creeks entered into an agreement with the commission to the Five Civilized Tribes for the allotment of their lands in September, 1897, which agreement was ratified by Congress, but defeated by the majority vote of the Creek people. Subsequently another agreement was entered into and ratified by their people, but not confirmed by Congress. In March last another agreement was effected and submitted to Congress, but as yet it has not been confirmed.

The Cherokees also entered into an agreement in February, 1899, which was ratified by their people and submitted to Congress to be ratified before March 4 of the same year. Subsequently their council extended the time of ratification by Congress to July 1, 1900, but no action was taken in reference to the same. In March last another agreement was entered into and submitted to Congress, but up to this time has failed of confirmation.

The Curtis act provides that the lands in these nations heretofore held in common under tribal laws shall be equally allotted to citizens thereof, making reservations for towns, schools, cemeteries, and other purposes, and also providing that mineral lands should be reserved for allotment and leased for a term of fifteen years under regulations of the Secretary of the Interior, and further, making it a penalty for any person to hold more than his pro rata share of the lands of the tribe until finally allotted to him. The act also abolished the Indian courts of these nations, giving full jurisdiction to the United States courts and directing that all rents and royalties due the tribes should be paid into the Treasury of the United States, under rules and regulations of the Secretary of the Interior, and that all moneys due from the United States Government should not, as previously, be paid to officers of the tribe for disbursement, but that all payments should be made by an officer of the Interior Department.

MINING.

Leases or licenses for the purpose of mining have in years past been granted by the tribal authorities of these nations under authority of their laws, which contracts covered a term of years.

The agreements entered into between these nations and the commission to the Five Civilized Tribes heretofore mentioned, as also those now pending before Congress, provided that all lands should be allotted absolutely to citizens, including any mineral found thereon, and protests have been filed with the Department by the authorities of the nations against the granting of any mineral leases as provided by section 13 of the Curtis act. In compliance with departmental directions, therefore, all interested parties were advised that applications for leases under said Curtis act would only be considered for the particular 640 acres upon which actual improvements had theretofore been made, or money expended in developing and operating mines under former tribal leases.

The Cudahy Oil Company, the Cherokee Oil and Gas Company, and Mr. Benjamin D. Pennington, in August last, filed applications for 290 oil leases of 640 acres each in the two nations, but in view of the protests of the tribal authorities against the granting of any mineral leases, the Department has not considered the same to the present time. Numerous other applications have also been made for coal, lead, and zinc in both the Creek and Cherokee nations, but, carrying out the policy of the Department, the same have not been considered, but simply placed on file in this office.

Therefore no formal mineral leases under the provisions of the act of Congress approved June 28, 1898, for a term of years, have been granted in either the Creek or Cherokee nations.

I would state, however, that the Kansas and Arkansas Valley Railway was given a permit by the Secretary of the Interior for a term of fifteen years from September 28, 1899, for the purpose of procuring gravel from the bars and bed of the Grand River in the Cherokee Nation, to be used as ballast and otherwise improving the property of the said railway. This permit provided that a royalty of 2 cents per cubic yard be paid the United States Indian agent for the benefit of the Cherokee Nation.

In the Cherokee Nation three permits have been granted, by authority of the Department, allowing parties to continue temporarily to mine coal for the purposes of shipment, where mines had formerly been operated under tribal leases. These parties were John Bullette, of Claremore, Ind. T., Taxanna Wooley, of Tulsa, Ind. T., and W. S. Edwards, of the Horsepen Coal and Mining Company, operating near Collinsville, on the line of railroad recently built to that point. The permit of Mr. Edwards, however, was afterwards revoked, by authority of the Department.

Also, under departmental authority, numerous citizens of these tribes having coal upon lands which they in good faith claim as their prospective allotments, and of which they are in actual possession, have been permitted to mine and sell same in limited quantities, for local consumption only.

In the Creek Nation, under the same circumstances as in the Cherokee Nation, a permit was granted Mr. E. H. Brown, of Dawson, Ind. T., to mine coal to ship, he having also formerly operated his mine near that place under tribal license of the Creek Nation.

A royalty, the same as prescribed in the Choctaw and Chickasaw nations, of 8 cents per ton mine run is paid to the United States Indian agent on all coal mined, and the amount so realized has been $3,856.01 for the Cherokee Nation and $3,023.27 for the Creek Nation from July 1, 1899, to June 30, 1900, which has been placed to the credit of the respective nations.

TRIBAL TAXES.

In the Cherokee Nation taxes are levied as follows:

Citizen merchants are taxed one-fourth of 1 per cent of the first cost of all merchandise as per bills of purchase.

They are also taxed 50 cents per head for all cattle introduced or purchased from noncitizens who have introduced them into the nation and 25 cents per head per annum grazing tax.

Peddlers are taxed 5 per cent of the amount of goods sold.

Noncitizens, traders in Canadian District (being that portion lying south of the Arkansas River) are not required to pay tax. This condition is the result of the operation of the treaty of 1866, under which the Southern (or Confederate) Cherokees returned to the Cherokee

Nation, settled in Canadian District, and were guaranteed certain privileges and rights, without reference to the Cherokee council, the right to select traders being one of such privileges.

Itinerant venders of drugs, nostrums, etc., are taxed $50 per month.

A tax of 20 cents per ton is levied upon prairie hay cut for sale or shipment.

The Creek tribal laws provide for the following taxes: On merchants, 1 per cent of first cost of goods or merchandise offered for sale; on physicians, $25 per annum; on lawyers, $25 per annum; the various other professionals and tradesmen are taxed amounts ranging from $6 to $250 per annum.

These taxes are paid to the United States Indian agent, Union Agency, and are by him placed to the credit of the tribe in the United States Treasury.

These tribal laws are still considered in force, and the Department has held that under the provisions of the act of Congress approved June 28, 1898 (30 Stat., 495), the tribal officers were prohibited from receiving same, and it became the duty of the Secretary of the Interior, under rules and regulations to be prescribed by him, to collect the revenues due the various nations, and deposit same to the credit of the respective tribes to which they belonged; therefore such taxes are paid to the United States Indian agent and deposited as stated.

Section 16 of the Curtis act provides:

That it shall be unlawful for any person, after the passage of this act, except as hereinafter provided, to claim, demand, or receive, for his own use or for the use of anyone else, any royalty on oil, coal, asphalt, or other mineral, or on any timber or lumber, or any other kind of property whatsoever, or any rents on any lands or property belonging to any one of said tribes or nations in said Territory, or for anyone to pay to any individual any such royalty or rents or any consideration therefor whatsoever; and all royalties and rents hereafter payable to the tribe shall be paid, under such rules and regulations as may be prescribed by the Secretary of the Interior, into the Treasury of the United States to the credit of the tribe to which they belong: *Provided*, That where any citizen shall be in possession of only such amount of agricultural or grazing lands as would be his just and reasonable share of the lands of his nation or tribe and that to which his wife and minor children are entitled, he may continue to use the same or receive the rents thereon until allotment has been made to him: *Provided further*, That nothing herein contained shall impair the rights of any member of a tribe to dispose of any timber contained on his, her, or their allotment.

The Department has held under this provision that the revenues due the nations should be collected by the Interior Department.

Section 2058 of the Revised Statutes of the United States also provides:

Each Indian agent shall, within his agency, manage and superintend intercourse with the Indians agreeably to law, and execute and perform such regulations and duties, not inconsistent with law, as may be prescribed by the President, Secretary of the Interior, Commissioner of Indian Affairs, or the Superintendent of Indian Affairs.

Noncitizens of the Creek Nation have endeavored to avoid these taxes, and collections have been made only after repeated notices that nonpayment would result in parties being liable to removal as intruders in the Indian country.

The lawyers located in this nation especially objected to the payment of this tax, claiming they were officers of the United States courts, and were exempt for the reason that, living in incorporated towns, the lands were segregated from the nation, and that the tribal laws, therefore, did not apply within such incorporated limits; also, that the

Curtis act did not authorize the Secretary of the Interior to collect such taxes.

The contention of these parties was submitted to the Department for consideration, and it was held that they were liable for the tax, and I was instructed accordingly. The attorneys, upon being advised of the decision of the Department, sought to have the inspector and Indian agent enjoined from collecting this tax, or removing them from the Territory for nonpayment. A hearing was had before Hon. John R. Thomas, judge, who held that the parties were liable, and sustained the action of the Department as to the validity of the tribal tax.

The case was appealed by the attorneys to the United States court of appeals in the Indian Territory, and the decision of the lower court was unanimously sustained (see Maxey *v.* Wright, decided January 6, 1900, 54 S. W. Rep., 807), the court holding in part that—

The act of Congress approved June 7, 1897 (30 Stat., 83) provides:

"That on and after January 1, 1898, the United States courts in the Indian Territory shall have original and exclusive jurisdiction and authority to try and determine all civil causes in law and equity thereafter instituted; * * * and the laws of the United States and the laws of Arkansas in force in the Territory shall apply to all persons therein, irrespective of race, the said courts exercising jurisdiction thereof as now conferred upon them in the trial of like causes."

While it is true that this act had the effect of abolishing the courts of the Indian tribes, which of course included those of the Creek Nation, and regulating all causes of action to the United States courts for trial, yet the executive and legislative departments of the Indian governments were retained, and the treaty provisions and intercourse laws and other statutes relating to the Indian Territory remained in full force. The full control of the Indian Department over those Indian tribes as they then existed was not interfered with, nor were the Indian statutes annulled, except so far as all jurisdiction was taken from their courts and transferred to those of the United States. The power to remove intruders for the causes assigned by treaty provisions or statutory law still remains as before in the Interior Department of the Government, and the act of Congress approved June 28, 1898, entitled, "An act for the protection of the people of the Indian Territory, and for other purposes" (30 Stat., 495), commonly called the Curtis bill, from beginning to end recognizes this continued authority of the Interior Department, and in many instances enlarges it.

The contention that the Creek Nation is not now an Indian reservation is not tenable. Whatever effect the Curtis bill may have had on the Creeks, it has not yet been carried into operation so far as it changes their title to their lands or their tribal relations to the United States. * * *

Nor does the fact that Congress, by the provisions of the Curtis bill, has provided for the creation of cities and towns in this nation, and for the extinguishment of the Indian title to the lands embraced within the limits of such municipal corporations, alter the case, because this provision of that bill has not yet been carried into effect, and the Indian title to such lands still remains in them, and it is yet their country. * * *

On the whole case we therefore hold that a lawyer who is a white man and not a citizen of the Creek Nation is, pursuant to their statute, required to pay for the privilege of remaining and practicing his profession in that nation the sum of $25; that if he refuse the payment thereof he becomes by virtue of the treaty an intruder, and that in such case the Government of the United States may remove him from the nation, and that this duty devolves upon the Interior Department. * * *

We are of the opinion, however, that the Indian agent, when directed by the Secretary of the Interior, may collect this money for the Creeks. The intercourse laws (sec. 2058, R. S., U. S.) provide that:

Each Indian agent shall, within his agency, manage and superintend the intercourse with the Indians, agreeably to law, and execute and perform such regulations and duties, not inconsistent with law, as may be prescribed by the President, the Secretary of the Interior, the Commissioner of Indian Affairs, or the Superintendent of Indian Affairs."

In this case the Indian agent was acting in strict accordance with directions and regulations of the Secretary of the Interior, in a matter clearly relating to intercourse with the Indians, and when it is remembered that up to the time that the United States courts were established in the Indian Territory the only remedy for the collection of this tax was by removal, that the Indian nations had no power to collect it except through the intervention of the Interior Department, it is quite clear that if in the best judgment of that Department it was deemed wise to take charge of the matter and collect this money and turn it over to the Indians, it has the power to do so under its superintending control of the Indians and the intercourse of white men with them granted by various acts of Congress; and in our opinion that power has not been taken away by any subsequent act of Congress or treaty stipulation. (Appendix No. 13, p. 152.)

An appeal was taken by these lawyers to the United States circuit court of appeals for-the eighth district, but which court has not as yet rendered an opinion.

From July 1, 1898, to June 30, 1899, but few remittances were received on account of taxes in the Creek Nation, there being no means of ascertaining what payments were due, or to enforce such payments, but about July 1, 1899, the Department appointed one revenue inspector for each of the Creek and Cherokee nations, each inspector having three assistant or district inspectors, whose duties are to ascertain the names of persons or firms throughout these two nations liable to the tax, see that payments are made, and to investigate and make reports concerning illegal timber cutting, introduction of cattle, etc.

In the Creek Nation from July 1, 1898, to June 30, 1899, before the appointment of the revenue inspectors, there was remitted to the United States Indian agent $4,913.63, while from July 1, 1899, to June 30, 1900, there has been collected from all sources $26,370.19, and the expense of the revenue inspectors in this nation during that time has been $4,884.52. The sources of revenue have been as follows:

Coal royalty	$3,023.27
Merchandise and occupation tax	18,811.27
Pasture tax	4,344.65
Seized lumber	191.00
Total	26,370.19

There are within the limits of the Creek Nation thirty-four towns, villages, or trading posts where those subject to the operation of the Creek license law are engaged in business. The list of persons residing within the limits of the Creek Nation who are subject to the operation of this law includes the names of 549 individuals or firms. These figures do not include Creek citizens, noncitizen Indians, or intermarried noncitizens.

The collection of this tax requires the constant attention of the revenue inspectors, as parties decline to remit until repeatedly requested, both orally and in writing, many contending that the receipts of the business in which they are engaged do not provide sufficient for their living expenses, but they desire to remain here until the country is opened for settlement. A few have closed their places of business rather than pay the required tax. Thus far no removals have been made from the Creek Nation for nonpayment of taxes.

The license law of the Creek Nation provides a tax on each banking establishment of one-half of 1 per cent of the capital stock invested, assessment to be made on the bank on account of the shares thereof. Under this law demand was made of all banks doing business for such tax, but the national banks refused to make payment, claiming they were exempt, and the question was therefore submitted by the Department to the Assistant Attorney-General for an opinion as to whether said tax could be collected, and in case of refusal whether there was

any legal remedy to enforce the collection thereof, and under date of
January 25, 1900, the Assistant-Attorney General rendered an opinion
which was approved by the Secretary of the Interior on the same date,
in which he held that an attempt to make the law on the Creek Nation
apply to national banks would come into conflict with the laws of the
United States, and that therefore said tax could not be collected.

Under the provisions of the Curtis Act, all former tribal grazing
leases in the Creek Nation were made void and terminated on April 1,
1899, and citizens were, therefore, allowed to rent their pro rata shares
of the lands of the tribe. Many large pastures or inclosed tracts were
therefore selected by citizens who rented such shares to cattlemen,
although in many instances such leases did not cover the entire pasture. In such instances, under authority of the Department, settlements were made with the cattlemen for the rent of such land not
selected by any citizen, and during the past year ended June 30, 1900,
$4,344.65 was so paid for the benefit of the tribe. The necessary
investigation of amounts so due has required considerable labor on the
part of the revenue inspector.

This work has also brought the inspectors into constant touch with
many citizens and others, and has been of material assistance in the
settlement of controversies constantly arising. Much time has also
been required by the inspectors to make investigations concerning the
unlawful cutting of timber, which is now practically under control.
During the past year $191 has been paid to the Indian agent for the
credit of the tribe for timber unlawfully cut and seized.

In the Cherokee Nation there was remitted from July 1, 1898, to
June 30, 1899, prior to the appointment of the revenue inspectors,
$3,150.87, while during the past year there has been collected from all
sources $19,455.05, and the expense of the revenue inspectors in this
nation during this time has been $5,833.01. The sources of revenue
have been as follows:

Coal royalty	$3,856.01
Merchandise and occupation tax	5,607.65
Hay royalty	4,474.88
Gravel royalty	100.00
Ferry tax	504.19
Cattle tax	1,956.00
Town lots	74.02
Seized lumber	250.00
Permit tax	2.00
Board of teachers at academies	2,330.77
Unexpended balance school fund	299.53
Total	19,455.05

There are 450 firms of citizens located in 82 towns and villages from
whom taxes have been collected, though many refuse to pay until
notified repeatedly and finally given a certain time to remit or close
their places of business.

In June, however, one W. C. Rogers, a mixed-blood Indian of the
Cherokee Nation, and well-to-do citizen, conducting several merchandise stores in said nation, refused to pay the required tax and his
place of business was closed, in compliance with Departmental instructions under date of September 22, 1899, to close the place of business
of any citizen of the Cherokee Nation who refused to pay the tax due
under regulations of the Department, after due notice had been given.
Mr. Rogers applied to the United States court for a temporary

restraining order against the officials of the Interior Department, and the same was granted, temporarily restraining them from interfering with his business. His store was therefore only actually closed three days.

The hearing on the merits of the case as to the authority of the Interior Department to close his store or collect this tax was had before Hon. Joseph A. Gill, United States judge for the northern district of the Indian Territory, at Vinita, on July 23 last, at which time the case was extensively argued and briefs filed, there appearing eight of the leading attorneys of the northern judicial district for the plaintiff, two of whom were paid attorneys for the Cherokee Nation, and United States District Attorney P. L. Soper appearing for the Government, and who made an extensive argument on the subject. Since that time the merchants generally in the Cherokee Nation have declined to make payment pending the result of this case.

On September 3, 1900, the court rendered its opinion in this case, making the injunction perpetual and holding that section 16 of the Curtis Act, authorizing the collection of "rents and royalties," did not include "taxes," and therefore the Secretary of the Interior had no authority to collect such from a Cherokee citizen.

The complete opinion is attached. (Appendix No. 14, p. 157.)

The tribal laws also provide for an introduction tax of 50 cents per head on cattle brought into the nation, with an additional annual grazing tax of 25 cents per head on all cattle so introduced.

During the past year there has been paid to the United States Indian agent $1,956 from this source.

Many questions and contentions have been made regarding the legality of this cattle tax, and prior to the passage of the Curtis Act it appears the nation collected little, if any, money from such source. It has been found by the revenue inspectors almost impracticable to ascertain the amount due or procure desired information in reference thereto, as interested parties use every means possible to avoid the payment of the tax, rendering it difficult to ascertain whether stock running at large was introduced, or native stock, upon which no tax is assessed.

The Cherokee tribal laws require the payment of 20 cents per ton on all hay shipped from the limits of the nation.

It appears prior to the passage of the Curtis Act the nation collected but little of this tax or royalty. During the year ending June 30, 1899, there was received by the Indian agent only $16.40 from this source, although much hay was shipped. After the appointment of the revenue inspectors, who gave this matter their personal attention, there was received from July 1, 1899, to June 30, 1900, $4,474.88.

Every means possible has been resorted to by noncitizens and others to avoid the payment of this tax. A noncitizen and resident of the Indian Territory was removed therefrom, under section 2149 of the Revised Statutes, for refusal to pay this hay royalty. Subsequently he returned and was arrested for so doing under section 2148 of the Revised Statutes, which provides:

If any person who has been removed from the Indian country shall thereafter at any time return or be found within the Indian country, he shall be liable to a penalty of one thousand dollars.

This case was tried before a jury, who were instructed by the court that the only question for determination was whether he had been removed and had returned, and as he was present during the trial, acknowledging on the witness stand that he had been removed, which fact was also corroborated by the Indian policeman who had removed him, there did not appear to be much doubt as to his guilt, but the jury could not agree. Subsequently the case against him was dismissed, and he again removed, but was permitted to return temporarily, owing to illness in his family. He has recently asked to be allowed to remain in the Indian Territory, promising a compliance with departmental regulations, and this request has been submitted to the Department for consideration.

The railroads, in compliance with a request from the Department, have issued orders to their station agents in the Cherokee Nation not to receive any hay for shipment until the royalty on same has been paid, and as a consequence payments are now promptly made by shippers.

Recently an action was also brought in the United States court before Hon. Joseph A. Gill, judge, seeking to enjoin the officers of the Department from collecting this hay tax, but no decision in the matter has yet been rendered by the court. Previously it was sought to recover hay seized by the Indian agent for nonpayment by replevin proceedings before the United States commissioner, but the matter was decided in favor of the Government, not permitting the plaintiff to procure possession of the hay.

In connection with the action of the Department in collecting the revenues of the Cherokee Nation, in December, 1899, the national council of the Cherokee Nation passed an act, which was approved by the principal chief on December 5, 1899, authorizing and requesting the Secretary of the Interior to collect all revenues due or which might become due to the Cherokee Nation under its tribal laws, and also authorizing the Secretary of the Interior to make such rules and regulations as he might deem advisable for the more certain and speedy collection of said revenues. This act, however, was disapproved by the President of the United States on January 6, 1900, for the reason that the Department held that the authority of the Secretary relative to the revenues of the Cherokee Nation is clearly defined in section 16 of the Curtis Act, and that no act of the Cherokee council could enlarge or modify the authority given by an act of Congress.

Much time of the revenue inspectors has also been spent in investigating reports and procuring evidence concerning illegal timber cutting in the Cherokee Nation.

EDUCATION.

The act of Congress approved June 28, 1898 (30 Stat., sec. 19, 495), provides:

That no payment of any moneys on any account whatever shall hereafter be made by the United States to any of the tribal governments or to any officer thereof for disbursement, but payments of all sums to members of said tribes shall be made under the direction of the Secretary of the Interior, by an officer appointed by him, and per capita payments shall be made direct to each individual in lawful money of the United States, and the same shall not be liable for the payment of any previously contracted obligations.

Under this provision the Secretary of the Interior assumed supervision of the schools of the Creek and Cherokee nations, under the direction of the superintendent of schools in the Indian Territory, with a supervisor located in each nation.

The Cherokees maintain 3 boarding schools, which are large, substantial, 3-story brick buildings, built at large expense. They also have a colored high school, and the enrollment of these 4 schools during the nine months of the past year has been 438, with an average attendance of 332, costing $45,755, or $137.81 per capita. They have also maintained, seven months of the year, 124 neighborhood or day schools, with an enrollment of 3,920 and an average attendance of 2,195, at a cost of $30,380, or $13.98 per capita, making a total enrollment of 4,358 pupils, with an average attendance of 2,527, at a cost of $76,135. It is estimated that there are about 8,340 Cherokee Indian children of school age.

In the Creek Nation there has been maintained nine months during the year 9 boarding and 55 neighborhood or day schools. The boarding schools have had an enrollment of 640 pupils, with an average attendance of 506, at a cost of $52,433.65, or $113.92 per capita, while at the neighborhood schools there has been an enrollment of 1,745, with an average attendance of 1,042, costing $13,223.42, or $12.68 per capita, making a total enrollment of 2,385 pupils attending all the schools, with an average attendance of 1,548, at an aggregate cost of $65.657.07.

The schools in the Creek and Cherokee nations are conducted under the tribal laws, and under the supervision of the general superintendent of schools in the Indian Territory, and supervisors, who also hold the examinations of teachers, and see that only competent persons receive appointments to such positions.

Appropriations are made by the respective councils of the nations for the maintenance of schools, and warrants are issued by the principal chiefs in accordance with their laws in payment of services of superintendents and other employees and support of the different schools. These warrants are approved by the supervisor of schools for each nation before being circulated, and the accounts for all expenditures are also investigated and approved in like manner. Warrants are paid by the United States Indian agent semiannually, from interest on funds of the tribes held in trust by the United States Government.

The agreements with these nations now pending before Congress make ample provisions for schools and the manner of conducting the same.

TOWN SITES.

No towns have been surveyed and platted in the Cherokee Nation under the provisions of the Curtis Act.

In the Creek Nation there have been two townsite commissions appointed, one for Muscogee and one for Wagoner, each commission consisting of three persons, one appointed by the Secretary of the Interior, one to represent the tribe, and one selected by the town. Both of the above-named towns were visited with disastrous fires, and the residents therefore asked that townsite commissions be appointed to survey and plat the same according to Government survey before rebuilding. The commission for Muscogee was appointed in April, 1899, consisting of Mr. Dwight W. Tuttle, of Connecticut, chairman; Mr. John Adams, appointed on behalf of the town, and Mr. Benjamin Marshal, a Creek citizen, representing the nation, appointed by the Secretary of the Interior, the principal chief declining to make the appointment under the terms of the Curtis Act.

The plat of Muscogee has been approved by the Department, and includes 2,444.76 acres. Appraisements have also been made and approved by the Secretary of the Interior. The appraisements of lots aggregates $236,136, and the expense of the commission to August 1, 1900, has been $15,022.57.

The law requires that all vacant or unimproved lots shall be sold at public auction at not less than their appraised value, while the holders of improved lots are permitted to purchase same at one-half of their appraised value, 10 per cent of which must be paid within two months from notice, and in the event of nonpayment lots are to be sold at auction. Such notices to holders have been issued by the commission, but on August 23, 1900, the principal chief of the nation, in conjunction with a citizen holder of a lot, made application to the United States court to have the commission enjoined from advertising or selling any of the lots, alleging illegality of the Curtis Act, and claiming the nation has not yet given consent for the sale of any lots or lands of the tribe. This application for injunction was granted temporarily by Hon. John R. Thomas, United States judge, on August 25, 1900, he holding practically that the Curtis Act is unconstitutional and that no action leading to the disposition of any of the property or lands of the tribe could be taken by the United States Government or by Congress without an agreement or the consent of the nation. The Department has therefore furloughed the members of the commission indefinitely without pay.

The commission at Wagoner was appointed in August, 1899, and consists of Dr. H. C. Linn; Mr. John H. Roark, on behalf of the town, and Mr. Tony Proctor, a Creek citizen, appointed by the chief of the tribe. The plat of this town has just been completed, although the appraisements have not yet been agreed upon by the members of the commission. The area of this town as surveyed and platted is 2,700 acres, and the expense of the commission to August 1, 1900, has been $9,967.16.

SMALLPOX.

Cherokee Nation.—While smallpox was reported early in the winter in the Choctaw Nation, it was not brought to the attention of this office to any extent until in the spring of 1900 in the Cherokee Nation, when it was reported among the Indians in the rural districts, about 18 miles east of Vinita, and before the danger was recognized there were about 65 cases reported in that vicinity.

Prompt steps were taken at once to look after the disease, and the board of health of the nation was given full charge of the supervision of the disease, and several United States policemen detailed to assist them in the enforcing of their orders. The principal chief directed the board to use every possible effort to eradicate the disease, and to cooperate with the Government officials of this Department.

While the disease was of a mild form, there was no doubt as to its being smallpox, and the exceptionally warm winter without question prevented the cases from being as serious as is usually the case.

It was stated that the most serious outbreak was in the Choctaw Nation, and this is probably true, considering the class of patients treated and the difficulty in quarantining towns and camps, but viewing the matter from the standpoint of length of time the disease raged it was quite serious in the Cherokee Nation, it only commencing in April, 1900, and there being treated after that time over 800 cases.

Considerable difficulty was experienced for a time over the methods and authority of the board in their action in preventing the spread of this disease, but the people soon realized the importance of the work of the board, and the disease was gradually stamped out.

The larger per cent of the cases treated in this nation were United States citizens, and the expense incident thereto will be paid from the appropriation made by Congress in the Indian appropriation act approved May 31, 1900, while the expense incurred in the treating of Cherokee citizens will be borne by the Cherokee Nation. The accounts, as submitted by the board of health, are now undergoing investigation prior to their submission to the Department.

The Indian agent, in his report submitted herewith, goes into detail concerning the work of suppressing the smallpox in this nation, and attention is invited thereto.

Creek Nation.—Under directions of the Department, the United States Indian agent, under supervision of this office, upon the breaking out of smallpox in the Creek Nation in November, 1899, immediately took charge of suppressing the disease, and placed Dr. F. B. Fite, a physician of Muscogee, in direct charge, and camps were established and other necessary steps taken to eradicate the epidemic, such as quarantining infected districts, vaccinating, etc. Dr. Fite, therefore, continued in charge of this work until about the middle of March, 1900, when the matter was turned over to the board of health of the Creek Nation, under the direction of the principal chief, and this board continued in charge until the disease was finally stamped out.

The outbreak in the Creek Nation was principally among Indians, and for that reason it was difficult to control; but the number of cases treated was quite small compared with the Choctaw and Cherokee Nation, therefore the expense incident thereto was considerably less.

The accounts for this indebtedness, like those for the other nations, are being investigated, and will in due time, when all are prepared for submission, be transmitted for the approval of the Department.

In connection with the epidemic in the Creek Nation, it is a notable fact that in the locality where smallpox raged the winter preceding, the expenses of which were authorized and paid by the Department, there was no smallpox during the recent epidemic, the disease being confined to entirely different districts.

Considerable trouble was experienced at times to procure the services of competent physicians to make necessary investigations or attend to cases in infected districts, owing to exposure to disease and a consequent loss of their own practice.

The United States Indian agent goes fully into the treatment of the disease in his report, and I would respectfully refer to the same.

The expense of suppressing the disease in incorporated towns was assumed by the towns in both the Creek and Cherokee nations.

CONSTITUTIONALITY OF THE CURTIS ACT.

On May 15, 1900, Hon. John R. Thomas, United States judge, in the case of John McGrath *v*. Lem Aldridge et al., involving possession of Cherokee lands—the defendant having taken possession of a part of the plaintiff's land, alleging in justification thereof that the latter was in possession of more than he was allowed by the Curtis Act—handed down the following opinion, holding that the Curtis law was in conflict with the Constitution of the United States—that no person shall be deprived of his property without due process of law—and therefore wholly inoperative to take away a portion of the citizen's holding upon the plea that he was holding more than his proportionate share of the tribal lands:

The agreed statement of acts presents the question of the right of a citizen not in possession of land in the Cherokee Nation to take possession of lands of the Cherokee Nation without reference to the fact that another party has it in his possession for the purpose of making a homestead.

This land of the Cherokee Nation was patented to them by the Government of the United States, and by virtue of the several treaties entered into between the Government of the United States and the Cherokee Nation it was provided that the Cherokee Nation should have the right of government in all domestic affairs. It is provided by the first treaty entered into between the Government of the United States and the Cherokee Nation, and the same provision has been ratified in each succeeding treaty, that no law passed by the Cherokee Nation should be in violation of the Constitution of the United States. If the Constitution of the United States of its own force does not become operative over all possessions of the United States, that matter has been disposed of by agreement, and it does not come within the same rule which is claimed to govern the island of Porto Rico on the one hand or the Philippine Islands on the other. This is a government of the people, by the people, and for the people, and the fundamental law governing a people governs every inch of their possessions.

The Constitution of the United States is put in force here. The Cherokee law provides, among other things, that citizens of the Cherokee Nation may go upon the public domain and make improvements, and that these improvements become an inheritable estate. It is provided by the constitution of the Cherokee Nation, and this is not in conflict with the Constitution of the United States, that the improvements made by a citizen of the Cherokee Nation are not subject to attachment or sale under execution. It is a vested property right. By provision of the fifth article of the amendments to the Constitution of the United States it is provided that a person shall not be deprived of life, liberty, or property without due process of law. The Supreme Court of the United States and other courts of last resort have decided that an act of Congress is not "due process of law." In order to be due process of law there must be an action brought in a court of competent jurisdiction, where the rights of the plaintiff are presented on one hand and the rights of defendant are presented by way of answer, and then the question at issue be determined judicially by the court. That has been decided to be due process of law. The Congress of the United States has endeavored in the seventeenth and eighteenth sections of the Curtis Act to say that citizens subject to the Constitution, its amenities and protection, may be deprived of property which the law of the Cherokee Nation and the Constitution of the United States authorizes them to hold and enjoy, without due process of law. This court decides that that can not legally be done.

The court further decides that one citizen can not take it upon himself to determine that another man has in his possession more than his proportionate share of the public domain of the Cherokee Nation. There is not a man alive to-day who can say what the proportionate share of a citizen of the Cherokee Nation is. That is a matter that can only be determined when allotment is made, or when the public domain has been measured—when it is known exactly how much there is of it, and when a census has been made and it is known to the single individual the number of Cherokee citizens. Then and not until then would it be possible to determine what the proportionate share of a Cherokee citizen is.

The court will not say that the Cherokee Nation, by proper process, might not proceed to condemn—if it were discovered after allotment that a man had in his possession more than his proportionate share—that the Cherokee Nation as a government and as the representative of this common property might not proceed to have this property condemned, giving compensation to the owner of the property for his improvements, and then throw it open for settlement or selection as a part of the public domain, but he can not be deprived of it without due process of law, and until it is determined that he has more than he is entitled to even the Cherokee Nation can not have him dispossessed. One citizen can not say: "Here, John Jones, you have more than you are entitled to. I have been lazy and improvident and have not tried to get a farm. You have gone to work and opened out this possession and made the improvement under the law. You have more than your share, and I am going to take it for my home." John Jones says: "You will not take it until I have been paid for my improvements."

The Curtis bill is very sweeping. It contains many provisions and is capable of many constructions. It is the first serious attempt the court has ever seen of Congress attempting to repeal an amendment of the Constitution by an act of Congress. But the court is of the opinion that the Curtis bill does not repeal the Constitution of the United States, nor any of its provisions, and is wholly inoperative, since the Cherokee Nation has not entered into a treaty authorizing the allotment of their common property.

What the condition of affairs might be if there had been a treaty entered into between the Cherokee Nation and the United States Government authorizing the allotment of their lands—disturbing the present title—is quite another thing. This land was bought and paid for by the Cherokee Indians with their own money and their own property. It was patented to them. It has been urged that Congress has the right to govern them as it sees fit; that they are wards of the Government, in other words, minors, and that the Government has the right to rule them; but it appears to me that that view would hardly be justified by law, and in fact the court thinks it could not be tolerated for a minute. These Indians were regarded as of age and able to contract when the Government bought their property from them, when they bought the Cherokee Strip and their lands in Georgia and Tennessee. The plea of infancy can only be pleaded by the infant and not by the other party. The Government can not plead that these are infants, since the Government by its own contract recognizes their right to contract.

On May 22 last I transmitted a copy of this opinion to the Department, which was referred to the Assistant Attorney-General for the Interior Department, who, under date of June 26, 1900, rendered an opinion, approved by the Department, wherein he expressed the opinion that the Department should proceed with the administration of the act, leaving the question of its constitutionality, and the authority to proceed thereunder, to be determined when it shall be raised in connection with some action taken in compliance with its requirements.

In this connection I would refer to the directions of the Department to the Muscogee town-site commission, through this office, to proceed with the sale of town lots under the provisions of the Curtis Act, and to the fact that an application for injunction was brought before Judge Thomas, and the same granted as stated in my report heretofore, referring to town sites in the Creek and Cherokee nations, the court again holding that the Curtis Act is unconstitutional.

Again on July 9, 1900, in an action brought before Judge Thomas at Muscogee, to restrain the officers of the Interior Department from interfering with the property of a Creek citizen, in a case where the Indian agent had taken steps to remove a fence from lands filed upon by another Creek citizen, a temporary order was granted, and the court virtually held that the Curtis Act was unconstitutional, and that no property of a citizen could be taken from him except by due process of law, that an act of Congress was not due process of law, and the said Curtis Act was inoperative because the Creek Nation had not entered into an agreement authorizing the allotment of their common property.

As yet, however, the case has not been heard on its merits, or the restraining order made permanent.

In this connection, and as one of the results of the decisions of Judge Thomas concerning the constitutionality of the Curtis act, I would respectfully quote herewith a copy of a newspaper item, which has been printed in a number of the local papers in the Territory, and daily papers of Kansas City and St. Louis, Mo., having circulation in this locality:

Court notes.—As the Curtis bill has been declared null and void, I hereby give notice to all Cherokee citizens that I will convene court in Claremore the first Monday in January, 1901, and all Cherokee citizens will govern themselves accordingly.— WATT STARR, *Judge, Cooweescoowee District.*

It would seem, however, that the United States Supreme Court, in the case of Stevens *v.* Cherokee Nation (174 U. S., p. 445), had practically passed upon the question of the constitutionality of the Curtis act. Although the case deals principally with the question of citizenship, the court quotes various sections of the Curtis act, and states:

* * * Conceding the constitutionality of the legislation otherwise, we need spend no time upon it.

Also:

* * * But it is "well settled that an act of Congress may supersede a prior treaty and that any questions that may arise are beyond the sphere of judicial cognizance, and must be met by the political department of the Government." (Thomas *v.* Gay, 169 U. S., 264,271, and cases cited.) * * *

The judgments in these cases were rendered before the passage of the act of June 28, 1898, commonly known as the Curtis act, and necessarily the effect of that act was not considered. As, however, the provision for an appeal to this court was made after the passage of the act, some observations upon it are required, and, indeed, the inference is not unreasonable that a principal object intended to be secured by an appeal was the testing of the constitutionality of this act, and that may have had controlling weight in inducing the granting of the right to such appeal.

The act is comprehensive and sweeping in its character, and notwithstanding the abstract of it in the statement prefixed to this opinion, we again call attention to its provisions. * * *

The twenty-sixth section provided that, after the passage of the act, "the laws of the various tribes or nations of Indians shall not be enforced at law or in equity by the courts of the United States in the Indian Territory;" and the twenty-eighth section, that after July 1, 1898, all tribal courts in the Indian Territory should be abolished.

The court concludes with the remark:

As we hold the entire legislation constitutional, the result is that all the judgments must be affirmed.

TRIBAL GOVERNMENTS.

Creek Nation.—The laws of this nation provide for the following officers:

Principal chief, second chief, auditor, superintendent of public instruction, private secretary to chief, janitor at capitol, and superintendents of six boarding and two orphan schools. The principal and second chief are each elected for four years by popular vote; the auditor, superintendent of public instruction, and janitor are selected by the national council; the private secretary is appointed by the principal chief, and the superintendents of boarding and orphan schools are appointed by the superintendent of public instruction.

The lawmaking body consists of a "House of Kings" (senate), with 47 members, and a "House of Warriors" (house), with 97 members, making what is known as their general council, and these members are elected by popular vote each four years, and who receive a compensation of $4 per diem and 10 cents per mile.

During the past fiscal year the council of the Creek Nation met in regular session in October and November, and the appropriation made by the council for its own expenses amounted to $22,281.15. In view of the fact that the newly elected principal chief took office on the 1st of December, he immediately called a special session of the council, and the appropriation made by such council for its own expenses amounted to $7,629.60, making the total expenses for the maintenance of council alone, for its two sessions, the same being in session about forty-seven days, of $29,910.75.

The other appropriations made by these councils for the general expenses of the Creek Nation amounted to $32,377.17, making a total for the support of the tribal government of $62,287.92, in addition to the appropriation of $88,338.97 made for schools.

As provided by the act of Congress approved June 7, 1897, all the acts of the Creek and Cherokee councils are required to be submitted to the President of the United States for executive action, and therefore all these appropriation acts and other laws passed by the Creek Nation have been submitted for executive action through this office, and report thereon made to the Department.

In this connection I would state that the council of the Creek Nation during the past fiscal year passed no laws which made any changes in their government, the only acts which were passed being appropriations, with the exception of two, one providing for the taking of the census, and another defining citizenship, which were disapproved by the President for the reason that they would be in direct conflict with the United States laws providing for the taking of the census and determining of citizenship in the Creek Nation by the commission to the Five Civilized Tribes.

Cherokee Nation.—The Cherokee laws provide for the following general officers: Principal chief, assistant chief, treasurer, auditor (each four years, elected by popular vote), three executive secretaries, and three members of the board of education, appointed by the principal chief.

Their lawmaking body consists of a senate, 18 members, and a council (or lower house) of 40 members, all elected every two years, who are allowed $3 per day while in attendance at the national council.

During the fiscal year ended June 30, 1900, the council of the Cherokee Nation was in regular session during November, 1899, and inasmuch as the new principal chief went into office on the 1st of December, a special session was called during that month. The appropriations made for the expenses of the November session amounted to $14,898.50 and of the December special session to $3,450.40, making a total for the councils of $18,348.90. In addition to these appropriations, acts were passed providing for the payment of the general officers and expenses of the Cherokee Nation, amounting to $12,199.36, making a total for the general expenses of the nation, without schools, of $30,548.26. The appropriations for the support of schools made by these councils amounted to $90,637.72.

The act of Congress approved June 7, 1897, also requires the submission of all acts of the Cherokee council to the President of the United States for executive approval, and therefore all of these appropriation and other acts were submitted to the Department through this office for such action.

Few acts were passed by the sessions of the Cherokee council above mentioned except appropriations. The more important of the acts other than appropriations were the following:

An act to extend the time allowed Congress to ratify the agreement dated January 4, 1899, which was approved by the President on December 22, 1899. An act for the purpose of disposing of certain jail property belonging to the nation, approved by the President on December 22, 1899. An act repealing section 49 of the Compiled Laws of the Cherokee Nation, regulating the manner of issuing warrants and the payment of interest thereon, which was approved January 5, 1900.   An act to make an investigation of the auditor's office, which was approved on January 13, 1900.

Choctaw Nation.—The tribal officers of the Choctaw Nation consist of the following: Principal chief, elected every two years, supreme court, national secretary, treasurer, auditor, attorney, and superintendent of public instruction.   They also have a complete judiciary and police system.

Their national council is composed of a senate and house of representatives, elected by popular vote—senators for two years and representatives for one year—all of whom receive $5 per diem while the national council is in session.

Under the agreement entered into between the Choctaw and Chickasaw and the United States, as ratified in section 29 of the act of Congress approved June 28, 1898, all acts of the Choctaw and Chickasaw nations in any manner affecting the laws of the tribe or individuals or the moneys or other property of the tribe or citizens thereof, except appropriations for the regular and necessary expenses of the governments of the respective tribes, shall not be of any validity until approved by the President of the United States.

Under this provision all acts of the Choctaw council are submitted to this office for transmission to the Department for Executive action, with the exception of the appropriation acts providing for the general expenses of the Choctaw government.

During the past fiscal year the Choctaw council submitted about thirty acts, covering different subjects, all of which were transmitted with reports.

The appropriations made by the Choctaw council, as shown by an act a copy of which they have furnished for my information, but which was not required to be submitted to the President, for the support of their tribal government, shows the sum of $10,000 having been appropriated for the expenses of their national council and about $7,590 for the general officers and expenses and about $19,900 for their tribal courts.

Chickasaw Nation.—The tribal officers of the Chickasaw Nation consist of the following: Governor, elected every two years; national secretary, treasurer, auditor, sheriffs, school superintendent, and a complete judiciary—supreme, district, and county courts—and police system.

Their legislature is composed of senators and representatives, elected every two years and every year, respectively, by popular vote, who receive $4 per diem while the council is in session.

The same law, as set out in the agreement heretofore referred to, provides for the submission of all Chickasaw acts excepting those made for the regular and necessary expenses of the tribal government.

During the past year there have been submitted about twenty acts of the Chickasaw legislature, which have been reported on by me and forwarded to the Department for Executive action, as provided by law.   These acts covered various subjects, but none of them materially changed their existing laws.

I have no data at hand showing the amounts appropriated for the expense of their tribal government, but from correspondence with parties who desire Chickasaw warrants paid it appears that their finances are in bad shape, doubtless caused by nonpayment of tribal taxes.

GENERAL.

The prime object of the Government, and the most important work to be accomplished in the Indian Territory, is the allotment of the lands in severalty of citizens of the Five Civilized Tribes.

The agreement with the Choctaw and Chickasaw provides that—

The United States shall put each allottee in possession of his allotment and remove all persons therefrom objectionable to the allottee.

Section 3 of the Curtis Act also provides in part as follows:

That any person being a noncitizen in possession of lands, holding the possession thereof under an agreement, lease, or improvement contract with either of said nations or tribes, or any citizen thereof, executed prior to January first, eighteen hundred and ninety-eight, may, as to lands not exceeding in amount one hundred and sixty acres, in defense of any action for the possession of such lands, show that he is and has been in peaceable possession of said lands, and that he has while in such possession made lasting and valuable improvements thereon, and that he has not enjoyed the possession thereof a sufficient length of time to compensate him for such improvements. Thereupon the court or jury trying said cause shall determine the fair and reasonable value of such improvements and the fair and reasonable rental value of such lands for the time the same shall have been occupied by such person, and if the improvements exceed in value the amount of rents with which such person should be charged the court, in its judgment, shall specify such time as will, in the opinion of the court, compensate such person for the balance due, and award him possession for such time unless the amount be paid by claimant within such reasonable time as the court shall specify. If the finding be that the amounts of rents exceed the value of the improvements, judgment shall be rendered against the defendant for such sum, for which execution may issue.

For years citizens of these nations have rented or leased lands to white persons, many in violation of tribal laws and without any authority whatever, and but few, if any, of these leases have been properly executed or conditions complied with, the Indians, especially full-bloods, having received practically nothing for the use of the lands, while the person now in possession claims protection under section 3, above quoted. Therefore the only manner by which the Indian can secure possession of his land is to institute suit in the United States court. Many Indians, being absolutely without means, are unable to give bond or employ attorneys to prosecute their claim, and therefore can not in any way obtain possession of their lands.

Indians are continually appealing to the Indian agent, and where it is shown that parties holding lands have no lease or contract whatever they are removed, as authorized by the Department. In other instances, however, the agent is powerless to assist the Indian, though the contract with the noncitizen may be illegal and made with some other Indian who has moved elsewhere.

Investigation has invariably demonstrated that the person in possession has not complied with his contract, and a settlement would show in every instance considerable due the Indian.

In this connection the Department has uniformly ruled that section 3, above quoted, must be administered by the court and not by the Department.

As a matter of fact, nearly every noncitizen in possession of Indian lands claims to have made "lasting and valuable improvements thereon" and that he has not enjoyed the possession thereof a sufficient length of time to compensate him for the improvements; and further, that he can only be removed by proceedings in court on the part of the Indian.

The United States court, by reason of crowded condition of the dockets, can not take up any of these cases for several years. In the meantime the Indian is deprived of possession of his lands.

To remedy this condition of affairs, I respectfully suggest and recommend that section 3 of the Curtis Act be modified to authorize the Secretary of the Interior to investigate such contracts, and where facts will warrant, that the noncitizen be removed, and that where he feels aggrieved with the findings he may appeal to the United States court to retain possession, giving bond therefor, thereby placing the burden upon him and not upon the Indian.

The commission to the Five Tribes, when making allotments, could, through their representatives in the field, make the necessary investigation, and where removals were desired of persons in possession "objectionable to the allottee," the same could be accomplished by the Indian agent through his police.

As it is expected that the work of allotment will begin next year in the Choctaw and Chickasaw nations, and as many citizens in the Creek Nation who have received certificates of allotment from the Commission to the Five Tribes are not able to secure possession of their lands, this matter is of the utmost importance in order that the work of allotment, and citizens placed in possession thereof, can proceed as rapidly as possible.

To enable the Indian agent to place allottees in possession and to remove unauthorized persons will require the entire aid of several policemen. The agent asks that his present force of 28 men, who receive $15 and $10 per month, be reduced to 11 members, the captain to receive $75 and 10 privates to receive $50 per month each, together with their necessary traveling expenses. As the complicated condition of affairs in the Indian Territory, compared with the ordinary duties of police on Indian reservations, will require the entire time of a limited number of police who should be men of discretion, I urgently recommend that Congress be asked to make provision for additional compensation for police, as above indicated.

Under existing laws Indians are also permitted to rent their proportionate share of tribal lands until allotments are made, and to also lease them thereafter.

A large majority of citizens are fully competent to protect their own interests in making leases or renting lands, but many of the citizens who are Indians by blood should be protected.

The vast number of improper lease contracts now in existence and the complications arising in the Indian getting possession of his lands, which will be repeated in new leases unless the Indian is protected to some extent, demonstrates the advisability of having some proper officer of the Government approve leases made by citizens of Indian blood, as is done in neighboring reservations.

The present condition of many of these Indians, who are ignorant and no few absolutely destitute, would seem to demand, as an act of humanity, that they at least receive protection from the Government in their dealings with white persons for some time to come, and which has not been accorded them in the past by their own governments. The AssistantAttorney-General has held, in a recent opinion, that the Secretary of the Interior was not required by law to approve leases or contracts, and I therefore urgently recommend that Congress be asked to authorize the Secretary of the Interior to approve contracts made between Indians by blood and white persons, where found desirable, so long as it is considered necessary for their protection, and that the Indian agent be directed to approve such contracts.

WHITE PERSONS.

It is estimated that there are at least 350,000 white people, not citizens of any tribe, in the Indian Territory, who came here with the consent of the Indians. They have erected their homes here, made farms, and, in many instances, erected substantial residences and fine business blocks in many towns throughout the Territory. All are required to pay a tax where engaged in business or profession for the benefit of the nation in which they are located.

In the Choctaw and Chickasaw nations such taxes are paid to the authorized agents of the nations. In the Creek and Cherokee nations such taxes as are prescribed by their laws have been received by the Indian agent under regulations of the Department.

The Choctaw laws fix a tax of $1\frac{1}{2}$ per cent upon the value of goods introduced for sale on merchants, and also 50 cents per ton on hay cut for sale or barter.

Cattle are not permitted to be introduced into the Choctaw Nation by their laws except during the months of November and December, and then only to be kept within feed pens and inclosures. A citizen is to be fined $5 per head for violation of this law, and noncitizens reported to the United States authorities for prosecution under section 2117 of the Revised Statutes or removal from the nation.

The Chickasaw laws provide for the payment of 1 per cent of capital employed on all merchants, but no tax on hay cut and disposed of. A tax of 25 cents per head is assessed on cattle introduced.

The Creek laws provide for a tax of 1 per cent of goods offered for sale, and no tax on hay cut, nor is any tax collected on cattle introduced.

The Cherokee tax their own citizens one-fourth of 1 per cent on first cost of goods where engaged in business, and also provide a royalty of 20 cents per ton on hay shipped from the nation, 50 cents per head on cattle introduced, and 25 cents per head annual grazing tax.

These taxes should be uniform throughout the Territory.

In the Choctaw and Chickasaw nations, where collections are made by tribal officers, noncitizens have combined together and nearly all refuse to pay the required tax, and the matter has been the subject of much correspondence between this office and the Department with officers of the nations and noncitizens. There have also been several removals from the limits of these nations of persons for nonpayment, and over 700 names of others refusing to pay have been submitted to the Department, although repeated notice has been given them that the Department and Assistant Attorney-General hold such taxes are valid so long as these tribal governments exist, which, under provision of their agreement, is to continue for eight years from March 4, 1898.

Nearly all of the noncitizens contend that these taxes are illegal, and are so advised by attorneys. It is also represented that the taxes are excessive, and that previous to the agreement they never were uniformly enforced, many "compromising" with collectors, and that but a small portion of amounts paid reached the treasuries of the respective nations.

In the Creek and Cherokee nations where collections are made by the Department there has been even more opposition, and few if any remittances have been made until police officers have been instructed to close places of business. Two removals from the Cherokee Nation have been made, and the legality of the collections by the Department continually contested in the courts.

No provision is made for the education of children of these white people, except in some instances where they have themselves provided schools, and while paying taxes to the Indian nations none of the money so paid is used for the benefit of their children.

In view of all these circumstances, and as officers of the Choctaw and Chickasaw nations are unable to collect taxes due, and to avoid the continual friction between whites and Indians, I respectfully renew the recommendations made in my last annual report—that the present system and rate of taxes be changed, and that in lieu thereof a uniform system of taxation be fixed upon noncitizens and others engaged in business, introducing stock, etc., to be collected by rules and regulations of the Department and used for the common good, including improvements of roads, education of children of noncitizens, after providing for necessary wants of Indians, including such allowance as may be found advisable for expenses of their governments, and that the property be attached for nonpayment instead of removals from the Territory, the only means of enforcing the payment of taxes. I believe such system would meet with general satisfaction so long as these tribal governments exist, or until this Territory shall become a State.

It has been considered that such changes would be a violation of the existing agreement with the Choctaw and Chickasaw nations, which provides that their governments shall continue for eight years. The agreement, however, states that such provisions "shall not be construed to be in any respect an abdication of Congress of power at any time to make needful rules and regulations respecting said tribes."

While these nations would undoubtedly prefer to collect and handle their own revenues, and would protest against any change, yet if the Government is to see that collections are made such measures as may seem most desirable to accomplish that end should be adopted. As heretofore stated, the tribal authorities are unable to collect the taxes, and the only penalty for nonpayment is removal.

In the Creek and Cherokee nations it is contended that the Curtis act does not authorize the Secretary of the Interior to collect revenues due such nations as prescribed by their tribal laws. The conditions are becoming more complicated in reference to this tax throughout the Territory, and certainly can not exist as at present for several years hence, and especially if the courts sustain the contention that taxes can not be collected after title passes to the noncitizen for town lots.

FINANCE.

The total amount of receipts, deposits, and disbursements made by the United States Indian agent, under supervision of this office, as shown in his more detailed report, aggregated $825,020.76 during the past fiscal year. The collections made from all sources by the agent for the Choctaw and Chickasaw nations during this time amounted to $150,728.98, and of this amount, as heretofore stated in this report, under the head of " Mining in the Choctaw and Chickasaw nations," $138,486.40 was for royalty on coal and asphalt.

From the revenues on such coal and asphalt, which by the agreement are to be used only for the education of children of Indian blood, there has been paid out in connection with the schools of the Choctaw Nation during the past fiscal year the sum of $92,881.95, as shown by the report of the superintendent of schools, and of this sum $59,362.15 was disbursed by the United States Indian agent and the balance by the Department on certified vouchers. In addition to this amount, claims for expenses of Choctaw schools prior to the time they were taken charge of by the United States, and since the ratification of the agreement, have been submitted to be paid by the Department direct, amounting to $12,571.67.

The compensation and expenses of the superintendent of schools and the several supervisors are remitted them direct from the Indian Office, they being disbursing officers, and I am not advised as to the proportions of the several funds from which they are paid.

There was also paid $69,710.08, on account of outstanding indebtedness of the Choctaw Nation, from the appropriation of $75,000 made by Congress from the funds in the United States Treasury belonging to said tribe.

The total amount of collections from all sources in the Creek Nation during the year was $26,370.19.

In the Cherokee Nation there was collected from all sources the sum of $19,455.05.

There has been paid the sum of $246,673.83 in retiring outstanding Creek warrants and $152,198.50 in interest on and retiring Cherokee warrants. For suppressing smallpox in the Creek Nation in the spring of 1899 $3,964.10 was also disbursed.

The Creek and Cherokee warrants are drawn by the principal chief of each nation, and are for the purpose of maintaining their governments and schools.

In view of the fact that these warrants are to be paid by a disbursing officer of the United States, and as a record of all appropriations is kept in this office when they are transmitted to the Department for executive action, under regulations of the Secretary of the Interior, the warrants issued by these two nations are required to be submitted to this office for examination and approval before being circulated. The warrants issued for expenses of schools are approved by the supervisors for the respective nations. Warrants issued for other and general purposes are approved by the United States Indian agent.

The Creeks have but a small outstanding indebtedness at present, as the interest on their funds in the United States Treasury, together with their revenues, nearly equals their annual expenditures.

The Cherokees, however, have an outstanding indebtedness of over $800,000 in warrants, which are held in various parts of the United States, from Maine to California, and draw interest at the rate of 6 per cent, while they receive but 5 per cent and less on their invested funds from the United States, which interest does not appear to be sufficient to meet their yearly expenditures and at the same time pay the interest on their outstanding indebtedness.

The Cherokees have four separate and distinct funds, and the large amount of outstanding warrants above mentioned applies in the main to the general fund. The interest on their school, orphan, and insane funds nearly covers the expenses under those heads.

I therefore renew my previous recommendation that Congress be asked to permit a sufficient amount of the funds of the Cherokee Nation to be withdrawn from the United States Treasury with which to pay all their outstanding indebtedness.

ROADS.

Throughout the Territory there are many roads or highways used by the general public and for the carrying of the mail.

In the allotment of lands it appears that no provision is made for such, consequently roads are continually being fenced by citizens. This has been the subject of much correspondence and investigation, and I therefore renew my previous recommendation that some legislation be enacted providing for roads, and suggest that 30 feet along each side of section lines, making a 60-foot highway, be reserved throughout the Territory for necessary roads. It is desirable that such be done before allotments are made.

ESTRAYS.

I also renew the recommendation submitted in my last annual report that Congress be asked to apply the "estray" laws of Arkansas, as set forth in Mansfield's Digest, to the Indian Territory.

NEW TIMBER LEGISLATION.

Heretofore the United States and tribal laws and the regulations of the Department prohibited the cutting of timber for the purposes of sale, or for any use except that of an Indian in improving his prospective allotment, but the last session of Congress passed an act providing for the procurement of timber and stone for domestic and industrial purposes in the Indian Territory, which act was approved on June 6, 1900, and is as follows:

AN ACT to provide for the use of timber and stone for domestic and industrial purposes in the Indian Territory.

Be it enacted by the Senate and House of Representatives of the United States of America in Congress assembled, That the Secretary of the Interior is authorized to prescribe rules and regulations for the procurement of timber and stone for such domestic and industrial purposes, including the construction, maintenance, and repair of railroads and other highways, to be used only in the Indian Territory, as in his judgment he shall deem necessary and proper, from lands belonging to either of the Five Civilized Tribes of Indians, and to fix the full value thereof to be paid therefor, and collect the same for the benefit of said tribes; and every person who unlawfully cuts, or aids, or is employed in unlawfully cutting, or wantonly destroys, or procures to be wantonly destroyed, any timber standing upon the land of either of said tribes, or sells or transports any of such timber or stone outside of the Indian Territory, contrary to the regulations prescribed by the Secretary, shall pay a fine of not more than five hundred dollars or be imprisoned not more than twelve months, or both, in the discretion of the court trying the same.

Under the provisions of said act the Secretary of the Interior, on July 14, 1900, issued regulations governing such procurement of timber and stone, and prescribed the forms of application, leases, etc. A copy of these regulations, which contains the forms mentioned, is attached. (Appendix No. 15, p. 161.)

NEW TOWN SITES.

The act of Congress approved May 31, 1900 (Indian appropriation act), provides:

That the Secretary of the Interior is hereby authorized, under rules and regulations to be prescribed by him, to survey, lay out, and plat into town lots, streets, alleys, and parks, the sites of such towns and villages in the Choctaw, Chickasaw, Creek, and Cherokee nations as may at that time have a population of two hundred or more.

As previously stated, there are in the Choctaw Nation 44, in the Chickasaw Nation 57, in the Cherokee Nation 29, and in the Creek Nation 11 towns, making an aggregate of 141 towns reported by the various postmasters as having a population of 200 people and over.

The agreement with the Choctaws and Chickasaws also provides that after present towns are surveyed and platted the remainder of the land shall be allotted equally among the citizens, and section 16 of the Curtis Act makes provision:

That where any citizen shall be in possession of only such amount of agricultural or grazing lands as would be his just and reasonable share of the lands of his nation or tribe, and that to which his wife and minor children are entitled, he may continue to use the same or receive the rents thereon until allotment has been made to him.

The act of May 31, 1900, also provides:

Upon the recommendation of the Commission to the Five Civilized Tribes the Secretary of the Interior is hereby authorized at any time before allotment to set aside and reserve from allotment any lands in the Choctaw, Chickasaw, Creek, or Cherokee nations, not exceeding one hundred and sixty acres in any one tract, at such stations as are or shall be established in conformity with law on the line of any railroad which shall be constructed, or be in process of construction, in or through either of said nations prior to the allotment of the lands therein, and this irrespective of the population of such town site at the time. Such town sites shall be surveyed, laid out, and platted, and the lands therein disposed of for the benefit of the tribe in the manner herein prescribed for other town sites.

Several railroads have been granted rights of way through the Indian Territory, the St. Louis, Oklahoma and Southern Railroad being the only one at present in the course of construction, and is being built from Sapulpa, Ind. Ter., across the Creek and Chickasaw nations to Denison, Tex.

Along the line of this railroad citizens and other interested parties have upon several instances, without authority, surveyed and platted town sites at proposed stations, making arrangements with citizens claiming such land as their prospective allotments to control such tracts.

In one instance in the Chickasaw Nation two citizens surveyed and platted into streets, blocks, and lots a town site of 1,280 acres from lands in their possession, claiming same as their prospective allotments, and rented or leased the same to parties desiring to build thereon.

Such lease contracts provided for payment of from $250 to $750 per lot, and in many instances no specified time of "rental" is mentioned, being practically a sale.

Upon my request, the United States attorney for the southern district, Mr. W. B. Johnson, brought suit to restrain these parties from so laying out towns on lands of the tribe and occupied by them as a farm. Hon. Hosea Townsend, United States judge for that district, upon the hearing of the case, held that as they were permitted to rent agricultural or grazing land no limitation was placed upon them and that they could rent the same in lots and for any purpose. Under the direction of the Department, the United States attorney has appealed from the decision of the court in this case.

As directed by the Department the various roads have been requested to file plats showing the location of the proposed stations along their

line of road, in order that 160 acres can be set aside at such place for
town sites as provided by law.

Much correspondence has been had on this subject, and the authorities of the various nations have protested against citizens speculating
in lands of the tribes by laying out and platting towns prior to allotment.   While such has been done heretofore in the building up of all
towns, such action on the part of citizens now appears to be prohibited
by law, as towns are to be confined to their present limits and all to be
laid out and platted exclusively by the Secretary of the Interior for
the benefit of the tribes.

It can not appear that if an Indian divides lands which he has in his
possession into blocks, lots, alleys, parks, etc., and sells or leases the
same, that it can be allotted to him as all lands are to be allotted after
appraisal according to value "considering their location." Therefore,
a small portion of a town would doubtless exceed in value such Indian's
pro rata share.   Furthermore, if towns are being continually built
up it must necessarily cause complication and delay in completing the
allotment.

I therefore suggest the advisability of additional legislation providing that until allotment citizens may rent their proportion of
"agricultural or grazing lands" for such purpose only.

CONCLUSION.

As previously stated, this Territory embraces nearly 20,000,000 acres,
owned in common by citizens of the various tribes, comprising Indians,
negroes, and intermarried whites, aggregating about 80,000 people,
within the borders of which are also located some 300,000 whites or
noncitizens who have no title to property and are without representation in the government of the Territory.

During the transitory period, until lands are appraised and allotted
by the commission to the Five Civilized Tribes, lands in town sites
disposed of, and tribal governments have become extinct, certain laws
of Arkansas are extended over the Indian Territory, federal laws apply
in other instances, and the Secretary of the Interior is charged by law
with enforcement of rules and regulations governing other matters.
Such a condition renders affairs so complicated that it is not surprising
when courts and eminent lawyers differ as to the proper construction
of the law, that people are frequently at a loss to determine what laws
apply, or who is authorized to enforce them.

The responsible and arduous duties required of the United States
Indian agent have been performed by the present incumbent, Mr. J.
Blair Shoenfelt, in a highly satisfactory manner.

The superintendent of schools, Mr. John D. Benedict, has also
proven himself amply qualified for his position in dealing with the
important work of education and in bringing about needed reforms
and properly conducting the Indian schools throughout the Territory.
He is assisted by an able corps of supervisors, one for each nation.

The annual reports of the United States Indian agent, superintendent
of schools, supervisors, and revenue inspectors are herewith submitted.

Very respectfully, your obedient servant,

J. GEO. WRIGHT,
United States Indian Inspector for the Indian Territory.

The SECRETARY OF THE INTERIOR.

Report of the Indian Inspector for Indian Territory, 1900.

OFFICE BUILDING OF UNION AGENCY, MUSKOGEE, IND. T. (SECOND FLOOR.)

REPORT OF UNITED STATES INDIAN AGENT AT UNION AGENCY.

UNITED STATES INDIAN SERVICE, UNION AGENCY,
Muscogee, Ind. T., August 31, 1900.

SIR: I have the honor to submit herewith my second annual report, referring to the work, progress, and events pertaining to affairs of this agency for the fiscal year ending June 30, 1900, as required by section 203, Regulations of the Indian Office, 1894.

This report aims only to give a general outline of the work accomplished during the year, and no attempt will be made to point out a way by which to "solve the Indian problem," but a brief recital of facts will be attempted, accompanied by tables giving industrial and financial statistics of general interest, with other information.

From all this it will be observed that the past year has been, to a certain extent, a prosperous one for the Indians of the Five Civilized Tribes.

LOCATION.

The agency is located at Muscogee, Ind. T., on the main line of the Missouri, Kansas and Texas Railway, about 100 miles south of the Kansas border, and 157 miles north of the State of Texas. Muscogee is a busy little town of about 6,000 population. There is also located here the commission to the Five Civilized Tribes, commonly known as the Dawes Commission. The United States court for the northern district of the Indian Territory has its headquarters here, and court is in session practically all the time. The offices of this agency, including the offices of the United States Indian inspector for the Indian Territory, the superintendent of schools for the Indian Territory, the revenue inspectors for the Creek and Cherokee nations, and the Creek school supervisor, are located on the second floor of a large three-story brick building and are rented from Mr. C. W. Turner. The Government owns no buildings at Muscogee.

CORRESPONDENCE.

There were received during the year 12,195 letters aside from those from the Department, all of which, with very few exceptions, were answered. More than 2,000 complaints were filed by citizens of the Five Tribes against noncitizens, covering almost every conceivable subject. A large majority of the complaints, however, were against white men, who in the past had intruded themselves upon the Indians and gained their confidence to a sufficient degree to secure possession of their prospective allotments, and after having secured possession refused to pay rent for the use of the land or vacate the same, thus preventing the Indian from receiving any rents or profits therefrom. Many of the Indians received no rent from their farms for the past year, as their tenants refused to pay, and when notified by this office to either vacate the premises occupied by them or show cause why they should not be removed, invariably presented as an answer to the complaint a dilapidated lead-pencil written contract, to the effect that they had leased the land for a period of years, and for the use thereof were to fence and erect improvements thereon, which, at the expiration of the contract, was to inure to the benefit of the Indian. An examination of these contracts disclosed that they were invariably in violation of tribal laws. More than seven-tenths of the noncitizens in possession of lands held by them under improvement contracts had not made the improvements agreed upon, and they had enjoyed the possession of the land for years without paying a single cent of rent either to the nation or any Indian citizen, and that the rents were far in excess of the value of the improvements made by them. Yet, despite the fact that the Indians were being imposed upon, this agency was powerless to aid them

53

in securing possession of their farms or allotments, on account of the provision contained in section 3 of the act of Congress, approved June 28, 1898 (30 Stat., 495), which is as follows:

"That any person being a noncitizen in possession of lands, holding the possession thereof under an agreement, lease, or improvement contract with either of said nations or tribes, or any citizen thereof, executed prior to January first, eighteen hundred and ninety-eight, may, as to lands not exceeding in amount one hundred and sixty acres, in defence of any action for the possession of said lands show that he is and has been in peaceable possession of such lands, and that he has while in possession made lasting and valuable improvements thereon, and that he has not enjoyed the possession thereof a sufficient length of time to compensate him for such improvements. Thereupon the court or jury trying said cause shall determine the fair and reasonable value of such improvements and the fair and reasonable rental value of such lands for the time the same shall have been occupied by such person, and if the improvements exceed in value the amount of rents with which persons should be charged, the court in its judgment shall specify such time as will, in the opinion of the court, compensate such person for the balance due, and award him possession for such time unless the amount be paid by claimant within such reasonable time as the court shall specify. If the finding be that the amount of rents exceed the value of the improvements, judgment shall be rendered against the defendant for such sum, for which execution may issue."

It will be observed that the court or jury trying or passing upon improvement contracts of noncitizens, referred to in said act of Congress, shall determine the fair and reasonable rental value of such lands for the time they shall have been occupied by such persons, and if the improvements exceed in value the amount of rents with which such persons should be charged, the court, in its judgment, shall specify such time as will, in the opinion of the court, compensate such person for the balance due, etc.

In order for the Indian citizen to secure possession of his land, it will be necessary for him to institute suit in the United States court. Many of the Indians are poor and unable to give bond as required by law, or employ attorneys to prosecute their claims before the court, and are therefore left helpless. In order to assist indigent Indians, I would recommend that section 3, referred to above, be so modified as to vest the power in some official of the Government under the direct supervision of the Department of the Interior to investigate and pass upon the validity of the improvement contracts held by noncitizens in the Indian Territory, entered into prior to the passage of said act of Congress, and if it be found upon examination that the rents exceed in value the improvements placed upon the selection or farm of the individual Indian citizens, that this office be authorized to remove all noncitizens in unlawful possession of lands belonging to any Indian of the Five Tribes, and that the allottee be placed in unrestricted possession of his allotment.

In my judgment, the only remedy to prevent a continuance of this unlawful occupation of Indian lands is for Congress to pass a rigid law to protect the Indian citizen against the encroachment of aggressive and grasping whites. Persons unlawfully in possession of Indian lands should be made to feel and understand that the Indians of the Five Civilized Tribes are still wards of the Government, and that the strong arm of the Interior Department can be evoked in order to secure them their rights—rights which have been granted to them by the Government of the United States under solemn treaties. It is of the highest importance that the lands of the Indians should be kept from further complication, at least until they shall have been allotted, and just and equitable laws should be passed governing contracts in this Territory. These contracts should be approved by a trusted agent of the Government in the Indian Territory before they shall have any force or be binding upon either party entering thereunto.

I have dwelt upon this subject at some length for the reason that it is one of the most important matters to be considered by the Department in solving the complex problem of placing the Indian allottee in possession of his selection of land.

The agreement between the United States and the Choctaw and Chickasaw nations, commonly known as the "Atoka agreement," provides that "the United States shall put each allottee in possession of his allotment and remove all persons therefrom objectionable to the allottee."

This section of the agreement is not specific, as it does not state how persons objectionable to the allottee shall be removed. Hundreds of allottees appeal to this agency urging the removal of persons occupying their prospective allotments.

The commission to the Five Civilized Tribes is about to establish a land office in the Choctaw and Chickasaw nations for the purpose of issuing certificates of selection of lands to allottees. I recommend that specific instructions be given as to the mean-

Report of the India   Inspector for Indian Territory. 1900.

ing of that part of the "Atoka agreement" above quoted, in reference to placing the allottee in possession of his allotment.

If the allottee is forced to file suit in the United States court in order to have intruders removed from his land, it will entail upon him an expense which he is unable to pay, and will also prevent him from acquiring immediate possession of his selection of land on account of the delay, which of necessity will occur where so many suits of like character are filed. This is a question of vital importance that will have to be met within the next year, and I therefore urge that some adequate method be provided for placing allottees in the nations mentioned in possession of their allotments with as little delay and friction as possible.

POPULATION.

There has been no material increase in the Indian population of the Five Tribes during the last fiscal year, although a large immigration has been coming into all parts of the Territory, composed of noncitizen farmers, merchants, and mechanics. The coal mining camps that were temporarily affected on account of the strike by the coal miners in the coal regions of the Choctaw Nation, in the mining towns or camps of Alderson, Hartshorne, Lehigh, Krebs, and Coalgate are again filling up, and upon every hand may be seen the evidence of renewed business activity.

No census of the Indian population has been taken during the year by this agency, but careful estimates of the total population of the Territory, compiled from the records of the commission to the Five Civilized Tribes, are given herewith and are probably as nearly accurate as can be estimated without making an actual enumeration.

Tribe.	Population.	Total.	Acres.
Choctaw Indians	16,000		
Choctaw freedmen	4,250		
		20,250	
Chickasaw Indians	6,000		a 11,338,985
Chickasaw freedmen	4,500		
		10,500	
Creek Indians	10,000		
Creek freedmen	6,000		
		16,000	3,040,000
Cherokee Indians	31,000		
Cherokee freedmen	4,000		
		35,000	5,031,351
Seminoles	3,000	3,000	366,000
Total		84,750	19,776,286

a Having about.

INDIAN POLICE.

The Indian police have rendered excellent service during the past year, and are very efficient; considering the small compensation which they receive. I desire to renew my recommendation made in my first annual report, that "a smaller number be employed and their allowance be made sufficient to keep them continually in the field."

At present the force consists of 1 captain, 2 lieutenants, 3 sergeants, and 22 privates, making a total of 28. They are stationed as follows: Cherokee Nation, 6; Choctaw Nation, 9; Creek Nation, 8; Chickasaw Nation, 4; Seminole Nation, 1.

It is suggested that in view of the new and changed conditions in the tribal governments, Congress be asked to reduce the police force in the Indian Territory to not to exceed 11 members; that they be paid a salary of $50 per month and actual and necessary traveling expenses, and that the captain be allowed $75 per month and like expenses. The compensation will then be sufficient to enable them to devote their entire time to the service. During the past year the force was almost constantly employed in making investigations upon complaints made by Indian citizens against intruders, many of whom the police were obliged to remove from the Territory under orders from your office to this agency.

Attention is invited to Exhibit A, which is a letter from J. W. Ellis, the present captain of the United States Indian police of this agency, wherein he mentions the duties of the police and makes suggestions which will, in his judgment, improve their efficiency.

Early in the year the following instructions were issued for the guidance of Indian police at this agency, and the force has been held to strict account for the proper observance of the same:

General rules and regulations for the guidance of Indian policemen.

1. Every member of the police force of this agency must render prompt obedience to superiors, conform strictly to the prescribed rules and regulations, be orderly and respectful in deportment, and refrain from profane, insolent, or vulgar language.

2. Must not only perform regular duty assigned, but be ready for special service at all times.

3. Indian police have no authority to deputize any person as their proxy or assistant.

4. No member shall be allowed to be concerned, directly or indirectly, in any compromise or arrangement between a party suspected of crime and the party alleged to have been injured.

5. No member shall drink intoxicating liquor under any circumstances.

6. No member shall maltreat or use unnecessary violence toward a prisoner or other person.

7. Charges against a member of the police force must be made to the agent by the injured parties.

8. No member of the force shall sell, barter, exchange or loan, or give away any clothes, arms, etc., that may be furnished by this agency, or that may be captured by him in the exercise of his duties.

9. All weapons captured by Indian policemen must be turned over to this office with a statement showing the circumstances and reasons for the capture.

10. Any member may be removed from office for intoxication; for willful noncompliance with rules or disobedience of orders; for violent, insolent, or vulgar language or behavior; for willfully maltreating prisoners or using unnecessary violence, or for committing a crime or misdemeanor or neglect of duty.

11. On the resignation, death, or discharge of a member of the police force, all Government property, except the uniform, must be returned to this office.

12. In all cases members of the police force must act in concert, and with coolness and firmness.

13. Indian police must keep this office at all times fully informed of persons introducing cattle, cutting or removing timber or prairie hay from the public domain, or committing any other unlawful acts.

14. Policemen will be especially vigilant in detecting and arresting perpetrators for stealing timber from the reservation, setting fire to prairies, selling intoxicating liquors or having them in possession, herding or driving cattle on or through any of the nations of the Five Tribes by noncitizens without permission.

15. The members of the police force should cooperate as far as possible with the local and Federal officers consistent with Federal and local law.

16. It has been ascertained that 5 per cent of the crime in the Indian Territory is directly traceable to intoxicating liquors. Indian policemen are instructed to keep vigilant watch against the introduction of intoxicating liquors. At express or freight offices you will, on having reasonable grounds of suspicion that certain particular packages contain intoxicating liquors, open and examine such suspicious packages, and if intoxicants are found you will immediately destroy the same and make full report thereof to this agency. In making these seizures of intoxicating liquors, you must make every search in the presence of the railroad or express agent, must not permit outside persons to be present under any pretext, must examine or search only such packages as there are reasonable grounds for suspecting contain intoxicants, and must handle all packages with proper care, remembering that Indian policemen are responsible for damage committed.

17. Indian police are furnished with commissions, which must be exhibited when authority is questioned.

18. While it is not expected nor desirable that Indian police should ask permission to absent themselves from their usual post-office addresses, it is expected that you will be required to report such absence to this agency for its information.

19. It is the duty of the Indian policemen to sustain the honor and good reputation of the force, and they must report any member of the force acting in such a way as to lower and degrade their credit and good standing.

20. Report also, immediately upon the receipt of this notice, what property you have belonging to the Government, as United States police shield or badge, arms, uniform, etc.

21. Acknowledge receipt of these instructions and carefully preserve them. Special instructions will be issued from time to time as occasion may require, copies of which will be furnished you.

SMALLPOX.

Cherokee Nation.—Early in the month of March last a report was received at this office, and also by the United States Indian inspector for the Indian Territory, that smallpox was raging in the Cherokee Nation, and upon request of the board of health of said nation they were given full charge to care for and treat patients afflicted with smallpox and to vaccinate all citizens of the Cherokee Nation who had been exposed and to take such other precautionary measures as they deemed advisable. Several United States Indian policemen were detailed to assist the board of health. Hon. Thomas M. Buffington, principal chief of the Cherokee Nation, issued an order to the Cherokee board of health instructing them to use all possible measures to eradicate the disease and to cooperate with the United States officials.

The first case that came to the attention of the board was that of Jeff Dick, an Indian, living 18 miles east of Vinita, and a neighbor of Dick's named Smith, both of whom afterwards died of confluent smallpox. These men contracted the disease from parties living near Joplin, Mo., and before it was recognized as smallpox large numbers were exposed, which resulted in 64 cases in that vicinity.

About this time smallpox appeared in other sections of the nation, and the Cherokee board of health, acting under directions and orders from the principal chief, called to their assistance several physicians, nurses, and guards. Mr. Frank C. Churchill, revenue inspector for the Cherokee Nation, informs me that he interviewed each member of the board of health, also numerous physicians acting under their direction, as well as others who were practicing their profession independently, and they all agreed that the eruptive disease was true smallpox beyond question, although it was disputed by other physicians residing in the nation, including some who had contracted the disease, and that all persons with whom he had talked upon the subject admitted that in most cases the disease had been of a very mild form, so mild in fact that many persons were not confined to their beds in consequence of it.

In the town of Claremore there were in all 343 cases, being double the number contracting the disease in the same area elsewhere. It appears that when the first cases were discovered, about January 1, the local board of health notified the town council, who ordered the homes of patients quarantined. This order was afterwards, however, revoked.

On the 5th of February the Cherokee board ordered the quarantine reestablished, and from the very first appearance of smallpox in the town it continued to spread, and on April 12 the national board established a quarantine camp just outside the town, where several tents were erected and a United States policeman put on guard, and most of the inhabitants of that vicinity vaccinated.

Much opposition to the action of the board of health was manifested in Claremore by a portion of the citizens, the newspapers, and some of the city officials, contending that the disease was not smallpox.

On the 19th of April I issued from this office the following letter, which was printed by the board and distributed through the town. The requests therein contained were generally respected, and from that time on the physicians in charge of the quarantine camp had no serious opposition. This notice was also issued and extensively circulated in the Creek and Choctaw nations, where smallpox was raging at the same time.

" *To whom it may concern:*

"Whereas an epidemic of smallpox is prevailing in certain localities of the Cherokee Nation, endangering the lives of its residents and citizens; and whereas the Cherokee national board of health of the Cherokee Nation have been authorized and directed by this office to employ every means in their power to check and eradicate this disease from your nation, therefore, I hereby order and direct every person living in such infected localities, or any person who may have been exposed thereto who may not have been successfully vaccinated within the last twelve months to submit to vaccination at once; and every house wherein victims of smallpox have resided to be fumigated, or destroyed by fire where the same can not be thoroughly disinfected by fumigation. The cooperation of every person for the maintenance or support of these directions is earnestly desired, yet opposition to them by anyone by counsel, advice, or resistance by physical force will not be tolerated."

The plan adopted by the board of health in treating smallpox patients, was to remove all persons found to be infected to a quarantine station, where they were held and treated until such time that it was deemed safe to permit them to return to their homes.

The stations consisted of tents when suitable buildings could not be procured, or, where it was found more economical and effective, the patients were quarantined at their homes, and when possible all persons who had been exposed were vaccinated, excepting in a few instances where the board was compelled to permit them to go without this important treatment, owing to the fact of the great prejudice that existed against vaccination. In some instances bloodshed was narrowly averted, so determined was the stand of certain persons against submitting to vaccination. In such cases the parties were held in quarantine until the disease had developed or that it was found that they were not afflicted by the contagion.

All infected houses and patients, with their effects, were thoroughly fumigated and disinfected. From the report of the board of health I found that 29 physicians, 6 Indian policemen, and 57 irregular employees, such as guards, nurses, cooks, etc., were employed, the entire expense of which, as reported by the secretary of the board, has been $19,454.48.

There were 817 cases of smallpox in the nation, 246 being Cherokee citizens and 571 being citizens of the United States.

Transmitted herewith and made part of this report (see Exhibit B) is a map of the Indian Territory, with points where quarantine was established indicated in colored ink.

The figures indicating the number of cases mentioned do not include those that were treated by private physicians, and the numbers refer entirely to those cases that came under the personal supervision and attendance of the Cherokee board of health.

The sentiment in the nation as to methods of procedure differed widely in the several towns when smallpox appeared, all the way from prompt action and cooperation with the board and other officials (as at Vinita, where the citizens without exception appeared to realize the importance of strict quarantine and vaccination), to points where there was open resistance, extending so far as to threaten the officials with violence should vaccination be attempted. I have no hesitancy in stating that the Cherokee medical board performed its duties faithfully under the trying circumstances.

It appears to be a well-established fact that smallpox develops and spreads more rapidly in cold than in warm weather. The past winter has been an exceptionally mild one, to which may possibly be attributed the very mild type of the disease, the death rate being only about 1 per cent of the cases reported. To what extent the fumigation of dwellings, bedding, and clothing has been effective it is impossible to determine, but I shall consider it very remarkable if persons are not contaminated thereby during the coming winter, thus causing another epidemic unless early precautions are taken.

Indifference to the proper precautions to be taken to prevent the spread of smallpox is very marked as a rule in the Cherokee Nation. Smallpox has been prevalent along the borders of the Cherokee Nation, as well as at Denison, Tex.; Coffeyville, Kans.; Joplin, Mo., and at other points.

The disease has been diagnosed as smallpox by a large number of educated and experienced physicians, and it has been clearly proven that it is highly contagious and that isolation and vaccination alone suppressed it.

Smallpox is loathsome in the extreme, many patients having suffered greatly from it, and the most zealous advocates of allowing it to spread will readily admit that it is not a disease one cares to contract.

Creek and Chickasaw nations.—Smallpox first made its appearance in the Creek Nation during the month of November, 1899. Many complaints were received at this office from various sections of the nation, and under orders from your office I placed Dr. Fite, of this town, in charge, with instructions to make a careful investigation and inform this agency whether or not smallpox existed, as reported, in the Creek Nation. The doctor visited Eufaula, Wagoner, Holdenville, and other towns and made a careful examination of the cases reported, and afterwards advised this office that there was no question as to the disease being smallpox.

I immediately issued an order to the physician to quarantine the towns and establish detention stations, which was done, and Dr. J. W. Lowe was placed in charge of the station at Holdenville, with orders to vaccinate all persons in that locality where there was any danger of the smallpox occuring and spreading. At this point we had 6 persons employed as guards. At Eufaula Dr. T, B. Benson was placed in charge of the camp established at that place and furnished with guards and policemen in order that he could enforce vaccination.

Information was received from Agent Patrick of the Sac and Fox Agency that smallpox was thought to exist near the western border of the Creek Nation, near his agency. Dr. Thompson, under directions of Dr. Fite, was at once sent to investigate the report. After a thorough investigation he returned to Muskogee and advised that no smallpox existed in that part of the Creek Nation. About this time all inmates of the jails were vaccinated.

On December 20 it was reported to this office that smallpox was raging at Colbert and other sections of the Chickasaw Nation. A committee of citizens residing at Colbert petitioned this agency for relief, and I at once sent Dr. Fite to that point, with directions to visit other sections of the Chickasaw Nation, and to take such measures as he deemed advisable to suppress it. He reported that the first case appeared at Colbert in December, about 3 miles east of the town, and in the family of one Pitman (colored), and that at the time of his arrival at Colbert there were 36 well-developed cases, and 9 deaths occurred, 8 of which were negroes and 1 white, and all afflicted were negroes, with the exception of 5 white persons.

There were 41 persons in the families of those who had the disease who had not yet developed it at the time of the doctor's visit. It was impossible to ascertain how many had been exposed outside of the families referred to. The town of Colbert is not incorporated, and having less than 200 inhabitants, could not legally do so. Its citizens had no funds for combating the disease except by public subscription. This they very magnanimously did, although the expenses were very heavy. Orders were issued requiring all persons to be vaccinated, and strict quarantine was established and other precautions necessary to stamp out the disease were taken.

At Kent, 12 miles east of Colbert, near Red River, one case was reported. This probably resulted from exposure with persons at Colbert who had the disease. At Chickasha the doctor found two well-developed cases. They were being quarantined and cared for by a committee and by public subscription. At this place the citizens of the town agreed, so far as they were concerned, to meet the expense and carry out such regulations as were necessary to combat the disease, but were powerless to enforce quarantine regulations, having no town government. In view of existing conditions I furnished them with a United States Indian policeman, who was directed to establish a strict quarantine and to hold all persons in that vicinity who had been exposed, and to compel others to submit to vaccination, and to take such other steps to prevent the spread of smallpox as were deemed necessary. This resulted in a complete stamping out of smallpox in the Chickasaw Nation so far as this office was advised.

Governor Johnston, of the Chickasaw Nation, promptly cooperated with this office, and aided very materially in stamping out this loathsome disease among his people.

On the 13th of March the work of suppressing smallpox in the Creek Nation was turned over to the board of health of the nation. Dr. Callahan, a resident member and president of the board, was placed in active charge, and reported from time to time the progress made toward controlling the disease. I have been unable to ascertain the exact date of the appearance of smallpox in the nation or just where it came from, but from the best evidence obtained it was brought here from some point in the Choctaw Nation to the town of Eufaula. From Eufaula it spread through the whole country west, where it was carried by pupils from the Eufaula High School. These pupils were allowed to go home after the fever developed, and through them it was spread throughout the country as far west as the Seminole Nation. These pupils were sent out from the Eufaula High School before it was generally known that smallpox existed at Eufaula.

The Indians have a marked fondness for visiting the sick, and it is very difficult to control them in this custom, no matter what the results may be. The suppression of smallpox in an enlightened community, where its character is understood and its direct results fully appreciated, is a task of no small magnitude, and one attended with a great many difficulties; but when undertaken among people whose intelligence is far below par, and who know but little and care still less about its loathsome character and dangerous results, and who are full of all sorts of superstition and prejudice, the undertaking is one of much greater proportion.

Dr. Callahan reports that the board of health had to fight every conceivable opposition from the beginning. The full-blood Indians and negroes are very ignorant and superstitious, and these characteristics have been so played upon by designing persons among them that in a number of cases they were armed and ready to defend themselves when any member of the medical board visited them. So prejudiced were they against vaccination and being taken to a detention camp that the physicians had to go through the country, hunt them up, and take them by force. This state of affairs necessitated an increase of help and caused an additional expense that would not have occurred under ordinary circumstances. Many of the more intelligent and influential men among the Indians themselves were opposed to our efforts toward suppressing smallpox, and these, with the number of quack doctors scattered throughout the country, caused no end of trouble. They excited and worked upon the prejudice of the people to such a degree that they threatened to massacre the entire crew at some of the quarantine stations.

The quack doctors charge that, by vaccinating the people, we were spreading the disease, and that any effort on the part of the medical board or this office to vaccinate should be stopped at all hazards. The president of the medical board reported 204 cases at 8 different camps, some of them of as virulent a form as could be imagined, others mild in character. So far as I have been able to find out, there were only 14 deaths from the disease in the Creek Nation. However, it is more than probable that others have died of the malady, as a great number were secreted in the woods in order to prevent the board of health from finding them.

The kind and humane treatment received by those who were detained in camps has convinced them of the correctness of the methods of handling the disease, and a great majority of them will be our strongest allies in another scourge of this character. Many of the full bloods were found in destitute circumstances, being without clothing or food; and in a number of instances entire families were stricken with the disease and no one was left to wait upon the sick, all of whom came under the care of the board of health and were well treated and fed upon good, nourishing food.

During the year 900 persons in all were vaccinated in the Creek Nation by the board of health. While the medical board was at work in the western part of the nation an outbreak of scarlet fever occurred in the Wetumka National Boarding School, and within five days after it made its appearance there were 38 cases well developed, some being very severe in character, and 4 of the pupils died. Prompt action was taken and the school was quarantined and the cases isolated, thus preventing the further spread of the disease. Considering the number of cases treated, the wide scope of country over which they were scattered, and the many difficulties encountered in caring for the invalids by Dr. Fite and Dr. J. O. Callahan, president of the board of health, I have no hesitancy in saying that they performed their duties faithfully under very trying circumstances.

Choctaw Nation.—Neither this office nor the board of health of the Choctaw Nation has been able to definitely locate the first case of smallpox, but as near as could be determined it first made its appearance at Hartshorne, a small mining town, during the month of June, 1899, and was called or termed "chicken pox," "Cuban itch," and "elephant itch." Shortly thereafter 8 cases were reported from Atoka. Upon investigation by this office, there were found 8 well-developed cases of smallpox.

I immediately wired Governor McCurtain, requesting that the board of health of the nation be placed in charge, and that they treat and care for all cases found and to take prompt action in suppressing the dread disease. Later I was informed by the governor that the board of health consisted of three reputable physicians; that they had no authority for doing other work than examining physicians; that there was no law creating a board of health or prescribing their duties, and that there were no hospitals in the country, and on account of the peculiar condition of affairs hospitals could not be built. However, later on it was decided that hospitals were not necessary, and that the few cases at Atoka could be easily taken care of, and I directed that detention camps be established and made as comfortable as possible.

In securing tents, fixtures, and food for these camps the board of health was compelled to work upon a credit basis. There were few Choctaw citizens who had the disease, and the nation had made no provision for their care, and at that time it was undecided as to whether the Choctaw Nation or the United States Government would take care of noncitizens. Under such circumstances, neither government having made an appropriation, it was a difficult matter to induce merchants to supply the camps with the necessary tents and subsistence. I finally succeeded in inducing Wolf & Co., of South McAlester, to furnish supplies for the various camps in the immediate neighborhood of South McAlester.

Early in November the Choctaw Nation made an appropriation of $10,000 for taking care of its citizens and issued national warrants. At that time I requested the board to make an estimate, as near as they possibly could, as to how long it would take to stamp out the smallpox, and about what expense would be incurred in caring for United States citizens afflicted with it. The board of health informed me that it was very uncertain as to what the expense would be, but that it would not be less than $50,000. They gave as their reason for the statement that the coal-mining towns were the hotbeds of the disease, and that the majority of the people of these places were citizens of the United States.

At mine No. 2, where several thousand miners were residing, there were found 17 cases the first day the board of health examined the town. They found that everybody in it had been exposed, and the only thing that could be done was to quarantine the entire place, and to effectively do so it was necessary to employ about 30 guards at $2 per day. The miners were nearly all negroes and were very ignorant, and in order to do anything with them we were compelled to use force to keep them within the quarantine line.

To give some idea as to the percentage of cases in these mining towns, where the population is continually changing, I have to say that up to January 1, 1900, out of

370 cases handled by the board of health 299 were at coal-mining camps, or were traced directly back to them.   It would appear, therefore, that at least 80 per cent of the cases were found in the mining camps.

During the month of November, 1899, the Choctaw general council passed a bill creating a board of health and prescribing their duties.   This bill was not approved by the President of the United States until the 18th of April, 1900, and, of course, was not effective until that date.   At the same time of the passage of the bill referred to, a bill was passed compelling vaccination among the Choctaw citizens.

Immediately after the passage of these bills, the board began the vaccination of Choctaw citizens.   Physicians were sent all over the country, and about 8,000 Choctaw citizens were vaccinated at the expense of the Choctaw government.   At the same time there were a large number of citizens vaccinated by physicians who were not employed by the board of health; one physician alone reports over 1,000 vaccinations.   As a consequence there were very few cases among the Choctaw Indians, especially the full bloods.

Dr. W. P. Hailey, secretary of the Choctaw medical board, informs me that if the board were empowered to enforce vaccination among the United States citizens without the danger of being drawn into a lawsuit, they (the medical board) would have had a smaller percentage of cases, and even those who had the disease would have had it in a modified form, as was the case in a few instances.

The number of cases treated by the board of health of the nation during the epidemic was over 1,000, of which 80 per cent were United States citizens, the death rate being about 2½ per cent.

Of the remaining cases about 20 per cent were of the confluent type, others discreet or in a very mild form.   The greatest percentage of deaths at any one place was at Allen, where, out of 9 cases, there were 4 deaths.

General.—A number of the towns in the Indian Territory have been incorporated, and where smallpox appeared in such towns the municipal authorities cared for the afflicted at the expense of the municipality.

INDIANS.

I have no complaint to make against the conduct of the Indians of the Five Civilized Tribes, no depredations being committed during the year.   There is every reason to believe that Indian depredations and disturbances in this country are at an end.

A few full-blood Indians in the Creek Nation, under the leadership of Chitto Harjo and Hotulka Fixico, are strenuously opposing the allotment of lands, and have banded together and refuse to appear before the commission to the Five Civilized Tribes to select their allotments.   These Indians are deluded with the hope or idea that there is a possibility of their securing the consent of the Government permitting them to return to their old customs and have their tribal government restored and live apart and separate from the rest of the world.   They claim that all the changes that have been required of the Creek people by the Government since the time of making their treaties were due to the connivance and work of the more intelligent class of Creeks and was not done at the instance of the United States Government, and quite a number of the more ignorant class of Indians, mostly full bloods, have been induced to believe the representations made to them, and from time to time conventions have been called to propagate this retrogressive sentiment among the Creek people.

The principal chief of the Creek Nation informs me that in the past much disturbance and violation of the peace and order among the Creek has been caused by this same element.   At times they would break out in open insurrection, attended with many casualties before it could be suppressed.

The present proposed policy of the Government to distribute the lands in severalty, instead of their being held in common, and having individual instead of tribal title, and the withdrawal of all the powers of government from the Indians with a view to establishing a government over them with relations of citizenship, has been the cause of this dissenting faction among the Creek people adopting the course they have.

I find from the records of the commission to the Five Civilized Tribes that a large majority of the Creek people have actually made selections of allotment and now hold certificates for such selections, and are anxious for the consummation of a treaty or agreement which will give them titles in fee simple for their allotments.   Other Indians are, as rapidly as possible, making selections of their allotments, and the only hindrance to the universal acceptance of allotment of lands in severalty by the Creek Indians is the influence exerted by the leaders of this dissenting faction, who term themselves the adherents of the "Hopothleyahola" treaty.

Early last spring this faction met in convention at Brush Hill, Ind. T., and appointed Chitto Harjo, Hotulka Fixico, and two others to go to Washington and present their protest against the changes in land tenure, and I understand that they are still in Washington, and that since their departure their followers have held numerous secret meetings and have elected a principal chief and other officers. They are now awaiting the return of the delegation from Washington. Letters received from the delegation at Washington by their followers have been extensively circulated. In these letters it was stated that they (the delegation) had defeated the agreement made between the commission to the Five Civilized Tribes and the Creek delegates, and that all that was required of them now was to select their officers and reestablish their old forms and customs of government, and they would then be recognized by the Washington authorities.

Such exaggerated and unfounded statements are causing some disturbance among the Creek; and even among those who have accepted the policy of the Government and selected their lands in severalty many are disposed to give credit to the unfounded representations made by this delegation now in Washington.

If these delegates representing the full bloods can be induced to make a correct report of the result of their mission, its futility, and the impossibility of stopping or delaying the carrying out of the present policy of the United States Government, their visit to Washington will not have been without wholesome results.

SCHOOLS.

It is gratifying to note the steady and rapid progress that has been made during the past year with the schools for the Indian children in the Indian Territory. Much interest is being manifested, and efficient and competent teachers are being employed.

In accordance with rules and regulations of the Secretary of the Interior, there has been appointed a superintendent of schools for the Indian Territory, also supervisors of schools for each nation, who are under the direction and supervision of the United States Indian inspector. It is the duty of said supervisors of schools to visit, from time to time, the several schools of the different tribes in the Indian Territory, and to make reports as to the efficiency of the teachers employed, as often as may be desired, to the Commissioner of Indian Affairs. They are also required to report upon the location and and the condition of each school in the Territory, the methods of instruction employed, and to make recommendations concerning the same.

It will be observed, therefore, that this agency has no supervision over the schools in the Indian Territory, and that full power and authority is vested in the superintendent of schools and the supervisors, under such rules and regulations as may be prescribed from time to time by the Secretary of the Interior.

From statistics furnished me by Superintendent Benedict, I am enabled to furnish an estimate of the number of school children in the Territory between the ages of 6 and 18 years. The estimate follows:

Nation.	Indians.	Negroes.	Whites.	Total.
Cherokee	8,340	950	10,000	19,290
Creek	1,850	1,300	3,500	6,650
Choctaw	4,000	1,000	16,000	21,000
Chickasaw	1,500	1,000	25,000	27,500
Seminole	400	400	100	900
Total school population	16,090	4,650	54,600	75,340

From which it will be observed that there are children of school age within the Indian Territory as follows:

Indian 16,090
Negro 4,650
White 54,600

Total 75,340

I am advised that the various nations have never built any local schoolhouses, except their boarding schools or academies. All the day or neighborhood schools in the Territory have been erected by private donation or subscription.

I also submit the number of schools and academies in the Indian Territory which are attended by Indian pupils only:

Nation.	Academies.	Day schools.
Cherokee	4	124
Creek	9	60
Choctaw	4	124
Chickasaw	5	14
Seminole	2	2

In addition to the above there are quite a number of mission schools, established by the various religious denominations, which are not under the control or supervision of either this office or the superintendent of schools, but are either under the direct control of the tribal authorities or conducted by the religious denominations.

Education is having its natural and inevitable effect on the Indians of the Five Tribes, as shown by the great improvement in their manner and method of living, the construction of their houses, and the cultivation of the soil.

FINANCIAL.

Choctaw and Chickasaw nations.—In my last annual report reference is made to the regulations prescribed by the Secretary of the Interior governing mineral leases and other matters in the Choctaw Nation, Indian Territory. Under the provisions of the act of June 28, 1898, these regulations provided, among other things, that the Indian agent for the Union Agency, Ind. T., should receive and receipt for all loyalties paid into his hands accompanied by a sworn statement. Moneys so collected are deposited with the assistant treasurer of the United States at St. Louis, Mo., to the credit of Treasurer of the United States, for the benefit of the Choctaw and Chickasaw nations, in the proportions of three-fourths to the Choctaw and one-fourth to the Chickasaw.

The regulations have been amended so as to fix the royalty on coal mined in the Indian Territory at 8 cents per ton of 2,000 pounds of mine-run coal, or coal as it is taken from the mines, including that which is commonly called "slack," instead of 10 cents per ton for screen coal, as heretofore. On asphalt 60 cents per ton for each and every ton produced weighing 2,000 pounds of refined, and 10 cents per ton for crude asphalt, the change in the regulations taking effect March 1, 1900.

The right was reserved, however, by the Secretary of the Interior in special cases to either reduce or advance the royalty on coal and asphalt on the presentation of facts which in his opinion make it to the interest of the Choctaw and Chickasaw nations; but the advance or reduction of the royalty on coal and asphalt in a particular case shall not modify the general provisions of these regulations fixing the minimum royalty as above set out.

A recent ruling of the Department, in which it is held that, under the provisions of the agreement of April 23, 1897, between the commission to the Five Civilized Tribes and the Choctaw and Chickasaw nations, as ratified by the act of Congress of June 28, 1898, the Indian agent was only required to collect royalties on coal and asphalt, such other royalties as may be due the nations, such as taxes on merchandise introduced and exposed for sale, permit and occupation taxes, rock royalty, etc., must be collected by the tribal authorities, as had been the custom prior to the passage of the act referred to.

The funds collected by the United States Indian agent on account of royalties on coal and asphalt mined, as stated above, are first deposited with the assistant treasurer of the United States to the credit of the Treasurer of the United States for the benefit of the Choctaw and Chickasaw nations, and afterwards disbursed by the United States Indian agent in payment of salaries of school teachers, employees, and the incidental expenses in connection with the management of the schools of the Choctaw Nation. The proportionate amount of the funds collected belonging to the Chickasaw Nation are held in the Treasury and not disbursed through this office, the Chickasaw managing their own schools and paying the expenses incident thereto out of the tribal funds through their treasury.

The principal coal-mine operators of the Choctaw Nation are:

The Choctaw, Oklahoma and Gulf Railroad Company, with headquarters at Little Rock, Ark., and mines at Alderson, Hartshorne, Gowen, and Wilburton.

The Osage Coal and Mining Company and the Atoka Coal and Mining Company, with mines at Lehigh, Coalgate, and Krebs, Ind. T., and headquarters at St. Louis, Mo. The two companies just mentioned are owned and controlled by one corporation.

The Kansas and Texas Coal Company, with mines at Krebs, Cherryvale, and Carbon, Ind. T., and near Jenson, Ark., with headquarters at St. Louis, Mo.

The Southwestern Coal and Improvement Company, with mines at Lehigh and Coalgate, Ind. T., with headquarters at Parsons, Kans.

The other coal-mine operators are J. B. McDougal, D. Edwards & Son, Samples Coal and Mining Company, Hailey Coal and Mining Company, McAlester Coal and Mining Company, the Ozark Coal and Mining Company, the Crescent Coal Company, Pat Harley, Perry Brothers, M. Perona, the Capital Coal and Mining Company, the Sans Bois Coal Company, McAlester Coal and Mineral Company; Devlin-Weir Coal Company, successors to Indianola Coal and Railway Company; Archibald Coal and Mining Company, now owned by William Busby; the Eastern Coal and Mining Company, the Turkey Creek Coal Company, the St. Louis and Galveston Coal and Mining Company, and other small operators, all having mines in the Choctaw Nation.

The asphalt mines, with one exception, are located near Dougherty, Chickasaw Nation, Ind. T. The names of the operators are: The Brunswick Asphalt Company, with headquarters at St. Louis, Mo.; the Caddo Asphalt Company, with headquarters at New York; the Elk Asphalt Company, with headquarters at Kansas City; the Rock Creek Natural Asphalt Company, with headquarters at Topeka, Kans.; the Moulton Asphalt and Mining Company, with headquarters at Coalgate, Choctaw Nation, Ind. T.

Below I give a statement in reference to the royalty collected by me for the Choctaw and Chickasaw nations from July 1, 1899, to June 30, 1900:

Coal royalty	$137,377.82
Asphalt royalty	1,108.58
Stone royalty	243.70
Rock royalty	859.40
Sale of town lots	11,139.48
Total collected and deposited	150,728.98

An increase over the amount collected for the past fiscal year of $37,597.76. This appreciable increase is accounted for by the opening up of a number of new mines and the further fact that no strikes have prevailed, as during the fiscal year ending June 30, 1899.

For comparison, I give below a statement of the royalties collected by me during the fiscal year ending June 30, 1900. (See last annual report.)

Coal royalty	$107,766.03
Asphalt royalty	1,295.32
Rock royalty	1,083.90
Miscellaneous receipts	2,985.97
Total	113,131.22

From the moneys collected by me on account of the royalty on coal and asphalt mined I disbursed in the payment of salaries of school-teachers employed and for incidental expenses in connection with the management of schools in the Choctaw Nation during the fiscal year ended June 30, 1900, $59,362.15. There are 5 academies in the Choctaw Nation, employing 60 persons and from 105 to 110 neighborhood school-teachers. These teachers and employees are paid for their services by this office, by means of a check drawn on the assistant treasurer of the United States at St. Louis, Mo. For further information in reference to the schools and how they are managed attention is invited to that part of my report marked "Schools."

PAYMENT OF CHOCTAW WARRANTS.

The act of Congress approved March 3, 1899 (30 Stat., 1099), provides:

"The Secretary of the Treasury is hereby authorized and directed to pay, from the funds in the Treasury belonging to the Choctaw Nation of Indians, outstanding warrants not exceeding in amount the sum of seventy-five thousand dollars: *Provided,* That before any of the said warrants are paid the Secretary of the Interior shall cause an investigation to be made to ascertain whether such warrants have been duly and legally issued and are a valid and subsisting obligation of said nation; and payment of the same shall be made by some official or employee designated for that purpose by the Secretary of the Interior."

In conformity with said act, the Secretary of the Interior caused the indebtedness of the Choctaw Nation to be investigated by Special Inspector J. W. Zevely, and

id investigation had been completed I was directed to pay certain warrants
d been favorably passed upon by the inspector, amounting to $69,710.08. The
nded balance of this fund, amounting to $5,289.92, has been returned to the
·y.   This payment was practically completed during the second quarter of
t fiscal year, but the holders of warrants continued to present and receive pay-
herefor to June 30, 1900.

CHEROKEE AND CREEK NATIONS.

·r the general provisions of the act of Congress approved June 28, 1900, the
ry of the Interior promulgated certain rules and regulations governing min-
ses, the collection and disbursement of revenues, etc., in the Cherokee and
lations.
·r these regulations the United States Indian agent is required to receive and
for all royalties, rents, taxes, and permits of whatsoever kind or nature that
due and payable to either of said nations.   These revenues, after having been
d, are deposited to the credit of the Treasurer of the United States with the
t treasurer of the United States at St. Louis, Mo., for the benefit of the tribe
·h it belongs.
·ated in my last annual report, the revenues due the Creek and Cherokee
arises principally from the taxes imposed upon merchants and others doing
s within the limits of their territories.
e are a few small coal mines in each nation. The output, however, is small and
alty realized is proportionately so.   In the Creek Nation there are 38 towns
out 600 traders; in the Cherokee Nation there are 82 towns and 454 traders.
ıerokee Nation imposes a tax of one-fourth of 1 per cent and the Creek
1 per cent on all merchandise introduced and offered for sale.   The Creek
also imposes an occupation tax per annum as follows:

in hides, peltry, furs, wool, pecans, and other country produce	$50
affording accommodation for fifty or more guests	150
affording accommodation for forty or more guests	75
affording accommodation for thirty or more guests	60
accommodating twenty or more guests	40
accommodating ten or less guests	24
g office	50
nd flouring mill	50
d cotton gin combined	50
gin alone	24
ill alone	24
and feed stable	50
able	24
r freight wagon or passenger hack other than those run by livery stables	
ıg tax as such	12
ry or harness establishment and boot and shoe shop	24
mith and wagon shop	24
ıre, cabinet, or work shop selling its own manufacture	24
ıce agent (life or fire)	50
ıg establishment, one-half of 1 per cent of capital stock invested, assess-	
: to be made on the bank on account of the shares thereof.	
ian or surgeon with certificate from the national board	25
. having diploma	25
ctor and builder	25
cting painter, brick or stone mason	24
ıently established photograph gallery	50
·r shop selling meats only	50
stand and restaurant	24
ll and planer	25
y establishment	24
·y	24
shop, one chair	12
dditional chair	6
op doing custom work only	24
ng establishment	24
ıaking and millinery establishment	24
· and confectionery	25
ade and ice cream stand	12

Undertaking establishment... $50
Gunsmith 12
Lawyer... 25
Tombstone and marble dealer... 25
Milk dairy.. 25
Shooting gallery.. 12
Billiard or pool hall 50
Revolving swing and merry-go-round.................................... 24
Peddler selling musical instruments, books, and ornamental trees and shrubs,
     per month 2
Peddler, 5 per cent of goods introduced for sale.
Menagerie and circus combined, per day................................ 25
Circus without menagerie, per day..................................... 10
Concert, in hall or tent, per day..................................... 5
Traveling photographer, per week...................................... 1

The total amount of royalty collected by me for the Creek Nation during the fiscal year ending June 30, 1900, is as follows:

Coal royalty $3,023.27
Merchandise and occupation tax 18,811.27
Pasture tax 4,344.65
Seized lumber.. 191.00
                                                            ───────
     Total... 26,370.19

as compared with $4,913.63 collected during the fiscal year 1899.

The following amounts of royalty were collected by me for the Cherokee Nation during the fiscal year 1900:

Coal royalty $3,856.01
Merchandise tax 5,607.65
Hay royalty 4,474.88
Gravel royalty... 100.00
Ferry tax... 504.19
Cattle tax.. 1,956.00
Town lots 74.02
Seized lumber... 250.00
Permit tax.. 2.00
Board of teachers at academies............................ 2,330.77
Unexpended balance of school fund 299.53
                                                           ───────
     Total.. 19,455.05

as compared with $3,150.87 collected during the fiscal year 1899. The increase in the amounts collected for the two nations is due to the efforts of the respective revenue collectors, Mr. Guy P. Cobb for the Creek Nation and Mr. Frank C. Churchill for the Cherokee Nation. These officers are assisted in their duties by district revenue inspectors.

GENERAL.

The total amount of money received, deposited, and disbursed by this office during the past fiscal year, as shown by the records, was $825,020.76.

As stated before, every remittance to this office must be accompanied by sworn statements in duplicate. One of these statements is filed with the United States Indian inspector for the Indian Territory, and the other is forwarded to Washington with the quarterly accounts. Attached to this report, and marked "Exhibit C," is the form of blank used by merchants in the Cherokee Nation in transmitting remittances to this office.

A similar form, marked "Exhibit D," is used by merchants in the Creek Nation.

The form of blank used in making remittance on account of royalty on coal in the Cherokee Nation is also given as an exhibit, marked "E."

A similar form to this blank is used by persons who remit on account of coal mined in the Creek Nation.

The form of blank used in connection with the payment of royalty on account of hay shipped from the Cherokee Nation is submitted as "Exhibit F."

The form of blank accompanying remittances for occupation tax due the Creek Nation is given, marked "Exhibit G."

All remittances are acknowledged. The form of acknowledgment of remittances on account of the payment of the taxes due on merchandise in the Creek and Çherokee nations are shown as exhibits " H " and " I;" on hay and coal, exhibits " H 1 " and " I 1," and occupation tax, " Exhibit D 1."

PAYMENT OF CREEK WARRANTS.

During the quarter ending September 30, 1899, I received for disbursement Creek funds amounting to $206,000. Out of this sum I paid and retired Creek warrants aggregating in amount $199,493.24, and $3,948.10 was used in paying expenses incurred by my predecessor, Agent Wisdom, in suppressing smallpox in the Creek Nation; the balance, $2,558.66, was returned to the Treasury.

During the quarter ending March 31, 1900, there was placed to my official credit $48,751 of Creek funds. Of this amount $47,180.59 was used in paying and retiring Creek warrants and $16 in paying an irregular employee (guard) for services rendered under direction of ex-Agent Wisdom during the smallpox epidemic which prevailed in the Creek Nation in 1899; the balance, $1,554.41, was returned to the Treasury.

From the above it will be noticed that the total amount disbursed in the payment of Creek warrants during the last fiscal year was $246,673.83, and in payment of expenses incurred in suppressing smallpox in the Creek Nation, $3,964.10.

Creek warrants are drawn by the principal chief. Those drawn against the school fund, however, must be approved by the United States school supervisor for the Creek Nation, and those drawn against the general fund must be approved by the United States Indian agent.

Checks in payment of these warrants are issued by the United States Indian agent on the Assistant Treasurer of the United States. As an exhibit to this report there is given, marked exhibits "M" and "N," facsimile of a Creek warrant and sample sheet of the Creek-warrant pay rolls.

PAYMENT OF CHEROKEE WARRANTS.

On April 28, 1900, in compliance with instructions from the Indian Office, I caused a notice to appear in the Cherokee Advocate, the official organ of the Cherokee Nation, stating that I would, at Muscogee, Ind. T., on Monday, May 16, 1900, and subsequent dates, until disbursement was completed, disburse the interest due the Cherokee Nation from the United States Government on their invested fund, amounting to $160,314.19; the said sum of $160,314.19 being applicable to warrants drawn on the respective funds as follows:

Warrants drawn on the general fund $89,687.16
Warrants drawn on the school fund 43,470.18
Warrants drawn on the orphan-asylum fund 23,043.26
Warrants drawn on the insane-asylum fund 4,113.59

Total 160,314.19

The notice also stated that the disbursement would be made under the laws of the Cherokee Nation in so far as they were not in conflict with the laws of the United States or the rules and regulations prescribed by the Department of the Interior and of the United States Treasury for the government of disbursing officers.

Before making a payment on any warrant the indorsement of the original payee is required. If the original payee is deceased, then the indorsement must be made by the legally appointed administrator or executor of the estate; certified copies of letters of administration must be furnished; powers of attorney were not recognized.

The advertisement then gave the number of each warrant to be paid and the fund upon which it was drawn. Interest on all outstanding warrants, whether for a full year or not, by reason of a recent act of the Cherokee council, was paid up to April 28, 1900.

The owner of a warrant was also required to furnish an affidavit to the effect that he was the legal holder of the same, and that it was drawn, to the best of his knowledge and belief, for a valuable consideration rendered the Cherokee Nation. The payment was continued to June 30, 1900. The recapitulatory statement shows that I have paid and retired—

461 general-fund warrants, with interest due thereon $48,251.44
278 school-fund warrants, with interest due thereon 41,048.36
90 orphan-fund warrants, with interest due thereon 19,431.85
43 insane-fund warrants, with interest due thereon 3,710.53

Total 112,442.18

I also paid the interest on 3,813 warrants, as follows:

51 insane-fund warrants	$229.91
387 school-fund warrants	1,736.78
3,375 general-fund warrants	37,789.63
Total	39,756.32

The total amount paid out in retiring warrants and paying interest was $152,198.50; the balance, $8,115.69, was returned to the Treasury.

All Cherokee warrants bear interest from the date of registration at the rate of 6 per cent per annum. It was found to be no small task to figure the interest on the 4,000 warrants presented for payment. There were about 4,500 warrants sent to this office at various times while the payment was in progress. Many of them, however, were not legally and technically indorsed, as is required by the regulations, and payment of interest for that reason was refused and the warrants returned to the holders.

Cherokee warrants are now held by individuals, corporations, and others at the uttermost ends of the United States. For instance, quite a number are owned by a lady living in Los Angeles, Cal.; the Municipal Savings Company, of Portland, Me., hold a number, and over $125,000 worth are held by one Wall street broker alone.

The rate of interest, 6 per cent, is considered high in the East, and for that reason, and the further fact that the United States officials now disburse Cherokee moneys, the value of the warrants in the open market has increased from about 90 to 98 and 99 cents, much to the gratification of school-teachers and the original holders.

No expense is necessarily attached to the collection of the interest due on the warrants, as they may be sent direct to this office, the interest figured thereon, and vouchers sent the holder for signature. When these vouchers have been returned to the agent's office, properly signed, a check drawn on the assistant treasurer of the United States at St. Louis, Mo., is sent to the owner of the warrants, and at the same time the warrants are returned to him. The amount of interest paid, however, and the date from and to which the interest is paid being first annotated on the back of the warrant or warrants, as the case may be.

During the recent payment there were filed in this office, either for the payment of the principal or the interest due thereon, over $800,000 worth of warrants. Warrants are gradually drifting into the hands of bankers and brokers in the East, and a ready sale for them in the open market can be found.

A careful estimate of the outstanding indebtedness of the Cherokee Nation, after the payment referred to had been completed, shows the debt of the nation to be a little over $800,000. The United States Government pays the Cherokee Nation, on account of interest on its invested funds, which are held in trust by it, at the rate of 3, 4, and 5 per cent per annum.

I recommend that Congress appropriate the sum of $800,000, or so much thereof as may be necessary, to pay the outstanding warrants of the Cherokee Nation that have been legally and properly issued.

I make this recommendation for the reason that the nation only receives interest at the rate of 3, 4, and 5 per cent, while it pays on its indebtedness an annual interest at the rate of 6 per cent.

A number of the warrants issued by the Cherokee Nation have been outstanding for more than five years. The amount due from the Government annually on the Cherokee invested funds is $163,000, which amount does not seem to be sufficient to pay the yearly indebtedness incurred in conducting the affairs of the nation, and for that reason it would seem that unless the appropriation referred to is made, the Cherokees will continue to remain in debt, and on this debt pay interest at the rate stated.

Special Inspector J. W. Zevely has submitted several reports and recommendations in the matter of Cherokee warrants to the Department. He concurs in my recommendation that the entire indebtedness of the nation should be paid off. There is attached as Exhibits O and P facsimile of a Cherokee warrant and sample sheet of Cherokee warrant pay roll.

TOWN LOTS IN THE CHOCTAW AND CHICKASAW NATIONS.

During the fiscal year closing June 30, 1900, there has been received at this office, on account of payment on town lots in the nations mentioned, $11,139.48.

Up to the present time in these two nations the plats of three towns only have been approved by the Secretary of the Interior. The towns are Colbert in the Chickasaw Nation and Sterrett and Atoka, in the Choctaw Nation.

After the plat of a town has been completed and approved, a notice of appraisement on improved lots is served upon the owners of improvements upon said lots by the town-site commission. A duplicate copy of this notice of appraisement is forwarded to this office, together with the town-site record book, and all persons are notified that they should remit for their lots to the United States Indian agent. When the remittance is received at this office, it is first entered into the cashbook and from there carried to the town-site record book.

The unimproved lots are sold at public auction to the highest bidder, who is required to pay for the same in four equal annual installments. The Department, however, has recently directed that the United States Indian agent for the Union Agency be present at the sale of unimproved lots and require the successful bidder to deposit with him 10 per cent of the purchase price, which shall be forfeited and become the property of the Choctaw and Chickasaw nations unless the purchaser shall pay the balance of the first installment in ten days from the date of sale. However, should any purchaser desire to pay the full amount of the first installment or the full purchase price at the time of the sale he is permitted to do so.

The owners of lots, either improved or unimproved, are allowed three years in which to pay for them. The first payment on improved lots must be made within sixty days from the date of the service of the notice of appraisement and the balance in three equal annual installments.

Patents for town lots in the Choctaw and Chickasaw nations are issued under joint hands of the respective executives of the Choctaw and Chickasaw nations. Before any patent can issue, it is necessary for this office to give said executives full information in reference thereto; in fact, all data in connection with the patents emanate from this office for the reason that the town-site record book is kept here and it could not be obtained from any other source. Exhibit N is a copy of the form of the patent to be used in these nations.

The form of blank used in connection with remittances to this office on account of improved and unimproved lots is shown as Exhibits O and P. The form of the acknowledgment or the receipt used is shown as Exhibit Q.

INDIAN GOVERNMENTS.

The Choctaw, Chickasaw, Cherokee, Creek, and Seminole Indian nations, commonly called the Five Civilized Tribes, occupy the major portion of what is known as "The Indian Territory." A small part of the Territory in the extreme northeast has been set apart for the Quapaw, Miami, Peoria, and other small tribes of Indians, and is known as the Quapaw Agency.

The total area of lands embraced within the Quapaw Agency is only 212,298 acres, and the total Indian population 1,448, as compared with 19,776,148 acres and about 81,000 Indians, freedmen, and 300,000 whites in the Five Nations.

The Five Civilized Tribes have, by treaty stipulations, the right of self-government, with certain limitations and conditions. No act of any of their legislatures or councils is effective until the same shall have been approved by the President of the United States.

The act of June 28, 1898 (the Curtis bill), abolished all the tribal courts in the Cherokee and Creek nations, but in no way deprived the councils of their rights to enact laws, subject to the approval of the President. The Cherokee, Creek, Choctaw, and Chickasaw nations have printed books of their laws, which have been carefully compiled and are written both in English and the language of the nation issuing them.

Cherokee Nation.—The power of the Cherokee government is divided into three distinct departments: the legislative, executive, and judicial. The national council of the Cherokee Nation is composed of its citizens, who are elected by popular vote, and convene annually on the first Monday in October, at the capital at Tahlequah, or in case of emergency it may be called together by the principal chief. No person can be an officer of the Cherokee Nation unless he is a citizen thereof. They are paid for their services out of funds belonging to the Cherokee Nation by means of a warrant issued by the principal chief. The supreme executive power of the nation is vested in the principal chief, who is styled "the principal chief of the Cherokee Nation." His term of office is for four years. The principal chief is assisted in his duties by the assistant principal chief, who is also elected by popular vote. The other officers are treasurer, auditor, and attorney-general.

Creek Nation.—The law-making power of this nation is lodged in a council, which consists of two houses—the house of kings and the house of warriors. The members of both houses are elected. No person can be a member of either house who is not a citizen of the Creek Nation. The style of the action of the council is: "Be it enacted by the national council of the Muskogee Nation." The highest executive power is known as the principal chief of the Muskogee Nation, who is elected for a term of four years, and has for his assistant the second chief of the Muskogee Nation, who is also elected and holds his office for the same term of years as the principal chief. The principal chief is invested with the reprieving and pardoning power, and is required to see that all laws of the nation are faithfully executed and enforced, and to make recommendations to the council that he deems necessary for the welfare of the nation. All the acts of the council are submitted to the principal chief for his approval or disapproval. The other officers of the nation are national treasurer, national interpreter, national auditor, international delegates, national translator, national license tax collector, national live stock inspector, and the national board of education. The national treasurer, national interpreter, and national translator are elected by the council for a term of four years. The other officers are nominated by the principal chief and confirmed by the national council. The council convenes annually at Okmulgee, the capital of the nation, and in case of emergency by a call from the principal chief.

Inasmuch as the act June 28, 1898, abolished the tribal courts of the Cherokee and Creek nations, no data will be given in reference to the former judicial systems of the two nations.

Choctaw Nation.—The powers of the government of the Choctaw Nation are divided into three distinct departments—legislative, executive, and judicial. The legislative power of the nation is vested in the general council, which consists of the senate and the house of representatives, and the style of their law is "Be it enacted by the general council of the Choctaw Nation assembled." No person can be a member of the council unless he is a citizen of the nation. The judicial system of the nation is vested in one supreme court, circuit, and county courts. The supreme executive power of the nation is vested in the principal chief, assisted by three subordinate district chiefs, who are elected for a term of two years. The other officers of the nation are national treasurer, national auditor, national agent, national inspector, and the national district collector.

Chickasaw Nation.—The government of the Chickasaw Nation, like that of the Choctaw Nation, is divided into three departments—the legislative, executive, and judicial. The legislative power of the nation is vested in two branches, one styled the senate and the other the house of representatives, and both together the legislature of the Chickasaw Nation. The style of the law is, "Be it enacted by the legislature of the Chickasaw Nation." The members of the legislature are elected by a popular vote for a term of two years. The executive power of the nation is vested in the chief magistrate, who is styled "The governor of the Chickasaw Nation." This officer is elected for a term of two years. The judicial powers of the nation consist of one supreme court, the district and such other courts as the legislature may from time to time ordain and establish. The other officers of the nation are national secretary, district attorney, national treasurer, auditor of public accounts, and the school superintendent.

The agreement entered into between the commission to the Five Civilized Tribes and the representatives of the Choctaw and Chickasaw nations at Atoka, Ind. T., April 23, 1897, and ratified by the act of June 28, 1898, permitted the continuance of the tribal courts, somewhat modified, for a period of eight years from the 4th day of March, 1898.

Seminole Nation.—The Seminole Nation has no printed laws, and I have no data at hand with which to give any information in reference thereto. The chief executive is known as "the governor of the Seminole Nation," and is elected for a term of four years. They have a council which is convened by the governor annually, or at such other times as in his judgment it may be deemed to the best interests of his people. They also have a national treasurer and auditor, who are appointed by the governor. The capitol is at Wewoka, Ind. T.

The agreement entered into between the commission to the Five Civilized Tribes and the Seminole commission, December 16, 1897, does not state when the tribal government shall cease to exist.

The governments of all the Five Tribes are modeled after those of the States of the Union.

BIOGRAPHICAL SKETCHES, RECOMMENDATIONS AND SUGGESTIONS MADE BY THE EXECUTIVES OF THE CHOCTAW, CREEK, CHICKASAW, AND SEMINOLE NATIONS.

The present executives of the Five Civilized Tribes of the Indian Territory are men of considerable influence among their people. It is thought that it will be interesting to give a brief sketch of their lives, and at the same time to embody in this report some of the recommendations and suggestions which they have made, at my request, that will ultimately be for the good of their people.

Johnston, governor, Chickasaw Nation.—Douglas H. Johnston, the present governor of the Chickasaw Nation, was born in the Choctaw Nation, Indian Territory, in 1856, and grew to manhood at South Canadian, and from there removed to the Chickasaw Nation in 1880. In 1884 he became contractor and superintendent of Bloomfield Seminary, which position he held continuously for thirteen years, and up to the time he was elected governor. Governor Johnston's administration began with the ratification of the "Atoka agreement," and his best efforts have been directed toward its strict enforcement. He has lent his aid toward rehabilitating the tribal government and correcting the abuses existing in his nation which the representatives of the United States Government have pointed out. The governor has endeavored to make his administration as economical and business-like as possible, and to protect the nation from citizenship frauds, and to preserve intact the tribal government. The governor makes the following recommendations and suggestions, which he thinks will be of material benefit both to citizens and noncitizens residing within the Chickasaw Nation:

First. The strict observance of the "Atoka agreement."

Second. Relief from citizenship frauds.

Third. The enforcement of the intercourse laws, in order that the tribal revenues may be collected.

In speaking of that part of the "Atoka agreement" in the matter of the collection of the tribal tax, the governor says that this is a subject in which his people are vitally concerned; "that their governments have been continued to this time in order that we may take such steps as may enable us to meet and face tribal extinction safely and without damage to tribal interests. In order that this can be done and our governments and public institutions continued, it is absolutely necessary that our tribal revenues be collected. The only means we have of collecting our revenues is by a strict enforcement of the intercourse laws; our statutes imposing what are known as tribal taxes, the payment of which is conditioned upon the compliance with which the noncitizens may enter the Indian country and to remain and do business therein. These laws have been held valid both by the courts and the Department, and I request that such noncitizens as refuse to comply with our laws imposing these taxes by the payment thereof be removed from the limits of the Indian country, under the laws of the United States governing trade and intercourse with the Indians."

The governor insists that this action by the United States is imperatively necessary, and adds further: "Notwithstanding the rulings of the courts and opinions of the Department, there is now throughout the Chickasaw Nation a united and organized plan to resist the payment of the tribal taxes, and unless those persons who have refused to pay and have been reported as intruders are summarily ejected from the Indian country, not only the Indian laws but the authority of the United States will be set at defiance."

Porter, chief, Creek Nation.—The principal chief of the Creek Nation, Hon. Pleasant Porter, was born in the Creek Nation, Indian Territory, about fifty-two years ago. He has long been recognized as one of the foremost men of this section and an advocate of progression; is broad and liberal in his ideas, and has served the nation as a delegate to Washington some fifteen or sixteen times. The chief was one of the members of the commission to negotiate several important treaties, notably the cession of Oklahoma and the recent agreement with the Dawes Commission. He has the following suggestions to make as to the best methods to be adopted in winding up the affairs of the Creek Nation:

First. The ratification of the Creek agreement.

Second. Some definite way of putting the allottee into possession of his lands.

Third. The early setting apart of the land that will be required for the present use and prospective growth of towns that now have a population of 200 or more.

Fourth. A uniform system of taxing noncitizen traders.

Fifth. The passing of a law compelling the fencing of lands rented for grazing purposes.

In the opinion of Chief Porter, it would be unfortunate to include the nations of the Indian Territory in any State or Territorial government, as he believes this would add another factor to the already difficult problem in the division of the landed and other interests of the Five Civilized Tribes; and, further, that the sooner the allotment is completed and the landed and other interests of the Creek Nation shall have been settled, the better; that the time only adds difficulties to the situations, and new ones are continually arising which could not have been aforeseen and provided for; that a period of transition is not the one in which the people are liable to prosper, and a settled condition of property and definite laws protecting the person and property is essential to the advancement and prosperity of any people; that he urges strongly the policy of laying aside all minor difficulties, in order to secure a solution of the vexed problems that now confront the Creek people. To use the language of the principal chief: "The present condition of the affairs of the nation are extremely unsatisfactory. A majority of the people have taken their allotments under the Curtis act. This and other laws of the United States renders it very difficult to put their allotments to practical use. Few have the means to fence their allotments, and consequently trespasses upon them are almost inevitable, and persons renting grazing privileges, in many instances, do not fence the grazing grounds rented to them, and animals placed upon them are able to commit trespasses upon the allotments of others, and the public domain unallotted, which is the source of a great deal of disturbance, and there being no adequate means in law to adjust these trespasses, it would be well to enact a law compelling the fencing of the lands rented for grazing purposes. It is suggested that a method of arbitration of all minor civil causes be adopted, making such arbitration final; this would be less burdensome to the people than carrying all such matters to the United States courts, or to the commissioner's court. The court facilities are very inadequate, making it necessary for the people to travel long distances and at a loss of much time, often over very trivial matters. If the Creek people are not to be entrusted with some limited measure of government, there should be more commissioner's courts established, so as to afford the means of settling causes easier and nearer home."

McCurtain, chief, Choctaw Nation.—Green McCurtain, the principal chief of the Choctaw Nation, though almost a full blood, and closely attached to the ways of his people, with keen and ever discerning foresight, enabling him to understand the inevitable fate that awaited the tribal government, advised his people to divide their common holdings and to prepare for the dissolution of the tribal government. In this he stood alone, and was truly a pioneer in the cause of his people's salvation. A man of loyal purpose and strong determinations, McCurtain began an advocacy of this policy that challenged the admiration of his friends and enemies alike, and which resulted in a signal triumph for both policy and advocate, and an agreement was made with the United States Government, largely at his instigation, by the Choctaw and Chickasaw, he being chosen as the chief executive of his nation—a vindication of his purposes, of which any statesman could well be proud.

Governor McCurtain's highest ambition is to see that his people get the protection afforded and promised them in the "Atoka agreement." He feels that the agreement affords the only practical solution of the Indian question, and for that reason, and others, counsels against any radical departure from its provisions, lest its main purposes be defeated. He is also vigilant and industrious in his efforts to protect his people against the frauds that threaten them, chief among which are the citizenship frauds.

Governor McCurtain has been sheriff of Skullyville County, district school trustee, district attorney, and treasurer of the nation. His family, the McCurtains, have always been prominent in national affairs.

The chief, in giving his views as to the best methods of winding up the affairs of the tribal government, recommends:

First. That a fair and equal division of all the common property be made in such a manner that it will protect all in their rights.

Second. The enforcement of the "Atoka agreement."

Third. The continuance of the tribal government for eight years, as provided for in the "Atoka agreement."

Fourth. The protection from fraudulent applications for citizenship.

Fifth. The enforcement of the tribal laws and the collection of the tribal taxes.

In reference to the collection of the tribal taxes, the chief has the following to say:

"I desire to call attention to that feature of the agreement relating to our government, and more particularly to our tribal taxes. I do not deem it necessary to discuss the importance of our taxes and their relation to our government. The tribal governments were continued by the agreement for a purpose material to the end therein sought, and should, therefore, be upheld. The tribal tax is one of the main stays of our government, and is not only important, but is absolutely indispensable to its continuance. The validity of the tribal tax has been discussed, reviewed, and litigated by the authorities, both judicial and departmental, and has in every instance been upheld. Not only have the taxes been held to be valid, but the decisions have invariably reasserted the authority of the Department of the Interior to enforce the payment of the same. It would seem that all that remains to be done is the actual collection of these taxes, and I would, therefore, suggest that vigorous steps be taken to execute the laws relating thereto. Notwithstanding the holdings of the courts and the Department favorable to these taxes, there is an organized opposition thereto among the noncitizens in this country, and unless dealt with in a positive manner and without delay this opposition will assume troublesome proportions."

Buffington, principal chief, Cherokee Nation.—Thomas M. Buffington was born October 19, 1855, at Cincinnati. Ark., and educated at Going Snake district schools, Cherokee Nation, Indian Territory.

In 1899 Mr. Buffington was elected to the judgeship of Delaware district, and in 1891 was called to the senate to represent the same district. He has served the nation in other capacities. In 1898 he was elected principal chief of the Cherokee Nation, which office he is now holding. Mr. Buffington is one of the tallest and best-built men in this section of the country, his height being 6 feet 7 inches. He was called to the highest position in the gift of his people at the most critical and delicate time in the history of his country.

Chief Buffington has displayed tact and firmness in the discharge of his duties. His relations with the United States officials in the Indian Territory have been exceedingly pleasant.

The chief is what may be termed a progressive Indian, and is in favor of making a treaty with the Dawes Commission with a view to winding up the affairs of the nation.

I regret to state that Chief Buffington has submitted no recommendations or suggestions that can be embodied in this report.

Brown, principal chief, Seminole Nation.—Hon. John F. Brown, known as "Governor Brown," is now and has been for the past fifteen years principal chief of the Seminole Nation. Governor Brown was born in Tahlequah, Ind. T., in the Cherokee Nation, October 23, 1843. He received a limited education in the district schools of the Cherokee Nation. During the war he served as first lieutenant in the First Creek Regiment. Immediately after the close of the war he moved to and joined his people, the Seminole. In 1865 Governor Brown was appointed a delegate to Washington, and was one of the signers of the famous 1866 treaty. The governor has also served his nation as delegate to Washington, as a member of the council, school superintendent, treasurer, and is now completing his fourth term as principal chief. The Seminole Nation, the governor says, is at the present time in a prosperous condition, satisfactory alike to the people and the Government at Washington, and that he can think of no suggestions that will improve their present or future prosperity, except to close the doors of the saloons dealing out whisky along the Seminole line bordering on Oklahoma. He recommends that his people be allowed to remain just as they are at present for as long a period as possible, and that they be given ample time for the opening up and cultivation of their lands. The governor adds that, with the establishment of the United States court, his people will necessarily become more familiar with its workings, learn to respect and appreciate its protecting influences, and that finally it will supersede and take the place of the tribal courts. The schools of the nation are in good working order and lend a powerful helping hand for good.

RAILROADS.

Under the provisions of the act of March 30, 1896 (29 Stat. L. P. A.), the St. Louis, Oklahoma and Southern Railroad Company have constructed and are now operating about 30 miles of their railroad between Sapulpa, a point on the St. Louis and San Francisco Railroad, to Okmulgee, the capital of the Creek Nation. The road is also in process of construction from Okmulgee, its present terminus, to Sherman, Tex. The contract for its completion requires that it be done by July 1, 1901, and when completed it is to be operated as a branch of the St. Louis and San Francisco Railway.

The Chicago, Rock Island and Pacific Railroad has completed a southwest branch line commencing near Chickasha, in the Indian Territory, and extending through the Kiowa, Apache, and Wichita reservations, Okla., a distance of about 75 miles.

The Fort Smith and Western Railway Company has been granted a right of way through the Choctaw and Creek nations by an act of Congress approved March 3, 1899. The maps of definite location of the line have been approved by the Acting Secretary of the Interior. I am not advised as to how much of the road has been constructed.

COLLECTION OF TRIBAL REVENUES.

Much opposition has been manifested during the past year to the collection of the tribal taxes due from noncitizens. There should be adopted a uniform system of taxing all persons doing business in the Indian Territory. If this is done it would, to a certain extent, remove the opposition and feeling against the payment of the tax, and lessen the work of this office in collecting it.

The payment of this tax, under certain conditions, allows noncitizens certain rights and privileges, and permits them to reside in the Indian Territory and do business therein.

In this connection I can not refrain from calling attention to some of the conditions prevailing, in order that the Department, and others interested, may derive an intelligent understanding of what the agents of the Government have to contend with in their efforts to carry out the Department's instructions directing the collection of tribal revenue.

Within the Indian Territory there are not less than 300,000 noncitizens who are engaged in the mercantile business and other pursuits, and who make every conceivable effort to avoid the payment of any tax. Especially is this true in regard to what is called "royalty on hay" in the Cherokee Nation. The Cherokee Nation by its laws imposes a tax of 20 cents per ton on all hay shipped from its limits. There is quite a demand for Indian Territory hay, and annually large shipments are made from the Cherokee Nation during the summer months, the royalty on which, if it were all collected, would be a source of considerable revenue. Despite all the past efforts of the Government officers of the Territory much of this royalty has not been collected for the reason that the intruder element, acting under advice of lawyers, have banded together to resist and prevent its collection. They have even gone so far as to intimidate and threaten the Indian policemen connected with this office when detailed for duty to assist the revenue inspectors. The timely removal from the Indian Territory of one of the leaders of the opposition to the payment of the hay tax has demonstrated that the tribal revenue can and will be collected, and has to a certain extent facilitated the work of collecting it and restored the confidence of the Cherokee, and leads them to believe that the Government will see that they are not deprived of this source of income and that ultimately they will receive the benefit therefrom.

Efforts have been made by hay shippers to prevent the collection of this tax or royalty by means of an injunction from the United States court, which has been invariably denied.

Last summer a number of lawyers in the northern district of the Indian Territory sought by injunction suit in the Federal courts to enjoin the agents of the Government from the collection of the occupation tax imposed upon them by the laws of the Creek Nation. In the case of Maxey et al. r. Wright et al., appealed to the court of appeals for the Indian Territory, it was held that the superintending control of the Interior Department over the Creek is in no wise abolished, but, on the contrary, all recent powers of the Department to remove from the Indian Territory, for the causes specified, by the treaties and the statutes, as they existed before the passage of the act, and that the bill, commonly called the "Curtis bill," from beginning to end recognizes this continued authority of the Interior Department and in many instances enlarged it.

The court further held that the Indian agent was acting in strict accordance with the directions of the Secretary of the Interior in a matter clearly relating to intercourse with the Indians, and that he had a right, under these regulations, to collect the revenue due the nation, and to remove therefrom as an intruder any person who failed to comply with the intercourse laws; and further, that the Indian statutes were not annulled, except that in so far as the jurisdiction was taken from them and transferred to the United States courts.

The above opinion, I understand, was concurred in by all the judges, and if this be true, the highest court of the Indian Territory has unanimously decided that the relations of the Interior Department to the Indian tribes in the Indian Territory are not only not changed by recent legislation, but its powers enlarged, then it would seem that there can be no question as to the authority of the Department to enforce the collection of the tribal tax and remove from the Territory all persons who may be there in violation of the law. Yet, in spite of this decision and others of a similar nature, the opposition to the collection of the tribal tax grows stronger, and many difficulties are encountered in attempting to collect it.

Last winter the governor of the Choctaw Nation complained that a number of noncitizens residing in his nation had failed or refused to pay the permit tax imposed by the Choctaw laws, and requested the removal of such persons from his nation.

Upon receipt of the governor's letter or complaint, the parties so complained of by the governor were then written the following letter:

"You are informed that the governor of the Choctaw Nation complains to this agency that you are a noncitizen residing in the Choctaw Nation, and that you have refused or failed to pay the permit tax as required by the Choctaw laws. The governor therefore reports you as an intruder in said nation and asks that you be removed from the limits of the same.

"You are hereby notified that the Department of the Interior holds that said tax is lawful and that said nation has the right to levy and collect the same from noncitizens residing in said nation, and all such noncitizens therein who refuse or fail to comply with the law imposing said tax upon them are subject to removal as intrud-

FERRY ACROSS THE ARKANSAS RIVER.

ers in an Indian country, under the provisions of section 2149, Revised Statutes of the United States.

"You are therefore directed to immediately pay said taxes to the authorized collectors for the Choctaw Nation, and you will inform me if you intend to comply with the said laws, and in case of your refusal to do so I will take the necessary steps to carry out the order of removal as above mentioned."

In one or two instances, no attention having been paid to the notice from this office, the persons complained of were removed from the Indian Territory. The removal of an intruder is always an unpleasant task, and was only resorted to in the last extremity.

In this connection I give below a copy of an editorial which recently appeared in the Chieftain, a paper published at Vinita, Ind. T. This editorial describes well the conditions that now exist, and the attitude of the persons who oppose and endeavor to thwart the Government officials in their efforts to collect the tribal taxes.

"Recent developments have revealed the attitude of the Government of the United States toward the Cherokee in a manner calculated to make the average Cherokee citizen open his eyes in astonishment. When the Curtis law was passed the Indians felt that their laws were abolished, their revenues cut off and their tribal existence suddenly and rudely ended; but if the Government, through the Interior Department, intends to enforce the collection of the taxes due the nation, and to protect the Indians in their land holdings and in various other ways, the future is a little bit brighter than the recent past. The fact is slowly beginning to dawn upon the Cherokee that the United States Government does not want to rob him nor to permit others to do so, but, on the other hand, proposes to see to it that he is protected as a tribe and as individuals.

"The Cherokee Nation has been the most beleaguered little government for the last quarter of a century on the globe. It has been mercilessly looted by its own citizens. Its grazing lands have been absolutely monopolized to the exclusion of the Indian settler by the cattlemen, some of them citizens by adoption and many of them white men from the States.

"These are the fellows who have opposed the Government at every step, and who are still opposing it and spending money to thwart every effort to do simple justice to the Indians. It is to be earnestly hoped the officials of the United States will not fail to take cognizance of the men who rallied around the accused in the trial that has been going on in this city this week at the United States court-house. The key to the whole situation could be found in that alone. What has prevented the allotment of land for the last decade or longer? It has unquestionably been the land monopolist, who did not want to give up the vast acreage of Indian land held and from which he was growing rich. Who is it that now boldly comes to the front and stands in the way of the Interior Department in its efforts to collect the revenue on hay? It is the same crowd of monopolists who have for many years hung upon the Indian country like a pack of hyenas. No wonder these men are ready to resist the collection of the royalty on hay. They know full well that it means the same on cattle, on merchandise, on coal, on the mineral and other products of the country, the heritage of the Cherokee Indians. The Government has at last reached the real battle ground in the settlement of affairs in the Cherokee Nation and at last come face to face with the real people who have all along stood in the way of the accomplishment of the purposes of the Government in dealing with the Indians. These fellows have hidden behind the real Indian and represented to the Government at Washington, through prepaid emissaries, that the Cherokee was opposed to allotment and every progressive movement. Who is it that is now resisting the payment of the Indian tax? Is it the Cherokee Indian? No. Although this is an Indian country (which they now deny), the Government is having no trouble with the Indians. It is the white man who has taken charge of the Indians' estate and who now disputes even with the United States Government itself as to whether he shall relinquish his hold upon it or not. The governor who a few days hence shall sit in the executive chair at Tahlequah is an Indian who comes from and who is in sympathy with the common Cherokee Indian. In him the United States officials here will find a safe ally. In him, we believe, the Interior Department will find a ready helper in unraveling the tangled skein of governmental complications in this country."

RECOMMENDATIONS.

I earnestly request that consideration be given to my recommendation in the matter of the reduction of the police force of this agency and to the increase of salary of the remaining members of the force, as outlined in this report.

I can not urge too strongly that some definite line of action be adopted in reference to putting allottees in possession of their allotments.

Congress should pass an act appropriating out of Cherokee funds a sufficient amount to pay the indebtedness of the nation.

A law should be passed compelling the Five Civilized Tribes of Indians to adopt a uniform system of taxing noncitizens residing and doing business within the limits of their nations.

There should be established a workhouse or reformatory, to be located at some suitable place in the Indian Territory, to be used as a place of confinement for a certain class of criminals, where they could be given the rudiments of an education.

Roads are in a deplorable condition in the Indian Territory, and I find that no provision has been made for the establishment of roads under the present system of allotting lands.

Many complaints were received at this agency during the year that roads were being fenced or turned, causing great annoyance and inconvenience to the traveling public. There seems to be no law providing for the establishment of highways or public roads, and I recommend that the commission to the Five Civilized Tribes be authorized to withhold from allotment 20 feet on each side of the center of the section line to be used as a highway, and, furthermore, that allottees be required to throw open all roads running through their selections on the section line where practicable.

In concluding this report permit me to say that I have endeavored to manage the affairs of this agency in a way that would be satisfactory to my superiors and beneficial to the great number of Indians under my charge.

I also desire to add that I am indebted to the employees of this agency for faithful service and earnest support in my efforts in behalf of these Indians; and especially am I indebted to Hon. J. George Wright, United States Indian inspector for the Indian Territory, for valuable aid and assistance.

With assurances of my appreciation for favors shown by your office during the year, I have the honor to be,

Very respectfully, your obedient servant,

J. BLAIR SHOENFELT,
United States Indian Agent.

The COMMISSIONER OF INDIAN AFFAIRS.

Report of the Indian Inspector for Indian Territory. 1900.

SUNDAY SCHOOL, INDIANS AND WHITE RENTERS.

REPORT OF SUPERINTENDENT OF SCHOOLS FOR INDIAN TERRITORY.

OFFICE OF SUPERINTENDENT OF SCHOOLS FOR INDIAN TERRITORY,
Muscogee, Ind. T., July 25, 1900.

DEAR SIR: I have the honor to submit my second annual report as Superintendent of the Schools in the Indian Territory, as follows:

PRELIMINARY.

For general information I venture a brief description of conditions as now existing in the Territory.

For the past sixty years or more the Five Civilized Tribes, viz, the Cherokee, Creek, Choctaw, Chickasaw, and Seminole, have owned all the land in the Territory, the members or citizens of each nation or tribe holding in common the tract of land conveyed by the United States to such tribe. The Indian population and total acreage are estimated about as follows:

Tribe or nation.	Population.	Acres of land.	Acres per capita.
Cherokee:			
Indians	30,000		
Freedmen	4,000		
Delaware	1,000		
Total	39,000	5,031,351	129
Creek:			
Indians	10,000		
Freedmen	6,000		
Total	16,000	3,040,000	190
Choctaw:			
Indians	16,000		
Freedmen	4,250		
Total	20,250	6,688,000	330
Chickasaw:			
Indians	6,000		
Freedmen	4,500		
Total	10,500	4,650,935	443
Seminole:			
Indians	1,500		
Freedmen	1,500		
Total	3,000	365,851	122

While the Choctaws and Chickasaws have more land per capita than the other nations, they have also a greater acreage of hilly, untillable land.

CLASSES OF INDIANS.

The Indian population may be divided into four classes, almost equal in number, viz: Full-bloods, half-breeds, freedmen, and intermarried whites, including those who possess but a small degree of Indian blood. Many of the Indians have fenced portions of the land belonging to their respective tribes, have built houses and developed farms. The greater portion of the land, however, remains undeveloped. In the work of making farms and cultivating the land, the "white" Indians, half-breeds, and negroes have been most active, while the full-bloods, as a rule, have been crowded back into the hills, where the restraints of civilization bear but lightly upon them.

FULL-BLOOD INDIANS.

In carrying on the work of education one of the most difficult tasks which confronts us is: How can we reach these full-bloods? They are to some extent nomadic in their habits of life, are governed largely by their prejudices and superstitions, and are naturally jealous of their white brethren who have steadily encroached upon their hunting grounds. They have nearly all adopted the white man's dress, but they are prone to hold tenaciously to many of the customs and modes of living of their ancestors. With some notable exceptions, they do not appreciate the need of education. A school may be started in a given neighborhood with good prospects, but before the end of the term the Indians of that vicinity may all migrate to some other settlement, leaving the teacher without pupils. Doubtless the plan now in vogue in some of the reservation day schools, of furnishing a noonday lunch to the pupils, would produce good results in some of these full-blood settlements, if we had suitable school buildings.

NEIGHBORHOOD SCHOOLS.

While the various Indian nations have expended large sums of money in erecting and maintaining a few boarding schools or academies, in which the children of favored citizens have been educated, free of charge, they have steadily and uniformly refused to build neighborhood school buildings. What is known as the "district school" in the States has received but little attention or encouragement here. There are no country or village schoolhouses in the Territory except such as have been erected by subscription or donation of funds. As a result of this policy it may well be imagined that almost every neighborhood school is conducted in a very cheaply-built, poorly-furnished house. Fully 90 per cent of these houses have no furniture, except the old-fashioned wooden benches.

CHANGING CONDITIONS.

During all these years each Indian nation has maintained its own political organization. Biennnially or quadrennially it has elected its own governor or chief, with full corps of officials. It has maintained its own legislature, composed of an upper and lower house, which has had full power to enact laws for the government of its citizens. It has maintained its own courts, vested with the authority to enforce these laws. It has maintained its own schools, with a code of laws and corps of school officials having absolute power to administer its educational affairs. For years past charges of reckless mismanagement of public affairs, corruption in office, and favoritism in the administration of public business have been so enormous and flagrant that the United States Government, by treaties and by act of Congress, finally determined to curtail the powers of these native officials. The act of June 28, 1898, commonly known as the Curtis Act, abolished their courts and substituted Federal courts in their stead. This act places the financial affairs of the various nations under the supervision of United States Government officials, places their schools under the supervision of the Secretary of the Interior, provides for individual allotment of their lands, and contains provisions tending toward an ultimate extinction of all tribal laws and governments. By reason of this act the Territory is now undergoing changes more important and far-reaching in their results than any ever before imposed upon the Indians. It may well be imagined that the natives, especially the full-bloods, are slow to understand these new requirements and hesitate to adapt their habits and modes of life to these new conditions and environments. The scope and meaning of some of the provisions of the Curtis Act are not readily grasped by the natives, while neither lawyers nor judges agree in their construction and application of these new laws. These conditions tend to create in the minds of the Indians feelings of dissatisfaction with the present state of affairs and feelings of doubt and uncertainty as to the final outcome.

The Federal officials are laboring earnestly and assiduously to protect the interests of the Indians, to fairly adjust their property rights in accordance with the new order of things, and Congress should speedily furnish whatever aid or relief is necessary to complete this enormous task. Owing to these peculiar conditions, the task of improving the educational work of the Territory is an extremely difficult one. Improvement implies change, and the Indians are, by nature, prone to resist changes. Oftentimes, when we find it necessary to make certain changes, we are informed that such changes can not be effected without violating the laws of the various Indian nations. Thus our efforts to improve educational conditions are frequently opposed, especially by that class of natives who are opposed to progress and improvement. Universal education is a greater necessity now among these people than ever before.

Tribal relations are being destroyed, tribal lands are being allotted in severalty, and each individual Indian will soon be expected to look out for himself, to depend upon his own resources, to act according to his own best judgment. These new relations and environments will not be understood or appreciated, these new responsibilities will not be easily borne, unless we succeed in improving the intellectual condition of these natives. We appreciate, I believe, the great importance of the task assigned to us, and while the limited control which we have over the schools of some of these nations prevents our inaugurating many radical reforms, yet we shall labor diligently to improve educational conditions in every possible way.

IMPROVED CONDITIONS.

As a result of our past year's work we can already note some improvements. When we entered upon our duties here, more than a year ago, it was openly charged that various native school boards were selling teachers' positions at from $10 to $25 each. No such charges were made during the past year. With but few exceptions the Indian school boards have cooperated with us heartily. Teachers are manifesting a livelier degree of interest in their work and are endeavoring to improve their qualifications. Some of the poorest teachers have been dropped, not having been able to pass reasonable examinations.

OUR SUMMER NORMALS.

Several months ago I applied to the authorities at Washington for an appropriation with which to conduct summer normal schools for the teachers of the Territory, but owing to the uncertain condition of the numerous bills then pending in Congress relating to Territorial affairs we were unable to secure any financial aid. Knowing something of the great value of normals and institutes to the teachers and to the schools, and knowing that the teachers of the Territory were specially in need of some normal training, we determined to accomplish something along that line. After consultation with the school supervisors and some of the tribal school officials it was agreed that such normals should be held during the month of June in the Cherokee, Creek, and Choctaw nations. These normals were held in the large academies, and a fee of $12 was collected from each teacher in attendance for board, room, and tuition for the term of four weeks. After paying actual cost of board the balance of the funds received was distributed among the instructors who were employed to conduct the recitations. The plan of boarding the teachers, of keeping them together in isolated academies for a month, was a new one, and it was not without some feelings of doubt and anxiety that we undertook this task. We succeeded, however, beyond our expectations. The teachers realized the need of improvement and were eager for the normals. Supervisors Coppock, Ballard, and McArthur spent the entire month of June in the normals of their respective nations and rendered valuable aid to the instructors who were employed during the term. Each of these supervisors taught some classes daily and were ever ready with valuable suggestions concerning school methods and management.

The Cherokee Normal was held at the Female Seminary, Tahlequah, and was attended by about 140 teachers.

The Creek Normal was held at the Eufaula High School, and enrolled about 60 teachers.

The Choctaw Normal was held at the Tushkahoma Female Academy, with an enrollment of about 100 teachers.

Besides the above, normals were also held in the Creek and Cherokee nations for the colored teachers, and were well attended.

The instruction given in all these summer schools was of a practical character, and we feel quite sure that the teachers who attended will enter upon their next year's work with improved methods of teaching and with higher ideals of education.

CHEROKEE SCHOOLS.

The Cherokee have doubtless made more progress in educational affairs than any other nation in the Territory. Their female seminary, male seminary, and orphan asylum are magnificent three-story brick buildings, upon which large sums of money have been expended. The annual closing exercises in these academies are always attended by large crowds of their citizens and are regarded as important events. During the past year the members of their board of education have shown a considerable degree of interest in the educational work of their nation, and as a rule Supervisor Coppock's advice and suggestions have been acted upon favorably by them.

One important change effected in their schools during the past year was the abolition of their winter vacation, which, in former years extended through the months of January and February. Now they have but a short Christmas vacation, and their school year closes before the hot season begins. A comparison of the cost of maintaining these academies during the fiscal year just closed with that of the preceding year shows an average saving of more than a dollar per month for each pupil in attendance.

CREEK SCHOOLS.

The Creeks have been somewhat lavish in the expenditure of funds for school purposes, but have not advanced very rapidly from an educational standpoint. They have more boarding schools than any other nation in the Territory (nine in number), yet not one pupil in a hundred ever reaches a high-school grade. By a law of the Creeks, a boarding school superintendent is declared to be an official of the nation, and therefore none but citizens of their own nation are eligible to these positions. When they had entire control of their own schools, it was not considered necessary that a boarding school superintendent should be an educated man, and it seems difficult yet to convince them that their educational affairs can not be successfully conducted by uneducated people. We have succeeded, however, in removing some of these superintendents who were charged with drunkenness and incompetency, and a healthier educational sentiment prevails now than was apparent a year ago. Through a careful, systematic checking of superintendents' accounts, Supervisor Ballard has reduced the annual expenses of these boarding schools over $5,000, at the same time improving the condition of the schools. Mr. Ballard has gained the confidence of the Creeks, has worked in harmony with the Creek officials and teachers, and they regret to hear that he is being transferred to another nation.

CHOCTAW NATION.

The schools of the Choctaw Nation are now maintained solely by the revenues derived from royalty on coal mined in that nation, as provided by the Atoka agreement and the so-called Curtis Act. The Atoka agreement contains the following provision:

"All coal and asphalt mines in the two nations (Choctaw and Chickasaw), whether now developed or to be hereafter developed, shall be operated and the royalties therefrom paid into the Treasury of the United States, and shall be drawn therefrom under such rules and regulations as shall be prescribed by the Secretary of the Interior."

Section 19 of the Curtis Act also contains the following provision:

"That no payment of any moneys on any account whatever shall hereafter be made by the United States to any of the tribal governments or to any officer thereof for disbursement, but payments of all sums to members of said tribes shall be made under direction of the Secretary of the Interior by an officer appointed by him."

Early in the year 1899 the Secretary of the Interior ruled that as the Atoka agreement and the act of Congress approved June 28, 1898, commonly known as the Curtis Act, provided for the gradual extinction of all tribal officers and of all of their governmental machinery, and that inasmuch as the provisions above quoted placed upon him the responsibility of the proper use and expenditure of these funds, that thereafter all appointments of employees in the schools maintained by the royalty fund should be made by him or under his direction. Acting under instructions, I attended a meeting of the Choctaw board of education, presided over by their principal chief, in April, 1899, and explained to them fully the rulings of the honorable Secretary. No objection whatever was made by any member of the board to our assuming entire control of their schools. The meeting was perfectly harmonious, and from that date (April 5, 1899) until the Choctaw council met in October following their board of education did not attempt to transact any school business, nor did they at any time question our authority to make appointments. During the summer I was in constant communication with the various members of their board and our proposed plans of work received their hearty indorsement. Public examinations were held by us in various parts of the nation and about 100 of the best available teachers were put in charge of their schools on the first of September. All went well until the Choctaw council met in October, when the politicians of that body, who had been accustomed to manipulating the schools in their own personal interests, caused us some annoyance by denying the right of the Secretary of the Interior to control the schools, by ordering their board of education to cease cooperating with us, and by threatening to withdraw their pupils from the academies. Hon. J. George Wright, United States Indian inspector, and the writer visited their council and endeavored to reason with them. We assured them that every effort would be exerted to build up their schools and tried to convince them that their action would simply result in injuring the interests of their own children. After the council adjourned school matters became comparatively quiet again, and I am pleased to note that their academies have had a larger attendance during the year and better teachers were employed than ever before, yet the cost of maintaining these academies has been materially reduced. Having had entire control of the Choctaw schools during the past year, we introduced some work along the line of manual training and domestic science, although we were hampered by the lack of the necessary tools and appliances. At first the pupils were not inclined to look with favor upon this departure from their accustomed routine and declared that they did not come to school to work. Before the year closed, however, many of the boys were proud of the various articles of furniture made by their own hands, such as tables, picture frames, stools, etc., while the girls at the close of school made a very creditable exhibit of their fine needlework.

I regret to report that on the 23d of June last the main building of Spencer Academy was destroyed by fire. A fire was started in the engine, as was customary, for the purpose of operating the steam pump, with which to fill a large tank with water. Sparks from the engine were blown through an open window, from which the bedding in one of the second-story rooms was set on fire. The flames spread rapidly, and as the building was a cheaply constructed, unplastered, frame structure it was impossible to save it. This building cost about $7,000, but could probably be replaced for about $5,000. This academy was destroyed by fire about three years ago and was rebuilt in 1898. The recent fire seems to have been purely accidental, and no blame attaches to any of the employees.

CHICKASAW SCHOOLS.

The five boarding schools were let by contract two or three years ago for a term of five years each by the Chickasaw authorities, and as they are maintained out of funds over which we have no control we have not been able to exercise much supervision over them. Reports received from that nation show that their schools are gradually getting more deeply in debt, and some of the superintendents or contractors of their boarding schools are unable to collect the moneys due them. Their school warrants are not worth their face value in cash, and unless some relief is supplied I fear that their schools will soon become financially embarrassed. Some arrangement should be made by which their share of the royalty fund could be used for the support of their schools. The school funds which the Chickasaws control are not sufficient to support the schools already established by them, yet it is said that the western half of their nation is almost entirely without school privileges.

Supervisor Simpson has been ever ready to assist and advise the Chickasaws upon school matters, but our limited authority in that nation has prevented our making much improvement in conditions.

I submit herewith a brief summary of statistics pertaining to the schools over which we exercise supervision, and for further information in detail I respectfully refer to the reports of the supervisors of the various nations which are presented herewith. A comparison of these statistics with those of former years will show that in the Cherokee, Creek, and Choctaw nations the expenses of maintaining schools have been materially reduced, while our system of examinations and supervision has enabled us to get rid of some incompetent employees and to improve the character of the work in many of the schools.

CHEROKEE SCHOOLS.

School.	Enrollment.	Average attendance.	Months of school.	Annual cost.	Average cost per pupil.	Number of employees.
Male seminary	120	80	9	$11,390.00	$131.75	
Female seminary	135	105	9	15,840.00	150.84	
Orphan Asylum	138	124	9	15,125.00	121.95	
Colored High School	45	23	9	3,400.00	147.78	
Total	438	332		45,755.00	137.81	
124 neighborhood schools	3,920	2,195	7	30,380.00	13.98	
Total	4,358	2,527		76,135.00		

CREEK SCHOOLS.

School.	Enrollment.	Average attendance.	Months of school.	Annual cost.	Average cost per pupil.	Nu of pl(
Eufaula	100	80	9	$7,784.76	$104.81	
Creek Orphan	60	55	9	6,562.16	130.22	
Euchee	80	58	9	6,668.15	123.76	
Wetumka	100	82	9	8,614.76	112.37	
Coweta	50	38	9	4,483.55	131.15	
Wealaka	50	39	9	3,909.48	115.37	
Tullahassee (colored)	100	80	9	8,057.88	108.22	
Pecan Creek (colored)	65	50	9	4,262.73	95.25	
Colored Orphan	35	24	9	2,000.18	104.15	
Total	640	506	....	52,483.65	113.92	
55 neighborhood schools	1,745	1,042	9	13,228.42	12.68	
Total	2,385	1,548	....	65,657.07	....	

CHICKASAW SCHOOLS.

School.	Enrollment.	Average attendance.	Months of school.	Annual cost.	Average cost per pupil.	Nu of pl(
Orphan Home	59	47	10	$6,500.00	$180.00	
Wahpanucka Male Institute	79	60	10	13,000.00	216.00	
Collins Female Institute	38	38	10	6,600.00	173.00	
Harley Male Institute	80	75	10	13,200.00	176.00	
Bloomfield Female Seminary	92	86	10	15,180.00	176.00	
Total	348	306	....	55,480.00	151.00	
17 neighborhood schools	489	386	10	36,115.00	93.00	
Total	837	692	....	92,595.00	....	

CHOCTAW SCHOOLS.

School.	Enrollment.	Average attendance.	Months of school.	Annual cost.	Average cost per pupil.	Nu of pl(
Jones Academy	110	81	9	$12,771.54	$157.67	
Spencer Academy	105	81	9	12,345.48	152.41	
Tushkahoma Female Academy	111	98	9	12,656.99	129.15	
Armstrong Male Orphan Academy	78	78	9	10,098.96	129.41	
Wheelock Female Orphan Academy	87	78	9	9,578.97	120.18	
Atoka Baptist Academy	58	55	9	5,569.10	101.25	....
Total	549	471	....	63,011.04	140.66	....
120 neighborhood schools	2,170	1,812	9	27,570.91	12.70	....
Total	2,719	2,283	....	90,581.95	....	....

NOTE.—In addition to the above cost, the sum of $2,300 was expended for repairs, hardwar(plies, and irregular labor.

SCHOOL CENSUS OF THE TERRITORY.

We have not had the necessary facilities for securing an accurate school cen(the Territory, but by the aid of our supervisors and teachers I have been ab compile the following estimate of the number of children between the ages of (18 years:

Nation.	Indians.	Negroes.	Whites.	'
Cherokee	8,340	950	10,000	
Creek	1,850	1,300	3,500	
Choctaw	4,000	1,000	16,000	
Chickasaw	1,500	1,000	25,000	
Seminole	400	400	100	
Total school population	16,090	4,650	54,600	

INDUSTRIAL AND MANUAL TRAINING.

My past year's experience in these Indian schools has led me to see the necessity of introducing some systematic work along the lines of industrial and ual training and domestic science.

It is high time that those who are responsible for the education of any class of children should realize that their educational training should be such as will prepare the children for the fullest enjoyment of the kind of life which they, in all human probability, are likely to lead. The purpose of the Government in educating children is to prepare them to become good citizens. It is true that one who is able to support himself and his family and is orderly in the community and obedient to the laws is a good citizen; but one who can do these things and in addition thereto can help other people to live by giving them employment, or who can add to the wealth of the world, is a still better citizen. Paupers, criminals, idlers, the sick, and the helpless are not useful citizens; but only those who are fitted for self-support, who are able to take care of money, who are able to buy and pay for the products of others, who are prepared to do a part in this commercial, industrial, mechanical world as now organized, are good citizens. To make such citizens is the aim of our best modern schools.

An education which fits for teaching, preaching, medicine, law, or for clerking in a store is good for those who follow those vocations; but all can not follow them. None of these vocations are constructive. It is only by work that all these material things that make our civilization so superior to all others have come into being. The work of the world must be done or we shall at once fall below the plane of civilization on which we are now living. It, therefore, is the function of these schools to train its pupils to work—to be able to learn how to build houses, how to furnish them, how to care for house and furniture, how to cook food so it will be both palatable and healthful as well as economical—how to make garments and how to mend them, and how to make and manage the machinery which is now so large a part of all our home and business life.

There is no difficulty in teaching these things to children and young people. There is nothing else that is so interesting to them, nor anything else in which their advancement is more marked. These matters are easily put in such form that the child or young person readily learns them. The great success of the manual-training and domestic-science schools of all places where established fully proves that these arts can be as readily taught as any other branches of our educational curricula. That German manufactures are found in every market at this dawn of the twentieth century is the result of establishing such schools in the Fatherland.

Nor need any one fear that pure education—mental discipline—will suffer by the founding of such schools. It has been proved beyond question that our men of large affairs are our men of greatest mental power; that business gives a mental training fully equal to that of the books; that the world around us and our minds are so interrelated that for most people there is no higher mental discipline possible than the discipline that comes in the lines of the preparation of the most useful and most helpful living.

It is a true saying, "As the twig is bent, the tree is inclined." It is also true that the bent given the child in his school days determines his inclination in after life. If his schooling is entirely in books, his inclination will be toward some bookish profession; and if we wish him to follow some more active vocation we must give him a more active training. If he is to be an agriculturist, he should be trained along the lines of farming and stock raising and the like. If he is to be a builder, he should be trained along the lines of mechanics and architecture. If he is to go to the head of some great business interest, he must be trained along the lines that pertain to that business. If he is to be a mechanic, it is better to give him a training of the hand that will fit him to do his work well and easily. Manual training is hand training and hand training is brain training, for the hand can only do the things which the brain has first thought out. To get the greatest brain training the hand also must be trained. The scientist has shown us that the brain tracts which control the nerves that extend to the hand are of very great area. There is no way to cultivate these brain tracts—to develop these brain cells—but by training the hand. Other things being equal, the man having the best hand training has the highest education. Those people which are foremost in the world's affairs have the highest hand training. The preeminence of the Greeks in the highest culture of the world for the past two thousand years is due largely to their wonderful hand training as shown in their temples, their columns, and their statuary. It is only what the hand does that endures. The human voice may speak words that will move the hearers to deeds of marvelous heroism. The voice of the singer may melt to tears or raise to loftiest ecstacy, but when the orator is absent or dead, and when the singer is silent, their powers are gone forever.

But let the hand be trained so that the words of the orator may be written down, cut in marble, or printed in books, let the song of the singer be written in music, and the words of the orator may thrill thousands who live in distant lands and the notes of the singer may send their sweet echo round the world.

It is only by the hand that man can give birth to his fullest thoughts and make them immortal. Does he think a beautiful edifice? If his hand is trained he can draw it upon paper, and other men with trained hands can erect it. Does he think out a new machine? The thought is worthless unless with trained hand he can work it out in metal and in wood, as did Fulton and Watt. Do beautiful forms flit through his brain? No one else can be charmed by their beauty unless, like Michael Angelo he can paint them on dome or canvas. "The artist sees in the wayside stone the angel form struggling to be free," but the angel will never enjoy its freedom till some one whose hands are skilled with mallet and chisel releases it from its bondage.

When it is realized how much of our health and wealth and life and happiness depend upon the skillful hands of some one, or rather of many, can any one doubt that there is need of hand training in the schools? Nor can this training wisely be delayed till later life. Unless those brain cells that connect with the delicate nerves of the hands and the fingers are used in youth they will not grow, and very early in the life of the youth it becomes impossible for them to be used. So the modern school gives the boy as well as the girl the needle and the knife to use, and later other delicate instruments that these nerve tracts may come into use, and may grow as the child grows. Boys need this training quite as much as girls. That the fingers of the average man are very much more awkward than those of the average woman is because in youth he did not receive the delicate training that she received. A baby boy's fingers are no more clumsy than a baby girl's, and if he is to be as deft as she he must have the same youthful training. Since steam and electricity have been harnessed to do the work of man, he needs a great dexterity of hand rather than great physical power.

Regarding domestic science—household arts—all that needs be said is: All the world eats and nearly all the world lives in houses. Probably 90 per cent of "all the ills that human flesh is heir to" have their origin in our food or in our unsanitary homes. Very many families fail to accumulate property—are kept always in poverty—because of wastefulness in cooking and in the other household matters, or because of sickness produced by faulty cooking and unwise eating or unhealthy home surroundings. There is enough of wisdom in the world to save people from this poverty and this sickness. And this wisdom can easily be put in a teachable form, and can be presented to girls so that they take great pleasure in learning it; nor is it more expensive than any other kind of schooling. It only needs that these schools be established and then all is so simple, so easy, and of such high value that everybody will wonder why these things were not always taught.

The teaching of these industrial arts does not in any way lessen the amount of scholarship acquired along the usual scholastic lines, but on the contrary is an aid to them. The rule is that those pupils who are most proficient in their literature, languages, mathematics, and sciences are also the ablest in their industrial arts and studies.

The work of the world must be done. It were better done by skilled than by unskilled hands. The vast majority of these children must do some kind of work of business. The school should train them for their life work. As these schools have heretofore been conducted their tendency has been to train away from work rather than toward work. The result is that work and business are distasteful to our Indian pupils. It is believed that an industrial schooling will change this matter greatly and that the lives of many can be made pleasant where otherwise they would be irksome.

SCHOOLS FOR NONCITIZENS OR WHITE CHILDREN.

I desire to renew the recommendation in my last annual report, to the effect that some provision be made for aiding the establishment of free schools for the white children of the Territory. About a dozen of the cities and villages of the Territory have attempted to establish free schools, but they are badly hampered by the fact that they can not levy tax upon any of the real estate in the Territory and have no power to issue bonds for building schoolhouses. All of the real estate is as yet vested in the Indians and is nontaxable. For this reason no land can be appropriated for school purposes. Outside of the incorporated cities there is no provision of law by which public-school districts can be organized; hence there are thousands of children scattered throughout the country and villages who are deprived of the privileges of free schools. The parents of these children are not responsible for the conditions which surround them, and until they can legally help themselves, Congress ought to be induced to furnish the necessary relief. While making commendable efforts to educate the far-away islanders of the sea, who are foreign to our civilization and who are not bound to us by any ties of race or relationship, our lawmakers should not

Report of the Indian Inspector for Indian Territory, 1900.

forget that here in the heart of own country are thousands of American boys and girls growing into American citizenship, who, by no fault of their parents, are deprived of the benefits of the American common school. Certainly, charity should in this, as in other instances, begin at home.

CHOCTAW AND CHICKASAW FREEDMEN.

In my last annual report I called attention to the fact that by the provisions of the act of Congress of June 28, 1898, the colored citizens of the Choctaw and Chickasaw nations are prevented from participating in school funds derived from royalties on coal and asphalt. These colored people are left without schools or school funds. Their children are growing up in ignorance. They could not legally tax themselves for the support of schools, even if they were able to bear the burden of such taxation. They are not permitted to attend any of the schools established for whites or Indians, and some provision should be made for their education.

CONCLUSION.

In closing I desire to testify to the earnestness and zeal manifested by our supervisors, whose annual reports are submitted herewith. They have encountered many difficulties and discouragements, but have at all times striven to do everything in their power to advance the educational interests of the Territory. We regret to lose Supervisor McArthur, who has recently been transferred to the reservation school at Pawhuska, Okla. His earnest, able efforts in behalf of the Choctaws justify us in assuring the authorities at Washington that he will always be found equal to any task that may be imposed upon him.

In the consideration of the many vexed questions that arise by reason of the peculiar conditions existing in the Territory, we have constantly received valuable aid from the Hon. J. George Wright, United States Indian inspector. His long experience in the Indian school service and his patient, constant devotion to duty have qualified him thoroughly for the position which he occupies.

The newspapers of the Territory must be recognized as a powerful auxiliary in the upbuilding of the educational work of the Territory. Their columns are always open to us, and almost without exception their editorials tend toward higher ideals in education.

Respectfully submitted.

JOHN D. BENEDICT,
Superintendent of Schools in Indian Territory.

The COMMISSIONER OF INDIAN AFFAIRS,
Washington, D. C.

ANNUAL REPORT OF THE SCHOOL SUPERVISOR FOR THE CREEK NATION, INDIAN TERRITORY.

OFFICE OF SUPERVISOR OF SCHOOLS FOR CREEK NATION,
Muscogee, Ind. T., June 16, 1900.

SIR: I have the honor to submit herewith my annual report of the school affairs in the Creek Nation for the scholastic year ending June 30, 1900.

There are 10 boarding schools and 55 neighborhood schools in the nation, all of which except 7 of the latter were in session from September 4, 1899, till May 11, 1900. These 7 neighborhood schools were discontinued April 10 on account of smallpox being prevalent in the neighborhoods.

The schools opened under unfavorable circumstances. Conditions were unsettled, the Indians were indifferent about sending their children to school, reports were circulated that the Creek council would make no appropriations for supporting the schools, and that the schools would close at the end of the first quarter; consequently the attendance during this quarter was not good.

The council made the appropriations, the schools continued, the Indians began to have confidence in our efforts, and the attendance during the remainder of the year was comparatively good.

BOARDING SCHOOLS.

Buildings.—The buildings at all of the boarding schools are in a fairly good condition. Repairs were made during the year and some additional buildings erected at several of the schools.

Superintendents.—The superintendents at all of these schools are Creek citizens, and, with the exception of two, they have been reasonably attentive to their duties and have been prompt in complying with requests of the supervisor.

Teachers.—Nearly all of the teachers were noncitizens, all of whom proved to be fairly successful in the work.

Health.—The health at several of the schools was not good. Many of the children were troubled with sore eyes during the early part of the year. Measles, pneumonia, and scarlet fever visited some of the schools. Several deaths occurred.

NEIGHBORHOOD SCHOOLS.

Buildings.—The buildings are not very good, many of them being log huts 12 by 14 feet, rudely constructed, well ventilated, poorly lighted, containing no furniture save some old style puncheon benches. A few of the buildings are frame box buildings in fairly good condition, but without suitable furniture. No supplies, such as maps, charts, and other necessary equipments for good schools, are found in any of the neighborhood schools. The buildings are erected and owned by the patrons of the school, and are used for church purposes as well as for school.

Teachers.—Of the 55 teachers, 20 are white, 13 Indian, and 22 negro. Many of the teachers, especially the Indians and colored citizens, have had no normal training and their scholarship is very limited.

Some of the white teachers are wide awake young men and women, who seem to be very much interested in building up these schools, yet the salary they receive (from $25 to $35 per month), and the inconveniences they find at their boarding places, do not offer much inducement for them to put forth the energy they would otherwise exert if surroundings were different.

Visitation.—I have visited all of the boarding schools and nearly all of the neighborhood schools. In many instances I took charge of classes and conducted the recitations and made suggestions to the teachers on the general management of the schools.

Normals.—During the month of June we had two successful normals, one at the Colored Orphan Home, the other at the Eufaula High School. More than one hundred teachers attended these normals, and good interest was manifested throughout.

Finances.—Aside from the regular school work, I have investigated all of the expenditures for the support of the schools, examined and approved all warrants issued against the school appropriations, and have kept a record of same, showing to whom issued, for what purpose, amount, date of issue, and date of my approval.

Following is a tabulated report of the Creek schools:

EUFAULA HIGH SCHOOL.

Employees.	Position.	Salary per month.	Race.	Age.	Single or married.	Birthplace.
A. L. Posey	Superintendent	a $600	Indian .	28	Married ..	Creek Nation.
Frank Shortall	Principal teacher	60	White ..	22	Single	Illinois.
Elizabeth A. Scott	Assistant teacher	45	....do ...	21	.....do	Cherokee Nation.
Francis Scott	....do	40	....do ...	23	.....do	Do.
Stella Blake	....do	40	....do ...	19	.....do	Missouri.
Mattie Fears	....do	35	....do ...	20	.....do	Texas.
Mrs. A. L. Posey	Matron	40	....do ...	26	Married ..	Arkansas.
Katherine Harris	Assistant matron	20	....do ...	21	Single	Do.
Robert Johnson	Cook	30	Negro ..	50	Married ..	Virginia.
Joe Grayson	Laborer	20	Indian .	24	Single	Arkansas.

a Per year.

Enrollment	100
Average attendance	80
Annual appropriation	$9,000.00
Amount expended	$7,784.76
Balance unexpended	$1,215.24

CREEK ORPHAN HOME.

Employees.	Position.	Salary per month.	Race.	Age.	Single or married.	Birthplace.
George W. Tiger.....	Superintendent........	a $600	Indian .	34	Married ..	Creek Nation.
P. A. Atkins.........	Principal teacher	50	White ..	25	Single	Kansas.
Anna Peterson	Assistant teacher	50	....do ...	24	.....do	Pennsylvania.
Anna Wright........	....do..............	50	....do ...	27	.....do	Virginia.
Mrs. L. B. Simpson...	Seamstress	35	....do ...	41	Widow ..	Kentucky.
Hepsey Jimboy......	Matron	30	Indian .	26	Single ...	Creek Nation.
J. Porter............	Cook	30	Negro ..	58	Married ..	Indian Territory.
Moss Byrde..........	Laborer	20	Indian .	29	.....do	Creek Nation.

a Per year.

Enrollment 60
Average attendance 55
Annual appropriation $6,666.66
Amount expended.. $6,562.16
Balance unexpended $104.50

WETUMKA BOARDING SCHOOL.

Employees.	Position.	Salary per month.	Race.	Age.	Single or married.	Birthplace.
J. S. Robison.........	Superintendent........	a $600	Indian .	42	Married ..	Creek Nation.
Mrs. J. S. Robison	Matron	25	....do ...	35	.....do	Do.
R. E. Cornelius	Principal teacher	50	White ..	26	.....do	Mississippi.
E. H. Bell...........	Assistant teacher	45	....do ...	20	Single ...	Texas.
Lena Benson	....do..............	40	Indian .	25	.....do	Creek Nation.
Hattie Benson.......	....do..............	35	....do ...	18	.....do	Do.
Dr. A. J. Hoover......	Physician	50	White ..	38	Married ..	North Carolina.
Mrs. A. J. Hoover	Music teacher	30	....do ...	26	.....do	Texas.
Clara Cornelius......	Boys' matron	20	....do ...	25	.....do	Mississippi.
Ada Carr...........	Girls' matron	20	Indian .	20	Single ...	Creek Nation.
J. K. Ditzler..........	Laborer	25	White ..	46	.....do	Ohio.
O. C. Ogeltree.......	Cook	25	....do ...	25	Married ..	Alabama.
Polly Chisholm.......	Laundress	10	Indian .	18	Single ...	Creek Nation.
Milly Harper	....do..............	10	....do ...	29	.....do	Do.

a Per year.

Enrollment 100
Average attendance 82
Annual appropriation.. $9,000.00
Amount expended.. $8,614.76
Balance unexpended... $385.24

EUCHEE BOARDING SCHOOL.

Employees.	Position.	Salary per month.	Race.	Age.	Single or married.	Birthplace.
W. A. Sapulpa	Superintendent........	a $500	Indian..		Widower .	Creek Nation.
G. C. Hughes........	Principal teacher	60	White ..		Married ..	Virginia.
Z. B. Hughes........	Assistant teacher	45	....do ...		.....do	West Virginia.
Dr. E. Keene........	Physician............	25	....do ...		Widow ..	Missouri.
Mrs. E. B. Hughes....	Matron	22	....do ...		Married ..	Arkansas.
Lulu E. Brown	Assistant matron	17	....do ...		Single ...	Illinois.
Mrs. Dotson..........	Cook	27	....do ...		Widow ..	Missouri.
Mrs. M. E. Howe.....	Laundress	17	....do ...		.....do	Wisconsin.
Cornelia Brown	Dining matron	17	....do ...	40	.....do	Missouri.
Gano Lee.............	Laborer	20	Indian..	58	Married ..	Creek Nation.

a Per year.

Enrollment 80
Average attendance 58
Annual appropriation $7,200.00
Amount expended $6,668.15
Balance unexpended... $531.85

COWETA BOARDING SCHOOL.

Employees.	Position.	Salary per month.	Race.	Age.	Single or Married.	Birthplace.
O. A. Morton	Superintendent	a$500.00	Indian	29	Married	Creek Nation.
Mrs. O. A. Morton	Principal teacher	50.00	White	28	....do....	Kansas.
Susanna Grimes	Assistant teacher	35.00	Indian	28	Single	Creek Nation.
S. J. Biggs	Matron	20.00	....do...	28	....do....	Do.
Emma Lynch	Assistant matron	22.50	White	29	Widow	Do.
Esther Miles	Cook	25.00	....do...	24	Single	Arkansas.
Alfred Olmsted	Laborer	22.50	....do...	31	....do....	Missouri.
Fannie Haynie	Laundress	22.50	....do...	39	Married	Washington, D. C.

a Per year.

Enrollment 50
Average attendance 38
Annual appropriation $4,500.00
Amount expended.. $4,483.55
Balance unexpended.. $16.45

WEALAKA BOARDING SCHOOL.

Employees.	Position.	Salary per month.	Race.	Age.	Single or married.	Birthplace.
E. E. Hardridge	Superintendent	a$500	Indian	36	Married	Creek Nation.
George C. Kindley	Principal teacher	55	White	34	Widower	Missouri.
Mabel Hall	Assistant teacher	35	....do...	26	Single	Iowa.
Mollie Jefferson	Matron	20	....do...	32	....do....	Arkansas.
Mrs. E. E. Hardridge	....do	20	Indian	31	Married	Creek Nation.
Lizzie Moore	....do	20	....do...	30	Single	Do.
W. I. Ellis	Cook	25	White	39	Married	Texas.
Mrs. W. I. Ellis	Laundress	18	....do...	34	....do....	Arkansas.
Walter Esco	Laborer	20	Indian	20	Single	Texas.

a Per year.

Enrollment 50
Average attendance 38
Annual appropriation $4,500.00
Amount expended.. $3,999.42
Balance unexpended.. $500.59

TULLAHASSEE BOARDING SCHOOL.

Employees.	Position.	Salary per month.	Race.	Age.	Single or married.	Birthplace.
B. H. Richards	Superintendent	a$600	Negro	38	Married	Creek Nation.
L. E. Willis	Principal teacher	50	....do...	28	....do....	Arkansas.
Laura A. Jackson	Assistant teacher	45	....do...	26	Single	Creek Nation.
E. D. Harrison	....do	40	....do...	22	....do....	Do.
Celia Roberts	....do	35	....do...	26	....do....	Do.
Mrs. B. H. Richards	Matron	35	....do...	33	Married	Do.
Mary Manuel	Laundress	20	....do...	42	Widow	Do.

a Per year.

Enrollment 100
Average attendance 80
Annual appropriation $9,000.00
Amount expended.. $8,057.88
Balance unexpended.. $942.12

FULL-BLOOD BOYS AT AN INDIAN BOARDING SCHOOL.

PECAN CREEK BOARDING SCHOOL.

Employees.	Position.	Salary per month.	Race.	Age.	Single or married.	Birthplace.
George H. Taylor....	Superintendent........	a $500	Negro	36	Married ..	Creek Nation.
W. R. Pamplin	Principal teacher.....	50	....do ...	20	Single	Illinois.
Mrs. M. L. Craw.....	Assistant teacher	40	....do ...	25	Married ..	Kansas.
Mrs. G. H. Taylor....	Matron	30	....do ...	30	.....do	Illinois.
Alice Tobler.........	Cook	15	....do ...	22	Single	Creek Nation.
James Long	Laborer	25	....do ...	32	Married ..	Do.

a Per year.

```
Enrollment.............................................................................   65
Average attendance ....................................................................   50
Annual appropriation .................................................................. $4,500.00
Amount expended....................................................................... $4,262.73
Balance unexpended.................................................................... $237.27
```

COLORED ORPHAN HOME.

Employees.	Position.	Salary per month.	Race.	Age.	Single or married.	Birthplace.
N. W. Perryman.....	Superintendent.......	a $500	Negro ..	31	Married ..	Creek Nation.
Howard Jenkins	Principal teacher.....	50	....do ...	28	Single	Missouri.
Jennie McIntosh....	Music teacher.........	30	....do ...	24	....do	Creek Nation.
Mrs. N. W. Perryman	Matron	25	....do ...	21	Married ..	Do.
Nettie Thompson....	Cook	12	....do ...	21	Single	Do.
Crum Island.........	Laborer	10	....do ...	18	.....do	Do.

a Per year.

```
Enrollment.............................................................................   35
Average attendance ....................................................................   24
Annual appropriation .................................................................. $3,333.33
Amount expended....................................................................... $2,000.18
Balance unexpended.................................................................... $1,333.15
```

SUMMARY.

School.	Appropriation.	Expenditure.	Unexpended.	Enrollment.	Average attendance.	Indian.	Negro.	White.	Total.
Eufaula	$9,000.00	$7,784.76	$1,215.24	100	80	2	1	7	10
Creek Orphan Home..	6,666.66½	6,562.16	104.50	60	55	3	1	4	8
Enchee...............	7,200.00	6,668.15	531.85	80	58	2	....	8	10
Wetumka	9,000.00	8,614.76	385.24	100	82	7	....	7	14
Coweta..............	4,500.00	4,483.55	16.45	50	38	3	....	5	8
Wealaka.............	4,500.00	3,999.48	500.52	50	39	4	....	5	9
Tullahassee	9,000.00	8,057.88	942.12	100	80	....	7	....	7
Colored Orphan	3,333.33¼	2,000.18	1,333.15	35	24	....	6	....	6
Pecan Creek, colored .	4,500.00	4,262.73	237.27	65	50	....	6	....	6
Neighborhood schools	16,842.00	13,223.42	3,618.58	1,745	1,042	13	22	20	55
Total	74,542.00	65,657.07	8,884.93	2,385	1,548	34	43	56	133

Approximate number of children in the Creek Nation between the ages of 5 and 18 years.

	Male.	Female.	Total.
Indian	700	750	1,450
Negro	600	700	1,300
White	1,300	1,450	2,750
Total	2,600	2,900	5,500

In concluding my report I desire to state that the cooperation of the Creek school superintendent and other Creek officials has been secured, and that a very harmonious feeling exists.

Very respectfully submitted.

CALVIN BALLARD,
School Supervisor Creek Nation.

Hon. JOHN D. BENEDICT,
Superintendent of Schools in Indian Territory.

REPORT OF CHEROKEE SCHOOL SUPERVISOR.

VINITA, IND. T., *July 10, 1900.*

SIR: I have the honor to submit my second annual report on educational matters in the Cherokee Nation.

I have devoted much of the past year to visitation of the schools and a consideration of their management, condition, and needs, and the facilities at hand for increasing their efficiency.

The system of schools is by Cherokee law under the control of a board of education, which is composed of three members, who are elected by the national council. The council determines the number of schools and appropriates funds for their support. The school board is authorized to conduct examinations, employ those who are properly qualified to teach, and to issue requisitions upon the chief for warrants against the school appropriations in favor of each teacher for the amount due him. The school board appoints three directors in each neighborhood where a school is established, whose duty it is to see that a suitable house is provided, with proper furnishings and fuel for the needs of the school.

At the close of a session the teacher makes a report, upon blanks furnished, giving the aggregate enrollment, the average attendance, the number of males and females, number of each under and above 10 years of age, and the number of days taught. This report is the basis upon which rests the requisition for a warrant to pay the teacher. It is signed by at least two of the local directors and its correctness is sworn to by the teacher. The salary of all teachers is fixed by act of the national council.

There are 124 ungraded neighborhood schools, 28 of which are denominated full-blood, and 15 for the freedmen are separate from the other schools. There are 4 boarding schools, the male seminary and female seminary at Tahlequah, the colored high school near Tahlequah, and an orphan home near Pryor Creek.

The Cherokee people have had schools for more than fifty years supported by public funds, in addition to various church mission schools. The number of schools has been increased from time to time, until at present 124 primary schools are maintained. The seminaries were founded by an act of council in 1846 and opened in 1850; the orphan asylum and colored high school were opened later. My observation upon the schools, buildings, appliances, and school laws has caused me to think there have been periods of school interest, when practical educators have guided in affairs and a time of general educational interest has prevailed, out of which has come new buildings and better schools. Then other periods of neglect and general inefficiency in management of educational matters have ensued, when schools have fallen into neglect and teachers were employed to draw the salaries. Inquiries among discreet citizens confirm this view. One of the periods of greatest incompetency in managing the school affairs of the nation occurred about the time the Secretary of the Interior decided to send representatives to the Indian Territory to supervise in school matters.

Upon coming to look over the situation here I learned that two members of the board had been recently changed, and the present members were gentlemen against whom no charges had been made of gross drunkenness and malfeasance in office. They were anxious to show what they could do by way of correcting abuses and improving the schools. I thought it best to advise with the board and encourage them in administering the schools in accordance with Cherokee law. We jointly conducted the examinations for teachers, and the board appointed teachers from those who received certificates and from graduates of the seminaries.

The national council in November elected two new members to the board. The present organization are Harvey W. C. Shelton, president; Thomas Carlile, secretary; Theodore Perry, member. These gentlemen have spent much time visiting schools during the term—February 2 to June 1. After a few weeks of visitation they unanimously came to the conclusion with me that one of the most urgent needs of the schools of the nation is a corps of trained teachers.

A SUMMER NORMAL.

We jointly signed a call for a summer teachers' normal, to be held at the female seminary building at Tahlequah, and at the same time a section of the colored high school for the colored teachers, from June 4 to 29, inclusive.

We agreed, in the appointments of teachers to be made, to give preference to those who should attend the normal, take the work, and pass creditably the examinations.

We employed a corps of competent instructors to aid in the normal. One hundred and forty applicants were enrolled at the seminary and 22 at the colored high school. The number in attendance and the evident benefit of the normal was

HOME OF UNEDUCATED INDIANS.

beyond everyone's expectation, as we had encountered intense and persistent opposition to the summer school. In addition to the branches taught in the common schools, we gave a course in theory and practice of teaching; one in psychology; model class instruction in first reader, number, and desk work, using 20 small children to practically demonstrate methods and results; a course in methods of teaching English and Latin for seminary teachers, and a daily counsel of teachers for the discussion of school affairs.

SCHOOLHOUSES.

There are, perhaps, 200 schoolhouses scattered through the territory of the nation; 124 are used each term for nation schools. In many of the others subscription schools are maintained a part of the time. Some of the houses are frame of suitable dimensions, lined and ceiled, with good floors and shingle roofs, and containing from six to eight windows. Many other houses are simple box structures, some of them cleated, and some with cracks open. Such houses mostly have four windows, the whole structure costing from $50 to $100. In the wooded sections many of the houses are of logs and contain one, two, or four windows. For bad weather the log houses are much more comfortable than the box houses. A few of them are supplied with manufactured desks, blackboards, and recitation seats. A great majority are defective in structure, having poor facilities for school work, being open so as to expose the children in severe weather, deficient in lighting, heating, and seating facilities. However, a new interest seems to have awakened, and more houses have been ceiled and otherwise repaired during the last year than for several years previous thereto. This is especially noticeable in full-blood neighborhoods. Perhaps a majority of the houses are used also for Sabbath school and church purposes.

BOOKS.

Most of the schoolbooks are supplied by the nation, $3,575 having been expended for that purpose last year, when a new list of text-books was adopted and introduced. Many of the schools are only partially supplied with books.

FINANCIAL.

An act of the Cherokee council appropriating funds for the support of schools, dated December 9, 1899, and approved by the President January 5, 1900, carried—

For 124 primary schools	$30, 380
For male seminary	11, 125
For female seminary	15, 125
For colored high school	3, 050
For orphan asylum	14, 525
For repairs on seminaries	1, 500
For medical attendance at seminaries	935
For medical attendance at colored high school	500
For medical attendance at orphan asylum	600
For salary and expenses of school board	2, 100
For deficiency appropriation for boarding schools	1, 357
For appropriation for books	3, 575
For education of blind	300
Total appropriation for school purposes	85, 072

CHEROKEE WARRANTS.

During the year it was made my duty to register and indorse all warrants issued by the nation against the school fund and the insane fund. In prosecution of this work I have looked carefully into the character and quality of service rendered or goods furnished, and have found generally the money has been prudently expended. I have been pleased to notice the officers of the nation and teachers are willing to cooperate for the betterment of the schools. They appreciate advice, suggestion, and guidance that will enable them to show faithfulness and good results in service and to merit credit for expenditures made.

SMALLPOX.

Early in January numerous cases of smallpox were reported from various parts of the nation. As the pupils gathered to the boarding schools word passed out rapidly that children were in school who had been exposed to the contagion. The medical board removed some from each seminary and placed them under quarantine. The effect was to have some pupils withdraw from school and many others were deterred from coming. A few of the neighborhood schools were closed on account of it. The general effect was to interfere with the enrollment and regular attendance of pupils. Nevertheless, the year's attendance and the work at the female seminary and the orphan asylum were fully up to the standard, and the male seminary and the colored high school were about the best for several years past.

One hundred and twenty-four primary schools are in session twelve weeks in the fall and sixteen weeks in the spring, or seven months in the year. The teachers are paid $35 per month of twenty days. The seminaries are in session nine months in the year.

The following statistics of general and scholastic population are the most reliable obtainable. I have made the school statistics from the term reports of the teachers. In estimating the general population, acting upon your suggestion, I addressed a blank to each of the neighborhood teachers, requesting them to furnish me a carefully prepared statement of the children in the neighborhood of school age, reporting separately male and female, Cherokee, white, and negro. I also secured the school census of Vinita and Claremore, the two largest towns in the nation. Using this data as a basis, I have estimated the remaining towns and communities of the nation and record the result of my calculations.

Cherokee primary schools for 1899–1900.

[From sworn reports of teachers.]

Number of mixed-blood schools, 109; negro, 15; total	124
Enrollment mixed-blood school	3,920
Males 2,012	
Females 1,908	
Average attendance	2,195
Attendance per cent of enrollment	56
Enrollment of boarding schools	395
Enrollment of 15 negro schools	948
Male 414	
Female 534	
Average attendance	559
Per cent of attendance	59

School children in Cherokee Nation.

Children from 6 to 8 years of Cherokee blood	8,340
Children from 6 to 18 years of negro blood	2,120
Children from 6 to 18 years of noncitizen white	9,552
Per cent of primary and boarding schools enrollment of citizen children	52
Per cent of average attendance of citizen children	30
Per cent of enrollment of negro children of whole number	45
Per cent of average attendance of negro children of whole number in Cherokee Nation	26

OTHER SCHOOLS.

Under law of Congress approved June 28, 1898, in the incorporated towns of Indian Territory, free public schools may be established and maintained under control of boards elected by the legal voters and supported by funds secured by taxation.

Vinita, Claremore, Nowata, Webbers Falls, and Muldron maintained graded schools the past year. Vinita and Claremore own their school buildings. In these towns free schools are permanently established, are equipped to do good work, are the pride of citizens, and hopefully lead in stable conditions of self-help that end in statehood. A few other towns have voted to establish free schools. A number of excellent church mission schools are maintained in the nation. Willie Halsell College, at Vinita, by the Methodist Episcopal Church South; Tahlequah Institute, by the Presbyterian Church; Cherokee Academy, by the Baptists, at Tahlequah; Chelsea Academy, at Chelsea, by the Presbyterians; and Skiatook Academy, by the Friends, at Skiatook. These institutions are positive educational forces in and near the neighborhoods where they are located. There is an academy at Pryor Creek, one at Afton, and one at Fairland, each supported by subscription, which supply certain educational needs of these growing towns.

I attended the commencement exercises of the Cherokee Orphan Asylum, the male and female seminaries, and the Colored High School. These are educational events of much importance to the Cherokees. The attendance of representative citizens was large; the exercises were creditable, and much school enthusiasm was manifested. There were four graduates from the male seminary and nine from the female seminary. I append a tabulated view of faculties, attendance, and expenses of these schools.

MALE SEMINARY.

Employees.	Position.	Salary.	Race.	Age.	Single or married.	Birthplace.	By whom appointed.
L. M. Logan	Principal teacher.	$900	White	47	Married	Tennessee	School board.
W. A. Thompson.	First assistant teacher.	675	Cherokee	32	...do...	Cherokee Nation.	Do.
R. L. Mitchell	Second assistant teacher.	450	...do...	26	Single	...do...	Do.
E. C. Alberty	Third assistant teacher.	450	...do...	33	Married	...do...	Do.
Wm. P. Thorne	Fourth assistant teacher.	450	...do...	26	...do...	...do...	Do.
J. R. Garrett	Steward	500	...do...	44	...do...	Missouri	National council.
Dr. C. M. Ross	Medical superintendent.	465	...do...	27	...do...	Cherokee Nation.	Do.

Enrollment 120
Average attendance 80
Per cent of attendance 66

Amount paid employees $3,890.00
Maintenance 7,500.00

Total cost 11,390.00
Cost per pupil per month 15.77

FEMALE SEMINARY.

Employees.	Position.	Salary.	Race.	Age.	Single or married.	Birthplace.	By whom appointed.
Miss A. F. Wilson.	Principal teacher.	$900	White	50	Single	Arkansas	School board.
Mrs. Harvey W. Shelton.	First assistant teacher.	675	Cherokee	30	Married	Cherokee Nation.	Do.
Miss Lillian Alexander.	Second assistant teacher.	450	...do...	20	Single	...do...	Do.
Miss Patsey Mayes.	Third assistant teacher.	450	...do...	22	...do...	...do...	Do.
Miss A. L. Morgan.	Fourth assistant teacher.	450	...do...	21	...do...	...do...	Do.
Miss Ella May Covel.	Fifth assistant teacher.	450	...do...	20	...do...	...do...	Do.
E. W. Buffington.	Steward	500	...do...	45	Married	...do...	National council.
Dr. C. M. Ross	Medical superintendent.	465	...do...	27	...do...	...do...	Do.

Enrollment 135
Average attendance 105
Per cent of attendance 77

Amount paid employees $4,840.00
Maintenance 11,500.00

Total cost 15,840.00
Cost per pupil per month 16.76

ORPHAN ASYLUM.

Employees.	Position.	Salary.	Race.	Age.	Single or married.	Birthplace.	By whom appointed.
Rev. J. F. Thompson.	Superintendent ..	$600	Cherokee	69	Married	Cherokee Nation.	National council.
S. F. Parks.......	Principal teacher.	720	....do	28	....do ...	Tennessee	Board of education.
G. T. Hampton...	First assistant teacher.	540	....do	23	Single ..	Cherokee Nation.	Do.
Fannie M.Browning.	Second assistant teacher.	405	....do	18	....do ...	.....do	Do.
Mrs.E. M.Thompson.	Third assistant teacher.	405	....do	36	Widow .	Texas	Do.
Dora Ward	Fourth assistant teacher.	405	....do	19	Single ..	Cherokee Nation.	Do.
Cherrie Edwardson.	Music teacher	450	....do	19	....do ...	.....do	Do.
Dr. J. L. Mitchell.	Medical superintendent.	600	....do	30	Married	.....do	National council.

Enrollment 138
Average attendance 124
Per cent of attendance 90

Amount paid employees... $4,125.00
Maintenance 11,000.00

Total cost.. 15,125.00
Cost per pupil per month.. 13.55

COLORED HIGH SCHOOL.

Employees.	Position.	Salary.	Race.	Age.	Single or married.	Birthplace.	By whom appointed.
Mrs. Fannie Lowery.	Teacher	$450	Negro ..	42	Married	Cherokee Nation.	Board of education.
George F. Nave...	Steward	300	....do ...	28	....do ...	.....do ...	National council.
Dr. Ed. W. Blake..	Medical superintendent.	500	White ..	26	Single ..	Missouri ..	Do.

Enrollment 45
Average attendance.. 23
Per cent of attendance.. 51

Amount paid employees... $1,250.00
Appropriation 2,150.00

Total cost.. 3,400.00
Cost per pupil per month.. 16.42

I record with pleasure my appreciation of your assistance and support in my efforts to promote the interests of education among the Cherokee people. I have also been ably supported by the newspapers, the clergymen, the business men, and the most intelligent class of citizens throughout the nation.

Respectfully submitted.

BENJAMIN S. COPPOCK,
Supervisor of Schools, Cherokee Nation.

Hon. J. D. BENEDICT,
Superintendent of Schools in Indian Territory.

REPORT OF CHOCTAW SCHOOL SUPERVISOR.

SOUTH MCALESTER, IND. T., *June 30, 1900.*

SIR: I have the honor to submit herewith my second annual report as school supervisor for the Choctaw Nation.

There are six boarding schools and 110 neighborhood schools in the Choctaw Nation.

The schools began the first Monday in September and continued until the 31st of May. A number of schools were late in organizing in the fall, and a number were not able to hold the pupils in school later than the beginning of April. There was much sickness in many of the neighborhoods, which interfered with the school work. Many of the children live a long distance from the school, and in bad weather are not able to attend. Considering the bad weather, the distance the children have to go in order to reach the schoolhouse, the uncomfortable buildings, and indifference upon the part of the patrons of the school, I believe that the schools in the Choctaw Nation have made as much progress as one could reasonably expect.

The boarding schools are poorly equipped. The employees in all of them worked under many difficulties, but accomplished much in the right direction.

Below is a list of the boarding schools:

WHEELOCK ACADEMY.

W. W. Appleton, Superintendent.

Employees.	Position.	Salary per month.
H. H. Sherman	Teacher	$55
Blanch Jarrell	....do	55
H. E. Appleton	Matron	50
Osella Byram	Seamstress	50
Sina Perdy	Cook	35
Nancy Brown	Laundress	20
James M. Land	Janitor	20

SPENCER ACADEMY.

Wallace B. Buts, Superintendent.

Employees.	Position.	Salary per month.
Cyrus H. Beery	Principal teacher	$100
Cynthia Raney	Assistant teacher	60
Gabe E. Parker	Teacher	50
Lizzie E. George	Music and primary teacher	35
Wallace W. Hibberd	Industrial teacher	50
Susan L. B. George	Matron	50
Sarah Hibberd	Seamstress	50
Kittie Hibberd	Assistant seamstress	35
Warren Buts	Engineer	50
John B. George	Cook	50
Lucinda Le Flore	Laundress	25

TUSHKAHOMA FEMALE INSTITUTE.

Charles F. Trotter, Superintendent.

Employees.	Position.	Salary per month.
Bell M. Wakefield	Principal teacher	$100
Fannie Pyle	Assistant teacher	60
R. Dayse King	....do	60
Annie R. Brown	Seamstress	50
Hattie Trotter	Matron	50
John Waters	Laundryman	40
Rose Graham	Cook	40

JONES ACADEMY.

W. A. Caldwell, Superintendent.

Employees.	Position.	Salary per month.
Lorenzo D. Stearns	Principal teacher	$100
Kate K. Knight	Assistant teacher	60
Effie L. Jackson	....do	60
James C. Caldwell	Industrial teacher	50
Lizzie B. Caldwell	Matron	50
Adda L. Stearns	Seamstress	50
Nellie M. Hibberd	Assistant seamstress	40
Andrew Long	Cook	50
J. B. Bucher	Engineer	50

ARMSTRONG ACADEMY.

Thomas W. Hunter, Superintendent.

Employees.	Position.	Salary per month.
Sam L. Morley	Principal teacher	$100
Soewillie Ikard	Assistant teacher	60
Carrie Hunter	Matron	50
Ida Folsom	Seamstress	40
Thomas C. Metcalf	Laundryman	35
George McBath	Cook	40

The school for orphans at Atoka is under the control of the Baptist Church. The following is approximately correct:

Choctaw children in school 2,154
Choctaw children in nation of school age.. 4,000
White children in nation.. 10,000
Negro children in nation of school age.. 1,000

The above is based on reports received from the various neighborhoods and towns in the Choctaw Nation.

I am, very respectfully,

E. T. McARTHUR,
School Supervisor for the Choctaw Nation.

Hon. JOHN D. BENEDICT,
Superintendent of Schools in Indian Territory.

List of neighborhood schools in Choctaw Nation.

Name.	Position.	Salary.	School at which employed.	When opened.	When closed.	No. of pupils in attendance.	No. of pupils in neighborhood.
J. F. Yandell	Teacher ..	$2	South Canadian....	Sept. 18	Apr. 20	8	60
S. P. Morris.............	....do	2	McAlester	Sept. 4	...do	17	43
Henry Wise.............	....do	2	South McAlester....	...do	May 31	11	20
H. W. Kennon.........	....do	25	Indianola	Oct. 2	Dec. 31	10	13
Augusta Heard.........	....do	30	Guertie	Sept. 4	Feb. 28	15	15
Alma Nash	....do	40	Savanna............	...do	Feb. 23	10	20
Lizzie Hatcher.........	....do	2	Calvin	Oct. 16	Nov. 7	10	10
Lucy Hatcher..........	....do	25	Little	Sept. 18	Feb. 2	13	13
Fannie Holmes.........	....do	25	Atwood............	...do	Feb. 28	12	17
H. Clay Kingsbury	....do	40	Coal Creek........	...do	May 18	6	29
May Featherstone.....	....do	2	Featherstone	Oct. 2	May 31	7	9
Lewis E. Christian	....do	2	Hartshorne	Sept. 4	May 18	7	12
A. Floyd..............	....do	2	Allen	...do	May 31	14	16
Robert E. Lee.........	....do	30	Boiling Spring......	Sept. 11	Mar. 31	20	21
Gus Merriman.........	....do	40	Summerfield	Oct. 2	May 31	23	20
Anna Hollard	....do	30	Springfield	Sept. 18	...do	17	21
L. B. Locke...........	....do	30	Salem	Nov. 28	..do	23	28
R. W. Carter..........	....do	45	Conser.............	Sept. 25	Apr. 16	22	40
D. J. Austin..........	....do	2	Red Oak	Sept. 1	May 31	10	21
Lucy Thomas..........	....do	35	Kulle Box	Sept. 4	..do	18	18
Ellis W. Thompson	....do	45	Big Lick	...do	Apr. 13	8	26
Robert Windsor	....do	40	Davenport.........	Nov. 27	Dec. 31	10	30
Lena Hallman	....do	40	Hochatown.........	Oct. 9	May 31	16	29
Hardie Wright	....do	35	Kulle Chito........	Nov. 9	Apr. 6	12	20
J. P. Hallman.........	....do	40	Stock Bridge.......	Sept. 11	Mar. 27	28	30
Frances M. Lyle.......	....do	2	Lyle Institute	Sept. 4	May 31	16	30
Mary P. Hotchkin.....	....do	30	Nunnah Takli......	...do	May 9	9	24
James M. White.......	....do	2	Brooken...........	Dec. 13	Feb. 28	15	11
Clara E. Hagood	....do	40	Cowlington	Sept. 18	May 31	21	25
Carrye Tennent	....do	45	Oak Lodge	Sept. 4	May 11	14	26
M. M. Ryan...........	....do	35	Bokoshe...........	Sept. 18	May 31	7	22
T. M. Wilson	....do	2	Cameron	Sept. 4	May 18	11	30
May J. Lynch	....do	30	Bethel.............	Nov. 13	May 31	11	26
Mrs. Theo. Belt........	....do	30	Milton.............	Oct. 2	..do	8	22
F. W. Carney.........	....do	25	Bennington	Sept. 4	Apr. 30	6	22
Lizzie Miller	....do	40	Howe	Oct. 2	May 31	13	25
Mattie B. Hagood	....do	30	Ward	Nov. 28	Mar. 19	14	15
Charles S. Christian....	....do	35	Tamaha	Sept. 4	Dec. 10	12	16
D. F. Jones...........	....do	40	Little Sans Bois ...	...do	May 31	12	12
Cora Lindsay..........	....do	35	Lenox..............	...do	...do	22	28
James A. Lynn........	....do	45	Bethel.............	...do	Jan. 12	22	28
Rufus H. Burrows.....	....do	35	Sans Bois..........	Oct. 23	May 31	11	14
John B. Holleman	....do	40	Stigler.............	Sept. 4	...do	21	24
J. J. Brown...........	....do	2	Whitefield	...do	...do	16	35
T. D. New	....do	2	Enterprise.........	Nov. 20	Mar. 23	18	18
Mary A. Smith........	....do	25	Cedar Chapel	Nov. 15	Apr. 16	11	23
T. H. Wheat..........	....do	40	Sans Bois..........	Sept. 4	Apr. 23	8	16
I. H. Windsor	....do	40	Cartersville	Sept. 25	May 31	15	29
Mamie J. Johnson.....	....do	35	Rock Creek	Sept. 24	Jan. 28	18	18
Mary Kennon	....do	30	Longtown..........	Sept. 4	May 31	18	21
Nettie Coleman	....do	2	Choate.............	Sept. 11	May 5	17	15
Mattie Huskey	....do	35	Kan Chito	Oct. 2	Mar. 8	10	20
J. A. Kirksey.........	....do	45	Bethel Hill	Sept. 4	May 31	19	49
L. A. Benton..........	....do	45	Mount Zion ...:....	...do	..do	9	20
Clarence W. Wilcher ..	....do	45	Kosoma............	Oct. 16	May 18	14	19
Joe Dukes.............	....do	45	Pleasant Hill.......	Sept. 4	Apr. 27	12	25
Loren D. Dukes........	....do	40	Post Oak Grove	Sept. 18	Mar. 18	14	20

List of neighborhood schools in Choctaw Nation—Continued.

Name.	Position.	Salary.	School at which employed.	When opened.	When closed.	No. of pupils in attendance.	No. of pupils in neighborhood.
G. H. Korns	Teacher ..	40	White Oak	Sept. 4	Dec. 21	16	20
S. A. Hamilton	....do	2	Poteau	....do ...	May 18	11	20
Laura Foster	....do	25	Oak Grove	Nov. 6	Jan. 31	11	11
Callie Stalcup	....do	40	Spring Chapel	Sept. 4	May 31	9	25
Elizabeth R. Alison	....do	40	Cold Spring	....do ...	....do ...	18	25
Emma Deshazo	....do	25	Goodland	Sept. 18	Apr. 25	7	19
W. E. Larecy	....do	35	Sugar Creek	Sept. 11	May 31	15	31
Bella McCallum	....do	2	Old Goodland	Sept. 18	....do ...	29	29
Ida Wallace	....do	30	Rock Hill	Sept. 4	May 28	7	15
Sue M. Oakes	....do	40	Grant	....do ...	May 31	10	21
Alice Deshazo	....do	25	Honey Spring	Dec. 4		22	27
Fannie Wiley	....do	30	Hibben	Oct. 2	May 31	18	26
Mrs. J. B. Herndon	....do	30	Pleasant Cove	Sept. 4	...do ...	18	50
Belle Hynson	....do	30	Sardis	Dec. 4	...do ...	11	19
Rose Hynson	....do	30	Pine Spring	Sept. 4	...do ...	18	45
Maggie Johns	....do	30	Oske Chito	Nov. 6	...do ...	14	15
Clara Charles	....do	35	Stringtown	Sept. 7	May 18	14	18
Sister Meugene	....do	2	Antlers	Sept. 4	May 31	38	38
Pitts Womack	....do	2	....do	....do ...	May 18	23	23
Maude P. Berry	....do	45	Chish Oktah	....do ...	May 31	15	18
N. V. Patterson	....do	45	Crowder Chapel	....do ...	Dec. 12	18	20
Leola Russel	....do	40	Bennington	....do ...	May 31	10	23
Clyde Carter	....do	2	Talihina	Oct. 2	Oct. 31	8	10
Alpha M. Saunders	....do	2	....do	Nov. 6	May 31	4	20
Lou J. Meroney	....do	45	Mount Pleasant	Sept. 4	...do ...	22	40
Tallilah Collier	....do	30	Doaksville	....do ...	...do ...	15	25
Bertha Whitehead	....do	45	Goodwater	....do ...	...do ...	31	40
Nettie Irvine	....do	45	Pleasant Hill	....do ...	...do ...	28	29
Wilson A. Shoney	....do	35	Kulli Tuklo	....do ...	...do ...	18	27
Ben Taylor	....do	40	Water Hole	....do ...	...do ...	20	26
Grace Kennon	....do	40	Lehigh	....do ...	May 25	10	16
Margery Morrison	....do	30	Gills	....do ...	May 31	12	16
Emma Gill	....do	40	Kiowa	....do ...	...do ...	20	26
B. I. Hill	....do	30	Salt Creek	....do ...	...do ...	16	10
Jabue Hogg	....do	35	Marysville	....do ...	...do ...	14	22
Maye Taffe	....do	25	Owl	Nov. 6	Mar. 31	9	9
A. J. Bristow	....do	35	Medical Spring	Sept. 4	Jan. 20	3	20
E. H. Rishel	....do	2	Atoka	....do ...	May 31	38	50
W. B. Merrell	....do	40	Red Oak	Oct. 2	Mar. 31	13	20
E. C. McBride	....do	40	Christian Hope	Oct. 16	May 31	15	20
Mrs. J. J. Read	....do	2	Wappanucka	Oct. 30	May 18	6	25
Inez Turnbull	....do	25	Mount Pleasant	Sept. 4	May 2	6	12
Florence Strickler	....do	25	Bokchito	Sept. 18	May 31	19	28
H. D. Neely	....do	2	Calvin Institute	Sept. 4	May 25	104	150
Monroe Thompson	....do	2	Choctaw Training School.	Sept. —	May 19	20	100
Mae Hamilton	....do	2	Caddo	Sept. 4	May 31	22	50
William P. Jones	....do	2	Scipio	Dec. 11	...do ...	16	16
Lillie M. Powers	....do	30	Buffalo Creek	Nov. 13	May 31	12	17
J. M. Stanley	....do	2	Legal	Nov. 6	May 18	9	15
Charles G. Strauss	....do	2	Living Land	Oct. 2	Nov. 24	21	25
Mollie E. Ogar	....do	40	Cedar	Jan. 8	Jan. 18	12	20
Lizzie Pollock	....do	2	Fortrims Chapel	Jan. 2	Jan. 22	7	7
Edwin Dukes	....do	30	Mountain Station	Jan. 15	May 31	18	42
Nellie Eubank	....do	2	Indianola	...do ...	...do ...	8	15
Joseph J. Jamison	....do	2	Caney	Jan. 2	Mar. 30	11	35
F. M. Abernathy	....do	2	Wilburton	Jan. 15	May 31	19	34
Dan Strawn	....do	2	Living Land	Jan. 27	...do ...	21	25
H. W. Kennon	....do	2	Bethlehem	Feb. 25	...do ...	9	9
James A. Lynn	....do	2	Tamaha	Jan. 15	May 18	11	16
Peter J. Hudson	....do	40	Sileana	Nov. 21	...do ...	16	39
Lee Galyean	....do	40	Bethel	Jan. 15		22	28
John M. Hudson	....do	2	Shady Point	Jan. 2	Apr. 20	5	11
Anna L. Hudson	....do	2	Blue Ridge	...do ...	May 31	9	9
Alice Terry	....do	2	Pine Hill	Mar. 12	Mar. 31	12	25
Bessie Welch	....do	2	Bengal	Apr. 2	Apr. 12	8	15
S. R. Hardy	....do	2	Caney	...do ...	May 31	11	35
T. D. Mullins	....do	2	Folsom	...do ...		9	20
S. G. Payte	....do	2	Nixon	...do ...	May 31	15	17

NOTE.—Where salaries are marked $2 the teachers received $2 per month per pupil.

REPORT OF CHICKASAW SCHOOL SUPERVISOR.

SULPHUR, IND. T., *June 25, :*

SIR: I submit herewith my report on the condition of schools with a census scholastic population of the Chickasaw Nation.

CITIZEN OR INDIAN SCHOOLS.

Twenty-two citizen schools were in operation during some part of the : academies, and 17 neighborhood or primary schools, with a total enrollment pupils.

The Chickasaw schools are entirely under the control of the tribal govern operated by the direction of a superintendent, elected by the legislature, and trustee for each school, who constitute the school board. These trustees are app by the superintendent and removed at his pleasure, without the advice or con anyone. The present superintendent is a half-blood, about 28 years of age, with education, but little force of character, and no experience in school work, and considered by many of the prominent men of his tribe to be totally unfit f position. The local trustees are mostly full-bloods who can speak very little E: but the majority of them are members of the Chickasaw legislature, who have ob a school for their locality through political influence.

PRIMARY SCHOOLS.

The primary schools are usually located in full-blood communities in the : far removed from the influences of civilization. The children in many ins speak Chickasaw entirely and hear nothing else, except during recitation, as of the teachers address them in that language outside of the schoolroom.

The schoolhouses are mostly small frame buildings furnished with a few board benches, with rarely a desk for writing on or for resting the children's upon, with no blackboards nor writing material of any sort; and many of houses are too filthy for swine to occupy, never having been cleaned since the: built, while many of the children are in squalor and rags. The teachers of schools have a very limited education, have never received any special prepa for their work, and are not required to pass any sort of an examination to tes fitness to teach, but are chosen solely by favoritism, preference being given to (asaw when the local trustee does not have a noncitizen friend who wants to The books are furnished by the superintendent at $25 per year to each school-books as were used in the States twenty-five years ago. Enrollment in 17 neig hood schools for this scholastic year is 489, with an average attendance of 386, approximate cost to the nation of $36,115, or an average cost of $93.54 per the children attending these schools each being allowed $8 per month for : This $8 per month is paid to persons who board these children in scrip or du on the nation. These persons being poor, are compelled to trade this scrip : some store—usually that of a half-blood—for provisions at from 25 to 50 per ce: count, and this paper must be presented to the auditing committee of the legis at its next annual meeting to be honored or disallowed, depending largely upc influence of the holder, to whom warrants are then issued, to be paid in turn at future time, whenever there is money in the treasury. Following is a tabl report of these primary schools:

Neighborhood schools.

Name of school.	Teachers.			Amount paid teachers.	Other expenses of the schools.	Months of school.	Number of Indian pupils enrolled.			Pupils in lower grades.	Average attendance.
	Male.	Female.	Total.				Male.	Female.	Total.		
Big Springs	1	....	1	$315	$686	7	10	7	17	17	11
Burris	1	....	1	450	1,270	10	12	7	19	19	15
Double Springs	1	....	1	450	2,470	10	32	18	50	50	30
Davis		1	1	450	2,310	10	19	15	34	34	28
Emet		1	1	450	2,630	10	18	17	35	35	32
H. Colbert		1	1	450	2,470	10	14	18	32	32	30
Kaneys	1	....	1	450	1,990	10	19	13	32	32	24
Lewis		1	1	450	870	10	3	8	11	11	10
McMillan		1	1	270	934	6	17	12	29	29	18
Pauls Valley		1	1	270	790	6	8	10	18	18	15
Potts		1	1	450	1,030	10	11	3	14	14	12
Red Springs	1	....	1	450	2,270	10	19	16	35	35	30
Sulphur Springs	1	....	1	450	2,290	10	17	18	35	35	25
Sulphur	1	....	1	90	60	2	10	11	21	21	18
Sandy Creek	1	....	1	450	2,470	10	18	19	37	37	30
Seeleys	1	....	1	450	2,070	10	18	17	35	35	25
Yellow Springs	1	....	1	450	2,710	10	23	12	35	35	23
Total	10	7	17	6,795	29,320	....	268	221	489	489	386

BOARDING SCHOOLS.

There are five boarding schools in operation in this nation, with an enrollment of 246 pupils, at an annual cost of $57,115, or $166.23 per pupil. These schools are let by contract on five-year terms, and only two of the five superintendents are competent to teach the common-school branches. By the terms of their contracts these superintendents receive a certain sum per year for instruction, board, medical attention, nursing, books, and laundering for a specified number of pupils, regardless of attendance, select all of their own teachers and subordinate help, employ their wives as matrons, and have unquestioned authority in the management of their schools; hence the discipline in several of the academies is very weak. The boys do pretty much as they please; besides, the sanitary conditions are almost entirely neglected. At one place I saw pigs, chickens, and boys contending for the occupancy of a recitation room, with the chances in favor of the pigs. The majority of these contractors are intermarried whites whose Indian wives are highly connected and who are of necessity men of large political influence to obtain these contracts; hence it often occurs that rumors of immorality and mismanagement of the schools are never investigated. Some of these superintendents are well-meaning men who do the best they can for the children, but others are unfit, morally and educationally, for the positions which they hold. Favoritism in the payment of warrants, I am informed, is the general practice with teachers and superintendents, many teachers being obliged to wait from one to two years to get their warrants cashed, or else sell them at a large discount, sometimes 50 per cent. Some of the superintendents of the academies tell me that they have not been able to get a cent of money on their school warrants from the Chickasaw treasurer since September 1, 1899, and have been compelled to buy provisions on time, agreeing to pay exorbitant prices therefor or else discount their warrants at the banks from 15 to 25 per cent to obtain money to pay running expenses. It is rumored that the outstanding warrants of the nation to-day amount to between $95,000 and $110,000, that the treasury is empty, and that money lenders are not anxious to buy school warrants at any price.

Stockraising on the ranges has been the principal employment in this country in the past, and very few of the people know anything else except the cowboy's trade and its attendant vices—drinking, consuming tobacco, and gambling. The ranges will be shortly all fenced up, the lands allotted, and people must turn their attention to agricultural pursuits; hence school studies and training should be shaped to that end. The prevailing idea has been, and is, to discourage all industrial work in these schools, allowing the boys to spend their leisure hours in idle sports and games of chance, and the girls in music and painting. The teachers and superintendents of these boarding schools, with one or two exceptions, know absolutely nothing of the principles of agriculture, botany, or horticulture; and at no place except the Orphans' Home are the boys taught to handle the plow or cultivator, ax or hoe, and only at this one school are the girls taught how to wash and mend their own clothes or cook a meal of victuals. The orphans are only required to labor one hour in the morning and one hour in the evening after schoolroom work is done, yet the repeal of this requirement is being strongly urged by some Chickasaw officials as being unjust and undignified. Following is a tabulated report of the academies:

ORPHANS' HOME.

Employees.	Position.	Salary.	Date of employment.	Race.	Age.	Single or married.	Birthplace.	By whom appointed.
W. S. Derrick	Superintendent	$1,500	Oct. 1,1899	White	52	Married	Missouri	Chickasaw school board.
Cora I. Fuller	Principal teacher	600	Sept. 1,1899	do	36	Single	Texas	Do.
Carrie Derrick	First assistant teacher	450	do	do	23	do	Arkansas	Do.
Willie B. Derrick	Music teacher	400	do	do	21	do	Indian Territory	Do.
Olla Studey	Matron	250	do	do	23	Married	Texas	Do.
D. S. Murby and wife	Cook	300						
	Laundress	250						
Place vacant	Workhand	192	Apr. 1,1898	White	24	Single	Tennessee	Do.

Yearly enrollment ... 59
Average daily attendance ... 47
Per cent of attendance ... 80
Appropriation ... $8,500.00
Amount paid employees ... 3,912.00
Maintenance ... 4,568.00
Average cost of pupil per month ... 9.76

BLOOMFIELD SEMINARY.

Employees.	Position.	Salary.	Date of employment.	Race.	Age.	Single or married.	Birthplace.	By whom appointed.
E. B. Hinshaw	Superintendent	$1,800	Sept. 1,1897	White		Married	Indiana	Contract with Chickasaw school board.
G. A. Nutt	First assistant teacher		Sept. 1,1899	do		do	Texas	Contractor.
A. E. Nutt	Second assistant teacher			do		Single	do	Do.
Libble Bennett	Music teacher			do		do	do	Do.
Mary Dobson	Art teacher			do		do	do	Do.
Mary Crutchfield	Elocution teacher			do		do	do	Do.
Mrs. E. B. Henshaw	Matron			do		Married	Indiana	Do.

Yearly enrollment ... 92
Average daily attendance ... 86
Appropriation ... $15,180
Amount paid employees (refused to give it).
Maintenance (refused to give it).
Average cost of pupil per month ... $16.50

HARLEY INSTITUTE.

Employees.	Position.	Salary.	Date of employment.	Race.	Age.	Single or married.	Birthplace.	By whom employed.
S. M. White	Superintendent		Oct., 1897	White		Married		Contract with Chickasaw legislature.
P. B. H. Shearer	Principal teacher		...do	...do		...do		By contractor.
Lulu White	First assistant teacher		Sept., 1899	...do		Single		Do.
Debble White	Second assistant teacher		...do	...do		...do		Do.
Joehana Engtwe	Music teacher		...do	...do		...do		Do.
Mrs. G. Shearer	Elocution teacher		Oct., 1897	...do		Married		Do.
Mrs. S. M. White	Matron		...do	Indian		...do		Do.

Yearly enrollment.
Average daily attendance. 80.00
Appropriation. 75.00
Amount paid employees (refused to give it). $13,200.00
Maintenance (refused to give it).
Average cost of pupil per month. $16.50

WAPANUCKA INSTITUTE.

Employees.	Position.	Salary.	Date of employment.	Race.	Age.	Single or married.	Birthplace.	By whom appointed.
C. A. Skean	Superintendent		Oct., 1897	White		Married	Tennessee	Contracted with Chickasaw board.
F. J. Newsome	Principal teacher		Sept., 1899	...do		Single	Texas	By contractor.
B. F. Harrison	First assistant teacher		...do	Indian		...do	Indian Territory	Do.
Thos. Benton	Second assistant teacher		...do	White		...do	Tennessee	Do.
Annie Cund	Music teacher		Oct., 1897	...do		...do	Texas	Do.
Mrs. C. A. Skean	Matron		...do	Indian		Married	Indian Territory	Do.

Yearly enrollment. 79
Average daily attendance. 60
Appropriation. $13,085
Amount paid employees (refused to give it).
Maintenance (refused to give it).
Average cost of pupil per month. $16.50

COLLINS INSTITUTE.

Employees.	Position.	Salary.	Date of employment.	Race.	Age.	Single or married.	Birthplace.	By whom appointed.
W. H. Jackson	Superintendent		Sept., 1897	White		Married	Mississippi	Contract with Chickasaw board.
Ruth Roach	Principal teacher		Sept., 1899	do		Single	Texas	Contractor.
Essie Glover	First assistant teacher		Jan., 1900	do		do	do	Do.
D. L. Swank	Music teacher		Sept., 1899	do		do	do	Do.
Mrs. W. H. Jackson	Matron		Sept., 1897	Indian		Married	Indian Territory	Do.

Yearly enrollment	88
Average daily attendance	38
Appropriation	$6,600
Amount paid employees (refused to give it).	
Maintenance (refused to give it).	
Average cost per pupil per month	$16.50

These schools were each described in detail in my report of September 16, 1899. In addition to the enrollment in the neighborhood schools and academies, the superintendent has issued certificates during the year to 175 Chickasaw children to attend noncitizen schools in this nation, each of which is entitled to receive from $8 to $14 per month, approximating $16,800; 5 academies, $57,115; 17 neighborhood schools, $36,115; total expense of schools for year 1899–1900, $110,030.

NONCITIZEN SCHOOLS.

The noncitizen population of this nation is composed largely of nomads and adventurers seeking to make a living or get wealth without hard labor. Many of them have come from Tennessee, Kentucky, and Mississippi, bringing with them a bitter prejudice against public schools, due somewhat to race distinction, but more largely to ignorance, hence the private school has been encouraged, and to-day it is almost impossible to find a village or hamlet where some bombastic individual has not been conducting a subscription school. This individual is known in the community as "The Professor." In nine cases out of ten these schools have proven a total failure because of the floating character of the population, not being able to pay the tuition of their children, and the lack of discipline and education on the part of the teacher. Failing in a few weeks in one community this would-be pedagogue moves on to a new field to repeat his failure there, while some one else hastens along to take the place vacated. With a very few exceptions the private and sectarian schools known here as colleges are doing no better work than the subscription schools. In view of this condition of uncertainty only four towns in this nation have had the courage to establish public schools. Purcell, Pauls Valley, Wynnewood, and Ardmore have elected school boards, levied a tax, and employed supervising principals and teachers; and while working under the most adverse circumstances in the way of protests from taxpayers, epidemics of scarlet fever and small-pox, have had marvelous success with their schools during the year just closed. Following is a tabulated report of these schools:

Report of noncitizen schools of the nation.

School.	Teachers employed. Male.	Female.	Amount paid teachers.	Other expenses of school.	Months of school.	White. Male.	Female.	Indian. Male.	Female.	Negro. Male.	Female.	Total.	High-school grades. Male.	Female.	Total.	Lower grades. Male.	Female.	Total.	Average attendance. Number.	Per cent.
Public schools of Ardmore	8	12	$4,460.00	$3,850.00	6	543	652	6	5	91	98	1,435	26	38	64	614	757	1,371	890	86
Public school of Wynnewood	3	5	1,535.00	407.00	4	191	175	8	7	39	86	456	3	6	9	285	212	447	325	......
Public school of Pauls Valley	3	4	1,720.00	1,290.00	8	185	199	8	10	...	...	402	14	16	30	179	193	372	321	80
Public schools of Purcell	4	9	4,030.00	9,452.00	8	300	225	15	20	40	61	662	20	43	63	335	264	599	512	......
Total	18	30	11,745.00	14,999.00	......	1,259	1,252	37	42	170	195	2,965	63	108	166	1,363	1,426	2,789	2,048	......
El Meta Christian College, Minco	...	5	1,594.00 (a)	2,690.00	9	24	22	18	18	18	...	82	12	17	29	30	28	58	60½	......
The Drexel School, Purcell	...	5	(a)	(b)	10	30	35	...	65	...	...	130	...	12	......	30	88	118	65	......
Hargrove College, Ardmore	3	5	3,420.00	190.00	9	85	80	14	10	...	...	189	8	10	......	91	80	171	140	82

a Mostly charitable work being done in this school by teachers.   b Can not be estimated. Much garden stuff raised on place.

The following is an estimate of the scholastic population of this nation between 5 and 18 years of age, obtained from teachers, postmasters, and others:

	Males.	Females.	Total.
Chickasaw children enrolled in national schools	459	376	835
Indians enrolled in El Meta and Hargrove colleges	29	28	57
Whites enrolled in El Meta and Hargrove colleges	78	88	166
Estimate of whites, from teachers, postmasters, and others	11,254	11,668	22,922
Estimate of Indians	568	692	1,260
Estimate of negroes	920	818	1,738
Total population	13,308	13,670	26,978
Chickasaw children as above	459	376	835
Counting one-half estimated Indians as Chickasaw	284	346	630
Total Chickasaw children	743	722	1,465
Choctaws			630

PRIVATE SCHOOLS.

A few private schools, notably, El Meta Christian College at Minco, Draper's School at Lime, Drexel School at Purcell, Clemmon's School at Davis, have been doing good work. I would commend in a special manner the thorough business-like work being done at El Meta Christian College. Not in thorough class-room work only, but in systematic business principles in every department of the school, good discipline, order, and cleanliness. In a land where shiftlessness, dirt, and disorder reign supreme in the schoolhouse this college is like an oasis in the desert. There is a great need of some authority to compel noncitizens and others who engage in teaching in this nation to show some evidence of fitness for the positions they seek, both moral and educational. I would also recommend that Choctaw children residing in the Chickasaw Nation be allowed the same amount per month for board as those who reside in their own nation.

Respectfully,

JOHN M. SIMPSON,
Supervisor of Schools, Chickasaw Nation.

Hon. JOHN D. BENEDICT,
Superintendent of Schools in Indian Territory.

REPORT OF REVENUE INSPECTOR FOR THE CHEROKEE NATION.

UNITED STATES INDIAN INSPECTION SERVICE,
Muscogee, Ind. T., June 30, 1900.

SIR: In compliance with your request, I have the honor to submit the following report for the fiscal year ending June 30, 1900:

As revenue inspector it is my duty under your instructions to supervise the collections of the various revenues due the Cherokee Nation, as directed, and see that the same are paid into the hands of the United States Indian agent at Muscogee, Ind. T., for credit to the tribe.

Upon assuming my duties July 1, 1899, there were appointed as my assistants three district revenue inspectors, who were immediately assigned to service by districts—Nos. 1, 2, and 3. Two of these district inspectors are now in service, one having resigned April 30, 1900.

On entering upon the duties of this office, I found no precedents and that, apparently, there had been no well-defined system of collecting the tribal revenues in the past when the same were collected by the tribal authorities, and up to that time the business had been conducted very much on the "go-as-you-please" plan and, if common report be true, the matter of collections wholly neglected in some sections. Many persons from whom revenues and taxes were due expressed themselves as ignorant of the requirements, often adding they had never been required to pay revenue before, and that under the old régime only a small part of the funds collected reached the tribal treasury. I found also that almost to a man those from whom revenue and taxes were due were averse to paying the nation anything, claiming that no revenues were needed by the nation, and further that there was no way to enforce payments. In the latter view of the situation interested parties were aided by attorneys and newspapers, who held that collections were unwarranted by law and illegal in fact, thus making the problem more complex and my duties the more difficult to execute. I set about inaugurating a system for collecting by first ascertaining from whom revenues were due, and to this end made an enumeration of the merchants doing business in the nation; also of coal operators, hay shippers, and introducers of cattle, etc., so far as the information could be obtained, these being the chief sources of revenue, of which I will speak in detail under their appropriate heads.

A strong sentiment has been created against the payment of tribal revenues, principally by persons who are not financially interested, but collections have been hindered and evaded thereby.

It is contended by newspapers and a class of agitators that the Cherokee revenue laws are unjust, in that they require a royalty on one commodity, hay as an illustration, and not on another, such as wheat, and some have in their zeal gone so far in trying to prejudice the public against the laws and regulations as to claim that the officers of the Interior Department are responsible for them; but a royalty of 20 cents per ton on hay does not appeal to the average mind as excessive, especially when the great bulk of the hay shipped from the nation is cut or shipped by men who have no ownership in the soil that produces this spontaneous crop; neither does the merchandise tax of one-fourth of 1 per cent on merchandise introduced and offered for sale seem oppressive, as the merchant purchasing $10,000 per annum is only required to pay $6.25 each quarter for the privilege of conducting his business in the nation, hence it must be conceded that noninterested persons who are now opposing the collections of tribal revenues with so much persistency and bitterness are doing so for the sake of opposing the administration of affairs generally rather than that the royalties and taxes are exorbitant or oppressive.

There have been cases where, acting under the advice of overzealous friends, parties have expended more money for so-called legal advice than their revenue or tax would have amounted to for a long period, had they paid it in accordance with the regulations.

I know of no one thing that emphasizes the oft-repeated assertion that "affairs in the Indian Territory are in a chaotic condition" so much as the attitude of those from whom revenues are due, and those who aid and abet them in evading payments of the same.

HAY ROYALTY.

No department of this office has attracted so much attention and comment by persons opposing the collection of revenues as the royalty on prairie hay.

The tribal laws and regulations of the Department require a royalty of 20 cents per ton on all hay shipped out of the nation. It was the first work taken up by me, and from July of last year to the present time it has required the utmost vigilance to collect the same, even from some of the large shippers, who had made repeated promises to pay all that was due.

It has been necessary to seize and impound in the custody of the United States Indian Agency thousands of tons of hay before shippers would pay the royalty, requiring activity and much travel from one shipping point to another.

Many of the shippers are noncitizens or intruders, and almost without exception the grass, when bought standing, is obtained at a nominal price, thus making the Cherokee Nation an attractive point for the operations of hay dealers.

During a portion of the year the railroads declined to ship hay until the royalty was paid, but recently certain railroads have instructed their agents to accept hay for shipment whether royalty was paid or not, which is construed by some of the shippers to mean that the railroads issuing such instructions will aid them in evading payments, or, at least, that the railroads are indifferent in the matter.

The revenues collected during the year prior to the appointment of revenue inspectors amounted to $16.40, and for the year now closing to $4,474.88, which is perhaps as potent an illustration as I can furnish as to what has been accomplished in this line.

The books of the treasurer of the Cherokee Nation show no receipts for hay during the last year of collections by the tribe itself, ending September 30, 1898.

MERCHANDISE TAX.

There is a merchandise tax of one-fourth of 1 per cent on all merchandise introduced and offered for sale in the Cherokee Nation, excepting in that section known as the Canadian district, where noncitizen merchants (under the treaty of 1866) are not required to pay this tax.

I have recently made an enumeration of merchants, and find there are 454 firms, located in 82 villages or trading posts, nearly every one of which has been visited during the year, and many of them quarterly, by myself or district inspectors. Parties have been furnished with the necessary blanks and instructed as to executing the same. Up to June 1 remittances from merchants were coming in regularly, when, acting under your instructions to close the place of business of any merchant refusing to pay the required tax, the store of W. C. Rogers, at Talala, was closed (on that date), after he had been repeatedly notified and had refused to make any payment.

He thereafter applied to the United States court, and a temporary restraining order against officers of the Interior Department from interfering with his business was issued by the court, and a hearing set for July 23, 1900. Since that time several merchants who had previously paid to a particular date, and promised to make payments quarterly, have refused or failed to do so.

The receipts from merchandise tax by the treasurer of the Cherokee Nation for their fiscal year closing September 30, 1898, as shown by his books, when revenues were collected by the tribal authorities, amount to $1,673.82. The receipts by the United States Indian agent from same source from September 30; 1898, to June 30, 1899, were $878.68. The receipts from July 1, 1899, to June 30, 1900, the period in which the revenue inspector has been on duty, amount to $5,607.65.

COAL ROYALTY.

There is a wide coal belt in the Cherokee Nation running from the Kansas line southward where coal is mined by what is known as the "stripping" process. Heretofore the collection of coal royalty has been conducted very loosely, and during the year prior to the appointment of revenue inspectors, there was paid into the hands of the Indian agent from this source only $239.71, while for the last year $3,856.01 has been collected, and I believe a system inaugurated that will bring larger sums in the future.

There are a large number of small coal operators in the nation, who sell coal by the measure, and it has taken considerable time and correspondence to impress upon these men the importance of paying the royalty.

The books of the Cherokee treasurer for the fiscal year of 1898 show receipts from "minerals," $251.22. There being no provision for royalty on other minerals, the item is presumed to refer to royalty on coal.

CATTLE TAX.

There is an introduction tax of 50 cents per head due on all cattle introduced into the nation; also an annual grazing tax of 25 cents per head on all introduced cattle. If collected, this tax would, in my opinion, exceed in amount all other taxes and revenues combined.

For a long time prior to the appointment of revenue inspectors no money has been received by the Cherokee treasurer from these sources. During the last year the sum of $1,956 has been collected.

There are many reasons why it is next to impossible to ascertain even the amount of taxes due, as cattlemen and others in possession of information have generally refused to give information as to the names of owners of introduced cattle, and as to whether cattle found running at large were introduced or native cattle. Cattle are introduced by railroads and frequently unloaded at night and from side tracks remote from town, where it is impossible for officers to see the cattle or obtain the names of witnesses, and many are driven into the nation at points where it is not easy to detect them. In addition to this, it is openly stated that the cattlemen are organized to evade the tax and withhold information concerning one another.

A contagious disease known as "Texas fever" has lately broken out among introduced cattle, which endangers other herds, and doubtless parties will be more willing in the future to furnish information concerning the introduction of cattle.

FERRY LICENSE.

License fees for ferries are required in the Cherokee Nation of $10 per annum on the Verdigris and Grand rivers and $25 on the Arkansas.

The ownership of these ferries appears to change very frequently, and I have had considerable difficulty in ascertaining the names of the operators, many of whom have been slow in making payments.

During the last year of collections by the Cherokee Nation itself, ending September 30, 1898, the Cherokee treasurer received $333. During the last fiscal year $504.19 has been collected from this source.

HOME OF CREEK FREEDMEN.

COTTON-PICKING TIME—CREEK FREEDMEN

TIMBER DEPREDATIONS.

For years the wanton destruction of timber has been going on in the nation.   During the past year numerous sawmills have been shut down, considerable lumber seized, and several persons arrested, some of whom were sent to jail and others have left the country.

At first public sentiment seemed to be against the prevention of timber cutting, it being thought that it would deprive citizens from cutting fuel, fence posts, and the like; but when it became understood that avenues were provided through your office for cutting timber for legitimate purposes, and that it was only intended to prevent the wholesale slaughter of timber by persons who had no right to it, and for commercial purposes, the action of the officers has been heartily approved by the Cherokee people at large.

Through the work performed by the revenue inspectors I believe the timber depredations are now under control, for the first time in a long period.

The following figures present the amounts collected in revenues from the sources mentioned under the three systems recently in operation:

Source.	For the year 1898, under Cherokee authority.	From September 30, 1898, to June 30, 1899.	From July 1, 1899, to June 30, 1900.
Hay		$16.40	$4,474.88
Merchandise	$1,673.82	878.68	5,607.65
Coal	251.22	239.71	3,856.01
Cattle			1,956.00
Ferries	333.00	344.71	504.19

The total receipts for the fiscal year from all sources have been $19,455.05.

I desire to acknowledge the courtesies and helpful suggestions received from you, the latter being specially valuable from your intimate knowledge of affairs in the Indian Territory.   I am also indebted to the United States Indian agent and the attaches of his office and that of your own for material assistance.

It is not claimed that all of the revenues have been collected, one year being too short a time in which to bring the new system into perfect working order, but on examination of the relative figures you will observe that the receipts have been increased during the past year in a large ratio, and I believe this branch of the service is in a fair way to show better results in the future.   You are fully aware of some of the difficulties which I have encountered.

In addition to my duties in the collection of revenues I have, acting under your directions, attended to numerous special investigations, which I trust have in some measure aided you in the administration of your office in this Territory, in which you are confronted with so many perplexing conditions.

Very respectfully, your obedient servant,

FRANK C. CHURCHILL,
Revenue Inspector for the Cherokee Nation.

Hon. J. GEORGE WRIGHT,
United States Indian Inspector for the Indian Territory.

REPORT OF REVENUE INSPECTOR FOR THE CREEK NATION.

UNITED STATES INDIAN INSPECTION SERVICE,
Muscogee, Ind. T., June 30, 1900.

SIR: Complying with your instructions to submit to you an annual report, showing the work done in connection with the collection of the Creek revenues by the revenue inspector and the district revenue inspectors for the Creek Nation during the year ending June 30, 1900, I have the honor to submit the following:

COLLECTION OF THE TRADER AND OCCUPATION TAX.

The collection of the tax imposed by the Creek license law was taken out of the hands of the tribal authorities by the act of June 28, 1898.   During the year ending June 30, 1899, the United States Indian agent collected the sum of $3,813.43, under the provisions of the said law.

When the work was taken up by the present force, the conditions existing were about as follows: A few traders were paying their tax regularly; many considered the tax had been abolished, and some new traders had come into the nation who had no knowledge of the existence of the tax. A majority of the lawyers within the limits of the Creek Nation had never paid tax as such, having avoided payment by claiming that they were officers of the United States court and therefore exempt by law. The lawyers refused to pay the tax and advised others to refuse. As a result of this action by the lawyers it was deemed advisable to enforce the collection of the tax in their case first.   They were duly served with demands for payment and threatened with removal in the event of their failure to pay, and thereupon they sought to obtain an injunction restraining the officers of the Department of the Interior from removing them from the limits of the Creek Nation.   Their prayer for injunction was denied by Hon. John R. Thomas, United States judge, and the position taken by the officers of the Department of the Interior was sustained.   This decision was sustained by the United States court of appeals of Indian Territory (Maxey v. Wright, 54 S. W. Reporter, 807) in the following language:

"On the whole case we therefore hold that a lawyer who is a white man and not a citizen of the Creek Nation is, pursuant to their statute, required to pay for the privilege of remaining and practicing his profession in that nation the sum of $25; that if he refuse the payment therefor he becomes by virtue of the treaty an intruder, and that in such a case the Government of the United States may remove him from the nation, and that this duty devolves upon the Interior Department.   Whether the Interior Department or its Indian agents can be controlled by the courts by the writs of mandamus and injunction is not material in this case, because, as we hold, an attorney who refuses to pay the amount required by the statute by its very terms becomes an intruder, whom the United States promises by the terms of the treaty to remove, and therefore in such cases the officers and agents of the Interior Department would be acting clearly and properly within the scope of their powers."

An appeal from this decision has been taken to the United States circuit court of appeals, where the case is now pending.

In August, 1899, after the decision of the lower court, those subject to the tax began making payments.

The method of collecting this tax has been as follows: At the beginning of each quarter the district inspectors have in their respective districts personally served upon all parties subject to this tax a ten days' demand for payment of taxes due, making semiweekly report to me showing service of the demand, changes in the list of taxpayers, and such other information as they have been able to secure. Fifteen days later, or as soon thereafter as practicable, a second peremptory demand calling for payment within five days has been served by the district inspectors upon all who failed to respond to the first demand, semiweekly report being made to me showing reason for failure to pay, if any, and giving other information.

At the expiration of the five days, or as soon thereafter as practicable, I have visited the various towns, accompanied by a district inspector, making personal demand for immediate payment from delinquents, and threatening the traders with the closing of their places of business, and those subject to an occupation tax with removal. Following this personal demand I have again called upon the delinquents, accompanied by a district revenue inspector and a force of Indian police, and either effected a settlement or closed their places of business, reporting for removal such delinquents as could not be satisfactorily closed.

Records are kept in my office made up from the reports of the district inspectors and the duplicate statements which accompany remittances to the United States Indian agent, that are used in making up delinquent lists, etc., and that afford a check upon the office of the United States Indian agent, so far as the revenues of the Creek Nation are concerned.

During the year ending June 30, 1900, the sum of $18,811.27 has been received by the United States Indian agent from those subject to this tax. Two places of business within the limits of the Creek Nation have been closed with the assistance of the Indian police, and a few business men have voluntarily closed their places of business rather than pay the taxes prescribed. No removals have been made on account of nonpayment of this tax.

The collection of this tax is opposed by nearly all who are subject thereto. At all times during the present year the taxpayers have expected relief from this tax, either by treaty, act of Congress, or decision of the court, and even now the lawyers represent that they are confident that they will secure a decision from the United States circuit court of appeals relieving them from the payment of this tax. As a result of this feeling the taxpayers have in many instances devoted their entire energy and ability to devising and inventing excuses for delay in paying their taxes, and there are some taxpayers who are in arrears at present.

In some localities within the limits of the Creek Nation various lines of business are overcrowded by people who are not at present making their living expenses, but who are striving to remain within the limits of the Creek Nation in order to take advantage of the opening up of this section of the country when the opening comes.

A large part of the business carried on within the limits of the Creek Nation is transacted by Creek citizens, noncitizen Indians, and intermarried noncitizens who have not been compelled to pay taxes.

COLLECTION OF RENTALS FROM CATTLEMEN AND OTHERS.

Leases from the Creek Nation on border pastures and other grazing land were terminated or abolished by the act of June 28, 1898. When work was commenced among the cattlemen it was found that many of the old pastures inclosed under the border pasture law contained tracts of land of inferior quality, owing to its roughness or to the fact that it was partially wooded, which remained unselected and which could not be leased by the cattlemen from individual citizens. Rent to the amount of $4,344.65 has been paid to the United States Indian agent during the year ending June 30, 1900, for the use of such land. The plan followed in outlining the settlements with cattlemen has been, first, to ascertain whether or not the pasture was all leased from individual citizens; if not found to be all leased, then to plat the pasture, check the plat with the leases submitted and the records of the commission of the Five Civilized Tribes, and base the settlement outlined on behalf of the Creek Nation on the amount of land not selected and not leased and the quality of the land covered by settlement, actual investigation as to the quality of the land being made by me when deemed necessary. The work has resulted in the collection of a considerable revenue for the Creek Nation, and settlements are outlined that should bring in $2,000 more for the use of lands during the season of 1899.

The work done along these lines has also been of material assistance in hastening the selection of land by Creek citizens, and has also assisted a large number of Creek citizens in collecting rents from their selections who, unassisted, would have failed to collect their rents. The cattle business, properly conducted, is, in my opinion, of great benefit to the Creek Nation. The cattle convert the grass into money, and while it is true that much of the resources so converted go to the benefit of outside parties, a considerable portion reaches the Indian citizens in the form of rent; another considerable portion reaches the agricultural farmer in the form of payment for corn, hay, etc., raised by him, and still another considerable portion goes to pay for help employed, and for the purpose of making improvements. Indirectly the merchants of the various towns are greatly benefited by the circulation of large sums of money which, without the cattle industry, they would not have.

Much of the land contained within the limits of the Creek Nation is unfit for any purpose other than that of grazing. This land will be to a large extent unselected after each individual citizen has made a selection of 160 acres. Under existing conditions the principal part of the grass growing on such lands is allowed to go to waste or is burned in the autumn. With proper legislation and regulations these lands could be made to yield a very considerable revenue to the Creek Nation.

At all times during the past year there have been limited numbers of cattle and horses running at large on the public domain of the Creek Nation. Many of these are owned by Creek citizens or intermarried noncitizens, or are native cattle owned by noncitizens, and cases which could not be reached under section 2117, Revised Statutes of the United States.

Numerous complaints have been received from citizens who have made selections, stating that others were grazing cattle on their selections without contract and without paying the citizen for the use of the grass. Under existing conditions it would seem that their proper remedy was through the United States courts, but owing to the poverty of the citizens and their inability to meet the expenses incident to litigation they have been afforded little relief.

WORK DONE IN CONNECTION WITH TIMBER.

This work has consisted, not in the collection of royalty, but in preventing the destruction of the timber assets of the Creek Nation. At the beginning of the year there were 13 sawmills, with a combined capacity of between 25,000 and 30,000 feet of lumber per day, operating on native timber, within the limits of the Creek Nation, sawing both for domestic and export purposes, and using walnut, cottonwood, and oak logs. Illegal timber cutting within the limits of the Creek Nation has been practically stopped, and at present little, if any, timber is being sawed except in accordance with the instructions of the Department of the Interior, and no lumber or timber is being exported.   The only revenue derived from this source during the year ending June 30, 1900, consists of $191 paid to the United States Indian agent for lumber and timber seized at Bristow, Catoosa, and Sapulpa.

ROYALTIES ON COAL.

This work has included the collection of royalty on coal and the prevention of illegal coal mining.   The amount of revenue derived from this source for the year ending June 30, 1899, was $3.   For the year ending June 30, 1900, the revenue has amounted to $3,023.27, and no coal is now being exported contrary to instructions.

In addition to the regular work outlined above, much has been done in preventing the cutting of hay on public domain.   Various investigations and reports have been made, covering a large variety of cases arising within the limits of the Creek Nation, but not directly yielding revenues, such as smallpox investigations, investigating the infringement of property rights along the St. Louis, Oklahoma and Southern Railroad, etc.

The total revenues collected for the year ending June 30, 1899, for the benefit of the Creek Nation amounted to $4,913.63; the total revenues for the year ending June 30, 1900, amounted to $26,370.19.   The total expense for salary, per diem, and traveling expenses for the revenue inspector and three district revenue inspectors for the year ending June 30, 1900, amounted to $4,884.52, leaving the net revenues for the year ending June 30, 1900, $21,485.67, showing an increase in the net revenues for the year ending June 30, 1900, over the net revenues for the year ending June 30, 1899, of $16,572.04.

There are within the limits of the Creek Nation 34 towns, villages, or trading posts where those subject to the operation of the Creek license law are engaged in business.   The list of persons residing within the limits of the Creek Nation who are subject to the operation of this law includes the names of 549 individuals or firms.   These figures do not include Creek citizens, noncitizen Indians, or intermarried noncitizens.

The work done by the revenue inspector and district revenue inspectors has brought them in personal contact with a majority of the people of all classes in the Creek Nation, and has enabled them to be of much service in explaining existing conditions to citizens and others, and in keeping the Department of the Interior in close touch with all classes of people in the Creek Nation.

Uncertainty in the minds of the people as to existing law, and as to authority for the enforcement of existing laws, has greatly impeded the work.

The three district revenue inspectors, W. A. Porter, A. E. McKellop, and James H. Alexander, have made report to the revenue inspector.   Their knowledge of the Creek language and their wide acquaintance with the residents of the Creek Nation have been of great service, and their work as a whole is deserving of commendation.   In my opinion, based on one year's work with them, it would have been very difficult to have improved upon the selection made at the time of their appointment.

Very respectfully, your obedient servant,

GUY P. COBB,
Revenue Inspector.

Hon. J. GEORGE WRIGHT,
    United States Indian Inspector for the Indian Territory.

This agreement by and between the Government of the United States, of the first
part, entered into in its behalf by the commission to the Five Civilized Tribes, Henry
L. Dawes, Tams Bixby, Frank C. Armstrong, Archibald S. McKennon, and Thomas
B. Needles, duly appointed and authorized thereunto, and the Government of the
Seminole nation in Indian Territory, of the second part, entered into on behalf of
said Government by its commission, duly appointed and authorized thereunto, viz:
John F. Brown, Okchan Harjo, William Cully, K. N. Kinkehee, Thomas West, and
Thomas Factor.

Witnesseth, that in consideration of the mutual undertakings herein contained,
it is agreed as follows:

All lands belonging to the Seminole tribe of Indians shall be divided into three
classes, designated as first, second, and third class, the first class to be appraised at
five dollars, the second class at two dollars and fifty cents, and the third class at one
dollar and twenty-five cents per acre, and the same shall be divided among the members
of the tribe so that each shall have an equal share thereof in value, so far as may
be, the location and fertility of the soil considered; giving to each the right to select
his allotment so as to include any improvements thereon, owned by him at the time,
and each allottee shall have the sole right of occupancy of the land so allotted to him,
during the existence of the present tribal government, and until the members of said
tribe shall have become citizens of the United States. Such allotments shall be made
under the direction and supervision of the Commission to the Five Civilized Tribes
in connection with a representative appointed by the tribal government, and the
chairman of said commission shall execute and deliver to each allottee a certificate
describing therein the land allotted to him.

All contracts for sale, disposition, or encumbrance of any part of any allotment
made prior to date of patent shall be void.

Any allottee may lease his allotment for any period not exceeding six years, the
contract therefor to be executed in triplicate upon printed blanks provided by the
tribal government, and before the same shall become effective it shall be approved
by the principal chief and a copy filed in the office of the clerk of the United States
court at Wewoka.

No lease of any coal, mineral, coal oil, or natural gas within said nation shall be
valid unless made with the tribal government by and with the consent of the allottee and approved by the Secretary of the Interior.

Should there be discovered on any allotment any coal, mineral, coal oil, or natural
gas, and the same should be operated so as to produce royalty, one-half of such
royalty shall be paid to such allottee and the remaining half into the tribal treasury
until extinguishment of tribal government, and the latter shall be used for the purpose of equalizing the value of allotments; and if the same be insufficient therefor,
any other funds belonging to the tribe upon extinguishment of tribal government
may be used for such purpose, so that each allotment may be made equal in value as
aforesaid.

The town site of Wewoka shall be controlled and disposed of according to the provisions of an act of the general council of the Seminole Nation, approved April 23,
1897, relative thereto; and on extinguishment of the tribal government, deeds of
conveyance shall issue to owners of lots as herein provided for allottees, and all lots
remaining unsold at that time, may be sold in such manner as may be prescribed by
the Secretary of the Interior.

Five hundred thousand dollars ($500,000) of the funds belonging to the Seminoles,
now held by the United States, shall be set apart as a permanent school fund for the
education of children of the members of said tribe, and shall be held by the United
States at five per cent interest, or invested so as to produce such amount of interest,
which shall be, after extinguishment of tribal government, applied by the Secretary
of the Interior to the support of Mekasuky and Emahaka academies, and the district

111

schools of the Seminole people; and there shall be selected and excepted from allotment three hundred and twenty acres of land for each of said academies and eighty acres each for eight district schools in the Seminole country.

There shall also be excepted from allotment one-half acre for the use and occupancy of each of twenty-four churches, including those already existing and such others as may hereafter be established in the Seminole country, by and with consent of the general council of the nation; but should any part of same at any time cease to be used for church purposes, such part shall at once revert to the Seminole people and be added to the lands set apart for the use of said district schools.

One acre in each township shall be excepted from allotment, and the same may be purchased by the United States upon which to establish schools for the education of children of noncitizens when deemed expedient.

When the tribal government shall cease to exist, the principal chief last elected by said tribe shall execute, under his hand and the seal of the nation, and deliver to each allottee, a deed conveying to him all the right, title, and interest of the said nation and the members thereof in and to the lands so allotted to him, and the Secretary of the Interior shall approve such deed, and the same shall thereupon operate as a relinquishment of the right, title, and interest of the United States in and to the land embraced in said conveyance, and as a guaranty by the United States of the title of said lands to the allottee; and the courts of said nation shall retain all the jurisdiction a relinquishment of his title to and interest in all other lands belonging to the tribe, except such as may have been excepted from allotment and held in common for other purposes. Each allottee shall designate one tract of forty acres, which shall, by the terms of the deed, be made inalienable and nontaxable as a homestead in perpetuity.

All moneys belonging to the Seminole remaining after equalizing the value of allotments as herein provided and reserving said sum of five hundred thousand dollars for school fund, shall be paid per capita to the members of said tribe in three equal installments, the first to be made as soon as convenient after allotment and extinguishment of tribal government, and the others at one and two years, respectively. Such payments shall be made by a person appointed by the Secretary of the Interior, who shall prescribe the amount of and approve the bond to be given by such person, and strict account shall be given to the Secretary of the Interior for such disbursements.

The " Loyal Seminole claim " shall be submitted to the United States Senate, which shall make final determination of same, and, if sustained, shall provide for payment thereof within two years from date hereof.

There shall hereafter be held, at the town of Wewoka, the present capital of the Seminole Nation, regular terms of the United States court as at other points in the judicial district of which the Seminole Nation is a part.

The United States agrees to maintain strict laws in the Seminole country against the introduction, sale, barter, or giving away of intoxicants of any kind or quality.

This agreement shall in no wise affect the provisions of existing treaties between the Seminole Nation and the United States except in so far as it is inconsistent therewith.

The United States courts now existing or that may hereafter be created in Indian Territory shall have exclusive jurisdiction of all controversies growing out of the title, ownership, occupation, or use of real estate owned by the Seminoles and to try all persons charged with homicide, embezzlement, bribery, and embracery hereafter committed in the Seminole country, without reference to race or citizenship of the persons charged with such crime, and any citizen or officer of said nation charged with any such crime, if convicted, shall be punished as if he were a citizen or officer of the United States; and the courts of said nation shall retain all the jurisdiction which they now have, except as herein transferred to the courts of the United States.

When this agreement is ratified by the Seminole Nation and the United States, the same shall serve to repeal all the provisions of the act of Congress approved June 7, 1897, in any manner affecting the proceedings of the general council of the Seminole Nation.

It being known that the Seminole Reservation is insufficient for allotments for the use of the Seminole people, upon which they, as citizens, holding in severalty, may reasonably and adequately maintain their families, the United States will make effort to purchase from the Creek Nation, at one dollar and twenty-five cents per acre, two hundred thousand acres of land, immediately adjoining the eastern boundary of the Seminole Reservation and lying between the North Fork and South Fork of the Canadian River, in trust for, and to be conveyed by proper patent by the United States to, the Seminole Indians, upon said sum of one dollar and twenty-five cents per acre being reimbursed to the United States by said Seminole Indians; the same to be allotted as herein provided for lands now owned by the Seminoles.

This agreement shall be binding on the United States when ratified by Congress, and on the Seminole people when ratified by the general council of the Seminole Nation.

In witness whereof the said commissioners have hereunto affixed their names at Muskogee, Indian Territory, this sixteenth day of December, A. D. 1897.

TAMS BIXBY,
FRANK C. ARMSTRONG,
ARCHIBALD S. McKENNON,
THOMAS B. NEEDLES,
Commission to the Five Civilized Tribes.

JOHN F. BROWN,
OKCHAN HARJO,
WILLIAM CULLY,
K. N. KINKEHEE,
THOMAS WEST,
THOMAS FACTOR,
Seminole Commission.

ALLISON L. AYLESWORTH,
Secretary.

A. J. BROWN,
Secretary.

APPENDIX NO. 2.

[PUBLIC—No. 162.]

AN ACT For the protection of the people of the Indian Territory, and for other purposes.

Be it enacted by the Senate and House of Representatives of the United States of America in Congress assembled, That in all criminal prosecutions in the Indian Territory against officials for embezzlement, bribery, and embracery the word "officer," when the same appears in the criminal laws heretofore extended over and put in force in said Territory, shall include all officers of the several tribes or nations of Indians in said Territory.

SEC. 2. That when in the progress of any civil suit, either in law or equity, pending in the United States court in any district in said Territory, it shall appear to the court that the property of any tribe is in any way affected by the issues being heard, said court is hereby authorized and required to make said tribe a party to said suit by service upon the chief or governor of the tribe, and the suit shall thereafter be conducted and determined as if said tribe had been an original party to said action.

SEC. 3. That said courts are hereby given jurisdiction in their respective districts to try cases against those who may claim to hold as members of a tribe and whose membership is denied by the tribe, but who continue to hold said lands and tenements notwithstanding the objection of the tribe; and if it be found upon trial that the same are held unlawfully against the tribe by those claiming to be members thereof, and the membership and right are disallowed by the commission to the Five Tribes, or the United States court, and the judgment has become final, then said court shall cause the parties charged with unlawfully holding said possessions to be removed from the same and cause the lands and tenements to be restored to the person or persons or nation or tribe of Indians entitled to the possession of the same: *Provided always,* That any person being a noncitizen in possession of lands, holding the possession thereof under an agreement, lease, or improvement contract with either of said nations or tribes, or any citizen thereof, executed prior to January first, eighteen hundred and ninety-eight, may, as to lands not exceeding in amount one hundred and sixty acres, in defense of any action for the possession of said lands show that he is and has been in peaceable possession of such lands, and that he has while in such possession made lasting and valuable improvements thereon, and that he has not enjoyed the possession thereof a sufficient length of time to compensate him for such improvements. Thereupon the court or jury trying said cause shall determine the fair and reasonable value of such improvements and the fair and reasonable rental value of such lands for the time the same shall have been occupied by such person, and if the improvements exceed in value the amount of rents with which such persons should be charged the court, in its judgment, shall specify such time as will, in the opinion of the court, compensate such person for the balance due, and award him possession for such time unless the amount be paid by claimant within such reasonable time as the court shall specify. If the finding be that the amount of rents exceed the value of the improvements, judgment shall be rendered against the defendant for such sum, for which execution may issue.

SEC. 4. That all persons who have heretofore made improvements on lands belonging to any one of the said tribes of Indians, claiming rights of citizenship, whose claims have been decided adversely under the Act of Congress approved June tenth, eighteen hundred and ninety-six, shall have possession thereof until and including

December thirty-first, eighteen hundred and ninety-eight; and may, prior to that time, sell or dispose of the same to any member of the tribe owning the land who desires to take the same in his allotment: *Provided*, That this section shall not apply to improvements which have been appraised and paid for, or payment tendered by the Cherokee Nation under the agreement with the United States approved by Congress March third, eighteen hundred and ninety-three.

Sec. 5. That before any action by any tribe or person shall be commenced under section three of this Act it shall be the duty of the party bringing the same to notify the adverse party to leave the premises for the possession of which the action is about to be brought, which notice shall be served at least thirty days before commencing the action by leaving a written copy with the defendant, or, if he can not be found, by leaving the same at his last known place of residence or business with any person occupying the premises over the age of twelve years, or, if his residence or business address can not be ascertained, by leaving the same with any person over the age of twelve years upon the premises sought to be recovered and described in said notice; and if there be no person with whom said notice can be left, then by posting same on the premises.

Sec. 6. That the summons shall not issue in such action until the chief or governor of the tribe, or person or persons bringing suit in his own behalf, shall have filed a sworn complaint, on behalf of the tribe or himself, with the court, which shall, as near as practicable, describe the premises so detained, and shall set forth a detention without the consent of the person bringing said suit or the tribe, by one whose membership is denied by it: *Provided*, That if the chief or governor refuse or fail to bring suit in behalf of the tribe then any member of the tribe may make complaint and bring said suit.

Sec. 7. That the court in granting a continuance of any case, particularly under section three, may, in its discretion, require the party applying therefor to give an undertaking to the adverse party, with good and sufficient securities, to be approved by the judge of the court, conditioned for the payment of all damages and costs and defraying the rent which may accrue if judgment be rendered against him.

Sec. 8. That when a judgment for restitution shall be entered by the court the clerk shall, at the request of the plaintiff or his attorney, issue a writ of execution thereon, which shall command the proper officer of the court to cause the defendant or defendants to be forthwith removed and ejected from the premises and the plaintiff given complete and undisturbed possession of the same. The writ shall also command the said officer to levy upon the property of the defendant or defendants subject to execution, and also collect therefrom the costs of the action and all accruing costs in the service of the writ. Said writ shall be executed within thirty days.

Sec. 9. That the jurisdiction of the court and municipal authority of the city of Fort Smith for police purposes in the State of Arkansas is hereby extended over all that strip of land in the Indian Territory lying and being situate between the corporate limits of the said city of Fort Smith and the Arkansas and Poteau rivers, and extending up the said Poteau River to the mouth of Mill Creek; and all the laws and ordinances for the preservation of the peace and health of said city, as far as the same are applicable, are hereby put in force therein: *Provided*, That no charge or tax shall ever be made or levied by said city against said land or the tribe or nation to whom it belongs.

Sec. 10. That all actions for restitution of possession of real property under this Act must be commenced by the service of a summons within two years after the passage of this Act, where the wrongful detention or possession began prior to the date of its passage; and all actions which shall be commenced hereafter, based upon wrongful detention or possession committed since the passage of this Act must be commenced within two years after the cause of action accrued. And nothing in this Act shall take away the right to maintain an action for unlawful and forcible entry and detainer given by the Act of Congress passed May second, eighteen hundred and ninety (Twenty-sixth United States Statutes, page ninety-five).

Sec. 11. That when the roll of citizenship of any one of said nations or tribes is fully completed as provided by law, and the survey of the lands of said nation or tribe is also completed, the commission heretofore appointed under Acts of Congress, and known as the "Dawes Commission," shall proceed to allot the exclusive use and occupancy of the surface of all the lands of said nation or tribe susceptible of allotment among the citizens thereof, as shown by said roll, giving to each, so far as possible, his fair and equal share thereof, considering the nature and fertility of the soil, location, and value of same; but all oil, coal, asphalt, and mineral deposits in the lands of any tribe are reserved to such tribe, and no allotment of such lands shall carry the title to such oil, coal, asphalt, or mineral deposits; and all town sites shall also be reserved to the several tribes, and shall be set apart by the commission hereto-

THE FIRST CHURCH IN INDIAN TERRITORY, BUILT BY COLONEL BELKNAP AT THE MILITARY
POST OF FORT GIBSON ABOUT 1845.

NATIONAL CEMETERY AT FORT GIBSON.

fore mentioned as incapable of allotment.   There shall also be reserved from allotment a sufficient amount of lands now occupied by churches, schools, parsonages,
charitable institutions, and other public buildings for their present actual and necessary use, and no more, not to exceed five acres for each school and one acre for each
church and each parsonage, and for such new schools as may be needed; also sufficient land for burial grounds where necessary.   When such allotment of the lands of
any tribe has been by them completed, said commission shall make full report thereof
to the Secretary of the Interior for his approval: *Provided*, That nothing herein contained shall in any way affect any vested legal rights which may have been heretofore granted by Act of Congress, nor be so construed as to confer any additional rights
upon any parties claiming under any such Act of Congress: *Provided further*, That
whenever it shall appear that any member of a tribe is in possession of lands, his
allotment may be made out of the lands allotted in his possession, including his home if the
holder so desires: *Provided further*, That if the person to whom an allotment shall
have been made shall be declared, upon appeal as herein provided for, by any of the
courts of the United States in or for the aforesaid Territory, to have been illegally
awarded rights of citizenship, and for that or any other reason declared to be not
entitled to any allotment, he shall be ousted and ejected from said lands; that all persons known as intruders who have been paid for their improvements under existing
laws and have not surrendered possession thereof who may be found under the provisions of this Act to be entitled to citizenship shall, within ninety days thereafter,
refund the amount so paid them, with six per centum interest, to the tribe entitled
thereto; and upon their failure so to do said amount shall become a lien upon all
improvements owned by such person in such Territory, and may be enforced by such
tribe; and unless such person makes such restitution no allotments shall be made to
him: *Provided further*, That the lands allotted shall be nontransferable until after
full title is acquired and shall be liable for no obligations contracted prior thereto by
the allottee, and shall be nontaxable while so held: *Provided further*, That all towns
and cities heretofore incorporated or incorporated under the provisions of this Act
are hereby authorized to secure, by condemnation or otherwise, all the lands actually
necessary for public improvements, regardless of tribal lines; and when the same can
not be secured otherwise than by condemnation, then the same may be acquired as
provided in sections nine hundred and seven and nine hundred and twelve, inclusive,
of Mansfield's Digest of the Statutes of Arkansas.

SEC. 12.   That when report of allotments of lands of any tribe shall be made to the
Secretary of the Interior, as hereinbefore provided, he shall make a record thereof,
and when he shall confirm such allotments the allottees shall remain in peaceable
and undisturbed possession thereof, subject to the provisions of this Act.

SEC. 13.   That the Secretary of the Interior is hereby authorized and directed from
time to time to provide rules and regulations in regard to the leasing of oil, coal, asphalt,
and other minerals in said Territory, and all such leases shall be made by the Secretary
of the Interior; and any lease for any such minerals otherwise made shall be absolutely
void.   No lease shall be made or renewed for a longer period than fifteen years, nor
cover the mineral in more than six hundred and forty acres of land, which shall conform as nearly as possible to the surveys.   Lessees shall pay on each oil, coal, asphalt,
or other mineral claim at the rate of one hundred dollars per annum in advance, for the
first and second years; two hundred dollars per annum, in advance, for the third and
fourth years, and five hundred dollars, in advance, for each succeeding year thereafter,
as advanced royalty on the mine or claim on which they are made.   All such payments
shall be a credit on royalty when each said mine is developed and operated and its
production is in excess of such guaranteed annual advanced payments; and all lessees
must pay said annual advanced payments on each claim, whether developed or undeveloped; and should any lessee neglect or refuse to pay such advanced annual royalty
for the period of sixty days after the same becomes due and payable on any lease,
the lease on which default is made shall become null and void, and the royalties paid
in advance shall then become and be the money and property of the tribe.   Where
any oil, coal, asphalt, or other mineral is hereafter opened on land allotted, sold, or
reserved, the value of the use of the necessary surface for prospecting or mining, and
the damage done to the other land and improvements, shall be ascertained under the
direction of the Secretary of the Interior and paid to the allottee or owner of the land,
by the lessee or party operating the same, before operations begin: *Provided*, That
nothing herein contained shall impair the rights of any holder or owner of a leasehold
interest in any oil, coal rights, asphalt, or mineral which have been assented to by act
of Congress, but all such interest shall continue unimpaired hereby, and shall be
assured to such holders or owners by leases from the Secretary of the Interior for the
term not exceeding fifteen years, but subject to payment of advance royalties as herein
provided, when such leases are not operated, to the rate of royalty on coal mined, and

the rules and regulations to be prescribed by the Secretary of the Interior, and preference shall be given to such parties in renewals of such leases: *And provided further,* That when, under the customs and laws heretofore existing and prevailing in the Indian Territory, leases have been made of different groups or parcels of oil, coal, asphalt, or other mineral deposits, and possession has been taken thereunder and improvements made for the development of such oil, coal, asphalt, or other mineral deposits, by lessees or their assigns, which have resulted in the production of oil, coal, asphalt, or other mineral in commercial quantities by such lessees or their assigns, then such parties in possession shall be given preference in the making of new leases, in compliance with the directions of the Secretary of the Interior; and in making new leases due consideration shall be made for the improvements of such lessees, and in all cases of the leasing or renewal of leases of oil, coal, asphalt, and other mineral deposits preference shall be given to parties in possession who have made improvements. The rate of royalty to be paid by all lessees shall be fixed by the Secretary of the Interior.

Sec. 14. That the inhabitants of any city or town in said Territory having two hundred or more residents therein may proceed, by petition to the United States court in the district in which such city or town is located, to have the same incorporated as provided in chapter twenty-nine of Mansfield's Digest of the Statutes of Arkansas, if not already incorporated thereunder; and the clerk of said court shall record all papers and perform all the acts required of the recorder of the county, or the clerk of the county court, or the secretary of state, necessary for the incorporation of any city or town, as provided in Mansfield's Digest, and such city or town government, when so authorized and organized, shall possess all the powers and exercise all the rights of similar municipalities in said State of Arkansas. All male inhabitants of such cities and towns over the age of twenty-one years, who are citizens of the United States or of either of said tribes, who have resided therein more than six months next before any election held under this Act, shall be qualified voters at such election. That mayors of such cities and towns, in addition to their other powers, shall have the same jurisdiction in all civil and criminal cases arising within the corporate limits of such cities and towns as, and coextensive with, United States commissioners in the Indian Territory, and may charge, collect, and retain the same fees as such commissioners now collect and account for to the United States; and the marshal or other executive officer of such city or town may execute all processes issued in the exercise of the jurisdiction hereby conferred, and charge and collect the same fees for similar services, as are allowed to constables under the laws now in force in said Territory.

All elections shall be conducted under the provisions of chapter fifty-six of said digest, entitled "Elections," so far as the same may be applicable; and all inhabitants of such cities and towns, without regard to race, shall be subject to all laws and ordinances of such city or town governments, and shall have equal rights, privileges, and protection therein. Such city or town governments shall in no case have any authority to impose upon or levy any tax against any lands in said cities or towns until after title is secured from the tribe; but all other property, including all improvements on town lots, which for the purposes of this Act shall be deemed and considered personal property, together with all occupations and privileges, shall be subject to taxation. And the councils of such cities and towns, for the support of the same and for schools and other public purposes, may provide by ordinance for the assessment, levy, and collection annually of a tax upon such property, not to exceed in the aggregate two per centum of the assessed value thereof, in manner provided in chapter one hundred and twenty-nine of said digest, entitled "Revenue," and for such purposes may also impose a tax upon occupations and privileges.

Such councils may also establish and maintain free schools in such cities and towns, under the provisions of sections sixty-two hundred and fifty-eight to sixty-two hundred and seventy-six, inclusive, of said digest, and may exercise all the powers conferred upon special school districts in cities and towns in the State of Arkansas by the laws of said State when the same are not in conflict with the provisions of this Act.

For the purposes of this section all the laws of said State of Arkansas herein referred to, so far as applicable, are hereby put in force in said Territory; and the United States court therein shall have jurisdiction to enforce the same, and to punish any violation thereof, and the city or town councils shall pass such ordinances as may be necessary for the purpose of making the laws extended over them applicable to them and for carrying the same into effect: *Provided,* That nothing in this Act, or in the laws of the State of Arkansas, shall authorize or permit the sale, or exposure for sale, of any intoxicating liquor in said Territory, or the introduction thereof into said Territory; and it shall be the duty of the district attorneys in said Territory and the officers of such municipalities to prosecute all violators of the laws of the United States relating to the introduction of intoxicating liquors into said Territory, or to their sale, or exposure for sale, therein: *Provided further,* That owners and holders of leases or improvements in any city or town shall be privileged to transfer the same.

Sec. 15. That there shall be a commission in each town for each one of the Chickasaw, Choctaw, Creek, and Cherokee tribes, to consist of one member to be appointed by the executive of the tribe, who shall not be interested in town property, other than his home; one person to be appointed by the Secretary of the Interior, and one member to be selected by the town. And if the executive of the tribe or the town fail to select members as aforesaid, they may be selected and appointed by the Secretary of the Interior.

Said commissions shall cause to be surveyed and laid out town sites where towns with a present population of two hundred or more are located, conforming to the existing survey so far as may be, with proper and necessary streets, alleys, and public grounds, including parks and cemeteries, giving to each town such territory as may be required for its present needs and reasonable prospective growth; and shall prepare correct plats thereof, and file one with the Secretary of the Interior, one with the clerk of the United States court, one with the authorities of the tribe, and one with the town authorities. And all town lots shall be appraised by said commission at their true value, excluding improvements; and separate appraisements shall be made of all improvements thereon; and no such appraisements shall be effective until approved by the Secretary of the Interior, and in case of disagreement by the members of such commission as to the value of any lot, said Secretary may fix the value thereof.

The owner of the improvements upon any town lot, other than fencing, tillage, or temporary buildings, may deposit in the United States Treasury, Saint Louis, Missouri, one-half of such appraised value; ten per centum within two months and fifteen per centum more within six months after notice of appraisement, and the remainder in three equal annual installments thereafter, depositing with the Secretary of the Interior one receipt for each payment, and one with the authorities of the tribe, and such deposit shall be deemed a tender to the tribe of the purchase money for such lot.

If the owner of such improvements on any lot fails to make deposit of the purchase money as aforesaid, then such lot may be sold in the manner herein provided for the sale of unimproved lots; and when the purchaser thereof has complied with the requirements herein for the purchase of improved lots he may, by petition, apply to the United States court within whose jurisdiction the town is located for condemnation and appraisement of such improvements, and petitioner shall, after judgment, deposit the value so fixed with the clerk of the court; and thereupon the defendant shall be required to accept same in full payment for his improvements or remove same from the lot within such time as may be fixed by the court.

All town lots not improved as aforesaid shall belong to the tribe, and shall be in like manner appraised, and, after approval by the Secretary of the Interior, and due notice, sold to the highest bidder at public auction by said commission, but not for less than their appraised value, unless ordered by the Secretary of the Interior; and purchasers may in like manner make deposits of the purchase money with like effect, as in case of improved lots.

The inhabitants of any town may, within one year after the completion of the survey thereof, make such deposit of ten dollars per acre for parks, cemeteries, and other public grounds laid out by said commission with like effect as for improved lots; and such parks and public grounds shall not be used for any purpose until such deposits are made.

The person authorized by the tribe or tribes may execute or deliver to any such purchaser, without expense to him, a deed conveying to him the title to such lands or town lots; and thereafter the purchase money shall become the property of the tribe; and all such moneys shall, when titles to all the lots in the towns belonging to any tribe have been thus perfected, be paid per capita to the members of the tribe: *Provided, however,* That in those town sites designated and laid out under the provisions of this Act where coal leases are now being operated and coal is being mined there shall be reserved from appraisement and sale all lots occupied by houses of miners actually engaged in mining, and only while they are so engaged, and in addition thereto a sufficient amount of land, to be determined by the appraisers, to furnish homes for the men actually engaged in working for the lessees operating said mines and a sufficient amount for all buildings and machinery for mining purposes: *And provided further,* That when the lessees shall cease to operate said mines, then, and in that event, the lots of land so reserved shall be disposed of as provided for in this Act.

SEC. 16. That it shall be unlawful for any person, after the passage of this Act, except as hereinafter provided, to claim, demand, or receive, for his own use or for the use of anyone else, any royalty on oil, coal, asphalt, or other mineral, or on any timber or lumber, or any other kind of property whatsoever, or any rents on any lands or property belonging to any one of said tribes or nations in said Territory, or for anyone to pay to any individual any such royalty or rents or any consideration therefor whatsoever; and all royalties and rents hereafter payable to the tribe shall be paid, under such rules and regulations as may be prescribed by the Secretary of the Interior, into the Treasury of the United States to the credit of the tribe to which they belong: *Provided*, That where any citizen shall be in possession of only such amount of agricultural or grazing lands as would be his just and reasonable share of the lands of his nation or tribe and that to which his wife and minor children are entitled, he may continue to use the same or receive the rents thereon until allotment has been made to him: *Provided further*, That nothing herein contained shall impair the rights of any member of a tribe to dispose of any timber contained on his, her, or their allotment.

SEC. 17. That it shall be unlawful for any citizen of any one of said tribes to inclose or in any manner, by himself or through another, directly or indirectly, to hold possession of any greater amount of lands or other property belonging to any such nation or tribe than that which would be his approximate share of the lands belonging to such nation or tribe and that of his wife and his minor children as per allotment herein provided; and any person found in such possession of lands or other property in excess of his share and that of his family, as aforesaid, or having the same in any manner inclosed, at the expiration of nine months after the passage of this Act, shall be deemed guilty of a misdemeanor.

SEC. 18. That any person convicted of violating any of the provisions of sections sixteen and seventeen of this Act shall be deemed guilty of a misdemeanor and punished by a fine of not less than one hundred dollars, and shall stand committed until such fine and costs are paid (such commitment not to exceed one day for every two dollars of said fine and costs), and shall forfeit possession of any property in question, and each day on which such offense is committed or continues to exist shall be deemed a separate offense. And the United States district attorneys in said Territory are required to see that the provisions of said sections are strictly enforced and they shall at once proceed to dispossess all persons of such excessive holding of lands and to prosecute them for so unlawfully holding the same.

SEC. 19. That no payment of any moneys on any account whatever shall hereafter be made by the United States to any of the tribal governments or to any officer thereof for disbursement, but payments of all sums to members of said tribes shall be made under direction of the Secretary of the Interior by an officer appointed by him; and per capita payments shall be made direct to each individual in lawful money of the United States, and the same shall not be liable to the payment of any previously contracted obligation.

SEC. 20. That the commission hereinbefore named shall have authority to employ, with approval of the Secretary of the Interior, all assistance necessary for the prompt and efficient performance of all duties herein imposed, including competent surveyors to make allotments, and to do any other needed work, and the Secretary of the Interior may detail competent clerks to aid them in the performance of their duties.

SEC. 21. That in making rolls of citizenship of the several tribes, as required by law, the Commission to the Five Civilized Tribes is authorized and directed to take the roll of Cherokee citizens of eighteen hundred and eighty (not including freedmen) as the only roll intended to be confirmed by this and preceding Acts of Congress, and to enroll all persons now living whose names are found on said roll, and all descendants born since the date of said roll to persons whose names are found thereon; and all persons who have been enrolled by the tribal authorities who have heretofore made permanent settlement in the Cherokee Nation whose parents, by reason of their Cherokee blood, have been lawfully admitted to citizenship by the tribal authorities, and who were minors when their parents were so admitted; and they shall investigate the right of all other persons whose names are found on any other rolls and omit all such as may have been placed thereon by fraud or without authority of law, enrolling only such as may have lawful right thereto, and their descendants born since such rolls were made, with such intermarried white persons as may be entitled to citizenship under Cherokee laws.

It shall make a roll of Cherokee freedmen in strict compliance with the decree of the Court of Claims rendered the third day of February, eighteen hundred and ninety-six.

Said commission is authorized and directed to make correct rolls of the citizens by blood of all the other tribes, eliminating from the tribal rolls such names as may have been placed thereon by fraud or without authority of law, enrolling such only as may have lawful right thereto, and their descendants born since such rolls were made, with such intermarried white persons as may be entitled to Choctaw and Chickasaw citizenship under the treaties and the laws of said tribes.

Said commission shall have authority to determine the identity of Choctaw Indians claiming rights in the Choctaw lands under article fourteen of the treaty between the United States and the Choctaw Nation concluded September twenty-seventh, eighteen hundred and thirty, and to that end they may administer oaths, examine witnesses, and perform all other acts necessary thereto and make report to the Secretary of the Interior.

The roll of Creek freedmen made by J. W. Dunn, under authority of the United States, prior to March fourteenth, eighteen hundred and sixty-seven, is hereby confirmed, and said commission is directed to enroll all persons now living whose names are found on said rolls, and all descendants born since the date of said roll to persons whose names are found thereon, with such other persons of African descent as may have been rightfully admitted by the lawful authorities of the Creek Nation.

It shall make a correct roll of all Choctaw freedmen entitled to citizenship under the treaties and laws of the Choctaw Nation, and all their descendants born to them since the date of the treaty.

It shall make a correct roll of Chickasaw freedmen entitled to any rights or benefits under the treaty made in eighteen hundred and sixty-six between the United States and the Choctaw and Chickasaw tribes and their descendants born to them since the date of said treaty and forty acres of land, including their present residences and improvements, shall be allotted to each, to be selected, held, and used by them until their rights under said treaty shall be determined in such manner as shall be hereafter provided by Congress.

The several tribes may, by agreement, determine the right of persons who for any reason may claim citizenship in two or more tribes, and to allotment of lands and distribution of moneys belonging to each tribe; but if no such agreement be made, then such claimant shall be entitled to such rights in one tribe only, and may elect in which tribe he will take such right; but if he fail or refuse to make such selection in due time, he shall be enrolled in the tribe with whom he has resided, and there be given such allotment and distributions, and not elsewhere.

No person shall be enrolled who has not heretofore removed to and in good faith settled in the nation in which he claims citizenship: *Provided, however,* That nothing contained in this Act shall be so construed as to militate against any rights or privileges which the Mississippi Choctaws may have under the laws of or the treaties with the United States.

Said commission shall make such rolls descriptive of the persons thereon, so that they may be thereby identified, and it is authorized to take a census of each of said tribes, or to adopt any other means by them deemed necessary to enable them to make such rolls. They shall have access to all rolls and records of the several tribes, and the United States court in Indian Territory shall have jurisdiction to compel the officers of the tribal governments and custodians of such rolls and records to deliver same to said commission, and on their refusal or failure to do so to punish them as for contempt; as also to require all citizens of said tribes, and persons who should be so enrolled, to appear before said commission for enrollment, at such times and places as may be fixed by said commission, and to enforce obedience of all others concerned, so far as the same may be necessary, to enable said commission to make rolls as herein required, and to punish anyone who may in any manner or by any means obstruct said work.

The rolls so made, when approved by the Secretary of the Interior, shall be final, and the persons whose names are found thereon, with their descendants thereafter born to them, with such persons as may intermarry according to tribal laws, shall alone constitute the several tribes which they represent.

The members of said commission shall, in performing all duties required of them by law, have authority to administer oaths, examine witnesses, and send for persons and papers; and any person who shall willfully and knowingly make any false affidavit or oath to any material fact or matter before any member of said commission, or before any other officer authorized to administer oaths, to any affidavit or other paper to be filed or oath taken before said commission, shall be deemed guilty of perjury, and on conviction thereof shall be punished as for such offense.

Sec. 22. That where members of one tribe, under intercourse laws, usages, or customs, have made homes within the limits and on the lands of another tribe they may retain and take allotment, embracing same under such agreement as may be made between such tribes respecting such settlers; but if no such agreement be made the improvements so made shall be appraised, and the value thereof, including all damages incurred by such settler incident to enforced removal, shall be paid to him immediately upon removal, out of any funds belonging to the tribe, or such settler, if he so desire, may make private sale of his improvements to any citizen of the tribe owning the lands: *Provided*, That he shall not be paid for improvements made on lands in excess of that to which he, his wife, and minor children are entitled to under this Act.

SEC. 23. That all leases of agricultural or grazing land belonging to any tribe made after the first day of January, eighteen hundred and ninety-eight, by the tribe or any member thereof shall be absolutely void, and all such grazing leases made prior to said date shall terminate on the first day of April, eighteen hundred and ninety-nine, and all such agricultural leases shall terminate on January first, nineteen hundred; but this shall not prevent individuals from leasing their allotments when made to them as provided in this Act, nor from occupying or renting their proportionate shares of the tribal lands until the allotments herein provided for are made.

SEC. 24. That all moneys paid into the United States Treasury at Saint Louis, Missouri, under provisions of this Act shall be placed to the credit of the tribe to which they belong; and the assistant United States treasurer shall give triplicate receipts therefor to the depositor.

SEC. 25. That before any allotment shall be made of lands in the Cherokee Nation, there shall be segregated therefrom by the commission heretofore mentioned, in separate allotments or otherwise, the one hundred and fifty-seven thousand six hundred acres purchased by the Delaware tribe of Indians from the Cherokee Nation under agreement of April eighth, eighteen hundred and sixty-seven, subject to the judicial determination of the rights of said descendants and the Cherokee Nation under said agreement. That the Delaware Indians residing in the Cherokee Nation are hereby authorized and empowered to bring suit in the Court of Claims of the United States, within sixty days after the passage of this Act, against the Cherokee Nation, for the purpose of determining the rights of said Delaware Indians in and to the lands and funds of said nation under their contract and agreement with the Cherokee Nation dated April eighth, eighteen hundred and sixty-seven; or the Cherokee Nation may bring a like suit against said Delaware Indians; and jurisdiction is conferred on said court to adjudicate and fully determine the same, with right of appeal to either party to the Supreme Court of the United States.

SEC. 26. That on and after the passage of this Act the laws of the various tribes or nations of Indians shall not be enforced at law or in equity by the courts of the United States in the Indian Territory.

SEC. 27. That the Secretary of the Interior is authorized to locate one Indian inspector in Indian Territory, who may, under his authority and direction, perform any duties required of the Secretary of the Interior by law, relating to affairs therein.

SEC. 28. That on the first day of July, eighteen hundred and ninety-eight, all tribal courts in Indian Territory shall be abolished, and no officer of said courts shall thereafter have any authority whatever to do or perform any act theretofore authorized by any law in connection with said courts, or to receive any pay for same; and all civil and criminal causes then pending in any such court shall be transferred to the United States court in said Territory by filing with the clerk of the court the original papers in the suit: *Provided*, That this section shall not be in force as to the Chickasaw, Choctaw, and Creek tribes or nations until the first day of October, eighteen hundred and ninety-eight.

SEC. 29. That the agreement made by the Commission to the Five Civilized Tribes with commissions representing the Choctaw and Chickasaw tribes of Indians on the twenty-third day of April, eighteen hundred and ninety-seven, as herein amended, is hereby ratified and confirmed, and the same shall be of full force and effect if ratified before the first day of December, eighteen hundred and ninety-eight, by a majority of the whole number of votes cast by the members of said tribes at an election held for that purpose; and the executives of said tribes are hereby authorized and directed to make public proclamation that said agreement shall be voted on at the next general election, or at any special election to be called by such executives for the purpose of voting on said agreement; and at the election held for such purpose all male members of each of said tribes qualified to vote under his tribal laws shall have the right to vote at the election precinct most convenient to his residence, whether the same be within the bounds of his tribe or not: *Provided*, That no person whose right to citizenship in either of said tribes or nations is now contested in original or appellate proceedings before any United States court shall be permitted to vote at said election: *Provided further*, That the votes cast in both said tribes or nations shall be forthwith returned duly certified by the precinct officers to the national secretaries of said tribes or nations, and shall be presented by said national secretaries to a board of commissioners consisting of the principal chief and national

Report of the Indian Inspector for Indian Territory, 1900.

THE ARKANSAS RIVER, LOW WATER.

secretary of the Choctaw Nation, the governor and national secretary of the Chickasaw Nation, and a member of the Commission to the Five Civilized Tribes, to be designated by the chairman of said commission; and said board shall meet without delay at Atoka, in the Indian Territory, and canvass and count said votes and make proclamation of the result; and if said agreement as amended be so ratified, the provisions of this Act shall then only apply to said tribes where the same do not conflict with the provisions of said agreement; but the provisions of said agreement, if so ratified, shall not in any manner affect the provisions of section fourteen of this Act, which said amended agreement is as follows:

This agreement, by and between the Government of the United States, of the first part, entered into in its behalf by the Commission to the Five Civilized Tribes, Henry L. Dawes, Frank C. Armstrong, Archibald S. McKennon, Thomas B. Cabaniss, and Alexander B. Montgomery, duly appointed and authorized thereunto, and the governments of the Choctaw and Chickasaw tribes or nations of Indians in the Indian Territory, respectively, of the second part, entered into in behalf of such Choctaw and Chickasaw governments, duly appointed and authorized thereunto, viz: Green McCurtain, J. S. Standley, N. B. Ainsworth, Ben Hampton, Wesley Anderson, Amos Henry. D. C. Garland, and A. S. Williams, in behalf of the Choctaw Tribe or Nation, and R. M. Harris, I. O. Lewis, Holmes Colbert, P. S. Mosely, M. V. Cheadle, R. L. Murray, William Perry, A. H. Colbert, and R. L. Boyd, in behalf of the Chickasaw Tribe or Nation.

ALLOTMENT OF LANDS.

Witnesseth, That in consideration of the mutual undertakings, herein contained, it is agreed as follows:

That all the lands within the Indian Territory belonging to the Choctaw and Chickasaw Indians shall be allotted to the members of said tribes so as to give to each member of these tribes so far as possible a fair and equal share thereof, considering the character and fertility of the soil and the location and value of the lands.

That all the lands set apart for town sites, and the strip of land lying between the city of Fort Smith, Arkansas, and the Arkansas and Poteau rivers, extending up said river to the mouth of Mill Creek; and six hundred and forty acres each, to include the buildings now occupied by the Jones Academy, Tushkahoma Female Seminary, Wheelock Orphan Seminary, and Armstrong Orphan Academy, and ten acres for the capitol building of the Choctaw Nation; one hundred and sixty acres each, immediately contiguous to and including the buildings known as Bloomfield Academy, Lebanon Orphan Home, Harley Institute, Rock Academy, and Collins Institute, and five acres for the capitol building in the Chickasaw Nation, and the use of one acre of land for each church house now erected outside of the towns, and eighty acres of land each for J. S. Murrow, H. R. Schermerhorn, and the widow of R. S. Bell, who have been laboring as missionaries in the Choctaw and Chickasaw nations since the year eighteen hundred and sixty-six, with the same conditions and limitations as apply to lands allotted to' the members of the Choctaw and Chickasaw nations, and to be located on lands not occupied by a Choctaw or a Chickasaw, and a reasonable amount of land, to be determined by the town-site commission, to include all court-houses and jails and other public buildings not hereinbefore provided for, shall be exempted from division. And all coal and asphalt in or under the lands allotted and reserved from allotment shall be reserved for the sole use of the members of the Choctaw and Chickasaw tribes, exclusive of freedmen: *Provided*, That where any coal or asphalt is hereafter opened on land allotted, sold, or reserved, the value of the use of the necessary surface for prospecting or mining, and the damage done to the other land and improvements, shall be ascertained under the direction of the Secretary of the Interior and paid to the allottee or owner of the land by the lessee or party operating the same, before operations begin. That in order to such equal division, the lands of the Choctaws and Chickasaws shall be graded and appraised so as to give to each member, so far as possible, an equal value of the land: *Provided further*, That the Commission to the Five Civilized Tribes shall make a correct roll of Chickasaw freedmen entitled to any rights or benefits under the treaty made in eighteen hundred and sixty-six between the United States and the Choctaw and Chickasaw tribes and their descendants born to them since the date of said treaty, and forty acres of land, including their present residences and improvements, shall be allotted to each, to be selected, held, and used by them until their rights under said treaty shall be determined, in such manner as shall hereafter be provided by act of Congress.

That the lands allotted to the Choctaw and Chickasaw freedmen are to be deducted from the portion to be allotted under this agreement to the members of the Choctaw and Chickasaw tribe so as to reduce the allotment to the Choctaws and Chickasaws by the value of the same.

That the said Choctaw and Chickasaw freedmen who may be entitled to allotments of forty acres each shall be entitled each to land equal in value to forty acres of the average land of the two nations.

That in the appraisement of the lands to be allotted the Choctaw and Chickasaw tribes shall each have a representative, to be appointed by their respective executives, to cooperate with the commission to the Five Civilized Tribes, or any one making appraisements under the direction of the Secretary of the Interior in grading and appraising the lands preparatory to allotment. And the land shall be valued in the appraisement as if in its original condition, excluding the improvements thereon.

That the appraisement and allotment shall be made under the direction of the Secretary of the Interior, and shall begin as soon as the progress of the surveys, now being made by the United States Government, will admit.

That each member of the Choctaw and Chickasaw tribes, including Choctaw and Chickasaw freedmen, shall, where it is possible, have the right to take his allotment on land, the improvements on which belong to him, and such improvements shall not be estimated in the value of his allotment. In the case of minor children, allotments shall be selected for them by their father, mother, guardian, or the administrator having charge of their estate, preference being given in the order named, and shall not be sold during his minority. Allotments shall be selected for prisoners, convicts, and incompetents by some suitable person akin to them, and due care taken that all persons entitled thereto have allotments made to them.

All the lands allotted shall be nontaxable while the title remains in the original allottee, but not to exceed twenty-one years from date of patent, and each allottee shall select from his allotment a homestead of one hundred and sixty acres, for which he shall have a separate patent, and which shall be inalienable for twenty-one years from date of patent. This provision shall also apply to the Choctaw and Chickasaw freedman to the extent of his allotment. Selections for homesteads for minors to be made as provided herein in case of allotment, and the remainder of the lands allotted to said members shall be alienable for a price to be actually paid, and to include no former indebtedness or obligation—one-fourth of said remainder in one year, one-fourth in three years, and the balance of said alienable lands in five years from the date of the patent.

That all contracts looking to the sale or incumbrance in any way of the land of an allottee, except the sale hereinbefore provided, shall be null and void. No allottee shall lease his allotment, or any portion thereof, for a longer period than five years, and then without the privilege of renewal. Every lease which is not evidenced by writing, setting out specifically the terms thereof, or which is not recorded in the clerk's office of the United States court for the district in which the land is located, within three months after the date of its execution, shall be void, and the purchaser or lessee shall acquire no rights whatever by an entry or holding thereunder. And no such lease or any sale shall be valid as against the allottee unless providing to him a reasonable compensation for the lands sold or leased.

That all controversies arising between the members of said tribes as to their right to have certain lands allotted to them shall be settled by the commission making the allotments.

That the United States shall put each allottee in possession of his allotment and remove all persons therefrom objectionable to the allottee.

That the United States shall survey and definitely mark and locate the ninety-eighth (98th) meridian of west longitude between Red and Canadian rivers before allotment of the lands herein provided for shall begin.

MEMBERS' TITLES TO LANDS.

That as soon as practicable, after the completion of said allotments, the principal chief of the Choctaw Nation and the governor of the Chickasaw Nation shall jointly execute, under their hands and the seals of the respective nations, and deliver to each of the said allottees patents conveying to him all the right, title, and interest of the Choctaws and Chickasaws in and to the land which shall have been allotted to him in conformity with the requirements of this agreement, excepting all coal and asphalt in or under said land. Said patents shall be framed in accordance with the provisions of this agreement, and shall embrace the land allotted to such patentee and no other land, and the acceptance of his patents by such allottee shall be operative as an assent on his part to the allotment and conveyance of all the lands of the Choctaws and Chickasaws in accordance with the provisions of this agreement, and as a relinquishment of all his right, title, and interest in and to any and all parts thereof, except the land embraced in said patents, except also his interest in the proceeds of all lands, coal, and asphalt herein excepted from allotment.

That the United States shall provide by law for proper records of land titles in the territory occupied by the Choctaw and Chickasaw tribes.

RAILROADS.

The rights of way for railroads through the Choctaw and Chickasaw nations to be surveyed and set apart and platted to conform to the respective acts of Congress granting the same in cases where said rights of way are defined by such acts of Congress, but in cases where the acts of Congress do not define the same then Congress is memorialized to definitely fix the width of said rights of way for station grounds and between stations, so that railroads now constructed through said nations shall have, as near as possible, uniform rights of way; and Congress is also requested to fix uniform rates of fare and freight for all railroads through the Choctaw and Chickasaw nations; branch railroads now constructed and not built according to acts of Congress to pay the same rates for rights of way and station grounds as main lines.

TOWN SITES.

It is further agreed that there shall be appointed a commission for each of the two nations. Each commission shall consist of one member, to be appointed by the executive of the tribe for which said commission is to act, who shall not be interested in town property other than his home, and one to be appointed by the President of the United States. Each of said commissions shall lay out town sites, to be restricted as far as possible to their present limits, where towns are now located in the nation for which said commission is appointed. Said commission shall have prepared correct and proper plats of each town, and file one in the clerk's office of the United States district court for the district in which the town is located, and one with the principal chief or governor of the nation in which the town is located, and one with the Secretary of the Interior, which shall be approved by him before the same shall take effect. When said towns are so laid out, each lot on which permanent, substantial, and valuable improvements, other than fences, tillage, and temporary houses, have been made, shall be valued by the commission provided for the nation in which the town is located at the price a fee-simple title to the same would bring in the market at the time the valuation is made, but not to include in such value the improvements thereon. The owner of the improvements on each lot shall have the right to buy one residence and one business lot at fifty per centum of the appraised value of such improved property, and the remainder of such improved property at sixty-two and one-half per centum of the said market value within sixty days from date of notice served on him that such lot is for sale, and if he purchases the same he shall, within ten days from his purchase, pay into the Treasury of the United States one-fourth of the purchase price, and the balance in three equal annual installments, and when the entire sum is paid shall be entitled to a patent for the same. In case the two members of the commission fail to agree as to the market value of any lot, or the limit or extent of said town, either of said commissioners may report any such disagreement to the judge of the district in which such town is located, who shall appoint a third member to act with said commission, who is not interested in town lots, who shall act with them to determine said value.

If such owner of the improvements on any lot fails within sixty days to purchase and make the first payment on same, such lot, with the improvements thereon, shall be sold at public auction to the highest bidder, under the direction of the aforesaid commission, and the purchaser at such sale shall pay to the owner of the improvements the price for which said lot shall be sold, less sixty-two and one-half per cent of said appraised value of the lot, and shall pay the sixty-two and one-half per cent of said appraised value into United States Treasury, under regulations to be established by the Secretary of the Interior, in four installments, as hereinbefore provided. The commission shall have the right to reject any bid on such lot which they consider below its value.

All lots not so appraised shall be sold from time to time at public auction (after proper advertisement) by the commission for the nation in which the town is located, as may seem for the best interest of the nations and the proper development of each town, the purchase price to be paid in four installments as hereinbefore provided for improved lots. The commission shall have the right to reject any bid for such lots which they consider below its value.

All the payments herein provided for shall be made under the direction of the Secretary of the Interior into the United States Treasury, a failure of sixty days to make any one payment to be a forfeiture of all payments made and all rights under the contract: *Provided*, That the purchaser of any lot shall have the option of paying the entire price of the lot before the same is due.

No tax shall be assessed by any town government against any town lot unsold by the commission, and no tax levied against a lot sold, as herein provided, shall constitute a lien on same till the purchase price thereof has been fully paid to the nation.

The money paid into the United States Treasury for the sale of all town lots shall be for the benefit of the members of the Choctaw and Chickasaw tribes (freedmen excepted), and at the end of one year from the ratification of this agreement, and at the end of each year thereafter, the funds so accumulated shall be divided and paid to the Choctaws and Chickasaws (freedmen excepted), each member of the two tribes to receive an equal portion thereof.

That no law or ordinance shall be passed by any town which interferes with the enforcement of or is in conflict with the laws of the United States in force in said Territory, and all persons in such towns shall be subject to said laws, and the United States agrees to maintain strict laws in the territory of the Choctaw and Chickasaw tribes against the introduction, sale, barter, or giving away of liquors and intoxicants of any kind or quality.

That said commission shall be authorized to locate, within a suitable distance from each town site, not to exceed five acres to be used as a cemetery, and when any town has paid into the United States Treasury, to be part of the fund arising from the sale of town lots, ten dollars per acre therefor, such town shall be entitled to a patent for the same as herein provided for titles to allottees, and shall dispose of same at reasonable prices in suitable lots for burial purposes, the proceeds derived from such sales to be applied by the town government to the proper improvement and care of said cemetery.

That no charge or claim shall be made against the Choctaw or Chickasaw tribes by the United States for the expenses of surveying and platting the lands and town sites, or for grading, appraising, and allotting the lands, or for appraising and disposing of the town lots as herein provided.

That the land adjacent to Fort Smith and lands for court-houses, jails, and other public purposes, excepted from allotment shall be disposed of in the same manner and for the same purposes as provided for town lots herein, but not till the Choctaw and Chickasaw councils shall direct such disposition to be made thereof, and said land adjacent thereto shall be placed under the jurisdiction of the city of Fort Smith, Arkansas, for police purposes.

There shall be set apart and exempted from appraisement and sale in the towns, lots upon which churches and parsonages are now built and occupied, not to exceed fifty feet front and one hundred feet deep for each church or parsonage: *Provided*, That such lots shall only be used for churches and parsonages, and when they ceased to be used shall revert to the members of the tribes to be disposed of as other town lots: *Provided further*, That these lots may be sold by the churches for which they are set apart if the purchase money therefor is invested in other lot or lots in the same town, to be used for the same purpose and with the same conditions and limitations.

It is agreed that all the coal and asphalt within the limits of the Choctaw and Chickasaw nations shall remain and be the common property of the members of the Choctaw and Chickasaw tribes (freedmen excepted), so that each and every member shall have an equal and undivided interest in the whole; and no patent provided for in this agreement shall convey any title thereto. The revenues from coal and asphalt, or so much as shall be necessary, shall be used for the education of the children of Indian blood of the members of said tribes. Such coal and asphalt mines as are now in operation, and all others which may hereafter be leased and operated, shall be under the supervision and control of two trustees, who shall be appointed by the President of the United States, one on the recommendation of the Principal Chief of the Choctaw Nation, who shall be a Choctaw by blood, whose term shall be for four years, and one on the recommendation of the Governor of the Chickasaw Nation, who shall be a Chickasaw by blood, whose term shall be for two years; after which the term of appointees shall be four years. Said trustees, or either of them, may, at any time, be removed by the President of the United States for good cause shown. They shall each give bond for the faithful performance of their duties, under such rules as may be prescribed by the Secretary of the Interior. Their salaries shall be fixed and paid by their respective nations, each of whom shall make full report of all his acts to the Secretary of the Interior quarterly. All such acts shall be subject to the approval of said Secretary.

All coal and asphalt mines in the two nations, whether now developed, or to be hereafter developed, shall be operated, and the royalties therefrom paid into the

Treasury of the United States, and shall be drawn therefrom under such rules and regulations as shall be prescribed by the Secretary of the Interior.

All contracts made by the National Agents of the Choctaw and Chickasaw Nations for operating coal and asphalt, with any person or corporation, which were, on April twenty-third, eighteen hundred and ninety-seven, being operated in good faith are hereby ratified and confirmed, and the lessee shall have the right to renew the same when they expire, subject to all the provisions of this Act.

All agreements heretofore made by any person or corporation with any member or members of the Choctaw or Chickasaw nations, the object of which was to obtain such member or members' permission to operate coal or asphalt, are hereby declared void: *Provided*, That nothing herein contained shall impair the rights of any holder or owner of a leasehold interest in any oil, coal rights, asphalt, or mineral which have been assented to by act of Congress, but all such interests shall continue unimpaired hereby and shall be assured by new leases from such trustees of coal or asphalt claims described therein, by application to the trustees within six months after the ratification of this agreement, subject, however, to payment of advance royalties herein provided for.

All leases under this agreement shall include the coal or asphaltum, or other mineral, as the case may be, in or under nine hundred and sixty acres, which shall be in a square as nearly as possible, and shall be for thirty years. The royalty on coal shall be fifteen cents per ton of two thousand pounds on all coal mined, payable on the 25th day of the month next succeeding that in which it is mined. Royalty on asphalt shall be sixty cents per ton, payable same as coal: *Provided*, That the Secretary of the Interior may reduce or advance royalties on coal and asphalt when he deems it for the best interests of the Choctaws and Chickasaws to do so. No royalties shall be paid except into the United States Treasury as herein provided.

All lessees shall pay on each coal or asphalt claim at the rate of one hundred dollars per annum, in advance, for the first and second years; two hundred dollars per annum, in advance, for the third and fourth years; and five hundred dollars for each succeeding year thereafter. All such payments shall be treated as advanced royalty on the mine or claim on which they are made, and shall be a credit as royalty when each said mine is developed and operated, and its production is in excess of such guaranteed annual advance payments, and all persons having coal leases must pay said annual advance payments on each claim whether developed or undeveloped: *Provided, however*, That should any lessee neglect or refuse to pay such advanced annual royalty for the period of sixty days after the same becomes due and payable on any lease, the lease on which default is made shall become null and void, and the royalties paid in advance thereon shall then become and be the money and property of the Choctaw and Chickasaw nations.

In surface, the use of which is reserved to present coal operators, shall be included such lots in towns as are occupied by lessees' houses—either occupied by said lessees' employees, or as offices or warehouses: *Provided, however*, That in those town sites designated and laid out under the provision of this agreement where coal leases are now being operated and coal is being mined, there shall be reserved from appraisement and sale all lots occupied by houses of miners actually engaged in mining, and only while they are so engaged, and in addition thereto a sufficient amount of land, to be determined by the town-site board of appraisers, to furnish homes for the men actually engaged in working for the lessees operating said mines, and a sufficient amount for all buildings and machinery for mining purposes: *And provided further*, That when the lessees shall cease to operate said mines, then and in that event the lots of land so reserved shall be disposed of by the coal trustees for the benefit of the Choctaw and Chickasaw tribes.

That whenever the members of the Choctaw and Chickasaw tribes shall be required to pay taxes for the support of schools, then the fund arising from such royalties shall be disposed of for the equal benefit of their members (freedmen excepted) in such manner as the tribes may direct.

It is further agreed that the United States courts now existing, or that may hereafter be created, in the Indian Territory shall have exclusive jurisdiction of all controversies growing out of the titles, ownership, occupation, possession, or use of real estate, coal, and asphalt in the territory occupied by the Choctaw and Chickasaw tribes; and of all persons charged with homicide, embezzlement, bribery, and embracery, breaches, or disturbances of the peace, and carrying weapons, hereafter committed in the territory of said tribes, without reference to race or citizenship of the person or persons charged with such crime; and any citizen or officer of the Choctaw or Chickasaw nations charged with such crime shall be tried, and, if convicted, punished as though he were a citizen or officer of the United States.

And sections sixteen hundred and thirty-six to sixteen hundred and forty-four, inclusive, entitled "Embezzlement," and sections seventeen hundred and eleven to seventeen hundred and eighteen, inclusive, entitled "Bribery and Embracery," of Mansfield's Digest of the laws of Arkansas, are hereby extended over and put in force in the Choctaw and Chickasaw nations; and the word "officer," where the same appears in said laws, shall include all officers of the Choctaw and Chickasaw governments; and the fifteenth section of the Act of Congress, entitled "An Act to establish United States courts in the Indian Territory, and for other purposes," approved March first, eighteen hundred and eighty-nine, limiting jurors to citizens of the United States, shall be held not to apply to the United States courts in the Indian Territory held within the limits of the Choctaw and Chickasaw nations; and all members of the Choctaw and Chickasaw tribes, otherwise qualified, shall be competent jurors in said courts: *Provided*, That whenever a member of the Choctaw and Chickasaw nations is indicted for homicide, he may, within thirty days after such indictment and his arrest thereon, and before the same is reached for trial, file with the clerk of the court in which he is indicted, his affidavit that he can not get a fair trial in said court; and it thereupon shall be the duty of the judge of said court to order a change of venue in such case to the United States district court for the western district of Arkansas, at Fort Smith, Arkansas, or to the United States district court for the eastern district of Texas, at Paris, Texas, always selecting the court that in his judgment is nearest or most convenient to the place where the crime charged in the indictment is supposed to have been committed, which courts shall have jurisdiction to try the case; and in all said civil suits said courts shall have full equity powers; and whenever it shall appear to said court, at any stage in the hearing of any case, that the tribe is in any way interested in the subject-matter in controversy, it shall have power to summon in said tribe and make the same a party to the suit and proceed therein in all respects as if such tribe were an original party thereto; but in no case shall suit be instituted against the tribal government without its consent.

It is further agreed that no act, ordinance, or resolution of the council of either the Choctaw or Chickasaw tribes, in any manner affecting the land of the tribe, or of the individuals, after allotment, or the moneys or other property of the tribe or citizens thereof (except appropriations for the regular and necessary expenses of the government of the respective tribes), or the rights of any persons to employ any kind of labor, or the rights of any persons who have taken or may take the oath of allegiance to the United States, shall be of any validity until approved by the President of the United States. When such acts, ordinances, or resolutions passed by the council of either of said tribes shall be approved by the governor thereof, then it shall be the duty of the national secretary of said tribe to forward them to the President of the United States, duly certified and sealed, who shall, within thirty days after their reception, approve or disapprove the same. Said acts, ordinances, or resolutions, when so approved, be published in at least two newspapers having a bona fide circulation in the tribe to be affected thereby, and when disapproved shall be returned to the tribe enacting the same.

It is further agreed, in view of the modification of legislative authority and judicial jurisdiction herein provided, and the necessity of the continuance of the tribal governments so modified, in order to carry out the requirements of this agreement, that the same shall continue for the period of eight years from the fourth day of March, eighteen hundred and ninety-eight. This stipulation is made in the belief that the tribal governments so modified will prove so satisfactory that there will be no need or desire for further change till the lands now occupied by the Five Civilized Tribes shall, in the opinion of Congress, be prepared for admission as a State to the Union. But this provision shall not be construed to be in any respect an abdication by Congress of power at any time to make needful rules and regulations respecting said tribes.

That all per capita payments hereafter made to the members of the Choctaw or Chickasaw nations shall be paid directly to each individual member by a bonded officer of the United States, under the direction of the Secretary of the Interior, which officer shall be required to give strict account for such disbursements to said Secretary.

That the following sum be, and is hereby, appropriated, out of any money in the Treasury not otherwise appropriated, for fulfilling treaty stipulations with the Chickasaw Nation of Indians, namely:

For arrears of interest, at five per centum per annum, from December thirty-first, eighteen hundred and forty, to June thirtieth, eighteen hundred and eighty-nine, on one hundred and eighty-four thousand one hundred and forty-three dollars and nine cents of the trust fund of the Chickasaw Nation erroneously dropped from the books of the United States prior to December thirty-first, eighteen hundred and forty, and restored December twenty-seventh, eighteen hundred and eighty-seven, by the award of the Secretary of the Interior, under the fourth article of the treaty of June twenty-second, eighteen hundred and fifty-two, and for arrears of interest at five per centum per annum, from March eleventh, eighteen hundred and fifty, to March third, eighteen hundred and ninety, on fifty-six thousand and twenty-one dollars and forty-nine cents of the trust fund of the Chickasaw Nation erroneously dropped from the books of the United States March eleventh, eighteen hundred and fifty, and restored December twenty-seventh, eighteen hundred and eighty-seven, by the award of the Secretary of the Interior, under the fourth article of the treaty of June twenty-second, eighteen hundred and fifty-two, five hundred and fifty-eight thousand five hundred and twenty dollars and fifty-four cents, to be placed to the credit of the Chickasaw Nation with the fund to which it properly belongs: *Provided,* That if there be any attorneys' fees to be paid out of same, on contract heretofore made and duly approved by the Secretary of the Interior, the same is authorized to be paid by him.

It is further agreed that the final decision of the courts of the United States in the case of the Choctaw Nation and the Chickasaw Nation against the United States and the Wichita and affiliated bands of Indians, now pending, when made, shall be conclusive as the basis of settlement as between the United States and said Choctaw and Chickasaw nations for the remaining lands in what is known as the "Leased District," namely, the land lying between the ninety-eighth and one hundredth degrees of west longitude and between the Red and Canadian rivers, leased to the United States by the treaty of eighteen hundred and fifty-five, except that portion called the Cheyenne and Arapahoe country, heretofore acquired by the United States, and all final judgments rendered against said nations in any of the courts of the United States in favor of the United States or any citizen thereof shall first be paid out of any sum hereafter found due said Indians for any interest they may have in the so-called leased district.

It is further agreed that all of the funds invested, in lieu of investment, treaty funds, or otherwise, now held by the United States in trust for the Choctaw and Chickasaw tribes, shall be capitalized within one year after the tribal governments shall cease, so far as the same may be legally done, and be appropriated and paid, by some officer of the United States appointed for the purpose, to the Choctaws and Chickasaws (freedmen excepted) per capita, to aid and assist them in improving their homes and lands.

It is further agreed that the Choctaws and Chickasaws, when their tribal governments cease, shall become possessed of all the rights and privileges of citizens of the United States.

ORPHAN LANDS.

It is further agreed that the Choctaw orphan lands in the State of Mississippi, yet unsold, shall be taken by the United States at one dollar and twenty-five cents ($1.25) per acre, and the proceeds placed to the credit of the Choctaw orphan fund in the Treasury of the United States, the number of acres to be determined by the General Land Office.

In witness whereof the said commissioners do hereunto affix their names at Atoka, Indian Territory, this the twenty-third day of April, eighteen hundred and ninety-seven.

GREEN McCURTAIN,
    Principal Chief.
J. S. STANDLEY,
N. B. AINSWORTH,
BEN HAMPTON,
WESLEY ANDERSON,
AMOS HENRY.
D. C. GARLAND,
    Choctaw Commission.

R. M. HARRIS,
    Governor.
ISAAC O. LEWIS,
HOLMES COLBERT,
ROBERT L. MURRAY,
WILLIAM PERRY,
R. L. BOYD,
    Chickasaw Commission.

FRANK C. ARMSTRONG,
    Acting Chairman.
ARCHIBALD S. McKENNON,
THOMAS B. CABANISS,
ALEXANDER B. MONTGOMERY,
Commission to the Five Civilized Tribes.
H. M. JACOWAY, Jr.,
    Secretary, Five Tribes Commission.

SEC. 30. That the agreement made by the Commission to the Five Civilized Tribes with the commission representing the Muscogee (or Creek) tribe of Indians on the twenty-seventh day of September, eighteen hundred and ninety-seven, as herein amended, is hereby ratified and confirmed, and the same shall be of full force and effect if ratified before the first day of December, eighteen hundred and ninety-eight, by a majority of the votes cast by the members of said tribe at an election to be held for that purpose; and the executive of said tribe is authorized and directed to make public proclamation that said agreement shall be voted on at the next general election, to be called by such executive for the purpose of voting on said agreement; and if said agreement as amended be so ratified, the provisions of this Act shall then only apply to said tribe where the same do not conflict with the provisions of said agreement; but the provision of said agreement, if so ratified, shall not in any manner affect the provisions of section fourteen of this Act, which said amended agreement is as follows:

This agreement, by and between the Government of the United States of the first part, entered into in its behalf by the Commission to the Five Civilized Tribes, Henry L. Dawes, Frank C. Armstrong, Archibald S. McKennon, Alexander B. Montgomery, and Tams Bixby, duly appointed and authorized thereunto, and the government of the Muscogee or Creek Nation in the Indian Territory of the second part, entered into in behalf of such Muscogee or Creek government, by its commission, duly appointed and authorized thereunto, viz, Pleasant Porter, Joseph Mingo, David N. Hodge, George A. Alexander, Roland Brown, William A. Sapulpa, and Conchartie Micco,

Witnesseth, That in consideration of the mutual undertakings herein contained; it is agreed as follows:

GENERAL ALLOTMENT OF LAND.

1. There shall be allotted out of the lands owned by the Muscogee or Creek Indians in the Indian Territory to each citizen of said nation one hundred and sixty acres of land. Each citizen shall have the right, so far as possible, to take his one hundred and sixty acres so as to include the improvements which belong to him, but such improvements shall not be estimated in the value fixed on his allotment, provided any citizen may take any land not already selected by another; but if such land, under actual cultivation, has on it any lawful improvements, he shall pay the owner of said improvements for same, the value to be fixed by the commission appraising the land. In the case of a minor child, allotment shall be selected for him by his father, mother, guardian, or the administrator having charge of his estate, preference being given in the order named, and shall not be sold during his minority. Allotments shall be selected for prisoners, convicts, and incompetents by some suitable person akin to them, and due care shall be taken that all persons entitled thereto shall have allotments made to them.

2. Each allotment shall be appraised at what would be its present value, if unimproved, considering the fertility of the soil and its location, but excluding the improvements, and each allottee shall be charged with the value of his allotment in the future distribution of any funds of the nation arising from any source whatever, so that each member of the nation shall be made equal in the distribution of the lands and moneys belonging to the nation, provided that the minimum valuation to be placed upon any land in the said nation shall be one dollar and twenty-five cents ($1.25) per acre.

3. In the appraisement of the said allotment, said nation may have a representative to cooperate with a commission, or a United States officer, designated by the President of the United States, to make the appraisement. Appraisements and allotments shall be made under the direction of the Secretary of the Interior, and begin as soon as an authenticated roll of the citizens of the said nation has been made. All citizens of said nation, from and after the passage of this Act, shall be entitled to select from the lands of said nation an amount equal to one hundred and sixty acres, and use and occupy the same until the allotments therein provided are made.

4. All controversies arising between the members of said nation as to their rights to have certain lands allotted to them shall be settled by the commission making allotments.

5. The United States shall put each allottee in unrestricted possession of his allotment and remove therefrom all persons objectionable to the allottee.

6. The excess of lands after allotment is completed, all funds derived from town sites, and all other funds accruing under the provisions of this agreement shall be used for the purpose of equalizing allotments, valued as herein provided, and if the same be found insufficient for such purpose, the deficiency shall be supplied from other funds of the nation upon dissolution of its tribal relations with the United States, in accordance with the purposes and intent of this agreement.

7. The residue of the lands, with the improvements thereon, if any there be, shall be appraised separately, under the direction of the Secretary of the Interior, and said lands and improvements sold in tracts of not to exceed one hundred and sixty acres to one person, to the highest bidder, at public auction, for not less than the appraised value per acre of land; and after deducting the appraised value of the lands, the remainder of the purchase money shall be paid to the owners of the improvement.

8. Patents to all lands sold shall be issued in the same manner as to allottees.

SPECIAL ALLOTMENTS.

9. There shall be allotted and patented one hundred and sixty acres each to Mrs. A. E. W. Robertson and Mrs. H. F. Buckner (nee Grayson) as special recognition of their services as missionaries among the people of the Creek Nation.

10. Harrell Institute, Henry Kendall College, and Nazareth Institute, in Muscogee, and Baptist University, near Muscogee, shall have free of charge, to be allotted and patented to said institutions or to the churches to which they belong, the grounds they now occupy, to be used for school purposes only and not to exceed ten acres each.

RESERVATIONS.

11. The following lands shall be reserved from the general allotment hereinbefore provided:

All lands hereinafter set apart for town sites; all lands which shall be selected for town cemeteries by the town-site commission as hereinafter provided; all lands that may be occupied at the time allotment begins by railroad companies duly authorized by Congress as railroad rights of way; one hundred sixty acres at Okmulgee, to be laid off as a town, one acre of which, now occupied by the capitol building, being especially reserved for said public building; one acre for each church now located and used for purposes of worship outside of the towns, and sufficient land for burial purposes, where neighborhood burial grounds are now located; one hundred sixty acres each, to include the building sites now occupied, for the following educational institutions: Eufaula High School, Wealaka Mission, New Yaka Mission, Wetumpka Mission, Euchee Institute, Coweta Mission, Creek Orphan Home, Tallahassee Mission (colored), Pecan Creek Mission (colored), and Colored Orphan Home. Also four acres each for the six court-houses now established.

TITLES.

12. As soon as practicable after the completion of said allotments the principa chief of the Muscogee or Creek Nation shall execute under his hand and the seal of said nation, and deliver to each of said allottees, a patent, conveying to him all the right, title, and interest of the said nation in and to the land which shall have been allotted to him in conformity with the requirements of this agreement. Said patents shall be framed in accordance with the provisions of this agreement and shall embrace the land allotted to such patentee and no other land. The acceptance of his patent by such allottee shall be operative as an assent on his part to the allotment and conveyance of all the land of the said nation in accordance with the provisions of this agreement, and as a relinquishment of all his rights, title, and interest in and to any and all parts thereof, except the land embraced in said patent; except, also, his interest in the proceeds of all lands herein excepted from allotment.

13. The United States shall provide by law for proper record of land titles in the territory occupied by the said nation.

TOWN SITES.

14. There shall be appointed a commission, which shall consist of one member appointed by the executive of the Muscogee or Creek Nation, who shall not be interested in town property other than his home, and one member who shall be appointed by the President of the United States. Said commission shall lay out town sites, to be restricted as far as possible to their present limits, where towns are now located. No town laid out and platted by said commission shall cover more than four square miles of territory.

15. When said towns are laid out, each lot on which substantial and valuable improvements have been made shall be valued by the commission at the price a fee-simple title to the same would bring in the market at the time the valuation is made, but not to include in such value the improvements thereon.

16. In appraising the value of town lots, the number of inhabitants, the location and surrounding advantages of the town shall be considered.

17. The owner of the improvements on any lot shall have the right to buy the same at fifty per centum of the value within sixty days from the date of notice served on him that such lot is for sale, and if he purchase the same he shall, within ten days from his purchase, pay into the Treasury of the United States one-fourth of the purchase price and the balance in three equal annual payments, and when the entire sum is paid he shall be entitled to a patent for the same, to be made as herein provided for patents to allottees.

18. In any case where the two members of the commission fail to agree as to the value of any lot they shall select a third person, who shall be a citizen of said nation and who is not interested in town lots, who shall act with them to determine said value.

19. If the owner of the improvements on any lot fail within sixty days to purchase and make the first payment on the same, such lot, with the improvements thereon (said lot and the improvements thereon having been theretofore properly appraised), shall be sold at public auction to the highest bidder, under the direction of said commission, at a price not less than the value of the lot and improvements, and the purchaser at such sale shall pay to the owner of the improvements the price for which said lot and the improvements thereon shall be sold, less fifty per centum of the said appraised value of the lot, and shall pay fifty per centum of said appraised value of the lot into the United States Treasury, under regulations to be established by the Secretary of the Interior, in four installments, as hereinbefore provided. Said commission shall have the right to reject a bid on any lot and the improvements thereon which it may consider below the real value.

20. All lots not having improvements thereon and not so appraised shall be sold by the commission from time to time at public auction, after proper advertisement, as may seem for the best interest of the said nation and the proper development of each town, the purchase price to be paid in four installments, as hereinbefore provided for improved lots.

21. All citizens or persons who have purchased the right of occupancy from parties in legal possession prior to the date of signing this agreement, holding lots or tracts of ground in towns, shall have the first right to purchase said lots or tracts upon the same terms and conditions as is provided for improved lots, provided said lots or tracts shall have been theretofore properly appraised, as hereinbefore provided for improved lots.

22. Said commission shall have the right to reject any bid for such lots or tracts which is considered by said commission below the fair value of the same.

23. Failure to make any one of the payments as heretofore provided for a period of sixty days shall work a forfeiture of all payments made and all rights under the contract; provided that the purchaser of any lot may pay full price before the same is due.

24. No tax shall be assessed by any town government against any town lot unsold by the commission, and no tax levied against a lot sold as herein provided shall constitute a lien on the same until the purchase price thereof has been fully paid.

25. No law or ordinance shall be passed by any town which interferes with the enforcement of or is in conflict with the constitution or laws of the United States, or in conflict with this agreement, and all persons in such towns shall be subject to such laws.

26. Said commission shall be authorized to locate a cemetery within a suitable distance from each town site, not to exceed twenty acres; and when any town shall have paid into the United States Treasury for the benefit of the said nation ten dollars per acre therefor, such town shall be entitled to a patent for the same, as herein provided for titles to allottees, and shall dispose of same at reasonable prices in suitable lots for burial purposes; the proceeds derived therefrom to be applied by the town government to the proper improvement and care of said cemetery.

27. No charge or claim shall be made against the Muscogee or Creek Nation by the United States for the expenses of surveying and platting the lands and town site, or for grading, appraising and allotting the land, or for appraising and disposing of the town lots as herein provided.

28. There shall be set apart and exempted from appraisement and sale, in the towns, lots upon which churches and parsonages are now built and occupied, not to exceed fifty feet front and one hundred and fifty feet deep for each church and parsonage. Such lots shall be used only for churches and parsonages, and when they cease to be so used, shall revert to the members of the nation, to be disposed of as other town lots.

29. Said commission shall have prepared correct and proper plats of each town, and file one in the clerk's office of the United States district court for the district in

which the town is located, one with the executive of the nation, and one with the secretary of the Interior, to be approved by him before the same shall take effect.
30. A settlement numbering at least three hundred inhabitants, living within a radius of one-half mile at the time of the signing of this agreement, shall constitute a town within the meaning of this agreement. Congress may by law provide for the government of the said towns.

CLAIMS.

31. All claims, of whatever nature, including the "Loyal Creek Claim" made under article 4 of the treaty of 1866, and the "Self Emigration Claim," under article 2 of the treaty of 1832, which the Muscogee or Creek Nation, or individuals thereof, may have against the United States, or any claim which the United States may have against the said nation, shall be submitted to the Senate of the United States as a board of arbitration; and all such claims against the United States shall be presented within one year from the date hereof, and within two years from the date hereof the Senate of the United States shall make final determination of said claim; and in the event that any moneys are awarded to the Muscogee or Creek Nation, or individuals thereof, by the United States, provision shall be made for the immediate payment of the same by the United States.

JURISDICTION OF COURTS.

32. The United States courts now existing, or that may hereafter be created in the Indian Territory, shall have exclusive jurisdiction of all controversies growing out of the title, ownership, occupation, or use of real estate in the territory occupied by the Muscogee or Creek Nation, and to try all persons charged with homicide, embezzlement, bribery and embracery hereafter committed in the territory of said Nation, without reference to race or citizenship of the person or persons charged with any such crime; and any citizen or officer of said nation charged with any such crime shall be tried and, if convicted, punished as though he were a citizen or officer of the United States; and the courts of said nation shall retain all the jurisdiction which they now have, except as herein transferred to the courts of the United States.

ENACTMENTS OF NATIONAL COUNCIL.

33. No act, ordinance, or resolution of the council of the Muscogee or Creek Nation in any manner affecting the land of the nation, or of individuals, after allotment, or the moneys or other property of the nation, or citizens thereof (except appropriations for the regular and necessary expenses of the government of the said nation), or the rights of any person to employ any kind of labor, or the rights of any persons who have taken or may take the oath of allegiance to the United States, shall be of any validity until approved by the President of the United States. When such act, ordinance, or resolution passed by the council of said nation shall be approved by the executive thereof, it shall then be the duty of the national secretary of said nation to forward same to the President of the United States, duly certified and sealed, who shall, within thirty days after receipt thereof, approve or disapprove the same, and said act, ordinance, or resolution, when so approved, shall be published in at least one newspaper having a bona fide circulation throughout the territory occupied by said nation, and when disapproved shall be returned to the executive of said nation

MISCELLANEOUS.

34. Neither the town lots nor the allotment of land of any citizen of the Muscogee Creek Nation shall be subjected to any debt contracted by him prior to the date his patent.
35. All payments herein provided for shall be made, under the direction of the secretary of the Interior, into the United States Treasury, and shall be for the benefit of the citizens of the Muscogee or Creek Nation. All payments hereafter to be made to the members of the said nation shall be paid directly to each individual member by a bonded officer of the United States, under the direction of the Secretary of the Interior, which officer shall be required to give strict account for such disbursements to the Secretary.
36. The United States agrees to maintain strict laws in the territory of said nation against the introduction, sale, barter, or giving away of liquors and intoxicants of any kind or quality.
37. All citizens of said nation, when the tribal government shall cease, shall become possessed of all the rights and privileges of citizens of the United States.

38. This agreement shall in no wise affect the provisions of existing treaties between the Muscogee or Creek Nation and the United States, except in so far as it is inconsistent therewith.

In witness whereof, the said Commissioners do hereunto affix their names at Muscogee, Indian Territory, this the twenty-seventh day of September, eighteen hundred and ninety-seven.

HENRY L. DAWES,
Chairman.
TAMS BIXBY,
Acting Chairman.
FRANK C. ARMSTRONG,
ARCHIBALD S. McKENNON,
A. B. MONTGOMERY,
Commission to the Five Civilized Tribes.
ALLISON L. AYLESWORTH,
Acting Secretary.
PLEASANT PORTER,
Chairman.
JOSEPH MINGO,
DAVID M. HODGE,
GEORGE A. ALEXANDER,
ROLAND (his x mark) BROWN,
WILLIAM A. SAPULPA,
CONCHARTY (his x mark) MICCO,
Muscogee or Creek Commission.
J. H. LYNCH,
Secretary.

Approved, June 28, 1898.

APPENDIX NO. 3.

REGULATIONS PRESCRIBED BY THE SECRETARY OF THE INTERIOR TO GOVERN MINERAL LEASES IN THE CHOCTAW AND CHICKASAW NATIONS, INDIAN TERRITORY, UNDER THE PROVISIONS OF THE AGREEMENT OF APRIL 23, 1897, BETWEEN THE COMMISSION TO THE FIVE CIVILIZED TRIBES AND THE SAID CHOCTAW AND CHICKASAW NATIONS AS RATIFIED BY ACT OF CONGRESS OF JUNE 28, 1898. (30 STAT., 495.)

MINERAL LEASES.

1. The agreement with the Choctaw and Chickasaw nations set out in section 29 of the act of Congress entitled "An act for the protection of the people of the Indian Territory, and for other purposes," approved June 28, 1898 (30 Stat., 495–510), which was duly ratified on August 24, 1898, provides that the leasing and operating of coal and asphalt lands in said nations shall be under the control of two trustees appointed by the President of the United States upon the recommendation of the executives of said nations, each of whom shall be an Indian by blood of the respective nation for which he may be appointed.

2. Each trustee to be appointed under the provisions of said agreement shall be required to file a bond, with two good and sufficient sureties or an approved trust or surety company, with the Secretary of the Interior in the penal sum of ten thousand dollars, conditioned for the faithful performance of his duties under said agreement as prescribed therein, and in accordance with these regulations. Said bonds shall be approved by the Secretary of the Interior before said trustees shall be permitted to enter upon their duties.

3. All applications must be made under oath, by parties desiring leases, to the United States Indian inspector located in the Indian Territory, upon blanks to be furnished by the inspector. Each party will be required to state that the application is not made for speculation, but in good faith for mining the mineral or minerals specified. A map must be filed with each application, showing the amount of land on each legal subdivision supposed to be underlaid with mineral and the quantity of mineral that can properly be mined. Applicants must furnish in detail any other information desired by the inspector regarding their prospective operations. All applications received by the inspector will, if satisfactory to him, be transmitted to said trustees for an immediate report to him of facts, and when they are returned he will transmit them to the Department, through the Commissioner of Indian Affairs.

with his recommendations. Applications by parties who do not themselves intend to operate mines upon the land applied for will be rejected by the inspector, subject to appeal, as provided hereafter in cases of controversies between applicants. Leases will not be transferable or negotiable, except with the consent of the Secretary, and any instrument with that purpose in view must be approved by him before it will become valid. No application will be received for any other mineral than coal and asphalt.

Should parties whose applications have been approved, and who have been so advised, fail to execute leases in accordance with these regulations within thirty days from notice, or to give good reason for such failure, the land applied for will be subject to lease by other parties. They should be so informed at time of notice of approval.

Said trustees shall at all times be under the direction and supervision of the inspector, and shall also make an examination from time to time, as often as it shall be deemed expedient, and at least once in every month, into the operations of all persons, corporations, or companies operating mines within said nations, with a view of ascertaining the quantity of mineral produced by each, the amount of royalty, if any, due and unpaid by each, and all other information necessary for the protection of the interests of the Choctaw and Chickasaw nations in the premises; and for this purpose all persons, corporations, or companies operating mines within the Choctaw and Chickasaw nations shall give said trustees access to any and all of their books and records necessary or required by them to be examined, and within fifteen days after the last day of each quarter said trustees shall make a joint report to the Secretary of the Interior, through the inspector, of all their acts under said agreement and these regulations.

4. All indentures of lease made by the trustees, as above provided, shall be in quadruplicate and shall contain a clear and full description by legal subdivisions of the tract or tracts of land covered thereby, not to exceed 960 acres, which legal subdivisions must be contiguous to each other. Said indentures of lease so executed shall be transmitted through the United States Indian inspector stationed in the Indian Territory to the Commissioner of Indian Affairs for submission to the Secretary of the Interior, for his approval, and no lease shall be valid until the same shall have been approved by the Secretary of the Interior.

5. Royalties shall be required of all lessees as follows, viz:

On coal, 8 cents per ton of 2,000 pounds on mine run, or coal as it is taken from the mines, including that which is commonly called "slack," which rate went into force and effect on and after March 1, 1900.

On asphalt, 60 cents per ton for each and every ton produced weighing 2,000 pounds, of refined, and 10 cents per ton on crude asphalt.

The right is reserved, however, by the Secretary of the Interior in special cases to either reduce or advance the royalty on coal and asphalt on the presentation of facts which, in his opinion, make it to the interest of the Choctaw and Chickasaw nations, but the advancement or reduction of royalty on coal and asphalt in a particular case shall not operate in any way to modify the general provisions of this regulation fixing the minimum royalty as above set out.

Provided, That all lessees shall be required to pay advanced royalties, as provided in said agreement, on all mines or claims, whether developed or not, to be "a credit on royalty when each said mine is developed and operated and its production is in excess of such guaranteed annual advanced payments," as follows, viz: One hundred dollars per annum in advance for the first and second years, two hundred dollars per annum in advance for the third and fourth years, and five hundred dollars in advance for each succeeding year thereafter; and that, should any lessee neglect or refuse to pay such advanced royalty for the period of sixty days after the same becomes due and payable on any lease, the lease on which default is made shall become null and void, and all royalties paid in advance shall be forfeited and become the money and property of the Choctaw and Chickasaw nations.

All advanced royalties as above defined shall apply from date of approval of each lease, and when any mine on a tract leased is operated royalty due shall be paid monthly as required until the total amount paid equals the first annual advanced payment, after which royalty due shall be credited on such payments; and the lessee shall operate and produce coal from each and every lease in not less than the following quantities: Three thousand tons during the first year from date of approval of lease, four thousand tons the second year, seven thousand tons the third year, eight thousand tons the fourth year, and fifteen thousand tons the fifth and each succeeding year thereafter.

6. All lessees of coal and asphalt on land allotted, sold, or reserved shall be required, before the commencement of operations, to pay to the individual owner the value of

the use of the necessary surface for prospecting and mining, including the right of
way for necessary railways and the damage done to the lands and improvement
and in case of disagreement, for the purpose of the ascertainment of the fair value of
the use of the land and the actual damage done, the owner of the land and the lessee
shall each select an arbitrator, who, together with such person as shall be appointed
or designated by the inspector located in the Indian Territory, shall constitute
board to consider and ascertain the amount that shall be paid by the lessee on accou
of use of the land and damage done, and the award of such board shall be final an
conclusive, unless the award be impeached for fraud. All timber and other material
taken by the lessee from land allotted, sold, or reserved for use in the erection of
buildings thereon, and in the mine or mines operated by him thereon, as for shorin
levels in coal mines, and so forth, shall be paid for by the lessee at the usual rates

7. Persons, corporations, and companies who, under the customs and laws of th
Choctaw and Chickasaw nations, have made leases with the national agents of sai
nations of lands therein for the purpose of mining coal or asphalt, and who, prior t
April 23, 1897, had taken possession of and were operating in good faith any mine o
coal or asphalt in said nation, shall be protected in their right to continue the oper
tion of such mines for the period and on the terms contained in the lease made t
said persons, corporations, or companies by such national agents, and shall have th
right, at the expiration of said term, to renew the lease of such mines, subject, how
ever, to all the provisions of the said agreement and of these regulations: *Provided*
That such persons, corporations, or companies shall, within sixty days after the exp
ration of their leases with the national agents of the Choctaw and Chickasaw nation
apply to the said trustees for a renewal of their leases under said agreement.

8. All leases made prior to April 23, 1897, by any person or corporation with an
member or members of the Choctaw or Chickasaw nations, the object of which wa
to obtain the permission of such member or members to operate coal or asphalt mine
within the said nations, are declared void by said agreement, and no person, corpora
tion, or company occupying any lands within either of said nations, under such indi
vidual leases, or operating coal or asphalt mines on such lands, under color of suc
leases, shall be deemed to have any right or preference in the making of any leas
or leases for mining purposes embracing the lands covered by such personal leases
by reason thereof; but parties in possession of such land who have made improve
ments thereon for the purpose of mining coal or asphalt shall have a preference righ
to lease the land upon which said improvements have been made, under the provi
sions of said agreement and these regulations.

9. Where two or more persons, corporations, or companies shall make applicatio
for the leasing of the same tract of land for mining purposes, and a controversy arise
between such persons, corporations, or companies as to the right of each to obtai
the lease of such land, it shall be the duty of the United States Indian inspecto
stationed in the Indian Territory to investigate into the rights of the parties an
determine as to which shall be given the right to lease the lands in controversy, sub
ject to appeal to the Commissioner of Indian Affairs, and from him to the Secretar
of the Interior.

Twenty days from notice of any decision by the United States inspector, or th
Commissioner of Indian Affairs, not interlocutory, will be allowed for appeal an
service of the same upon the opposite party, whether notice of the decision is give
by mail or personally. When notice is given by the inspector by mail it should b
by registered letter.

In cases pending on appeal before the Commissioner of Indian Affairs, or th
Department, argument may be filed at any time before the same is reached in orde
for examination, and copy of the same shall be served upon the opposite party, an
he shall be allowed ten days for reply and to serve the same.

Proof of personal service of appeal or argument shall be the written acknowledg
ment of the person served or the affidavit of the person who served the same attache
thereto, stating the time, place, and manner of service. All notices shall be serve
upon the attorneys of record.

Proof of service by registered letter shall be the affidavit of the person mailing the
letter, attached to a copy of the post-office receipt.

No leases will be executed where a conflict exists, until the matter has been finally
adjudicated by the Department, in case of appeal.

10. All lessees will be required to keep a full and correct account of all their operations under leases entered into under said agreement and these regulations, and their
books shall be open at all times to the examination of said trustees, of the United
States Indian inspector stationed in the Indian Territory, and such other officer or
officers of the Indian department as shall be instructed by the Secretary of the Inte-

rior or the Commissioner of Indian Affairs to make such examination; but, except as to the said trustees and the United States Indian inspector located in the Indian Territory, no lessee will be held to have violated this regulation for refusing to permit an examination of his books by any person unless such person shall produce written instructions from the Secretary of the Interior or from the Commissioner of Indian Affairs requiring him to make such an examination, and said lessees shall make all their reports to said United States Indian inspector, and they shall be subject to any instructions given by him.

11. All royalties, including advanced royalties, as provided for in said agreement and in these regulations, shall be payable in lawful money of the United States, or exchange issued by a national bank in the United States, to the United States Indian agent at the Union Agency in the Indian Territory, who shall be at all times under the direction and supervision of the United States Indian inspector for the Indian Territory.   The advanced royalties are payable one hundred dollars on the filing of the application, which may be made by a certified check on any national bank of the United States payable to the order of the United States Indian agent, which check shall be retained by the United States Indian inspector until the application is approved; one hundred dollars in one year thereafter; two hundred dollars in two years thereafter; two hundred dollars in three years thereafter, and five hundred dollars on the fourth and each succeeding year until the end of the term thereof. All monthly royalties shall be accompanied by a sworn statement in duplicate by the person, corporation, or company making the same as to the output of the mine of such person, corporation, or company for the month for which royalties may be tendered.   One part of said sworn statement shall be filed with the United States Indian agent, to be transmitted to the Commissioner of Indian Affairs, and the other part thereof shall be filed with the United States Indian inspector located in the Indian Territory.

12. The said United States Indian agent shall receive and receipt for all royalties paid into his hands when accompanied by a sworn statement as above provided, but not otherwise; and all royalties received by him shall be, as soon as practicable, deposited with the United States subtreasurer at St. Louis, in like manner as are deposited moneys known in the regulations of the Indian Office as miscellaneous receipts, Class III, with a statement showing the proportionate shares of each of the Choctaw and Chickasaw nations.

13. All royalties collected and deposited by the United States Indian agent, as above set forth, shall be held to the credit of the Choctaw and Chickasaw nations in their respective proportions, and shall be subject to disbursement by the Secretary of the Interior for the support of the schools of the Choctaw and Chickasaw nations in accordance with said agreement.

14. All lessees under said agreement and these regulations will be required to give bond, with two good and sufficient sureties or an approved surety company, for the faithful discharge of their obligations under their leases in such penalty as shall be prescribed in each case by the Secretary of the Interior, and until such bond is filed by the lessee and approved and accepted by the Secretary of the Interior no rights or interests under any lease shall accrue to such lessee.

15. The right to alter or amend these regulations is reserved.

E. A. HITCHCOCK,
Secretary of the Interior.

DEPARTMENT OF THE INTERIOR,
Washington, D. C., May 22, 1900.

APPENDIX NO. 4.

APPLICATION FOR MINERAL LEASE.

[May 22, 1900.]

To the United States Indian Inspector located in the Indian Territory:

—— ——, desiring to avail —— of the provisions of section twenty-nine of the act of Congress of June 28, 1898 (30 Stat., 495), entitled "An act for the protection of the people of the Indian Territory, and for other purposes," hereby make— application to lease, for the purpose of mining ——, the following tract of land, viz: —— section ——, in township ——, of range ——, in the —— Nation, containing ——— acres, more or less, the attached map showing the amount of land on each legal subdivision supposed to be underlaid with ———, and the quantity that can probably be mined; and ——— solemnly ——— that this application is made in good faith, and with no other object than that of mining the mineral specified.

———— ————.

Sworn to and subscribed before me this ——— day of ———, 190—.

———— ————.

———— ————.

Washington, D. C., ———, 190—.
Approved:
———— ————,
    Secretary.

APPENDIX NO. 5.

ADDITIONAL INFORMATION TO ACCOMPANY APPLICATION FOR MINING LEASE IN THE CHOCTAW AND CHICKASAW NATIONS, INDIAN TERRITORY.

——— ———, of ———, makes the following statements, under oath, to accompany his application attached hereto, dated ———, for the purpose of mining ——— in the ——— Nation, covering the following-described land: ———.

1. The applicant has filed ——— other applications for leases to mine ——— in addition to the one herein asked, and is interested in ——— other ——— leases in the Indian Territory, known as the ———.

2. That he does not intend to sell or transfer this application or the lease arising therefrom; that there is no agreement, open or secret, whereby the applicant is to sell, assign, transfer to, or consolidate this application or the lease arising therefrom with any other person or corporation whatsoever, but that the applicant proposes to operate the mines covered by his application for himself, or in case of a company or corporation for said company or corporation.

3. Applicant has heretofore had ——— national contract with the Choctaw and Chickasaw nations covering the land herein described. Under same, mines have been operated by the applicant on this tract for ——— years, such operations having been commenced on or about ——— by sinking a shaft or slope ——— feet, and has taken therefrom about ——— tons of ———, and has expended $——— in improvements on said tract, comprising: ———.

4. That the applicant will, within ——— months after formal lease is duly approved and delivered to him, commence active operations; that the applicant has ——— dollars now on hand for such operations, and that the applicant has good reasons to believe that he or it will produce from said mine ——— tons of ——— during the first year from the date of the approval of the lease; that he or it will produce ——— tons during the second year, and ——— tons during the third year, and that there is embraced within the tract applied for, from the best obtainable information, ——— tons of workable ———, and, in case of coal applications, there are ——— veins of coal on said tract, each vein ——— inches in thickness, with a pitch about ——— degrees; applicant further states that ——— acres of the tract applied for are underlaid with ———, as shown by the plat.

5. That the applicant will exercise no rights or privileges whatever under the application herein described, nor commence operations, until the lease shall have been duly approved and delivered to him.

6. That the applicant is a resident of ——— and engaged in the business of ———, and has had ——— years' experience in coal (or ———) business in company with ——— at ———, and that there are ——— other persons interested in this application or lease if granted, their names and post-office addresses as follows: ———. If the applicant is a corporation, the members interested in or composing the same are as follows: ———.

7. There is submitted herewith in connection with said application a certified check for $100, payable to the United States Indian agent, the same to be applied as advanced royalty on the lease applied for as required by the regulations of the Secretary of the Interior.

(When the applicant is a corporation, the following should be filled out.)

8. Applicant is a corporation organized under the laws of the State of ———, with a capital stock of ——— dollars; that there has been subscribed and paid into the

treasury of the corporation, and now held subject to bona fide mining operations, the sum of —— dollars thereof.

The applicant's post-office is ——.

—— ——.
—— ——.
—— ——.
—— ——.

Subscribed and sworn to before me this —— day of ——, 190—.

NOTE.—When the applicant is a corporation, the application and this affidavit must be signed by the proper officer thereof.

Plat accompanying should show land applied for, by legal subdivisions, according to United States surveys, amount underlaid with mineral, veins of coal, etc., and any improvements, railroads, etc. that may be on the land.

If applicant has not heretofore operated under national contract, the word "No" should be inserted, in the first line of section 3, and the latter clause of said section should be stricken out. If so operated, the word "shaft" or "slope" should be stricken out, as the case may be, unless mines have been operated by both, in which case the depth of each should be stated.

Each applicantion should be confined to tracts underlaid with mineral so far as possible, and not exceed 960 acres in area. A less number of acres, however, will be considered.

APPENDIX NO. 6.

[Transferable and negotiable only with the consent of the Secretary of the Interior.]

[Write all names and addresses in full.]

[June 15, 1900.]

INDIAN TERRITORY COAL MINING LEASE (CHOCTAW AND CHICKASAW NATIONS).

Indenture of lease, made and entered into in quadruplicate, on this —— day of ——, A. D. 190—, by and between —— and —— as mining trustees of the Choctaw and Chickasaw nations, parties of the first part, and ——, of ——, county of ——, State of ——, part— of the second part, under and in pursuance of the provisions of the act of Congress approved June 28, 1898 (30 Stat., 495), the agreement set out in section twenty-nine thereof, duly ratified on August 24, 1898, and the rules and regulations prescribed by the Secretary of the Interior on May 22, 1900, relative to mining leases in the Choctaw and Chickasaw nations.

Now, therefore, this indenture witnesseth that the parties of the first part, for and in consideration of the royalties, covenants, stipulations, and conditions hereinafter contained and hereby agreed to be paid, observed, and performed by the part— of the second part, —— executors, administrators, or assigns, do hereby demise, grant, and let unto the part— of the second part, —— executors, administrators, or assigns, the following-described tract of land, lying and being within the —— Nation, and within the Indian Territory, to wit: The ——, of section ——, of township [1] ——, of range [2] ——, of the Indian meridian, and containing —— acres, more or less, for the full term of —— years from the date hereof, for the sole purpose of prospecting for and mining coal ——.

In consideration of the premises the part— of the second part hereby agree— and bind —— executors, administrators, or assigns, to pay or cause to be paid to the United States Indian agent for the Union Agency, Indian Territory, as royalty, the sums of money as follows, to wit:

On the production of all mines developed and operated under this lease the sum of —— cents per ton of 2,000 pounds on mine-run, or coal as it is taken from the mines, including that which is commonly called "slack."

And all said royalties accruing for any month shall be due and payable on or before the twenty-fifth day of the month succeeding.

And the part— of the second part further agree— not to hold the land described for speculative purposes, but in good faith for mining the mineral specified.

And the part— of the second part further agree— and bind —— executors, administrators, or assignees, to pay or cause to be paid to the United States Indian agent for the Union Agency, Indian Territory, as advanced royalty on each and every mine or claim within the tract of land covered by this lease, the sums of money as follows, to wit: One hundred dollars per annum, in advance, for the first and second years; two hundred dollars per annum, in advance, for the third and fourth years;

---

[1] State whether north or south.   [2] State whether east or west.

and five hundred dollars per annum, in advance, for the fifth and each succeeding year thereafter of the term for which the lease is to run, it being understood and agreed that said sums of money to be paid as aforesaid shall be a credit on royalty should the part— of the second part develop and operate a mine or mines on the lands leased by this indenture, and the production of such mine or mines exceed such sums paid as advanced royalty as above set forth; and further, that all advanced royalties as above defined shall apply from date of approval of each lease, and when any mine is operated royalty due shall be paid monthly as required until the total amount paid equals the first annual advanced payment, after which royalty due shall be credited on such payments; and the part— of the second part agree— and bind ——— executors, administrators, or assigns to operate and produce coal from each and every lease of not less than the following quantities: Three thousand tons during the first year from date of approval of lease; four thousand tons the second year; seven thousand tons the third year; eight thousand tones the fourth year; and fifteen thousand tons the fifth and each succeeding year thereafter; and it is further agreed that should the part— of the second part neglect or refuse to pay such advanced annual royalty for the period of sixty days after the same becomes due and payable under this lease, then this lease shall be null and void, and all royalties paid in advance shall become the money and property of the Choctaw and Chickasaw tribes of Indians, subject to the regulations of the Secretary of the Interior aforesaid.

The part— of the second part further covenant— and agree— to exercise diligence in the conduct of the prospecting and mining operations, and to open mines and operate the same in a workmanlike manner to the fullest possible extent on the above-described tract of land; to commit no waste upon said land or upon the mines that may be thereon, and to suffer no waste to be committed thereon; to take good care of the same, and to surrender and return the premises at the expiration of this lease to the parties of the first part in as good condition as when received, ordinary wear and tear in the proper use of the same for the purposes hereinbefore indicated, and unavoidable accidents, excepted, and not to remove therefrom any buildings or improvements erected thereon during said term by ——— the part— of.the second part, but said buildings and improvements shall remain a part of said land and become the property of the owner of the land as a part of the consideration for this lease, in addition to the other considerations herein specified—except engines, tools, and machinery, which shall remain the property of the said part— of the second part; that ——— will not permit any nuisance to be maintained on the premises, nor allow any intoxicating liquors to be sold or given away to be used for any purposes on the premises, and that ——— will not use the premises for any other purpose than that authorized in this lease, nor allow them to be used for any other purpose; that ——— will not, at any time during the term hereby granted, assign, transfer, or sublet ——— estate, interest, or term in said premises and land or the appurtenances thereto to any person or persons whomsoever without the written consent thereto of the parties of the first part being first obtained, subject to the approval of the Secretary of the Interior.

And the said part— of the second part further covenant— and agree— that ——— will keep an accurate account of all mining operations, showing the whole amount of coal mined or removed, and that there shall be a lien on all implements, tools, movable machinery, and other personal chattels used in said prospecting and mining operations, and upon all such coal obtained from the land herein leased, as security for the monthly payment of said royalties.

And the part— of the second part agree— that this indenture of lease shall be subject in all respects to the rules and regulations heretofore or that may be hereafter prescribed, under the said act of June 28, 1898, by the Secretary of the Interior relative to mineral leases in the Choctaw and Chickasaw nations; and said part— of the second part expressly agree— to pay to said United States Indian agent any additional rate of royalty that may be required by the Secretary of the Interior during the term this lease shall be in force and effect; and further, that should the part— of the second part, ——— executors, administrators, or assigns, violate any of the covenants, stipulations, or provisions of this lease, or fail for the period of thirty days to pay the stipulated monthly royalties provided for herein, then the Secretary of the Interior shall be at liberty, in his discretion, to avoid this indenture of lease, and cause the same to be annulled, when all the rights, franchises, and privileges of the part— of the second part, ——— executors, administrators, or assigns, hereunder shall cease and end, without further proceedings.

The part— of the second part ——— firmly bound for the faithful compliance with the stipulations of this indenture by and under the bond made and executed by the part— of the second part as principal— and ——— as suret— entered into the ——— day of ———, and which is on file in the Indian Office.

In witness whereof, the said parties of the first and second parts have hereunto set their hands and affixed their seals the day and year first above mentioned.

[1] Witnesses:

———— ———— as to ———— ————, [SEAL.] [2]
Trustee for Choctaw Nation.
———— ———— as to ———— ————, [SEAL.]
Trustee for Chickasaw Nation.

———— ————} as to ———— ————. [SEAL.]

———— ————} as to ———— ————. [SEAL.]

———— ————} as to ———— ————. [SEAL.]

———— ————} as to ———— ————. [SEAL.]

———— ————} as to ———— ————. [SEAL.]

No. ————
Department of the Interior,
Washington, D. C.
COAL LEASE.

Mining Trustees.

TO

OF

Sec. ————, Tp. ————, Range ————,
in the ———— Nation, Indian Territory.
Dated ————, 190—.
Expires ————, 19—.
DEPARTMENT OF THE INTERIOR,
U. S. INDIAN SERVICE, UNION AGENCY,
Muscogee, Ind. T., ————, 190—
Respectfully forwarded to the Commissioner of Indian Affairs for consideration with my report of even date.

————
Indian Inspector

DEPARTMENT OF THE INTERIOR,
OFFICE OF INDIAN AFFAIRS,
Washington, D. C. ————, 190—
Respectfully submitted to the Secretary of the Interior with favorable recommendation.

————
Commissioner.

DEPARTMENT OF THE INTERIOR,
Washington, D. C., ————, 190—
Approved:

————
Secretary of the Interior.

APPENDIX NO. 7.

[Transferable and negotiable only with the consent of the Secretary of the Interior.]

[Write all names and addresses in full.]

[June 15, 1900.]

INDIAN TERRITORY ASPHALT MINING LEASE (CHOCTAW AND CHICKASAW NATIONS).

Indenture of lease, made and entered into in quadruplicate, on this ———— day of ————, A. D. 190—, by and between ———— and ———— as mining trustees of the Choctaw and Chickasaw nations, parties of the first part, and ————, of ————, county of ————, State of ————, part— of the second part, under and in pursuance of the provisions of the act of Congress approved June 28, 1898 (30 Stat., 495), the agreement set out in section twenty-nine thereof duly ratified on August 24, 1898, and the rules and regulations prescribed by the Secretary of the Interior on May 22, 1900, relative to mining leases in the Choctaw and Chickasaw nations.

Now, therefore, this indenture witnesseth, that the parties of the first part, for and in consideration of the royalties, covenants, stipulations, and conditions hereinafter contained and hereby agreed to be paid, observed, and performed by the part— of the second part, ———— executors, administrators, or assigns, do hereby demise, grant, and let unto the part— of the second part, ———— executors, administrators, or assigns, the following-described tract of land, lying and being within the ———— Nation, and within the Indian Territory, to wit: The ————, of section ————, of township [3]————,

[1] Two witnesses to each signature, including signatures of trustees.
[2] Stamps are required by the act of June 13, 1898, to be placed on leases as follows, viz: Leases for one year, 25 cents; for more than one year and not exceeding three years, 50 cents; and for more than three years, $1. Lessees must furnish stamps for all leases.
[3] State whether north or south.

of range [1] ——, of the Indian meridian, and containing —— acres, more or less, for the full term of —— years from the date hereof for the sole purpose of prospecting for and mining asphalt ——.

In consideration of the premises the part— of the second part hereby agree— and bind —— executors, administrators, or assigns to pay or cause to be paid to the United States Indian agent for the Union Agency, Indian Territory, as royalty, the sums of money as follows, to wit: —— cents per ton for each and every ton of asphalt produced weighing 2,000 pounds of refined, and —— cents per ton on crude asphalt.

And all said royalties accruing for any month shall be due and payable on or before the twenty-fifth day of the month succeeding.

And the part— of the second part further agree— not to hold the land described for speculative purposes, but in good faith for mining the mineral specified.

And the part— of the second part further agree— and bind —— executors, administrators, or assigns to pay or cause to be paid to the United States Indian agent for the Union Agency, Indian Territory, as advanced royalty on each and every mine or claim within the tract of land covered by this lease the sums of money as follows, to wit: One hundred dollars per annum, in advance, for the first and second years; two hundred dollars per annum, in advance, for the third and fourth years; and five hundred dollars per annum, in advance, for the fifth and each succeeding year thereafter, of the term for which this lease is to run, it being understood and agreed that said sums of money to be paid as aforesaid shall be a credit on royalty should the part— of the second part develop and operate a mine or mines on the lands leased by this indenture, and the production of such mine or mines exceed such sums paid as advanced royalty as above set forth; and further, that all advanced royalties as above defined shall apply from date of approval of each lease, and when any mine is operated royalty due shall be paid monthly as required until the total amount paid equals the first annual advanced payment, after which royalty due shall be credited on such payments; and further, that should the part— of the second part neglect or refuse to pay such advanced annual royalty for the period of sixty days after the same becomes due and payable under this lease, then this lease shall be null and void, and all royalties paid in advance shall become the money and property of the Choctaw and Chickasaw tribes of Indians, subject to the regulations of the Secretary of the Interior aforesaid.

The part— of the second part further covenant— and agree— to exercise diligence in the conduct of the prospecting and mining operations, and to open mines and operate the same in a workmanlike manner to the fullest possible extent on the above-described tract of land; to commit no waste upon said land or upon the mines that may be thereon, and to suffer no waste to be committed thereon; to take good care of the same, and to surrender and return the premises at the expiration of this lease to the parties of the first part in as good condition as when received, ordinary wear and tear in the proper use of the same for the purposes hereinbefore indicated, and unavoidable accidents, excepted, and not to remove therefrom any buildings or improvements erected thereon during said term by ——, the part— of the second part, but said buildings and improvements shall remain a part of said land and become the property of the owner of the land as a part of the consideration for this lease, in addition to the other considerations herein specified—except engines, tools, and machinery, which shall remain the property of the said part— of the second part; that —— will not permit any nuisance to be maintained on the premises, nor allow any intoxicating liquors to be sold or given away to be used for any purpose on the premises, and that —— will not use the premises for any other purpose than that authorized in this lease, nor allow them to be used for any other purpose that —— will not, at any time during the term hereby granted, assign, transfer, or sublet —— estate, interest, or term in said premises and land or the appurtenances thereto to any person or persons whomsoever without the written consent thereto of the parties of the first part being first obtained, subject to the approval of the Secretary of the Interior.

And the said part— of the second part further covenant— and agree— that —— will keep an accurate account of all mining operations, showing the whole amount of asphalt mined or removed, and that there shall be a lien on all implements, tools, movable machinery, and other personal chattels used in said prospecting and mining operations, and upon all such asphalt obtained from the land herein leased, as security for the monthly payment of said royalties.

And the part— of the second part agree— that this indenture of lease shall be subject in all respects to the rules and regulations heretofore or that may be hereafter

---

[1] State whether east or west.

prescribed, under the said act of June 28, 1898, by the Secretary of the Interior relative to mineral leases in the Choctaw and Chickasaw nations; and said part— of the
second part expressly agree— to pay to said United States Indian agent any additional rate of royalty that may be required by the Secretary of the Interior during
the term this lease shall be in force and effect; and further, that should the part— of
the second part, ——— executors, administrators, or assigns, violate any of the covenants, stipulations, or provisions of this lease, or fail for the period of thirty days to
pay the stipulated monthly royalties provided for herein, then the Secretary of the
Interior shall be at liberty, in his discretion, to avoid this indenture of lease and
cause the same to be annulled, when all the rights, franchises, and privileges of the
part— of the second part, ——— executors, administrators, or assigns hereunder shall
cease and end without further proceedings.

The part— of the second part ——— firmly bound for the faithful compliance with
the stipulations of this indenture by and under the bond made and executed by the
part— of the second part as principal— and ——— as suret— entered into the ———
day of ———, and which is on file in the Indian Office.

In witness whereof, the said parties of the first and second parts have hereunto
set their hands and affixed their seals the day and year first above mentioned.

[1]Witnesses:

——— ——— as to ——— ———,   [SEAL.][2]
                          Trustee for Choctaw Nation.

——— ——— as to ———————,   [SEAL.]
                          Trustee for Chickasaw Nation.

——— ———} as to ——— ———.   [SEAL.]

——— ———} as to ——— ———.   [SEAL.]

——— ———} as to ——— ———.   [SEAL.]

——— ———} as to ——— ———.   [SEAL.]

——— ———} as to ——— ———.   [SEAL.]

No. ———
Department of the Interior,
Washington, D. C.

ASPHALT LEASE.

Mining Trustees,

TO

OF

Sec. ———, Tp. ———, R. ———, in the
Nation, Indian Territory.

Dated ———, 190—.

Expires ———, 19—.

DEPARTMENT OF THE INTERIOR,
U. S. INDIAN SERVICE, UNION AGENCY,
Muskogee, Ind. T., ——— 190—.

Respectfully forwarded to the Commissioner of Indian Affairs for consideration
with my report of even date.

———————,
Indian Inspector.

DEPARTMENT OF THE INTERIOR,
OFFICE OF INDIAN AFFAIRS,
Washington, D. C., ——— 190—.

Respectfully submitted to the Secretary
of the Interior with favorable recommendation.

———————,
Commissioner.

DEPARTMENT OF THE INTERIOR,
Washington, D. C., ——— 190—.

Approved:

———————,
Secretary of the Interior.

[1]Two witnesses to each signature, including signatures of trustees.
[2]Stamps are required by the act of June 13, 1898, to be placed on leases as follows, viz: Leases for
one year, 25 cents; for more than one year and not exceeding three years, 50 cents; and for more
than three years, $1. Lessees must furnish stamps for all leases.

APPENDIX NO. 8.

BOND.

[May 22, 1900.]

Know all men by these presents, that[1] ——, of ——, as principal—, and ——, of ——, as surety, are held and firmly bound unto the United States of America in the sum of —— dollars, lawful money of the United States, for the payment of which, well and truly to be made, we bind ourselves, and each of us, our heirs, successors, executors, and administrators, jointly and severally, firmly by these presents.

Sealed with our seals and dated —— day of ——.

The condition of this obligation is such, that whereas the above-bounden —— as principal—, entered into —— certain indenture— of lease, dated —— with —— and —— mining trustees of the Choctaw and Chickasaw nations, for the lease of a certain tract of land located in the —— Nation, Indian Territory, for the purpose of prospecting for and mining —— for the period of —— years.

Now, if the above-bounden —— shall faithfully carry out and observe all the obligations assumed in said indenture— of lease by ——, and shall observe all the laws of the United States, and regulations made or which shall be made thereunder, for the government of trade and intercourse with Indian tribes, and all the rules and regulations that have been or may be prescribed by the Secretary of the Interior, under the act of June 28, 1898 (30 Stat., 495), relative to mining leases in the Choctaw and Chickasaw nations, in the Indian Territory, then this obligation shall be null and void; otherwise, to remain in full force and effect.

Signed and sealed in the presence of[2]—

—— ——   —— ——.   [L. S.][3]
—— ——   —— ——.   [L. S.]
—— ——   —— ——.   [L. S.]
—— ——   —— ——.   [L. S.]
—— ——   —— ——.   [L. S.]
—— ——   —— ——.   [L. S.]

Department of the Interior, Washington, D. C.

BOND

OF

——————

Lessee— of ——————

in the ——————

Nation, Ind. T., for mining purposes.

Washington, D. C., ——, 180—.

Approved:

Secretary.

APPENDIX NO. 9.

MINERAL LEASES, CHOCTAW AND CHICKASAW NATIONS.

DEPARTMENT OF THE INTERIOR,
OFFICE OF THE ASSISTANT ATTORNEY-GENERAL,
Washington, May 11, 1900.

The SECRETARY OF THE INTERIOR.

SIR: I am in receipt of your request for an opinion as to whether the Secretary of the Interior has power, under the agreement between the United States and the

---

[1] The Christian names and residences of principals.
[2] There must be at least two witnesses to all signatures, though the same two persons may witness all.
[3] A seal must be attached by some adhesive substance to the signatures of principals and sureties.

Choctaw and Chickasaw tribes, approved by act of June 28, 1898 (30 Stat., 495), to authorize the leasing of lands for mining substances other than coal and asphalt.

Said agreement provides that the lands of those tribes shall be allotted to the members thereof; that "all coal and asphalt" shall be reserved for the sole use of the members of such tribes; that patents shall issue conveying to the allottees all the interest of the Choctaw and Chickasaw in and to the allotted land, "excepting all coal and asphalt" in and under said land, and that the acceptance of such patent shall operate as a relinquishment by the allottee of all his right in all the lands of the Choctaw and Chickasaw except that embraced in his patent and "except his interest in the proceeds of the lands, coal and asphalt, herein excepted from allotment."

In the paragraph relating to leases it is provided that "all coal and asphalt" shall remain and be the common property of the members of the tribes; that the revenue from "coal and asphalt" shall be used for the education of children of the members of said tribes; that such "coal and asphalt mines as are now in operation, and all others which may hereafter be leased and operated, shall be under the supervision and control of two trustees;" that "all coal and asphalt mines in the two nations" shall be operated and the royalties therefrom paid into the Treasury of the United States and drawn therefrom under rules and regulations prescribed by the Secretary of the Interior; and that all contracts made by the national agents for operating "coal and asphalt" which were being operated in good faith April 23, 1897, be ratified and confirmed.

It is there provided as follows:

"All agreements heretofore made by any person or corporation with any member or members of the Choctaw or Chickasaw nations, the object of which was to obtain such member's or members' permission to operate coal or asphalt, are hereby declared void: *Provided*, That nothing herein contained shall impair the rights of any holder or owner of a leasehold interest in any oil, coal rights, asphalt, or mineral which have been assented to by act of Congress, but all such interests shall continue unimpaired hereby and shall be assured by new leases from such trustees of coal or asphalt claims described therein by application to the trustees within six months after the ratification of this agreement, subject, however, to payment of advance royalties herein provided for.

"All leases under this agreement shall include the coal or asphaltum, or other mineral, as the case may, in or under nine hundred and sixty acres, which shall be in a square form as nearly as possible, and shall be for thirty years."

The agreement then fixes the royalty to be paid on coal and asphalt, with the proviso that the Secretary of the Interior may reduce or advance the royalties on "coal and asphalt" when he deems it to the best interest of the Indians to do so.

The fact that no substance except coal and asphalt is mentioned in connection with the allotment of lands to individuals and the patent to the allottee shows clearly that it was not intended to retain as the property of the tribe or to except from the conveyance to the allottee any substance other than coal and asphalt that might be in or under the land allotted. The care exercised to specifically mention "coal and asphalt" in every declaration as to reservations for the common benefit of the members of the tribes, and to omit therefrom the mention, specifically or generally, by the use of the phrase "other mineral," of any other substance is significant, and clearly demonstrates an intention to limit such reservations to the substances specifically mentioned—that is, coal and asphalt.

To make productive the property or things thus declared to be, and reserved from allotment as, the common property of the members of the tribes, provision was made for granting privileges or leases for mining these substances. All these provisions except two mention specifically and only "coal and asphalt." Nothing in said agreement was to impair "the rights of any holder or owner of a leasehold interest in any oil, coal rights, asphalt or mineral, which have been assented to by act of Congress," and such interests were to be "assured by new leases from such trustees of coal or asphalt claims described therein." This provision does not apply generally, but is limited to the class of leases described; that is, those which had been assented to by act of Congress, so that there is yet no general provision as to any substances other than coal or asphalt. Immediately following the provision last referred to is the statement:

"All leases under this agreement shall include the coal or asphaltum or other mineral, as the case may be, in or under nine hundred and sixty acres, which shall be in a square form as nearly as possible, and shall be for thirty years."

This is the first and only time the word "mineral" appears in said agreement in connection with any general provision relating to leases for mining purposes, and if there is any authority for giving a lease for mining any substance other than coal and asphalt, except as an assurance of rights under a lease of oil or other mineral assented to by act of Congress, it rests upon the phrase "other mineral," injected into this clause defining the extent of the territory to be covered by a lease for mining purposes. It being possible that some leasehold interests had been theretofore assented to by Congress involving the right to mine other mineral, and it being deemed advisable to avoid any misunderstanding as to claims of that class, the phrase "other mineral" was inserted where it is found. It was certainly never intended by the insertion of this phrase in the sentence defining the extent of leases to enlarge all the provisions preceding it and to authorize leases for mining substances which it is clearly intended shall go with the title to the land to the respective allottees.

After a careful consideration of this matter, I am of opinion, and advise you, that there is no authority, under the provisions of said agreement, for giving leases for the purpose of mining any substance other than coal and asphalt, except as an assurance of rights under a lease of oil or other mineral, assented to by act of Congress.

Very respectfully,

WILLIS VAN DEVANTER,
Assistant Attorney-General.

Approved, May 11, 1900.
    E. A. HITCHCOCK, *Secretary.*

APPENDIX NO. 10.

DEPARTMENT OF THE INTERIOR,
OFFICE OF THE ASSISTANT ATTORNEY-GENERAL,
Washington, March 10, 1900.

The SECRETARY OF THE INTERIOR.

SIR: You have submitted for my "opinion in the matter therein dealt with" a letter of the Commissioner of Indian Affairs of July 22, 1899, in which he discusses certain questions propounded by the United States Indian inspector for the Indian Territory relative to mining leases in said Territory.

These questions arise under the act of June 28, 1898 (30 Stat., 495, 505), and the agreement with the Choctaw and Chickasaw nations therein recited and thereby ratified.

This agreement made provision for the allotment of land in severalty to the members of said nations, and the conveyance to the individual of all the title of the nations in the land allotted "excepting all coal and asphalt in or under said land." All coal and asphalt were to "remain and be the common property of the members of the Choctaw and Chickasaw tribes."

Further provisions of the agreement necessary to be noticed here are as follows:

"Such coal and asphalt mines as are now in operation and all others which may hereafter be leased and operated shall be under the supervision and control of two trustees * * * each of whom shall make full report of all his acts to the Secretary of the Interior quarterly. All such acts shall be subject to the approval of the Secretary of the Interior.

"All coal and asphalt mines of the two nations, whether now developed or to be hereafter developed, shall be operated and the royalty therefrom paid into the Treasury of the United States, and shall be drawn therefrom under such rules and regulations as shall be prescribed by the Secretary of the Interior.

"All contracts made by the national agents of the Choctaw and Chickasaw nations for operating coal and asphalt, with any person or corporation, which were on April twenty-third, eighteen hundred and ninety-seven, being operated in good faith are hereby ratified and confirmed, and the lessee shall have the right to renew the same when they expire, subject to all the provisions of this act.

"All agreements heretofore made by any person or corporation with any member or members of the Choctaw and Chickasaw nations the object of which was to obtain such member's or members' permission to operate coal and asphalt are hereby declared void. * * *

"All leases under this agreement shall include the coal or asphaltum, or other mineral as the case may be, in or under nine hundred and sixty acres, which shall be in a square as nearly as possible and shall be for thirty years. * * * No royalties shall be paid except into the United States Treasury as herein provided."

Under these provisions three different companies applied for asphalt leases of certain lands in the Chickasaw Nation, and upon examination it was found that in several instances the same tracts were embraced in two of the applications and that one tract, the SE. ¼ of sec. 21, T. 1 S., R. 3 E., was included in all three of them.

The Davis Mining Company is composed of Chickasaw citizens who obtained a charter, better spoken of as a license, from the Chickasaw Nation March 4, 1895, authorizing them, for a period of twenty years, to prospect for, mine, and sell all minerals, gases, oil, coal, and asphaltum within a certain territory described by metes and bounds which embraced the individual claims of the persons comprising said company, which was a copartnership and not a corporation. This company never conducted any active mining operations, but September 12, 1895, leased to W. A. Dennis and associates "all the asphaltum and petroleum under and upon the private claim and improvements" of the parties comprising said Davis Mining Company, naming them, "situated within the boundary lines of the Davis Mining Company charter" for the life of said charter. September 16, 1895, Dennis and his associates transferred to the Rock Creek Natural Asphalt Company, a corporation organized under the laws of Kansas, all rights, titles, and privileges granted them by the lease from the Davis Mining Company.

June 14, 1897, the Rock Creek Natural Asphalt Company, the Davis Mining Company assenting thereto, granted and leased to C. O. Baxter and his associates "all the lime rock asphaltum situated under and upon the territory" described in the lease from the Davis Mining Company to Dennis, for a period of ten years. June 28, 1898, Baxter transferred all his rights under that lease to the Gilsonite Roofing and Paving Company, a corporation organized under the laws of Missouri.

The Indian inspector made a statement of the facts in the controversy between these three parties, and said:

"The question is now submitted as to whether the application of the Davis Mining Company to this whole tract should be considered and a lease granted them in view of the fact that they had obtained the original charter and leased it to these parties, although never putting any improvements on the lands themselves.

"Second, whether the Rock Creek Natural Asphalt Company should be granted a lease, inasmuch as they had gone upon the lands described, although not upon that portion covered by mine No. 4, which they subleased to the Gilsonite people; or,

"Whether the Rock Creek Natural Asphalt Company should be given a lease upon the tracts where they have placed their improvements, and the Gilsonite Roofing and Paving Company a lease covering their improvements, as shown by the applications of each."

The Commissioner of Indian Affairs discusses the questions upon the assumption that the facts are as set forth in the report of the Indian inspector. He points out that the divisional line between the Choctaw and Chickasaw nations is political merely and does not divide the interests of the respective nations in the lands they own in common; that the Choctaw Nation owns an undivided three-fourths interest in lands within the political boundaries of the Chickasaw Nation, and the Chickasaw Nation owns an undivided one-fourth interest in the lands within the political boundaries of the Choctaw Nation; that it is not claimed that the Choctaw Nation gave its assent to the Chickasaw act, under which the Davis Mining Company received its license, and concludes that it was not competent for the Chickasaw Nation alone to authorize citizens of that nation to engage in mining operations within that nation, and that companies organized under said law of the Chickasaw Nation had no authority to enter upon said lands for the purpose of mining without the consent of the Choctaw Nation. He holds that the license of the Davis Mining Company, not being a lease from individual citizens and not being a contract with national agents of the Choctaw and Chickasaw nations—the Chickasaw Nation not having assented to or become a party thereto—was neither confirmed nor nullified by the agreement with these nations, set forth in the act of June 28, 1898, supra, but was invalid from the beginning. As a result of this conclusion he holds that "the rights of the parties must be determined according to their equities under the regulations or dependent upon the improvements on the land, the party occupying and improving the land being entitled to the benefit thereof."

After the matter reached this Department some of the parties asked to be allowed to present oral argument, but afterwards it was agreed by all interests that the case should be submitted upon printed briefs, and the Rock Creek Asphalt Company and the Gilsonite Roofing and Paving Company have filed briefs.

The charter or license upon which the Davis Mining Company bases its claim was obtained under the provisions of an act of the Chickasaw legislature approved December 21, 1885, and the amendment thereto of September 24, 1887. (Constitution, Laws, and Treaties of the Chickasaw Nation, 1899, p. 188.)

The act of 1886 authorized resident citizens to form corporate companies to engage in developing coal mines, and to transport, ship, or sell coal beyond the limits of the nation. They were to first file a written application for a charter, designating the place of operations with the name of the company, and what they wished to develop and work, and file a bond for the faithful observance of the laws of the nation and the payment of the tax on all coal mines. Such companies were authorized "to contract with capitalists, to prospect for, develop, and work coal mines as provided for in this act, and to maintain and to operate the same." They were required to pay to the Chickasaw Nation monthly one-half cent per bushel on all coal mined. The amendment of 1887 made the act include petroleum, natural gas, and asphaltum making the royalty thereon 2 per cent on all gross sales of such products.

As pointed out by the Commissioner of Indian Affairs, the Choctaw and Chickasaw nations are joint owners of the lands occupied by them respectively, the Choctaw holding a three-fourths interest in the lands occupied by the Chickasaw and the Chickasaw holding a one-fourth interest in those occupied by the Choctaw. Because of this joint interest it was held that both nations should join in the agreement ratified by the act of June 28, 1898, by which a change in the tenure of their lands was to be effected. The leases or contracts ratified and confirmed by said agreement were those made by the "national agents of the Choctaw and Chickasaw nations," and not those made by the representative of one nation alone. It was not intended by that agreement to recognize any contract or lease made by one of these nations alone through its representatives. As said by the Commissioner of Indian Affairs, it is not shown or claimed that the Choctaw Nation ever gave its assent to the Chickasaw act under which the Davis Mining Company claims existence. I am of opinion that no claim based upon that act is entitled to recognition under the agreement. If a charter or license granted under that act is affected by said agreement it is not by way of ratification or confirmation, and hence no claim to a preference right to a lease of ground covered by a charter issued under said Chickasaw law can be successfully asserted by virtue of any provision of said agreement. The matter of leasing mineral lands is fully covered by the provisions of said agreement, and unless an applicant claiming a preference right to a lease can bring himself within its provisions and the regulations issued thereunder his claim must fall. The Davis Mining Company, not having a lease that comes within the confirmatory provisions of said agreement, has no preference right to a lease for the land in question.

Neither of the other applicants claims to hold under a contract made directly with the national agents of the Choctaw and Chickasaw nations or either of them, and hence neither has any claim falling within the confirmatory provisions of the agreement ratified in 1898. They, in each instance, went upon the land in pursuance of and under the authority of the license to the Davis Mining Company. That license being given without authority, conferred no right upon the Davis Mining Company, and that company could not grant any right which it never had.

Even if it be admitted that parties who are in possession of lands under such license, lease, or contract as those presented here may have a right that should be recognized, the fact still remains that neither of these parties is entitled under those instruments to exclusive possession of the lands in question. The license to the Davis Mining Company was to mine "all minerals, gases, oils, coal, and asphaltum or all minerals known to the law." The lease to Dennis, transferred by him to the Rock Creek Natural Asphalt Company, was of "all the asphaltum and petroleum" under and upon the same land, and the lease to Baxter, transferred to the Gilsonite Roofing and Paving Company, was of "all the lime rock asphaltum" under and upon said land. In this instrument a right was reserved to the Rock Creek Company "to use any and all lime rock asphalt for its own use and to do its own mining." If these instruments are to be consulted to determine the rights of these applicants the conclusion would be that neither is entitled to a preference right as against the other to a lease by reason of possession, because neither has a right to the exclusive possession of the tract in controversy between them. In no phase of the case can either of these applicants successfully assert a preference right to a lease of said lands by reason of the instruments under which they went upon it. I concur in the conclusion reached by the Indian Office that these parties are upon the land in question without any right to be there recognized by the law, and that neither of them can as a matter of legal right demand a lease thereof.

In paragraph 9 of the regulations governing mineral leases in the Choctaw and Chickasaw nations it is provided that persons or corporations who have under the customs and laws of the Choctaw and Chickasaw nations made leases with the national agents for mining coal, asphalt, or other minerals, and who, prior to April 23, 1897, had taken possession of and were operating any such mine in good faith, should be protected in the right to continue the operation thereof and have the right to renew the same. A further provision of said paragraph is as follows:

" * * * and all corporations which, under charters obtained in accordance with the laws of the Chickasaw Nation, had entered upon and improved, and were occupying and operating, any mine of coal, asphalt, or other mineral, within said Chickasaw Nation, shall have a preference right to lease the mines occupied and operated by such corporations, subject to all the general provisions of said agreement and of these regulations: *Provided*, That should there arise a controversy between two or more of such corporations, the respective rights of each shall be determined after an investigation by the inspector located in the Indian Territory, subject to appeal to the Commissioner of Indian Affairs, and from him to the Secretary of the Interior."

In paragraph 10 of said regulations it is pointed out that all leases made prior to April 23, 1897, by individual members of said nation were, according to the agreement, declared void, and hence that no preference right could be asserted by reason of such a lease and then it is said "but parties in possession of mineral lands who have made improvements thereon for the purpose of mining shall have a perference right to lease the land upon which said improvements have been made, under the provisions of said agreement and these regulations."

While these provisions of the regulations as to claims not based upon a lease ratified by said agreement are not specifically authorized by any provision of the law, yet the Department having charge of the matter of mineral leases had the authority to adopt the plan to the end that parties who had in good faith expended money in the development of mining claims might secure the benefit of such expenditures. These applicants, not having any claim to the land which is confirmed and ratified by said agreement, the granting of a lease rests in the sound discretion of the mineral trustees acting under and in conformity with the regulations and subject to the approval of the Secretary of the Interior. There being a controversy as to a part of the land, the right to a lease of the tract thus in controversy or to the different subdivisions thereof, should be considered and determined in the mode prescribed by the regulations, and in accordance therewith. If, upon the investigation by the inspector, as provided in the regulations, no reason is disclosed for refusing a lease to either of these parties for land not claimed by the other, the application should be allowed to that extent, and as to the land about which there is a controversy, the facts as to possession and improvements should be ascertained to determine the equities of the parties, to the end that each may be given a lease to cover, if possible, the ground upon which he has in good faith made improvements.

In the same letter the inspector says:

" I am requested to submit the following questions for consideration:

" First. Does the act of Congress and the treaty referred to abrogate and nullify the charters granted by the Chickasaw Nation where the charter members had not up to April 23, 1897, taken actual possession of and developed the mines?

" Second. In cases where these chartered companies had leased the mines claimed to other parties who took possession under such leases and developed the mines and were in possession of the mines, operating the same in good faith, on April 23, 1897, which has the preference right to make the lease from the mining trustees?

" Third. In cases where the Indian chartered company leased to so-called capitalists and the capitalists in turn subleased the mining claims to other parties, who took possession under such leases, developed the mines, and were operating the same in good faith on April 23, 1897, which is entitled to obtain the lease?

" Fourth. Is any person or corporation entitled under the Curtis bill and the treaty to the preference right to a lease who had not developed a mine and was not in actual possession and in good faith operating the same on April 23, 1897?

" Fifth. Is it lawful for any person or corporation under any of the leases above referred to entered into before the adoption of the treaty to pay royalty to the lessors?"

He does not say who made the request, nor does he state that the questions are involved in any matter pending for adjudication. In so far as those questions, except the last, are not answered in the discussion herein of the specific case submitted, the answer would, as pointed out by the inspector, depend in large degree upon the facts in each individual case. Under these circumstances I would respectfully suggest that no specific answer be given to these hypothetical questions thus submitted.

As to the last question, there can be but one answer, and that is found in the agreement. All coal and asphalt is to remain and be the common property of the members of the tribe; the royalties from all coal and asphalt mines are to be paid into the treasury of the United States, and finally it is specifically said: "No royalties shall be paid except into the United States Treasury as herein provided."

In view of these provisions it is not lawful for any person or corporation to pay royalty under any lease to any one, except to the proper officer of the United States.

The papers submitted are herewith returned.

Very respectfully,

WILLIS VAN DEVANTER,
Assistant Attorney-General.

Department of the Interior, March 10, 1900.
Approved:
    E. A. HITCHCOCK, *Secretary.*

APPENDIX NO. 11.

FIVE CIVILIZED TRIBES—PERMIT TAX.

DEPARTMENT OF THE INTERIOR,
OFFICE OF THE ASSISTANT ATTORNEY-GENERAL,
Washington, July 13, 1900.

The SECRETARY OF THE INTERIOR.

SIR: I am in receipt by your reference, with request for an opinion upon the legal matters presented therein, of a letter from the Indian inspector assigned to the Indian Territory, setting forth that certain parties doing business in towns in the Indian Territory have refused to pay the permit tax or license fee imposed by the laws of the several nations, this refusal being based upon the claim that they have purchased town lots and by such purchase have acquired the right to reside within the limits of the nation in which such lots are situated, and upon the further claim that section 14 of the act of June 28, 1898, confers or recognizes such a right of residence within the limits of incorporated cities and towns in the Territory.

The question is not directly as to the right of these people, not citizens, to occupy the property they have bought, but is as to their right to carry on a business in one of those nations without first obtaining a permit therefor as required by the laws of the nation. The right of these nations or tribes to prescribe regulations requiring those not citizens engaging in business within the nation to pay a permit tax or license fee has been recognized by this Department and sustained by the courts. In the case of Maxey *v.* Wright, decided January 6, 1900 (54 S. W. Rep., 807), the court of appeals of Indian Territory upheld the right of the Creek Nation to require the payment of such a tax or fee and the power of this Department to take charge of the matter, collect the money and turn it over to the Indians or in case of refusal of any one to pay the same to enforce the penalty of removal prescribed by laws of the nation.

It seems that many persons engaged in business in these nations, especially in the Choctaw and Chickasaw nations, have become purchasers of town lots at sales made under the provisions of the act of June 28, 1898 (30 Stat., 495), and now refuse to pay the tax or fee imposed by the laws of the nations upon noncitizens carrying on business there. Their position is not clearly set forth in the papers submitted, but it seems to be that a lot so purchased is no longer the property of the tribe and that the owner may conduct upon such lot any business that he may see fit to engage in. The purchase of a town lot does not make the purchaser a citizen of the nation within whose boundaries such town may be located, nor does it necessarily operate to confer upon him a license to follow a pursuit in disregard of the laws of the nation requiring a noncitizen to secure a permit before engaging in such business. In the case of Maxey *v.* Wright, supra, the court declared it unnecessary then to decide as to the effect of the law of June 28, 1898, authorizing the sale of lands in cities and towns, upon this question saying:

"Nor does the fact that Congress by the provisions of the Curtis bill has provided for the creation of cities and towns in this nation and the extinguishment of the Indian title to the lands embraced within the limits of such municipal corporations alter the case because this provision of that bill has not been carried into effect. The Indian title to such lands still remains in them and it is yet their country. What effect the provision of this statute relating to cities and towns, when fully consummated, may have we do not now decide."

Important changes have been made both as to the conduct of the internal affairs of these nations and as to their relations with the outside world. These changes are largely the result of the law of June 28, 1898, supra, which, among other things, provides a plan by which lands in cities and towns may be sold to others than citizens of the nation. As said before, a purchase of such lands does not, however, give the purchaser any special privilege or benefit in the matter of engaging in business in such nation. Such a purchaser bought the property with a knowledge of the provisions of the tribal law and the conditions imposed thereby upon anyone wishing to engage in business in such nation, and that he could remain within the boundaries of such nation and occupy the property thus purchased only in conformity to and compliance with the laws of that nation.

The contention that the purchase of a town lot in one of these nations exonerates a noncitizen, wishing to engage in trade or business, from compliance with the laws of such nation and gives him a license to engage in business there in defiance of such laws can not be sustained. A noncitizen has in this respect the same status after such purchase as he had before, and must afterwards, as before, meet the requirements of law if he desires to engage in business there. He is also subject to the same penalty for refusal to comply with the law after such purchase as he was before.   If there is any hardship in the matter, it does not grow out of conditions arising subsequently to his purchase, as there has been no change in the laws of any of said nations in this respect since provision was made for the sale of town lots.   He voluntarily placed himself in the position he occupies and must bear the incident responsibilities. The question as to the powers and duties of this Department in the premises is necessarily presented.   Relative to that question the court, in the case of Maxey v. Wright, supra, used the following language:

"On the whole case we therefore hold that a lawyer who is a white man, and not a citizen of the Creek Nation is, pursuant to their statute, required to pay for the privilege of remaining and practicing his profession in that nation the sum of $25; that if he refuse the payment thereof, he becomes by virture of the treaty an intruder, and that in such case the Government of the United States may remove him from the nation; and that this duty devolves upon the Interior Department. Whether the Interior Department or its Indian agents can be controlled by the courts by the writs of mandamus and injunction is not material in this case, because as we hold, an attorney who refuses to pay the amount required by the statute by its very terms becomes an intruder, whom the United States promises by the terms of the treaty to remove, and therefore in such cases the officers and agents of the Interior Department would be acting clearly and properly within the scope of their powers."

At another place the court said:

"We are of the opinion, however, that the Indian agent, when directed by the Secretary of the Interior, may collect this money for the Creeks. * * * In this case the Indian agent was acting in strict accordance with the directions and regulations of the Secretary of the Interior in a matter clearly relating to intercourse with the Indians.   And when it is remembered that up to the time that the United States courts were established in the Indian Territory the only remedy for the collection of this tax was by removal, and that the Indian nations had no power to collect it except through the intervention of the Interior Department, it is quite clear that if in the best judgment of that Department it was deemed wise to take charge of the matter, and collect this money, and turn it over to the Indians, it had the power to do so, under the superintending control of the Indians and the intercourse of white men with them granted by various acts of Congress; and in our opinion that power has not been taken away by any subsequent act of Congress or treaty stipulation."

The powers and duties of this Department in the premises are so fairly set forth and defined by this language as to justify its adoption by the Department as a correct statement thereof.   The statements are as applicable now as when that decision was rendered, and are as true of all the nations as of the Creek.

Section 14 of the act of June 28, 1898, authorizes the incorporation of cities and towns in the Indian Territory, making the provisions of Mansfield's Digest of the Statutes of Arkansas applicable, and further provides as follows:

"All elections shall be conducted under the provisions of chapter fifty-six of said digest entitled 'Elections,' so far as the same may be applicable; and all inhabitants of such cities and towns, without regard to race, shall be subject to all laws and ordinances of such city or town governments, and shall have equal rights, privileges, and protection therein.   Such city or town governments shall in no case have any authority to impose upon or levy any tax against any lands in said cities or towns until after title is secured from the tribe; but all other property, including all improvements on town lots, which for the purposes of this act shall be deemed and considered personal property, together with all occupations and privileges, shall be subject to taxation.   And the councils of such cities and towns, for the support of the same and for school and other public purposes, may provide by ordinance for the assessment, levy, and collection annually of a tax upon such property, not to exceed in the aggregate two per centum of the assessed value thereof, in manner provided in chapter one hundred and twenty-nine of said digest, entitled 'Revenue,' and for such purposes may also impose a tax upon occupations and privileges."

These are provisions for establishing and maintaining municipal governments enacted to meet the changed conditions in the Territory, and while they recognize the right of persons not citizens of the tribe or nation to reside in such towns, to participate in such governments, to enjoy the benefits and protection thereof, and also their liability to contribute by payment of taxes to the expenses of such government, they do not relieve such persons from observance of and compliance with the laws of the nation.   The payment of a license fee imposed by a municipal government upon a certain occupation would not relieve one of the obligation to pay a like fee imposed by the State government.   While the relations between these municipal governments and the Indian Nation are perhaps not precisely the same as those ordinarily existing between a city and the State, yet they are so similar that the same rule obtains. As said before, the question is not as to the right of noncitizens to reside in these towns, but is as to their right to carry on a business in the nation in violation of the laws thereof. The provisions of said section 14 do not, in my opinion, operate to relieve inhabitants of cities and towns in these nations from the payment of the permit tax or fee prescribed by the laws of the nation in which such city or town may be located.

The papers submitted are herewith returned.

Very respectfully,

WILLIS VAN DEVANTER,
Assistant Attorney-General.

Approved:

THOS. RYAN, *Acting Secretary.*
JULY 13, 1900.

APPENDIX NO. 12.

[Extract of Indian appropriation act for the fiscal year 1901, approved May 31, 1900, as far as it pertains to legislation concerning Indian Territory.]

COMMISSION TO THE FIVE CIVILIZED TRIBES.

For salaries of four commissioners, appointed under acts of Congress approved March third, eighteen hundred and ninety-three, and March second, eighteen hundred and ninety-five, to negotiate with the Five Civilized Tribes in the Indian Territory, twenty thousand dollars: *Provided,* That the number of said commissioners is hereby fixed at four. For expenses of commissioners, and necessary expenses of employees, and three dollars per diem for expenses of a clerk detailed as special disbursing agent by Interior Department, while on duty with the commission, shall be paid therefrom; for clerical help, including secretary of the commission and interpreters, five hundred thousand dollars, to be immediately available; for contingent expenses of the commission, four thousand dollars; in all, five hundred and twenty-four thousand dollars: *Provided further,* That this appropriation may be used by said commission in the prosecution of all work to be done by or under its direction as required by statute.

That said commission shall continue to exercise all authority heretofore conferred on it by law. But it shall not receive, consider, or make any record of any application of any person for enrollment as a member of any tribe in Indian Territory who has not been a recognized citizen thereof, and duly and lawfully enrolled or admitted as such, and its refusal of such applications shall be final when approved by the Secretary of the Interior: *Provided,* That any Mississippi Choctaw duly identified as such by the United States commission to the Five Civilized Tribes shall have the right, at any time prior to the approval of the final rolls of the Choctaws and Chickasaws by the Secretary of the Interior, to make settlement within the Choctaw-Chickasaw country, and on proof of the fact of bona fide settlement may be enrolled by the said United States commission and by the Secretary of the Interior as Choctaws entitled to allotment: *Provided further,* That all contracts or agreements looking to the sale or incumbrance in any way of the lands to be allotted to said Mississippi Choctaws, shall be null and void.

TOWN SITES.

To pay all expenses incident to the survey, platting, and appraisement of town sites in the Choctaw, Chickasaw, Creek, and Cherokee nations, Indian Territory, as required by sections fifteen and twenty-nine of an act entitled "An act for the protection of the people of the Indian Territory, and for other purposes," approved June twenty-eighth, eighteen hundred and ninety-eight, for the balance of the current year and for the year ending June thirtieth, nineteen hundred and one, the same to be immediately available, sixty-seven thousand dollars, or so much as may be necessary: *Provided,* That the Secretary of the Interior is hereby authorized, under rules and regulations to be prescribed by him, to survey, lay out, and plat into town lots, streets, alleys, and parks, the sites of such towns and villages in the Choctaw, Chickasaw, Creek, and Cherokee nations, as may at that time have a population of two hundred or more, in such manner as will best subserve the then present needs and the reasonable prospective growth of such towns. The work of surveying, laying out, and platting such town sites shall be done by competent surveyors, who shall prepare five copies of the plat of each town site which, when the survey is approved by the Secretary of the Interior, shall be filed as follows: One in the office of the Commissioner of Indian Affairs, one with the principal chief of the nation, one with the clerk of the court within the territorial jurisdiction of which the town is located, one with the commission to the Five Civilized Tribes, and one with the town authorities, if there be such. When in his judgment the best interests of the public service require, the Secretary of the Interior may secure the surveying, laying out, and platting of town sites in any of said nations by contract.

Hereafter the work of the respective town-site commissions provided for in the agreement with the Choctaw and Chickasaw tribes ratified in section twenty-nine of the act of June twenty-eighth, eighteen hundred and ninety-eight, entitled "An act for the protection of the people of the Indian Territory, and for other purposes," shall begin as to any town site immediately upon the approval of the survey by the Secretary of the Interior, and not before.

The Secretary of the Interior may, in his discretion, appoint a town-site commission consisting of three members for each of the Creek and Cherokee nations, at least one of whom shall be a citizen of the tribe and shall be appointed upon the nomination of the principal chief of the tribe. Each commission, under the supervision of the Secretary of the Interior, shall appraise and sell for the benefit of the tribe the town lots in the nation for which it is appointed, acting in conformity with the provisions of any then existing act of Congress or agreement with the tribe approved by Congress. The agreement of any two members of the commission as to the true value of any lot shall constitute a determination thereof, subject to the approval of the Secretary of the Interior, and if no two members are able to agree the matter shall be determined by such Secretary.

Where in his judgment the public interests will be thereby subserved, the Secretary of the Interior may appoint in the Choctaw, Chickasaw, Creek, or Cherokee Nation a separate town-site commission for any town, in which event as to that town such local commission may exercise the same authority and perform the same duties which would otherwise devolve upon the commission for that nation. Every such local commission shall be appointed in the manner provided in the act approved June twenty-eighth, eighteen hundred and ninety-eight, entitled "An act for the protection of the people of the Indian Territory."

The Secretary of the Interior, where in his judgment the public interests will be thereby subserved, may permit the authorities of any town in any of said nations, at the expense of the town, to survey, lay out, and plat the site thereof, subject to his supervision and approval, as in other instances.

As soon as the plat of any town site is approved, the proper commission shall, with all reasonable dispatch and within a limited time, to be prescribed by the Secretary of the Interior, proceed to make the appraisement of the lots and improvements, if any, thereon, and after the approval thereof by the Secretary of the Interior, shall, under the supervision of such Secretary, proceed to the disposition and sale of the lots in conformity with any then existing act of Congress or agreement with the tribe approved by Congress, and if the proper commission shall not complete such appraisement and sale within the time limited by the Secretary of the Interior they shall receive no pay for such additional time as may be taken by them, unless the Secretary of the Interior, for good cause shown, shall expressly direct otherwise.

The Secretary of the Interior may, for good cause, remove any member of any town-site commission, tribal or local, in any of said nations, and may fill the vacancy thereby made, or any vacancy otherwise occurring, in like manner as the place was originally filled.

It shall not be required that the town-site limits established in the course of the platting and disposing of town lots and the corporate limits of the town, if incorporated, shall be identical or coextensive, but such town-site limits and corporate limits shall be so established as to best subserve the then present needs and the reasonable prospective growth of the town, as the same shall appear at the times when such limits are respectively established: *Provided, further,* That the exterior limits of all town sites shall be designated and fixed at the earliest practicable time, under rules and regulations prescribed by the Secretary of the Interior.

Upon the recommendation of the Commission to the Five Civilized Tribes the Secretary of the Interior is hereby authorized at any time before allotment to set aside and reserve from allotment any lands in the Choctaw, Chickasaw, Creek, or Cherokee nations, not exceeding one hundred and sixty acres in any one tract, at such stations as are or shall be established in conformity with law on the line of any railroad which shall be constructed or be in process of construction in or through either of said nations prior to the allotment of the lands therein, and this irrespective of the population of such town site at the time. Such town sites shall be surveyed, laid out, and platted, and the lands therein disposed of for the benefit of the tribe in the

manner herein prescribed for other town sites: *Provided further*, That when
any tract of land shall be set aside as herein provided which is occupied by a mem
of the tribe, such occupant shall be fully compensated for his improvements there
under such rules and regulations as may be prescribed by the Secretary of
Interior.

Nothing herein contained shall have the effect of avoiding any work hereto
done in pursuance of the said act of June twenty-eighth, eighteen hundred
ninety-eight, in the way of surveying, laying out, or platting of town sites, apprai
or disposing of town lots in any of said nations, but the same, if not heretofore can
to a state of completion, may be completed according to the provisions hereof.

*   *   *   *   *   *   *

CHICKASAW INCOMPETENT FUND.

That the Secretary of the Interior be, and he is hereby, authorized and direc
to pay out and distribute in the following manner the sum of two hundred and
teen thousand six hundred and seventy-nine dollars and forty-eight cents, wh
amount was appropriated by the act of June twenty-eighth, eighteen hundred
ninety-eight, and credited to the "incompetent fund" of the Chickasaw Indian Nat
on the books of the United States Treasury, namely: First, there shall be paid
such survivors of the original beneficiaries of said fund and to such heirs of decea
beneficiaries as shall, within six months from the passage of this act, satisfacto
establish their identity in such manner as the Secretary of the Interior may presci
and also the amount of such fund to which they are severally entitled, their resp
tive shares; and second, so much of said fund as is not paid out upon claims satis
torily established as aforesaid shall be distributed per capita among the member
said Chickasaw Nation, and all claims of beneficiaries and their respective heirs
participation in said incompetent fund not presented within the period afores
shall be, and the same are hereby, barred.

APPENDIX NO. 13.

In the United States court of appeals in the Indian Territory.

N. B. MAXEY, ET AL., APPELLANTS,

v.

J. GEO. WRIGHT, UNITED STATES INDIAN INSPECTOR, ET AL., APPELLEES.

} No. 267.

Appeal from the United States court for the northern district of the Indian Te
tory, at Muscogee, Hon. John R. Thomas, judge presiding.

William T. Hutchings, for appellants; P. L. Soper, United States attorney,
L. F. Parker, jr., assistant United States attorney, for appellees.

OPINION.

CLAYTON, J.

This is an action brought in equity in the United States court at Muscogee, Ind.
to enjoin J. George Wright, United States Indian inspector for the Indian Territc
and J. Blair Shoenfelt, United States Indian agent for the Five Civilized Tribes, fi
collecting from plaintiffs, who are all noncitizens of the Creek Nation and attorn
at law, residing in the Creek Nation, and practicing law in said court, an occupat
tax imposed on them by virtue of the laws of the Creek Nation, which, among ot
things, provides that a tax of $25 per annum shall be collected from each law
residing and practicing their profession in the Creek Nation who is not a citizer
the Creek or Seminole Nation. To the complaint the following demurrer was fi

"Comes now the said defendants, by Pliny L. Soper, United States attorney
the northern district of the Indian Territory, and demurs to the complaint of pl
tiffs, and for ground therefor states:

"First. That the court has no jurisdiction of the subject-matter of the action.

"Second. That the complaint does not state facts sufficient to constitute a caus
action against these defendants, or for which any equitable relief may be grante

The court below sustained this demurrer, and, plaintiffs refusing to plead furtl
the cause was dismissed. Exception to the sustaining of the demurrer and dismi
of the complaint were duly saved and the cause regularly appealed to this court.

It is contended by the appellants: First, that the Creek Nation has no power to enforce this tax on a citizen of the United States residing in that nation, because it is claimed that the Creek Nation is not possessed of such sovereign powers as would permit it to levy a tax upon the person or occupation of any other than its own citizens, and to support this contention we are cited to the opinion of Attorney-General Wirt on the right of the Cherokee Nation to impose a tax on traders (1 Opns. Att. Gen., 645). This opinion was rendered in 1824, at which time, by virtue of the treaties then existing between the Cherokee Nation and the United States, the Cherokee Nation had relinquished that right. That opinion is based exclusively on the treaty of 1785. The Attorney-General says:

"The time has passed away in which it would be tolerated to treat these people as we please, because we are Christians and they are heathens. If the tax is to be resisted we must find some solid ground for that resistance which law and reason will support, and which we can justify both toward God and man. If, by the treaties into which they have entered with us, they have debarred themselves from imposing this tax, they can not justly complain if we insist on the fulfillment of these treaties and the withdrawal of the tax as far as it shall be found in conflict with their own stipulations. * * *

"Now, the stipulation of the treaty of 1785 is that 'the United States in Congress assembled shall have the sole and exclusive right of regulating the trade with the Indians, and managing all their affairs in such manner as they think proper.' The right thus conferred on the United States is sole and exclusive; consequently neither the Cherokee nor any other nation had the right thereafter to touch the subject which was thus solely and exclusively given to the United States. What was the right thus solely and exclusively given to the United States? The right of regulating the trade with the Indians. What does this mean? The right of regulating the conduct of the citizens of the United States in carrying on this trade? This can not be the meaning, because this right the United States had before, and it required no treaty to give it to them. The treaty meant to give a right which did not exist before, and this could only be the right to prescribe the whole system of regulations, on both sides, under which the trade should be carried on. * * *

"But if it were conceded that the Cherokee Nation might prohibit this trade altogether it would not follow that they might, under these treaties, tolerate it under such regulations as they might institute, for, whether the power of the entire prohibition has been given to Congress or not, the sole and exclusive power of regulation has been given to them; and so long as these treaties remain in force it seems manifest that the Indians have no power to interfere with those regulations, either by addition or subtraction. And what is a tax upon persons authorized by Congress to trade without it but a new and distinct regulation superinduced upon the regulations provided by Congress?"

It is clear that the Attorney-General founds his opinion upon the fact, as he finds it, that the Cherokee Nation had "debarred themselves from imposing this tax."

But no such stipulation and abrogation of rights can be found in any treaty between the United States and the Creeks; but, upon the contrary, in all of their treaties with the Government, and more especially by the treaty of 1856 (Revision of Indian Treaties, 111), they have carefully guarded their sovereignty and their right to admit, and consequently to exclude, all white persons, except such as are named in the treaty. Article 15 of the treaty reads as follows:

"ARTICLE 15. So far as may be compatible with the Constitution of the United States, and the laws made in pursuance thereof regulating trade and intercourse with the Indian tribes, the Creek and Seminole shall be secured in the unrestricted right of self-government and full jurisdiction over persons and property within their respective limits, excepting, however, all white persons, with their property, who are not by adoption or otherwise members of either the Creek or Seminole tribe, and all persons not being members of either tribe found within their limits shall be considered intruders and be removed from and kept out of the same by the United States agents for said tribes, respectively (assisted, if necessary, by the military), with the following exceptions, viz: Such individuals, with their families, as may be in the employment of the Government of the United States; all persons peaceably traveling or temporarily sojourning in the country, or trading therein under license from the proper authorities of the United States, and such persons as may be permitted by the Creek and Seminole, with the assent of the proper authorities of the United States, to reside within their respective limits without becoming members of either of said tribes."

The last clause of the article of the treaty above set out clearly confers upon the Creek Nation the power of admitting into their territory, with the consent of the proper authorities of the United States, such "other persons" than those named by it, and if it has that power, it is equally clear that it may prescribe all reasonable terms upon the compliance of which such persons may be admitted or excluded; more especially so when it is remembered that by the provision of the same treaty it is provided that "So far as compatible with the Constitution of the United States, and the laws made in pursuance thereof regulating trade and intercourse with the Indian tribes, the Creek * * * shall be secure in the unrestricted right of self-government," and, further, that all such persons as may be in the Creek Nation without the consent of that nation are deemed to be intruders, and pledges itself to remove them.

Attorneys practicing in the United States courts are not persons who come within the exceptions, for they are not "in the employment of the Government of the United States," or "persons peaceably traveling or temporarily sojourning in the country, or trading therein under license from the proper authority of the United States."

Article 7 of the treaty between the United States and the Choctaw and Chickasaw nations (11 Stat. L., 613) is, upon the question here involved, identical with article 15 of the Creek treaty. And the question as to whether these nations had the power to enforce their permit laws was passed upon by Attorney-General Wayne McVeagh in 1881. He says:

"The validity of such permits is recognized by the concluding clause of article 7 of the treaty of June 22, 1831, which is not inconsistent with the terms of the later treaty." (17 Op. Atty. Gen., 134.)

Upon the same subject Attorney-General Phillips, in 1884, says:

"In absence of treaty of statutory provision to the contrary, the Choctaw and Chickasaw nations have power to regulate their own rights of occupancy, and to say who shall participate, and upon what conditions, and hence may require permits to reside in the nations from citizens of the United States and levy a pecuniary exaction therefor.

"The clear result of all the cases, as restated in 95 U. S., 526, is 'the right of the Indians to their occupancy is as sacred as that of the United States to the fee.'

"I add, that so far as the United States recognize political organizations among Indians, the right of occupancy is a right in the tribe or nation. It is, of course, competent for the United States to disregard such organizations and treat Indians individually, but their policy has generally been otherwise. In such cases presumptively they remit all questions of individual right to the definition of the nation as being purely domestic in character. The practical importance here of this proposition is that in the absence of express contradictory provisions by treaty, or by statutes of the United States, the nation (and not a citizen) is to declare who shall come within the boundaries of its occupancy and under what regulations and conditions. * * *

"(a) Article 7, 1855, secured to the Choctaw and Chickasaw, among other things, 'the unrestricted right of self-government and free jurisdiction over persons and property within their respective limits, excepting, however, all persons or their property who are not by birth, adoption or otherwise, citizens or members of either tribe,' etc.

"I submit that whatever this may mean it does not limit the right of these tribes to pass upon the question who (of persons indifferent to the United States, i. e., neither employees nor objectionable) shall share their occupancy and upon what terms. That is a question which all private persons are allowed to decide for themselves; and even with animals, not men, have a certain respect paid to the instinct which in this respect they share with man. The serious words 'jurisdiction' and 'self-government' are scarcely appropriate to the right of a hotel keeper to prescribe rules and charges for persons who become his fellow-occupants. It is, therefore, improbable that the above proposition in the treaty of 1855 has any relation to this plain natural right and natural instinct of an Indian nation." (18 Op. Atty. Gen., 36-37.)

We fully agree with these opinions, and hold, therefore, that unless since the ratification of the treaty of 1856 there has been a treaty entered into or an act of Congress passed repealing it, that the Creek Nation had the power to impose this condition or occupation tax, if it may be so called, upon attorneys at law, white men, residing and practicing their profession in the Indian Territory. And, inasmuch as the Government of the United States, in the treaty, had declared that all persons not authorized by its terms to reside in the Creek Nation should be deemed to be intruders, and had obligated itself to remove all such persons from the Creek Nation, the remedy to enforce this provision of the treaty was a removal by the United States from the Creek Nation of the delinquent as an intruder. Whether the Creek Nation, since the establishment of the courts in the Indian Territory and of the passage of the so-called Curtis bill, could recover the amount specified by the Creek statute by a proper action in the courts is not necessarily now a question for us to decide, because the treaty provides a remedy, and whether this remedy is exclusive of the courts or only cumulative is not material. The superintending control of the Interior Department over the Creeks is nowhere abolished, but on the contrary all recent legislation has confirmed and even enlarged it, leaving all of the powers of that Department of the Government to remove from the Indian Territory for the causes specified by the treaties and the statutes as they existed before that time.

The act of Congress approved June 7, 1897 (30 Stat. L., 83), provides:

"That on and after January 1, 1898, the United States courts in the Indian Territory shall have original and exclusive jurisdiction and authority to try and determine all civil causes in law and equity thereafter instituted, * * * ; and the laws of the United States and the laws of Arkansas in force in the Territory shall apply to all persons therein, irrespective of race, the said courts exercising jurisdiction thereof as now conferred upon them in the trial of like causes."

While it is true that this act had the effect of abolishing the courts of the Indian tribes, which of course included those of the Creek Nation, and of relegating all causes of action to the United States courts for trial, yet the executive and legislative departments of the Indian governments were retained, and the treaty provisions and intercourse laws and other statutes relating to the Indian Territory remained in full force. The full control of the Indian Department over these Indian tribes as they then existed was not interfered with, nor were the Indian statutes annulled, except in so far as that all jurisdiction was taken from their courts and transferred to those of the United States. The power to remove intruders for the causes assigned by treaty provisions or statutory law still remains, as before, in the Interior Department of the Government; and the act of Congress approved June 28, 1898, entitled, "An act for the protection of the people in the Indian Territory, and for other purposes" (30 Stat. L., 495), commonly called the Curtis bill, from beginning to end, recognizes this authority of the Interior Department, and in many instances enlarges it.

The contention that the Creek Nation is not now an Indian reservation is not tenable. Whatever effect the Curtis bill may have upon the Creek, it has not yet been carried into operation so far as it changes their title to their lands or their tribal relations to the United States. The mere fact that the Creek are, at some future time, to hold their lands in severalty, instead of in the name of the nation, or in common, is not incompatible with and does not change the legislation which gives to them the exclusive right of occupancy of their country; nor can it be successfully maintained that because the United States at one time bought from the tribe of Indians who first occupied that country, thereby extinguishing the then Indian title to this land, and afterwards sold it to the Creek, giving to them a fee simple title thereto, that therefore it is not in possession of the Creek as an Indian reservation. When the Government, in 1825, bought the lands from the Osage, who occupied them under the "original Indian title," they became a part of the public domain, subject to be appropriated by the Government and set aside for Indian reservations, or for any other purpose which it might designate. And by the act of Congress of May 28, 1830 (4 Stat. L., 411), Congress authorized the President to set it apart for the reception of such tribes of Indians as might be willing to exchange for it the lands where they then resided and remove upon them. The statute is as follows:

"That it shall and may be lawful for the President of the United States to cause so much of any territory belonging to the United States west of the river Mississippi not included in any State or organized Territory, and to which the Indian title has been extinguished, as he may judge necessary, to be divided into a suitable number of districts, for the reception of such tribes or nations of Indians as may choose to exchange the lands where they now reside, and remove there; and to cause each of said districts to be so described by natural or artificial marks as to be easily distinguished from every other."

Clearly this is a reservation of so much of the lands as the President might thereafter designate for the purpose set forth in the statute, and pursuant to the statute the change was afterwards made by which the Creek surrendered their right of occupancy of the lands they then held in Alabama for those which they now possess. The land was conveyed to them with the limitation that they should not alienate it without the consent of the United States. By numerous treaties, the statutes, including the intercourse laws, their right to the exclusive occupancy of the country was assured to them. No white men, except such as were allowed to go upon other Indian reservations, were permitted to enter the Creek Nation. By the most solemn pledges they were to be protected from the intrusion of white men.

But, whether strictly an Indian reservation or not, the Creek nation is so far clothed with sovereign powers as that the treaties made between it and the United States, until abrogated, are binding, and, as already shown, the treaty provides that, as to all but the classes of persons therein designated, the Creek nation is clothed with the power to admit white men or not, at its option, which, as we hold, gave it the right to impose conditions. Nor does the fact that Congress, by the provision of the Curtis bill, has provided for the creation of cities and towns in this nation and the extinguishment of the Indian title to the lands embraced within the limits of such municipal corporations alter the case, because this provision of that bill has not yet been carried into effect. The Indian title to such lands still remains in them and it is yet their country. What effect the provision of this statute relating to cities and towns, when fully consummated, may have we do not now decide.

But it is claimed that because Congress has enacted a statute establishing United States courts in the Creek Nation, and as attorneys practicing in such courts are officers thereof, therefore they are excluded from the provisions of the treaty.

First, because they are officers; and,

Second, because as courts can not perform their duties without the aid of attorneys, they are therefore a necessary and constituent part of it; and if taxed, they might refuse to pay and leave the country, or be removed therefrom by the agent, and as every man charged with crime is entitled to be heard in the courts by counsel, he would thus be deprived of this constitutional right.

In Ex parte Yale (25 Cal., 241) the Supreme Court says:

"An officer, as defined by Webster, is 'a person who performs any public duty.' An attorney at law is not such an officer. And in our opinion he is not an officer in the constitutional sense of the term and does not hold a public trust. On this point we agree with Justice Crocker and Norton in Cohen v. Wright (22 Cal., 293).

Mr. Justice Platt, in a case relating to the oath of an attorney (20 Johns, 492), says:

"The point is simply whether an attorney or counselor holds an office of public trust in the sense of the Constitution. * * * In my judgment an attorney and counselor does not hold an office, but exercises a privilege or franchise. As attorneys or counselors they perform no duties in behalf of the Government—they execute no public trust."

Cooley on Taxation (576) says:

"Practitioners of law and medicine are not uncommonly taxed a specific sum upon the privilege of pursuing their calling for a year or other specified time. Such a tax is not a poll tax, and may therefore be levied when poll taxes are forbidden. Sometimes the tax is graded by the supposed value of the privilege. The right to impose an occupation tax on practitioners of law has been much contested, as being in effect a tax on the privilege of seeking justice in the courts; but it has, nevertheless, been sustained without only faint dissent."

To the same effect see Longville r. State, 4 Tex. App., 312; Simmons v. State, 12 Mo., 271; State r. Hubbard, 3 O., 63; Young r. Thomas, 17 Fla. 170; Cousins v. State, 50 Ala., 115; Wright r. Atlanta, 54 Ga., 645; Stuart r. Potts, 49 Miss., 749; Tiedeman on Police Powers, 84-101; Weeks on Attorneys, 41, 2d ed.

In Ex parte Williams (31 Tex. Crim. Reports, 262) the court says:

"But, conceding them to be officers, still that would be no ground for exemption from taxation. * * * But in the second place, the contention that the legislature may cripple or destroy the judicial department is more plausible than sound. * * * The objection goes to the existence of the power, rather than to any probability of its exercise. It is, indeed, an objection that could be urged against any exercise of the taxing power. Thus, the legislature ought not to have the power to tax land, for fear it might confiscate; nor personal property, because the tax imposed might exceed its value; nor any occupation, business, or pursuit, because they could be taxed out of existence, and the livelihood of many be destroyed. * * * There is certainly no force in the proposition that by the imposition of this tax some defendant may be deprived of counsel. The presumption is absolute, says Judge Dederick in the Tennessee 'Lawyers Tax Cases,' that all good citizens will obey their State's laws, and pay the taxes imposed. There will always be lawyers who obey the law and pay their occupation tax. The person accused of crime will always be within reach of lawyers in a position to defend him by reason of having paid their tax. Until the criminal can show that he has actually been deprived of legal counsel by reason of this occupation tax, the lawyer can not interpose this plea, that can only inure to the benefit of the defendant. It is a defense peculiarly personal, and this court would not declare the occupation tax law unconstitutional on the ground that some criminal might be deprived of counsel by reason of the law, although no such case arose, or ever will arise. This contention is utterly without foundation, for the reason that this provision was put in the bill of rights not to operate under contingencies but upon actual occurrences; and we have none such here. Many reasons could be urged against this position, but it is deemed so frail that it is not necessary to deal with it further than to draw a plain parallel. We might with equal propriety charge the legislature with murder because some person gets snake bitten and can get no whisky to drink for it and dies, on account of the legislature imposing an occupation tax on liquor dealers, as to say that a criminal is deprived of the right of appearing by counsel on account of the legislature placing an occupation tax on lawyers, or might with some propriety accuse the legislature with murder because some person dies on account of a tax on traveling physicians. The cases are about on a par."

We agree with the authorities and hold that attorneys at law are not relieved from the payment of the amount required by the Creek statute for the privilege of remaining and practicing their profession in the Creek Nation because of the fact that they are lawyers.

On the whole case, we therefore hold that a lawyer who is a white man and not a citizen of the Creek Nation is, pursuant to their statute, required to pay for the privilege of remaining and practicing his profession in that nation the sum of $25; that if he refuse the payment thereof he becomes, by virtue of the treaty, an intruder, and that in such a case the Government of the United States may remove him from the nation, and that this duty devolves upon the Interior Department.

Whether the Interior Department or its Indian agents can be controlled by the courts by the writs of mandamus and injunction is not material in this case, because, as we hold, an attorney who refuses to pay the amount required by the statute by its very terms becomes an intruder, whom the United States promises by the terms of the treaty to remove, and therefore in such cases the officers and agents of the Interior Department would be acting clearly and properly within the scope of their powers.

The complaint challenges the right of the Indian agent to collect this tax, but at the hearing before us this point was waived by appellants in open court, because, as stated by their counsel, the object of the suit was to get a judicial determination of the question as to whether under the law they were liable at all.

We are of the opinion, however, that the Indian agent, when directed by the Secretary of the Interior, may collect this money for the Creeks. The Intercourse Laws (sec. 2058, R. S. U. S.) provide that:

"Each Indian agent shall, within his agency, manage and superintend the intercourse with the Indians agreeably to law, and execute and perform such regulations and duties, not inconsistent with law, as may be prescribed by the President, the Secretary of the Interior, the Commissioner of Indian Affairs, or Superintendent of Indian Affairs."

In this case the Indian agent was acting in strict accordance with directions and regulations of the Secretary of the Interior, in a matter clearly relating to intercourse with the Indians, and when it is remembered that up to the time that the United States courts were established in the Indian Territory, the only remedy for collection of this tax was by removal, that the Indian nations had no power to collect it except through the intervention of the Interior Department, it is quite clear that if in the best judgment of that Department it was deemed wise to take charge of the matter and collect this money and turn it over to the Indians, it had power to do so under its superintending control of the Indians, and the intercourse of white men with them, granted by various acts of Congress; and in our opinion that power has not been taken away by any subsequent act of Congress or treaty stipulation.

The decree of the court below, sustaining the demurrer to the complaint and dismissing the case, is affirmed.

APPENDIX NO. 14.

OPINION OF JUDGE GILL.

In the United States court in the Indian Territory, northern district, sitting at Vinita.

W. C. ROGERS, PLAINTIFF, }
v. }
FRANK CHURCHILL, J. GEORGE WRIGHT, AND J. BLAIR SHOENFELT, }
Defendants. }

STATEMENT OF CASE.

This is a complaint in equity in which the plaintiff, W. C. Rogers, seeks to enjoin the defendants, Frank C. Churchill, J. George Wright, and J. Blair Shoenfelt, from collecting the tax claimed to be due the Cherokee Nation from the plaintiff as a merchant.

The facts in the case, as shown by the pleadings and the evidence, briefly stated, are substantially as follows: The plaintiff, W. C. Rogers, is a Cherokee citizen by birth, and is a merchant and trader in the Cherokee Nation, having a business at three different points therein, namely, one at Talala, carrying a general stock of merchandise of about $20,000; one at Vera and one Skiatook, each carrying a stock of about $8,000. Said stocks of merchandise consist of fruits, groceries, dry goods, clothing, hats, caps, etc.

That the defendant, Frank C. Churchill, is an employee of the Interior Department of the United States. Defendant J. George Wright is the duly appointed, qualified, and acting United States Indian inspector for the Indian Territory, and defendant J. Blair Shoenfelt is the duly appointed, qualified, and acting Indian agent for the Union Agency in the Indian Territory, and that as such officers and employees they perform such acts and services as may be directed by the said Department of the Interior and the laws of the United States.

The tax in controversy arises under article 2, "Trade and intercourse," and is found in the Compiled Laws of the Cherokee Nation, 1892, sections 582 to 589, inclusive.

The evidence taken shows that the defendants, acting as officers and employees of the Un ted States, served notice upon the plaintiff, W. C. Rogers, that he would be required to pay the tax due the Cherokee Nation to them, in accordance with certain rules and regulations adopted by the Secretary of the Interior in reference to the collection of taxes due the Cherokee Nation, and the plaintiff was repeatedly notified by said officers to pay said tax; that plaintiff failed to pay any attention to these notices, and failed to report, pay, or tender any part of the tax.

That on or about the 1st day of June, 1900, the defendants, acting in their official capacity, and acting through the Indian police, closed up the store of the plaintiff at Talala and held possession of the same for a period of five days, during which time the plaintiff was unable to trade or do business therein.

It is also in evidence that the Secretary of the Interior, acting under the general provisions of the act of Congress approved June 28, 1898, commonly known as the "Curtis bill," under the head of "Royalties, rents, etc.," in paragraph 13, provided:

"That the United States Indian agent shall receive and receipt for all royalties paid into his hands when accompanied by the sworn statement as provided in the proceeding regulation, but not otherwise, and it shall also be his duty to collect, under the supervision and direction of the United States Indian inspector for the Indian Territory, all rents, permits, revenues, and taxes, of whatsoever kind or nature that may be due and payable to any Indian tribe or tribes to which these regulations may apply, as provided for by the laws of such tribe or tribes."

And further provided in paragraph 14, as follows:

"The rents and permits, taxes, and revenues provided for by the foregoing regulation to be collected by the United States Indian agent shall be due and payable to him in lawful money of the United States at the time when such rents, permits, taxes, and revenues would, under the laws of the particular nations, have been due and payable to the authorities of said nations had not the act of June 28, 1898, and especially section 16 thereof, been passed."

Upon the closing of said store the plaintiff brought his action to this court for the purpose of restraining defendants, or any of them, or anyone acting under them, from interfering with or attempting to interfere with the possession of said stock of goods, and praying that this order be made perpetual. A temporary injunction issued in pursuance of said bill and prayer, and this case came on to be heard on the pleadings and evidence on July 23, 1900, with the understanding that the submission of the case should be final as to this court.

OPINION.

The case at bar presents some very peculiar features, and the law applicable thereto is in an unsatisfactory condition. The matter, reduced from the lengthy argument and presentation on either side, resolves itself into two principal questions:

First. Is there a traders' tax authorized by law to be assessed against and collected from a Cherokee citizen, doing a general merchandise business in the Cherokee Nation in the Indian Territory, since the adoption of the Curtis Act on June 28, 1898?

Second. If such a tax is authorized and collectible, does the law authorize the Interior Department to collect it?

I.

An examination of the Cherokee laws, article 2, entitled "Trade and intercourse," shows that such trade and intercourse and such law applied only to the Indian citizen, and the only penalty for the infraction of such law was punishment by a fine or by a fine and imprisonment, as the same should be found by the Cherokee courts. No provision was made in said article for the enforcement of the collection of the taxes other than by fine or by fine and imprisonment, to be imposed in the Cherokee courts, and in those alone.

Section 28 of the Curtis bill abolished all the tribal courts in the Indian Territory and prohibited any officers of said courts from performing any act theretofore authorized by any law in connection with said courts. If the said article 2 of the Cherokee laws is to stand at all, as being not annulled and a valid law, it is one which provides punishment for its infraction merely by a fine, or by a fine and imprisonment, and by this means alone, except that where a party fails to obtain a receipt for a tax and post it in his place of business, as provided by section 589 of said article, the sheriff of the district is to close his store and report such offender, that he may be proceeded against criminally. A careful examination of said article does not reveal any method whereby the offender's goods may be reached, or whereby any lien whatever is created or attaches to the goods, or whereby any punishment can be inflicted upon the offending party except in the Cherokee courts.

It is a rule well established that all statutes imposing taxes are to be followed strictly; that the manner of laying the tax, the time and manner of collection, and all the means pointed out toward effecting the object to be attained, namely, the collection of the tax, are to be followed with exactitude, and a failure to follow the law, either in the assessment or as to the means to be used to collect it, may upon resistance avoid the tax.

It may be safely stated in a brief way that the United States, by acts of Congress and treaties with the Cherokees, gave to the Cherokee the right to regulate internal affairs of the Cherokee Nation in respect to trade as to its own citizens, and that acting under the treaties and statutes the act above referred to as article 2, "Trade and intercourse," Compiled Laws of the Cherokee Nation, was in all respects legal and in conformity with the rights of the nation in reference to taxing its own citizens doing business within its boundaries. It may also be stated without question that the United States have the authority at any time, by statute, to alter and change the laws of the Cherokee Nation—in fact, Congress has often exercised this right, although at times its power to do so has been questioned. It may also be safely stated that the Secretary of the Interior, and the Commissioner of Indian Affairs, and the President, by various acts of Congress, have been authorized to exercise at times a wide discretion in the control of Indian affairs, and this has at all times been exercised for the good of the Indians themselves; and where the Secretary of the Interior or the Commissioner of Indian Affairs are given, under a statute, discretion with reference to carrying out its provisions they are the sole judges of the use or abuse of that discretion; but the Secretary of the Interior and the Commissioner of Indian Affairs must in their action have behind them some substantive law of Congress upon which to base their action.

By the act of June 28, 1898, Congress took away the right of the Cherokee Nation, as well as the right of the other tribes with whom agreements were not consummated, to exercise judicial functions through their tribal courts, and consequently took away from the Cherokee Nation all power to impose the penalties prescribed in article 2, "Trade and intercourse," with reference to the enforcing of the collection of said revenues, and said nation is at this time impotent to enforce in any way the collection of said traders' tax. It might be said that, in view of this state of affairs, it was the moral duty of Congress to prescribe some method whereby these revenues could be collected, inasmuch as they had rendered the nation powerless to collect them; but with the question of morals this court has nothing to do, nor has it anything to do with the policy of the Government in relation to controlling the Indian affairs. By said Curtis bill Congress provided that this Cherokee statute could not be enforced at law or in equity in the United States courts. By said act it authorized and directed, as to rents and royalties on the leasing of oil, coal, asphalt, and other mineral lands in said Territory, that the Secretary should make rules and regulations and collect all moneys due, and provided that anybody else undertaking to collect such royalties should be guilty of a misdemeanor, but nowhere in said statute did it specifically authorize the Secretary of the Interior to collect the taxes due under the laws of the several nations.

II.

Prior to the enactment of the Curtis bill there was no statute authorizing the Secretary of the Interior to enter the Cherokee Nation and collect the taxes due by Cherokee statutes, and if there be any statute of the United States authorizing the Secretary of the Interior or the Commissioner of Indian Affairs, or any of their officers, to enter the Cherokee Nation and collect such tax, it has not been cited to the court, nor is the court itself aware of such law. It is, however, claimed that section 2058, Revised Statutes of the United States, confers such authority upon the

Indian agent. That statute says that the "Indian agent shall within his agency manage and superintend the intercourse with the Indians agreeably to law, and perform such regulations and duties not inconsistent with law as may be prescribed by the President, the Secretary of the Interior, the Commissioner of Indian Affairs, or the Superintendent of Indian Affairs." In the opinion of the court this section relates to intercourse with the Indians; that is, intercourse of the tribe with noncitizens of the tribe, and has no bearing upon intercourse among citizens of a tribe, and therefore does not apply to the case at bar.

Does the statute of the United States giving the Secretary of the Interior certain discretion—viz, section 2058, Revised Statutes of the United States—authorize him to prescribe how the laws of the Cherokee Nation shall be carried into force and effect by rules and regulations, when such laws themselves prescribe a different method of procedure? In other words, can the Secretary of the Interior make rules and regulations to carry into force and effect a Cherokee law in a different manner and by a process different from that prescribed by the law under which he undertakes to act? Or, to put it more strongly, can the Secretary of the Interior, by rules and regulations, amend the Cherokee statute by prescribing the mode of its enforcement, and in that way assume to exercise the powers of Congress in that regard? It is the opinion of the court that this power does not rest in the Secretary of the Interior. That the Secretary of the Interior may make rules and regulations not inconsistent with laws, in relation to the control and regulation of the Indians and Indian affairs with noncitizens of a tribe, can not be disputed; but he is not authorized to make law. If the Secretary, without a substantive statute to that end, may come into the Cherokee Nation and, acting upon a Cherokee statute, seek to control the effect of that statute by assuming the duties of the Cherokee officers under that statute, all that he could do would be to proceed in the manner prescribed by the statute, which would require him, if he found an Indian doing business and trading within the limits of the Cherokee Nation without the license prescribed by law, to close his business and report him to the tribal court in the district in which he was doing business for his failure to comply with the law, which tribal court no longer has any existence and can perform no duties in reference thereto. To hold that the Secretary can collect this tax or close the business of an Indian trading in the Cherokee Nation is to hold that he has absolute, unqualified, undisputed, autocratic sway over the interior trade of the nation by its citizens. This court does not believe that such power vests in the Secretary of the Interior as the law now stands, as to the Cherokee Nation.

In 1890, by the act of Congress of that year, the Constitution of the United States was put in force and effect in the Cherokee and other Indian nations of the Five Civilized Tribes. This was reiterated in the act of June, 1897, and the courts of the United States given absolute jurisdiction both in law and equity over all citizens, irrespective of race, color, or previous condition, and the laws of the United States were extended over the Cherokee Nation. The Constitution of the United States provides in specific terms (article 5, amendments to the Constitution), "That no person shall be deprived of life, liberty, or property without due process of law," and this right has, since 1890, been given to the Indians of this nation. By "due process of law" is meant the right to contest any attempt to deprive a person of his life, liberty, or property in the courts having jurisdiction. By reason of the act of June 28, 1898, it would seem that the right to contest the collecting of this tax, by trial in any court, has been taken absolutely away from Indians trading in the Cherokee Nation; consequently there is no legal method by which the tax imposed by a Cherokee statute can be enforced. Certainly the term "by due process of law" does not include any other method than the method pointed out by the law itself. The Secretary of the Interior is authorized to make rules and regulations within the law, and not inconsistent with the law, but he can not make the law, nor change it, nor alter its force or effect, nor can he take from or add to the law, and, except this law be changed in some way, it can not at this time be enforced as the law itself prescribes. Had Congress designed that the Secretary of the Interior should collect the tribal taxes, it would have said so in specific terms—in terms as specific and clear as are used in authorizing the Secretary of the Interior to collect rents and royalties. It can not be successfully contended that the terms "royalties and rents" include the term "tax," as those terms have a meaning separate and distinct from the terms "tax" and "revenue."

The court holds that the temporary injunction heretofore granted restraining the defendants from interfering with the store and business of the plaintiff in Talala shall be, and the same is hereby, made perpetual.

There having been no attempt on the part of these defendants to close or interfere with the business of plaintiff at Vera and Skiatook, or to remove the plaintiff from the Territory, that part of the prayer of the bill is refused.

To which judgment of the court defendants except.

In the United States court for the Indian Territory, northern district, at Vinita.

W. C. ROGERS, PLAINTIFF,

v.

J. GEORGE WRIGHT, J. BLAIR SHOENFELT, AND FRANK CHURCHILL,
defendants.

ORDER.

On this 8th day of June, A. D. 1900, in open court at Vinita, is presented the complaint of the plaintiff, duly verified, praying for an injunction restraining the defendants, their servants, agents, and employees, from in any manner undertaking to collect of the plaintiff any tribal tax, and from interfering with the plaintiff in his business at Talala, Cherokee Nation, at Vera, Cherokee Nation, and at Skiatook, Cherokee Nation, and from undertaking to remove the plaintiff from the Cherokee Nation as a means of forcing the payment by him of tribal taxes claimed by defendants to be owing by him to the Cherokee Nation, said complaint having been heretofore filed in this court; and also comes the plaintiff, by J. S. Davenport, L. F. Parker, jr., and William Mollette and W. H. Kornegay, his attorneys, and files a motion asking the court to set a day for the hearing in this on the application for a temporary restraining order, and also asking that defendants be restrained pending the hearing as asked for in the complaint, and the matters and things set forth being by the court seen and heard; and, it appearing therefrom that plaintiff is entitled to equitable relief by way of injunction, it is considered and ordered that defendants J. George Wright, J. Blair Shoenfelt, and Frank Churchill, and each of them, their servants, agents, and employees, be restrained from in any manner interfering with the plaintiff's business as a merchant at Talala, Ind. T., at Vera, Ind. T., and at Skiatook, Ind. T., and that they and each of them be restrained from in any manner endeavoring to collect tribal taxes of the plaintiff by reason of such mercantile business, and that they and each of them be restrained from removing the plaintiff from the Cherokee Nation by reason of the nonpayment of said tribal taxes, claimed to be due the Cherokee Nation as set forth in the complaint; and that this order shall become effectual upon the execution of a good and sufficient bond by the plaintiff in the sum of $2,000, payable to the defendants, to answer for the damages that may accrue to them by reason of the injunction herein, and that the injunction herein be subject to the further order of the court. It is further ordered that each of the defendants show cause at the United States court room at Vinita, at 10 o'clock a. m. of July 7, A. D. 1900, why the injunction herein should not be made perpetual. And thereupon comes the plaintiff herein and files a bond as required, with William Little and James C. Hall as sureties, and said bond is adjudged good and sufficient, and it is ordered that the injunction do now become effectual.

JOSEPH A. GILL, *Judge Presiding.*

UNITED STATES OF AMERICA, *Indian Territory, Northern District, ss:*

I, Charles A. Davidson, clerk of the United States court for the northern district of the Indian Territory, do hereby certify the foregoing to be a true copy of an order made by said court on the 8th day of June, 1900, as appears from the records now on file in my office.

Witness my hand and seal of said court at Vinita this the 8th day of June, 1900.

CHARLES A. DAVIDSON, *Clerk.*
By T. A. CHANDLER, *Deputy.*

APPENDIX NO. 15.

REGULATIONS GOVERNING THE PROCUREMENT OF TIMBER AND STONE FOR DOMESTIC AND INDUSTRIAL PURPOSES IN THE INDIAN TERRITORY, AS PROVIDED IN THE ACT OF JUNE 6, 1900 (PUBLIC NO. 174).

1. The United States Indian agent for the Union Agency is hereby authorized and directed to enter into a contract or contracts, upon applications made in the form of affidavits, upon blanks prescribed, when approved by the Secretary of the Interior, with any responsible person, persons, or corporation for the purchase of timber or stone from any of the public lands belonging to any of the Five Civilized Tribes, and to collect, on or before the end of each month, the full value of such

timber or stone as the Secretary of the Interior shall hereafter determine should be paid; and the timber and stone so procured under such contracts may be used for "domestic and industrial purposes, including the construction, maintenance, and repair of railroads and other highways," within the limits of the Indian Territory only.

Applications must be presented to the United States Indian inspector located in the Indian Territory and by him forwarded, with his recommendation, through the Commissioner of Indian Affairs, to the Department.

Applicants must state the quality and quantity of timber or stone proposed to be cut or quarried, the purpose or purposes for which and the place or places where said timber and stone are to be used, as the case may be, the amount considered just and reasonable to be paid by them, and their reasons for such conclusion. Each application must be accompanied by the affidavits of two disinterested persons, corroborating specifically all the statements of the applicant; and the inspector is hereby authorized to require any other information as to the value of the timber or stone, or to show the good faith of the applicant.

2. Before any timber shall be cut or any stone taken from any of the lands belonging to any of the Five Civilized Tribes, the person, persons, or corporation desiring to secure such timber or stone shall enter into a contract or contracts with said Indian agent, in accordance with the form hereto attached, which contract, however, shall not be of force until the Secretary of the Interior shall have indorsed his approval thereon: *Provided*, That each such person, persons, or corporation shall give bond (form attached hereto) in a sufficient sum, to be fixed by the Secretary of the Interior, with two good and sufficient sureties, or an approved surety company, as surety, conditioned for the faithful performance of the stipulations of the contract or contracts, and also conditioned for the faithful observance of all of the laws of the United States now in force or that may hereafter be enacted, and the regulations now prescribed or that may hereafter be prescribed by the Secretary of the Interior relative to any and all matters pertaining to the affairs of any of the Five Civilized Tribes.

3. The moneys so collected shall be placed to the credit of the tribe or tribes to which the land belongs from which such timber or stone was procured, as miscellaneous receipts, class three, "not the result of the labor of any member of such tribe;" but no timber or stone shall be taken from any land selected by any citizen of any of the Five Civilized Tribes as his prospective allotment without his consent, and only from such land being cleared, or to be cleared, for cultivation, and not until a contract shall have been entered into by the said United States Indian agent and the person, persons, or corporation desiring to procure such timber or stone, and the same shall have been approved.

The price to be paid under such contract shall be satisfactory to such prospective allottee, and shall be held by the Indian agent and paid to said allottee after final allotment to him shall have been made: *Provided*, That the provisions of this section shall apply to all tracts now in possession of any citizens of any of the Five Civilized Tribes who intend to include such tracts in their prospective allotments, and the money derived from the sale of timber or stone taken from any such tracts shall be held by the Indian agent until such time as allotment of the tract or tracts from which such timber or stone was taken shall have been made, at which time the money so held shall be paid by the Indian agent to the citizen taking such tract or tracts as his allotment: *And provided further*, That the Indian agent shall be required to keep an accurate list, by legal subdivision, of the land from which such timber or stone was taken, and also an accurate list of the amount of money derived from the sale of timber or stone taken from each such legal subdivision. Value of timber and stone taken from unappraised selected lands must be added to the appraisement when made.

4. The contract or contracts entered into by said Indian agent with any person, persons, or corporation shall describe the land from which the timber or stone is to be taken by legal subdivisions, and if any contractor shall take timber or stone from any land other than that covered by his contract he shall be liable to forcible removal from the Indian Territory and suit on his bond, and such unlawful taking of timber and stone shall work also a forfeiture of his contract.

5. The act of Congress under which these rules are promulgated provides that "every person who unlawfully cuts, or aids, or is employed in unlawfully cutting, or wantonly destroys, or procures to be wantonly destroyed, any timber standing upon the land of either of said tribes, or sells or transports any of such timber or stone outside the Indian Territory, contrary to the regulations prescribed by the Secretary, shall pay a fine of not more than five hundred dollars, or be imprisoned not more than twelve months, or both, in the discretion of the court trying the same."

The Indian agent for the Union Agency shall see that any person, persons, or corporation who procures timber or stone from any of the lands belonging to any of the Five Civilized Tribes, under and in accordance with the provisions of the act of Congress approved June 6, 1900 (Public No. 174), and these regulations, employs Indians in the cutting and removal of said timber and in the quarrying and removal of said stone whenever practicable on the same terms as other labor, Indians to have the preference over white men.

The Department reserves the right to amend these regulations and to advance the price to be paid for timber or stone to be taken under any contract if it be shown that the amount stipulated in the contract is less than the "full value," or to cancel any contract for failure to pay promptly the amounts due, or for any other good and sufficient cause, after due notice to the party or parties in interest, giving the right to show cause, within ten days from service of such notice, why this action should not be taken.

W. A. JONES,
Commissioner of Indian Affairs.

WASHINGTON, D. C., *July 14, 1900.*
Approved:
THOS. RYAN, *Acting Secretary.*

FORM OF APPLICATION.

——— ———,
———, 1900.

I hereby apply for permission to enter into a contract with the United States Indian agent at Muscogee, Indian Territory, for the purchase of ([1]) ——— located on the ([2]) ———.

Such timber or stone is to be used at ———.

I consider that the timber is worth on the stump the following prices, to wit: ———, and that the stone is worth the following price per cubic yard, to wit: ———.

I base my opinion as to the values above stated upon the following facts: ([3])———.

Subscribed and sworn to before me, ——— ———, this ——— day of ———, 19—.

——— ———,

——— ——— and ——— ———, being by me first duly sworn, upon their oaths state, each for himself, that he is well acquainted with the land above described and with the quantity and quality of the timber and stone thereon, and with the place or places where it is proposed to use the above-mentioned material, and also with the values and prices of stone and timber in the vicinity of the place from which it is proposed to take and where it is proposed to use such material, and with the cost of removing and transporting timber and stone, and with all the facts stated by the applicant above named, and knows that the facts stated by him are true and correct in every particular.

——— ———.
——— ———.

Subscribed and sworn to before me, a ——— for the ———, at my office in ———, this ——— day of ———, ———.

——— ———,
———.

FORM OF INDIAN TERRITORY TIMBER AND STONE CONTRACT.

——— Nation.

[Write all names and addresses in full.]

This agreement, made and entered into in quadruplicate at the Union Agency, Muscogee, Indian Territory, this ——— day of ———, 19—, by and between ——— ———, United States Indian agent for the Union Agency, party of the first part, and ——— ———, of ———, part— of the second part, under and in pursuance of the provisions of the act of Congress approved June 6, 1900 (Public No. 174), and the rules and regulations prescribed by the Secretary of the Interior on July 14, 1900, relative to the procurement of timber and stone from any of the lands belonging to

---

[1] Insert amount, kind, and character of timber or stone, or both, desired.
[2] Insert description of land.
[3] State distance from place where material is to be procured to place where it is to be used, cost of transportation, etc., market price of material where it is to be used, and any other facts which may be of aid in arriving at a conclusion.

timber or stone as the Secretary of the Interior shall hereafter determine should be paid; and the timber and stone so procured under such contracts may be used for "domestic and industrial purposes, including the construction, maintenance, and repair of railroads and other highways," within the limits of the Indian Territory only.

Applications must be presented to the United States Indian inspector located in the Indian Territory and by him forwarded, with his recommendation, through the Commissioner of Indian Affairs, to the Department.

Applicants must state the quality and quantity of timber or stone proposed to be cut or quarried, the purpose or purposes for which and the place or places where said timber and stone are to be used, as the case may be, the amount considered just and reasonable to be paid by them, and their reasons for such conclusion. Each application must be accompanied by the affidavits of two disinterested persons, corroborating specifically all the statements of the applicant; and the inspector is hereby authorized to require any other information as to the value of the timber or stone, or to show the good faith of the applicant.

2. Before any timber shall be cut or any stone taken from any of the lands belonging to any of the Five Civilized Tribes, the person, persons, or corporation desiring to secure such timber or stone shall enter into a contract or contracts with said Indian agent, in accordance with the form hereto attached, which contract, however, shall not be of force until the Secretary of the Interior shall have indorsed his approval thereon: *Provided*, That each such person, persons, or corporation shall give bond (form attached hereto) in a sufficient sum, to be fixed by the Secretary of the Interior, with two good and sufficient sureties, or an approved surety company, as surety, conditioned for the faithful performance of the stipulations of the contract or contracts, and also conditioned for the faithful observance of all of the laws of the United States now in force or that may hereafter be enacted, and the regulations now prescribed or that may hereafter be prescribed by the Secretary of the Interior relative to any and all matters pertaining to the affairs of any of the Five Civilized Tribes.

3. The moneys so collected shall be placed to the credit of the tribe or tribes to which the land belongs from which such timber or stone was procured, as miscellaneous receipts, class three, "not the result of the labor of any member of such tribe;" but no timber or stone shall be taken from any land selected by any citizen of any of the Five Civilized Tribes as his prospective allotment without his consent, and only from such land being cleared, or to be cleared, for cultivation, and not until a contract shall have been entered into by the said United States Indian agent and the person, persons, or corporation desiring to procure such timber or stone, and the same shall have been approved.

The price to be paid under such contract shall be satisfactory to such prospective allottee, and shall be held by the Indian agent and paid to said allottee after final allotment to him shall have been made: *Provided*, That the provisions of this section shall apply to all tracts now in possession of any citizens of any of the Five Civilized Tribes who intend to include such tracts in their prospective allotments, and the money derived from the sale of timber or stone taken from any such tracts shall be held by the Indian agent until such time as allotment of the tract or tracts from which such timber or stone was taken shall have been made, at which time the money so held shall be paid by the Indian agent to the citizen taking such tract or tracts as his allotment: *And provided further*, That the Indian agent shall be required to keep an accurate list, by legal subdivision, of the land from which such timber or stone was taken, and also an accurate list of the amount of money derived from the sale of timber or stone taken from each such legal subdivision. Value of timber and stone taken from unappraised selected lands must be added to the appraisement when made.

4. The contract or contracts entered into by said Indian agent with any person, persons, or corporation shall describe the land from which the timber or stone is to be taken by legal subdivisions, and if any contractor shall take timber or stone from any land other than that covered by his contract he shall be liable to forcible removal from the Indian Territory and suit on his bond, and such unlawful taking of timber and stone shall work also a forfeiture of his contract.

5. The act of Congress under which these rules are promulgated provides that "every person who unlawfully cuts, or aids, or is employed in unlawfully cutting, or wantonly destroys, or procures to be wantonly destroyed, any timber standing upon the land of either of said tribes, or sells or transports any of such timber or stone outside the Indian Territory, contrary to the regulations prescribed by the Secretary, shall pay a fine of not more than five hundred dollars, or be imprisoned not more than twelve months, or both, in the discretion of the court trying the same."

It is further agreed that said timber shall be cut and removed and that said stone shall be quarried and removed from said land as soon as practicable after the date of this contract, so that no depreciation in value or waste may accrue to said party of the first part by reason of unnecessary delay in the removal of said timber or stone, provided that the terms of this contract shall not extend beyond the period of one year from the date hereof, and the timber or stone procured under this contract may be used within the limits of the Indian Territory only for "domestic and industrial purposes, including the construction, maintenance, and repair of railroads and other highways."

It is further understood and agreed by the part— of the second part that this agreement is void and of no effect unless approved by the Secretary of the Interior.

The part— of the second part further agree— that this agreement shall in all respects be subject to the rules and regulations heretofore or that may hereafter be prescribed under the said act of June 6, 1900, by the Secretary of the Interior relative to the procurement of timber and stone from any of the lands belonging to any of the Five Civilized Tribes, and to pay to the United States Indian agent for the Union Agency the full value of the timber or stone hereinbefore mentioned, in accordance with the provisions hereof.

The part— of the second part ——— firmly bound for the faithful compliance with the stipulations of this agreement by and under the bond made and executed by the part— of the second part as principal— and ——— ———, as suret— entered into the ——— day of ———, and which is on file in the office of the Commissioner of Indian Affairs.

In witness whereof, the said parties of the first and second parts have hereunto set their hands and affixed their seals the day and year first above written.

Witnesses:[1]

$$\left. \begin{array}{c} \underline{\quad\quad} \ \underline{\quad\quad} \end{array} \right\}$$ as to ——— ———, [SEAL.][2]

U. S. Indian Agent.

$$\left. \begin{array}{c} \underline{\quad\quad} \ \underline{\quad\quad} \end{array} \right\}$$ as to ——— ———. [SEAL.]

$$\left. \begin{array}{c} \underline{\quad\quad} \ \underline{\quad\quad} \end{array} \right\}$$ as to ——— ———. [SEAL.]

$$\left. \begin{array}{c} \underline{\quad\quad} \ \underline{\quad\quad} \end{array} \right\}$$ as to ——— ———. [SEAL.]

---

[1] Two witnesses to each signature, including signature of agent.
[2] Stamps are required by the act of June 13, 1898. Party of second part must furnish stamps.

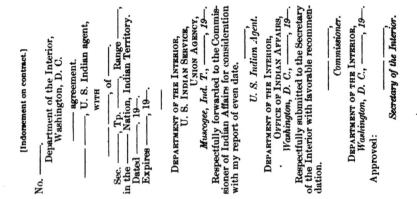

[Indorsement on contract.]

No. ———:

Department of the Interior,
Washington, D. C.

——— agreement.

———, U. S. Indian agent,
WITH
———, of ———,
Sec. ———, Tp. ———, Range ———.
in the ——— Nation, Indian Territory.
Dated ——— 19—.
Expires ——— 19—.

DEPARTMENT OF THE INTERIOR,
U. S. INDIAN SERVICE,
UNION AGENCY,
Muscogee, Ind. T., ———, 19—.

Respectfully forwarded to the Commissioner of Indian Affairs for consideration with my report of even date.

U. S. Indian Agent.

DEPARTMENT OF THE INTERIOR,
OFFICE OF INDIAN AFFAIRS,
Washington, D. C., ———, 19—.

Respectfully submitted to the Secretary of the Interior with favorable recommendation.

Commissioner.

DEPARTMENT OF THE INTERIOR,
Washington, D. C., ———, 19—.

Approved:

Secretary of the Interior.

any of the Five Civilized Tribes, and the timber or stone procured under the provisions of this contract and the rules and regulations heretofore or that may hereafter be prescribed by the Secretary of the Interior;

Witnesseth, that the said party of the first part agrees to sell to said part— of the second part timber or stone of the kind or kinds hereinafter specified, standing, fallen, lying, or being on lands within the limits of the ———— Nation, which said lands are described as follows, to wit: The ———— of section ————, of township (¹) ————, of range (²) ————, of the Indian meridian, and containing ———— acres, more or less.

The part— of the second part agree— to cut and remove the timber or quarry and remove the stone hereinafter mentioned from within the above-described limits, and agree— to employ Indian labor in the cutting and removal of the timber and the quarrying and removal of the stone in preference to other labor on equal terms, whenever suitable Indian labor can be obtained.

For and in consideration of the foregoing, the said part— of the second part also agree— to pay to the United States Indian agent for the Union Agency, for the benefit of the ———— tribe of Indians, for all such timber cut and stone quarried on said described lands, at the following rates, to wit:

Merchantable saw timber, i. e., timber capable of being manufactured into lumber, as follows:

For walnut timber, ———— per thousand feet; for cypress timber, ———— per thousand feet; for ash timber, ———— per thousand feet; for oak timber, ———— per thousand feet; for pine timber, ———— per thousand feet; for cottonwood timber, ———— per thousand feet, and for ———— timber, ———— per thousand feet.

Telegraph poles.

Cedar, four to five inch top, eight to ten inch bottom, ———— feet long, ———— cents each.

Cedar, six-inch top, twelve-inch bottom, ———— feet long, ———— cents each.

Cedar, ———— inch top, ———— inch bottom, ———— feet long, ———— cents each.

Oak, four to five inch top, eight to ten inch bottom, ———— feet long, ———— cents each.

Oak, six-inch top, twelve-inch bottom, ———— feet long, ———— cents each.

Oak, ———— inch top, ———— inch bottom, ———— feet long, ———— cents each.

Piling.

Cedar, ———— cents per foot; oak, ———— cents per foot, running measure.

Railroad cross-ties (bridge, hewn, or sawed).

Oak (post, bur, white, red, and black), ———— cents each.

Pine, ———— cents each.

Cedar, bois d'arc, walnut, mulberry, sassafras, and red or slippery elm, ———— cents each.

Black locust and coffee bean, ———— cents each.

Railroad switch ties.

Oak (post, white, bur, red, and black), ———— cents each.

Pine, ———— cents each.

Fence posts.

———— cents each.

Cord wood.

———— dollar— per cord.

Stone.

———— dollar— per cubic yard.

It is agreed that full payment shall be made for said timber or stone before any of it is removed from the land hereinbefore described, and title to said timber or stone shall not vest in the part— of the second part until full payment shall have been made therefor.

---

¹ State whether north or south.   ² State whether east or west.

It is further agreed that said timber shall be cut and removed and that said stone shall be quarried and removed from said land as soon as practicable after the date of his contract, so that no depreciation in value or waste may accrue to said party of the first part by reason of unnecessary delay in the removal of said timber or stone, provided that the terms of this contract shall not extend beyond the period of one year from the date hereof, and the timber or stone procured under this contract may be used within the limits of the Indian Territory only for "domestic and industrial purposes, including the construction, maintenance, and repair of railroads and other highways."

It is further understood and agreed by the part— of the second part that this agreement is void and of no effect unless approved by the Secretary of the Interior.

The part— of the second part further agree— that this agreement shall in all respects a subject to the rules and regulations heretofore or that may hereafter be prescribed under the said act of June 6, 1900, by the Secretary of the Interior relative to the procurement of timber and stone from any of the lands belonging to any of the Five Civilized Tribes, and to pay to the United States Indian agent for the Union Agency the full value of the timber or stone hereinbefore mentioned, in accordance with the provisions hereof.

The part— of the second part ———— firmly bound for the faithful compliance with the stipulations of this agreement by and under the bond made and executed by the part— of the second part as principal— and ———— ————, as suret— entered into the ———— day of ————, and which is on file in the office of the Commissioner of Indian Affairs.

In witness whereof, the said parties of the first and second parts have hereunto set their hands and affixed their seals the day and year first above written.

Witnesses: [1]

> } as to ———— ————,   [SEAL.] [2]
>
>   *U. S. Indian Agent.*
>
> } as to ———— ————.   [SEAL.]
>
> } as to ———— ————.   [SEAL.]
>
> } as to ———— ————.   [SEAL.]

[1] Two witnesses to each signature, including signature of agent.
[2] Stamps are required by the act of June 13, 1898.   Party of second part must furnish stamps.

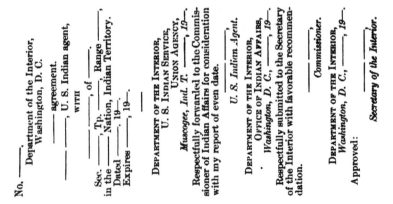

I appreciate the many kindnesses shown me by yourself and the United S
Indian inspector. I await your further commands.
Very respectfully, your obedient servant,

J. W. ELLIS,
Captain United States Indian Police for Indian Territo

Hon. J. BLAIR SHOENFELT,
United States Indian Agent, Muscogee, Ind. T.

EXHIBIT C.

The delivery of this blank is intended as a demand for payment of all taxes d
Make statement in duplicate.
Taxes should be paid to periods ending March 31, June 30, September 30,
December 31.

Department of the Interior, United States Indian Service.

To J. BLAIR SHOENFELT,
United States Indian Agent, Muscogee, Indian Territory:

1. My name is John R. McIntosh.
2. I am a member of the firm of Milam and McIntosh Hdwe. and Imp. Co.
3. Kind of business, hardware and implements.
4. Place of business, Chelsea.
5. Commenced business 1895.
6. Taxes are paid with this remittance from Oct. 1, 1899, to Dec. 31, 1899.
7. Amount of merchandise received and offered for sale by said firm during
time, $1,302.46.
8. On which the tax of one-fourth of one per cent amounts to $3.35.

JOHN R. McINTOSH,
Member of the Fir

I, John R. McIntosh, of Chelsea, I. T., solemnly swear that the sum of three
$\frac{25}{100}$ dollars ($3.25), forwarded herewith in accordance with the foregoing staten
is the correct and entire amount due from Oct. 1, 1899, to Dec. 31, 1899, to
Cherokee Nation, Indian Territory, as a tax on merchandise, and the same is
and complete payment of all taxes so due to the date last above mentioned, and
no goods or merchandise have been received or offered for sale by us, either dis
or indirectly, during the period from Oct. 1, 1899, to Dec. 31, 1899, except as set
above.

JOHN R. McINTOS

Subscribed and sworn to before me this Jan. 10, 1900.

[NOTARY SEAL.]   JOHN D. SCOTT, Notary Pub

(Indorsed:) Cherokee Nation. Merchandise tax. Sworn statement accompar
remittance of Milam and McIntosh, at Chelsea, I. T., for period commencing O
1899, and ending Dec. 31, 1899. $3.25. Duplicate sworn statement forwarde
U. S. Indian inspector ——, 190—. No. 243. Received Jan. 16, 1900. Offi
U. S. Indian agent, Muscogee, Ind. Ter.
R. S. U. S., section 5392. Every person who, having taken an oath before a
petent tribunal, officer, or person, in any case in which a law of the United S
authorizes an oath to be administered, that he will testify, declare, depose, or ce
truly, or that any written testimony, declaration, deposition, or certificate by
subscribed is true, willfully and contrary to such oath states or subscribes any mat
matter which he does believe to be true, is guilty of perjury, and shall be puni
by a fine of not more than two thousand dollars, and by imprisonment, at hard la
not more than five years; and shall, moreover, thereafter be incapable of giving
timony in any court of the United States until such time as the judgment against
is reversed.
Section 5393. Every person who procures another to commit any perjury is g
of subornation of perjury, and punishable as in the preceding section prescribed

---

EXHIBIT D.

Make statement in duplicate.
Taxes should be paid to periods ending March 31, June 30, September 30,
December 31.

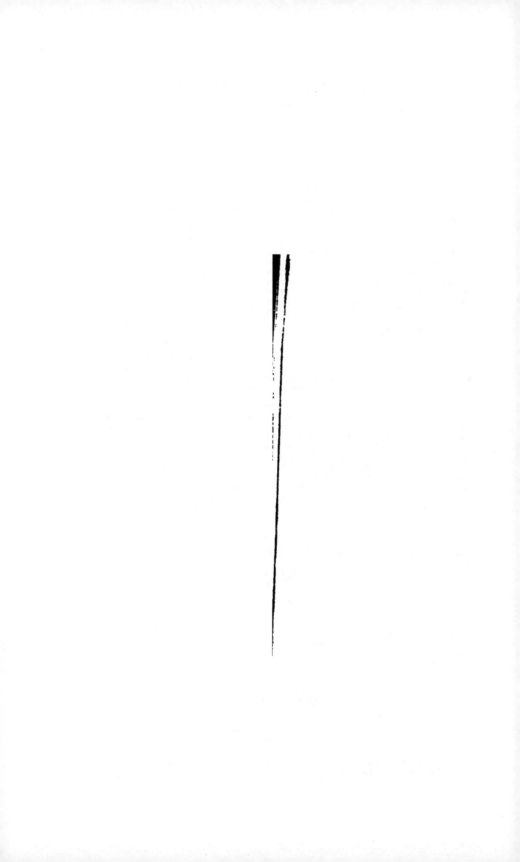

Deparment of the Interior, United States Indian Service.

To J. BLAIR SHOENFELT,
United States Indian Agent, Muscogee, Indian Territory:

1. My name is C. G. Moore.
2. I am a member of the firm C. G. Moore.
3. Kind of business, drugs.
4. Place of business, Eufaula.
5. Commenced business Dec. 20, 1897.
6. Date from and to which taxes are now paid, Jan. 1, 1900, to March 31, 1900.
7. Original cost of merchandise offered for sale by said firm during such time, $2,020.
8. On which the tax of one per cent amounts to ($20.20) twenty and $\frac{20}{100}$ dollars.

C. G. MOORE, *Member of the Firm.*

I, C. G. Moore, of Eufaula, I. T., solemnly swear that the sum of twenty and $\frac{20}{100}$ dollars ($20.20), forwarded herewith in accordance with the foregoing statement, is the correct and entire amount due from me to the Creek Nation, Indian Territory, as a tax on merchandise, and the same is full and complete payment of all taxes so due to the date last above mentioned, and that no goods or merchandise have been received or offered for sale by me, either directly or indirectly, during the period from Jan. 1, 1900, to March 31, 1900, except as set forth above.

C. G. MOORE.

Subscribed and sworn to before me this 21st day of May, 1900.

[NOTARY SEAL.]   R. L. SIMPSON, *Notary Public.*

(Indorsed:) Creek Nation. Merchandise tax. Sworn statement accompanying remittance of C. G. Moore, at Eufaula, I. T., for period commencing Jan. 1, 1900, and ending Mch. 31, 1900. $20.20. Duplicate sworn statement forwarded to U. S. Indian inspector ———, 190—. No. 535. Received Jan. 16, 1900. Office of U. S. Indian agent, Muscogee, Ind. Ter.

R. S. U. S., section 5392. Every person who, having taken an oath before a competent tribunal, officer, or person, in any case in which a law of the United States authorizes an oath to be administered, that he will testify, declare, depose, or certify truly, or that any written testimony, declaration, deposition, or certificate by him subscribed is true, wilfully and contrary to such oath states or subscribes any material matter which he does not believe to be true, is guilty of perjury, and shall be punished by a fine of not more than two thousand dollars, and by imprisonment, at hard labor, not more than five years; and shall, moreover, thereafter be incapable of giving testimony in any court of the United States until such time as the judgment against him is reversed.

Section 5393. Every person who procures another to commit any perjury is guilty of subornation of perjury, and punishable as in the preceding section prescribed.

EXHIBIT D 1.

All remittances should be made to U. S. Indian agent, accompanied by statements in duplicate.

DEPARTMENT OF THE INTERIOR,
UNITED STATES INDIAN SERVICE,
OFFICE OF UNITED STATES INDIAN AGENT,
Union Agency, Muscogee, Indian Territory, May 23, 1900.

VILLIAM T. HUTCHINGS,
Muscogee, Indian Territory.

SIR: I acknowledge receipt from you of check for $6.25, the same being in payment of your occupation tax as a lawyer, doing business at Muscogee, Creek Nation, from April 1, 1900, to June 30, 1900, as per statement accompanying remittance.

Very respectfully,

J. BLAIR SHOENFELT, *U. S. Indian Agent.*

EXHIBIT E.

To comply with conditions of permit royalties should be made promptly.

DEPARTMENT OF THE INTERIOR,
UNITED STATES INDIAN SERVICE,
Dawson, I. T., May 31, 1900.

Bullette and Heffelfinger, of Dawson, solemnly swear that we have mined 425 tons of coal from the Cherokee Nation, Indian Territory, at Dawson, during the period commencing May 16, 1900, and ending May 31, 1900, subject to a tax of ten cents per ton, and amounting to thirty-four dollars, which amount is herewith enclosed. And I further state the above quantity of coal is all that I have mined, directly or indirectly, within the limits of the Cherokee Nation during the period stated, and that the same was mined in accordance with a permit granted to ———, under date of ———, 190—.

J. W. CORWIN, Weigher.

Sworn to and subscribed before me this 31 day of May, 1900.
[NOTARY SEAL.]   WM. P. MOORE, <i>Notary Public.</i>

The above statement must be filled out in duplicate and sworn to before an officer authorized to administer oaths.
Remit direct to U. S. Indian agent.

(Indorsed:) Cherokee Nation. Coal tax. Sworn statement accompanying remittance of Bullette and Heffelfinger, Dawson, for period May 16, 1900, and ending May 31, 1900. $34.00. Duplicate sworn statement forwarded to U. S. Indian inspector ———, 190—. No. 773. Received June 11, 1900. Office of the U. S. Indian agent, Muscogee, Ind. Ter.

EXHIBIT F.

Remittances must be accompanied by sworn statements in duplicate.

DEPARTMENT OF THE INTERIOR,
UNITED STATES INDIAN SERVICE,
Vinita, Ind. Ter., Jan. 15, 1900.

D. T. Hall, of Vinita, solemnly swear that I have shipped 117 tons of hay from the Cherokee Nation, Indian Territory, from Vinita station during the period commencing Jan. 10, 1900, and ending Jan. 15, 1900, subject to a tax of twenty cents per ton, and amounting to 23.40 dollars, which amount is herewith enclosed. And I further state that the above quantity of hay is all that I have purchased, cut, or shipped directly or indirectly from the limits of the Cherokee Nation since July 1, 1898, to this date, on which the royalty is unpaid.

D. T. HALL.

Subscribed and sworn to before me this 15 day of Jan., 1900.
[NOTARY SEAL.]   W. L. CHAPMAN, <i>Notary Public.</i>

Hay shipped in cars numbered M. K. T., 32170; M. K. T., 11123; M. K. T., 7292; K. C. and L., 1621; C. O. and G., 33167; P. M. and O., 1121.

(Indorsed:) Cherokee Nation. Hay tax. Sworn statement accompanying remittance of D. T. Hall, Vinita, for period Jan. 10, 1900, and ending Jan. 15, 1900. $23.40. Duplicate sworn statement forwarded to U. S. Indian inspector ——— 190—. No. 275. Received Jan. 18, 1900, office U. S. Indian agent, Muscogee, Ind. Ter.

EXHIBIT G.

Quarters end March 31, June 30, September 30, and December 31.

DEPARTMENT OF THE INTERIOR,
UNITED STATES INDIAN SERVICE,
Muskogee, I. T., May 1, 1900.

I do hereby certify that I have been or will be engaged in the occupation of attorney at law at my regular place of business, at Muskogee, I. T., Creek Nation, Indian Territory, during the period commencing April 1, 1900, and ending June 30, 1900, and that I have paid J. Blair Shoenfelt, U. S. Indian agent, according to the laws of the Creek Nation, the sum of ($6.25) six and $\frac{25}{100}$ dollars, in payment of the tax for the above-mentioned period.

WM. T. HUTCHINGS.

Make all checks and drafts payable to U. S. Indian agent.

(Indorsed:) Creek Nation. Occupation tax. Sworn statement accompanying remittance of Wm. T. Hutchings, Muskogee, for period commencing April 1, 1900, and ending June 30, 1900. $6.25. Duplicate sworn statement forwarded to U. S. Indian inspector ———, 190—. No. 321. Received May 23, 1900. Office of U. S. Indian agent, Muscogee, Ind. Ter.

EXHIBIT H.

All remittances should be made to U. S. Indian agent, accompanied by statements in duplicate.

DEPARTMENT OF THE INTERIOR,
UNITED STATES INDIAN SERVICE,
OFFICE OF UNITED STATES INDIAN AGENT,
Union Agency, Muskogee, Indian Territory, May 23, 1900.

C. G. MOORE, *Eufaula, Indian Territory.*

SIR: I acknowledge receipt from you of check for $20.20, the same being in payment of tax on merchandise offered for sale by you in the Creek Nation from January 1st, 1900, to March 31, 1900, as per sworn statements accompanying remittance.

Very respectfully,

J. BLAIR SHOENFELT, *U. S. Indian Agent.*

EXHIBIT H 1.

DEPARTMENT OF THE INTERIOR,
UNITED STATES INDIAN SERVICE,
Union Agency, Muskogee, Indian Territory, January 18, 1900.

D. T. HALL, *Vinita, I. T.*

SIR: I acknowledge the receipt from you of Saint Louis exchange for $23.40, the same being tendered in payment of the royalty on hay shipped from the Cherokee Nation by you from January 10th to 15th, 1900, as per sworn statements accompanying the remittance.

Very respectfully,

J. BLAIR SHOENFELT,
U. S. Indian Agent.

EXHIBIT L

All remittances should be made to U. S. Indian agent, accompanied by statements in duplicate.

DEPARTMENT OF THE INTERIOR,
UNITED STATES INDIAN SERVICE,
OFFICE OF UNITED STATES INDIAN AGENT,
Union Agency, Muskogee, Indian Territory, Jan. 16, 1900.

MILAM & McINTOSH, *Chelsea, I. T.*

GENTLEMEN: I acknowledge receipt from you of St. Louis exchange for $3.25, the same being in payment of tax on merchandise offered for sale by you in the Cherokee Nation from October 1st to December 31st, 1899, as per sworn statements accompanying remittance.

Very respectfully,

J. BLAIR SHOENFELT,
U. S. Indian Agent.

EXHIBIT I 1.

DEPARTMENT OF THE INTERIOR,
UNITED STATES INDIAN SERVICE,
Union Agency, Muskogee, Indian Territory, June 11, 1900.

BULLETTE AND HEFFLEFINGER,
Claremore, Indian Territory.

SIRS: I acknowledge the receipt from you of Saint Louis exchange for $34.00, the same being tendered in payment of royalty on coal mined by you in the Cherokee Nation from May 16th to 31st, 1900, as per sworn statements accompanying the remittance.

Very respectfully,
(Signed)

J. BLAIR SHOENFELT,
U. S. Indian Agent.

EXHIBIT Q.

THE CHOCTAW AND CHICKASAW NATIONS, INDIAN TERRITORY.

To all to whom these presents come, greeting:

Whereas a certain commission, heretofore appointed and acting under authority of section twenty-nine of the act of Congress approved June 28, 1898 (30 Stat., 495), surveyed and platted the town of ——, —— Nation, Indian Territory; and

Whereas the plat of said town was approved by the Secretary of the Interior, on the —— day of ——, and was duly placed on file; and

Whereas the said commission has awarded the real estate described hereinbelow to ——, who has deposited —— dollars, the full amount of the purchase price, with the United States Indian agent, at ——, Indian Territory, and is, therefore, entitled to a patent:

Now, therefore, we, the undersigned, the principal chief of the Choctaw Nation and the governor of the Chickasaw Nation, do, by virtue of the power and authority vested in us by the aforesaid twenty-ninth section of said act of Congress of the United States, hereby grant, sell, and convey unto the said —— ——, —— heirs and assigns forever, all the right, title, and interest of the Choctaw and Chickasaw nations, aforesaid, in and to lot— numbered ——, in block— numbered ——, in the town of ——, —— Nation, Indian Territory, and according to the plat thereof on file as aforesaid, saving and excepting from this conveyance, however, all coal and asphalt.

In witness whereof, we, the principal chief of the Choctaw Nation and the governor of the Chickasaw Nation, have hereunto set our hands and caused the great seal of our respective nations to be affixed at the dates hereinafter shown.

Date: ——, 190—.

[SEAL.]

——— ———,
Principal Chief of the Choctaw Nation.

Date: ——, 190—.

[SEAL.]

——— ———,
Governor of the Chickasaw Nation.

(Indorsed:) Patent. Choctaw and Chickasaw nations to ——, lot— No. ——, block— No.——, town of ——, Indian Ter., —— Nation. Filed for record at request of ——, book ——, page ——, on the —— day of ——, 190—, at —— o'clock — m.

EXHIBIT R.

This statement must be forwarded in duplicate with remittance.

DEPARTMENT OF THE INTERIOR,
UNITED STATES INDIAN SERVICE,
Atoka, Indian Territory, May 24th, 1900.

J. BLAIR SHOENFELT,
United States Indian Agent, Muskogee, Indian Territory.

SIR: I do hereby certify that the following-described lots, situated in the town of Atoka, Choctaw Nation, Indian Territory, having been appraised by the Choctaw town-site commission, and the value of the lots having been fixed by said commission at figures named:

Lot No.	Block No.	Appraised value.	Per cent. (50 per cent or 62½ per cent).	Which amounts to—	Amount of this payment.
4	40	$200.00	62½	$125.00	$62.50
5	40	225.00	50	112.50	56.25
8	40	175.00	62½	109.38	54.69
Total					173.44

I do hereby tender to you the sum of $173.44, the same being 1st and 2nd payment thereon in accordance with said appraisement by said town-site commission.

Very respectfully,

JULIUS C. FOLSOM.

My post-office address is Atoka, I. T.

No. 1000 A Exhibit- O.   EXECUTIVE DEPARTMENT OF THE CHEROKEE NATION.

General Fund warrants must be approved by
U. S. Indian Agent.

Tahlequah, C. N., January 196 0

Hon. JOE M. LAHAY, Treasurer C. N.

PAID

Pay to the order of Johnson Williams the sum of

One Thousand 00/100 Dollars

out of the GENERAL FUND as per an act of appropriation, dated August 17,
1897, and approved by the President of the United States, October 10,
1899, and this shall be your warrant for the same.

J M B Springston
PRINCIPAL CHIEF.

Registered G. B. Cunningham
ASSISTANT SECRETARY.

WITH INTEREST AT THE RATE OF 6 PER CENT PER ANNUM FROM DATE UNTIL ADVERTISED FOR PAYMENT.

$1000.00

| 44326 | Indian Office.
Incl. No. 11 | 1900 |

Received Payment on
this warrant.

Remittances must be made to the United States Indian agent by postal or express money order or St. Louis exchange.

The signature should correspond with name given on notice of appraisement.

(Indorsed:) Improved town lots, Choctaw and Chickasaw nations, Indian Territory. Statement accompanying remittance of Julius C. Folsom, P. O. address at Atoka, Ind. Ter., the same being 1st and 2nd payment on appraised value of town lots in Atoka, Ind. Ter. $173.44. Duplicate statement forwarded to U. S. Indian Inspector ————, 1900. No. 594. Received May 25, 1900. Office of U. S. Indian Agent, Muscogee, Ind. Ter.

This statement must be forwarded in duplicate with remittance.

DEPARTMENT OF THE INTERIOR,
UNITED STATES INDIAN SERVICE,
Sterrett, Indian Territory, Oct. 1st, 1900.

J. BLAIR SHOENFELT,
United States Indian Agent, Muskogee, Indian Territory.

SIR: I do hereby certify that the following-described lots, situated in the town of Sterrett, Choctaw Nation, Indian Territory, having been sold to me by the Choctaw town-site commission at prices named:

Lot No.	Block No.	Sold for—	Amt. of this payment.
1	125	25.00	6.2
2	125	25.00	6.2
3 (fractional)	125	20.00	5.0
4	125	25.00	6.2
5	125	25.00	6.25
6	125	25.00	6.25
Total		145.00	36.25

I do hereby tender to you the sum of $36.25, the same being the first payment thereon in accordance with said sale by said town-site commission.

Very respectfully,

EVERETT E. TAYLOR.

My post-office address is Sterrett, I. T.

Remittances must be made to the United States Indian agent by postal or express money order or St. Louis exchange.

The signature should correspond with name given to town-site commission when lots were originally purchased.

(Indorsed:) Unimproved town lots. Choctaw and Chickasaw nations, Indian Territory. Statement accompanying remittance of Everett E. Taylor, P. O. address at Sterrett, Ind. Ter., the same being first payment on sale value of town lot in Sterrett, Ind. Ter. $36.25. Duplicate statement forwarded to U. S. Indian inspector ————, 1900. No. 50. Received Oct. 2, 1899. Office of U. S. Indian agent, Muscogee, Ind. Ter.

EXHIBIT S.

All remittances should be made to U. S. Indian agent, accompanied by statements in duplicate.

DEPARTMENT OF THE INTERIOR, UNITED STATES INDIAN SERVICE,
OFFICE OF UNITED STATES INDIAN AGENT,
Union Agency, Muskogee, Indian Territory, May 25, 1900.

JULIUS C. FOLSOM,
Atoka, Indian Territory:

I acknowledge receipt from you of postal money order for $173.44, the same being the first and second payments on lot 4, block 40; lot 5, block 40; lot 8, block 40, Atoka, Choctaw Nation, Indian Territory, as per statements accompanying remittance.

Very respectfully,

J. BLAIR SHOENFELT, *U. S. Indian Agent.*

C

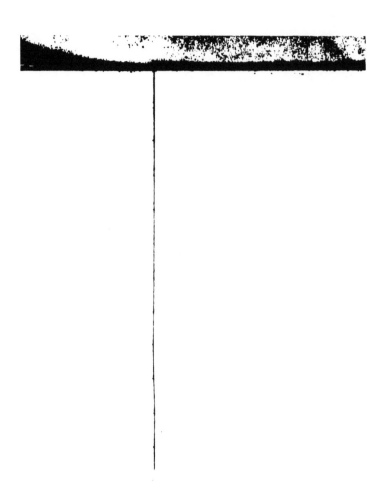

ANNUAL REPORT

OF THE

United States Indian Inspector for the Indian Territor

TOGETHER WITH

THE REPORTS OF THE INDIAN AGENT IN CHARGE OF THE UNION
AGENCY, THE SUPERINTENDENT AND SUPERVISORS
OF SCHOOLS, AND REVENUE INSPECTORS
IN THAT TERRITORY,

TO THE

SECRETARY OF THE INTERIOR

FOR THE

FISCAL YEAR ENDED JUNE 30, 1901.

WASHINGTON:
GOVERNMENT PRINTING OFFICE.
1901.

CONTENTS.

EXISTING LEGISLATION.

In the last annual report of the inspector, covering the fiscal year ended June 30, 1900, an outline of the existing legislation at that time was given.

During the past fiscal year Congress has enacted considerable important legislation affecting the work of the adjustment of affairs in the Indian Territory.

Briefly, reference is herein made to the general laws governing the Territory, together with the new legislation referred to above.

The Seminole Nation effected an agreement with the United States under date of December 16, 1897, which was duly ratified by Congress on July 1, 1898, and no material changes have been made in the political condition of said nation during the past year. A copy of this agreement is attached as Appendix No. 1, page 157.

The agreement negotiated by the Commission to the Five Civilized Tribes with the Choctaw and Chickasaw nations is embodied in section 29 of the act of Congress approved June 28, 1898 (30 Stat., 495). The entire act, which includes what is known as the Curtis Act proper, which affected the Creek and Cherokee nations, is shown by Appendix No. 2, page 159.

In the Indian appropriation act approved May 31, 1900 (30 Stat., 221), Congress authorized the Secretary of the Interior to lay out and survey all towns in the Indian Territory having a population of 200 or more, thus taking this work out of the hands of the townsite commissions as contemplated by the act of June 28, 1898, supra, the work of the several commission being thereby limited to making appraisements after the plats of the town-sites are completed and approved. An extract showing the provisions of the legislation above referred to is attached as Appendix No. 3, page 178.

The act of June 6, 1900 (31 Stat., 660), prohibited the cutting of timber in the Indian Territory, except as authorized under rules and regulations promulgated by the Secretary of the Interior. A copy of this act, with existing rules and regulations, is submitted as Appendix No. 4, page 179.

The agreement with the Creek Nation, entered into by the Commission to the Five Civilized Tribes and an authorized commission on the part of the nation, under date of March 8, 1900, was duly ratified by Congress, with certain amendments, on March 1, 1901 (31 Stat., 861), which act of Congress, except section 36, was accepted and ratified by the national council of the Creek Nation on May 25, 1901, and on June 25, 1901, the President issued his proclamation declaring the same duly ratified and that the provisions had become law according to the terms thereof. The full text of this agreement as finally ratified, together with the proclamation of the President, is shown by Appendix No. 5, page 185.

On the same date, viz, March 1, 1901, Congress ratified a similar agreement with the Cherokees, but the same was rejected by the members of the tribe at a special election called for the purpose of passing upon the same by a vote of 2,323 for and 3,346 against.

Congress also on March 3, 1901 (31 Stat., 1447), by amendment to section 6, of chapter 119, United States Statutes at Large, volume 24, bestowed United States citizenship upon every Indian in the Indian Territory. This act, together with a quotation from the original act, is shown by Appendix No. 6, page 194.

Certain new legislation affecting the Territory was also embodied in the regular Indian appropriation act of March 3, 1901 (31 Stat., 1058–1075), the most important of which pertained to the granting of rights of way for telephone and telegraph lines through Indian lands and also through the lands of the Five Civilized Tribes. An extract of this legislation, together with a paragra h contained in the same act concerning the submission of the acts of the tribal councils, and the removal and appointment of townsite commissioners, is also submitted as Appendix No. 7, page 195.

DUTIES OF THE INSPECTOR.

Section 27 of the Curtis Act, approved June 28, 1898 (30 Stat., 495), provided:

That the Secretary of the Interior is authorized to locate one Indian inspector in Indian Territory, who may, under his authority and direction, perform any duties required of the Secretary of the Interior by law relating to affairs therein.

I was detailed and assigned to this duty on August 17, 1898, establishing headquarters at Muskogee, assuming a supervisory control, under direction of the Secretary of the Interior, over the affairs of the Union Indian Agency, and dealing with such other matters as come within the jurisdiction of the Department, save those within the province of the Commission to the Five Civilized Tribes in the Territory.

The inspector exercises supervision and general direction over the following officials of the Department within the Territory: United States Indian agent, Union Agency; superintendent of schools in the Indian Territory; one school supervisor for each of the Choctaw, Chickasaw, Creek, and Cherokee nations, under the immediate direction of the superintendent; the revenue inspector for the Creek Nation; the revenue inspector for the Cherokee Nation; the mining trustees for the Choctaw and Chickasaw nations; one townsite commission for each of the Choctaw and Chickasaw nations, and at present local commissions for each of the towns of Muskogee and Wagoner, in the Creek Nation, and others which may hereafter be created; supervising engineer of town sites, and twelve surveying parties.

Reports, recommendations, and requests for instructions or indications of policies, emanating from any of the above officials, pass through the office of the inspector, who is required to submit his views with such recommendations as he deems proper for the benefit of the Department, through the Commissioner of Indian Affairs, in passing upon matters under consideration. He is also required from time to time to keep the Department informed as to the progress of all work and the general conditions in the Territory in the different branches or departments of his office. The work of the several townsite commissions and the establishment of exterior limits, and the details of surveying and platting towns, as required by the act of May 31, 1900, supra, has been particularly under the direction of the inspector.

By reason of the perplexing conditions and the fact that the laws applicable to the Territory are susceptible of different constructions, even by eminent lawyers and jurists, and the continual increase of the duties of the inspector, the year just closed has met more complications, and it has been a more difficult task to deal with the numerous questions involved, the necessary reports to the Department, etc., than the year previous.

SUBJECTS DISCUSSED.

The different matters handled during the year and discussion phases of the work are given in detail following, and for conve the subjects are divided, with subdivisions by nations and others priate, as follows: Seminole Nation; mining; town sites; tribal nues; schools; new agreements; timber and stone; finances; w payments; miscellaneous; recommendations.

SEMINOLE NATION.

The carrying out of the agreement with the Seminoles, as sho Appendix No. 1, has not required any particular attention c inspector. The general winding up of their affairs, as requi said agreement, I am informed, is progressing as rapidly and sa torily as possible under the supervision of the Commission to the Civilized Tribes.

No matters of consequence have been before the inspector o Indian agent during the year in said nation, with the exception of investigations required concerning the grazing and holding of within the limits of the nation by noncitizens without authority.

MINING.

CHOCTAW AND CHICKASAW NATIONS.

Coal and asphalt in these nations are to be reserved from allo and remain the common property of the tribes.

Leases or national contracts made by authority of the nations ing mines actually in operation on the date of the signing of the ment, April 23, 1897, were ratified and confirmed. Other leases said agreement are made under rules and regulations of the Secre of the Interior.

The mining trustees, one for each nation, represent the interes the tribes and supervise mines in operation under direction of Department and this office, execute leases when applications approved by the Secretary of the Interior, and perform such duties as are required of their position. A change in the personr the trustees was made during the year. Mr. L. C. Burris, the tr on the part of the Chickasaw Nation, retiring on account of exp term, and Mr. Charles D. Carter being appointed in his stead.

The inspector, by authority of the Department, has during the conferred and consulted with the United States mine inspector fol Indian Territory concerning the coal fields. Mr. Luke W. Br who has been the mine inspector for several years past, resigne the close of the fiscal year to engage in other business. His serv had been highly satisfactory to the Department.

There has been considerable activity in the coal mines of the Ch Nation during the past year, and the coal output, as compared the previous years, has increased, as will be seen by a compai statement of such output, shown below: July 1, 1898, to June 30, 1 1,404,442 tons; July 1, 1899, to June 30, 1900, 1,900,127 tons; July 1900, to June 30, 1901, 2,398,156 tons.

The policy pursued by the Department in the matter of grantin both coal and asphalt leases has been such as has discouraged applic

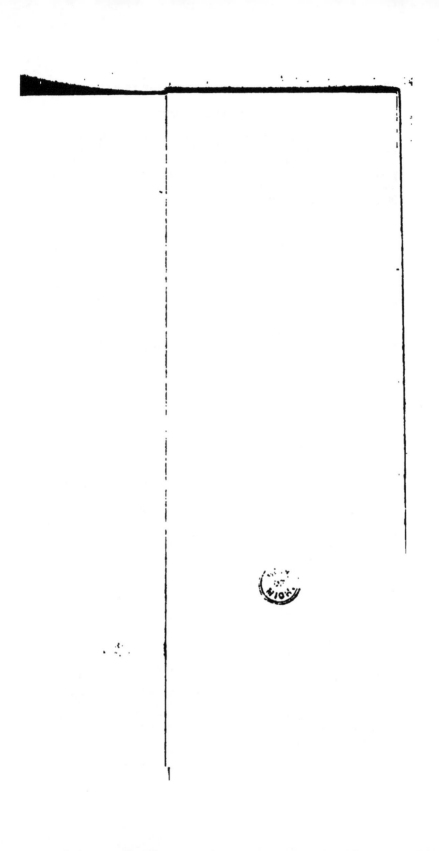

ns for speculative purposes, and the satisfactory effect of this policy
s been shown by the large decrease in the number of applications
ed. Applicants are required to furnish satisfactory evidence of good
ith, financial strength, and experience and ability of the parties
terested to successfully carry on mining operations. The form of
uses now prescribed, together with the forms of application, require
guaranty of a specific output each year.

Under the provisions of the agreement the following coal leases have
en entered into by the mining trustees and approved by the Secre-
ry of the Interior, all in the Choctaw Nation:

Name.	Number.	Date of approval.
ring the fiscal year ended June 30, 1899:		
Choctaw, Oklahoma and Gulf Rwy.	30	Mar. 1, 1899
John F. McMurray.	8	Apr. 27, 1899
ring the fiscal year ended June 30, 1900:		
D. Edwards & Son	3	Aug. 22, 1899
McKenna, Amos & Amos (since canceled)	1	Oct. 24, 1899
McAlester Coal Mining Co.	2	Feb. 19, 1900
Choctaw Coal and Mining Co.	3	May 4, 1900
Sans Bois Coal Co	6	June 25, 1900
ring the fiscal year ended June 30, 1901:		
Central Coal and Coke Co. (since canceled)	1	Aug. 27, 1900
William Busby.	1	Sept. 6, 1900
Samples Coal and Mining Co	1	Oct. 4, 1900
McAlester-Galveston Coal Mining Co.	1	Oct. 18, 1900
H. Newton McEvers.	1	Do.
Degnan & McConnell.	3	Nov. 16, 1900
Folsom-Morris Coal Mining Co.	1	Nov. 22, 1900
Ozark Coal and Rwy. Co.	1	Dec. 8, 1900
St. Louis-Galveston Coal Mining Co	2	Jan. 14, 1901
Missouri, Kansas and Texas Coal Co.	1	Feb. 12, 1901
Osage Coal and Mining Co.	7	May 7, 1901
Atoka Coal and Mining Co	7	Do.
Devlin-Wear Coal Co	1	June 17, 1901
Total number leases	81	

Of the above, Messrs. McKenna, Amos & Amos and the Central
al and Coke Company, after repeated attempts to operate and addi-
nal prospecting, having ascertained the quality of the coal was such
to make mining operations on the lands covered by their leases
profitable, requested that they be permitted to relinquish such
uses, which permission was granted by the Department and the leases
nceled.

The following is a list of companies and parties who are still oper-
ing under national contracts: Kansas and Texas Coal Company,
uthwestern Coal and Improvement Company, Hailey Coal and Min-
g Company, Turkey Creek Coal Company, Capital Coal and Mining
mpany, J. B. McDougall, M. Perona, R. Sarlls, Perry Brothers,
ston Coal Company. A limited quantity of coal has been taken out
r local consumption by a few other small operators under informal
rmits granted by authority of the Department.

I attach as an exhibit, marked "A" for the ready reference of the
partment, a map of the Choctaw Nation, showing the location of the
proved leases above referred to, together with the approximate
ation of the several operators under tribal contracts.

The asphalt leases are all located in the Chickasaw Nation, and owing
the limited number of the same, no map is submitted.

The rate of royalty on coal, as changed by the Department to take
ect March 1, 1900, 8 cents per ton, mine run, has remained the same

during the entire fiscal year, and all royalties have been paid at that rate.

Several of the prominent operators in February last petitioned the honorable Secretary to amend the regulations concerning royalties to be paid on coal so as to exempt a class commonly known as "boiler coal," used in generating steam and for other mechanical purposes in the operation of the mines. An argument, stating in detail the contention of the operators in this matter, was prepared and filed by Mr. R. M. McDowell, the general manager of the Osage and Atoka companies at St. Louis, but after due consideration by the Department, together with a report of the mining trustees, and accompanying reports of the principal chief of the Choctaw Nation and the governor of the Chickasaw Nation, who opposed such request, the Department denied the petition of the operators and declined to make any change in existing regulations. The language of the Department in passing upon this matter is quoted below:

While the twenty-ninth section of said act of June 28, 1898, gives the Secretary of the Interior power to reduce or advance royalties on coal and asphalt, the Department considers the amount of royalty now required fair, and that the regulations are in accordance with the law, which requires royalty on all coal mined.

The question of competition and its effects on the different companies operating in the Indian Territory is one for the companies and not for the Department.

Concurring in the recommendation of the Commissioner, you are directed to promptly advise all coal operators in the Choctaw and Chickasaw nations that they must pay royalty on all coal taken from mines by them, regardless of whether the coal produced is sold or is used for operating purposes.

Although another year has passed, the asphalt industry in the Indian Territory is still in its infancy, none of the mines having been developed to any extent, and the outputs under leases granted extremely small. The holders of present leases, however, attempt to explain this matter by reason of the fact that the mines are invariably located at some distance from railroad transportation, and it requires considerable effort to establish markets for this particular class of asphaltum, and also by reason of the fact that experiments have demonstrated that complicated machinery is necessary to properly separate the rock asphalt.

The rate of royalty to be paid on asphaltum also remains the same as during the previous fiscal year. viz, 60 cents per ton on refined and 10 cents per ton on crude.

The following leases for the purpose of mining asphalt have been entered into and approved:

Name.	No.	Date of approval.
During the fiscal year ended June 30, 1900:		
Brunswick Asphalt Co.	1	Mar. 20, 1900
Caddo Asphalt Co.	1	Apr. 21. 1900
Elk Asphalt Co	1	May 3, 1900
During the fiscal year ended June 30, 1901:		
Downard Asphalt Co	1	Oct. 18, 1900
M. & A. Schneider	1	Nov. 23, 1900
Tar Spring Asphalt Co.	1	May 13, 1901
Total number leases	6	

One or two other companies claiming to be operating under tribal charters or contracts have operated to a very limited extent during the year.

The Department, since the granting of the leases above named, has declined to approve any further applications, owing to the undeveloped state of the asphalt industry, but I have been given authority to grant informal permits generally to parties desiring to mine asphaltum, thereby allowing competition and not restricting operations to any particular individual or company.

All royalties due are remitted monthly to the United States Indian agent at Union Agency, and with these remittances the operators submit a sworn statement showing the output of their mines during the months for which the remittance is made. Their books are subject to inspection at all times, and the mining trustees, under the agreement, are required to report quarterly concerning all their operations. In such reports they furnish a statement of the output of each mine, as ascertained by them from personal inspection. This statement is compared in this office with the records of payments to the United States Indian agent and in this manner a systematic check is kept upon the amounts due from the several companies.

During the past fiscal year the royalties collected on account of coal and asphalt in the Choctaw and Chickasaw Nations have amounted to:

Coal royalty $198,449.35
Asphalt royalty 1,214.20

Total 199,663.55

This represents the actual amount paid to the United States Indian agent during the year and will not exactly agree with the report of the output in tons for the year, by reason of the fact that there were numerous payments made which could not properly be chargeable to the yearly output, as various settlements were made on account of back royalties. etc., as a systematic settling up of all accounts was made during that time.

A comparative statement showing the total collected for the years previous is given below: July 1, 1898, to June 30, 1899, $110,145.25; July 1, 1899. to June 30, 1900, $138,486.40; July 1, 1900, to June 30, 1901, $199,663.55.

The assignments or transfers which were referred to in my last annual report, made by the Choctaw, Oklahoma and Gulf Railway Company, of certain of their approved leases to other mining companies, were disapproved by the Department after being considered. The form of lease now used specifically provides that such lease shall not be transferred or assigned except with the consent of the Secretary of the Interior.

Applications for leases under the agreement are made direct to the inspector and no leases are entered into until such applications have been submitted to and approved by the Department. A copy of the regulations of May 22, 1900, which are still in effect, together with a copy of the present forms of application, leases, etc., are attached as Appendixes No. 8 to 13, pages 196, 205, 206, 207, 210, 212.

From the foregoing it will be noted that there are at present 79 approved coal leases in effect, and 6 approved asphalt leases, making a total of 85, and that there are 10 operators who are still mining under national and tribal contracts.

For further details concerning the leases, operations, etc., in the Choctaw and Chickasaw nations, attention is respectfully invited to the accompany report of the mining trustees.

The royalties arising from coal and asphalt in both the Chocta:
Chickasaw nations are placed to the credit of the two tribes i
relative amounts respectively due them and held for educational
poses in accordance with the provisions of the agreement.

CREEK NATION.

Under the provisions of the Curtis Act no formal leases have
entered into by the Department covering mineral lands in the '
Nation. Several informal permits have been granted to parties
citizens and noncitizens, allowing them to strip coal in small q
ties on lands selected by Indians as their prospective allotr
with the consent of such Indians, upon which coal royalty has
paid to the United States Indian agent at the rate of 8 cents pe
the same as in the Choctaw and Chickasaw nations, which royalt
ing the year has amounted to $4,128.22, as against $3,023.27 f(
previous year, showing an increase of $1,104.95.

The recently ratified agreement with the Creek Nation do(
reserve mineral lands, and inasmuch as the Department has d(
that it will be necessary for said lands to be taken cognizance
the Commission to the Five Civilized Tribes in the making of th
appraisements and the distribution of allotments, all coal p(
heretofore issued in the Creek Nation have since been canceled.

It has been held that inasmuch as coal, oil, or other minera
stances in place are a part of the realty, and as Indian citizer
only dispose of their allotments before the expiration of five
from the date of the ratification of the agreement, on May 25,
with the consent of the Secretary of the Interior, the citizer
attempts to make a lease by the provisions of which he dispo
the coal or other mineral in or under his allotment illegally att
to dispose of part of the fee, unless such disposal is made wi
consent of the Secretary of the Interior.

In June last there was considerable agitation near the town (
Fork, in the Creek Nation, concerning the discovery of wh(
believed to be a valuable flowing oil well. Investigation of the n
however, developed the fact that the reports concerning the sam(
much exaggerated, and that it would require a considerable f
expenditure of money to ascertain the character and quantity o
oil. The matter was reported to the Department, and the h
above referred to concerning coal, oil, and other leases was the se(
of such oil agitation, and it was held, as above stated, that any
for the purpose of extracting such oil would not be recognized
Department.

CHEROKEE NATION.

It having been determined by the Department, as mentioned
report for the previous fiscal year, that no leases would be made
the provisions of section 13 of the Curtis Act, no applications fo
eral leases in the Cherokee Nation during the year have been rec

One permit, referred to in my last annual report, was grant
the Secretary of the Interior for fifteen years from September 28
to the Kansas and Arkansas Valley Railroad Company, for the p
of procuring gravel from the bars and bed in the Grand River
Cherokee Nation to be used as ballast and otherwise improvii

property of said railroad, which permit provided for a royalty of 2 cents per cubic yard to be paid for the benefit of the nation. This is still in effect.

No other permits of this character have been granted during the year.

The same as in the Creek Nation, there have been several informal permits granted to both citizens and noncitizens to mine coal in the Cherokee Nation, the royalty upon which has been paid to the United States Indian agent at the rate of 8 cents per ton, and has amounted during the year to $6,326.87, as against $3,856.01 for the previous year, showing an increase of $2,470.86.

The coal mined in the Cherokee Nation lies near the surface and is mined by the stripping process. No other mining operations of any character have been carried on during the year in the Cherokee Nation.

The applications referred to in my last report of the Cudahy Oil Company, the Cherokee Oil and Gas Company, and Mr. Benjamin D. Pennington for a large number of oil leases of 640 acres each have not as yet been approved, and the same are still pending before the Department. Recently, however, the Department has asked to be fully advised respecting the situation of the lands covered by certain applications, upon which they claim to have valuable improvements, and to the end that all parties in interest may be heard, thirty days were granted the oil companies, the Cherokee Nation, and the Delaware Indians within which to make any showing they desired in writing. I was also requested at the same time to make an examination and report upon the present state of occupancy by the company or individual Indians covering certain of these lands in the Cherokee Nation, which report has been submitted.

TOWNSITES.

COMMISSIONS.

Attention is invited to the agreement with the Choctaw and Chickasaw nations pertaining to town sites, as shown by Appendix No. 2, and to section 15 of the Curtis Act proper, as shown by the same appendix, which contains the townsite provisions applicable to the Creek Nation up to the ratification of the new agreement, and also applicable to the Cherokee Nation.

Under the provisions of this legislation the work of surveying and platting of towns in the Choctaw and Chickasaw nations was contemplated to be performed by two commissions, one for each nation. These commissions were appointed by the Department, and about June 1, 1899, commenced their work.

Mr. J. A. Sterrett, of Ohio, was appointed chairman of the Choctaw Commission, and Mr. B. S. Smiser was appointed by the principal chief on the part of the nation.

Mr. Samuel N. Johnson, of Kansas, was appointed chairman of the Chickasaw Commission, and the governor of that nation appointed Mr. Wesley B. Burney.

Since commencing this work in June, 1899, the Choctaw Commission has surveyed, platted, and appraised the town of Sterrett, which town site had an area of 485 acres, including the cemetery, with a population of 800, the work costing $3,235.35. They also completed the same work at the town of Atoka, which town site has an area of 277.18 acres, with a population of about 1,200, at a total cost of $1,768.94. They also have been engaged, after the completion of the work at Atoka on November 6, 1899, the remainder of the time until about June 1, 1901, at the town of South McAlester, at which town the work cost, approximately, after deducting an estimated amount chargeable to the supervision of the platting of the towns of Guertie, Kiowa, Calvin, and Poteau, which work was done under the supervision of the commission at the expense of the towns, $12,000.

The four towns last above named, Guertie, Kiowa, Calvin, and Poteau, prepared plats of their town sites under the supervision of the commission at their own expense, which plats have been approved by the Department, and appraisements made by this commission, who report an expense of approximately $5,000, chargeable to the work of establishing the limits of these four towns, supervising the surveying, platting, and appraising the same. This commission, about June 30 last, completed its appraisements at South McAlester and Poteau.

The Chickasaw Commission, after commencing in 1899, surveyed, platted, and appraised the town of Colbert, having an area of 129.77 acres and a population of something over 200, at an expense of $4,029.38. This work was completed about August 29, 1899, after which time the commission was engaged to February 14, 1901, in platting the town of Ardmore, which townsite has an area of 2,262.14 acres, including the cemetery, and a population of about 6,000, which work cost, up to the date of the furlough of the commission, approximately, $16,000.

It was ascertained that the plat of the town of Ardmore, as prepared by this commission, was inaccurate, and that it was necessary to make an entire resurvey of the town, and the commission was therefore, on February 14, 1901, indefinitely furloughed and no further service performed by such commission during the remainder of the fiscal year. The chairman of this commission, Mr. Samuel N. Johnson, was relieved by the Department. The surveying and platting of the town was done by direction of the honorable Secretary of the Interior under the existing legislation contained in the act of Congress approved May 31, 1900, which provides:

* * * the Secretary of the Interior is hereby authorized, under rules and regulations to be prescribed by him, to survey, lay out, and plat into town lots, streets, alleys, and parks, the sites of such towns and villages in the Choctaw, Chickasaw, Creek, and Cherokee nations, as may at that time have a population of 200 or more, in such manner as will best subserve the then present needs and the reasonable prospective growth of such towns.

In April, 1899, a commission was appointed for the town of Muskogee, in the Creek Nation; under the provisions of the Curtis Act, consisting of Mr. Dwight W. Tuttle, of Connecticut, chairman, Mr. John Adams, on behalf of the town, and Mr. Benjamin Marshall, representing the nation.

The plat of the Muskogee townsite, as prepared by this commission, was approved June 4, 1900, and the appraisements made under the provisions of the Curtis Act, which provides that all unimproved lots shall be sold at public auction. An application was made to the United States court by a citizen holder of an unimproved lot, in conjunction with the principal chief, for a restraining order enjoining the commission from advertising and selling any of the lots, alleging illegality of the Curtis Act, and claiming that the nation had not given consent for the sale of any lots or lands of the tribe. This injunction was granted on August 25, 1900, temporarily, by Hon. John R. Thomas,

United States judge, and subsequently made permanent. In view of such injunction the Muskogee Commission was, about September 1, 1900, indefinitely furloughed, and no further action taken looking to the disposal of the lots within the town during the year.

The area of the Muskogee townsite is 2,444.76 acres, and the expenses of the commission, up to the time of its furlough, was $15,843.68.

In August, 1899, a similar commission was appointed for the town of Wagoner, in the Creek Nation, consisting of Mr. H. C. Linn, chairman, Mr. J. H. Roark, on behalf of the town, and Mr. Tony Proctor, on behalf of the tribe.

The plat of this townsite was approved on October 19, 1900, and the appraisements made and completed, but owing to the action of the court in the case of the Muskogee town site no steps were taken to sell or dispose of the lots under the provisions of the Curtis Act, and the commission was, on April 23, 1901, indefinitely furloughed, and no further steps taken during the fiscal year concerning this townsite.

The area of this townsite is 2,700 acres, and up to the date of the furlough of the commission, the work had cost $16,946.70.

Immediately upon the ratification of the recent Creek agreement, steps were taken to reinstate the Muskogee and Wagoner commissions, and they commenced their services in rescheduling and appraising such townsites under the provisions of such agreement on July 1, 1901.

No commissions have been appointed in the Cherokee Nation.

CHANGES MADE BY ACT OF MAY 31, 1900.

Owing to the number and size of towns in the Indian Territory, Congress in the Indian appropriation act for the fiscal year 1900, approved May 31, 1900 (31 Stat., 221, see Appendix No. 3), modified the Choctaw and Chickasaw agreement and the Curtis Act proper, authorizing the Secretary of the Interior to lay out and survey all townsites in the Indian Territory having a population of 200 or more, thus taking this work out of the hands of the townsite commissions, as contemplated by the act of June 28, 1898, the work of such commissions being thereby limited particularly to making appraisements after the plats of townsites are completed and approved.

Provision was also made in the act of May 31, 1900, supra, for the setting aside by the Secretary of the Interior, upon the recommendation of the Commission to the Five Civilized Tribes, of new townsites along the line of the railroads which shall be constructed or are in process of construction through the Territory.

This act also gave the Secretary authority to secure the surveying and platting of townsites by contract, and also authorized him to permit the authorities of any town to survey and plat its own town site at the expense of the town, subject to his supervision and approval.

The removal of any member of a town-site commission, whether tribal or local, in any of the nations, was authorized to be made by the Secretary of the Interior for good cause.

The exterior limits of all towns were required by said act to be designated and fixed at the earliest practicable date under rules and regulations to be prescribed by the Secretary of the Interior, and in order that this work might commence, steps were taken immediately after the passage of this act to organize a force of surveying parties for this work.

On August 16, 1900, the executives of both the Choctaw and Chickasaw nations filed a protest against the action of the Department in its efforts to carry out the provisions of the act of May 31, 1900, in regard to town-site matters in said nations, in which protest they contended at considerable length that such action was illegal and void.   This protest was, on September 4, 1900, duly considered by the Department, and I was advised:

> The Department has given due consideration concerning the validity of the town-site provisions in said act of May 31, 1900, and it is clearly of the opinion that no good reason is shown why the provisions of said act should not be executed.   It is manifestly the duty of this Department to enforce the legislative will as expressed in an act of Congress, unless duly restrained by judicial authority.
> The Department does not concede that the provision of said act of May 31, 1900, is * * * a violation of the agreement contained in section 29 of the act of Congress approved June 28, 1898 (30 Stat., 495).   It is the province of the legislative department to make the law, and of the executive department to enforce it in accordance with legislative will.

The most important ruling during the year concerning the work of appraisement by the commissions was in connection with the question of considering trees, orchards, etc., as "permanent, valuable, and substantial improvements, other than tillage, fences, and temporary houses," within the meaning of the agreement with the Choctaw and Chickasaw nations.   It was held, after due consideration by the Department, that there was no doubt that the law contemplated that the land upon which trees were planted in good faith and which were in a thrifty condition, and such as would enhance the value of the lots upon which they were grown, should be considered as substantially and valuably improved.

WORK PERFORMED, GENERAL.

Shortly before the passage of the act of May 31, 1900, the several townsite commissions in the Indian Territory had been placed under my direct supervision by the Department, and I was directed, after the passage of said act, to make recommendations concerning and take steps to carry out the provisions of the same.

To carry out the provisions of said act of May 31, 1900, and sections 15 and 29 of the Curtis Act, an appropriation was made in the regular Indian appropriation bill of $67,000; adding to this amount the unexpended balance of previous appropriations, there was available for the townsite work in the Indian Territory for the current year about $80,000.

As stated above, steps were immediately taken to establish the exterior limits of all towns having a population of 200 or more.   A supervising engineer and, as rapidly as possible, surveyors were appointed and placed in the field in charge of parties, and the work of establishing the exterior limits was first begun in the Choctaw and Chickasaw nations.

It was first the purpose of the Department to detach from the two commissions in the Choctaw and Chickasaw nations the tribal members of such commissions, utilizing them to accompany the surveyors and assisting in the establishment of such exterior limits, thereby allowing the nations representation in such work.   The authorities of both tribes, however, considering, as heretofore referred to, the act

Segregations made by the Hon. Secretary of the Interior, upon the recommendation of the Commission to the Five Civilized Tribes, along the line of the newly constructed St. Louis, Oklahoma and Southern Railroad.

Creek Nation:	Acres.	Chickasaw Nation:	Acres.
Alabama	80	Ada	160
Beggs	160	Bryant (now Millcreek)	155.45
Henrietta	157.13	Francis	160
Mounds	160	Gray	80
Okmulgee	160	Helen	156.09
Wetumka	160	Madill	160
Winchell	160	Ravia	160
Yager (now Foster)	120	Roff	160
		Scullin	120
		Woodville	160

STATUS OF INTERIOR SURVEYS AND PLATTING.

CHOCTAW NATION.

Plats made and approved.

	Population.	Area.		Population.	Area.
		Acres.			*Acres.*
Antlers	800	182.5	Poteau	1,200	645
Cameron	300	155	Redoak	209	132.5
Caddo	1,200	400	Tamaha	313	142.3
Enterprise	552	107.5	Talihina	400	210.59
Grant	250	131.22	Whitefield	354	100.57
Hoyt	284	97.5			

All of these plats were submitted prior to the close of the fiscal year, but only six were approved up to June 30, the remaining five being approved within a few days after the 1st of July.

Field work completed but plats not approved.

	Population.	Area.		Population.	Area.
		Acres.			*Acres.*
Canadian	554	197.5	Stigler	300	102.33
Cowlington	235	157.5	Spiro	600	225.7
Durant	3,500	1,284	Wister	360	149.78
Howe	1,000	326.7	Wapanucka	215	180
Heavener	250	175.64			

Work of surveying and platting under progress.

	Population.	Area.
		Acres.
Coalgate	2,600	785
Lehigh	3,000	1,050
McAlester	750	759.07

Yet to be surveyed and platted.—Allen, Hartshorne, Krebs, Wilburton.

Surveyed, platted, and appraised under town-site commission.

	Population.	Area.		Population.	Area.
		Acres.			*Acres.*
Atoka	1,200	277.18	Kiowa	250	365
Calvin	250	160	Sterrett	800	485
Guertie	225	160	South McAlester	4,000	2,902.27

CHICKASAW NATION.

Plats made and approved.—Woodville.

Field work complete but plats not approved.

	Population.	Area.		Population.
		Acres.		
Ardmore	6,000	2,262.14	Marietta	1,150
Berwyn	237	191.25	Minco	662
Cumberland	340	173.98	McGee	250
Chickasha	3,500	1,248.7	Pauls Valley	2,000
Duncan	1,500	1,010.07	Pontotoc	264
Dougherty	417	243.13	Paoli	225
Emet	300	170	Rush Springs	490
Johnson	230	90	Silo	400
Lebanon	218	164.92		

Work of surveying and platting under progress.

	Population.	Area.		Population.
		Acres.		
Connerville	217	180	Leon	240
Comanche	600	436.93	Marlow	1,214
Erin Springs	204	110	Wynnewood	2,993
Earl	240	125	Purcell	3,000
Davis	2,000	531.85		

Yet to be surveyed and platted.

	Population.	Area		Population.
		Acres.		
Cornish	210	190.28	Orr	215
Center	510	195	Purdy	200
Durwood	250	140	Ryan	900
Hickory	292	170	Stonewall	240
Kemp	230	120	Sulphur	2,000
Lonegrove	215	195	Tishomingo	500
Mannsville	215	175	Terral	500
Oakland	800	321.25		

Surveyed, platted, and appraised under townsite commission.—Colbert, population area, 129.77 acres.

Towns along the line of the St. Louis, Oklahoma and Southern Railroad, p by Mr. L. F. Parker under contract; plats completed but not yet approved, Woodville: Ada, Bryant (now Millcreek), Francis, Gray, Helen, Madill, Roff, Scullin, and Woodville.

CREEK NATION.

The plats of the towns of Wagoner and Muskogee, which had prepared by the respective commissions, have been approved. plat of the townsite of Mounds, one of the new towns along the li the St. Louis, Oklahoma and Southern Railroad, was also appr the same having been platted under contract, as heretofore referre by Mr. L. F. Parker. The other towns in the Creek Nation, o contract with Mr. Parker, were surveyed and platted during the but the plats had not yet been submitted to and approved by Department at the close of the year. These towns are as foll Alabama, Beggs, Henrietta, Okmulgee, Holdenville, Wetu Winchell, and Yager (now Foster).

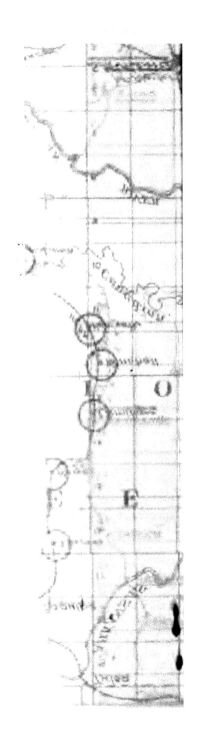

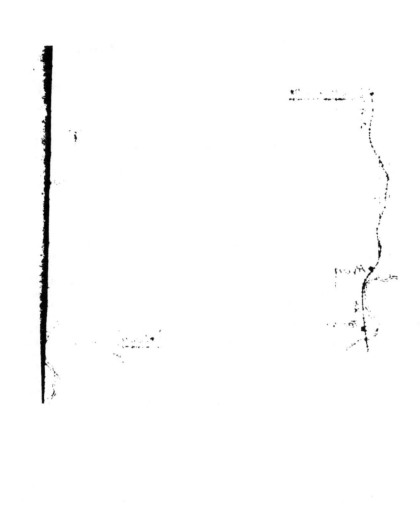

No other steps, with the exception of the establishment of the terior boundaries, were taken during the year to survey and plat wnsites in the Creek Nation.

CHEROKEE NATION.

Owing to the fact that all available surveyors were engaged in the hoctaw and Chickasaw nations during the year, and by reason of the ending agreement with this nation, no steps were taken to survey nd plat any town in the Cherokee Nation of which the exterior limits ere established during the year.

SUMMARY.

For more detailed information concerning the work performed, and he status of the same, I would respectfully invite attention to the eport of the supervising engineer submitted herewith.

A map of the Indian Territory has been prepared showing all the owns thus far ascertained to have a population of 200 or more, and lso the new townsites along the St. Louis, Oklahoma and Southern Railroad, and upon this map the progress of the work on June 30, 1901, is shown, to which map, as showing the location of the towns nd the status and progress of the work on that date, attention is par-icularly invited. (See Exhibit B.)

The townsite appropriation for the fiscal year, including unexpended balances from the previous year, as heretofore stated, was approximately $80,000. The expenses of the four townsite commissions while they were on duty during the year have been paid from this fund: The Muskogee Townsite Commission until they were furloughed, September 1, 1900; the Chickasaw Commission until February 14, 1901; the Wagoner Commission until April 23, 1901, and the Choctaw Commission all the year.

On June 30, 1901, there were twelve surveying parties in the field, a supervising engineer, four draftsmen, and two clerks, besides the Choctaw Commission, and the expense of photolithographing plats by the Department being paid from this fund, which practically exhausted the same, leaving a balance of only a few hundred dollars at the close of the year.

In addition to the work of the commissions, and referring to the statements previously given, the following has been accomplished with he above expenditure:

Exterior limits established in the Choctaw Nation, 25 towns; Chicka-aw Nation, 42 towns; Creek Nation, 8 towns; Cherokee Nation, 29 owns; a total of 104 towns.

Probably 25 towns in the different nations, which had prior to that ime been reported by postmasters and mayors as having a population f 200 or more, upon being visited by surveyors were ascertained to ot have the required population.

The field work of surveying and platting 20 towns in the Choctaw Nation was completed during the year, with 3 under way on June 0. The field work of surveying and platting 27 towns in the Chicka-aw Nation, including 10 under contract with Mr. L. F. Parker, here-ofore referred to, was completed during the year, with 9 under way n June 30. The platting of 9 townsites, under contract in the Creek

Nation, was also completed, making a total of 56 towns during year.

The cost of the work of surveying and platting town sites, after exterior limits were established, has varied a great deal, according the accessibility of the town, location of the site, general condi and the topography of the ground; the towns in almost every inst having been built up without regard to provision being made for str regularly sized lots, blocks, etc., resulting in a great deal of irregula As an example of the character of work performed, and to show complications arising and the way the work is finally platted, a of the unapproved plat of the town of McGee, in the Chickasaw Na is submitted as Exhibit C.

There have also been a great many delays and complications wi have arisen by reason of errors in the approved plats of rail grounds, and discrepancies in the location thereof, where such gro come within the townsite limits.

It is probably safe to say that the work of surveying and plat has cost on an average about $3.50 per acre, but as the work gresses and the surveying parties become more familiar with experienced in the particular class of work of surveying towns wh are already built up, the expense is materially reduced, as will noted by the cases cited in the supervising engineer's report.

Several attempts have been made under that provision of the act May 31, 1900, which authorizes the Secretary of the Interior to al towns to survey and plat their own townsites at the expense of s towns, by the citizens and authorities of towns in the Choctaw Chickasaw nations to make such surveys at their own expense, un the direction of the Department, but such attempts have in ne every instance proven a failure, as incompetent surveyors have b engaged and the work both carelessly and inaccurately done, result in the surveyors of the Department being required to make en resurveys of such towns. There have been, however, a few excepti to this rule, viz, Calvin, Guertie, Kiowa, and Poteau, in the Choc Nation. The plats of these four towns, after being corrected in mi details, were allowed to pass and approved by the Department.

When plats of townsites are approved a number of photolithograp copies of each are made, which are placed on sale at a nominal pr sufficient to pay for the cost of the same, which allows the reside of the towns to procure official copies of such plats.

TRIBAL REVENUES.

By laws enacted by the councils and legislatures of the several trib noncitizens residing and doing business within the tribal limits of respective nations are required to pay certain amounts for the pr lege of so doing. The only penalty, however, for failure or refu to pay such tribal taxes or permits is removal by the Interior Dep ment, under section 2149, Revised Statutes of the United States.

This has caused constant friction between noncitizens and tr authorities, and in view of the continued refusal of such noncitizen comply with these laws, recommendations have heretofore been m and urged that the attention of Congress be called to the condition the Territory as respecting taxes.

An appropriation was embodied in the Indian appropriation

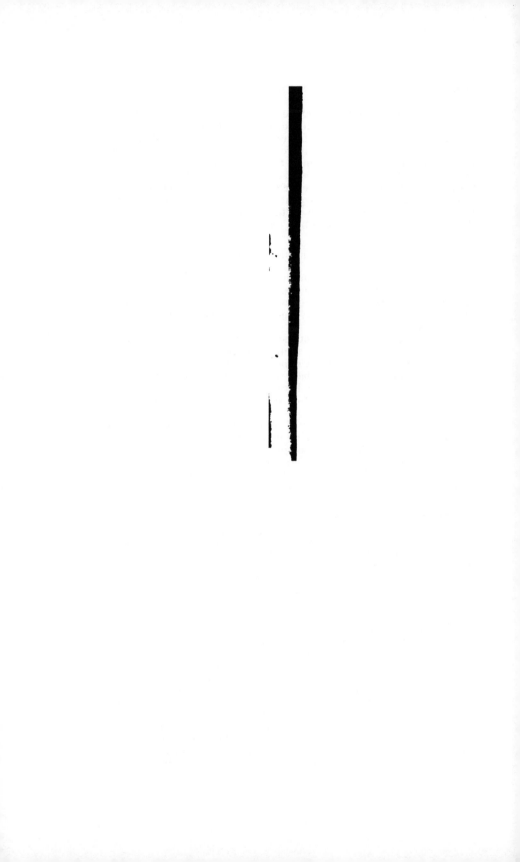

for the fiscal year 1902 of $5,000 to enable the Secretary of the Interior to investigate and report to Congress whether it is practicable to provide a system of taxation of personal property, occupations, franchises, etc., in the Indian Territory sufficient to maintain a system of free schools for all the children of the Territory. In order to ascertain information desired the Department has appointed Mr. Frank C. Churchill, who has heretofore been the revenue inspector for the Cherokee Nation, and it is urgently recommended that some action to relieve the present situation pertaining to the tribal permit laws in the Indian Territory be taken by Congress at as early a date as practicable.

CHOCTAW AND CHICKASAW NATIONS.

There has been no change in the tribal laws of the Choctaw and Chickasaw nations during the past year which affect the permits required from noncitizens residing and doing business within the limits of such nations, and my last annual report outlined in detail the several classes of permits.

Under the existing agreement the tribal authorities collect the revenues and taxes, as required by their respective laws, but have no way of enforcing payment except by appealing to the Interior Department. Noncitizens in both nations have at all times, to a certain extent, refused to comply with tribal laws, claiming exemption for various technical reasons, and every effort possible is made to avoid the payment of these assessments.

At different times the names of numerous parties were submitted by me to the Department as having been reported by the tribal authorities for refusal or failure to comply with the laws, with the request that authority be granted for their removal from the nations in which they resided and the Indian Territory, in accordance with the provisions of section 2149 of the Revised Statutes of the United States, which provides:

The Commissioner of Indian Affairs is authorized and required, with the approval of the Secretary of the Interior, to remove from any tribal reservation any person being therein without authority of law, or whose presence within the limits of the reservation may, in the judgment of the Commissioner, be detrimental to the peace and welfare of the Indians, and may employ for the purpose such force as may be necessary to enable the agent to effect the removal of such person.

The complaints of the executives of both the Choctaw and Chickasaw nations became so numerous that the Department, on August 13, 1900, requested an official opinion from the Attorney-General as to the powers and authority of the Interior Department in the matter of the collection of permit taxes imposed by the laws of the respective nations in the Indian Territory upon noncitizens engaged in various pursuits in said nations. This opinion was rendered on September 7, 1900, to the effect that, under the provisions of sections 2147 to 2150, inclusive, of the Revised Statutes of the United States, it is the duty of the Interior Department, within any of the Indian nations of the Indian Territory, to remove all persons of the classes forbidden by treaty or law who are there without Indian permit or license, and also to close all business which requires a permit or license and is being carried on without one, and to remove all cattle being pastured on the public lands without such permit or license where the same is required.

It was also held by the honorable Attorney-General that the act of

June 28, 1898, which embodies the agreement with the Choctaw and Chickasaw nations, does not either deprive these nations of the power to enact such legislation or exempt purchasers of town or city lots from its operation, and even if the Indian title to the lots sold has been extinguished, and conceding that the statutes authorize the purchase of such lots by an outsider and recognizes his right to do so, the result is still the same, for the legal right to purchase land within an Indian nation gives a person no right of exemption from the laws of such nation, nor does it authorize him to do any act in violation of the treaties with such nation; that the laws requiring a permit to reside or carry on a business in the Indian country existed long before this act was passed; that if any outsider saw proper to purchase a lot under such act of Congress he did so with full knowledge of the fact that he could occupy it for residence or business only by the consent of the Indians. The full text of this opinion is shown by Appendix No. 14, page 213.

The Department in advising me of such opinion directed that public notice be given embodying the holding of the Attorney-General, which notice was given September 18, 1900, as follows:

To whom it may concern:

In compliance with instructions from the honorable Secretary of the Interior, notice is hereby given to all noncitizens residing or located in the Choctaw and Chickasaw nations that the tribal taxes as prescribed by the laws of said nations are held to be legal, and that parties refusing to pay the same are liable to removal from the limits of said nations.

All persons liable for such taxes refusing to pay the same to the duly authorized agents of the Choctaw and Chickasaw nations within ten (10) days from this date, or as soon thereafter as demand for same is made, will be reported to the Department as directed.

The principal chief of the Choctaw Nation and the governor of the Chickasaw Nation have been advised to report the names of all persons refusing or declining to make such payment on demand after the expiration of ten days from September 18, 1900.

The letter from the honorable Secretary of the Interior on this subject is as follows:

DEPARTMENT OF THE INTERIOR,
Washington, September 12, 1900.

THE UNITED STATES INDIAN INSPECTOR FOR THE INDIAN TERRITORY,
Muskogee, Ind. Ter.

SIR: Referring to your several communications requesting authority to remove certain parties from the Chickasaw and Choctaw nations upon the request of the executives thereof, for the reason that said parties have failed and refused to pay the tribal taxes due said nations for permission to reside and carry on business therein, you are advised that on the 13th ultimo the Department requested an opinion from the Attorney-General "as to the duties, powers, and authority of this Department in the matter of the collection of permit taxes imposed by the laws of the respective Indian nations in the Indian Territory, known as the Five Civilized Tribes, upon noncitizens engaged in various pursuits within the territorial limits of such nations." The Attorney-General was requested to answer the following questions:

"Have these nations the right to require noncitizens to pay a permit tax or license fee for the privilege of engaging in business within their boundaries?

"Does the provision of the act of June 28, 1898, allowing other than citizens to purchase town lots occupied by them, constitute a recognition by Congress of their right to be and remain in such nation and have the effect of relieving them from the payment of the permit tax?

"Does the actual purchase of a town or city lot, sold under the provisions of the act of June 28, 1898, relieve a noncitizen from the payment of such tax or fee?

"Can a noncitizen be lawfully permitted to hold and pasture cattle upon the lands of such nation without paying the tax prescribed by the nation for such privilege?

"Has this Department authority under the law to remove a noncitizen who refuses to pay such tax?

"Has it authority in the case of a merchant refusing to pay such tax to close his place of business or to remove his stock of merchandise beyond the limits of the nation?

"Did the Indian Territory, by reason of the provisions of the act of June 28, 1898, authorizing the sale of town lots to noncitizens, cease to be Indian country, so that the provisions of sections 2147–2150, Revised Statutes, do not apply thereto?

"Will the lands of any nation in which a town or city is located cease to be Indian country, so as to remove them from the jurisdiction and operation of these tribal laws, when the lots in such town or city shall have been sold under the provisions of said act of 1898?

"What is the full scope of the authority and duty of this Department in the premises under the treaties with these nations and the laws of the United States regulating trade and intercourse with the Indians?"

On the 7th instant the Attorney-General rendered his opinion, pursuant to said request, in which he held among other things, that under the provisions of sections 2147 to 2150, inclusive, of the Revised Statutes of the United States, "the authority and duty of the Interior Department is, within any of these Indian nations, to remove all persons of the classes forbidden by treaty or law who are there without Indian permit or license; to close all business which requires a permit or license and is being carried on there without one; and to remove all cattle being pastured on the public land without Indian permit or license, where such license or permit is required."

The Attorney-General suggests, however, that on account of the number of persons engaged in business, and the large interests involved, "public notice be first given to all persons residing or carrying on business without an Indian permit or license, where for such residence or business such permit is required, that unless such permit or license be obtained by a short day to be named such persons will be removed and such business closed; and in case of cattle pastured without permission, where permission is required, such cattle will be removed from within the nation."

You are therefore directed to cause public notice to be given as suggested by the Attorney-General, and you will fix the time therein at ten days from the date thereof, after which all such persons failing to pay the tribal taxes will be removed from the nation and their places of business will be closed, and that cattle being pastured on the public land without the payment of the tribal tax will be removed from the particular nation in which they are being pastured.

If at the expiration of said ten days any person, persons, or corporation has failed or refused to comply with the requirements in said notice you will report the names of such persons to the Department, in order that action may be taken under the provisions of sections 2147 to 2150, inclusive.

In view of the opinion rendered by the Attorney-General the Department expresses the hope that it will be unnecessary to resort to summary measures as above indicated.

A copy of said opinion of the Attorney-General is inclosed.

Respectfully,

E. A. HITCHCOCK, *Secretary.*

With reference to the status of persons having purchased town lots, the honorable Attorney-General, in his opinion of September 7, referred to by the honorable Secretary of the Interior, states in part as follows:

"Nor does the act of June 28, 1898 (30 Stat., 495), either deprive these nations of the power to enact such legislation or exempt purchasers of town or city lots from its operation; * * * and even if the Indian title to the particular lots sold has been extinguished, and conceding that the statute authorizes the purchase of such lots by any outsider, and recognizes his right to do so, the result is still the same, for the legal right to purchase land within an Indian nation gives to the purchaser no right of exemption from the laws of such nation, nor does it authorize him to do any act in violation of the treaties with such nation. These laws requiring a permit to reside or carry on business in the Indian country existed long before and at the time this act was passed. If any outsider saw proper to purchase a town lot under this act of Congress he did so with full knowledge that he could occupy it for residence or business only by permission from the Indians. * * * All that this act does in this respect is to give the consent of the United States to such purchase, with the assumption that the purchaser if he wishes to occupy will comply with the local laws, just as in other cases. The United States might sell lands which it holds in a State, but it would be a strange contention that this gave the purchaser any immunity from local laws or local taxation. The case is much like that of a Federal license to manufacture and sell spirituous liquors, which while good as against the United States confers no right where such manufacture and sale are forbidden. This act was passed with the full knowledge of these laws of the Indian nations, approved by the President and having the full force of laws, and had Congress intended to nullify these laws, or take away the power to enact them, or to exempt the purchasers of lots or any other persons from their operation, it is quite safe to say it would have done so by provisions very different from those in the act of 1898.''

As above quoted, the Department expresses the hope that it will be unnecessary to resort to summary measures, as indicated in the letter of the honorable Secretary, in view of the opinion rendered by the Assistant Attorney-General for the Interior Department to the same effect, public notice of which has heretofore been given.

Very respectfully,

J. GEO. WRIGHT,
United States Indian Inspector for Indian Territory.

MUSKOGEE, IND. T., *September 18, 1900.*

Copies of the same were given to the public press and a supply furnished the executives of both nations to be delivered to the parties refusing to comply with the tribal laws.

After this information was made public and persons fully advised, in reference thereto the causes of complaint in many instances were removed and payments made. It was, however, necessary in a few cases to require more aggressive action on the part of the Department, and in some aggravated cases the removal of persons made under the provisions of the section of the Revised Statutes above quoted.

There has been considerable litigation in the Chickasaw Nation which has arisen from the action taken by the Department in enforcing the collection of merchandise permits and the closing of stores in the town of Ardmore, where several merchants still declined to comply with the requirements of the tribal laws. Consequently authority was obtained for their removal, and on October 13, 1900, the United States Indian agent, through the Indian police, closed the stores of several of these merchants in this town pending settlement. Application was then made to Hon. Hosea Townsend, United States judge for the southern district, for relief, and a temporary order was issued restraining the inspector and other officials and employees from closing up the places of business or storehouses of the parties named or any other merchants in the town of Ardmore. The merchants owning the stores closed subsequently made settlement with the Chickasaw authorities, with the exception of one 'man, Mr. Jake Bodovitz, who, having refused, was removed from the Chickasaw Nation and the Indian Territory. There has been no resistance whatever to the carrying out of the orders of the Department by the people interested, except to test the right and authority of the Interior Department in a legal way to do so.

After the restraining order had been issued concerning the closing of stores a suit was brought by Mr. Bodovitz, the gentleman above named, suing myself and other officers for $10,000 damages by reason of the closing of his business and his removal from the Territory. This suit, together with the final hearing on the application for injunction, was taken under advisement by the court and attorneys representing both sides directed to file briefs. The Department requested the Attorney-General to detail one of the law clerks of his office on the case for the purpose of briefing the same, which brief was prepared and filed by Mr. F. E. Hutchins of the Department of Justice. (A copy of this brief is shown by Appendix No. 15, p. 216.)

In view of the new phase of the question presented by the passage of the act of March 3, 1901, bestowing United States citizenship upon all Indians in the Indian Territory, further arguments on this point were desired by the court. Therefore, upon the request of the Departnent, the Attorney-General detailed Mr. P. L. Soper, the United States attorney for the northern district, to assist Mr. W. B. Johnson, the United States attorney for the southern district, in these cases at Ardmore, owing to the fact that a decision in that case would to a certain extent establish a precedent upon which similar action could be taken in the Creek and Cherokee nations. The hearing of this case was finally reached in the latter part of June, 1901. Upon the conclusion of the arguments the court orally expressed his views but reserved his opinion, which has not yet been rendered.

Concerning the question of taxes on cattle introduced into the Choctaw and Chickasaw nations, steps have been and are being taken to enforce the laws in that regard, and notices have been prepared by the United States Indian agent with my approval, and sent to the executives of both nations for service upon parties complained of, allowing them a reasonable time to comply with the requirements before taking action with reference to their removal.

During the entire year, by authority of the Department, there have been three persons removed from the limits of the Choctaw Nation on account of noncompliance with tribal laws, and six from the Chickasaw Nation. Some of these parties returned to the Territory immediately after removal, and the attention of the United States district attorneys of the proper district has been called to the cases in each instance, with the request that they be prosecuted for violation of section 2148 of the Revised Statutes of the United States, which provides:

If any person who has been removed from the Indian country shall thereafter at any time return or be found within the Indian country, he shall be liable to a penalty of one thousand dollars.

Several indictments on this score have been procured, but no cases in the Choctaw and Chickasaw nations have yet been reached and decided.

Owing to the fact that permit taxes in the Choctaw and Chickasaw nations are collected by the tribal authorities, I am unable to furnish any data concerning the amounts paid in these two nations.

CREEK NATION.

A new permit law was enacted by the national council of the Creek Nation in November, 1900, and was duly approved by the President of the United States. This law reduced the amount on goods and merchandise introduced and offered for sale from 1 per cent of the first cost of such goods to one-half of 1 per cent. Other assessments on physicians, lawyers, and other professionals or tradesmen remain practically the same as before.

This permit law provided specifically that parties desiring to engage in any manner of business in the Creek Nation must get permission from the United States Government and pay to the United States Indian agent at Union Agency the amount fixed, quarterly, and that should any person refuse to pay such amount he should be reported to the United States authorities for removal.

In my last annual report attention was invited to the test case instituted by noncitizen attorneys in the Creek Nation concerning the legality of the Creek tribal taxes, which case was entitled Maxey v. Wright, and was decided by the United States court of appeals in the

Indian Territory affirming a decision of the lower court sustaining the position of the Government (54 S. W. Rep., 807).   This opinion was given in full as an appendix to my last report.   This case was appealed from the court of appeals in the Indian Territory to the United States circuit court of appeals for the eighth district at St. Louis, and affirmed by said court.

In view of the decision in this case and the passage and approval of the new permit law, heretofore referred to, not so much radical opposition has been encountered in the collection of the tribal taxes in the Creek Nation during the year, and it has been necessary to take arbitrary action in but two cases, these parties being removed under the provisions of section 2149 of the Revised Statutes of the United States for refusal to pay.   In these cases the parties immediately returned after removal, and suits were instituted in the United States court for violation of the provisions of section 2148 of the Revised Statutes.   When brought to trial before Hon. Joseph A. Gill, judge of the United States court for the northern district of Indian Territory, in May last, both defendants, Dr. D. M. Pate and Mr. J. J. Sisson, entered pleas of guilty, which were accepted by the court, and upon the payment of all back taxes and the costs in the respective cases such cases were stricken from the docket.   The action in these two cases has had its effect, and at the present time so much difficulty is not being experienced in the collection of the Creek revenues.

The taxes in the Creek Nation, as heretofore stated, are collected by the Government, and a revenue inspector, the same as for the previous year, has been employed to ascertain payments due and to take such other steps necessary to cause payments to be promptly made to the United States Indian agent   During the previous years the revenue inspector had the assistance of three district inspectors, but after the work had been systematized the services of these assistant inspectors were dispensed with.

The expenses of the revenue inspector are paid from the collections made, as authorized by a recent act of the Creek national council.

There are at present, as shown by the report of the revenue inspector, within the limits of the Creek Nation 38 towns, villages, or trading posts where those subject to the operation of the Creek permit law are engaged in business, and the list of persons subject to the operation of such law include the names of 827 individuals or firms.

There has been collected from all sources in the Creek Nation from July 1, 1900, to June 30, 1901, the sum of $30,827.60, arising as follows:

Coal royalty	$4,128.22	Timber royalty	$4,313.50
Pasture and cattle revenues	1,950.00	Insurance	909.01
Merchandise	14,247.98		
Occupation	5,109.37	Total	30,827.60
Stone royalty	169.52		

The expenses of the revenue inspector for this year aggregate $4,230.82, leaving, after deducting this amount and exchange of $52.32, a net balance of $26,544.46 to the credit of the nation.

The similar expenses of the revenue inspector for the preceding year amounted to $4,884.52, showing a decrease in expenditures for the past year; and the following comparative statement, showing the total amounts collected for fiscal years 1899, 1900, and 1901, shows a material increase in the receipts: July 1, 1898, to June 30, 1899,

14,913.63; July 1, 1899, to June 30, 1900, $26,370.19; July 1, 1900, to June 30, 1901, $30,827.60.

The funds which are deposited to the credit of the tribe on account of revenues collected, as above, are used in the payment of the outstanding indebtedness of the nation, which payments are made semiannually by the United States Indian agent, together with the general interest funds of the tribe.

The new agreement with the Creeks, which went into effect May 25, 1901, does not in any material way modify the tribal tax laws, with the exception that cattle grazed upon lands regularly selected by Creek citizens are not liable to tribal taxes, but when cattle are introduced into the Creek Nation and grazed on land not selected by Creek citizens, the Secretary of the Interior is authorized to collect from the owners thereof a reasonable grazing tax for the benefit of the tribe. The agreement also provides that there should be no permit tax upon noncitizens for the privilege of renting lands for agricultural purposes.

While the results of the collection of tribal taxes in the Creek Nation have been gratifying, it has required constant diligence on the part of the revenue inspector, and, while payments have in the end been made, it has been necessary to repeatedly request parties to make the same, as such payments are usually delayed as long as possible. The revenue inspector has therefore been compelled to keep in close touch with the business of each particular noncitizen engaged in business in the nation, visiting all parties personally from time to time and giving them notice by use of the mails.

CHEROKEE NATION.

In the existing tribal tax laws in the Cherokee Nation no changes have been made within the past year. As noted in my last report, the Department held that under the provisions of the act of Congress approved June 28, 1898 (30 Stat., 495), which act still remains in force in the Cherokee Nation, in view of the fact that no agreement has been ratified in said nation, the tribal authorities in this nation are prohibited from receiving or collecting revenues required to be paid under their laws, and it therefore became the duty of the Secretary of the Interior, under rules and regulations to be prescribed by him, to collect such revenues and place the same to the credit of the tribe. The same as in the Creek Nation, in order to see that these revenues were properly paid to the United States Indian agent, a revenue inspector for the Cherokee Nation has been employed, whose duty has been similar to the inspector for the Creek Nation. As their services were deemed no longer necessary, the district inspectors employed during the previous year were dispensed with also in the Cherokee Nation.

The laws of the Cherokee Nation provide for a tax on merchandise introduced by Indian citizens, which is different in that regard from the laws of any other of the Five Civilized Tribes. During the summer of 1900 there was much opposition to this merchandise tax from Cherokee citizens, and as will be seen by reference to my last annual report, the authority of the Department to enforce the collection of this tax from Cherokee citizens was tested in the United States court by a case brought by one W. C. Rogers, which case was decided on September 3, 1900, by Hon. Joseph A. Gill, United States judge for the northern district of the Indian Territory, and a perpetual injunc-

Indian Territory affirming a decision of the lower court sustaining the position of the Government (54 S. W. Rep., 807). This opinion was given in full as an appendix to my last report. This case was appealed from the court of appeals in the Indian Territory to the United States circuit court of appeals for the eighth district at St. Louis, and affirmed by said court.

In view of the decision in this case and the passage and approval of the new permit law, heretofore referred to, not so much radical opposition has been encountered in the collection of the tribal taxes in the Creek Nation during the year, and it has been necessary to take arbitrary action in but two cases, these parties being removed under the provisions of section 2149 of the Revised Statutes of the United States for refusal to pay. In these cases the parties immediately returned after removal, and suits were instituted in the United States court for violation of the provisions of section 2148 of the Revised Statutes. When brought to trial before Hon. Joseph A. Gill, judge of the United States court for the northern district of Indian Territory, in May last, both defendants, Dr. D. M. Pate and Mr. J. J. Sisson, entered pleas of guilty, which were accepted by the court, and upon the payment of all back taxes and the costs in the respective cases such cases were stricken from the docket. The action in these two cases has had its effect, and at the present time so much difficulty is not being experienced in the collection of the Creek revenues.

The taxes in the Creek Nation, as heretofore stated, are collected by the Government, and a revenue inspector, the same as for the previous year, has been employed to ascertain payments due and to take such other steps necessary to cause payments to be promptly made to the United States Indian agent During the previous years the revenue inspector had the assistance of three district inspectors, but after the work had been systematized the services of these assistant inspectors were dispensed with.

The expenses of the revenue inspector are paid from the collections made, as authorized by a recent act of the Creek national council.

There are at present, as shown by the report of the revenue inspector, within the limits of the Creek Nation 38 towns, villages, or trading posts where those subject to the operation of the Creek permit law are engaged in business, and the list of persons subject to the operation of such law include the names of 827 individuals or firms.

There has been collected from all sources in the Creek Nation from July 1, 1900, to June 30, 1901, the sum of $30,827.60, arising as follows:

Coal royalty	$4,128.22	Timber royalty	$4,313.50
Pasture and cattle revenues	1,950.00	Insurance	909.01
Merchandise	14,247.98		
Occupation	5,109.37	Total	30,827.60
Stone royalty	169.52		

The expenses of the revenue inspector for this year aggregate $4,230.82, leaving, after deducting this amount and exchange of $52.32, a net balance of $26,544.46 to the credit of the nation.

The similar expenses of the revenue inspector for the preceding year amounted to $4,884.52, showing a decrease in expenditures for the past year; and the following comparative statement, showing the total amounts collected for fiscal years 1899, 1900, and 1901, shows a material increase in the receipts: July 1, 1898, to June 30, 1899,

ources during the year from July 1, 1900, to June 30, 1901, are given
in the following statement:

Merchandise	$2,437.47	Town lots	$10.02
Cattle revenues	1,127.25	School revenue	2,321.19
Hay royalty	6,469.17	Telephones	10.50
Coal royalty	6,326.87		
Ferry charters	200.00	Total	19,392.65
Gravel	490.18		

The expenses of the revenue inspector for the Cherokee Nation are
also paid from the moneys collected, and such expenses for the year
aggregate the sum of $4,038.34, while the expenses for the previous
year were $5,833.01, showing a considerable decrease.

After deducting the expenses of the revenue inspector and the
amount paid for exchange, $37.13, a net balance of $15,317.18 is left
to the credit of the nation.

The following comparative statement is given, showing the amounts
received for the fiscal years 1899, 1900, and 1901: July 1, 1898, to June
30, 1899, $3,150.87; July 1, 1899, to June 30, 1900, $19,455.05; July
1, 1900, to June 30, 1901, $19,392.65.

An examination of the above statement indicates a falling off of the
revenue for the year of $62.40, but owing to the decrease in expenses
it results in an actual net increase of $1,695.14, which, under the
circumstances and in view of the disturbed conditions in the Cherokee
Nation, the holding of the courts concerning revenues due from Indian
citizens, and the general public sentiment relative to the same, is
deemed an exceptionally creditable showing.

The net amount deposited to the credit of the nation is disbursed by
the United States Indian agent semiannually, together with the other
interest funds of the tribe, in the payment of the outstanding indebtedness of the nation.

Attention is respectfully invited to the reports of the revenue
inspectors for both the Creek and Cherokee nations herewith submitted.

SCHOOLS.

CHOCTAW AND CHICKASAW NATIONS.

Attention is respectfully invited to the report of Mr. John D. Benedict, superintendent of schools in the Indian Territory, who has
charge of the details in connection with Indian schools, making his
reports through the inspector to the Department.

The revenues arising from the royalties on coal and asphalt in these
nations are used, as provided in the agreement with said nations, for
the education of children of Indian blood of the members of said tribes.

The agreement further provides that such royalties shall be paid
into the Treasury of the United States and shall be drawn out under
rules and regulations prescribed by the Secretary of the Interior.

As stated in my last annual report, the schools of the Choctaw Nation
were taken charge of by the Government under rules and regulations
promulgated by the Department, and the control of same was continued throughout the year under such regulations. The authorities
of the nation questioned the right of the Interior Department to assume
entire control of their schools under that provision of the agreement

which provides that the royalties arising from coal and asphalt shall be drawn out of the Treasury under rules and regulations of the Secretary of the Interior, and several conferences have been had between the Government and tribal officials in order that some arrangement might be made whereby the schools would be jointly managed, and an agreement has recently been entered into between the principal chief of the Choctaw Nation and the superintendent of schools, approved by the honorable Secretary of the Interior, placing such schools jointly in charge of the United States school supervisor and a representative on the part of the tribal Government; their acts, however, to be subject to the supervision and instructions of the Department through the superintendent of schools.

The superintendent reports in the Choctaw Nation that the work has progressed satisfactorily, and that the boarding schools in this nation will now compare favorably with the average high school in the States; that much has been accomplished in both manual training and industrial work; that the increased interest in educational matters is shown by the fact that the boarding schools have been crowded and that a larger number of neighborhood schools have been maintained than before.

Contracts are made with the superintendents of boarding schools for the maintenance of the pupils at a certain fixed rate per pupil, and the other employees of the schools are paid stipulated monthly salaries.

The neighborhood or day school teachers are paid in most instances a stipulated salary, but in some instances, where the schools are mixed, a certain amount per pupil is paid. The payments of sums due under contracts with the boarding-school superintendents are made on certified vouchers by the Department, and the other expenses are paid by the United States Indian agent at Union Agency.

There have been maintained during the year in the Choctaw Nation five boarding schools or academies; two of these are orphan academies, at which a number of pupils remain the entire year. The school year at each of these academies is nine months, and there has been a total enrollment of 525 pupils, an average attendance of 430, at a total cost of $58,469.84, or $135.98 per capita.

There has also been maintained during the nine months of the year 161 neighborhood or day schools in the Choctaw Nation, with an enrollment of 2,879 pupils, an average attendance of 1,924, at a cost of $34,391.02, or $17.87 per capita.

In addition to these day schools in the Choctaw Nation, there has been an enrollment of 305 Choctaw pupils in day schools in the Chickasaw Nation, the pupils being of Choctaw blood and residing within the limits of the Chickasaw Nation and attending private schools. Teachers of these pupils are paid $2 per month per pupil, making a total expenditure for Choctaw pupils in the Chickasaw Nation of $3,147.70.

The total enrollment of Choctaw pupils, including academies and day schools, is 3,709, with an average attendance of 2,555, and a total cost of $96,008.56.

In the Chickasaw Nation their schools have been entirely under the control of the tribal authorities, and maintained from their own funds other than such as arise from the coal and asphalt royalties. The Government did not take charge or interfere with such schools so long as they were maintained at the expense of the tribe, and as the tribe still declined to consider that the Department had any legal right to exercise supervision over their schools, even if paid from the coal and asphalt royalties, no action was taken concerning the matter until an agreement was entered into, after considerable negotiation, between the honorable Secretary of the Interior and the governor of the Chickasaw Nation on April 11, 1901, which agreement is set forth in full in the superintendent's report.

Under such agreement or regulations the schools are now to be controlled by a board of examiners, one of whom shall be designated by the Secretary of the Interior. Mr. John D. Benedict, the present superintendent of schools, was designated by the Department as such member, and the matter of preparing for the opening of such schools for the year commencing in September, 1901, has been given consideration.

These regulations provide that the school officials appointed by the Secretary of the Interior shall have access to the schools in the Chickasaw Nation for the purpose of advising as to the character and conduct of the employees, course of study, etc., and that there should be friendly cooperation with such school officials on the part of the officials and officers of the Chickasaw Nation; also that no person shall be eligible to teach in such nation who has not been examined by this board, and that no act of said board shall be effective for such purpose unless concurred in by each and every member thereof, and that the outstanding warrants of the Chickasaw Nation legally issued for labor performed or goods furnished for school purposes since the ratification of the agreement were to be paid from the coal and asphalt funds now in the hands of the United States, and that such funds should thereafter be applied for the maintenance of their schools under these regulations.

The report of the superintendent shows that liberal appropriations have been made by the Chickasaw Nation for the maintenance of their schools, and that during the year there were maintained five boarding schools, but owing to the fact that these schools, as stated above, have not been under the charge of the Government, the data and statistics could only be procured through the tribal authorities, and such have only been partially furnished to this time, and therefore the total enrollment and cost of such boarding schools in the Chickasaw Nation can not be given. Such information as has been procured is shown in the superintendent's report.

There have also been maintained probably about twenty neighborhood or day schools, concerning which no information has been received.

CREEK NATION.

The United States Government, under the provisions of section 19 of the act of Congress approved June 28, 1898, had only assumed a supervisory control over the schools in the Creek Nation prior to the ratification of the recent agreement on May 25, 1901.

During the year this nation maintained 9 boarding schools—6 for Indian children and 3 for freedmen or colored children. They also have 64 neighborhood schools, 41 of which are for Indians and 23 for negroes.

The superintendent states that the attendance at some of these schools has been materially reduced during the last year, principally from two causes—smallpox and dissatisfaction among the full-bloods concerning the allotment of lands.

The total enrollment of the 9 boarding schools was 591, an average attendance of 450, costing $50,470.40, or $112.16 per capita, while at the 64 neighborhood schools there has been an enrollment of 2,070, with an average attendance of 957, costing $17,788.28, or $18.58 per capita, making a total enrollment of 2,661 pupils, an average attendance of 1.407, and a total cost of $68,258.68.

The expense of the maintenance of the Creek schools is provided for by direct appropriations of the national council, which appropriations are submitted to and approved by the President of the United States; and warrants for the payment of the indebtedness are issued upon requisitions duly approved by the tribal school superintendent and the Federal supervisor, which warrants are paid semiannually from the funds of the tribe by the United States Indian agent.

The recently ratified agreement with the Creek Nation places the direct control of their schools in the hands of the tribal superintendent of education and the United States supervisor, acting jointly, subject to the rules and regulations of the honorable Secretary of the Interior. Such regulations are now being considered by the Department, and schools for the coming year will be conducted in accordance therewith.

CHEROKEE NATION.

Supervision has also been had over the schools in the Cherokee Nation, under provisions of section 19 of the act of June 28, 1898, there being no ratified agreement with said nation; and the examination and appointment of all teachers and employees are made by the tribal board of education and the United States supervisor acting jointly.

The superintendent states that there is more interest discernible in educational work in the Cherokee Nation, and that the supervisor has visited all the various neighborhood schools from time to time.

This nation provides for the expenses of its schools in the same manner as the Creek Nation, by appropriations of its national council and warrants in payment of such expenses are issued by the principal chief and in due time paid by the United States Indian agent in the same manner.

These warrants, as well as those in the Creek Nation, are approved by the supervisor of schools for each nation before being circulated.

The Cherokees during the year maintained three boarding schools and one colored high school. The enrollment of these four schools has been 686, with an average attendance of 455, at a total cost of $48,275, or $106.10 per capita. They have also maintained during seven months of the year 124 neighborhood or day schools, with an enrollment of 4,153, an average attendance of 2,356, costing $34,460, or $14.63 per capita, making a total enrollment of 4,839 pupils for the nation, a total average attendance of 2,811, and a total annual expenditure of $82,735.

NEW AGREEMENTS.

CREEK.

On March 8, 1900, there was negotiated in the city of Washington an agreement between the authorized representatives of the Creek (or Muskogee) tribe of Indians, and the Commission to the Five Civilized

Tribes, which was presented to Congress for ratification, and after certain amendments was, by the act of March 1, 1901 (31 Stat., 861), ratified and confirmed.

This act provided that the agreement should be in full force and effect when ratified by the Creek national council; that the principal chief, as soon as practicable after the ratification of the agreement by Congress, should call an extra session of his council and lay before it the agreement and the act of Congress ratifying it, and if the agreement be ratified by said council, as provided in the constitution of the nation, the act of the council should be transmitted to the President of the United States, whereupon the President should issue his proclamation declaring the same duly ratified, and that all the provisions of the agreement had become law according to the terms thereof. It also provided that such ratification by the national council should be made within ninety days from March 1, 1901.

The principal chief convened the national council of the Creek Nation in special session of May 7, 1901, and by an act of said council approved by the principal chief on May 25, 1901, the agreement as ratified by Congress was accepted and confirmed by the Creek tribe, with the exception that section thirty-six of the agreement concerning Seminoles residing in the Creek Nation and Creeks residing in the Seminole Nation was passed upon separately and specifically, as provided by the terms of said section, and rejected, thereby eliminating said section from the agreement.

The act of the national council above referred to was submitted to the President of the United States by the honorable Secretary of the Interior, and the President on June 25, 1901, issued his proclamation declaring the agreement duly ratified. (See Appendix No. 5.)

Attention is respectfully invited to the terms of said agreement, as shown by the same appendix, and reference is only made in this report to a few of the provisions of the same and to such matters which have thus far been receiving the attention of the inspector.

Owing to the fact that the agreement was ratified and the proclamation issued at the close of the fiscal year, few steps had been taken to June 30 for carrying out its provisions.

All allotments which had been made to Creek citizens by the Commission to the Five Civilized Tribes prior to the ratification of the agreement, as to which there was no contest and which did not include public property or were not otherwise affected, were confirmed. By the provisions of section 7 such allotted lands could not be sold by the allottee or his heirs before the expiration of five years from the ratification of the agreement, except with the approval of the Secretary of the Interior. This section also provided that each citizen shall select from his allotment 40 acres of land for a homestead, which could not be alienated for twenty-one years. Up to the close of the year no deeds to land have been issued nor any formal requests made by Creek citizens, through this office, to approve any sales of allotments made to them. Numerous informal inquiries are made, however, from time to time by both Indians and others asking information concerning their right to dispose of their allotments.

Section 8 of the agreement provides that the Secretary of the Interior shall, through the United States Indian agent, after the ratification of the agreement, put each citizen in possession of his land and remove therefrom all persons objectionable to him, but to the close of the year no action had been taken to carry out the provisions of this section. The same, however, is now receiving attention, in view of the fact that requests for steps of this kind are beginning to be made, and public notice issued to interested parties inviting their attention to this provision.

The provisions of the act of Congress approved May 31, 1900, pertaining to townsite matters in the Indian Territory, which authorized the Secretary of the Interior to lay out, survey, and plat townsites, was incorporated in section 10 of the agreement, but provision was made that all townsites having a population of 200 or more shall be surveyed and platted, and others may be.

Section 11 provides that persons in rightful possession of town lots having improvements thereon other than temporary buildings, fencing, and tillage, have the right to purchase the lots at one-half of the appraised value.

Section 12 provides that any person having the right of occupancy of a residence or business lot, or both, in a town, whether improved or not, and owning no other lot or land therein, can purchase such lot at one-half of the appraised value.

Section 13 provides that a person holding lands within a town, occupied by him as a home, and also any person who had at the time of the signing of the agreement purchased any lot, tract, or parcel of land from any person in legal possession at the time, could purchase the lots embraced in same at one-half of the appraised value, not, however, exceeding 4 acres.

Section 14 provides that all lands not otherwise provided for, unimproved, should be sold at public auction, but that any person having the right of occupancy to such lands to be sold could purchase one-fourth of the lots into which such land had been subdivided at two-thirds of their appraised value.

Under the provisions of this townsite legislation, the Muskogee and Wagoner townsite commissions which had surveyed and platted these two towns under the provisions of the Curtis act were reinstated on July 1, 1901, and immediately commenced the work of rescheduling and appraising the land in such towns under the provisions of the agreement.

No other steps had as yet been taken up to the close of the year to carry out the provisions of this legislation. The boundaries of all towns having a population of 200 or over, however, had before the passage of the agreement been established under the provisions of the act of May 31, 1900.

Section 33 of the agreement provided that no funds belonging to the tribe should be used or paid out for any purpose without the consent of the tribe expressly given through its national council, except as provided in said agreement. In order to provide for the necessary expenses of the collection of the tribal revenues or taxes, the national council, by an act approved May 25, 1901, authorized the Secretary of the Interior to pay the expenses incident to the collection of such revenues from the receipts therefrom.

Section 37 provides that Creek citizens may rent their allotments, as selected, for a term not exceeding one year, and inasmuch as it was currently reported that citizens were making leases of all characters for longer terms, the matter was submitted to the Department, and I have been advised that such leases will not in any way be recognized by the Department as legal.

This same section provides that cattle grazed upon selected allotments of citizens shall not be liable to any tribal tax, but where cattle are introduced into the Creek Nation and grazed on lands not so selected, the Secretary of the Interior is authorized to collect from the owners thereof a reasonable grazing tax for the benefit of the tribe. Regulations concerning the collection of this tax upon cattle grazed upon what is known as the public domain, or land not selected as allotments, are being prepared and considered.

The Department, in considering the effect of section 38, concerning the disposal of timber by Creek allottees, has held that any citizen of the Creek Nation who holds an allotment regularly selected before the Commission to the Five Civilized Tribes is authorized to dispose of the timber thereon. The same section, however, provides that timber taken from lands not so selected must be under contract prescribed by the Secretary of the Interior.

Section 40 provides that the Creek school fund shall be used under the direction of the Secretary of the Interior for the education of Creek citizens, and the Creek schools shall be conducted under rules and regulations prescribed by him, under direct supervision of the Creek school superintendent and a supervisor appointed by the Secretary, and under Creek laws. It also provides that all accounts for expenditures shall be examined and approved by said superintendent and supervisor and also by the general superintendent of Indian schools in the Indian Territory. If said superintendent and supervisor fail to agree upon any matter under their direction or control, it shall be decided by said general superintendent, subject to appeal to the Secretary. The regulations concerning education under the provisions of this legislation have not as yet been promulgated.

Prior to the ratification of the agreement, all acts of the national council of the Creek Nation were required, under the provisions of an act of Congress approved June 7, 1897, to be submitted to the President of the United States for executive action.

Section 42 of the agreement, however, excepts the general appropriations for the necessary incidental and salaried expenses of the Creek government, and such acts do not now require the approval of the President.

Under the provisions of this agreement it is provided that the tribal government of the Creek Nation shall not continue longer than March 4, 1906, the same date that the agreement with the Choctaw and Chickasaw nations provides for the winding up of the tribal affairs of those nations.

CHEROKEE.

On April 9, 1900, an agreement similar to the one negotiated with the Creek Nation was negotiated by a commission representing the Cherokee Nation and the Commission to the Five Civilized Tribes. This agreement was ratified, with certain amendments, by an act of Congress approved March 1, 1901. It provided in said act that the agreement should be in full force and effect if ratified by a majority of the votes cast by members of the Cherokee tribe at a general election held for that purpose.

This election was held on April 29, 1901, and upon the canvass of the votes the agreement was defeated by a majority of the votes cast, there being 2,323 for and 3,346 against, and therefore such agreement did not become law.

Immediately after the rejection of this agreement the Cherokee council authorized the appointment of another commission to negotiate with the Commission to the Five Civilized Tribes looking to the entering into of a new agreement, but this act was disapproved by the President of the United States, it not being deemed advisable to consider the entering into of a new agreement at that particular time.

CHOCTAW AND CHICKASAW.

The national council of the Choctaw Nation and the national legislature of the Chickasaw Nation authorized the negotiation of a supplemental agreement with the Commission to the Five Civilized Tribes, which agreement was entered into on February 7, 1901, the purpose of the same being to fix a date for the closing of the tribal rolls and to adjust certain complications concerning townsite matters brought about by the act of May 31, 1900. This agreement was submitted to Congress, but to date has failed of ratification.

TIMBER AND STONE.

The act of Congress approved June 6, 1900 (31 Stats., 660), is as follows:

AN ACT to provide for the use of timber and stone for domestic and industrial purposes in the Indian Territory.

Be it enacted by the Senate and House of Representatives of the United States of America in Congress assembled, That the Secretary of the Interior is authorized to prescribe rules and regulations for the procurement of timber and stone for such domestic and industrial purposes, including the construction, maintenance, and repair of railroads and other highways, to be used only in the Indian Territory, as in his judgment he shall deem necessary and proper, from lands belonging to either of the Five Civilized Tribes of Indians, and to fix the full value thereof to be paid therefor, and collect the same for the benefit of said tribes; and every person who unlawfully cuts, or aids, or is employed in unlawfully cutting, or wantonly destroys, or procures to be wantonly destroyed, any timber standing upon the land of either of said tribes, or sells or transports any of such timber or stone outside of the Indian Territory, contrary to the regulations prescribed by the Secretary of the Interior, shall pay a fine of not more than five hundred dollars, or be imprisoned not more than twelve months, or both, in the discretion of the court trying the same. (31 Stat., 660.)

Regulations have been promulgated under the provisions of this legislation, and attention is invited to Appendix No. 4 for a copy of the same now in effect.

Under said regulations numerous applications have been received, the most of which were for the general cutting of timber to be sold in neighboring towns for local consumption and other applications for the cutting of large pine timber for the use of the mines.

After carefully considering the advisability of granting applications of a general character, the Department finally decided to not approve such applications, in view of the fact that the timber was being estimated by the Commission to the Five Civilized Tribes and the value of the same was necessary to be considered in the appraisement, and the cutting would be a continual source of embarrassment and complication in the final allotment of lands; and further, owing to the scattered condition of such timber, it was impracticable to procure a description of each 40-acre tract and the quantity of timber taken therefrom as contemplated by the regulations; therefore the Department on April 27, 1901, suspended the general regulations restricting the cutting of timber in the Territory for the present to props and caps for mines and ties and piling for railroads.

There have been but few complaints of aggravated cases of timber cutting in the Indian Territory during the past year, the law being plain and as a general rule well understood by all concerned.   In a few instances, in the Choctaw and Chickasaw nations particularly, several parties, undoubtedly under a misconception of the law, have cut timber for use of the mines, etc., but the matter being looked into and upon notice from me, their sawmills were immediately shut down and the cutting stopped, and I have been recently authorized to accept settlement from these parties for timber cut at the rate of $1 per 1,000 feet.

During the year, under the provisions of the regulations referred to, only three contracts have been entered into by the United States Indian agent upon applications which were submitted to and approved by the Department; all of these contracts being for the purchase of timber for ties and piling for use in the construction of new railroads through the Territory.   A list of these contracts is given below: Osgood and Johnson, of St. Elmo, Ill., approved December 11, 1900, covering 200,000 ties to be procured from the Creek and Chickasaw nations, for use in the construction of the St. Louis, Oklahoma and Southern Railroad.   William N. Jones, of Fayetteville, Ark., approved May 7, 1901, for 450,000 ties, to be procured from the lands of the Choctaw and Chickasaw nations, to be used in the construction of the Western Oklahoma Railroad through said nations.   Mr. Bernard Corrigan, of Kansas City, Mo., approved May 20, 1901, for 8,000 cubic yards of sandstone, and 100,000 linear feet of timber for piling, and 500,000 feet B. M. of timber for bridges in the Choctaw and Chickasaw nations for the Western Oklahoma Railroad.

The rates to be paid for timber and stone procured under the above contracts was fixed by the Department at 10 cents each for cross-ties, 15 cents each for switch ties, $12 per 1,000 linear feet for timber for piling, $1 per 1,000 feet, B. M., for timber for bridges, and 10 cents per cubic yard for stone.

The Department has considered, and I have been advised, that the timber regulations should be so construed as to permit Indian citizens in possession of their pro rata shares of the lands of the tribe, or prospective allotments, which they were clearing in good faith for cultivation, to sell or dispose of timber cut in such clearing, as stove wood or cord wood, to any person needing the same for domestic use in the Territory.

Whenever parties were advised, however, of this holding, they were informed that this construction should not be abused or made a pretext for the indiscriminate cutting of timber, and that where it was ascertained that parties were cutting or selling large merchantable timber in commercial quantities purely for speculative purposes, steps would be taken immediately looking to the prosecution of such parties under the provisions of the law.

The act of June 6, 1900, supra, still remains applicable to all portions of the Indian Territory, with the exception of the allotted lands in the Creek Nation, the recently ratified agreement with such nation changing the law in that regard, section 38 of the same providing:

After any citizen has selected his allotment, he may dispose of any timber th but if he dispose of such timber, or any part of the same, he shall not th select lands in lieu thereof, and his allotment shall be appraised as if in the co when selected.

No timber shall be taken from lands not so selected, and disposed of without payment of a reasonable royalty thereon, under contract to be prescribed by the Secretary of the Interior.

FINANCES.

RECEIPTS.

All coal and asphalt royalties, payments for all town lots, together with the amount paid for timber and stone in the Territory, and tribal revenues in the Creek and Cherokee nations, are collected by the United States Indian agent for the Union Agency, under rules and regulations of the Department and direction of the inspector.

The total amount of receipts during the year commencing July 1, 1900, and ending June 30, 1901, as shown by the report of the Indian agent, submitted herewith, from the various sources, is as follows:

Choctaw and Chickasaw:

Coal and asphalt	$199, 663. 55	
Town lots	25, 140. 91	
Timber and stone	11, 449. 20	
Total		$236, 253. 6

Creek:

Coal	$4, 128. 22	
Pasture and cattle	1, 950. 00	
Merchandise and occupation	19, 357. 35	
Timber and stone	4, 483. 02	
Insurance	909. 01	
Total		30, 827. 60

Cherokee:

Coal	$6, 326. 87	
Hay	6, 469. 17	
Merchandise	2, 437. 47	
School revenues	2, 321. 19	
Cattle	1, 127. 25	
Gravel	490. 18	
Ferries	200. 00	
Telephone	10. 50	
Town lots	10. 02	
Total		19, 392. 65

Seminole:

Stone		7.71
Sale of townsite plats		32. 40
Grand total		286, 514. 02

The statement below, giving the totals for the previous year as compared with the above, shows an increase in the amounts collected of $89,959.80:

Creek Nation	$26, 370. 19
Cherokee Nation	19, 455. 05
Choctaw and Chickasaw nations	150, 728. 98
Total	196, 554. 22

DISBURSEMENTS.

The expenses incurred in the maintenance of the schools of the Choctaw Nation are paid from the coal and asphalt royalties belonging to said nation, and the larger per cent of the disbursements of this kind are made by the United States Indian agent at Union Agency.

No disbursements on account of schools in the Chickasaw Nation were made during the year.

The Indian agent has also, during the year, paid the expenses incurred in the suppression of smallpox in the several nations in the Indian Territory during the epidemic in the winter of 1899 and the spring of 1900.

Since January 1, 1901, he has also paid all expenses, with the exception of the salaries of the commissions and the supervising engineer, incurred in connection with the townsite work in the Indian Territory, and also paid the other incidental expenses of both his office and the inspector's, together with payments from time to time of the semiannual interest funds of the Creek and Cherokee nations, which are applied upon the outstanding warrant indebtedness, a small payment of Choctaw warrants, and also other minor miscellaneous payments.

The total disbursed during the year under the different heads is shown below:

Warrant payments, Creek	$138, 788. 93
Warrant payments, Choctaw, general	4, 130. 78
Warrant payments, Choctaw school certificates	607. 70
Schools, Choctaw	57, 278. 33
Townsites	37, 263. 08
Smallpox	41, 328. 56
Office, incidental	23, 924. 18
Creek indigents	828. 00
Paid exchange	142. 96
Total	304, 292. 52

WARRANT PAYMENTS.

CHEROKEE.

It is customary, and by reason of a tribal law requiring the interest to be paid annually, for the United States Indian agent to make the payment of outstanding Cherokee warrants on April 28 of each year.

In April, 1901, the principal chief called the election upon the pending agreement for April 29, and inasmuch as the agreement, if ratified, would have carried an appropriation for the settlement of all the outstanding indebtedness of the Cherokee Nation, the payment was postponed until after action was taken upon the agreement; therefore no payment of Cherokee warrants was made during the fiscal year. An advertisement, however, was prepared at the close of the fiscal year after the agreement had been rejected for a payment to commence July 1, 1901, which payment is now in progress, and during which it is proposed to disburse the available sum of $215,157.22.

The Cherokees have four separate and distinct funds, viz, general, school, orphan, and insane.

The amounts applicable to the school, orphan, and insane funds are practically sufficient to pay the warrants issued under these funds. While there is an outstanding indebtedness under the general fund of from $700,000 to $800,000, the amount applicable to this fund is not sufficient to meet the annual tribal expenditures and at the same time pay interest on their outstanding indebtedness.

Attention has heretofore been invited, in my last annual report, concerning the fact that this large outstanding indebtedness of the Cherokee Nation draws interest at the rate of 6 per cent, while they only receive 5 per cent on their invested funds from the United States, and it has been recommended that Congress permit the withdrawal of a sufficient amount of their general invested funds to take up the outstanding indebtedness under this head, which recommendation is respectfully renewed.

The payments of the warrants under the general fund, now in progress, will practically retire all warrants outstanding up to warrant No. A-46, dated May 21, 1894.

Since November 1, 1899, the Department has required that all warrants issued by the principal chief of the Cherokee Nation shall be forwarded to this office for examination against the appropriations and records, and approval by the United States Indian agent so far as they pertain to the general fund, and the school supervisor so far as they pertain to the school, orphan, and insane funds. In this manner a systematic check is kept of the outstanding indebtedness of the Cherokee Nation at all times, and greatly facilitates the payments made by the agent.

CREEK.

All warrants issued by the principal chief of the Creek Nation are, as in the Cherokee Nation, forwarded to this office for examination and approval.

The interest on the invested fund of the Creek Nation is practically sufficient to pay the current expenses of the tribal government of said nation, with the assistance of the revenue collected on account of tribal taxes, coal, etc.

In August and September, 1900, the United States Indian agent made a payment of outstanding warrants of the Creek Nation, and a second payment was made, commencing in January, 1901, and extending along the remainder of the year, making a total disbursement of $138,788.93.

CHOCTAW.

The balance remaining of the appropriation of $75,000 made by Congress from the general fund of the Choctaw Nation, as available during the year, amounted to $5,289.92, and the United States Indian agent has disbursed from such fund, in the payment of warrants approved by the Department, as required by law, the sum of $4,130.78, leaving an amount available under this fund of $1,159.14.

I have been authorized to investigate and report other warrants sufficient to utilize the balance of this fund.

The agent has also, during the year, under his original instructions, paid the sum of $607.70 on account of old school warrants or certificates issued by the nation for the education of pupils of Indian blood after the ratification of the agreement on June 28, 1898, and prior to the date the Government took control of their schools.

CHICKASAW.

On April 11, 1901, regulations were promulgated by the Department, which were assented to by the tribal authorities of the Chickasaw Nation, concerning the control of their schools and the disbursement of the coal and asphalt royalties applicable for educational purposes in that nation. Under such regulations I was instructed to examine and report concerning the outstanding school indebtedness of the Chickasaw Nation in order that steps could be taken to pay the same. This investigation at the close of the year had not been completed, information having been requested of the tribal authorities concerning the number, date, amount, and other information pertaining to the warrants issued for school purposes since the ratification of the agreement, together with a statement or list of those paid by the tribal authorities, and evidence as to the validity of such as remained unpaid. This information has not yet been procured and therefore it has been impossible to make an intelligent report concerning the outstanding school indebtedness in the Chickasaw Nation, and no payments of this kind were made during the past fiscal year.

CHICKASAW INCOMPETENT FUND.

The Indian appropriation act approved May 31, 1900, made provision for the disbursement of what is known as the "incompetent fund" of the Chickasaw Nation, amounting to $216,679.48. This act required that there should first be paid to such survivors of the original beneficiaries of such fund and to such heirs of deceased beneficiaries as should within six months from the passage of the act satisfactorily establish their identity in such manner as the Secretary of the Interior might prescribe; the remainder of such fund as should not be paid out upon these claims, satisfactorily established, to be distributed per capita among the members of the Chickasaw Nation.

Under instructions of the Department, as will be seen by reference to my last annual report, these claims were submitted to the United States Indian agent for the Union Agency, and within the date allowed for the filing of the same 243 were presented, claiming an aggregate amount of $180,000. The agent has had considerable difficulty in ascertaining the facts concerning these claims, and has but recently been enabled to secure sufficient information to make an intelligent report on the same, which report has, since the close of the fiscal year, been made. Detailed information concerning these matters is set forth in the agent's report.

FORT SILL MILITARY WOOD RESERVE.

During the previous fiscal year the ninety-eighth meridian of west longitude, between the Red and Canadian rivers, being the boundary between the Chickasaw Nation, Indian Territory, and the Kiowa and Comanche, and Wichita Indian reservations in Oklahoma Territory, was surveyed and definitely marked, as required by the provisions of the act of Congress approved June 28, 1898. The survey of this meridian developed the fact that it was originally erroneously marked, and therefore the same was reestablished, throwing the line westward and materially changing the boundary of the Chickasaw Nation—throwing a small portion of the southwest corner of said nation into the Kiowa and Comanche reservations, and a strip commencing at a point some 25 miles north of the southwest corner, and growing in width to about 2 or 3 miles at the northwest corner of the nation, was taken from the reservations named in Oklahoma and thrown into the Chickasaw Nation.

By Executive order of June 4, 1892, a portion of the Kiowa and Comanche Indian Reservation was set apart as a wood reserve for the military post of Fort Sill, Okla. The relocation of the ninety-eighth meridian, as above referred to, moving the boundary line westward, threw a portion of the original wood reserve within the limits of the Chickasaw Nation, contrary to the intention in setting apart said wood reserve.

In February, 1901, there was considerable conflict between the authorities of the military post at Fort Sill and Indian citizens of the Chicasaw Nation who were attempting to locate and settle upon the lands thrown into the Chickasaw Nation by the relocation of the boundary, but which lands were originally within the wood reserve, and in order that these conflicts might be avoided the matter was taken up with the Department, with the recommendation that the original Executive order be so modified as to make the eastern boundary of said wood reserve coincident with the new ninety-eighth meridian as surveyed and marked pursuant to law, and an Executive order was issued on March 9, 1901, to this effect.

TRIBAL GOVERNMENTS AND ACTS OF THEIR COUNCILS.

In my last annual report the organization of the respective political governments of the Five Civilized Tribes was fully discussed, and information touching the several branches of such governments was furnished, and it is therefore not deemed necessary to repeat the same in this report.

Approximately the expenses of such governments, obtained from information derived from the acts of the legislative bodies of the same, are as follows, not, of course, including the appropriations made for schools. The items given for the Choctaw and Chickasaw nations are more approximate than those of the Creek and Cherokee nations, for the reason that the appropriations for the necessary expenses of the governments of these two nations are not required to be submitted for approval, but are believed to be reasonably accurate from the information at hand:

Creek Nation:
Appropriations for general officers and expenses..................... $10,450.00
For one regular and one special session of council.................. 32,413.70

Total... 42,863.70

Cherokee Nation:
General officers and expenses.................................... 6,480.00
One regular and one special session of council..................... 19,077.70
Expenses of elections... 3,759.70

Total... 29,317.40

Report of Indian Inspector for Indian Territory. 1901.

MEMBERS OF SO-CALLED "SNAKE BAND" OF CREEK INDIANS.

Choctaw Nation:
Geneneral officers, including tribal courts, etc $67,000.00
One regular and one special session of council 12,000.00

Total 79,000.00

Chickasaw Nation:
General officers and expenses 25,000.00
Legislature.. 6,000.00

Total 31,000.00

Under the Choctaw and Chickasaw agreements all acts of the national council of the Choctaw Nation and the national legislature of the Chickasaw Nation, except the appropriations for the regular and necessary expenses of the government of the respective tribes, are required to be submitted to the President of the United States for executive action, who shall within thirty days after reception approve or disapprove the same, and no act shall be of any validity until approved by the President.

In the Creek and Cherokee nations, the act of Congress approved June 7, 1897 (30 Stat., 60-84), requires that all acts except resolutions for adjournment be submitted for Executive action to the President of the United States, and such acts shall not take effect if disapproved by him or until thirty days after their passage. It was held under this legislation that acts must be either approved or disapproved by the President within thirty days after their passage. This provision was modified, however, by the Indian appropriation act approved March 3, 1901, see Appendix No. 7, allowing the President thirty days after reception of such acts to approve or disapprove the same. It was also modified by the ratification of the Creek agreement, which provides that all acts of the Creek national council shall be of no validity until approved by the President, except appropriations for the necessary incidental and salaried expenses of the Creek government.

Under the provisions of the law above referred to and by direction of the honorable Secretary of the Interior, the acts of the national councils of the Creek, Cherokee, Choctaw, and Chickasaw nations, with the exceptions noted, are submitted to this office and the same are forwarded with reports thereon to the Department.

SO-CALLED SNAKE UPRISING.

During the winter of 1900-1901 certain full-blood Creek Indians, belonging to the most ignorant and superstitious class, and being radical in their desires for a maintenance of past tribal relations and customs, formed what is known as the "Snake Band," with a Creek Indian by the name of Chitto Harjo, or Snake, as the nominal leader. An organization was perfected with the election of a principal chief and other tribal officers, and attempts were made to establish a Creek national government in opposition to the recognized one. Councils were held, and, owing to the threatening attitude of the Indians, it was for a time feared serious trouble would ensue. Notices were posted throughout the Creek Nation warning Indians from having anything to do whatever with the recognized tribal government, and also threatening punishment to Indians who employed white men as farmers or tenants. The so-called principal chief appointed what are known as light horsemen, who were armed, and their action culminated in intimi-

dating parties located in isolated places and the vicinity of their operations.   It was finally deemed the most expedient course, in order to
have a moral effect, to enforce existing law and quell any disturbances
that might arise, to ask the assistance of the military, and therefore,
at the request of the honorable Secretary of the Interior and the honorable Attorney-General, upon the representation of officers of both
departments in the Indian Territory, the War Department ordered one
troop of United States cavalry at Fort Reno to the Creek Nation to
assist the civil authorities in making arrests of Indians for whom warrants had been issued.

The United States marshal for the northern district, together with
a commissioner from the United States court, with the escort of the
troops, went to the scene of the disturbance and a large number of
these Indians were placed under arrest without serious difficulty.

These Indians were brought to Muskogee, placed in jail, and upon
being arraigned before the United States court and pleading guilty to
the charge of conspiracy, and taking an oath promising to obey the
laws of the United States and recognize the authorized government of
the Creek Nation, and to keep the peace, they were, by Hon. John R.
Thomas, presiding judge, paroled pending good behavior, and allowed
to return to their homes.   This resulted in effectually quieting the
uprising and breaking up the organization, and the presence of the
troops in the Territory, without doubt, was a great assistance in
preventing probable bloodshed.

Owing to the general disturbed conditions arising from this organization and other matters, it was deemed best to retain the presence of
the troops in the Territory, and such troops have been and are still
within the Territory, but have been withdrawn from the Creek Nation
and are now located at old Fort Gibson.

UNITED STATES CITIZENSHIP CONFERRED UPON MEMBERS OF THE FIVE CIVILIZED TRIBES.

Congress, by the act of March 3, 1901 (31 Stat., 1447), by the
amendment to section 6 of chapter 119 of United States Statutes at
Large, volume 24, bestowed United States citizenship upon every
Indian in the Indian Territory.   (See Appendix No. 6.)

The passage of this act caused much comment and difference of
opinion as to its effect, but as yet no cases involving this question
have been up in the court, with the exception of a case in the Chickasaw
Nation, where the attorneys contended that by reason of this act noncitizens were no longer subject to the tribal revenue or permit laws.

TELEPHONE AND TELEGRAPH LINES.

Provision was made in the Indian appropriation act approved March
3,1901, see Appendix No. 7, authorizing the Secretary of the Interior
to grant rights of way, in the nature of an easement, for telephone
and telegraph lines through any Indian reservation and through any
lands held by any Indian tribe or nation in the Indian Territory.
Regulations were promulgated under this legislation by the Department on March 26, 1901, a copy of which is hereto attached as Appendix
No. 16, p. 224.   These regulations do not contemplate that applications
for rights of way shall be made through the inspector and therefore I
have no information of any action taken in regard thereto.

APPROPRIATIONS.

The Indian appropriation act of May 31. 1900, carried an appropriation of $15,280 for the incidental expenses of the inspector's and Indian agent's office in the Indian Territory for the fiscal year 1901. This appropriation act, as heretofore referred to in my report under the head of "Townsites," also appropriated $67,000 to carry on the townsite work in the Territory during the year.

The act of March 3, 1901, making appropriations for the fiscal year 1902, carried a sum of $18,000 for the incidental expenses of the inspector's and agent's office in the Indian Territory, and also made an appropriation of $150,000 to provide for town-site work.

QUAPAW AGENCY.

Matters affecting the Quapaw Agency, not coming under the head of the Five Civilized Tribes, are not regularly considered under the supervision of the inspector, but I have been called upon during the year to make one investigation of a matter pertaining to that agency.

Complaints were made to the Department by the superintendent of the Seneca school and the acting United States Indian agent that noncitizens were grazing stock upon the lands of the Seneca reserve in violation of section 2117 of the Revised Statutes of the United States, without the consent of the Department, his office, or the Indians. I was requested to make an investigation concerning the same, which was done, and the matter reported to the Department and brought to the attention of the United States district attorney for the northern district. Indian Territory, for the prosecution of the offending parties.

RECOMMENDATIONS.

The unsettled condition of affairs throughout the Indian Territory must necessarily continue during the transitory period until towns are surveyed, platted, and lots therein disposed of, citizens enrolled, lands appraised and allotted, and the several tribal governments, with their various laws, extinguished.

When it is considered that this Territory contains some 19,000,000 acres, rich in mineral deposits, and is also an exceptionally fine agricultural country, portions of which are specially adapted to the raising of cotton, which fact has induced some 300,000 or more white persons, or noncitizens, to locate here, all seeking to take advantage of the opportunities presented, together with the constant building and construction of new railroads, thereby continually changing conditions, the work of ascertaining and enrolling some 80,000 proper citizens of the various tribes, allotting lands to same under existing agreements; surveying, platting, and disposing of lots in about 140 towns; the enforcing of certain acts of Congress (with the various constructions placed on same and consequent litigation), together with the various tribal laws still recognized, and the final winding up of the affairs of the several nations, is difficult to realize by those not familiar with the requirements and duties involved upon the officers of the various departments of the Government in the Indian Territory.

In every instance, in considering the duties required of the Interior Department, executing the laws and required regulations, action taken only after matters are submitted with full explanation, the same carefully considered in turn both by the honorable Commissioner of Indian Affairs and the honorable Secretary of the Interior, and in many instances by the latter submitted to the honorable Assistant Attorney-General for the Interior Department, or the honorable Attorney-General, for an opinion on the legal questions involved, and the duties of the Department in reference thereto; and in many other instances after having been passed upon by the United States courts in the Indian Territory.

The most important and desired work to be accomplished in the Indian Territory at this time by the Government and all interested parties is the allotment of lands in severalty to the citizens of the Five Civilized Tribes and the final winding up of their affairs.

The existing agreements with the various tribes under which this work is to be accomplished provide that all lands shall be appraised and so allotted that each individual will receive his equal share in the value of the same, to be equalized either in lands or moneys of the tribe.

Being directed to submit such suggestions and recommendations as are deemed desirable for the betterment of the conditions existing in the Indian Territory, I would respectfully suggest that the most desirable change would be additional legislation with the various tribes, if necessary, providing for a more simple manner of allotments of lands than the present agreements provide.

Were lands allotted giving to each citizen a specific and equal number of acres without appraisement, permitting him to make selection where desired, and the balance or surplus lands remaining sold for the benefit of all, as is and always has been done by the Government among all Indians throughout the country, and where as much difference in quality of lands exists as here, it would seem apparent to any familiar with the difficulty, if not impracticability, by reason of the fact that values of lands are constantly changing throughout the Territory, owing to extensive improvements made by railroads and building up of towns, which could not be foreseen, that the work of completing these allotments would be accomplished in a much shorter time, and finally more satisfactory to interested citizens than under existing law.

As set forth in detail in this report, the tribal permit laws are different in each of the nations, and cause constant friction between noncitizens and Indians, as also much litigation in the courts. I therefore renew my previous recommendation that a uniform system of taxation throughout the Territory be provided by Congress, the same to be used for general purposes for all concerned, including improvement of roads and education of some 50,000 children of noncitizens. Under direction of the honorable Secretary of the Interior, an investigation is now being made, authorized by Congress, for the purpose of ascertaining whether it will be practicable to levy taxes throughout the Territory for such purposes.

I respectfully renew my previous recommendation that Congress be asked to permit a sufficient amount of the funds of the Cherokee Nation to be withdrawn from the United States Treasury with which to pay their outstanding indebtedness, which aggregates at this time about $800,000 in warrants, which warrants draw interest at the rate of 6 per cent, while the nation receives but 5 per cent and less on invested funds from the United States.

In the various existing agreements providing for allotments of lands no provision is made for roads throughout the Territory, and as selections are made by citizens for lands which they propose taking as allotments, roads are being continually fenced by citizens or renters, causing much trouble and endless complaint.   I therefore recommend that some legislation be enacted providing for roads, and suggest 30 feet along each side of section lines be reserved from allotment for such purpose throughout the Territory.

In the Cherokee, Choctaw, and Chickasaw nations there is no provision of law at present providing for segregating land for townsite purposes where there are less than 200 people, except along the lines of new railroads, as provided for by the act of Congress approved May 31, 1900.   There are a large number of such towns, or small communities, for which some provision should either be made, or they be advised that such lands will be allotted.   Information concerning the status of each of these places is now being procured and will be submitted at a later date, with specific recommendations in reference thereto.

In the Creek Nation, by provision of the recent agreement, the Indian agent is required to place allottees in possession of their lands and to remove persons located thereon objectionable to such allottee. He is also required to constantly investigate matters in different parts of the Territory and frequently remove noncitizens from the Territory, under orders of the Department.   The only force available for such purpose is the Indian police, who are now allowed by Congress $15 per month for officers and $10 per month for privates.   The agent asks that he be authorized to employ a limited number of policemen and that he be authorized to pay $75 per month for the captain and $50 per month each for privates, together with their necessary traveling expenses, to enable him to procure suitable men.   In view of the complicated conditions and the duties required, I urgently recommend that Congress be asked to make provision for this additional compensation for pay of police.

It is much desired by all in the Territory that Congress enact a law for the protection and preservation of game, which is much needed and which I urgently recommend.

CONCLUSION.

I beg to express my appreciation of the support of the Department, as also of the Office of Indian Affairs, in the consideration of matters pertaining to the Territory with which I am required to deal.

I am pleased to report that the arduous and perplexing duties, under existing conditions, of the Indian agent, superintendent and supervisors of schools, revenue inspectors, and other officers, together with the clerical force connected with this office, have been cheerfully and faithfully performed.

I also desire to state that the several United States attorneys in the Indian Territory—Mr. P. L. Soper of the northern, Mr. W. B. Johnson of the southern, and Mr. J. H. Wilkins of the central judicial districts—have at all times, when requested, willingly represented the Department in the courts and have rendered valuable service in presenting the Government's position and construction of various laws on questions involved.   Mr. Soper, especially, having had more questions on construction of law to contend with in his district, which comprises the Creek and Cherokee nations, has devoted much time and labor in preparing exhaustive arguments and briefs in matters presented to the courts for judicial determination. By reason, however, of the large amount of work required of these attorneys in their own departments, it is difficult for them to give the time required to properly represent the Interior Department in numerous cases constantly arising in the courts.

There has been less friction between the tribal authorities and the Department than heretofore, and a more satisfactory understanding has existed where the executives of the different nations have conferred with officials of the Department. This is especially true in the Creek Nation, where frequent conferences are held with the principal chief, Hon. P. Porter, on questions arising affecting his people, and matters amicably adjusted and understood.

Very respectfully, your obedient servant,

J. GEO. WRIGHT,
United States Indian Inspector for the Indian Territory.

The SECRETARY OF THE INTERIOR.

REPORT OF UNITED STATES INDIAN AGENT AT UNION AGENCY.

MUSKOGEE, IND. T., *September 3, 1901.*

SIR: In compliance with instructions, I have the honor to herewith submit this, my third annual report of the affairs at this agency for the fiscal year ended June 30, 1901, in which I have incorporated certain statistical information.

By way of preface, in order that a clearer conception may be had of the volume and character of business coming before this agency for attention and adjudication, I shall briefly call attention to the area and population of the territory over which this agency exercises jurisdiction; the source and method of government, and the vast forward strides that have been made in the matter of development of the Indian Territory, and the increase in population by these Five Nations in the last decade.

In 1890 the total population of the Indian Territory was 178,000, of which 50,000 were Indians.

In 1900 the population of the Indian Territory, according to the Twelfth Census, is 391,960, of which about 70,000 are Indians, showing an increase in the total population of 117 per cent.

The area of the Indian Territory is 33,000 square miles, an area greater than that contained in any one of the States of Connecticut, Delaware, Maine, Maryland, Massachusetts, and an area equal to that of Indiana, and has a greater population than any one of the States of Montana, Idaho, Nevada, North Dakota, Arizona, South Dakota, Wyoming, Utah, Washington, or the Territory of New Mexico. If a State it would be entitled to two Senators and two Congressmen.

During the fiscal year ended June 30, 1901, there has been disbursed, by this office $304,292.52, and collected and deposited (less exchange of $142.96) to the credit of the Treasurer of the United States on account of royalties and from sale of town-site maps $286,371.06, and in addition I have also deposited unexpended balances of Government funds, or, in other words, returned it to the Treasurer, the sum of $46,028.35; total, $636,691.93.

Below I give a statement of the disbursements made and for what expended:

To pay salaries of school-teachers in the Choctaw Nation and incidental expenses in connection with the management of Choctaw schools	$57,278.33
Paid Choctaw warrants out of the $75,000 appropriated by the act of Congress of March 3, 1899 (30 Stats.,1099)	4,130.78
Paid Choctaw warrants issued to school-teachers in Choctaw Nation for services rendered prior to the Government's taking charge of the schools of the Choctaw Nation, and after the passage of the act of June 28, 1898	607.70
Paid expenses in connection with town-site work	37,263.08
Paid expenses in connection with the suppression of the spread of smallpox in the Indian Territory	41,328.56
Paid Creek warrants	138,788.93
Incidental expenses in connection with the management of the office and payment of salaries of employees	23,924.18
Paid Creek indigents	828.00
Paid exchange	142.96
Total	304,292.52

Hereafter in this report I will, in the mention of the nations, give the total amount of royalty collected for each and the source from which it arose.

LOCATION.

As heretofore stated in my former annual report, the agency is located at Muskogee, Ind. T., on the main line of the Missouri, Kansas and Texas Railway, about 100 miles south of the Kansas line, and 157 miles north of the State of Texas.

The offices of the Indian agent are on the second floor in what is known as the Masonic building, and are owned by and rented from Messrs. C. W. Turner et al., of Muskogee. In the same building, and on the same floor, are the offices of the United States Indian inspector for the Indian Territory; the superintendent of schools in Indian Territory; the supervisor of schools for the Creek Nation; the revenue inspectors for the Cherokee and Creek nations, and the supervising engineer for Indian Territory town-site surveys.

It is proper to add that at this place the Government owns no buildings.

53

CORRESPONDENCE.

The correspondence at this agency during the past fiscal year was voluminous, and is constantly increasing. The numerous remittances require acknowledgment, and complaints are constantly being made to this office against intruders, and other matters are brought to my attention requiring very careful consideration. The correspondence embraces almost every conceivable topic. I try in every instance to give a satisfactory answer to all inquiries and explain the laws and conditions as well as I can to every inquirer.

INDIAN POLICE.

The Indian police force at this agency has been reduced from 1 captain, 2 lieutenants, 3 sergeants, and 22 privates, to 1 captain, 2 lieutenants, and 8 privates.

As a rule the police have been faithful and obedient, prompt and energetic in the suppression of crime, and in informing this office of the names of persons who commit unlawful acts within their respective districts.

The compensation for captains and lieutenants is $15 per month and for privates $10 per month.

I have restationed these policemen so as to render the most efficient service, considering the limited number.

I renew my recommendation heretofore made that the captain be allowed a salary of $100 per month, and the lieutenants and privates a salary of $50 per month and their actual and necessary expenses while traveling on official business under orders. If the salaries just mentioned are paid to the policemen, I think that a more efficient service can be had, and better men can be secured to fill the places.

FINANCIAL.

CHOCTAW AND CHICKASAW NATIONS.

In my former reports reference is made to the regulations prescribed by the Secretary governing mineral leases in the Choctaw and Chickasaw nations, Indian Territory, under provisions of the act of June 28, 1898.

The regulations provide, among other things, that the Indian agent for the Union Agency, Ind. T., shall receive and receipt for all royalties paid into his hands when accompanied by sworn statements, and when so collected to be deposited with the assistant treasurer of the United States, St. Louis, Mo., to the credit of the Treasurer of the United States for the benefit of the Choctaw and Chickasaw nations.

The royalty on coal is at the rate of 8 cents per ton of 2,000 pounds of mine-run coal, or coal as it is taken from the mines, including that which is commonly called slack.

On asphalt, 60 cents per ton for each and every ton produced weighing 2,000 pounds for refined, and 10 cents per ton for crude asphalt.

Any other royalties due these nations, such as tax on merchandise, permit, occupation, and tax on cattle, are collected by the tribal authorities, as was the custom prior to the passage of the act of June 28, 1898.

The revenue derived from royalty on coal and asphalt, or so much as is necessary, is used for the education of children of Indian blood of the members of the Choctaw and Chickasaw tribes (freedmen excepted).

Upon my requisition, the Indian Office places to my official credit with the assistant treasurer of the United States, out of the asphalt and coal royalties, certain sums of money, and I use this in paying the salaries of school-teachers employed in the academies and neighborhood schools of the Choctaw Nation. The Chickasaw Nation has, up to the present time, managed their own schools, and this office does not, therefore, pay any of the employees or teachers connected therewith.

The mining trustees of the Choctaw and Chickasaw nations are appointed by the President of the United States, one upon the recommendation of the principal chief of the Choctaw Nation and one upon the recommendation of the governor of the Chickasaw Nation, each of whom shall be members of the Choctaw and Chickasaw nations, respectively. Their salaries are paid by the respective nations and they are required to make reports of all their acts to the Secretary of the Interior quarterly. No lease entered into by them is valid until the same shall have been approved by the Secretary of the Interior.

I give below a list of the leases that have been entered into by the mining trustees.

date of the approval of the same, and the person, firm, or corporation operat-
same:

COAL.

Name of lessor.	Number of leases.	Date of approval by Secretary of the Interior.
Oklahoma and Gulf Rwy. Co	30	Mar. 1, 1899
eMurray	8	Apr. 27, 1899
1s & Son	3	Aug. 22, 1899
, Amos & Amosa	1	Oct. 24, 1899
Coal Mining Co	2	Feb. 19, 1900
Coal and Mining Co	3	May 4, 1900
Coal Co	6	June 25, 1900
al and Coke Co. a	1	Aug. 27, 1900
iusby	1	Sept. 6, 1900
oal and Mining Co	1	Oct. 4, 1900
and Galveston Coal Mining Co	1	Oct. 18, 1900
a McEvers	1	Oct. 18, 1900
McConnell	3	Nov. 16, 1900
orris Coal Mining Co	1	Nov. 22, 1900
l and Railway Co	1	Dec. 8, 1900
ialveston Coal Mining Co	2	Jan. 14, 1901
Kansas and Texas Coal Co	1	Feb. 12, 1901
l and Mining Co	7	May 7, 1901
l and Mining Co	7	May 7, 1901
n-Wear Coal Co	1	June 17, 1901
l number of leases	81	

ASPHALT.

	Number of leases.	Date of approval
t Asphalt Co	1	Mar. 20, 1900
phalt Co	1	Apr. 21, 1900
lt Co	1	May 3, 1900
Asphalt Co	1	Oct. 18, 1900
hneider	1	Nov. 25, 1900
t Asphalt Co	1	May 13, 1900
l number of leases	6	

a The two leases above noted have been canceled.

are other mining operators in the Choctaw and Chickasaw nations, Indian
, operating under what are known as national contracts, and a few other
erators that have neither leases nor contracts. This last-mentioned class do
business, and the royalties received from them are therefore small. A list
two classes of mine operators follows:
J. B. McDougal, Kansas and Texas Coal Company, Southwestern Coal and
ment Company, Hailey Coal and Mining Company, Pat Harley, Perry
, M. Perona, Caston Coal Company, Capitol Coal and Mining Company,
. Denman, Turkey Creek Coal Company, Choctaw Mining and Mercantile
v, C. G. Adkins, Mrs. Mary A. Ford, Fitchburg Coal and Mining Company,
ie Watkins.
It: Gilsonite Roofing and Paving Company, Rock Creek Natural Asphalt
y, and George D. Moulton.
I give a statement in reference to the royalty collected by me for the Choc-
Chickasaw nations from July 1, 1900, to June 30, 1901:
oyalty, $198,449.35; asphalt royalty, $1,214.20; total, $199,663.55; as com-
ith coal royalty, $137,377.82; asphalt royalty, $1,108.58; total, $138,486.40,
during the fiscal year ended June 30, 1900, showing an increase of $61,177.15.
has also been collected by me for the benefit of the Choctaw and Chickasaw
luring the period ended June 30, 1901, the following amounts arising from
res named:

	$25,090.91
	50.00
lty	122.29
ralty	11,326.91
grand total of	236,253.66
exchange	53.51
	236,200.15

is the net amount I have deposited to the credit of the Treasurer of the
tates for the benefit of the Choctaw and Chickasaw nations.

TOWN LOTS.

Section 29 of the act of June 28, 1898, provides that the owner of improvements on each lot shall have the right to buy one residence and one business lot at 50 per centum of the appraised value of such improved property, and the remainder of such improved property at 62½ per centum of the said market value within sixty days from the date of notice served on him; if he purchase same he shall within ten days pay into the Treasury of the United States one-fourth of the purchase price, and the balance in three equal annual installments, and when the entire sum is paid he shall be entitled to a patent to the same.

The instructions to the town-site commission for the Choctaw and Chickasaw nations states that the United States Indian agent for the Union Agency will be charged with the collecting and accounting for the purchase money on all lots in each town. Among other things, he is directed to notify the town-site commissioners at the proper time of all defaults in the first payment on improved lots.

In accordance with this law and the regulations all payments on account of town lots in the Choctaw and Chickasaw nations are made to me, and this is the source from which the royalty mentioned above as town lots is derived.

After the town-site commissioners for the Choctaw and Chickasaw nations have finished the town-site record book of any particular town, the same is filed in this office, together with the original notices of appraisement showing the time of service of said notices. The town-site commission instructs all persons upon whom these notices have been served to make remittances to this office on account of any payments they may desire to make on account of town lots that have been appraised to them.

I have now in my possession the town-site record books of Colbert, Chickasaw Nation; Sterrett, Atoka, Calvin, Guertie, Kiowa, South McAlester, and Poteau. Choctaw Nation.

Remittances from these towns are being constantly received. It is my duty to see that these remittances are made within the time required by law, that the amount remitted is the correct amount due, and that the person who remits the same is the proper person to do so. The blanks to accompany these remittances have been prepared in this office, and are supplied upon application.

Unimproved lots are sold by the town-site commissioners of the Choctaw and Chickasaw nations, after proper advertisement has been published, stating therein the time and places that said lots will be offered for sale, and when sold the schedule of the sale is sent to this office.

Under date of March 22, 1900, the Indian Office directed that the Indian agent be present at the sale of unimproved town lots in the Choctaw and Chickasaw nations, and receive and receipt for any payments made to him. The Department requires the successful bidder to deposit with him (the Indian agent), at the time of the sale, 10 per centum of the purchase price, which shall be forfeited and be and become the property of the Choctaw and Chickasaw nations unless the said purchaser shall pay the balance of the first installment, one-fourth of the sale price of the lot, within ten days from the date of sale.

Acting under these instructions, I have, whenever unimproved town lots have been sold in any town of the Choctaw and Chickasaw nations, detailed one or more of my clerks to attend said sale and collect the 10 per centum required, or receive any other amount of the purchase price that the successful bidder may pay.

In a recent ruling of the Department it was held that "while it was true that section 29 of the act of June 28, 1898 (30 Stat., 495), provides that a failure for sixty days to make one payment to be a forfeiture of all payments made and all rights under the contract, it is not believed the failure to make payment when due of itself works a forfeiture; that until such time as proper action shall have been taken declaring a forfeiture, the purchaser would have the right to make the payment, and the agent would be justified in accepting the same." However, before doing so, I have been directed to notify the authorities of the Choctaw and Chickasaw nations of the payments that have not been made within the time required by law, for the purpose of seeing whether, as such authorities, they had any objections to my accepting said payments. This requires considerable correspondence between myself and the respective executives of the Choctaw and Chickasaw nations. As yet no definite policy has been decided upon by said executives as to this matter.

This office insists upon a strict compliance with the law requiring that remittances on town lots shall be made within the time prescribed, but in special cases, or where the circumstances are such that the remittances can not well be made, it is thought, rather than work a hardship upon any person or deprive them of any vested rights, that some discretion should be used in accepting payments not made within the time required by law.

Section 29 of the act referred to provides that the commissioners shall locate, within a suitable distance from each town site, not to exceed 5 acres, to be used as a cemetery, and when any town had paid to me $10 per acre therefor it shall be entitled to a patent to the same, and shall dispose of same at reasonable prices in suitable lots for burial purposes, the proceeds of such sale to be applied by the town government to the proper care and improvement of said cemetery.

The $50 remittance referred to above under the head cemeteries, was received from the town of Kemp, Chickasaw Nation.

TIMBER AND STONE.

Under date of July 14, 1900, the Department promulgated regulations governing the procurement of timber and stone for domestic and industrial purposes in the Indian Territory, as provided in the act of June 6, 1900 (Public No. 174).

These regulations require that the Indian agent for the Union Agency enter into a contract upon application in the form of affidavits upon blanks prescribed, when approved by the Secretary of the Interior, with any responsible person, persons, or corporations for the purchase of timber or stone from any of the public lands belonging to any of the Five Civilized Tribes, and to collect on or before the end of each month the full value of such timber or stone as the Secretary of the Interior shall hereafter determine should be paid. The moneys collected are to be placed to the credit of the tribe or tribes to which the lands belong from which such timber or stone was secured, but no timber or stone shall be taken from any lands selected by any citizen of any of the Five Civilized Tribes as his prospective allotment without his consent, and only from such land being cleared or to be cleared for cultivation, and not until a contract shall have been entered into by the United States Indian agent and the persons or corporation desiring to procure such timber or stone. The price to be paid under such contract to be satisfactory to the prospective allottee, providing that the provisions of this section shall not apply to all tracts now in possession of any citizen of any of the Five Civilized Tribes who intend to include such tracts in their prospective allotments. The moneys so derived to be deposited with the assistant treasurer of the United States at St. Louis, Mo., and when the tract or tracts from which the said timber or stone was taken shall have been allotted, the Secretary of the Interior shall cause to be paid to the citizen or citizens taking the said tract or tracts as his or her allotments if found to be entitled to such moneys.

I am also required to keep an accurate list by legal subdivision of the lands from which said timber or stone is taken, and also a correct list of all moneys derived from the sale of all timber or stone taken from each legal subdivision. The value of the timber and stone taken from unappraised selected land must be added to the appraisement when made.

I have entered into contracts with the following-named persons and corporations, under the regulations referred to: W. N. Jones, Fayetteville, Ark., approved May 7, 1901; Osgood & Johnson, St. Elmo, Ill., approved December 11, 1900; Bernard Corrigan, Kansas City, Mo., approved May 20, 1901; Missouri, Kansas and Texas Railway Company, approved July 20, 1901.

The royalty to be paid on timber and stone taken under these contracts has been fixed by the honorable Secretary of the Interior.

In order to properly account for any moneys that come into my hands on account of any stone or timber removed from the lands of the Five Civilized Tribes, I have prepared a record book which shows the following:

First. Name of person with whom contract has been entered into.

Second. Date of approval of contract by Secretary of Interior.

Third. Address of persons securing the contract.

Fourth. Date of contract, and whether for timber or stone removed.

Fifth. Date when remittance was received at this office.

Sixth. The period in which the timber or stone was removed, and the legal subdivisions of the land from which it was taken.

Seventh. The number of pieces of timber or yards of stone, as the case may be; the rate, amount remitted; from which nation removed, and the name of the allottee of the land from which the timber or stone was taken, together with a blank in which to insert the date of the patent to the citizen when the same shall have been issued, and a column for remarks.

There has also been prepared an index book, showing the number of townships in each nation. It is found that the Choctaw Nation had 360 townships; the Chickasaw Nation, 260; the Creek Nation, 165; the Cherokee Nation, 220, and the Seminole Nation, 30.

After the remittance has been properly entered into the record book from the cash book, it is then taken to the index book and the township and section of the township from which the timber or stone was taken annotated therein, together with the number of pieces of timber or yards of stone removed.

In this way, by reference to these books, one can see at a glance the number of pieces of timber or yards of stone that have been taken from any tract of land in the Indian Territory.

I find it no small task to keep these records.

As mentioned above, there have been received at this office, under the regulations above referred to, remittances to the amount of $122.29 on account of the royalty on stone taken from the lands of the Choctaw and Chickasaw nations. The royalty on timber removed from the lands of these nations amounted to $11,326.91.

SALARIES OF SCHOOL TEACHERS.

From the moneys collected by me on account of the royalty on coal and asphalt mined I disbursed in the payment of salaries of school teachers employed and for incidental expenses connected with the management of schools in the Choctaw Nation during the fiscal year ended June 30, 1901, $57,278.33.

There are four academies in the Choctaw Nation, employing about 50 persons. In addition to the above, I pay the salaries of about 150 neighborhood school teachers. These teachers are paid by me by checks drawn on the assistant treasurer of the United States at St. Louis, Mo.

PAYMENT OF CHOCTAW WARRANTS.

The act of Congress of March 3, 1899 (30 Stats., 1099), appropriated $75,000 out of the Choctaw moneys held in trust by the United States to pay outstanding warrants, when found to have been issued for a valid and subsisting obligation of said nation.

In my last annual report I stated that I had disbursed out of this $75,000 the sum of $69,710.08, leaving a balance on hand of $5,289.92.

During the fiscal year ended June 30, 1901, I have disbursed out of this $5,289.92 the sum of $4,130.78, in payment of certain Choctaw warrants favorably passed upon by the Department and ordered paid. This leaves an unexpended balance of the $75,000 the sum of $1,159.14.

In addition to the warrants that have been paid out of the $75,000 referred to above, I have also disbursed $607.70 in payment of warrants issued to school teachers in the Choctaw Nation for services rendered prior to the Government's taking charge of the schools of the Choctaw Nation, and after the passage of the act of June 28, 1898. These last-mentioned warrants were paid from royalties collected by me on account of coal and asphalt mined.

TOWN-LOT PATENTS.

Patents to town lots in the Choctaw and Chickasaw nations, under the provisions of the act of Congress of June 28, 1898 (30 Stats., 495), issue under the joint hands of the principal chief of the Choctaw Nation and the governor of the Chickasaw Nation, and convey the title to said lots, save and except, however, all coal and asphalt therein. These patents are filled out in this office and forwarded to the respective named executives to be dated, signed, and the great seals of the nations impressed thereon. So far there has been issued 445 patents conveying town lots in the towns in the Choctaw and Chickasaw nations, as follows:

Colbert, Chickasaw Nation	24
Kiowa, Choctaw Nation	42
Sterrett, Choctaw Nation	129
Atoka, Choctaw Nation	9
South McAlester, Choctaw Nation	140
Guertie, Choctaw Nation	62
Calvin, Choctaw Nation	36
Poteau, Choctaw Nation	2
Total	445

When these patents have been returned to this office properly signed by the executives, the date of the signing of the same by the said executives is duly recorded in the town-site record book opposite to each particular lot conveyed. They are then delivered to the proper parties without cost to them.

CHEROKEE NATION.

Under the general provisions of the act of Congress of June 28, 1898, the Secretary of the Interior promulgated certain rules and regulations governing mineral eases and the disbursement and collection of revenue in the Cherokee Nation. Under these rules and regulations the United States Indian agent is required to receive and receipt for all royalties, rents, taxes, and permits of whatever kind and nature that may be due and payable to the Cherokee Nation. Such revenue is deposited to the credit of the Treasurer of the United States with the assistant treasurer of the United States at St. Louis, Mo., for the benefit of the Cherokee Nation.

ROYALTIES.

I give below a detailed statement of the royalties collected by me during the fiscal year ended June 30, 1901, for the Cherokee Nation:

Coal royalty	$6,326.87	School revenue	$2,321.19
Hay royalty	6,469.17	Telephone tax	10.50
Ferry tax	200.00		
Merchandise royalty	2,437.47	Total collected	19,392.65
Cattle tax	1,127.25	Less exchange	37.13
Travel royalty	490.18		
Town lots, proceeds	10.02		19,355.52

Which sum is the net amount deposited to the credit of the Cherokee Nation, as compared with $19,455.05 for the fiscal year ended June 30, 1900, a decrease of $62.40.

The Cherokee Nation imposes a tax of one-fourth of 1 per cent on all merchandise introduced and offered for sale in the Cherokee Nation.

Joseph A. Gill, judge of the United States court for the northern district of the Indian Territory, in a recent decision held that the Department of the Interior could not enforce this law against citizens of the Cherokee Nation by blood who are doing business within the limits of said nation. Therefore, this merchandise tax is collected now only from noncitizen merchants.

The royalty on coal is at the rate of 8 cents per ton on all coal mined, including that which is commonly called slack. No extensive coal operators are at work in this nation, and for that reason the coal royalty collected in this nation is not anywhere near as much as that collected for the Choctaw and Chickasaw nations.

The Cherokee law imposes a tax of 20 cents per ton on all hay shipped from its limits. This royalty is collected by this office, and is mentioned above. The total amount received under this head for the fiscal year ended June 30, 1901, is $6,469.17.

Persons who have introduced and held cattle in the Cherokee Nation, in accordance with the laws of said nation, pay an introduction tax of 25 cents per head, and the total revenue arising from this source for the past year is, as stated above, $1,127.25.

License to operate ferries is granted by the treasurer of the nation. On the Arkansas and Canadian rivers the annual tax is $25 per annum; on the Illinois, Grand, Verdigris, and Neosho rivers the tax is $10 per annum. The total receipts arising from this source during the past fiscal year is, as stated above, $200.

Under date of September 28, 1898, the honorable Secretary of the Interior granted a permit to the Kansas and Arkansas Valley Railway Company to take and remove gravel from the bars and beds of grand River within the limits of certain described territory. This land lies close to the mouth of the Grand River, and near Fort Gibson, Ind. T. The Secretary fixed the rate of royalty on such gravel removed at the rate of 2 cents per cubic yard, measured when loaded upon the cars of said railway company, the royalty thereon to be paid to this office monthly. There has been collected during the past fiscal year from this source, for the benefit of the Cherokee Nation, $490.18.

The Cherokee laws, which were in full force and effect prior to the passage of the act of June 28, 1898, provided that the town commissioner could sell lots in the towns of said nation. A number of lots were sold in this nation, and after the passage of the act of June 28, 1898, which abolished his office, certain persons, although not solicited to do so, paid into this office and completed payments on their lots $10.02 during the fiscal year just ended.

Under date of June 27, 1901, the Indian Territory Telephone Company paid into his office $10.50, that being the amount of revenue due the Cherokee Nation from said company, at the rate of one-half of 1 per cent of the net proceeds derived from the operation of said telephone company during the period ending June 1, 1901.

The Cherokee law provides that pupils of the male and female seminaries and the colored high school shall pay before entering said schools the sum of $5 per month for board in three regular installments, the first one-third at the beginning of the term and the other two-thirds at stated periods in advance.

There has been collected and remitted to this office on this account, and termed "school revenue," $2,321.19.

CHEROKEE WARRANTS.

No payment of Cherokee warrants was made during the fiscal year ended June 30, 1901.

The last payment of Cherokee warrants took place April 28, 1900. It was the original intention to make another payment on the same day of the next succeeding year.

A clause in the agreement negotiated between the Commission to the Five Civilized Tribes and the Cherokee Tribe of Indians at the city of Washington on the 9th day of April, 1900, and which, before becoming a law, must be ratified by a majority of votes cast by said tribe at an election held for that purpose within ninety days of the approval of the act by the President of the United States, provided that the Secretary of the Interior shall cause to be paid all just indebtedness of said tribe existing at the date of the ratification of this agreement. The principal chief proclaimed by proclamation that on April 29, 1901, the members of said tribe should decide by vote whether or not the agreement should be ratified or rejected. Inasmuch as the whole indebtedness could have been paid at once if said treaty had been ratified, it was decided to not make a payment on April 28, 1901, but await the result of the vote in reference to the ratification or rejection of the treaty. Later, by a count of the votes cast, it was ascertained that the treaty had been rejected. Thereupon I issued an advertisement stating that on July 1, 1901, I would disburse the sum of $211,657.22 of Cherokee moneys in payment of certain Cherokee warrants, a copy of which advertisement is given below:

Notice is hereby given, that I, J. Blair Shoenfelt, United States Indian agent and disbursing officer, acting under instructions from the Honorable Secretary of the Interior, at my office in Muskogee, Indian Territory, will, on July 1, 1901, and subsequent days until disbursement is completed, disburse the interest due the Cherokee Nation from the United States Government on their invested funds, amounting to $211,657.22. The said sum of $211,657.22 is applicable to the payment of warrants drawn on the respective funds as follows:

Warrants drawn on—

General fund	$110,401.19
School fund	64,558.49
Orphan asylum fund	31,712.35
Insane asylum fund	4,984.19
	211,657.22

The said disbursement will be made under the laws of the Cherokee Nation, in so far as they do not conflict with the rules and regulations prescribed by the Department of the Interior and the United States Treasury for the government of disbursing officers.

By the terms of the act of the Cherokee Council, approved by the President of the United States on January 5, 1900, interest on outstanding Cherokee warrants became due and payable annually. Interest on Cherokee warrants has been paid up to April 28, 1900. Upon warrants which are hereby advertised for payment and cancellation all interest will be paid. The interest on all warrants issued prior to April 27, 1900, will be paid. Interest will not be paid on warrants issued subsequently to that date, for the reason that it is not deemed to be due, and these warrants should not be presented.

In making this payment the indorsement of the original payee will be required before either the interest or principal will be paid; or, if the original payee is deceased, then the indorsement of the legally appointed administrator or executor of the estate will be necessary. Certified copies of the letters of administration must be furnished in cases where indorsements are made by administrators. Powers of attorney will not be recognized.

In the payment of the principal and interest the present legal holder of the warrant will be required to receipt for the same over his signature.

The following warrants, if legally issued for a valuable consideration to the Cherokee Nation, will be paid:

Insane asylum fund.—E 24, and interest thereon to April 3, 1899, this warrant having been heretofore advertised for payment on that date. E 40, 41, 50, 52, and 73, and interest due thereon to April 28, 1900, these warrants having been heretofore advertised for payment on that date. Also warrants E 76 to E 117, inclusive; E 251 to E 256, inclusive; and D 3 and 4, and the interest due thereon to June 22, 1901.

Orphan asylum fund.—F 142, 153, 167, and 179, and interest due thereon to April 3, 1899, these warrants having heretofore been advertised for payment on that date. Warrants C 33 and 40, and the interest due thereon to April 28, 1900, these two warrants having been heretofore advertised for payment on that date. Also warrants numbered from C 41 to C 121, inclusive, and the interest due thereon to June 22, 1901.

School fund.—K 471, and interest due thereon to April 3, 1899, this warrant having been heretofore advertised for payment on that date; and K 224, A 9, 22, 81, and 89, and interest due thereon to April 28, 1900, these warrants having been heretofore advertised for payment on that date. Also warrants numbered from K 245 to K 248, inclusive; A 121 to 281, inclusive; and B 1 to 223, inclusive, and the interest due thereon to June 22, 1901.

General fund.—Warrants C 762, 767, 768, 769, 770, 773, 774, 1148, 1149, D 40, 42, 46, 51, 65, 73, 84, 95, 98, 115, 116, 117, 119, 135, 149, 152, 158, 159, 168, 176, 178, 203, 204, 228, 231, 240, 243, O 33, 45, 47, 52, 65, 66, 67, 71, 83, 87, 93, 95, 98, 110, and 128, and the interest due thereon to April 3, 1899, these warrants having been heretofore advertised for payment on that date. Also warrants C 1162, 1165, 1166, 1168, 1173, 1190, D 265, 270, 280, O 198, 200, 203, 219, 224, 263, 264, 265, 266, 307, 330, 356, 367, and 374, and interest due thereon to April 28, 1900, these warrants having been heretofore advertised for payment on that date. Also

the following warrants: A 1 to A 45, inclusive; D 361 to D 506, inclusive; C 1198 to C 1388, inclusive; C 1393 to C 1462, inclusive; O 690 to O 748, inclusive, and interest due thereon to June 22, 1901.
Warrants should not be presented for payment prior to July 1, 1901.
If any further information is desired apply to the United States Indian agent, Union Agency, Muscogee, Ind. T.

The payment has been in progress since the 1st of July, and will be practically completed by September 1, 1901.

CREEK NATION.

During the fiscal year ended June 30, 1901, there was collected for the Creek Nation $30,827.60, arising from the following sources:

Coal royalty	$4,128.22
Pasture tax	1,950.00
Merchandise tax	14,247.98
Occupation tax	5,109.37
Stone royalty	169.52
Timber royalty	4,313.50
Insurance	909.01
Total	30,827.60
Less exchange	52.32
Net amount deposited	30,775.28
As compared with	26,370.19
Collected for the fiscal year ended June 30, 1900, or an increase of	4,457.41

Prior to January 1, 1901, the Creek Nation imposed a tax of 1 per cent on all merchandise introduced and exposed for sale within its limits.

At the October, 1900, session of the national council a permit law was passed, which law was approved by the principal chief on November 5, 1900, and was afterwards approved by the President of the United States on November 22, 1900.

Following is the law in full:

PERMIT LAW.

Be it enacted by the National Council of the Muskogee Nation:

SECTION 1. That all persons who are not citizens by blood of the Muskogee Nation, or who have not been adopted by the Muskogee Nation, and whose names do not appear on authenticated rolls of the Muskogee Nation, who shall desire to engage in any manner of business in the Muskogee Nation shall obtain the consent of the United States Government, and shall pay to the United States Indian agent, at Union Agency, Muskogee, Indian Territory, for the benefit of the Muskogee Nation, the annual permit tax hereinafter fixed; the same to be paid quarterly, in advance in all cases, except where based on the cost of goods offered. Quarters to begin January first, April first, July first, and October first of each year.

All legitimate business houses of whatsoever character or capacity engaged in the sale of all manner of dry goods, groceries, provisions, hardware, lumber, drugs, millinery, leather goods, or any other article known or designated as merchandise, shall pay an annual tax of one-half of 1 per cent of the first cost of all goods offered for sale, excepting such goods as have been actually produced in the Muskogee Nation or shall have been bought within the limits of the nation from a trader who shall have previously paid this tax of one-half of 1 per cent of such goods; all payments to be accompanied by sworn statements, said statements to be verified by personal inspection by a proper inspector of the original invoices or the books of the trader.

The rate of taxation on all other classes of business shall be as follows:

On each dealer in hides, peltries, furs, wool, pecans, and other country produce	$50.00
On each hotel affording accommodations for 30 or more guests	36.00
On each hotel affording accommodations for 20 or more guests	24.00
On each hotel affording accommodations for less than 20 guests	12.00
On each printing office	12.00
On each oil, grist, or flouring mill	24.00
On each cotton gin	24.00
On each livery and feed stable	24.00
On each feed stable or yard	12.00
On each dray or freight wagon or passenger hack other than those owned by livery stables paying as such	12.00
On each blacksmith or wagon shop	12.00
On each insurance agent (life or fire)	50.00
On each physician having certificate from the National Medical Board	25.00
On each dentist having diploma	25.00
On each butcher shop selling meat only	24.00
On each restaurant or lunch counter (stand)	12.00
On each laundry or laundry agency	12.00
On each barber shop	12.00
On each bakery and confectionery or lemonade and ice-cream stand	12.00
On each merry-go-round	24.00
On each gunsmith, tinsmith, locksmith, or watch repairer	12.00
On each lawyer	25.00
On each tombstone or marble dealer	12.00
On each shooting gallery	12.00
On each billiard and pool table	5.00
On each show or concert in hall or tent, per day	5.00
On each circus without menagerie, per day	10.00
On each circus and menagerie combined, per day	25.00
On each banking establishment one-half of one per cent of capital stock invested—assessment to be made on the bank on account of the shares thereof.	
On each peddler, street or travelling vendor, 5 per cent of goods offered for sale.	
On each establishment selling nonintoxicating ales, tonics, meads, or any other form of drink intended as a substitute for malt or spirituous liquors	100.00

SEC. 2. Should any person refuse to pay the tax herein provided when due and when demand is made, or should any person refuse to permit a personal inspection to be had of original invoice-books, etc., such person shall be reported to the proper authorities for removal from the Muskogee Nation.

Failure to pay within ten days after tax is due and demand has been made shall constitute a refusal to pay.

SEC. 3. This act shall become a law upon the approval of the President of the United States, and shall be in full force and effect from and after January 1, 1901.

All laws heretofore enacted by the national council of the Muskogee Nation, relating to permit tax, which are in conflict with this act, are hereby repealed.

SEC. 4. All classes of business in operation or which may hereafter be established in this nation, not included in the above list, shall be assessed by the principal chief, subject to the approval of the United States Indian agent.

There was collected from merchants and other persons pursuing occupations in the Creek Nation during the fiscal year ended June 30, 1901, as stated above, the sum of $19,357.35.

Rent to the amount of $1,950, as shown above, has been paid to me during the past year by cattlemen for use of certain pastures which had not been selected by any individual Creek citizen as his or their prospective allotments.

Under the act of June 6, 1900, there were paid into this office on account of timber and stone removed from the lands of the Creek Nation, the sum of $4,483.02. This timber and stone was used principally in the construction of the St. Louis, Oklahoma and Southern Railroad, said line of railway running from Sapulpa in a southerly direction through the lands of the Creek and Chickasaw nations to Sherman, Tex.

I have heretofore given under the head Chickasaw and Choctaw nations, the manner of caring for moneys received from these sources.

It will be noted in the above that I have mentioned as revenue $901.01 under the head insurance. This was the amount that was collected by the principal chief of the Creek Nation from certain insurance companies and turned over to me as the amount paid for damages done by fire to certain buildings belonging to the Creek Nation, and occupied and used by the colored orphan asylum.

Royalty on coal, as stated above, amounted to $4,128.22. The principal mines are located at or near Howard, on the line of the St. Louis and San Francisco Railway. The rate of royalty on coal mined is the same in the Creek Nation as in the Choctaw and Chickasaw nations, viz: 8 cents per ton on all coal mined, including that which is commonly called slack.

To assist in the collection of revenue for the Cherokee and Creek nations, there have been appointed by the Secretary of the Interior two revenue inspectors, Guy P. Cobb for the Creek Nation, and Frank C. Churchill for the Cherokee Nation, and their salaries and expenses paid from moneys collected for the benefit of the respective nations.

All remittances, without reference to the source, or from whom received, are accompanied by statements in duplicate. One copy of these statements is given to the revenue inspectors for the Cherokee and Creek nations for their information and guidance.

SALE OF TOWN-SITE MAPS.

There have been placed on file in this office photolithographic copies of the town-site maps of the towns of Muskogee, Wagoner, and Mounds, Creek Nation, Ind. T., and of Woodville, Chickasaw Nation, Ind. T., with directions to sell same in the open market, as follows: Mounds and Woodville, 40 cents each; Wagoner and Muskogee, 50 cents each.

During the fiscal year ended June 30, 1901, I have disposed of the following maps in the towns named:

Muskogee, 59, at 50 cents each	$29.50
Wagoner, 5, at 50 cents each	2.50
Mounds, 1, at 40 cents	.40
Total	32.40

I have sold no map of the town of Woodville, Chickasaw Nation.

This $32.40, referred to, has been by me deposited with the Assistant Treasurer of the United States to the credit of the Treasurer of the United States for the benefit of the fund, "Town-site commissioners, Indian Territory, 1901."

PAYMENT OF EXPENSES INCURRED IN CONNECTION WITH TOWN-SITE WORK IN THE INDIAN TERRITORY.

Acting under directions of the Department, and since January 1, all expenses connected with the town-site work in the Indian Territory, except the salaries of the town-site commissioners and the supervising engineer, are paid by this office. There re twelve surveying parties in the field and the salaries of the surveyors, transitmen, hainmen, rodmen, etc., are paid monthly. I also pay the salaries of such employees i this office and that of the United States Indian inspector who do town-site work. 'his includes draftsmen and clerks. Up to June 30, 1901, as stated in the opening f this report, I disbursed out of the townsite fund to pay expenses of the character ientioned above $37,283.08. Inasmuch as the surveyors are constantly traveling 'om town to town and have a good many irregular employees, this necessarily in-reases the work done by this office to a very considerable extent.

CREEK INDIGENTS.

The act of the national council of the Muskogee Nation, approved by the princi-al chief of said nation November 5, 1900, and by the President December 3, 1900, ppropriated $7,236 to be paid to 201 Creek indigents at the rate of $3 per month per erson. The Creek national council determine who are indigents and the principal hief of the nation furnishes me with a list of the names certified to him as being 'reek indigents by said council, and I pay these indigents the $3 per month they re allowed by the act of their council just above referred to. Up to June 30 I have isbursed in the payment of Creek indigents for the amount due them for the quarter nding March 3, 1901, $828, as heretofore stated in this report.

PAYMENT OF CREEK WARRANTS.

During the fiscal year ended June 30, 1901, I received for disbursement Creek noneys, aggregating $140,301.91, under the following heads, to wit:

ndian moneys, proceeds of labor, Creek	$15,693.26
Fulfilling treaties with the Creeks	50,447.35
Interest on Creek general fund	74,161.30
	140,301.91

Of this $140,301.91, $138,788.93 was used to pay warrants drawn by the principal chief of the Creek Nation to pay expenses incurred in the management of the affairs of the tribe. This leaves an unexpended balance of $1,512.98, under the fund, inter-est on Creek general fund.

This unexpended balance is to be used in paying certain Creek warrants heretofore advertised, and which have not yet been presented.

In this connection, it is proper to add that I have recently been advised by the honorable Commissioner of Indian Affairs that there are available for disbursement Creek funds aggregating $95,000, and I have issued an advertisement notifying the public that a payment of Creek warrants will begin at this agency on September 2, 1901, and continue until the said sum of $95,000 is completely disbursed. After this disbursement has been completed, it will leave the Creek Nation in debt to the extent only of about $6,000.

SMALLPOX.

In my last annual report I referred to the outbreak of smallpox throughout the Indian Territory and the work this office did in connection with the boards of health of the Choctaw, Cherokee, and Creek nations in suppressing the same.

The act of Congress approved May 31, 1900, contained the following clause:

Fifty thousand dollars, or so much thereof as may be necessary, to be immediately available, in payment of liabilities already incurred, and for an amount necessary to be expended in suppressing the spread of smallpox in the Indian Territory among those residents of said Territory not members of an Indian tribe or nation therein, all accounts to be first carefully examined and approved by the secretary of the Interior as just and reasonable.

CHEROKEE NATION.

In this nation the total expense was found to be, after a careful examination, $18,756.25; of this amount $2,198.88 was for supplies furnished in connection with the suppression of the spread of smallpox; $681.67 of this amount was paid from Cherokee funds, and the balance, $1,517.21, from the $50,000 appropriated by the act of Congress, supra.

The total expense of this nation on account of the employment of irregular labor, such as doctors, guards, physicians, and nurses, was $16,557.37; of this amount $5,120.54 was paid from Cherokee funds, and $11,397.33 from the $50,000 appropri-ated by the act of Congress.

All of the expenses incurred in this nation, save and except $39.50, has been paid. This $39.50 is due to some guards who rendered service, but who have not yet applied for payment, they having doubtless left the country, and the amount due each so small that they have never taken the trouble to collect it.

The nationality of each person cared for when afflicted with smallpox was kept, in order that the expense incurred in treating white persons could be paid from the $50,000, and the Indian citizens from the funds belonging to the tribe to which they belonged. This was done for the reason that the amount appropriated by the act of Congress referred to was only available to pay the expenses of treating and caring for persons not members of any Indian tribe or nation.

CREEK NATION.

The total expense of suppressing the spread of smallpox in the Creek Nation was $15,741.74. Of this amount, $3,853.32 was used in payment of supplies furnished; payable from Creek funds, $3,060.84; from the $50,000 appropriated by the act of Congress, $792.48. The balance of the $15,741.74, viz, $11,888.42, was reserved to pay irregular labor, such as doctors, nurses, guards, etc. Of this amount I have disbursed the following sums for the purposes stated:

Payable from Creek funds	$8,077.71
From the $50,000 appropriated by the act of Congress	3,734.96
	11,812.67

Leaving yet to be paid the sum of $75.75. This balance is due to certain persons who performed services as guards, and who have never applied for payment of same.

The proportion of expenses in the Creek Nation was ascertained in the same manner as in the Cherokee Nation; that is, with reference to the total expenses of the camps and the number of Indian citizens and noncitizens treated therein.

CHOCTAW NATION.

After a very careful examination of all the accounts presented in this nation it was found that the total expenses that could be paid out of the $50,000 appropriated by the act of Congress referred to was $30,572.17. Of this amount $15,014.90 was in payment of supplies furnished, and the balance, $15,557.27, to pay irregular labor, such as guards, physicians, nurses, etc.

The supplies in each one of these nations were paid for under departmental instructions, by means of a certified voucher issued by me and forwarded to the Indian Office for examination and certification to the Treasury Department for payment direct to the claimant.

Persons irregularly employed, such as guards, doctors, nurses, etc., were paid direct by this office, by means of checks drawn on the assistant treasurer of the United States, said checks being handed direct to the persons who performed the service after they had signed the proper vouchers therefor.

All of the moneys reserved to pay irregular labor in the Choctaw Nation, save $2,559.25, has been disbursed. This amount will be paid to persons entitled to receive payment as soon as they can be located and the correctness of their claims ascertained.

From the above it will be seen that the total expense incurred in suppressing the spread of smallpox is as follows:

Cherokee Nation.	
From Cherokee funds	$5,814.46
From $50,000 appropriated by Congress	12,941.79
Creek Nation:	
From Creek funds	11,197.81
From $50,000 appropriated by Congress	4,543.93
Choctaw Nation:	
Approved for payment from the $50,000 appropriated by Congress	30,572.17
Total	65,070.16

Of this amount there has actually been paid for the purposes mentioned in this report $62,395.66, leaving a balance yet to be disbursed of $2,674.50.

From the above it will be noted that the total amount disbursed and yet to be paid out of the $50,000 in the three nations is $48,057.89, leaving a balance available of this sum of $1,942.11.

It is thought proper to add that all accounts, either for supplies furnished or for work done in connection with the suppression of the spread of smallpox in the Cherokee, Creek, and Choctaw Nations, were first carefully examined in this office and that of the United States Indian inspector for the Indian Territory before they were submitted to the Department for approval.

It was found, upon examination and after very careful consideration, that it was necessary, in many instances, to reduce, for various reasons, the claims of physicians and others connected with this work.

In the case of supplies furnished, the prices charged were found to be in excess of those usually charged in commercial circles for like articles, and in every instance a reduction was made.

SEMINOLE NATION.

In my annual report for the fiscal year ended June 30, 1899, I stated that in December, 1897, the Seminole Nation and the Commission to the Five Civilized Tribes, otherwise known as the Dawes Commission, entered into an agreement which provided for the allotment of their lands and the establishment of a United States court at Wewoka in said nation, and gave to the United States court exclusive jurisdiction of all controversies growing out of the ownership, occupation, or use of real estate owned by the Seminoles, and to try persons charged with homicide, embezzlement, bribery, and embracery committed in the Seminole country, without reference to the citizenship of the person charged with such crime.

I added that the Seminole Indian courts are allowed to retain the jurisdiction as they now have, except as is transferred to the United States courts, and for the gradual extinguishment of the tribal government.

By reason of this agreement, which was afterwards ratified by Congress, the Seminoles are not under the provisions of the act of Congress of June 28, 1898, and the Indian agent does not receive or disburse any of their moneys, it being done by tribal officers.

However, under the provisions of the act of June 6, 1900, governing the procurement of timber and stone for domestic and industrial purposes in the Indian Territory, there was paid into this office $7.71 on account of royalty on 257.14 yards of stone at 3 cents per yard. This money was afterwards deposited by me with the assistant treasurer of the United States to the credit of the Treasurer of the United States for the benefit of the Seminole Nation.

The Seminoles, as I stated above, manage their own affairs, and this agency has little to do with them, except to assist in the enforcement of their tribal revenue laws and the collection of taxes. I have one policeman stationed in this nation, and he cooperates with and assists the principal chief of said nation, Hon. John F. Brown, in enforcing intercourse laws when directed to do so by this office.

CREEK AGREEMENT.

The act of Congress approved March 1, 1901 (Public, 112), ratified and confirmed an agreement with the Muskogee or Creek Tribe of Indians entered into between the Commission to the Five Civilized Tribes and the said tribe of Indians at the city of Washington on the 8th day of March, 1901, with certain amendments, and the same was to be in full force and effect when ratified by the Creek national council. On May 25, 1901, by a majority of votes, the Creek national council, then in session for that purpose, ratified and confirmed said agreement as therein amended, and it became law by the terms thereof. Announcement of the same was made by the President of the United States by means of a proclamation dated at the city of Washington on the 25th day of June, 1901.

This agreement provides for the general allotment of lands, and confirms selections of citizens heretofore made and who held certificates of said selections issued by the Commission to the Five Civilized Tribes. It also provides for the laying out and platting of town sites of all towns having a present population of 200 or more.

The titles to lands are to be conveyed by a deed issued by the principal chief and to be approved by the Secretary of the Interior, which shall serve as a relinquishment to the grantee all right, title, and interest of the United States in and to the lands embraced in his deed. All deeds, when so executed and approved, shall be filed in the office of the Commission to the Five Civilized Tribes and there recorded without expense to the grantee, and such records shall have like effect as other public records.

A certain number of acres are set aside for the boarding schools of the Creek Nation and certain other mission societies; one acre each for six established courthouses with improvements thereon; one acre each for all churches and schools outside of towns, now regularly used as such.

The act also permits municipal corporations in the Creek Nation, with the approval of the Secretary of the Interior, to issue bonds and borrow money thereon for sanitary purposes, and for the construction of sewers, lighting plants, waterworks, and schoolhouses, subject to all of the provisions of law of the United States in force in the organized territory of the United States in reference to municipal indebtedness and issuance of bonds for public purposes, and said laws were to be in force in this nation and made applicable to the cities and towns therein, the same as if specially enacted in reference thereto.

The agreement also provides for the settlement of all just claims of the Creek Nation against the United States.

The agreement also provides that the Commission to the Five Civilized Tribes shall make, at the earliest time practicable, a complete roll of all citizens of said Creek Nation, and when completed the same to be approved by the Secretary of the Interior.

The United States agrees to pay all of the expense incident to the surveying, platting, and disposition of town lots, and of allotments of all lands under the provisions of the agreement, except where town authorities have been or may be duly authorized to survey and plat their respective towns at the expense of such towns.

Section 37 provides that Creek citizens can rent their allotments when selected for a term not exceeding one year and after receiving title thereto, without restriction, if adjoining allottees are not injured thereby, and cattle grazing thereon shall not be liable to any tribal tax, but when cattle are introduced into the Creek Nation and grazed on lands not selected by Creek citizens, the Secretary of the Interior is authorized to collect from the owners thereof a reasonable grazing tax for the benefit of the tribe. Section 2117 of the Revised Statutes of the United States shall not apply to Creek lands.

A citizen of the Creek Nation having his allotment may dispose of any timber thereon, but if he dispose of such timber or any part of same he shall not thereafter select other lands in lieu thereof. His allotment shall be appraised as if in condition when selected. The timber is not to be taken from lands not selected without payment of royalty thereon under contract to be prescribed by the Secretary of the Interior.

All teachers are to be appointed under and by direction of the superintendent of Creek schools and the supervisor of the Creek Nation, preference to be given to Indian citizens in the employment of teachers. The expense of running the schools is to be appropriated by the Creek national council, not to exceed the sum of $76,468.40. But in the event of failure to make such appropriation the Secretary may direct the use of a sufficient amount of the school fund to be used in the payment of the expense necessary to the efficient conduct of the schools, strict account thereof to be rendered to him and the principal chief.

The United States agrees to maintain strict laws in the Creek Nation against the introduction, sale, barter, or giving away of liquors or intoxicants of any kind whatsoever. The tribal government of the Creek Nation is not to continue longer than March 4, 1906, subject to such further legislation as may be deemed proper.

Section 8 of this agreement provides that the Secretary of the Interior shall, through the United States Indian agent in said Territory, immediately after the ratification of the agreement, put each citizen who has made selection of his allotment in unrestricted possession of his land and remove therefrom all persons objectionable to him; and when any citizen shall thereafter make selection of his allotment as herein provided and receive certificate therefor, he shall be immediately thereupon placed in possession of his land.

The honorable Secretary of the Interior has recently directed that I proceed in this matter by giving public notice to all persons in possession of land and having no lease with a citizen who has filed on or selected the same to remove therefrom not later than October 1, 1901.

CHEROKEE AGREEMENT.

The Cherokee agreement negotiated between the Commission to the Five Civilized Tribes and the Cherokee tribe of Indians at the city of Washington on the 9th day of April, 1900, and ratified by the act of Congress of March 1, 1901, with certain amendments, failed to become a law for the reason that at an election held for the purpose of ratifying or rejecting the same a majority of the votes cast were against the ratification of said treaty. This places the Cherokee Nation under the provisions of the act of June 28, 1898, otherwise known as the Curtis Act.

EDUCATION.

The increase of interest in the upbuilding of educational matters in the Indian Territory is due largely to the untiring efforts of Mr. John D. Benedict, superintendent of schools in the Indian Territory, assisted by the various supervisors of the several nations in this agency.

The educational work of the Territory has moved along quietly during the past year. A better understanding has been reached between the Government school officials and the tribal officials of the Territory, and all are working harmoniously now.

Superintendent Benedict and his supervisors have devoted a good share of their time to visiting schools in all parts of the Territory, and they always receive a cordial welcome from the Indians.

Smallpox and other contagious diseases at times attack the schools, and the attendance is often very materially reduced thereby. Parents, too, are often indifferent about sending their children regularly to school. It seems hard to convince many Indians of the evils of absenteeism.

The general interest in educational matters is on the increase, however, and the summer normal schools for teachers which have just been held in each nation will not only prepare the teachers for better work, but will doubtless create a livelier interest in the educational work of the Territory. The report of the superintendent shows that a larger number of schools were maintained during the past year than ever before. The school finances are also much better managed than formerly. Instead of having to wait from one to two years for their pay, as in former times, teachers are now beginning to receive their salaries with reasonable promptness.

CHICKASAW INCOMPETENT CLAIMS.

The Indian appropriation act (Public—No. 131) approved May 31, 1900, contained the following provision:

That the Secretary of the Interior be, and is hereby, authorized and directed to pay out and distribute in the following manner the sum of two hundred and sixteen thousand six hundred and seventy-nine dollars and forty-eight cents, which amount was appropriated by the act of June twenty-eighth, eighteen hundred and ninety-eight, and credited to the "incompetent fund" of the Chickasaw Nation on the books of the United States Treasury, namely: First, there shall be paid to such survivors of the original beneficiaries of said fund and to such heirs of deceased beneficiaries as shall, within six months from the passage of this act, satisfactorily establish their identity in such manner as the Secretary of the Interior may prescribe, and also the amount of such fund to which they are severally entitled, their respective shares; and, second, so much of said fund as is not paid out upon claims satisfactorily established as aforesaid shall be distributed per capita among the members of the Chickasaw Nation, and all claims of beneficiaries and their respective heirs for participation in said incompetent fund not presented within the period aforesaid shall be, and the same are hereby, barred.

The Commissioner of Indian Affairs, under date of July 17, 1900, called my attention to the fact that it is the duty of the persons who claim to be entitled to share in the distribution of the above amount to satisfactorily establish their identity in such manner as the Secretary of the Interior might prescribe, and that the Secretary of the Interior is authorized and directed to pay to each person who shall establish his identity the portion of the fund to which he is entitled.

In order that the provisions of the act above quoted could be carried out, I was directed to issue a notice to be published in the newspapers of the Chickasaw Nation, both in English and Chickasaw language, as was necessary to notify all persons that evidence tending to establish the identity and claims of Chickasaw incompetents, or the descendants of those incompetents who are dead, would be received at this agency up to and including October 31, 1900. I inserted in said notice that the Chickasaw Nation had the right to file evidence rebutting that filed by any particular claimant, and that after October 31, 1900, papers in each case would be forwarded to the Department for such action thereon as was deemed appropriate.

I was also directed to notify by mail the governor of the Chickasaw Nation of the filing of each claim, giving the date, name of the beneficiary, the amount of the claim, and that the proper representative of the nation would be allowed to examine any evidence which might be filed in this office in relation to any of said cases; also to file evidence against the allowance of any particular claim, and further, that after October 31, 1900, I was to carefully examine each case and make report and recommendation thereon, this report to be submitted to the Indian Office and by it to be transmitted to the Department with appropriate recommendations. A copy of said notice is given herewith:

DEPARTMENT OF THE INTERIOR,
UNITED STATES INDIAN SERVICE,
Union Agency, Muskogee, Ind. T., July 23, 1900.

Notice to Chickasaw citizens:

The Indian appropriation act approved May 31, 1900, contains the following provision:
"That the Secretary of the Interior be, and is hereby, authorized and directed to pay out and distribute in the following manner the sum of two hundred and sixteen thousand six hundred and seventy-nine dollars and forty-eight cents, which amount was appropriated by the act of June twenty-eighth, eighteen hundred and ninety-eight, and credited to the 'incompetent fund' of the Chickasaw Nation on the books of the United States Treasury, namely: First, there shall be paid to

such survivors of the original beneficiaries of said fund and to such heirs of deceased beneficiaries as shall, within six months from the passage of this act, satisfactorily establish their identity in such manner as the Secretary of the Interior may prescribe, and also the amount of such fund to which they are severally entitled, their respective shares; and, second, so much of said fund as is not paid out upon claims satisfactorily established as aforesaid shall be distributed per capita among the members of said Chickasaw Nation, and all claims of beneficiaries and their respective heirs for participation in said incompetent fund not presented within the period aforesaid shall be, and the same are hereby, barred."

It will be observed that it is made the duty of the claimants to satisfactorily establish their identity n such manner as the Secretary of the Interior may prescribe, and that the Secretary of the Interior is authorized and directed to pay to each person who shall establish his identity the portion of the fund to which he is entitled.

Notice is hereby given that evidence tending to establish the identity of claims of Chickasaw incompetents, or descendants of those incompetents, who are dead, will be received at the Union Agency up to and including October 31, 1900, and all such evidence should be addressed to the United States Indian agent, Union Agency, Muscogee, Ind. T.

The Chickasaw Nation has a right to file evidence rebutting that filed by particular claimant, and for that purpose shall be allowed to examine any evidence which may be submitted pertaining to any claimant.

Parties forwarding any claims should set forth in detail treaty, laws, and relationship upon which claims are based and the amount claimed.   Before such claims can be considered it will be necessary for parties to satisfactorily establish their claims to such amounts independent of any payments heretofore made by the Chickasaw authorities in 1889, or at any other time.

After October 31 parties having submitted claims will be duly notified of the time when they can personally appear before the United States Indian agent for the purpose of furnishing any additional desired information or proof.

J. BLAIR SHOENFELT,
United States Indian Agent for the Five Civilized Tribes.

It was the intention of this office to take oral testimony in the matter of claims of persons to share in the incompetent fund, but the Indian Office advised me later that it was not contemplated by the Department that oral testimony should be taken, but that it was expected and intended that claimants should establish their identity to the satisfaction of the Secretary of the Interior by written evidence in the form of affidavits or depositions, or such documentary evidence as they might be able to supply, and further, that no evidence in support of the claim of any alleged incompetent could be received or considered after the 30th of November, 1900, and I should at once notify each person who claims to be an incompetent or descendant of an incompetent, and who has given me notice of such claim, that they would be required to file evidence upon which they rely in support of their claims in this office prior to the date mentioned, to wit, November 30, 1900, this notice to be given publicity in the same manner as I gave the original notice. A copy of this supplementary notice herewith:

DEPARTMENT OF THE INTERIOR, UNITED STATES INDIAN SERVICE,
Union Agency, Muskogee, Ind. T., October 15, 1900.

SUPPLEMENTAL NOTICE TO CHICKASAW CITIZENS.

The Indian appropriation act approved May 31, 1900, contains the following provision:

"That the Secretary of the Interior be, and is hereby, authorized and directed to pay out and distribute in the following manner, the sum of two hundred and sixteen thousand six hundred and seventy-nine dollars and forty-eight cents, which amount was appropriated by the act of June twenty-eighth, eighteen hundred and ninety-eight, and credited to the 'incompetent fund' of the Chickasaw Indian Nation on the books of the United States Treasury, namely: First, there shall be paid to such survivors of the original beneficiaries of said fund and to such heirs of deceased beneficiaries as shall within six months after the passage of this act satisfactorily establish their identity in such manner as the Secretary of the Interior may prescribe, and also the amount of such fund to which they are severally entitled, their several shares; and second, so much of said fund as is not paid out upon claims satisfactorily established as aforesaid shall be distributed per capita among the members of said Chickasaw Nation, and all claims of beneficiaries and their respective heirs for participation in said incompetent fund not presented within the period aforesaid shall be, and the same are hereby, barred."

It will be observed that it is made the duty of the claimants to satisfactorily establish their identity in such manner as the Secretary of the Interior may prescribe, and the Secretary of the Interior is authorized and directed to pay to each person who shall establish his identity the portion of the fund to which he is entitled.

Notice is hereby given that evidence in the form of affidavits or depositions or such documentary evidence as claimants may be able to supply tending to establish the identity of claims of Chickasaw incompetents, or descendants of those incompetents who are dead, will be received at the Union Agency up to and including November 30, 1900, and not later; and all such evidence should be addressed to the United States Indian agent, Union Agency, Muskogee, Ind. T.

The Chickasaw Nation has the right to file evidence rebutting that filed by any particular claimant, and for that purpose shall be allowed to examine any evidence which may be submitted pertaining to any claim.

Parties forwarding claims should set forth in detail treaty, laws, and relationship upon which claims are based and the amount claimed, and it will be necessary for parties to satisfactorily establish their claims to such amounts independent of any payment heretofore made by the Chickasaw authorities in 1889 or at any other time.

I will not appear at any time or place in the Chickasaw Nation for the purpose of taking oral testimony in connection with these claims, but all claims must be satisfactorily established in the manner above indicated, and same, together with the testimony pertaining thereto, must be filed in my office on or before November 30, 1900, as above stated. This is in pursuance of a recent order of the Department.

J. BLAIR SHOENFELT,
United States Indian Agent for Five Civilized Tribes.

There have been filed in this office 243 claims, aggregating in amount something over $175,000.

The proof submitted was in the form of affidavits and not depositions. A number of the claimants offered no proof as to their identity except their own statement "that they believe they were the only living heirs of the original incompetents."

Under the provisions of the treaty of 1834, for the purpose of dividing their lands, the Chickasaws were divided into three classes, to wit, competents, incompetents, and orphans.

The competents were those persons who could obtain a certificate of their competency and ability to attend to their own affairs, and the incompetents were those persons who could not obtain such certificates. The competency and incompetency of such persons was passed upon by a commission under the provisions of article 4 of the treaty of 1834. Such persons as could not obtain such certificates as to their competency were placed upon a separate roll, known as the "incompetent roll," and their lands were disposed of by the Government of the United States, and the consideration resulting therefrom was to be held by the Government until such time as the chiefs in council might see fit to recommend that it be paid to the claimants.

The records in some of these claims were voluminous and were very difficult of solution, and in order that fraud might not be perpetrated upon the nation, but that justice might be done, I took each case up separately and arrived at my conclusion only after a careful examination of all the evidence submitted.

An examination of the records of the 1899 payment showed that at that time in a great majority of cases different persons applied and different relationships were established to that now claimed, and to persons entirely different to those now claiming a portion of the fund was paid to them as heirs of incompetents.

While it is not contended that the 1889 records were conclusive, and that the persons establishing their identity at that time were in truth and fact heirs of the incompetents, however, in view of the fact that such proceedings were had openly and in the presence of a commission duly appointed by the Chickasaw Nation for that purpose, I am of the opinion, as stated in a number of my conclusions, that they are entitled to a fair consideration.

A comparison of the incompetent roll of 1834 with the rolls of the Chickasaw Indians of 1818 develops a condition as regards many of the claims which would seem to me to render them impossible of establishment. The incompetent roll of 1834 is merely a list of names and amounts without information as to the sex or family relationship, while the 1818 roll, made sixteen years before that time, is made up by families and contains full and complete information.

A great many of the original affidavits filed in support of claims are couched in practically almost the identical language, and contain essentially the same statements.

It was contended on the part of the Chickasaw Nation that many of the persons who gave testimony are known as "standing witnesses," ready to testify for a consideration. I did not permit such statements to influence my judgment in passing upon the claims.

Many of the witnesses afterwards made statements, in the form of supplementary affidavits, that the statements made by them were neither read nor interpreted to them.

As before stated, the work of examining and reporting on these claims required a great deal of work in itself and was a monumental task. I had to examine the rolls and records carefully and compare them, and so prepare my report as to enable the Department to pass intelligently upon each claim.

SNAKE UPRISING.

In my last annual report I mentioned that a few full-blood Indians in the Creek Nation, under the leadership of Chitto Harjo and Hotulka Fixico, were strenuously opposing the allotment of lands, and had banded together and refused to appear before the Commission to the Five Civilized Tribes to select their allotments. These Indians were deluded with the hope that there was a possibility of their securing the consent of the Government to permit them to return to their old customs and have their tribal governments restored, and live apart and separate from the rest of the world. From time to time they banded together in conventions and made speeches, and endeavored to propagate this retrogressive sentiment among other Creek Indians. They did all they could to oppose the policy of the Government in reference to the allotment of the lands in severalty and the giving of an individual title instead of holding the land in common.

It has been and is the custom of the Commission to the Five Civilized Tribes to issue what are termed certificates of selections. These disaffected Indians did all

" Every person, other than an Indian, who, within the limits of any tribe with whom the United States has existing treaties, hunts, or traps, or takes and destroys any peltries or game, except for subsistence in an Indian country, shall forfeit all the traps, guns, and ammunition in his possession used, or procured to be used for that purpose, and all peltries so taken, shall be liable in addition to a penalty of five hundred dollars."

Attention is also invited to section 1923 of Mansfield's Digest of the Statutes of Arkansas, which is as follows:

" It shall be unlawful for any person, with intent to kill, maim, or paralyze any fish or other water animals, to cast, drop, or otherwise deposit in any river, creek, lake, or pond, or in any other stream or body of water within this State, any explosive material or substance, or any intoxicating or stupify-ing liquid, drug, vegetable, or fruit, or to take from any river, creek, lake, pond, or other stream or body of water within this State, any fish so stupefied, intoxicated, or killed."

Section 1925 of Mansfield's Digest of the Statutes of Arkansas provides that any person found guilty of violating the provisions of section 1923 shall be fined for each offense not less than $5 nor more than $20.

In order to properly protect the game of this Territory, I suggest that the residents of each town who are interested in the preservation of game organize themselves into a club, with the object and purpose of preventing the unlawful, wanton, and indiscriminate destruction of game. Such clubs should, through their presidents and secretaries, immediately notify this agency whenever any non-residents are found hunting or fishing in their vicinity.

This office, when so notified, will direct that the parties complained of be arrested and prosecuted in accordance with the provisions of section 2137, supra.

The hearty cooperation of all persons interested in this matter will be appreciated.

These notices I have caused to be posted at conspicuous places in the post-offices in the Indian Territory and in the post-offices in the towns of the States bordering on this reserve, namely, Missouri, Kansas, Oklahoma, Texas, and Arkansas. After the issuance of this letter a number of the Indian police of this agency made some arrests and confiscated the guns and game found in the possession of the parties thus arrested. The guns so taken, in a number of instances, after investigation have been returned to the parties from whom they were taken, but not until they had promised to leave the Territory and not again enter it without permission.

I respectfully recommend that a stringent law be passed to protect the game in the Indian Territory.

RAILROADS.

The Fort Smith and Western Railroad Company were granted their charter to construct its line of railway through the Indian Territory by the act of Congress of March 3, 1899. It now has 20 miles of its line under construction. This portion of line runs from Coal Creek to the junction on the line of the Kansas City and Southern Railroad. The eastern terminus of this road is at Fort Smith, Ark., and it is pro-posed to extend it westward through the Choctaw and Creek nations to a point in Oklahoma not yet known.

Muskogee and Western Railroad Company.—The Muskogee and Western Railroad Company was chartered under the laws of Oklahoma Territory for the purpose of constructing a line of railroad from Fort Gibson, Cherokee Nation, through Muskogee, and thence westward into Oklahoma Territory to a point at or near El Reno. The first three sections of the proposed line of railway have been submitted to the Depart-ment and have been approved. In connection with the building of this road the company proposes the erection of a bridge over the Arkansas River at a point near the mouth of Grant River and about 5 miles distant from Muskogee. Authority for the erection of this bridge has been obtained from the War Department, and the contract for its erection has been let.

Ozark and Cherokee Central Railroad Company.—The Ozark and Cherokee Central Railroad Company has not yet begun the construction of its line in the Territory, its work having been confined to the building of the line between Fayetteville, Ark., and thence westward to the Cherokee line. It has submitted maps showing its definite right of way through the Cherokee and Creek nations as far as Muskogee, Ind. T. They expect to have the road completed to Tahlequah by June 1, 1902.

Missouri, Kansas and Texas Railway Company.—The Missouri, Kansas and Texas Railway Company has under construction 2.27 miles of road from what is known as the Samples mine, near McAlester, to the Redmond mine, and the offshoot from this mine to the Archibald coal mines, about 1.14 miles. These short lines are con-structed under the original charter of September 25, 1865, and the authority of the Secretary of the Interior of May 13, 1901.

Arkansas and Choctaw Railroad Company.—The Arkansas and Choctaw Railroad Company completed no additional mileage during the past fiscal year, but during the present fiscal year they will have completed 75 miles additional, and have under contract another line in the Choctaw Nation to the western line of the Chicka-saw Nation. Bids have been asked for and contract is to be awarded August 26 of this year. This road is constructed under and by virtue of the provisions of the act of Congress (Public—23) approved January 28, 1899. It is thought that the entire road, 325 miles in length, will have been completed and put in operation within a year and a half.

Chicago, Rock Island and Pacific Railway Company.—The Chicago, Rock Island and Pacific Railway Company has constructed no new line in the Indian Territory during the past fiscal year. It is thought possible, however, it will construct an eastward line from Chickasha during the present fiscal year.

St. Louis and San Francisco Railway Company.—The St. Louis and San Francisco Railway Company has, during the year ended June 30, 1901, completed 160.75 miles of new road through the Creek, Seminole, and Chickasaw nations. This completes the extension of their line from Sapulpa, Creek Nation, to Sherman, Tex., known as the Red River Division. The company now has under construction what is known as the Miami Cut-off, from Miami to Afton, 13.56 miles. This line of road is being completed under the name of the Kansas City, Fort Scott and Memphis Railroad Company, under charter of March 27, 1901.

EXECUTIVES OF THE FIVE CIVILIZED TRIBES.

There has been no change of executive officials of the five Indian tribes of this agency since my last report. P. Porter, principal chief of the Creek Nation, when the council is not in session, has his executive office at Muskogee, Ind. T. G. W. Dukes, principal chief of the Choctaw Nation, when council is not in session, has his executive office at Talihina, Ind. T. D. H. Johnston, governor of the Chickasaw Nation, when council is not in session, has his executive office at Emet, Ind. T. T. M. Buffington, principal chief of the Cherokee Nation, maintains his executive office at Tahlequah at all times, although he resides at Vinita, Ind. T. John F. Brown, governor of the Seminole Nation, has his executive office at Wewoka, its capital. The relations between these respective officers and this office have been friendly, and they have cooperated with me, and I with them, to enforce the tribal laws of their respective nations.

RECOMMENDATIONS.

I again renew my recommendation that the salaries of the Indian police at this agency be increased as outlined in this report.

Recommendation is again made that Congress appropriate out of Cherokee funds a sufficient amount to pay the entire indebtedness of that nation.

A uniform system of taxing noncitizens residing and doing business in the Indian Territory should be adopted.

A road law should be passed.

I recommend that a stringent law be passed by Congress to protect the game of the Indian Territory.

CONCLUSION.

I take pleasure in stating that the employes of this office have rendered faithful and efficient service.

To the Hon. J. George Wright, United States Indian inspector for the Indian Territory, whose long experience in the Indian service and his familiarity with the conditions of this Territory constitute him a most efficient officer, I am especially indebted for valuable advice and assistance.

I am also indebted to Mr. J. W. Zevely, special inspector, for aid and assistance rendered in connection with the payment of Cherokee and Creek warrants.

I assure the Indian Office of my appreciation of courtesies shown during the past year.

I have the honor to be, very respectfully, your obedient servant,

J. BLAIR SHOENFELT,
United States Indian Agent.

The COMMISSIONER OF INDIAN AFFAIRS.

REPORT OF SUPERINTENDENT OF SCHOOLS FOR INDIAN TERRITORY.

OFFICE OF SUPERINTENDENT OF SCHOOLS IN INDIAN TERRITORY,
Muskogee, Ind. T., August 15, 1901.

SIR: I have the honor to submit my third annual report, as follows: I think it may be safely stated that our work during the past year has proceeded more harmoniously than during any previous year. Friendlier relations have been maintained between the school officials representing the Government and those representing the various tribes.

For some time after we first entered upon our work here in the Territory the tribal officials were inclined to deny our right to exercise any control over their schools. Each nation had its own corps of school officials, who were very jealous of their positions. Whenever changes were proposed by us looking toward a betterment of school conditions we were sure to be confronted with some tribal law or custom which would be urged as a bar against any reforms which we might suggest. The tribal school officials, whether competent or not, were entirely satisfied with their own management of affairs and were inclined to resent any interference with their right to control school matters according to their own pleasure.

With but few exceptions they manifested a much greater interest in securing good positions for their relatives and personal or political friends than in the welfare of their children.

By the aid of a liberal supply of patience, however, we have been able to effect many changes and improvements, and to convince the tribal officials that in the upbuilding of the schools there is abundant work for all of us.

INDIAN SCHOOLS.

Our jurisdiction is limited to the Indian schools of the Territory, although we are always ready to assist and cooperate with the various schools established for white children in every possible manner.

In many neighborhoods we have combined forces by bringing Indian and white children into the same schools. In neighborhoods where there are a sufficient number of Indian children to justify us in establishing schools for them we employ the teachers. Indian children attend such schools free of cost, and the white children are permitted to attend upon the payment of a reasonable tuition. In other neighborhoods, where the whites are largely in the majority, they establish private or public schools and we pay tuition for the few Indians who attend their schools. This plan has, with but few exceptions, worked well, and has resulted in establishing schools in neighborhoods where neither race could muster enough pupils to justify the maintenance of a school without the cooperation of the other. None of the Indian academies or boarding schools admit pupils who do not belong to their own tribe or nation.

The following is a summary of statistics of the Indian schools:

School.	Enrollment.	Average attendance.	Months of school.	Annual cost.	Average cost per pupil.	Number of employees.
CHICKASAW SCHOOLS. a						
Orphan Home	54	51	10	$4,747.31	$171.44	8
Wapanucka Institute	80	60	6	7,800.00	130.00	7
Collins Institute	49	40	10	6,400.00	160.00	7
Harley Institute b	106	72	10			13
Bloomfield Seminary b		92	10	14,025.00	152.44	
Total		351				

a Chickasaw superintendent of schools failed to make any report on neighborhood schools.
b Superintendent failed to make complete report.

CHEROKEE FEMALE ACADEMY, TAHLEQUAH.

Report of Indian Inspector for Indian Territory, 1901.

JONES ACADEMY CHOCTAW NATION.

Schools.	Enroll-ment.	Average attend-ance.	Months of school.	Annual cost.	Average cost per pupil.	Num-ber of em-ploy-ees.
CHOCTAW SCHOOLS.						
Jones Academy	142	101	9	$14,755.75	$146.10	13
Tushkahoma Academy	123	99	9	14,351.86	144.97	13
Armstrong Academy	97	87	9	12,253.97	140.85	9
Wheelock Academy	108	92	9	11,606.26	126.18	8
Atoka Baptist Academy	55	51	9	6,500.00	107.84	....
Total	525	430	....	58,469.84	135.98	43
161 neighborhood schools	2,879	1,924	....	34,391.02	17.87	169
47 neighborhood schools a	305	201	....	3,147.70	15.66	47
Total	3,709	2,555	....	96,008.56	....	259
CHEROKEE SCHOOLS.						
Male seminary	232	137	9	14,875.00	108.57	8
Female seminary	221	136	9	14,825.00	109.41	8
Orphan asylum	179	147	9	15,125.00	103.24	8
Colored high school	54	35	9	3,450.00	98.57	3
Total	686	455	....	48,275.00	106.10	27
124 neighborhood schools	4,153	2,356	7	34,460.00	14.68	124
Total	4,839	2,811	....	82,735.00	....	151
CREEK SCHOOLS.						
Eufaula	114	96	9	8,772.46	b 91.38	11
Creek orphan	62	55	9	5,722.64	104.95	7
Euchee	79	55	8	7,255.17	131.90	9
Wetumka	84	62	9	7,988.50	128.04	11
Coweta	51	39	9	3,991.37	102.34	7
Wealaka	35	24	8	3,259.76	135.82	8
Tallahassee (colored)	92	67	9	7,206.20	107.54	8
Pecan Creek (colored)	50	35	9	3,261.11	93.26	5
Colored orphan	24	17	9	3,061.19	180.07	5
Total	591	450	....	50,470.40	112.16	71
64 neighborhood schools	2,070	957	9	17,788.28	18.58	64
Total	2,661	1,407	....	68,258.68	....	135

a Choctaws who attended public and private schools in the Chickasaw Nation and whose tuition was paid at the rate of $2 per month for each pupil. Clothing and shoes are furnished free of charge to pupils in Choctaw academies, in addition to board and rooms.
b About 10 per cent of the enrollment was day students, for whom the only expenditure was cost of books and tuition.

DENOMINATIONAL SCHOOLS.

The various religious denominations were the pioneers in the educational work of this country. Soon after this Territory was given to the Five Civilized Tribes, missionaries representing the various churches came across the Mississippi River and established little missions wherein the Indian children were gathered and instructed in religion and the elements of an English education.

The religious idea was so thoroughly stamped by them upon the educational work of the Territory that, even to this day, nearly every Indian thinks a school is not complete unless devotional exercises and the study of the Bible are included in its curriculum. In the establishment of day schools in remote country districts we frequently receive letters from the old Indian parents saying: "Please send us a good, Christian teacher. We want Sunday-school in our schoolhouse." The world may perhaps never know what hardships these missionaries endured, what dangers they encountered, nor what sacrifices they made, but the fact remains that to them belongs the credit of not only having established the first schools and churches in the Territory, but also that of having firmly implanted in the mind of the Indian the love of, and desire for, religion and education.

Their little missions were first established and maintained by their church boards, together with such contributions as they could secure from benevolent people "back in the States." After years of unselfish toil, the various Indian councils or legislatures were induced to make annual appropriations to these schools, which, in many instances, enabled the missionaries to enlarge their buildings and increase their teaching force.

In the language of an educated Indian, who was detailing some of these facts of educational history:

Finally, there came a time when the Indians thought they were smart enough to manage their own schools. They took control of these schools and appointed members of their own tribe to manage them. As long as they retained control no material improvement was made.

It soon became evident that under Indian control these mission schools (which had developed into boarding schools) would not supply the educational demands of the Territory, and the churches instead of abandoning the work entirely to the Indians established other schools, some of which are now regarded as being the best educational institutions in the Territory. Their influence for good is apparent throughout every part of the Territory, and their richest harvests are yet to be garnered.

Whites and Indians are admitted to these denominational schools upon equal terms and are taught in the same classes. While they have fixed rates of tuition, yet some of them are educating children of poor parentage free of charge.

The following statement concerning the educational work of the Presbyterian Church in the Indian Territory was prepared by President A. G. Evans, of Henry Kendall College:

Missionaries of the American Board of Missions accompanied some of the tribes when they first came to the Indian Territory. These conducted valuable schools for a number of years. Among the stations where work of this kind was done Old Dwight and Park Hill in the Cherokee Nation were prominent. Good, early work was also done in the Choctaw Nation at Wheelock and Spencer and in the Creek Nation, at Old Tallahassee. The civil war interrupted this work, most of which had previously been handed over by the American board to the care of the Presbyterian board. After the war the Creek and Choctaw nations made contracts with the Presbyterian Board of Foreign Missions to conduct some of their schools. Under this arrangement the missionary board paid for the teaching and the nations for the expense of board, etc. Between 1880 and 1890 the foreign board transferred all such work to the home board. Tallahassee, Wealaka, Nuyaka, New Spencer, and Wheelock were conducted in this way, and the excellence of the work they did is best shown by the very large number of their pupils who are among the most progressive and influential of all the Indian citizens to-day. About 1885 the attention of the Presbyterian board was called to the terribly destitute condition of the white renters in the Indian Territory. Schools for both Indian and white children were organized at a number of points. Among these may be mentioned Muskogee, Tahlequah, Park Hill, Elm Spring, Old Dwight, Tulsa, Red Fork, Pleasant Hill, and McAlester. As soon as provision was made for towns to incorporate and organize school boards some of these were dropped. Some, on the other hand, by simply attempting to respond to the urgent demands upon them, developed into institutions doing much more advanced work than was originally intended. At present the Presbyterian Church is carrying on the Nuyaka school under contract with the Creek Nation. Students are all Creek Indians, and do work in the grade classes as other Indian schools do. A day school for white and Indian children is maintained at Park Hill, in the Cherokee Nation. At Elm Spring and Old Dwight are schools where, in addition to day schools, white and Indian, a limited number of boarders are taken and do some industrial work. At Dwight there is a small farm, where the boys are trained in farm work and allowed to help pay their way by this means. The school at Tahlequah has developed into the Tahlequah Institute, which has accommodations for a number of boarders as well as a large number of day scholars, both white and Indian. Work is done here from the lowest grades up to the academic course. At Muskogee, where the work was first organized by Miss Alice Robertson as a home training school for Indian girls, the pressure of the demand has been so great that it has gradually developed more advanced classes, until in 1894 it was organized as a college, now called "Henry Kendall College." Its curriculum is up to the standard of the best colleges. Connected with it are an academic department and a preparatory school, which provide a full course from the fifth grade to the college entrance. The college has graduated 17 students, of whom 9 were Indians and 8 white. It is open to students of both sexes and has during the past year in all its departments had about 200 students. It has 12 regular teachers and accommodations for about 70 boarders.

Rev. Charles Van Hulse kindly furnishes the following statement concerning the work of the Catholic Church in the Territory:

As soon as the Right Rev. Bishop Meerschaert was appointed the first vicar apostolic of Oklahoma and Indian Territory in 1891, he founded Nazareth Institute in Muskogee. He gave charge of it to the Sisters of St. Joseph, who, under the supervision of Rev. W. H. Ketcham (an Indian by blood himself, and who is at the present time director of the Catholic Indian bureau in Washington, D. C.), made it a successful institution. The first year it was a day school only. The second year accommodations were made for boarders, both girls and boys, the girls boarding with the sisters and the boys with the priest, who is principal of the school. Since then, every year new improvements have been made. In 1900 the Sisters of St. Joseph of St. Doris (Carondelet) took charge of the school.

A school both for day scholars and girl boarders was founded in Vinita by the Right Rev. Bishop Meerschaert in 1894. The school is in charge of the Sisters of Mount Carmel, of New Orleans, La., under the direction of a priest.

In 1899 a day school was founded in Tulsa, also in charge of the Sisters of Mount Carmel, of New Orleans.

There are schools also in Antlers, in charge of the Sisters of St. Rosa of Lima (boarders and day scholars); in Krebs, in charge of the Sisters of Mercy (boarders and day scholars); in Coalgate and in Lehigh, in charge of the Benedictine Sisters; in Ardmore, in charge of the Sisters of Mercy (boarders and day scholars); in Purcell and in Chickasha, in charge of the Sisters of St. Francis (day school only).

All those schools have been established for the different Indian tribes. White children are admitted also.

Among the leading educational institutions established by the Methodist Episcopal Church are Spaulding Institute at Muskogee, Willie Halsell College at Vinita, and Hargrove College at Ardmore. These schools are well managed, and are all doing good work.

The Baptists have reason to be proud of the work being done by Bacone University, near Muskogee; by their Cherokee Academy at Tahlequah, and by other mission schools located in various parts of the Territory.

I have not been able to secure complete statistics from all of these denominational schools, but the following summary will furnish some information concerning their good work:

SCHOOL HERD, NUYAKA, CREEK NATION—PRESBYTERIAN MISSION.

Name of school	Location	President or principal	By whom established	When established	Receipts				Expenditures		
					Church	Tuition	Other sources	Total	Teachers' salaries	Other expenses	Total
Hargrove College	Ardmore	Thos. G. Whitten	Methodist Church	1895	$100	$650	$340	$1,090	$490	$500	$990
St. Josephs	Chickasha	Sister Mary Cosma	Rev. Father Isadore	1900					3,209	2,732	5,941
Tahlequah Institute	Tahlequah	Chas. A. Peterson	Presbyterian Church	1888	3,430	2,010		5,440	3,209	2,782	2,832
Cherokee Academy	...do	J. C. Park	American Baptist Home Mission Society.	1896	2,469	254		2,723	1,700	1,132	
Whitaker Orphan Home	Pryor Creek	W. T. Whitaker	W. T. Whitaker	1897			878	878		1,050	1,050
Dwight Mission	Marble	F. L. Schaub	Presbyterian Church	1835	2,306	94		2,400	1,524	875	2,399
Chelsea Academy	Chelsea	G. A. Bearden	Cumberland Presbyterian Church.			940		940	900	40	940
St. Agnes	Antlers	Sister M. Eugenia	Father Ketcham	1897							
Episcopal School	Lehigh	Geo. Biller, Jr	Geo. Biller, Jr	1899		500		500	400	100	500
Willie Halsell College	Vinita	Theo. F. Brewer	Methodist, Episcopal Church South.	1886		3,000		3,000	3,000		3,000
Nazareth Institute	Muskogee	Charles Van Hulse	Sisters of St. Joseph.	1891	125	300	232	657	300	125	425
Henry Kendall College	...do	A. Grant Evans	Presbyterian Board Home Missions.	1894	9,500	4,500		14,000	6,500	7,500	14,000
Friends School	Hillside	Eva Watson	Orthodox Friends.	1886	1,000	160		1,160	1,110	50	1,160
Spaulding Institute	Muskogee	C. M. Coppedge	Methodist Episcopal Church South.	1881		3,100	2,200	5,300	3,500	1,800	5,300
Total					18,930	15,508	3,650	38,088	22,623	15,904	38,527

Denominational schools, Indian Territory—Continued.

Name of school.	Teachers. Males.	Teachers. Females.	Number months school.	Value of buildings and grounds.	Enrollment. Whites. M.	Whites. F.	Indians. M.	Indians. F.	Total. M.	Total. F.	Average attendance. Whites. M.	Whites. F.	Indians. M.	Indians. F.	Total. M.	Total. F.
Hargrove College	4	5	9	$18,000	85	90	7	15	92	105	47	51	4	8	51	59
St. Josephs		3	8		43	56	14	1	57	57	34	44	11	1	45	45
Tahlequah Institute	1	6	9	8,000	26	29	56	85	82	114	15	18	32	54	47	72
Cherokee Academy	1	3	9	6,000	36	25	52	49	88	74	16	11	23	23	39	84
Whitaker Orphan Home		1	9	8,000	15	15			15	15	11	11			11	11
Dwight Mission	1	2	10	10,000	32	30	21	10	53	40	11	10	7	8	18	13
Chelsea Academy		2	9	2,000	60	56		2	60	67	49	86		2	49	88
St. Agnes	1	2	8		31	24	21	22	52	46	11	8	10	9	21	17
Episcopal School	1	1	9		35	15	21		55	15	25	10			25	10
Willie Halsell College	4	5	9	60,000	30	25	36	38	66	63	21	17	25	28	46	45
Nazareth Institute			9	7,000	68	67	33	18	91	85	58	50	18	15	73	65
Henry Kendall College	5	9	9	45,000	70	40	37	25	107	65	59	29	16	19	87	48
Friends School	1	3	9	6,000	33	82	28	36	61	68	12	16	16	22	28	88
Spaulding Institute	2	6	9	45,000	49	118	28	32	64	150	35	75	16	20	45	96
Total	20	50	125	205,000	613	621	310	383	923	964	401	386	184	204	585	560

PUBLIC SCHOOLS.

ne act of Congress approved June 28, 1898, commonly known as the Curtis Act,
ains the following provisions relative to the establishment of public schools in
Territory:

ch city or town governments (incorporated cities and towns only) shall in no case have any
ority to impose upon or levy any tax against any lands in said cities or towns until after title is
red from the tribe; but all other property, including all improvements on town lots which for the
oses of this act shall be deemed and considered personal property, together with all occupations
privileges, shall be subject to taxation. And the councils of such cities and towns, for the sup-
of the same and for schools and other public purposes, may provide by ordinance for the assess-
t, levy, and collection annually of a tax upon such property not to exceed in the aggregate two
entum of the assessed value thereof, in manner provided in chapter one hundred and twenty-
of said digest (Arkansas Statutes), entitled "Revenue," and for such purposes may also impose
: upon occupations and privileges.
ch councils may also establish and maintain free schools in such cities and towns, under the pro-
ns of sections sixty-two hundred and fifty-eight to sixty-two hundred and seventy-six inclusive
id digest, and may exercise all the powers conferred upon special school districts in cities and
us in the State of Arkansas by the laws of said State, when the same are not in conflict with the
isions of this act.

rior to the passage of this act there was no provision of law whatever for the
blishment of public schools anywhere in the Territory; even now no public
ools can be organized except in the incorporated cities and towns.

he act above quoted limits taxation in these cities and towns to 2 per cent per
um for all purposes.

hen it is remembered that up to this time no taxes could be levied, except upon
onal property, occupations, and privileges, and that the personal property is
ely composed of cheaply built stores and houses, it can readily be seen that that
ion of the 2 per cent tax set aside for school purposes must be totally inade-
e to the needs of the schools in every such city or town. By this law, too, all
pations are subject to double taxation, inasmuch as they are taxed by the tribal
orities.

he following is a list of the incorporated cities and towns in the Territory, together
h the population of each as shown by the United States official census of 1900,
ough in nearly every town the population has very largely increased since this
us was taken:

Population of the incorporated towns of Indian Territory, 1900.

Towns.	Popula-tion.	Towns.	Popula-tion.	Towns.	Popula-tion.
r....................	268	Eufaula	757	Pauls Valley	1,467
n....................	606	Fairland	499	Peoria	144
nore	5,681	Fort Gibson	617	Pontotoc	366
lesville	698	Gans	136	Poteau	1,182
ryn	273	Grove	314	Pryorcreek	495
jacket	303	Hanson	182	Purcell	2,277
xhe	158	Hartshorne............	2,352	Purdy	200
ow	626	Heavener	234	Ravia	128
lo	930	Hickory	262	Rush Springs..........	518
eron	316	Holdenville	749	Salisaw................	965
diah	522	Howe..................	626	Sapulpa	891
nea.................	241	Johnson	204	Silo...................	246
otah	805	Kemp	221	South McAlester	3,479
sca.................	566	Lehigh	1,500	Spiro	543
kasha..............	3,209	Lenapah	154	Sterrett...............	575
more	855	Leon	221	Stilwell...............	779
gate................	2,614	Longrove..............	215	Sulphur Springs.......	1,198
nsville.............	376	McAlester	646	Tahlequah	1,482
anche..............	547	McGee................	209	Tamaha	237
erville..........,...	189	Mannsville	198	Thackerville	154
ish.................	307	Marietta...............	842	Tulsa	1,390
ington.............	272	Marlow................	1,016	Vian	296
berland............	343	Miami	1,527	Vinita	2,339
s...................	1,846	Muldrow	465	Wagoner	2,372
cherty	437	Muskogee.............	4,254	Webbers Falls	211
zan	1,164	Nowata................	498	Welch	834
nt	2,969	Oakland...............	701	Westville	296
....	225	Oologah	308	Wister	313
ore	192	Orr	222	Wyandotte	224
t	342	Paoli	234	Wynnewood...........	1,907

Denominational schools, Indian Territory—Continued.

Name of school.	Teachers.		Number months school.	Value of buildings and grounds.	Enrollment.						Average attendance.					
	Males.	Females.			Whites.		Indians.		Total.		Whites.		Indians.		Total.	
					M.	F.	M.	F.	M.	F.	M.	F.	M.	F.	M.	F.
Hargrove College	4	5	9	$18,000	85	90	7	15	92	105	47	51	4	8	51	59
St. Josephs		3	8		43	56	14	1	57	57	34	44	11	1	45	45
Tahlequah Institute	1	6	9	8,000	26	29	56	85	82	114	15	18	32	64	47	72
Cherokee Academy	1	3	9	6,000	26	25	62	49	88	74	16	11	23	23	39	74
Whitaker Orphan Home		1	9	8,000	15	15			15	15	16	11			11	11
Dwight Mission	1	2	9	10,000	32	30	21	10	53	40	11	10	7	8	18	13
Chelsea Academy		2	10	2,000	60	56		2	60	57	49	36		2	49	88
St. Agnes	1	2			31	24	21	22	52	46	11	8	10	9	21	17
Episcopal School		1	8		85	15			85	15	26	10			26	10
Willie Halsell College	1		9	50,000	30	26	36	38	66	63	21	17	25	28	46	45
Nazareth Institute	4	5	9	7,000	68	67	23	18	91	85	66	60	18	15	78	66
Henry Kendall College	5	9	9	45,000	70	40	37	25	107	65	59	29	28	19	87	48
Friends School	1	8	9	6,000	33	32	28	36	61	68	12	16	16	22	28	38
Spaulding Institute	2	6	9	45,000	49	118	15	32	64	150	35	75	10	20	45	96
Total	20	50	125	206,000	618	621	310	383	923	954	401	386	184	204	566	590

Public schools, Indian Territory—Continued.

Towns.	Average attendance.							
	Whites.		Indians.		Negroes.		Total.	
	M.	F.	M.	F.	M.	F.	M.	F.
Muskogee..........	180	190	....	....	70	112	250	302
Rush Springs	43	52	3	1	....	....	46	53
Marietta	75	100	9	7	....	....	84	107
Ardmore	352	403	6	7	65	90	423	500
Chickasha	163	156	1	....	23	30	187	186
Marlow	134	146	1	3	....	....	135	149
Pauls Valley.......	130	116	....	....	....	....	130	116
Purcell	150	203	6	9	23	36	179	248
Claremore	88	78	....	....	....	....	88	78
Nowata	48	41	24	20	....	....	72	61
South McAlester ...	137	153	4	7	27	34	168	194
Tulsa	82	90	17	20	12	13	111	123
Eufaula	28	36	4	5	15	25	47	66
Checotah	58	65	9	12	....	....	67	77
Muldrow..........	60	70	8	12	....	....	68	82
McAlester..........	56	59	8	9	....	....	64	68
Vinita..............	65	59	63	66	24	48	152	173
Total.........	1,849	2,017	163	178	259	388	2,271	2,583

While about twenty of these towns have endeavored to organize public schools, yet their limited funds have been a constant source of embarrassment to them. The small fund which they have been able to realize from taxation in most instances has been but scantily sufficient to pay teachers' salaries, leaving them powerless to build and equip suitable school buildings. The great majority of these towns are as yet absolutely unable to even raise sufficient money by taxation to employ the necessary teachers. As I have already said, the unincorporated towns and villages, many of which are springing up in all parts of the Territory, are absolutely powerless in the matter of establishing free schools. This is indeed a pitiable condition of affairs, and one for which the people of the Territory are in no way responsible.

Some members of Congress claim that it would be establishing a bad precedent for Congress to appropriate money for the support of these schools. Two objections are urged by them, viz:

They say that the general policy of the Government has been that the State or Territory should maintain its own schools.

They also say that there are many localities throughout the States where the people are too poor to properly maintain public schools, and that if Congress should appropriate money in aid of public schools in the Territory it would soon be deluged with petitions to appropriate money for these poor localities in the States.

To the first objection it may be said that Congress has, from time to time, ever since the organization of our Government, donated large tracts of land, amounting to millions of acres, for the support of schools. Many of our Presidents have recommended that Congress appropriate money directly from the United States Treasury for this purpose.

Jefferson repeatedly urged that Congress should devote its surplus revenues derived from duties on imports to the building up of free schools in the young States and Territories.

Grant, in his annual message of 1871, said: "Educational interests may well be served by the grant of the proceeds of the sale of land to settlers."

Hayes, in 1880, said: "The acts of Congress, from time to time, donating public lands to the several States and Territories in aid of educational interests have proved to be wise measures of public policy, resulting in great and lasting benefit."

Arthur, in 1881, said: "A large portion of the public domain has been from time to time devoted to the promotion of education. There is now special reason why, by setting apart the proceeds of its sales of public lands, or by some other course, the Government should aid the work of education."

President Harrison, in his first annual message, said: "The interest of the General Government in the education of the people found an early expression, not only in the thoughtful and sometimes warning utterances of our ablest statesmen, but in liberal appropriations from the common resources for the support of education in the new States. No one will deny that it is of the gravest national concern that those who hold the ultimate control of all public affairs should have the necessary intelligence wisely to direct and determine them. National aid to education has heretofore taken the form of land grants, and in that form the constitutional power of Congress to promote the education of the people is not seriously questioned. I do not think it can be successfully questioned when the form is changed to that of a direct grant of money from the public Treasury."

President McKinley, in his second annual message, strongly recommended that Congress make some provision for the education of the 30,000 white children in the Indian Territory.

In reply to the second objection above stated it would seem to be sufficient to say that Congress is responsible for the helpless condition of the white settlers of the Territory and should, in some way, remove this condition of helplessness. In this connection, it should be remembered, also, that the negroes of the Territory, except the colored citizens of the Creek and Cherokee nations, have no funds with which to educate their children, and some provision should be made which will enable them to maintain schools for their children.

PRIVATE SCHOOLS.

In many of the smaller towns of the Territory private or subscription schools for whites are maintained during a portion of each year. In a few cases earnest, enthusiastic teachers have gone into these villages and have organized fairly good schools, but they are usually unable to secure suitable buildings and furniture, and many of their patrons are too poor to pay the tuition of their children. It too often happens that incompetent teachers, those who have failed in examination or have been unable to secure good positions, drift into these towns and "keep" school as long as the people will allow them to remain. Their terms are usually short, however, and such schools change teachers several times during the year.

Private schools, Indian Territory.

Name of school.	Location.	President or principal.	By whom established.	When established.	Receipts.		
					Tuition.	Other sources.	Total.
Caddo High School	Caddo	J. J. Scarborough .	People of Howe.	1889..	$520	....	$520
The Public School.	Howe........	John Begley......			265	....	265
Westville School ..	Westville	C. B. Rhodes......	C. B. Rhodes	1901..			
El Meta Christian College.	Minco ,.......	Meta Chestnutt...	Meta Chestnutt..	1894..	1,848	$1,923	3,771
Pryor Creek Academy.	Pryor Creek .	H. S. Bruce	Stock company.	....	1,200	....	1,200
Total				....	3,833	1,923	5,756

Name of school.	Expenditures.			Teachers.		Number months school.	Value of buildings and grounds.
	Teachers' salaries.	Other expenses.	Total.	M.	F.		
Caddo High School..........	$555	$88	$643	1	1	9	....
The Public School..........	265	....	265	1	1	10	$500
Westville School				1	1	4	400
El Meta Christian College...	1,200	2,385	3,585	1	3	9	5,000
Pryor Creek Academy	1,200	....	1,200	2	2	9	2,000
Total	3,220	2,473	5,693	6	8	41	7,900

Name of school.	Enrollment.						Average attendance.					
	Whites.		Indians.		Total.		Whites.		Indians.		Total.	
	M.	F.	M.	F.	M.	F.	M.	F.	M.	F.	M.	F.
Caddo High School	41	48	30	23	71	71	14	10	13	14	27	24
The Public School	40	32	.....	.....	40	32	35	25	.....	.....	35	25
Westville School												
El Meta Christian College ..	47	48	15	13	62	61	33	48	10	12	43	55
Pryor Creek Academy	69	71	17	21	86	92	31	32	8	9	39	41
Total..................	197	199	62	57	259	256	113	110	31	35	144	145

Report of Indian Inspector for Indian Territory, 1901.

SCHOOL BUILDING, EUFAULA, CREEK NATION.

OUR SUMMER NORMALS.

It was with some feeling of doubt that we attempted to organize summer normal schools for the teachers of the various nations of the Territory a year ago. We realized the great need of such schools, but as they were new to the Territory we did not know how many teachers would endeavor to attend. The normals held in the Cherokee, Creek, and Choctaw nations during the summer of 1900 proved so helpful to the teachers that it seemed necessary only to announce the dates and places of holding this year's normals to insure good attendance at each. Our first normal in the Cherokee Nation left such a good impression upon the people that their council, at its annual session, in October last, passed a law making it obligatory upon their board of education to hold a four-weeks' normal every summer thereafter. The session just closed at Tahlequah was attended by 154 teachers, and was characterized by good, earnest work upon the part of all present. The three members of the Cherokee board were in attendance nearly every day, and did everything in their power to make the normal as successful as possible. In that nation a separate normal was held for colored teachers, with an attendance of 18.

The Creek normal, held at Eufaula, enrolled, this summer, 74 teachers. A separate normal was also held in this nation for colored teachers, in which 50 teachers were enrolled.

The Choctaw normal, just closed, was held at Jones Academy with an attendance of 155 teachers.

Our supervisors (each in his own nation) were in constant attendance at these normals and devoted their time faithfully to directing and supervising the work.

We continued the plan adopted last year of bringing the teachers together in a boarding school, where they are furnished with board, room, and tuition for a term of four weeks for $12 each. This plan has succeeded well. It not only enables those present to concentrate their attention and efforts upon their work, but it affords the teachers an opportunity for getting better acquainted and for exchanging views informally upon the many questions which confront them in the school work. Our teachers are most certainly manifesting a commendable interest in the great task of improving the educational work of the Territory.

As a specimen of Indian English and eloquence, I quote the following speech, delivered at the Choctaw normal, during general exercises, by Robert Lee, a full-blood Choctaw:

You belong to a white race and I belong to an Indian race, but when reflect back years ago and when look upon this body of teachers with a pleasant faces and blue eyes, I say, "Amen, welcome my white friends, welcome."

The normal is the grandest, the bravest, and the profoundest thing ever started in the Indian Territory, and when I look over these teachers I found about twenty-four Indians who expect to teach his coming year. Most of the teachers are young ladies, and when I see these black-haired and black-eyed, my heart thrilled with a gladness and joy and I say, "Welcome, my white friend." If it had not been for you these girls would not have been here. Welcome Texas, welcome Arkansas, welcome Nebraska, welcome Ohio, welcome Missouri, welcome Illinois and Wisconsin. Years ago at the time of the discovery of America, we the Indian people, or our ancestors rather, know nothing of education, know nothing of Bible, know nothing of work, and your ancestors and my ancestors were enemies. They fought each other, they killed each other because the Indian believed that this grand old country, lying in the north temperate zone, extending from the Arctic Ocean to the Gulf of Mexico, touching the Pacific Ocean and the Atlantic Ocean, was belong to them, and said, "Strange people shall not have our hunting ground." The war began, but Indians have nothing to fight with and your ancestors killed a thousands of my people, they shed the precious blood of my people, they have taken a poor innocent babies from their mother's arms and drown them in the rivers, they force them to move to the west, they force them to cross Mississippi River and drown half of them in that river, they make them settle down in this wild country at that time known as Indian Territory, they killed our chief, Poshimataha, they killed our warriors, Arvatayatabee, Moshalitabee, Ashakatabee, and many others, but to-day, in the year of our Lord 1901, and in the name of our great God, you and I are coworkers and the same as one.

The Indian children of to-day are taught to be a prejudice against the white people. I am sorry to say, but it is true, when I was a boy I was taught to be a prejudice against the white people, but to-day I can not help but like you people. I love you people because you have taught me how to love my people and my country; you have taught me how to make living; you have taught me how to work; you have showed me a true living God and taught me how to worship Him, and when I look upon uneducated Choctaws I feel the burden of responsibility upon my shoulder and on the shoulders of these uneducated ones, and I feel like get down on my knees before this body of teachers and say: "O. teachers, establish the normal more firm and strong in the Indian Territory and help me, or help us, to educate these uneducated Choctaws, that they may get out this state lethargy and be a better citizen, and be a lover of their homes and their country." I say again I feel like get down on my knees and beg you teachers do all in your power to educate these uneducated Choctaws, that we may bring them into a higher standpoint or a higher civilization. If I should ask the question, "What is the teacher's duty?" no doubt some will say: "The teacher's duty is to teach you to read and write," but, my fellow-teachers, we, the Indian people, need more than that. I am a believer of fashion. It is the duty of every woman to make herself beautiful and attractive as she possibly can. "Handsome is as handsome does," but she is much handsomer if well dressed. The time never ought to come in this country when you can tell a farmer's wife or daughter simply by the garments she wears. Say to every teacher, every girl and woman, no matter what material of your dress may be, no matter how cheap and coarse it is, cut it and make it in fashion. To adorn ourselves seems to be a part of our nature and this desire seems to be everywhere and in everything. I sometimes thought that desire for beauty covers the earth with flowers. It is this desire that paints the wings of moths, tints the chamber of the shell, and gives the bird its plumage. O, teachers, daughters, and wives, if you would be loved adorn yourself; if you would be adored be beautiful, and when you go out to teach my people if you have girls in your school teach them that fashion is the essential thing; teach them how to be a good work; teach them how to be a lady, and above all teach them how to be a good wife and mother. And men if you have boys in your school teach them that laboring is not disgrace as they generally believe that it is disgrace for man to work. You don't have to work with them, but teach them how to swing the axes. If you know how, teach them how to be good workers; teach them how to be a good carpenter; teach them how to be a farmer; teach them how to be an honest man; teach them how to be a good citizen, and above all teach them how to be a good husband and good father; teach them how to beautify their homes with plants, flowers, and vines. Remember that everything of beauty tends to the elevation of man; every little morning-glory whose purple bosom is thrilled with the amorous kisses of the sun is tend to put a blossom in your heart. Teach them that every flower about a house certifies to the refinement of somebody. Every vine climbing, blossoming, tells of love and joy. There is no happiness in the schoolhouse not filled with love and kindness. There is no happiness in a home not filled with a love. Teach them that where husband hate wife, where wife hates husband, where children hate their parents and each other, there is a "hell" upon earth. Teach them that Indian Territory is the finest country ever occupied by Indians. We have 31,000 square miles of land—over 20,000,000 acres. Upon these plains we can raise enough to feed 15,000,000 people. Beneath these prairies were hidden million of ages ago by that old miser, the sun 20,000 square miles of coal. Think of all this force willed and left to us by the dead morning of the world. Think of the fireside of the future, around which will sit the fathers, mothers, and children of the years to come. Think of the sweet and happy faces, loving and tender eyes that will glow and gleam in the sacred light of these flames. Indian Territory, the finest country in the West the finest country for a normal, as it contains first-class teachers from all parts of the country.

The following resolutions, prepared and adopted by the teachers at the close of the Choctaw Normal, will show something of the spirit now manifested by the teachers.

Whereas, in order to properly extend to Supt. J. D. Benedict, Supervisor Calvin Ballard, Superintendent Butz, of Jones Academy, the instructors, and others who have contributed directly or indirectly to the unparalleled success of the Choctaw Normal, our thanks and appreciation for their efforts to place the teachers of the Choctaw Nation upon a higher plane of teaching, we, the teachers of the Choctaw Normal, adopt the following resolutions:

1. That we express our appreciation and confidence in the masterly manner in which Superintendent Benedict is managing the schools, and for his untiring efforts and kindly counsel in this great educational cause.

2. That in Supervisor Calvin Ballard we have found a polished gentleman, a thorough educator and to him we are personally indebted for the great success of this normal in all its bearings. We appreciate his untiring energy, his devotion to the work, and his kindly care and consideration for our every welfare. We pledge him our hearty and willing cooperation in his arduous labor of building up a more efficient school system in the Choctaw Nation.

3. That we tender our heartfelt thanks to the instructors Professors—Beck, Bayne, and Puntenny—for their wise directions and careful instructions. We will ever hold them in the highest esteem and the memory of our association with them will always be an inspiration to press onward toward the goal. We desire, also, to extend to Mrs. Bayne our appreciation for the excellent music furnished.

4. That we extend to Superintendent Butz, of Jones Academy, and his assistants our hearty and sincere thanks for the free use of the buildings and grounds, and for the assiduous way they have looked after and provided for the reception and comforts of all, during the normal.

5. That a copy of these resolutions be furnished to Supt. J. D. Benedict, Supervisor Calvin Ballard and to each of the instructors of the Choctaw Normal, and that the papers of the Choctaw Nation be requested to publish the same.

J. Y. COLLINS, *Chairman;*
L. B. LOCKE, *Secretary;*
MISS SUE M. OAKES,
MISS CARRIE TENNENT,
MISS LOU J. MERONEY,
Committee on Resolutions.

We were unable to get a normal school started last year in the Chickasaw Nation, but this summer, at a rather late date, a normal was finally announced and, under the direction of Supt. E. B. Hinshaw, of Bloomfield Academy, about 30 of the Chickasaw teachers met at Tishomingo and spent four weeks very profitably in study. Having made the start we shall expect good results another year in this nation.

SCHOOL VISITATION.

I am a thorough believer in personal visitation and close supervision of schools. Rural schools, especially, are in constant need of the advice and encouragement of competent supervisors. The patrons are always pleased to know that the school officials are actually visiting their little schools. They are ever ready to receive and carry out suggestions concerning the education of their children. Soon after the schools opened last fall I addressed the following letter to each of the supervisors:

To School Supervisors.

I addressed to you a letter about a year ago urging the importance of giving close attention to the neighborhood schools of your nation. I desire now to renew that recommendation with emphasis. The crops are nearly all gathered, and the children ought to be in school. These neighborhood schools have heretofore been sadly neglected, and by personal visitation and inspection you can assist very materially in building them up. Where the buildings are in bad condition, a suggestion from you to the right party should have great weight. You should see that each teacher keeps a daily register, showing the attendance of each pupil, and if the attendance is not good you should urge upon the pupils, teachers, local trustees, and citizens the importance of sending their children to school regularly. In the present shifting, changing condition of affairs it may sometimes occur that the school

TUSHKAHOMMA FEMALE INSTITUTE, CHOCTAW NATION.

house is not located in the proper place. By acquainting yourself with each neighborhood you can advise the citizens upon this matter. Schoolhouses should always be built on well-drained ground and within reach of pure drinking water. In your visits to these schoolhouses you should not criticise the teacher in the presence of the school. Too much fault-finding is apt to discourage rather than encourage the teacher and pupils. You should remain in each school long enough to get some definite knowledge as to its condition and the character of the work done by the teacher. You should carefully note the manner of conducting recitations, and during the intermission make such suggestions to the teacher as will tend to secure better work upon his or her part. You should devote the greater part of your time from now until next June to visiting these neighborhood schools. I shall endeavor to visit and inspect all the boarding schools during the year, but shall not be able to visit many day schools. I desire that you hereafter make a monthly report to me, beginning at the end of the present month, somewhat after the form inclosed herewith. Each report should contain a list of the schools visited by you during the month and the date of the visit, together with such suggestions as to needed changes as you may find necessary to submit.

Much good has already resulted from the visits of the supervisors, and the knowledge which has been gained thereby of the actual condition and needs of the rural schools, will, I hope, enable us to accomplish still better results in the future.

CHEROKEE SCHOOLS.

The teachers and other school employees of the Cherokee Nation are examined by the Cherokee board of education and Supervisor Coppock, acting together. After examination the teachers are assigned to the various schools of the nation by the board, subject to the approval of the supervisor. A healthier interest is plainly discernible in the educational work of this nation. Their council enacted a wise law at its last annual session by which the long winter vacation which had been customary in their neighborhood schools was abolished.

Supervisor Coppock has visited nearly all the schools of that nation during the past year, and his encouraging words to the pupils, teachers, and parents are always helpful.

CREEK SCHOOLS.

The Creek Nation maintains 9 boarding schools, 6 for Indian children and 3 for children of their freedmen. They also have 64 neighborhood schools, 41 of which are Indian schools and 23 are for negro children. The attendance in some of these schools was materially reduced during the past year, principally from two causes, viz, smallpox, and the dissatisfaction which arose among the full-bloods concerning the individual allotment of lands. Creek citizens are still retained as superintendents of these boarding schools (except Nuyaka). Some of the superintendents are careless in their work, and neglect to take the necessary precaution against the introduction of smallpox and other contagious diseases into their schools.

The treaty recently made between the Creeks and the Federal Government places the direct control of their schools in the hands of the Creek superintendent of education and our supervisor, acting jointly, subject, however, to the rules and regulations of the Interior Department. Miss Alice M. Robertson is just closing her first year's work as supervisor of the Creek schools. The work was not entirely new to her, as she was born and reared among these Indians and had taught in a number of Indian schools. She is deeply interested in the welfare of the Creeks, and has labored earnestly to improve the condition of their schools.

I regret that the treaty above mentioned reserved but 40 acres of land for each of these boarding schools. After deducting yards, barn lots, and orchards but little land is left for cultivation. Every one of these schools should have a good, large farm, which, properly managed, would furnish nearly all the provisions needed for the maintenance of the school.

CHOCTAW SCHOOLS.

We have had entire control of the Choctaw schools during the past year and the school work of that nation has progressed satisfactorily, except that some of the officials who were opposed to surrendering entire control have been inclined to encourage a spirit of dissatisfaction among their people. In order to remove all cause for dissatisfaction, I have recommended that their school authorities be recognized to some extent hereafter. The work in the boarding schools of this nation will now compare very favorably with the average high schools of the States.

Some good work has been accomplished in manual training and industrial work during the past year. The girls have made very good progress in sewing, embroidery work, and housekeeping.

The boys have taken quite a lively interest in learning to use tools, and the tables, picture frames, etc., which they have made are evidence of their skill in handiwork.

The increased interest in educational matters in this nation is shown by the facts that the boarding schools have been crowded to their utmost limits, and a larger number of neighborhood schools have been maintained than ever before. The 170 or more teachers of this nation have kept Supervisor Ballard very busy during the past year, and his patience and tact in dealing with the Indians have made him many friends among the Choctaws.

CHICKASAW SCHOOLS.

Until within the past few months the Chickasaw authorities have steadily refused to admit that we had any legal right to exercise supervision over their schools, inasmuch as they were endeavoring to maintain them out of funds over which we had no control.

This made it impossible for us to do much effective work for the schools of that nation, and for this reason the services of our Chickasaw supervisor were dispensed with some time ago.

The schools of this nation were gradually getting more deeply in debt, and their financial condition finally became so serious that it was necessary that their authorities make some concessions in order that their schools might receive the benefit of their share of the coal royalty funds, the expenditure of which the honorable Secretary of the Interior was made responsible for by the terms of the act of Congress of June 28, 1898. After some considerable negotiation between the honorable Secretary of the Interior and the governor of the Chickasaw Nation, the following agreement was made relative to the disbursement of this royalty fund:

As applicable to the disbursement of the Chickasaw coal and asphaltum royalty fund for educational purposes in that nation, the following regulations are hereby approved by the Secretary of the Interior and the Chickasaw Nation by its governor:

1. That a board of examiners, one of whom shall be designated by the Secretary of the Interior, shall be appointed by the duly constituted authority or authorities of the Chickasaw Nation, among whose duties shall be that of examining applicants to teach in said nation, with a view to ascertaining their qualification in every respect for the performance of that duty.

2. That, after the close of the present scholastic year, to wit, June 30, 1901, no person shall be eligible to teach in the schools of the Chickasaw Nation who has not been examined by such board of examiners and received a certificate from such board as to his mental, moral, and other qualifications to teach, which certificate shall expire one year from the date thereof.

3. That no act of said board shall be effective for any purpose unless concurred in by each and every member thereof.

4. That said board of examiners shall have authority, and it shall be their duty, to revoke and cancel the certificate of any teacher who may by said board be found guilty of any act of immorality or of any conduct which, in the judgment of the board, renders such teacher an unfit person to have charge of a school or be associated therewith as a teacher, and it shall be the duty of said board to take jurisdiction of any complaint in that behalf which may be made in writing against such teacher. And the decision of said board relative thereto shall forthwith be reported to the board of education for said Chickasaw Nation, for appropriate action.

5. The school officials appointed by the Secretary of the Interior for the Indian Territory shall at all times have access to the schools of the Chickasaw Nation for the purpose of advising as to the character and conduct of school employees, course of study, methods of teaching, sanitation and discipline, and friendly cooperation with such school officials, so as aforesaid appointed by the Secretary of the Interior, on the part of the school officials, teachers and other officers of the Chickasaw Nation in the betterment of such schools is assured by said nation, and any information that may be desired by the Secretary of the Interior, or his representative, as to the condition or conduct of such schools will at all times be cheerfully furnished.

6. That the outstanding warrants of the Chickasaw Nation legally issued, for the service performed or material furnished for school purposes, in accordance with school laws of the Chickasaw Nation since the ratification of the Atoka agreement, shall be paid without unnecessary delay by a disbursing officer, designated by the Secretary of the Interior, out of the Chickasaw coal and asphaltum royalty fund now in the hands of the United States, so far as the same will apply, and such school warrants as may hereafter be legally issued for such service or such material for school purposes, in accordance with such laws, shall in like manner be paid out of such fund as shall hereafter come into the hands of the United States, so far as the same will apply, annually, semiannually, or quarterly, as the Secretary of the Interior may determine best, so long as these regulations shall be observed by the Chickasaw Nation.

WASHINGTON, D. C., April 11, 1901.
Approved:

E. A. HITCHCOCK,
Secretary of the Interior.
D. H. JOHNSTON,
Governor Chickasaw Nation.

This fund now amounts to about $100,000, but it is feared that it is not sufficient to liquidate the entire school indebtedness of that nation.

The Chickasaws deserve credit for their liberal appropriations for educational purposes, but their annual expenses are in excess of their ability to pay. Some of the school employees have been unable to get any money upon their warrants for the past two years without heavily discounting them. Not only are the children in their academies boarded and educated at the expense of the nation, but for several years past the nation has undertaken to pay the board of children who attend their neighborhood schools. Under this agreement many parents receive pay for boarding their own children at home. Their annual expenses should be curtailed and arrangements made so that the contractors who maintain their boarding schools and the teachers of the nation may receive their pay more promptly.

WAPANUCKA INSTITUTE.

aployee and position.	Salary.	Race.	Age.	Single or married.	Birthplace.	By whom appointed.
som, principal teacher.....	$600	White ..	30	Single	Tex	C. A. Skean.
k, assistant teacher.........	300	....do ...	48	.....do	.....do	Do.
ton, instrumental music ...	300	....do ...	25	.....do	.....do	Do.
ed, piano instructor........	210	....do ...	22	.....do	.....do	Do.
tiels, cook	240	....do ...	40	.....do	Ind. T	Do.
, laborer....................	150	....do ...	25	.....do	.....do	Do.
d, laundress................	240	....do ...	40	.....do	.....do	Do.

of months of school........	6
daily attendance	60
of attendance	75
nrollment...................	80
ation	$9,600
paid employees.............	$2,040
ance	$5,760
cost of pupil per month	$21.67

COLLINS INSTITUTE.

aployee and position.	Salary.	Race.	Age.	Single or married.	Birthplace.	By whom appointed.
es, principal teacher	$400	White ..	25	Single	Tenn	W. H. Jackson.
Jackson, primary teacher ..	200	....do ...	19	Married ..	Tex	Do.
. Jackson, music teacher ...	350	....do ...	21	Single	Ind. T	Do.
rand, cook	300	Negro ..	28	.....do	Tex	Do.
dges, laundryman	250	White ..	45	Married ..	Mo	Do.
tin, wood chopper	120	....do ...	44	.....do	Mo	Do.
kson, laborer...............	200	....do ...	20	.....do	Ind. T	Do.

of months of school........	10
daily attendance	40
of attendance..............	82
nrollment.................	49
ation	$6,400
paid employees	$1,820
ance.....................	$4,580
cost of pupil per month....	$16

ORPHANS' HOME.

aployee and position.	Salary.	Race.	Age.	Single or married.	Birthplace.	By whom appointed.
rick, superintendent.......	$1,500	White ..	53	Married ..	Mo	Chickasaw superintendent of schools.
'uller, principal teacher....	600	....do ...	38	Single		Do.
errick, assistant teacher....	500	....do ...	24	.....do		Do.
rrick, music teacher.......	400	....do ...	22	.....do		Do.
ampbell, seamstress	250	....do ...	36	.....do		Do.
phy, cook	300	....do ...	40	Married ..		Do.
well, laundress	250	....do ...	22	Single		Do.
dom, farmer	200	....do ...	53	Married ..		Do.

of months of school........	10
daily attendance	50.5
of attendance	94
nrollment.................	54
ation	$10,000.00
paid employees............	$4,000.00
ance	$4,747.31
cost of pupil per month....	$17.32

MANUAL TRAINING.

iave introduced manual training in all of the boarding schools over which we
ad entire control, and in some others. The Indian boys and girls take an
in the work, and with the limited facilities at hand we believe that a fairly
ginning has been made along this line.

inual training is of value and importance to the pupils of a city high school,
much greater value is it to these Indian boys and girls, every one of whom is
ner of a tract of land which needs improvements and development in order to

make it productive. These schools will produce far better results when manual training, together with industrial training, shall become an important part of every course of study.

THE SCHOOL AND THE HOME.

Education is by no means confined to the schoolroom. One of our great writers has said that it is a continuing process, beginning with the cradle and ending with the grave. Every teacher of experience is a witness to the fact that the influence of the home is a powerful factor in the education of every child.

While there are many refined and cultured homes among the Indians of the Territory, yet there are many homes, especially among the poor, unlettered full-blood element, where education receives but little encouragement or cooperation. This fact makes the task of educating these children a slow one. Many of the lessons learned in school, many of the habits formed there, are forgotten and neglected when the children return to their homes.

It would be a blessing to these people if we could secure as their teachers strong-minded men and women. They need teachers whose influence would not be confined to the little rustic schoolroom, but who would be able to render the much-needed assistance in the improvement of homes, the development and cultivation of farms, and in the care of orchards and live stock.

Their former mode of living and environment have been the direct opposite of that which now confronts them. Their tribal relations are well-nigh abolished, their hunting grounds destroyed, and a new life, a new civilization, faces them. Their habits of life, their inclinations, their customs can not all be changed in a day. With proper assistance, however, they may be led to direct their energies along new lines. They can be led to see that the same amount of energy expended by them in tramping over the hills in search of snakeroot would bring them better financial results if expended in planting and cultivating crops. They might easily learn that the time and energy expended in hunting game would insure them more meat if devoted to raising pigs and calves. They should not be allowed to remain objects of charity, but should be taught that they should return an equivalent for everything which they receive from their neighbors.

I submit herewith the annual reports of the supervisors for the Creek, Cherokee, and Choctaw nations. I have no report from the Chickasaw Nation, for the reason that the office of supervisor for that nation was discontinued on the 1st day of June.

I am under renewed obligations to you, sir, for the assistance and encouragement which I have constantly received from your Department in my work here in the Territory, and also take pleasure in acknowledging the valuable aid and support given me by the Hon. J. George Wright, United States Indian Inspector for the Indian Territory.

Respectfully submitted.

JOHN D. BENEDICT,
Superintendent of Schools in Indian Territory.

The SECRETARY OF THE INTERIOR.

REPORT OF CREEK SCHOOL SUPERVISOR.

OFFICE OF SCHOOL SUPERVISOR FOR CREEK NATION,
MUSKOGEE, IND. T., *August 15, 1901.*

SIR: I have the honor to present the following annual report as supervisor of schools for the Creek Nation:

It is impossible to obtain reliable data as to the population of the Creek Nation The estimate given me by their principal chief is, however, 10,000 Creek Indians and 4,500 Creek negroes. The Creek school fund, used exclusively for educational purposes for these people, amounts annually to $76,468.40. Of this amount $63,300 is annually required for the maintenance of the ten boarding schools, leaving a balance of $13,168.40 for the support of neighborhood schools.

As a matter of actual fact the above amount is increased each year by special appropriations made by the Creek council. The amount appropriated for school purposes at the last annual session of the Creek council was $88,900.

The present school system of the Creeks is largely the work of their first superintendent of education, whose initial public service was in this capacity, from 1869 to 1872 It may not be out of place in this connection to speak of the comparative newness of educational work among the Creeks as contrasted with that of their neighbors, the Choctaws and Cherokees, who had a number of Indian graduates of Eastern

THE BEST DAY SCHOOLHOUSE, CREEK NATION.

THE WORST SCHOOLHOUSE, CREEK NATION

colleges before the first log-cabin school was established among the Creeks. When the Creek school system was inaugurated by Pleasant Porter, who as chief executive of the Creeks continues the unwearying interest in educational affairs he has manifested throughout his public life, an apportionment at the rate of two-thirds for Indian and one-third for negro citizens was deemed the fair proportion, and it is upon this basis that the schools are carried on. The increase of population is more rapid among the negroes than among the Indians, and there is from them a constant pressure for additional neighborhood schools, for the establishment of which there are no funds available. In several instances I have found that the local trustees have allowed negro children to attend the Indian school where there was no negro school within a long distance. In these cases the race distinction was kept quite marked by separate seats and separate classes. One very remote negro community sent in through their Indian town chief a petition reporting a considerable number of citizen children, at the same time requesting the appointment of a full-blood Indian teacher. The negroes insist upon teachers of their own race. I was very much surprised when, after a whole day of driving, I found a negro instead of an Indian school. In two instances I have found an Indian child attending a negro neighborhood school.

From the accompanying statistics it will be seen that the average citizen attendance in the neighborhood schools the past year was 2,070, as against 1,745 the preceding year, a gain of about 18 per cent. This gain is exceedingly encouraging when it is remembered that the past year has been a very trying one for the schools. With allotment of lands in process, an objected-to enrollment going on, and with an unratified treaty pending, the minds of many were filled with restless distrust. This culminated in the setting up of a rival government by the Chitto Harjo faction, who claimed authority from the Great Father at Washington to go back to "the old treaty," under which there were no schools. As the result of one of the first edicts of the Chitto Harjo council a great many children were taken out of school, and the schools in four neighborhoods were entirely broken up.

The almost unprecedented prevalence of disease and death greatly affected the attendance at school. The Creeks are a people of intense emotions and in a period of political excitement they brood over the future with a vague and unreasoning terror which leads to sickness and death. Then the bereaved family keep the children at home. Not a community has escaped smallpox, and in some localities there have been epidemics of measles and mumps, while meningitis and pneumonia have been unusually frequent and fatal. At least a third of the teachers had smallpox during the year; one of our most promising young Indian teachers died of it. At Wealaka boarding school there were two deaths from it, but usually it was in a mild form, leaving no permanent disfigurement of its victim. Its appearance in a school was very naturally followed by a panic and the withdrawal of pupils. I was myself very much afraid of it at first, but after frequent exposure came at last to consider myself "immune" and paid no attention to it. The Creeks, especially the full bloods, cling to many old customs. One of these is the building of a house of hewed logs, roofed with oaken boards, over a grave, as a habitation for the departed spirit, which it is believed hovers near the body after death. The Creeks have no fear of the dead, but a desire to keep their loved ones still near them. Near each home is the group of tiny cabins built over the graves of their lost ones. In my journeyings I saw few of these family grave yards without newly built houses of the dead.

From all this it will be seen that an increase of 18 per cent the past year is a very hopeful indication, especially as the adoption in the Creek schools of the report blanks prepared by you for general use in Indian Territory schools has secured a great gain in completeness and accuracy of reports. This will be realized from a comparison of specimen reports herewith submitted.

Heretofore the grade of the school and the pay of the teacher were based upon the average attendance shown by the quarterly reports of the teacher. It was tacitly understood that the reports were to be padded if the average could not otherwise be kept up. Even yet I find the exercise of some vigilance necessary. I have found babies of 2 and 3 years carried to school to help out the average and because otherwise an older sister would have had to stay at home too, to care for them. Where every pupil is reported in detail it is much easier to detect inaccuracy of report.

Some time since various complaints reached me as to the work of a teacher whom I believed to be faithful and conscientious. She was charged with incompetence, neglect of duty, etc. I spent a day in the neighborhood going from house to house to try to discover the difficulty. I took two quarterly reports with me and after asking questions as to attendance, etc., showed the reports and told them that the teacher had written, asking instructions because of the trouble. Several school patrons then owned up that the trouble was a settlement quarrel as to where the school should be held. Neither the east side nor the west side was willing to see the house of the other side occupied by the school. An adjustment of the schoolhouse question settled the complaints against the teacher.

Noncitizen whites are allowed to attend the Indian, and noncitizen negroes the colored schools upon payment of a tuition fee of $1 a month, one-fourth of this amount being used for local school purposes and the remainder going to the teacher. The accompanying statistics show that the past year the enrollment was 1,054 Indians, 349 whites, 1,016 citizen and 90 noncitizen negroes. The average attendance of this enrollment was: Indian, 43 per cent; white, 48 per cent; citizen negro, 49 per cent; noncitizen negro, 58 per cent. The conditions already described largely account for the small average in Indian attendance. On the other hand the negroes are far more gregarious than the Indians, and the greater compactness of their settlements has made the schools accessible to a greater number. Very few negroes belonged to the Chitto Harjo faction. A comparison of reports from the boarding schools, to which noncitizens are never admitted, shows at the Indian schools an average of 76 per cent of the number authorized by law, while the negro average was only 64 per cent. Indians send their children to boarding school to learn English, as they are very ambitious in that direction. The present allotment and segregation of land will probably scatter the negro population and changes will doubtless occur. The advantage the negro has over the Indian by his knowledge of English is not evinced by any corresponding literary achievement. Negroes are content to leave school with less accomplished. Our school system offers the same advantages to both races, but the most advanced pupils are in the Indian schools and are mostly young people with whom the English is an acquired language. The tendency of the negroes is to early marriage and settlement in life, and they are more likely to be kept at work by their parents. Another reason may be that as a rule the Indians have had more competent teachers. Only recently are they beginning to realize that "State-raised" negroes whose pretentious claims were supported principally by showy attire, flashy jewelry, and a smattering of piano playing may possibly not have been the best guides for youth. A very hopeful indication in this direction, however, is the very evident satisfaction that the more progressive negroes show in the sifting process that there is in the present system of teachers' examinations.

As instructed by you, I took a description of all neighborhood schools I visited. Not trusting the exactness of the feminine eye I took a tapeline with me, and the dimensions given in the condensed statistics of schoolhouses are interior measurements. There is a greater diversity of buildings among the Indian than among the negro schools. Five Indian schools are held in painted frame church buildings. Several have desks. On the other hand, 11 Indian schools are held in log cabins, while for the negro schools not one log cabin remains in use. As the Indians have the best, so they have the worst buildings. The very worst is the Okfuskey school, near Eufaula, a cabin of small, rough logs, plastered with mud, with earthen floor, and no windows. The only light comes in through the open door. Only a stone's throw from this cabin is a very good box-house church, ceiled inside, with good glass windows and comfortable benches. The pious church members will not allow the use of their sacred edifice for school purposes, and there is no law compelling the providing of better buildings, the only stipulation being that a suitable building shall be provided and the supply of fuel, etc., necessary, furnished by the patrons of the school. In some communities great pride is taken in the school, and improvements are made from time to time. Usually schoolhouses are isolated in their location. Not infrequently they are broken into and books stolen or destroyed. In one Indian neighborhood a white family refused to pay tuition for their children and yet demanded that they be allowed to continue going to school. When denied they broke into the schoolhouse, broke not only window panes, but sash as well, broke the slates, opened up the books and poured all the ink over their pages, etc. The schoolhouse was repaired, a new supply of books gotten, and barred wooden shutters placed over the windows. Again the door was broken down and the same wanton destruction repeated. This white family was not of the ordinary "renter" class, but of those nomads who wander perpetually in wagons, ostensibly seeking a location, but really from an aversion to settled toil. After the second destruction of the school property such pointed suggestions were made to this family by the Indians that they hastily moved on.

A parallel instance occurred a little later in another school. The most common abuse of school property is the "shooting out" of the window panes. This is usually ascribed to cowboys and to passers through the country. With the constantly increasing improvement in the direction of law and order we may hope that the school districts will be encouraged to greater efforts for good schoolhouses, and that they may be better equipped for school purposes. In almost all neighborhoods the "mah hah kah chuk ko," the schoolhouse, is the "mek ku sup kah chuk ko," the "prayer house " (church), as well, and its primary purpose being for religious gatherings the furniture is with special reference to that use, consisting usually of long wooden benches of crude domestic manufacture.

The Creeks are of an intensely religious nature. From time immemorial their customs and beliefs, their social and political life, all centered in a devout worship of the unseen. From their faith in the Great Spirit the transition to a belief in the Christian God is of such easy acceptance that the two are often inextricably blended in their minds. Not infrequently, even in the homes of native exhorters whose Christian sincerity can not be doubted, I have noticed the "sok pof ke tah," the hollow tube through which the "he lis hi yah," the medicine man, chants his prayers, seeking to appease offended spirits of evil, or imploring the kindly aid of spirits of good. With a people of such profound religious beliefs church comes first of all, and if one or the other must suffer, the church is preferred to the school. So few buildings are provided with desks that the teaching of writing or drawing is attended with great difficulty.

Very helpful to our school work the past year was the largely increased appropriation for neighborhood schools made by the last annual Creek council. This enabled us to increase the salary of each teacher $5 a month, so that after that act went into effect we paid $30, $35, and $40 a month to neighborhood school-teachers. The Creeks as a whole are very liberal in school matters, and the present council deserves to be held in high estimation for their liberal and progressive attitude toward school appropriations.

The expenditure for neighborhood schools in salaries of teachers and for books and other school supplies during the past year was $17,788.28, or an amount of $8.59 for each citizen student enrolled during the year.

In the boarding schools the total expenditure was $50,420.40 for an average attendance of 450, or 112.16 per pupil.

I do not attempt to give any statistics as to amounts expended or students in attendance in schools in the incorporated towns of the nation, nor to more than refer to the fact that a large number of the more well-to-do Creek citizens are educating their children at their own expense, sending them not only to the private schools of the Territory, but each year an increasing number is found in educational institutions in the States. Some of the most generous givers to promising young academies and colleges in the Creek Nation have been Creek citizens.

There is no possibility of obtaining any reliable data as to the "subscription schools" for renter whites found in many localities where large tracts of land have been leased for agricultural purposes. These schools are most numerous after the cotton-picking season in the winter until field work begins again in the early spring, and then in midsummer after crops are "laid by" until cotton picking begins again. During the past year I visited quite a number of such schools. From the difficulties under which they are carried on they average in grade of work done far below our Creek schools. Even these schools are invaluable, however, to these hard-working white people, and the scanty draught from the "Pierian Spring" keeps alive many noble aspirations that would otherwise perish. Individual ownership of land will have the effect of enabling better arrangements for occupation of agricultural lands, and we may expect a consequent drifting out of the illiterate, restless whites to whom the unsettled conditions here made this an inviting haven. From the influence of this class has come much of the petty lawlessness which has filled the Territory jails with youthful criminals and given to this country an undeservedly bad name.

The summer normal schools so successfully inaugurated by my predecessor were continued this year at Eufaula and Muskogee, these places having been selected by vote of the teachers. The tuition paid enabled us to secure excellent instructors. Each year there is a greater appreciation of the benefit of normal instruction and a corresponding improvement in work and in interest. This year quite a number of young people, notably more advanced students of the Eufaula High School, availed themselves of the exceptional opportunity for self-improvement, though not intending to teach. The Eufaula normal for Indian and white students enrolled 75, 60 taking the teachers' examination, of whom 46 passed and received certificates. Forty-five colored teachers took the examinations at Muskogee, 27 receiving certificates. While the attendance was 25 per cent greater this year than last, certificates were issued this year to only 64 per cent of those who were examined as against 86 per cent who obtained certificates last year. Each year the examination is more rigid with the anticipated effect of improving the personnel of our teaching force. Less attention is also paid to reviews preparatory to examination and more to methods of teaching. Much time was given to pedagogical instruction, and there was abundant opportunity for discussion and comparison of methods and for interchange of suggestion and helpful experience. At Eufaula practical illustrations of schoolroom work with primary students were given. Two classes of young children afforded an effective object lesson, one class being of English-speaking children and the other non-English-speaking full-bloods.

It may be interesting to note the nativity of students at these normals. At Eufaula there were from Indian Territory, 22; Arkansas, 16; Missouri, 7; Texas, 4; Pennsylvania, 2; Kansas, 2; Iowa, 2; Illinois, 2; Alabama, 1; Kentucky, 1; South Dakota, 1; Georgia, 1; West Virginia, 1, and Mississippi, 1. At Muskogee, Ind. T., 13; Texas, 5; Kansas, 4; Missouri, 4; Ohio, 3; Tennessee, 3; Louisiana, 3; Arkansas, 2; South Carolina, 2; Alabama, 2, and Mississippi, Maryland, Georgia, and District of Columbia, each 1.

This normal work as inaugurated by my predecessor is having the anticipated result in improving the class of teachers and consequently the quality of work done in the schools.

If it were possible to pay teachers' salaries in cash instead of giving them warrants, which are only paid semiannually, we should be able to secure still better teachers. As it is we have some very noble men and women teaching in our neighborhood schools. Many instances of privation, of self-denial, and devotion to duty have come to my knowledge. I know of teachers who have made tactful, helpful suggestions as to improved home life, of their visiting the sick, watching by the dying and comforting the sorrowing. In some instances they have had an influence for good in their community as uplifting as quiet and unostentatious.

Many miles from railway and post-office I found one of these teachers, an Indian, from whom I had not expected much. I found him in an old log cabin, which bore everywhere evidences of his efforts to make it tenable for the school. On the rude "puncheon" seats were grouped wide-awake Indian boys and girls whose constant trustful looks up into the teacher's face told the story of his influence over them. After the regular routine had been gone through with—in a manner that alike surprised and delighted me—with the completion of recitations, books were put away in the cupboard the teacher had made. Having no singing books, he had fastened large sheets of newspaper together, and on this improvised scroll had printed in large letters the hyms he taught them. I confess that their singing of "Abide with me, fast falls the eventide," was more beautiful in sentiment than it was perfect in harmony. After reciting texts of scripture, with reverently bowed heads, they joined in the Lord's prayer. I know not the creed of this teacher, but of this I am sure, that his work in training head and heart and hand entitles him to a place among the world's unrecognized heroes.

In visiting neighborhood schools, I try to surprise the teacher by reaching the schoolhouse before 9 or after 3 o'clock on my first visit. There has been a tendency to shorten the day at both ends, and to give an unauthorized Friday half-holiday. Detection in this breach of duty is usually sufficient admonition. A striking fact is that of the 12 teachers whom I found absent from duty without a satisfactory excuse, not one made a high enough average in examination to secure a certificate to teach next year. Experience shows that the best qualified teachers are most faithful in their work.

So much was said at the meeting of Indian-school employees, which I recently attended at Buffalo, in regard to the relative success of white and Indian teachers. that I would like to say that some of my best neighborhood school-teachers are Indians. An Indian teacher, whose English training has come from good white teachers, makes a capital teacher. I know of one young woman thus trained who makes her pupils understand thoroughly every English sentence in their text-books. She tells them the meaning in Creek and requires them to give the words in both languages. She is careful to speak always to them in English, only using the Creek for purposes of explanation. They write the English words and sentences constantly, but never write any Indian. Most of the Indians who have dropped out of our teaching force have been compelled to do so from lack of knowledge of English, and this is the result of having had teachers who were content to teach mechanically. I hope much from some of the students now in our Indian schools.

An attempt was made the past year to secure better results by grading the boarding schools. As the recently ratified Creek treaty stipulates that the Creek government shall cease to exist in 1906, statehood and a different school system are thus foreshadowed. In our school work we can not strive so much for a permanent system as for the accomplishment of work most needed in the present. To this end industrial training is of the highest importance. Very few of the rising generation may hope for professional occupations, but each young Creek will have a farm.

The Creeks of long ago were a very industrious people, and skilled in primitive manufactures. The men tilled the ground and wrought in wood and metal and the women wove fabrics of cotton and wool on rude upright looms like those still used

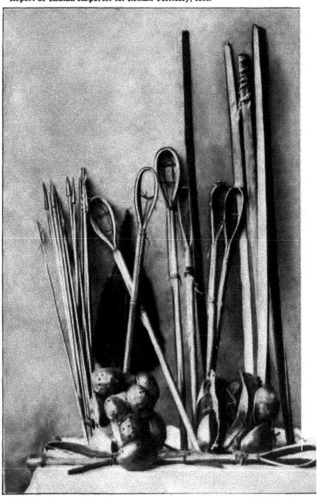

CREEK BOWS AND ARROWS, BALL STICKS, TURTLE SHELLS, FEATHER FAN, E

Report of Indian Inspector for Indian Territory. 190L.

CREEK NATIVE INDUSTRIES—BASKETRY.

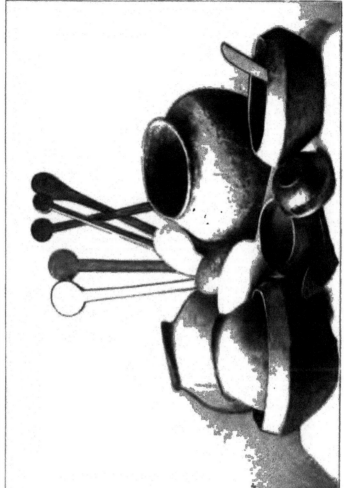

CREEK NATIVE INDUSTRIES—POTTERY AND SPOONS.

by the Navaho. The women also made garments of buckskin, their beadwork was of unique beauty, and they were skilled in pottery and basketry. It is scarcely to be wondered at that articles bought from the trader are rapidly superseding these native manufactures in which so much of slow and patient toil is required. A few years ago native pottery was in general use. Scarce a woman is now living who can make it. The stone jar from the trader's store has largely taken the place of the great olla-shaped earthen "Ahl kus wah," standing in the chimney corner with its generous supply of "sofkey," the national dish made from corn which is both food and drink to the Creeks. In my travel among the people the past year I have given especial attention to native industries because of the very general consideration which this question is receiving in connection with manual training. While many Creek women still understand basketry it does not seem practicable to revive this industry. The material they use is long flexible strips split from the outer surface of cane stalks. In the Creek Nation the herds of cattle have long since destroyed the formerly dense cane brakes, and only in remote wilds of the Choctaw Nation can the bamboo-like growth be found.

It is not uncommon to find Indian homes where the furniture is practically all of domestic manufacture. The skill thus manifested indicates that the Creeks would readily adapt themselves to mechanic arts, and is a great argument for manual training in their schools.

The limited funds available at the various boarding schools has seemed to require that student labor should be directed to daily necessity and such distasteful drudgery as wood chopping and dish washing. Of creative industry—the fascinating evolution of a perfected article of use or beauty our schools have had practically nothing.

In some of the boarding schools teachers have interested themselves in teaching needlework, and with very creditable results. I have introduced plain sewing in a number of neighborhood schools with so encouraging a degree of success that I hope to greatly increase this work the coming year.

My duties as supervisor have been divided between office and field work. In office work there is the handling of a considerable correspondence, sending out report blanks and examining reports and accounts as received, keeping records, sending out school supplies, etc. Under your instructions I have tried whenever practicable to be at the office on Saturday, that teachers and others desiring personal interviews might be able to find me. Examination of reports and accounts has required much office work. All such papers receive the joint consideration of the Creek superintendent of education and myself, and upon our requisition, sent through you to the principal chief, warrants for the payment of school indebtedness are issued. Before being sent out from the executive office these warrants come to me for comparison as to clerical correctness, for record and approval.

By the use of the neostyle I have been able to send out frequent circular letters to the teachers, and thus have been able to keep in closer touch with them at a saving of individual correspondence.

I hope the following year to have my work still further systemized, that more time may be spent in the field and less in the office. The past year 166 days were spent in the field, and 180 visits paid to schools. The schools are so scattered that ordinarily but two can be visited in a day, and frequently but one. Often a whole day must be consumed in reaching a neighborhood.

Your instructions of November 27 last directed me to spend all the time possible among the people, acquainting myself with their conditions, and trying to help all that I could in their local work. The Creeks are a people of strong social instincts, who delight to congregate for friendly gatherings, the purposes of which vary according to the community or the season of the year. From their widely scattered homes they come at certain times, bringing all the family, and camping out around the church or the dance square. A large percentage of the Creeks are communicants in either Baptist or Methodist churches, and most of these congregations every fourth week hold a "church meeting," usually assembling on Friday afternoon. Tents are pitched and great log fires made. Ample supplies of food are brought by the members, who, in some cases also bring dishes, cooking utensils, etc. It is, however, a matter of great church pride to have as complete a camp house as possible built beside the church. Sometimes there are several buildings fitted up for this social life of the church. A long shed is provided for a dining room. The men care for their horses, get wood and water, and sit around in groups to talk while the women prepare the meals. The children, who in pleasant weather have the best time of all, play merrily about.

When the meal is ready men and women sit on opposite sides of the table, and the more conservative elderly women will never eat until the men have finished. Some Indian families—the greater proportion probably—have adopted white people's methods of preparing food. At these meetings it is interesting to note the various styles of cookery. At one where the bill of fare was especially varied in Indian cookery there was squirrel soup thickened with pounded corn, venison slowly browned over coals, turkey baked with rice, roasted sweet potatoes, "blue dumplings," a mixture of corn and beans prepared with lye, which is esteemed a special delicacy, wholesome and palatable native bread baked over the coals, and great bowls of sofkey. As one "to the manner born," I confined myself to the Indian dishes, to the great amusement and pleasure of my hospitable entertainers. In white people's cookery there was chicken and pork, biscuit, light bread, pies, cakes, preserved peaches, and canned blackberries.

The repast finished, the leading church members go into the church or under the bough-covered booth and begin to sing, the sound of the singing being the signal for devotional service. Men and women sit on different sides. The preaching service is always long, never less than two sermons being preached, and usually three or four. During prayer all kneel, and all the church members, "me ku sa pul ke," or "praying people," pray audibly at the same time, the leader, however, continuing after all other voices have ceased. With most it is a cardinal belief that in the church rests a power to forgive sin, and at these monthly meetings those who have transgressed are brought up for trial. The culprit usually confesses standing before the congregation. The presiding minister, after eliciting this confession and a plea for pardon, admonishes the sinner, submits the question to the congregation, and upon their vote restores the repentant one to full communion. A hymn is sung and all shake hands with the restored.

It is hard for white people to appreciate this literal interpretation of the gospel injunction to forgive until "seventy times seven," and to understand how a minister who has been openly intoxicated is shortly after preaching again with the same acceptance as before.

I have never attended one of the dances of the Creeks. Recently, however, my school inspection took me near one of the town squares where the people were gathering for an all-night "stomp" dance. Here the smoke arose from many camp fires. In the center all grass and vegetation had been removed from the ground, leaving the brown earth bare and soft. Around this square were grouped booths thickly thatched with leafy branches of trees. On posts of the booth hung the deerskin drum, the medicine rattle, and the turtle-shell anklets to be used by the dancers. Near by stood great cone-shaped jars of antique native pottery filled with the medicine drink, a dark decoction of "mek ko ho yah ne chah." Each year the "he lis hi yah," the medicine man, makes a new seat to be used in his spirit rites, and many of these queer little benches, hewn out of the oak, were carefully ranged about the medicine man, for no one dare move or take them away. At one end of the square two groups of young men laid their ball sticks in opposite rows, matching themselves for a rival contest in the athletic game of which they are so fond. Some were stripped to the waist, but none in the old time ball costume of necklace and breechcloth. I spent some little time visiting the different family camps, finding few of the many children had attended school lately. Still fewer could read, and none seemed to understand English. I estimated about 200 people were there. I saw not a negro and no other white person. Nearly all the Indians were full-bloods. I find many such communities as this back from the railroads where few white people penetrate. Yet right across the sacred limits of this town square runs a line of numbered stakes tracing the right of way of a soon to be built railway.

It was long after dark when I reached the hospitable Indian home where I was expected to spend the night. The comfortable, roomy house was of hewed logs, with stone fireplaces, and a separate building for cooking and eating. The room prepared for me was indeed inviting, with its clean bed, abundant towels, pitcher of fresh cistern water, and great bouquets of roses on table and mantel. All Creeks eat in the open air whenever possible, and the supper table was spread on the porch. The spoons and forks were of plated silver, and the supper was well cooked and nicely served. There was home-cured ham, eggs, biscuit, butter, radishes fresh from the garden, and an abundance of rich cream for strawberries and coffee. My hostess was a full-blood whose education had been just six months in a mission school where special attention had been given to domestic training. Coming from an industrious and thrifty full-blood family, she had improved her meager opportunity to the utmost. In the morning her three boys, of whom she is justly proud, mounted their ponies and convoyed me to the neighborhood school, three miles away, I was en route to inspect. Very bright little fellows they were, bidding fair to become fine scholars.

Many times the past year I have been dependent upon full-blood families for food and shelter. Always I have been cordially received and the best they had bestowed upon me.

s diverged from strictly school matters because in order to understand
ions one must know living conditions also.
er last, the official term of Mr. Alex McIntosh, the Creek superinten-
:ion, having expired, Mr. James R. Gregory was elected as his successor.
1as brought to his work a due appreciation of its importance, and while
ave differed on administrative points, our relations have been extremely
we have worked without disagreeable friction.   He is a representative
idical class of Creeks and was the first to seek United States citizenship
olishment of courts in the Territory.   He is a veteran of the civil war, in
red as a Federal volunteer, and is a great sufferer from rheumatism con-
· service.   He has thus been unable to give as much personal attention
of schools as is contemplated by the Creek law.   Whenever he has been
chools I have found him a very valuable coadjutor.
on, I desire to express my appreciation of the valuable work done by my
Mr. Calvin Ballard.   The affairs of the office had been so thoroughly
s to make it comparatively easy for me to go on with the work as
1im.   I found his selection of teachers to have been extremely judicious,
ebted to him for giving me helpful replies to many inquiries.
am I indebted to you for constant help.   I appreciate the advantage
r supervisors which I have in occupying an office in the same building
I have turned to you in every difficulty and perplexity, never failing
ired instructions.   To this, more than to any other cause, is due any
:ess which may have attended my efforts during the past year.
y submitted.

ALICE M. ROBERTSON, *Supervisor.*

D. BENEDICT,
·intendent of Schools in Indian Territory.

Creek neighborhood schools (Indian).

Teacher.	Race.	Citizens.		Whites.		Remarks.
		En-rolled.	Aver-age.	En-rolled.	Aver-age.	
... John A. Denny	White ..	41	15	7	3	
... William Withrow......	....do ...	15	6	......	......	Discontinued.
... V. E. Hill	....do ...	47	21	8	2	
... Jas. Sulphur	Indian .	22	8	......	......	
... A. W. Barnett..........	....do ...	16	8	......	......	Do.
... W. S. Owen	White ..	25	6	21	7	Do.
... Rose Paul	....do ...	16	10	1	1	Do.
... Cooper Dawson..........	....do ...	27	13	18	9	
... C. B. Weirick	....do ...	17	7	6	2	1st and 2d quarters.
... R. D. Love	....do ...	14	10	4	2	3d and 4th quarters.
... L. Morton	Indian .	28	10	3	2	
... Harrie Blake	White ..	27	17	......	......	
... J. T. Turpin.............	....do ...	20	8	15	3	1st and 2d quarters.
... W. I. Brodie	....do ...	13	6	21	6	2d and 3d quarters.
... H. M. Harjo...........	Indian .	25	15	......	......	
... L. G. McIntosh..........	....do ...	10	8	2	1	Discontinued.
... G. Hughes	White ..	13	11	2	2	
... H. D. Alexander......	Indian .	17	6	5	3	
... M. J. Berryhill..........	....do ...	39	14	6	2	
... Nancy Scott............	....do ...	21	9	......	......	
... S. Reinhardt..........	White ..	30	7	21	5	
... R. D. Love	....do ...	18	4	......	......	Discontinued. Snake faction.
... Rose Paul	....do ...	12	9	25	16	2d and 3d quarters.
... Johnson King.........	Indian .	21	14	......	......	Discontinued.
... J. N. Blackwell	White ..	27	9	10	5	Do.
·a . H. A. Walker	....do ...	7	3	2	2	Do.
... C. B Weirick	....do ...	15	8	42	20	3d and 4th quarters.
... Robt. Francis..........	Indian .	24	9	......	......	
... H. G. Simpson	White ..	47	15	14	6	
... B. Phillips	....do ...	22	5	6	3	1st quarter.
... F. Lindley.............	....do ...	17	6	2	2	
... .do	....do ...	21	10	7	6	Do.
... C. Ratcliffe	....do ...	16	11	21	17	
... Mary Long	Indian .	25	12	......	......	

Creek boarding schools—Continued.

WETUMKA BOARDING SCHOOL.

Employees.	Position.	Salary per month.	Race.	Age.	Single or married.	Birthplace.
A. L. Posey	Superintendent	[1]$600	Indian	29	Married	Creek Nation.
James P. Atkins	Principal teacher	50	White	26	Single	Kansas.
Fannie M. Bridges	Assistant teacher	45	...do...	21	...do...	Missouri.
Belle Meagher	...do	40	Indian	20	...do...	Creek Nation.
Koga McIntosh	...do	40	...do...	22	...do...	Do.
Susanne Barnett	...do	35	...do...	20	...do...	Do.
Mrs. A. L. Posey	Matron	40	White	27	Married	Arkansas.
Mrs. E. M. Perryman	Assistant matron	35	Indian	36	Widow	Creek Nation.
Kate Dougherty	Cook	30	White	25	Single	Kansas.
Nancy McIntosh	Laundress	20	Indian	50	Widow	Creek Nation.
William Posey	Laborer	25	...do...	22	Single	Do.

[1] Per annum.

Average enrollment: Boys, 46; girls, 38; average attendance 62
Annual appropriation $9,000.00
Amount expended 7,938.50
Average per capita cost 126.04

EUCHEE BOARDING SCHOOL.

Employees.	Position.	Salary per month.	Race.	Age.	Single or married.	Birthplace.
Wm. A. Sapulpa	Superintendent	[1]$600	Indian	41	Widower	Creek Nation.
Harry H. Bell	Principal	50	White	21	Single	Kansas.
Frances M. Scott	Assistant teacher	45	...do...	25	...do...	Cherokee Nation.
Lucile Byrd	...do	40	Indian	19	...do...	Creek Nation.
Tookah Ross	Matron	25	...do...	27	Widow	Cherokee Nation.
M. Brown	...do	25	White	25	Single	Arkansas.
M. LeGrand	Cook	20	...do...	26	...do...	Missouri.
E. Smith	Laundress	20	...do...	24	Married	
J. Smith	Laborer	25	...do...	27	...do...	

[1] Per annum.

Average enrollment: Boys, 41; girls, 38; average attendance 55
Annual appropriation $7,200.00
Amount expended 7,255.17
Average per capita cost (eight months) 131.90

The greatly increased expense because of smallpox and pneumonia necessitated closing the school for lack of funds.

CREEK ORPHAN HOME.

Employees.	Position.	Salary.	Race.	Age.	Single or married.	Birthplace.
Johnson E. Tiger	Superintendent	[1]$500	Indian	25	Married	Creek Nation.
Anna M. Peterson	Principal teacher	50	White	25	Single	Pennsylvania.
Anna Belle Wright	Assistant teacher	45	...do...	27	...do...	West Virginia.
Lena B. Tiger	Matron	35	Indian	26	Married	Creek Nation.
Susie Biggs	Assistant matron	30	...do...	29	Single	Do.
L. B. Simpson	Seamstress	30	White	41	Widow	Kentucky.
J. H. Nance	Cook	20	Negro	30	Married	

[1] Per annum.

Average enrollment: Boys, 30; girls, 32; average attendance 55
Annual appropriation $6,666.66
Amount expended 5,722.64
Average cost per capita 104.96

Creek boarding schools—Continued.

WEALAKA BOARDING SCHOOL.

Employees.	Position.	Salary per month.	Race.	Age.	Single or married.	Birthplace.
E. Hardridge.........	Superintendent......	1$500	Indian..	37	Married ..	Creek Nation.
o. C. Kindley.........	Principal teacher....	50	White ..	35	Widower .	Missouri.
ıbel Hall.............	Assistant teacher	45	....do ...	27	Single	Iowa.
ıllie Jefferson.........	Matron	20	....do ...	82	....do ...	Arkansas.
ıma Kindley.........	....do	20	....do ...	24	....do ...	Do.
W. Cash..............	Cook................	25	....do ...	25	Married ..	
ınnie Haynie.........	Laundress	20	....do ...	40	Widow ...	District Columbia.
ılter Esco	Laborer..............	25	Negro ..	21	Single	Texas.

1 Per annum.

ʼerage enrollment: Boys, 16; girls. 19; average attendance.................................... 24
ınual appropriation $4,500.00
ınount expended.. 3,259.76
r capita cost (eight months).. 135.82

There were two deaths from smallpox and one from meningitis at this school, and it was entirely ɔken up by disease.

COWETA BOARDING SCHOOL.

Employees.	Position.	Salary per month.	Race.	Age.	Single or married.	Birthplace.
ı. H. Alexander	Superintendent......	1$500	Indian..	28	Married ..	Creek Nation.
ɔn R. Price..........	Principal teacher	50	White ..	23	Single	Illinois.
ıtharyn Blake.......	Assistant teacher	45	....do ...	22	....do ...	Missouri.
.M. Alexander.......	Matron..............	25	Indian..	27	Married ..	Creek Nation.
ıdeline Jacker	Laundress...........	20	....do ...	24	Single	Michigan.
.lliam Caton	Laborer..............	20	White ..	30	....do ...	
ınie K. Cox..........	Cook................	25	Indian..	35	Married ..	Creek Nation.

1 Per annum.

ɛʼrage enrollment: Boys, 26: girls, 25; average attendance 39
ınual appropriation $4,500.00
ıount expended... 3,991.37
ıt per capita... 102.34

Colored boarding schools.

TULLAHASSEE.

Employees.	Position.	Salary per month.	Race.	Age.	Single or married.	Birthplace.
ı. Lewis	Superintendent......	1$600	Negro ..	34	Married ..	Indian Territory.
ward Jenkins.......	Principal teacher	60	....do ...	29	Single	Missouri.
ıes Clark	Assistant teacher	45	....do ...	24	....do ...	Louisiana.
ıra A. Jackson......	....do..............	40	....do ...	27	....do ...	Kansas.
ı Maud L. Craw	....do..............	40	....do ...	26	Married ..	Indian Territory.
ora F. Lewis.........	Matron	40	....do ...	30	....do ...	Do.
ın Marshall.........	Cook	25	....do ...	21	Single	Do.
ıes Long	Laborer..............	25	....do ...	33	Married ..	Do.

1 Per annum.

ʼrage enrollment: Boys, 38; girls, 54; average attendance.................................... 67
ıual appropriation $9,000.00
ount expended... 7,206.20
t per capita... 107.54

Colored boarding school—Continued.

BECAN CREEK BOARDING SCHOOL.

Employees.	Position.	Salary per month.	Race.	Age.	Single or married.	Birthplace.
J. P. Davidson.........	Superintendent......	¹$500	Negro ..	50	Married ..	Indian Territory
A. H. Mike.............	Principal teacher....	50	....do ...	26	Single	Do.
Celia S. Roberts........	Assistant teacher	40	....do ...	27	.....do	Do.
Mrs. J. Davidson........	Matron	30	....do ...	48	Married ..	Do.
Emma Island...........	Cook	20	....do ...	34	Single	Do.

¹ Per annum.

Average enrollment: Boys, 19; girls, 31; average attendance................................... 35
Annual appropriation $4,500.00
Amount expended.. 3,264.11
Cost per capita..:... 93.26

COLORED ORPHAN HOME.

Employees.	Position.	Salary per month.	Race.	Age.	Single or married.	Birthplace.
Geo. H. Taylor.........	Superintendent......	¹$500	Negro ..	37	Married ..	Indian Territory.
Wm. R. Pamplin.......	Principal teacher....	50	....do ...	21	Single	Illinois.
Florence Pamplin.....	Assistant teacher	40	....do ...	28	.....do	Do.
Mrs. G. H. Taylor......	Matron..............	25	....do ...	31	Married ..	Do.
Sarah Foster...........	Cook	15	....do ...	25	Widow ...	Indian Territory.

¹ Per annum.

Average enrollment, 24; boys, 11; girls, 13; average attendance............................... 17
Annual appropriation $3,333.33
Amount expended.. 3,061.19
Cost per capita.. 180.00

The destruction by fire of the boys' building and contents added to the cost here.

REPORT OF CHEROKEE SCHOOL SUPERVISOR.

VINITA, IND. T., *July 11, 1901.*

SIR: I have the honor to submit my third annual report on education in the Cherokee Nation for the year ending June 30, 1901.

General harmony has been maintained with the officials, the school board, and the teachers employed by the nation, in efforts to promote desired results. In supervision of school work I have had constant regard for acts of council and the constitution and laws of the Cherokee people.

The past year has been one of ceaseless activity in efforts to come into personal touch with the educational forces of the nation; to gather information at first hands; to see the teachers, the schools, and people, and to have the best use made of the available facilities.

I have spent many weeks in the visitation of schools, observing methods of instruction, the supply and the need of accommodation and appliances for effective work, and the disposition of neighborhoods to receive the advantages offered to their children. Some of the difficulties observed result from lack of appreciation of the benefits of education on the part of citizen parents and of renters, a desire to have a teacher employed holding the same political views or religious creed as prevails in the neighborhood, or a favorite of one or two influential families, or lack of books, blackboards, desks, or seats. None of these causes are generally prevalent, but in the aggregate they have caused light attendance, small interest, and failure to secure good results at several schools.

More difficult to manage has been the prevalence of smallpox, measles, and mumps. These causes have interfered with the attendance and school work of numerous neighborhoods and of the seminaries. In most of the communities there exists a good wholesome educational interest. Another feature which has interfered with neighborhood schools has been the general prosperity of the Cherokee people. Good crops and good prices have urged farmers to thrift and a command of all their forces to raise and secure all possible products, as cotton, cotton seed, corn, wheat. hay, potatoes, cattle, hogs, and poultry. In the aggregate, the returns for the year have been large, and numbers of children were kept from school to do home work. Several schools were practically abandoned during strawberry picking and cotton and corn gathering.

PRIMARY SCHOOLS.

The schools are in session twelve weeks in the fall and sixteen in the spring. They may.be known as 30 full-blood, 80 mixed, and 14 negro schools. The teachers are paid a uniform price of $35 per month. The aggregate enrollment of pupils for the fall term was in the 124 schools 3,962, with an average attendance of 2,351, or 59.3 per cent of enrollment. In the spring term the enrollment was 4,153, with an average attendance of 2,361, or 56.8 per cent of the enrollment. In the fall term there were 28 schools that enrolled 40 or more pupils each, averaging 52.7 to the school and maintaining 59 per cent of their enrollment. There were 19 schools that each enrolled less than 18 pupils and averaging only 14.8 to the school; the average attendance at these schools was 62 per cent of their enrollment.

The average attendance at the primary schools for the year of 7 months was 2,356, and the aggregate cost was $34,460, or $14.63 per pupil, a cost of $2.09 per month. Of the above amount $2,000 was for schoolbooks. No account is taken of the cost of new houses, repairs on houses, or for blackboards, desks, stoves, maps, or other supplies furnished by the school patrons during the year.

HIGH SCHOOLS.

The nation maintains four high schools—the male seminary, the female seminary, the orphan asylum, and the colored high school. These are boarding schools, and each includes a primary and an intermediate department. In the high school departments there were enrolled at the male seminary 66, of whom 5 were graduated; at the female seminary 49 were enrolled and 7 were graduated; at the orphan asylum 4 were enrolled and none were graduated; at the colored high school none were enrolled.

In all departments there were enrolled: At the male seminary 232, and the average attendance was (9 months) 137; at the female seminary 221, and an average of 135.5; at the orphan asylum 179, with an average of 146.5; at the colored high school 54 were enrolled, with an average attendance of 35. These four high schools have been maintained the past year at a cost of $49,442, or about one and one-half times the cost of the 124 day schools.

The aggregate enrollment at the boarding schools was 686, with an average attendance of 454, or 66 per cent of enrollment; 119 were in the high school departments. In the past two years there has been a decided gain in these schools in regard to attendance and amount and quality of work done. The classes graduated were better prepared than those of last year. The commencement exercises were most creditable and satisfactory. The orations were carefully prepared and well pronounced. They were heard by large audiences of intelligent, cultivated people. They are important educational factors in the year's work. They gratify parents and awaken worthy ambitions among the numerous pupils engaged in preparatory work. Like good results were obtained from the closing exercises of the two schools which had no graduates.

Special attention is given to filling up and strengthening the work of the high school departments. A comparative view of attendance and cost will indicate certain gains at each school.

Female seminary:
    Average attendance last year (9 months).. 105
    Cost per pupil.. $150.85
    Average attendance this year.. 135.5
    Cost per pupil.. $109.41
Male seminary.
    Average attendance last year (9 months) 80
    Cost per pupil.. $142.37
    Average attendance this year... 137
    Cost per pupil.. $108.57
Orphan Asylum:
    Average attendance last year (9 months) 124
    Cost per pupil.. $122.00
    Average attendance this year... 146.5
    Cost per pupil.. $103.24
Colored high schools:
    Average attendance last year (9 months).. 23
    Cost per pupil... $147.89
    Average attendance this year... 35
    Cost per pupil. $96.57

OTHER SCHOOLS.

The incorporated towns of Vinita, Claremore, Nowata, and Muldrow maintain good graded schools which are supported by local taxation. Graded schools are supported by subscription at Bluejacket, Afton, Fairland, Prior Creek, and Webbers Falls. A number of excellent schools are maintained in the nation by the churches. At Vinita, Willie Halsell College by the Methodist Episcopal Church South and St. Mary's Institute by the Catholic Church; at Chelsea, an academy by the Presbyterian Church; at Skiatook, an academy by the Friends; at Tahlequah, an academy by the Baptists and Tahlequah Institute by the Presbyterians; at Dwight an academy by the Presbyterian Church. There are numerous subscription schools of a more or less temporary character found scattered through the nation.

THE SUMMER NORMAL.

Last year I reported that the members of the school board had "spent much time visiting schools," that "after a few weeks of visitation they unanimously came to the conclusion with me that one of the most urgent needs of the schools of the nation is a corps of trained teachers. We jointly signed a call for a summer teachers' normal, to be held at the female seminary building at Tahlequah and one for colored teachers at the colored high school. We agreed in the appointments of teachers to be made to give preference to those who should attend the normal, take the work and pass creditably the examinations."

Similar arrangements were made this summer. A competent corps of instructors were employed. We enrolled 154 at the female seminary and 18 at the colored normal.

The common-school branches were taught and reviewed. Every attendant took a course in theory and practice of teaching. Teachers applying for positions in the high schools took a special course in psychology. All took methods in primary work, in which seat work and recitations were daily exemplified in the use of several young pupils. Gaining by the experience of last year, teachers who came in studiously applied themselves from the start. They showed the spirit of those who believe industry and merit will win. One period daily was devoted to round-table work. Papers were prepared and discussions held on numerous practical questions that arise in the experience of the schoolroom.

A fair examination was given on six subjects at the close of the normal, viz: Arithmetic, grammar, history, geography, primary work, and theory and practice. Of those examined we secured for the preferred list of eligibles for appointment 105 and 13 from the negro normal. All these go to their schools with a month's good special training for their work. In selecting teachers for most important and desirable places the normal grade and the applicant's record as a teacher were considered. The good results from last year's normal were quite noticeable through the year's school work. Still better results are expected to follow from this summer's work.

THE NATIONAL SCHOOL BOARD.

Under the laws of the nation this board consists of three members, who serve for three years, one of whom is elected by the council each year. They are bonded administrative officers of the entire school system. They determine the qualifications of teachers, appoint the same, revoke appointments for cause, establish and discontinue schools according to law, appoint local directors for primary schools, receive sworn term reports from teachers and issue requisitions for warrants thereon for the teachers' pay, organize the high schools and supervise the same, settle quarterly with the stewards on their financial conduct of these schools, issue requisitions for their warrants, and report annually in detail to the council all of their official transactions for the year.

The present board is doing many times as much work as there is any evidence previous boards have done. Office records of past years are scant and unreliable when any pretense was made of keeping records. They are not serviceable in making any kind of report. At present the board keeps and has ready for my inspection and use a record of teachers' examinations, a record of attendance and term reports of each of the high schools, a financial record giving all requisitions for funds, a record of all primary teachers' appointments with enrollment and average attendance of each school each term, a record of schoolbooks purchased and of their distribution to schools, a minute book of the board's official proceedings, and a letter book containing copies of important letters. They also keep on file all teachers' examination papers with grades thereon and all vouchers and papers pertaining to settlements with the stewards of the high schools.

CHEROKEE WARRANTS.

I have continued to register and indorse warrants issued by the nation against the school fund, the orphan fund, and the insane fund. In every instance I have looked up the basis of the warrant as to its legality, provision for its payment by appropriation, and the value rendered the nation whether in service or merchandise, as determined by current market values. All requisitions upon which warrants are based, with laws and acts of council pertinent thereto, have been submitted to me with the warrants drawn under authority thereof.

I have approved all warrants submitted except school warrants Nos. 793B, 801B, and 826B, which were returned to the principal chief with a record of my reasons for refusing to approve them.

FINANCIAL.

An act of the Cherokee council appropriating funds for the support of schools the current year was approved by the principal chief December 5, and by the President December 28, 1900. Other appropriations were made and the bills together carried—

128 primary teachers	$31,360.00
Female seminary, general expenses	14,425.00
Repairs on female seminary buildings	600.00
Deficiency bills	363.33
Male seminary, general expenses	14,475.00
Deficiency bills	3,548.86
Repairs on buildings	250.00
Desks	350.00
Fifth assistant teacher	142.00
Medical superintendent at the male and female seminaries	933.33
Colored high school, general expenses	3,450.00
Deficiency	366.42
General deficiency, bills against school	353.24
Schoolbooks	2,000.00
Support of Cherokees at the International School for the Blind at Fort Gibson, Ind. T.	800.00
Salaries and expenses of members of the school board	2,200.00

The deficiency appropriations were required mainly by act of council moving the beginning of fiscal year up from November 20 to January 1, following:

Orphan asylum, general expenses	$15,125.00
Deficiency bills and accounts	660.25
Insane asylum, general expenses	2,692.00
Medical superintendent	233.33
Deficiency bills and accounts	321.88
Total charges against the school fund	75,117.18
Total charges against orphan fund	15,785.25
Total charges against insane fund	3,247.21

MALE SEMINARY.

Employee and position.	Salary.	Race.	Age.	Single or married.	Birthplace.	By whom appointed.
L. M. Logan, principal teacher	$900	White	48	Married	Tennessee	Board of education.
J. L. Harnage, first assistant	675	Cherokee	28	Single	Texas	Do.
Jean Finley, second assistant	450	....do....	26	.....do....	Cherokee Nation.	Do.
Geo. A. Cox, third assistant	450	....do....	24	.....do....	.....do....	Do.
W. P. Thorne, fourth assistant	450	....do....	27	Married	......do....	Do.
Mrs. L. M. Logan, fifth assistant	450	White	38	.....do....	Texas	Do.
J. R. Garrett, steward	500	Cherokee	45	.....do....	Missouri	National council.
Dr. C. M. Ross, medical superintendent.	465	....do....	28	.....do....	Cherokee Nation.	Do.

Enrollment	232
Average attendance	137
Per cent of attendance	59
Salaries of faculty, steward, and physician	$4,275.00
Other expenses	$10,600.00
Cost per pupil	$108.57
Cost per pupil per month	$12.06

FEMALE SEMINARY.

Employee and position.	Salary.	Race.	Age.	Single or married.	Birthplace.	By whom appointed.
Miss Florence Wilson, principal teacher.	$900	White ...	51	Single	Arkansas .	Board of education.
Mrs. Mae Shelton first assistant teacher.	675	Cherokee	31	Married ..	Cherokee Nation.	Do.
Miss Lillian Alexander, second assistant teacher.	450	....do	21	Single	......do	Do.
Miss Minta Foreman, third assistant teacher.	450	....do	23	.....do	......do	Do.
Miss Dannie Ross, fourth assistant teacher.	450	....do	23	.....do	......do	Do.
Mrs. Sallie G. Pendleton, fifth assistant teacher.	450	....do	26	Married ..	Alabama .	Do.
E. W. Buffington, steward	500	....do	46	.....do	Cherokee Nation.	National council.
Dr. C. M. Ross, medical superintendent.	465	....do	28	.....do	......do	Do.

```
Enrollment .......................................................................................  221
Average attendance ..............................................................................  135.5
Per cent of attendance ..........................................................................  61.3
Salaries of faculty, steward, and physician .....................................................  $4,275.00
Other expenses ..................................................................................  $10,550.00
Cost per pupil ..................................................................................  $109.41
Cost per pupil per month ........................................................................  $12.15
```

ORPHAN ASYLUM.

Employee and position.	Salary.	Race.	Age.	Single or married.	Birthplace.	By whom appointed.
Rev. J. F. Thompson, superintendent.	$600	Cherokee	60	Married ..	Cherokee Nation.	National council.
E. C. Alberty, principal teacher ...	720	....do	34	.....do	......do	School board.
W. A. Thompson, first assistant teacher.	540	....do	33	.....do	......do	Do.
Miss Flora Lindsey, second assistant teacher.	405	....do	23	Single	......do	Do.
Mrs. Eugenia M. Thompson, third assistant teacher.	405	....do	37	Widow ...	Texas	Do.
R. R. Eubanks, fourth assistant teacher.	405	....do	22	Single	Cherokee Nation.	Do.
Miss Cherie Edmonson, music teacher.	450	....do	20	.....do	......do	Do.
Dr. J. A. Patton, medical superintendent.	600	....do	28	Married ..	......do	National council.

```
Enrollment .......................................................................................  179
Average attendance ..............................................................................  146.5
Per cent of attendance ..........................................................................  82
Salaries of superintendent, faculty, and physician ..............................................  $4,125.00
Other expenses ..................................................................................  $11,000.00
Cost per pupil per month ........................................................................  11.43
```

COLORED HIGH SCHOOL.

Employee and position.	Salary.	Race.	Age.	Single or married.	Birthplace.	By whom appointed.
Mrs. Fannie Lowery, teacher	$450	Negro ...	43	Married ..	Cherokee Nation.	Board of education.
Geo. F. Nave, steward.............	300	....do	29	.....do	......do	National council.
Dr. Otto Rodgers, medical superintendent.	500	Cherokee	26	Single	......do	Board of education.

```
Enrollment .......................................................................................  54
Average attendance ..............................................................................  35
Per cent of attendance ..........................................................................  64.8
Salaries of teacher, steward, and physician .....................................................  $1,250.00
Other expenses ..................................................................................  $2,200.00
Cost per pupil ..................................................................................  $98.57
Cost per pupil per month ........................................................................  $10.8
```

The special gains of the year are the increased attendance and diminished cost of pupils at the high schools; better discipline and more thorough work, coupled with stronger confidence of the patrons in these institutions; the establishment of a summer normal upon principles and with rules that make for confidence and efficiency of teachers, assuring the recognition of merit and successful work while largely decreasing the baleful influence of politics, favoritism, and relationship by eliminating incompetent and irresponsible teachers from the list of appointments.

There has been a gain in educational spirit and purpose throughout the nation. For these and other good results I would accord due credit to the officials, teachers, and public-spirited citizens of the nation who have contributed to the volume of effort and interest that has made possible the success attained in the year's work.

For your intelligent direction and constant support and encouragement I return thanks.

Very respectfully, BENJAMIN S. COPPOCK,
Supervisor of Schools, Cherokee Nation, Ind. T.

Hon. JOHN D. BENEDICT,
Superintendent of Schools in Indian Territory.

REPORT OF CHOCTAW SCHOOL SUPERVISOR.

SOUTH MCALESTER, IND. T., *August 12, 1901.*

DEAR SIR: I have the honor to submit my annual report as school supervisor for the Choctaw Nation for the fiscal year ending June 30, 1901.

In the Choctaw Nation there are 5 academies and about 160 day or neighborhood schools. The academies are Jones and Armstrong for boys and Tuskahoma and Wheelock for girls and the Atoka Baptist Academy for boys and girls. These academies are managed under the contract plan, the superintendents furnishing the pupils food, clothing, text-books, and all things necessary for the comfort of the pupils. Armstrong and Wheelock academies are for orphans. At the Baptist academy the church board owns the building, and pays the teachers and other employees. About 90 pupils are cared for at each of these academies.

Jones and Tuskahoma are three-story brick buildings similar in structure and each will accommodate 110 children. They are both heated by steam and Jones is lighted by electricity. Armstrong is a two-story brick building heated by stoves and lighted by lamps. Wheelock is a two-story frame building heated by steam, and lamps are used for lighting.

There are needed repairs at all of these buildings, reports of which have been submitted by the superintendents of the schools.

So far as practicable, a uniform course of study has been followed. The superintendents are practical schoolmen, all having had actual experience in schoolroom work. Manual labor has been one of the prominent features. The boys are taught the use of tools, and seem to take quite an interest in making various articles. The girls are taught how to cook and to do general housework; besides, are taught sewing and fancy needlework. We hope to be better equipped for work on these lines next year.

The teachers and other employees have been satisfactory, and taking all things in consideration, this has been a very successful year in the academies.

DAY OR NEIGHBORHOOD SCHOOLS.

There have been about 160 day or neighborhood schools in operation during the year. This includes the small towns and villages in which live but few Choctaw children. Most of these schools were opened September 1, 1900, and many of them continued for nine months. Several of them were discontinued in March and April on account of smallpox and poor attendance.

During the year I visited about 140 of these schools, traveling several hundred miles over rough and mountainous country. I made a careful record of my visits, noting the condition of the buildings and surroundings in general, the efficiency of the teacher, and the general tone of the school. In many of these visits, especially in the full-blood settlements, I had public meetings of the patrons, and through an interpreter I explained to them the purpose of my visits. The schools are quite a distance apart and in many instances I have traveled 20 miles to find one small school. Many children have to go 2, 3, and sometimes 5 miles to school. The buildings are mostly small; many of them simply log huts without furniture, save a few old-style puncheon benches, and without maps, charts, blackboard, and other necessary equipments with which to conduct a successful school.

Great care was taken in the selection of teachers, and considering the poorly equipped buildings, the many sacrifices they had to make from the surrounding conditions, the teachers have done remarkably well.

One of the prominent features in the educational work of the Territory and especially in the Choctaw Nation is the summer normals for teachers. We had a very successful normal with an enrollment of 155, about 20 of whom are Choctaws. We had three experienced normal instructors who did systematic work, and the reports are that our normal compares favorably with some of the best normals of the States.

Following is a tabulated statement of the Choctaw schools:

WYNE WARD ACADEMY.

[Enrollment, 142; average attendance, 101; days attendance, 27,689.]

Employee and position.	Race.	Age.	Single or married.	Birthplace.	Appointed.	Relieved.	Salary. Month.	Received.
L. D. Stearns, superintendent	W.		M.		1900. Sept. 15	1900. Nov. 24	(¹)	$2,774.68
George Beck, principal teacher	W.	62	M.	Eng	do	1901. June 14	$100.00	900.00
James N. Wilson, first assistant	W.	22	S.	Mo	do	do	60.00	540.00
Cynthia Rainey, second assistant	W.	28	S.	Mo	do	do	60.00	540.00
Helen Severs, third assistant	I.	19	S.	Ind. T	do	do	40.00	360.00
Adda L. Stearns, matron	W.	40	M.	Ill	do	1900. Nov. 30	50.00	176.67
Alabama M. Fuller, assistant matron	W.	62	W.	Ark	do	1901. June 14	40.00	360.00
Sarah Hibberd, seamstress	W.	50	M.	N.Y	do	do	50.00	450.00
Helen Hibberd, assistant seamstress	W.	19	S.	Mich	do	do	40.00	360.00
Warren Butz, engineer	W.	28	S.	Ill	do	Jan. 31	50.00	276.67
Albert Rader, engineer	W.	23	S.	Ill	1901. Feb. 1	June 14	50.00	223.33
Frances J. Pamplin, cook	A.	53	S.	Ill	1900. Sept. 15	do	50.00	450.00
Mary F. Pamplin, laundress	A.	27	W.	Ill	do	do	40.00	360.00
John D. Plunket, laborer	W.	32	M.	Ind. T	do	do	35.00	315.00
Wallace Butz, superintendent	W.		S.	Ill	Dec. 1	do	(²)	6,349.30
Laura Collison, matron	W.	40	W.	Ill	do	do	50.00	320.10
Total								14,755.75

¹ Died. ² Contract.

TUSKAHOMA FEMALE ACADEMY.

[Enrollment, 123; average attendance, 99, days attendance, 29,293.]

Employee and position.	Race.	Age.	Single or married.	Birth-place.	Appointed.	Relieved.	Salary.	Received.
					1900	1901		
Charles F Trotter, superintendent	W.		M.	Ind	Sept. 15	June 14	(1) $100	$900.00
Robert A. Bayne, principal teacher	W.	41	M.	Ohio	do	do	60	540.00
Etta A. Bayne, assistant teacher	W.	40	M.	Ohio	do	do	35	305.00
Varina L. Jackson, assistant teacher	W.	35	S.	Tex	do	do	60	540.00
B Dayse King, assistant teacher	W.	24	M.	Miss	do	do	50	450.00
Hattie Trotter, matron	W.	29	S.	Ind Ter.	do	do	40	360.00
Julia Falconer, assistant matron	I.	20	S.	Ark	do	do	40	360.00
Kate Griffin, seamstress	W.	25	S.	Tenn	Sept. 25	Apr. 30	40	301.33
Mrs. M. E. Hogshead, assistant seamstress	W.	52	W.	Ark	Sept. 15	June 14	40	450.00
Turk Holman, engineer	W.	33	M.	Mo	do	do	50	450.00
Minnie E. May, cook	W.	25	M.	Ind	do	do	50	450.00
Jesse G. May, laundryman	W.	31	M.	Ark	do	do	35	360.00
Andrew Holman, janitor	W.	47	W.	Ark	do	do	35	315.00
Pauline Fewell, assistant seamstress	W.	20	S.	Miss	May 1	do	40	58.67
Total								

ARMSTRONG MALE ACADEMY.

[Enrollment, 97; average attendance, 87; days attendance, 25,164.]

Employee and position.	Race.	Age.	Single or married.	Birth-place.	Appointed.	Relieved.	Salary.	Received.
					1900.	1901.		
Sam L. Morley, superintendent	W.		S.	Ind. T	Sept. 15	June 30	(1) $100	$2,276.98
Gabe E. Parker, principal teacher	I.	21	M.	Ind. T	do	June 14	60	540.00
Edwin O. Clark, assistant teacher	I.	22	S.	Ind. T	do	Nov. 30	50	540.00
Susie E. Sloan, assistant teacher	I.	24	S.	Minn	Dec. 8	June 14	50	162.04
Jennie A Clark, assistant teacher	W.	24	S.	Ind. T	Sept. 15	do	40	125.00
Donn Gardner, matron	W.	18	S.	Tex	do	do	40	450.00
May Morley, assistant matron	I.	30	S.	Ind. T	do	do	40	360.00
Ida Folsomn, seamstress	A.	24	S.	Tex	do	do	40	450.00
George McBath, cook	W.	37	S.	Ark	do	Jan. 21	35	360.00
Thomas G. Metcalf, laundryman					1901.			228.67
Sarah Young, laundress	A.	27	W.	Ind. T	Feb. 1	June 14	85	96.88
					1900.			
Robert O. Knight, janitor	W.	29	S.	Ala	Sept. 16	do	85	315.00
Total								

1 Contract.

WHEELOCK FEMALE ACADEMY.

[Enrollment, 108; average attendance, 92; days attendance, 26,711.]

	Race.	Age.			Birth place.	Appointed.	Relieved.	Compensation.	Amount received.
W. W. Appleton, superintendent	W.		M.	M.		1900. Sept. 15	1901. June 30	(1)	$4,818.26
Alpha M. Saunders, principal teacher	W.	20	F.	s.	Tex.	do	June 14	$60	540.00
Sue M. Oakes, assistant teacher	I.	22	F.	s.	Ind. T.	do	do	55	495.00
Mary E. Appleton, matron	W.	35	F.	M.	Ohio.	do	do	50	450.00
Margaret Mitchell, seamstress	W.	27	F.	s.	Mo.	do	do	50	450.00
Sina Perly, cook	A.	49	F.	M.	Ind. T.	do	do	35	315.00
Elizabeth Frazier, laundress	A.	40	F.	M.	do	do	do	25	225.00
Albert Byrd, janitor	A.	22	M.	s.	do	do	do	35	315.00
Total									11,608.26

ATOKA BAPTIST ACADEMY.

[Enrollment, 55; average attendance, 51; days attendance, 14,121.]

	Race.	Age.			Birth place.	Appointed.	Relieved.		Compensation.	Amount received.
E. H. Riehel, superintendent	W.	47	M.	M.	Mo.	1900. Sept. 1	1901. May 31	Ill	(1)	$5,500.00
Total										

1 Contract.

Other employees appointed by church board.

NEIGHBORHOOD SCHOOLS.

Teacher.	School.	Race.	Age.	Single or married.	Birth place.	Appointed.	Relieved.	Enrollment.	Days of school.	Days attendance.	Compensation.	Amount received.
Allson, Elizabeth R	Cold Spring	W.	53	M.	Mo.	1900. Sept. 1	1901. May 31	25	184	2,142	$40	$356.00
Austin, D. J	Allen	W.	56	M.	Mo.	Sept. 10	Apr. 26	24	161	2,699	35	284.83
Albright, Katherine C	Bokoshe	W.	21	S.	Miss.	do	Jan. 31	10	92	737	40	177.68
Do	do					1901. Feb. 1	Apr. 19	10	59	237	30	79.00

NEIGHBORHOOD SCHOOLS—Continued.

Teacher	School	Race	Age	Single or married	Birthplace	Appointed	Relieved	Enrollment	Days of school	Days attendance	Compensation	Amount received
Ater, Allan C.	Canadian	W.	39	M.	Ohio	1900 Sept. 1	1901 Apr. 26	27	135	2,517	82	$307.70
Alexander, H. J.	Wadesville	L.	27	M.	Ind. T.	Oct. 1	Mar. 31	18	112	1,452	2	154.70
Austin, Male	Coal Creek	W.	23	S.	Ark.	Dec. 10	1900 Dec. 31	9	18	57	30	21.29
Abernathy, F. M	Wilburton	W.	47	M.		Sept. 1	Dec. 21	20	80	1,177	2	128.30
Burgoyne, May	Big Lick	W.	26	S.	Ill	do	1901 May 31	29	183	2,697	45	405.00
Belt, Mrs. Theo.	Milton	W.	30	M.	La	Sept. 1	Apr. 19	19	153	1,266	30	225.64
Benton, L. A.	Kulli Chito	L.	37	S.	N.Y.	do	May 31	26	194	3,244	45	400.50
Burrows, Rufus H	Middle Sans Bois	W.	43	M.	S.C.	do	1900 Oct. 31	8	37	206	35	70.00
Do	Vireton		21	S.	Ga.	Nov. 1	May 10	16	99	1,082	30	187.74
Baldwin, W. J	Big Hill	W.	20	S.	Ill	Sept. 1	Mar. 31	29	134	1,667	45	315.00
Battenberg, Francile	Sorrell	W.				Sept. 10	Feb. 8	6	102	778	30	146.67
Do	Tuskahoma					1901 Feb. 27	May 31	12	67	565	30	92.14
Brown, J. J	Stock Bridge	W.	27	S.	Ark	1900 Sept. 10	do	19	186	2,018	40	348.00
Bohanan, Wm. J	Post Oak Grove	L.	38	M.	Ind. T.	Dec. 10	1901 Mar. 31	15	82	790	2	101.90
Brasel, Irene	Wilburton	W.	20	S.	Ind. T	1901 Jan. 7	Feb. 11	10	28	174	35	41.98
Do	do					Feb. 26	Apr. 5	10	29	60	36	44.68
Brower, Lulu	Enterprise	W.	23	S.	Md	Feb. 1	May 30	15	85	625	2	66.90
Brewer, Ruby	Tallihina	W.	17	S.	Ark	Mar. 11	May 24	10	66	258	2	39.70
Coleman, Minnie	Buffalo Creek	W.	20	S.	Ind. T	1900 Sept. 1	1900 Sept. 16	13	10	108	30	16.00
Coleman, Nettie	Short Mountain	L.	22	S.	Tex	do	Nov. 23	11	55	351	40	110.67
Christian, Charles S.	Antlers	W.	21	S.	Mo		1901 May 3	16	168	1,248	2	135.30
Christian, Lewis E	Hartshorne	W.	43	M.	Mo	do	May 17	7	165	763	2	81.00
Crouthamel, A. H	Cowlington	W.	24	M.	Penn	do	Mar. 24	11	178	1,840	30	209.00
Carney, F. W	Kennady	W.	52	S.	Tenn	Oct. 15	Apr. 19	11	127	615	30	135.45
Crumpecker, Dilla M	Oak Grove	W.	10	S.	Tex	Oct. 1	Dec. 31	4	72	848	30	105.45

Name	Post office	Color	Age	Sex	Where born	Date began	Date ended					Amount
Cummings, T	Sittle	L.	19	S.	Ind. T	1900 Oct. 15	May 31	4	72	711	2	117.20
Davis, Emison E	Kiowa	W.	31	M.	Mo.	Sept. 1	May 8	19	171	2,358	40	330.23
Dukes, Edwin	Mountain Station	L.	20	S.	Ind. T	..do	Sept. 30	11	20	148	35	85.00
Dickerson, J. H.	Cox Chapel	W.	47	M.	Mo.	Sept. 10	Apr. 16	11	170	1,238	30	251.45
Doyle, Nannie E	Pleasant Valley	W.	19	S.	Ind. T	Nov. 19	Mar. 22	5	82	366	2	36.40
Doyle, Stella	Round Hill	W.	18	S.	Ind. T	1901 Jan. 7	Mar. 4	13	39	404	25	49.19
Deshazo, Alice	Honey Springs	W.	20	S.	Mo.	Feb. 11	May 31	27	75	1,600	2	168.80
Dwight, S. E.	Cedar Chapel	L.	22	S.	Ind. T	Apr. 9	..do	14	39	422	2	45.60
Eubank, Nellie	Indianola	W.	25	M.	Tex	1900 Oct. 1	May 10	10	156	1,321	2	131.90
Emery, W. B	Mount Pleasant	W.	34	M.	Mo.	Sept. 1	Oct. 26	14	36	115	30	55.16
Do	Blue Spring					Nov. 12	May 6	16	122	1,285	30	174.81
Emery, Mrs. Icie	Rock Spring	W.	21	M.	Miss	Sept. 1	May 18	9	55	206	30	78.00
Do	do					Nov. 19	Apr. 30	5	112	566	2	60.10
Everett, Mrs. Jessie L	Medical Springs	W.	38	W.	Ind. T	Sept. 1	May 31	20	189	1,809	30	270.00
Eifert, Bettie	Long Mountain	W.	21	S.	Ind. T	Sept. 10	Oct. 5	9	20	106	30	25.84
Eastman, H. P.	Durant	W.	39	M.	Tex	Sept. 1	May 17	21	185	2,168	2	235.10
Ervin, Ida	Brooken	W.	26	S.	Mo.	1901 Jan. 21	May 24	7	90	303	2	34.70
Ervin, Amanda	Hoyt	W.	30	S.	Mo.	Feb. 11	Feb. 28	2	12	16	2	1.50
Fulsom, Cloe A	Stringtown	L.	21	S.	Ind. T	1900 Sept. 1	May 31	12	188	1,801	35	315.00
Featherston, May	Featherston	W.	24	S.	Tex	Sept. 10	May 24	21	168	1,655	30	239.49
Fordyce, Lulu	Choate	W.	22	S.	Kans	1901 Jan. 1	May 17	12	99	724	30	136.45
Folsom, John N	Pleasant Hill	L.		M.		Jan. 15	May 31	20	99	1,610	2	176.10
Gay, Wm	South McAlester	W.	61	M.	Ire.	1900 Sept. 17	May 10	14	161	1,619	2	165.20
Green, Belle	Bethel	W.	28	S.	Ala.	Sept. 1	Jan. 31	11	99	256	40	
Do	do					1901 Feb. 1	Mar. 26		80	280		255.16
Garrett, Ethel	Wister	W.	26	S.	Ark.	1900 Oct. 1	Mar. 8	6		62	2	21.40
Garland, J. G	Ellis Chapel	W.	56	M.	Ire.	1901 Feb. 18	May 31	13	75	922	2	84.50
Holdsworth, Katie	Tushkahoma	W.	21	S.	Mo.	1900 Sept. 1	Sept. 14	10	10	78	35	18.67
Do	Lehigh					Sept. 17	Apr. 30	11	172	713	35	261.83

NEIGHBORHOOD SCHOOLS—Continued.

Teacher.	School.	Race.	Age.	Single or married.	Birthplace.	Appointed.	Relieved.	Enrollment.	Days of school.	Days attendance.	Compensation.	Amount received.
Homidy, Emma	Rock Creek	W		W	Penn	1900. Sept. 1	1901. May 31	16	192	2,053	$75	$315.00
Hallman, J. P.	Water Hole	W	55	M	Ga	do	Mar. 11	14	125	973	36	269.59
Hatcher, Lizzie	Cedar Chapel	W	23	S	Tex	Sept. 24	Dec. 31	19	63	740	30	95.06
Hogg, Jay	Marysville	W	27	M	Mo	Sept. 1	May 31	16	190	1,754	30	315.00
Hynson, Mrs. Rose	Pine Spring	W	34	S	Ill	do	do	19	191	2,069	55	315.00
Hynson, Belle	Pleasant Hill	W	23	M	Tex	do	do	16	191	1,567	55	270.00
Halleman, John B	Stigler	W	28	M	Ala	do	do	25	193	2,163	40	360.00
Hotchkin, Mary P	Nunnih Takalo	W	20	S	Tex	do	1900. Dec. 21	11	20	241	30	96.71
Do	Coal Creek					1901. Jan. 7	Feb. 28	9	34	221	30	54.19
Harrison, W. H	Little Sans Bois	I	20	S	Ind. T	1900. Sept. 1	1900. May 31	21	191	1,815	45	406.00
Herndon, Mrs. J. B	Pleasant Cove	W	32	W	Tenn	Sept. 1	May 30	18	181	1,742	35	362.35
Hallman, Lena	Hochatown	W	22	M	Ga	Sept. 10	May 31	23	187	2,559	40	348.00
Hamilton, S. A	Potean	W	32	S	Mich	Sept. 1	May 31	17	150	1,573	2	171.20
Hibbard, Katherine	Calvin	W	18	S	Ill	Sept. 17	Jan. 31	8	93	571	2	59.70
Holland, Anna	Conser	W	23	M	Ill	Oct. 1	May 24	26	188	2,919	45	406.00
Hill, B. T	Sardis	W	50	W	Ill	Sept. 1	do	22	162	2,430	2	257.60
Hankins, Mrs. C. M	Kon Chito	W	26	W	Miss			21	189	2,865	30	263.23
Hamilton, Mrs. Mae	Pleasant Hill	W	28	M	Tex	do	1901. Jan. 11	26	66	1,154	2	123.90
Herndon, Elnora	Short Mountain	W	20	S	Tex	Nov. 26	Jan. 31	9	44	104	30	65.00
Hower, Jessie	Frazier	W	20	S	Ill	Oct. 22	May 31	14	151	1,230	30	218.68
Hatcher, Lucy	Roberta	W	23	S	Tex	1901. Jan. 1	Mar. 31	3	62	166	2	16.00
Irvine, Nettie	Pleasant Hill	W	38	W	Tex	1900. Sept. 1	Jan. 31	16	107	1,126	45	225.00
Do	do					1901. Feb. 1	May 31		85	909	35	140.00
Jones, D. F	Toloke	W	29	M	Ark	1900. Sept. 1	do 3	17	190	2,046	40	346.67
Johns, Maggie	Oaka Chito	I	20	S	Tex	do	May 10	16	174	1,683	30	242.90
Jeter, Hattie	Oakerville	I	23	M	Ind. T	Oct. 16	May 31	7	143		2	61.80
Jackson, Mrs. W. L	Lenox	W	29		Mo	Oct. 1	May 31	18	173	1,080	40	320.00

Name	School	Color	Age	Sex	State	Date of appointment	Date of commencing	No. (a)	No. enrolled	Aggregate	Rate	Amount
Do	do						Apr. 6		40	297	35	77.00
Do	do					1901. Feb. 1	May 10	30	25	50	2	16.90
Kirksey, J. A.	Bethel Hill	W.	54	M.	Ala.	Apr. 8	Sept. 21	9	194	2,402	45	400.00
Kennon, Mattie	Bower	W.	18	S.	Ohio.	Sept. 12	Dec. 21	21	69	591	30	96.42
Lynch, May J	Boel	W.	22	S.	Ill.	Sept. 1	May 31	21	128	1,421	35	98.00
Larcey, W. E.	Sugar reek	W.	22	S.	Ark.	Sept. 1	Mar. 31	17	189	2,746	35	315.00
La Rue, Margarette	Sixty Pot	W.	24	S.	Mo.	...do	Mar. 22	12	139	1,447	30	201.29
La Rue, Lettuce	Ellis Chapel	L.	19	S.	Mo.	Sept. 17	Nov. 30	14	50	306	25	65.94
Lee, Robert E	Bing Spring	W.	22	S.	Miss.	Sept. 1	May 31	15	176	2,039	35	298.06
Larmour, Mary	Guertie		22	S.	Ill.	...do	Jan. 31		103	850	35	175.00
Do	do					Feb. 1	May 31		85	675	30	120.00
Lewis, Maye	Atwood	I.	20	S.	Ind. T	900. Oct. 1	Feb. 18	11	97	651	30	139.29
Lee, L. B.	Salem	W.	25	S.	Ark.	Sept. 1	Jan. 31	21	94	1,208	40	200.00
Do	do						May 31					120.00
Lindsey, Hattie	Salem	W.	24	S.	Ark.	1901. Feb. 1	May 31	1,267		85	30	120.00
Do	Doaksville	I.	24	S.	Ind. T		Sept. 30	144	11	20	40	40.00
Lyle, Frances M	Tamaha	W.	28	S.	S. C.	900. Sept. 1	Dec. 13	493	12	48	30	65.81
Latt, J. H	Grant	W.	35	M.	Ala.	...do	May 24	1,802	19	185	40	350.97
Langston, Geo. W	Frink	W.	18	S.	Tex.	Sept. 1	May 21	1,142	14	140	2	112.70
Lacy, W. S.	Redoak	W.	24	S.	Miss.	Feb.	Feb. 20	422	5	114	25	141.25
Do	Cameron					...do	Jan. 31	1,144	19	100	45	225.00
Lynn, J. A.	Tallihina	W.	30	M.	Ind.	901. Feb. 1	May 17	677	19	75	40	141.94
Morrison, Margery	Gills	W.	26	S.	Ohio.	900. Oct. 1	Dec. 21	755	24	59	2	83.40
Do	do					Sept. 1	Dec. 31	2,315		81	35	814.09
Miller, Lizzie	Howe	W.	30	S.	Miss.	901. Jan. 1	Apr. 26	1,385	17	109	40	200.00
Do	do					900. Sept. 1	Jan. 31	1,005		41	30	120.00
Merriman, Gus	Summerfield	W.	27	S.	Ark.	Feb. 1	May 31	462	18	34	45	82.74
Do	Panshawe					90. Sept. 1 / Nov. 26	Oct. 26 / Dec. 21	96	8	20	2	11.20

NEIGHBORHOOD SCHOOLS—Continued.

Teacher.	School.	Race.	Age.	Single or married.	Birthplace.	Appointed.	Relieved.	Enrollment.	Days of school.	Days attendance.	Compensation.	Amount received.
Merriman, Gus	Summerfield					1901. Jan. 21	1901. May 31	1,314	18	95	$45	$196.97
Morris, S. P.	McAlester	W.	46	M.	Tenn.	1900. Sept. 1	do	2,593	25	171	45	380.00
Miller, Alice M.	Hibben	W.	32	S.	Miss.	do	May 10	1,296	19	164	40	382.90
Meroney, Lou J.	Mount Pleasant	W.	49	S.	Ga.	Sept. 1	May 31	26	31	3,519	45	405.00
Moore, Lizzie	Ward	L.	18	W.	Miss.	do	Mar. 10	13	194	1,656	25	208.06
Mahoney, Mary	Antlers	W.	21	S.	Ireland	do	May 10	33	176	8,189	2	322.30
McClaren, Ethel	Honey Springs	W.	20	S.	Mo.	do	Nov. 10	13	38	49	35	70.30
McBride, E. C.	Christian Hope	W.	31	W.	do	do	Apr. 30	21	168	2,424	40	320.00
McClure, Mrs. C. L.	Choate	L.	34	S.	N. Y.	do	Dec. 31	12	56	251	40	120.00
McCurtain, Lou	Oak Lodge	I.	18	W.	Ind. T	do	Apr. 26	15	169	1,463	40	314.67
McArthur, Mary O.	Goodland	W.	32	S.	Tex.	do	Apr. 7	15	127	889	30	186.77
McCallum, Bella	Old Goodland	W.	35	S.	Ark.	do	Oct. 18	24	33	831	45	69.68
Morgan, John J	Zion	W.		M.	Ill.	Nov. 1	Dec. 22	15	33	383	2	46.90
Do	do					1901. Jan. 1	May 31	7	108	960	25	125.00
Murray, J. I	Redoak	W.	24	S.	Ark.	1900. Oct. 18	Dec. 21		43	138	2	14.30
McCaslan, Annie R	Ellis Chapel	W.	21	S.	Tex.	1901. Jan. 7	Feb. 6	13	96	1,027	2	106.80
Morrison, Mrs. B. R.	Spiro	W.	29	M.	Tenn.	Jan. 7	May 17	7	44	159	2	17.20
Mitchell, Mattie	Redoak	L.	22	S.	Ark.	do	Mar. 7	16	48	716	2	78.60
McElroy, Elma.	Reichert	W.	25	S.	Ind. T	Feb. 11	Apr. 25	89	171	11,890	2	1,818.90
Neely, H. D.	Durant	W.	20	M.	Ill.	Sept. 1	May 24	19	168	1,778	30	235.16
Noah, D. S.	Albion	L.		M.	Ind. T	Oct. 1	May 31					
Nichols, J. E.	Bennington	W.	32	S.	Tenn.	1900. Nov. 26	Mar. 31	15	65	914	2	95.60
Oakley, Cyrus K	Coal Creek	W.	19	S.	Ark.	Sept. 1	Sept. 30	9	20	92	40	40.00
Do	Pine Ridge					Oct. 22	Nov. 22	12	22	167	30	31.68
Do	Wolf Creek					Dec. 5	May 31	14	84	901	30	176.13
Oakes, Virgia	Rock Hill	L.	19	S.	Ind. T	Sept. 1	do	11	198	1,479	30	270.00
Overstreet, Dora	Short Mountain	L.	21	S.	Ind. T	1901. Feb. 1	do	11	82	428	25	97.58
Owen, C. D.	Turkey Creek	W.	27	M.	Ark.	do	do	10	81	628	2	57.50
Paxson, Anna L.	Chish Oktah	L.	50	S.	Ill.	1900. Sept. 1	do	32	189	8,874	45	405.00
Phipps, M. L.	Whitefield	W.	35	M.	Miss.	do	do	19	175	2,050	2	280.00

Name	Place	Race	Age	Sex	State	Date	Date					Amount
Powe, Grace.	Walnut Grove	W.	26	S.	N.C.	do. 29	Oct. 26	9	85	296	25	45.97
Do	Old Goodland					Oct.	May 31	24	145	1,843	46	316.00
Philbeck, R. E.	Enterprise	W.	23	S.	Ark	Sept. 1	Jan. 31	15	104	1,087	2	115.90
Powers, Lillie M	Sileans	W.	22	S.	Tex	do.	May 31	11	180	1,163	30	267.09
Petty, W. H	Albany	W.	31	M.	Tenn	Dec. 1	Mar. 12	7	67	211	2	38.20
Price, John R	Center Hill	W.	22	S.	Ill	1901. Jan. 7	Mar. 29	7	60	291	2	32.50
Perry, Estella	Hill Chapel	W.	24	S.	Ind. T	1900. Dec. 1	Apr. 5	9	90	677	2	74.50
Russell, Leola	Bennington	W.	29	S.	S.C.	Sept. 1	May 31	23	182	1,506	40	356.71
Read, Mrs. J J	Wapanucka	W.	46	S.	S.C.	do.	May 30	15	181	983	2	110.50
Blabel, E. H	Atoka	W.	47	M.	Ill	do.	May 24	42	186	4,352	2	473.10
Ryan, M. M	Cartersville	W.	40	M.	Ky	do.	Jan. 30	16	108	821	40	200.00
Riner, Lillian	Sulphur Spring	L.	19	M.	Ind. T	Sept. 11	May 31	22	180	2,737	30	270.00
Read, Mrs. Inez	Caney	L.	23	S.	Ind. T	Sept. 1	May 31	4	112	2,306	30	94.40
Redman, Clara.	Bylngton	W.	18	S.	Ark	Nov. 12	Mar. 15	9	79	345	2	49.40
Byan, M. M	Cartersville	W.	25	M.	Ark	1901. Feb. 1	May 10	12	68	436	30	98.87
Sullivan, E. P	Dunlap.					Jan. 1	May 31	8	44	786	2	78.00
Strawn, Dan	Living Land.	W.	20	S.	Ark	1900. Sept. 1	May 20	21	138	1,574	40	287.59
Stoney, Wilson A	Kulli Tukio	L.	28	M.	Ind. T	do.	May 31	19	192	1,727	40	380.00
Strickler, Florence.	Bokchito	W.	20	S.	Ind. T	do.	do.	17	182	1,909	35	316.00
Session, John H.	White Oak	W.	19	S.	Ark	do.	Mar. 8	11	108	1,950	40	287.74
Staton, Mrs. June H	Crowder Chapel	W.	24	W.	Iowa	do.	Mar. 31	20	127	1,488	40	270.42
Stalcup, Callie.	Spring Chapel	W.	36	S.	Tenn	Jan.	Jan. 31	18	107	447	45	225.00
Do	do	W.	36	S.	Tenn	1901. Feb. 1	Apr. 30		22	288	35	106.00
Scarborough, James J	Caddo	W.	37	M.	N.C.	1900. Sept. 1	May 14	42	176	3,408	2	457.50
Smith, Lucy H.	Springfield	W.	20	S.	Ill	do.	Dec. 31	18	76	657	40	160.00
Stanley, J. M.	Legal	W.	60	M.	Va	Sept. 10	do. 19	11	160	1,032	35	253.28
Shepherd, Myrtle	Globe.	W.	19	S.	Mo	do.	Mar. 1	634	13	113	30	164.00
Strother, B. M.	Utica	W.	26	S.	Tex	Sept. 29	Mar. 1	968	16	100	30	162.90
Sumter, Mrs. Serena.	Black Jack	L.	23	M.	Ind. T	Oct. 15	Feb. 28	598	16	91	2	124.30
Sherred, J. M., jr	Davenport.	L.	20	S.	Ind. T	Nov. 12	Dec. 7	512	13	20	2	32.40
Sull, Emma C.	Long Creek.	W.	25	S.	Mo	1901. Mar. 12	May 25	458	13	60	2	47.00
Sexton, H. J	Mountain Station	L.	28	S.	Ind. T	1900. Dec. 1	Apr. 25	1,012	16	99	2	111.40
Sigwig, J. F.	Brooken	W.	40	M.	Tex	Nov. 26	Dec. 31	47	7	19	2	4.70
Thomas, Lucy	Kulli Box	L.	22	S.	Ind. T	Sept. 10	May 30	2,766	21	191	40	380.00
Thompson, Ella W.	Beach Creek	L.	23	S.	Ind. T	Sept. 10	Oct. 29	647	21	36	35	57.24
Thornburgh, Etta	Doaksville	W.	22	S.	Mo	Oct. 15	Apr. 26	1,268	13	130	2	156.90

NEIGHBORHOOD SCHOOLS—Continued

Teacher.	School.	Race.	Age.	Single or married.	Birth-place.	Appointed.	Relieved.	Enrollment.	Days of school.	Days attendance.	Compensation.	Amount received.
						1901.	1901.					
Underwood, I.T	Sterrett	W	38	M.	Va	Feb. 27	May 31	658	13	66	82	981.50
Vaughn, L.D	Lenox	I	28	M.	Ind. T	Oct. 29	Apr. 15	1,680	18	117	2	169.60
Windsor, I.H	Sans Bois	W	30	M.	Mo	Sept. 1	Jan. 31	746	18	102	40	200.00
Do	do					Feb. 1	May 10	406		70	30	115.16
Wheat, T.H	Calvin	W	41	M.	Miss	Sept. 1	Sept. 6	28	8	6	2	2.80
Do	Reichert					Sept. 8	Jan. 21	715	16	94	80	181.32
Do	Alikchi					Feb. 1	Apr. 12	887	8	51	35	84.00
						1900.						
White, J.M	Brooken	W	39	M.	Ill	Sept. 10	Nov. 20	7	46	234	2	25.20
Wilkins, A.J	Thessalonian	I	24	S.	Ind. T	Oct. 1	Nov. 16	12	20	80	2	8.90
Do	Cedar				Ind. T	Nov. 26	Apr. 8	15	90	945	2	99.80
Williams, Katherine	Good Spring	I	29	S.	Ind. T	Oct. 22		16	101	1,114	2	116.10
Ward, Mrs. J.L	Limestone	W	36	M.	Australia	Oct. 1		7	164	997	2	99.10
						1901.						
Walker, Ella	Tamaha	I	21	S.	Ind. T	Feb. 7	May 31	14	99	1,065	2	114.60
Whitehead, Bertha	Goodwater	W	34	S.	Mo	Sept. 1	...do	25	192	2,730	45	406.00
Yandell, J.F	Alikchi	W	30	S.	Tex	...do	Jan. 31	11	104	601	45	225.00
Zufall, Pearl	Nunnih Takali	W	21	S.	Ind. T	Jan. 7	Feb. 1	11	20	160	30	25.28
Total								2,879		228,285		34,391.02

Academies.	Number of employees.			Enrollment.	Days attendance.	Average attendance.	Expenses.	Cost per pupil per month.
	M.	F.	Total.					
Jones	5	8	13	142	27,689	101	$14,755.75	$16.23
Armstrong	5	4	9	97	25,184	87	12,253.97	14.82
Tushkahoma	5	8	13	123	26,973	99	14,351.86	16.11
Wheelock	2	6	8	108	26,711	92	11,608.26	13.28
Atoka Baptist				55	14,121	51	5,500.00	11.98
Total	17	26	43	525	120,678		58,469.84	

NEIGHBORHOOD SCHOOLS.

Number of schools	161
White teachers:	
Male	59
Female	76
Indian teachers:	
Male	15
Female	19
Total number of teachers	169
Total days' attendance	228,285
Total cost	$34,891.02

In concluding my report, I wish to thank you for the many valuable suggestions and the help you have given me. I also desire to thank the teachers, employees, and school officials for their cooperation in our efforts.

I wish also to express my gratitude to the people of the Choctaw Nation, and especially to the citizens, for the kindness and hospitality they have shown me during my visits throughout the nation.

This report is very respectfully submitted.

CALVIN BALLARD,
School Supervisor, Choctaw Nation.

Hon. JOHN D. BENEDICT,
Superintendent of Schools for the Indian Territory.

REPORT OF THE REVENUE INSPECTOR FOR THE CREEK NATION.

MUSCOGEE, IND. T., *July 1, 1901.*

SIR: Complying with instructions to submit to you an annual report showing the work done by the revenue inspector in connection with the collection of the revenues of the Creek Nation, I have the honor to respectfully submit the following:

TRADER AND OCCUPATION TAX.

The total amount of funds received by the United States Indian agent during the fiscal year ending June 30, 1900, from this source was $18,811.27. The amount received from the same source during the fiscal year ending June 30, 1901, is $19,357.35.

The method of collecting the tax during the year just ended has been as follows:

At the beginning of each quarter written demand has been made on all persons subject to this tax requiring payment to the United States Indian agent within ten days, and such demand has been followed up by personal demand made upon delinquents by the revenue inspector, or district revenue inspector, at or near the expiration of the ten days specified in the written demand.

Records are kept in my office, made up from information secured by personal investigation, and the duplicate statements which accompany remittances to the United States Indian agent, affording a systematic check on all work done by this office and all moneys received by the United States Indian agent so far as the revenues of the Creek Nation are concerned.

During the present year the permit law of the Creek Nation has been revised, reducing the tax on merchandise offered for sale from 1 per cent to one-half of 1 per cent, exempting such goods as have been actually produced in the Muskogee Nation, or shall have been bought within the limits of the Creek Nation, from traders who shall have previously paid the tax on such goods, and reducing the tax levied on a majority of the occupations subject to the operation of the Creek permit law.

A copy of said law as revised, now in force, is as follows:

Be it enacted by the national council of the Muskogee Nation:

SECTION 1. That all persons who are not citizens by blood of the Muskogee Nation, or who have not been adopted by the Muskogee Nation, and whose names do not appear on authenticated rolls of the Muskogee Nation, who shall desire to engage in any manner of business in the Muskogee Nation, shall obtain the consent of the United States Government, and shall pay to the United States Indian agent at Union Agency, Muscogee, Ind. T., for the benefit of the Muskogee Nation, the annual permit tax hereinafter fixed, the same to be paid quarterly, in advance in all cases, except where based on the cost of goods offered. Quarters to begin January 1, April 1, July 1, and October 1 of each year.

All legitimate business houses of whatsoever character or capacity engaged in the sale of all manner of dry goods, groceries, provisions, hardware, lumber, drugs, millinery, leather goods, or any other articles known or designated as merchandise, shall pay an annual tax of one-half of 1 per cent of the first cost of all goods offered for sale, excepting such goods as have been actually produced in the Muskogee Nation, or shall have been bought within the limits of the nation from a trader who shall have previously paid this tax of one-half of 1 per cent of such goods, all payments to be accompanied by sworn statements, said statements to be verified by personal inspection by a proper inspector of the original invoices or the books of the trader.

The rate of taxation on all other classes of business shall be as follows:

On each dealer in hides, peltries, furs, wool, pecans, and other country produce	$50.00
On each hotel affording accommodations for 30 or more guests	36.00
On each hotel affording accommodations for 20 or more guests	24.00
On each hotel affording accommodations for less than 20 guests	12.00
On each printing office	12.00
On each oil, grist, or flouring mill	24.00
On each cotton gin	24.00
On each livery and feed stable	24.00
On each feed stable or yard	12.00

)n each dray or freight wagon or passenger hack other than those owned by livery stables paying as such..	$12.00
)n each blacksmith or wagon shop	12.00
)n each insurance agent (life or fire)	50.00
)n each physician having certificate from the national medical board.......................	25.00
)n each dentist having diploma	25.00
)n each butcher shop selling meat only...	24.00
)n each restaurant or lunch stand..	12.00
)n each laundry or laundry agency...	12.00
)n each barber shop..	12.00
)n each bakery and confectionery or lemonade and ice-cream stand........................	24.00
)n each merry-go-round..	12.00
)n each gunsmith, tinsmith, locksmith, or watch repairer	12.00
)n each lawyer...	25.00
)n each tombstone or marble dealer	12.00
)n each shooting gallery	12.00
)n each billiard and pool table..	5.00
)n each show or concert in hall or tent, per day...	5.00
)n each circus without menagerie, per day..	10.00
)n each circus and menagerie combined, per day...	25.00
)n each banking establishment one-half of 1 per cent of capital stock invested, assessment to be made on the bank on account of the shares thereof.	
)n each peddler, street or traveling vendor, 5 per cent of goods offered for sale.	
)n each establishment selling nonintoxicating ales, tonics, meads, or any other form of drink intended as a substitute for malt or spirituous liquors	100.00

SEC. 2. Should any person refuse to pay the tax herein provided when due and when demand is made, or should any person refuse to permit a personal inspection to be had of original invoices, books, etc., such person shall be reported to the proper authorities for removal from Muskogee Nation.

Failure to pay within ten days after tax is due and demand has been made shall constitute a refusal to pay.

SEC. 3. This act shall become a law upon the approval of the President of the United States, and shall be in full force and effect from and after January 1, 1901.

All laws heretofore enacted by the national council of the Muskogee Nation relating to permit tax which are in conflict with this act are hereby repealed.

SEC. 4. All classes of business in operation, or which may hereafter be established in this nation, not included in the above list shall be assessed by the principal chief, subject to the approval of the United States Indian agency.

Approved, November 5, 1900.

P. PORTER, *Principal Chief.*

Approved by William McKinley, November 22, 1900.

At all times during the past year the collection of this tax has been actively resisted by many of the persons subject to the operation thereof.

During the early part of the year this resistance was based on the undecided appeal in the case of Maxey *v.* Wright, then pending before the United States circuit court of appeals.

After the appeal was decided in this case adversely to the taxpayers, it was found necessary to remove from the limits of the Creek Nation and the Indian Territory, for nonpayment of Creek permit taxes, Dr. D. M. Pate, of Checotah, Ind. T., and J. . Sisson, of Tulsa, Ind. T., both of whom returned and were prosecuted under section 2148 of the Revised Statutes of the United States; and, pending action of the Department of Justice in their cases, the resistance to the operation of the Creek permit law was based on the undecided condition of such cases. Settlement was had in these cases on the 27th day of May, 1901, both Dr. Pate and Mr. Sisson entering a plea of guilty before Hon. Joseph A. Gill, judge of the United States court for the northern district of the Indian Territory.

Prior to such settlement, and on the 3d day of March, 1901, legislation was enacted by the United States Congress declaring all Indians in the Indian Territory citizens of the United States; and on the 25th day of May, 1901, an agreement between the Creek Nation and the United States, affecting conditions in the Creek Nation, was ratified, since which time and up to the present the resistance to the operation of the Creek permit law is based upon the provisions of the act of March 3 and the Creek agreement, the taxpayers claiming that the act which made the members of the Creek tribe or nation citizens of the United States destroyed the right of the Creek Nation to impose or receive the taxes imposed by the Creek permit law, and that that part of the Creek agreement which provides a method whereby noncitizens may acquire title to part of the Creek lands implies consent to noncitizens to reside within the Creek Nation in such a degree as to prevent such noncitizens becoming intruders subject to removal under United States statutes; and an effort is now being made by the legal advisers of many of the taxpayers to perfect an organization to resist the operation of the Creek permit law through the United States courts.

During the past year those paying permit taxes based upon the cost of goods offered for sale have, as a rule, paid with a reasonable degree of promptness, while many of those subject to tax levied on occupations have at all times been in arrears.

Among such delinquents the most noticeable cases are among lawyers.

I attribute the failure on the part of the lawyers to comply with the law to the fact that they have at all times been able to advance some trivial or technical ground for delay, and to the fact that a large number of the lawyers engaged in practice within the limits of the Creek Nation are in very poor circumstances financially; and some, perhaps, actually unable to earn or borrow sufficient money to pay the Creek permit tax.

There are at present within the limits of the Creek Nation 38 towns, villages, or trading posts where those subject to the operation of the Creek license law are engaged in business.

The list of persons subject to the operation of the Creek permit law includes the names of 827 individuals or firms doing business within the limits of the Creek Nation.

COLLECTION OF RENTALS FROM CATTLEMEN AND OTHERS.

Rent to the amount of $1,950 has been paid to the United States Indian agent during the past year by cattlemen on that part of their inclosed pastures which had not been selected by individual Creek citizens as their prospective allotment.

The plan followed in outlining the settlements with cattlemen has been to ascertain whether or not the pasture was all leased from individual citizens. If it was not found to be all leased, then to check the plat with the leases submitted and the records of the Commission to the Five Civilized Tribes, and to base the outline of settlement on behalf of the Creek Nation on the amount of land not selected and not leased and the quality of the land covered by settlement.

The amount derived from this source during the fiscal year ending June 30, 1900, was $4,344.65, and the decrease in the amount collected during the past year is accounted for by the fact that many additional selections have been filed in the inclosed pastures during the past year, and that many pastures used during the preceding year have not been occupied; and while the work done along these lines has not resulted in a very great income to the Creek people, it has materially assisted in hastening the selection of land by Creek citizens, and has also assisted a large number of Creek citizens in locating accurately their section and collecting the rents from the same, and has enabled me to become familiar with many of the methods that are now being followed by speculators and others in endeavoring to secure control of the future disposition of the lands of the Creek Nation.

In connection with the cattle industry I would respectfully call your attention to certain conditions existing in the Creek Nation at the present time.

At all times during the past year a limited number of horses, cattle, and other live stock have been permitted to run at large within the limits of the Creek Nation, and have been a source of many complaints in cases where crops belonging to citizens or leasers were damaged by such stock.

I am advised that the fence law of the State of Arkansas is followed by the United States court in such cases, and that under that law it is necessary for the owner of the crop to have such crop inclosed with a hog-proof fence in order to maintain a claim for damages to such crop by live stock.

In some sections of the Creek Nation all crops are so inclosed. In other sections no particular effort is made to so inclose the crops, but an understanding is had among most of the occupants of the land that all stock shall be kept up, and when stock is permitted to run at large in these districts it is driven out of the neighborhood with the assistance of dogs and sometimes firearms, to the material injury of the owner of such stock; and the owner refrains from appealing to the United States court, preferring to bear his loss rather than incur the enmity of his neighbors. I would respectfully recommend that the advisability of establishing a uniform and effective fence law be considered.

The cattle industry is of great importance to this section of the country at present, owing to the fact that much of the land of the Creek Nation is not of a superior quality, but admirably adapted to grazing purposes, and were the cattle industry disturbed and driven from the Creek Nation, many of the individual citizens would be unable to secure any income from the lands embraced in their allotments. On the other hand, a large portion of the lands contained within the limits of the Creek Nation is admirably adapted to agricultural puposes and will eventually be placed in cultivation, and a law compelling the owners of live stock to keep such live stock confined would materially aid and hasten the development of the agricultural districts of the Creek Nation.

A large majority of the cattlemen prefer to keep their cattle confined, and do so under existing conditions, and, generally speaking, the owner of live stock is better able to keep his stock confined than the Indian allottee or immigrant leaser is to fence his crop. Any legislation contemplated, affecting the conditions outlined above, should, in my opinion, make provision for roads.

TIMBER AND STONE ROYALTY.

The work done in this connection has been principally under the regulations of the honorable Secretary of the Interior, promulgated under the act of June 6, 1900, and in connection with timber and stone secured for construction purposes by the St. Louis, Oklahoma and Southern Railroad and their contractors and subcontractors.

The amount received by the United States Indian agent during the past year from these sources is $4,483.02.

Many small timber depredations have been investigated, and some few prosecutions had in cases where small quantities of timber have been illegally cut or destroyed; but no considerable quantity of timber has been illegally cut, and none, so far as I am advised, shipped from the limits of the Creek Nation.

ROYALTY ON COAL.

The amount received for the benefit of the Creek Nation as royalty on coal mined during the past year is $4,128.22.

The principal mines are located at Howard, 3 miles east of Tulsa, and in the vicinity of Henryetta, and have been operated under temporary permits.

There are many valuable coal deposits within the limits of the Creek Nation, and oil has been discovered in several localities, notably in the vicinity of Red Fork, and much speculation is at present being indulged in with a view to controlling the future disposition of the mineral deposits.

In addition to the regular work outlined above, much has been done in preventing illegal coal mining, the cutting of hay, and the grazing of stock on the public domain, and a large variety of investigations and reports have been made covering illegal land holdings, town-site speculations, status and population of sites sought to be segregated for town-site purposes, effect of segregation, and such other matters as you have seen fit to assign me.

The total moneys received by the United States Indian agent for the benefit of the Creek Nation are as follows:

Coal royalty	$4,128.22
Pasture and cattle tax	1,950.00
Timber and stone royalty	4,483.02
Merchandise and occupation tax	19,357.35
Insurance	909.01
	30,827.60
Less exchange	52.32
Total	30,775.28

The total receipts for the preceding fiscal year were $26,370.19.

The total expenses for the past year for salary and per diem, and traveling expenses, clerical assistance, etc., amounted to $4,230.82, including amount paid for office furniture.

The similar expense for the preceding fiscal year amounted to $4,884.52, showing an increase in receipts and a decrease in expenditures for the past year as compared with the preceding year.

During the past year all of the district revenue inspectors for the Creek Nation have resigned, leaving the revenue inspector no assistance in performing field work. Authority has been granted to employ clerical assistance, and one clerk has been employed, one half of whose time has been devoted to office work with the revenue inspector of the Creek Nation, relieving the revenue inspector of much of the detail office work and materially aiding in the general work.

Very respectfully,

GUY P. COBB, *Revenue Inspector.*

Hon. J. GEO. WRIGHT,
   U. S. Indian Inspector for Indian Territory.

REPORT OF THE REVENUE INSPECTOR FOR THE CHEROKEE NATION.

MUSCOGEE, IND. T., *July 1, 1901.*

SIR: I have the honor to submit the following report, as revenue inspector for the Cherokee Nation, for the fiscal year ending June 30, 1901.

Acting under your instructions, my duty is the supervision of the payment of the revenues, royalties, and taxes due the Cherokee Nation into the hands of the United States Indian agent at Muscogee, Ind. T., for credit to the nation.

The principal sources of revenue in the Cherokee Nation are from a tax of one-fourth of 1 per cent on merchandise introduced and offered for sale; an introduction tax of 50 cents per head and a grazing tax of 25 cents per head on cattle introduced into the nation; a royalty of 20 cents per ton on hay shipped from the nation; a royalty of 8 cents per ton on coal mined in the nation; ferry licenses; and a royalty of 2 cents per cubic yard on gravel taken from the banks of Grand River.

At the commencement of the present fiscal year there were on duty and acting under my direction two district revenue inspectors, both of whom resigned in September last, since which time I have been alone in the performance of the field work.

Beginning with July 20, 1900, authority was granted me to employ a revenue clerk in conjunction with the revenue inspector for the Creek Nation, we occupying the same office, the remuneration of such clerk being paid equally from the accounts of the revenue inspectors for the Cherokee and Creek nations. We were fortunate in securing the services as clerk of an efficient stenographer and typewriter at $75 per month. This arrangement has proved very satisfactory and economical, and under this plan the correspondence, at times quite voluminous, has been promptly attended to and the records of remittances checked up daily, and frequent comparisons made with the books of the United States Indian agent, who is the custodian of all funds.

The business year has been one of various vicissitudes in the Cherokee Nation, involving public questions somewhat disturbing in their character, both legal and political, all bearing more or less on the question of revenues and taxes and public sentiment concerning the same, and I may add that each successive change has made collections more uncertain and difficult. The interruptions and unrest following Judge Gill's decision, hereinafter referred to, and the discussion and disposal of the proposed agreement between the nation and the United States have been the most important features that I have encountered with reference to my duties.

Some of the Cherokee citizens appreciate that the loose and extravagant methods which have been in vogue in the management of the financial affairs of the Cherokee Nation, when under their own untrammeled control, have created a heavy floating debt for the nation, which demands that all of their fixed revenues be collected.

Few well-informed Cherokees deny this as individuals, but it is a deplorable fact that whenever a contest has arisen over the collection of moneys due the nation a large class of prominent Cherokees have invariably been found in sympathy with and arrayed against the collection of all tribal revenues. This is emphasized by the appearance in court as counsel for the defense of paid attorneys of the Cherokee Nation, arguing against the collection of taxes due the nation when legal questions have arisen.

I referred in my last report to the case of W. C. Rogers, a Cherokee citizen, whose store at Talala was closed by me under your instructions in June, 1900, for nonpayment of the merchandise tax of one-fourth of 1 per cent on goods introduced and offered for sale by him. Rogers refused to pay the tax and declared himself opposed to the collection of revenues by officers of the United States Government.

The attempt to force Rogers to pay his tax engendered considerable feeling among the Cherokee merchants throughout the nation, and a fund was raised among these citizen merchants to prosecute the case in the courts, the amount of which, I am credibly informed, was $500, a sum, by the way, doubtless in excess of what the taxes of the contributors would have been had they been sufficiently patriotic to have paid the taxes due their own people without contest.

They secured from the Hon. Joseph A. Gill, judge of the United States court, a temporary restraining order, preventing the officers of the Government from interfering with the business of Rogers in this matter, which order was made perpetual in the following September, after lengthy arguments, at Vinita, Ind. T.

The court found that the officers of the United States had no authority to enforce collection of merchandise tax from Cherokee citizens, but was, of course, silent concerning other phases of the general subject.

Since that time the merchandise tax has been demanded from noncitizen merchants only, and I should state that this class does not include many of the larger merchants; hence the receipts from this source are materially lessened, the loss falling, of course, upon the Cherokee Nation itself.

I regret to report that a considerable number of the noncitizen merchants of the nation were in arrears at the close of the fiscal year; some, however, will make payment very soon. The number of merchants, while constantly changing in personnel, is not materially increased from last year.

I have made specific demands for payment before a certain day on several merchants that have not yet responded. Indeed, I am of the opinion that it is not their intention to do so, and I feel that I have exhausted every means at my command to secure payment; and if payment is brought about in quite a number of cases it will be the result of more drastic measures than I am at present authorized to employ.

The receipts for merchandise tax during the year have been $2,437.47.

CATTLE TAX.

Under the old laws of the Cherokee Nation there is a tax of 50 cents per head on all cattle introduced into the nation, and an annual grazing tax of 25 cents per head on such introduced cattle.

All cattle laws enacted by the Cherokee Nation have always been more or less disregarded by the cattlemen, and at the time of the appointment of the revenue inspector for the Cherokee Nation these laws were practically a dead letter.

At the November session of the Cherokee council in 1900 the law in relation to the introduction of cattle was practically reenacted, and was approved by the President December 27, 1900, and is as follows, being Cherokee senate bill No. 5:

AN ACT To prevent the introduction of cattle into the Cherokee Nation.

Whereas the introduction of cattle into the Cherokee Nation from the various States and Territories of the United States brings a disease known as Texas fever, for the prevention and cure of which no adequate remedy has been found; and

Whereas the introduction of cattle into the Cherokee Nation and the promiscuous grazing of same upon the pub ic domain during certain seasons has practically destroyed the home industry of native cattle and placed the farmers at the mercy of the larger cattle dealers: Therefore,

Be it enacted by the national council, That it shall be unlawful for any person to introduce cattle of any kind whatever into the Cherokee Nation from any State or Territory of the United States or any other Indian Territory for the purpose of holding or grazing them upon the public domain of the Cherokee Nation, whether the same be inclosed or otherwise: *Provided,* that citizens of the Cherokee Nation may introduce cattle between the 1st day of December and the 28th day of February of the following year by paying 50 cents per head for each and every head of cattle so introduced.

Be it further enacted, That it shall be the duty of the principal chief of the Cherokee Nation to report all violations of the above section to the Indian agent at Muscogee, Ind. T., or other proper authority of the United States, with the request that said violators of said section may be proceeded against as provided in section 2117 of the Revised Statutes of the United States, and that they and the cattle so introduced in violation of said section be removed from without the limits of the Cherokee Nation.

Be it further enacted, That all moneys collected under the provisions of this act, after paying the necessary expenses, shall be placed by the Indian agent to the credit of the school fund of the Cherokee Nation.

Approved by principal chief November 28, 1900.

Approved by President December 27, 1900.

Compared with former years the business of introducing cattle into the Cherokee Nation is on the wane and the raising of improved grades of cattle in the nation on the increase.

While there are many thousands of introduced cattle in the nation, they are now held in comparatively small lots, the greater part of which are kept within inclosures, and I am of the opinion that a less number are at present ranging on the public domain than in any previous year.

The collection of the prescribed taxes has been found to be extremely difficult, and it is impossible, in some instances, to ascertain when, where, and by whom certain cattle were introduced, for, as a rule, persons who have witnessed the unloading of cattle at railroad stations and their introduction overland are possessed of very imperfect memories, an infirmity which affects witnesses in cattle matters more than any other class with which I have come in contact.

Citizens will often complain of the damage done to crops by cattle owned by non-residents and noncitizens, and at the same time dare not or will not furnish proof as to who actually introduced the cattle into the nation.

One scheme of evading the introduction tax is for cattlemen residing in Texas, Arkansas, and elsewhere to ship them to the nation, unload them at the cattle yards of the railroad, and there sell them to other parties, when controversy immediately arises as to who introduced the cattle—the party who put them into the cattle yards or the one who took them out.

The introduction of cattle out of season, infected as they frequently are with Texas fever, is a constant menace to reputable farmers who are building up herds of high grade native cattle.

Up to February 28, the quarantine limit, I have succeeded in securing the payment of the introduction tax on several hundred head of cattle. Since that time the matter of furnishing proof concerning the introduction of cattle has been in the hands of the principal chief, as provided in the act above quoted, so far as I have been advised.

The receipts during the year from this source have been $1,127.25.

TIMBER.

In my last annual report to you I stated that it was my belief that the matter of preventing the destruction of timber in the Cherokee Nation was well in had. I now confirm that statement.

The policy of the Department on this subject seems to be well understood, and the prosecutions in the courts of the United States commissioners in the past have had a very wholesome influence.

While I have been called upon to investigate numerous complaints, it is gratifying for me to be able to report that they were in most cases found to be of a comparatively trivial nature when the facts were obtained.

The importance of following up the matter of timber regulations I regard as of considerable importance to the nation, as good timber is none too abundant, resulting from its wholesale slaughter years ago.

HAY ROYALTY.

There is a royalty of 20 cents per ton due on all hay shipped from the Cherokee Nation.

As reported last year, this still continues to be one of the most hotly contested sources of revenue with which I have had to contend, although I am pleased to report to you that the arrangements for its collection have not hitherto been so complete.

The legality of enforcing this royalty is still questioned, and two cases are now in the courts, one growing out of a seizure of a carload of hay at Bluejacket, Ind. T., followed by a writ of replevin in favor of S. W. Kelley.

This case was heard before United States Commissioner Don Carlos, at Vinita, Ind. T., and argued at great length. The court found that hay could only be surrendered on the payment of royalty, from which appeal was taken to the United States court, and the matter is now pending.

The other case referred to is in the form of injunction proceedings against myself and others, restraining the officers of the Government from seizing or otherwise interfering with hay offered for shipment by Fred L. Kelley.

My understanding is that the court refused to grant an injunction in this case, and the case was appealed to the appellate court, and final hearing has not been had.

The hay industry in the Cherokee Nation has already grown to great proportions, and, with the decline of the cattle business, large areas are devoted to this crop that were formerly used for grazing; at least 25 immense storage barns have been erected at points along the several railroads during the present year, nearly all of which are owned by noncitizens of the Cherokee Nation.

Something over one year ago, nearly all the railroads operating in the Cherokee Nation issued an order to their agents not to receive hay for shipment unless the royalty was paid, and less hay has escaped payment of royalty during the last year than heretofore; at the same time it has been found necessary to be specially alert at railroad competing points, it being quite common for shippers to represent to one railroad company that they can ship by another railroad without payment of royalty. Another method resorted to by hay shippers is, whenever a new station agent is appointed, and changes have been numerous during the past year, to rush in large shipments before the new agent becomes acquainted with the regulations, when shippers will endeavor to avoid payment; several hundred dollars have been secured this year by following up such cases vigorously.

The receipts during the year from hay royalty have been $6,470.17.

COAL ROYALTY.

There is a royalty of 8 cents per ton on all coal mined in the Cherokee Nation.

Numerous permits to strip coal for local consumption and neighborhood use have been issued by your office, and most of the coal mined, although taken out in very small quantities, has been accounted for by these small operators. While the receipts from this class are not large, the wisdom of closely watching operations, especially for the purpose of ascertaining that parties have authority to strip coal from particular land, is apparent.

Coal is shipped in commercial quantities from two points only, namely, Dawson and Collinsville; the latter point being the most important.

During the last week of June I spent several days in Collinsville checking up the shipments from that point, with the view of informing myself as to the exact amount

of coal shipped.   For obvious reasons I am unable to furnish figures at this time, but
I am satisfied that it is the intention of shippers to comply with the regulations, and
the data at hand will be carefully gone over in the near future. ·
The receipts from coal royalty during the year have been $6,326.87.

FERRY LICENSE.

Section 739 of the laws of the Cherokee Nation is as follows:

Any person desirous of keeping a public ferry shall first be required to obtain a license for that purpose from the national treasurer, and for which he shall pay annually, in advance, the following tax,
to wit: For a ferry on the Arkansas and the Canadian rivers, the sum of $25 per annum; on the Illinois,
Grand, Verdigris, and "Neosho" rivers, the sum of $10 per annum.

I have made diligent inquiry into this subject from time to time, and have secured
the payment of several license fees.   Exact information concerning the owners of ferryboats is hard to obtain, for the reason that the boats frequently change ownership
and some of the ferries are operated in season of high water only.   My observation is
that no list of ferry operators would be correct as to names for many months in
succession.
The receipts during the year from this source have been $200.

ROYALTY ON GRAVEL.

You will observe in the appropriate place herein that the sum of $490.18 has been
collected as a royalty on gravel during the past year.
This item of revenue arises from 2 cents per cubic yard for gravel taken from the
banks of the Grand River near Fort Gibson, by the Missouri Pacific Railway Company, to be used as ballast for the tracks of that road.
While the amount from this source is not large up to the present time, I am informed
by the officers of the railroad that it is the policy of the company to use a considerable quantity in the future.
The gravel is easy of access and of excellent quality for the purpose, and the supply
is almost unlimited.
While the railroad is constantly improving its tracks, the Cherokee Nation is likely
to receive an income from this material in future.

SUMMARY OF RECEIPTS.

Merchandise tax	$2,437.47	
Cattle tax	1,127.25	
Royalty on hay	6,469.17	
Royalty on coal	6,326.87	
Ferries	200.00	
Gravel	490.18	
		$17,050.94

The following items have been received and placed to the credit of the Cherokee Nation:

School revenues	$2,321.19	
Town lots	10.02	
Telephone	10.50	
		$2,341.71
		19,392.65
Less exchange charged during the year		37.13
Total		19,355.52

EXPENSES FOR THE FISCAL YEAR.

First quarter, 1901	$1,269.15
Second quarter, 1901	925.09
Third quarter, 1901	870.74
Fourth quarter, 1901	873.36
Total	4,088.34

Again I have to report that I do not claim that all of the revenues due the Cherokee Nation have been collected, but I entertain the hope that, in the opinion of my
superiors, it is from no lack of diligence or zeal on my part.
Had I been permittted to secure payment from Cherokee merchants of the merchandise tax it would have increased considerably the total receipts.

The expenses of my office, which include the clerical assistance referred to, have been decreased during the year to the amount of $4,038.34, a reduction of $1,794.67, while the adverse circumstances which I have explained to some extent have resulted in a falling off of the receipts of $62.40 from the sum reported for the last fiscal year, by which you will observe an actual net increase over last year of $1,695.14. Doubtless the small deficit in receipts over last year will be offset by funds now in transit.

CONCLUSION.

In addition to the duties incident to the collection of the various revenues, I have, as you are aware, spent considerable time during the year in making special investigations and reports under your direction, including the subject of excessive holdings of lands which is now in the hands of the courts.

So far as I am advised, every communication received at my office has received a prompt reply, and the receipts of revenues at the office of the United States Indian agent have been checked up and compared daily with my own records.

While the duties have at times been somewhat arduous and delicate, I have endeavored to perform every service to the best of my ability, with the one purpose of complying strictly with the regulations and making the best possible showing for the Cherokee Nation, that needs and should receive every dollar that is due from revenues and taxes.

The foregoing summary, though briefly and imperfectly told, I trust will enable you to form a correct opinion as to conditions touched upon, in the Cherokee Nation, so far as I have been called upon to interest myself therein.

As indicated herein, the nature of my work has been such that I have been called upon to make frequent examinations of the accounts of the United States Indian agent regarding Cherokee affairs, where every courtesy has been extended to me by him and his efficient assistants.

With the hope that my labors have in some measure lightened the burdens of your very arduous position in the Indian Territory, and with thanks for courtesies received at your hands,

I have the honor to be, very respectfully,

FRANK C. CHURCHILL,
Revenue Inspector.

Hon. J. GEO. WRIGHT,
  U. S. Indian Inspector for the Indian Territory.

REPORT OF THE MINING TRUSTEES FOR THE CHOCTAW AND CHICKASAW NATIONS.

MCALESTER, IND. T., *August 17, 1901.*

SIR: In compliance with the request in your letter of August 2, 1901, we submit herewith a report covering the work of our office for the fiscal year ended June 30, 1901.

COAL AND ASPHALT.

The coal under our jurisdiction is entirely within the Choctaw Nation. It commences in the northeastern edge, adjoining Arkansas, and extends westerly a distance of 90 miles; the greatest width of this belt is 35 miles. There is also a field of coal extending from Haileyville southwesterly to and including what is known as the Coalgate and Lehigh fields. The average thickness of this coal is 4 feet.

The asphalt beds lie almost altogether within the Chickasaw Nation. It is impossible to give definite limits, but asphalt has been found at points covering the entire center of that nation.

OPERATORS.

The two following statements give the names of individuals and companies who are now mining coal and asphalt in the Choctaw and Chickasaw nations (1) under leases approved by the Department and (2) under tribal contracts:

Operators under approved leases.

Name of operator.	Mines at —.	Principal office.
Atoka Coal and Mining Co	Lehigh, Ind T	St. Louis, Mo.
Brunswick Asphalt Co	Dougherty, Ind. T	Do.
Busby, William	Archibald, Ind. T	Parsons, Kans.
Choctaw Coal and Mining Co	Sutter, Ind. T	Sutter, Ind. T.
Choctaw, Oklahoma and Gulf R. R. Co	Alderson, Hartshorne, and Gowen, Ind. T	Little Rock, Ark.
Degnan & McConnell	Wilburton, Ind. T	Wilburton, Ind. T.
Devlin-Wear Coal Co	Poteau, Ind. T	Topeka, Kans.
D. Edwards & Son	McAlester and Kiowa, Ind, T.	McAlester, Ind. T.
Folsom-Morris Coal Mining Co	Lehigh, Ind. T	Ardmore, Ind. T.
Milby and Dow Coal and Mining Co.[1]	Dow, Ind. T	Houston, Tex.
Mexican Gulf Coal and Transportation Co.[1]	Howe, Ind. T	Howe, Ind. T.
McAlester Coal Mining Co	Buck, Ind. T	New York City.
McMurray, John F	Archibald, Ind. T	S. McAlester, Ind. T.
McAlester and Galveston Coal Mining Co.	McAlester, Ind. T	McAlester, Ind. T.
McEvers, H. Newton	do	Do
Ola Coal and Mining Co.[1]	Ola, Ind. T	Ola. Ind. T.
Osage Coal and Mining Co	Krebs, Ind. T	St. Louis, Mo.
Ozark Coal and Rwy. Co	Panama, Ind. T	Panama, Ind. T.
St. Louis and Galveston Coal and Mining Co.	Lehigh, Ind. T	St. Louis, Mo.
Samples Coal and Mining Co	McAlester, Ind. T	McAlester, Ind. T.
Wilburton Coal and Mining Co.[1]	Wilburton, Ind. T	Wilburton, Ind. T.

[1] Operations of these four companies carried on under contract on approved leases of Choctaw, Oklahoma and Gulf Railroad Company.

Operators under tribal contracts.

Name of operator.	Mines at—	Principal office.
Adkins, Charles G.[1]	Cameron, Ind. T	Cameron, Ind. T.
Bache & Denman[1]	Red Oak, Ind. T	Alderson, Ind. T.
Caston Coal Co	Wister, Ind. T	McAlester, Ind. T.
Capital Coal and Mining Co	Savanna, Ind. T	Savanna, Ind. T.
Choctaw Mining and Mercantile Co	do	Do.
Gilsonite Roofing and Paving Co	Dougherty, Ind. T	St. Louis, Mo.
Hailey Coal and Mining Co	Haileyville, Ind. T	Haileyville, Ind. T.
Kansas and Texas Coal Co	Carbon, Ind. T	St. Louis, Mo.
Moulton, George D	Antlers, Ind. T	Coalgate, Ind. T.
McDougall, J. B	Coalgate, Ind. T	Do.
Perona, Mike	Savanna, Ind. T	Savanna, Ind. T.
Perry Brothers	Coalgate, Ind. T	Coalgate, Ind. T.
Rock Creek Natural Asphalt Co	Dougherty, Ind. T	Topeka, Kans.
Southwestern Coal and Improvement Co.	Coalgate, Ind. T	Parsons, Kans.
Turkey Creek Coal Co	Hughes, Ind. T	Hughes, Ind. T.

[1] Operations by these two parties in nature of prospecting.

NOTE.—Operations by George D. Moulton by permission of Department.

COAL ACREAGE LEASED.

The total number of acres of land covered by approved coal leases in the Choctaw Nation is 73,740, and the total approximate number of acres of coal covered by these leases is 69,585, as shown by the following statement:

Name of lessee.	Number of leases.	Number acres land leased.	Number acres coal leased (approximate).
Atoka Coal and Mining Co.	7	6,580	6,580
Busby, William	1	960	730
Choctaw Coal and Mining Co	3	2,880	2,880
Choctaw, Oklahoma and Gulf R. R. Co.	30	28,800	27,096
D. Edwards & Son	3	2,880	2,880
Degnan & McConnell	3	2,880	2,365
Devlin-Wear Coal Co.	1	960	720
Folsom-Morris Coal Mining Co.	1	960	960
Missouri, Kansas and Texas Coal Co	1	960	960
McMurray, John F	8	7,680	7,040
McAlester Coal Mining Co	2	1,240	1,240
McEvers, H. Newton	1	280	280
McAlester and Galveston Coal Mining Co.	1	480	309
Osage Coal and Mining Co.	7	6,680	6,680
Ozark Coal and Rwy. Co.	1	960	833
St. Louis-Galveston Coal and Mining Co	2	1,920	1,480
Samples Coal and Mining Co.	1	960	872
Sans Bois Coal Co	6	5,680	5,680
Total	79	73,740	69,585

ASPHALT ACREAGE LEASED.

The total number of acres of land covered by approved aphalt leases in the Chickasaw Nation is 4,320 and the total approximate number of acres of asphalt covered by these leases is 3,860, as shown by the following statement:

Name of lessee.	Number of leases.	Number acres land leased.	Number acres asphalt leased (approximate).
Brunswick Asphalt Co	1	960	500
Caddo Asphalt Mining Co	1	960	960
Downard Asphalt Co	1	360	360
Elk Asphalt Co	1	960	960
M. & A. Schneider.	1	960	960
Tar Spring Asphalt Co	1	120	120
Total	6	4,320	3,860

COAL CONTROLLED BY NATIONAL CONTRACTS.

In the Choctaw Nation there are approximately 16,440 acres of coal controlled by parties under national contracts, and the following statement shows the acreage of each operator:

Name of operator.	Mines at—	Number acres (approximate).
Caston Coal Co	Wister, Ind. T.	960
Capital Coal and Mining Co	Savana, Ind. T.	500
Choctaw Mining and Mercantile Co.	...do	800
Hailey Coal and Mining Co.	Haileyville, Ind. T.	800
Kansas and Texas Coal Co.	Carbon, Ind. T.	1,660
McDougall, J. B	Coalgate, Ind. T.	800
Perona, Mike	Savana, Ind. T.	160
Perry Brothers.	Coalgate, Ind. T.	800
Southwestern Coal and Improvement Co.	...do	9,000
Turkey Creek Coal Co	Hughes, Ind. T.	960
Total		16,440

NOTE.—National contracts do not give metes and bounds of tracts covered thereby; hence, the above acreage is approximate.

The following statement shows the different railroads running through the coal lds of the Choctaw Nation and the number of approved leases reached by each lroad, as well as the number of individuals and companies operating under national ntracts:

ssouri, Kansas and Texas Railroad:
  (a) Total number of approved leases... 24
  (b) Operators under national contracts 7
                                               — 31

)ctaw, Oklahoma and Gulf Railroad:
  (a) Total number of approved leases... 38
  (b) Operators under national contracts 3
                                               — 41

nsas City Southern Railroad:
  (a) Total number of approved leases... 4
  (b) Operators under national contracts 0
                                               — 4

Louis and San Francisco Railroad:
  (a) Total number of approved leases... 1
  (b) Operators under national contracts 0
                                               — 1

[n the foregoing statement, we have accredited each lease to that railroad to which is connected by switch, or through which the railroad runs.
A large percentage of the leases on the Choctaw, Oklahoma and Gulf Railroad are developed.
There are several leases near one or more railroads; but they are undeveloped, ! not reached by a railroad, and are not, therefore, included in the foregoing state-!nt.
There are several leases approved for asphalt, and two companies operating asphalt der charters, near the Gulf, Colorado and Santa Fe Railroad, in the Chickasaw .tion; but the leases are undeveloped, and operations under charters are limited.) reference is made, therefore, to asphalt in the foregoing statement.

ROYALTY ON COAL.

The Atoka agreement ratified national contracts under which parties were mining il in the Choctaw Nation on April 23, 1897, and from July 1, 1898, to January 1, !9, coal mining operations were conducted under national contracts. The royalty id during this period was the royalty fixed in the national contracts, or one-half it a bushel of 85 pounds.
The Atoka agreement provides that the royalty on coal mined in the Choctaw and iickasaw nations shall be 15 cents per ton of 2,000 pounds on all coal mined. The reement also empowers the Secretary of the Interior to reduce or advance the rate royalty on coal whenever it is deemed best for the interests of the two nations to so.
December 12, 1898, upon petition of the coal operators of the Choctaw Nation the :retary reduced the rate of royalty from 15 cents per ton on all coal mined to 10 its per ton on coal screened over meshes 1 inch square. This rate became effective inary 1, 1899, and was the rate until March 1, 1900. In February, 1900, the coal !rators again petitioned the Secretary to reduce the rate of royalty to 6$\frac{3}{4}$ cents per i on run-of-mine coal. After consideration of the matter the Secretary fixed the e of royalty at 8 cents per ton on all coal mined, including slack. This rate :ame effective March 1, 1900, and is the rate now in effect.
Each one of the foregoing petitions was submitted to us for our recommendations, i each time we protested against a reduction of the existing rate of royalty, and)mitted written arguments in support of our views. We are satisfied, however, th the present rate, and hope it will not be disturbed.

ROYALTY ON ASPHALT.

The rate of royalty on asphalt was definitely fixed by the Department on August 1899, and is 60 cents per ton on refined, and 10 cents per ton on crude, asphalt; l this rate is now in effect.

EXAMINATION OF BOOKS OF COAL AND ASPHALT OPERATORS.

The regulations of the Department require that the mining trustees shall—

ke an examination from time to time, as often as it shall be deemed expedient, and at least once every month, into the operations of all persons, corporations, or companies operating mines within 'said nations, with a view of ascertaining the quantity of mineral produced by each, the amount of alty, if any, due and unpaid by each, and all other information necessary for the protection of the erests of the Choctaw and Chickasaw nations in the premises; and for this purpose all persons, porations, or companies operating mines within the Choctaw and Chickasaw nations shall give d trustees access to any and all of their books and records necessary or required by them to be imined. * * *

With a view of determining the total amount of coal or asphalt mined and the total amount of royalty due the nations by coal or asphalt operators we go either to the operators' mines or to their principal offices at least once each month and examine their mining books and records. The result of our monthly examinations is embodied in a quarterly report to the Secretary of the Interior, through Inspector Wright's office, which report shows the actual amount of coal or asphalt mined and the actual amount of royalty due the nations by each operator for each one of the three months covered by our report. The amounts of royalty reported by us are compared in the office of the United States Indian agent at Muscogee with the amounts of royalty paid by each operator. By this system of checking the Choctaw and Chickasaw nations receive the proper royalty on the output of each coal and asphalt mine in the two nations.

The following statements on pages 13, 14, and 15 show the total amounts of coal and asphalt mined and the total amounts of royalty paid by each coal and asphalt operator in the Choctaw and Chickasaw nations during the fiscal year ended June 30, 1901:

Statement showing total amount of coal mined and royalty paid by each operator in Choctaw Nation, Ind. T., for fiscal year ended June 30, 1901, at 8 cents a ton.

Name of operator.	Coal mined (tons).	Royalty paid.
Atoka Coal and Mining Co	309,195	$24,785.59
Adkins, Charles G	1,277.7	102.21
Archibald Coal and Mining Co	200	16.01
Bache & Denman	1,729.7	138.37
Busby, William	9,024	721.92
Capital Coal and Mining Co	11,789	989.12
Caston Coal Co	3,351.2	268.09
Choctaw Coal and Mining Co	25,583.25	2,046.66
Choctaw Mining and Mercantile Co	17,920	1,433.60
Choctaw, Oklahoma and Gulf R. R. Co	469,671	37,573.68
Crescent Coal Co	9,024.4	721.95
Degnan & McConnell	120,806	9,664.48
Devlin-Wear Coal Co	68,914.3	5,513.14
Edwards & Son, D	26,753.5	2,140.28
Folsom-Morris Coal Mining Co	265	21.30
Hailey Coal and Mining Co	54,843	4,387.45
Harley, Pat	1,506	120.48
Kansas and Texas Coal Co	121,853.8	9,748.29
Mexican Gulf Coal and Transportation Co	96,057.7	7,684.61
Milby & Dow Coal and Mining Co	77,398.7	6,191.49
McAlester Coal Mining Co	75,754	6,060.33
McAlester Coal and Mineral Co	53,011.45	4,240.90
McAlester and Galveston Coal Mining Co	1,812	144.96
McEvers, H. Newton	2,166.5	173.34
McDougall, J. B	56,408	4,512.67
McMurray, John F	1,088.5	87.06
Ola Coal and Mining Co	64,956.12	5,196.53
Osage Coal and Mining Co	262,406.9	20,992.71
Ozark Coal and Railway Co	30,490.25	2,439.22
Perona, Mike	3,308.25	264.66
Perry Brothers	44,986.4	3,598.90
Samples Coal and Mining Co	38,746	3,099.60
Southwestern Coal and Impr. Co	185,064.9	14,805.15
St, Louis-Galveston Coal and Mining Co	8,550.5	684.04
Turkey Creek Coal Co	9,503	760.34
Wilburton Coal and Mining Co	132,793.2	10,623.46
Total	2,398,156.02	191,852.50

Statement showing total amount of asphalt mined and royalty paid by each operator in the Choctaw and Chickasaw nations for the fiscal year ended June 30, 1901, at 10 cents a ton.

Name of operator	Asphalt mined.	Royalty paid.
	Tons.	
Brunswick Asphalt Co	96	$9.60
Caddo Asphalt Mining Co	0	0
Downard Asphalt Co	0	0
Elk Asphalt Co	0	0
Gilsonite Roofing and Paving Co	1,232	123.20
Moulton, George D	1,064	106.40
Rock Creek Natural Asphalt Co	1,100.97	110.10
Schneider, M. & A	0	0
Tar Spring Asphalt Co	0	0
Total	3,492.97	349.30

Statement showing total amount of asphalt mined and royalty paid, etc.—Continued.

RECAPITULATION.

Mineral.	Amounts mined.	Royalty paid.
	Tons.	
Coal	2,398,156.02	$191,852.50
Asphalt	3,492.97	349.30
Total	2,401,648.99	192,201.80

INFORMAL COAL-MINING PERMITS.

Under a ruling of the Department, dated January 18, 1900, informal coal-mining permits are granted to parties to mine coal in the two nations. Under these permits parties may mine coal for home use and for local trade, but they are required to pay each month a royalty of 8 cents a ton on coal mined by them, in accordance with the regulations of the Department.

These permits are not granted until the mining trustees have personally examined the coal and are satisfied that it does not exist in quantities sufficient to warrant parties in incurring the expense of leasing and operating it; and, after these permits have been granted, if the vein of coal develops into a workable vein, the permits are revoked.

The following permits have been issued upon our recommendation:

Name.	Address.	Remarks.
Ford, Mrs. M. A	Ardmore, Ind. T	
Reeder, Joel G	Folsom, Ind. T	
Watkins, Leslie	Spiro, Ind. T	Revoked account of coal developing into workable vein.

The following statements show the applications and the leases that have passed through our office and have been acted on by the Department:

Applications reported by mining trustees.

Name of applicant.	Mineral.	Claims applied for.	Claims recommended.
Adkins, Charles G	Coal	1	1
Atoka Coal and Mining Co	do	8	8
Bache & Denman	do	2	2
Bond, R. I	do	1	1
Brunswick Asphalt Co	Asphalt	1	1
Capital Coal and Mining Co	Coal	2	2
Chambers, Thomas H	do	1	1
Chickasaw Asphalt Co	Asphalt	[1]1	
Essen Coal Co	Coal	1	1
Folsom-Morris Coal Mining Co	do	2	2
Kansas and Texas Coal Co	do	10	10
Kilpatrick, R. H	do	2	2
Mahan, J. P	do	1	1
Missouri, Kansas and Texas Coal Co	do	2	2
Morton, John S	do	1	1
Morton Coal Co	do	1	1
McAlester Coal Co	do	1	1
McDougall, J. B	do	1	1
McEvers, H. Newton	do	1	1
McAlester and Galveston Coal Mining Co	do	1	1
Osage Coal and Mining Co	do	7	7
Perry Brothers	do	2	1
Reeder, Joel G	do	[2]1	
Rock Creek Natural Asphalt Co	Asphalt	1	1
Rodgers, A. K	Coal	1	1
Sans Bois Coal Co	do	4	4
Tar Spring Asphalt Co	Asphalt	1	1
Turkey Creek Coal Co	Coal	2	1
Washington & Cruce	Asphalt	1	1
Williams, Boone	do	1	1
Total		62	58

[1] Returned to be amended.   [2] Mining permit recommended.

Applications approved by Department and forwarded to mining trustees for execution of leases.

Name of applicant.	Mineral.	Applications approved.
Atoka Coal and Mining Co.[1]	Coal	7
Devlin-Wear Coal Co	....do	1
Downard Asphalt Co	Asphalt	1
Folsom-Morris Coal Mining Co	Coal	1
Hopkins, Stuart N	....do	1
Kansas and Texas Coal Co.[1]	....do	4
Missouri, Kansas and Texas Coal Co.	....do	1
McEvers, H. Newton	....do	1
McAlester and Galveston Coal Mining Co.	....do	1
Osage Coal and Mining Co.[1]	....do	7
Rodgers, A. K	....do	1
Sans Bois Coal Co.[2]	....do	4
Schneider, M. & A	Asphalt	1
Tar Spring Asphalt Co	....do	1
. Total		32

[1] Heretofore operated under national contracts.
[2] New leases approved in exchange for four others canceled.

Applications disapproved by Department.

Name of applicant.	Mineral.	Applications disapproved.	Remarks.
Atoka Coal and Mining Co.	Coal	1	
Bond, R. I	....do	1	
Brewer Mining Co.	....do	1	
Brown, Charles W	Asphalt	1	
Folsom-Morris Coal Mining Co.	Coal	1	
Kansas and Texas Coal Co	....do	3	
Mahan, J. P	....do	1	
Missouri, Kansas and Texas Coal Co.	....do	1	
Milby and Dow Coal and Mining Co.	....do	5	Tracts applied for covered by national contract of Southwestern Coal and Improvement Co.
Reeder, Joel G	....do	1	Mining permit granted.
Schneider, M. & A	Asphalt	1	
Southwestern Coal and Improvement Co.	Coal	10	To continue operations under national contract.
Turkey Creek Coal Co.	....do	2	
Washington & Cruce	Asphalt	1	
Total		30	

Leases executed by mining trustees and forwarded to Department.

Name of lessee.	Mineral.	Number leases.	To Department.
Atoka Coal and Mining Co.[1]	Coal	7	Apr. 8, 1901
Busby, William	....do	1	Aug. 14, 1901
Central Coal and Coke Co.	....do	1	July 27, 1900
Devlin-Wear Coal Co	....do	1	Mar. 18, 1901
Downard Asphalt Co	Asphalt	1	Oct. 1, 1900
Folsom-Morris Coal Mining Co.	Coal	1	Nov. 5, 1900
Hopkins, Stuart N	....do	1	Sept. 25, 1900
Missouri, Kansas and Texas Coal Co	....do	1	Jan. 27, 1901
McAlester and Galveston Coal Mining Co	....do	1	Sept. 27, 1900
McEvers, H. Newton	....do	1	Do.
Osage Coal and Mining Co.[1]	....do	7	Apr. 8, 1901
Sans Bois Coal Co.[2]	....do	4	June 21, 1901
Schneider, M. & A	Asphalt	1	Nov. 8, 1900
Tar Spring Asphalt Co	....do	1	Apr. 8, 1901
Total		29	

[1] Heretofore operated under national contracts.
[2] New leases approved in exchange for four others canceled.

Leases approved by Department.

Name of lessee.	Mineral.	Number leases.	Date approved.
Atoka Coal and Mining Co[1]	Coal	7	May 7, 1901
Busby, William	...do	1	Sept. 6, 1900
Central Coal and Coke Co	...do	1	Aug. 27, 1900
Devlin-Wear Coal Co	...do	1	June 17, 1901
Degnan & McConnell[1]	...do	3	Nov. 16, 1900
Downard Asphalt Co	Asphalt	1	Oct. 18, 1900
Folsom-Morris Coal Mining Co	Coal	1	Nov. 22, 1900
Missouri, Kansas and Texas Coal Co	...do	1	Feb. 12, 1901
McAlester and Galveston Coal Mining Co	...do	1	Oct. 18, 1900
McEvers, H. Newton	...do	1	Do.
Osage Coal and Mining Co[1]	...do	7	May 7, 1901
Ozark Coal and Railway Co	...do	1	Dec. 8, 1900
Samples Coal and Mining Co	...do	1	Oct. 4, 1900
St. Louis-Galveston Coal and Mining Co[1]	...do	2	Jan. 14, 1901
Schneider, M. & A	Asphalt	1	Nov. 23, 1900
Tar Spring Asphalt Co	...do	1	May 13, 1901
Total		31	

[1] Heretofore operated under national contracts.

Leases disapproved by Department.

Name of lessee.	Mineral.	Leases.	Date disapproved.	Remarks.
Crescent Coal Co	Coal	3	Feb. 26, 1901	To continue operations under national contract.

NOTE.—This company has since failed. All its improvements have been sold, and the mine is now closed.

RECAPITULATION OF FOREGOING STATEMENTS.

Applications reported by mining trustees:
(a) For coal 56
(b) For asphalt 6
— 62

Applications recommended by mining trustees:
(a) For coal 53
(b) For asphalt 5
— 58

Applications approved by Department:
(a) For coal 29
(b) For asphalt 3
— 32

Applications disapproved by Department:
(a) For coal 27
(b) For asphalt 3
— 30

Leases executed by mining trustees and forwarded to the Department:
(a) For coal 26
(b) For asphalt 3
— 29

Leases approved by Department:
(a) For coal 28
(b) For asphalt 3
— 31

Leases disapproved by department:
(a) For coal 3
(b) For asphalt 0
— 3

The following leases were approved by the Department previous to July 1, 1900:

Name of lessee.	Mineral.	Leases.	Date approved.
Brunswick Asphalt Co	Asphalt	1	Mar. 20, 1900
Caddo Asphalt Mining Co	...do	1	Apr. 21, 1900
Choctaw Coal and Mining Co	Coal	3	May 4, 1900
Choctaw, Oklahoma and Gulf R. R. Co	...do	30	Mar. 1, 1899
Edwards & Son, D	...do	3	Aug. 22, 1899
Elk Asphalt Co	Asphalt	1	May 13, 1900
McAlester Coal Mining Co	Coal	2	Feb. 19, 1900
McKenna, Amos & Amos	...do	1	Oct. 24, 1899
McMurray, John F	...do	8	Apr. 23, 1899
Sans Bois Coal Co	...do	6	June 25, 1900
Total		56	

RECAPITULATION.

Leases approved previous to July 1, 1900...   56
Leases approved during fiscal year ended June 30, 1901...............................   31

    Total leases approved June 30, 1901   87
Leases canceled during above periods...   2

    Total leases in effect June 30, 1901   85

Classified as to mineral:
    Coal leases...   79
    Asphalt leases..   6

    Total..   85

LESSEES SUBLEASING APPROVED LEASES.

The Choctaw, Oklahoma and Gulf Railroad Company has subleased 11 of its 30 approved coal leases to other companies, but the title to the 11 leases still vests in the Choctaw, Oklahoma and Gulf Railroad Company, and that company is held responsible for the payment of all royalties accruing on coal mined by the sublessee companies.

Efforts were made to have the Department approve the assignments to the sublessee companies of the said 11 leases, but the assignments were disapproved by the Department on March 2 and 5, 1901. The assignments were as follows:

Name of assignee.	Choctaw lease assigned (No.).
Milby & Dow Coal and Mining Co.................	6 and 7
Wilburton Coal and Mining Co..	20 and 21
Ola Coal and Mining Co...	22 and 23
Mexican Gulf Coal and Transportation Co.......................................	24, 25, 26, 27, and 28

TIMBER FOR MINES.

Under instructions of Inspector Wright, we advised all mine operators on February 5, 1901, that they might procure the necessary timbers for their mines from citizens of any of the Five Civilized Tribes, provided the citizens procured the timbers from land legally in their possession for allotment purposes, and which they were clearing in good faith without entering into contract or paying royalty therefor, as required by the regulations of the Department.

March 9, 1901, under instructions of Inspector Wright, the foregoing instructions were modified, and all mine operators were advised as follows:

* * * You will be allowed to procure only props and ties from citizens who are actually clearing land selected by them for allotments. * * *
You will not be allowed to cut any pine or merchantable timber out of which to make your props and ties. (Merchantable timber is timber large enough to be sawed into lumber.)

Afterwards, under further instructions of Inspector Wright, each coal and asphalt operator in the Choctaw and Chickasaw Nation was advised that the regulations theretofore issued by the Department under the act of June 6, 1900, had been suspended, and that applications would no longer be received under the same except for props and caps for mines and for ties and pilings for railroads. They were further advised:

The cutting of large merchantable timber for general commercial and industrial purposes, including the building of houses for mine operators and other purposes requiring such large timber, will not hereafter be permitted in Indian Territory. Mine operators must make arrangements to procure such timber as they require outside of the Territory, except small timbers for props and caps, which can be procured from Indian citizens who are clearing their lands in good faith; and when such small timbers as they require for props and caps can not be procured from Indians they will have to enter into contract for same.

APPROVED COAL LEASES CANCELED BY DEPARTMENT.

The following approved coal leases have been canceled by the Department:

Name of lessee.	Leases.	Date approved.	Date canceled.
Central Coal and Coke Co.....................................	1	Aug. 27, 1900	June 14, 1901
McKenna, Amos & Amos......................................	1	Oct. 24, 1899	Aug. 28, 1900
Total.......................................	2		

After approval by the Department of the foregoing leases, the lessees thoroughly prospected the tracts, but found it unprofitable to operate mines thereon on account of the poor quality of the coal, and at the special request of the lessees the leases were canceled.

APPROVED LEASES NOT OPERATED.

In our special report of June 3, 1901, and in our two last quarterly reports, we gave the names of parties who have approved leases but have not begun operations thereon. We submit below a statement showing such lessees:

Name of lessee.	Mineral.	Leases held.	Leases not operated.	Date approved.
Caddo Asphalt Mining Co	Asphalt	1	1	Apr. 21, 1900
Choctaw Coal and Mining Co	Coal	·3	1	May 13, 1900
Choctaw, Oklahoma and Gulf R. R. Co	....do	30	14	Mar. 1, 1899
Downard Asphalt Co	Asphalt	1	1	Oct. 18, 1900
Elk Asphalt Co	....do	1	1	May 13, 1900
Missouri, Kansas and Texas Coal Co	Coal	1	1	Feb. 12, 1901
McMurray, John F.	....do	8	7	Apr. 23, 1899
Sans Bois Coal Co	....do	6	6	June 25, 1900
Schneider, M. & A	Asphalt	1	1	Nov. 23, 1900
Tar Spring Asphalt Co	....do	1	1	May 13, 1901
Total		53	34	

COMPLAINTS.

During the year we have investigated and made written reports on various complaints. Most of these complaints were by individuals against coal operators, although some were by coal operators against individuals.

In most instances the complaints by individuals against coal operators were for damages to the surface of land caused by sinking slopes or shafts, by the construction of railroad switches, and by other improvements necessary in the operation of coal mines. Our practice in investigating these complaints was to get all parties together at some convenient point, generally at the point where the damages were alleged to have been done, and after hearing both sides to suggest as a remedy the payment by the coal operator to the complainant of such amount as we thought equitable. The results of our investigation were always reported to Inspector Wright. We have been able thus far to settle all complaints referred to us.

The complaints by coal operators have generally been against strikers—men who will not mine themselves and are unwilling for anyone else to mine. These strikers live in the different mining camps and usually have been previously employed by the coal operators. Their methods are insidious and it is difficult at times to catch up with them. Their general practice is to persuade miners to stop work, and while their persuasions are not always accompanied by threats, still threats are often made, and their methods of persuasion are sometimes so forceful that they amount to threats. On account of the presence of these striking miners in the different mining camps, many coal operators can not employ as many men as they need. As a result their output is curtailed and the nations sustain heavy losses in royalty.

Our investigations of the cases referred to us have shown that the complaints of the operators were well founded, and we have recommended to the Department that striking miners be removed from the lands leased to the operators by the Department.

Complaints can best be investigated on the ground where the damages were done and when all parties interested can be gotten together; yet it has taken a great deal of our time to dispose of them on account of the distance to the mining camps and the difficulty in getting the parties together.

CONTESTS.

Previous to the adoption of the Atoka agreement companies and individuals had operated coal mines in the Choctaw Nation under national contracts. Under the agreement all contracts under which operations were being carried on in good faith on April 23, 1897, were confirmed and the rights of the parties holding them protected. Unfortunately the national contracts did not describe by metes and bounds the lands they covered. In the Chickasaw Nation the legislature had given charters to different parties, and while under the charters metes and bounds were given, yet it was found that these grants were excessively large, amounting in each instance to thousands of acres.

Under national contracts in the Choctaw Nation parties had claimed 1 mile in every direction from each coal discovery, but as there was no limit to the number of discoveries a citizen might have or a company might lease, it was but natural that when the Department issued rules and regulations requiring coal leases to be described by legal subdivisions there should arise many contests as to the prior rights to lease certain tracts. In some of these contests large amounts were involved and much time and labor were spent in hearing and disposing of such contests.

All these contests have been settled, however, and lines of agreement have been established, so that no further trouble is expected from this source. In all contests we have made investigations and written reports with our recommendations to Inspector Wright.

Respectfully,

NAPOLEON B. AINSWORTH,
Trustee, Choctaw Nation.
CHARLES D. CARTER,
Trustee, Chickasaw Nation.

Mr. J. GEO. WRIGHT,
United States Indian Inspector, Muscogee, Ind. T.

SUPERVISING ENGINEER, INDIAN TERRITORY TOWNSITES,
Muskogee, Ind. T., August 19, 1901.

SIR: I have the honor to transmit herewith the annual report of the supervising engineer for the fiscal year ending June 30, 1901.

Very respectfully,

H. V. HINCKLEY, *Supervising Engineer.*

The U. S. INDIAN INSPECTOR FOR THE INDIAN TERRITORY,
Muskogee, Ind. T.

ANNUAL REPORT OF SUPERVISING ENGINEER.

The supervising engineer of town-site surveys in the Indian Territory has the honor of submitting the following report of work done under his supervision during the year ending June 30, 1901:

PRELIMINARIES.

He assumed the duties of the office June 4, 1900. During the months of June and July he made recommendations as to how the work should be done, prepared "copy" for instructions to surveyors, blank forms for town-boundary reports, and drawing for stencils for marking town-boundary posts; checked and corrected the plats of Calvin and Guertie, which had been sent in by the Choctaw town-site commission, etc.

SURVEYORS REPORT FOR DUTY.

The following is a list of surveyors and the dates when they reported for duty: John G. Joyce, jr., July 13, 1900; John F. Fisher, July 14, 1900; Elmer E. Colby, July 21, 1900; Henry M. Tinker, Aug. 14, 1900; Mortimer Z. Jones, Aug. 15, 1900; Joseph T. Payne, Sept. 1, 1900; Frank Hackelman, Sept. 3, 1900; Carson E. Phillips, Nov. 28, 1900; Mark Kirkpatrick, Dec. 14, 1900; Sidney T. Emerson, Dec. 28, 1900; Frank H. Boyd, Mar. 7, 1901; Charles L. Wood, Mar. 22, 1901.

During July and August Surveyors Colby and Fisher made partial tracings of the land office township plats on file in office of the Commission to the Five Civilized Tribes (the Department being unable to furnish copies of these plats) for use of the surveyors in establishing town boundaries and did other miscellaneous preliminary work.

Surveyor Joyce was detailed to resurvey and replat the town of Wagoner, Creek Nation, which had been surveyed and platted by the Wagoner town-site commission, and later to check and plat the town of South McAlester, which was being surveyed by the Choctaw town-site commission. His services were rendered to the town-site commissions during the last five months of 1900. On the 2d day of January, 1901, he was detailed to check the plat of the town of Ardmore, Chickasaw Nation, and the field work and plat proving to be extremely defective he was instructed to resurvey and replat the town.

BOUNDARY WORK COMMENCED.

On the 6th of August, 1900, the supervising engineer, with Surveyors Colby and Fisher, proceeded to the town of Chickasha, in the Chickasaw Nation, and commenced the establishment of exterior limits of the towns along the Chicago, Rock Island and Pacific Railway. The following tables, numbered 1 to 9, inclusive, show the details of acreages, cost of boundary work, dates of completion, etc.:

(All west of "first guide meridian west.")

[Towns reported to have 200 or more people.   Act May 31, 1900; Public—131.]

Town.[1]	Completed or population counted.	Boundary. Acres.	Cost. Dollars.	Cost. Per acre.	Surveyor.	Population.	Acres per capita.	Estimate for surveying and platting.	Acres (included in column 3) for cemetery.[2]	Date of approval of exterior limits. Remarks.
1	2	3	4	5	6	7	8	9	10	11
Chickasha	Sept. 1, 1900	1,248.70	190.83	$0.15	Colby	3,000	0.42	$125.00	30.2	Nov. 18, 1900.
Comanche	Sept. 5, 1900	436.98	167.91	.39	Tinker	600	.73	500.00	5	Oct. 26, 1900.
Duncan	Aug. 25, 1900	1,011.70	187.74	.19	...do	1,500	.67	800.00	5	Do.
Duncan, amended	Jan. 14, 1901	1,010.22								Feb. 12, 1901.
Loco	Aug. 20, 1900				Fisher	127				Population short. Not bounded.
Marlow	Aug. 28, 1900	960.00	90.49	.10	Colby	1,214	.80	350.00	12.27	Oct. 26, 1900.
Minco	Aug. 30, 1900	287.00	100.23	.35	Fisher	622	.46	200.00	5	Do.
Ninnekah	Aug. 13, 1900				...do	140				Population short. Not bounded.
Rush Springs	Aug. 22, 1900	380.00	116.86	.30	...do	490	.78	300.00	9.97	Oct. 26, 1900.
Ryan	Aug. 29, 1900	435.89	166.82	.39	Jones	900	.48	350.00	5	Do.
Terral	Sept. 6, 1900	290.00	109.70	.39	...do	500	.56	200.00	5	Do.
Total		5,088.24	1,128.58	.22		8,826	.57	42,825.00	77.46	

[1] Boundary work completed.
[2] "Cemetery," under the law 5 acres only; balance in lots.
[3] Total of the towns that have been bounded.
[4] Estimates in column 9 were of dates given in column 2 and were for supervision and tracing only, the towns having expressed a desire to survey and plat themselves at their own expense.

TABLE No. 2.—*Status of boundary work in Chickasaw Nation, June 30, 1901.*

SANTA FE DIVISION.[1]

(From "first guide meridian west" to a line 5 miles west of St. Louis, Oklahoma and Southern Railway.)

[Towns reported to have 200 or more people. Act May 31, 1900; public—131.]

Town.	Completed or population counted.	Boundary. Acres.	Boundary. Cost. Dollars.	Boundary. Cost. Per acre.	Surveyor.	Population.	Acres per capita.	Estimate for surveying and platting.	Acres (included in column 8) for cemetery.[3]	Date of approval of exterior limits. Remarks.
1	2	3	4	5	6	7	8	9	10	11
Ardmore	Sept. 18, 1900	190.06	(²)	(⁴)	Joyce	287	0.80	$600.00	(²)	Bounded and platted together.
Berwyn	July 1, 1901	191.25	135.50	$0.71	Payne				5	Dec. 19, 1900.
Berwyn amended					(Office)					Not yet submitted.
Center	Nov. 1, 1900	195.00	90.68	.46	Payne	510	.38	600.00	5	Dec. 20, 1900.
Cornish	Sept. 15, 1900	190.28	90.75	.48	Jones	210	.91	350.00	5	Feb. 15, 1901.
Davis	Oct. 24, 1900	531.85	187.34	.35	Fisher	2,000	.27	1,600.00	7.5	Dec. 17, 1900.
Dougherty	Sept. 28, 1900	243.13	96.85	.40	Hackelman	417	.57	750.00	5	Jan. 31, 1901.
Durwood	Sept. 25, 1900	140.00	91.00	.65	Tinker	250	.56	400.00	5	Dec. 15, 1900.
Earl	Sept. 14, 1900	125.00	60.00	.48	do	240	.50	350.00	5±	Dec. 13, 1900.
Erin Springs	Jan. 24, 1901	110.00	42.85	.39	Phillips	204	.39	300.00		Mar. 23, 1901.
Hart	Nov. 1, 1900				Payne	106				Population short. Not bounded.
Johnson	Dec. 18, 1900	90.00	60.00	.67	do	230	.39	500.00	5	Feb. 7, 1901.
Lebanon	Oct. 11, 1900	164.92	72.85	.44	Jones	218	.76	500.00	5	Dec. 19, 1900.
Leon	Sept. 28, 1900	165.00	93.10	.56	do	240	.69	400.00	5	Dec. 20, 1900.
Lonegrove	Sept. 15, 1900	195.00	59.75	.31	Payne	197				Population short.
Do	June 17, 1901	330.00	91.80	.28	Tinker	215	.91	600.00	5	Not yet approved. Not bounded.
Marietta	Oct. 5, 1900				Jones	1,160	.29	600.00	10	Jan. 12, 1901.
Maxwell	Oct. 22, 1900				Payne	172				Population short. Not bounded.
Mannsville	Sept. 19, 1900	175.00	96.25	.54	Tinker	215	.81	560.00	5	Dec. 15, 1900.
McGee	Oct. 25, 1900	122.50	158.75	$1.30	Payne	250	.49	850.00	5	Dec. 17, 1900.
Midland	Oct. 23, 1900				do	185				Population short. Not bounded.
McMillan	Oct. 6, 1900				Jones	135				Do.
Nebo	Oct. 1, 1900				Hackelman	86				Do.
Orr	Sept. 21, 1900	185.00	92.00	.50	Jones	215	.86	460.00	5	Dec. 20, 1900.
Paoli	Jan. 11, 1901	85.48	218.22	$2.56	Payne	225	.38	300.00	4.48	Apr. 11, 1901.
Purcell	Sept. 29, 1900	1,206.50	392.55	.33	Colby	3,000	.40	8,000.00	5	Not yet approved.
Pauls Valley	Sept. 21, 1900	946.83	211.12	.22	Fisher	2,000	.47	2,900.00	[4]12	Dec. 17, 1900.
Springer	Sept. 14, 1900				Payne	115				Population short. Not bounded.
Sulphur	Oct. 10, 1900	948.14	213.23	.22	Fisher	1,500	.68	2,900.00	7	Not yet approved.
Tussy	Sept. 8, 1900				Tinker	185				Population short. Not bounded.
Wayne	Sept. 21, 1900				Colby	168				Do.
Wynnewood	do	767.50	206.50	.27	Hackelman	2,998	.25	2,600.00	15	Dec. 15, 1900.
Total		7,108.86	2,761.39	.39		17,712	.40	20,560.00	180.98	

[1] Boundary work completed.
[2] Cemetery, under the law, 5 acres; balance in lots.
[3] See Table No. 12.
[4] Including old cemetery (lots) in town.

[a] Including 13 miles of line run in timber.
[b] Subdivision work, $1.96; boundary, 59 cents; total, $2.55.

TABLE No. 3.—*Status of boundary work in Chickasaw Nation June 30, 1901.*

FRISCO DIVISION.[1]

(All within 5 miles on either side of the St. Louis, Oklahoma, and Southern Railway.)

[Towns reported to have 200 or more people. Act May 31, 1900; Public—131.]

Town.	Completed or population counted.	Boundary. Acres.	Cost. Dollars.	Cost. Per acre.	Surveyor.	Population.	Acres per capita.	Estimate for surveying and platting.	Acres (included in column 3) for cemetery.	Date of approval of exterior limits. Remarks.
1	2	3	4	5	6	7	8	9	10	11
Ada	Jan. 14, 1901	2 569.90	207.73	$0.37	Payne	1,150	0.49	3 $1,800.00	4 10	Feb. 6, 1901.
Bryant 3		156.45			Dawes Commission.			3 $85.00		Oct. 26, 1900.
Colbert		129.77			Chickasaw Townsite Commission.	200	.65			Aug. 14, 1899. 5
Colbert cemetery		5.00			...do					
Cliff	Oct. 8, 1900				Tinker	196				Apr. 12, 1900. 6 Population short. Not bounded.
Do	June 26, 1901				...do	166		3 $85.00		Do.
Francis		160.00			Dawes Commission.					Oct. 26, 1900.
Gray		60.00			...do					Do.
Helen		156.09			...do			3 $85.00		Do.
Hickory	June 26, 1901	170.00	101.14	.59	Payne	250	.68	3 $85.00		Not yet submitted.
Flirt	June 29, 1901				...do	50		500.00		Population short. Not bounded.
Madill		160.00			Dawes Commission.			3 $85.00		Jan. 5, 1901.
Oakland	June 27, 1901	321.25	152.30	.47	Tinker	800	.40	1,200.00	5	Not yet submitted. Not bounded.
Oakman	June 29, 1901				Payne	90		3 $85.00		Population short.
Ravia	Feb. 23, 1901	3 326.39	110.20	.34	Phillips	500	.65			Apr. 20, 1900. Not bounded.
Regan	Oct. 1, 1900				Hackelman	119				Population short.
Roff	Dec. 31, 1900	3 595.00	188.90	.82	Payne	600	.99	3 $800.00	5	Feb. 6, 1901. Not bounded.
Russett	Sept. 26, 1900				Tinker	100		3 $85.00		Population short. Not bounded.
Scullin		120.00			Dawes Commission.					Oct. 26, 1900.
Tishomingo	June 4, 1901	175.00	146.94	.84	Fisher	850	.50	700.00	5	Not yet submitted.
Woodville		160.00			Dawes Commission.			3 $85.00		Oct. 26, 1900.
Total		8,273.86	907.21			4,660		5,180.00	20	
Total 7		2,147.64	907.21	.42		8,650	.59	4,565.00	20	

1 Boundary work completed.
2 Including areas previously selected by Dawes Commission.
3 L. F. Parker, contract approved November 17, 1900, $75 per town.
4 Cemetery under the law, 5 acres; balance in lots.
5 Now Mill Creek.
6 Not under the act above cited—Act June 28, 1898; Public—162.
7 Bounded under direction of the supervising engineer. Six towns only.

TABLE No. 4.—*Status of boundary work in Chickasaw Nation June 30, 1901.*

EASTERN DIVISION.[1]

(East of a line 5 miles east of the St. Louis, Oklahoma and Southern Railway.)

[Towns reported to have 200 or more people. Act May 31, 1900; Public—181.]

Town.	Completed or population counted.	Boundary.	Cost.		Surveyor.	Population.	Acres per capita.	Estimate for surveying and platting.	Acres (included in column 3) for cemetery.	Date of approval of exterior limits. Remarks.
		Acres.	Dollars.	Per acre.						
1	2	3	4	5	6	7	8	9	10	11
Connerville	Nov. 2, 1900	180	77.04	$0.43	Fisher	217	0.83	$500.00	5	June 1, 1901.
Cumberland	Oct. 12, 1900	174.80	80.40	.46	Tinker	340	.50	500.00	5	Dec. 19, 1900.
Cumberland (amended)	June 29, 1901	173.98			...do					Not yet approved.
Emet	Oct. 6, 1900	170	136.00	.80	...do	300	.57	500.00	0	Dec. 16, 1900.
Kemp	Oct. 23, 1900	120	91.85	.77	Hackelman	220	.52	350.00	5	Do.
Pontotoc	Oct. 6, 1900	195	102.90	.53	...do	264	.74	600.00	5	Do.
Silo	Oct. 17, 1900	195	80.00	.41	Tinker	400	.49	500.00	5	Do.
Stonewall	Oct. 19, 1900	117.50	94.70	.81	Hackelman	240	.49	450.00	5	Do.
Total		1,151.48	662.89	.58		1,991	.57	3,400.00	30	

[1] Boundary work completed.

WESTERN DIVISION.[1]

(West of "fourth guide meridian east.")

[Towns reported to have 200 or more people. Act May 31, 1900; Public—131.]

Town.	Completed or population counted.	Boundary. Acres.	Cost. Dollars.	Cost. Per acre.	Surveyor.	Population.	Acres per capita.	Estimate for surveying and platting.	Acres (included in column 9) for cemetery.	Date of approval of exterior limits. Remarks.
1	2	3	4	5	6	7	8	9	10	11
Alderson	(²)				Hackelman	196				Coal twn. Not bounded.
Allen	Oct. 24, 1900	120	62.67	$0.52	Payne	285	$0.51		5	Not bounded.
Do	June 29, 1901	182.50	112.95	.62	Hallman	800	.23	$400.00	5	Not yet app rod.
Antlers	Dec. 24, 1900	277.18			Choctaw Townsite Commission.	1,200	.23	500.00	5	Feb. 8, 1901. See Table No. 15.³
Calvin	Nov. 7, 1900	160	179.24	.45	Halliday	200	.90		0	See Table No. 15.
Caddo	Nov. 14, 1900	400	121.15	.61	Tucker	1,200	.33	1,000.00	5	Feb. 9, 1901.
Colian	May 14, 1901	197.50		.29	Mil m	554	.36	750.00	0	Jan. 8, 1901.
Coalgate	Nov. 19, 1900	412.50	119.38	.24	Fisher	2,700	.15	1,500.00	5	Not yet submitted. Feb. 4, 1901.
—		1,284	810.34		Tinker	3,500	.37	3,000.00	0	See Table No. 15.
—ie		160			Halliday	200	.80			See Table No. 15.
Hartshorne	(²)									Coal twn. Not bounded. Coal town.
Krebs	Dec. 7, 1900	380	142.20	.43	Tinker	1,500	.22	1,000.00	0	Not yet app rod. See Table No. 15.
Kiowa		365			Halliday	210	1.71		5	Not yet su i ted. See Table No. 15.
Lehigh	May 10, 1900	500	166.00	.33	Fisher	3,000	.17	1,700.00	5	Not yet su i ted. See Table No. 15.
McAlester		759.07			Kirkpatrick	646		1,800.00	5	See Table No. 15.
Phillips	(²)				Hackelman	167				Coal town. Not bounded.
Savanna	Oct. 27, 1900				Choctaw Townsite Commission.	800	.60		5	In short. Not bounded. See Table No. 15.³
Sterret		⁵485	89.10	.50	do	3,479				
South McAlester	Nov. 9, 1900	2,902.27			Fisher	3,479	.88	600.00	5	See Table No. 15.³
—la		180				215	.84		5	Apr 23, 1901.
Total		8,715.02	1,308.08	⁵.37		20,596	⁵.26	12,250.00	55	

[1] Boundary work completed.
[2] Coal towns. Not bounded. Inspectors instructions Apr. 24, 1901.
[3] Act June 28, 1898.
[4] No boundary report submitted till after June 30, 1901.
[5] Nine towns only.

TABLE No. 6.—*Status of boundary work in Choctaw Nation June 30, 1901.*

EASTERN DIVISION.[1]

(East of fourth guide meridian east.)

Act May 31, 1900; Public—131.]

[Towns reported to have 200 or more people.

Town.	Completed or population counted.	Boundary.	Cost.		Surveyor.	Population.	Acres per capita.	Estimate for surveying and platting.	Acres (included in column 3) for cemetery.	Date of approval of exterior limits. Remarks.
		Acres.	Dollars.	Per acre.						
1	2	3	4	5	6	7	8	9	10	11
Bokoshe	Dec. 7, 1900				Payne	160				Population short. Not bounded.
Brooken	Nov. 24, 1900				Hackelman	180				Do.
Cameron	Dec. 14, 1900	155.00	135.27	$0.87	Payne	300	0.52	$500.00	5	Feb. 21, 1901.
Cavanal	Nov. 12, 1900				do	45				Population short. Not bounded.
Cowlington	Dec. 12, 1900	157.50	61.15	.39	do	285	.69	700.00	5	Feb. 7, 1901.
Enterprise	Nov. 22, 1900	107.50	95.75	.89	Hackelman	352	.31	600.00	5	Feb. 15, 1901.
Fanshawe	Oct. 24, 1900				Jones	115				Population short. Not bounded.
Goodwater	Oct. 26, 1900				Hackelman	38				Do.
Grant	Mar. 22, 1901	131.22	81.80	.62	do	250	.52	300.00	0	Apr. 11, 1901.
Goodland	Feb. 20, 1901				do	160				Population short. Not bounded.
Hoyt	Dec. 1, 1900	97.50	63.82	.65	do	294	.34	350.00	5	Feb. 15, 1901.
Howe	Dec. 6, 1900	326.53	203.27	.62	do	1,000	.33	1,000.00	5	Feb. 6, 1901.
Howe, supplemental	Mar. 20, 1901	.17			Jones					Apr. 8, 1901.
Heavener	Dec. 1, 1900	175.64	88.65	.50	do	250	.70	750.00	5	Feb. 23, 1901.
Oaklodge	Dec. 21, 1900				do	75				Population short. Not bounded.
Poteau	Oct. 24, 1900	645.00	(3)		Payne	1,200	.54	289.40	5	See Table No. 16.
Red Oak	Nov. 15, 1900	132.50	115.80	.87	McCarthy	209	.63	500.00	5	Dec. 15, 1900.
Reichert	Dec. 21, 1900				do	100				Population short. Not bounded.
Shady Point	Dec. 30, 1900				do	162				Do.
Spiro	Feb. 27, 1901	225.00	114.92	.51	Payne	600	.37	600.00	5	Feb. 15 and Apr. 8, 1901.
Spiro, supplemental	Dec. 6, 1900	102.33	67.66	.66	do	300	.34	360.00	4.83	Apr. 9, 1901.
Sigler	Dec. 10, 1900	210.09	187.17	.89	do	400	.52	750.00	5	Feb. 15, 1901.
Talihina	May 10, 1901	210.59			Hackelman					Feb. 6 and Apr. 9, 1901.
Talihina, amended	Nov. 17, 1900				Fisher					June 4, 1901.
Thomasville	Dec. 12, 1900				do					Town abandoned.
Tamaha	May 18, 1901	142.30	70.50	.49	Jones	315	.45	450.00	5	Feb. 5, 1901.
Wilburton	Nov. 6, 1900	275.38	129.44	.47	Hackelman	3,000	.09	900.00		Not yet approved.
Wister	June 13, 1901	149.56	100.62	.67	Jones	360	.41	600.00	4.56	June 22, 1901.
Wister, supplemental		.22			do					June 12, 1901.
Witteville	Nov. 20, 1900				Payne	25				Population short. Not bounded.
Whitefield	Nov. 28, 1900	100.57	86.50	.86	Hackelman	354	.28	850.00	5	Feb. 12, 1901.
Total		3,135.41	1,601.72	.70		9,409	.34	8,989.40	69.89	

[1] Boundary work completed.   [3] No boundary survey.

[Towns reported to have 200 or more people. Act May 31, 1900; Public—131.]

Town.	Completed or population counted.	Boundary. Acres.	Boundary. Cost. Dollars.	Boundary. Per acre.	Surveyor.	Population.	Acre per capita.	Estimate for surveying and platting.	Acres (included in column 3) for cemetery.	Date of approval of exterior limits. Remarks.
1	2	3	4	5	6	7	8	9	10	11
Alabama		80.00			Dawes Commission.			$885.00		Oct. 28, 1900.
Boggs										
Bristow	Dec. 25, 1900	160.00	93.94	$0.26	do.			$85.00		Do.
Choska	Dec. 19, 1900	365.00	27.66	.24	Tinker.	900	0.40	800.00	5	Feb. 12, 1901.
Checotah	Dec. 18, 1900	115.00	141.22	.35	Phillips.	350	.33	1,200.00	5	Feb. 16, 1901.
Coweta		403.75			Fisher.	1,000	.40			do.
Clarksville	Dec. 17, 1900	147.50	47.65	.32	Phillips.	400	.37	400.00	5	June 21, 1901.
Eufaula	Jan. 3, 1901	347.63	171.70	.50	Fisher.	1,000	.35	1,100.00	5	Not yet approved.
Eufaula, supplemental	June 13, 1901	78.12	67.00	.86	Boyd.		.08	600.00		Not bounded.
Gibson										Feb. 7, 1901.
Holdenville	Dec. 17, 1900	429.79	102.71	.24	Jones.	1,700	.25	$400.00	5	Oct. 26, 19..
Henryetta		157.18			Dawes Commission.			$85.00		
Mounds		160.00						(b)		Do.
Muskogee	Apr. 7, 1900	2,444.76				5,000	.49	$85.00	74.76	June 4, 1900.
Okmulgee	Jan. 3, 1901	415.00	79.81	.19	do.	900	.46	$1,000.00	5	Feb. 6, 1901.
Sapulpa	Jan. 1, 1901	501.25	152.65	.30	do.	1,500	.33	800.00	5	Feb. 15, 1901.
Tulsa	Dec. 19, 1900	654.64	152.00	.23	do.	1,700	.38	1,300.00	40	Feb. 21, 1901.
Wagoner	Aug. 27, 1900	2,700.00			Wagoner townsite commission.					Oct. 10, 1900.
Winchell		160.00			Dawes Commission.			$85.00		Oct. 28, 1900.
Wetumka		160.00			do.			$85.00		Do.
Yager		120.00			do.			$85.00		Do.
Total		9,599.51	1,039.24	.30		144.50	.35	8,196.00	154.76	

1 Boundary work completed.
2 L. F. Parker, contract ($75 per town).
3 All improvements owned by two allottees—on their own lands.
4 Creek treaty (act March 1, 1901; Public—No.112), section 22, says Coweta and Gibson may be surveyed. No instructions.
5 See Table No. 17.
6 Now Fowler.

TABLE No. 8.—*Status of boundary work in Cherokee Nation June 30, 1901.*

SOUTHERN DIVISION.[1]

(Townships 9 to 19 north, inclusive.)

[Towns reported to have 200 or more people. Act May 31, 1900; Public—131.]

Town.	Completed or population counted.	Boundary. Acres.	Cost. Dollars.	Cost. Per acre.	Surveyor.	Population.	Acres per capita.	Estimate for surveying and platting.	Acres (included in column 3) for cemetery.	Date of approval of exterior limits. Remarks.
1	2	3	4	5	6	7	8	9	10	11
Briartown	Dec. 21, 1900					62				Population short. Not bounded.
Fort Gibson	Feb. 19, 1901	258.85	117.70	0.45	Phillips	625	0.41	$800.00	11.25	
Gans	Feb. 5, 1901				Tinker	150				Do.
Hanson	Mar. 14, 1901	95.00	88.56	93	Tinker	210	45	350.00	5	
Muldrow	Mar. 21, 1901	206.56	114.73	56	do	465	44	500.00	10	
Sallisaw	Mar. 8, 1901	257.78	68.58	82	do	1,000	26	900.00	10	
Stilwell	Mar. 30, 1901	142.08	110.74	78	do	1,000	24	400.00	5	
Tahlequah	Apr. 19, 1901	507.50	213.87	42	do	1,500	33	2,500.00	20	
Westville	Apr. 4, 1901	117.50	87.35	74	do	875	31	350.00	5	
Webbers Falls	Feb. 23, 1901	75.50	66.87	88	do	211	36	450.00	0	
Vian	Mar. 2, 1901	188.12	85.70	46	do	350	54	500.00	5.62	
Total		1,847.37	968.65	52		5,848	33	6,750.00	71.87	

[1] Boundary work completed. No boundaries yet approved. Nothing done toward surveying and platting.

TABLE No. 9.— Status of boundary work in Cherokee Nation June 30, 1901.

NORTHERN DIVISION.[1]

(Townships 20 to 29 north, inclusive.)

[Towns reported to have 200 or more people. Act May 31, 1900: Public—131.]

Town.	Completed or population counted.	Boundary.			Surveyor.	Population.	Acres per capita.	Estimate for surveying and platting.	Acres (included in column 3) for cemetery.	Date of approval of exterior limits. Remarks.
		Acres.	Cost.							
			Dollars.	Per acre.						
1	2	3	4	5	6	7	8	9	10	11
Adair	Jan. 23, 1901	150.00	87.84	$0.58	Fisher	300	0.50	$450.00	5	
Afton	Feb. 28, 1901	296.25	110.15	.37	do	600	.49	750.00	7.50	
Bartlesville	Jan. 9, 1901	297.09	87.95	.29	Tinker	1,000	.30	800.00	5	
Blue Jacket	Feb. 22, 1901	141.25	77.12	.43	Fisher	300	.61	500.00	5	
Collinsville	Apr. 16, 1901	270.00	104.80	.39	do	1,100	.25	600.00	10	
Catoosa	Apr. 6, 1901	165.00	96.49	.59	do	250	.66	500.00	7.50	
Choteau	Jan. 10, 1901	130.00	57.18	.44	do	250	.52	300.00	5	
Chelsea	Mar. 28, 1901	345.10	91.38	.27	do	700	.49	900.00	8.19	
Centralia	Feb. 13, 1901	177.50	91.86	.52	do	400	.44	500.00	5	
Claremore	Feb. 8, 1901	545.00	130.40	.24	Tinker	1,000	.55	1,300.00	15	
Fairland	Mar. 20, 1901	280.00	155.07	.41	Fisher	600	.38	600.00	10	
Grove	Mar. 19, 1901	185.88	76.58	.68	do	450	.41	500.00	10	
Lenapah	Jan. 22, 1901	117.50	85.97	.73	Tinker	205	.58	300.00	5	
Nowata	Jan. 3, 1901	380.00	112.25	.31	do	900	.40	700.00	20	
Oolagah	Jan. 28, 1901	170.00	86.95	.51	do	394	.55	500.00	5	
Pryor Creek	Jan. 17, 1901	269.37	87.31	.32	Fisher	600	.45	800.00	10	
Ramona	Apr. 22, 1901	110.00	69.22	.63	do	200	.56	300.00	5	
Talala	Jan. 16, 1901	137.50	72.81	.53	Tinker	210	.65	400.00	5	
Vinita	Feb. 5, 1901	772.48	240.13	.31	Fisher*	2,500	.31	2,500.00	83.73	
Welch	Feb. 20, 1901	118.75	47.42	.40	do	330	.36	300.00	5	
Total		5,028.67	1,968.33	.39		12,201	.41	13,500.00	176.92	

[1] Boundary work completed. No boundaries yet approved. Nothing done toward surveying and platting.

6854—01——10

MISCELLANEOUS.

Township plats.—The partial tracings from the township plats frequently proved to be insufficient; for example, where the towns had spread over into other sections or townships, or had cemeteries in other townships, or where the towns were located in townships other than shown on the General Land Office map of the Territory, dated 1899; for example, Collinsville and Centralia. In most of such cases additional tracings have had to be made from the plats on file with the Dawes Commission.

Population.—Some towns proved to be only a trifle short on population at the time of the surveyors' first visit, and in such cases, if the indications were favorable, word was left with the proper parties to notify the inspector whenever they reached the 200 limit, and they have then been bounded; for example, Lone Grove, Allen, and Ramona.

Sickness.—One transitman has been the victim of smallpox, and at least four of the surveyors have had malarial fever with chills, two of them being very sick at this time.

Frisco division.—The establishment of the limits of the towns within 5 miles on each side of the St. Louis, Oklahoma and Southern Railway, was delayed until after the completion of that road, so that these towns might adjust themselves to the new conditions before being bounded. After the completion of the road some of these towns had less than 200 people.

Boundary posts.—Exterior limits of the town sites have been marked sometimes by stones or by posts either plain or painted white, but in general with oak posts 4 by 4 inches by 5 feet, painted white and lettered in black, per cut.

Notices.—Notice of establishment of limits of each town which has been bounded under the supervision of this office has been posted in the post-office of that town, as follows:

Notice is hereby given that the town-site limits of Blue Jacket, Cherokee Nation, Ind. T., have this day been determined and will include the following lands, to wit:

	Section.	Township.	Range.	Acres.
W. ¼ of E. ¼ of NW. ¼ of NE. ¼ of SE. ¼ of	20	27 N	21 E	2.50
W. ¼ of NE. ¼ of SW. ¼ of NE. ¼ of SE. ¼ of	20	27 N	21 E	1.25
W. ¼ of NW. ¼ of NE. ¼ of SE. ¼ of	20	27 N	21 E	5.00
NW. ¼ of SW. ¼ of NE. ¼ of SE. ¼ of	20	27 N	21 E	2.50
S. ¼ of S. ¼ of NE. ¼ of SE. ¼ of	20	27 N	21 E	10.00
E. ¼ of E. ¼ of NW. ¼ of SE. ¼ of	20	27 N	21 E	10.00
SE. ¼ of SE. ¼ of	20	27 N	21 E	40.00
E. ¼ of E. ¼ of SW. ¼ of SE. ¼ of	20	27 N	21 E	10.00
S. ¼ of SW. ¼ of SW. ¼ of	21	27 N	21 E	5.00
W. ¼ of NW. ¼ of NW. ¼ of	28	27 N	21 E	20.00
NE. ¼ of NE. ¼ of	29	27 N	21 E	40.00
E. ¼ of E. ¼ of NW. ¼ of NE. ¼ of	29	27 N	21 E	10.00
SW. ¼ of SE. ¼ of NW. ¼ of NE. ¼ of	29	27 N	21 E	2.50
E. ¼ of E. ¼ of NW. ¼ of SE. ¼ of NE. ¼ of	29	27 N	21 E	2.50
W. ¼ of NE. ¼ of SE. ¼ of NE. ¼ of	29	27 N	21 E	5.00
Park				
W. ¼ of NE. ¼ of SW. ¼ of NE. ¼ of	29	27 N	21 E	5.00
E. ¼ of NW. ¼ of SW. ¼ of NE. ¼ of	29	27 N	21 E	5.00
Cemetery				
S. ¼ of SE. ¼ of NE. ¼ of SE. ¼ of	28	27 N	21 E	5.00
Total, including park and cemetery				181.25
Total, excluding park and cemetery				166.25

The boundaries have been marked, and parties erecting improvements outside of these limits will so at their own risk, as there is no provision protecting residents of the town in their holdings cept within the town-site limits.

JOHN F. FISHER,
Surveyor.
HARRY A. ROBERTS,
Transitman.
H. V. HINCKLEY,
Supervising Engineer.

' That hereafter it shall be unlawful for any person to destroy, deface, change, or remove to another ace any section corner, quarter-section corner, or meander post on any Government line of survey, or to cut down any witness tree, or any tree blazed to mark the line of a Government survey, to deface, change, or remove any monument or bench mark of any Government survey. That y person who shall offend against any of the provisions of this paragraph shall be deemed guilty a misdemeanor, and upon conviction thereof in any court shall be fined not exceeding two hundred and fifty dollars or be imprisoned not more than one hundred days. All fines accruing under is paragraph shall be paid into the Treasury, and the informer in each case of conviction shall be id the sum of twenty-five dollars." (29 Stats., 343.)
Violations of this statute will be vigorously prosecuted.
Posted February 22, 1901.

These notices or description sheets and the accompanying explanatory plats have en made out and submitted in quintuplicate. The report sheets per sample herewith (Centralia), with full letters of explanation, have been made in triplicate.

INDIAN TERRITORY TOWN SITES.

GEO. WRIGHT,
United States Indian Inspector for Indian Territory.
SIR: I have to report that the limits of the town of Centralia, in the Cherokee Nation, have been ablished in accordance with the five copies, hereto attached, of notice, plat, and description, the iginals of which have been posted in the post-office in said town.
Commenced February 8, 1901; completed February 13, 1901; delay, rain, one day.
This town is located about 22 miles northwest from Vinita station, which is on the Frisco and Katy ilways.
The cost of establishing these limits is as follows:
Wages, $84.86; limit posts, etc., $7.00; total, $91.86; area, 177.5 acres. Cost of bounding (per acre), 52 nts. Topography of town, rolling prairie; condition of town, fairly good; estimated cost of surveying town, $500; estimated time necessary to survey town, forty days.
This town does not desire to be surveyed at once at its own expense.
The present plat of the town may be of some use as basis for new one.
Estimated population, 400.
Respectfully,

H. V. HINCKLEY,
Supervising Engineer.

MUSKOGEE, IND. T., *June 22, 1901.*

Fourteen standard boundary posts painted and lettered.

Towns now having 190 or more people, and new towns springing up, may soon ave 200 people, and so have to be bounded, and it may be decided to establish nits for some of the coal-mining towns which have been temporarily passed. (See able No. 5.)
Delays.—The principal cause of delay in the establishment of exterior limits has en that section and quarter-section corner stones have frequently been found loose lowed up) or missing entirely. In one case a section corner was found in the undation of a residence. In such cases it has been necessary to run several miles line to reestablish the corners, and at quite a number of towns the cost of the unedary work has been more than doubled by the cause above stated. Much of e cost is also due to the amount of subdivision work necessary to keep the limits own to a reasonable minimum.

BOUNDARY WORK—SUMMARY.

Counting Surveyor Joyce's time, from January 2, 1901, the twelve surveyors (averaging their time) have been at work eight months and two days, and in that time the terior limits of all towns of 200 or more people in the Indian Territory have been tablished; the field work of surveying and platting has been completed at 56 towns, clusive of town site commission towns, 31 town plats have been checked in the fice, and 17 plats altogether have been approved.
Table No. 10 shows that 107 towns have been bounded, inclusive of Poteau and rdmore, which were bounded and platted together; McAlester, the boundary of hich was not reported till after June 30, 1901; and Choska, abandoned; and exclusive of Dawes Commission and town-site commission towns, and that 35,537.42 acres ave been segregated at a cost of $13,440.94, or approximately 38 cents per acre.

The estimated population of these towns is 88,737, and the area, including cemeteries, is about 0.40 acre per capita. The estimate for surveying and platting these towns is $86,444.92.

These estimates are low for the towns on the Rock Island, for the reason that most of these towns had engaged surveyors to survey the towns, at the expense of the towns, but have made failure of it. (See note 2 under Table No. 1.) The estimates for some of the towns on the St. Louis, Oklahoma and Southern Railway are high for the, reason that when the estimates went in, the supervising engineer was not advised as to what towns were included in the Parker contract.

TABLE No. 10.—*Summary of boundary work,*[1] *June 30, 1901 (limited strictly to the work under the supervising engineer, and to towns actually bounded).*

[Towns reported to have 200 or more people. Act May 31, 1900. Public—131.]

Nation.	Division.	Number of towns.	Acres.	Cost.		Population.	Acres per capita.	Estimates for surveying and platting.
				Dollars.	Per acre.			
Chickasaw	Rock Island	8	5,038.24	1,128.58	0.22	8,826	0.57	$2,825.00
Do	Santa Fe	[2]22	9,365.62	3,561.39	.38	23,312	.40	26,595.62
Do	Frisco	6	2,147.54	907.21	.38	3,650	.59	4,585.00
Do	Eastern	7	1,151.48	662.89	.57	1,991	.57	3,400.00
Choctaw	Western	[3]10	4,365.57	1,503.03	.34	14,350	.30	12,250.00
Do	Eastern	[4]16	3,135.41	1,701.72	.54	9,409	.33	8,939.40
Creek		[5]9	3,457.62	1,039.24	.30	9,450	.37	7,600.00
Cherokee	Southern	9	1,847.37	908.55	.49	5,548	.33	6,750.00
Do	Northern	20	5,028.67	1,968.33	.39	12,201	.41	13,500.00
Total		[6]107	35,537.42	13,440.94	.38	88,737	.40	86,144.92

[1] Work completed.
[2] Includes Ardmore. No separate boundary report. Assumed cost of bounding, $800. Population, 5,600.
[3] Includes McAlester. No separate boundary report. Assumed cost of bounding, $200.
[4] Includes Poteau. No separate boundary report. Assumed cost of bounding, $100.
[5] Includes Choska—abandoned.
[6] Boundary reports prepared for 104 towns only.

SURVEYING AND PLATTING.

Surveying and platting at the expense of the towns has in many cases proved a failure, because the contracts have been awarded to the lowest bidders regardless of their qualifications and without bond for the satisfactory completion of the work. The work has therefore been carelessly done and but half done, and the surveyor has generally been paid in full prior to the inspection of the work by a representative of the Department. The following towns, however, are excepted from the above statement, viz: Calvin, Guertie, and Kiowa, surveyed by William P. Halliday, and Poteau, surveyed by John McCarthy. The plats of these towns were allowed to pass after being checked and corrected, while McAlester, Grant, Chickasha, Marlow, Rush Springs, and Comanche had to be resurveyed.

ROCK ISLAND DIVISION.

[Act May 31, 1900. Public—131.]

Towns.	Estimates for surveying and platting, Table No. 1.	Actual cost.			Work completed.		Surveyor.	Date of approval. Remarks.
		Acres.	Dollars.	Per acre.	Field.	Office.		
1	2	3	4	5	6	7	8	9
Chickasha	(1)$125.00	1,248.70	(*)1,319.33	$1.05	June 5,1901	June 30,1901	Colby	
Comanche	500.00	436.93			June 30,1901		do	
Duncan	800.00	1,011.70			June 20,1901	June 30,1901	do	
Marlow	350.00	960.00					do	
Minco	200.00	297.00	501.46	1.74	June 25,1901		Jones	
Rush Springs	300.00	380.00			June 6,1901	June 30,1901	Colby	
Ryan	350.00	435.39					do	
Terrel	200.00	280.00					do	
Total	2,825.00	5,089.72	1,814.79	1.18				

1 Estimates were for supervision and tracing only, the towns having proposed to make the surveys at their own expense.

* Cost to the United States, exclusive of amounts paid by towns for incomplete and inaccurate surveys.

TABLE No. 12.—*Status of surveying and platting in Chickasaw Nation June 30, 1901.*

SANTA FE DIVISION.

[Act May 31, 1900. Public—131.]

Towns.	Estimates for surveying and platting, Table No. 2.	Acres.	Actual cost.		Work completed.		Surveyor.	Date of approval. Remarks.
			Dollars.	Per acre.	Field.	Office.		
1	2	3	4	5	6	7	8	9
Ardmore	¹$6,025.52	2,262.11	²$6,035.52	$2.67	June 26, 1901	June 30, 1901	Joyce	Not yet approved.
Berwyn	600.00	191.25	660.00	3.45	June 21, 1901	...do	Wood	Do.
Center	600.00	195.00			Nothing done	Nothing done		
Cornish	350.00	190.28			...do	...do		
Davis	1,600.00	531.85			...do	...do		
Dougherty	750.00	243.13			June 24, 1901	...do	Wood.	
Durwood	400.00	140.00			Nothing done	...do		
Earl	350.00	125.00	270.91	2.16	Incomplete.	...do	Tinker.	
Erin Springs	300.00	110.00			...do	...do	Wood.	
Johnson	500.00	90.00			...do	...do	Hackelman	Do.
Lebanon	500.00	164.92	180.00	1.09	June 16, 1901	Incomplete.	Emerson.	
Leon	400.00	165.00			May 31, 1901	June 30, 1901	Boyd	D
Longrove	600.00	195.00			Incomplete.	Nothing done		
Marietta	640.00	330.00	790.00	2.39	Nothing done	...do	Tinker.	
Mannsville	500.00	175.00			May 21, 1901	June 28, 1901	Hackelman	
Metie	350.00	122.50			Nothing done	Incomplete.		
Orr	460.00	185.00			June 26, 1901	Nothing done	Hackelman	Do.
Pwoll	300.00	85.48	217.53	2.90	Nothing done	June 39, 1901	Hackelman	
Purcell	3,400.00	1,206.50			June 3, 1901	Nothing done	Phillips.	
Pauls Valley	2,900.00	946.83	2,523.61	2.67	Nothing done	June 30, 1901	Phillips.	Do.
Sulphur	2,900.00	948.14			June 11, 1901	Nothing done	Phillips.	Do.
Wynnewood	2,600.00	767.50			Incomplete.	...do	Phillips.	
Total	26,595.52	9,370.52	10,707.97	2.61				

¹ No estimate prior to this resurvey. Includes 5 acres cemetery. ² Exclusive of $16,000 previously spent (by Chickasaw town-site commission) on firstsurvey.

TABLE No. 13.—*Status of surveying and platting in Chickasaw Nation June 30, 1901.*

FRISCO DIVISION.

[Act May 31, 1900. Public—131.]

Towns.	Estimates for surveying and platting. Table No. 3.	Acres.	Actual cost.		Work completed.		Surveyor.	Date of approval. Remarks.
			Dollars.	Per acre.	Field.	Office.		
1	2	3	4	5	6	7	8	9
Ada..........	$1,300.00	559.90			May —,1901	Nothing done		
Bryant²......	85.00	155.45			Feb. —,1901	do		
Colbert......	⁴4,029.38	134.77	⁴4,029.38	$29.90			Chickasaw town-site commission.	Aug. 14, 1899.
Francis......	85.00	160.00			Feb. —,1901	Incomplete.	(³)	
Gray.........	85.00	90.00			Jan. 29,1901	do	(³)	
Helen........	85.00	156.09			June 30,1901	Nothing done	(³)	
Hickory......	500.00	170.00			Nothing done	do		
Madill.......	85.00	160.00			June 22,1901	do	(³)	
Oakland......	1,200.00	321.95			Nothing done	do		
Ravia........	85.00	326.39			June 30,1901	do	(³)	
Roff.........	800.00	595.00			do	do		
Scullin......	85.00	120.00			do	do	(³)	
Tishomingo...	700.00	175.00			Nothing done	do		
Woodville....	85.00	160.00	95.00	.59	Dec. 19,1900	Jan. 3,1901	(³)	Jan. 31, 1901.
Total.......	9,209.38	3,273.85	4,124.38					

1 L. F. Parker contract, approved November 17, 1900.
2 Now Millcreek.
3 No estimate prior to survey.
4 Includes expenses of appraisement and sale of town property.

TABLE No. 14.—*Status of surveying and platting in Chickasaw Nation June 30, 1901.*

EASTERN DIVISION.

[Act May 31, 1900. Public—131.]

Towns.	Estimates for surveying and platting, Table No.4.	Acres.	Actual cost.		Work completed.			Surveyor.	Date of approval. Remarks.
			Dollars.	Per acre.	Field.	Office.			
1	2	3	4	5	6	7		8	9
Connerville	$500.00	180.00			Incomplete.	Nothing done		Emerson	
Cumberland	500.00	173.94	405.00	$2.33	May 11, 1901	June 30, 1901		do	
Emet	500.00	170.00	420.00	2.17	May 6, 1901	do		do	
Kemp	350.00	120.00			Nothing done	Nothing done			
Pontotoc	600.00	195.00			June 20, 1901	do		Hackelman	
Silo	500.00	195.00	220.00	1.13	May 20, 1901	June 17, 1901		Emerson	
Stonewall	450.00	117.50			Incomplete.	Nothing done		do	
Total	3,400.00	1,151.44	1,045.00						
Three towns	1,500.00	538.98	1,045.00	1.94					

WESTERN DIVISION.

[Act May 31, 1900. Public—181.]

Town.	Estimates for surveying and platting. Table No. 5.	Acres.	Actual cost.		Work completed.		Surveyor.	Date of approval. Remarks.
			Dollars.	Per acre.	Field.	Office.		
1	2	3	4	5	6	7	8	9
Allen	$400.00	120.00			Incomplete	Nothing done	Payne	Being surveyed and platted.
Antlers	500.00	182.50	711.29	$3.89	Feb. 4, 1901	May 21, 1901	Hackelman	June 7, 1901.
Ato'a	(1)	277.18	1,768.94	6.50			Choctaw town-site commission.	Feb. 23, 1900.
Calvin	(1)	160.00			June 30, 1900		Halliday	Nov. 8, 1900.
Caddo	1,000.00	400.00	1,192.07	2.98	Mar. 22, 1901	May 21, 1901	Emerson	June 7, 1901.
Canadian	750.00	197.50			June 6, 1901	Incomplete	Boyd	
Coalgate	1,500.00	412.50	3,064.16	2.39	Incomplete		Hackelman	Being surveyed and platted.
Durant	3,000.00	1,294.10			June 7, 1901	June 30, 1901	Kirkpatrick	
Guertie	(1)	160.00			July 12, 1900		Halliday	Nov. 2, 1900.
Krebs	1,000.00	380.00			Nothing done			Boundary not yet approved.
Kiowa	(1)	365.00			Sept. 7, 1900		Halliday	Nov. 2, 1900.
Lehigh	1,700.00	500.00			Nothing done		Jones	Being surveyed and platted.
McAlester	1,800.00	759.07			One-half done		Kirkpatrick	Do.
Sterrett	(1)	485.00	3,285.32	6.74			Choctaw town-site commission.	Aug. 28, 1899.
South McAlester	(1)	2,902.27	12,000.00	4.14	Dec. 12, 1901	Dec. 14, 1901	...do	Feb. 14, 1901.
Wapanucka	600.00	180.00	431.61		June 19, 1901	Incomplete	Payne	
Total	12,250.00	8,715.02	22,406.39	3.94				

1 Commissioners' salaries included.   2 At expense of the town.   3 Those towns only which are completed.

TABLE No. 16.—*Status of surveying and platting in Choctaw Nation, June 30, 1901.*

EASTERN DIVISION.

[Act May 31, 1900. Public—131.]

Town.	Estimates for surveying and platting, Table No. 6.	Acres.	Actual cost. Dollars.	Actual cost. Per acre.	Work completed. Field.	Work completed. Office.	Surveyor.	Date of approval.	Remarks.
1	2	3	4	5	6	7	8	9	
Cameron	$500.00	155.00	494.35	$3.19	Apr. 13, 1901	June 18, 1901	Payne	Not yet approved.	
Cowlington	200.00	157.50			Apr. 30, 1901	Incomplete.	do	Do.	
Enterprise	600.00	107.50	163.00	1.52	May 20, 1901	June 17, 1901	Hackelman	June 4, 1901.	
Grant	300.00	131.22	250.70	1.91	May 18, 1901	May 21, 1901	do	Not yet approved.	
Hoyt	350.00	97.50	165.00	1.68	May 10, 1901	June 17, 1901	do	Do.	
Howe	1,000.00	326.70	1,427.95	1.37	Apr. 5, 1901	June 18, 1901	Jones		
Heavener	750.00	175.64			May 18, 1901	Incomplete.	Payne		
Poteau	¹239.40	645.00	²239.40	.37	May 13, 1901	May 21, 1901	McCarthy	June 4, 1901.	
Redoak	500.00	182.50	361.71	2.73	Jan. 23, 1901	May 14, 1901	Emerson	June 7, 1901.	
Spiro	600.00	225.70			Mar. 13, 1901		Payne	Survey completed. Plat delayed.	
Stigler	350.00	102.33	199.00	1.94	Apr. 19, 1901	June 17, 1901	Hackelman	Not yet approved.	
Talihina	750.00	210.59	622.05	2.95	Mar. 7, 1901	May 21, 1901	do	June 4, 1901.	
Tamaha	450.00	142.30	255.00	2.07	Apr. 11, 1901	June 17, 1901	do	Not yet approved.	
Whitefield	350.00	100.57	221.00	2.20	May 1, 1901	do	do	Do.	
Wilburton	900.00	275.58						Coaltown. Not yet surveyed.	
Wister	600.00	149.78			May 10, 1901	Incomplete.	Jones		
Total	8,999.40	3,135.41	4,429.16	³1.92					

¹ Estimate made to conform to cost.   ² Cost to the United States. Surveyed and platted at expense of the town.

³ Total cost of completed surveys divided by acres in those towns.

[Act May 31, 1900. Public—131.]

Town.	Estimates for surveying and platting. Table No. 7.	Acres.	Actual cost. Dollars.	Per acre.	Work completed. Field.	Office.	Surveyor.	Date of approval. Remarks.
Alabama	$85.00	80.00			Feb. —, 1901	Incomplete	(3)	Held on account station grounds.
Beggs	85.00	160.00			Jan. 21, 1901	do	(3)	Do.
Bristow	800.00	800.00			Nothing done	Nothing done		
Checotah	1,200.00	365.00			do	do		
Coweta	(3)	403.75			do	do		
Clarksville	400.00				do	do		
Eufaula	1,700.00	147.50			do	do	(4)	Do.
Foster	85.00	425.75			Feb. —, 1901	Incomplete		
Gibson	(3)	120.00			Nothing done	Nothing done		
Holdenville	400.00				June 27, 1901	Incomplete	(3)	Do.
Henryetta	85.00	429.79			Feb. 1, 1901	do	(3)	Jan. 3, 1901.
Mounds	85.00	157.13	$80.00	$0.50	Dec. 8, 1900	Dec. 18, 1900	Muscogee town-site commission.	June 4, 1900.
Muscogee		160.00 ... 2,441.76	15,842.68	6.48	Apr. 7, 1900	Apr. 7, 1900		
Okmulgee	1,000.00	415.00			June 15, 1901	Incomplete	(4)	Held on account station grounds.
Sapulpa	800.00	501.25			Nothing done	Nothing done		
Tulsa	1,300.00	654.58			do	do	Wagoner town-site commission.	Oct. 10, 1900.
Wagoner		2,700.00	16,946.70	6.28	Aug. 27, 1900	Aug. 27, 1900		
Winchell	85.00	160.00			Apr. —, 1901	Incomplete	(3)	Held on account station grounds.
Wetumka	85.00	160.00			Jan. 24, 1901	do	(3)	Do.
Total	8,195.00	9,484.51						

1 No towns surveyed and platted, except Wagoner and Muscogee and those along the St. Louis, Oklahoma and Southern Railway.
2 L. F. Parker, contract ($75 per town).
3 Treaty says may be surveyed. No instructions.
4 Including commissioners' salaries.

Draftsmen.—The following draftsmen reported for duty on the dates given: Samuel A. Cobb, February 12, 1901; William G. Rawles, February 14, 1901; Andrew N. Darrow, March 14, 1901; Harry T. Kerr, March 18, 1901. They have, therefore, been on duty an average time of four months and one day.

Delays.—If the work of surveying and platting the towns has progressed slowly, the two principal causes of delay have been: First, the extreme irregularity with which most of the towns have been built up (see plat of McGee herewith); second, complications as to railroad right of way and station grounds, errors in railroad plats, and confliction of plats.

These conditions have to be straightened out, and in numerous cases it has become necessary to prepare amended plats for the railroads to file to eliminate the discrepancies before town plats could be completed.

COST OF SURVEYING AND PLATTING.

In June, 1900, the supervising engineer advised the inspector that the expense of surveying and platting all towns in the Indian Territory should not exceed $3 per acre. That estimate was intended to include the cost of establishing the exterior limits. The estimate in Table No. 10 for surveying and platting is $2.43 per acre. The actual cost per acre for bounding the towns is 38 cents, making the total estimated cost $2.81 per acre.

Most of the surveyors were inexperienced at town-site work. That they are cutting down the cost of the work as they become more experienced is illustrated by the following:

		Per acre.
Hackelman	Antlers	$3.89
	Talihina	2.96
	Grant	1.91
	Emet	1.52
Emerson	Red Oak	2.73
	Caddo	2.98
	Cumberland	2.33
	Silo	1.13

Although the cost of boundary work has been more than was anticipated, and although the total cost of bounding, surveying, and platting to date is nearly $4 per acre, it is believed that the work can be completed within the estimate.

SUMMARY.

Tables 11 to 17, inclusive, show the progress of the field and office work in connection with the surveying and platting of the towns. No instructions have been received to survey and plat the towns in the Cherokee Nation. Assuming that such orders are forthcoming, the work of surveying and platting all the towns in the Indian Territory having at present 200 or more people can be completed with the present force probably not later than October 1, 1902.

SUGGESTIONS.

In closing, it may not be improper for the supervising engineer to make two suggestions:

First. In platting the town sites provision has been made for section-line roads to enter the towns, but there is no road law in force in the Indian Territory, and the section-line roads are, therefore, prospective. Congress might be asked to provide that 30 feet on each side of every section line should be reserved in the deeds and dedicated to public use.

Second. There is an apparent unfairness in the several acts of Congress, which provide for the surveying and platting of such towns only as have a population of 200 or more, at the same time providing for the segregation of 160 acres at stations on new railroads. The result is that towns are laid out where there are no people, while towns of 196 people are passed by.

In the judgment of the supervising engineer all towns, however small, should be segregated, surveyed, and platted, except in cases where the buildings are owned by the prospective allottee or where arrangements are or can be otherwise made to protect the owners of the improvements.

This agreement, by and between the Government of the United States, of the first part, entered into in its behalf by the commission to the Five Civilized Tribes, Henry L. Dawes, Tams Bixby, Frank C. Armstrong, Archibald S. McKennon, and Thomas B. Needles, duly appointed and authorized thereunto, and the Government of the Seminole Nation in Indian Territory, of the second part, entered into on behalf of said government by its commission, duly appointed and authorized thereunto, viz, John F. Brown, Okchan Harjo, William Cully, K. N. Kinkehee, Thomas West, and Thomas Factor;

Witnesseth that, in consideration of the mutual undertakings herein contained, it is agreed as follows:

All lands belonging to the Seminole tribe of Indians shall be divided into three classes, designated as first, second, and third class, the first class to be appraised at five dollars, the second class at two dollars and fifty cents, and the third class at one dollar and twenty-five cents per acre, and the same shall be divided among the members of the tribe so that each shall have an equal share thereof in value, so far as may be, the location and fertility of the soil considered; giving to each the right to select his allotment so as to include any improvements thereon owned by him at the time, and each allottee shall have the sole right of occupancy of the land so alloted to him during the existence of the present tribal government, and until the members of said tribe shall have become citizens of the United States. Such allotments shall be made under the direction and supervision of the commission to the Five Civilized Tribes in connection with a representative appointed by the tribal government, and the chairman of said commission shall execute and deliver to each allottee a certificate describing therein the land allotted to him.

All contracts for sale, disposition, or encumbrance of any part of any allotment made prior to date of patent shall be void.

Any allottee may lease his allotment for any period not exceeding six years, the contract therefor to be executed in triplicate upon printed blanks provided by the tribal government, and before the same shall become effective it shall be approved by the principal chief and a copy filed in the office of the clerk of the United States court at Wewoka.

No lease of any coal, mineral, coal oil, or natural gas within said nation shall be valid unless made with the tribal government, by and with the consent of the allottee and approved by the Secretary of the Interior.

Should there be discovered on any allotment, any coal, mineral, coal oil, or natural gas, and the same should be operated so as to produce royalty, one-half of such royalty shall be paid to such allottee and the remaining half into the tribal treasury until extinguishment of tribal government, and the latter shall be used for the purpose of equalizing the value of allotments; and if the same be insufficient therefor, any other funds belonging to the tribe, upon extinguishment of tribal government, may be used for such purpose, so that each allotment may be made equal in value as aforesaid.

The town site of Wewoka shall be controlled and disposed of according to the provisions of an act of the general council of the Seminole Nation, approved April 23, 1897, relative thereto; and on extinguishment of the tribal government, deeds of conveyance shall issue to owners of lots as herein provided for allottees; and all lots remaining unsold at that time may be sold in such manner as may be prescribed by the Secretary of the Interior.

Five hundred thousand dollars ($500,000) of the funds belonging to the Seminoles, now held by the United States, shall be set apart as a permanent school fund for the education of children of the members of said tribe, and shall be held by the United States at five per cent interest, or invested so as to produce such amount of interest, which shall be, after extinguishment of tribal government, applied by the Secretary of the Interior to the support of Mekasuky and Emahaka academies and the district schools of the Seminole people; and there shall be selected and excepted from allotment three hundred and twenty acres of land for each of said academies and eighty acres each for eight district schools in the Seminole country.

There shall also be excepted from allotment one-half acre for the use and occupancy of each of twenty-four churches, including those already existing and such others as may hereafter be established in the Seminole country, by and with consent of the general council of the nation, but should any part of same, at any time, cease to be used for church purposes, such part shall at once revert to the Seminole people and be added to the lands set apart for the use of said district schools.

One acre in each township shall be excepted from allotment, and the same may be purchased by the United States upon which to establish schools for the education of children of noncitizens when deemed expedient.

When the tribal government shall cease to exist, the principal chief, last elected by said tribe, shall execute, under his hand and the seal of the nation, and deliver to each allottee a deed conveying to him all the right, title, and interest of the said nation and the members thereof, in and to the lands so allotted to him, and the Secretary of the Interior shall approve such deed, and the same shall thereupon operate as a relinquishment of the right, title, and interest of the United States in and to the land embraced in said conveyance, and as a guaranty by the United States of the title of said lands to the allottee; and the acceptance of such deed by the allottee shall be a relinquishment of his title to and interest in all other lands belonging to the tribe, except such as may have been excepted from allotment and held in common for other purposes. Each allottee shall designate one tract of forty acres, which shall, by the terms of the deed, be made inalienable and nontaxable as a homestead in perpetuity.

All moneys belonging to the Seminoles remaining after equalizing the value of allotments as herein provided, and reserving said sum of five hundred thousand dollars for school fund, shall be paid per capita to the members of said tribe in three equal installments, the first to be made as soon as convenient after allotment and extinguishment of tribal government, and the others at one and two years, respectively. Such payments shall be made by a person appointed by the Secretary of the Interior, who shall prescribe the amount of and approve the bond to be given by such person, and strict account shall be given to the Secretary of the Interior for such disbursements.

The "Loyal Seminole claim" shall be submitted to the United States Senate, which shall make final determination of same, and, if sustained, shall provide for payment thereof within two years from date hereof.

There shall hereafter be held at the town of Wewoka, the present capital of the Seminole Nation, regular terms of the United States Court as at other points in the judicial district of which the Seminole Nation is a part.

The United States agrees to maintain strict laws in the Seminole country against the introduction, sale, barter, or giving away of intoxicants of any kind or quality.

This agreement shall in no wise affect the provisions of existing treaties between the Seminole Nation and the United States, except in so far as it is inconsistent therewith.

The United States courts now existing, or that may hereafter be created in Indian Territory, shall have exclusive jurisdiction of all controversies growing out of the title, ownership, occupation, or use of real estate owned by the Seminoles; and to try all persons charged with homicide, embezzlement, bribery, and embracery hereafter committed in the Seminole country, without reference to race or citizenship of the persons charged with such crime, and any citizen or officer of said nation charged with any such crime, if convicted, shall be punished as if he were a citizen or officer of the United States, and the courts of said nation shall retain all the jurisdiction which they now have, except as herein transferred to the courts of the United States.

When this agreement is ratified by the Seminole Nation and the United States, the same shall serve to repeal all the provisions of the act of Congress approved June 7, 1897, in any manner affecting the proceedings of the general council of the Seminole Nation.

It being known that the Seminole Reservation is insufficient for allotments for the use of the Seminole people, upon which they, as citizens, holding in severalty, may reasonably and adequately maintain their families, the United States will make effort to purchase from the Creek Nation, at one dollar and twenty-five cents per acre, two hundred thousand acres of land, immediately adjoining the eastern boundary of the Seminole Reservation, and lying between the North Fork and South Fork of the Canadian River, in trust for, and to be conveyed by proper patent by the United States to, the Seminole Indians, upon said sum of one dollar and twenty-five cents per acre being reimbursed to the United States by said Seminole Indians; the same to be allotted, as herein provided for lands now owned by the Seminoles.

This agreement shall be binding on the United States when ratified by Congress, and on the Seminole people when ratified by the general council of the Seminole Nation.

In witness whereof the said commissioners have hereunto affixed their names at Muskogee, Indian Territory, this sixteenth day of December, A. D. 1897.

TAMS BIXBY,	JOHN F. BROWN,
FRANK C. ARMSTRONG,	OKCHAN HARJO,
ARCHIBALD S. McKENNON,	WILLIAM CULLY,
THOMAS B. NEEDLES,	K. N. KINKEHEE,
Commission to the Five Civilized Tribes.	THOMAS WEST,
	THOMAS FACTOR,
	Seminole Commission.
ALLISON L. AYLESWORTH,	A. J. BROWN,
Secretary.	*Secretary.*

APPENDIX NO. 2.

[PUBLIC—No. 162.]

AN ACT For the protection of the people of the Indian Territory, and for other purposes.

Be it enacted by the Senate and House of Representatives of the United States of America in Congress assembled, That in all criminal prosecutions in the Indian Territory against officials for embezzlement, bribery, and embracery the word "officer," when the same appears in the criminal laws heretofore extended over and put in force in said Territory, shall include all officers of the several tribes or nations of Indians in said Territory.

SEC. 2. That when in the progress of any civil suit, either in law or equity, pending in the United States court in any district in said Territory, it shall appear to the court that the property of any tribe is in any way affected by the issues being heard, said court is hereby authorized and required to make said tribe a party to said suit by service upon the chief or governor of the tribe, and the suit shall thereafter be conducted and determined as if said tribe had been an original party to said action.

SEC. 3. That said courts are hereby given jurisdiction in their respective districts to try cases against those who may claim to hold as members of a tribe and whose membership is denied by the tribe, but who continue to hold said lands and tenements notwithstanding the objection of the tribe; and if it be found upon trial that the same are held unlawfully against the tribe by those claiming to be members thereof, and the membership and right are disallowed by the commission to the Five Tribes, or the United States court, and the judgment has become final, then said court shall cause the parties charged with unlawfully holding said possessions to be removed from the same and cause the lands and tenements to be restored to the person or persons or nation or tribe of Indians entitled to the possession of the same: *Provided always,* That any person being a noncitizen in possession of lands, holding the possession thereof under an agreement, lease, or improvement contract with either of said nations or tribes, or any citizen thereof, executed prior to January first, eighteen hundred and ninety-eight, may, as to lands not exceeding in amount one hundred and sixty acres, in defense of any action for the possession of said lands show that he is and has been in peaceable possession of such lands, and that he has while in such possession made lasting and valuable improvements thereon, and that he has not enjoyed the possession thereof a sufficient length of time to compensate him for such improvements. Thereupon the court or jury trying said cause shall determine the fair and reasonable value of such improvements and the fair and reasonable rental value of such lands for the time the same shall have been occupied by such person, and if the improvements exceed in value the amount of rents with which such persons should be charged the court, in its judgment, shall specify such time as will, in the opinion of the court, compensate such person for the balance due, and award him possession for such time unless the amount be paid by claimant within such reasonable time as the court shall specify. If the finding be that the amount of rents exceed the value of the improvements, judgment shall be rendered against the defendant for such sum, for which execution may issue.

SEC. 4. That all persons who have heretofore made improvements on lands belonging to any one of the said tribes of Indians, claiming rights of citizenship, whose claims have been decided adversely under the act of Congress approved June tenth, eighteen hundred and ninety-six, shall have possession thereof until and including

December thirty-first, eighteen hundred and ninety-eight; and may, prior to that time, sell or dispose of the same to any member of the tribe owning the land who desires to take the same in his allotment: *Provided,* That this section shall not apply to improvements which have been appraised and paid for, or payment tendered by the Cherokee Nation under the agreement with the United States approved by Congress March third, eighteen hundred and ninety-three.

SEC. 5. That before any action by any tribe or person shall be commenced under section three of this act, it shall be the duty of the party bringing the same to notify the adverse party to leave the premises for the possession of which the action is about to be brought, which notice shall be served at least thirty days before commencing the action by leaving a written copy with the defendant, or, if he can not be found, by leaving the same at his last known place of residence or business with any person occupying the premises over the age of twelve years, or, if his residence or business address can not be ascertained, by leaving the same with any person over the age of twelve years upon the premises sought to be recovered and described in said notice; and if there be no person with whom said notice can be left, then by posting same on the premises.

SEC. 6. That the summons shall not issue in such action until the chief or governor of the tribe, or person or persons bringing suit in his own behalf, shall have filed a sworn complaint, on behalf of the tribe or himself, with the court, which shall, as near as practicable, describe the premises so detained, and shall set forth a detention without the consent of the person bringing said suit or the tribe, by one whose membership is denied by it: *Provided,* That if the chief or governor refuse or fail to bring suit in behalf of the tribe then any member of the tribe may make complaint and bring said suit.

SEC. 7. That the court in granting a continuance of any case, particularly under section three, may, in its discretion, require the party applying therefor to give an undertaking to the adverse party, with good and sufficient securities, to be approved by the judge of the court, conditioned for the payment of all damages and costs and defraying the rent which may accrue if judgment be rendered against him.

SEC. 8. That when a judgment for restitution shall be entered by the court the clerk shall, at the request of the plaintiff or his attorney, issue a writ of execution thereon, which shall command the proper officer of the court to cause the defendant or defendants to be forthwith removed and ejected from the premises and the plaintiff given complete and undisturbed possession of the same. The writ shall also command the said officer to levy upon the property of the defendant or defendants subject to execution, and also collect therefrom the costs of the action and all accruing costs in the service of the writ. Said writ shall be executed within thirty days.

SEC. 9. That the jurisdiction of the court and municipal authority of the city of Fort Smith for police purposes in the State of Arkansas is hereby extended over all that strip of land in the Indian Territory lying and being situate between the corporate limits of the said city of Fort Smith and the Arkansas and Poteau rivers, and extending up the said Poteau River to the mouth of Mill Creek: and all the laws and ordinances for the preservation of the peace and health of said city, as far as the same are applicable, are hereby put in force therein: *Provided,* That no charge or tax shall ever be made or levied by said city against said land or the tribe or nation to whom it belongs.

SEC. 10. That all actions for restitution of possession of real property under this Act must be commenced by the service of a summons within two years after the passage of this Act, where the wrongful detention or possession began prior to the date of its passage; and all actions which shall be commenced hereafter, based upon wrongful detention or possession committed since the passage of this Act must be commenced within two years after the cause of action accrued. And nothing in this Act shall take away the right to maintain an action for unlawful and forcible entry and detainer given by the Act of Congress passed May second, eighteen hundred and ninety (Twenty-sixth United States Statutes, page ninety-five).

SEC. 11. That when the roll of citizenship of any one of said nations or tribes is fully completed as provided by law, and the survey of the lands of said nation or tribe is also completed, the commission heretofore appointed under Acts of Congress, and known as the "Dawes Commission," shall proceed to allot the exclusive use and occupancy of the surface of all the lands of said nation or tribe susceptible of allotment among the citizens thereof, as shown by said roll, giving to each, so far as possible, his fair and equal share thereof, considering the nature and fertility of the soil, location, and value of same; but all oil, coal, asphalt, and mineral deposits in the lands of any tribe are reserved to such tribe, and no allotment of such lands shall carry the title to such oil, coal, asphalt, or mineral deposits; and all town sites shall also be reserved to the several tribes, and shall be set apart by the commission heretofore mentioned as incapable of allotment. There shall also be reserved from allotment a sufficient amount of lands now occupied by churches, schools, parsonages, charitable institutions, and other public buildings for their present actual and necessary use, and no more, not to exceed five acres for each school and one acre for each church and each parsonage, and for such new schools as may be needed; also sufficient land for burial grounds where necessary. When such allotment of the lands of any tribe has been by them completed, said commission shall make full report thereof to the Secretary of the Interior for his approval: *Provided,* That nothing herein contained shall in any way affect any vested legal rights which may have been heretofore granted by Act of Congress, nor be so construed as to confer any additional rights upon any parties claiming under any such Act of Congress: *Provided further,* That whenever it shall appear that any member of a tribe is in possession of lands, his allotment may be made out of the lands in his possession', including his home if the holder so desires: *Provided further,* That if the person to whom an allotment shall have been made shall be declared, upon appeal as herein provided for, by any of the courts of the United States in or for the aforesaid Territory, to have been illegally accorded rights of citizenship, and for that or any other reason declared to be not entitled to any allotment, he shall be ousted and ejected from said lands; that all persons known as intruders who have been paid for their improvements under existing laws and have not surrendered possession thereof who may be found under the provisions of this Act to be entitled to citizenship shall, within ninety days thereafter, refund the amount so paid them, with six per centum interest, to the tribe entitled thereto; and upon their failure so to do said amount shall become a lien upon all improvements owned by such person in such Territory, and may be enforced by such tribe; and unless such person makes such restitution no allotments shall be made to him: *Provided further,* That the lands allotted shall be nontransferable until after full title is acquired and shall be liable for no obligations contracted prior thereto by the allottee, and shall be nontaxable while so held: *Provided further,* That all towns and cities heretofore incorporated or incorporated under the provisions of this Act are hereby authorized to secure, by condemnation or otherwise, all the lands actually necessary for public improvements, regardless of tribal lines; and when the same can not be secured otherwise than by condemnation, then the same may be acquired as provided in sections nine hundred and seven and nine hundred and twelve, inclusive, of Mansfield's Digest of the Statutes of Arkansas.

SEC. 12. That when report of allotments of lands of any tribe shall be made to the Secretary of the Interior, as hereinbefore provided, he shall make a record thereof, and when he shall confirm such allotments the allottees shall remain in peaceable and undisturbed possession thereof, subject to the provisions of this Act.

SEC. 13. That the Secretary of the Interior is hereby authorized and directed from time to time to provide rules and regulations in regard to the leasing of oil, coal, asphalt, and other minerals in said Territory, and all such leases shall be made by the Secretary of the Interior; and any lease for any such minerals otherwise made shall be absolutely void. No lease shall be made or renewed for a longer period than fifteen years, nor cover the mineral in more than six hundred and forty acres of land, · which shall conform as nearly as possible to the surveys. Lessees shall pay on each oil, coal, asphalt, or other mineral claim at the rate of one hundred dollars per annum, in advance, for the first and second years; two hundred dollars per annum, in advance, for the third and fourth years, and five hundred dollars, in advance, for each succeeding year thereafter, as advanced royalty on the mine or claim on which they are made. All such payments shall be a credit on royalty when each said mine is developed and operated and its production is in excess of such guaranteed annual advanced payments; and all lessees must pay said annual advanced payments on each claim, whether developed or undeveloped; and should any lessee neglect or refuse to pay such advanced annual royalty for the period of sixty days after the same becomes due and payable on any lease, the lease on which default is made shall become null and void, and the royalties paid in advance shall then become and be the money and property of the tribe. Where any oil, coal, asphalt, or other mineral is hereafter opened on land allotted, sold, or reserved, the value of the use of the necessary surface for prospecting or mining, and the damage done to the other land and improvements, shall be ascertained under the direction of the Secretary of the Interior and paid to the allottee or owner of the land, by the lessee or party operating the same, before operations begin: *Provided,* That nothing herein contained shall impair the rights of any holder or owner of a leasehold interest in any oil, coal rights, asphalt, or mineral which have been assented to by act of Congress, but all such interest shall continue unimpaired hereby, and shall be assured to such holders or owners by leases from the Secretary of the Interior for the term not exceeding fifteen years, but subject to payment of advance royalties as herein provided, when such leases are not operated, to the rate of royalty on coal mined, and the rules and regulations to be prescribed by the Secretary of the Interior, and preference shall be given to such parties in renewals of such leases: *And provided further,* That when, under the customs and laws heretofore existing and prevailing in the Indian Territory, leases have been made of different groups or parcels of oil, coal, asphalt, or other mineral deposits, and possession has been taken thereunder and improvements made for the development of such oil, coal, asphalt, or other mineral deposits, by lessees or their assigns, which have resulted in the production of oil, coal, asphalt, or other mineral in commercial qualities by such lessees or their assigns, then such parties in possession shall be given preference in the making of new leases, in compliance with the directions of the Secretary of the Interior; and in making new leases due consideration shall be made for the improvements of such lessees, and in all cases of the leasing or renewal of leases of oil, coal, asphalt, and other mineral deposits preference shall be given to parties in possession who have made improvements.   The rate of royalty to be paid by all lessees shall be fixed by the Secretary of the Interior.

Sec. 14. That the inhabitants of any city or town in said Territory having two hundred or more residents therein may proceed, by petition to the United States court in the district in which such city or town is located, to have the same incorporated as provided in chapter twenty-nine of Mansfield's Digest of the Statutes of Arkansas, if not already incorporated thereunder; and the clerk of said court shall record all papers and perform all the acts required of the recorder of the county, or the clerk of the county court, or the secretary of state, necessary for the incorporation of any city or town, as provided in Mansfield's Digest, and such city or town government, when so authorized and organized, shall possess all the powers and exercise all the rights of similar municipalities in said State of Arkansas.   All male inhabitants of such cities and towns over the age of twenty-one years, who are citizens of the United States or of either of said tribes, who have resided therein more than six months next before any election held under this Act, shall be qualified voters at such election.   That mayors of such cities and towns, in addition to their other powers, shall have the same jurisdiction in all civil and criminal cases arising within the corporate limits of such cities and towns as, and coextensive with, United States commissioners in the Indian Territory, and may charge, collect, and retain the same fees as such commissioners now collect and account for to the United States; and the marshal or other executive officer of such city or town may execute all processes issued in the exercise of the jurisdiction hereby conferred, and charge and collect the same fees for similar services, as are allowed to constables under the laws now in force in said Territory.

All elections shall be conducted under the provisions of chapter fifty-six of said digest, entitled "Elections," so far as the same may be applicable; and all inhabitants of such cities and towns, without regard to race, shall be subject to all laws and ordinances of such city or town governments, and shall have equal rights, privileges, and protection therein.   Such city or town governments shall in no case have any authority to impose upon or levy any tax against any lands in said cities or towns until after title is secured from the tribe; but all other property, including all improvements on town lots, which for the purposes of this Act shall be deemed and considered personal property, together with all occupations and privileges, shall be subject to taxation. And the councils of such cities and towns, for the support of the same and for school and other public purposes, may provide by ordinance for the assessment, levy, and collection annually of a tax upon such property, not to exceed in the aggregate two per centum of the assessed value thereof, in manner provided in chapter one hundred and twenty-nine of said digest, entitled "Revenue," and for such purposes may also impose a tax upon occupations and privileges.

Such councils may also establish and maintain free schools in such cities and towns under the provisions of sections sixty-two hundred and fifty-eight to sixty-two hundred and seventy-six, inclusive, of said digest, and may exercise all the powers conferred upon special school districts in cities and towns in the State of Arkansas by the laws of said State when the same are not in conflict with the provisions of this Act.

For the purposes of this section all the laws of said State of Arkansas herein referred to, so far as applicable, are hereby put in force in said Territory; and the United States court therein shall have jurisdiction to enforce the same, and to punish any violation thereof, and the city or town councils shall pass such ordinances as may be necessary for the purpose of making the laws extended over them applicable to them and for carrying the same into effect: *Provided,* That nothing in this Act, or in the laws of the State of Arkansas, shall authorize or permit the sale, or exposure for sale, of any intoxicating liquor in said Territory, or the introduction thereof into said Territory; and it shall be the duty of the district attorneys in said Territory and the officers of such municipalities to prosecute all violators of the laws of the United States relating to the introduction of intoxicating liquors into said Territory, or to their sale, or exposure for sale, therein: *Provided further*, That owners and holders of leases or improvements in any city or town shall be privileged to transfer the same.

SEC. 15. That there shall be a commission in each town for each one of the Chickasaw, Choctaw, Creek, and Cherokee tribes, to consist of one member to be appointed by the executive of the tribe, who shall not be interested in town property, other than his home; one person to be appointed by the Secretary of the Interior, and one member to be selected by the town. And if the executive of the tribe or the town fail to select members as aforesaid, they may be selected and appointed by the Secretary of the Interior.

Said commissions shall cause to be surveyed and laid out town sites where towns with a present population of two hundred or more are located, conforming to the existing survey so far as may be, with proper and necessary streets, alleys, and public grounds, including parks and cemeteries, giving to each town such territory as may be required for its present needs and reasonable prospective growth; and shall prepare correct plats thereof, and file one with the Secretary of the Interior, one with the clerk of the United States court, one with the authorities of the tribe, and one with the town authorities. And all town lots shall be appraised by said commission at their true value, excluding improvements; and separate appraisements shall be made of all improvements thereon; and no such appraisement shall be effective until approved by the Secretary of the Interior, and in case of disagreement by the members of such commission as to the value of any lot, said Secretary may fix the value thereof.

The owner of the improvements upon any town lot, other than fencing, tillage, or temporary buildings, may deposit in the United States Treasury, Saint Louis, Missouri, one-half of such appraised value; ten per centum within two months and fifteen per centum more within six months after notice of appraisement, and the remainder in three equal annual installments thereafter, depositing with the Secretary of the Interior one receipt for each payment, and one with the authorities of the tribe, and such deposit shall be deemed a tender to the tribe of the purchase money for such lot.

If the owner of such improvements on any lot fails to make deposit of the purchase money as aforesaid, then such lot may be sold in the manner herein provided for the sale of unimproved lots; and when the purchaser thereof has complied with the requirements herein for the purchase of improved lots he may, by petition, apply to the United States court within whose jurisdiction the town is located for condemnation and appraisement of such improvements, and petitioner shall, after judgment, deposit the value so fixed with the clerk of the court; and thereupon the defendant shall be required to accept same in full payment for his improvements or remove same from the lot within such time as may be fixed by the court.

All town lots not improved as aforesaid shall belong to the tribe, and shall be in like manner appraised, and, after approval by the Secretary of the Interior, and due notice, sold to the highest bidder at public auction by said commission, but not for less than their appraised value, unless ordered by the Secretary of the Interior; and purchasers may in like manner make deposits of the purchase money with like effect, as in case of improved lots.

The inhabitants of any town may, within one year after the completion of the survey thereof, make such deposit of ten dollars per acre for parks, cemeteries, and other public grounds laid out by said commission with like effect as for improved lots; and such parks and public grounds shall not be used for any purpose until such deposits are made.

The person authorized by the tribe or tribes may execute or deliver to any such purchaser, without expense to him, a deed conveying to him the title to such lands or town lots; and thereafter the purchase money shall become the property of the tribe; and all such moneys shall, when titles to all the lots in the towns belonging to any tribe have been thus perfected, be paid per capita to the members of the tribe: *Provided, however*, That in those town sites designated and laid out under the provisions of this Act where coal leases are now being operated and coal is being mined there shall be reserved from appraisement and sale all lots occupied by houses of miners actually engaged in mining, and only while they are so engaged, and in addition thereto a sufficient amount of land, to be determined by the appraisers, to furnish homes for the men actually engaged in working for the lessees operating said mines and a sufficient amount for all buildings and machinery for mining purposes: *And provided further*, That when the lessees shall cease to operate said mines, then, and in that event, the lots of land so reserved shall be disposed of as provided for in his Act.

Sec. 16. That it shall be unlawful for any person, after the passage of this Act, except as hereinafter provided, to claim, demand, or receive, for his own use or for the use of anyone else, any royalty on oil, coal, asphalt, or other mineral, or on any timber or lumber, or any other kind of property whatsoever, or any rents on any lands or property belonging to any one of said tribes or nations in said Territory, or for anyone to pay to any individual any such royalty or rents or any consideration therefor whatsoever; and all royalties and rents hereafter payable to the tribe shall be paid, under such rules and regulations as may be prescribed by the Secretary of the Interior, into the Treasury of the United States to the credit of the tribe to which they belong: *Provided,* That where any citizen shall be in possession of only such amount of agricultural or grazing lands as would be his just and reasonable share of the lands of his nation or tribe and that to which his wife and minor children are entitled, he may continue to use the same or receive the rents thereon until allotment has been made to him: *Provided further,* That nothing herein contained shall impair the rights of any member of a tribe to dispose of any timber contained on his, her, or their allotment.

Sec. 17. That it shall be unlawful for any citizen of any one of said tribes to inclose or in any manner, by himself or through another, directly or indirectly, to hold possession of any greater amount of lands or other property belonging to any such nation or tribe than that which would be his approximate share of the lands belonging to such nation or tribe and that of his wife and his minor children as per allotment herein provided; and any person found in such possession of lands or other property in excess of his share and that of his family, as aforesaid, or having the same in any manner inclosed, at the expiration of nine months after the passage of this Act, shall be deemed guilty of a misdemeanor.

Sec. 18. That any person convicted of violating any of the provisions of sections sixteen and seventeen of this Act shall be deemed guilty of a misdemeanor and punished by a fine of not less than one hundred dollars, and shall stand committed until such fine and costs are paid (such commitment not to exceed one day for every two dollars of said fine and costs), and shall forfeit possession of any property in question, and each day on which such offense is committed or continues to exist shall be deemed a separate offense. And the United States district attorneys in said Territory are required to see that the provisions of said sections are strictly enforced and they shall at once proceed to dispossess all persons of such excessive holding of lands and to prosecute them for so unlawfully holding the same.

Sec. 19. That no payment of any moneys on any account whatever shall hereafter be made by the United States to any of the tribal governments or to any officer thereof for disbursement, but payments of all sums to members of said tribes shall be made under direction of the Secretary of the Interior by an officer appointed by him; and per capita payments shall be made direct to each individual in lawful money of the United States, and the same shall not be liable to the payment of any previously contracted obligation.

Sec. 20. That the commission hereinbefore named shall have authority to employ, with approval of the Secretary of the Interior, all assistance necessary for the prompt and efficient performance of all duties herein imposed, including competent surveyors to make allotments, and to do any other needed work, and the Secretary of the Interior may detail competent clerks to aid them in the performance of their duties.

Sec. 21. That in making rolls of citizenship of the several tribes, as required by law, the Commission to the Five Civilized Tribes is authorized and directed to take the roll of Cherokee citizens of eighteen hundred and eighty (not including freedmen) as the only roll intended to be confirmed by this and preceding Acts of Congress, and to enroll all persons now living whose names are found on said roll, and all descendants born since the date of said roll to persons whose names are found thereon; and all persons who have been enrolled by the tribal authorities who have heretofore made permanent settlement in the Cherokee Nation whose parents, by reason of their Cherokee blood, have been lawfully admitted to citizenship by the tribal authorities, and who were minors when their parents were so admitted; and they shall investigate the right of all other persons whose names are found on any other rolls and omit all such as may have been placed thereon by fraud or without authority of law, enrolling only such as may have lawful right thereto, and their descendants born since such rolls were made, with such intermarried white persons as may be entitled to citizenship under Cherokee laws.

It shall make a roll of Cherokee freedmen in strict compliance with the decree of the Court of Claims rendered the third day of February, eighteen hundred and ninety-six.

Said commission is authorized and directed to make correct rolls of the citizens by blood of all the other tribes, eliminating from the tribal rolls such names as may have been placed thereon by fraud or without authority of law, enrolling such only as may have lawful right thereto, and their descendants born since such rolls were made, with such intermarried white persons as may be entitled to Choctaw and Chickasaw citizenship under the treaties and the laws of said tribes.

Said commission shall have authority to determine the identity of Choctaw Indians claiming rights in the Choctaw lands under article fourteen of the treaty between the United States and the Choctaw Nation concluded September twenty-seventh, eighteen hundred and thirty, and to that end they may administer oaths, examine witnesses, and perform all other acts necessary thereto and make report to the Secretary of the Interior.

The roll of Creek freedmen made by J. W. Dunn, under authority of the United States, prior to March fourteenth, eighteen hundred and sixty-seven, is hereby confirmed, and said commission is directed to enroll all persons now living whose names are found on said rolls, and all descendants born since the date of said roll to persons whose names are found thereon, with such other persons of African descent as may have been rightfully admitted by the lawful authorities of the Creek Nation.

It shall make a correct roll of all Choctaw freedmen entitled to citizenship under the treaties and laws of the Choctaw Nation, and all their descendants born to them since the date of the treaty.

It shall make a correct roll of Chickasaw freedmen entitled to any rights or benefits under the treaty made in eighteen hundred and sixty-six between the United States and the Choctaw and Chickasaw tribes and their descendants born to them since the date of said treaty and forty acres of land, including their present residences and improvements, shall be allotted to each, to be selected, held, and used by them until their rights under said treaty shall be determined in such manner as shall be hereafter provided by Congress.

The several tribes may, by agreement, determine the right of persons who for any reason may claim citizenship in two or more tribes, and to allotment of lands and distribution of moneys belonging to each tribe; but if no such agreement be made, then such claimant shall be entitled to such rights in one tribe only, and may elect in which tribe he will take such right; but if he fail or refuse to make such selection in due time, he shall be enrolled in the tribe with whom he has resided, and there be given such allotment and distributions, and not elsewhere.

No person shall be enrolled who has not heretofore removed to and in good faith settled in the nation in which he claims citizenship: *Provided, however,* That nothing contained in this Act shall be so construed as to militate against any rights or privileges which the Mississippi Choctaws may have under the laws of or the treaties with the United States.

Said commission shall make such rolls descriptive of the persons thereon, so that they may be thereby identified, and it is authorized to take a census of each of said tribes, or to adopt any other means by them deemed necessary to enable them to make such rolls. They shall have access to all rolls and records of the several tribes, and the United States court in Indian Territory shall have jurisdiction to compel the officers of the tribal governments and custodians of such rolls and records to deliver same to said commission, and on their refusal or failure to do so to punish them as for contempt; as also to require all citizens of said tribes, and persons who should be so enrolled, to appear before said commission for enrollment, at such times and places as may be fixed by said commission, and to enforce obedience of all others concerned, so far as the same may be necessary, to enable said commission to make rolls as herein required, and to punish anyone who may in any manner or by any means obstruct said work.

The rolls so made, when approved by the Secretary of the Interior, shall be final, and the persons whose names are found thereon, with their descendants thereafter born to them, with such persons as may intermarry according to tribal laws, shall alone constitute the several tribes which they represent.

The members of said commission shall, in performing all duties required of them by law, have authority to administer oaths, examine witnesses, and send for persons and papers; and any person who shall willfully and knowingly make any false affidavit or oath to any material fact or matter before any member of said commission, or before any other officer authorized to administer oaths, to any affidavit or other paper to be filed or oath taken before said commission, shall be deemed guilty of perjury, and on conviction thereof shall be punished as for such offense.

Sec. 22. That where members of one tribe, under intercourse laws, usages, or customs, have made homes within the limits and on the lands of another tribe they may retain and take allotment, embracing same under such agreement as may be made between such tribes respecting such settlers; but if no such agreement be made the improvements so made shall be appraised, and the value thereof, including all damages incurred by such settler incident to enforced removal, shall be paid to him immediately upon removal, out of any funds belonging to the tribe, or such settler, if he so desire, may make private sale of his improvements to any citizen of the tribe owning the lands: *Provided*, That he shall not be paid for improvements made on lands in excess of that to which he, his wife, and minor children are entitled to under this Act.

SEC. 23. That all leases of agricultural or grazing land belonging to any tribe made after the first day of January, eighteen hundred and ninety-eight, by the tribe or any member thereof shall be absolutely void, and all such grazing leases made prior to said date shall terminate on the first day of April, eighteen hundred and ninety-nine, and all such agricultural leases shall terminate on January first, nineteen hundred: but this shall not prevent individuals from leasing their allotments when made to them as provided in this Act, nor from occupying or renting their proportionate shares of the tribal lands until the allotments herein provided for are made.

SEC. 24. That all moneys paid into the United States Treasury at Saint Louis, Missouri, under provisions of this Act shall be placed to the credit of the tribe to which they belong; and the assistant United States treasurer shall give triplicate receipts therefor to the depositor.

SEC. 25. That before any allotment shall be made of lands in the Cherokee Nation, there shall be segregated therefrom by the commission heretofore mentioned, in separate allotments or otherwise, the one hundred and fifty-seven thousand six hundred acres purchased by the Delaware tribe of Indians from the Cherokee Nation under agreement of April eighth, eighteen hundred and sixty-seven, subject to the judicial determination of the rights of said descendants and the Cherokee Nation under said agreement. That the Delaware Indians residing in the Cherokee Nation are hereby authorized and empowered to bring suit in the Court of Claims of the United States, within sixty days after the passage of this Act, against the Cherokee Nation, for the purpose of determining the rights of said Delaware Indians in and to the lands and funds of said nation under their contract and agreement with the Cherokee Nation dated April eighth, eighteen hundred and sixty-seven; or the Cherokee Nation may bring a like suit against said Delaware Indians; and jurisdiction is conferred on said court to adjudicate and fully determine the same, with right of appeal to either party to the Supreme Court of the United States.

SEC. 26. That on and after the passage of this Act the laws of the various tribes or nations of Indians shall not be enforced at law or in equity by the courts of the United States in the Indian Territory.

SEC. 27. That the Secretary of the Interior is authorized to locate one Indian inspector in Indian Territory, who may, under his authority and direction, perform any duties required of the Secretary of the Interior by law, relating to affairs therein.

SEC. 28. That on the first day of July, eighteen hundred and ninety-eight, all tribal courts in Indian Territory shall be abolished, and no officer of said courts shall thereafter have any authority whatever to do or perform any act theretofore authorized by any law in connection with said courts, or to receive any pay for same; and all civil and criminal causes then pending in any such court shall be transferred to the United States court in said Territory by filing with the clerk of the court the original papers in the suit: *Provided*, That this section shall not be in force as to the Chickasaw, Choctaw, and Creek tribes or nations until the first day of October, eighteen hundred and ninety-eight.

SEC. 29. That the agreement made by the Commission to the Five Civilized Tribes with commissions representing the Choctaw and Chickasaw tribes of Indians on the twenty-third day of April, eighteen hundred and ninety-seven, as herein amended, is hereby ratified and confirmed, and the same shall be of full force and effect if ratified before the first day of December, eighteen hundred and ninety-eight, by a majority of the whole number of votes cast by the members of said tribes at an election held for that purpose; and the executives of said tribes are hereby authorized and directed to make public proclamation that said agreement shall be voted on at the next general election, or at any special election to be called by such executive for the purpose of voting on said agreement; and at the election held for such purpose all male members of each of said tribes qualified to vote under his tribal laws shall have the right to vote at the election precinct most convenient to his residence, whether the same be within the bounds of his tribe or not: *Provided*, That no person whose right to citizenship in either of said tribes or nations is now contested in original or appellate proceedings before any United States court shall be permitted to vote at said election: *Provided further*, That the votes cast in both said tribes or nations shall be forthwith returned duly certified by the precinct officers to the national secretaries of said tribes or nations, and shall be presented by said national secretaries to a board of commissioners consisting of the principal chief and national secretary of the Chocktaw Nation, the governor and national secretary of the Chickasaw Nation, and a member of the Commission to the Five Civilized Tribes, to be designated by the chairman of said commission; and said board shall meet without delay at Atoka, in the Indian Territory, and canvass and count said votes and make proclamation of the result; and if said agreement as amended be so ratified, the provisions of this Act shall then only apply to said tribes where the same do not conflict with the provisions of said agreement; but the provisions of said agreement, if so ratified, shall not in any manner affect the provisions of section fourteen of this Act, which said amended agreement is as follows:

This agreement, by and between the Government of the United States, of the first part, entered into in its behalf by the Commission to the Five Civilized Tribes, Henry L. Dawes, Frank C. Armstrong, Archibald S. McKennon, Thomas B. Cabaniss, and Alexander B. Montgomery, duly appointed and authorized thereunto, and the governments of the Choctaw and Chickasaw tribes or nations of Indians in the Indian Territory, respectively, of the second part, entered into in behalf of such Choctaw and Chickasaw governments, duly appointed and authorized thereunto, viz: Green McCurtain, J. S. Standley, N. B. Ainsworth, Ben Hampton, Wesley Anderson, Amos Henry, D. C. Garland, and A. S. Williams, in behalf of the Choctaw Tribe or Nation, and R. M. Harris, I. O. Lewis, Holmes Colbert, P. S. Mosely, M. V. Cheadle, R. L. Murray, William Perry, A. H. Colbert, and R. L. Boyd, in behalf of the Chickasaw Tribe or Nation.

ALLOTMENT OF LANDS.

Witnesseth, That in consideration of the mutual undertakings, herein contained, it is agreed as follows:

That all the lands within the Indian Territory belonging to the Choctaw and Chickasaw Indians shall be allotted to the members of said tribes so as to give to each member of these tribes so far as possible a fair and equal share thereof, considering the character and fertility of the soil and the location and value of the lands.

That all the lands set apart for town sites, and the strip of land lying between the city of Fort Smith, Arkansas, and the Arkansas and Poteau rivers, extending up said river to the mouth of Mill Creek; and six hundred and forty acres each, to include the buildings now occupied by the Jones Academy, Tushkahoma Female Seminary, Wheelock Orphan Seminary, and Armstrong Orphan Academy, and ten acres for the capital building of the Choctaw Nation; one hundred and sixty acres each, immediately contiguous to and including the buildings known as Bloomfield Academy, Lebanon Orphan Home, Harley Institute, Rock Academy, and Collins Institute, and five acres for the capitol building in the Chickasaw Nation, and the use of one acre of land for each church house now erected outside of the towns, and eighty acres of land each for J. S. Murrow, H. R. Schermerhorn, and the widow of R. S. Bell, who have been laboring as missionaries in the Choctaw and Chickasaw nations since the year eighteen hundred and sixty-six, with the same conditions and limitations as apply to lands allotted to the members of the Choctaw and Chickasaw nations, and to be located on lands not occupied by a Choctaw or a Chickasaw, and a reasonable amount of land, to be determined by the town-site commission, to include all court-houses and jails and other public buildings not hereinbefore provided for, shall be exempted from division. And all coal and asphalt in or under the lands allotted and reserved from allotment shall be reserved for the sole use of the members of the Choctaw and Chickasaw tribes, exclusive of freedmen: *Provided*, That where any coal or asphalt is hereafter opened on land allotted, sold, or reserved, the value of the use of the necessary surface for prospecting or mining, and the damage done to the other land and improvements, shall be ascertained under the direction of the Secretary of the Interior and paid to the allottee or owner of the land by the lessee or party operating the same, before operations begin. That in order to such equal division, the lands of the Choctaws and Chickasaws shall be graded and appraised so as to give to each member, so far as possible, an equal value of the land: *Provided further*, That the Commission to the Five Civilized Tribes shall make a correct roll of Chickasaw freedmen entitled to any rights or benefits under the treaty made in eighteen hundred and sixty-six between the United States and the Choctaw and Chickasaw tribes and their descendants born to them since the date of said treaty, and forty acres of land, including their present residences and improvements, shall be allotted to each, to be selected, held, and used by them until their rights under said treaty shall be determined, in such manner as shall hereafter be provided by act of Congress.

That the lands allotted to the Choctaw and Chickasaw freedmen are to be deducted from the portion to be allotted under this agreement to the members of the Choctaw and Chickasaw tribe, so as to reduce the allotment to the Choctaws and Chickasaws by the value of the same.

That the said Choctaw and Chickasaw freedmen who may be entitled to allotments of forty acres each shall be entitled each to land equal in value to forty acres of the average land of the two nations.

That in the appraisement of the lands to be allotted the Choctaw and Chickasaw tribes shall each have a representative, to be appointed by their respective executives, to cooperate with the commission to the Five Civilized Tribes, or any one making appraisements under the direction of the Secretary of the Interior in grading and appraising the lands preparatory to allotment. And the land shall be valued in the appraisement as if in its original condition, excluding the improvements thereon.

That the appraisement and allotment shall be made under the direction of the Secretary of the Interior, and shall begin as soon as the progress of the surveys, now being made by the United States Government, will admit.

That each member of the Choctaw and Chickasaw tribes, including Choctaw and Chickasaw freedmen, shall, where it is possible, have the right to take his allotment on land, the improvements on which belong to him, and such improvements shall not be estimated in the value of his allotment. In the case of minor children, allotments shall be selected for them by their father, mother, guardian, or the administrator having charge of their estate, preference being given in the order named, and shall not be sold during his minority. Allotments shall be selected for prisoners, convicts, and incompetents by some suitable person akin to them, and due care taken that all persons entitled thereto have allotments made to them.

All the lands allotted shall be nontaxable while the title remains in the original allottee, but not to exceed twenty-one years from date of patent, and each allottee shall select from his allotment a homestead of one hundred and sixty acres, for which he shall have a separate patent, and which shall be inalienable for twenty-one years from date of patent. This provision shall also apply to the Choctaw and Chickasaw freedman to the extent of his allotment. Selections for homesteads for minors to be made as provided herein in case of allotment, and the remainder of the lands allotted to said members shall be alienable for a price to be actually paid, and to include no former indebtedness or obligation—one-fourth of said remainder in one year, one-fourth in three years, and the balance of said alienable lands in five years from the date of the patent.

That all contracts looking to the sale or incumbrance in any way of the land of an allottee, except the sale hereinbefore provided, shall be null and void. No allottee shall lease his allotment, or any portion thereof, for a longer period than five years, and then without the privilege of renewal. Every lease which is not evidenced by writing, setting out specifically the terms thereof, or which is not recorded in the clerk's office of the United States court for the district in which the land is located, within three months after the date of its execution, shall be void, and the purchaser or lessee shall acquire no rights whatever by an entry or holding thereunder. And no such lease or any sale shall be valid as against the allottee unless providing to him a reasonable compensation for the lands sold or leased.

That all controversies arising between the members of said tribes as to their right to have certain lands allotted to them shall be settled by the commission making the allotments.

That the United States shall put each allottee in possession of his allotment and remove all persons therefrom objectionable to the allottee.

That the United States shall survey and definitely mark and locate the ninety-eighth (98th) meridian of west longitude between Red and Canadian rivers before allotment of the lands herein provided for shall begin.

MEMBERS' TITLES TO LANDS.

That as soon as practicable, after the completion of said allotments, the principal chief of the Choctaw Nation and the governor of the Chickasaw Nation shall jointly execute, under their hands and the seals of the respective nations, and deliver to each of the said allottees patents conveying to him all the right, title, and interest of the Choctaws and Chickasaws in and to the land which shall have been allotted to him in conformity with the requirements of this agreement, excepting all coal and asphalt in or under said land. Said patents shall be framed in accordance with the provisions of this agreement, and shall embrace the land allotted to such patentee and no other land, and the acceptance of his patents by such allottee shall be operative as an assent on his part to the allotment and conveyance of all the lands of the Choctaws and Chickasaws in accordance with the provisions of this agreement, and as a relinquishment of all his right, title, and interest in and to any and all parts hereof, except the land embraced in said patents, except also his interest in the proceeds of all lands, coal, and asphalt herein excepted from allotment.

That the United States shall provide by law for proper records of land titles in the territory occupied by the Choctaw and Chickasaw tribes.

RAILROADS.

The rights of way for railroads through the Choctaw and Chickasaw nations to be surveyed and set apart and platted to conform to the respective acts of Congress granting the same in cases where said rights of way are defined by such acts of Congress, but in cases where the acts of Congress do not define the same then Congress is memorialized to definitely fix the width of said rights of way for station grounds and between stations, so that railroads now constructed through said nations shall have, as near as possible, uniform rights of way; and Congress is also requested to fix uniform rates of fare and freight for all railroads through the Choctaw and Chickasaw nations; branch railroads now constructed and not built according to acts of Congress to pay the same rates for rights of way and station grounds as main lines.

TOWN SITES.

It is further agreed that there shall be appointed a commission for each of the two nations. Each commission shall consist of one member, to be appointed by the executive of the tribe for which said commission is to act, who shall not be interested in town property other than his home, and one to be appointed by the President of the United States. Each of said commissions shall lay out town sites, to be restricted as far as possible to their present limits, where towns are now located in the nation or which said commission is appointed. Said commission shall have prepared correct and proper plats of each town, and file one in the clerk's office of the United States district court for the district in which the town is located, and one with the principal chief or governor of the nation in which the town is located, and one with the Secretary of the Interior, be approved by him before the same shall take effect. When said towns are so laid out, each lot on which permanent, substantial, and valuable improvements, other than fences, tillage, and temporary houses, have been made, shall be valued by the commission provided for the nation in which the town is located at the price a fee-simple title to the same would bring in the market at the time the valuation is made, but not to include in such value the improvements thereon. The owner of the improvements on each lot shall have the right to buy one residence and one business lot at fifty per centum of the appraised value of such improved property, and the remainder of such improved property at sixty-two and one-half per centum of the said market value within sixty days from date of notice served on him that such lot is for sale, and if he purchases the same he shall, within ten days from his purchase, pay into the Treasury of the United States one-fourth of the purchase price, and the balance in three equal annual installments, and when the entire sum is paid shall be entitled to a patent for the same. In case the two members of the commission fail to agree as to the market value of any lot, or the limit or extent of said town, either of said commissioners may report any such disagreement to the judge of the district in which such town is located, who shall appoint a third member to act with said commission, who is not interested in town lots, who shall act with them to determine said value.

If such owner of the improvements on any lot fails within sixty days to purchase and make the first payment on same, such lot, with the improvements thereon, shall be sold at public auction to the highest bidder, under the direction of the aforesaid commission, and the purchaser at such sale shall pay to the owner of the improvements the price for which said lot shall be sold, less sixty-two and one-half per cent of said appraised value of the lot, and shall pay the sixty-two and one-half per cent of said appraised value into United States Treasury, under regulations to be established by the Secretary of the Interior, in four installments, as hereinbefore provided. The commission shall have the right to reject any bid on such lot which they consider below its value.

All lots not so appraised shall be sold from time to time at public auction (after proper advertisement) by the commission for the nation in which the town is located, as may seem for the best interest of the nations and the proper development of each town, the purchase price to be paid in four installments as hereinbefore provided for improved lots. The commission shall have the right to reject any bid for such lots which they consider below its value.

All the payments herein provided for shall be made under the direction of the Secretary of the Interior into the United States Treasury, a failure of sixty days to make any one payment to be a forfeiture of all payments made and all rights under the contract: *Provided*, That the purchaser of any lot shall have the option of paying the entire price of the lot before the same is due.

No tax shall be assessed by any town government against any town lot unsold by the commission, and no tax levied against a lot sold, as herein provided, shall constitute a lien on same till the purchase price thereof has been fully paid to the nation.

The money paid into the United States Treasury for the sale of all town lots shall be for the benefit of the members of the Choctaw and Chickasaw tribes (freedmen excepted), and at the end of one year from the ratification of this agreement, and at the end of each year thereafter, the funds so accumulated shall be divided and paid to the Choctaws and Chickasaws (freedmen excepted), each member of the two tribes to receive an equal portion thereof.

That no law or ordinance shall be passed by any town which interferes with the enforcement of or is in conflict with the laws of the United States in force in said Territory, and all persons in such towns shall be subject to said laws, and the United States agrees to maintain strict laws in the territory of the Choctaw and Chickasaw tribes against the introduction, sale, barter, or giving away of liquors and intoxicants of any kind or quality.

That said commission shall be authorized to locate, within a suitable distance from each town site, not to exceed five acres to be used as a cemetery, and when any town has paid into the United States Treasury, to be part of the fund arising from the sale of town lots, ten dollars per acre therefor, such town shall be entitled to a patent for the same as herein provided for titles to allottees, and shall dispose of same at reasonable prices in suitable lots for burial purposes, the proceeds derived from such sales to be applied by the town government to the proper improvement and care of said cemetery.

That no charge or claim shall be made against the Choctaw or Chickasaw tribes by the United States for the expenses of surveying and platting the lands and town sites, or for grading, appraising, and allotting the lands, or for appraising and disposing of the town lots as herein provided.

That the land adjacent to Fort Smith and lands for court-houses, jails, and other public purposes, excepted from allotment shall be disposed of in the same manner and for the same purposes as provided for town lots herein, but not till the Choctaw and Chickasaw councils shall direct such disposition to be made thereof, and said land adjacent thereto shall be placed under the jurisdiction of the city of Fort Smith. Arkansas, for police purposes.

There shall be set apart and exempted from appraisement and sale in the towns, lots upon which churches and parsonages are now built and occupied, not to exceed fifty feet front and one hundred feet deep for each church or parsonage: *Provided*, That such lots shall only be used for churches and parsonages, and when they ceased to be used shall revert to the members of the tribes to be disposed of as other town lots: *Provided further*, That these lots may be sold by the churches for which they are set apart if the purchase money therefor is invested in other lot or lots in the same town, to be used for the same purpose and with the same conditions and limitations.

It is agreed that all the coal and asphalt within the limits of the Choctaw and Chickasaw nations shall remain and be the common property of the members of the Choctaw and Chickasaw tribes (freedmen excepted), so that each and every member shall have an equal and undivided interest in the whole; and no patent provided for in this agreement shall convey any title thereto. The revenues from coal and asphalt, or so much as shall be necessary, shall be used for the education of the children of Indian blood of the members of said tribes. Such coal and asphalt mines as are now in operation, and all others which may hereafter be leased and operated, shall be under the supervision and control of two trustees, who shall be appointed by the President of the United States, one on the recommendation of the Principal Chief of the Choctaw Nation, who shall be a Choctaw by blood, whose term shall be for four years, and one on the recommendation of the Governor of the Chickasaw Nation, who shall be a Chickasaw by blood, whose term shall be for two years; after which the term of appointees shall be four years. · Said trustees or either of them, may, at any time, be removed by the President of the United States for good cause shown. They shall each give bond for the faithful performance of their duties, under such rules as may be prescribed by the Secretary of the Interior. Their salaries shall be fixed and paid by their respective nations, each of whom shall make full report of all his acts to the Secretary of the Interior quarterly. All such acts shall be subject to the approval of said Secretary.

All coal and asphalt mines in the two nations, whether now developed, or to be *hereafter* developed, shall be operated, and the royalties therefrom paid into the

Treasury of the United States, and shall be drawn therefrom under such rules and regulations as shall be prescribed by the Secretary of the Interior.

All contracts made by the National Agents of the Choctaw and Chickasaw nations for operating coal and asphalt, with any person or corporation, which were, on April twenty-third, eighteen hundred and ninety-seven, being operated in good faith are hereby ratified and confirmed, and the lessee shall have the right to renew the same when they expire, subject to all the provisions of this Act.

All agreements heretofore made by any person or corporation with any member or members of the Choctaw or Chickasaw nations, the object of which was to obtain such member or members' permission to operate coal or asphalt, are hereby declared void: *Provided*, That nothing herein contained shall impair the rights of any holder or owner of a leasehold interest in any oil, coal rights, asphalt, or mineral which have been assented to by act of Congress, but all such interests shall continue unimpaired hereby and shall be assured by new leases from such trustees of coal or asphalt claims described therein, by application to the trustees within six months after the ratification of this agreement, subject, however, to payment of advance royalties herein provided for.

All leases under this agreement shall include the coal or asphaltum, or other mineral, as the case may be, in or under nine hundred and sixty acres, which shall be in a square as nearly as possible, and shall be for thirty years. The royalty on coal shall be fifteen cents per ton of two thousand pounds on all coal mined, payable on the 25th day of the month next succeeding that in which it is mined. Royalty on asphalt shall be sixty cents per ton, payable same as coal: *Provided*, That the Secretary of the Interior may reduce or advance royalties on coal and asphalt when he deems it for the best interests of the Choctaws and Chickasaws to do so. No royalties shall be paid except into the United States Treasury as herein provided.

All lessees shall pay on each coal or asphalt claim at the rate of one hundred dollars per annum, in advance, for the first and second years; two hundred dollars per annum, in advance, for the third and fourth years; and five hundred dollars for each succeeding year thereafter. All such payments shall be treated as advanced royalty on the mine or claim on which they are made, and shall be a credit as royalty when each said mine is developed and operated, and its production is in excess of such guaranteed annual advance payments, and all persons having coal leases must pay said annual advanced payments on each claim whether developed or undeveloped: *Provided, however*, That should any lessee neglect or refuse to pay such advanced annual royalty for the period of sixty days after the same becomes due and payable on any lease, the lease on which default is made shall become null and void, and the royalties paid in advance thereon shall then become and be the money and property of the Choctaw and Chickasaw nations.

In surface, the use of which is reserved to present coal operators, shall be included such lots in towns as are occupied by lessees' houses—either occupied by said lessees' employees, or as offices or warehouses: *Provided, however*, That in those town sites designated and laid out under the provision of this agreement where coal leases are now being operated and coal is being mined, there shall be reserved from appraisement and sale all lots occupied by houses of miners actually engaged in mining, and only while they are so engaged, and in addition thereto a sufficient amount of land, to be determined by the town-site board of appraisers, to furnish homes for the men actually engaged in working for the lessees operating said mines, and a sufficient amount for all buildings and machinery for mining purposes: *And provided further*, That when the lessees shall cease to operate said mines, then and in that event the lots of land so reserved shall be disposed of by the coal trustees for the benefit of the Choctaw and Chickasaw tribes.

That whenever the members of the Choctaw and Chickasaw tribes shall be required to pay taxes for the support of schools, then the fund arising from such royalties shall be disposed of for the equal benefit of their members (freedmen excepted) in such manner as the tribes may direct.

It is further agreed that the United States courts now existing, or that may hereafter be created, in the Indian Territory shall have exclusive jurisdiction of all controversies growing out of the titles, ownership, occupation, possession, or use of real estate, coal, and asphalt in the territory occupied by the Choctaw and Chickasaw tribes: and of all persons charged with homicide, embezzlement, bribery, and embracery, breaches, or disturbances of the peace, and carrying weapons, hereafter committed in the territory of said tribes, without reference to the race or citizenship of the person or persons charged with such crime; and any citizen or officer of the Choctaw or Chickasaw nations charged with such crime shall be tried, and, if convicted, punished as though he were citizen or officer of the United States.

And sections sixteen hundred and thirty-six to sixteen hundred and forty-four, inclusive, entitled "Embezzlement," and sections seventeen hundred and eleven to seventeen hundred and eighteen, inclusive, entitled "Bribery and Embracery," of Mansfield's Digest of the laws of Arkansas, are hereby extended over and put in force in the Choctaw and Chickasaw nations; and the word "officer," where the same appears in said laws, shall include all officers of the Choctaw and Chickasaw governments; and the fifteenth section of the Act of Congress, entitled "An Act to establish United States courts in the Indian Territory, and for other purposes," approved March first, eighteen hundred and eighty-nine, limiting jurors to citizens of the United States, shall be held not to apply to United States courts in the Indian Territory held within the limits of the Choctaw and Chickasaw nations; and all members of the Choctaw and Chickasaw tribes, otherwise qualified, shall be competent jurors in said courts: *Provided*, That whenever a member of the Choctaw and Chickasaw nations is indicted for homicide, he may, within thirty days after such indictment and his arrest thereon, and before the same is reached for trial, file with the clerk of the court in which he is indicted, his affidavit that he can not get a fair trial in said court; and it thereupon shall be the duty of the judge of said court to order a change of venue in such case to the United States district court for the western district of Arkansas, at Fort Smith, Arkansas, or to the United States district court for the eastern district of Texas, at Paris, Texas, always selecting the court that in his judgment is nearest or most convenient to the place where the crime charged in the indictment is supposed to have been committed, which courts shall have jurisdiction to try the case; and in all said civil suits said courts shall have full equity powers; and whenever it shall appear to said court, at any stage in the hearing of any case, that the tribe is in any way interested in the subject-matter in controversy, it shall have power to summon in said tribe and make the same a party to the suit and proceed therein in all respects as if such tribe were an original party thereto; but in no case shall suit be instituted against the tribal government without its consent.

It is further agreed that no act, ordinance, or resolution of the council of either the Choctaw or Chickasaw tribes, in any manner affecting the land of the tribe, or of the individuals, after allotment, or the moneys or other property of the tribe or citizens thereof (except appropriations for the regular and necessary expenses of the government of the respective tribes), or the rights of any persons to employ any kind of labor, or the rights of any persons who have taken or may take the oath of allegiance to the United States, shall be of any validity until approved by the President of the United States. When such acts, ordinances, or resolutions passed by the council of either of said tribes shall be approved by the governor thereof, then it shall be the duty of the national secretary of said tribe to forward them to the President of the United States, duly certified and sealed, who shall, within thirty days after their reception, approve or disapprove the same. Said acts, ordinances, or resolutions, when so approved, shall be published in at least two newspapers having a bona fide circulation in the tribe to be affected thereby, and when disapproved shall be returned to the tribe enacting the same.

It is further agreed, in view of the modification of legislative authority and judicial jurisdiction herein provided, and the necessity of the continuance of the tribal governments so modified, in order to carry out the requirements of this agreement, that the same shall continue for the period of eight years from the fourth day of March, eighteen hundred and ninety-eight. This stipulation is made in the belief that the tribal governments so modified will prove so satisfactory that there will be no need or desire for further change till the lands now occupied by the Five Civilized Tribes shall, in the opinion of Congress, be prepared for admission as a State to the Union. But this provision shall not be construed to be in any respect an abdication by Congress of power at any time to make needful rules and regulations respecting said tribes.

That all per capita payments hereafter made to the members of the Choctaw or Chickasaw nations shall be paid directly to each individual member by a bonded officer of the United States, under the direction of the Secretary of the Interior, which officer shall be required to give strict account for such disbursements to said Secretary.

That the following sum be, and is hereby, appropriated, out of any money in the Treasury not otherwise appropriated, for fulfilling treaty stipulations with the Chickasaw Nation of Indians, namely:

For arrears of interest, at five per centum per annum, from December thirty-first, eighteen hundred and forty, to June thirtieth, eighteen hundred and eighty-nine, on one hundred and eighty-four thousand one hundred and forty-three dollars and nine cents of the trust fund of the Chickasaw Nation erroneously dropped from the books of the United States prior to December thirty-first, eighteen hundred and forty, and *restored* December twenty-seventh, eighteen hundred and eighty-seven, by the award

:retary of the Interior, under the fourth article of the treaty of June twenty-
ighteen hundred and fifty-two, and for arrears of interest at five per centum
n, from March eleventh, eighteen hundred and fifty, to March third, eighteen
and ninety, on fifty-six thousand and twenty-one dollars and forty-nine
he trust fund of the Chickasaw Nation erroneously dropped from the books
ited States March eleventh, eighteen hundred and fifty, and restored Decem-
:y-seventh, eighteen hundred and eighty-seven, by the award of the Secre-
le Interior, under the fourth article of the treaty of June twenty-second,
hundred and fifty-two, five hundred and fifty-eight thousand five hundred
ty dollars and fifty-four cents, to be placed to the credit of the Chickasaw
ith the fund to which it properly belongs: *Provided,* That if there be any
' fees to be paid out of same, on contract heretofore made and duly approved
cretary of the interior, the same is authorized to be paid by him.
:ther agreed that the final decision of the courts of the United States in the
e Choctaw Nation and the Chickasaw Nation, against the United States and
ita and affiliated bands of Indians, now pending, when made, shall be con-
the basis of settlement as between the United States and said Choctaw and
w nations for the remaining lands in what is known as the "Leased District,"
he land lying between the ninety-eighth and one hundredth degrees of west
and between the Red and Canadian rivers, leased to the United States by
' of eighteen hundred and fifty-five, except that portion called the Cheyenne
ahoe country, heretofore acquired by the United States, and all final judg-
idered against said nations in any of the courts of the United States in favor
ited States or any citizen thereof shall first be paid out of any sum hereafter
: said Indians for any interest they may have in the so-called leased district.
rther agreed that all of the funds invested, in lieu of investment, treaty
otherwise, now held by the United States in trust for the Choctaw and
w tribes, shall be capitalized within one year after the tribal governments
e, so far as the same may legally be done, and be appropriated and paid, by
:er of the United States appointed for the purpose, to the Choctaws and
ws (freedmen excepted) per capita, to aid and assist them in improving their
d lands.
:ther agreed that the Choctaws and Chickasaws, when their tribal govern-
ise, shall become possessed of all the rights and privileges of citizens of the
ates.

ORPHAN LANDS.

:ther agreed that the Choctaw orphan lands in the State of Mississippi, yet
lall be taken by the United States at one dollar and twenty-five cents ($1.25)
and the proceeds placed to the credit of the Choctaw orphan fund in the
of the United States, the number of acres to be determined by the General
ce.
ess whereof the said commissioners do hereunto affix their names at Atoka,
rritory, this the twenty-third day of April, eighteen hundred and ninety-

GREEN McCURTAIN, *Principal Chief.*	R. M. HARRIS, *Governor.*
J. S. STANDLEY,	ISAAC O. LEWIS,
N. B. AINSWORTH,	HOLMES COLBERT,
BEN HAMPTON,	ROBERT L. MURRAY,
WESLEY ANDERSON,	WILLIAM PERRY,
AMOS HENRY,	R. L. BOYD,
D. C. GARLAND,	*Chickasaw Commission.*
Choctaw Commission.	

FRANK C. ARMSTRONG,
Acting Chairman.

ARCHIBALD S. McKENNON,
THOMAS B. CABANISS,
ALEXANDER B. MONTGOMERY,
Commission to the Five Civilized Tribes.

H. M. JACOWAY, Jr.,
Secretary, Five Tribes Commission.

That the agreement made by the Commission to the Five Civilized Tribes
:ommission representing the Muscogee (or Creek) tribe of Indians on the
venth day of September, eighteen hundred and ninety-seven, as herein

amended, is hereby ratified and confirmed, and the same shall be of full force and effect if ratified before the first day of December, eighteen hundred and ninety-eight, by a majority of the votes cast by the members of said tribe at an election to be held for that purpose; and the executive of said tribe is authorized and directed to make public proclamation that said agreement shall be voted on at the next general election, to be called by such executive for the purpose of voting on said agreement; and if said agreement as amended be so ratified, the provisions of this Act shall then only apply to said tribe where the same do not conflict with the provisions of said agreement; but the provisions of said agreement, if so ratified, shall not in any manner affect the provisions of section fourteen of this Act, which said amended agreement is as follows:

This agreement, by and between the Government of the United States of the first part, entered into in its behalf by the Commission to the Five Civilized Tribes, Henry L. Dawes, Frank C. Armstrong, Archibald S. McKennon, Alexander B. Montgomery, and Tams Bixby, duly appointed and authorized thereunto, and the government of the Muscogee or Creek Nation in the Indian Territory of the second part, entered into in behalf of such Muscogee or Creek government, by its commission, duly appointed and authorized thereunto, viz, Pleasant Porter, Joseph Mingo, David N. Hodge, George A. Alexander, Roland Brown, William A. Sapulpa, and Conchartie Micco,

Witnesseth, That in consideration of the mutual undertakings herein contained, it is agreed as follows:

GENERAL ALLOTMENT OF LAND.

1. There shall be allotted out of the lands owned by the Muscogee or Creek Indians in the Indian Territory to each citizen of said nation one hundred and sixty acres of land. Each citizen shall have the right, so far as possible, to take his one hundred and sixty acres so as to include the improvements which belong to him, but such improvements shall not be estimated in the value fixed on his allotment, provided any citizen may take any land not already selected by another; but if such land, under actual cultivation, has on it any lawful improvements, he shall pay the owner of said improvements for same, the value to be fixed by the commission appraising the land. In the case of a minor child, allotment shall be selected for him by his father, mother, guardian, or the administrator having charge of his estate, preference being given in the order named, and shall not be sold during his minority. Allotments shall be selected for prisoners, convicts, and incompetents by some suitable person akin to them, and due care shall be taken that all persons entitled thereto shall have allotments made to them.

2. Each allotment shall be appraised at what would be its present value, if unimproved, considering the fertility of the soil and its location, but excluding the improvements, and each allottee shall be charged with the value of his allotment in the future distribution of any funds of the nation arising from any source whatever, so that each member of the nation shall be made equal in the distribution of the lands and moneys belonging to the nation, provided that the minimum valuation to be placed upon any land in the said nation shall be one dollar and twenty-five cents ($1.25) per acre.

3. In the appraisement of the said allotment, said nation may have a representative to cooperate with a commission, or a United States officer, designated by the President of the United States, to make the appraisement. Appraisements and allotments shall be made under the direction of the Secretary of the Interior, and begin as soon as an authenticated roll of the citizens of the said nation has been made. All citizens of said nation, from and after the passage of this Act, shall be entitled to select from the lands of said nation an amount equal to one hundred and sixty acres, and use and occupy the same until the allotments therein provided are made.

4. All controversies arising between the members of said nation as to their rights to have certain lands allotted to them shall be settled by the commission making allotments.

5. The United States shall put each allottee in unrestricted possession of his allotment and remove therefrom all persons objectionable to the allottee.

6. The excess of lands after allotment is completed, all funds derived from town sites, and all other funds accruing under the provisions of this agreement shall be used for the purpose of equalizing allotments, valued as herein provided, and if the same be found insufficient for such purpose, the deficiency shall be supplied from other funds of the nation upon dissolution of its tribal relations with the United States, in accordance with the purposes and intent of this agreement.

7. The residue of the lands, with the improvements thereon, if any there be, shall be appraised separately, under the direction of the Secretary of the Interior, and

17. The owner of the improvements on any lot shall have the right to buy the same at fifty per centum of the value within sixty days from the date of notice served on him that such lot is for sale, and if he purchase the same he shall, within ten days from his purchase, pay into the Treasury of the United States one-fourth of the purchase price and the balance in three equal annual payments, and when the entire sum is paid he shall be entitled to a patent for the same, to be made as herein provided for patents to allottees.

18. In any case where the two members of the commission fail to agree as to the value of any lot they shall select a third person, who shall be a citizen of said nation and who is not interested in town lots, who shall act with them to determine said value.

19. If the owner of the improvements on any lot fail within sixty days to purchase and make the first payment on the same, such lot, with the improvements thereon (said lot and improvements thereon having been theretofore properly appraised), shall be sold at public auction to the highest bidder, under the direction of said commission, at a price not less than the value of the lot and improvements, and the purchaser at such sale shall pay to the owner of the improvements the price for which said lot and the improvements thereon shall be sold, less fifty per centum of the said appraised value of the lot, and shall pay fifty per centum of said appraised value of the lot into the United States Treasury, under regulations to be established by the Secretary of the Interior, in four installments, as hereinbefore provided. Said commission shall have the right to reject a bid on any lot and the improvements thereon which it may consider below the real value.

20. All lots not having improvements thereon and not so appraised shall be sold by the commission from time to time at public auction, after proper advertisement, as may seem for the best interest of the said nation and the proper development of each town, the purchase price to be paid in four installments, as hereinbefore provided for improved lots.

21. All citizens or persons who have purchased the right of occupancy from parties in legal possession prior to the date of signing this agreement, holding lots or tracts of ground in towns, shall have the first right to purchase said lots or tracts upon the same terms and conditions as is provided for improved lots, provided said lots or tracts shall have been theretofore properly appraised, as hereinbefore provided for improved lots.

22. Said commission shall have the right to reject any bid for such lots or tracts which is considered by said commission below the fair value of the same.

23. Failure to make any one of the payments as heretofore provided for a period of sixty days shall work a forfeiture of all payments made and all rights under the contract; provided that the purchaser of any lot may pay full price before the same is due.

24. No tax shall be assessed by any town government against any town lot unsold by the commission, and no tax levied against a lot sold as herein provided shall constitute a lien on the same until the purchase price thereof has been fully paid.

25. No law or ordinance shall be passed by any town which interferes with the enforcement of or is in conflict with the constitution or laws of the United States, or in conflict with this agreement, and all persons in such towns shall be subject to such laws.

26. Said commission shall be authorized to locate a cemetery within a suitable distance from each town site, not to exceed twenty acres; and when any town shall have paid into the United States Treasury for the benefit of the said nation ten dollars per acre therefor, such town shall be entitled to a patent for the same, as herein provided for titles to allottees, and shall dispose of same at reasonable prices in suitable lots for burial purposes; the proceeds derived therefrom to be applied by the town government to the proper improvement and care of said cemetery.

27. No charge or claim shall be made against the Muscogee or Creek Nation by the United States for the expenses of surveying and platting the lands and town site, or for grading, appraising and allotting the land, or for appraising and disposing of the town lots as herein provided.

28. There shall be set apart and exempted from appraisement and sale, in the towns, lots upon which churches and parsonages are now built and occupied, not to exceed fifty feet front and one hundred and fifty feet deep for each church and parsonage. Such lots shall be used only for churches and parsonages, and when they cease to be so used, shall revert to the members of the nation, to be disposed of as other town lots.

29. Said commission shall have prepared correct and proper plats of each town, and file one in the clerk's office of the United States district court for the district in which the town is located, one with the executive of the nation, and one with the *Secretary* of the Interior, to be approved by him before the same shall take effect.

30. A settlement numbering at least three hundred inhabitants, living within a radius of one-half mile at the time of the signing of this agreement, shall constitute a town within the meaning of this agreement. Congress may by law provide for the government of the said towns.

CLAIMS.

31. All claims, of whatever nature, including the "Loyal Creek Claim" made under article 4 of the treaty of 1866, and the "Self Emigration Claim," under article 12 of the treaty of 1832, which the Muscogee or Creek Nation, or individuals thereof, may have against the United States, or any claim which the United States may have against the said nation, shall be submitted to the Senate of the United States as a board of arbitration; and all such claims against the United States shall be presented within one year from the date hereof, and within two years from the date hereof the Senate of the United States shall make final determination of said claim; and in the event that any moneys are awarded to the Muscogee or Creek Nation, or individuals thereof, by the United States, provision shall be made for the immediate payment of the same by the United States.

JURISDICTION OF COURTS.

32. The United States courts now existing, or that may hereafter be created in the Indian Territory, shall have exclusive jurisdiction of all controversies growing out of the title, ownership, occupation, or use of real estate in the territory occupied by the Muscogee or Creek Nation, and to try all persons charged with homicide, embezzlement, bribery and embracery hereafter committed in the territory of said Nation, without reference to race or citizenship of the person or persons charged with any such crime; and any citizen or officer of said nation charged with any such crime shall be tried and, if convicted, punished as though he were a citizen or officer of the United States; and the courts of said nation shall retain all the jurisdiction which they now have, except as herein transferred to the courts of the United States.

ENACTMENTS OF NATIONAL COUNCIL.

33. No act, ordinance, or resolution of the council of the Muscogee or Creek Nation in any manner affecting the land of the nation, or of individuals, after allotment, or the moneys or other property of the nation, or citizens thereof (except appropriations for the regular and necessary expenses of the government of the said nation), or the rights of any person to employ any kind of labor, or the rights of any persons who have taken or may take the oath of allegiance to the United States, shall be of any validity until approved by the President of the United States. When such act, ordinance, or resolution passed by the council of said nation shall be approved by the executive thereof, it shall then be the duty of the national secretary of said nation to forward same to the President of the United States, duly certified and sealed, who shall, within thirty days after receipt thereof, approve or disapprove the same, and said act, ordinance, or resolution, when so approved, shall be published in at least two newspapers having a bona fide circulation throughout the territory occupied by said nation, and when disapproved shall be returned to the executive of said nation.

MISCELLANEOUS.

34. Neither the town lots nor the allotment of land of any citizen of the Muscogee or Creek Nation shall be subjected to any debt contracted by him prior to the date of his patent.

35. All payments herein provided for shall be made, under the direction of the Secretary of the Interior, into the United States Treasury, and shall be for the benefit of the citizens of the Muscogee or Creek Nation. All payments hereafter to be made to the members of the said nation shall be paid directly to each individual member by a bonded officer of the United States, under the direction of the Secretary of the Interior, which officer shall be required to give strict account for such disbursements to the Secretary.

36. The United States agrees to maintain strict laws in the territory of said nation against the introduction, sale, barter, or giving away of liquors and intoxicants of any kind or quality.

37. All citizens of said nation, when the tribal government shall cease, shall become possessed of all the rights and privileges of citizens of the United States.

38. This agreement shall in no wise affect the provisions of existing treaties between

the Muscogee or Creek Nation and the United States, except in so far as it is inconsistent therewith.

In witness whereof, the said Commissioners do hereunto affix their names at Muscogee, Indian Territory, this the twenty-seventh day of September, eighteen hundred and ninety-seven.

HENRY L. DAWES,
Chairman.
TAMS BIXBY,
Acting Chairman.
FRANK C. ARMSTRONG,
ARCHIBALD S. McKENNON,
A. B. MONTGOMERY,
Commission to the Five Civilized Tribes.
ALLISON L. AYLESWORTH,
Acting Secretary.
PLEASANT PORTER,
Chairman.
JOSEPH MINGO,
DAVID M. HODGE,
GEORGE A. ALEXANDER,
ROLAND (his x mark) BROWN,
WILLIAM A. SAPULPA,
CONCHARTY (his x mark) MICCO,
Muscogee or Creek Commission.
J. H. LYNCH,
Secretary.

Approved, June 28, 1898.
(Creek agreement, Sec. 30 of "Curtis Act" not ratified by tribe. See appendix No. 5.)

APPENDIX NO. 3.

PORTION OF THE ACT OF MAY 31, 1900 (31 STAT., 221), IN REGARD TO TOWN-SITE MATTERS IN THE INDIAN TERRITORY.

To pay all expenses incident to the survey, platting, and appraisement of town sites in the Choctaw, Chickasaw, Creek, and Cherokee nations, Indian Territory, as required by sections fifteen and twenty-nine of an act entitled "An Act for the protection of the people of the Indian Territory, and for other purposes," approved June twenty-eighth, eighteen hundred and ninety-eight, for the balance of the current year and for the year ending June thirtieth, nineteen hundred and one, the same to be immediately available, sixty-seven thousand dollars, or so much as may be necessary: *Provided,* that the Secretary of the Interior is hereby authorized, under rules and regulations to be prescribed by him, to survey, lay out, and plat into town lots, streets, alleys, and parks, the sites of such towns and villages in the Choctaw, Chickasaw, Creek, and Cherokee nations, as may at that time have a population of two hundred or more, in such manner as will best subserve the then present needs and the reasonable prospective growth of such towns. The work of surveying, laying out, and platting such town sites shall be done by competent surveyors, who shall prepare five copies of the plat of each town site which, when the survey is approved by the Secretary of the Interior, shall be filed as follows: One in the office of the Commissioner of Indian Affairs, one with the principal chief of the nation, one with the clerk of the court within the territorial jurisdiction of which the town is located, one with the Commission to the Five Civilized Tribes, and one with the town authorities, if there be such. Where in his judgment the best interests of the public service require, the Secretary of the Interior may secure the surveying, laying out, and platting of town sites in any of said nations by contract.

Hereafter the work of the respective town-site commissions provided for in the agreement with the Choctaw and Chickasaw tribes ratified in section twenty-nine of the Act of June twenty-eighth, eighteen hundred and ninety-eight, entitled "An Act for the protection of the people of the Indian Territory, and for other purposes," shall begin as to any town site immediately upon the approval of the survey by the Secretary of the Interior and not before.

The Secretary of the Interior may in his discretion appoint a town-site commission consisting of three members for each of the Creek and Cherokee nations, at least one of whom shall be a citizen of the tribe and shall be appointed upon the nomination of the principal chief of the tribe. Each commission, under the supervision of the Sec-

ary of the Interior, shall appraise and sell for the benefit of the tribe the town lots
the nation for which it is appointed, acting in conformity with the provisions of
y then existing act of Congress or agreement with the tribe approved by Congress.
e agreement of any two members of the commission as to the true value of any lot
all constitute a determination thereof, subject to the approval of the Secretary of
: Interior, and if no two members are able to agree the matter shall be determined
such Secretary.

Where in his judgment the public interests will be thereby subserved, the Secre-
y of the Interior may appoint in the Choctaw, Chickasaw, Creek, or Cherokee
tion a separate town-site commission for any town, in which event as to that town
h local commission may exercise the same authority and perform the same duties
iich would otherwise devolve upon the commission for that nation. Every such
al commission shall be appointed in the manner provided in the Act approved
ne twenty-eighth, eighteen hundred and ninety-eight, entitled "An Act for the
otection of the people of the Indian Territory."

The Secretary of the Interior, where in his judgment the public interests will be
reby subserved, may permit the authorities of any town in any of said nations, at
: expense of the town, to survey, lay out, and plat the site thereof, subject to his
pervision and approval, as in other instances.

As soon as the plat of any town site is approved, the proper commission shall, with
reasonable dispatch and within a limited time, to be prescribed by the Secretary
the Interior, proceed to make the appraisement of the lots and improvements, if
y thereon, and after the approval thereof by the Secretary of the Interior, shall,
der the supervision of such Secretary, proceed to the disposition and sale of the lots
conformity with any then existing act of Congress or agreement with the tribe
proved by Congress, and if the proper commission shall not complete such appraise-
ant and sale within the time limited by the Secretary of the Interior, they shall
ceive no pay for such additional time as may be taken by them, unless the Secre-
ry of the Interior for good cause shown shall expressly direct otherwise.

The Secretary of the Interior may, for good cause, remove any member of any
wn-site commission, tribal or local, in any of said nations, and may fill the vacancy
ereby made or any vacancy otherwise occurring in like manner as the place was
iginally filled.

It shall not be required that the town-site limits established in the course of the
atting and disposing of town lots and the corporate limits of the town, if incorpo-
ted, shall be identical or coextensive, but such town-site limits and corporate limits
all be so established as to best subserve the then present needs and the reasonable
ospective growth of the town, as the same shall appear at the times when such
nits are respectively established: *Provided further,* That the exterior limits of all
wn sites shall be designated and fixed at the earliest practicable time under rules
d regulations prescribed by the Secretary of the Interior.

Upon the recommendation of the Commission to the Five Civilized Tribes the Sec-
tary of the Interior is hereby authorized at any time before allotment to set aside
d reserve from allotment any lands in the Choctaw, Chickasaw, Creek, or Cherokee
tions, not exceeding one hundred and sixty acres in any one tract, at such stations
are or shall be established in conformity with law on the line of any railroad which
all be constructed or be in process of construction in or through either of said nations
ior to the allotment of the lands therein, and this irrespective of the population of
ch town site at the time. Such town sites shall be surveyed, laid out, and platted,
d the lands therein disposed of for the benefit of the tribe in the manner herein
escribed for other town sites: *Provided further,* That whenever any tract of land
all be set aside as herein provided which is occupied by a member of the tribe,
ch occupant shall be fully compensated for his improvements thereon under such
les and regulations as may be prescribed by the Secretary of the Interior.

Nothing herein contained shall have the effect of avoiding any work heretofore
ne in pursuance of the said Act of June twenty-eighth, eighteen hundred and
nety-eight, in the way of surveying, laying out, or platting of town sites, appra sing
disposing of town lots in any of said nations, but the same, if not heretofore car-
d to a state of completion, may be completed according to the provisions hereof.

APPENDIX NO. 4.

GULATIONS GOVERNING THE PROCUREMENT OF TIMBER AND STONE, FOR DOMESTIC
AND INDUSTRIAL PURPOSES, IN THE INDIAN TERRITORY, AS PROVIDED IN THE ACT OF
JUNE 6, 1900. (31 STAT., 660.)

1. The United States Indian agent for the Union Agency is hereby authorized and
rected to enter into a contract or contracts, upon applications, made in the form of

affidavits, upon blanks prescribed, when approved by the Secretary of the Interior. with any responsible person, persons, or corporation for the purchase of timber or stone from any of the public lands belonging to any of the Five Civilized Tribes, and to collect, on or before the end of each month, the full value of such timber or stone as the Secretary of the Interior shall hereafter determine should be paid; and the timber and stone so procured under such contracts may be used for "domestic and industrial purposes, including the construction, maintenance, and repair of railroads and other highways," within the limits of the Indian Territory only.

Applications must be presented to the United States Indian inspector located in the Indian Territory and by him forwarded, with his recommendation, through the Commissioner of Indian Affairs, to the Department.

Applicants must state the quality and quantity of timber or stone proposed to be cut or quarried, the purpose or purposes for which and the place or places where said timber and stone are to be used, as the case may be, the amount considered just and reasonable to be paid by them, and their reasons for such conclusion. Each application must be accompanied by the affidavits of two disinterested persons, corroborating specifically all the statements of the applicant, and the inspector is hereby authorized to require any other information as to the value of the timber or stone, or to show the good faith of the applicant.

2. Before any timber shall be cut or any stone taken from any of the lands belonging to any of the Five Civilized Tribes, the person, persons, or corporation desiring to secure such timber or stone shall enter into a contract or contracts with said Indian agent, in accordance with the form hereto attached, which contract, however, shall not be of force until the Secretary of the Interior shall have indorsed his approval thereon: *Provided*, That each such person, persons, or corporation shall give bond (form attached hereto) in a sufficient sum, to be fixed by the Secretary of the Interior. with two good and sufficient sureties, or an approved surety company, as surety, conditioned for the faithful performance of the stipulations of the contract or contracts, and also conditioned for the faithful observance of all of the laws of the United States now in force or that may hereafter be enacted, and the regulations now prescribed or that may hereafter be prescribed by the Secretary of the Interior relative to any and all matters pertaining to the affairs of any of the Five Civilized Tribes.

3. The moneys so collected shall be placed to the credit of the tribe or tribes to which the land belongs from which such timber or stone was procured, as miscellaneous receipts, class three, "not the result of the labor of any member of such tribe:" but no timber or stone shall be taken from any land selected by any citizen of any of the Five Civilized Tribes as his prospective allotment without his consent, and only from such land being cleared, or to be cleared, for cultivation, and not until a contract shall have been entered into by the said United States Indian agent and the person, persons, or corporation desiring to procure such timber or stone, and the same shall have been approved.

The price to be paid under such contract shall be satisfactory to such prospective allottee: *Provided*, That the provisions of this section shall apply to all tracts now in possession of any citizens of any of the Five Civilized Tribes who intend to include such tracts in their prospective allotments, and the money derived from the sale of timber or stone taken from any such tracts shall be deposited in the United States Treasury, St. Louis, Mo., to the credit of the Secretary of the Interior and subject to his check in his official capacity only, and when the tract or tracts from which such timber or stone was taken shall have been allotted, the Secretary of the Interior shall pay the money so deposited to the citizen or citizens taking the said tract or tracts as his or their allotment, if found to be entitled to said money: *And provided further*, That the Indian agent shall be required to keep an accurate list, by legal subdivision, of the land from which such timber or stone was taken, and also an accurate list of the amount of money derived from the sale of timber or stone taken from each such legal subdivision. Value of timber and stone taken from unappraised selected lands must be added to the appraisement when made.

4. The contract or contracts entered into by said Indian agent with any person, persons, or corporation shall describe the land from which the timber or stone is to be taken by legal subdivisions, and if any contractor shall take timber or stone from any land other than that covered by his contract he shall be liable to forcible removal from the Indian Territory and suit on his bond, and such unlawful taking of timber and stone shall work also a forfeiture of his contract.

5. The act of Congress under which these rules are promulgated provides that "every person who unlawfully cuts, or aids, or is employed in unlawfully cutting, or wantonly destroys, or procures to be wantonly destroyed, any timber standing upon the land of either of said tribes, or sells or transports any of such timber or stone outside *the* Indian Territory, contrary to the regulations prescribed by the Secretary, shall *pay a fine of* not more than five hundred dollars, or be imprisoned not more than *twelve months*, or both, in the discretion of the court trying the same."

The Indian agent for the Union Agency shall see that any person, persons, or corporation who procures timber or stone from any of the lands belonging to any of the Five Civilized Tribes, under and in accordance with the provisions of the act of Congress approved June 6, 1900 (31 Stat., 660), and these regulations, employs Indians in the cutting and removal of said timber and in the quarrying and removal of said stone whenever practicable on the same terms as other labor, Indians to have the preference over white men.

The Department reserves the right to amend these regulations and to advance the price to be paid for timber or stone to be taken under any contract if it be shown that the amount stipulated in the contract is less than the "full value," or to cancel any contract for failure to pay promptly the amounts due, or for any other good and sufficient cause, after due notice to the party or parties in interest, giving the right to show cause, within ten days from service of such notice, why this action should not be taken.

W. A. JONES,
Commissioner of Indian Affairs.

WASHINGTON, D. C., *February 14, 1901.*
Approved:
THOS. RYAN, *Acting Secretary.*

Amendment to the regulations of the Interior Department governing the procurement of timber and stone for domestic and industrial purposes in the Indian Territory, dated February 14, 1901, promulgated under the act of Congress approved June 6, 1900. (31 Stat., 660.)

Applications will not be received for the present under said regulations, except for props and caps for mines and ties and pilings for railroads, and said regulations are suspended, except as above modified.

This amendment approved by Secretary of the Interior April 27, 1901.

————

AN ACT To provide for the use of timber and stone for domestic and industrial purposes in the Indian Territory.

Be it enacted by the Senate and House of Representatives of the United States of America in Congress assembled, That the Secretary of the Interior is authorized to prescribe rules and regulations for the procurement of timber and stone for such domestic and industrial purposes, including the construction, maintenance, and repair of railroads and other highways, to be used only in the Indian Territory, as in his judgment he shall deem necessary and proper, from lands belonging to either of the Five Civilized Tribes of Indians, and to fix the full value thereof to be paid therefor, and collect the same for the benefit of said tribes; and every person who unlawfully cuts, or aids, or is employed in unlawfully cutting, or wantonly destroys, or procures to be wantonly destroyed, any timber standing upon the land of either of said tribes, or sells or transports any of such timber or stone outside of the Indian Territory, contrary to the regulations prescribed by the Secretary, shall pay a fine of not more than five hundred dollars, or be imprisoned not more than twelve months, or both, in the discretion of the court trying the same. (31 Stat., 660.)

Approved, June 6, 1900.

————

FORM OF APPLICATION.

————————,
————, 1900.

I hereby apply for permission to enter into a contract with the United States Indian agent at Muscogee, Indian Territory, for the purchase of (¹) ———— located on the (²) ————.

Such timber or stone is to be used at ————.

I consider that the timber is worth on the stump the following prices, to wit, ————, and that the stone is worth the following price per cubic yard, to wit, ————.

I base my opinion as to the value above stated upon the following facts: (³) ————.

Subscribed and sworn to before me, ———— ————, this ———— day of ————, 19—.

———— ————,
————————.

————————————————————————

¹ Insert amount, kind, and character of timber or stone, or both desired.
² Insert description of land.
³ State distance from place where material is to be procured to place where it is to be used, cost of transportation, etc., market price of material where it is to be used, and any other facts which may be of aid in arriving at a conclusion.

—— —— and —— ——, being by me first duly sworn, upon their oaths, state, each for himself, that he is well acquainted with the land above described and with the quantity and quality of the timber and stone thereon, and with the place or places where it is proposed to use the above-mentioned material, and also with the values and prices of stone and timber in the vicinity of the place from which it is proposed to take and where it is proposed to use such material, and with the cost of removing and transporting timber and stone, and with all the facts stated by the applicant above named, and knows that the facts stated by him are true and correct in every particular.

—— ——.
—— ——.

Subscribed and sworn to before me, a —— for the ——, at my office in ——. this —— day of ——, ——.

—— ——,
—— ——.

FORM OF INDIAN TERRITORY TIMBER AND STONE CONTRACT.

—— Nation.

(Write all names and addresses in full.)

This agreement, made and entered into in quadruplicate at the Union Agency, Muskogee, Indian Territory, this —— day of ——, 19—, by and between —— ——, United States Indian agent for the Union Agency, party of the first part, and —— ——, of ——, part— of the second part, under and in pursuance of the provisions of the act of Congress approved June 6, 1900 (Public—No. 174), and the rules and regulations prescribed by the Secretary of the Interior on February 14, 1901, relative to the procurement of timber and stone from any of the lands belonging to any of the Five Civilized Tribes, and the timber or stone procured under the provisions of this contract and the rules and regulations heretofore or that may hereafter be prescribed by the Secretary of the Interior:

Witnesseth that the said party of the first part agrees to sell to said part— of the second part timber or stone of the kind or kinds hereinafter specified, standing, fallen, lying, or being on lands within the limits of the —— Nation, which said lands are described as follows, to wit: The —— section of ——, of township (^{1})——, of range (^{2})——, of the Indian meridian, and containing —— acres, more or less.

The part— of the second part agree— to cut and remove the timber or quarry and remove the stone hereinafter mentioned from within the above-described limits, and agree— to employ Indian labor in the cutting and removal of the timber and the quarrying and removal of the stone in preference to other labor on equal terms, whenever suitable Indian labor can be obtained.

For and in consideration of the foregoing, the said part— of the second part also agree— to pay to the United States Indian agent for the Union Agency, for the benefit of the —— tribe of Indians, for all such timber cut and stone quarried on said described lands, at the following rates, to wit:

MERCHANTABLE SAW TIMBER, I. E., TIMBER CAPABLE OF BEING MANUFACTURED INTO LUMBER, AS FOLLOWS:

For walnut timber, —— per thousand feet: for cypress timber, —— per thousand feet; for ash timber, —— per thousand feet; for oak timber, —— per thousand feet; for pine timber, —— per thousand feet; for cottonwood timber, —— per thousand feet, and for —— timber, —— per thousand feet.

TELEGRAPH POLES.

Cedar, four to five inch top, eight to ten inch bottom, —— feet long, —— cents each.

Cedar, six-inch top, twelve-inch bottom, —— feet long, —— cents each.

Cedar, —— inch top, —— inch bottom, —— feet long, —— cents each.

^{1}State whether north or south. ^{2}State whether east or west.

[Indorsements on contract.]

No. ——.

DEPARTMENT OF THE INTERIOR.
WASHINGTON, D. C.

—— AGREEMENT.

—— ——, U. S. Indian Agent,
WITH
—— ——, of ——.

Sec. ——, Tp. ——, Range ——, in the
—— Nation, Indian Territory.
Dated ——, 19—.
Expires——, 19—.

DEPARTMENT OF THE INTERIOR.
U. S. INDIAN SERVICE.
UNION AGENCY,
MUSKOGEE, I. T., ——, 19—.
Respectfully forwarded to the Commissioner
of Indian Affairs for consideration with my
report of even date.

——— ———,
U. S. Indian Agent.

DEPARTMENT OF THE INTERIOR.
OFFICE OF INDIAN AFFAIRS,
WASHINGTON, D. C., ——, 19—.
Respectfully submitted to the Secretary of
the Interior with favorable recommendation.

——— ———,
Commissioner.

DEPARTMENT OF THE INTERIOR.
WASHINGTON, D. C., ——, 19—.
Approved:

——— ———,
Secretary of the Interior.

FORM OF BOND.

Know all men by these presents, That we, (¹) —— ——, of ——, as principals, and —— ——, of ——, and —— ——, of ——, as sureties, are held and firmly bound unto the United States of America in the sum of —— dollars, lawful money of the United States, for the payment of which, well and truly to be made, we bind ourselves and each of us, our heirs, successors, executors, and administrators, jointly and severally, firmly by these presents.

Sealed with our seals and dated the —— day of ——, 19—.

The condition of this obligation is such, That whereas the above-bounden ——, —— as principal—, —— entered into a certain agreement dated ——, 19—, with the United States Indian agent for the Union Agency, for the purchase of ——, to be procured from (²) the ——, said —— to be used in the Indian Territory only for "domestic and industrial purposes, including the construction, maintenance, and repair of railroads and other highways."

Now, if the above-bounden —— —— shall faithfully carry out and observe all the obligations assumed in said agreement by —— ——, and shall observe all the laws of the United States and regulations made or which shall be made thereunder for the government of trade and intercourse with the Indian tribes, and the rules and regulations that have been or may be prescribed by the Secretary of the Interior under the act of Congress approved June 6, 1900 (Public, No. 174), relative to the procurement of timber and stone from lands belonging to any of the Five Civilized Tribes in the Indian Territory, then this obligation shall be null and void, otherwise to remain in full force and effect.

Signed and sealed in the presence of (³)

———— ————.
———— ————.
———— ————.
———— ————.

———— ————. [L. S.] (⁴)
———— ————. [L. S.]
———— ————. [L. S.]
———— ————. [L. S.]

¹ The Christian names and residences of principals, and of the sureties, where personal sureties are given, of whom there must be two.
² Give description of land.
³ There must be at least two witnesses to all signatures, though the same two persons may witness all.
⁴ A seal must be attached by some adhesive substance to the signatures of principals and sureties.

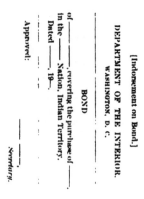

APPENDIX NO. 5.

[PUBLIC—No. 112.]

AN ACT To ratify and confirm an agreement with the Muscogee or Creek tribe of Indians, and for other purposes.

Be it enacted by the Senate and House of Representatives of the United States of America in Congress assembled, That the agreement negotiated between the Commission to the Five Civilized Tribes and the Muscogee or Creek tribe of Indians at the city of Washington on the eighth day of March, nineteen hundred, as herein amended, is hereby accepted, ratified, and confirmed, and the same shall be of full force and effect when ratified by the Creek national council. The principal chief, as soon as practicable after the ratification of this agreement by Congress, shall call an extra session of the Creek national council and lay before it this agreement and the Act of Congress ratifying it, and if the agreement be ratified by said council, as provided in the constitution of said nation, he shall transmit to the President of the United States the act of council ratifying the agreement, and the President of the United States shall thereupon issue his proclamation declaring the same duly ratified, and that all the provisions of this agreement have become law according to the terms thereof: *Provided,* That such ratification by the Creek national council shall be made within ninety days from the approval of this Act by the President of the United States.

This agreement by and between the United States, entered into in its behalf by the Commission to the Five Civilized Tribes, Henry L. Dawes, Tams Bixby, Archibald S. McKennon, and Thomas B. Needles, duly appointed and authorized thereunto, and the Muskogee (or Creek) tribe of Indians, in Indian Territory, entered into in behalf of said tribe by Pleasant Porter, principal chief, and George A. Alexander, David M. Hodge, Isparhecher, Albert P. McKellop, and Cub McIntosh, delegates, duly appointed and authorized thereunto,

Witnesseth that in consideration of the mutual undertakings herein contained it is agreed as follows:

DEFINITIONS.

1. The words "Creek" and "Muskogee," as used in this agreement, shall be deemed synonymous, and the words "Creek Nation" and "tribe" shall each be deemed to refer to the Muskogee Nation or Muskogee tribe of Indians in Indian Territory. The words "principal chief" shall be deemed to refer to the principal chief of the Muskogee Nation. The words "citizen" or "citizens" shall be deemed to refer to a member or members of the Muskogee tribe or nation of Indians. The words "The Dawes Commission" or "commission" shall be deemed to refer to the United States Commission to the Five Civilized Tribes.

GENERAL ALLOTMENT OF LANDS.

2. All lands belonging to the Creek tribe of Indians in the Indian Territory, except town sites and lands herein reserved for Creek schools and public buildings, shall be appraised at their true value, excluding only lawful improvements on lands in

actual cultivation. The appraisement shall be made under direction of the Dawes Commission by such number of committees, with necessary assistance, as may be deemed necessary to expedite the work, one member of each committee to be appointed by the principal chief; and if the members of any committee fail to agree as to the value of any tract of land, the value thereof shall be fixed by said commission. Each committee shall make report of its work to said commission, which shall from time to time prepare reports of same, in duplicate, and transmit them to the Secretary of the Interior for his approval, and when approved one copy thereof shall be returned to the office of said commission for its use in making allotments as herein provided.

3. All lands of said tribe, except as herein provided, shall be allotted among the citizens of the tribe by said commission so as to give each an equal share of the whole in value, as nearly as may be, in manner following: There shall be allotted to each citizen one hundred and sixty acres of land—boundaries to conform to the Government survey—which may be selected by him so as to include improvements which belong to him. One hundred and sixty acres of land, valued at six dollars and fifty cents per acre, shall constitute the standard value of an allotment, and shall be the measure for the equalization of values; and any allottee receiving lands of less than such standard value may, at any time, select other lands, which, at their appraised value, are sufficient to make his allotment equal in value to the standard so fixed.

If any citizen select lands the appraised value of which, for any reason, is in excess of such standard value, the excess of value shall be charged against him in the future distribution of the funds of the tribe arising from all sources whatsoever, and he shall not receive any further distribution of property or funds of the tribe, until all other citizens have received lands and money equal in value to his allotment. If any citizen select lands the appraised value of which is in excess of such standard value, he may pay the overplus in money, but if he fail to do so, the same shall be charged against him in the future distribution of the funds of the tribe arising from all sources whatsoever, and he shall not receive any further distribution of property or funds until all other citizens shall have received lands and funds equal in value to his allotment; and if there be not sufficient funds of the tribe to make the allotments of all other citizens of the tribe equal in value to his, then the surplus shall be a lien upon the rents and profits of his allotment until paid.

4. Allotment for any minor may be selected by his father, mother, or guardian, in the order named, and shall not be sold during his minority. All guardians or curators appointed for minors and incompetents shall be citizens.

Allotments may be selected for prisoners, convicts, and aged and infirm persons by their duly appointed agents, and for incompetents by guardians, curators, or suitable persons akin to them, but it shall be the duty of said commission to see that such selections are made for the best interests of such parties.

5. If any citizen have in his possession, in actual cultivation, lands in excess of what he and his wife and minor children are entitled to take, he shall, within ninety days after the ratification of this agreement, select therefrom allotments for himself and family aforesaid, and if he have lawful improvements upon such excess he may dispose of the same to any other citizen, who may thereupon select lands so as to include such improvements; but, after the expiration of ninety days from the ratification of this agreement, any citizen may take any lands not already selected by another; but if lands so taken be in actual cultivation, having thereon improvements belonging to another citizen, such improvements shall be valued by the appraisement committee, and the amount paid to the owner thereof by the allottee, and the same shall be a lien upon the rents and profits of the land until paid: *Provided*, That the owner of improvements may remove the same if he desires.

6. All allotments made to Creek citizens by said commission prior to the ratification of this agreement, as to which there is no contest, and which do not include public property, and are not herein otherwise affected, are confirmed, and the same shall, as to appraisement and all things else, be governed by the provisions of this agreement; and said commission shall continue the work of allotment of Creek lands to citizens of the tribe as heretofore, conforming to provisions herein; and all controversies arising between citizens as to their right to select certain tracts of land shall be determined by said commission.

7. Lands allotted to citizens hereunder shall not in any manner whatsoever, or at any time, be incumbered, taken, or sold to secure or satisfy any debt or obligation contracted or incurred prior to the date of the deed to the allottee therefor and such lands shall not be alienable by the allottee or his heirs at any time before the expiration of five years from the ratification of this agreement, except with the approval of the Secretary of the Interior.

Each citizen shall select from his allotment forty acres of land as a homestead which shall be nontaxable and inalienable and free from any incumbrance whatever for twenty-one years, for which he shall have a separate deed, conditioned as above: *Provided,* That selections of homesteads for minors, prisoners, convicts, incompetents, and aged and infirm persons, who can not select for themselves, may be made in the manner herein provided for the selection of their allotments; and if, for any reason, such selection be not made for any citizen, it shall be the duty of said commission to make selection for him.

The homestead of each citizen shall remain, after the death of the allottee, for the use and support of children born to him after the ratification of this agreement, but if he have no such issue, then he may dispose of his homestead by will, free from limitation herein imposed, and if this be not done, the land shall descend to his heirs according to the laws of descent and distribution of the Creek Nation, free from such limitation.

8. The Secretary of the Interior shall, through the United States Indian agent in said Territory, immediately after the ratification of this agreement, put each citizen who has made selection of his allotment in unrestricted possession of his land and remove therefrom all persons objectionable to him; and when any citizen shall thereafter make selection of his allotment as herein provided, and receive certificate therefor, he shall be immediately thereupon so placed in possession of his land.

9. When allotment of one hundred and sixty acres has been made to each citizen, the residue of lands, not herein reserved or otherwise disposed of, and all the funds arising under this agreement shall be used for the purpose of equalizing allotments, and if the same be insufficient therefor, the deficiency shall be supplied out of any other funds of the tribe, so that the allotments of all citizens may be made equal in value, as nearly as may be, in manner herein provided.

TOWN SITES.

10. All towns in the Creek Nation having a present population of two hundred or more shall, and all others may, be surveyed, laid out, and appraised under the provisions of an act of Congress entitled "An act making appropriations for the current and contingent expenses of the Indian department and for fulfilling treaty stipulations with various Indian tribes for the fiscal year ending June thirtieth, nineteen hundred and one, and for other purposes," approved May thirty-first, nineteen hundred, which said provisions are as follows:

"That the Secretary of the Interior is hereby authorized, under rules and regulations to be prescribed by him, to survey, lay out, and plat into town lots, streets, alleys, and parks the sites of such towns and villages in the Choctaw, Chickasaw, Creek, and Cherokee nations, as may at that time have a population of two hundred or more, in such manner as will best subserve the then present needs and the reasonable prospective growth of such towns. The work of surveying, laying out, and platting such town sites shall be done by competent surveyors, who shall prepare five copies of the plat of each town site which, when the survey is approved by the Secretary of the Interior, shall be filed as follows: One in the office of the Commissioner of Indian Affairs, one with the principal chief of the nation, one with the clerk of the court within the territorial jurisdiction of which the town is located, one with the Commissioner to the Five Civilized Tribes, and one with the town authorities, if there be such. Where in his judgment the best interest of the public service require, the Secretary of the Interior may secure the surveying, laying out, and platting of town sites in any of said nations by contract.

"Hereafter the work of the respective town-site commissions provided for in the agreement with the Choctaw and Chickasaw tribes ratified in section twenty-nine of the act of June twenty-eighth, eighteen hundred and ninety-eight, entitled 'An act for the protection of the people of the Indian Territory, and for other purposes,' shall begin as to any town site immediately upon the approval of the survey by the Secretary of the Interior and not before.

"The Secretary of the Interior may in his discretion appoint a town-site commission consisting of three members for each of the Creek and Cherokee nations, at least one of whom shall be a citizen of the tribe and shall be appointed upon the nomination of the principal chief of the tribe. Each commission, under the supervision of the Secretary of the Interior, shall appraise and sell for the benefit of the tribe the town lots in the nation for which it is appointed, acting in conformity with the provisions of any then existing act of Congress or agreement with the tribe approved by Congress. The agreement of any two members of the commission as to the true value of any lot shall constitute a determination thereof, subject to the approval of the Secretary of the Interior, and if no two members are able to agree the matter shall be determined by such Secretary.

"Where in his judgment the public interests will be thereby subserved, the Secretary of the Interior may appoint in the Choctaw, Chickasaw, Creek, or Cherokee Nation a separate town-site commission for any town, in which event as to that town such local commission may exercise the same authority and perform the same duties which would otherwise devolve upon the commission for that nation. Every such local commission shall be appointed in the manner provided in the act approved June twenty-eighth, eighteen hundred and ninety-eight, entitled 'An act for the protection of the people of the Indian Territory.'

"The Secretary of the Interior, where in his judgment the public interests will be thereby subserved, may permit the authorities of any town in any of said nations, at the expense of the town, to survey, lay out, and plat the site thereof, subject to his supervision and approval, as in other instances.

"As soon as the plat of any town site is approved, the proper commission shall, with all reasonable dispatch and within a limited time, to be prescribed by the Secretary of the Interior, proceed to make the appraisement of the lots and improvements, if any, thereon, and after the approval thereof by the Secretary of the Interior, shall, under the supervision of such Secretary, proceed to the disposition and sale of the lots in conformity with any then existing act of Congress or agreement with the tribe approved by Congress; and if the proper commission shall not complete such appraisement and sale within the time limited by the Secretary of the Interior, they shall receive no pay for such additional time as may be taken by them, unless the Secretary of the Interior for good cause shown shall expressly direct otherwise.

"The Secretary of the Interior may, for good cause, remove any member of any town-site commission, tribal or local, in any of said nations, and may fill the vacancy thereby made, or any vacancy otherwise occurring, in like manner as the place was originally filled.

"It shall not be required that the town-site limits established in the course of the platting and disposing of town lots and the corporate limits of the town, if incorporated, shall be identical or coextensive, but such town-site limits and corporate limits shall be so established as to best subserve the then present needs and the reasonable prospective growth of the town, as the same shall appear at the times when such limits are respectively established: *Provided further*, That the exterior limits of all town sites shall be designated and fixed at the earliest practicable time under rules and regulations prescribed by the Secretary of the Interior.

"Upon the recommendation of the Commission to the Five Civilized Tribes the Secretary of the Interior is hereby authorized at any time before allotment to set aside and reserve from allotment any lands in the Choctaw, Chickasaw, Creek, or Cherokee nations, not exceeding one hundred and sixty acres in any one tract, at such stations as are or shall be established for any such town, on the line of any railroad which shall be constructed or be in process of construction in or through either of said nations prior to the allotment of the lands therein, and this irrespective of the population of such town site at the time. Such town sites shall be surveyed, laid out, and platted, and the lands therein disposed of for the benefit of the tribe in the manner herein prescribed for other town sites: *Provided further*, That whenever any tract of land shall be set aside as herein provided which is occupied by a member of the tribe, such occupant shall be fully compensated for his improvements thereon under such rules and regulations as may be prescribed by the Secretary of the Interior: *Provided*, That hereafter the Secretary of the Interior may, whenever the chief executive or principal chief of said nation fails or refuses to appoint a town-site commissioner for any town or to fill any vacancy caused by the neglect or refusal of the town-site commissioner appointed by the chief executive or principal chief of said nation to qualify or act, in his discretion appoint a commissioner to fill the vacancy thus created."

11. Any person in rightful possession of any town lot having improvements thereon, other than temporary buildings, fencing, and tillage, shall have the right to purchase such lot by paying one-half of the appraised value thereof, but if he shall fail within sixty days to purchase such lot and make the first payment thereon, as herein provided, the lot and improvements shall be sold at public auction to the highest bidder, under direction of the appraisement commission, at a price not less than their appraised value, and the purchaser shall pay the purchase price to the owner of the improvements, less the appraised value of the lot.

12. Any person having the right of occupancy of a residence or business lot, or both, in any town, whether improved or not, and owning no other lot or land therein, shall have the right to purchase such lot by paying one-half of the appraised value thereof.

13. Any person holding lands within a town occupied by him as a home, also any

person who had at the time of signing this agreement purchased any lot, tract, or parcel of land from any person in legal possession at the time, shall have the right to purchase the lot embraced in same by paying one-half of the appraised value thereof, not, however, exceeding four acres.

14. All town lots not having thereon improvements, other than temporary buildings, fencing, and tillage, the sale or disposition of which is not herein otherwise specifically provided for, shall be sold within twelve months after their appraisement, under direction of the Secretary of the Interior, after due advertisement, at public auction to the highest bidder at not less than their appraised value.

Any person having the right of occupancy of lands in any town which has been or may be laid out into town lots, to be sold at public auction as above, shall have the right to purchase one-fourth of all the lots into which such lands may have been divided at two-thirds of their appraised value.

15. When the appraisement of any town lot is made upon which any person has improvements as aforesaid, said appraisement commission shall notify him of the amount of said appraisement, and he shall, within sixty days thereafter, make payment of ten per centum of the amount due for the lot, as herein provided, and four months thereafter he shall pay fifteen per centum additional, and the remainder of the purchase money in three equal installments, without interest.

Any person who may purchase an unimproved lot shall proceed to make payment for same in such time and manner as herein provided for the payment of sums due on improved lots, and if in any case any amount be not paid when due, it shall thereafter bear interest at the rate of ten per centum per annum until paid. The purchaser may in any case at any time make full payment for any town lot.

16. All town lots purchased by citizens in accordance with the provisions of this agreement shall be free from incumbrance by any debt contracted prior to date of his deed therefor, except for improvements thereon.

17. No taxes shall be assessed by any town government against any town lot remaining unsold, but taxes may be assessed against any town lot sold as herein provided, and the same shall constitute a lien upon the interest of the purchaser therein after any payment thereon has been made by him, and if forfeiture of any lot be made all taxes assessed against such lot shall be paid out of any money paid thereon by the purchaser.

18. The surveyors may select and locate a cemetery within suitable distance from each town, to embrace such number of acres as may be deemed necessary for such purpose, and the appraisement commission shall appraise the same at not less than twenty dollars per acre, and the town may purchase the land by paying the appraised value thereof; and if any citizen have improvements thereon, other than fencing and tillage, they shall be appraised by said commission and paid for by the town. The town authorities shall dispose of the lots in such cemetery at reasonable prices, in suitable sizes for burial purposes, and the proceeds thereof shall be applied to the general improvement of the property.

19. The United States may purchase, in any town in the Creek Nation, suitable land for court-houses, jails, and other necessary public buildings for its use, by paying the appraised value thereof, the same to be selected under the direction of the department for whose use such buildings are to be erected; and if any person have improvements thereon, other than temporary buildings, fencing, and tillage, the same shall be appraised and paid for by the United States.

20. Henry Kendall College, Nazareth Institute, and Spaulding Institute, in Muskogee, may purchase the parcels of land occupied by them, or which may have been laid out for their use and so designated upon the plat of said town, at one-half of their appraised value, upon conditions herein provided; and all other schools and institutions of learning located in incorporated towns in the Creek Nation may, in like manner, purchase the lots or parcels of land occupied by them.

21. All town lots or parts of lots, not exceeding fifty by one hundred and fifty feet in size, upon which church houses and parsonages have been erected, and which are occupied as such at the time of appraisement, shall be properly conveyed to the churches to which such improvements belong gratuitously, and if such churches have other adjoining lots inclosed, actually necessary for their use, they may purchase the same by paying one-half the appraised value thereof.

22. The towns of Clarksville, Coweta, Gibson Station, and Mounds may be surveyed and laid out in town lots and necessary streets and alleys, and platted as other towns, each to embrace such amount of land as may be deemed necessary, not exceeding one hundred and sixty acres for either, and in manner not to include or interfere with the allotment of any citizen selected prior to the date of this agreement, which survey may be made in manner provided for other towns; and the appraisement of the town lots of said towns may be made by any committee appointed

for either of the other towns hereinbefore named, and the lots in said towns may be disposed of in like manner and on the same conditions and terms as those of other towns. All of such work may be done under the direction of and subject to the approval of the Secretary of the Interior.

TITLES.

23. Immediately after the ratification of this agreement by Congress and the tribe, the Secretary of the Interior shall furnish the principal chief with blank deeds necessary for all conveyances herein provided for, and the principal chief shall thereupon proceed to execute in due form and deliver to each citizen who has selected or may hereafter select his allotment, which is not contested, a deed conveying to him all right, title, and interest of the Creek Nation and of all other citizens in and to the lands embraced in his allotment certificate, and such other lands as may have been selected by him for equalization of his allotment.

The principal chief shall, in like manner and with like effect, execute and deliver to proper parties deeds of conveyance in all other cases herein provided for. All lands or town lots to be conveyed to any one person shall, so far as practicable, be included in one deed, and all deeds shall be executed free of charge.

All conveyances shall be approved by the Secretary of the Interior, which shall serve as a relinquishment to the grantee of all the right, title, and interest of the United States in and to the lands embraced in his deed.

Any allottee accepting such deed shall be deemed to assent to the allotment and conveyance of all the lands of the tribe, as provided herein, and as a relinquishment of all his right, title, and interest in and to the same, except in the proceeds of lands reserved from allotment.

The acceptance of deeds of minors and incompetents, by persons authorized to select their allotments for them, shall be deemed sufficient to bind such minors and incompetents to allotment and conveyance of all other lands of the tribe, as provided herein.

The transfer of the title of the Creek tribe to individual allottees and to other persons, as provided in this agreement, shall not inure to the benefit of any railroad company, nor vest in any railroad company, any right, title, or interest in or to any of the lands in the Creek Nation.

All deeds when so executed and approved shall be filed in the office of the Dawes Commission, and there recorded without expense to the grantee, and such records shall have like effect as other public records.

RESERVATIONS.

24. The following lands shall be reserved from the general allotment herein provided for:

(a) All lands herein set apart for town sites.

(b) All lands to which, at the date of the ratification of this agreement, any railroad company may, under any treaty or act of Congress, have a vested right for right of way, depots, station grounds, water stations, stock yards, or similar uses connected with the maintenance and operation of the railroad.

(c) Forty acres for the Eufaula High School.

(d) Forty acres for the Wealaka Boarding School.

(e) Forty acres for the Newyaka Boarding School.

(f) Forty acres for the Wetumka Boarding School.

(g) Forty acres for the Euchee Boarding School.

(h) Forty acres for the Coweta Boarding School.

(j) Forty acres for the Creek Orphan Home.

(i) Forty acres for the Tallahassee Colored Boarding School.

(k) Forty acres for the Pecan Creek Colored Boarding School.

(l) Forty acres for the Colored Creek Orphan Home.

(m) All lands selected for town cemeteries, as herein provided.

(n) The lands occupied by the university established by the American Baptist Home Mission Society, and located near the town of Muskogee, to the amount of forty acres, which shall be appraised, excluding improvements thereon, and said university shall have the right to purchase the same by paying one-half the appraised value thereof, on terms and conditions herein provided. All improvements made by said university on lands in excess of said forty acres shall be appraised and the value thereof paid to it by the person to whom such lands may be allotted.

(o) One acre each for the six established Creek court-houses with the improvements thereon.

(p) One acre each for all churches and schools outside of towns now regularly used as such.

All reservations under the provisions of this agreement, except as otherwise provided herein, when not needed for the purposes for which they are at present used, shall be sold at public auction to the highest bidder, to citizens only, under directions of the Secretary of the Interior.

MUNICIPAL CORPORATIONS.

25. Authority is hereby conferred upon municipal corporations in the Creek Nation, with the approval of the Secretary of the Interior, to issue bonds and borrow money thereon for sanitary purposes, and for the construction of sewers, lighting plants, waterworks, and schoolhouses, subject to all the provisions of laws of the United States in force in the organized Territories of the United States in reference to municipal indebtedness and issuance of bonds for public purposes; and said provisions of law are hereby put in force in said nation and made applicable to the cities and towns therein the same as if specially enacted in reference thereto.

CLAIMS.

26. All claims of whatsoever nature, including the "Loyal Creek claim" under article four of the treaty of eighteen hundred and sixty-six, and the "Self-emigration claim" under article twelve of the treaty of eighteen hundred and thirty-two, which the tribe or any individual thereof may have against the United States, or any other claim arising under the treaty of eighteen hundred and sixty-six, or any claim which the United States may have against said tribe, shall be submitted to the Senate of the United States for determination; and within two years from the ratification of this agreement the Senate shall make final determination thereof; and in the event that any sums are awarded the said tribe, or any citizen thereof, provision shall be made for immediate payment of same.

Of these claims the "Loyal Creek claim," for what they suffered because of their loyalty to the United States Government during the civil war, long delayed, is so urgent in its character that the parties to this agreement express the hope that it may receive consideration and be determined at the earliest practicable moment.

Any other claim which the Creek Nation may have against the United States may be prosecuted in the Court of Claims of the United States, with right of appeal to the Supreme Court; and jurisdiction to try and determine such claim is hereby conferred upon said courts.

FUNDS OF THE TRIBE.

27. All treaty funds of the tribe shall hereafter be capitalized for the purpose of equalizing allotments and for the other purposes provided in this agreement.

ROLLS OF CITIZENSHIP.

28. No person, except as herein provided, shall be added to the rolls of citizenship of said tribe after the date of this agreement, and no person whomsoever shall be added to said rolls after the ratification of this agreement.

All citizens who were living on the first day of April, eighteen hundred and ninety-nine, entitled to be enrolled under section twenty-one of the act of Congress approved June twenty-eighth, eighteen hundred and ninety-eight, entitled "An act for the protection of the people of the Indian Territory, and for other purposes," shall be placed upon the rolls to be made by said commission under said act of Congress, and if any such citizen has died since that time, or may hereafter die, before receiving his allotment of lands and distributive share of all the funds of the tribe, the lands and money to which he would be entitled, if living, shall descend to his heirs according to the laws of descent and distribution of the Creek Nation, and be allotted and distributed to them accordingly.

All children born to citizens so entitled to enrollment up to and including the first day of July, nineteen hundred, and then living, shall be placed on the rolls made by said commission; and if any such child die after said date the lands and moneys to which it would be entitled, if living, shall descend to its heir according to the laws of descent and distribution of the Creek Nation, and be allotted and distributed to them accordingly.

The rolls so made by said commission, when approved by the Secretary of the Interior, shall be the final rolls of citizenship of said tribe, upon which the allotment of all lands and the distribution of all moneys and other property of the tribe shall be made, and to no other persons.

[Muscogee Agreement.]

PROCLAMATION.

Whereas the act of Congress entitled "An act to ratify and confirm an agreement with the Muscogee or Creek tribe of Indians and for other purposes," approved on the first day of March, nineteen hundred and one, contains a provision as follows:

"That the agreement negotiated between the Commission to the Five Civilized Tribes and the Muscogee or Creek tribe of Indians, at the city of Washington on the eighth day of March, nineteen hundred, is hereby amended, ratified, and confirmed, and the same shall be of full force and effect when ratified by the Creek national council. The principal chief, as soon as practicable after the ratification of this agreement by Congress, shall call an extra session of the Creek national council and lay before it this agreement and the act of Congress ratifying it, and if the agreement be ratified by said council, as provided in the constitution of said nation, he shall transmit to the President of the United States the act of council ratifying the agreement, and the President of the United States shall thereupon issue his proclamation declaring the same duly ratified, and that all the provisions of this agreement have become law according to the terms thereof: *Provided*, That such ratification by the Creek national council shall be made within ninety days from the approval of this act by the President of the United States."

And whereas the principal chief of the said tribe has transmitted to me an act of the Creek national council entitled "An act to ratify and confirm an agreement between the United States and the Muscogee Nation of Indians of the Indian Territory," approved the twenty-fifth day of May, nineteen hundred and one, which contains a provision as follows:

"That said agreement, amended, ratified, and confirmed by the Congress of the United States, as set forth in said act of Congress approved March 1, 1901, is hereby accepted, ratified, and confirmed on the part of the Muscogee Nation and on the part of the Muscogee or Creek tribe of Indians constituting said nation, as provided in said act of Congress and as provided in the constitution of said nation, and the principal chief is hereby authorized to transmit this act of the national council ratifying said agreement to the President of the United States as provided in said act of Congress."

And whereas paragraph thirty-six of said agreement contains a provision as follows:

"This provision shall not take effect until after it shall have been separately and specifically approved by the Creek national council and by the Seminole general council; and if not approved by either, it shall fail altogether and be eliminated from this agreement without impairing any other of its provisions."

And whereas there has been presented to me an act of the Creek national council entitled "An act to disapprove certain provisions relating to Seminole citizens in the agreement between the Muscogee Nation and the United States, ratified by Congress March 1, 1901," approved the twenty-fifth day of May, nineteen hundred and one, by which the provisions of said paragraph thirty-six are specifically disapproved:

Now, therefore, I, William McKinley, President of the United States, do hereby declare said agreement, except paragraph thirty-six thereof, duly ratified, and that all the provisions thereof, except said paragraph thirty-six, which failed of ratification by the Creek national council, became law according to the terms thereof upon the twenty-fifth day of May, nineteen hundred and one.

In witness whereof I have hereunto set my hand and caused the seal of the United States to be affixed.

Done at the city of Washington this twenty-fifth day of June, in the year of our Lord one thousand nine hundred and one and of the independence of the United States the one hundred and twenty-fifth.

[SEAL.]

WILLIAM McKINLEY.

By the President:

DAVID J. HILL, *Acting Secretary of State.*

APPENDIX NO. 6.

[PUBLIC—No. 173.]

AN ACT To amend section six, chapter one hundred and nineteen, United States Statutes at Large numbered twenty-four.

Be it enacted by the Senate and House of Representatives of the United States of America in Congress assembled, That section six of chapter one hundred and nineteen of the United States Statutes at Large numbered twenty-four, page three hundred and ninety, is hereby amended as follows, to wit: After the words "civilized life," in line thirteen of said section six, insert the words "and every Indian in Indian Territory."

Approved, March 3, 1901.

Section 6, chapter 119, 24th Statutes, is quoted below:

"That upon the completion of said allotments and the patenting of the lands to said allottees, each and every member of the respective bands or tribes of Indians to whom allotments have been made shall have the benefit of and be subject to the laws, both civil and criminal, of the State or Territory in which they may reside; and no Territory shall pass or enforce any law denying any such Indian within its jurisdiction the equal protection of the law.

And every Indian born within the territorial limits of the United States to whom allotments shall have been made under the provisions of this act, or under any law or treaty, and every Indian born within the territorial limits of the United States who has voluntarily taken up, within said limits, his residence separate and apart from any tribe of Indians therein, and has adopted the habits of civilized life, and every Indian in Indian Territory is hereby declared to be a citizen of the United States, and is entitled to all the rights, privileges, and immunities of such citizens, whether said Indian has been or not, by birth or otherwise, a member of any tribe of Indians within the territorial limits of the United States, without in any manner impairing or otherwise affecting the right of any such Indian to tribal or other property."

APPENDIX NO. 7.

[Extracts from Indian appropriation act for fiscal year 1902, approved March 3, 1901 (31 Stat., 1447), so far as it pertains to legislation in the Indian Territory.]

* * * To enable the Secretary of the Interior to investigate and report to Congress at its next session whether it is practicable to provide a system of taxation of personal property, occupations, franchises, and so forth, in the Indian Territory sufficient to maintain a system of free schools to all the children of the Indian Territory, five thousand dollars

* * * That hereafter the Secretary of the Interior may, whenever the chief executive of the Choctaw or Chickasaw Nation refuses or fails to appoint a town-site commissioner for any town, or to fill any vacancy caused by the neglect or refusal of the town-site commissioner appointed by the chief executive of the Choctaw or Chickasaw Nation to qualify or act, in his discretion, appoint a commissioner to fill the vacancy thus created.

* * * That no act, ordinance, or resolution of the Creek or Cherokee tribes, except resolutions for adjournment, shall be of any validity until approved by the President of the United States. When such acts, ordinances, or resolutions passed by the council of either of said tribes shall be approved by the principal chief thereof, then it shall be the duty of the national secretary of said tribe to forward them to the President of the United States, duly certified and sealed, who shall, within thirty days after their reception, approve or disapprove the same. Said acts, ordinances, or resolutions when so approved, shall be published in at least two newspapers having a bona fide circulation in the tribe to be affected thereby, and when disapproved shall be returned to the tribe enacting the same.

* * * That the Secretary of the Interior is hereby authorized and empowered to grant a right of way, in the nature of an easement, for the construction, operation, and maintenance of telephone and telegraph lines and offices for general telephone and telegraph business through any Indian reservation, through any lands held by an Indian tribe or nation in the Indian Territory, through any lands reserved for an Indian agency or Indian school or for other purposes in connection with the Indian service, or through any lands which have been allotted in severalty to any individual Indian under any law or treaty, but which have not been conveyed to the allottee with full power of alienation, upon the terms and conditions herein expressed. No such lines shall be constructed across Indian lands, as above mentioned, until authority therefor has first been obtained from the Secretary of the Interior, and the maps of definite location of the lines shall be subject to his approval. The compensation to be paid the tribes in their tribal capacity and the individual allottees for such right of way through their lands shall be determined in such manner as the Secretary of the Interior may direct, and shall be subject to his final approval; and where such lines are not subject to State or Territorial taxation the company or owner of the line shall pay to the Secretary of the Interior, for the use and benefit of the Indians, such

annual tax as he may designate, not exceeding five dollars for each ten miles of line so constructed and maintained; and all such lines shall be constructed and maintained under such rules and regulations as said Secretary may prescribe; but nothing herein contained shall be so construed as to exempt the owners of such lines from the payment of any tax that may be lawfully assessed against them by either State, territorial, or municipal authority; and Congress hereby expressly reserves the right to regulate the tolls or charges for the transmission of messages over any lines constructed under the provisions of this act: *Provided*, That incorporated cities and towns into or through which such telephone or telegraphic lines may be constructed shall have the power to regulate the manner of construction therein, and nothing herein contained shall be so construed as to deny the right of municipal taxation in such towns and cities.

APPENDIX NO. 8.

REGULATIONS PRESCRIBED BY THE SECRETARY OF THE INTERIOR TO GOVERN MINERAL LEASES IN THE CHOCTAW AND CHICKASAW NATIONS, INDIAN TERRITORY, UNDER THE PROVISIONS OF THE AGREEMENT OF APRIL 23, 1897, BETWEEN THE COMMISSION TO THE FIVE CIVILIZED TRIBES AND THE SAID CHOCTAW AND CHICKASAW NATIONS, AS RATIFIED BY ACT OF CONGRESS OF JUNE 28, 1898. (30 STAT., 495.)

MINERAL LEASES.

1. The agreement with the Choctaw and Chickasaw nations set out in section 29 of the act of Congress entitled "An act for the protection of the people of the Indian Territory, and for other purposes," approved June 28, 1898 (30 Stat., 495–510), which was duly ratified on August 24, 1898, provides that the leasing and operating of coal and asphalt lands in said nations shall be under the control of two trustees appointed by the President of the United States upon the recommendation of the executives of said nations, each of whom shall be an Indian by blood of the respective nation for which he may be appointed.

2. Each trustee to be appointed under the provisions of said agreement shall be required to file a bond, with two good and sufficient sureties or an approved trust or surety company, with the Secretary of the Interior in the penal sum of $10,000, conditioned for the faithful performance of his duties under said agreement as prescribed therein, and in accordance with these regulations. Said bonds shall be approved by the Secretary of the Interior before said trustees shall be permitted to enter upon their duties.

3. All applications must be made under oath, by parties desiring leases, to the United States Indian inspector located in the Indian Territory, upon blanks to be furnished by the inspector. Each party will be required to state that the application is not made for speculation, but in good faith for mining the mineral or minerals specified. A map must be filed with each application, showing the amount of land on each legal subdivision supposed to be underlaid with mineral and the quantity of mineral that can properly be mined. Applicants must furnish in detail any other information desired by the inspector regarding their prospective operations. All applications received by the inspector will, if satisfactory to him, be transmitted to said trustees for an immediate report to him of facts, and when they are returned he will transmit them to the Department, through the Commissioner of Indian Affairs, with his recommendations. Applications by parties who do not themselves intend to operate mines upon the land applied for will be rejected by the inspector, subject to appeal, as provided hereafter in cases of controversies between applicants. Leases will not be transferable or negotiable, except with the consent of the Secretary, and any instrument with that purpose in view must be approved by him before it will become valid. No application will be received for any other mineral than coal and asphalt.

Should parties whose applications have been approved, and who have been so advised, fail to execute leases in accordance with these regulations within thirty days from notice, or to give good reason for such failure, the land applied for will be subject to lease by other parties. They should be so informed at time of notice of approval.

Said trustees shall at all times be under the direction and supervision of the inspector, and shall also make an examination from time to time, as often as it shall be deemed expedient, and at least once in every month, into the operations of all persons, corporations, or companies operating mines within said nations, with a view of ascertaining the quantity of mineral produced by each, the amount of royalty, if any, due and unpaid by each, and all other information necessary for the protection of the interests of the Choctaw and Chickasaw nations in the premises; and for this purpose all persons, corporations, or companies operating mines within the Choctaw and Chickasaw nations shall give said trustees access to any and all of their books and records necessary or required by them to be examined, and within fifteen days after the last day of each quarter said trustees shall make a joint report to the Secretary of the Interior, through the inspector, of all their acts under said agreement and these regulations.

4. All indentures of lease made by the trustees, as above provided, shall be in quadruplicate and shall contain a clear and full description by legal subdivisions of the tract or tracts of land covered thereby, not to exceed 960 acres, which legal subdivisions must be contiguous to each other. Said indentures of lease so executed shall be transmitted through the United States Indian inspector stationed in the Indian Territory to the Commissioner of Indian Affairs, for submission to the Secretary of the Interior for his approval, and no lease shall be valid until the same shall have been approved by the Secretary of the Interior.

5. Royalties shall be required of all lessees as follows, viz:

On coal, 8 cents per ton of 2,000 pounds on mine run, or coal as it is taken from the mines, including that which is commonly called "slack," which rate went into force and effect on and after March 1, 1900.

On asphalt, 60 cents per ton for each and every ton produced weighing 2,000 pounds, of refined, and 10 cents per ton on crude asphalt.

The right is reserved, however, by the Secretary of the Interior in special cases to either reduce or advance the royalty on coal and asphalt on the presentation of facts which, in his opinion, make it to the interest of the Choctaw and Chickasaw nations, but the advancement or reduction of royalty on coal and asphalt in a particular case shall not operate in any way to modify the general provisions of this regulation fixing the minimum royalty as above set out:

Provided, That all lessees shall be required to pay advanced royalties, as provided in said agreement, on all mines or claims, whether developed or not, to be "a credit on royalty when each said mine is developed and operated and its production is in excess of such guaranteed annual advanced payments," as follows, viz: One hundred dollars per annum in advance for the first and second years, $200 per annum in advance for the third and fourth years, and $500 in advance for each succeeding year thereafter; and that, should any lessee neglect or refuse to pay such advanced royalty for the period of sixty days after the same becomes due and payable on any lease, the lease on which default is made shall become null and void, and all royalties paid in advance shall be forfeited and become the money and property of the Choctaw and Chickasaw nations.

All advanced royalties as above defined shall apply from date of approval of each lease, and when any mine on a tract leased is operated royalty due shall be paid monthly as required until the total amount paid equals the first annual advanced payment, after which royalty due shall be credited on such payments; and the lessee shall operate and produce coal from each and every lease in not less than the following quantities: Three thousand tons during the first year from date of approval of lease; 4,000 tons the second year; 7,000 tons the third year; 8,000 tons the fourth year, and 15,000 tons the fifth and each succeeding year thereafter.

6. All lessees of coal and asphalt on land allotted, sold, or reserved shall be required, before the commencement of operations, to pay to the individual owner the value of the use of the necessary surface for prospecting and mining, including the right of way for necessary railways and the damage done to the lands and improvements; and in case of disagreement, for the purpose of the ascertainment of the fair value of the use of the land and the actual damage done, the owner of the land and the lessee shall each select an arbitrator, who, together with such person as shall be appointed or designated by the inspector located in the Indian Territory, shall constitute a board to consider and ascertain the amount that shall be paid by the lessee on account of use of the land and damage done, and the award of such board shall be final and conclusive unless the award be impeached for fraud. All timber and other materials taken by the lessee from land allotted, sold, or reserved for use in the erection of buildings thereon, and in the mine or mines operated by him thereon, as for shoring levels in coal mines, etc., shall be paid for by the lessee at the usual rates.

7. Persons, corporations, and companies who, under the customs and laws of the Choctaw and Chickasaw nations, have made leases with the national agents of said nations of lands therein for the purpose of mining coal or asphalt, and who, prior to April 23, 1897, had taken possession of and were operating in good faith any mine of coal or asphalt in said nation, shall be protected in their right to continue the operation of such mines for the period and on the terms contained in the lease made to

said persons, corporations, or companies by such national agents, and shall have the right, at the expiration of said term, to renew the lease of such mines, subject, however, to all the provisions of the said agreement and of these regulations: *Provided,* That such persons, corporations, or companies shall, within sixty days after the expiration of their leases with the national agents of the Choctaw and Chickasaw nations, apply to the said trustees for a renewal of their leases under said agreement.

8. All leases made prior to April 23, 1897, by any person or corporation with any member or members of the Choctaw or Chickasaw nations, the object of which was to obtain the permission of such member or members to operate coal or asphalt mines within the said nations, are declared void by said agreement, and no person, corporation, or company occupying any lands within either of said nations under such individual leases, or operating coal or asphalt mines on such lands under color of such leases, shall be deemed to have any right or preference in the making of any lease or leases for mining purposes embracing the lands covered by such personal leases, by reason thereof; but parties in possession of such land who have made improvements thereon for the purpose of mining coal or asphalt shall have a preference right to lease the land upon which said improvements have been made, under the provisions of said agreement and these regulations.

9. Where two or more persons, corporations, or companies shall make application for the leasing of the same tract of land for mining purposes, and a controversy arises between such persons, corporations, or companies as to the right of each to obtain the lease of such land, it shall be the duty of the United States Indian inspector stationed in the Indian Territory to investigate into the rights of the parties and determine as to which shall be given the right to lease the lands in controversy, subject to appeal to the Commissioner of Indian Affairs, and from him to the Secretary of the Interior.

Twenty days from notice of any decision by the United States inspector, or the Commissioner of Indian Affairs, not interlocutory, will be allowed for appeal and service of the same upon the opposite party, whether notice of the decision is given by mail or personally. When notice is given by the inspector by mail it should be by registered letter.

In cases pending on appeal before the Commissioner of Indian Affairs, or the Department, argument may be filed at any time before the same is reached in order for examination, and copy of the same shall be served upon the opposite party, and he shall be allowed ten days for reply and to serve the same.

Proof of personal service of appeal or argument shall be the written acknowledgement of the person served or the affidavit of the person who served the same attached thereto, stating the time, place, and manner of service. All notices shall be served upon the attorneys of record.

Proof of service by registered letter shall be the affidavit of the person mailing the letter attached to a copy of the post-office receipt.

No leases will be executed where a conflict exists until the matter has been finally adjudicated by the Department, in case of appeal.

10. All lessees will be required to keep a full and correct account of all their operations under leases entered into under said agreement and these regulations, and their books shall be open at all times to the examination of said trustees, of the United States Indian inspector stationed in the Indian Territory, and such other officer or officers of the Indian department as shall be instructed by the Secretary of the Interior or the Commissioner of Indian Affairs to make such examination; but, except as to the said trustees and the United States Indian inspector located in the Indian Territory, no lessee will be held to have violated this regulation for refusing to permit an examination of his books by any person unless such person shall produce written instructions from the Secretary of the Interior or from the Commissioner of Indian Affairs requiring him to make such an examination, and said lessees shall make all their reports to said United States Indian Inspector, and they shall be subject to any instructions given by him.

11. All royalties, including advanced royalties, as provided for in said agreement and in these regulations, shall be payable in lawful money of the United States, or exchange issued by a national bank in the United States, to the United States Indian agent at the Union Agency in the Indian Territory, who shall be at all times under the direction and supervision of the United States Indian inspector for the Indian Territory. The advanced royalties are payable $100 on the filing of the application which may be made by a certified check on any national bank of the United State payable to the order of the United States Indian agent, which check shall be retained by the United States Indian inspector until the application is approved; $100 in one year thereafter; $200 in two years thereafter; $200 in three years thereafter, and $50 on the fourth and each succeeding year until the end of the term thereof. All

monthly royalties shall be accompanied by a sworn statement, in duplicate, by the person, corporation, or company making the same as to the output of the mine of such person, corporation, or company for the month for which royalties may be tendered. One part of said sworn statement shall be filed with the United States Indian agent, to be transmitted to the Commissioner of Indian Affairs, and the other part thereof shall be filed with the United States Indian inspector located in the Indian Territory.

12. The said United States Indian agent shall receive and receipt for all royalties paid into his hands when accompanied by a sworn statement as above provided, but not otherwise, and all royalties received by him shall be, as soon as practicable, deposited with the United States subtreasurer at St. Louis, in like manner as are deposited moneys known in the regulations of the Indian office as miscellaneous receipts, Class III, with a statement showing the proportionate shares of each of the Choctaw and Chickasaw nations.

13. All royalties collected and deposited by the United States Indian agent, as above set forth, shall be held to the credit of the Choctaw and Chickasaw nations in their respective proportions, and shall be subject to disbursement by the Secretary of the Interior for the support of the schools of the Choctaw and Chickasaw nations in accordance with said agreement.

14. All lessees under said agreement and these regulations will be required to give bond, with two good and sufficient sureties or an approved surety company, for the faithful discharge of their obligations under their leases in such penalty as shall be prescribed in each case by the Secretary of the Interior, and until such bond is filed by the lessee and approved and accepted by the Secretary of the Interior no rights or interests under any lease shall accrue to such lessee.

15. The right to alter or amend these regulations is reserved.

E. A. Hitchcock,
Secretary of the Interior.

Department of the Interior,
Washington, D. C., May 22, 1900.

FORMS.

Application for Mineral Lease.

(May 22, 1900.)

To the United States Indian Inspector
Located in the Indian Territory:

—— —— desiring to avail —— of the provisions of section twenty-nine of the act of Congress of June 28, 1898 (30 Stats., 495), entitled "An act for the protection of the people of the Indian Territory, and for other purposes," hereby make— application to lease, for the purpose of mining ——, the following tract of land, viz: —— —— section —— in township —— of range —— in the —— Nation, containing —— acres, more or less, the attached map showing the amount of land on each legal subdivision supposed to be underlaid with —— and the quantity that can probably be mined; and —— solemnly —— that this application is made in good faith, and with no other object than that of mining the mineral specified.

—— ——.

Sworn to and subscribed before me this —— day of ——, 190—.

—— ——,
—— ——.

Washington, D. C., —— ——, 190—.
Approved:

——,
Secretary.

[Transferable and negotiable only with the consent of the Secretary of the Interior.]

(Write all names and addresses in full.)

(May 22, 1900.)

Indian Territory Asphalt Mining Lease (Choctaw and Chickasaw Nations).

Indenture of lease, made and entered into in quadruplicate on this —— day of ——, A. D. 190-, by and between —— —— and —— ——, as mining trustees of the Choctaw and Chickasaw nations, parties of the first part, and —— ——, of ——, county of ——, State of ——, part- of the second part, under and in pursuance of the provisions of the act of Congress approved June 28, 1898 (30 Stats., 495), the agreement set out in section twenty-nine thereof, duly ratified on August 24, 1898, and the rules and regulations prescribed by the Secretary of the Interior on May 22, 1900, relative to mining leases in the Choctaw and Chickasaw nations.

Now, therefore, this indenture witnesseth: That the parties of the first part, for and in consideration of the royalties, covenants, stipulations, and conditions hereinafter contained and hereby agreed to be paid, observed, and performed by the part-of the second part, ——, executors, administrators, or assigns do hereby demise, grant, and let unto the part- of the second part, —— executors, administrators, or assigns, the following-described tract of land, lying and being within the —— Nation and within the Indian Territory, to wit: The —— —— of section ——, of township [1] ——, of range [2] ——, of the Indian meridian, and containing —— acres, more or less, for the full term of —— years from the date hereof for the sole purpose of prospecting for and mining asphalt —— ——.

In consideration of the premises, the part- of the second part hereby agree- and bind —— executors, administrators, or assigns to pay or cause to be paid to the United States Indian agent for the Union Agency, Indian Territory, as royalty, the sums of money as follows, to wit: —— cents per ton for each and every ton of asphalt produced weighing 2,000 pounds of refined and —— cents per ton on crude asphalt.

And all said royalties accruing for any month shall be due and payable on or before the twenty-fifth day of the month succeeding.

And the part- of the second part further agree- not to hold the land described for speculative purposes, but in good faith for mining the mineral specified.

And the part- of the second part further agree- and bind —— executors, administrators, or assigns to pay or cause to be paid to the United States Indian agent for the Union Agency, Indian Territory, as advanced royalty on each and every mine or claim within the tract of land covered by this lease, the sums of money as follows, to wit: One hundred dollars per annum, in advance, for the first and second years; two hundred dollars per annum, in advance, for the third and fourth years, and five hundred dollars per annum, in advance, for the fifth and each succeeding year thereafter of the term for which this lease is to run, it being understood and agreed that said sums of money to be paid as aforesaid shall be a credit on royalty should the part- of the second part develop and operate a mine or mines on the lands leased by this indenture and the production of such mine or mines exceed such sums paid as advanced royalty as above set forth; and further, that all advanced royalties as above defined shall apply from date of approval of each lease, and when any mine is operated royalty due shall be paid monthly as required until the total amount equals the first annual advanced payment, after which royalty due shall be credited on such payments; and further, that should the part- of the second part neglect or refuse to pay such advanced annual royalty for the period of sixty days after the same becomes due and payable under this lease, then this lease shall be null and void, and all royalties paid in advance shall become the money and property of the Choctaw and Chickasaw tribes of Indians, subject to the regulations of the Secretary of the Interior aforesaid.

The part- of the second part further covenant- and agree- to exercise diligence in the conduct of the prospecting and mining operations, and to open mines and operate the same in a workmanlike manner to the fullest possible extent on the above-described tract of land; to commit no waste upon said land or upon the mines that may be thereon, and to suffer no waste to be committed thereon; to take good care of the same, and to surrender and return the premises at the expiration of this lease to the parties of the first part in as good condition as when received, ordinary wear and tear in the proper use of the same for the purposes hereinbefore indicated and unavoidable accidents excepted, and not to remove therefrom any buildings or improvements erected thereon during said term by —— ——, the part- of the second part, but said buildings and improvements shall remain a part of said land and become the property of the owner of the land as a part of the consideration for this lease, in addition to the other considerations herein specified, except engines, tools, and machinery, which shall remain the property of the said part- of the second part; that —— will not permit any nuisance to be maintained on the premises, nor allow any intoxicating liquors to be sold or given away to be used for any purposes on the premises, and that —— will not use the premises for any other purpose than that authorized in this lease, nor allow them to be used for any other purpose; that —— will not at any time during the term hereby granted assign or transfer —— estate, interest, or term in said premises and land or the appurtenances thereto to any person or persons whomsoever without the written consent thereto of the parties of the first part being first obtained, subject to the approval of the Secretary of the Interior.

And the said part- of the second part further covenant- and agree- that —— will keep an accurate account of all mining operations, showing the whole amount of asphalt mined or removed, and that there shall be a lien on all implements, tools, movable machinery, and other personal chattels used in said prospecting and mining

---

[1] *State* whether north or south.   [2] State whether east or west.

ions and upon all such asphalt obtained from the land herein leased as
y for the monthly payment of said royalties.

the part- of the second part agree- that this indenture of lease shall be sub-
all respects to the rules and regulations heretofore or that may be hereafter
bed under the said act of June 28, 1898, by the Secretary of the Interior rela-
mineral leases in the Choctaw and Chickasaw nations; and further, that
the part- of the second part, —— executors, administrators, or assigns,
any of the covenants, stipulations, or provisions of this lease, or fail for the
of thirty days to pay the stipulated monthly royalties provided for herein,
1e Secretary of the Interior shall be at liberty, in his discretion, to avoid this
ure of lease and cause the same to be annulled, when all the rights, fran-
and privileges of the part- of the second part, —— executors, adminis-
, or assigns hereunder, shall cease and end without further proceedings.
. the part- of the second part —— firmly bound for the faithful compliance
1e stipulations of this indenture by and under the bond made and executed
part- of the second part as principal- and —— —— as suret- entered into
— day of ——, ——, and which is on file in the Indian Office.
itness whereof the said parties of the first and second parts have hereunto set
ands and affixed their seals the day and year first above mentioned.
nesses :

—— —— as to, —— ——,　　[SEAL.]²
Trustee for Choctaw Nation.

—— —— as to ——,　　[SEAL.]
Trustee for Chickasaw Nation.

—— —— } as to —— ——.　　[SEAL.]

—— —— } as to —— ——.　　[SEAL.]

—— —— } as to —— ——.　　[SEAL.]

—— —— } as to —— —-.　　[SEAL.]

—— —— } as to —— ——.　　[SEAL.]

——

EPARTMENT OF THE INTERIOR,

WASHINGTON, D. C.

ASPHALT LEASE.

Mining Trustees.

TO

OF

——, Tp.——, R.——, in the

Nation, Indian Territory.

—— ——, 190-.

¡ —— ——, 19—.

DEPARTMENT OF THE INTERIOR,
U. S. INDIAN SERVICE,
UNION AGENCY,
Muscogee, I. T.,——, *190-.*

Respectfully forwarded to the Commissioner of Indian Affairs for consideration
with my report of even date.

—— ——,
Indian Inspector.

DEPARTMENT OF THE INTERIOR,
OFFICE OF INDIAN AFFAIRS,
Washington, D. C.,——, *190-.*

Respectfully submitted to the Secretary
of the Interior with favorable recommendation.

—— ——,
Commissioner.

DEPARTMENT OF THE INTERIOR,
Washington, D. C.,——, *190-.*

Approved:

—— ——,
Secretary of the Interior.

witnesses to each signature, including signatures of trustees.
s are required by the act of June 13, 1898, to be placed on leases as follows, viz: Leases for
, 25 cents; for more than one year and not exceeding three years, 50 cents; and for more
1e years, $1. Lessees must furnish stamps for all leases.

[Transferable and negotiable only with the consent of the Secretary of the Interior.]

(Write all names and addresses in full.)

(May 22, 1900.)

INDIAN TERRITORY COAL MINING LEASE (CHOCTAW AND CHICKASAW NATIONS).

Indenture of lease, made and entered into in quadruplicate, on this —— day of ———, A. D. 190-, by and between —— —— and —— ——, as mining trustees of the Choctaw and Chickasaw nations, parties of the first part, and —— ——, of ———, county of ———, State of ———, part- of the second part, under and in pursuance of the provisions of the act of Congress approved June 28, 1898 (30 Stats., 495), the agreement set out in section twenty-nine thereof duly ratified on August 24, 1898, and the rules and regulations prescribed by the Secretary of the Interior on May 22, 1900, relative to mining leases in the Choctaw and Chickasaw nations.

Now, therefore, this indenture witnesseth, that the parties of the first part, for and in consideration of the royalties, covenants, stipulations, and conditions hereinafter contained and hereby agreed to be paid, observed, and performed by the part- of the second part, —— executors, administrators, or assigns, do hereby demise, grant, and let unto the part- of the second part, —— executors, administrators, or assigns, the following described tract of land, lying and being within the —— Nation, and within the Indian Territory, to wit: The —— —— of section ———, of township[1] ———, of range[2]———, of the Indian meridian, and containing —— acres, more or less, for the full term of —— years from the date hereof, for the sole purpose of prospecting for and mining coal —— ——.

In consideration of the premises the part- of the second part hereby agree- and bind —— executors, administrators, or assigns to pay or cause to be paid to the United States Indian agent for the Union Agency, Indian Territory, as royalty, the sums of money as follows, to wit:

On the production of all mines developed and operated under this lease the sum of —— cents per ton of 2,000 pounds on mine run, or coal as it is taken from the mines, including that which is commonly called "slack."

And all said royalties accruing for any month shall be due and payable on or before the twenty-fifth day of the month succeeding.

And the part- of the second part further agree- not to hold the land described for speculative purposes, but in good faith for mining the mineral specified.

And the part- of the second part further agree- and bind —— —— executors, administrators, or assigns to pay or cause to be paid to the United States agent for the Union Agency, Indian Territory, as advanced royalty on each and every mine or claim within the tract of land covered by this lease the sums of money as follows, to wit: One hundred dollars per annum, in advance, for the first and second years; two hundred dollars per annum, in advance, for the third and fourth years, and five hundred dollars per annum, in advance, for the fifth and each succeeding year thereafter of the term for which this lease is to run, it being understood and agreed that said sums of money to be paid as aforesaid shall be a credit on royalty should the part- of the second part develop and operate a mine or mines on the lands leased by this indenture, and the production of such mine or mines exceed such sums paid as advanced royalty as above set forth; and further that all advanced royalties as above defined shall apply from date of approval of each lease, and when any mine is operated royalty due shall be paid monthly as required until the total amount paid equals the first annual advanced payment, after which royalty due shall be credited on such payments; and the part- of the second part agree- and bind —— —— executors, administrators, or assigns to operate and produce coal from each and every lease of not less than the following quantities: Three thousand tons during the first year from date of approval of lease; four thousand tons the second year; seven thousand tons the third year; eight thousand tons the fourth year, and fifteen thousand tons the fifth and each succeeding year thereafter; and it is further agreed that should the part- of the second part neglect or refuse to pay such advanced annual royalty for the period of sixty days after the same becomes due and payable under this lease, then this lease shall be null and void, and all royalties paid in advance shall become the money and property of the Choctaw and Chickasaw tribes of the Indians, subject to the regulations of the Secretary of the Interior aforesaid.

The part- of the second part further covenant- and agree- to exercise diligence in

---

[1] State whether north or south.   [2] State whether east or west.

the conduct of the prospecting and mining operations, and to open mines and operate the same in a workmanlike manner to the fullest possible extent on the above-described tract of land; to commit no waste upon said land or upon the mines that may be thereon, and to suffer no waste to be committed thereon; to take good care of the same, and to surrender and return the premises at the expiration of this lease to the parties of the first part in as good condition as when received, ordinary wear and tear in the proper use of the same for the purposes hereinbefore indicated and unavoidable accidents excepted, and not to remove therefrom any buildings or improvements erected thereon during said term by ——— ———, the part– of the second part, but said buildings and improvements shall remain a part of said land and become the property of the owner of the land as a part of the consideration for this lease, in addition to the other considerations herein specified—except engines, tools, and machinery, which shall remain the property of the said part– of the second part; that ——— will not permit any nuisance to be maintained on the premises, nor allow any intoxicating liquors to be sold or given away to be used for any purposes on the premises, and that ——— will not use the premises for any other purpose than that authorized in this lease, nor allow them to be used for any other purpose; that ——— will not at any time during the term hereby granted assign or transfer ——— estate, interest, or term in said premises and land or the appurtenances thereto to any person or persons whomsoever without the written consent thereto of the parties of the first part being first obtained, subject to the approval of the Secretary of the Interior.

And the said part– of the second part further covenant– and agree– that——— will keep an accurate account of all mining operations, showing the whole amount of coal mined or removed, and that there shall be a lien on all implements, tools, movable machinery, and other personal chattels used in said prospecting and mining operations, and upon all such coal obtained from the land herein leased, as security for the monthly payment of said royalties.

And the part– of the second part agree– that this indenture of lease shall be subject in all respects to the rules and regulations heretofore or that may be hereafter prescribed under the said act of June 28, 1898, by the Secretary of the Interior relative to mineral leases in the Choctaw and Chickasaw nations; and, further, that should the part– of the second part, ——— executors, administrators, or assigns, violate any of the covenants, stipulations, or provisions of this lease, or fail for the period of thirty days to pay the stipulated monthly royalties provided for herein, then the Secretary of the Interior shall be at liberty, in his discretion, to avoid this indenture of lease, and cause the same to be annulled, when all the rights, franchises, and privileges of the part– of the second part, ——— executors, administrators, or assigns, hereunder shall cease and end, without further proceedings.

The part– of the second part ——— firmly bound for the faithful compliance with the stipulations of this indenture by and under the bond made and executed by the part– of the second part as principal– and ——— as suret– entered into the ——— day of ———, and which is on file in the Indian Office.

In witness whereof, the said parties of the first and second parts have hereunto set their hands and affixed their seals the day and year first above mentioned.

[1] Witnesses:

——— ———	as to ——— ———,	[SEAL.][2]
	Trustee for Choctaw Nation.	
——— ———	as to ——— ———,	[SEAL.]
	Trustee for Chickasaw Nation.	
——— ——— }	as to ——— ———.	[SEAL.]
——— ——— }	as to ——— ———.	[SEAL.]
——— ——— }	as to ——— ———.	[SEAL.]
——— ——— }	as to ——— ———.	[SEAL.]
——— ——— }	as to ——— ———.	[SEAL.]

[1] Two witnesses to each signature, including signatures of trustees.
[2] Stamps are required by the Act of June 13, 1898, to be placed on leases as follows, viz: Leases for one year, 25 cents; for more than one year and not exceeding three years, 50 cents; and for more than three years, $1. Lessees must furnish stamps for all leases.

DEPARTMENT OF THE INTERIOR,
U. S. INDIAN SERVICE,
UNION AGENCY,
Muscogee, I. T., ———— ————, *190*—.
Respectfully forwarded to the Commissioner of Indian Affairs for consideration with my report of even date.

Indian Inspector.

DEPARTMENT OF THE INTERIOR,
OFFICE OF INDIAN AFFAIRS,
Washington, D. C., ———— , *190*—.
Respectfully submitted to the Secretary of the Interior with favorable recommendation.

Commissioner.

DEPARTMENT OF THE INTERIOR,
Washington, D. C., ———— , *190*—.
Approved:

Secretary of the Interior.

No.———

DEPARTMENT OF THE INTERIOR,
WASHINGTON D. C.

COAL LEASE.

Mining trustees,

TO

OF

Sec. ——, Twp. ——, Range ——,
in the ———— Nation, Indian Territory.
Dated ———— , 190—.
Expires ———— , 19—.

BOND.

(May 22, 1900.)

Know all men by these presents, that [1] ———— ————, of ———— ————, as principal- and ———— ————, of ———— ————, as surety, are held and firmly bound unto the United States of America in the sum of ———— dollars, lawful money of the United States, for the payment of which, well and truly to be made, we bind ourselves, and each of us, our heirs, successors, executors, and administrators, jointly and severally, firmly by these presents.

Sealed with our seals, and dated ———— day of ————.

The condition of this obligation is such, that whereas the above-bounden ———— ———— as principal-, entered into ———— certain indenture- of lease, dated ———— ————, with ———— and ———— ————, mining trustees of the Choctaw and Chickasaw nations, for the lease of a certain tract of land located in the ———— Nation, Indian Territory, for the purpose of prospecting for and mining ———— for the period of ———— years.

Now, if the above-bounden ———— ———— shall faithfully carry out and observe all the obligations assumed in said indenture- of lease by ———— ————, and shall observe all the laws of the United States, and regulations made or which shall be made thereunder, for the government of trade and intercourse with Indian tribes, and all the rules and regulations that have been or may be prescribed by the Secretary of

———
[1] The Christian names and residences of principals.

the Interior, under the act of June 28, 1898 (30 Stat., 495), relative to mining leases in the Choctaw and Chickasaw nations, in the Indian Territory, then this obligation shall be null and void, otherwise to remain in full force and effect.

Signed and sealed in the presence of [1]—

————— —————.   ————— —————.   [L. S.] [2]
————— —————.   ————— —————.   [L. S.]
————— —————.   ————— —————.   [L. S.]
————— —————.   ————— —————.   [L. S.]
————— —————.   ————— —————.   [L. S.]
————— —————.   ————— —————.   [L. S.]

DEPARTMENT OF THE INTERIOR,
WASHINGTON, D. C.

BOND
OF

Lessee—— of ——————Nation,

in the ——————

Indian Territory, for mining purposes.

WASHINGTON, D. C., ————, 190—.

Approved:

——————
Secretary.

OATH.

We, the undersigned, mining trustees of the Choctaw and Chickasaw nations, Indian Territory, do solemnly swear that the leases hereunto annexed, numbered ——, to ——, were made by us personally with ——— ——, of —— ——; that we have made the same fairly, without any benefit or advantage to ourselves, severally or jointly, or allowing any such benefit or advantage corruptly to the said —— —— (for mining purposes in the said nations), or any other person or persons.

——————————,
Trustee, Choctaw Nation.

——————————,
Trustee, Chickasaw Nation.

Subscribed and sworn to before me at ——·this —— day of ——, 190-.

——————————,
Notary Public.

My commission expires ——, ——.

——————

APPENDIX NO. 9.

APPLICATION FOR MINERAL LEASE.

(May 22, 1900.)

To the United States Indian inspector located in the Indian Territory:

——————, desiring to avail —— of the provisions of section twenty-nine of the act of Congress of June 28, 1898 (30 Stat., 495), entitled "An act for the protection of the people of the Indian Territory, and for other purposes," hereby make application to lease, for the purpose of mining —— the following tract of land,

——————

[1] There must be at least two witnesses to all signatures, though the same two persons may witness all.

[2] A seal must be attached by some adhesive substance to the signatures of principals and sureties.

viz: —— —— section ——, in township ——, of range ——, in the —— Nation, containing —— acres, more or less, the attached map showing the amount of land on each legal subdivision supposed to be underlaid with —— and the quantity that can probably be mined; and —— solemnly —— that this application is made in good faith, and with no other object than that of mining the mineral specified.

Sworn to and subscribed before me this —— day of ——, 190–.

—————,

WASHINGTON, D. C., ——, 190–.
Approved.

—————,
Secretary.

APPENDIX NO. 10.

ADDITIONAL INFORMATION TO ACCOMPANY APPLICATION FOR MINING LEASE IN THE CHOCTAW AND CHICKASAW NATIONS, INDIAN TERRITORY.

—— ——, of —— ——, makes the following statements, under oath, to accompany his application attached hereto, dated ——, for the purpose o fmining —— in the —— Nation, covering the following described land: —— ——.

1. The applicant has filed —— other applications for leases to mine ——, in addition to the one herein asked, and is interested in —— other —— leases in the Indian Territory, known as the —— ——.

2. That he does not intend to sell or transfer this application or the lease arising therefrom; that there is no agreement, open or secret, whereby the applicant is to sell, assign, transfer to, or consolidate this application or the lease arising therefrom with any other person or corporation whatsoever, but that the applicant proposes to operate the mines covered by his application for himself, or, in case of a company or corporation, for said company or corporation.

3. Applicant has heretofore had —— national contract with the Choctaw and Chickasaw nations covering the land herein described. Under same mines have been operated by the applicant on this tract for —— years, such operations having been commenced on or about —— by sinking a shaft or slope —— feet, and has taken therefrom about —— tons of ——, and has expended $—— in improvements on said tract, comprising —— ——.

4. That the applicant will, within —— months after formal lease is duly approved and delivered to him, commence active operations; that the applicant has —— dollars now on hand for such operations, and that the applicant has good reasons to believe that he or it will produce from said mine —— tons of —— during the first year from the date of the approval of the lease; that he or it will produce —— tons during the second year, and —— tons during the third year, and that there is embraced within the tract applied for, from the best obtainable information, —— tons of workable ——, and, in case of coal applications, there are —— veins of coal on said tract, each vein —— inches in thickness, with a pitch of about —— degrees; applicant further states that —— acres of the tract applied for are underlaid with ——, as shown by the plat.

5. That the applicant will exercise no rights or privileges whatever under the application herein described, nor commence operations, until the lease shall have been duly approved and delivered to him.

6. That the applicant is a resident of —— and engaged in the business of ——, and has had —— years' experience in coal (or ——) business, in company with —— ——, at ——, and that there are —— other persons interested in this application or lease, if granted; their names and post-office addresses are as follows: —— ——. If the applicant is a corporation, the members interested in or composing the same are as follows: —— ——.

7. There is submitted herewith in connection with said application a certified check for $100, payable to the United States Indian agent, the same to be applied as advanced royalty on the lease applied for, as required by the regulations of the Secretary of the Interior.

(When the applicant is a corporation the following should be filled out:)

8. Applicant is a corporation organized under the laws of the State of ——, with

a capital stock of ——— dollars; that there has been subscribed and paid into the treasury of the corporation and now held subject to bona fide mining operations the sum of ——— dollars thereof.

The applicant's post-office is ——— ———.

        ——— ———.
        ——— ———.
        ——— ———.

Subscribed and sworn to before me this ——— day of ———, 190-.

        ——— ———.

NOTE.—When the applicant is a corporation the application and this affidavit must be signed by the proper officer thereof.

Plat accompanying should show land applied for, by legal subdivisions according to United States surveys, amount underlaid with mineral, veins of coal, etc., and any improvements, railroads, etc., that may be on the land.

If applicant has not heretofore operated under national contract, the word "No" should be inserted in the first line of section 3, and the latter clause of said section should be stricken out. If so operated, the word "shaft" or "slope" should be stricken out, as the case may be, unless mines have been operated by both, in which even that depth of each should be stated.

Each application should be confined to tracts underlaid with mineral, so far as possible, and not exceed 960 acres in area. A less number of acres, however, will be considered.

APPENDIX NO. 11.

[Transferable and negotiable only with the consent of the Secretary of the Interior.]

(Write all names and addresses in full.)

(June 15, 1900.)

INDIAN TERRITORY COAL-MINING LEASE (CHOCTAW AND CHICKASAW NATIONS).

Indenture of lease, made and entered into in quadruplicate on this ——— day of ———, A. D. 190-, by and between ——— ——— and ——— ———, as mining trustees of the Choctaw and Chickasaw nations, parties of the first part, and ——— ———, of ———, county of ———, State of ———, part- of the second part, under and in pursuance of the provisions of the act of Congress approved June 28, 1898 (30 Stats., 495), the agreement set out in section twenty-nine thereof duly ratified on August 24, 1898, and the rules and regulations prescribed by the Secretary of the Interior on May 22, 1900, relative to mining leases in the Choctaw and Chickasaw nations.

Now, therefore, this indenture witnesseth: That the parties of the first part, for and in consideration of the royalties, covenants, stipulations, and conditions hereinafter contained and hereby agreed to be paid, observed, and performed by the part- of the second part, ——— executors, administrators, or assigns, do hereby demise, grant, and let unto the part- of the second part, ——— executors, administrators, or assigns, the following-described tract of land, lying and being within the ——— Nation and within the Indian Territory, to wit, the ——— ———, of section ———, of township[1] ———, of range[2] ———, of the Indian meridian, and containing ——— acres, more or less, for the full term of ——— years from the date hereof, for the sole purpose of prospecting for and mining coal ——— ———.

In consideration of the premises, the part- of the second part hereby agree- and bind ——— executors, administrators, or assigns, to pay or cause to be paid to the United States Indian agent for the Union Agency, Indian Territory, as royalty, the sums of money as follows, to wit:

On the production of all mines developed and operated under this lease the sum of ——— cents per ton of 2,000 pounds on mine run or coal as it is taken from the mines, including that which is commonly called "slack;" and all said royalties accruing for any month shall be due and payable on or before the twenty-fifth day of the month succeeding.

And the part- of the second part further agree- not to hold the land described for speculative purposes, but in good faith for mining the mineral specified.

And the part- of the second part further agree- and bind- ——— executors, administrators, or assigns to pay or cause to be paid to the United States Indian agent for the Union Agency, Indian Territory, as advanced royalty on each and every mine or

---

[1] State whether north or south.   [2] State whether east or west.

claim within the tract of land covered by this lease, the sums of money as follows, to wit, one hundred dollars per annum, in advance, for the first and second years; two hundred dollars per annum, in advance, for the third and fourth years, and five hundred dollars per annum, in advance, for the fifth and each succeeding year thereafter of the term for which this lease is to run, it being understood and agreed that said sums of money to be paid as aforesaid shall be a credit on royalty should the part-of the second part develop and operate a mine or mines on the lands leased by this indenture, and the production of such mine or mines exceed such sums paid as advanced royalty as above set forth; and, further, that all advanced royalties as above defined shall apply from date of approval of each lease, and when any mine is operated royalty due shall be paid monthly as required until the total amount paid equals the first annual advanced payment, after which royalty due shall be credited on such payments; and the part- of the second part agree- and bind- —— —— executors, administrators, or assigns to operate and produce coal from each and every lease of not less than the following quantities: Three thousand tons during the first year from date of approval of lease, four thousand tons the second year, seven thousand tons the third year, eight thousand tons the fourth year, and fifteen thousand tons the fifth and each succeeding year thereafter; and it is further agreed that should the part- of the second part neglect or refuse to pay such advanced annual royalty for the period of sixty days after the same becomes due and payable under this lease, then this lease shall be null and void, and all royalties paid in advance shall become the money and property of the Choctaw and Chickasaw tribes of Indians, subject to the regulations of the Secretary of the Interior aforesaid.

The part- of the second part further covenant- and agree- to exercise diligence in the conduct of the prospecting and mining operations, and to open mines and operate the same in a workmanlike manner to the fullest possible extent on the above-described tract of land; to commit no waste upon said land or upon the mines that may be thereon, and to suffer no waste to be committed thereon; to take good care of the same, and to surrender and return the premises at the expiration of this lease to the parties of the first part in as good condition as when received, ordinary wear and tear in the proper use of the same for the purposes hereinbefore indicated and unavoidable accidents excepted, and not to remove therefrom any buildings or improvements erected thereon during said term by —— ——, the part- of the second part, but said buildings and improvements shall remain a part of said land and become the property of the owner of the land as a part of the consideration for this lease, in addition to the other considerations herein specified, except engines, tools, and machinery, which shall remain the property of the said part- of the second part; that —— will not permit any nuisance to be maintained on the premises, nor allow any intoxicating liquors to be sold or given away to be used for any purpose on the premises, and that —— will not use the premises for any other purpose than that authorized in this lease, nor allow them to be used for any other purpose; that —— will not at any time during the term hereby granted assign, transfer, or sublet —— estate, interest, or term in said premises and land or the appurtenances thereto to any person or persons whomsoever without the written consent thereto of the parties of the first part being first obtained, subject to the approval of the Secretary of the Interior.

And the said part- of the second part further covenant- and agree- that —— will keep an accurate account of all mining operations, showing the whole amount of coal mined or removed, and that there shall be a lien on all implements, tools, movable machinery, and other personal chattels used in said prospecting and mining operations and upon all such coal obtained from the land herein leased as security for the monthly payment of said royalties.

And the part- of the second part agree- that this indenture of lease shall be subject in all respects to the rules and regulations heretofore or that may be hereafter prescribed under the said act of June 28, 1898, by the Secretary of the Interior relative to mineral leases in the Choctaw and Chickasaw nations; and said part- of the second part expressly agree- to pay to said United States Indian agent any additional rate of royalty that may be required by the Secretary of the Interior during the term this lease shall be in force and effect; and further, that should the part- of the second part, —— or executors, administrators, or assigns, violate any of the covenants, stipulations, or provisions of this lease, or fail for the period of thirty days to pay the stipulated monthly royalties provided for herein, then the Secretary of the Interior shall be at liberty, in his discretion, to avoid this indenture of lease and cause the same to be annulled, when all the rights, franchises, and privileges of the part- of the second part, —— executors, administrators, or assigns hereunder, shall cease and end without further proceedings.

The part- of the second part —— firmly bound for the faithful compliance with the stipulations of this indenture by and under the bond made and executed by the part- of the second part, as principals, and ———————, as suret-, entered into the —— day of ———, and which is on file in the Indian Office.

In witness whereof the said parties of the first and second parts have hereunto set their hands and affixed their seals the day and year first above mentioned.

Witnesses:[1]

——— ——— as to ——— ———,   [SEAL.][2]
                    Trustee for Choctaw Nation.
——— ——— as to ——— ———,   [SEAL.]
                    Trustee for Chickasaw Nation.
}as to ——— ———.   [SEAL.]
}as to ——— ———.   [SEAL.]
}as to ——— ———.   [SEAL.]
}as to ——— ———.   [SEAL.]
}as to ——— ———.   [SEAL.]

APPENDIX NO. 11.

DEPARTMENT OF THE INTERIOR,
U. S. INDIAN SERVICE, UNION AGENCY,
Muscogee, I. T., ————, 190-.

Respectfully forwarded to the Commissioner of Indian Affairs for consideration with my report of even date.

————,
Indian Inspector.

DEPARTMENT OF THE INTERIOR,
OFFICE OF INDIAN AFFAIRS,
Washington, D. C., ————, 190-.

Respectfully submitted to the Secretary of the Interior with favorable recommendation.

————,
Commissioner.

DEPARTMENT OF THE INTERIOR,
Washington, D. C., ————, 190-.

Approved.

————,
Secretary of the Interior.

No. ——
Department of the Interior,
Washington, D. C.

COAL LEASE.

Mining Trustees,

TO

OF

Sec. ——, Tp. ——, Range ——, in
the —— Nation, Indian Territory.

Dated ————, 190-.
Expires ————, 19-.

[1] Two witnesses to each signature, including signatures of trustees.
[2] Stamps are required by the act of June 13, 1898, to be placed on leases as follows, viz: Leases for one year, twenty-five cents; for more than one year and not exceeding three years, fifty cents; and for more than three years, one dollar. Lessees must furnish stamps for all leases.

6854—01——14

APPENDIX NO. 12.

[Transferable and negotiable only with the consent of the Secretary of the Interior.]

(Write all names and addresses in full.)

(June 15, 1900.)

INDIAN TERRITORY ASPHALT MINING LEASE (CHOCTAW AND CHICKASAW NATIONS).

Indenture of lease made and entered into in quadruplicate, on this ———— day of ————, A. D. 190–, by and between ———— ———— and ———— as mining trustees of the Choctaw and Chickasaw nations, parties of the first part, and ———— of ————, county of ————, State of ————, part– of the second part, under and in pursuance of the provisions of the act of Congress approved June 28, 1898 (30 Stats., 495), the agreement set out in section 29 thereof duly ratified on August 24, 1898, and the rules and regulations prescribed by the Secretary of the Interior on May 22, 1900, relative to mining leases in the Choctaw and Chickasaw nations.

Now, therefore, this indenture witnesseth, that the parties of the first part, for and in consideration of the royalties, covenants, stipulations, and conditions hereinafter contained and hereby agreed to be paid, observed, and performed by the part– of the second part, ————, executors, administrators, or assigns, do hereby demise, grant, and let unto the part– of the second part, ———— executors, administrators, or assigns, the following-described tract of land, lying and being within the ———— Nation, and within the Indian Territory, to wit: The ———— ———— of section ———— of township[1] ————, of range[2] ————, of the Indian meridian, and containing ———— acres, more or less, for the full term of ———— years from the date hereof for the sole purpose of prospecting for and mining asphalt ———— ————.

In consideration of the premises the part– of the second part hereby agree– and bind ———— executors, administrators, or assigns, to pay or cause to be paid to the United States Indian agent for the Union Agency, Ind. T., as royalty, the sums of money as follows, to wit: ———— cents per ton for each and every ton of asphalt produced weighing 2,000 pounds, of refined, and ———— cents per ton on crude asphalt.

And all said royalties accruing for any month shall be due and payable on or before the twenty-fifth day of the month succeeding.

And the part– of the second part further agree– not to hold the land described for speculative purposes, but in good faith for mining the mineral specified.

And the part– of the second part further agree– and bind ———— executors, administrators, or assigns, to pay or cause to be paid to the United States Indian agent for the Union Agency, Ind. T., as advanced royalty on each and every or mine claim within the tract of land covered by this lease the sums of money as follows, to wit: One hundred dollars per annum, in advance, for the first and second years; two hundred dollars per annum, in advance, for the the third and fourth years, and five hundred dollars per annum, in advance, for the fifth and each succeeding year thereafter, of the term for which this lease is to run, it being understood and agreed that said sums of money to be paid as aforesaid shall be a credit on royalty should the part– of the second part develop and operate a mine or mines on the lands leased by this indenture, and the production of such mine or mines exceed such sums paid as advanced royalty as above set forth; and further, that all advanced royalties as above defined shall apply from date of approval of each lease, and when any mine is operated royalty due shall be paid monthly as required until the total amount paid equals the first annual advanced payment, after which royalty due shall be credited on such payments; and further, that should the part– of the second part neglect or refuse to pay such advanced annual royalty for the period of sixty days after the same becomes due and payable under this lease, then this lease shall be null and void, and all royalties paid in advance shall become the money and property of the Choctaw and Chickasaw tribes of Indians, subject to the regulations of the Secretary of the Interior aforesaid.

The part– of the second part further covenant– and agree– to exercise diligence in the conduct of the prospecting and mining operations, and to open mines and operate the same in a workmanlike manner to the fullest possible extent on the above-described tract of land; to commit no waste upon said land or upon the mines that may be thereon, and to suffer no waste to be committed thereon; to take good care of the same, and to surrender and return the premises at the expiration of this lease to the

———— ————

[1] State whether north or south.　　　　　[2] State whether east or west.

parties of the first part in as good condition as when received, ordinary wear and tear in the proper use of the same for the purposes hereinbefore indicated, and unavoidable accidents, excepted, and not to remove therefrom any buildings or improvements erected thereon during said term by ———— ————, the part- of the second part, but said buildings and improvements shall remain a part of said land and become the property of the owner of the land as a part of the consideration for this lease, in addition to the other considerations herein specified—except engines, tools, and machinery, which shall remain the property of the said part- of the second part; that ———— will not permit any nuisance to be maintained on the premises, nor allow any intoxicating liquors to be sold or given away to be used for any purposes on the premises, and that ———— will not use the premises for any other purposes than that authorized in this lease, nor allow them to be used for any other purpose; that ———— will not at any time during the term hereby granted assign, transfer, or sublet ———— estate, interest, or term in said premises and land or the appurtenances thereto to any person or persons whomsoever without the written consent thereto of the parties of the first part being first obtained, subject to the approval of the Secretary of the Interior.

And the said part- of the second part further covenant- and agree- that ———— will keep an accurate account of all mining operations, showing the whole amount of asphalt mined or removed, and that there shall be a lien on all implements, tools, movable machinery, and other personal chattels used in said prospecting and mining operations, and upon all such asphalt obtained from the land herein leased, as security for the monthly payment of said royalties.

And the part- of the second part agree- that this indenture of lease shall be subject in all respects to the rules and regulations heretofore or that may be hereafter prescribed, under the said act of June 28, 1898, by the Secretary of the Interior relative to mineral leases in the Choctaw and Chickasaw nations; and said part- of the second part expressly agree- to pay to said United States Indian agent any additional rate of royalty that may be required by the Secretary of the Interior during the term this lease shall be in force and effect; and further, that should the part- of the second part, ———— executors, administrators, or assigns, violate any of the covenants, stipulations, or provisions of this lease, or fail for the period of thirty days to pay the stipulated monthly royalties provided for herein, then the Secretary of the Interior shall be at liberty, in his discretion, to avoid this indenture of lease, and cause the same to be annulled, when all the rights, franchises, and privileges of the part- of the second part, ———— executors, administrators, or assigns hereunder shall cease and end, without further proceedings.

The part- of the second part ———— firmly bound for the faithful compliance with the stipulations of this indenture by and under the bond made and executed by the part- of the second part as principal- and ———— ———— as suret- entered into the ———— day of ————, ————, and which is on file in the Indian Office.

In witness whereof, the said parties of the first and second parts have hereunto set their hands and affixed their seals the day and year first above mentioned.

[1] Witnesses:

———— ———— as to ———— ————,   [SEAL.][2]
                              Trustee for Choctaw Nation.
———— ———— as to ———— ————,   [SEAL.]
                              Trustee for Chickasaw Nation.
———— ————} as to ———— ————.   [SEAL.]
———— ————} as to ———— ————.   [SEAL.]
———— ————} as to ———— ————.   [SEAL.]
———— ————} as to ———— ————.   [SEAL.]
———— ————} as to ———— ————.   [SEAL.]

[1] Two witnesses to each signature, including signatures of trustees.
[2] Stamps are required by the act of June 13, 1898, to be placed on leases, as follows, viz: Leases for one year, 25 cents, for more than one year and not exceeding three years, 50 cents, and for more than three years, $1. Lessees must furnish stamps for all leases.

DEPARTMENT OF THE INTERIOR,
U. S. INDIAN SERVICE, UNION AGENCY,
Muscogee, Ind. T., ——, 190-.
Respectfully forwarded to the Commissioner of Indian Affairs for consideration with my report of even date.

Indian Inspector.

No. ——
Department of the Interior,
Washington, D. C.

ASPHALT LEASE.

Mining Trustees,

TO

DEPARTMENT OF THE INTERIOR,
OFFICE OF INDIAN AFFAIRS,
Washington, D. C., ——, 190-.
Respectfully submitted to the Secretary of the Interior with favorable recommendation.

Commissioner.

OF

DEPARTMENT OF THE INTERIOR,
Washington, D. C., ——, 190-.
Approved:

Secretary of the Interior.

Sec. ——, Tp. ——, Range ——, in the —— Nation, Indian Territory.
Dated ——, ——, 190-.
Expires ——, ——, 190-.

APPENDIX No. 13.

BOND.

(May 22, 1900.)

Know all men by these presents that [1] —— ——, of —— ——, as principal-, and —— ——, of —— ——, as surety, are held and firmly bound unto the United States of America in the sum of —— dollars, lawful money of the United states, for the payment of which, well and truly to be made, we bind ourselves and each of us, our heirs, successors, executors, and administrators, jointly and severally, firmly by these presents.

Sealed with our seals and dated —— day of ——.

The condition of this obligation is such that whereas the above-bounden ——
——, as principal-, entered into —— certain indenture- of lease, dated ——
——, with —— —— and —— ——, mining trustees of the Choctaw and Chickasaw nations, for the lease of a certain tract of land located in the —— Nation, Indian Territory, for the purpose of prospecting for and mining —— for the period of —— years.

Now, if the above-bounden —— —— shall faithfully carry out and observe all the obligations assumed in said indenture- of lease by —— ——, and shall observe all the laws of the United States, and regulations made or which shall be made there-

---

[1] The Christian names and residences of principals.

under, for the government of trade and intercourse with Indian tribes, and all the rules and regulations that have been or may be prescribed by the Secretary of the Interior, under the act of June 28, 1898 (30 Stat., 495), relative to mining leases in the Choctaw and Chickasaw nations, in the Indian Territory, then this obligation shall be null and void; otherwise to remain in full force and effect.

Signed and sealed in the presence of —[1]

————— —————, ————— —————. [L. S.][2]
————— —————, ————— —————. [L. S.]
————— —————, ————— —————. [L. S.]
————— —————, ————— —————. [L. S.]
————— —————, ————— —————. [L. S.]
————— —————, ————— —————. [L. S.]

Department of the Interior, Washington, D. C.

BOND

OF

Lessee_ of

in the Nation, Indian Territory, for mining purposes.

WASHINGTON, D. C., ———, 190-.

Approved:

——————
Secretary.

APPENDIX NO. 14.

DEPARTMENT OF JUSTICE,
Washington, D. C., September 7, 1900.

The honorable the SECRETARY OF THE INTERIOR.

SIR: I have the honor to reply to your note of August 13, 1900, requesting my official opinion upon several questions there stated arising from conditions now existing in the Indian country occupied by the Five Civilized Tribes of Indians, and which conditions are stated, in substance, thus:

Without referring specially to the tax legislation of these Indian nations, they generally require that persons not citizens or members of any Indian tribe who reside or carry on certain kinds of business within their limits shall procure and pay for a permit or license to do so.

Many persons of this description have bought, under the act of Congress referred to below, lots in the towns and cities in these nations, and many of them are engaged in mercantile, professional, and other kinds of business and refuse to pay such tax, claiming, among other reasons, that the act of Congress referred to in authorizing the sale of such lots to persons not Indians or connected with any tribe has recognized this right to so purchase and to reside and carry on business on said lots and has exempted them from such tax.

In addition to this vast herds of cattle, owned by persons not citizens of such nation nor connected with any Indian tribe, are by their owners kept and grazed upon the public lands of these nations, and the owners refuse to pay the tax imposed on account thereof; and the questions propounded relate chiefly to the power and duty of the Department of the Interior to inforce payment of these taxes, and to remove from the limits of such nation, as intruders, those who refuse payment

---

[1] There must be at least two witnesses to all signatures, though the same two persons may witness all.
[2] A seal must be attached by some adhesive substance to the signatures of principals and sureties.

thereof. On account of the number of persons, the vast amount of property, and the consequences involved, the question is, as you suggest, one of great magnitude and importance.

Without referring specially to the different treaties with these Indian nations, it may be stated that they provide that all persons not citizens of such nations or members of any Indian tribe found within the limits of such nation should be considered as intruders and be removed from and kept out of the same by the United States. From this class of intruders are excepted the employees of the Government and their families and servants; employees of any internal improvement company; travelers and temporary sojourners; those holding permits from any of the Indian tribes to remain within their limits, and white persons who, under their laws, are employed as "teachers, mechanics, or skilled in agriculture."

It is apparent, therefore, that save the excepted classes no one not a citizen or member of a tribe, can be lawfully within these limits, without Indian permission, and equally apparent that all may be so with such permission. And it follows that the same power that can refuse or grant such permission can equally impose the terms on which it is granted.

So far as concerns the Choctaw and Chickasaw nations (and the same rule applies to the others), this question was passed upon by my predecessor, Attorney-General Wayne McVeagh, who held (17 Ops, 134) that such permit and license laws with their tax were valide and must be enforced. The same doctrine was held by Acting Attorney-General Phillips (18 Ops., 34). Both these opinions are cited by the court of appeals of Indian Territory, in Maxey v. Wright (54 S. W. Repr., 807), which distinctly affirms the validity of this legislation. I quite agree with these opinions and have no doubt that it is competent for those Indian nations to prescribe the terms here being considered upon which they will permit outsiders to reside or carry on business within their limits.

Nor does the act of June 28, 1898 (30 Stat., 495), either deprive these nations of the power to enact such legislation or exempt purchasers of town or city lots from its operation.

This was also decided in the case last referred to. So far as affects any question here, that statute provides a plan for the organization of cities and towns, for the sale of town and city lots, and the extinguishment of the Indian title. This last has not yet been consummated, but, as said by the court in Maxey v. Wright, supra, decided January 6, 1900, "The Indian title to such lands still remains in them and it is yet their country."

But, however this may be, and, even if the Indian title to the particular lots sold has been extinguished, and conceding that the statute authorizes the purchase of such lots by any outsider and recognizes his right to do so, the result is still the same, for the legal right to purchase land within an Indian nation gives to the purchaser no right of exemption from the laws of such nation, nor does it authorize him to do any act in violation of the treaties with such nation. These laws requiring a permit to reside or carry on business in the Indian country existed long before and at the time this act was passed. And if any outsider saw proper to purchase a town lot under this act of Congress he did so with full knowledge that he could occupy it for residence or business only by permission from the Indians. I do not say that Congress might not violate its treaty promises and authorize the outside world to enter upon and occupy the lands of the Indians without their consent, but do say that provisions very different from any contained in this act would be required to justify the imputation of any such intention. All that this act does in this respect is to give the consent of the United States to such purchase, with the assumption that the purchaser, if he wishes to occupy, will comply with the local laws, just as in other cases. The United States might sell lands which it holds in a State, but it would be a strange contention that this gave the purchaser any immunity from local laws or local taxation. The case is much like that of a Federal license to manufacture and sell spirituous liquors, which, while good as against the United States, confers no right where such manufacture and sale are forbidden. This act was passed with the full knowledge of these laws of the Indian nations, approved by the President and having the full force of laws, and, had Congress intended to nullify these laws or take away the power to enact them, or to exempt the purchasers of lots or any other persons from their operation, it is quite safe to say it would have done so by provisions very different from those in the act of 1898.

The treaties and laws of the United States make all persons, with a few specified exceptions, who are not citizens of Indian nations or members of an Indian tribe, and are found within an Indian nation without permission intruders there, and require their removal by the United States. This closes the whole matter, absolutely excludes all but the excepted classes, and fully authorizes these nations to absolutely exclude outsiders or to permit their residence or business upon such terms as they may choose to impose, and it must be borne in mind that citizens of the United States have, as such, no more right or business to be there than they have in any foreign nation, and can lawfully be there at all only by Indian permission, and that their right to be or remain or carry on business there depends solely upon whether they have such permission.

As to the power or duty of your Department in the premises there can hardly be a doubt. Under the treaties of the United States with these Indian nations this Government is under the most solemn obligation, and for which it has received ample consideration, to remove and keep removed from the territory of these tribes all this class of intruders who are there without Indian permission. The performance of this obligation, as in other matters concerning the Indians and their affairs, has long been devolved upon the Department of the Interior. This power and duty are affirmed in the two opinions referred to, and as directly in Maxey *v.* Wright, supra. In that case it was said, on page 812:

Upon the whole case we therefore hold that a lawyer, who is a white man and not a citizen of the Creek Nation, is, pursuant to their statutes, required to pay for the privilege of remaining and practicing his profession in that nation the sum of $25, and if he refuses the payment thereof he becomes, by virtue of the treaty, an intruder, and that in such a case the Government of the United States may emove him from the nation, and that this duty devolves upon the Indian Department.

And in another place:

We are of the opinion, however, that the Indian agent, when directed by the Secretary of the Interior, may collect this money from the Creeks. * * * In this case the Indian agent was acting in strict accordance with directions and regulations of the Secretary of the Interior in a matter clearly relating to intercourse with the Indians.

That the United States has the power to perform its treaty stipulations in this regard can not be doubted, and as already said, and in the opinions referred to and above quoted, the execution of that power and duty devolves upon the Interior Department. This power of removal is expressly conferred by Revised Statutes, sections 2147 to 2150, inclusive, with the right to use the military force of the United States when necessary for its accomplishment. And a power of this nature carries with it the duty of its exercise.

But as to persons other than purchasers of town or city lots, residing or carrying on business thereon, no question arises under the above act of 1898, and persons who are pasturing cattle upon, or otherwise occupying part of the public domain of either of these Indian nations without permission from the Indian authorities, are simply intruders and should be removed, unless they obtain such permit and pay the required tax or permit or license fee.

In one of the questions submitted you ask whether your Department has "authority in the case of a merchant refusing to pay such tax to close his place of business or to move his stock of merchandise beyond the limits of the nation?"

To this I answer, your Department may and should remove such merchant unless he has a permit to reside or remain there, and close his place of business and his business, unless he has a permit to carry it on, in all places where such permit is required by law. The question of the right to remove his stock of merchandise beyond the limits of the Indian nation is a different and more doubtful one. While he has no right to remain or carry on business there without a permit to do so, his want of right to keep his goods there, or the right of the Department to remove them, is not so clear. While the law excludes him and authorizes his removal, it does not do so expressly, at least, as to his goods. And, as the whole evil which is sought to be remedied is so done by the removal of the owner and the closing of his business, it is recommended that his goods be permitted to remain if he so desire.

Your question whether the lands of any Indian nation in which a town or city is situated will cease to be Indian country, etc., when the lands in such town or city are sold, is not involving any present existing question, or one which I am authorized to answer.

Your last question asks: "What is the full scope of the authority and duty of the Department of the Interior in the premises under the treaties with these nations and the laws of the United States regulating trade and intercourse with the Indians?"

As applicable to the cases here in hand, which is as far as I, am authorized to answer the question, and which is designed also as a comprehensive answer to all the other questions save the one last referred to above, it may be said generally that the authority and duty of the Interior Department is, within any of these Indian nations, to remove all persons of the classes forbidden by treaty or law who are there without Indian permit or license, to close all business which requires a permit or license and is being carried on there without one, and to remove all cattle being pastured on the public land without Indian permit or license where such license or permit is required; and this is not intended as an enumeration or summary of all the powers or duties of your Department in this direction.

In view of the number of persons, the magnitude of the interests involved, and also as tending to a more ready and better adjustment of the difficulties, it is suggested that public notice be first given to all persons residing or carrying on business without an Indian permit or license where, for such residence or business, such permit is required, that unless such permit or license be obtained by a short day, to be named, such persons will be removed and such business closed, and, in cases of cattle pastured without permission where permission is required, such cattle will be removed from within the nation.

I return herewith the printed copy of the constitution and laws of the Chickasaw Nation transmitted with your note.

Respectfully,

JOHN W. GRIGGS,
Attorney-General.

APPENDIX NO. 15.

United States court, southern district, Indian Territory.

A. KLOSKI ET AL. ⎫
    v.   ⎬
JACK ELLIS ET AL. ⎭

BRIEF FOR DEFENDANTS.

Because the Secretary of the Interior deems the matters involved in this case of great importance in the administration of Indian affairs in his Department, and has requested that a brief therein be prepared in this Department, this brief is prepared under the direction of the Attorney-General and submitted, in addition to that of the United States attorney in charge of the case.

In this case, brought to restrain the defendants from closing the business of certain persons within said district who refuse to pay certain tribal taxes, the court directs that briefs be filed upon the following points, viz:

1. Is there any specific act of Congress specially authorizing the Secretary of the Interior to close the place of business of any noncitizen merchant exposing goods for sale without a permit as required by the section above referred to and by the treaty of 1866?

2. In the absence of any specific act of Congress, has the Secretary of the Interior general authority or discretion to make rules and regulations where there is no specific law authorizing him to do so?

3. As to section 2058 of the Revised Statutes of the United States, which authorizes the Secretary of the Interior to prescribe rules and regulations "not inconsistent with law," is such intended to authorize him to make such rules and regulations where there is no law on the subject, or forbidding him to do so, or is he only authorized to make such rules and regulations not inconsistent with some specific law authorizing him to take such action?

GENERAL CONSIDERATIONS.

Before considering directly the questions propounded some general observations will tend to elucidate the whole subject.

For obvious reasons it has long been the policy of the Government in its treaties with Indian tribes, its laws in relation to the Indians, and in its legislation as to Indian reservations, to isolate the Indians from the white people, to keep them together by themselves, and to not only prevent their intrusion among the whites, but to especially prevent the intrusion of whites among the Indians. Except as to a few specified cases, not only has been and is this the general policy of the Government upon its own account, but it is so because of its treaty obligations which require it to prevent the intrusion of unauthorized persons and unlicensed traders within Indian reservations or the Indian Territory. The most, if not all, of our Indian treaties have expressly stipulated that the United States shall prevent all such intrusions and shall remove all such unauthorized intruders.

This is a duty which the United States has, by various acts of legislation and otherwise, undertaken to perform. And all its acts in this respect are to be construed with reference to this policy and this duty and its attempted performance, and for the faithful performance of which it has received more than ample consideration. I need to no more than allude to what the Supreme Court has often said, that these Indians are the wards of the nation; that having in various ways reduced them to a state of dependency, we are bound to give them all that practicable protection which their dependent condition demands.

THE CHOCTAW AND CHICKASAW TREATIES OF 1855 AND 1866.

By Article VII of the treaty of 1855 it is provided that, "So far as may be compatible with the Constitution of the United States and the laws made in pursuance thereof regulating trade and intercourse with the Indian tribes, the Choctaws and

Chickasaws *shall be secured* in the unrestricted right of self-government and full juris-diction over persons and property within their respective limits," excepting as to persons and property of those not citizens or members of either tribe.

The continuance in force of this article and the independence and autonomy of the Choctaw and Chickasaw nations are recognized all through the treaty of 1866, and especially by Article XLV of that treaty, and are still recognized as in force by all branches of the Government, and those nations continue to make their own laws and carry on their government under this article.

This, of itself and without anything more, makes this Indian country, as to the people of the United States, a foreign and sovereign country into which they can not go, and with whose people they can not trade except by permission of the local authorities and upon such terms as those authorities may prescribe, for this is inher-ent in and essential to that self-government conferred by this article. But even this is not all. By this article the United States has agreed to secure and protect this self-government which necessarily carries with it this right of exclusion of outsiders.

But this right and duty to exclude all outsiders, resident or traders, does not depend alone upon this autonomy and sovereignty of the Indian nations, but is expressly stipulated in the treaty of 1886. As amended upon its ratification Article XLIII provides:

The United States promise and agree that no white person, except officers, agents, and employees of the Government, and of any internal improvement company or persons traveling through or tem-porarily sojourneying in the said nations or either of them, shall be permitted to go into said Terri-tory, unless formally incorporated and naturalized by the joint action of the authorities of such nations into one of the said nations of Choctaws and Chickasaws according to their laws, customs, or usages.

And Article XXXIX, as amended on ratification, stipulates that—

No person shall expose goods or other articles for sale as a trader without a permit.

These are stipulations of the United States and are aimed against its own citizens, and are for the protection of the Indians, and they must be performed, if at all, by the United States, whose promises they are. And one of the questions here involved, but as to which there can be no doubt, is whether this Government has the power to perform these, its treaty obligations; and the other is whether the means by which it has attempted this performance are lawful; and these would seem to be the only questions in the case.

Under the Constitution this treaty is of itself as much the law of the land and of the same force and efficacy as any statute, and no other legislation was needed in order to both authorize and make it the duty of the Executive branch of the Gov-ernment—charged with the execution of all Federal laws—to execute these provi-sions and prevent the intrusion of outsiders into the Indian Territory, and to prevent unlicensed trading there, and to this end to close all such business.

STATUTES IN PART PERFORMANCE OF TREATY OBLIGATIONS.

While this treaty is, under the Constitution, quite sufficient in itself to authorize and make it the duty of the Executive to enforce these stipulations and close up and prevent unlicensed trading business, yet Congress has added statutes equally plain and emphatic, and has done all that legislation can do to perform the treaty obliga-tions of the Government, and there can be no kind of doubt that this legislation was intended to authorize, and was thought quite sufficient to authorize, the exclusion from and the prevention of unlicensed trading in the Indian Territory. Of the many provisions, any of which would entirely warrant the prevention and the closing of unlicensed business in the Indian Territory, or such business without a local permit when such is required, but few will be cited here, for these are quite sufficient.

But, in order to a proper understanding of this legislation, it must be remembered that, under the provision above referred to, these Indian nations were, as to the ques-tions here involved, independent and sovereign nations, with full power to exclude or permit, upon just such terms as they chose, the residence or the transaction of business within their borders by any outside person. This being so, it is simply of course that the United States could no more authorize such residence or business than it could in the case of any other sovereign nation. It may, of course, give its own authority or consent to its own citizens, but to be effectual the consent of the Indian authorities is requisite. For example, the United States may authorize or license certain persons to trade or carry on business in this Territory, but if, as in this case, the local laws of the nation require a permit and the payment of a tax for this, such requirement must be complied with. In other words, the consent or license of the United States is merely to trade or carry on business there according to and in com-pliance with local laws. Indeed, the United States could not authorize any such business in violation of local laws.

Therefore, if Revised Statutes, section 2128, applies to these Indian *nations*, it merely authorizes the persons described to trade in such manner and upon such terms as are prescribed by the laws of those nations, and could do nothing more. And when the treaty of 1866 provided, as it did, that "no person shall expose goods or other articles for sale as a trader without a permit," it is impossible to suppose that Congress intended to authorize such business without a permit, or in violation of the tribal law which required it.

But, passing this without further elaboration, Revised Statutes, section 2129, is quite as conclusive:

> No person shall be permitted to trade with any of the Indians in the Indian country without a license therefor from a superintendent of Indian affairs, or Indian agent, or subagent.

For the reasons above stated, even such a license could authorize such business only upon compliance with the local laws of that country, and as the plaintiffs in this case did not have such license, and as the local laws required a permit from the Indian authorities, their business was in violation of the laws of both the United States and the Indian nations; and the only question is whether the means adopted by the Government for its suppression, in performance of its treaty obligations and in pursuance of its settled policy, were lawful. This is the ultimate question in the case, and to the solution of which all the other questions tend.

THE GENERAL POWER OF THE EXECUTIVE BRANCH OF THE GOVERNMENT TO EXECUTE THE LAWS.

It is a grave mistake to suppose that the executive branch of the Government requires any special authorization by Congress to execute the national laws.

On the contrary, such execution is within the power and duty of the Executive independently of any express authority from Congress.

"The executive power shall be vested in a President of the United States of America."

That is, the whole executive power of the nation is vested in the President. But in a vast government and governmental machine like ours it is impossible for the President to himself perform all of these duties, and therefore the performance of many of them is, by law, confided to departments and other officers. Still, the executive acts of these are the exercise of executive functions, and are, in theory and in law, the acts of the President in his executive capacity under the Constitution. Congress may or may not prescribe these executive duties to be performed, or the manner or detail of their performance, but even in the absence of such legislation it is none the less the province and duty of the President to perform all necessary executive acts of the Government. And unless the manner or detail of such performance be prescribed by law, these are within his discretion, so that they are appropriate and reasonable and not in violation of any law. In other words—and this is the main point—the executive authority is derived from the Constitution and not from Congress, and must be exercised whether Congress prescribes the manner or detail thereof or not.

"He shall take care that the laws be faithfully executed."

Here, too, his authority is from the Constitution and not from Congress. And here, too, Congress may or may not or only partially prescribe the manner and detail of the execution of the laws.

But in the absence of such legislation, and to the extent that the law does not prescribe the manner or detail of such execution, this is necessarily left to the Executive discretion; and the President, Department, Bureau, or officer to whom such execution of the law upon a particular subject is by law, committed, may adopt any appropriate, adequate, and reasonable mode or means not violative of any law.

Therefore it is that the President, by and through the Department having, by law, charge of the Indian affairs, may execute and enforce the treaty and statutory laws forbidding trading in the Indian Territory without a permit, even though Congress had made no provision as to the manner of doing so, and in doing this might adopt any reasonable, appropriate, and adequate means not in violation of law, for neither the power, duty, nor means of the Executive in seeing that the laws be faithfully executed is at all dependent upon whether Congress has or has not prescribed the manner or detail of such execution. Congress may prescribe the manner or means of such execution, but to the extent that it does not do so the Executive, or that branch of it to which the subject is confided, must do it.

From all this it necessarily follows that the real question involved in this case is not so much whether there is any express statutory provision specifically directing or authorizing the mode adopted by the Department of the Interior for suppressing illegal trading in the Indian Territory as it is whether that mode is in violation of any existing law; the point being that, unless Congress has prescribed an exclusive mode, or has forbidden this one—and clearly it has done neither—then the Department having charge of the matter may well adopt the means it has chosen.

Indeed, in the face of the above treaty and statutory provisions absolutely forbidding all trading in the Indian Territory without a permit from both the Indian and the United States authorities, it seems passing strange that the question whether this Government has the power to stop and prevent the illegal business thus prohibited should be seriously propounded. And yet this is really the only question in this case, for it is this illegal business only which the Government seeks to stop or close, and no objection is made to the means adopted for this purpose; but the whole contention is that the Government has no power to stop it at all. Hence, as before said, the only question is whether the Government has the power to prevent a business expressly made illegal by both treaty and statutory provisions, and such a question may well excite surprise in the legal or judicial mind.

If these general observations are correct, it follows that the proper Executive Department may execute and enforce Federal laws in the premises by proper means without any other authorization than the laws themselves. And this brings us to the questions of whether in this case this has been attempted by the proper Department and by proper means, and to the direct consideration of

THE SPECIFIC QUESTIONS PROPOUNDED.

I. The first of these questions must be answered in the negative. There is no act of Congress expressly and in terms authorizing the Secretary of the Interior to close the place of business of any merchant in the Indian Territory, nor, in the case of very many and perhaps the most of the duties imposed upon him by law and his office, is there any act expressly authorizing him to perform such duties in the particular case, nor directing the manner or detail of such performance. Whatever power the Secretary has in this direction, in this case and in very many others, is derived from general laws, his powers and duties as an executive officer, and his power and duty as such to execute the laws relative to matters within his Department.

The whole subject of Indian affairs and intercourse with the Indians has been, from an early day, devolved by law upon the Department of the Interior, which has since had and now has entire control of that subject, together with the execution of the laws relating thereto; and the entire authority and control of the Government over these matters is exercised by that Department, and whatever the Government may do in this direction may be and is done by and through that Department; and if the Government can stop, prevent, or close illegal business in the Indian Territory, it can do so by and through that Department.

II. I am not certain that I fully understand the scope and meaning of this question, or the reason therefor; for, as will be seen, there is "specific law authorizing the Secretary of the Interior to" make rules and regulations, but I assume that by the question it is intended to inquire whether the Secretary has "general authority or discretion to make rules and regulations" concerning the particular business involved in this case, viz, the business of trading with the Indians without permit, and the closing such business "where there is no specific law authorizing him to do so," and that it has relation to the general power of the Secretary in case the first question is answered in the negative, but I answer the question in both aspects.

This question must be answered in the affirmative, for very many reasons, a few of which will be stated here.

Revised Statutes, section 441, provides that—

The Secretary of the Interior is charged with the supervision of public business relating to the following subjects * * *

Third. The Indians.

Sec. 463. The Commissioner of Indian Affairs shall, under the direction of the Secretary of the Interior. and agreeably to such regulations as the President may prescribe, have the management of all Indian affairs and of all matters arising out of Indian relations.

And section 2058:

Each Indian agent shall, within his agency, manage and superintend the intercourse with the Indians, agreeably to law, and execute and perform such regulations and duties not inconsistent with law, as may be prescribed by the President, the Secretary of the Interior, the Commissioner of Indian Affairs, or the Superintendent of Indian Affairs.

These provisions are so broad and comprehensive that they could hardly have been made more so, and clearly embrace the whole subject of governmental control of and dealing with the Indians, including intercourse with them and the execution of the laws relating to them. Not only this, but all through the very many acts relating to the Indians and their affairs there is the complete recognition that, except in a·few cases where a duty is devolved upon the President or some other officer, the entire subject of Indian affairs is devolved upon the Department of the Interior and the Secretary, its head. And his authority is just as broad, comprehensive, and complete as it is with reference to the other subjects committed to him by the same section, for it is conferred in the same words, the whole section being as follows:

The Secretary of the Interior is charged with the supervision of public business relating to the following subjects:
First. The census, when directed by law.
Second. The public lands, including mines.
Third. The Indians.
Fourth. Pensions and bounty lands.
Fifth. Patents for inventions.
Sixth. The custody and distribution of publications.
Seventh. Education.
Eighth. Government Hospital for the Insane
Ninth. Columbian Asylum for the Deaf and Dumb.

Is it possible to seriously suppose that the head of an Executive Department of the Government, charged with the supervision of and exercising the entire executive power of the Government as to such vast and varied subjects, with such infinite ramifications and details, is yet without power to make needful rules and regulations for the performance of that duty and without which such performance would be an utter impossibility? Such power is absolutely necessary, and is inherent in every executive officer charged with a, supervision or direction which involves discretion or judgment as to the manner or detail of execution. And when Congress has charged the head of an Executive Department of the Government with the entire supervision and administration of such vast, varied, intricate, and difficult subjects as are the nine mentioned in this section, and has not itself made all needful rules and regulations directing the manner and detail of the performance of his duties, it is quite safe to say that, even without any express provision therefor, it has given him the power to perform such duties, the proper and appropriate means, the chief and most appropriate of which are rules and regulations. It would be most idle to suppose that Congress in charging the Secretary with such duties as these, intended to withhold from him the best, most usual, appropriate, and effective means for their performance—the power to make needful, proper, and lawful rules and regulations concerning it. On the contrary, it is quite safe to say that Congress desired and intended the fullest, best, and most efficient performance and administration of those duties, and to that end conferred upon the Secretary, along with the devolution of the duties, the proper appropriate and adequate means for their performance not inconsistent with existing law. Otherwise we must suppose that Congress intended to impose the duties, but to withhold the best and, in fact, the only means for their performance, for it is absolutely impossible that all these duties could be properly and efficiently performed without other rules and regulations than those which Congress has prescribed.

It follows, and necessarily, that even had Congress not expressly authorized such rules and regulations, the power to make them would have still existed as an adjunct to and one of the proper and appropriate means for the performance of the duties imposed. But this express authorization, while not necessary, except by way of greater certainty, was quite proper for that purpose, and removed all question as to the power. The uniform practice of all the departments to make such rules under the same authority, with the express and tacit assent of every branch of the Government, is itself quite sufficient proof of the power, and the fact that such authority exists even without any express grant will be of use in considering the next question, if, indeed, it be needed.

III. The third and remaining question is this:

Third. As to section 2058 of the Revised Statutes of the United States, which authorizes the Secretary of the Interior to prescribe rules and regulations "not inconsistent with law," is such intended to authorize him to make such rules and regulations where there is no law on the subject, or forbidding him to do so, or is he only authorized to make such rules and regulations not inconsistent with some specific law *authorizing him to take such action?*

The latter part of this question, which I have italicized, seems to leave the meaning somewhat uncertain. Does the latter part of the question inquire whether he is authorized to make only such rules, etc., as are not inconsistent with the law authorizing him to make rules—"to take such action"—or to inquire whether he is authorized to make only such rules, etc., as are not inconsistent with some specific existing law? In the latter case, the expression "authorizing him to take such action" would refer, not to the law authorizing him to make rules, but to some existing law upon the same subject as that to which his rules relate, and this would restrict such rules to those which should affirmatively consist or agree with some existing law, and would change the expression from "not inconsistent with" into "consist with," and would not authorize any rules where there was no law on the subject or with which they might agree. It is assumed that the latter is meant, for it is not perceived how, in the former sense, the question could arise in this case, or how it could be material. But I answer the question generally.

Section 2058, referred to in the question, is not the only one conferring general power upon the Secretary to make rules, etc. In addition to the sections before quoted, placing the control of Indian affairs in the hands of the Secretary of the Interior, and giving him thereby the implied power to make rules, etc., for the performance of the duties imposed upon him, Revised Statutes, section 161, expressly authorizes such head of a department "to prescribe regulations not inconsistent with law for the government of his department."

What, then, is the meaning of this expression "not inconsistent with law," which limits alike the power of all the heads of departments, and generally in every other case where the power is conferred at all, to make rules and regulations?

Whether expressed or not, all of these, and also all other grants of power to make rules, etc., are subject to the same limitation that they are "not inconsistent with law." For even if Congress has the power—which may well be doubted—to authorize anyone to make rules and regulations inconsistent with, contrary to, or in violation of law, it is not to be supposed that it intends to do so.

But a general grant of this power might leave it open to possible claim that the power was without any such limitation, and authorized the making of rules without reference to, or even contrary to, existing law. To avoid this, and for greater certainty, this limitation is generally, but not always, expressed. For example, it is not expressed in section 463, above quoted, and in other instances; but there can be no doubt that it is implied wherever there is or may be any law other than such rules upon the subject.

But when this limitation is expressed, it is generally but not always in the same language, but in words of the same meaning—"not inconsistent with law," or "not contrary to law," "not repugnant to law," or some similar expression expressing the whole object of the limitation, viz, the subjection of such rules and regulations to existing law. Indeed, it is the whole and only purpose of this limitation to restrict an otherwise unlimited grant of power, to one to make only such rules and regulations as are not inconsistent with, contrary to, or in violation of existing law.

This being so, the meaning of the term "not inconsistent with law" is certain. It means just what it says—not inconsistent with, contrary to, or in violation of law; the subjection of rules, etc., to legislative law. And this goes far toward answering the specific question, which is, as I understand it,

Whether such rules, etc., must affirmatively, consist with, agree with, or be in accord with some specific legislative law, or, on the other hand, may be prescribed where there is no such law on the subject, or none forbidding such rules.

While the answer to this may not at first blush be obvious, it is believed to be none the less certain; and especially when considered in view of the fact that the sole purpose of the limitation is to avoid the apparent authorization of rules which will be an infraction of or in disagreement with existing law.

First, the meaning of the words "not inconsistent with" is far from being the same as "consistent with." It may mean, and in many cases does mean, much more. Hence Congress, instead of using the term "consistent with law," has used the proper words, "not inconsistent with law" to express its idea of being not contrary to or in disagreement with law. "Consistent with" necessarily implies some existing thing with which the thing in question may consist or agree. And so, also, does "inconsistent with;" for one thing can not be either consistent or inconsistent with what does not exist. But "not inconsistent with" has a meaning very different from either. For a thing is equally "not inconsistent with" what does not exist and with what does exist, but is not in disagreement with the thing in question. This is alike the definition of the lexicographers and the popular idea of the meanings of the words. A rule or regulation can not be inconsistent with law when there is no law upon the subject. It may be not consistent with law, but can not be inconsistent with law, for inconsistency means disagreement, which can not be where there is nothing with which to disagree.

If there be no law upon a given subject, then a rule or regulation upon that subject can not possibly be inconsistent with law. Had Congress intended to authorize only such rules, etc., as are consistent with law, doubtless it would have said so; but when Congress has used instead, as often as it has in various statutes, the expression "not inconsistent with law," which has an entirely different meaning, every court is bound to presume that this was done purposely and in view of its different meaning.

Hence the limitation is not that such rules shall consist or agree with some existing law, but that they shall not be inconsistent with any such law; and this want of inconsistency, or noninconsistency, may be because there is no law on the subject and therefore no inconsistency, or because the rules are not inconsistent with such law as there is.

But not only does the ordinary and proper meaning of the words require this construction, but, as will be seen, it is really only "where there is no law on the subject" that rules and regulations are authorized at all or are of any use or force. In this matter, as in most others, Congress has itself prescribed many of the rules and regulations for performing the duties imposed; but in matters of such magnitude, variety, and infinity of detail as those committed to the Interior Department, or even to the Indian Affairs branch of it, it is simply impossible that Congress should prescribe all the rules and regulations needful in the premises, and it does not attempt to do so. But it is only where it has not done so that the Secretary is authorized to make any rule at all; that is, as the question suggests, "where there is no law on the subject." And this is so in all cases where rules, etc., are authorized, for where there is any law on the subject that itself is the rule and regulation, and none that the subordinate can make can alter or change it. And, to the extent that any rule or regulation consists or agrees with the law, it is the law, and not the regulation, which governs, and the latter is without force. It is only where the rule goes beyond the law—or does something as to which the law is silent, supplies what is omitted from the law; in other words, "where there is no law on the subject"—that rules and regulations have any place or any force, and it is simply because Congress, while prescribing some of many of the rules and regulations for the performance of certain duties, can not always, by a general law, prescribe all of them, that persons charged with such performance are sometimes authorized to make others. But it will be noted that it is only where the law itself has not prescribed them that any such rules can be made or be of any force. To illustrate: Section 162, Revised Statutes, requires that certain Departments and Bureaus shall for one portion of the year be kept open for business at least eight hours a day and for another portion ten hours; but by section 161 each head of a Department is authorized to prescribe rules and regulations, etc. Now, because the law is silent on the subject there can be no doubt that, under this grant of power, each head of a Department may make rules fixing the particular hours between which such places must be kept open; but it is only because the law is silent that he could do so. It is equally certain that had no law fixed the number of hours which such places should be opened, such Secretary might have made rules prescribing the reasonable time therefor; but here, too, only because the law was silent.

It will be seen on reflection that it is only "where there is no law on the subject" that any rules or regulations can be made or be of any force. Their only purpose or object is to supply what is needful, but not prescribed by the general law, and to meet cases unforeseen and therefore not provided for. The limitation prescribed is that they shall not be inconsistent with law. There is no requirement that these rules, etc., shall be consistent with law, which is or may be a very different thing, and which requirement would render the power substantially or entirely worthless; for, so far as a rule consists with, agrees with, or corresponds to the law it is needless and of no force, for the superior law takes its place. Certainly Congress has not so often used this expression for the mere futile purpose of authorizing rules consistent or agreeing with already existing laws. On the contrary, the obvious intention has been to authorize rules, etc., where the law has failed to do so, but not inconsistent with the law where it has spoken. The law may direct a certain thing to be done and prescribe, with more or less of detail, what may or may not be done in performance, and always it is only where and to the extent that the law has not done this that other rules and regulations can do so.

Another illustration will suffice. By section 17 of the judiciary act of 1789 (1 Stat. 73, 83) the courts of the United States are authorized to make rules, "which rules are not repugnant to the laws of the United States." This is of course the same as "not inconsistent," and shows the sense in which Congress uses the term. And by section 917, Revised Statutes, the Supreme Court may prescribe rules "not inconsistent with any law of the United States" for the practice of the courts. The use of the word "any" only emphasizes and makes clear the fact that it is some existing specific law with and to which the rules may not be inconsistent or "repugnant," and more clearly shows that "inconsistent" is used as synonymous with "repugnant." It can not be considered that in these two sections, meaning precisely the same thing, it was intended by one that no rules should be made except such as actually consisted with some existing law, and in the other that any rules might be made which were not "repugnant" to existing law. This is again emphasized in section 918, by which the circuit and district courts are authorized to make rules "not inconsistent with any law of the United States." And everywhere, it is believed, the word is used in the same and the only proper sense as equivalent to "repugnant." It is believed that all this is quite sufficient to support the following

PROPOSITIONS.

I. The Secretary of the Interior, being by law charged with the governmental administration of Indian affairs, may, without any other authority than that of the law which imposes the duty, make all reasonable, proper, and appropriate rules and regulations for the performance of that duty wherever and to the extent that the law has not done so; id est, not inconsistent with law.

II. But the Secretary of the Interior is also by law expressly authorized to make such rules and regulations.

III. In either case, and whether such power be expressly conferred or not, the limitation is that such rules and regulations shall be not inconsistent with law; and this means only that they shall not be repugnant to any existing law, and does not mean that there must actually be any law with which they must consist or agree, nor does it forbid such rules, etc., where there is no law on the subject.

These propositions, if correct, would seem to answer the questions suggested. But I desire, with permission, to submit two other points not involved in those questions, but which are in the case at bar.

First. The case may be decided either way, no matter which way these questions are answered, or whether the Secretary has or has not power to make any rules or regulations.

For if the trading by the plaintiffs in the Indian Territory without a license or permit from the United States and Indian authorities is illegal, and if the Government has power to prevent or close such illegal business, and if the Secretary of the Interior in this respect represents or exercises the power of the Government—that is, acts by its authority—then he may prevent or close such illegal business quite irrespective of any power to make rules, etc., and equally irrespective of whether he has made any or has not. While, on the other hand, if such business is not illegal, and the Secretary, representing and acting for the Government, has no power to prevent or close it, then no rules which he could make would give him such power.

Second. In our Government, its three coordinate branches are, in the exercise of their restrictive functions, quite independent of each other, save only that the judicial branch may inquire whether any act of either of the others is in violation of any constitutional or statutory law, and, if so, to declare it void. Can it go any further? Therefore when the executive does an act which is certainly within his executive competency, the judiciary can question it only upon the ground that it is in violation of some law, but not at all because there is no act of Congress expressly authorizing it, if it be an executive act which the nation can do; for in such case the Executive represents and exercises the sovereign power of the nation, which does not wait upon or require any warrant from any source to exercise its functions. In other words, whatever is within the executive power of this Government that the Executive may do, and without any other warrant than the Constitution which conferred the power. So that whatever is within the executive competency of the Government that the President may do, even when Congress is silent on the subject. The Constitution has not conferred executive power upon Congress and Congress can confer none upon the President. The Constitution conferred it all upon the President, and there is none left, and none which Congress can confer. True, Congress may say what, in the exercise of this power, the Executive may do, and, to a certain extent, what he may not do—may regulate the exercise of the power, but can not confer any; and the Executive requires no other warrant than the Constitution itself for the performance of any act legitimately within the executive competency of the Government. Therefore it is that the judiciary can question the Executive only upon two grounds, viz, that his act is not the exercise of Executive power or is in violation of law.

That the control of the Indians and Indian affairs, including the intercourse of white people, is a legitimate executive function is not only beyond all question, but is distinctly recognized by Congress, which has delegated the whole subject to an executive department. Therefore it is that, even if there had been no law forbidding the intercourse or trading of whites with the Indians on their reservations or the Indian Territory, still if the executive department having the Indians in charge found this to be harmful to the Indians or seriously detrimental to its administration of those affairs, there can be no question that it might prohibit and prevent it, just as it might the introduction of firearms or intoxicating liquors, and for the same reason. And in such case the judicial branch of the Government could not question the executive for its want of power or legislative warrant, but only upon the ground that its act was in violation of some law.

Much more is all this true when the Executive acts in pursuance of legislative authority and his acts are in execution of positive law. Our treaty, the Indian law, and the law of Congress all equally forbid the unauthorized trading of whites within this Indian territory. Not only is it the power and duty of the Executive to see that this law be faithfully executed, but, as the law stands, there is no other power that can do so; and when the Executive attempts to perform this plain duty is it within the judicial competency to question the act, save only to inquire whether his act is in violation of any law? With deference, it is submitted that it is not; and it is further submitted that the whole case depends simply upon whether the action of the Interior Department and its agents, in attempting to close this illegal business, has been in violation of any law.

Respectfully submitted.

F. E. HUTCHINS,
Special Assistant to the Attorney-General.

APPENDIX NO. 16.

REGULATIONS OF THE DEPARTMENT OF THE INTERIOR UNDER SECTION 3 OF THE ACT OF MARCH 3, 1901, CONCERNING RIGHT OF WAY FOR A TELEPHONE AND TELEGRAPH LINE THROUGH ANY LANDS HELD BY AN INDIAN TRIBE OR NATION IN THE INDIAN TERRITORY, THROUGH ANY LANDS RESERVED FOR AN INDIAN AGENCY OR INDIAN SCHOOL OR FOR OTHER PURPOSE IN CONNECTION WITH THE INDIAN SERVICE, OR THROUGH ANY LANDS WHICH HAVE BEEN ALLOTTED IN SEVERALTY.

DEPARTMENT OF THE INTERIOR, OFFICE OF INDIAN AFFAIRS,
Washington, D. C., March 15, 1901.

The following regulations are prescribed under section 3 of the act of March 3, 1901 (Public—No. 137), granting right of way for a telephone and telegraph line through any Indian reservation, through any lands held by an Indian tribe or nation in the Indian Territory, lands reserved for an Indian agency or Indian school or for other purpose in connection with the Indian Service, or allotted lands:

1. Section 3 of the act of Congress approved March 3, 1901, entitled "An act making appropriations for the current and contingent expenses of the Indian Department and for fulfilling treaty stipulations with various Indian tribes for the fiscal year ending June thirtieth, nineteen hundred and two, and for other purposes," is as follows:

SEC. 3. That the Secretary of the Interior is hereby authorized and empowered to grant a right of way, in the nature of an easement, for the construction, operation, and maintenance of telephone and telegraph lines and offices for general telephone and telegraph business through any Indian reservation, through any lands held by an Indian tribe or nation in the Indian Territory, through any lands reserved for an Indian agency or Indian school or for other purpose in connection with the Indian Service, or through any lands which have been allotted in severalty to any individual Indian under any law or treaty, but which have not been conveyed to the allottee with full power of alienation, upon the terms and conditions herein expressed. No such lines shall be constructed across Indian lands, as above mentioned, until authority therefor has first been obtained from the Secretary of the Interior, and the maps of definite location of the lines shall be subject to his approval. The compensation to be paid the tribes in their tribal capacity and the individual allottees for such right of way through their lands shall be determined in such manner as the Secretary of the Interior may direct and shall be subject to his final approval; and where such lines are not subject to State or Territorial taxation the company or owner of the line shall pay to the Secretary of the Interior, for the use and benefit of the Indians, such annual tax as he may designate, not exceeding five dollars for each ten miles of line so constructed and maintained; and all such lines shall be constructed and maintained under such rules and regulations as said Secretary may prescribe. But nothing herein contained shall be so construed as to exempt the owners of such lines from the payment of any tax that may be lawfully assessed against them by either State, Territorial, or municipal authority; and Congress hereby expressly reserves the right to regulate the tolls or charges for the transmission of messages over any lines constructed under the provisions of this act: <i>Provided,</i> That incorporated cities and towns into or through which such telephone or telegraphic lines may be constructed shall have the power to regulate the manner of construction therein, and nothing herein contained shall be so construed as to deny the right of municipal taxation in such towns and cities. * * *

2. No company or individual is authorized to construct a telephone or telegraph line across Indian lands as mentioned in the foregoing section of the act of March 3, 1901, until authority therefor has first been obtained from the Secretary of the Interior.

3. Any company or individual desiring to obtain such permission must file an application therefor in this office, for transmission to the Secretary of the Interior. Such application should, in as particular a manner as possible, describe the route of

the proposed telephone or telegraph line within the lands named in the above section and must be accompanied, in the case of a company or corporation, by—

First. A copy of its articles of incorporation, duly certified to by the proper officer of the company under its corporate seal, or by the secretary of the State or Territory where organized.

Second. A copy of the State or Territorial law under which the company was organized, with the certificate of the governor or secretary of the State or Territory that the same is the existing law.

Third. When said law directs that the articles of association or other papers connected with the organization be filed with any State or Territorial officer, the certificate of such officer that the same have been filed according to law, with the date of the filing thereof.

Fourth. When a company is operating in a State or Territory other than that in which it is incorporated, the certificate of the proper officers of the State or Territory is required that it has complied with the laws of that State or Territory governing foreign corporations to the extent required to entitle the company to operate in such State or Territory.

Fifth. The official statement, under seal of the proper officer, that the organization has been completed; that the company is fully authorized to proceed with the construction of the line of telephone or telegraph according to the existing law. (Form 1.)

Sixth. An affidavit by the president, under the seal of the company, showing the names and designations of its officers at the date of the filing of the proofs. (Form 2.)

Seventh. Satisfactory evidence of the good faith of the company and its financial ability in the matter of the construction of the proposed line.

4. It is further provided in said section that maps of definite location of the lines shall be subject to the approval of the Secretary of the Interior.

5. All maps of location presented for approval under said section 3 should be filed with this office and should be drawn on tracing linen and in duplicate.

6. Where the proposed line is greatly in excess of 20 miles, separate maps should be filed in 20-mile sections.

7. Where grounds are required for office purposes, the exact location of the same should be noted upon the maps of location, but separate plats of such grounds must be filed and approved.

8. The scale of maps showing the line of route should be 2,000 feet to an inch. The maps may, however, be drawn to a larger scale when necessary; but the scale must not be so greatly increased as to make the map inconveniently large for handling. Plats of grounds required for office purposes should be drawn on a scale of 50 feet to an inch, and must be filed separately from the line of route. Such plats should show enough of the line of route to indicate the position of the tract with reference thereto.

9. The termini of the line of route should be fixed by reference of course and distance to the nearest existing corner of the public survey. The map, engineer's affidavit, and president's certificate (Forms 3 and 4) should each show these conditions. A tract for grounds for office purposes must be similarly referenced and described on the plat.

10. In filing maps of location for approval under said section 3, the same should be accompanied by the affidavit of the president or other principal officer of the company, defining the purpose, intent, and financial ability of the company in the matter of the construction of the proposed line. Further, each map should be accompanied by evidence of the service of an exact copy thereof, and the date of such service upon (1) in case of allottees, or in case of a reservation, the agent in charge; (2) in case of the Five Civilized Tribes, upon the principal chief or secretary of such tribe or nation.

11. No action will be taken upon such map until the expiration of twenty days from the date of such service.

12. A company will not be permitted to proceed with the construction of any portion of its line until the map showing the location thereof has first been approved by the Secretary of the Interior.

13. When a line of telephone or telegraph is constructed, an affidavit of the president setting forth the fact must be filed in this office in duplicate. If a change from the route indicated upon the approved map of location is found to be necessary, on account of engineering difficulties or otherwise, new maps and field notes of the changed route must be filed and approved, and a right of way upon such changed lines must be acquired, damages ascertained, and compensation paid on account thereof, in all respects as in the case of the original location, before construction can be proceeded with upon such changed line.

14. Upon the approval of the map of definite location specific directions will be given in the matter of the acquirement of the right of way and determination of damages occasioned by the construction of the line.

15. The conditions on different reservations throughout the country are so varied that it is deemed inadvisable to prescribe definite rules in the matter of determining the tribal compensation and damages for right of way. As a rule, however, the United States Indian agent, or a special United States Indian agent, or Indian inspector will be designated to determine such compensation and damages, subject to the approval of the Secretary of the Interior.

16. Telephone and telegraph companies should not independently attempt to negotiate with the individual occupants and allottees for right of way and damages. When the lands are not attached to an agency, some proper person will be designated to act with the allottee in determining the individual damages. Where such lands are attached to an Indian agency, the United States Indian agent or other proper person connected with the Indian Service will be designated to act with and for the allottees or occupants in the matter of determining individual damages for right of way, subject to the approval of the Secretary of the Interior.

17. No company having secured a right of way under the provisions of this section will be permitted to lease or enter into any arrangements with any other company or individual for the use of any poles or fixtures erected and maintained by virtue of authority granted under this section without first obtaining the consent of the Secretary of the Interior.

18. The foregoing regulations shall be observed, so far as applicable, by any individual seeking to procure a right of way for the construction of telephone and telegraph lines under the provisions of this section, and particularly as to the purpose, intent, and financial ability of the applicant.

19. If in the administration of said section cases are found which are not covered by these regulations, such cases will be disposed of according to their respective merits under special instructions, or supplemental regulations embracing cases of that character will be adopted as may seem necessary.

Very respectfully,

W. A. JONES,
Commissioner.

DEPARTMENT OF THE INTERIOR, *March, 26, 1901.*

Approved.

E. A. HITCHCOCK, *Secretary.*

Forms for proof of organization of company and verification of maps of location.

(1)

I, —— ——, secretary (or president) of the —— company, do hereby certify that the organization of said company has been completed; that the company is fully authorized to proceed with the construction of the line according to the existing laws of the State (or Territory), and that the copy of the articles of association (or incorporation) of the company herewith (or heretofore filed in the Department of the Interior) is a true and correct copy.

In witness whereof I have hereunto set my name and the corporate seal of the company.

[SEAL.]

—— ——,
—— of the —— Company.

(2)

State of ——,
   County of ——, *ss:*

—— ——, being duly sworn, says that he is the president of the —— company, and that the following is a true list of the officers of the said company, with the full name and official designation of each, to wit: (Here insert the full name and official designation of each officer.)

[SEAL OF COMPANY.]

—— ——,
President of the Company.

(3)

State of ——,
    County of ——, *ss:*
    —— ——, being duly sworn, says he is the chief engineer of (or is the person employed to locate) the line of telephone and telegraph of the —— company; that the location of the line of route of said lines from —— to ——, a distance of —— miles, was made by him or under his direction as surveyor employed by the company and under its authority, commencing on the —— day of ——, 19—, and ending on the —— day of ——, 19—; and that such survey is accurately represented on the accompanying map.

                                                —— ——,
                                              —— ——.

Sworn and subscribed to before me this —— day of ——, 19—.
[SEAL.]
                                            —— ——,
                                            Notary Public.

(4)

    I, —— ——, do hereby certify that I am the president of the —— company; that —— ——, who subscribed the foregoing affidavit, was employed to make the survey by the said company; that the survey of line of route of the company's lines, as accurately represented on the accompanying map, was made under authority of the company; that the said line of route so surveyed and as represented on the said map was adopted by the company by resolution of its board of directors on the —— day of ——, 19—, as the definite location of the telephone and telegraph line from —— to ——, a distance of —— miles; and that the map has been prepared to be filed for the approval of the Secretary of the Interior, in order that the company may obtain the benefits of the third section of the act of Congress approved March 3, 1901 (Public—No. 137), entitled "An act making appropriations for the current and contingent expenses of the Indian Department and for fulfilling treaty stipulations with various Indian tribes for the fiscal year ending June thirtieth, nineteen hundred and two, and for other purposes."

Attest:
                                    President of the —— *Company.*
—— ——,
    Secretary.
[SEAL OF THE COMPANY.]

O

ANNUAL REPORT

OF THE

United States Indian Inspector for the Indian Territo

TOGETHER WITH

THE REPORTS OF THE INDIAN AGENT IN CHARGE OF THE UNION
AGENCY, THE SUPERINTENDENT AND SUPERVISORS
OF SCHOOLS, AND REVENUE INSPECTOR
IN THAT TERRITORY,

TO THE

SECRETARY OF THE INTERIOR

FOR THE

FISCAL YEAR ENDED JUNE 30, 1902.

———◄•●•►———

WASHINGTON:
GOVERNMENT PRINTING OFFICE.
1902.

CONTENTS.

4 CONTENTS.

ANNUAL REPORT

OF THE

UNITED STATES INDIAN INSPECTOR FOR THE INDIAN TERRITORY.

MUSKOGEE, IND. T., *September 3, 1902.*

SIR: I have the honor to submit my fourth annual report of the work of the United States Indian inspector for Indian Territory, covering the fiscal year ended June 30, 1902, respectfully inviting attention to the attached reports of the several officers under my supervision, which show in detail the business transacted by them respectively.

INTRODUCTORY.

The various acts of Congress and agreements with the different tribes of Indians in Indian Territory provide for the valuation and distribution, among the several individual members of each tribe, of the property of such Indians, comprising the entire Indian Territory, a tract of more than 19,000,000 acres, upon which have sprung up in the neighborhood of 150 towns having a population ranging from 200 to 7,000 inhabitants, and a large number of smaller villages.

The duty of carrying out this work has been imposed by Congress upon the Secretary of the Interior. A large portion of the same is carried on through the Commission to the Five Civilized Tribes, who have direct supervision of procuring a correct roll of Indians entitled to participate in such distribution, and to appraise and allot the lands of the various nations. All other matters requiring the attention of the Secretary of the Interior are handled directly from the Department or through the several officers in the field under his direction.

The work incident to the settling of these conditions has brought forth many new, intricate, and, in a number of cases, extremely perplexing and annoying legal questions, the solution of which has first fallen to the Interior Department; and oftentimes where such decisions are not considered final by law they are taken to the courts, both in and out of the Territory, in mandamus and injunction suits, and in some instances damage cases have been brought against the inspector and other officers where they have performed the duties required of them by instructions from the Secretary of the Interior.

The condition of the work of the inspector's office and others connected therewith at the close of the fiscal year was gratifying, the same having progressed during the entire year with more dispatch and in a more satisfactory manner than at any time previous.

This report, it is believed, will show that the work in all its branches is well in hand, particularly that part pertaining to the disposition of the town sites and the leasing of mineral lands.

The duties of the inspector in complying with instructions have constantly increased, necessitating the employment of additional clerical force, engineers, and other assistants from time to time, in order to expeditiously and properly prosecute the work. All matters requiring attention have been handled as rapidly as possible consistent with efficiency and economy. Due credit should be given, in reviewing the work of the year, to the several officers and employees connected with this office, and the faithfulness and energy of all are acknowledged and appreciated.

Brief mention will be made of the population of the Territory and the number of members of the Indian tribes. According to the Twelfth Census, completed during the fiscal year ended June 30, 1901, the total population, including whites, Indians, and negroes, was 391,960, about 84,000 of this number being members of the Five Civilized Tribes.

The population of these tribes, including freedmen, with the exception of the Seminoles, with the area of each nation, is approximately as follows:

Tribe.	Population.	Area.
		Acres.
Choctaw	20,250	11,338,95
Chickasaw	11,500	
Creek	15,000	3,040,00
Cherokee	35,000	5,081,35
Seminole	2,757	366,00
Total	84,507	19,776,25

Reference is made to my last annual report for more detailed statements of the population of the Territory and the nations thereof.

The opportunity presented for investment and the extensive railroad building have, during the year just closed, brought large numbers of people of all classes from the surrounding States and Territories to the Indian Territory; therefore the total population as ascertained by the last census has since materially increased.

In order to give an intelligent review of the conditions and the work performed, the present laws governing affairs in the Territory are briefly mentioned below.

EXISTING LEGISLATION.

By the act of March 3, 1893, Congress created the Commission to the Five Civilized Tribes to negotiate with the several nations of the Indian Territory, looking either to the individualization of their lands or the cession of the same to the United States.

The first agreement to be made and ratified by both parties was with the Seminole Nation, which was dated December 16, 1897, and ratified by Congress on July 1, 1898. A copy of this agreement is submitted as Appendix No. 1, page 141.

By the act approved June 28, 1898 (30 Stat., 495), commonly known as the Curtis Act, provision was made for the allotment of the lands and the general winding up of the tribal affairs of the Choctaw, Chickasaw, Creek, and Cherokee nations, no agreements having been secured up to that time which had been ratified by both Congress and these tribes.   To this act, however, was appended an agreement with the Choctaws and Chickasaws which had been entered into on April 23, 1897, and an agreement which had been entered into with the Creeks on September 27, 1897.

The Choctaw and Chickasaw agreement was, on August 24, 1898, ratified by the Indians, but the Creek agreement was rejected, which left the Curtis Act proper, sections 1 to 28, applicable to the Creek and Cherokee nations.

The Curtis Act proper and the agreement with the Choctaws and Chickasaws are shown by Appendix No. 2, page 143.

Afterwards, on March 8, 1900, the Commission entered into another agreement with the Creek Indians, which was, by the act of March 1, 1901 (31 Stat., 861), ratified by Congress and in due time by the National Council of the Creek Nation. (See Appendix No. 3, page 158.)

A supplemental agreement with the Creek Nation was ratified by Congress on June 30, 1902 (32 Stat. 500), and the same has since the close of the fiscal year been confirmed by the National Council of the Creek Nation, and according to the terms thereof the President issued his proclamation on August 8, 1902, stating that such supplemental agreement became law on July 26, 1902.   A copy of this agreement is submitted as Appendix No. 4, page 166.

Up to the close of the fiscal year no agreement had as yet been entered into with the Cherokee Nation which had been ratified by both Congress and the tribe, and that nation was, therefore, still subject to the general provisions of the Curtis Act, approved June 28, 1898.   However, on July 1, 1902 (32 Stat., 716), at the close of the last session of Congress, an act was passed to provide for the allotment of the lands of the Cherokee Nation, for the disposition of town sites, etc., which was to become effective when ratified by a majority of the whole number of votes cast by the legal voters of the Cherokee Nation at an election to be held within forty days from the passage of such act.   This election was held on August 7, 1902, and the act ratified. This supplemental agreement is submitted as Appendix No. 5, page 171.

The Indian appropriation act approved May 31, 1900 (31 Stat., 221), modified the provisions of the Curtis Act and the Choctaw and Chickasaw agreement concerning the surveying and platting of town sites, and authorized the Secretary of the Interior to make such surveys at all towns having a population of 200 or more, thus taking this work out of the hands of the several town-site commissions, as before provided.   An extract showing the provisions of this legislation is attached as Appendix No. 6, page 180.

The cutting of timber and procurement of stone in the Indian Territory are governed by the act of June 6, 1900 (31 Stat., 660), except that the Creek agreement, ratified since the passage of this act, permits Indian citizens who have selected their allotments to dispose of the timber thereon.   A copy of the rules and regulations of the Department governing the procurement of timber and stone is submitted as Appendix No. 7, page 181.

Certain new legislation affecting the Territory was embodied in the Indian appropriation act of March 3, 1901 (31 Stat., 1447), the most important of which pertained to the granting of rights of way for telephone and telegraph lines through Indian lands. An extract showing the provisions pertaining to Indian Territory is submitted as Appendix No. 8, page 187, and a copy of the regulations relative to telephone lines as Appendix No. 9, page 188.

The Indian appropriation act of May 27, 1902 (32 Stat., 245), also contained considerable legislation concerning the Territory, and provided for the surveying and platting of small towns having a population of less than 200 inhabitants. It also made an appropriation of $15,000 for the purpose of removing intruders and placing allottees in unrestricted possession of their allotments, but provided that it shall be unlawful to remove or deport any person from the Indian Territory who is in lawful possession of any lots or parcels of land in any city or town in the Territory which has been designated as a town site under existing laws and treaties. Provision was also made for the new western judicial district of the Indian Territory. An extract showing this legislation is attached as Appendix No. 10, page 192.

By an act approved May 19, 1902 (32 Stat., 200), Congress provided that any incorporated city or town in the Indian Territory having a population of 2,000 or more might issue bonds and borrow money thereon for the construction of sewers and waterworks and the building of schoolhouses. A copy of this act is shown on page 45 of this report.

A general railroad act, practically repealing all previous acts and authorizing the taking of grounds for the construction of railroads by condemnation proceedings, was passed on February 28, 1902 (32 Stat., 43). A copy of this act is submitted as Appendix No. 11, page 195.

DUTIES OF THE INSPECTOR.

On August 17, 1898, I was detailed and assigned to duty in the Indian Territory, with instructions to establish headquarters at Muskogee. This assignment was made in accordance with the provisions of section 27 of the Curtis Act, approved June 28, 1898 (30 Stat., 495), which provides that the Secretary of the Interior is authorized to locate one Indian inspector in the Indian Territory, who may under his authority and direction perform any duties required of the Secretary of the Interior by law relating to affairs therein.

The inspector, under the direction of the Secretary of the Interior, exercises supervision and general direction over the United States Indian agent at Union Agency, the superintendent of schools in Indian Territory with his corps of school supervisors, the revenue inspector for the Creek, Cherokee, and Chickasaw nations, the mining trustees of the Choctaw and Chickasaw nations, the several town-site commissions, and the office and field force engaged in the work of surveying and platting town sites.

The above-mentioned branches of the inspector's office practically handle all matters coming within the jurisdiction of the Department in the Territory, except such as belong to the Commission to the Five Civilized Tribes.

All correspondence to and from the Department with any of the above officials passes through the office of the inspector, who is required to submit his views and recommendations bearing on the subjects at issue. These reports are forwarded through the Commissioner of Indian Affairs, who in turn transmits them to the Secretary of the Interior, with his report and recommendation. The inspector also from time to time advises the Department of matters requiring its attention, and keeps it informed as to the general status of affairs.

SEMINOLE NATION.

Matters in this nation continue to progress satisfactorily, and there is little to be reported or said concerning the same. I understand the Commission to the Five Civilized Tribes has practically completed the allotments to these Indians, and their roll of citizenship having heretofore been submitted and approved, conditions in this nation are far more advanced than in any other.

Only one matter of importance has been before the inspector's office during the year in the Seminole Nation and that was a contract which had been entered into between the Seminole Nation, through its principal chief, with the consent of the allottee, and a lime manufacturing company for the use of stone from certain lands for the purpose of making lime. This contract was being considered at the close of the year, not having been finally passed upon at that time.

Quite an important change, from a political standpoint, occurred in this nation just after the close of the fiscal year. Hon. John F. Brown, who has managed the affairs of the nation successfully for many years, as principal chief, being defeated for reelection, and the new principal chief, Hon. Hulputta Micco, taking charge.

MINING.

CHOCTAW AND CHICKASAW NATIONS.

The coal mines of these two nations are practically all located in the Choctaw Nation, and the asphalt deposits are almost entirely confined to the limits of the Chickasaw Nation. The agreement with these two nations provides that coal and asphalt shall be reserved from allotment and remain the common property of the tribes, and under such agreement no mining operations are carried on except for the two minerals above mentioned.

The funds received on account of royalties for coal and asphalt mined are paid to the United States Indian agent, at Union Agency, for the credit of the Choctaws and Chickasaws, and disbursed under the direction of the Secretary of the Interior for the education of the children of Indian blood of said tribes.

As contemplated by the agreement, practically all of the operations which have heretofore been carried on under national contracts are now under formal leases, entered into by the mining trustees and approved by the Department, with good and sufficient bonds for the faithful performance by the lessee of the stipulations of such leases, the payment of royalties, etc.

These formal leases have been made with the parties holding tribal contracts as rapidly as such contracts expire, the agreement providing that where mines were being operated in good faith under the authority of the Indian tribes on the date of the signing of such agreement, April 23, 1897, such contracts upon their expiration would be subject to renewal under the provisions of such agreement.

But few leases, except such as were in the nature of renewals of old national contracts, have been made during the year, the policy of the Department being to discourage speculative applications. Applicants for leases of either coal or asphalt lands are required to furnish evidence of their ability, both from the standpoint of knowledge of the business and financial strength, to operate the properties should they be granted a lease.

Provision is made for two mining trustees, to be appointed by the

President upon the recommendation of the executive of each tribe. Such trustees enter into leases on behalf of the tribes, and inspect and generally supervise the operations under the direction of the Secretary of the Interior through this office. During the year these positions have been filled by Mr. Napoleon B. Ainsworth for the Choctaw Nation and Mr. Charles D. Carter for the Chickasaw Nation. A report of such trustees, showing in detail the work performed by them, accompanies this report, to which attention is invited.

The trustees are also required by law to submit reports quarterly of their actions, which reports are promptly transmitted to and filed with the Secretary of the Interior. In these reports they show the result of their examination of the records and books of the several mining companies, which statements are compared in this office with the record of payments received by the United States Indian agent for verification.

The coal industry of the Indian Territory seems to steadily push forward and the output continues to increase, as noted from the following comparative statement:

	Tons.
July 1, 1898, to June 30, 1899	1,404,442
July 1, 1899, to June 30, 1900	1,900,127
July 1, 1900, to June 30, 1901	2,398,154
July 1, 1901, to June 30, 1902	2,735,365

Applications for coal or asphalt leases are made direct to the inspector, who is required to procure such additional information concerning the applicants, etc., as he deems proper. The applications are then referred to the trustees for an inspection of the tracts applied for, careful consideration, report, and recommendation, after which they are forwarded by the inspector to the Department, through the Indian Office, with his report and recommendation. When approved by the honorable Secretary of the Interior, leases are entered into by the trustees for a period of thirty years, and the forms now prescribed require a specific guaranty that not less than a certain tonnage will be mined each year.

Following is a list of the coal and asphalt leases granted during the year ended June 30, 1902.

Name.	Number.	Date of approval.
COAL.		
Arkansas-McAlester Coal Co. (new)	1	Oct. 1, 1901
Thomas H. Chambers (new)	1	Dec. 9, 1901
Turkey Creek Coal Co. (renewal national contract)	1	Mar. 18, 1902
Southwestern Coal and Improvement Co. (renewal national contract)	10	Apr. 4, 1902
Essen Coal Co. (new)	1	Apr. 12, 1902
Bache & Denman (new)	1	Apr. 22, 1902
Kansas and Texas Coal Co. (renewal national contract)	4	June 13, 1902
Atoka Coal and Mining Co. (renewal national contract)	1	Do.
Capital Coal and Mining Co. (renewal national contract)	1	June 16, 1902
Hailey Coal and Mining Co. (renewal national contract)	2	June 17, 1902
McDougall Co. (renewal national contract)	1	June 18, 1902
Le Bosquet Coal and Mining Co. (new)	1	Do.
ASPHALT.		
Choctaw Asphalt Co	1	Apr. 22, 1902
Total number leases granted during the year	26	

In addition to the one formal asphalt lease which has been granted as above indicated, I have, by specific authority of the Department, and as mentioned in my last report, granted several informal permits to mine coal and asphalt, the purpose in granting these permits being to encourage the discovery and development of coal and asphalt, with a view to ultimately granting leases to those who, in pursuance of such permits, in good faith entered upon the work of discovery and development, demonstrated the character of the mineral, and otherwise brought themselves within the rules, regulations, and terms upon which leases have been granted under the provisions of the agreement.

The pending supplemental agreement with the Choctaws and Chickasaws, ratified by Congress July 1, 1902 (32 Stat., 641), to become effective upon its acceptance and ratification by the tribes, and to be voted on at an election to be called not later than November 1, 1902, prohibits the making of any additional coal or asphalt leases after the final ratification thereof. The Department has therefore instructed that no further applications be received at this time, and that all now pending be transmitted for consideration.

All permit holders were notified that those entitled thereto should present their applications for formal leases at an early date, in view of the proposed inhibition of further leases in the pending supplemental agreement. Such permit holders have all filed their formal applications. which are being considered by the Department.

A statement showing all coal and asphalt leases which have been entered into under the provisions of the agreement, and which were in effect on June 30, 1902, is respectfully given below:

Name.	Number.	Date of approval.
COAL.		
Choctaw, Oklahoma and Gulf Railroad Co.	30	Mar. 1, 1899
John F. McMurray.	8	Apr. 27, 1899
D. Edwards & Son	2	Aug. 22, 1899
Arkansas-McAlester Coal Co. (by transfer)	1	Do.
McAlester Coal Mining Co.	2	Feb. 19, 1900
Choctaw Coal and Mining Co.	3	May 4, 1900
Sans Bois Coal Co.	2	June 25, 1900
William Busby.	1	Sept. 6, 1900
Samples Coal and Mining Co	1	Oct. 4, 1900
McAlester-Galveston Coal Mining Co.	1	Oct. 18, 1900
H. Newton McEvers.	1	Do.
Degnan & McConnell.	3	Nov. 16, 1900
Folsom-Morris Coal Mining Co.	1	Nov. 22, 1900
Ozark Coal and Railway Co.	1	Dec. 8, 1900
St. Louis-Galveston Coal and Mining Co.	2	Jan. 14, 1901
Missouri, Kansas and Texas Coal Co.	1	Feb. 12, 1901
Osage Coal and Mining Co.	7	May 7, 1901
Atoka Coal and Mining Co	7	Do.
Devlin-Wear Coal Co.	1	June 17, 1901
Sans Bois Coal Co.	4	Aug. 5, 1901
Arkansas-McAlester Coal Co.	1	Oct. 1, 1901
Thomas H. Chambers.	1	Dec. 9, 1901
Turkey Creek Coal Co	1	Mar. 18, 1902
Southwestern Coal and Improvement Co.	10	Apr. 4, 1902
Essen Coal Co.	1	Apr. 12, 1902
Bache & Denman	1	Apr. 22, 1902
Kansas and Texas Coal Co.	4	June 13, 1902
Atoka Coal and Mining Co	1	Do.
Capital Coal and Mining Co	1	June 16, 1902
Hailey Coal and Mining Co.	2	June 17, 1902
McDougall Co.	1	June 18, 1902
Le Bosquet Coal and Mining Co	1	Do.
Total number coal leases in effect June 30, 1902	104	
ASPHALT.		
Brunswick Asphalt Co	1	Mar. 20, 1900
Elk Asphalt Co	1	May 3, 1900
Downard Asphalt Co	1	Oct. 18, 1900
M. & A. Schneider.	1	Nov. 23, 1900
Tar Spring Asphalt Co.	1	May 13, 1901
Choctaw Asphalt Co	1	Apr. 22, 1902
Total number asphalt leases in effect June 30, 1902	6	

For the convenient reference of the Department I submit, as an exhibit (marked A), a map of the Choctaw Nation, showing the location of the coal leases in that nation. There is also shown the approximate location of the operations which are still being carried on under old tribal contracts where such contracts have not yet been converted into formal leases under the agreement. The number of asphalt leases being so limited, no map showing the location of the same is submitted.

Referring to the report for the previous fiscal year, giving a list of coal leases granted up to that time, it will be noted that one of the approved leases of Messrs. D. Edwards & Son has been transferred, with the consent of the mining trustees and the approval of the Department, to the Arkansas-McAlester Coal Company.

The Department also permitted the Sans Bois Coal Company to exchange 4 of its original approved leases for the same number of leases covering other lands, it having been ascertained that the coal under a portion of the leases first granted could not be operated. This explains the statement showing that this company has only 2 leases approved in 1900 and 4 approved in 1901.

The asphalt lease of the Caddo Asphalt Company has, upon the request of such company, been surrendered and canceled, they having failed to find asphaltum of such quality and in such quantities that it could be profitably mined.

On June 30, 1901, as shown by the report for the year ending on that date, there were 10 companies or parties still operating under national contracts. Of these 10 all but 4 have since been granted formal leases. Of these 4 3 have continued operations, 2 (M. Peroni and R. Sarlls) under informal permits, their national contracts having been submitted and found to be defective and invalid, the other being Messrs. Perry Brothers, whose applications have been considered and passed upon since the close of the fiscal year. The fourth operator, the Caston Coal Company, has abandoned all of its operations.

The rate of royalty paid on both coal and asphalt has remained the same during the entire year, viz, 8 cents per ton, mine run, for coal, and 60 cents per ton on refined or 10 cents per ton on crude asphalt.

The total amount of royalty collected on account of coal and asphalt in the Choctaw and Chickasaw nations during the year has amounted to $245,848.01 coal royalty and $1,513.35 asphalt royalty, making a total of $247,361.36.

The figures given above show the actual amount collected by the United States Indian agent for these accounts, but such amounts will not agree with the report of the output in tons, there being quite large payments made from time to time on account of back royalty, as will be referred to hereafter. The general settling up of these old matters resulted in the collection of almost $20,000, which, together with the advanced royalty paid on all leases in effect, accounts for the discrepancy between the reports of the output and moneys received.

The total coal and asphalt royalties collected for the fiscal years 1899, 1900, 1901, and 1902 are shown by the following comparative statement:

July 1, 1898, to June 30, 1899 .... $110,145.25
July 1, 1899, to June 30, 1900 .... 138,486.40
July 1, 1900, to June 30, 1901 .... 199,663.55
July 1, 1901, to June 30, 1902 .... 247,361.36

There has been considerable correspondence with the Department and the several mine operators in the matter of the final settlement of all old amounts due on account of back royalties, which amounts were ascertained from various sources. The one which has required the most attention and which has finally been closed was the amounts due from the several operators in 1898. These operators paid royalty on all coal mined up to January 1, 1899 (at which date the royalty was fixed by regulation of the Secretary of the Interior at 10 cents per ton), at the rate prescribed by their tribal or national contracts, viz, one-half cent per bushel, or 12½ cents per ton.

The agreement with the Choctaws and Chickasaws provided for a royalty on coal of 15 cents per ton, but authorized the Secretary of the Interior to reduce or advance the same, as he deemed best for the interests of the Indians. In settling up old accounts it was ascertained that operators had paid at the rate of 12½ cents per ton during the year 1898, while the law required a rate of 15 cents per ton. The matter was submitted to the Department, and after being considered I was advised that the rate of 15 cents per ton should be collected, and directed to call upon all operators for the amounts due during such period. Proper statements were prepared and all companies called upon, and in due time the amounts charged were paid. which settled up all back royalty claims and, as stated heretofore, the records and books are now carefully checked each quarter and it is promptly ascertained whether all amounts due are paid.

But little progress has been made during the year in the operation of the asphalt mines of the Indian Territory. The lessees continue to prospect and experiment, but the results are unsatisfactory, one company reporting that although they had believed asphalt existed in paying quantities where they desired to mine and they had expended considerable money in preparing to operate, still, after further investigation it was proven to them that it was not worth while to pursue the matter further; that they believed the asphalt in the Territory is in small pockets, and that this assumption is warranted by the finding of other companies. They therefore have withdrawn from the Indian Territory field and will procure their asphalt in the future from the island of Cuba.

There are a number of coal leases in the Choctaw Nation covering lands where incorporated towns are in existence at this time. The lease of the McAlester-Galveston Coal Mining Company covers a portion of the town of McAlester. This company attempted to make some new openings in the streets and at other points which were objectionable to the residents and authorities of the town. Therefore, in October, 1901, application was made by the incorporated town of McAlester to the United States court of the central district, Indian Territory, for an order restraining the company from opening a shaft in the street, and Hon. William H. H. Clayton, United States judge for that district, after a hearing, granted the injunction, holding that inasmuch as the area of the land in controversy was within the limits of a town it was the duty of the company to have made application to have the land where it desired to operate reserved for its use, under the provisions of the agreement. It was further held that even if the plat of the town site had been prepared and approved, the court would recognize any existing streets to the extent of preventing the obstruction of the same.

The forms of application, lease, etc., in use at the present time, together with a copy of the existing rules and regulations governing mineral leases in the Choctaw and Chickasaw nations, are attached as Appendix No. 12, page 200.

CREEK NATION.

Coal has never been extensively mined in the Creek Nation and in most instances is found in shallow veins near the surface.   Considerable coal, however, has recently been discovered along the line of the St. Louis and San Francisco Railroad in said nation.

The agreement with the Creek Nation, as ratified by the act of Congress approved March 1, 1901 (31 Stat., 861), and by the tribe on May 25, 1901, makes no provision for the leasing of mineral lands and does not reserve any of such land from allotment.

The agreement provides, however, that Indian citizens can not dispose of their allotments within five years, except with the consent of the Secretary of the Interior, and as coal, oil, and other minerals are considered part of the realty, the Department has held that an Indian citizen can not mine coal or other mineral and dispose of the same without the consent of the Department.

It was not believed by the Department to be desirable, owing to the present conditions, to permit Indians to mine coal until they have received absolute title to their land, but in a few instances where parties had been mining coal in good faith under permits granted prior to the ratification of the agreement, they have been permitted to continue upon the written consent of the Indian allottee and with the understanding that a royalty of eight cents per ton was to be paid into the United States Treasury through the United States Indian agent at Union Agency, and held to the credit of the land upon which the coal was mined, the same as is done in the case of the money collected for timber and stone under the provisions of the regulations governing such matters, said money to be eventually paid the allottee.   But few of these permits have been granted, and the amount of money which has been collected on account of the coal mined thereunder amounted during the year to $2,761.20.

The operations carried on under the conditions above mentioned have been on a small scale, the coal as a general rule being mined by what is known as the stripping process, and principally used for local consumption.

No other mining in the Creek Nation has been carried on during the year.   During the first part of the year, however, there was some little excitement over the matter of the discovery of what was believed to be valuable oil deposits at Red Fork and Tulsa in the Creek Nation, but inasmuch as the Department held that any leases for the purpose of extracting oil would be invalid and could not be recognized or permitted, the prospecting and drilling for oil in these towns was not resumed until about the latter part of June 1902, after the lots had been appraised, amounts due paid, and deeds issued.

CHEROKEE NATION.

The provisions of section 13 of the Curtis Act authorized the making of mineral leases in the Cherokee Nation, but the Department has declined to generally receive any application for leases under such section, in view of the various pending agreements.

Under the provisions of such legislation, however, the Secretary of the Interior, as mentioned in previous reports, granted a permit for fifteen years to the Kansas and Arkansas Valley Railroad Company for the purpose of procuring gravel from the bars and bed of the Grand River in the Cherokee Nation, which permit is still in effect. A royalty of 2 cents per cubic yard is paid for the benefit of the nation for all gravel taken out under this permit.

A number of informal permits have been granted to both citizens and noncitizens to mine coal, principally for local consumption. This coal is mined on a small scale, and a royalty of 8 cents per ton is paid to the United States Indian agent, which amounted during the year to $5,339.57, as against $6,326.87 for the previous year. As in the Creek Nation, coal has never been extensively mined, being shallow and mined by the stripping process.

In previous reports I have mentioned the fact that the Cherokee Oil and Gas Company and other parties in 1899 had made application for a large number of oil and gas leases, covering tracts in the Cherokee Nation which they claimed to have improved and taken possession of under authority of tribal leases granted by the Cherokee Nation prior to the passage of the Curtis Act. The applications of the Cherokee Oil and Gas Company, after having been carefully considered by the Department and full examination of the tracts applied for being made and reports submitted, were finally passed upon May 12, 1902, and twelve of these applications were approved. All other applications of this company were severally and collectively rejected and denied, with the exception that they were allowed sixty days to present further proof concerning one particular application where they claimed to have sunk a well at a cost of $5,000. The formal leases covering the land described in the said twelve applications which were approved were duly executed by the company and the Secretary of the Interior under date of June 7, 1902.

These leases were granted under section 13 of the act of June 28, 1898, in pursuance of the preference right given by that section to those who or whose grantors have, under the customs and laws heretofore existing and prevailing in the Cherokee Nation, obtained leases of land containing oil, taken possession thereunder, made improvements, and developed and produced oil in commercial quantities. They cover a period of fifteen years, with rate of royalty of 10 per cent of the value of all crude oil extracted, each lease being for 640 acres.

Under similar conditions the Cudahy Oil Company, upon an application made in 1899, was granted one oil and gas lease since the close of the year.

TOWN SITES.

SURVEYS.

During the fiscal year ended June 30, 1901, the exterior limits of practically all the towns in the Indian Territory having more than 200 people were established, and a number of interior surveys completed. The work which has been under way during the past year has been almost entirely surveying and platting these towns into lots, blocks, and streets after the limits had once been determined upon.

These surveys have been made in accordance with the provisions of the legislation applicable to the several tribes, as modified by the act of May 31, 1900 (31 Stat., 221—see Appendix No. 6), which authorized the Secretary of the Interior to lay out and survey all town sites in the Indian Territory having a population of 200 or more, and all of the work which has been performed during the year has been at towns with 200 or more inhabitants, with the exception of the smaller towns in the Creek Nation specifically provided for by the agreement with that nation and at a few new town sites set aside upon the recommendation of the Commission to the Five Civilized Tribes under the provisions of this same act of May 31, 1900.

To carry on the town-site work the Indian appropriation act approved March 3, 1901, for the fiscal year 1902 provided $150,000. This fund is used not only in making surveys but in the appraisements and all other work in connection with the final disposition of town-site matters in the Choctaw, Chickasaw, Creek, and Cherokee nations.

While the act of May 31, 1900, supra, authorized the Secretary of the Interior to secure the surveying and platting of towns by contract, this plan was not followed in any way during the year. During the previous year a number of towns were platted under contract by Mr. L. F. Parker, as mentioned in my last report. The work has been carried on by the employment of town-site surveyors, and there have been engaged during the year from ten to twelve parties, consisting of a surveyor in charge, with transitman, chainmen, rodmen, and other necessary employees. In some of the larger towns, in order to expedite the work, more than one transit party has been furnished a surveyor, where the work would permit the use of such increased force.

There have been some changes in the field forces during the year. It has been the plan where employees have shown themselves particularly competent to promote them to more responsible places, thus making the service more efficient. The following, however, is a list of the office and field forces that were employed at the close of the year, so far as the surveys proper are concerned, not including chainmen, rodmen, and other irregular employees of this class:

Supervising engineer.—H. V. Hinckley.
Assistant supervising engineer.—John G. Joyce, jr.
Draftsmen.—Harry T. Kerr, Samuel A. Cobb, William G. Rawles.
Surveyors.—Charles L. Wood, Frank F. Sweet, William E. McElree, C. E. Phillips, John F. Fisher, Samuel P. Matthews, Mark Kirkpatrick, E. E. Colby, J. T. Payne, J. Gus Patton.
Transitmen.—Julian Burney, Henry M. Tinker, Charles L. Grimes, Merritt A. Howerton, J. Frank Ryan, John G. Hough, Earl Miller, Charles B. Stebbins, A. H. Collins, A. J. Gardenhire (irregular), William P. Danford (irregular).

I regret to report the death in the early part of the year of Mr. Mortimer Z. Jones, a surveyor appointed from Kansas. Mr. Jones was an energetic and efficient employee, and was taken ill with typhoid-malarial fever while engaged in the work at Lehigh, in the Choctaw Nation, and died at that place.

It was found to be necessary to fix a certain standard of accuracy up to which the several surveyors must gauge their work in platting town sites, and therefore, after some correspondence with the Department, the following limit of error was adopted, which has proven satisfactory:

First. Discrepancies between any angle and the governing distance shall not exceed two (2) minutes.

Second. The discrepancy in the angles of any block shall not exceed four (4) minutes, regardless of the number of sides to the block.

Third. No discrepancy will be allowed in excess of four-tenths ($\frac{4}{10}$) of a foot in the length of any 300-foot block, or six-tenths ($\frac{6}{10}$) in the length of any block.

Fourth. No discrepancy will be allowed in excess of one (1) foot in any street line or base line across any town site.

The most serious complications that have been dealt with during the year have been the accurate location and platting of grounds claimed by railroad companies within the several town sites which have been surveyed. It has been difficult to procure necessary and satisfactory information, and plats which have been filed and prepared by the railroad companies have, as a general rule, been seriously incomplete and inaccurate, requiring the submission and approval of supplemental and amended plats, which has caused considerable annoyance and delay.

The plan adopted by the Department during the previous year of making photolithographic copies of all plats has been continued, one original plat being submitted to and approved by the Department, photolithographic copies thereof made to file with the various officers, in compliance with the provisions of the law, and other copies being offered for sale to the public at a price sufficient to pay the cost of photolithographing. This plan enables the residents of towns to procure official copies of such plats which are absolutely accurate and duplicates of the original.

In the Cherokee Nation the towns had at one time been laid out by the tribal authorities and the right of occupancy to lots disposed of by the nation. In establishing the limits of these towns under the provisions of the act of May 31, 1900, it was held by the Department that the question of the area originally included within the town sites as laid out by the Cherokee Nation was not to be considered; that under the law the criterion by which to determine the limits to be given each town site was the present needs and reasonab'e prospective growth of the town. Therefore, in determining the limits of Cherokee towns the original boundaries were not followed.

The interior subdivisional surveys of all towns having a population of 200 or more, in the Choctaw, Chickasaw. and Cherokee nations, and all towns in the Creek Nation, were practically completed on June 30, 1902, and the following is a statement showing the towns surveyed prior to the beginning of this fiscal year, those surveyed during the fiscal year, those under way at the close thereof, and the ones still remaining.

A progress map showing the status of the surveys on June 30, 1902, has been prepared. This map shows the location of each of the towns mentioned hereafter, and is submitted as Exhibit B.

Attention is respectfully invited to the report of the supervising engineer, which is also submitted.

CHOCTAW NATION.

Surveyed and platted by town-site commission prior to the passage of the act of May 31, 1900.

Town.	Population.	Area.	Town.	Population.	Area.
		Acres.			*Acres.*
Atoka	1,200	277.18	Kiowa	250	360
Calvin	250	160	South McAlester	4,000	2,902.27
Guertle	225	160	Sterrett	800	485

Surveyed and platted during fiscal year 1901, by the Secretary of the Interior, under direction of the inspector.

Town.	Population.	Area.	Town.	Population.	Area.
		Acres.			*Acres.*
Antlers	800	182.5	Hoyt	284	97.5
Caddo	1,200	400	Poteau	1,200	645
Cameron	300	155	Redoak	209	132.5
Canadian	554	197.5	Spiro	600	225.78
Cowlington	235	157.5	Stigler	300	102.33
Durant	3,500	1,284	Talihina	400	210.59
Enterprise	552	107.5	Tamaha	313	142.3
Grant	250	131.22	Wapanucka	215	180
Heavener	250	175.64	Wister	360	149.78
Howe	1,000	326.7	Whitefield	354	100.37

Surveyed and platted during fiscal year 1902, by the Secretary of the Interior, under direction of the inspector.

Town.	Population.	Area.	Town.	Population.	Area.
		Acres.			*Acres.*
Allen	235	120	Lehigh	3,000	1,050
Coalgate	2,600	785	McAlester	750	759.07
Durant (addition)		40	Wapanucka (addition)	1,300	245
Haileyville	1,500	681.05	Wilburton	3,000	275.58

Surveying and platting under progress.

Town.	Population.	Area.
		Acres.
Hartshorne	2,300	848.11

The above shows the disposition of all the towns in the Choctaw Nation which were considered up to June 30, 1902, as having a population of 200 or more inhabitants. No action has been taken concerning the town of Krebs, which was shown in my report for the year 1901, inasmuch as it is a coal town and its status has not yet been determined.

In addition to the above towns, the Department has approved, just at the close of the year, the recommendations of the Commission to the Five Civilized Tribes for the segregation of new town sites along the line of the newly constructed Arkansas and Choctaw Railroad through the Choctaw Nation, as follows. The advice concerning the approval of these town sites was not received in time to commence the work of platting them during the past year, but the same is now under way.

Town.	Area.	Town.	Area.
	Acres.		*Acres.*
Bennington	140	Harrington	45
Boswell	160	New Bokchito	45
Fort Towson	160	Purnell	89.39
Garvin	120	Soper	90
Gilbert	100	Valliant	120
Hugo	160		

The Department has also approved the recommendation of the Commission to the Five Civilized Tribes for the segregation of a tract for town-site purposes along the line of the Missouri, Kansas and Texas Railroad Company in the Choctaw Nation, as follows:

Town.	Population.	Area.
Stringtown	164	*Acres.* 62.5

CHICKASAW NATION.

Surveyed and platted by town-site commission prior to the passage of the act of May 31, 1900.

Town.	Population.	Area.
Colbert...	275	*Acres.* 129.77

Surveyed and platted during fiscal year 1901, by the Secretary of the Interior, under direction of the inspector.

Town.	Population.	Area.	Town.	Population.	Area.
		Acres.			*Acres.*
Ardmore	6,000	2,282.14	Marietta	1,150	330
Berwyn	237	191.25	Minco..................	622	285.35
Cumberland...........	340	173.98	McGee.................	250	122.5
Chickasha.............	3,500	1,246.19	Pauls Valley..........	2,000	946.83
Duncan	1,500	1,010.07	Pontotoc.............	264	195
Dougherty	417	243.13	Paoli..................	225	85.48
Emet	300	170	Rush Springs	490	380
Johnson	230	90	Silo	400	195
Lebanon	218	164.92			

In addition to the above, the surveying of the following new towns in the Chickasaw Nation, along the line of the St. Louis, Oklahoma and Southern Railroad, was done by Mr. L. F. Parker, under contract, during the year 1901:

Town.	Area.	Town.	Area.
	Acres.		*Acres.*
Ada...........................	559.9	Madill..........................	160
Bryant (now Mill Creek).............	155.45	Ravia	326.39
Francis	160	Roff	595
Gray	80	Scullin	120
Helen.........................	156.09	Woodville	160

It having been shown that there was no necessity for a town site at the station of Gray, the segregation made was, during the year, canceled, and therefore the plat of this town site will not be submitted for approval.

Surveyed and platted during fiscal year 1902, by the Secretary of the Interior, under direction of the inspector.

Town.	Population.	Area.	Town.	Population.	Area.
		Acres.			*Acres.*
Addington	300	145.4	Marlow	1,214	960
Connerville	317	180	Kemp	230	120
Comanche	600	437.04	Orr	215	185
Earl	240	125	Purcell	3,000	1,110.68
Elmore	225	145	Purdy	200	116.5
Erin Springs	204	110	Ryan	900	485.39
Davis	2,000	581.46	Stonewall	240	117.5
Center	510	196	Sugden	350	149.18
Cornish	210	190.28	Terral	500	280
Leon	240	165	Wynnewood	2,993	767.5

Surveying and platting under progress.

Town.	Population.	Area.	Town.	Population.	Area.
		Acres.			*Acres.*
Oakland	900	343.75	Tishomingo	1,200	55

Towns over 200 yet to be surveyed and platted.

Town.	Population.	Area.	Town.	Population.	Area.
		Acres.			*Acres.*
Durwood	250	140	Mannsville	215	175
Hickory	292	170	Sulphur	2,000	948.14
Lonegrove	215	195			

The four towns first above named have been delayed by reason of the fact that they are located in close proximity to railroads which are being or have recently been constructed. The work at the town of Sulphur has been postponed, owing to the fact that the supplemental agreement, not yet ratified by the tribes, provides for a reservation on account of the mineral springs at this point.

In addition to the above list of towns yet to be surveyed and platted should be added the following towns along new railroads, which have been set aside upon the recommendation of the Commission to the Five Civilized Tribes:

Town.	Area.	Town.	Area.
	Acres.		*Acres.*
Blue (now Milburn)	160	Mead	80

CREEK NATION.

Surveyed and platted prior to and during fiscal year 1901.

Town.	Area.	Town.	Area.
By town-site commission:	*Acres.*	Under contract by L. F. Parker—Ctd.	*Acres.*
Muskogee	2,444.76	Mounds	160
Wagoner	2,700	Okmulgee	415
Under contract by L. F. Parker:		Holdenville	429.7
Alabama	80	Wetumka	160
Beggs	160	Winchell	160
Henryetta	157.13	Foster (Yager P. O.)	120

Surveyed and platted during fiscal year 1902, by the Secretary of the Interior, under direction of the inspector.

Town.	Population.	Area.	Town.	Population.	Area.
		Acres.			*Acres.*
Bixby	85	80	Inola		160
Bristow	900	385	Kellyville		80
Coweta	200	85	Lee	25	45
Checotah	1,000	503.75	Red Fork	200	160
Clarksville	400	147.5	Sapulpa	1,500	501.25
Eufaula	1,000	431.38	Tulsa	1,700	654.58
Gibson Station		160	Wildcat	200	158

The segregations for the towns of Gibson Station, Inola, and Kellyville were made upon the recommendation of the Commission to the Five Civilized Tribes under the provision of that portion of the act of May 31, 1900, providing for towns along railroads, which act was embodied in section 10 of the Creek agreement. These segregations were made without regard to the population, and I have no accurate information as to the number of people at these places.

From the above it will be noted that the surveys are entirely completed within the Creek Nation, and the list includes all small towns, as the agreement specifically provided that all, without regard to population, might be surveyed.

CHEROKEE NATION.

Surveyed and platted during fiscal year 1902, by the Secretary of the Interior, under direction of the inspector.

Town.	Population.	Area.	Town.	Population.	Area.
		Acres.			*Acres.*
Adair	300	150	Lenapah	203	118.12
Afton	1,200	532.5	Muldrow	500	210.5
Bartlesville	1,000	342.44	Nowata	900	375.63
Blue Jacket	350	196.25	Oolagah	308	170
Chelsea	1,000	452.59	Pryor Creek	600	365
Catoosa	250	165	Ramona	200	110
Collinsville	1,100	270	Stilwell	600	164.22
Claremore	1,000	657.5	Sallisaw	1,000	257.78
Centralia	400	177.5	Talala	300	170
Choteau	250	130	Vian	400	220.62
Fairland	600	240	Vinita	2,500	946.23
Grove	500	210	Webbers Falls	250	80.5
Gans	215	115	Westville	750	179.99
Hanson	210	95	Welch	330	160

Surveying and platting under progress.

Town.	Population.	Area.	Town.	Population.	Area.
		Acres.			*Acres.*
Fort Gibson	1,200	412.65	Tahlequah	1,800	632.5

The surveys of Fort Gibson and Tahlequah were finished shortly after the close of the fiscal year, which completes all the towns in the Cherokee Nation having a population of two hundred or more inhabitants.

SMALL TOWNS.

The act of May 31, 1900, as stated, only authorized the surveying and platting of towns having a population of two hundred or more inhabitants, and with the exception of the Creek Nation, where such act was amended by the ratification of the agreement with this tribe, the only work that has been done was at these larger places.

The Indian appropriation act for the year 1903, approved May 27, 1902 (32 Stat., 245), provided, however, for the surveying and platting of all small towns, as follows:

That the limits of such towns in the Cherokee, Choctaw, and Chickasaw nations, having a population of less than two hundred people, as in the judgment of the Secretary of the Interior should be established, shall be defined as early as practicable by the Secretary of the Interior in the same manner as provided for towns having over two hundred people under existing law, and the same shall not be subject to allotment; that the land so segregated and reserved from allotment shall be disposed of in such manner as the Secretary of the Interior may direct by a town-site commission, one member to be appointed by the Secretary of the Interior, and one by the executive of the nation in which such land is located; the proceeds arising from the disposition of such lands to be applied in like manner as the proceeds of other lands in town sites.

At the close of the fiscal year, under the provisions of the legislation above quoted, I had caused practically all the small towns and post-offices in the Choctaw, Chickasaw, and Cherokee nations to be visited by surveyors and transitmen, and reports as to population, existing conditions, etc., made, which reports have been transmitted to and considered by the Department since the close of the year. There are about 440 of these smaller towns and post-offices, but it is not believed that it will be necessary to establish or survey town sites at more than 60 towns in the Chickasaw Nation, 25 in the Choctaw Nation, and 20 in the Cherokee Nation.

APPRAISEMENTS.

There have been three commissions engaged in the work of appraising town sites practically the entire year.

In the Choctaw Nation, during the first part of the year, the commission consisted of the same two members that had been engaged in the work during the previous year, namely, Mr. J. A. Sterrett, of Ohio, and Mr. Butler S. Smiser, representing the nation. In October, however, Mr. Smiser resigned, and Mr. Thomas W. Hunter was appointed in his stead, and the commission continued with this personnel the remainder of the year.

In the Chickasaw Nation, during the early part of the year, there was no commission. Mr. Arthur W. Hefley was afterwards appointed as chairman of this commission, vice the former chairman, Mr. Samuel N. Johnson, and Mr. Wesley B. Burney, on the part of the tribe, having been reinstated, the work of this commission again commenced, and has since continued.

On July 1, 1901, the two commissions, one for the town of Wagoner and one for the town of Muskogee, in the Creek Nation, were reappointed under the provisions of the agreement with that tribe. These commissions at once entered upon the work of completing the reappraisements of these two towns, which work was finally finished about the 1st of September. The chairmen of these two commissions, Mr. Dwight W. Tuttle and Mr. Henry C. Linn, were appointed as members of the commission for the Creek Nation, and Mr. George A. Alexander was appointed the third member, on behalf of the tribe, and this commission has continued the remainder of the year.

There has been no commission appointed in the Cherokee Nation.

The work was somewhat delayed in the Choctaw and Chickasaw nations during the early part of the fiscal year, owing to the attitude of the executives of these tribes relative to permitting the Indian members of the commissions to proceed with the work of appraising towns which had been platted under the act of May 31, 1900, they having protested, as referred to in my last annual report, against this work proceeding, contending that it was a violation of the strict terms of their agreement. These executives finally instructed the Indian members of these two commissions to decline to proceed with the work, after which these two commissioners were removed by the Department under the authority contained in the Indian appropriation act approved March 3, 1901. After this action and several conferences with the representatives of the two tribes, it was agreed that the work of appraisement should proceed. The tribal members of these two commissions were reappointed, which appointments were accepted by the Department, and the work has since that time been pushed as rapidly as possible.

As to the power and authority of the Secretary of the Interior to determine matters over which the town-site commissions fail to agree, I have to respectfully submit an opinion of Hon. William H. H. Clayton, the United States judge of the central district, Indian Territory (see Appendix No. 13, p. 211), upon a case which was brought before him, where the two members of the town-site commission for the Choctaw Nation failed to agree as to what should be classed an improvement in an instance known as the Allen Wright case, where a certain reservoir was in question. The Department held, with the chairman of the commission, that such reservoir should be considered as a permanent and substantial improvement, and the court held that the action of the Secretary of the Interior in this case was final and not subject to review.

The pending supplemental agreement with the Choctaws and Chickasaws provides that occupants or purchasers of lots in town sites upon which no improvements were made prior to the ratification of the act by Congress, which was July 1, 1902, shall pay the full appraised value of such lot instead of the percentage named in the Atoka agreement. If this supplemental agreement is ratified by the tribes, it will be necessary for the town-site commissions in the Choctaw and Chickasaw nations, in making their appraisements, to ascertain whether the improvements were made before or after July 1 last.

After the appraisement of any town site is made and approved, the proper commission serves a notice upon each owner, advising him of the amount of appraisement and the time within which he must pay the proper per cent. In the Creek Nation the first payment of 10 per cent must be paid within sixty days from service of notice, the second payment of 15 per cent within four months thereafter, and the remainder of the purchase money in three equal annual installments without interest. It is provided, however, that in case any amount be not paid when due, the same shall thereafter bear interest at the rate of 10 per cent per annum until paid.

In the Choctaw and Chickasaw nations the first payment of 25 per cent must be made within sixty days from notice, and the balance in three equal annual installments.

These payments are all made to the United States Indian agent at Union Agency, and it requires a large amount of detailed clerical work to properly handle and receive the same.

The amount collected by the Indian agent from this source during the year was $157,188.53 for the Choctaw and Chickasaw nations and $80,536.56 for the Creek Nation, a total of $237,725.39.

As referred to in my last annual report, the act of May 31, 1900, so modified the then existing legislation that the work of town-site commissions could not commence as to any town until after the approval of the plat thereof. Therefore, the work of the several commissions during the year just closed has been entirely that of making appraisements.

A progress map, showing the status of the appraisements on June 30, 1902, has been prepared, and is submitted as Exhibit C.

CHOCTAW NATION.

In the Choctaw Nation at the close of the fiscal year the work of appraisement was practically up with the surveys. This commission had before the commencement of the past fiscal year appraised the towns of Atoka, Calvin, Guertie, Kiowa, South McAlester, and Sterrett.

A complete list of the towns which they have appraised up to June 30, 1902, including the above, showing the acreage and the total amount of the appraisements at each town, is respectfully shown below:

Completed prior to June 30, 1901.

Town.	Area.	Appraisement.	Town.	Area.	Appraisement.
	Acres.			*Acres.*	
Atoka	277.18	a $40,786.00	Kiowa	360	a $2,050.00
Calvin	160	1,949.00	South McAlester	2,902.27	233,668.00
Guertie	160	a 808.00	Sterrett	485	a 5,282.50

a Amount of appraisement covers improved property only.

Completed during fiscal year ended June 30, 1902.

Town.	Area.	Appraisement.	Town.	Area.	Appraisement.
	Acres.			*Acres.*	
Allen	120	$5,031.	Hoyt	97.5	$2,174.00
Antlers	182.5	13,450.	McAlester	759.07	57,348.00
Canadian	197.5	7,401.	Poteau	645	44,195.00
Cowlington	157.5	3,366.	Redoak	132.5	4,759.00
Cameron	155	5,496.	Stigler	102.33	2,934.30
Caddo	400	70,	Talihina	210.59	3,673.00
Enterprise	107.5	3,595.	Tamaha	142.3	4,157.00
Grant	131.22	4,266.00	Whitefield	100.57	3,327.00
Howe	326.7	14,440.60	Wister	149.78	1,045.00

The commission at the close of the year was engaged in the work of making the appraisements at the following towns:

Town.	Area.
	Acres.
Heavener	175.64
Spiro	225.78
Wilburton	275.56

Of towns having a population of 200 or more in the Choctaw Nation, the commission has the following yet to appraise:

Town.	Area.	Town.	Area.
	Acres.		*Acres.*
Durant	1,324	Coalgate	785
Lehigh	1,050	Hartshorne	848.11
Wapanucka	425	Haileyville	681.05

In addition to the above, after the surveys are completed and the plats approved, the commission will have yet to appraise a number of town sites set aside upon the recommendation of the Commission to the Five Civilized tribes (see report under Surveys, p. 20), and also a few other small towns that have been found since the close of the year to contain more than 200 inhabitants, but where the area has not yet been determined, as also such coal towns as it is finally determined to survey.

The Choctaw commission has, in addition to its regular work of appraising towns, sold the vacant lots in the towns of South McAlester, McAlester, Canadian, and Poteau, and also the default lots at Atoka.

CHICKASAW NATION.

The work of the new Chickasaw commission was hardly gotten under way until about January, 1902, since which time it has been given every facility to push the work of appraisement, in view of the large number of towns in that nation, some of which are quite large. It has been furnished with additional clerical force, and has had the work going on in several towns at one time.

The following is a list of towns appraised by this Commission up to June 30, 1902, including the one town, Colbert, which was appraised in 1899, showing the amount of the appraisments and the area of each:

Appraised prior to June 30, 1901.

Town.	Area.	Appraisement.
	Acres.	
Colbert	129.77	a $3,200.00

a Amount of appraisement covers improved property only.

Appraised during fiscal year 1902.

Town.	Area.	Appraisement.	Town.	Area.	Appraisement.
	Acres.			*Acres.*	
Ardmore	2,262.14	$322,818.00	Marlow	960	$62,753.00
Chickasha	1,246.19	203,412.00	Minco	285.35	20,888.00
Cumberland	173.98	4,697.00	Marietta	330	49,954.00
Emet	170	5,520.00	Rush Springs	380	33,861.80
Johnson	90	4,111.00	Silo	195	2,375.00
Lebanon	164.92	4,862.00	Woodville	160	27,583.00
McGee	122.5	5,403.00			

At the close of the fiscal year the Commission had under way and had practically completed the apprasements at the following towns:

Town.	Area.	Town.	Area.
	Acres.		Acres.
Addington	145.4	Ryan	435.30
Comanche	437.04	Sugden	149.18
Duncan	1,010.07	Terral	280
Pauls Valley	946.83		

The Commission has the following towns having a population of 200 or more yet to appraise:

Town.	Area.	Town.	Area.
	Acres.		Acres.
Berwyn	191.25	Lonegrove	195
Center	195	Mannsville	175
Cornish	190.28	Oakland	862.75
Connerville	180	Orr	185
Dougherty	248.18	Purcell	1,110.68
Davis	581.46	Pontotoc	195
Durwood	140	Paoli	85.48
Elmore	145	Purdy	116.25
Earl	125	Stonewall	117.5
Erin Springs	110	Tishomingo	545
Hickory	170	Wynnewood	767.5
Kemp	120	Sulphur	948.14
Leon	165		

In addition to the above, the Commission will have the towns along the St. Louis, Oklahoma and Southern Railroad, platted under contract (see page 21), except Woodville, which has already been appraised; such other new towns along the lines of railroads which have been or may be set aside upon the recommendation of the Commission to the Five Civilized Tribes, and some few others where it may be ascertained that the population is over 200 yet to appraise.

It will be noted from the above statements that the majority of the larger towns in the Chickasaw Nation have been completed. The Commission has, in addition to this appraisement work proper, sold the unimproved lots in a few of the smaller towns and prepared for the sales at Ardmore, Chickasha, and Marietta, which took place during July last.

CREEK NATION.

As stated above, the work of the two separate Commissions appointed under the provisions of the agreement with the Creek Nation to complete the work at Wagoner and Muskogee was practically completed by the 1st of September. Since that time the Commission for this nation has been engaged in pushing the appraisements at other towns, the plats of which have been approved.

I respectfully submit below a list of the towns in the Creek Nation where the appraisements had been made up to June 30, 1902, showing the total amount of the appraisement of each town site and the acreage thereof:

THE HOME OF A CREEK FULL BLOOD.

Completed during fiscal year ended June 30, 1902.

Town.	Area.	Appraisement.	Town.	Area.	Appraisement.
	Acres.			*Acres.*	
Muskogee	2,444.76	$241,370.20	Holdenville	429.79	$102,810.00
Wagoner	2,700	159,475.00	Kellyville	80	6,712.00
Alabama	80	7,292.00	Mounds	160	27,004.00
Beggs	160	24,486.00	Okmulgee	415	82,571.00
Bixby	80	7,187.00	Redfork	160	18,128.00
Bristow	385	63,217.50	Tulsa	654.58	107,173.30
Foster (Yager post-office)	120	6,922.00	Wetumka	160	33,941.00
Henryetta	157.13	24,295.00	Winchell	160	8,333.00

The Commission, in addition to the above, had the work at the following towns practically completed, and had planned for the sales of vacant lots during July at all the towns along the St. Louis, Oklahoma and Southern Railroad from Mounds to Holdenville and at Muskogee and Wagoner:

Town.	Area.	Town.	Area.
	Acres.		*Acres.*
Eufaula	431.38	Inola	160
Checotah	503.75	Gibson Station	160

The commission has the following towns still to appraise:

Town.	Area.	Town.	Area.
	Acres.		*Acres.*
Sapulpa	501.25	Lee	45
Clarksville	147.5	Wildcat	158
Coweta	85		

Of the towns yet to appraise, only one, Sapulpa, is of any size. The commission is now engaged in obtaining preliminary information at all of these towns.

The agreement with the Creek Nation provides for numerous classes of holdings and recognizes in certain cases the right of parties to purchase unimproved lots. This has caused considerable conflict of interests, and will necessitate the hearing of a large number of contests in the Creek towns, which will delay the work of this Commission to some extent.

At the stations of Mounds to Foster, inclusive, along the line of the St. Louis, Oklahoma and Southern Railroad in the Creek Nation, certain lands were set aside as new town sites upon the recommendation of the Commission to the Five Civilized Tribes. In appraising these tracts it was held by the Department that only two classes of holdings, under the provisions of the law, should be recognized; one being improved property, and the other being lots held as a home in connection with valuably improved lots, not to exceed four acres.

This construction of the law caused numerous protests and complaints from parties who claimed to own the occupancy right to unimproved lots in these towns, but after careful consideration the Department declined to change its decision in the matter, holding that after the segregation of the land for town-site purposes parties could not legally sell the right of occupancy to any unimproved property therein, but that where improvements had been erected in good faith the parties erecting the same should be protected. Since the close of the fiscal year, and at the time these unimproved lots were offered for sale at public auction, application was made to Hon. Charles W. Raymond, United States judge for the western district of Indian Territory, for an injunction restraining the town-site commission from selling any of these lots, but after hearing the argument of the parties interested the injunction was denied and the sale proceeded.

CHEROKEE NATION.

None of the surveys in the Cherokee Nation were finally completed and the plats approved until the latter part of the year, and owing to this fact, and the further fact that there was considerable legislation pending affecting this tribe, no town-site commission was appointed in this nation, and therefore no appraisements have been made.

Since the passage and ratification of the act of July 1, 1902, providing for the allotment of the lands and disposition of town-sites in the Cherokee Nation, it is expected that steps will at once be taken to appoint a commission and push the appraisements to early completion.

TOWN-LOT DEEDS.

No appraisements having been made in the Cherokee Nation, no titles to town lots in that nation have passed.

In the Creek Nation a large number of town-lot deeds have been issued. The agreement with this nation provides that all conveyances shall be approved by the Secretary of the Interior, which approval shall serve as a relinquishment to the grantee of all right, title, or interest of the United States in and to the lands embraced in his deed. Therefore all deeds to lots in this nation are submitted to the Department, and the following is a brief statement of the plan of procedure:

When full payment for any lot in the Creek Nation has been made to the United States Indian agent, he at once, in addition to furnishing the owner of the lot with a final receipt, issues a statement or certificate in duplicate, one of which he forwards to the principal chief of the Creek Nation and one to this office, setting forth the fact that the party named has made full payment for the lots described in accordance with the appraisement made by the town-site commission, and is entitled to a deed therefor. The deed is then drawn by the principal chief and transmitted to this office, where the duplicate certificate of final payment issued by the Indian agent is attached, and the deed is carefully checked and transmitted to the Department for the approval of the Secretary of the Interior, as required by law.

The agreement also provides that the Commission to the Five Civilized Tribes shall record all deeds; therefore when the deeds are approved by the Department they are forwarded to the Commission to be recorded, and the Commission in turn transmits them to the principal chief to be delivered to the grantee.

In the Choctaw and Chickasaw nations the agreement does not provide that deeds shall be approved by the Secretary of the Interior, and therefore when full payment for any lots in these nations is made, the deeds are drawn in the office of the United States Indian agent and transmitted to the principal chief of the Choctaw Nation and the governor of the Chickasaw Nation for execution and return.   After they are received by the agent, properly executed, they are forwarded to the parties entitled to the same.

A form of deed in use in the Creek Nation is submitted as Appendix No. 14, page 213. and a similar form applying to the Choctaw and Chickasaw nations as Appendix No. 15, page 214.

TRIBAL REVENUES.

The conditions, so far as the tribal revenues are concerned, have continued practically the same during the past year as for the year previous.   The laws enacted by the tribal authorities have attempted to fix and prescribe certain permit or other taxes to be assessed against noncitizens residing and doing business within the Indian Territory, but the only method of enforcing these tribal taxes, as a general rule, has been by the removal of the parties declining to pay, under the provisions of section 2149 of the Revised Statutes of the United States.

In the Creek and Cherokee nations these revenues have been entirely collected by the Secretary of the Interior, through the United States Indian agent at Union Agency, all payments being made to such agent and deposited to the credit of the respective tribes with the Treasurer of the United States.

In the Choctaw and Chickasaw nations, however, their agreement permits them to continue to collect their own revenues as prescribed by their laws.

The parties affected by these tribal taxes throughout the Indian Territory have felt that they should not be required to pay the same, claiming that the public generally received no benefit from such taxes, and the noncitizens have repeatedly refused to comply with these laws. Numerous cases have been before the United States courts, and the matter of providing an equitable system of taxation for the Indian Territory has been brought to the attention of the Department, and Congress authorized the Secretary of the Interior to make an investigation and report concerning the matter, which was made by Mr. Frank C. Churchill, formerly revenue inspector for the Cherokee Nation, who was appointed a special agent for this purpose, who urgently recommended that some action be taken to relieve the present situation.

Previous to the fiscal year just closed there had been two revenue inspectors, one for the Creek Nation and one for the Cherokee Nation; but, as stated above, Mr. Churchill was appointed a special agent, and owing to the state of the work it was not believed necessary to have two inspectors in the Creek and Cherokee nations, and therefore the work in the Cherokee Nation was also assigned to Mr. Guy P. Cobb, the inspector for the Creek Nation.

At the close of the fiscal year, the work of collecting the cattle tax in the Chickasaw Nation having been turned over to the Government by the tribe, as will be hereafter referred to, was also placed in charge of Mr. Cobb, so that at the end of the year he was the revenue inspector for the Creek, Cherokee, and Chickasaw nations.   His report is respectfully submitted and attention invited thereto.

CHOCTAW AND CHICKASAW NATIONS.

The tribal authorities have continued to collect, with varied success, the tribal revenues and permits exacted of noncitizens residing and doing business within the limits of these nations, and where such non-citizens have failed or refused to pay the amounts demanded the executives have reported such fact to this office, after which the matter was looked into by the United States Indian agent and recommendations were in due time made to the Department for the removal of the parties complained of by the tribes. A number of removals were made during the year, and had their effect in assisting in the collection of these revenues.

In some instances, however, the parties removed would return to the Territory, and upon such cases being reported the matter was referred to the United States district attorneys with the request that steps be taken to prosecute them for returning to the Territory in violation of law after having been removed.

These removals have been made under the provisions of section 2149 of the Revised Statutes of the United States, it having been held by the Attorney-General of the United States, in an opinion rendered September 7, 1900, and which was submitted with my last annual report, that it was the duty and authority of the Interior Department, within any Indian nation of the Indian Territory, to remove all persons of the classes forbidden by treaty or law who were in such nation without permit or license.

As during the previous year, the matter of the right of the Department to assist in the collection of these tribal taxes has been before the United States courts in a number of cases, and it has been held that the only action that could be taken was removal, under the provisions of the statute above quoted.

There has been so much litigation and agitation over the matter of these tribal revenues that Congress saw fit to legislate concerning the same, and in the last Indian appropriation act, approved May 27, 1902, the following is embodied:

That it shall hereafter be unlawful to remove or deport any person from the Indian Territory who is in lawful possession of any lots or parcels of land in any town or city in the Indian Territory which has been designated as a town site under existing laws and treaties, and no part of this appropriation shall be used for the deportation or removal of any such person from the Indian Territory.

The question of collecting the taxes on cattle introduced in the Choctaw and Chickasaw nations has, however, received considerable attention, and in a number of cases where the tribal authorities were unable to collect the amounts due, the Department authorized the removal of the cattle and the owners thereof.

In the Chickasaw Nation, owing to the unsuccessful manner in which the cattle taxes were being collected, the tribe, through its national legislature, authorized and requested the Government to take the matter in charge, the expense of such work to be paid from the collections made, and an act was passed to this effect, which was approved by the President of the United States, and regulations were promulgated thereunder. A copy of these regulations is respectfully submitted as Appendix No. 16, page 215.

As before mentioned, Mr. Guy P. Cobb, the revenue inspector for the Creek and Cherokee nations, was also assigned to the duty of looking after the payments in the Chickasaw Nation, and four assistants or district inspectors were employed. These regulations provide that there shall be levied an annual privilege or permit tax of 25 cents per head on horses, cattle, and mules, and 5 cents per head on sheep and goats, with certain exceptions for family use.

Collections under the direction of the Secretary of the Interior began about June 21, and up to June 30, 1902, there was paid to the United States Indian agent at Union Agency and placed to the credit of the tribe from this source the sum of $1,160.75.

When these regulations were promulgated during the month of June, they were distributed among the cattlemen of the Chickasaw Nation, and the general impression was that the tax would be more promptly and readily paid since the Government had taken charge of the matter than heretofore.

CREEK.

The revenues from noncitizens residing in the Creek Nation have been collected by the United States Indian agent during the year, in accordance with the provisions of the permit law enacted by the national council of that nation in 1900. During most of the year there has been but little trouble in this connection, the taxes having been quite promptly paid until about the time of the passage of the Indian appropriation act of May 27, 1902, heretofore referred to, which provided that it would be unlawful to remove any noncitizens who were in lawful possession of any lots or parcels of land in any incorporated or regularly established town in the Indian Territory when the parties owing these privilege or occupancy taxes declined to further pay the same.

A few removals were previously made during the year, of physicians and other parties who declined to comply with the tribal laws.

There was collected from July 1, 1901, to June 30, 1902, for the benefit of the Creek Nation, the total sum of $97,733.35. Of this amount $80,536.56 was on account of payments for town lots.

The following statement shows the sources from which the remainder of the amount collected, $17,196.79, was derived:

Coal royalty	$2,761.20
Merchandise	5,317.08
Occupation	3,049.44
Pasture and cattle revenues	5,087.25
Sale of court-house	981.82
Total	17,196.79

The expenses of the revenue-inspection service chargeable to the Creek Nation for the year aggregates $2,814.57, payable from the funds collected, as shown by the statement above. The similar expenses of the revenue inspector for the preceding year were $4,230.82, showing a material decrease in the expenditures for the past year. This decrease was brought about by the fact that the work in the Creek and Cherokee nations was carried on under the supervision of one inspector instead of two, as for the year previous.

The following comparative statement, showing the amounts collected for the several fiscal years, is respectfully submitted. The amount given for the fiscal year just closed only includes the items properly considered tribal revenue, and not the amount collected for town lots.

From July 1, 1898, to June 30, 1899	$4,913.63
From July 1, 1899, to June 30, 1900	26,370.19
From July 1, 1900, to June 30, 1901	30,827.60
From July 1, 1901, to June 30, 1902	17,196.79

It will be noted from the statement of the revenues collected during the year that one of the largest items is on account of pasture and cattle revenues. The Creek agreement provides that when cattle are introduced into the Creek Nation and grazed on lands not selected by Indians, the Secretary of the Interior is authorized to collect from the owners thereof a reasonable grazing tax for the benefit of the tribe, and therefore, under the provisions of this law, the following regulations were promulgated by the Department on July 23, 1901:

That parties desiring to introduce or graze cattle upon the public domain of the Creek Nation shall first make application to the United States Indian inspector for the Indian Territory, and shall pay to the United States Indian agent, Union Agency, the rate of one dollar per head for cattle desired to be grazed thereon, which amount shall be paid prior to the time the cattle are so introduced; and that a description of such cattle, including the brands, together with any other desired information, shall be furnished; and that parties so introducing cattle shall agree to take such measures as may be necessary to prevent cattle so introduced from infringing upon the lands of adjoining allottees.

Where cattle are confined to fenced inclosures or pastures, part of which has been selected and leased by individual citizens, a grazing tax on the unselected portion of such pasture shall be based on a full, fair rental; provided that such rental shall in no case be less than fifteen cents per acre; and provided further, that in instances where any or all of the provisions herein enumerated are not complied with, such cattle shall be removed from the limits of the Creek Nation by the Indian agent, and the amount previously paid for grazing privileges shall be forfeited.

The total amount received from this source during the year was $5,087.25.

The efforts of the revenue inspector in procuring a large amount due on account of the grazing of these cattle on the public domain have been particularly successful, and have necessitated his constant care and numerous long trips to remote and interior parts of the nation.

While the tribal tax laws have not been repealed, still, as Congress has prohibited the removal of persons in possession of town lots from the Indian Territory, as the law at present stands, it is practically impossible to collect any tribal taxes, except in cases similar to the cattle revenues, above referred to, where the parties liable do not reside within the limits of regularly established towns.

CHEROKEE.

As before stated, the work of looking after the collection of the revenues in the Cherokee Nation has also been part of the duties of the former revenue inspector for the Creek Nation. These revenues have been collected from noncitizens during the year, paid to the United States Indian agent, and by him placed to the credit of the tribe. The courts having heretofore held that the taxes prescribed by the Cherokee tribal laws affecting citizens of that nation could not be enforced, the only collections made have been from noncitizens. The principal source of revenue in the Cherokee Nation has been the royalty on hay, and this has been secured without any particular difficulty, the railroads transporting such hay having instructed their local agents not to bill the same until evidence had been presented that the royalty thereon had been paid.

The amount received in the Cherokee Nation from the several sources during the year, from July 1, 1901, to June 30, 1902, are given in the following statement:

Merchandise	$3,375.66
Coal royalty	5,339.57
Hay royalty	7,422.31
Timber	461.00
Gravel	236.52
Ferry charters	225.00
Total	17,060.06

The proportionate part of the expenses of the revenue inspector chargeable to the Cherokee Nation is paid from the moneys collected, and such expenses for the year aggregate the sum of $2,598.84, while the same expenses for the previous year were $4,038.34.   This decrease is due to the fact that one inspector looked after both the Creek and Cherokee nations, where two men were previously employed.

A comparative statement showing the amounts collected for previous fiscal years is given below:

July 1, 1898, to June 30, 1899 .... $3, 150. 87
July 1, 1899, to June 30, 1900 .... 19, 455. 05
July 1, 1900, to June 30, 1901 .... 19, 392. 65
July 1, 1901, to June 30, 1902 .... 17, 060. 08

SCHOOLS.

CHOCTAW AND CHICKASAW NATIONS.

The schools in these two nations have during the past year been maintained from the royalties derived from coal and asphalt, the agreement providing that such money shall be used only for the education of children of Indian blood, and disbursed under such rules and regulations as may be prescribed by the Secretary of the Interior.

In the Choctaw Nation the schools have been practically under the entire control of the United States Government, an arrangement having been made whereby the schools were to be jointly in charge of the United States school supervisor and a representative on the part of the tribal government, their acts, however, to be subject to the approval of the Department, through the general superintendent of schools for Indian Territory.

Mr. John D. Benedict, the superintendent of schools in Indian Territory, has had entire charge of the details in connection with the educational work, and his report, discussing every phase of the subject, is transmitted, and attention is respectfully invited thereto.   Reference is also made to the reports of the several supervisors, submitted by the superintendent, which reports take up in detail the work in each nation.

The superintendent reports that while the past year has been a remarkably quiet one in educational matters, it has been by far the most successful of any since the Department assumed a supervisory control over the schools of the Indian Territory.

The tribal officials are now almost without exception working in harmony with the Federal officials in endeavoring to secure better educational facilities.

The expenses of the maintenance of the schools of the Choctaw Nation are paid by the United States Indian agent at Union Agency, by the usual official checks upon the assistant treasurer of the United States at St. Louis, Mo.   These checks are drawn upon the pay rolls and accounts as submitted and certified to by the school supervisor and tribal representative, and approved by Superintendent Benedict.   The employees of boarding schools and day-school teachers are carried as Government employees, with the exception that contracts are entered into with superintendents of boarding schools for the maintenance of the pupils attending such schools.   The payments of the accounts of the superintendents are made direct by the Department on certified vouchers.

There are still five boarding schools maintained in the Choctaw Nation, two of which are orphan academies. During the year there have also been maintained 190 day schools and a number of small neighborhood boarding schools; also several schools where Choctaw pupils reside within the limits of the Chickasaw Nation, where the teachers are paid a certain amount per pupil. The total enrollment of all the above schools during the year was 4,788, at a total cost of $113,485.65.

In the Chickasaw Nation there have been maintained four boarding schools, one of which is an orphan academy, and 16 day schools, with a total enrollment of 939 pupils, costing $84,257.85.

The past year is the first one that the expenses of the schools in the Chickasaw Nation have been paid from the coal and asphalt royalties, and this action was taken in view of the agreement entered into between the Secretary of the Interior and the governor of the Chickasaw Nation in April, 1901, referred to in my last annual report. Practically the only charge the Government has of these schools, however, is the matter of the qualifications of the teachers to be employed, and as they still practically control the same, paying their own expenses by means of warrants, which warrants are afterwards taken up and paid by the Government from their funds, the results which have been accomplished by the Chickasaw schools are not as satisfactory as the Choctaw, as the expenses have been exceptionally large when the number of pupils receiving the benefit of educational facilities is taken into consideration, and it would therefore appear to be necessary and desirable that some radical changes in the matter of the schools in the Chickasaw Nation be adopted during the next school year. In considering the expenses of the Chickasaw schools, it should also be remembered that the pupils in this nation are not furnished with clothing or shoes. These articles are supplied in the Choctaw Nation, and still the schools are run at a much less expense.

The superintendent in his report states that the greatest difficulty to contend against in the establishment of day schools is the scarcity of suitable schoolhouses, it having been customary in each of the nations to require the neighborhood to erect and furnish its own school building.

CREEK NATION.

The schools of this nation are jointly in the control of a tribal superintendent and a Federal supervisor, both acting under rules and regulations prescribed by the Secretary of the Interior, which rules are in the form of an agreement entered into between the principal chief of the Creek Nation and the superintendent of schools in Indian Territory and approved by the Department. The full text of these rules is shown by the report of Superintendent Benedict, herewith submitted.

The expense of maintaining these schools is paid upon appropriations made by the national council by warrants drawn by the principal chief, which warrants are semiannually taken up and paid by the United States Indian agent from the proper funds of the tribe. These warrants are issued by the principal chief upon a joint requisition of the tribal superintendent and the Federal supervisor, approved by the superintendent of schools in Indian Territory.

During the past fiscal year the Creek Nation has maintained 10 boarding schools, 7 for Indian children and 3 for freedmen or colored children. Two of these 10 schools are orphan homes. There have also been maintained 52 day schools. The total enrollment of these schools has been 2,754, at a total cost of $72,102.26.

CHEROKEE NATION.

The conditions, so far as educational matters are concerned, remain practically the same in the Cherokee Nation, the Government only assuming a supervisory control over their schools, under the provisions of section 19 of the Curtis Act.

A school supervisor in the Cherokee Nation, acting under the direction of the superintendent of schools in Indian Territory, spends his entire time in visiting and inspecting the schools, assisting in the examination of applicants for appointment as teachers, and passing upon and approving warrants issued by the principal chief in the payment of the expenses of such schools.

The expenses of these schools are provided for by acts of the national council appropriating certain amounts for the maintenance thereof. Requisitions are made by the tribal board of education upon the principal chief, and upon such requisitions he issues his warrants, which, as stated above, are approved by the Federal school supervisor before being circulated.

The new agreement which has since the close of the fiscal year been ratified by the Cherokee tribe provides for joint control of their schools, and such schools will be maintained during the coming school year under the provisions of such new legislation, which is set out in full in the report of the superintendent.

There have been 4 boarding schools maintained by the Cherokee Nation during the year, 1 being an orphan academy and 1 a colored high school; also 140 day schools, all having a total enrollment of 5,383 pupils, maintained at a total cost of $98,054.

NEW AGREEMENTS.

CREEK.

A supplemental agreement with the Creek Nation was ratified by Congress on June 30, 1902 (32 Stat., 500), which was to become of full force and effect if ratified by the Creek council on or before September 1, 1902. Since the close of the fiscal year, on July 26, 1902, the national council ratified and confirmed this supplemental agreement, and in accordance with the terms thereof the President of the United States, on August 8, 1902, issued his proclamation declaring that the same had become law on the date ratified by the tribe.

A copy of this supplemental agreement, together with a copy of the proclamation of the President, is shown by Appendix No. 4, page 116.

This supplemental agreement provides that all lands subject to allotment shall be appraised at not to exceed $6.50 per acre, instead of at their true value, as provided by the original agreement.

Provision was made for the descent and distribution of lands and moneys of deceased Indians, in accordance with chapter 49 of Mansfield's Digest of the Statutes of Arkansas.

Provision was also made for the enrollment of children born up to and including May 25, 1901, and living upon that date.

The first legislation providing for public highways or roads is contained in this supplemental Creek agreement, which provides for such roads, 3 rods in width, along section lines, and at other places where the necessity demands, upon the payment of damages.

The supplemental agreement provides a penalty for the desecration of cemeteries, and also where cemeteries have been set aside for towns that the town authorities shall not be authorized to dispose of the lots therein until payment has been made to the Creek Nation therefor.

Provision was also made that all lands designated as parks upon the plat of any town site shall be paid for within one year, at the rate of $20 per acre.

It is also provided that allotted lands can not be alienated by the allottee or his heirs before the expiration of five years from the date of the approval of this supplemental agreement, except with the consent of the Secretary of the Interior; that the 40-acre homestead shall not be alienated for twenty-one years from the date of the deed therefor.

Provision is made that Creek citizens may rent their allotments, for strictly nonmineral purposes, for a term not to exceed one year for grazing purposes only, and for a period of not to exceed five years for agricultural purposes, and that leases for longer periods and for mineral purposes may be made with the approval of the Secretary of the Interior.

CHEROKEES.

All agreements heretofore entered into between the Commission to the Five Civilized Tribes and the Cherokee Indians having failed of ratification, Congress, on July 1, 1902 (32 Stat., 716), passed an act to provide for the allotment of the lands of this nation, for the disposition of town sites, and for other purposes. This act provided, however, that the same should not be of any validity until ratified by a majority of the whole number of votes cast by the legal voters of the Cherokee Nation at an election to be called by the principal chief within ten days after the passage of this act and to be held within thirty days thereafter.

This election was duly held on August 7, 1902, and the votes were canvassed and counted by the Cherokee council at a special session, resulting in the ratification of this act. The result of such election was proclaimed on August 12, 1902.

Attention is respectfully invited to the terms of this agreement (see Appendix No. 5, page 171), and reference is briefly made to certain particular and important provisions thereof.

The lands subject to allotment shall be appraised at their true value, consideration not being given to the location of the land, timber, or improvements thereon, or any mineral deposits thereunder.

The Commission to the Five Civilized Tribes shall allot to each citizen, as soon as practicable after the approval of the citizenship roll by the Secretary of the Interior, land equal in value to 110 acres of the average allottable lands. Forty acres of this allotment shall be selected as a homestead, and shall be inalienable during the lifetime of the allottee, not to exceed twenty-one years from the date of his certificate of allotment. The remainder of this allotment can not be alienated by the allottee or his heirs before the expiration of five years from the date of the ratification of this act.

It is made unlawful after ninety days from the ratification of this act for any member of the Cherokee tribe to hold more lands in value than that of 110 acres of average allottable land for himself and each member of his family, and a penalty for the violation of this law is provided.

The United States Indian agent at Union Agency is required under the direction of the Secretary of the Interior to place allottees in possession of their allotments and remove objectionable persons therefrom.

Provision is made that the roll of citizenship shall be made as of September 1, 1902, and no applications for enrollment shall be received after October 31, 1902.

It is also provided that the school fund of the Cherokee Nation shall be used under the direction of the Secretary of the Interior for the education of children of Cherokee citizens, and such schools shall be conducted under rules and regulations to be prescribed by him, and be under the supervision of the Federal supervisor and the tribal school board.

Public highways or roads two rods in width may be established along all section lines without compensation being paid therefor, and other public roads may be established where necessary for the public good, the actual value of the land to be determined and paid.

Provision is made for the holding of both improved and unimproved property, under certain conditions, in towns which have been surveyed and platted under the provisions of previous legislation, all lots to be appraised in the usual manner by a town-site commission.

The act further provides that the Secretary of the Interior shall cause to be paid all just indebtedness of the Cherokee tribe existing at the date of the ratification of such act which may have been lawfully contracted, as also warrants drawn by authority of law hereafter and prior to the dissolution of the tribal government, such payments to be made from any funds in the United States Treasury belonging to such tribe.

Cherokee citizens may rent their allotments when selected for a term not to exceed one year for grazing purposes only, and for a period not to exceed five years for agricultural purposes, and leases for longer periods and for mineral purposes may also be made with the approval of the Secretary of the Interior.

The provisions of section 13 of the Curtis Act, providing for the leasing of mineral lands, shall not apply to the Cherokee Nation.

CHOCTAW AND CHICKASAW.

Congress also, on July 1, 1902, ratified a supplemental agreement with the Choctaw and Chickasaw nations, embodying numerous important provisions affecting these two tribes. This supplemental agreement, however, is only to become effective when ratified by a majority of the votes cast at an election which has been called for September 25, 1902.

The most important provisions of this supplemental agreement are the disposition of certain citizenship questions, the fixing of a standard allotment of land equal in value to 320 acres of the average allottable lands to be given to each citizen by blood, and land equal in value to 40 acres of average allottable land to each Choctaw and Chickasaw freedman, the sale of the coal and asphalt lands, and the cession to the

United States of a certain tract of land for a Government reservation at Sulphur Springs, in the Chickasaw Nation.

Attention is respectfully invited to the text of this supplemental agreement, which is submitted as Appendix No. 17, page 271.

TIMBER AND STONE.

The law governing the cutting of timber and procurement of stone from the lands of the Five Civilized Tribes has not been changed during the year, and the regulations promulgated under the provisions of the act of Congress approved June 6, 1900 (31 Stat., 660), are still in effect. Attention is respectfully invited to a copy of these regulations submitted with this report as Appendix No. 7, page 181.

The law provides a fine of not more than $500 or imprisonment for not more than twelve months. or both, in the discretion of the court, for the cutting of timber or procurement of stone in violation of the regulations above mentioned.

The regulations provide that parties desiring to cut timber or procure stone must make application to the inspector for permission to enter into contract with the United States Indian agent at Union Agency. Such applications are forwarded by me for the consideration of the Department, and. if approved, the Indian agent is directed to enter into contract, and after the approval of such contract the parties are authorized to cut the timber or procure the stone, and not before.

No applications of a general character for the cutting of timber for local domestic purposes have been received during the year, it having been considered by the Department, as mentioned in my last annual report, that it was inadvisable to make such contracts for the reasons stated, and the general regulations still remain suspended, except where timber is absolutely necessary for the construction of railroads and for props and caps for mines.

A list of the contracts made under the provisions of this legislation is respectfully given below. These contracts are made for a term of one year from their date, and the list only includes such as were in effect during the fiscal year for which this report is made:

Name	Material to be procured.	Amount.	Date of contract.
Osgood & Johnson	Railroad ties	200,000	Sept. 15,1900
William N. Jones	Cross-ties	400,000	Apr. 22,1901
	Switch ties	50,000	
Bernard Corrigan	Piling............linear feet..	100,000	
	Bridge timber............feet B. M..	500,000	Mar. 29,1901
	Sandstone.......... cubic yards..	8,000	
Missouri, Kansas and Texas Ry. Co..	Stone for ballast purposes, cubic yards.	200,000	June 22,1901
Gulf, Colorado and Santa Fe Ry. Co...	....do......	100,000	Aug. 1,1901
Vernon E. Steen	Piling............linear feet..	200,000	Sept. 16,1901
	Bridge timber............feet B. M..	2,000,000	
Angus McLeod	Piling............linear feet..	10,000	Sept. 27,1901
	Switch ties	600	
Central Coal and Coke Co	Cross ties	600,000	Sept. 21,1901
	Switch ties	2,000	
Kenefick Construction Co	Bridge timber............feet B. M..	2,500,000	
	Piling............linear feet..	90,000	Jan. 23,1902
	Cross-ties	475,000	
	Switch ties	2,760	
A McLeod & Co.	Bridge timber. ....feet B. M..	500,000	
	Piling............linear feet..	40,000	Feb. 28,1902
	Cross-ties..	100,000	
	Switch ties	1,000	
St. Louis and San Francisco R. R. Co.	Stone for ballast purposes. cubic yards.	750,000	Apr. 15,1902
John Simpson	Numerous mine timbers		June 21,1902

The last two contracts were entered into during the year, but were not finally approved until after June 30.

A number of contracts above mentioned expired during the year. The Missouri, Kansas and Texas Railway Company, upon the expiration of its contract, at its request was granted permission to renew the same for one year, which renewal has been properly made.

The contracts which have been entered into provide for the following rates to be paid for timber and stone procured thereunder, viz: 10 cents each for cross-ties; 15 cents each for switch ties; $12 per 1,000 linear feet for timber for piling; $1 per 1,000 feet board measure for timber for bridges; 10 cents per cubic yard for stone for masonry, and one-half cent per cubic yard for stone for ballast purposes. Mine timbers are paid for at prices ranging from 20 cents to $1 per 100 for props, 20 cents per 100 for pit ties, 15 cents per 100 for cap pieces, and $14 and $20 per 100 for cross bars, according to the size and length of the different timbers.

Contractors are not permitted to enter the inclosures or go upon land actually in possession of and claimed in good faith as the prospective allotments of Indian citizens and cut timber or procure stone without their consent, and unless they can procure the consent of the Indian citizens to allow them to take timber from such land, they must confine their operations to the public domain.

The amounts due under the respective contracts are paid to the United States Indian agent at Union Agency, who is required to keep an accurate list by legal subdivisions of the land from which such timber and stone have been taken, which money is placed to the credit of the particular tracts of land from which the same was procured, to be, after allotment, paid to the citizen or citizens receiving such land, if in the final equalization it is found that they are entitled to said money. The total amount collected in all nations from this source during the year was $74,977.37.

The act of June 6, 1900, and the regulations promulgated thereunder, do not apply, however, to allotted lands in the Creek Nation, the agreement with such nation providing that after any citizen has selected his allotment, he may dispose of the timber thereon. No timber, however, can be taken from lands not so selected without the payment of a reasonable royalty thereon, under contract to be prescribed by the Secretary of the Interior.

These regulations have been so construed by the Department as to permit Indian citizens in possession of lands claimed in good faith as their prospective allotments, and where they are clearing the same for cultivation, to dispose of the surplus timber as stove wood or cord wood only, for local consumption, and to otherwise utilize the timber from such clearing in erecting fences, buildings, or other permanent improvements on their land.

Parties, however, on being advised in reference to these matters, are cautioned against the indiscriminate cutting of timber for speculative purposes, and informed that they will not be permitted to sell or dispose of large merchantable timber in commercial quantities.

The effect of this legislation is now generally understood throughout the Territory, and there are few if any complaints that parties are violating the law. Where reports are made that parties are wantonly cutting timber in violation of these regulations, steps are at once taken to look into the matter, and if the facts show that the parties complained of are guilty, the matter is at once referred to the proper officers of the United States court for attention.

The question of the right of Seminole citizens who have taken their allotments to dispose of the timber thereon and ship the same from the limits of the Indian Territory was brought to the attention of the Department, and I was advised on June 14, 1902, that inasmuch as the Seminole agreement makes no specific provision concerning the cutting of timber, and as the act of June 6, 1900, supra, pertains to all of the five civilized tribes, there was no law authorizing the shipment of timber cut from the allotments of the Seminoles to points outside of the Territory, and that the regulations promulgated under the act above referred to are applicable to the Seminole equally with the other nations of the Territory.

FINANCE.

RECEIPTS.

The work of the office of the United States Indian agent incident to the collection of the royalties and other moneys due the tribes has materially increased during the year. These moneys are collected by him under rules and regulations of the Department and the direction of the inspector and placed to the credit of the Treasurer of the United States for the benefit of the respective tribes.

The handling of this money requires a large amount of detailed clerical work. Practically all is remitted through the mails and comes in all forms—postal money orders, bank exchange, personal checks, express orders, and currency.

The largest number of remittances is received on account of payments on town lots, such property being owned by so many different individuals and payments being made in installments. This occasions a great many small remittances, all of which must be properly credited to the particular lot for which payment is made. Formal receipts for all moneys paid are promptly forwarded by mail.

As shown by the report of the Indian agent, submitted herewith, the following is a statement of the receipts from the various sources as indicated, during the year commencing July 1, 1901, and ending June 30, 1902:

Choctaw and Chickasaw:		
Coal and asphalt	$247,361.36	
Town lots	157,188.83	
Timber and stone	74,516.37	
Chickasaw:		$479,066.56
Cattle tax		1,160.75
Creek:		
Coal royalty	$2,761.20	
Merchandise	5,317.08	
Occupation	3,049.44	
Pasture and cattle revenues	5,087.25	
Sale of court-house	981.82	
Town lots	80,536.56	
Cherokee:		97,733.35
Merchandise	3,375.68	
Coal royalty	5,339.57	
Hay royalty	7,422.31	
Timber	461.00	
Gravel	236.52	
Ferry charters	225.00	
		17,060.08
Sale of town-site plats		73.20
Total		595,093.94

Deducting from the total amount collected the amount paid for exchange, $335.84, the net amount deposited is shown to be $594,758.10.

Comparing the totals given with the amounts collected during the previous year, as shown by the following, it will be noted that there is an increase of $308,579.92.

Receipts during the year 1901.

Choctaw and Chickasaw nations	$236,253.66
Creek Nation	30,827.60
Cherokee Nation	19,392.65
Seminole Nation	7.71
Sale of town-site plats	32.40
Total	286,514.02

DISBURSEMENTS.

The total amount of disbursements by the United States Indian agent at Union Agency during the year commencing July 1, 1901, and ending June 30, 1902, under the several heads, is shown by the following statement:

Warrant payments:	
Creek	$130,890.13
Choctaw, general	485.70
Choctaw school certificates	188.10
Chickasaw	129,590.40
Cherokee	201,623.84
Schools, Choctaw	64,854.24
Expenses, town site	84,890.60
Smallpox	1,505.32
Creek indigents	5,249.50
Destitute Cherokees and expenses	13,751.32
Exchange	335.84
Office incidentals and miscellaneous	24,684.28
Total	658,049.27

The total disbursements for the fiscal year ended June 30, 1901, were $304,292.52, which, compared with the amount disbursed during the year just closed, shows an increase of $353,756.75.

From the above itemized statement of the disbursements made it will be noted that, as during the previous years, the Indian agent has paid the expenses incurred in the maintenance of the schools of the Choctaw Nation, made certain disbursements to retire outstanding warrants of the several tribes, paid the larger part of the expenses of the town-site work, and numerous other miscellaneous items.

WARRANT PAYMENTS.

CHEROKEE.

As referred to in my last annual report, steps had been taken at that time by the United States Indian agent to disburse the available sum of $215,157.22 in the payment of interest upon and retiring certain outstanding Cherokee warrants. This payment proceeded during the first part of the fiscal year, and there was disbursed of the amount above given the total sum of $201,623.84.

This payment covered warrants issued against the four funds of the Cherokee Nation, viz: General, school, orphan, and insane.

The outstanding indebtedness of the Cherokee Nation draws interest at the rate of 6 per cent per annum, while their invested funds only pay them 5 per cent, but the act of July 1, 1902, which has only recently been ratified by the Cherokee tribe, provides that the Secretary of the Interior shall cause to be paid all just indebtedness of the tribe existing at the date of ratification of the act, and also all warrants drawn by authority of law thereafter and prior to the dissolution of the tribal government. This matter is now receiving the consideration of the Department.

Prior to the close of the fiscal year an advertisement had been issued for a payment to commence on July 1, 1902, which payment is now in progress, and during which it is proposed to disburse the sum of $148,232.79, interest on their invested funds, which was available prior to the ratification of the act of July 1, 1902.

This payment will practically retire all of the general fund indebtedness outstanding up to warrant No. F 7, dated December 17, 1894.

CREEK.

There have been two payments of Creek warrants made by the United States Indian agent during the past fiscal year—one in September, 1901, and one in February, 1902—aggregating a total disbursement of $130,890.13. Just at the close of the fiscal year a payment, to commence July 10, 1902, to disburse the sum of $36,839.07 was advertised, which payment is now being made.

The Creek Nation has no large outstanding indebtedness, the interest on their invested funds being practically sufficient to maintain their tribal government and schools, with the assistance of the revenues collected by the United States Indian agent on account of tribal taxes, etc.

CHOCTAW.

My last report showed the sum of $1,159.14 as the balance remaining of the appropriation of $75,000 made by Congress in 1899, from the general fund of the Choctaw Nation, for the payment of certain outstanding warrants at that time.

I have been authorized to investigate and transmit to the Department sufficient warrants which could be paid under this appropriation to exhaust the remainder thereof. There are but few of these old warrants still outstanding, and as they are presented they are carefully looked into and reported to the Department.

The agent has disbursed from this appropriation during the year, in the payment of warrants certified to him by me, after the same were approved by the Department, $485.70, leaving a balance at the close of the fiscal year yet available under this fund of $673.44.

I have also certified to the agent during the year, and he has paid under his original instructions, certain old school warrants or certificates of the Choctaw Nation, issued by them prior to the time the Government took control of their schools, and since their agreement was ratified, amounting to $188.10. These school warrants were paid from the fund derived from the royalties on coal and asphalt.

CHICKASAW.

Under the regulations promulgated during the fiscal year 1901, the outstanding warrants of the Chickasaw Nation, issued in the operation *of their* schools, were to be paid from the royalties collected on

account of coal and asphalt.   Under instructions from the Department
I made an extensive investigation of the outstanding school indebtedness of the Chickasaw Nation up to August 31, 1901, and furnished a
report of the warrants which I believed should be paid.   This report
aggregated about $130,000, and after its approval by the Department
the United States Indian agent was directed to pay the warrants investigated by me and shown by the list which had been approved by the
Department.   This payment was made and a total amount of $129,590.40
disbursed.

An investigation of additional warrants to be paid, issued since
August 31, 1901, was made just at the close of the past fiscal year,
and it is expected that a second payment will be made soon.

MUNICIPAL BONDS.

Section 25 of the Creek agreement, as ratified by the act of Congress
approved March 1, 1901 (31 Stat., 861), provides:

Authority is hereby conferred upon municipal corporations in the Creek Nation,
with the approval of the Secretary of the Interior, to issue bonds and borrow money
thereon for sanitary purposes, and for the construction of sewers, lighting plants,
waterworks, and schoolhouses, subject to the provisions of the laws of the United
States in reference to municipal indebtedness and issuance of bonds for public purposes; and said provisions of law are hereby put in force in said nation and made
applicable to the cities and towns therein the same as if specially enacted in reference
thereto.

This section, it will be noted, authorized municipal corporations in
the Creek Nation only, with the approval of the Secretary of the
Interior, to issue bonds for waterworks, schools, and other public
improvements.   Under this section the city of Muskogee voted a bond
issue of $175,000, which issue was, after due consideration, approved
by the honorable Secretary of the Interior.

The town of Okmulgee held an election and authorized the issuance
of bonds for school purposes in the sum of $20,000, which was
approved by the Department.

The town of Checotah also voted for an issuance of bonds for school
purposes, in the sum of $10,000, which has not yet been finally passed
upon.

The town of Wagoner voted for an issue of bonds in the sum of
$100,000 for waterworks, and $15,000 for the purchase of certain school
buildings.   The Department declined to give its approval to the waterworks bonds for this town, but stated upon certain conditions that it
would approve the issue of $15,000 for school purposes.   Prior to the
time that the town of Wagoner furnished the additional evidence
required by the Department concerning its school-bond issue, Congress
passed the following act governing the issuance of bonds for municipal
purposes, which was approved on May 19, 1902 (32 Stat., 200), and
which applies to the Indian Territory as a whole.

AN ACT for the protection of cities and towns in the Indian Territory, and for other purposes.

*Be it enacted by the Senate and House of Representatives of the United States of America
in Congress assembled,* That any incorporated city or town in the Indian Territory having a population of two thousand or more, is hereby authorized to issue bonds and borrow money thereon, to be used for the construction of sewers and waterworks and
the building of schoolhouses, such bonds not to exceed an amount, the interest on
which at five per centum per annum would be liquidated by a tax of five mills upon
the dollar of valuation of the taxable property in such city or town, to be ascertained
by the last assessment for the purpose of taxation; and that before such bonds shall

be issued, the same shall be authorized by a two-thirds majority of the qualified voters of such city or town, voting at an election held for that purpose, notice of which shall be published for four consecutive weeks prior thereto in a newspaper of general circulation published in such municipality: *Provided*, That such bonds shall not be issued until it shall be made to appear to the satisfaction of the judge of the United States court for the judicial district in which such municipality is located, by petition of the mayor and council thereof, that all the requirements of this section have been complied with, who shall thereupon cause to be entered upon the minutes of his court a judgment or decree reciting the facts as he finds them to be: *Provided*, however, that before any election shall be held for the purposes herein named, a census shall be taken, and the population of said municipality ascertained by some suitable person or persons, appointed for that purpose by the said judge of the district court, who shall make a sworn return to said judge, showing the number of inhabitants thereof, and that the judgment or decree shall set forth the population and taxable wealth of the municipality, and said order or decree shall be printed on said bond, and made a part thereof, and shall be final and conclusive against said municipality in any litigation on said bonds.

Sec. 2. That such bonds shall contain all necessary and usual provisions expressing the contract, shall be signed by the mayor and countersigned by the treasurer of such municipality, who shall keep a proper record of such bonds. Said bonds shall not bear a rate of interest exceeding 5 per centum per annum, payable semiannually, and none of said bonds shall be sold at less than their par value.

Sec. 3. That any municipality incurring any indebtedness for the purposes provided for in this act shall, by ordinance which shall be irrepealable, provide for the collection of an annual tax sufficient to pay the interest on such bonds, as the same falls due, and also to pay and discharge the principal thereof within twenty years from the date of contracting the same: *Provided*, That if any municipality shall have the authority under any special act to issue its bonds, the amount of the bonds issued under the special act shall be first deducted, and there shall only be issued under this act such additional bonds as shall not exceed the limit provided in this act.

This act provides that towns having a population of 2,000 or more are authorized to issue bonds for public improvements not to exceed an amount the interest of which at 5 per centum per annum would be liquidated by a tax of 5 mills on the dollar of the valuation of the taxable property of such city or town. The act also provides the manner of holding elections to vote upon such bond issues, and instead of requiring that the same meet the approval of the Secretary of the Interior, it is provided that the judge of the United States court for the judicial district in which such municipality is located shall pass upon the same.

In view of the fact that the election concerning the Wagoner school bonds was held prior to the passage of this act, the authorities of this town urgently requested that the Secretary of the Interior give his approval to such bonds under the provisions of the legislation contained in the Creek agreement, first above quoted, but the Department held that the town of Wagoner, having a population of over 2,000, the provisions of the act of May 19, 1902, were mandatory, and that they must now proceed under such act.

The town of Checotah, having a population of less than 2,000 inhabitants, is not affected by the act of May 19, 1902, and therefore has submitted the matter of its bond issue to the Department, under the provisions of section 25 of the Creek agreement.

NEW RAILROAD LEGISLATION.

The various acts of Congress governing the construction of railroads through the Indian Territory have heretofore provided that companies desiring to build such railroads should make application to the Department for permission to survey and locate their lines, and after such survey was made the maps of definite location and plats of station grounds selected should be filed with and approved by the Secretary of the Interior.

Provision was made for the settlement of damages by reason of the construction of such roads in case amicable adjustment could not be made, by the appointment of referees, etc., all matters being under the direction of the Department.

The authority granted by Congress through these various acts for the construction of railroads only applied to Indian lands, and therefore, after the disposition of some of the town sites through the Indian Territory, whereby the title passed from the tribe to individual owners of town lots, the question of the authority of railroad companies to construct their lines through such town sites became a serious one.

An act was passed by Congress and approved February 28, 1902 (32 Stat. 43), entitled "An act to grant a right of way through the Oklahoma Territory and the Indian Territory to the Enid and Anadarko Railroad Company, and for other purposes," which act made general provision for the construction of railroads through any lands held by any Indian tribe or nation, person or municipality, or through any lands in the Indian Territory, which have been or may hereafter be allotted, whether the same have or have not been conveyed to the allottee. This act does not provide that permission to locate lines shall be obtained from the Department, nor does it provide that the plats of such lines be approved by the Secretary of the Interior, although it is required that such plats be filed with the Department, and also the United States Indian agent and the principal chief or governor of any tribe through whose lands its line may run.

The act also provides that in case of a failure of the railroad company to make amicable settlement with any individual owner, occupant, allottee or tribe, steps may be taken in the United States courts to condemn the lands sought to be acquired, and all compensation and damages to be paid shall be determined by a board of referees to be appointed by such court and to act under its direction.

A copy of this act has been submitted as Appendix No. 11, page 195, to which attention is respectfully invited.

APPROPRIATIONS.

The Indian appropriation act for the fiscal year 1902, approved March 3, 1901, appropriated $18,000 for the incidental expenses of the Indian service in the Indian Territory, and the same act provided an appropriation of $150,000 to carry on the town-site work.

The act of May 27, 1902, making appropriations for the fiscal year 1903, carried the same sum of $18,000 for incidental expenses in the Territory; also an additional sum of $50,000 to carry on the town-site work, and $15,000 for the purpose of removing intruders and placing allottees in unrestricted possession of their allotments.

TRIBAL GOVERNMENTS.

There has been no change in the tribal governments of the Five Civilized Tribes during the past fiscal year. Such tribal governments, under the provisions of the present legislation are to exist not longer than March 4, 1906.

The executives of these tribes during the year have been Hon. P. Porter, principal chief of the Creek Nation; Hon. T. M. Buffington, principal chief of the Cherokee Nation; Hon. G. W. Dukes, principal chief of the Choctaw Nation; Hon. D. H. Johnston, governor of the Chickasaw Nation, and Hon. John F. Brown, principal chief of the Seminole Nation.

Since the close of the fiscal year elections have been held in the Choctaw, Chickasaw, and Seminole nations, and there will be changes in these three nations during the current year. A successor to Principal Chief Brown, of the Seminole Nation, Hon. Hulputta Micco, has already assumed his duties.

The national councils or legislatures of these tribes have met in compliance with their tribal laws and made appropriations for the expenses of the national governments of the respective nations and passed such acts or resolutions as were deemed by them to be proper.

In the Choctaw, Chickasaw, and Creek nations all acts of the national councils must be submitted to and approved by the President of the United States before they are of any validity, except appropriations for the necessary incidental and salaried expenses of the tribal governments.

In the Cherokee Nation all acts or resolutions of the national council are required to be submitted to and approved by the President.

The agreement with the Seminole Nation does not require that the acts of the council of that nation receive Executive approval.

By direction of the Department, the tribal authorities submit the acts passed by the national councils to this office, after which they are transmitted with my report to the Secretary of the Interior.

DESTITUTE CHEROKEE INDIANS.

The attention of the Department was called in February last, through the principal chief of the Cherokee Nation and the United States Indian agent, to the destitute circumstances of certain full-blood Cherokee Indians, and after careful consideration the Department placed to the credit of the United States Indian agent certain funds derived from the collection of royalties, etc., belonging to the Cherokee Nation, and I was directed to instruct the agent to make payments to each family that showed to his satisfaction they were in need of relief. The Department authorized me to employ persons who were familiar with the conditions in the Cherokee Nation to procure information concerning the circumstances of these Indians, and, acting under these instructions, with my cooperation, the agent placed two paying parties in the field, and disbursed a total sum of $13,067 in relieving these Indians.

For more information concerning this matter I respectfully refer to the report of the United States Indian agent.

REMOVING INTRUDERS FROM CREEK ALLOTMENTS.

Section 8 of the Creek agreement, ratified by the act of Congress approved March 1, 1901, provides that the Secretary of the Interior shall, through the United States Indian agent at Union Agency, put each citizen who has made selection of his allotment in unrestricted possession of the same, and remove therefrom all persons objectionable to him.

In July, 1901, by direction of the Department, I issued a public notice advising all parties residing upon the allotments of Creek

Indians of the provisions of this law, and that they must arrange, either by lease or otherwise, with the Indian citizen to remain upon his land; failing to do which, if complaint is made, the United States Indian agent would carry out the provisions of this law.

The agent has given a large part of his time and attention to these complaints, they being very numerous, and it was finally necessary in November and December last for him to place a squad of Indian police in the field for the purpose of putting these allottees in possession of their land. Action was only taken in cases where formal complaint had been filed and the objectionable parties had been given an opportunity to remove or answer the complaint, and removals were only made in aggravated cases, the majority of the complaints being satisfactorily settled.

There were no funds available to pay the expenses of placing Creek citizens in possession of their allotments, except the regular Indian Territory appropriation, which was only sufficient to maintain the inspector's and agent's offices, and therefore during the year the agent was unable to take action in all of the cases brought before him; but in the Indian appropriation act approved May 27, 1902, provision was made for the sum of $15,000 to pay such expenses.

SULPHUR SPRINGS.

The attention of the Department has been frequently called for some time past, by outside interested parties, to the mineral springs located at and near the town of Sulphur, in the Chickasaw Nation. These matters were referred to me for investigation and report, and, after carefully looking into the same and visiting the place, I recommended, if the tribes would agree to the setting aside of the land for that purpose, that these springs be reserved from the public domain or private control. The matter received the careful consideration of the Department and was referred to Congress with the supplemental agreement of the Choctaws and Chickasaws with certain recommendations, which agreement as finally ratified by the act of Congress approved July 1, 1902, provides that the two tribes shall sell and convey to the United States a tract or tracts of land at and in the vicinity of Sulphur, not exceeding 640 acres, to be selected under the direction of the Secretary of the Interior and to embrace all the natural springs in and about said village, and so much of the streams adjacent thereto as may be deemed necessary. This reservation is to be paid for at the rate of $20 per acre, and until otherwise provided by law the Secretary of the Interior may, under the rules prescribed for that purpose, regulate and control the use of the water of said springs and creeks and the temporary use and occupation of the lands ceded. It is further provided that it is the intention of this law that in future the land and improvements on this reservation shall be conveyed by the United States to such Territorial or State organization as may exist at the time the conveyance is made.

The setting aside of the lands at Sulphur, however, will not become effective if the supplemental agreement above referred to fails of ratification by the tribes at the election which is to be held September 25, 1902.

QUAPAW AGENCY.

Only one matter of any importance at the Quapaw Agency has been brought to the attention of the inspector during the year, the small tribes under this agency not being regularly considered as being within his jurisdiction.

This case was one of the propriety of approving a certain mining lease made by M. E. Douthat and wife, for themselves and minor children, Quapaw Indians, covering their allotments. I personally visited the Quapaw Agency, conferred with the superintendent and acting agent concerning the matter, and in due time submitted my report thereon to the Department.

CONCLUSION.

The complicated condition of affairs in the Indian Territory will necessarily continue until the present work of allotting lands and disposing of town lots is completed and the various tribal governments with their laws are extinguished.

The greatest need of the Territory at this time is educational facilities for noncitizens. This subject, however, has had the attention of the Department and Congress.

In view of the recent supplemental agreements with the several tribes, which have had the careful consideration of the Department before being submitted to and ratified by the last session of Congress, no recommendations for additional legislation are made at this time, the work to be performed being to carry out the provisions of these agreements. I do, however, respectfully invite attention to the urgent need for some provision being made requiring deeds, mortgages, etc., to be recorded.

A bill introduced at the last session of Congress providing for the protection and preservation of game in the Indian Territory failed to become a law. Such a law is much needed and desired by all, and I therefore respectfully recommend that the matter be again submitted for the consideration of Congress.

In closing this report, I desire to state that I am under renewed obligations to the Department and the Office of Indian Affairs for the support given me and prompt consideration of matters affecting the Territory pertaining to my duties.

My official relations during the year with the numerous Federal officials in the Territory, as well as the executives of the Five Civilized Tribes, have been particularly harmonious and pleasant, and I beg to express my appreciation of the numerous courtesies received from each.

Very respectfully, your obedient servant,

J. GEO. WRIGHT,
United States Indian Inspector for Indian Territory.

The SECRETARY OF THE INTERIOR.

ANNUAL REPORT OF UNITED STATES INDIAN AGENT, UNION AGENCY, IND. T.

MUSKOGEE, IND. T., *September 4, 1902.*

Complying with instructions, I have the honor to submit herewith this, my fourth annual report of the affairs at this agency, the same being for the fiscal year ended June 30, 1902.

The Indian agent at Union Agency has charge of what are known as the Five Civilized Tribes of Indians, viz, Cherokees, Choctaws, Chickasaws, Creeks, and Seminoles.

During the fiscal year ended June 30, 1874, the several agencies of the Five Civilized Tribes were consolidated into one union agency, which was located at Muskogee, Ind. T., and the headquarters of the agency have remained at this place ever since that date.

The Five Civilized Tribes embrace practically all of the Indian Territory, except a small section of country in the extreme northeastern corner set apart for the Quapaw, Modoc, and other small bands of Indians who are in charge of a superintendent of schools.

There are 33,000 square miles of land in the Indian Territory, and, as stated in my annual report for the fiscal year ended June 30, 1901, it has an area greater than that contained in any of the States of Connecticut, Delaware, Maine, Maryland, Massachusetts, and an area equal to that of Indiana, and has a greater population than any of the States of Montana, Idaho, Nevada, North Dakota, Arizona, South Dakota, Wyoming, Utah, Washington, or the Territory of New Mexico.

The population of the Indian Territory, according to the Twelfth Census, in 1900, was 391,960, of which about 70,000 are Indians, and during the ten years intervening between 1890 and 1900 the increase of population was 117 per cent.

During last year there were produced in the Indian Territory 4,500,000 bushels of wheat, corn, and oats, 4,000,000 bushels of vegetables, 60,000 bales of cotton, and 175,000 tons of hay, valued at $1,000,000. It is claimed that the Indians alone own over 800,000 head of cattle. The majority of the cattle held in the Indian Territory are owned by noncitizens.

The coal fields of the Indian Territory are being developed rapidly and the output is increasing from year to year. It is estimated that during the fiscal year ended June 30, 1902, approximately 2,800,000 tons of coal were mined.

The constant influx of whites into the Territory during the years 1901 and 1902 has very materially increased the population. This settling up of the country by whites is due to the fact that the Government is endeavoring, through the Commission to the Five Civilized Tribes, by agreements with the Indians, to have them abandon their tribal forms of government and segregate their lands by allotment, instead of holding them in common, as has been the custom. By various acts of Congress, United States courts have been established in the Territory, and as far as practicable, in accordance with agreements, the Indian courts have been abolished.

The Indian Territory has been divided into four judicial districts, the northern district comprising the Quapaw agency and all of the Cherokee Nation, except the southwest corner; the western district, the southwest corner of the Cherokee Nation, all of the Creek and Seminole nations, and the northwest corner of the Choctaw Nation; the central district, all of the Choctaw nation, except the northwest corner; and the southern district, all of the Chickasaw Nation.

It is thought proper to here briefly refer to the Commission to the Five Civilized Tribes and the work it has under its charge in the Indian Territory. This Commission is commonly known as the Dawes Commission, having taken its name from its venerable chairman, the Hon. Henry L. Dawes, of Massachusetts. The Commission was originally appointed under the provisions of the act of March 3, 1893, and was authorized to enter into negotiations with the Five Civilized Tribes—

For the purpose of the extinguishment of the national or tribal title to any lands within the Indian Territory now held by any and all such nations or tribes, either by cession of the same or some part thereof to the United States, or by the allotment and division of the same in severalty among the

51

Indians of said nations or tribes, respectively, as may be entitled to the same, or by such other method as may be agreed upon between the several nations or tribes aforesaid, or each of them, and the United States, with a view of such adjustment on a basis of justice and equity as may, with the consent of such nations or tribes of Indians, so far as may be necessary, be requisite and suitable to enable the ultimate creation of a State or States of the Union, which shall embrace the lands within the said Indian Territory.

The Commission has succeeded in making agreements with the Choctaw and Chickasaw, Seminole and Creek, and lately with the Cherokee tribes of Indians, all of which have been ratified by Congress and said nations.

To give an idea of the scope and extent of the Commission's work, there is quoted below an extract from its annual report for the fiscal year ended June 30, 1901, which reads as follows:

To allot them land upon any other principle than equality of value would remedy none of the evils arising from the unequal distribution of land, which has so long existed, while to apply this principle as the law provides involves one of the largest, most intricate, and difficult undertakings in which our Government has ever been engaged.

Various bills have been introduced in Congress with reference to making the Indian Territory a State. Many are in favor of its coming in as it now is, while others are advocating the union with the Territory of Oklahoma, and the admission of these two Territories as one State. There is no question, the number of inhabitants and the area only being considered, but that these two Territories should be admitted as one State. However, considering the anomalous condition of affairs, and the fact that the Government is now engaged in the duty of breaking up the tribal relations and alloting the lands, it is not thought to be expedient or wise for the Indian Territory to be admitted at this time.

DUTIES OF THE INDIAN AGENT.

The duties of the Indian agent at this agency are vastly different from those of an agent at other Indian reservations, and there is briefly mentioned some of the work that the agent here is required to perform. This will be alluded to now in a general way, but later on, so far as the work done and moneys collected are concerned, it will be referred to by nations.

In addition to regulating trade and intercourse between the Indians and whites, the agent is required by the act of June 28, 1898 (30 Stat., 495), to collect the royalty on all coal and asphalt mined in the Choctaw and Chickasaw nations, and to collect the royalty on all timber or stone removed from any of the lands of the Five Civilized Tribes in the Indian Territory.

For the Cherokee and Creek nations the agent collects the royalty on all coal mined, and also collects the tax from noncitizen traders residing and doing business in said nations, and all other royalties, such as the collection of hay, ferry, and other permits.

Under the law and regulations of the Department all payments on town lots in the Indian Territory must be made direct to this office. The citizens of 48 towns are now remitting to this office, either in full or partial payments on their lots. The magnitude of this work can only be realized by those familiar with it. However, in order to give a fair idea of it, it is only necessary to say that in each town there is an average of 2,000 lots. Proper entries in reference to these remittances are first made upon the cashbook and then taken to the different town-site record books, and after any lot in the Choctaw and Chickasaw nations has been fully paid for a patent conveying the same is filled out by this office and submitted to the executives of the Choctaw and Chickasaw nations for signature, after which it is returned to me for transmittal to the person entitled to receive the same. In the Creek Nation, after a lot has been fully paid for, advice of such payment is made to the principal chief of the Creek Nation and to the honorable Secretary of the Interior as well. The principal chief, after such advice, issues a deed conveying said lot and forwards the same to the Secretary of the Interior for his approval, after which it is sent to the Commission to the Five Civilized Tribes to be recorded, and by the Commission forwarded to the principal chief for delivery to the person entitled to receive the same.

The Indian agent pays all warrants drawn by the principal chief of the Creek and Cherokee nations and all school-fund warrants drawn by the Chickasaw authorities.

In substance this office acts as the treasurer for the Choctaw, Cherokee, Creek, and Chickasaw tribes of Indians. The agent personally devotes a great deal of time to the hearing of complaints made by Indians against noncitizens and adjusting their differences. Section 8 of the Creek agreement requires that each citizen be placed in unrestricted possession of his allotment, and that objectionable persons be removed therefrom, and the agent also performs such other duties as may be required of him from time to time by the Department in connection with the management of the affairs of the Five Civilized Tribes of Indians.

During the fiscal year ending June 30, 1902, the following sums of money were received and disbursed by me:

RECEIPTS.

Received from the Indian Office, account requisitions	$692,224.62
Royalties collected, account Choctaw and Chickasaw nations	479,066.56
Royalties collected, account Cherokee Nation	17,060.08
Royalties collected, account Creek Nation	97,733.35
Cattle tax collected for Chickasaw Nation	1,160.75
From sale of town-site maps	73.20
Total	1,287,318.56

DISBURSEMENTS.

Paid expenses in connection with the town-site work in the Indian Territory	84,890.60
Paid salary of Indian agent	2,500.00
Paid salaries of Indian police	1,829.68
Paid tolls on official telegrams	63.98
Paid salaries of employees and incidental expenses incurred in connection with the management of the agency	18,358.24
Paid rent of offices and agent's residence	1,650.00
Paid Choctaw warrants issued to school-teachers in the Choctaw Nation, for services rendered prior to the Government's taking charge of the schools of the Choctaw Nation, and after the passage of the act of June 28, 1898	188.10
Paid Choctaw warrants, act of March 3, 1899	485.70
Paid salaries of employees and incidental expenses incurred in connection with management of Choctaw schools	64,854.24
Paid Chickasaw warrants	129,590.40
Paid Cherokee warrants	201,623.84
Paid Creek warrants	130,890.13
Paid Creek indigents	5,249.50
Paid destitute Cherokee Indians, and incidental expenses incurred in making said payments	13,751.32
Paid expenses incurred in connection with the suppression of the spread of smallpox in the Indian Territory, from the $50,000 appropriated by the act of May 21, 1900	1,502.22
For same purpose, out of Creek funds	3.10
Paid per diem and mileage of witnesses in attendance before the Commission to the Five Civilized Tribes, and expenses of Cherokee Commission	282.38
Deposit of royalties collected account Choctaw, Chickasaw, Cherokee, and Creek nations	594,684.90
Deposited funds received on account of sale of town-site maps	73.20
Paid exchange	335.84
Deposit of unexpended balances	34,408.15
Deposits by agent	103.04
Total	1,287,318.56

CORRESPONDENCE.

The correspondence at this agency during the past fiscal year has increased considerably on account of the numerous payments made on town lots, all of which have to be acknowledged. Many inquiries are made with reference to the valuation of lots and to whom the same are appraised, and in addition miscellaneous correspondence requires time and attention. Every communication received is answered or referred to the proper officer for attention. The letters received average 200 a day, and those sent out average about 500 a day.

INDIAN POLICE.

The Indian police force at this agency was reduced at the beginning of the past fiscal year to 1 captain, 2 lieutenants, and 8 privates, but later was increased by the appointment of 5 additional privates. They have been so stationed as to render the most efficient service, considering the area of the territory and the limited number.

I have previously recommended in my former reports that the salaries of the Indian police at this agency be increased, but Congress has failed to make an appropriation for this purpose, and the salaries, therefore, of the Indian police continue as they were heretofore, namely, captains and lieutenants $15, and privates $10 per month.

The Indian police carry out the orders of the Indian agent, and assist the deputy United States marshals in making arrests and suppressing the whisky traffic, and act as peace officers. The force under my command at this agency during the past fiscal year has rendered efficient service.

PLACING CREEK ALLOTTEES IN POSSESSION OF THEIR ALLOTMENTS.

The noncitizen element of the Indian Territory, it is claimed, originally came here upon the tacit consent and by the permission of the Indian. Prior to the allotment of the Creek Nation these noncitizens improved farms for a great many of the Creek citizens under contracts and leases, many of them ranging from four to twenty years; and when the allotment finally took place these noncitizens were loath to give up the lands which they had improved and made, in many instances, into respectable farms. Of course, after receiving a certificate showing selections of their lands as allotments the Indian citizens clamored to be put in possession thereof, and in order to place such allottees in possession of their allotments without unnecessary delay the following provision was inserted in the recent Creek agreement:

> The Secretary of the Interior shall, through the United States Indian agent in said Territory immediately after the ratification of this agreement, put each citizen who has made selection of his allotment in unrestricted possession of his land, and remove therefrom all persons objectionable to him; and when any citizen shall thereafter make selection of his allotment as herein provided and receive certificate therefor he shall be immediately thereupon so placed in possession of his land.

After the ratification of the agreement referred to, the Secretary of the Interior directed that this office place Creek citizens in possession of their allotments, and remove therefrom all objectionable persons.

Upon complaint of Creek citizens to this office that they could not get possession of their allotments, and after investigation of the complaint, the following letter was issued and mailed to all persons against whom complaints were made:

> Complaint has been made by —— —— for —— ——, who has filed on the E. ½ of SE. ¼ and NW. ¼ of SE. ¼ of W. ½ of NW. ¼ of NE. ¼, and E ½ of NE. ¼ of NW. ¼ of section 5, township 16, range 11 to the effect that you are in possession of such land without the consent of the allottee, and unrestricted possession of such land has been requested under the provisions of section 8 of the Creek agreement, which provides as follows:
>
> "The Secretary of the Interior shall, through the United States Indian agent * * * put each citizen who has made selection of his allotment in unrestricted possession of his land, and remove therefrom all persons objectionable to him * * *."
>
> In accordance with such provision the honorable Secretary of the Interior has directed me to place Creek citizens in unrestricted possession of the lands selected by them, and to remove from such lands all persons other than tenants of the allottees.
>
> You are therefore respectfully advised that if you are in unlawful possession of the above-mentioned land you are subject to removal therefrom, and you are directed to vacate same or show cause to this office within ten days from date of receipt of this letter why you should not be removed.

It will be noted that this order permitted the person complained of a reasonable time in which to answer said complaint, and if an answer was submitted it was considered in connection with the original complaint of the Creek citizen, and if no good reason existed why it should not be done, an order was placed in the hands of a United States Indian policeman connected with this agency, directing that the party complained of be removed from the allotment in question and the allottee placed in possession thereof.

Up to and including June 30, 1902, there has been received in this office 399 complaints of this character. Of this number 204 have been settled satisfactorily to all parties interested. There are yet 195 of these cases to be considered and acted upon.

Congress failed to provide means to carry out the provisions of this section of the agreement, and owing to the very limited amount of money that I could use out of the appropriation set apart for this agency to pay traveling and incidental expenses the efforts of this office to place Creek allottees in possession of their allotments were hampered to a considerable extent. Realizing this condition of affairs, Congress, in the Indian bill for the fiscal year ended June 30, 1903, appropriated $15,000 for the purpose of removing intruders from the Indian Territory and placing allottees in possession of their allotments, to be immediately available, and to be expended under direction of the Secretary of the Interior. A portion of this $15,000 has recently been placed to my official credit, and the work of removing intruders and placing allottees in possession of their allotments will, during the present fiscal year, be pushed with vigor.

Section 8 of the Creek agreement, it will be noted, only required that the allottee be placed in possession of his allotment, and made no provision for his future protection. Therefore, in the recent Creek supplemental agreement it was modified so as to require the Secretary of the Interior, through the United States Indian agent, to protect the allottee in his right to possession against any and all persons claiming under any lease, agreement, or conveyance not in conformity to law.

ROADS.

Many complaints have been made to this office by Indian citizens of the change of roads without their consent. The allotment of the lands to the Indians, and the endeavor of most of the citizens to arrange their fences so as to conform with section lines, have, in many instances, changed the established roads. It has been the practice of this office, where parties desired to change a road and place it on a township, section and quarter-section line, to require them to file a petition setting forth the necessity for such change, accompanied by diagram showing the route of the old road and the proposed new road.   After such petition has been received, a competent attaché of the office, or a policeman, is directed to investigate the matter and report whether or not such change as is contemplated would materially interfere with the traveling public, and if it is found that such change would be beneficial to the public generally, an order is issued authorizing the change as petitioned for and set forth in the diagram; provided, however, always, that the new road be made equally as good as the old, and that guideboards be placed in conspicuous places, advising the public of such change.

There is an erroneous idea prevalent throughout the country that there is a law in existence requiring all roads to be placed upon section lines.   I know of no such law, yet where it is found necessary to change a road, an effort is made to have the new road placed upon township, section, or quarter-section lines.   The recent Creek supplemental agreement has the following on this subject:

> Public highways, or roads 3 rods in width, being 1½ rods on each side of the section line, may be established along all section lines without any compensation being paid therefor; and all allottees, purchasers, and others shall take the title to such lands subject to this provision.   And public highways or roads may be established elsewhere whenever necessary for the public good, the actual value of the land taken elsewhere than along section lines to be determined under the direction of the Secretary of the Interior, while the tribal government continues, and to be paid by the Creek Nation during that time; and if buildings or other improvements are damaged in consequence of the establishment of such public highways or roads, whether along section lines or elsewhere, such damages, during the continuance of the tribal government, shall be determined and paid in the same manner.

FINANCIAL.

CHOCTAW AND CHICKASAW NATIONS

The regulations prescribed by the Secretary of the Interior under the provisions of the act of June 28, 1898 (30 Stats., 495), provide, among other things, that the Indian agent for the Union Agency, Ind. T., shall receive and receipt for all royalties paid into his hands when accompanied by sworn statements, and when so collected, to be deposited with the assistant treasurer of the United States, St. Louis, Mo., to the credit of the Treasurer of the United States, for the benefit of the Choctaw and Chickasaw nations.

The royalty on coal has been fixed at 8 cents per ton of 2,000 pounds on mine-run coal, or coal as it is taken from the mines, including that which is commonly called slack.

On asphalt, 60 cents per ton for each and every ton produced weighing 2,000 pounds, for refined, and 10 cents per ton for crude asphalt.

The revenue thus derived, or so much as is necessary, is used for the education of children of Indian blood of the members of the Choctaw and Chickasaw tribes (freedmen excepted).

To look after the mineral royalties in the Choctaw and Chickasaw nations there have been appointed by the President of the United States, upon the recommendation of the principal chief of the Choctaw Nation and the governor of the Chickasaw Nation, what are known as mineral trustees, one of whom shall be a member of the Choctaw tribe of Indians and one of the Chickasaw tribe of Indians, and their salaries are paid by the respective nations.   The mining trustees are required to make reports of all their acts to the Secretary of the Interior, quarterly, and to enter into leases, but no lease is valid until the same shall have been approved by the Secretary of the Interior.

I give below a list of the leases that have been entered into by the mining trustees, and the date of the approval of same, and the name of the person, firm, or corporation operating the lease, up to and including June 30, 1902.

COAL.

Name of lessor.	Number of leases.	Date of approval.
Choctaw, Oklahoma and Gulf Rwy. Co.	30	Mar. 1, 1899
John F. McMurray	8	Apr. 27, 1899
D. Edwards & Son a	3	Aug. 22, 1899
McKenna, Amos & Amos b	1	Oct. 24, 1899
McAlester Coal Mining Co.	2	Feb. 19, 1900
Choctaw Coal and Mining Co.	3	May 4, 1900
Sans Bois Coal Co	6	June 25, 1900
Central Coal and Coke Co. b	1	Aug. 27, 1900
William Busby	1	Sept. 6, 1900

a One of these leases transferred to Arkansas-McAlester Coal Co.
b The two leases noted canceled.   Total number of leases in force, 104.

COAL—Continued.

Name of lessor.	Number of leases.	Date of approval.
Samples Coal and Mining Co	1	Oct. 4, 1900
McAlester and Galveston Coal Mining Co	1	Oct. 18, 1900
H. Newton McEvers	1	Do.
Degnan & McConnell	3	Nov. 16, 1900
Folsom-Morris Coal Mining Co	1	Nov. 22, 1900
Ozark Coal and Railway Co	1	Dec. 8, 1900
St. Louis-Galveston Coal Mining Co	2	Jan. 14, 1901
Missouri, Kansas and Texas Coal Co.	1	Feb. 12, 1901
Atoka Coal and Mining Co.	7	May 7, 1901
Osage Coal and Mining Co.	7	Do.
The Devlin-Wear Coal Co.	1	June 17, 1901
Arkansas-McAlester Coal Co	1	Oct. 1, 1901
Thomas H. Chambers	1	Dec. 9, 1901
Turkey Creek Coal Co	1	Mar. 18, 1902
Southwestern Coal and Improvement Co.	10	Apr. 4, 1902
Essen Coal Co.	1	Apr. 12, 1902
Franklin Bache and Heber Denman	1	Apr. 22, 1902
Kansas and Texas Coal Co.	4	June 13, 1902
Atoka Coal and Mining Co	1	Do.
Capital Coal and Mining Co	1	June 16, 1902
Halley Coal and Mining Co.	2	June 17, 1902
McDougall Co.	1	June 18, 1902
Le Bosquet Coal Co	1	Do.
Total number of leases	106	

ASPHALT.

	Number of leases.	Date of approval.
Brunswick Asphalt Co.	1	May 20, 1900
Caddo Asphalt Co. a	1	Apr. 21, 1900
Elk Asphalt Co.	1	May 3, 1900
Downard Asphalt Co.	1	Oct. 18, 1900
M. & A. Schneider.	1	Nov. 23, 1900
Tar Spring Asphalt Co	1	May 13, 1900
Choctaw Asphalt Co	1	Apr. 22, 1902
Total number of leases.	7	

a The lease above noted has been canceled. Total number of leases in force, 6.

There are also a few parties still mining under national contracts and informal permits, but practically all payments now received are from operators having formal leases.

Herewith is a statement in reference to coal and asphalt royalties collected by me for the Choctaw and Chickasaw nations from July 1, 1901, to June 30, 1902.

Coal royalty	$245,848.01
Asphalt royalty	1,513.35
Total	247,361.36

For the sake of comparison there is given herewith a statement in reference to the coal, asphalt, and other mineral royalties collected by myself and predecessor in office from June 28, 1898 (30 Stats., 495), the date of the passage of the Curtis act, under the provisions of which act this royalty is collected to June 30, 1899, and from July 1, 1899, to June 30, 1900, and from July 1, 1900, to June 30, 1901:

From June 28, 1898, to June 30, 1899:

Coal royalty	$107,766.03
Asphalt royalty	1,295.32
Rock royalty	1,083.90
Total	110,145.25

From July 1, 1899, to June 30, 1900:

Coal royalty	137,377.82
Asphalt royalty	1,108.58
Total	138,486.40

From July 1, 1900, to June 30, 1901:

Coal royalty	198,449.35
Asphalt royalty	1,214.20
Total	199,663.55

In order to give the total royalty collected from the above sources, I again tabulate the coal, asphalt, and other mineral royalties collected from June 28, 1898, to June 30, 1902:

June 28, 1898, to June 30, 1899	$110,145.25
July 1, 1899, to June 30, 1900	138,486.40
July 1, 1900, to June 30, 1901	199,663.55
July 1, 1901, to June 30, 1902	247,361.36
Total	695,656.56

There have also been collected by me for the benefit of the Choctaw and Chickasaw nations during the period ended June 30, 1902, the following amounts, arising from the sources named:

Town lots	$157,188.83
Timber	73,619.30
Stone	897.07
Total	231,705.20
To which add the coal, asphalt, and other mineral royalties collected during the fiscal year ended June 30, 1902, viz	247,361.36
Making a grand total of	479,066.56
Less exchange	218.40
Leaving net amount to be deposited	478,848.16

CHOCTAW AND CHICKASAW NATIONS.

TOWN LOTS.

Under the provisions of the act of June 28, 1898 (30 Stats., 495), the owners of improvements on town lots in the Choctaw and Chickasaw nations, after notices of appraisement in connection with said lots have been served upon them by the town-site commission, pay for said lots to this office. The first payment is to be made within sixty days from the date the notices of appraisement are served, and the balance due to be paid in three equal annual installments; and when any lot is fully paid for, patent conveying the same, which is filled out in this office, is transmitted to the executives of the Choctaw and Chickasaw nations for signature. The Indian agent is also required to notify the town-site commissioners at the proper time of all defaults of first payment on improved lots.

The town-site record books of towns in the Choctaw and Chickasaw nations, after having been properly prepared, are filed in this office, and when payments are made on town lots they are first entered in the cashbook and from there taken to the town-site record books. I now have in my possession the following town-site record books:

Choctaw Nation.—Sterrett, Kiowa, Atoka, Calvin, Guertie, South McAlester, Grant, Poteau, Caddo, Red Oak, Talihina, Canadian, Wister, Antlers, Cameron, Howe, Hoyt, Enterprise, McAlester, Whitefield, Tamaha, Cowlington, and Stigler.

Chickasaw Nation.—Lebanon, Cumberland, McGee, Johnson, Emet, Silo, Colbert, Woodville, Ardmore, Chickasha, Marietta, Minco, and Rush Springs.

Remittances from these towns are received daily. It is incumbent on this office to see that these remittances are made within the time required by law, and that the person who remits the same is the proper person to make payments thereon. Blanks have been prepared to accompany these remittances and are furnished upon application to this office or by the town-site commissioners.

Unimproved lots are sold by the Choctaw and Chickasaw town-site commissioners, after proper advertisement has been published, and when sold the schedule of the sale is sent to this office.

The Department has directed that the Indian agent be present at the sale of unimproved town lots in the Choctaw and Chickasaw nations and receive and receipt for any payments made to him, the successful bidder to deposit with the Indian agent at the time of the sale 10 per cent of the purchase price, which shall be forfeited and be and become the property of the Choctaw and Chickasaw nations unless the said purchaser shall pay the balance of the first installment, one-fourth of the sale price of the lot, within ten days from the date of the sale. If desired, however, the successful bidder may make full payment on the lot.

Acting under these instructions, I have, whenever unimproved town lots have been sold in any town in the Choctaw and Chickasaw nations, detailed one or more of my clerks to attend said sale and receive and receipt for any money that may be paid them.

The total amount paid into this office on account of the sale of town lots during the fiscal year ended June 30, 1902, was $157,188.83.

TIMBER AND STONE.

The Department has heretofore promulgated regulations governing the procurement of timber and stone for domestic and industrial purposes in the Indian Territory, as provided in the act of June 6, 1900 (Public No. 174).

These regulations require that the Indian agent enter into a contract, to be approved by the Secretary of the Interior, with any responsible person, persons, or corporations, for the purchase of timber or stone from any of the public lands belonging to any of the Five Civilized Tribes, and to collect the full value of such timber or stone as the Secretary of the Interior shall determine should be paid therefor. The moneys so collected are to be placed to the credit of the tribe or tribes to which the lands belong from which such timber or stone was secured, no timber or stone to be removed from any land selected by any citizen of any of the Five Civilized Tribes as his prospective allotment without his consent. The moneys collected from this source are to be deposited with the assistant treasurer of the United States at St. Louis, Mo., and when the tract or tracts from which the said timber or stone was taken shall have been allotted, the Secretary of the Interior shall cause to be paid to the citizen or citizens taking the said tract or tracts as his or her allotment if found to be entitled to the moneys so collected.

The regulations require that I keep an accurate list by legal subdivisions of the lands from which said timber or stone is taken, and also a correct list of all moneys derived from the sale of all timber or stone taken from each legal subdivision. The value of the timber and stone taken from unappraised selected land must be added to the appraisement when made.

The following contracts with the persons and corporations named have been entered into under the requirements referred to:

Name and address.	Date of contract.
Osgood & Johnson, St. Elmo, Ill.	Dec. 11, 1900
W. N. Jones, Fayette, Ark.	May 7, 1901
Bernard Corrigan, Kansas City, Mo.	May 20, 1901
Missouri, Kansas and Texas Rwy. Co., St. Louis, Mo.	July 20, 1901
Gulf, Colorado and Santa Fe Rwy. Co., Galveston, Tex.	Sept. 21, 1901
Vernon E. Steen, Sherman, Tex.	Oct. 14, 1901
Angus McLeod, Neosho, Mo.	Oct. 23, 1901
Central Coal and Coke Co., Kansas City, Mo.	Oct. 29, 1901
Kenefick Construction Co., Clinton, Iowa.	Mar. 14, 1902
A. McLeod & Co., Neosho, Mo.	Apr. 30, 1902

In addition to entering into contracts with the above-mentioned firms and corporations, the honorable Secretary of the Interior, under date of September 28, 1898, granted a permit to the Kansas and Arkansas Railway Company, with headquarters at St. Louis, Mo., to take and remove gravel from the bars and beds of the Grand River, within the limits of certain described territory. This land lies close to the mouth of the Grand River and near Fort Gibson, Ind. T. The rate of royalty fixed on such gravel removed is at the rate of 2 cents per cubic yard, measured when loaded on the cars of said railway company.

The royalty to be paid on timber and stone taken under these contracts has been fixed by the honorable Secretary of the Interior. In my last annual report I referred to the manner of caring for these royalties.

The amount collected from this source during the fiscal year ended June 30, 1902, was $73,619.30 for the Choctaw and Chickasaw nations, and $461 for the Cherokee Nation; total, $74,080.30.

SALARIES OF SCHOOL-TEACHERS.

The royalty collected on account of coal and asphalt mined in the Choctaw and Chickasaw nations is used in the payment of salaries of school-teachers and the incidental expenses incurred in the management of the schools.

The salaries of the teachers employed in the Choctaw Nation, in addition to a few other teachers who reside in the Chickasaw Nation and who teach Choctaw pupils of Indian blood, and the incidental expenses incurred in the management of the schools are paid by this office.

There are employed in the four academies in the Choctaw Nation about 55 persons, and the neighborhood school-teachers in the Choctaw Nation, including a few neighborhood school-teachers in the Chickasaw Nation who teach Choctaw pupils of Indian blood, aggregate about 175. These teachers are paid by this office upon vouchers approved by the supervisors of schools for the Choctaw and Chickasaw nations, respectively, and the superintendent of schools of the Indian Territory, by means of checks drawn on the assistant treasurer of the United States at St. Louis, Mo.

The total sum disbursed for the purposes mentioned amounted during the fiscal year ended June 30, 1902, to $64,854.24.

PAYMENT OF CHOCTAW WARRANTS.

Out of the $75,000 appropriated by the act of Congress of March 3, 1899 (30 Stat., 1099), I have heretofore disbursed prior to July 1, 1901, $73,840.86, and during the fiscal year ended June 30, 1902, in payment of warrants, I disbursed the sum of $485.70, leaving a balance yet to be disbursed of $673.44.

In addition to the warrants that have been paid out of the $75,000 referred to above, I have also disbursed the sum of $188.10 in payment of warrants issued to school-teachers in the Choctaw Nation for services rendered prior to the Government taking charge of the schools of said nation, and after the passage of the act of June 28, 1898. These last-mentioned warrants were paid from royalties collected by me on account of coal and asphalt mined.

PAYMENT OF CHICKASAW WARRANTS.

Under date of April 11, 1901, the honorable Secretary of the Interior and Hon. D. H. Johnson, governor of the Chickasaw Nation, entered into certain agreements relative to the disbursement of a proportionate share of the fund arising on account of the royalty on coal and asphalt mined in the Choctaw and Chickasaw nations. It is to be remembered that the royalty arising from the mining of these two minerals is to be used for school purposes only. Paragraph 6 of this agreement provides as follows:

That the outstanding warrants of the Chickasaw Nation, legally issued for the service performed for material furnished for school purposes, in accordance with school laws of the Chickasaw Nation since the ratification of the Atoka agreement, shall be paid without unnecessary delay by disbursing officers, designated by the Secretary of the Interior, out of the Chickasaw coal and asphaltum royalty fund now in the hands of the United States, so far as the same will apply, and such school warrants as may hereafter be legally issued for such service, or such material for school purposes, in accordance with such laws, shall in like manner be paid out of such funds as shall hereafter come into the hands of the United States, so far as the same will apply annually, semiannually, or quarterly, as the Secretary of the Interior may determine best, so long as these regulations shall be observed by the Chickasaw Nation.

Some time after the issuance of these regulations, the Secretary of the Interior directed the United States Indian inspector for the Indian Territory to make an investigation and report as to what Chickasaw school-fund warrants should be paid. The inspector thereupon made such investigation and submitted an itemized report of warrants that had been issued in payment of services rendered or supplies furnished the schools of the Chickasaw Nation from June 28, 1898, to August 31, 1901. This report was approved, and I was directed to disburse the sum of $133,299.26 of Chickasaw school moneys in payment of the warrants that had been approved by the Department.

Under date of January 14, 1902, in order to give publicity to the payment, I issued the following notice:

Notice is hereby given that I, J. Blair Shoenfelt, United States Indian agent and disbursing officer, acting under instructions from the honorable Secretary of the Interior, at my office at Muskogee, Ind. T., will, on February 1, 1902, and subsequent days until disbursement is completed, pay all Chickasaw school-fund warrants that have been issued in payment for services rendered or supplies furnished from June 28, 1898, to August 31, 1901, that have been examined and approved by me for payment.

In making the payment the indorsement of the original payee will be required, or, if the payee is deceased then the indorsement of the legally appointed administrator or executor of the estate will be necessary. Copies of letters of administration must be furnished in cases where indorsements are made by administrators. Powers of attorney will not be recognized under any circumstances.

The holders of the class of warrants that are advertised for payment should present them to this office at the earliest date practicable, submitting list in duplicate, showing number of warrant payee, and amount

If any further information is desired, apply to the United States Indian agent, Muskogee, Ind. T.

The payment commenced promptly in February and was practically completed by March 31, but holders of some of the warants not having presented them during the months of February and March, payment was continued to June 30, 1902.

Of the $133,299.26 received for disbursement, I paid out the sum of $129,590.40 and returned to the Treasury $3,708.86.

CHICKASAW CATTLE TAX.

Under date of June 3, 1902, the honorable Acting Secretary of the Interior promulgated regulations governing the introduction by noncitizens of live stock in the

Chickasaw Nation, Ind. T.   Under these regulations noncitizens introducing or holding cattle within the limits of the Chickasaw Nation must pay an annual permit tax on all stock so introduced and held within the limits of the said nation, as follows: On cattle, horses, and mules, 25 cents per head, and on sheep and goats, 5 cents per head; provided, that there shall be exempt from taxation, when used and owned by the head of the family, 2 cows and calves, and one team consisting of 2 horses or mules, or 1 horse and 1 mule.   Such permit tax shall be payable to the United States Indian agent at Union Agency, and the money so collected to be deposited to the credit of the Treasurer of the United States with the assistant treasurer of the United States at St. Louis, Mo., for the benefit of the Chickasaw Nation.

Section 7 of the regulations referred to provides:

Authorized agents of the Interior Department will make necessary investigations and reports and see that proper remittances are forwarded.

Since the issuance of these regulations, up to and including June 30, 1902, there was collected from this source $1,160.75.

TOWN-LOT PATENTS.

Patents to town lots in the Choctaw and Chickasaw nations, under the provisions of the act of Congress of June 28, 1898 (30 Stat., 495), issue under the joint hands of the principal chief of the Choctaw Nation and the governor of the Chickasaw Nation, and convey the title to said lots, save and except, however, all coal and asphalt therein.   These patents are filled out in this office and forwarded to the respective named executives to be dated, signed, and to have the great seals of the nations impressed thereon.   Up to June 30, 1902, I have prepared and submitted to the executives of the nations named 898 patents conveying town lots in the Choctaw and Chickasaw nations, as follows:

	Patents.
Choctaw Nation:	
Atoka	21
Antlers	18
Cameron	2
Caddo	15
Calvin	64
Guertie	64
Grant	60
Howe	20
Kiowa	67
Poteau	67
Red Oak	21
South McAlester	184
Sterrett	184
Talihina	31
Wister	25
Chickasaw Nation:	
Colbert	35
Cumberland	2
Emet	7
Lebanon	2
Silo	7
Woodville	2

When these patents are returned to this office properly signed by the executives and the great seals of the nations impressed thereon, the date of such signing is duly recorded in the town-site record book opposite each particular lot conveyed, and the patents are then delivered to the parties entitled to receive them, without cost.

CREEK NATION.

Collected for the benefit of the Creek Nation during the period commencing June 28, 1898, and ending June 30, 1899	$4,913.63
From July 1, 1899, to June 30, 1900	26,370.19
From July 1, 1900, to June 30, 1901	30,827.60
From July 1, 1901, to June 30, 1902	97,733.35
Total	159,844.77

The sum of money collected during the fiscal year ended June 30, 1902, arose as follows:

Coal royalty	$2,761.29
Town lots	80,586.56
Merchandise tax	5,317.08
Pasture and grazing tax	5,087.25
Occupation tax	3,049.44
Sale court-house, furniture, and fixtures	981.82
Total	97,733.35
Less exchange	78.80
Net amount deposited	97,654.55

During the fiscal year ended June 30, 1901, the merchandise and occupation tax collected amounted to $19,357.35, as compared with $8,366.52 collected during the fiscal year ended June 30, 1902.

The Indian appropriation act for the fiscal year ending June 30, 1903, (32 Stats., 245) contains the following provision:

* * * *Provided, however,* That it shall hereafter be unlawful to remove or deport any person from the Indian Territory who is in lawful possession of any lots or parcels of land in any town or city in the Indian Territory which has been designated as a town site under existing laws and treaties, and no part of this appropriation shall be used for the deportation or removal of any such person from the Indian Territory.

Prior to the passage of this act of Congress, the only way to enforce the collection of the tribal tax was by removal of the person who refused to pay the same from the Indian Territory. This power having now to a large extent been taken away from the Indian agent, on account of most of the merchants owning town lots, a great many of them have refused to pay the tax, and the agent is powerless to collect it, he having no way to enforce the law. This practically nullifies the Indian laws, although they are still in force, but of no effect.

The decrease is further accounted for by the fact that the Creek Nation formerly imposed a tax of 1 per cent on all merchandise introduced and offered for sale within its limits, but at the October, 1899, session of the Creek national council a law was passed, which law was approved by the principal chief of the Creek Nation on November 5, 1900, and by the President on November 22, 1900, reducing the tax to one-half of one per cent on all merchandise introduced and offered for sale. Under the provisions of the act of the Creek council referred to, as stated above, there was collected on account of tax on merchandise and on occupation permits the sum of $8,366.52 during the fiscal year ended June 30, 1902.

The royalty on coal in the Creek Nation is the same as in the Choctaw and Chickasaw nations, i. e., 8 cents per ton on mine-run coal, including that which is commonly called "slack." On the coal produced in said nation, there was remitted to this office during the past fiscal year, as royalty thereon, the sum of $2,761.20.

Section 37 of the Creek agreement (31 Stats., 861) provides as follows:

Creek citizens may rent their allotments when selected for a term not exceeding one year, and after receiving title thereto without restriction, if adjoining allottees are not injured thereby, and cattle grazed thereon shall not be liable to any tribal tax, but when cattle are introduced into the Creek Nation and grazed on lands not selected by citizens, the Secretary of the Interior is authorized to collect from the owners thereof a reasonable grazing tax for the benefit of the tribe. * * *

During the fiscal year ended June 30, 1902, as stated above, there was collected on account of the rent of unselected land, and for grazing purposes, under the provisions of the Creek agreement just above quoted, the sum of $5,087.25. When cattle were grazed upon unselected lands, $1 per head for such cattle so introduced and ranged was charged.

A recent act of the Creek council authorized the sale of the court-houses and furniture and fixtures pertaining thereto belonging to the Creek Nation, since the Creek courts having been abolished, there no longer existed any necessity therefor. A number of these court-houses and their furniture and fixtures were sold, and the proceeds of said sales were remitted to this office by the principal chief of the Creek Nation, amounting to $981.82, as stated above.

A number of the towns in the Creek Nation have been platted and appraised by the Creek town-site commission and payments are being made in accordance with such appraisements.

Payments on lots situated in the following towns in the Creek Nation are now being received: Alabama, Beggs, Bristow, Foster (Yeager post-office), Henryetta, Mounds, Muskogee, Okmulgee, Red Fork, Tulsa, Wetumka, Wagoner.

During the fiscal year ended June 30, 1902, I received on account of the sale of town lots in the Creek Nation the sum of $80,536.56. To assist in the collection of this revenue there has been appointed an inspector for the Cherokee and Creek nations, and Mr. Guy P. Cobb has acted as such inspector during the past fiscal year. All remittances must be accompanied by statements in duplicate. One copy of these statements is given to the revenue inspector of the Cherokee and Creek nations for his information and guidance and the other copy sent to the Department with my quarterly accounts.

DEEDS TO LOTS.

Up to August 11, 1902, 992 deeds have been issued by the principal chief of the Creek Nation, upon advices from this office that full payments had been made thereon conveying lots in the towns mentioned, as follows:

Beggs	9
Bristow	51
Henryetta	8
Holdenville	82
Mounds	35
Muskogee	474
Okmulgee	65
Red Fork	135
Tulsa	9
Wagoner	119
Wetumka	14
Total	992

While it would appear that only 992 deeds have been issued up to the date mentioned, the principal chief advises me that in many instances a single deed will convey as many as four or five lots.

CREEK INDIGENTS.

The act of the national council of the Muskogee Nation, approved by the principal chief of said nation on November 5, 1900, and by the President December 3, 1900, appropriated $7,236 to be paid to 201 Creek indigents, at the rate of $3 per month to each person. The Creek national council determined who were indigents, and the principal chief of the nation furnished me with a list of names certified to by said council as being Creek indigents, and I pay these indigents the $3 per month they are allowed by the act of the Creek council just above referred to. During the fiscal year ended June 30, 1901, I disbursed out of Creek funds to pay Creek indigents the amounts due them, the sum of $828.

During the fiscal year ended June 30, 1902, there was disbursed for this purpose the sum of $5,249.60.

It will be noted from the above, therefore, that the total disbursed for this purpose during the fiscal years mentioned was $6,077.60, leaving an unexpended balance of the appropriation yet to be disbursed of $1,158.40.

This money belongs to the Creek Indians, and is paid from their fund denominated "Indian moneys, proceeds of labor, Creek," and is derived on account of royalties, etc., collected for the benefit of the Creek Nation.

PAYMENT OF CREEK WARRANTS.

During the fiscal year ended June 30, 1902, I received for disbursement in payment of Creek warrants Creek Indian moneys aggregating $133,352.05 under the following heads, to wit:

"Indian moneys, proceeds of labor, Creek"	$8,642.53
"Interest on Creek general fund"	74,741.12
"Fulfilling the treaties with the Creeks"	49,968.40

Of this sum, $130,890.13 was used to pay warrants drawn by the principal chief of the Creek Nation to pay expenses incurred in connection with the management of the affairs of the tribe. The unexpended balance of above sum, designated as "Interest on Creek general fund," was deposited to the credit of the Treasurer of the United States at the close of the fiscal year ended June 30, 1902, but the same will be returned in order to pay certain Creek warrants that have been advertised for payment, but have not been presented.

The Commissioner of Indian Affairs has recently advised that the sum of $36,839.07 was available after July 1, 1902, for the purpose of paying Creek warrants, and directed that I issue an advertisement stating that I would exhaust said amount, as far as practicable, in paying Creek warrants that should be retired. In accordance with these instructions, the following notice was issued:

Notice is hereby given that I, J. Blair Shoenfelt, United States Indian agent and disbursing officer acting under instructions will, at my office in Muskogee, Ind. T., on July 10, 1902, and subsequent days until disbursement is completed, disburse the sum of $36,839.07 of Creek moneys in payment of the indebtedness of the Creek Nation, as evidenced by warrants drawn by the principal chief of said nation.

Warrants to be paid are as follows:

All Creek warrants heretofore advertised for payment, and general fund warrants Nos. 320 to 402, inclusive; school fund warrants Nos. 741 to 980, inclusive.

The said disbursement will be made under the laws of the Creek Nation, in so far as they are not in conflict with the laws of the United States, or the rules and regulations prescribed by the Department of the Interior and of the United States Treasury for the government of disbursing officers.

In making this payment the indorsement of the original payee will be required before a warrant is paid, or if the original payee is deceased, then the indorsement of the legally appointed administrator or executor of the estate will be required.

Certified copies of letters of administration must be furnished, showing the appointment of the administrator or executor, as the case may be.

Powers of attorney will not be recognized; the present legal holder of the warrant will in all cases be required to receipt for the same over his own signature.

Warrants will be received and filed for payment on and after July 8, 1902.

LEASING OF CREEK ALLOTMENTS.

The adoption of the Creek supplemental agreement of June 30 last (32 Stats., 500), by the Creek council, and later the proclamation of the President declaring it in full force and effect, and binding on all citizens and others affected thereby, and the beginning of the issuance of title to allottees thereunder has stimulated the real estate agent to renewed activity, and contracts are being made with Creek citizens for various uses of their lands in direct conflict with the letter and spirit of the agreement, the same being also evasive and misleading.

Paragraph 17 of the recent supplemental agreement modifies section 37 of the agreement ratified by the act of March 1, 1901, and, as amended, is reenacted to read as follows:

> Creek citizens may rent their allotments, for strictly nonmineral purposes, for a term not to exceed one year for grazing purposes only and for a period not to exceed five years for agricultural purposes, but without any stipulation or obligation to renew the same. Such leases for a period longer than one year for grazing purposes and for a period longer than five years for agricultural purposes, and leases for mineral purposes may also be made with the approval of the Secretary of the Interior, and not otherwise. Any agreement or lease of any kind or character violative of this paragraph shall be absolutely void and not susceptible of ratification in any manner, and no rule of estoppel shall ever prevent the assertion of its invalidity. Cattle grazed upon leased allotments shall not be liable to any tribal tax, but when cattle are introduced into the Creek Nation and grazed on lands not selected for allotment by citizens, the Secretary of the Interior shall collect from the owners thereof a reasonable grazing tax for the be efit of the tribe, and section 2117 of the Revised Statutes of the United States shall not hereafter apply to Creek lands.

Leases are being made for a period of five years which purport to be for agricultural purposes, but upon close examination and careful reading of such contracts as have been presented to this office it is clearly seen that the prime object is to secure possession of the citizen's allotment, by making to him a first payment of one-half year's rent for his allotment of 160 acres, at rates of from 15 to 25 cents per acre per annum. In many instances the leases provide for improvements to be made upon such land, the same to be paid for out of the stipulated rental, while others provide that all improvements placed thereon by the lessee shall be removed at the expiration of five years.

It is evident, however, that any considerable improvements that may be placed on these allotments will, at the expiration of the term of five years, exhaust all rents accruing under the contract, thus giving the use of 160 acres to the lessee for that period for a few dollars and depriving the allottee of his rent.

Some leases are being made in conformity with the terms of the agreement and lessees are observing such terms in good faith.

The allotments of incompetents, minors, and convicts in many instances have been taken possession of by unscrupulous persons claiming to have rented or purchased them from the allottees, or some one claiming to represent them.

Some remedial measure should be adopted to prevent the continuance of such unlawful practices above cited, and make clear a way for the legitimate leasing and renting of Creek allotments, especially the allotments of such allottees who are incompetent to transact and manage their own affairs.

I am protecting the full-blood Creeks who can, as a rule, neither read nor write the English language, and are more liable to be imposed upon than those of mixed blood.

The Creeks have accepted the policy of the Government in good faith, and every effort has been made, where complaints were made, to place Indians in unrestricted possession of their distributive share of the lands allotted to them, thus providing a way whereby the individual citizen might utilize for his personal benefit, by a well-guarded system of renting and leasing, the highest productive capacity of his share of the profits.

I have endeavored to impress upon Creek citizens who have taken their allotments that, inasmuch as they have willingly consented to the wish of the Government that their tribal government be abolished, and they having accepted citizenship under the protection of the United States giving and guaranteeing to them all their property interests and advancing them to a higher plane socially as well as politically, that the

Government would see that their rights and interests were protected so far as it was possible to do so, in order that they might reap the full benefits from their allotments.

CHEROKEE NATION.

Under the general provisions of the act of Congress of June 28, 1898 (32 Stats., 495), the Indian agent is required to receive and receipt for all payments of royalties, rents, taxes, and permits of whatever kind and nature that may be due and payable to the Cherokee Nation, and when collected such revenue is deposited to the credit of the Treasurer of the United States with the assistant treasurer of the United States at St. Louis, Mo., for the benefit of the Cherokee Nation.

ROYALTIES.

Since the passage of the act referred to, the following sums of money have been collected for the benefit of the Cherokee Nation:

From June 28, 1898, to June 30, 1899	$3,150.87
From July 1, 1899, to June 30, 1900	19,455.05
From July 1, 1900, to June 30, 1901	19,392.65
From July 1, 1901, to June 30, 1902	17,060.08
Total	59,058.65

The money collected for the benefit of the Cherokee Nation during the fiscal year ended June 30, 1902, arose as follows:

Merchandise royalty	$3,375.68
Coal royalty	5,339.57
Hay royalty	7,422.31
Gravel royalty	236.52
Timber royalty	461.00
Ferry tax	225.00
Total	17,060.08
Less exchange	26.79
Net amount deposited	17,033.29

The merchandise tax referred to above is collected from noncitizen merchants doing business in the Cherokee Nation, Indian Territory. The tax is at the rate of one-fourth of 1 per cent on all merchandise introduced and offered for sale within the limits of the said nation. This merchandise tax was originally collected from citizens and noncitizens alike, but recently the Hon. Joseph A. Gill, judge of the United States court for the northern district of the Indian Territory, in an opinion, held that the Department of the Interior could not enforce the collection of this tax from citizens of the Cherokee Nation by blood, who are residing and doing business therein; therefore this tax is now only collected from noncitizen merchants. The total amount collected, as will be noted above, account of merchandise tax, was $3,375.68.

The royalty on coal is at the rate of 8 cents per ton on all coal mined, including that which is commonly called "slack." There are no extensive coal mines in the Cherokee Nation, and the royalty from this source is therefore small, amounting to, as noted above, $5,339.57.

The Cherokee Nation impose a tax of 20 cents per ton on all hay shipped from within its limits. The total amount received from this source during the fiscal year ended June 30, 1902, was $7,422.31.

The honorable Secretary of the Interior, under date of September 28, 1898, granted a permit to the Kansas and Arkansas Valley Railway Company to take and remove gravel from the bars and beds of Grand River, within the limits of certain described territory. This land lies close to the mouth of the Grand River, and near Fort Gibson, Ind. T. The Secretary fixed the rate of royalty on such gravel removed at the rate of 2 cents per cubic yard, measured when loaded upon the cars of said railway company, the royalty thereon to be paid to this office monthly. There has been collected by me during the past fiscal year from this source, for the benefit of the Cherokee Nation, $236.52.

Under date of March 14, 1902, the honorable Acting Secretary of the Interior approved a contract entered into by and between the United States Indian agent for the Union Agency, Ind. T., and the Kenefick Construction Company, under the provisions of the act of Congress approved June 6, 1900, relative to the procurement of timber and stone from any of the lands belonging to any of the Five Civilized Tribes in the Indian Territory. The lands from which this timber and stone were to be removed is mentioned specifically in the contract, and lies in the Cherokee and Creek nations. Under the provisions of this contract the timber and stone so removed is paid for into this office.

The Kenefick Construction Company removed, up to June 30, 1902, such a number of ties and timber from the Cherokee Nation that the royalty thereon amounted to $461.

Where ferries are operated on the Arkansas and Canadian rivers in the Cherokee Nation an annual tax of $25 is charged. On the Illinois, Grand, Verdigris, and Neosho rivers the tax is at the rate of $10 per annum. The total receipts arising from this source during the past fiscal year was, as stated above, $225.

CHEROKEE WARRANT PAYMENT.

During the fiscal year ended June 30, 1902, I received for disbursement $215,157.22 of Cherokee moneys, under the following heads, to be used in paying the interest on certain Cherokee warrants advertised for payment, and interest on other outstanding warrants of said nation, all of which were issued by the principal chief thereof:

General fund	$110,401.19
School fund	64,559.49
Orphan asylum fund	31,712.35
Insane asylum fund	4,984.19
Indian moneys proceeds of labor, Cherokee	3,500.00
Total	215,157.22
Disbursed out of this amount	201,623.84
And returned to the Treasury unexpended balances amounting to	13,533.38

Under the following heads, to wit:

Interest on Cherokee school fund	116.75
Interest on orphan asylum fund	12,684.19
Interest on insane asylum fund	461.47
Indian moneys, proceeds of labor, Cherokee	270.97
Total	13,533.38

For further information on this subject see my advertisement of June 22, 1901, incorporated in my last annual report.

On such warrants as were paid and retired the interest was computed to the date of the publication of the advertisement, which was published in the Cherokee Advocate, the official organ of the Cherokee Nation, on Saturday, June 22, 1901.

The interest was computed and paid on all warrants issued prior to April 27, 1900, and such interest was paid up to April 28, 1901. No interest was paid on any warrants issued after April 28, 1900, except such as were paid and retired. A recent ruling of the Department, however, directs that the interest on all outstanding warrants, whether for a year or less, must be paid up to April 28 of any given year, provided a payment takes place.

I have recently been directed by the Department to make another payment of Cherokee warrants, and in accordance with said instructions have issued the following advertisement, which was published in the Cherokee Advocate, June 21, 1902:

Notice is hereby given that I, J. Blair Shoenfelt, United States Indian agent and disbursing officer, acting under instructions from the honorable Secretary of the Interior, at my office in Muskogee, Ind. T., will, on July 1, 1902, and subsequent days until disbursement is completed, disburse the interest due the Cherokee Nation from the United States Government on their invested funds, amounting to $148,232.79.

The said sum of $148,232.79 is applicable to the payment of warrants on the respective funds, as follows:

Interest on Cherokee Nation or general fund	$70,429.21
Interest on Cherokee orphan fund	31,418.15
Interest on Cherokee school fund	42,716.70
Interest on Cherokee asylum fund	3,668.73
Total	148,232.79

The said disbursement will be made under the laws of the Cherokee Nation, in so far as they are not in conflict with the rules and regulations prescribed by the Department of the Interior, and of the United States Treasury, for the government of disbursing officers.

By the terms of an act of the Cherokee council, approved by the President January 5, 1900, interest on outstanding Cherokee warrants became payable annually. Interest on Cherokee warrants has been paid up to April 28, 1901.

Upon warrants which are hereby advertised for payment and cancellation all interest will be paid. The interest on all warrants issued prior to April 27, 1902, will be paid, whether for a year or less.

In making this payment the indorsement of the original payee will be required before either the interest or principal will be paid, or, if the original payee is deceased, then the indorsement of the legally appointed administrator or executor of the estate will be necessary. Certified copies of the letters of administration must be furnished in cases where indorsements are made by administrators. Powers of attorney will not be recognized.

In the payment of principal and interest the present legal holder of the warrant will be required to receipt for the same over his own signature.

The following warrants, if legally issued for valuable consideration to the Cherokee Nation, will be paid and retired:

Insane asylum fund.—E 73 and interest due thereon to April 28, 1900; D 3 and 4 and the interest due thereon to June 22, 1901, these warrants having heretofore been advertised for payment on that date. Also D 5 to D 47, inclusive, and interest due thereon to June 21, 1902.

Orphan asylum fund.—C 44 and C 120 and interest due thereon to June 22, 1901, these two warrants having heretofore been advertised for payment on that date. Also warrants C 122 to C 212, inclusive, and interest due thereon to June 21, 1902.

School fund.—A 81 and interest due thereon to April 28, 1900, this warrant having heretofore been advertised for payment on that date. Also warrants K 245, K 246, K 247, and K 248; A 205, A 245, and B 88, and interest due thereon to June 22, 1901. Also warrants B 224 to B 384, inclusive, and interest due thereon to June 21, 1902.

General fund.—Warrants C 762, 767, 768, 769, 770, 774; D 46, 65, 73, 84, 98, 115, 116, 117, 119, 134, 135, 149, 158, 159, 168, 178; O 33, 45, 52, 65, 66, 67, 71, 82, 83, 87, 93, 95, 110, and 128, and the interest due thereon to April 3, 1899, these warrants having heretofore been advertised for payment on that date. Also warrants C 1162, 1165, 1166, 1168, 1173; D 263, 270, 290; O 203, 219, 224, 263, 264, 265, 266, 307, and interest due thereon to April 28, 1900, these warrants having heretofore been advertised for payment on that date. Also C 1229, 1333, 1361, 1419, 1427, 1437; O 718, 737; D 451, 456, A 22 and 31, and interest due thereon to June 22, 1901, these warrants having heretofore been advertised for payment on that date. Also the following warrants: A 46 to A 125, A 127 to A 193; C 1464, 1465, 1466, 1469, 1470 to 1478, inclusive; C 165; D 1 to 137, 139 to 155, 161, 167, 168, 169; F 1 to 6, and interest due thereon to June 21, 1902. Warrants should not be presented for payment prior to July 1, 1902.

If any further information is desired, apply to the United States Indian agent, Union Agency, Muskogee, Ind. T.

In order that the public may appreciate the enormity of the task incident to paying of Cherokee warrants and interest due thereon, it is only necessary for me to remark that the warrants are handled nine times in this office before payment of interest or principal is made. First, the warrants are checked when handed in by the owner or bank having them for collection; second, they are examined and put in order, with reference to the fund from which they are payable; third, they are compared with the records in this office furnished by the Cherokee authorities, to see that they have been properly and legally issued and are valid and outstanding obligations against the Cherokee Nation; fourth, the interest is figured; fifth, the first calculation is checked; sixth, the data in reference to the warrant on which interest is paid is entered on a subvoucher; seventh, this subvoucher is checked, added up, and carried to the pay roll proper in the sum aggregate; eighth, the interest paid on the warrant is annotated on the back thereof, and if retired, it is so marked; and ninth, the warrants on which interest only is figured are returned to the owner. One thousand and thirty-four warrants were paid and retired under the advertisement made under date of June 22, 1901, and the interest was paid on 5,004 warrants. My account of this payment has been carefully checked in the Office of the Commissioner of Indian Affairs and the Auditor for the Interior Department at Washington, D. C., and it is gratifying to state that only one error was made in computing interest.

Cherokee warrants, on account of the fact that the Government now pays them, and the interest due thereon, have advanced in price from 85 cents to 98 cents, flat.

The warrants are rarely presented by the persons in whose favor they were originally issued, but are almost invariably sent through some bank for collection.

When the Cherokee authorities had the matter of the payment of these warrants in hand, the price of the warrants went as low as 75 cents.

PAYMENT TO DESTITUTE CHEROKEE INDIANS.

The principal chief of the Cherokee Nation having advised this office that a large number of full-blood Cherokee Indians were in destitute and needy circumstances, and the report of the chief having been forwarded to me by the Department, and the matter having been carefully considered, I was directed to relieve this destitution by making a small per capita distribution of money among said destitute Indians. This distribution of money was made during the months of April, May, and June. I received for disbursement $15,000, and out of this sum disbursed to relieve destitution $13,067, paid incidental expenses incurred in connection with said payment $684.32, and returned to the Treasury $1,248.68.

I had two paying parties in the field during the period mentioned above. Prior to the said parties going into the field I issued the following circular letter, in order that those interested might be fully advised:

To whom it may concern:

Notice is hereby given that I will be at the following-named places in the Cherokee Nation, Indian Territory, on the dates mentioned, for the purpose of distributing funds in my hands, to relieve needy and destitute Cherokee full-blood Indians who live in the vicinity of the towns named:

Party No. 1.

Saline court-house, April 15 to 18, inclusive.
Moodys, April 22 to 24, 1902, inclusive.
Kansas, noon, April 25 to 26, 1902, inclusive.
Spavinaw, April 29 to May 2, 1902, inclusive.
Whitmore, May 6 to 9, 1902, inclusive.
Goingsnake court-house, May 12 to 16, 1902, inclusive.
Zena, May 19 to 22, 1902, inclusive.

Party No. 2.

Remy, April 23 to 25, 1902, inclusive.
Swimmer. April 28 to 30, 1902, inclusive.
Stilwell, May 2. 3, and 5, 1902, inclusive.
Campbell, May 6 to 9, 1902, inclusive.
McKee, May 12 to 14, 1902, inclusive.
Marble, May 16 to 18, 1902, inclusive.
Bunch, May 19 to 23, 1902 inclusive.
Cookson, May 26 to 29, 1902, inclusive.
White Oak, June 3, 1902.
Catoosa, June 4, 1902, commencing at noon.
Bartlesville, June 6, 1902.
Such Cherokee full-bloods as are in destitute circumstances and desire to participate in the distribution of this fund should present themselves at any one of the towns named on dates given.
For further information on this subject address the United States Indian Agent, Muskogee, Ind. T.

The newspapers throughout the Indian Territory very kindly copied this notice.
The pay rolls on which these payments were made show that 4,189 persons actually received money. The paying parties report that the full-blood Cherokees were in very destitute circumstances, and while the amounts paid to heads of families were small, I am satisfied it relieved them from want and destitution, and tided them along so that they could put in their crops.
It is to be remembered that this distribution of money was not moneys appropriated by the United States, but was moneys actually belonging to the Cherokee tribe of Indians, which had been collected by this office for them from noncitizens, account of royalties on hay, merchandise tax, etc.

PAYMENT PER DIEM AND MILEAGE TO WITNESSES BEFORE THE DAWES COMMISSION AND EXPENSES OF CHEROKEE CITIZENSHIP COMMISSION.

The President, on January 20, 1902, approved the act of the Cherokee council making provision for the representation of the Cherokee Nation before the Commission to the Five Civilized Tribes, in connection with the work of completing the roll of citizens of the Cherokee Nation, and for other purposes.
This act provides for attorneys to represent the interests of the nation, and at the same time gives the Commission authority to summon before it witnesses, and to allow such witnesses 10 cents per mile and $2 per diem while actually in attendance before the Commission.
This act also provides for the payment of the current and contingent expenses of the Commission and fixes the salaries of the attorneys and provides for the employment and pay of a stenographer, and also authorizes the attorneys, when necessary, to engage the services of some persons in serving subpoenas upon witnesses.
The salaries of the attorneys and stenographer and the incidental expenses incurred by the Commission in connection with its work were originally paid by warrants drawn by the principal chief of the Cherokee Nation, but this appropriation having become exhausted the Commissioner of Indian Affairs, under date of June 18, 1902, advised me that the Department, under date of June 14, 1902, authorized and directed the Indian Office to place to my official credit, as Indian moneys, the sum of $2,000 for the payment of fees and necessary expenses incurred by the Cherokee Nation in the defense of citizenship cases before the Dawes Commission and that requisition for the amount mentioned above had been issued, in order that it might be in my hands before the close of the citizenship rolls on July 1.
During the quarter ended June 30. 1902, out of the fund just mentioned, I made the following disbursements:

Paid per diem and mileage of witnesses	$93.00
Paid incidental expenses of the Commission	189.38
Total	282.38

And returned to the Treasurer the unexpended balance of said fund amounting to $1,717.62.

SEMINOLE NATION.

In December, 1897, the Seminole Nation and the Commission to the Five Civilized Tribes, otherwise known as the Dawes Commission, entered into an agreement which provided for the allotment of their lands and the establishment of a United States court at Wewoka, the capital of said nation, and gave the United States courts exclusive jurisdiction over all controversies growing out of the ownership, occupation, or use of real estate owned by the Seminole Nation, and to try persons charged with homicide, embezzlement, bribery, and embracery committed in the Seminole country, without reference to the citizenship of the persons charged with such crimes. The Seminole Indian courts were allowed to retain their jurisdiction as they had to prior to the ratification of such agreement, except such cases as would be tried in the United States court, and the agreement also provided for the gradual extinguishment of the tribal government.

No revenues or royalties of any character have been collected by me for the benefit of the Seminole Nation during the fiscal year ended June 30, 1902. The Commission to the Five Civilized Tribes has completed the enrollment of the Seminole Nation, and has also practically completed the allotment of their lands in severalty.

The principal chief of the Seminole Nation has frequently complained to this office that noncitizens have introduced and held cattle in the Seminole Nation. These complaints are then sent to an Indian policeman, stationed at Wewoka, Seminole Nation, for investigation and report, and if it is found that said cattle are being held within the limits of said nation contrary to law, then an order issued directing that they be removed therefrom.

The office has enforced the intercourse laws of the Seminole Nation, and aided in assisting the chief in the execution of the Seminole laws whenever it was called upon to do so.

The advanced state of the Seminole Nation at this time is largely due to the wisdom and foresight of its late principal chief, the Hon. John F. Brown, who has been succeeded as such principal chief by Hon. Hulputta Micco.

SALE OF TOWN-SITE MAPS.

There have been placed on file in this office photolithographic copies of the town-site maps of the towns of Muskogee, Mounds, and Wagoner, in the Creek Nation, Indian Territory, and Centralia, Choteau, Collinsville, Chelsea, Catoosa, Lenapah, Nowata, Ramona, Vinita, and Welch, in the Cherokee Nation, and Woodville, in the Chickasaw Nation.

I am directed to dispose of these maps at prices fixed by the Department and to deposit the proceeds of the sale of same to the credit of the United States for the benefit of the fund "Town-site commissioners for Indian Territory."

There has been received for the fiscal year ended June 30, 1902, on account of the sale of town-site maps of the towns mentioned, the sum of $73.20.

PAYMENT OF EXPENSES INCURRED IN CONNECTION WITH TOWN-SITE WORK IN THE INDIAN TERRITORY.

Acting under instructions of the Department since January 1, 1901, all expenses incurred in connection with the town-site work in the Indian Territory, except the salaries of the town-site commissioners and the supervising engineer for the Indian Territory town-site surveys, are paid by this office. There are approximately about 100 people connected with this work who receive pay through this office, such as surveyors, transitmen, chainmen, and rodmen, all of whom are paid monthly. I also pay the salaries of such employees in this office, and that of the United States Indian inspector, who do town-site work. This includes draftsmen and clerks. Up to June 30, 1902, as stated in the opening of this report, I disbursed out of the town-site fund, to pay expenses of the character mentioned above, $84,890.60. This amount includes $238.51 in payment of expenses incurred during the fiscal year ended June 30, 1901. In addition to paying the salaries of the employees mentioned, I also pay the traveling expenses of the surveyors, and such other incidental expenses as the purchase of stakes, axes, office rent, etc. The preparation of the vouchers on which the payment of the expenses mentioned above is made involves considerable work by the office.

SETTLEMENT OF SMALLPOX CLAIMS.

In my previous annual report I referred to the outbreak of smallpox throughout the Indian Territory, prevalent during the fall and winter of 1899 and the winter and spring of 1900, and the work this office did in connection with the boards of health of the Choctaw, Cherokee, and Creek nations in suppressing the same. The act of May 31, 1900, appropriated $50,000, to be immediately available, in payment of liabilities already incurred, and for amount necessary to be expended in suppression of smallpox in the Indian Territory among those resident in the said Territory not members of any tribe or nation therein.

The expenses incurred in suppressing this disease in the Cherokee and Creek nations have all been practically paid. In the Choctaw Nation the expenses incurred have been paid, except certain claims that have been disallowed, pending further proof as to the merits of the same. The total sum paid during the fiscal year ended June 30, 1902, from the $50,000 appropriated by the act of Congress referred to, was $1,502.32, and from the fund "Indian moneys proceeds of labor, Creek," $3.10.

Part of the expenses incurred in connection with the suppression of this disease in the Cherokee and Creek nations was paid from funds belonging to said nations, as the $50,000 appropriated could not be used where the afflicted were members of any Indian tribe; hence the charge of $3.10, noted above, from Creek Indian moneys.

PRESERVATION OF GAME IN THE INDIAN TERRITORY.

In my last annual report I referred to the unlawful and indiscriminate killing of game in the Indian Territory, and that the practice of persons living in adjoining States entering the Indian Territory for the purpose of hunting had become so common that complaints were being constantly made to this office to put a stop to it; that the noncitizens did not confine themselves to killing just what game they needed, but slaughtered deer and wild turkeys by the wholesale and shipped them to their homes, and that they also trespassed upon the allotments of Indian citizens and individual holdings of Indian citizens without their consent and much to their annoyance. I issued a circular letter calling attention to section 2137 of the Revised Statutes of the United States, which prohibits any person, other than an Indian, from hunting or trapping, taking, or destroying any peltries or game, except for subsistence, in an Indian country; and also to section 1923 of Mansfield's Digest of the Statutes of Arkansas, which makes it unlawful for any person to kill, maim, or paralyze any fish or other water animals, etc.; and also to section 1925 of the same digest, which provides for a penalty for violating the provisions of section 1923.

Later on I directed the Indian police connected with this agency to arrest noncitizen hunters and to confiscate any game that they might have in their possession, together with any guns, ammunition, etc., and report such arrests and confiscation promptly to this office. Owing to the very limited number of Indian police in the Indian Territory but few arrests of this character were made, and my efforts to preserve the game were, for that reason, to a large extent futile.

Citizens and noncitizens alike becoming indignant at the practice of citizens from the adjacent States entering the Indian Territory and killing the game, presented the matter to Congress, with the view of having a rigid game law passed, as was recommended in my previous annual report; but although a bill was prepared by the attorneys of the Indian Territory and introduced in Congress in this connection, it failed of passage.

Something should be done, and I again renew my former recommendation that Congress pass proper game laws to protect the game in the Indian Territory.

EXECUTIVES OF THE FIVE CIVILIZED TRIBES.

It is thought proper to here express the very high appreciation of the ability and character of the Hon. Pleasant Porter, principal chief of the Creek Nation, whose untiring efforts, statesmanlike qualities, and marked ability have been so conspicuously displayed in the past year or two, as principal chief of the Creek Nation, in advancing and promoting the interests of said nation.

The relation of this office with the Hon. G. W. Dukes, principal chief of the Choctaw Nation; the Hon. D. H. Johnson, governor of the Chickasaw Nation; the Hon. John F. Brown, principal chief of the Seminole Nation; and the Hon. T. M. Buffington, principal chief of the Cherokee Nation, have been very friendly, and they have cooperated with me and I with them in enforcing the laws of their nations, and have discharged the duties of their respective offices, I think, with great ability.

The only change that has occurred in the executives of the Five Civilized Tribes was the recent retirement of the Hon. John F. Brown, principal chief of the Seminole Nation, by the election of the Hon. Hulputta Micco.

SCHOOLS.

At present the teachers of the Choctaw Nation are paid quarterly for services rendered by means of my official check, while the teachers employed in the Cherokee, Creek, and Chickasaw nations are paid by means of tribal warrants. Educational advantages consistent with the prospective growth of the Territory should be provided for. It is a lamentable fact that at the present time public schools can be organized only within the limits of incorporated towns, and as the tribal relations are soon to be abolished, tribal schools will also, sooner or later, of necessity be discontinued, and unless some relief is provided the rural districts and small towns of the Indian Territory will be left with no schools, and there is no law under which they may be established.

TAXATION TO PROVIDE SCHOOLS IN THE INDIAN TERRITORY.

The Indian appropriation act of March 3, 1901 (31 Stat., 1058–1074), contains the ollowing provision:

To enable the Secretary of the Interior to investigate and report to Congress at its next session whether it is practicable to provide a system of taxation of personal property, occupation, franchises, etc., in the Indian Territory, sufficient to maintain a system of free schools to all the children of the Indian Territory, $5,000.

Under the clause of the act referred to, Mr. Frank C. Churchill, formerly revenue inspector for the Cherokee Nation, was appointed by the honorable Secretary of the Interior to investigate and make a report as to the practicability of providing a system of taxation on personal property, occupation, franchises, etc., in the Indian Territory sufficient to maintain a system of free schools for the benefit of the children within the limits of the Indian Territory.

On the 14th day of March, 1902, a report was submitted by Mr. Churchill, after careful investigation, in which he recommends that tribal taxes within the limits of the Five Civilized Tribes be abolished, as they seem to be incomplete, unequal, and difficult of collection, and that a uniform system be established, to correspond with what is commonly known as "State tax," in lieu thereof.

At the time of submitting the report there was in the Indian Territory 560 post-offices, with 108 incorporated towns and 42 small towns not incorporated, which have been or are to be surveyed and platted, but in which, at the time report was submitted, no tax could be legally levied.

It is recommended that the continuance of the tribal schools—that is, schools managed in whole or in part by the Cherokees, Chickasaws, Choctaws, Creeks, and Seminoles—indefinitely with any semblance of tribal control would be against the best interests of the Indian children, as well as a great waste of tribal funds, and that the school funds belonging to the several tribes in the Indian Territory should, as early as possible, be put beyond the reach of tribal officials, for the reason that the schools are not provided for all the Indian children; that many of the Indian children now provided with school privileges receive such privileges through political favoritism and corrupt influences, to the exclusion of others quite as worthy; that the expense thereby created is far too great for the advantages received, and much greater than it would be were the schools conducted judiciously and honestly, and that the present boarding-school system is faulty and expensive.

Reference is also made to the illiteracy and crime prevailing in the Indian Territory, and much of this illiteracy and crime is attributed to the fact that the citizens of the Territory have so few educational advantages. It seems to be the consensus of opinion that no objection would be raised by any person to the attendance at the same school of Indian and white children, as that custom now prevails largely throughout the Indian Territory, but that separate schools should be provided for negroes.

In order to promote greater interest in educational matters, and, next to compulsory education, found to be necessary in many of the best States where common schools are thoroughly established, a moderate tax system for schools would prove to be the best incentive to a proper interest in education, and tend to increase and develop such an interest, on the ground that nothing so emphasizes the real value of a thing as positive evidence that it costs something in money and effort.

It seems that the increase in population in the Indian Territory in the last decade was 117.5 per cent, and that everything indicates that this increase will continue, and in a greater ratio, and provisions should be made for an acreage income for the use of all lands leased by Indians that would put this phase of the general question of an income for schools and other purposes first and foremost. While it might be contended that such a suggestion might be interpreted as a recommendation for tax upon the Indian lands, such is not the case; but, however, a provision making the validity of all leases and their use in courts as evidence contingent upon such lease being recorded, and an acreage income actually paid in advance for the full term of the lease, is intended; and upon this income from the people of the Territory would have to depend very largely the support of schools and other expenses incident to its development.

There are upward of 100,000 persons of school age residents of the Indian Territory without free schools, and nearly $400,000 of Indian funds are expended annually for the maintenance of tribal schools, in which only from 12,000 to 15,000 pupils are enrolled. Only about 30 of the towns authorized to do so have raised a tax for schools, amounting to about $50,000, and there is not less than $50,000,000 of taxable property, to which additions are being made almost hourly, upon which a tax of one-half of 1 per cent would net $250,000, an occupation tax would yield $125,000, and a poll tax not less than $100,000, to which $200,000 should be added for taxes upon railroads, telegraph, telephone, and other corporations and franchises to correspond with the above amount. A small acreage income from land lease, and plans, as outlined, would net about $100,000, the total of these items being $675,000, and that amount can be raised without proving a burden or hardship upon any person.

Recommendation is made that 30 school districts should be established at once, under the direction of the Secretary of the Interior, together with the necessary subdivisions, and that all legislation, in the nature of things, should be, in a sense, preliminary, and be added to and enlarged upon with the development of the Territory, and that once provided for and actually put in operation, the real value of good schools to a new country will be recognized and cheerfully maintained by the peopl e.

RAILROADS.

With the increase of population, and the consequent increase of trade, railroads have been quick to take advantage of the situation, and many new lines of road are being built through the Indian Territory.

The Kansas City, Fort Scott and Memphis Railway Company, recently acquired by the St. Louis and San Francisco Railroad Company, constructed, during the fiscal year ended June 30, 1902, 13.096 miles of railroad between Miami and Afton, Ind. T., known as the "Miami Cut-off," thus shortening their line between Kansas City and Oklahoma and Texas points.

The general manager of the Fort Smith and Western Railroad Company advises, under date of August 11, 1902, that his company is now operating 63 miles of their own line, which has been built and put in operation during the past fiscal year from Coal Creek to Crowder City, Ind. T., the latter mentioned town being a junction point with the Missouri, Kansas and Texas Railroad; that the route taken by the line of railway is through the very best part of the Choctaw Nation, and that the management confidently look forward to a good business.

During the fiscal year ended June 30, 1902, the Missouri, Kansas and Texas Railroad completed its Edwards and Krebs branches, making a total mileage of 5.11 miles built by this company. These were branches built to coal mines to facilitate the transaction of its coal business.

The Kiowa, Chickasha and Fort Smith Railroad Company, operated by the Santa Fe System, constructed a line of railway in connection with the Gulf, Colorado and Santa Fe Railway Company from Pauls Valley, Ind. T., to Lindsay, in the Chickasaw Nation, Indian Terrftory, a distance of 24 miles, and the Santa Fe System has other lines of railway in process of construction, but not completed.

The Arkansas Western Railroad Company completed its line of road from Heavener, Ind. T , eastward into Arkansas, a distance of about 12 miles.

During the fiscal year ended June 30, 1902, the Choctaw, Oklahoma and Western Railroad Company, a branch of the Choctaw, Oklahoma and Gulf Railroad Company now absorbed by the Chicago, Rock Island and Pacific Railway Company, constructed and put in operation a line of railway from Ardmore Junction, near Hartshorne, Ind. T., on its main line, to Ardmore, Ind. T., a distance of 117.65 miles, and in addition built a number of branch lines and spurs to mines, aggregating 5.86 miles.

The Arkansas and Choctaw Railroad has recently been acquired by the St. Louis and San Francisco Railroad Company, and I have been advised that the said Arkansas and Choctaw Railroad Company constructed or partially constructed during the year ended June 30, 1902, within the Indian Territory 167.4 miles of railroad, and of this amount of mileage 79 miles were completely constructed and ready for operation prior to June 30, 1902, and the remainder, to wit, 88.4 miles, have been graded, but not completely constructed ready for operation.

The Ozark and Cherokee Central Railway Company has completed 75 miles of its line from Fayetteville, Ark., to Tahlequah, Ind. T., and trains are now being operated over the same. The company now has under process of construction 70 miles of railroad, from Tahlequah to Okmulgee, via Muskogee, Ind. T., and expects to have this 70 miles completed and ready for operation by November 1, 1902.

The act of Congress granting right of way through the Oklahoma and Indian Territories to the Enid and Anadarko Railroad Company and for other purposes, approved February 28, 1902, requires, among other things, that correct maps, showing the lines of railroad in sections of 25 miles each and all lands taken under the act, shall be filed in the Department of the Interior and with the United States Indian agent for the Indian Territory, and with the principal chief or governor of any nation through which the lines of railroad may be located or in which said lines are situated.

Under the provisions of this act and former acts of Congress there has been filed in this office during the fiscal year ended June 30, 1902, 65 maps.

CREEK SUPPLEMENTAL AGREEMENT.

The act of Congress approved June 30, 1902 (32 Stats., 500), ratifies and confirms a supplemental agreement with the Creek tribe of Indians. Said act provides that—

All lands belonging to the Creek tribe of Indians in the Indian Territory, except town sites and land reserved for Creek schools and churches, railroads, and town cemeteries, in accordance with the provisions of the act of Congress approved March 1, 1901, shall be appraised at not to exceed $6.50 per acre, excluding only lawful improvements on lands in actual cultivation, said appraisement to be made under the direction and supervision of the Commission to the Five Civilized Tribes, and the descent and distribution of land and money provided for shall be in accordance with chapter 49 of Mansfield's Digest of the Statutes of Arkansas, now in force in the Indian Territory: *Provided,* That only citizens of the Creek Nation, male and female, and their Creek descendants, shall inherit lands of the Creek Nation: *And provided further,* That if there be no person of Creek citizenship to take the descent and distribution of said estate, then the inheritance shall go to noncitizen heirs in the order named in said chapter 49.

The supplemental agreement also provides how the rolls of citizenship shall be completed and what names shall be added thereto.

Reference has heretofore been made to the clause in the agreement providing for roads in the Creek Nation.

All funds of the Creek Nation not needed for equalization of allotments, including the Creek school fund, is to be paid out under the direction of the Secretary of the Interior per capita to the citizens of the Creek Nation on the dissolution of the Creek tribal government.

Each citizen is required to select from his allotment 40 acres of land as a homestead, which shall be and remain nontaxable, inalienable, and free from any incumbrance whatever for twenty-one years from the date of the deed therefor, and a separate deed shall be issued to each allottee for his homestead, in which this condition shall appear.

Creek citizens are permitted to rent their allotments, for strictly nonmineral purposes, for a term not to exceed one year for grazing purposes only, and for a period not to exceed five years for agricultural purposes.

Cattle grazed upon leased allotments shall not be liable to any tribal tax, but when cattle are introduced into the Creek Nation and grazed on lands not selected for allotment by citizens, the Secretary of the Interior shall collect from the owners thereof a reasonable grazing tax for the benefit of the tribe.

Before cattle are introduced into the Creek Nation to be grazed upon either lands not selected for allotment or upon lands allotted or selected for allotment, the owner thereof shall first obtain a permit from the United States Indian agent authorizing the introduction of such cattle.

CHEROKEE AGREEMENT.

The act of Congress approved July 1, 1902 (32 Stats., 716), provides for the allotment of lands in the Cherokee Nation, with the disposition of town sites therein, and for other purposes, which act was later ratified, as required, by a majority of the voters of the Cherokee Nation.

The Commission to the Five Civilized Tribes is required to allot to each citizen of the Cherokee Nation land equal in value to 110 acres of the average allottable lands of the Cherokee Nation, to conform as nearly as may be to the areas and boundaries established by the Government survey, which land may be selected by each allottee so as to include his improvements, and each member of the tribe shall designate as a homestead out of said allotment land equal in value to 40 acres, which shall be inalienable during the lifetime of the allottee, not exceeding twenty-one years from the date of the certificate of allotment. All lands allotted, except such land as is set apart for homestead purposes, shall be alienable in five years after the issuance of the patent.

Allotment certificates issued by the Dawes Commission shall be conclusive evidence of the right of an allottee to the tract of land described therein, and the United States Indian agent shall, under the direction of the Secretary of the Interior, upon application of the allottee, place him in possession of his allotment, and remove therefrom all persons objectionable to him, and the acts of the Indian agent hereunder shall not be controlled by the writ or process of any court.

Exclusive jurisdiction is conferred upon the Commission to the Five Civilized Tribes, under the direction of the Secretary of the Interior, to determine all matters relative to the appraisement and the allotment of lands.

The following lands are reserved from allotment:

(*a*) All lands set apart for town sites by the provisions of the act of Congress of June twenty-eight, eighteen hundred and ninety-eight, (Thirtieth Statutes, page four hundred and ninety-five), the provisions of the act of Congress of May thirty-first, nineteen hundred (Thirty-first Statutes, page two hundred and twenty-one), and by the provisions of this act.

(b) All lands to which, upon the date of the ratification of this act, any railroad company may, under any treaty or act of Congress, have a vested right of way, depots, station grounds, water stations, stock yards, or similar uses only, connected with the maintenance and operation of the railroad.

(c) All lands selected for town cemeteries, not to exceed twenty acres each.

(d) One acre of land for each Cherokee schoolhouse not included in town sites or herein otherwise provided for.

(e-l inc.) Four acres for Willie Halsell College at Vinita, Baptist mission school at Tahlequah, Presbyterian school at Tahlequah, Park Hill mission school south of Tahlequah, Elm Springs mission school at Barren Fork, Dwight mission school at Sallisaw, Skiatook mission near Skiatook, and Lutheran mission school on Illinois River north of Tahlequah.

(m) Sufficient ground for burial purposes where neighborhood cemeteries are now located not to exceed three acres each.

(n) One acre for each church house outside of towns.

(o) The square now occupied by the capitol building at Tahlequah.

(p) The grounds now occupied by the national jail at Tahlequah.

(q) The grounds now occupied by the Cherokee Advocate printing office at Tahlequah.

(r-s) Forty acres each for the Cherokee male and female seminaries near Tahlequah.

(t) One hundred and twenty acres for the Cherokee Orphan Asylum on Grand River.

(u-v) Forty acres each for the colored high school in Tahlequah district and the Cherokee Insane Asylum.

(w) Four acres for the school for blind, deaf, and dumb children near Fort Gibson.

The acre so reserved for any church or schoolhouse in any quarter section of land shall be located where practicable, in a corner of such quarter section adjacent to the section lines thereof.

Provided, That the Methodist Episcopal Church South may, within twelve months after the ratification of this act, pay ten dollars per acre for the one hundred and sixty acres of land adjacent to the town of Vinita, and heretofore set apart by act of the Cherokee National Council for the use of said church for missionary and educational purposes, and now occupied by Willie Halsell College (formerly Galloway College), and shall thereupon receive title thereto; but if said church fail so to do it may continue to occupy said one hundred and sixty acres of land as long as it uses same for the purposes aforesaid.

Provision is made for the closing of the citizenship rolls and the addition of certain names thereon.

The Cherokee school fund is to be used, under the direction of the Secretary of the Interior, for the education of children of Cherokee citizens, and the Cherokee schools are to be conducted under rules prescribed by him according to Cherokee laws.

Public highways or roads two rods in width, being one rod on each side of the section line, may be established along all section lines without any compensation being paid therefor, and all allottees, purchasers, and others shall take the title to such lands subject to this provision; and public highways or roads may be established elsewhere whenever necessary for the public good, the actual value of the land taken elsewhere than along section lines to be determined under the direction of the Secretary of the Interior, while the tribal government continues, and to be paid by the Cherokee Nation during that time; and if buildings or other improvements are damaged in consequence of the establishment of such public highways or roads, whether along section lines or elsewhere, such damages, during the continuance of the tribal government, shall be determined and paid for in the same manner.

Provision is also made for the reservation and setting aside of lands for town-site purposes, either where towns have heretofore been established or may be established.

The tribal government of the Cherokee Nation shall not continue longer than March 4, 1906.

The collection of all revenues of whatsoever character belonging to the tribe shall be made by an officer appointed by the Secretary of the Interior, and all funds of the tribe and all moneys accruing under the provisions of this act shall be paid out under the direction of the Secretary of the Interior, and when required for per capita payments shall be paid directly to each individual by an appointed officer, under the direction of the Secretary of the Interior.

The Secretary of the Interior shall cause to be paid all just indebtedness of said tribe existing at the date of the ratification of the act, which may have been lawfully contracted, and warrants therefor drawn by authority of law are to be paid, as are also warrants drawn by authority of law hereafter and prior to the dissolution of the tribal government out of funds belonging to the tribe. Said payments are to be made by the Secretary of the Interior or an officer appointed by him for that purpose.

Cherokee citizens may rent their allotments when selected for a term not to exceed one year for grazing purposes only, and for a period not to exceed five years for agricultural purposes, but without any stipulation or obligation to renew the same; but leases for a period longer than one year for grazing purposes and for a period longer than five years for agricultural purposes and for mineral purposes may also be made with the approval of the Secretary of the Interior and not otherwise. Any agreement or lease of any kind or character violative of this section shall be absolutely void and not susceptible of ratification in any manner, and no rule of estoppel shall ever prevent the assertion of its invalidity. Cattle grazed upon leased allotments shall not be liable to any tribal tax, but when cattle are introduced into the Cherokee Nation and grazed on lands not selected as allotments by citizens, the Secretary of the Interior shall collect from the owners thereof a reasonable grazing tax for the benefit of the tribe, and section two thousand one hundred and seventeen of the Revised Statutes of the United States shall not hereafter apply to Cherokee lands.

CHOCTAW AND CHICKASAW AGREEMENT.

The act of Congress approved July 1, 1902 (32 Stats., 641), confirms the agreement with the Choctaw and Chickasaw tribes of Indians, and for other purposes, but the same is not effective nor binding until ratified by a majority of the voters of the

Choctaw and Chickasaw nations. The date of voting for the ratification or rejection of this agreement will take place at various points throughout the Choctaw and Chickasaw nations on September 25, 1902.

RECOMMENDATIONS.

Having in mind the large number of white children who have no school advantages, I recommend that a system of taxation be adopted sufficient to maintain a system of free schools, as outlined in this report, and in accordance with the suggestions made by Mr. Frank C. Churchill, special agent on taxation for free schools in the Indian Territory, in his report to the Secretary of the Interior, and that Congress provide means by which the rural districts and small towns of the Territory may be provided with schools.

I most earnestly recommend that an asylum for the care of insane white people, or, in other words, citizens of the United States, be founded in this Territory, and that the same be supported by Congressional legislation or appropriations, as it is estimated that the number of insane, exclusive of Indians, in the Indian Territory at this time is some 300 or more, upon the assumption that there are about 500,000 non-citizen residents in the Territory, and for the further reason that there is no asylum in said Territory where they could be cared for.

I have heretofore stated in this report that, in my opinion, a law should be passed to protect the game of the Indian Territory.

In this report reference is made to the unfortunate condition of affairs in the Indian Territory on account of the lack of road laws, and to remedy this evil, legislation on this subject was incorporated in the recent Creek supplemental agreement and in the agreement made with the Cherokee tribe of Indians, ratified by the acts of Congress approved June 30, 1902 and July 1, 1902, respectively, and recommendation is made that similar legislation be had for the Choctaw and Chickasaw nations.

CONCLUSION.

I have attended to the affairs of this agency to the very best of my ability, and I trust in such a manner as to meet with the approval of the Department.

I am under renewed obligations to Hon. J. George Wright, United States Indian inspector for the Indian Territory, for valuable aid and assistance rendered me.

I must express my appreciation of the cordial support and courtesy shown me by your office.

I have the honor to be, very respectfully, your obedient servant,

J. BLAIR SHOENFELT,
United States Indian Agent.

The COMMISSIONER OF INDIAN AFFAIRS.

REPORT OF SUPERINTENDENT OF SCHOOLS FOR INDIAN TERRITORY.

OFFICE OF SUPERINTENDENT OF SCHOOLS IN INDIAN TERRITORY,
Muskogee, Ind. T., July 30, 1902.

SIR: I have the honor to submit my fourth annual report as superintendent of the schools of Indian Territory, together with the annual reports of the supervisors of the Cherokee, Creek, Choctaw, and Chickasaw nations, as follows:

The past year has been a remarkably quiet one in educational matters, and by far the most successful of any since the Department assumed supervisory control over the Indian schools of this Territory.

The tribal officials, who formerly administered their own school affairs as they pleased, seem now convinced that it was necessary to make some changes in order that their schools might accomplish better results, and at this time they are, almost without exception, working in harmony with us in endeavoring to secure better educational facilities for the children of the various tribes.

It is pleasing to note, too, that a healthier educational sentiment prevails than formerly. Parents manifest more interest in the educational welfare of their children, and teachers devote their spare time more earnestly to fitting themselves for better work. These improved conditions are due in great measure to our personal visitation, our educational meetings, and our summer normals for teachers. There still remains much to be done, however, especially in neighborhoods remote from railroads, where schoolhouses are scarce and as a rule are cheaply constructed and entirely unfurnished.

The greatest difficulty which we have to contend against in the establishment of day schools is the scarcity of suitable schoolhouses. It has always been customary in every nation to require each neighborhood to erect and furnish its own school building. No public funds have ever been used for this purpose, and no funds are now available for erecting or furnishing such buildings.

The somewhat unsettled condition of affairs throughout the Territory renders it difficult as yet to maintain day schools throughout the entire school year. The people are somewhat shifting in disposition, many of them moving from one neighborhood to another in search of more suitable lands for allotment. Not until these conditions become more settled and some means provided by which better buildings can be secured will the day schools accomplish the work which ought to be done in them.

Another difficulty in any attempt to build up permanent day schools in the Territory is encountered by reason of the uncertainty as to the future of the tribal schools.

The leading members of each tribe assert that when the tribal existence of their governments is terminated all their schools are to be abandoned and their tribal school moneys are to be distributed per capita among the members of each tribe or nation. If this be true, the educational problem of the Territory will then become a still more serious one. The Indian children of the Territory will then need as good school facilities as now, but if the lands are not to be subject to taxation, how are their schools to be maintained? This seems to be an important question, which, pending the final winding up of the tribal affairs of the Territory, ought not to be overlooked.

To distribute the school funds pro rata among the members of the various tribes and to provide no method by which school funds could be raised would practically mean to destroy all educational facilities. While the process of tearing down tribal institutions is going on some attention should be given to the matter of providing some means by which the educational training of the children may be continued.

SCHOOL LAWS AND REGULATIONS.

So many questions have arisen as to the manner of conducting the schools of the various nations that I have deemed it advisable to present here copies of the provisions of law under which we are working.

Cherokee Nation.—The Cherokee schools are under the immediate control of the Cherokee board of education and our supervisor of schools for that nation. The board consists of three members, elected by the council of the nation. D. E. Ward, of Tahlequah; Thomas Carlisle, of Campbell post-office, and A. S. Wyly, of Tahlequah, are the present members. The board has an office in Tahlequah, where the members and Supervisor B. S. Coppock frequently meet for consultation and the transaction of school business.

A recent act of Congress contains the following provisions concerning the schools of the Cherokee Nation:

SEC. 32. The Cherokee school fund shall be used, under the direction of the Secretary of the Interior, for the education of children of Cherokee citizens, and the Cherokee schools shall be conducted under rules prescribed by him according to Cherokee laws, subject to such modifications as he may deem necessary to make the schools most effective and to produce the best possible results; said schools to be under the supervision of a supervisor appointed by the secretary and a school board elected by the national council.

SEC. 33. All teachers shall be examined by said supervisor, and said school board and competent teachers and other persons to be engaged in and about the schools with good moral character only shall be employed; but where all qualifications are equal, preference shall be given to citizens of the Cherokee Nation in such employment.

SEC. 34. All moneys for carrying on the schools shall be appropriated by the Cherokee national council, not to exceed the amount of the Cherokee school fund; but if the council fail or refuse to make the necessary appropriations, the Secretary of the Interior may direct the use of a sufficient amount of the school fund to pay all necessary expenses for the efficient conduct of the schools, strict account therefor to be rendered to him and the principal chief.

SEC. 35. All accounts for expenditures in carrying on the schools shall be examined and approved by said supervisor, and also by the general superintendent of Indian schools in the Indian Territory, before payment thereof is made.

SEC. 36. The interest arising from the Cherokee orphan fund shall be used, under the direction of the Secretary of the Interior, for maintaining the Cherokee Orphan Asylum for the benefit of the Cherokee orphan children.

If ratified next month by the nation, the above-quoted provisions of law will constitute the basis for the future conduct of the Cherokee schools.

In the Cherokee Nation two general classes of certificates are issued to teachers upon examination, termed "Class A" and "Class B."

Applicants for "Class A" certificates are examined in orthography, penmanship, reading, arithmetic, algebra, grammar, geography, United States history, theory and practice, primary work, physiology, and civil government.

Teachers who receive a general average of 90 per cent in the above-named branches, with no branch below 75 per cent, receive certificates valid for two years. Those attaining a general average of not less than 80 per cent, with no subject below 65 per cent, receive one-year certificates.

Applicants for "Class B" certificates are examined in the above-named branches, omitting algebra, physiology, and civil government.

Teachers for the seminaries and orphan academy are usually selected from the list of those holding "Class A" certificates.

Those holding "Class B" certificates are eligible to positions in the primary or neighborhood schools.

Special certificates styled "Class C" are sometimes issued to those teachers who understand both Cherokee and English, and who are to teach in full-blood neighborhoods.

About 20 teachers are employed in the seminaries and orphan academy of this nation, at salaries ranging from $45 to $100 per month, for nine months in each year.

About 140 primary or neighborhood teachers are employed at the uniform salary of $35 per month.

The teachers of this nation are paid in Cherokee warrants, which are not usually convertible into cash (except by sale at a discount) until about six months after date of issue.

Creek Nation.—The schools of the Creek Nation are now being conducted under the following rules and regulations:

1 That so far as practicable the rules for the Indian school service, 1898, and the regulations concerning education in the Indian Territory heretofore promulgated by the Secretary shall apply in the government of the Creek schools.

2 All teachers in the boarding schools and day schools shall be examined and appointed by the superintendent of public instruction for the Creek Nation and the supervisor of schools for the Creek Nation. All boarding-school superintendents and other necessary employees in the boarding schools shall be appointed by the superintendent of public instruction for the Creek Nation and the supervisor of schools for the Creek Nation, and no person shall be employed who is not competent to perform the duties of the position to which he or she may be appointed. In the appointment of superintendents, teachers, and other school employees preference shall be given citizens of Indian blood, where they are competent to pass the necessary examinations and are otherwise duly qualified and suitable for such positions.

The supervisor of schools shall at all times be under the direction and supervision of the superintendent of schools for the Indian Territory.

3. That the superintendent of schools in the Indian Territory shall have the right to disapprove any appointment made as above, for good cause, and remove any school employee for incompetency.

immorality, or other just cause, after due investigation, subject, however, to an appeal to the Honorable Secretary of the Interior.

4. That the salaries of superintendents, teachers, and other school employees, shall be fixed by the Secretary of the Interior, and the number of all employees shall be fixed by the Secretary of the Interior.

5. The superintendent of each boarding school shall, under the direction of the superintendent of public instruction and the supervisor of schools, purchase at the lowest obtainable price such provisions as may be needed for the maintenance of the school of which he is superintendent, and he shall keep a complete and accurate book account of all purchases; provided, that the superintendent of public instruction and the supervisor of schools for Creek Nation may, when so directed by the Secretary of the Interior, take bids for furnishing the necessary provisions for such boarding schools, and shall award the contract for furnishing such provisions to the lowest responsible bidder.

6. That at the end of each quarter, and within ten days thereafter, the superintendent of each boarding school shall submit an itemized report to the superintendent of public instruction and the supervisor of schools, showing in detail the articles purchased by him for such school and the prices thereof. The superintendent of public instruction and the supervisor of schools shall carefully examine such report and shall issue a joint requisition upon the principal chief of the Creek Nation for warrants in favor of all parties from whom proper purchases shall have been made, which requisition shall be approved by the superintendent of schools in Indian Territory, and shall be his voucher for the issuance of warrants in payment of said indebtedness.

7. The supervisor of schools shall file with the Indian agent for the Union Agency duplicate copies of all requisitions issued at the time of the filing of original requisitions with the principal chief of the Creek Nation.

8. All teachers shall be required to make quarterly reports, and their salaries and the salaries of other school employees shall be audited and paid as provided in sections six and seven above.

9. The supervisor of schools and the superintendent of public instruction for the Creek Nation shall purchase such books and supplies as may be needed for the day schools, subject to the direction of the superintendent of schools in Indian Territory.

10. The annual expense of each boarding school shall not exceed the amount appropriated therefor.

11. The superintendent of schools in Indian Territory shall fix regular times and places of meeting for the supervisor of schools and the superintendent of public instruction for the Creek Nation for the transaction of business which properly belongs to them, and he may notify them to hold special meetings whenever, in his opinion, it becomes necessary to do so.

12. The superintendent of schools in Indian Territory shall prepare and formulate rules and regulations fixing the duties of the various employees in the Creek schools and providing for the proper conduct and management of said schools, which shall not take effect until approved by the Secretary of the Interior.

13. That the superintendent of each boarding school shall be required to give a bond for the faithful performance of his duties and for the proper care of all school property within his control, the amount of said bond to be fixed by the Secretary of the Interior.

14. Whenever the superintendent of public instruction for the Creek Nation and the supervisor of schools shall fail to agree upon any matter under their direction or control, it shall be decided by the superintendent of schools in Indian Territory, subject to an appeal to the Secretary of the Interior.

15. That at the close of each scholastic year each of the national boarding schools shall be inspected by a competent architect, at a compensation to be agreed upon by the superintendent of public instruction and the supervisor of the nation, subject to the approval of the superintendent of schools; and should it be found that any of these buildings are in need of repairs or additional buildings are needed, the necessary estimates, including a detailed, itemized estimate of labor and material, together with plans and specifications, if necessary, shall be furnished to the superintendent of public instruction and the supervisor of schools, and if approved by the superintendent of schools in Indian Territory estimates for such repairs shall be submitted by the superintendent of schools to the national council, in order that the necessary appropriations may be made.

When such appropriations are made the superintendent of schools in Indian Territory shall invite bids for the performance of such work by printed posters publicly displayed or by advertisements in newspapers, and he shall let the contract therefor to the lowest and most satisfactory bidder.

When the repairs have been completed and inspected a requisition shall be made in the matter, as indicated in section 6 of the proposed regulations concerning education in the Creek Nation.

The above and foregoing regulations have been agreed upon by us, subject to the approval of the honorable Secretary of the Interior

P. PORTER,
Principal Chief, Creek Nation.

JOHN D. BENEDICT,
Superintendent of Schools in Indian Territory.

Approved August 27, 1901.

THOS. RYAN,
Acting Secretary of the Interior.

For positions in the Creek schools all teachers are examined in orthography, reading, penmanship, arithmetic, grammar, geography, United States history, physiology, and primary work.

A general average of 85 per cent is required for a first grade certificate valid for two years.

A general average of 75 per cent for a second grade and 65 per cent for a third grade certificate is required, each valid for one year.

About 20 teachers are employed in the Creek boarding schools, at salaries ranging from $40 to $65 per month for a term of nine months, with board and room included.

About 65 teachers are employed in the neighborhood schools of this nation at salaries ranging from $25 to $40 per month. About 7 of those employed in the boarding schools and 20 of those employed in the neighborhood schools are colored teachers.

The teachers of this nation are paid quarterly in Creek warrants which are not redeemable in cash until about six months after date of issue.

Mr. J. R. Gregory, of Inola, Ind. T., is the present Creek superintendent. Miss Alice Robertson, supervisor for the Creek Nation, resides at Muskogee.

The summer normal for the Chickasaw Nation did not begin until July 7, and is now in session at Tishomingo, with an attendance of about 80 teachers.

SCHOOLS FOR WHITE CHILDREN.

I can not refrain from again calling attention to the deplorable condition of the white children of this Territory, considered from an educational standpoint.

The Indian Territory has a greater population than any other Territory within the boundaries of the United States, greater even than any one of the eight smallest States in the Union. Of the half million people now residing here at least four-fifths are whites, who have come from the various States and have settled here with the intention of making this Territory their future home. They are found in every village and neighborhood, and are engaged in various kinds of business. They do not differ in anywise from the average citizen of the States, possessing the same love of home, family, and country as the average American citizen. The wonderful growth of many of the towns is due to their enterprise, and the development of the thousands of farms now being platted and allotted will depend in very large measure upon their labor.

Outside of the incorporated towns of the Territory there is no provision of law whatever by which a public school district may be organized or taxes levied for any purpose.

During the past winter Hon. Frank C. Churchill, special agent for the Interior Department, made a thorough investigation of educational conditions in this Territory and submitted an elaborate report thereon.

CHOCTAW AND CHICKASAW FREEDMEN.

In my former reports I have called attention to the educational needs of the negro citizens of the Choctaw and Chickasaw nations.

The Atoka agreement, which was entered into between these two nations and the Federal Government in 1898, expressly provides that their freedmen shall not be entitled to any part of the coal royalties, which now constitute the school funds of these two nations. As a result of this provision, the children of about 4,000 colored Choctaw citizens and about the same number of colored Chickasaws are left entirely without any educational facilities. They are not able to pay for the education of their children in private schools, and consequently these children are growing up in dense ignorance.

STATISTICS.

I have called upon all the schools of the Territory to furnish some statistics concerning their enrollment, attendance, income, and cost of maintenance, but after repeated requests for such information I am able to present only a fragmentary report. This is due to several causes, viz:

First. We have no means for taking a school census of the Territory.

Second. Many of the private and denominational schools keep no daily register of attendance.

Third. Many of the schools change teachers several times during the year.

Fourth. Many of the schools continue in session but a fractional part of the school year, and when called upon for information their teachers have gone to their homes in the States, leaving no school records of any value.

The teachers of the Indian schools are, however, now required to make quarterly reports; hence we are able to present reasonably complete statistics from the tribal schools. In making comparisons of the cost of the Indian schools of the various nations, it should be remembered that in the Choctaw academies clothing is furnished to all pupils free of charge in addition to the board, tuition, medical attendance, and books furnished to the academy pupils of the other nations.

During the year nine small boarding schools were established in the Choctaw Nation for the benefit of those children who resided in sparsely settled neighborhoods, remote from schools. These little boarding schools have proven to be quite popular among the Choctaw people, as they were the means of gathering in quite a good many full-blood children who never before attended schools of any kind. As shown by Supervisor Ballard's report, 257 children were enrolled in these small schools during the year.

since the ratification of the Atoka agreement, shall be paid without unnecessary delay by a disbursing officer, designated by the Secretary of the Interior, out of the Chickasaw coal and asphaltum royalty funds now in the hands of the United States, so far as the same will apply, and such school warrants as may hereafter be legally issued for such service or such material for school purposes, in accordance with such laws, shall in like manner be paid out of such fund as shall hereafter come into the hands of the United States, so far as the same will apply, annually, semiannually, or quarterly, as the Secretary of the Interior may determine best, so long as these regulations shall be observed by the Chickasaw Nation.

Washington, D. C., April 11, 1901.

Approved.

E. A. HITCHCOCK,
Secretary of the Interior.
D. H. JOHNSTON,
Governor Chickasaw Nation.

Under this agreement the following board of examiners was appointed: John D. Benedict, of Muskogee; E. B. Hinshaw, of Kemp; and George Bourland, of Ardmore.

Two grades of certificates are issued to the teachers of the Chickasaw Nation, although either grade is valid for but one year.

A first-grade certificate requires a general average of 80 per cent, with no branch below 65 per cent, in the following branches, viz: Orthography, reading, penmanship, arithmetic, grammar, geography, United States history, physiology, algebra, physics, botany, rhetoric, civil government, and theory and practice.

Applicants for second-grade certificates omit the last six branches above named, and are required to make a general average of 75 per cent, with no branch below 60 per cent.

Teachers in the Chickasaw boarding schools are employed by the contractors who manage such schools. Day school-teachers receive $45 per month in Chickasaw warrants, which warrants are not usually paid within a year from date of issue.

OUR SUMMER NORMALS.

The increased interest manifested by teachers in our summer normals augurs well for the future of these schools. During the month of June normals were in session for four weeks in the Creek, Cherokee, and Choctaw nations, and much good work was accomplished along the line of fitting teachers for better school work. Those in attendance evinced great interest in the work by continuous hard study and by close attention to the development of improved methods of teaching.

Forty-nine teachers were enrolled in the Creek normal, 167 in the Cherokee normal, and 165 in the Choctaw normal. Our former plan of bringing the teachers of each nation together at a boarding school, centrally located, and furnishing them board, room, and tuition for four weeks at the uniform charge of $12 each, was continued this year with increased success. This plan enables the teachers to become better acquainted with each other, and during intermissions much time is well spent in informally exchanging opinions upon the many vexed questions which confront them in their daily school work.

The great majority of our teachers have had no professional training, except such as we have been able to give them in these summer normals. Those who were really desirous of preparing themselves for better work were prompt in taking advantage of the opportunities for improvement offered through these summer normals, while those who were poorly fitted for teaching and manifested no interest in their work, no desire to qualify themselves for better teaching, have gradually dropped out of the profession.

By means of our examinations we have been able to weed out the sluggards, and the testimony of prominent educators who have visited our normals substantiates the statement that the teachers in our Indian schools are now equally as good as can be found in any of the Western States.

In the selection of teachers we have steadily adhered to the merit system, and teachers have finally learned that the permanency of their positions depends upon the amount of zeal and efficiency displayed by them in their school work.

One interesting feature of this year's normal work was the special lecture courses given by Prof. Joseph Carter and Mrs. Carter. Their practical talks upon manual training, nature study, agriculture, and domestic science were thoroughly appreciated by all who heard them and were very inspiring and helpful to our teachers.

In addition to the normals above mentioned separate summer schools were held at Tahlequah and Muskogee for the colored teachers of the Cherokee and Creek nations. Twenty-three negro teachers were enrolled at Tahlequah and 49 at Muskogee. Their summer terms were characterized by the same earnestness and zeal which pervaded the larger normals, where white and Indian teachers attended together.

Denominational schools, Indian Territory.

Name of school	Location	President or principal	By whom established	When established	Receipts — Church	Tuition	Other sources	Total	Expenditures — Teachers' salaries	Other expenses	Total
Dwight Mission	Marble	F. L. Schaub	Presbyterian Church	1835	$2,100.00	$116.00		$2,216.00	$1,300.00	$215.00	$1,515.00
Cherokee Academy	Tahlequah	W. J. Pack	American Baptist Home Mission Society	1886		600.00	$850.00	1,450.00	1,650.00	1,200.00	2,850.00
Friends' School	Hillside	Eva Watson	Orthodox Friends	1888							
Hargrove College	Ardmore	Thos. G. Whitten	Methodist Church	1895	1,000.00	385.12	1,300.45	2,685.57	862.50	1,750.00	2,612.50
Henry Kendall College	Muskogee	A. Grant Evans	Presbyterian Board Home Missions	1894	8,500.00	5,250.00		13,750.00	7,600.00	6,500.00	14,000.00
Nazareth Institute	do	Jos. Van Hulse	Sisters of St. Joseph	1891							
Spaulding Institute	do	Theo. F. Brewer	Methodist Episcopal Church South	1881		1,500.00	3,000.00	4,500.00	3,359.00	500.00	4,459.00
St. Joseph's	Chickasha	Sister Mary Cosma	Rev. Father Isadore	1900		581.35	718.35	1,299.70	480.00	372.40	852.40
Tahlequah Institute	Tahlequah	Chas. A. Peterson	Presbyterian Church	1888	2,800.44	2,228.43		5,028.87	3,600.00	1,428.87	5,028.87
Whitaker Orphan Home	Pryor Creek	W. T. Whitaker	W. T. Whitaker	1897	400.00		2,296.41	2,296.41	500.00	1,796.41	2,296.41
Willie Halsell College	Vinita	C. L. Browning	Methodist Episcopal Church South	1896		2,700.00		3,100.00	2,860.00		2,800.00
Indian University	Bacone	J. H. Scott	Baptist Church		518.94	595.70	5,525.86	6,640.40	5,800.00	840.40	6,640.40
Total					15,319.28	13,906.60	13,681.07	42,906.95	28,451.50	14,593.08	43,044.58

Name of school	Teachers — Male	Female	Number months school	Value of buildings and grounds	Enrollment — Whites M	Whites F	Indians M	Indians F	Total M	Total F	Average attendance — Whites M	Whites F	Indians M	Indians F	Total M	Total F
Dwight Mission	1	3	8	$6,000	24	21	23	14	47	35						
Cherokee Academy	2	3	9	4,000	53	45	55	34	108	79					46	35
Friends' School		3	9	6,000	35	36	26	31	61	67					29	35
Hargrove College	3	5	9	30,000	78	66										
Henry Kendall College	5	10	9	50,000	42	53	24	23	102	89	15	16	14	19		
Nazareth Institute		5	9	7,000	85	82	33	52	71	134	58	43	20	21	78	65
Spaulding Institute		3	8	50,000	74	79	8	6	118	44	40	45	25	17	66	62
St. Joseph's	2	8	9	5,000	26	32			82	91						
Tahlequah Institute	1	6	10	7,000	38	30	56	59	86	90	20	24	39	42	59	60
Whitaker Orphan Home		2	9	10,000	80	74			80	74	30	25			30	60
Willie Halsell College	3	8	9	50,000	44	49	28	20	76	69	60	60	28		60	60
Indian University	3	2	9	35,000												
Total	21	55	107½	260,000	581	577	282	256	863	835						

Indian schools.

Schools.	Enrollment.	Average attendance.	Months of school.	Annual cost.	Average cost per pupil.	Number of employees.
CHEROKEE SCHOOLS.						
Male seminary	239	154	9	$16,890.00	$109.32	9
Female seminary	263	179	9	19,180.00	107.15	12
Orphan academy	180	150	9	20,402.00	136.01	11
Colored high school	62	41.6	9	4,377.00	105.22	4
140 day schools	4,639	2,728	7	37,205.00	a 1.95	140
Total	5,383	3,252.6		98,054.00		176
CREEK SCHOOLS.						
Eufaula	112	70	8½	7,879.09	112.55	11
Creek Orphan Home	67	60	8½	6,397.59	106.62	9
Euchee	143	65.3	8½	6,219.44	95.68	9
Wetumka	156	90	8½	8,509.21	94.54	12
Coweta	67	41	8½	4,005.39	97.69	8
Wealaka	64	45	8½	4,520.67	100.45	8
Nuyaka	97	81	8½	5,200.00	69.13	10
Tullahassee (colored)	116	71	8½	8,430.78	118.74	8
Pecan Creek (colored)	65	42	8½	3,972.47	92.37	5
Orphan home (colored)	45	31.8	8½	3,498.37	112.85	4
52 day schools	1,822	744	8½	13,469.25	a 2.12	52
Total	2,754	1,341.1		72,102.26		136
CHOCTAW SCHOOLS.						
Armstrong Academy	111	97.85	9	15,501.39	156.28	11
Wheelock Academy	94	79.41	9	12,063.64	150.53	10
Tushkahoma Academy	125	110	9	15,086.27	138.03	12
Jones Academy	123	103.11	9	15,154.09	146.00	12
Atoka Baptist Academy	56	49.4	9	6,125.45	124.00	10
190 day schools	3,074	2,082	9	38,843.18	a 2.12	190
Small boarding schools	257	205	5	7,015.13	34.22	12
Choctaw tuition pupils in Chickasaw Nation	948			3,706.50		
Total	4,788			113,485.65		
CHICKASAW SCHOOLS.						
Orphans' home	67	56	10	8,779.41	175.59	8
Bloomfield Seminary	109	90	10	14,479.75	160.88	6
Collins Institute	40	37	5	5,920.00	160.00	8
Harley Institute	110	78.5	10	9,900.00	126.11	9
16 day schools	613		9	45,178.69		19
Total	939			84,257.85		50

a Per month.

Chickasaw day schools.

Teacher.	School.	Post-office address.	Race.	Salary.	Amount received.	Enrollment. M.	Enrollment. F.	Expenses.	Days attendance.
W. E. Finley	Kaney	Brownville	White	$45.00	$427.50	13	9	$1,616.97	4,798
E. W. Thompson	McMillan	McMillan	do	45.00	427.50	15	13	1,568.00	4,825
W. O. Harris	Sulphur	Guy	do	65.00	650.00	42	54	5,829.00	18,993
Thenia Jennings a	do	do	Indian	35.00	350.00				
Fannie Hooper	Red Springs	Conway	White	45.00	337.50	21	14	3,173.00	7,327
W. H. Allison a	do	do	do	45.00	90.00				1,947
Annie McCarty	Sulphur Sp'gs	Ada	Indian	45.00	450.00	22	16	3,308.63	9,727
Lulu Bynum	Emet	Emet	do	45.00	427.50	19	24	2,803.61	8,044
Mrs. Berta Manley	Seeley	Connorville	do	45.00	427.50	28	10	3,254.93	6,951
Geo. H. Priest	Yellow Sp'gs	Jesse	White	45.00	427.50	25	11	3,584.64	10,677
C. J. Moore	Roff	Roff	do	75.00	750.00	39	32	5,147.30	15,288
Fannie Reynolds a	do	do	do	40.00	100.00				
Brownie Davis	Burris	Tishomingo	do	45.00	427.50	16	5	1,262.87	3,722
Nell Hudnall	Davis	Davis	do	45.00	427.50	16	20	2,779.94	8,239
Lottie McCarty	Colbert	Franks	Indian	45.00	427.50	22	13	3,009.97	8,452
Mary Goforth	Sandy Creek	Wiley	do	45.00	427.50	19	18	3,068.58	9,970
Loula Kemp	Double Sp'gs	Mead	do	45.00	427.50	16	10	2,193.98	6,516
Mamie Burris	Lewis Reel	Reagaw	do	45.00	337.50	13	16	1,377.27	3,461
Jas. O. Modbette	Kemp	Kemp	White	45.00	427.50	10	12	1,200.00	2,500
Total					7,767.50	336	277	45,178.69	131,437

a Assistant teachers.

I am under renewed obligations to your Department, sir, for the interest manifested in our work, and for your hearty support in all matters with which we have had to deal.

It is with pleasure, also, that I acknowledge our indebtedness to the Hon. J. George Wright, United States Indian inspector, for his patient and timely assistance and advice upon all matters of importance connected with our work.

Respectfully submitted.

JOHN D. BENEDICT,
Superintendent of Schools in Indian Territory.

The COMMISSIONER OF INDIAN AFFAIRS.

REPORT OF THE CREEK SCHOOL SUPERVISOR.

OFFICE OF SCHOOL SUPERVISOR FOR CREEK NATION,
Muskogee, Ind. T., July 15, 1902.

SIR: The fourth annual report of the supervisor of Creek schools is herewith submitted.

The duties of this office are outlined in the following extract from the Creek treaty:

The Creek school fund shall be used, under direction of the Secretary of the Interior, for the education of Creek citizens, and the Creek schools shall be conducted under rules and regulations prescribed by him, under direct supervision of the Creek school superintendent and a supervisor appointed by the Secretary, and under Creek laws, subject to such modifications as the Secretary of the Interior may deem necessary to make the schools most effective and to produce the best possible results.

All teachers shall be examined by or under direction of said superintendent and supervisor, and competent teachers and other persons to be engaged in and about the schools with good moral character only shall be employed, but where all qualifications are equal preference shall be given to citizens in such employment.

All moneys for running the schools shall be appropriated by the Creek national council, not exceeding the amount of the Creek school fund, seventy-six thousand four hundred and sixty-eight dollars and forty cents; but if it fail or refuse to make the necessary appropriations the Secretary of the Interior may direct the use of a sufficient amount of the school funds to pay all expenses necessary to the efficient conduct of the schools, strict account thereof to be rendered to him and to the principal chief.

All accounts for expenditures in running the schools shall be examined and approved by said superintendent and supervisor, and also by the general superintendent of schools in Indian Territory, before payment thereof is made.

If the superintendent and supervisor shall fail to agree upon any matter under their direction or control, it shall be decided by said general superintendent, subject to appeal to the Secretary of the Interior, but his decision shall govern until reversed by the Secretary.

The school law of the Creek Nation to which reference is made above is as follows:

That there be and is hereby created the office of superintendent of public instruction, who shall be elected by the national council at its regular session, and who shall hold this office for a term of two years. He shall be installed in the same manner as other executive officers, and until such installation he shall not be competent to perform the functions of his office. He shall have his office in the national capitol building and shall be present at the sessions of the national teachers' institute. He shall be subject to laws regarding impeachment. He shall have authority to adopt rules and regulations not inconsistent with the laws of the Muskogee Nation for the government of schools established and maintained by the nation; to authenticate his actions by the use of a seal; to make requisition on the executive department for funds necessary to the support of the school; to prescribe and enforce a course of study in the several schools and furnish a series of text-books, one of which shall be the Bible; to prescribe and enforce rules for the examination of teachers and for the admission of pupils to the national boarding schools and such other high schools as may hereafter be established; to appoint teachers for the primary schools and superintendents for the boarding and high schools, but the superintendents so appointed shall select and employ their own teachers; he shall examine applicants for the position of teachers and grant certificates according to qualifications; to revoke for immorality, incompetence, or intemperance all certificates of whatsoever grade; to remove or discontinue any primary school which does not maintain a daily average of thirteen pupils during the winter months, and fifteen during the summer months.

The superintendent of public instruction shall appoint to each school three respectable citizens as a board of trustees, who shall hold their office during their good behavior, but shall not be entitled to any compensation. The superintendent of public instruction shall have complete control and supervision of all the school and educational interests of the nation at large, subject to such direction as may be imposed by law. The superintendent of public instruction shall keep a correct record of all his transactions in a suitable book, which shall be open to anyone for inspection; he shall report to the principal chief on or before the 15th day of September of each year a statement of the condition of the schools of the Muskogee Nation, accompanying his report with a tabular statement showing the number of schools in operation, number of children attending the same, the amount of unexpended appropriation, if any; make estimates of funds required for support of schools the coming year, that the council may have information upon which to base an appropriation; furnish blanks necessary to enable teachers and trustees to make their reports; to purchase the text-books and distribute the same upon requisition of teachers. When a neighborhood shall make application to the superintendent he shall grant permission for the establishment of a school, provided there are not less than 15 pupils, and if a suitable school building with necessary fixtures be provided within six weeks after such permission is given he shall assign a teacher to the same. The superintendent shall report at the close of each scholastic term to the principal chief the condition and progress of each school under his supervision, together with such suggestions and recommendations as he believes will improve the schools, which report or transcript thereof shall be furnished annually to the national council of the Muskogee Nation within three days after the meeting of the regular session thereof.

The superintendent of public instruction shall receive an annual salary of $800 and shall execute a bond of $2,000 for a faithful performance of the duties of his office.

Approved, November 5, 1896.

From the act above given it will be seen that the power of the Creek superintendent of public instruction was very great, and as the position had been one controlled entirely by political interest it will be readily inferred how much of reform had become necessary in Creek school matters. The kindly tact of my predecessor and my own great affection for the people among whom almost my whole life has been passed have not entirely averted friction in the bringing about of required changes. It is to the credit of the Creek people that when they have understood the advantages of changes they have accepted them in the spirit in which they were made.

The Creek council, at its regular session, passed the customary appropriations for boarding schools, amounting in the aggregate to $63,300, thus leaving the balance, which they appropriated for the neighborhood schools, of only $13,148.40, as against $25,000 appropriated the preceding year before the treaty became effective. I have, therefore, to report a decrease in the number of neighborhood schools. The total number last year was 65, with a total enrollment of 2,070 pupils. This year the total number of schools has been 56, with an enrollment of 1,822 pupils, the decrease of 14 per cent in the number of schools showing a corresponding decrease of 12 per cent in the number of pupils enrolled. This decrease is confined to Indian attendance. The colored schools were the same this year as last, and the enrollment in these schools for the negroes was practically unchanged from last year.

Like the preceding year, the past has been marked by conditions unfavorable to the schools. While smallpox has been less prevalent, few neighborhoods have entirely escaped it. In one of my visitations the mother of a large family met me at the gate with complaints that the neighbors "fussed so" she had been compelled to keep her children out of school until they should recover from "the bumps," though a part of them felt so well they wanted to go to school just the same. "The bumps" being a local name for smallpox, I did not go farther than the gate, although from frequent exposure I have lost fear of the disease. Scarlet fever, measles, and mumps have all been epidemic in certain localities, and cases of pneumonia have been frequent and fatal.

The greatest suffering of the people has been, however, from the terrible drought of last summer, with the consequent failure of all crops but cotton. Many Indians, instead of being able to hire help to pick their cotton, were compelled to keep their children out of school for this work. In the spring the same need led to keeping the children out to help in planting. In many cases parents, because of scant food supply and consequent lack of means to purchase both food and clothing, were unable to send their children to school. This failure of crops has been a terrible setback to the people. While they have struggled through without any outside aid and have thus escaped the baneful after effects of temporary pauperism, they have undergone many privations. In visiting their homes, very seldom did I find the "ohl kus wah" beside the fireplace with its ever ready food and drink, the "sofkey," though the most prized of all Creek native food, a sort of soup made from pounded corn. The great wooden mortars in which the corn is beaten for this dish stood idly inverted. The trim little log smokehouses, usually so carefully locked to keep safe the family supply of home-cured bacon, stood almost invariably open this year, showing bare salting benches and empty racks. Usually a little flour was most of the food supply of the family. Yet the people kept up their courage and were as kindly as ever. In one place I shared the family dinner of bread and greens, to which I was welcomed with such unaffected cordiality that I could not but think of the proverb of King Solomon about the "dinner of herbs where love is." Most serious financially was the loss for lack of food of horses, hogs, and poultry. Often near the roadside I saw lying gaunt carcasses of starved horses, so thin that even the buzzards left them untouched. Hardier cattle managed to "rustle" through. In previous famine years wild game afforded much subsistence to the people. White people have practically destroyed this food supply. Where a few years ago herds of deer were numerous and prairie chickens flocked in thousands, not even a hoofmark in the clay nor a stray feather fluttering in the wind is now seen.

As in the storied days of Hiawatha, so too to these people with the famine came "the cold and cruel winter," a winter of very unusual severity, for which the people were ill prepared. More than once the deep drifted snow, so unusual in our southern latitude, practically suspended the whole system of neighborhood schools. This spring and summer there has been a greater demand than ever for Indian Territory pasturage for Texas cattle starved out there by continued drought. Thousands of allotments have been leased for pasture and a number of schoolhouses have been entirely inclosed. One school was necessarily closed after it was found unsafe for the children to attempt crossing the pasture. At other schools the attendance suffered much this spring from the same cause.

In some cases objection to the teacher has hurt the attendance. One neighborhood was dissatisfied with their teacher because he did not go to church. One teacher who had done fairly good work for several years married a full-blood girl for the sake of her quarter section of land. The courtship in this case was through an interpreter, as neither could speak the language of the other. She soon became dissatisfied and returned to her people. An attempt on his part to bring her back with a drawn revolver infuriated the neighborhood, and the trustees sent for me. After hearing both sides, the teacher not attempting to deny the use of the revolver "to scare her," I suggested his immediate resignation. Shortly after, it developed that he was the leader of a band of horse thieves—men who were thought to be industrious renters of Indian lands, but who added to their incomes by robbing their neighbors. This case has been the one exception of entire unworthiness.

The greatest obstacle to successful work in our neighborhood schools is the presence of a preponderant population of illiterate whites. While the Indian day schools have all been open to this class of people upon the payment of $1 a month tuition, their enrollment for the past year has been only 404, with an average attendance of 142. A majority of this small number would not pay the tuition, and when told, after repeated failures, that they must pay, left school and tried to injure the teacher in the community. The example of the dominant race in its neglect of schools is far stronger than can be the precept of the teacher. Of all the wrongs, real or imaginary, which the Indians have suffered at the hands of the white man, none can compare with this insidious undermining of what was good in their tribal existence by the presence of this mass of ignorant and too often vicious and criminal people. Good people are not usually willing to stay where there is so little opportunity for the education of their children.

I have been pleased to note attempts at improvement of school property in a number of neighborhoods. The Okfuskey school, reported last year as the worst building in the nation, now has a good floor and a glass window. The miserable box house at Carrs Creek having been destroyed by fire from the stovepipe, which went up through a hole in the chimneyless roof, has been replaced by a large frame building.

The surveying, setting apart, and properly marking, by the Dawes Commission, of the acre stipulated by treaty for each school has been a helpful step. The implied permanence of the school building will encourage its protection and improvement. This work was admirably done, the surveyors in charge using especial care to place each acre to the best advantage for school purposes.

With the rapid progress of allotment of Creek lands has come the change of home and the scattering out of many people who were closely grouped. This shifting of population will require some readjustment of school districts. New towns springing up with the projection and construction of new railroads are also causing changes in the homes of the people. The entire surface of the country seems undergoing a change. One prairie, where two years ago I drove for nearly 15 miles without passing a house, I found this spring with newly made farms almost touching each other for the entire distance, most of them being occupied by white renters.

A large number of noncitizen negroes are also coming into the Creek Nation. The statements as to illiterate whites from outside largely apply also to this outside negro population.

Statistics of boarding schools show a marked increase in attendance. It is to be regretted that this attendance is so irregular. The enrollment at the Indian boarding schools was 707, as against 602 last year. This is an excess of 35 per cent above the legal number of pupils, but the average attendance was only 448, or about 14 per cent less than the prescribed number. In the colored boarding schools, with an authorized number of 185, there has been an enrollment of 226 and an average of 144, an enrollment of 22 per cent more and an average of 23 per cent less than is authorized.

Among the negroes have been some crude attempts at educational institutions growing out of ill-advised individual ambition. Some months ago, having seen earnest appeals in different newspapers in this section of country for help for an Indian industrial school, I went to visit it, being the more desirous of seeing it because that very community had refused the previous year to allow the establishment of a national school. I found the school to be the private enterprise of a comparatively ignorant, "state-raised" negro, whose industrial plan was raising cotton by child labor on Indian land. His students present, with the exception of three Indian day pupils, were all negroes, although he informed me that some white children attended the school. He made a speech to his pupils telling them that he

would ask me to talk to them because I was a visitor, but saying that neither I nor any other Government person had anything to do with their school. They wanted neither aid nor supervision, because in the schools under Government control there was a division of the races, and as God had made all people alike they ought all to go to school together. I desired to see the boarding department of the school, but was not allowed to do so. I was convinced that there was no opportunity for observing any rules of decency in the wretched building I did not go into.

A severe blow to any enlargement of farm training or of greater efforts toward at least partial self-support of the boarding schools has been that provision of the Creek treaty which cuts down the land allowed to each school to 40 acres.

EUFAULA BOARDING SCHOOL.

This school is commandingly situated on a picturesque eminence just within the corporation line of the town of Eufaula. Outcropping rocks render it unfit for agriculture, and so only 5 acres are reserved here, the remaining 35 being a small portion of the large and productive farm 3 miles away, once the property of the school, but taken from it by the treaty.

In other years about one-half the school was in the primary department, which was this year done away with, it having been determined to make this school of a higher grade than the others. A white superintendent having been placed in charge, disappointed applicants for the position of superintendent were unsparing in efforts to break the school up. Under these circumstances an average attendance of 70 per cent was quite as good as could have been anticipated. The gain in quality of work done was very marked. A baseball team at this school has distinguished itself by fine playing, vanquishing all opposing teams and making such fame for itself that nearly all the members were offered paying positions for the summer.

I regret to lose from this school Mr. Frank Shortall, who has been a most faithful and efficient principal, but leaves us for a wider sphere of labor elsewhere.

WETUMKA.

This school has probably never had a more successful year. At the same time that the attendance has been greatly increased the cost of the school has been diminished. Careful attention to out of school work has been given here to both boys and girls. This spring individual garden plots were given the students and prizes offered to those who should be most successful. This experiment was a very great success, arousing much interest and pride on the part of the young farmers.

EUCHEE.

The high personal regard I feel for the estimable Creek citizen who is superintendent of this school makes me regret exceedingly that I can not speak in higher commendation of the work of the school. No perceptible advance has been made here except in economy of management. Lack of water supply is a very great drawback, and there have been other peculiar and annoying difficulties.

NUYAKA.

This school is conducted under the auspices of the Presbyterian Board of Home Missions in accordance with the terms of a contract by which the Creek Nation pays annually $70 each for 80 pupils, it being understood that this payment covers only expenses for subsistence, etc., the board of home missions employing and paying the superintendent and teachers. This school is on the cottage plan, its 80 pupils being in three separate homes, each with its distinctive family life, but all attending school together, and details of students for outdoor work coming from the different homes. While this system is much more expensive the possibilities for development of the individual are so much greater as to justify it. The school farm, garden, and orchard are in excellent condition. A fine poultry yard is a means of practical and valuable instruction. The school has a good milk and butter supply, though dairying is not taught as I should like to see it taught. In the girls' cottages I was shown some exquisite embroidery and lace work which was being taught. Having expressed a preference for more practical plain sewing and mending, various girls with evident pride showed me the garments they were wearing which they had made and laundered themselves. From the sewing closets large baskets were brought out that I might see the partly finished week's mending. The patching and darning were all that I could ask in careful neatness. One great advantage at thi school is the contented spirit of the students and the consequent fewer changes. More stress is laid upon use of the English language here, where all employees are white, than we have been able to secure in the other boarding schools.

WEALAKA.

This school has kept a higher average the past year and made good progress. An especially interesting industrial feature had been inaugurated here, that of nursery work in the planting, grafting, and budding of young fruit trees. The departure of Mr. George C. Kindley, the efficient principal teacher by whom this work was undertaken, practically ended it. Mr. Kindley is now in school work in the Philippines.

COWETA.

Good progress has been made at this school. The superintendent is the grandson of the first constitutional chief of the Creek Nation and his parents were educated in mission schools. He himself completed his mission-school training by three years at Carlisle and some time spent there on the outing system. He is one who says "come" to the school boys and he has the place in fine condition.

CREEK ORPHAN HOME.

The record of this school has been very creditable to its young Indian superintendent. Orphan children are sent here more to find a home than to go to school, and are younger and more dependent than in other schools. Some attention should be paid to the property rights of these orphans and their allotments of land be so managed that some values might accrue to them and not be absorbed entirely by selfish kins people or unauthorized guardians. Unless something of this sort is done additional appropriation should be made for this school to purchase clothing for the children and to cover the additional expense of maintaining a home for them during the summer months when the other schools are closed.

TULLAHASSEE.

I regret that this school has not made as good a record this year as last. The attendance is far below what it should be, and the general neatness and order have not been so good as last year.

PECAN CREEK.

This school has been excellently managed. Order, cleanliness, and economy have been ruling characteristics.

I deeply regret the death of the principal teacher, William Rutherford Pamplin, a young man whose fine ability and scholarship, exemplary character, and high purpose all promised a brilliant future.

COLORED ORPHAN HOME.

This school has labored under great difficulty because of lack of a boys' dormitory, the one which was destroyed by fire last year not having been replaced. The school has been much fuller than for years past. What has been said as to the property rights of Creek orphan children would apply here also.

A severe blow to this school was the sudden death from heart failure of the efficient matron, Mrs. Maggie Sango.

As in preceding years, two summer normal schools were held, one at Eufaula for white and Indian, and the other at Muscogee for colored teachers. At Eufaula 51 teachers were in attendance, and 93 per cent of those who took the examinations made a passing grade. At Muscogee 41 were examined, 87 per cent passing. As showing the origin of these teachers it may be interesting to note their birthplaces. At Eufaula there were from Indian Territory, 11; Missouri, 10; Arkansas, 8; Illinois, 4; Kansas, Tennessee, Kentucky, Georgia, and Texas, each 2, and Virginia, South Dakota, Alabama, Oregon, and France, each 1. Two were Americans born in Turkey of missionary parents. At Muscogee there were from Texas, 10; Mississippi and Indian Territory, each 5; Arkansas, 4; Tennessee, 3; Kentucky, Louisiana, and Kansas, each 2, and North Carolina, Missouri, Ohio, New York, Maryland, District of Columbia, South Carolina, and Alabama, each 1.

A comparison of the numbers given this year with those of last will show a decreased attendance, but a larger percentage of those who passed the examinations.

Report of Indian Inspector for the Indian Territory, 1902.

NUYAKA MISSION SCHOOL CREEK NATION.

It will also be noticed that the attendance from Indian Territory is much smaller. As it becomes generally understood that there is neither fear nor favor shown in these examinations, poorer teachers have dropped out and given up the effort. While it is a matter of sincere regret to me that so few Creek citizens are able to pass the examinations for teachers, nothing else could be expected. An incontrovertible proof of past deficiencies in educational work is the fact that a number of those who held the highest positions in the boarding schools have dropped entirely out because they could not obtain even third-grade certificates. What could be expected of pupils trained by such teachers? At first there was a disposition to question the fairness of examinations, but as all examination papers were retained the correctness of grades given was easily demonstrated and the eyes of the unbelieving were opened. One member of the Creek council whose very worthy young daughter, educated in the national schools, failed utterly on examination told me that the teachers they had had should be serving terms in the penitentiary for the wrong they had done the people through their incompetence. It has been encouraging to see with how little friction the improvement in grade of teachers has been progressing.

In the Creek Nation the number of teachers required is so much smaller than in the others that the financial question becomes a serious one. Normal instructors are paid from the tuition collected, and as the same amount of tuition is charged in the different nations, it will be seen that the others have a decided advantage pecuniarily. A generous gift from Mrs. William Thaw, of Pittsburg, Pa., enabled us to have a full corps of teachers, without which our very successful work would have been quite incomplete. To teach primary methods with non-English-speaking pupils a class of full-blood children was brought from their homes in the country. The presence of Mr. and Mrs. Carter was most helpful and inspiring. The work as outlined by them was a revelation to many of our teachers and will be of inestimable value to them in helping them to do more than simply follow the trite routine of the printed page. With the quick memories of Indian children very frequently pupils know every lesson in a reader before they have studied it, simply from hearing the recitations of other classes. To no class of children can nature study appeal more strongly or by judicious and interested teachers be more helpfully taught than to Indian pupils. Much more attention was paid to teaching reading than in previous normals. This was done because of the stress you have laid upon the importance of better work in this direction than we have had in our schools.

A series of evening entertainments was a pleasant feature of the Eufaula normal. Music, recitations, and informal lectures on American, European, and oriental travel were agreeably instructive and restful. A visit and excellent talk from the principal chief of the Creek Nation was also very helpful. Nor would I fail to allude to the inspiration in the presence and suggestions of Supervisor Beck and yourself.

The heavy cost of provisions this year making it impossible to find anyone willing to assume the financial responsibility of the boarding department of the Eufaula normal I was forced to take it myself. While this was something of a burden, I am not sorry to have had this care of purchasing supplies and planning and ordering meals, etc., for it has given me an actual experience as to what may be done in our boarding schools that will quite repay the additional labor.

The past year, in the performance of duty in this nation, I have spent one hundred and seventy-eight days in the field, and have traveled by team 2,722 miles and by rail 4,456 miles, in all 7,178 miles. The expenses of my office have been as follows:

Salary and per diem	$1,856.00
Traveling expenses	453.40
Office expenses	90.60
Total	2,400.00

The severe weather of the winter prevented my doing as much school visiting as I should otherwise have done, because it was not just to the schools to visit them on days when it was impossible for the children to get there. Most of the children in the neighborhood schools have long distances to go to school and could not get there through the severe storms of last winter. Through April and May heavy rains raised the streams so that I often found them impassable. Sometimes I sat on the bank and waited for a creek to run down; sometimes I got very wet in the deep water; only once did I get into water that was swimming. The most annoying difficulty in visiting schools is the constant changing of roads consequent upon the taking of allotments. I have had to open and shut as many as 30 pasture gates in one day's driving.

In my visitation of neighborhood schools the past year I was glad to find much greater faithfulness on the part of teachers. They were much more careful to begin on time and not to close before time than last year.

Not nearly so many complaints of teachers have come to me from patrons of these neighborhood schools, and on the other hand the work of the teachers has been far more frequently commended. It is a great pleasure to me to see that the people seem to have greater confidence that the intention of the Government in directing the management of their schools is to make them better, and I am therefore much more hopeful of the success of the work for the coming year.

The Creek superintendent, Mr. Gregory, and myself have worked together quite pleasantly the past year. There has been far less of friction in all directions than last year.

The greatest gain of the year has been in the financial management of the boarding schools. A comparison of this year's reports with those of last year will show that with the enormous increase in the price of provisions and with an increased attendance of students the average cost is less than last year. I hope for much better results the coming year with the promise of abundant crops and cheaper food.

Thanking you for ever-helpful counsel in every difficulty and perplexity with which I have gone to you, and with a full realization of the fact that to you more than to myself is due largely any success of the work of Creek schools during the past year, the preceding report is respectfully submitted.

ALICE M. ROBERTSON, *Supervisor.*

Hon. JOHN D. BENEDICT,
  Superintendent of Schools in Indian Territory.

School statistics, Creek Nation.

EUFAULA.

Name of employee.	Position.	Race.	Age.	Salary per month.	Amount received.	Months employed.
William H. Lester	Superintendent	White	65	$50.00	$500.00	10
Frank Shortall	Principal teacher	do	24	65.00	552.50	8½
Anna M. Peterson	Assistant teacher	do	26	50.00	425.00	8½
Elizabeth A. Scott	do	do	23	45.00	382.50	8½
Sallie Maxey	do	do	21	45.00	382.50	8½
Celia Lester	Matron	do	55	30.00	255.00	8½
C. M. Perryman	do	Indian	36	30.00	232.50	7½
Alice H. Palmer	do	White	27	30.00	54.00	1¾
Sarah Foster	Cook	Negro	30	25.00	212.50	9½
Saladin Lafavor	Laborer	Indian	26	25.00	162.50	6½
H. McIntosh	do	do	20	25.00	50.00	2
Hepsy McIntosh	Laundress	do	60	20.00	170.00	8½

Number enrolled:

Males 53
Females 59

    Total 112

Average attendance 70
Total salaries paid $3,379.00
Total other expenses $4,500.09
Annual cost per pupil $112.55
Cost per pupil per month $13.24

WETUMKA.

Name of employee.	Position.	Race.	Age.	Salary per month.	Amount received.	Months employed.
James P. Atkins	Superintendent	White	27	$50.00	$500.00	10
C. G. Goodwin	Principal teacher	do	25	55.00	467.50	8½
Anna Belle Wright	Assistant teacher	do	28	45.00	382.50	8½
F. Gladys Bridges	do	do	22	45.00	382.50	8½
Susanne Barnett	do	Indian	21	45.00	157.50	3½
Lucy H. Smith	do	White	21	45.00	204.00	4½
Belle M. Atkins	Matron	Indian	21	30.00	255.00	8½
Jennie Duncan	do	White	35	30.00	255.00	8½
O. Ogletree	Cook	do	30	35.00	280.00	8
A. J. Stice	Laundress	do	40	20.00	170.00	8½
Douglass Collins	Laborer	Indian	21	20.00	180.00	9
Charles March	do	White	23	20.00	180.00	9

Number enrolled:

Males 86
Females 70

Total 156

Average attendance 90
Total salaries paid $3,414.00
Total other expenses $5,095.21
Annual cost per pupil $94.54
Cost per pupil per month $11.12

EUCHEE.

Name of employee.	Position.	Race.	Age.	Salary per month.	Amount received.	Months employed.
Wm. A. Sapulpa..........	Superintendent	Indian	42	$50 00	$600.00	12
Harry H. Bell.............	Principal teacher.....	White	22	55.00	467.50	8½
Dannie Ross.............	Assistant teacher.....	Indian	29	45.00	382.50	8½
Susanna Grimes..........	.....do	....do	30	40.00	340.00	8½
Susie J. B. Sapulpa.....	Matron	...do	30	25.00	212.50	8½
Tooka S. Ross	...do	...do	26	25.00	212.50	8½
....	Cook			20.00	180.00	9
....	Laundress			20.00	180.00	9
....	Laborer			20.00	180.00	9

Number enrolled:

Males 72
Females 71

Total... 143

Average attendance 65½
Total salaries paid $2,785.00
Total other expenses $3,434.44
Annual cost per pupil $95.68
Cost per pupil per month $11.25

CREEK ORPHAN HOME.

Name of employee.	Position.	Race.	Age.	Salary per month.	Amount received.	Months employed.
Johnson E. Tiger	Superintendent	Indian	26	$50.00	$600.00	12
Bruce McKinley	Principal teacher	White	27	50.00	425.00	8½
Mabel Hall	Assistant teacher....	....do	28	45.00	382.50	8½
Lena B. Tiger............	Matron	Indian	27	30.00	360.00	12
Ida B. Holcomb	...do	White	34	30.00	240.00	8
Lillie Benson	...do	Indian	24	30.00	15.00	½
Mollie Jefferson	Seamstress	White	32	30.00	240.00	8
Mollie Robinson	Cook	Negro	50	25.00	237.50	9½
M. Checote	Laundress..........	Indian	30	16.00	144.00	9
....	2 laborers..........	....do		40.00	360.00	9

Number enrolled:

Males 35
Females 32

Total... 67

Average attendance 60
Total salaries paid $3,004.00
Total other expenses $3,393.59
Annual cost per pupil $106.62
Cost per pupil per month $11.23

COWETA.

Name of employee.	Position.	Race.	Age.	Salary per month.	Amount received.	Months employed.
Samuel J. Checote	Superintendent	Indian	35	$11.66	$458.34	11
John R. Price.............	Principal teacher	White	24	50.00	425.00	8½
Lucile Byrd..............	Assistant teacher....	Indian	20	45.00	382.50	8½
Annie Checote	Matron	....do	30	25.00	212.50	8½
S. W. Dorsey	...do	White	38	25.00	112.50	4½
Amanda Davis............	...do	...do	30	25.00	50.00	2
Alma W. Allen	Laundress	...do	40	16.00	144.00	9
Fannie J. Haynie.........	Cook	...do	35	20.00	170.00	8½
Martin Kanard	Laborer	Indian	21	20.00	170.00	8½

Number enrolled:
Males 3
Females 34

Total 6

Average attendance 4
Total salaries paid $2,124.84
Total other expenses $1,880.55
Annual cost per pupil $97.48
Cost per pupil per month $11.50

WEALAKA.

Name of employee.	Position.	Race.	Age.	Salary per month.	Amount received.	Months employed.
Henry M. Harjo	Superintendent	Indian	35	$41.66	$458.34	11
Geo. C. Kindley	Principal teacher	White	36	50.00	175.00	7½
W. D. Atkins	....do	....do	30	50.00	250.00	5
Lillian Lee	Assistant teacher	....do	26	45.00	382.50	8½
Katie M. Harjo	Matron	Indian	25	25.00	212.50	8½
Emma Kindley	....do	White	24	25.00	212.50	8½
Zare Jackson	Cook	....do	50	20.00	170.00	8½
Mrs. Z. Jackson	Laundress	....do	45	16.00	136.00	8½
Albert Stake	Laborer	Indian	25	20.00	200.00	10

Number enrolled:
Males 33
Females 31

Total 64

Average attendance... 45
Total salaries paid.. $2,196.84
Total other expenses... 2,323.83
Annual cost per pupil.. 100.45
Cost per pupil per month... 11.81

TULLAHASSEE (COLORED).

Name of employee.	Position.	Race.	Age.	Salary per month.	Amount received.	Months employed.
Philip A. Lewis	Superintendent	Negro	35	$50.00	$600.00	12
S. B. Gilliam	Principal teacher	....do	50	60.00	510.00	8½
J. D. Knox	Assistant teacher	....do	40	45.00	382.50	8½
Hattie Davidson	....do	....do	40	40.00	340.00	8½
Celia Roberts Mike	....do	....do	28	40.00	340.00	8½
Elzora F. Lewis	Matron	....do	31	30.00	255.00	8½
Ellen Marshall	Cook	....do	21	25.00	212.50	8½
....	2 laborers.	....do	....	20.00	360.00	9

Number enrolled:
Males.. 51
Females.. 65

Total 116

Average attendance 71
Total salaries paid.. $3,100.00
Total other expenses... 5,330.73
Annual cost per pupil.. 118.74
Cost per pupil per month... 14.20

PECAN CREEK (COLORED).

Name of employee.	Position.	Race.	Age.	Salary per month.	Amount received.	Months employed.
J. P. Davidson	Superintendent	Negro	50	$41.66	$500.00	12
W. R. Pamplin	Principal teacher	....do	22	50.00	285.00	6½
M. L. Craw	Assistant teacher	....do	27	40.00	140.00	3½
M. L. Craw	Teacher	....do	27	50.00	250.00	5
Mrs. J. P. Davidson	Matron	....do	49	30.00	255.00	8½
Emma Island	Cook	....do	35	20.00	180.00	9

Number enrolled:
```
    Males ...................................................................  32
    Females..................................................................  33
    Total....................................................................  65
```

```
Average attendance ..........................................................  42
Total salaries paid..........................................................  $1,610.00
Total other expenses.........................................................  2,362.47
Annual cost per pupil .......................................................  92.87
Cost per pupil per month ....................................................  10.80
```

COLORED ORPHAN HOME.

Name of employee.	Position.	Race.	Age.	Salary per month.	Amount received.	Months employed.
A. G. W. Sango.............	Superintendent	Negro	35	$41.66	$500.00	12
Mattie G. Key	Teacher	...do	28	40.00	340.00	8¼
Maggie Sango.............	Matron	...do	25	25.00	137.50	5¼
Nellie McGee	.....do	...do	40	25.00	75.00	3
Cynthia Tolliver..........	Cook	...do	45	15.00	145.00	9

Number enrolled:
```
    Males ...................................................................  19
    Females..................................................................  26
    Total....................................................................  45
```

```
Average attendance ..........................................................  31¼
Total salaries paid .........................................................  $1,197.50
Total other expenses.........................................................  2,300.87
Annual cost per pupil .......................................................  112.85
Cost per pupil per month ....................................................  13.15
```

NUYAKA.

Number enrolled:
```
    Males ...................................................................  48
    Females .................................................................  49
    Total....................................................................  97
```

```
Average attendance ..........................................................  81
Cost to Creek Nation:
    Annually ................................................................  $5,600.00
    Annually per scholar.....................................................  69.13
    Per scholar per month....................................................  7.68
```

Employees are appointed and paid by the Presbyterian Board of Home Missions.

Day schools.

Teacher.	School.	Post-office address.	Race.	Age.	Monthly salary.	Amount received.	Days taught.	Enrollment Indians M.	Enrollment Indians F.	Enrollment White M.	Enrollment White F.	Days attendance Indians M.	Days attendance Indians F.	Days attendance Whites (aver. age).
John A. Denny	Alabama	Amatola	White	33	$30.00	$30.00	40	10	6	1	1	51	89	30
A. P. Stephenson	do	do	do	45	30.00	90.00	59	11	11			392	228	
Lloyd C. Johnson	do	Welcetka	do	25	30.00	112.50	67	10	6	15	12	278	98	12¼
Y. E. Hill	Arbeka	Fame	do	28	40.00	340.00	180	15	23	6	5	1,377	2,615	5½
Johnson R. King	Artussie	Eufaula	Indian	22	30.00	255.00	180	14	24			868	1,141	11
Cooper Dawson	Bonds switch	Chevotah	White	22	30.00	135.00	91	5	5	15	11	265	302	14
W. T. Brodie	do	do	do	28	30.00	70.50	50	10	1	11	5	119	40	9
Alice H. Palmer	Carrs Creek	do	do	26	35.00	105.00	70	10	5	6	7	208	213	30½
Cooper Dawson	do	do	do	25	35.00	110.00	66	12	14	14	29	676	345	
Harrie Blake	do	do	do	24	35.00	295.00	175	12	7			1,665	1,429	12
R. D. Lore	Chevotah	Henryetta	do	21	25.00	272.50	154	13	3	14	18	900	705	2
Rose Marcum	Coal Creek	Okmulgee	Indian	24	35.00	50.00	44	12	13	2	2	214	15	
Lucy H. Smith	Cnseetah	Eufaula	White	21	35.00	81.00	48	10	12			288	456	
Alice H. Palmer	Eufaula	do	do	26	35.00	132.00	56	10	12			208	529	6
Cora Ethel Fair	do	do	do	19	35.00	255.00	180	13	14	22	14	788	714	
L. A. Benton	Fishertown	Chevotah	Indian	28	35.00	138.00	100	13	9			1,471	1,409	9
Mattie Edna Fair	Fish Pond	Bearden	White	25	25.00	30.00	18	6	4	9	12	404	345	9
Sallie Reinhardt	Gentry's	Chevotah	do	24	30.00	255.00	177	9	6	1	9	43	16	5
Annie Wright	Grave Creek	Manda	Indian	25	30.00	196.00	150	7	9	6	6	565	340	4
Liliorn Morton	Hillabee	Thurman	do	35	30.00	290.00	178	14	4	7	8	1,560	476	3
M. J. Berryhill	Honey Creek	Okmulgee	Indian	24	35.00	297.50	150	10	10	12	7	334	436	14
Ginnie B. Welfick	Hitchita	Hitchita	do	36	30.00	162.50	115	4	4	4	2	470	310	4
Hettie D. Alexander	Kellyville	Kellyville	White	26	35.00	297.50	180	23	8			1,722	318	
Nancy M. Scott	Middle Creek	Wetumka	Indian	25	40.00	270.00	178	17	17	1		630	601	
Coral Lee Wright	Okfuskee	Eufaula	do	30	40.00	340.00	180	6	15	17	11	815	1,717	7
Clara Reinhardt	Okmulgee	Okmulgee	White	23	30.00	282.50	175	8	6	13	16	630	797	20
Cornelia Ratcliff	Pecan Grove	Holdenville	do	30	30.00	255.00	127	8	5			906	496	
George W. Coachman	Red Fork	Red Fork	do	20	25.00	165.00	176	10	5	10	6	843	560	6
Elmer Finley	Salt Spring	Wetumka	Indian	23	30.00	245.00	176	12	5	7	5	704	327	4
Pearl Pearson	Sudham	Sudham	White	28	30.00	270.00	175	13	10			1,310	1,071	
Charles Agee	Stone Bluff	Stone Bluff	do	30	30.00	285.00	176	14	10			1,286	972	
Alice M. Barnett	Thlewarthley	Watsonville	Indian	19	25.00	60.00	45	10	7			172	165	
Lula M. Carr	Thlewarthley No. 2	Wetumka	do	22	30.00	116.00	98	8	6	8	3	838	416	4
W. T. Brodie	Salt Creek	do	White	28	30.00	62.50	50	7	10	1	1	172	270	2
Addie B. Carr	Thlapthlokko	do	Indian	35	30.00	213.00	161	9	3			540	1,198	
Rachel C. Goat	do	Holdenville	do	35	35.00	297.50	170	3	9	8	3	1,066	392	
Lewis C. Johnson	Tiger Creek	Henryetta	White	24	35.00	290.00	170	15	6	1	1	1,126	1,599	11
Dora Johnson	Turkabatchee	Eufaula	do	24	36.00	292.50	178	12	10	18	10	828	1,165	
Ada M. Thurman	Tuskegee	Mounds	do	30	25.00	95.00	70	11	16			251	312	12
Jennie D. Pitman	Twin Mounds	Wewoka	Indian	22	25.00	25.00	20	8	8	11	13			
Leontine Whiteside	Wewoka	Muskogee	White											

Enrollment	791
Average attendance	309
Months of school	8½
Paid for teachers' salaries	$7,737.00
Average cost of tuition per pupil	$25.03
Average cost of tuition per pupil per month	$2.90

Day schools (colored).

Teacher	School	Post-office address	Race	Age	Monthly salary	Amount received	Days taught	Enrollment Citizens M	Citizens F	Noncitizens M	Noncitizens F	Days attendance Citizens M	Citizens F	Noncitizens (average)
M. W. Bl n	Ash Creek	Ridge	Negro	25	$30.00	$30.00	22	5	12			73	184	
Ida M. Kibler	do	do	do	23	30.00	53.00	42	10	19			285	464	
M. M. son	do	do	do	24	30.00	107.25	68	9	30	6	8	675	1,317	7
J. M. Dude	Black Jack	Muskogee	do	42	30.00	287.50	177	24	29	4	8	963	1,986	
Maud V. Jones	Blue Creek	Clarksville	do	40	40.00	340.00	180	22	29	5	3	2,913	2,364	7
Rumella Kinchin	Brush Hill	Brush Hill	do	23	35.00	220.00	178	11	40	3		1,470	1,542	2
dr H. Mike	Cane Creek	Lee	do	34	35.00	297.50	180	20	18	1		738	2,244	
E. L. Thurman	Coal Creek	Ridge	do	28	30.00	285.00	176	19	15			1,664	1,177	
lh I Grayson	Coon Creek	Eufaula	do	35	30.00	262.50	177	22	22	3	3	2,383	2,356	
1 Mr Sims	Cherryville	Lee	do	19	30.00	162.50	128	12	17	9	6	508	779	3
Nancy E. dson	Durant	Muskogee	do	30	30.00	201.00	160	14	8	4		892	779	
Sallie Worall	Eufaula	Pufaula	do	21	25.00	231.00	165	7	21			1,931	1,694	
Jennie V. Kh	Little River	Holdenville	do	30	30.00	297.50	180	28	25	2	8	1,931	1,694	2
I. H. el.	New sh	Tullahassee	do	25	30.00	255.00	90	24	21	4	7	1,152	680	5
dy E. Bailey	rdse	Okmulgee	do	22	35.00	122.50	77	13	21	7	4	348	2,416	6
S. E. th	do Agee	do	do	26	35.00	160.00	100	8	9			1,199	495	
N.E. Mo	Old Agecy	Muskogee	do	23	40.00	265.00	137	16	16			1,689	1,445	
William l q	Salt Creek	Beggs	do	27	35.00	80.50	41	27	31			691	639	
I. H. Parker	do	Gatersville	do	26	30.00	272.50	90	29	25			1,997	1,862	
P. B. l.Hu wh	om	Muskogee	do	36	35.00	112.50	76	25	18			470	608	
s. E. Marchant		Catoosa	do	26	35.00	175.00	108	24	34		7	1,600	1,983	
efrl Armstead	Spring Hill	Choska	do	23	25.00	245.00	177	29	22	1		1,831	3,123	4
F. D. Harrison	Spring Wiley	Ridge	do	25	30.00	255.00	176	14	24	8		1,677	2,465	
La E. des	Sugar Syke		do	25	30.00	255.00	180	15	24			1,346	1,508	
B. F. Sykes	Wild Cat	Wild Oat	do	40	30.00	247.50	171	24	13	17	11	2,779	2,281	1
Gertrude E. Burden	Nw Springs	Inola	do	26	35.00	297.50	172	13	16	2	2	1,463	1,970	

Enrollment	1,031
Average attendance	436
Months of school	8½
Paid for teachers' salaries	$5,782.25
Average cost of tuition per pupil	$13.15
Average cost of tuition per pupil per month	$1.50

REPORT OF CHEROKEE SCHOOL SUPERVISOR.

TAHLEQUAH, IND. T., *July 15, 1902.*

SIR: I have the honor to submit my fourth annual report as supervisor of schools for the Cherokee Nation.

A gain over previous years has been made in the number of schools, the proficiency of teachers, and the enrollment of pupils. The national council has been generous in appropriations; the chief and other officials, along with the school board, have labored to promote Cherokee educational interests. I think they evince more personal and tribal pride in their schools than in any other one feature of their national life. They accept any reasonable suggestions looking to their improvement.

For three years the gain has been constant, as will be shown in this report. In pursuance of your instructions, I have spent as much time as could be spared from office duties in the visitation of schools, encouraging teachers, pupils, and neighborhoods. Some of the visits have been very timely and necessary. In the aggregate much good has been accomplished by these studies in the field.

For two days past I have been in session with the national school board, considering the various schools and neighborhoods. We have agreed to discontinue certain schools on account of small attendance and lack of interest, and have agreed upon the establishment of an equal number of schools in other localities. Many petitions for new schools are on file in the board's office. No school is discontinued that makes an average attendance of 15 in the fall term and 18 in the spring term; and no school is established unless the neighborhood provide a suitable house with proper furnishings.

I have urged the Cherokee board to visit schools. They have devoted much time to this useful work, encouraging teachers and pupils, while promoting educational interests in the neighborhoods. The Cherokee Nation is divided into three educational districts, each one of which is under the immediate charge of a member of the school board. They each have 45 schools to visit; they study the condition and need of the neighborhoods, the capabilities and fitness of teachers, and secure such information as will aid in determining how to wisely locate the various teachers when appointments are made. Two members of the board visited all of their schools during the spring term; the other one failed to reach a few schools on account of high waters and pressure of office work.

PRIMARY SCHOOLS.

More and better work than heretofore has been done in the neighborhood schools. Good results of last year's normal training are in evidence. Better teaching, better attendance of pupils, better interest in education may be noted. Eleven new schools were established last term. There are at present 140. Schools were in session a fall term of three months, with an enrollment of 4,227 and an average monthly attendance of 2,641. The spring term continued four months, with an enrollment of 4,948 and an average monthly attendance of 2,794. The aggregate monthly enrollment for the year of seven months was 4,639; the average attendance for the same was 2,728, or 58.8 per cent of enrollment.

The cost of these schools was $37,205, or $1.95 per pupil per month. Teachers are paid a uniform salary of $35 per month. The steady gain in the primary schools is shown partly by the enrollment of the spring term, which in 1900 was 3,920; in 1901, 4,153; and in 1902, 4,948—a gain in two years of 1,028. The per cent of attendance this year was slightly better than in any previous year.

Of the primary schools, 15 are for colored pupils, and attended by negroes only; 28 are attended by full-blood Cherokee-speaking pupils, in neighborhoods where very little English is known or used in the homes. Some full bloods attend various other schools. English-speaking mixed bloods constitute the balance of the enrollment. Adding the attendance of high schools and primary schools, there were last year in Cherokee schools 5,692 pupils, or more than 62 per cent of the population from 6 to 20 years of age.

HIGH SCHOOLS.

The four high schools of the nation were each in session nine months the past year, with an aggregate enrollment of 744, a gain over last year of about 58, and an average attendance of 525, a gain of 71 over last year. The aggregate cost was $60,849.78, an excess over last year of $11,407.78. The increased expense was caused mainly by larger average attendance and by higher prices of all necessities, which resulted from the prevailing drought of the year. A noticeable item is the collection for board at *these institutions*, which was $11,934.85 for the year. This amount has been placed *to the credit* of the school fund. I ask your attention to the gain in number of *pupils* doing high-school work. Last year I reported 119, of whom 12 were graduated. I am now able to report 197, of whom 18 were graduated. This is the largest number ever graduated in one year from the Cherokee high schools. I can not learn that these schools were ever in better condition than at this time. I may add there are 244 pupils in the fifth and sixth years' work. I am sure the preparatory work was never so well done as last year.

IMPROVEMENTS.

Last council appropriated funds to buy some chemical and physical apparatus for both the male and female seminaries. This apparatus has been secured, and their use will aid in teaching these subjects. Each school carries a $50 subscription list of newspapers and magazines, which are used in current topics. One thousand dollars were given for repairs and purchase of furniture at the female seminary, $500 for repairs at the male seminary, and $2,350 for repairs at the orphan asylum. Contractors are now making necessary repairs, and when the schools open in September the buildings will be much recovered from wear and hard service.

THE SUMMER NORMAL.

From June 4 to July 2 was held, in two sections, our third summer school for teachers. The division for Cherokees at the female seminary enrolled 167, and was taught by a very able and experienced corps of instructors. The division of 23 colored teachers, held at the national capitol, was in every way very successful.

No feature of the work since I came has been more helpful, encouraging, and directly useful in promoting a proper educational spirit in this country than this month's service with 190 teachers, mostly Cherokee citizens, gathered from every neighborhood and from representative families of the nation. Their influence will reach thousands of the Cherokee children. The importance of this is indicated by the fact shown by official reports that the Cherokee children of school age are more than those of the other four civilized tribes combined, excluding negroes.

The most excellent and highly satisfactory work of this year could not have been done without the preparation given by the two previous normals. In addition to instruction in the art of teaching primary work and common-school branches, we gave algebra, physiology, civil government, and physics.

A class of 40, all of whom were graduates of some institution, or holders of a last year's first-grade certificate, took the work leading to a Class A, first grade, two years' certificate. Twenty-five were successful. Thirty-three secured first-grade Class B certificates. These certificates were attested by myself and countersigned by you, and thus made valid in all the territory of your jurisdiction. One hundred and forty of the 148 who took the examinations received certificates. Of those who passed 121 were citizens and 19 were noncitizens. Of the 23 enrolled at the colored section 14 were citizens and 9 noncitizens. Twenty-two received certificates. The surprise at both sections was the large per cent of those examined who were able to pass, and generally with good grades. However, the grades were earned and the tests given were fair and impartial. The commendable results grew out of the methods, the spirit, and hard work of the normal. The promptness and regularity of attendance, the interest, the faithful study, the earnestness of purpose shown throughout the month, and the generally satisfactory results secured, I have not seen surpassed. Everybody cooperated. Your timely suggestions and assistance, and the labors of your Professor and Mrs. Carter materially contributed to best results. Eight of our teachers were excused to attend other normals. Most of them took summer work at the University of Chicago, to better fit them to teach in our high schools.

In addition to the month's training and review of studies, a very satisfactory result was the securing of enough teachers for all of our schools; not a school was left for a supply teacher. Those depending upon favoritism, political pull, or personal influence were not appointed for next year, and are not upon the list of eligibles. The moral educational effect of this fact is very important, as it turns the attention of teachers to merit, hard work, and successful teaching as their guaranty of future employment. It eliminates the most unhappy blight hitherto known to Cherokee schools.

ITEMS OF GAINS.

Increase in—

Number of pupils doing high-school work	78
Number enrolled in high schools	58
Number of graduates	6
Number enrolled in the normal	17
Number of pupils in primary schools	796
Average attendance	433
Enrollment in all schools	853

A reduction from $2.09 to $1.95 in the cost per pupil per month in the primary schools. All teachers selected upon merit by impartial tests, and better qualified than heretofore. A good working understanding between the school board and myself.

Three years ago the average attendance at the male seminary was 78; last year it was 154.5. In the same time the average attendance at the female seminary increased from 105 to 179; at the orphan asylum from 110 to 150; and at the colored high school from 20 to 41.6.

There has been a saving of 30 per cent in the per capita cost to the nation of attending pupils, and a decided gain in the efficiency of the educational work done.

CHEROKEE WARRANTS.

I have continued to register and indorse warrants issued by the nation against the school fund, the orphan fund, and the insane fund. In every instance I have looked up the warrant as to its legality, provision for its payment by appropriation, and the value rendered the nation, whether in service or merchandise, as determined by current market values. All requisitions upon which warrants are based, with laws and acts of council pertaining thereto, have been submitted to me, with the warrants drawn under authority thereof. Aggregate amount of appropriations for which warrants may be drawn during the current year against these three funds is $106,625.15. My duty in connection with these expenditures involves a very considerable amount of painstaking labor, but it is an added safeguard to the funds, and guaranty of proper disbursements.

FINANCIAL.

An act of the Cherokee council appropriating funds for the support of schools the current year was approved by the principal chief December 6, 1901, and by the President January 24, 1902. It carried the following sums:

140 primary teachers	$34,300.00
Male seminary, all purposes	17,525.00
Female seminary, all purposes	21,615.00
Colored high school, all purposes	3,877.15
School books for primary school	2,650.00
Medical superintendent at seminaries	933.00
Support of blind at blind school at Fort Gibson	300.00
Salaries and expenses of school board	2,600.00
Orphan asylum, for furniture	1,000.00
Orphan asylum, for repairs	2,350.00
Orphan asylum, other expenses	16,200.00
Insane asylum, all expenses	3,275.00
Total charges against the school fund	83,800.15
Total charges against the orphan fund	19,550.00
Total charges against the insane fund	3,275.00

I append tables showing attendance, instructors, and cost of each of the schools of the nation.

MALE SEMINARY.

Employee.	Position.	Race.	Age.	Salary per month.	Amount received.	Months employed.
L. M. Logan	Principal teacher	White	49	$100.00	$900.00	9
R. L. Mitchell	First assistant teacher	Cherokee	28	75.00	675.00	9
E. V. Allen	Second assistant teacher	White		50.00	200.00	4
S. J. Bross	do	do		50.00	250.00	5
W. P. Thorne	Third assistant teacher	Cherokee	28	50.00	450.00	9
R. R. Eubanks	Fourth assistant teacher	do	23	50.00	450.00	9
Mrs. L. M. Logan	Fifth assistant teacher	White	39	50.00	450.00	9
J. R. Garrett	Steward	Cherokee	46	41.66	500.00	12
Dr. C. M. Ross	Medical superintendent	do	29	38.75	465.00	12

Number of pupils enrolled	239
Average attendance	154¼
Total salaries paid	$4,340.00
Total other expenses	$12,550.00
Annual cost per pupil	$109.32
Cost per pupil per month	$12.15

FEMALE SEMINARY.

Employee.	Position.	Race.	Age.	Salary per month.	Amount received.	Months employed.
Etta J. Rider	Principal teacher	White		$100.00	$900.00	9
Mrs. Mae Shelton	First assistant teacher	Cherokee.	32	75.00	300.00	4
Lillian Alexander	....do	....do	22	75.00	375.00	5
Minta Foreman	Second assistant teacher	....do	24	50.00	450.00	9
Flora Lindsey	Third assistant teacher	....do		50.00	450.00	9
Maymie Starr	Fourth assistant teacher	....do		50.00	75.00	1½
Eldee Starr	....do	....do		50.00	375.00	7½
Mineola Ward	Fifth assistant teacher	....do		50.00	450.00	9
Josie Duncan	Matron	....do		50.00	250.00	5
Minnie Beuge	....do	....do		50.00	250.00	5
E. W. Buffington	Steward	....do	47	41.66	500.00	12
Dr. C. M. Ross	Medical superintendent	....do	29	38.75	465.00	12

Number of pupils enrolled 268
Average attendance 179
Total salaries paid $4,840.00
Total other expenses 14,340.00
Annual cost per pupil $107.15
Cost per pupil per month $11.91

ORPHAN ASYLUM.

Employee.	Position.	Race.	Age.	Salary per month.	Amount received.	Months employed.
J. F. Thompson	Superintendent	Cherokee.	61	$50.00	$300.00	6
J. H. Dannenberg	....do	....do		50.00	300.00	6
E. C. Alberty	Principal teacher	....do	35	80.00	720.00	9
R. Bruce Garrett	First assistant teacher	....do		60.00	540.00	9
Mary Gulager	Second assistant teacher	....do		45.00	270.00	6
Carrie Mayes	....do	....do		45.00	135.00	3
Eugenia Thompson	Third assistant teacher	....do	38	45.00	405.00	9
Martha L. Morgan	Fourth assistant teacher	....do		45.00	405.00	9
Cherrie Edmonson	Music teacher	....do	21	50.00	450.00	9
J. A. Patton	Medical superintendent	....do	29	50.00	300.00	6
Walter Smith	....do	....do		50.00	300.00	6

Number of pupils enrolled 180
Average attendance 150
Total salaries paid $4,125.50
Total other expenses $16,277.13
Annual cost per pupil $136.01
Cost per pupil per month $15.11

COLORED HIGH SCHOOL.

Employee.	Position.	Race.	Age.	Salary per month.	Amount received.	Months employed.
H. H. Bryant	Teacher	Colored		$50.00	$450.00	9
George F. Nave	Steward	....do	30	25.00	150.00	6
Ned Mackey	....do	....do		25.00	150.00	6
C. M. Ross	Medical superintendent	Cherokee.	29	41.66	333.34	8
Otto Rodgers	....do	....do	26	41.66	166.66	4

Number of pupils enrolled 62
Average attendance 41.6
Total salaries paid $1,250.00
Total other expenses $3,127.15
Annual cost per pupil $105.22
Cost per pupil per month $11.70

	Male seminary.	Female seminary.	Orphan asylum.	Colored high school.	Total in schools.
High school department:					
Seniors	8	11	....	....	19
Juniors	7	17	....	....	24
Sophomores	23	27	4	....	54
Freshmen	42	35	10	13	100
Number in high-school work	80	90	14	13	197
Intermediate grades:					
Sixth grade	26	38	18	11	93
Fifth grade	54	63	22	12	151
Number in intermediate work	80	101	40	23	244
Primary work:					
Fourth year	51	40	36	11	138
Third year	16	21	20	7	64
Second year	9	9	19	8	45
First year	3	2	51	....	56
Number in primary work	79	72	126	26	303
Number in each school	239	263	180	62	a 744

a Total attendance at the four high schools.

Day schools.

FALL TERM.

Teacher.	School.	Post-office address.	Race.	Age.	Salary.	Amount received.	Days taught.	Enrollment.			Average attendance.	Days attendance.
								Males.	Females.	Aggregate.		
CASADIAN DISTRICT.												
Bettie Eiffert	Webbers Falls	Webbers Falls	Cherokee		$35.00	$105.00	60	14	19	33	29	1,740
Lulu B. Smith	Gerrin	do	do		35.00	105.00	60	13	14	27	17	1,020
Julia Russell	New Hope	do	White		35.00	105.00	60	11	12	23	14	840
Fannie Sixkiller	Union Chapel	Muskogee	Cherokee	21	35.00	96.25	60	14	7	21	8	440
Lillie Cunningham	Starvilla	Starvilla	do	22	35.00	105.00	60	19	24	43	22	1,320
Gussie Sanders	Prairie Gap	Texanna	do	20	35.00	105.00	60	12	9	21	15	900
C. C. Brown	Beck	Faun	White		35.00	106.00	60	16	15	31	18	1,080
Birdie Harris	Ettowa	do	Cherokee		35.00	52.50	30	3	3	6	2	60
J. H. Plunkett	Texanna	Texanna	White		35.00	105.00	60	11	11	22	12	720
Mary F. Russell	Bennett	Bennett		35	35.00	105.00	60	20	15	35	28	1,680
Callie Sevier	McDaniel	Webbers Falls	Cherokee	22	35.00	106.00	60	13	13	26	9	640
COOWEESCOOWEE DISTRICT.												
Mrs. M. J. Browning	Vinita	Vinita	Cherokee	29	38.00	105.00	60	17	20	37	29	1,740
Anna E. Lyons	do	do	do		38.00	106.00	60	31	21	52	38	2,280
Mrs. Lizzie K. Athey	do	do	do		38.00	105.00	60	15	11	26	21	1,200
Ione Harlin	Chelsea	Chelsea	do		38.00	105.00	60	26	20	45	40	2,400
Mrs. L. J. Ross	Catale	Catale	do		38.00	105.00	60	18	8	26	18	1,080
Pearl Drew	West Point	Woodey	do		38.00	105.00	60	12	18	30	21	1,260
Grace Phillips	Oologah	Oologah	do		38.00	105.00	60	28	27	55	45	2,700
Susie Phillips	Nowata	Nowata	do		38.00	105.00	60	47	51	98	90	6,400
Kate Carselowey	Adair	Adair	do		35.00	105.00	60	17	19	36	30	1,740
N. H. Vaun	Gooee Neck	Lenapah	Colored		35.00	105.00	60	19	30	49	24	1,440
Abbie Wagoner	Lightning Creek	Hayden	do		35.00	105.00	60	34	32	66	38	2,580
Corrinne Alberty	Brushy Creek	Choteau	do		35.00	105.00	60	27	28	55	43	2,700
Cherrie Riley	Browning Spring	Pryorcreek	Cherokee		35.00	105.00	60	13	17	30	17	1,020
Jane Anna Ballard	Pryor Creek	do	do	26	35.00	105.00	60	38	22	60	42	2,520
Savola Mitchell	Tovey	Centralia	do		35.00	105.00	60	11	16	27	18	1,080
Bessie Scrimshire	Pawpaw	Whitecak	do		35.00	101.50	58	21	21	87	22	1,320
Hattie Eaton	Claremore	Claremore	do		35.00	105.00	60	10	16	26	16	928
Jemale Ross	do	do	do	20	35.00	103.25	59	25	16	41	28	1,380
Josephine Howard	Justice	Bartlesville	do		35.00	108.25	59	25	14	39	24	1,416
Lenora Grey	Sugar Mound	Foyil	do	26	35.00	96.25	55	10	18	28	21	1,155
Maggie Parks	Payne	Foyil	do		35.00	105.00	60	11	20	31	21	1,260
Ada Sanders	Hickory Creek	Lenapah	Colored		35.00	105.00	60	24	19	43	31	1,860

Day schools—Continued.

FALL TERM—Continued.

Teacher.	School.	Post-office address.	Race.	Age.	Salary.	Amount received.	Days taught.	Males.	Females.	Aggregate.	Average attendance.	Days attendance.
DELAWARE DISTRICT.												
Alice Thornton	Mitchell Springs	Maysville, Ark	Cherokee		$35.00	$105.00	60	13	12	25	17	1,020
Steve W. Peck	Pineville	do	do		35.00	105.00	60	16	14	30	19	1,140
James Ward	Minnehaha	Kansas	do		35.00	105.00	60	16	12	28	18	1,060
Levi Gritts	Osequah	Eucha	do	41	35.00	105.00	60	10	18	28	16	960
Walter Fox	Honey Creek	Grove	do	28	35.00	105.00	60	24	28	52	29	1,740
Ellen Gladney	Grove	do	do		35.00	105.00	60	20	30	50	38	2,280
Lucinda Ballard	Victory	Afton	do		35.00	105.00	60	13	18	31	17	1,020
Juliette Smith	Eutopia	Big Cabin	do	22	35.00	99.75	57	13	9	22	19	1,063
Olevia Mitchell	Blue Jacket	Blue Jacket	do		35.00	106.00	60	12	12	24	19	1,380
Mrs. Carrie Washbourn	Delaware Town	Eucha	do		35.00	106.00	60	12	12	24	19	1,140
Henrietta French	Moore	Vinita	Colored		35.00	106.00	60	37	48	85	28	1,560
Lula James	Vinita	do	do		35.00	106.00	60	21	26	47	64	3,840
Eugenia Eubanks	Aurora	Fairland	Cherokee	19	35.00	106.00	60	9	12	21	17	1,020
Flossie Carsclowey	Afton	Afton	do	20	35.00	106.00	60	13	11	24	16	960
R. L. Huggins	Ketchum	Ketchum	White		35.00	106.00	60	14	10	24	20	1,200
Maude Ward	Fairland	Fairland	Cherokee	21	35.00	106.00	60	20	28	48	40	2,400
Mollie Randolph	Olympus	Grove	do		35.00	106.00	60	21	15	36	24	1,440
William Flemming	Hickory Grove	Fairland	White		35.00	103.25	59	15	16	31	19	1,121
Allen F. Small	Ballard	Echo	do		35.00	106.00	60	15	17	32	26	1,560
Kate Zimmerman	Carsclowey	Vinita	do		35.00	106.00	60	14	11	25	13	1,780
FLINT DISTRICT.												
Emma Foreman	Elm Grove	Elm	Cherokee		35.00	105.00	60	19	23	42	18	1,080
Laura Padden	Rock Springs	Stillwell	do		35.00	105.00	60	19	19	38	19	1,140
Allie Pack	Bethel	do	do		35.00	106.00	60	10	18	28	10	600
Hattie Johnson	Dalouagah	do	do		35.00	61.25	35	5	16	21	13	465
Nellie Silk	Cochran	do	do	19	35.00	105.00	60	17	14	31	15	900
Sarah McCoy	Round Spring	Bunch	do		35.00	105.00	60	13	12	25	15	900
Sarah Fletcher	Chuculate	do	do		35.00	105.00	60	18	18	26	16	1,080
Bessie E. Rodgers	Rocky Mount	Stillwell	do		35.00	105.00	60	18	18	36	18	780
Alice Holland	Hum	do	do		35.00	105.00	60	21	17	88	22	1,320
George A. Cox	Stillwell	do	do		35.00	105.00	60	19	18	82	20	1,200
William Gott	Walnut Grove	Bunch	do	61	30.00	98.00	56	12	12	24	15	840

GOING SNAKE DISTRICT.

Name	School	Post Office	Race	No.									Amount
Mary Davis	Oak Grove	Tolu, Ark	Cherokee		85.00	106.00	80	10	16	26	14		840
James Bates	Hern	Westville	White	71	85.00	106.00	80	17	21	38	19		1,140
Inez Matherson	Shiloh	Stillwell	Cherokee		85.00	106.00	80	15	26	40	30		1,900
Nannie Watts	Peevine	Baron	do	21	85.00	106.00	80	12	16	31	17		1,020
Bertie Couch	Tom Devine	Westville	do		85.00	106.00	80	16	12	21	22		1,320
Josie Duncan	Fairfield	Baron	do		85.00	106.00	80	9	17	21	8		480
George W. Smith	Stony Point	Stillwell	do	28	85.00	106.00	80	14	12	28	16		960
W. W. Smith	Mulberry	Baron	White	25	85.00	106.00	80	11	11	28	13		780
Nora Holt	Baptist	Baptist	Cherokee	29	85.00	106.00	80	26	12	38	19		1,140
James M. Crutchfield	Kansas	Kansas	do		85.00	106.00	80	14	11	25	11		1,020
Mary Wolfe	Tyners Valley	Westville	do	28	85.00	106.00	80	19	7	28	11		660
Gean Finley	Taylor	Chance	do	29	85.00	106.00	80	15	28	28	27		1,320
George Meeker	Green	Westville	do	24	85.00	106.00	80	11	11	22	16		660
Della James	Ballard Creek	Baptist	do	25	85.00	106.00	80	11	17	22	20		960
Daisy Harris	Whitmire	Baron	do		85.00	78.75	45	13	11	24	15		675

ILLINOIS DISTRICT.

Name	School	Post Office	Race	No.									Amount
Bessie B. Howard	Three Rivers	Fort Gibson	Cherokee	18	85.00	106.00	80	15	10	26	14		840
Flora Thornton	Fort Gibson	do	do	41	85.00	106.00	80	21	14	35	21		1,280
W. H. Fields	do	do	Colored		85.00	106.00	80	24	41	65	24		2,040
Charles W. Willey	Manard	Manard	Cherokee		85.00	106.00	80	32	9	41	24		1,440
Harriet Skates	Watie	Fort Gibson	Colored		85.00	106.00	80	18	18	36	22		1,740
Emma Ingram	Bragg	Braggs	Colored		85.00	106.00	80	19	14	33	38		1,320
Anne E. Chase	Greenleaf	do	Cherokee	20	85.00	106.00	59	17	25	42	19		1,080
Anna E. Sevier	Campbell	Campbell	do	22	85.00	108.25	80	11	11	22	11		681
Piercie Foreman	Terrell	Vian	Cherokee	41	85.00	106.00	80	7	9	16	24		660
Joanna Duncan	Vian	do	do		85.00	106.00	80	25	26	51	29		1,440
Lulu E. Vann	Sand Town	do	Colored		85.00	106.00	80	17	25	42	21		1,280
Jennie Barns	McKey	McKey	do		85.00	106.00	80	17	13	30	10		600
Henry W. Moore	Young	do	Cherokee		85.00	106.00	80	13	7	27	10		600
Mary Hubbard	Garfield	Garfield	do		85.00	106.00	80	13	14	33	21		
T. C. Pyle	White Oak	Cookson	White	46	85.00	106.00	80	14	19	33	21		1,280

SALINE DISTRICT.

Name	School	Post Office	Race	No.									Amount
Ella Mae Covel	Water Mill	Spavinaw	Cherokee	22	85.00	106.00	80	12	10	22	11		660
Avery Vann	Lynches Prairie	Chaffee	Colored		85.00	106.00	80	39	32	71	35		2,100
Florence Ross	Oceola	Locustgrove	Cherokee	21	85.00	106.00	80	16	6	22	16		900
Arthur Sanders	Cedar Bluff	do	do	21	85.00	106.00	80	10	11	21	11		900
Emma Berry	Arcadia	Rose	do		85.00	106.00	80	18	14	32	8		480
Callie Ridge	Rose	do	do		85.00	106.00	80	11	16	27	16		900
Ell Toney	Wycliffe	do	do	22	85.00	106.00	80	10	8	18	11		660
Laura Patrick	Elm	Elm	do		85.00	106.00	80	30	17	47	21		1,280

SEQUOYAH DISTRICT.

Name	School	Post Office	Race	No.									Amount
Mrs. W. S. Scott	Muldrow	Muldrow	Cherokee		85.00	106.00	80	29	18	47	31		1,900
Emma Winfield	Red Land	Redland	Colored		85.00	106.00	80	15	12	27	19		1,140
John Rodgers	Hanson	Hanson	Cherokee	40	85.00	106.00	80	16	16	32	17		1,020

Day schools—Continued.

FALL TERM—Continued.

Teacher.	School.	Post-office address.	Race.	Age.	Salary.	Amount received.	Days taught.	Enrollment.				Days attendance.
								Males.	Females.	Aggregate.	Average attendance.	
SEQUOYAH DISTRICT—continued.												
Nannie Taylor	Roastingear	Uniontown, Ark	Cherokee	20	$35.00	$105.00	60	3	13	16	11	660
None Adair	Adair	Adair	do	24	35.00	105.00	60	17	15	32	15	900
Alma Nash	Advance	Muldrow	do		35.00	105.00	60	6	10	16	14	840
M. J. Swimmer	Belfonte	Long	do		35.00	105.00	60	14	17	31	21	1,260
Daisy D. Starr	Sweet Town	Sallsaw	do		35.00	105.00	60	11	10	21	8	480
TAHLEQUAH DISTRICT.												
Mollie Adair	Eureka	Eureka	Cherokee		35.00	105.00	60	20	15	35	18	1,080
Belle Cunningham	Blue Springs	Gideon	do	21	35.00	105.00	60	10	11	21	11	660
Bertha Morgan	Swimmer	do	do		35.00	105.00	60	4	10	14	13	780
Bessie Wyly	North Tahlequah	Tahlequah	do		35.00	105.00	60	31	15	46	27	1,620
Emma Finley	East Tahlequah	do	do		35.00	38.50	22	7	12	19	9	198
Frances V. Ross	Ball Hill	do	do		35.00	105.00	60	18	12	30	15	900
Columbia R. Gourd	Bug Tucker	Moody	do		35.00	105.00	60	13	5	18	17	420
Bessie Triplett	Double Springs	Tahlequah	do		35.00	105.00	60	13	12	25	16	900
Letitia Wilson	Grand View	do	do		35.00	105.00	60	18	6	21	16	780
Nannie Hatfield	Hart	Moody	do		35.00	105.00	60	9	9	18	10	600
Roweanna Harmage	Crittenden	Crittenden	do		35.00	105.00	60	13	19	32	17	1,020
J. H. Covel	Union	Tahlequah	do	20	35.00	64.75	37	16	20	36	20	740
W. H. Balentine, jr	Caney	Welling	do		35.00	61.25	35	15	3	18	7	245
Mrs. Fanny Lowery	Tahlequah	Tahlequah	do		35.00	105.00	60	16	27	43	31	1,860
B. D. Andrews	Four-mile Branch	do	Colored		35.00	92.75	53	26	20	46	21	1,113
W. H. Balentine, sr	Parkhill	Parkhill	Cherokee		35.00	61.25	35	8	9	17	12	420
Minnie Benge	Downing	Peggs	do		35.00	106.00	60	20	28	48	23	1,380
Lovey Davis	Flint Ridge	Melvin	Colored		35.00	105.00	60	15	16	31	20	1,200

SPRING TERM.

Teacher.	School.	Post-office address.	Race.	Age.	Salary.	Amount received.	Days taught.	Males.	Females.	Aggregate.	Average attendance.	Days attendance.
CANADIAN DISTRICT.												
Hattie Starr	New Hope	Webbers Falls	Cherokee		$35.00	$140.00	40	19	21	40	18	1,440
Lizzie Stegall	Starville	Starville	do		35.00	70.00	20	12	17	29	16	660
Mary Hubbard	Prairie Gap	Texanna	do		35.00	140.00	40	15	13	28	13	980
John H. Plunkett	Texanna	do	White		35.00	140.00	40	28	16	44	14	1,440

Teacher	School	Post office	Nation									
Mary F. Russell	Bennett	Bennett	do	35	35.00	136.50	78	26	25	61	24	1,872
Ellie Sevier	McDaniel	Webbers Falls	Cherokee	22	35.00	140.00	80	8	10	18	8	640
C. C. Brown	Buck	Faun	White		35.00	134.75	77	18	23	41	17	1,309
Julia Russell	Brushy Mount	Texanna		21	35.00	140.00	80	15	21	36	21	1,680
A. L. Grisham	Gerrin	Webbers Falls	do		35.00	140.00	80	17	17	34	19	1,520
Mrs. Mae Shelton	Webbers Falls	Muskogee	Cherokee	32	35.00	140.00	80	15	22	37	27	2,160
Jennie Glass	Union Chapel	Briartown	do	20	35.00	140.00	80	17	16	32	16	1,200
Ollie Griffin	Briartown	Briartown	do	20	35.00	131.25	75	18	26	44	25	1,875

___ DISTRICT.

Teacher	School	Post office	Nation									
Mrs. M. J. Browning	Vinita	Vinita	do		35.00	40.00	80	14	20	34	24	1,920
Mrs. Lizzie K. Alhey	do	do	do	29	35.00	140.00	80	13	18	26	19	1,520
___ E. Lyons	do	do	do	30	35.00	140.00	80	25	22	47	31	2,640
Maggie Parks	Chelsea	Chelsea	do		35.00	44.00	80	21	26	47	33	2,480
L. J. R ___	Catale	Catale	do		35.00	140.00	80	14	12	26	18	1,440
K. Pearl Drew	West Point	Oolly	do		35.00	18.00	80	18	23	39	18	1,440
Grace Phillips	Oologah	Oologah	do		35.00	140.00	80	32	36	68	36	8,840
Suda Phillips	Nowata	Nowata	do	20	35.00	0.00	80	25	22	47	48	2,880
___lla Mitchell	Torcey	Centralia	do		35.00	44.00	80	10	11	21	16	1,280
Olevia Mitchell	Pawpaw	Whiteoak	do		35.00	140.00	80	20	18	38	16	1,280
Jennie F. Ross	Claymore	Clai ___ re	do		35.00	140.00	79	25	16	41	23	1,840
Bessie Scrimosbire	do	do	do		35.00	138.25	80	18	8	26	17	1,343
Jennie ___	Justice	Bartlesville	do		35.00	140.00	80	11	11	39	25	2,000
Eli Toney	Sugar Mound	Foyil	do		35.00	140.00	80	13	18	29	17	1,360
George V ___ nt	Payne	Whitecak	White		35.00	140.00	79	30	19	32	20	1,600
J. A. Hensley	Whitecak	Collinsville	Cherokee		35.00	134.25	80	24	32	62	41	2,289
Lulu James	Collinsville	Kinnison	do	25	35.00	18.00	80	18	25	47	40	8,200
Robert Fields	___ Neck	___h	Colored		35.00	140.00	74	23	15	38	19	1,520
W. H. ___ in	Hic-kory Creek	do	do		35.00	29.50	80	28	17	40	50	2,712
Corinne Alberty	Lightning Creek	Hayden	do		35.00	140.00	80	29	38	66	61	4,080
Abbie ___	Brushy Creek	Choteau	Cherokee		35.00	44.00	80	19	30	61	55	2,800
Emma Winfield	Nowata	Nowata	do		35.00	18.00	80	24	30	48	37	2,980
Callie Burns	Adair	Adair	do	41	35.00	140.00	80	20	22	46	26	2,880
Emma Scott	___	Pryor Creek	do	26	35.00	18.00	80	18	11	42	23	2,240
J ___ ___ Duncan	Browning Springs	do	do		35.00	140.00	80	32	33	29	20	1,600
Jan ___ ___ Ballard	Pryor Ceek		do		35.00	140.00	80			65	45	3,600

DELAWARE DISTRICT.

Teacher	School	Post office	Nation									
Alice Thornton	Mitchell Springs	Maysville, Ark	Cherokee		35.00	120.75	69	18	10	28	14	966
Steve W. Peck	Pineville	do	do	20	35.00	18.00	80	14	17	31	26	2,090
Shorey W. ___	Minnehaha	___	do		35.00	18.00	80	14	12	26	14	1,120
___ Smith	Osequah	___m	do		35.00	140.00	80	10	14	24	18	1,040
Sadie B. Sanders	Honey Creek	Grove	do	22	35.00	70.00	40			41	24	1,920
Mrs. A. L. Ballard	Grove	do	do		35.00	140.00	80	20	20	40	30	1,200
Lucinda Ballard	Victory	Afton	do	29	35.00	18.00	75	11	27	20	17	1,360
Juliette Smith	Eutopia	Big ___	do		35.00	181.25	80	11	22	27	18	976
___ Finley	Bluejacket	Bluejacket	do		35.00	18.00	80	11	11	32	26	2,090
Mrs. Minnie Henry	Delaware Town	Eucha	do	28	35.00	18.00	80	11	16	25	19	1,520
B. W. ___ill	Aurora	Fairland	do		35.00	140.00	80	12	12	27	19	960
Eugenia Eubanks	Afton	A ___din	do		35.00	18.00	80			24	12	

Day schools—Continued.

SPRING TERM—Continued.

Teacher.	School.	Post-office address.	Race.	Age.	Salary.	Amount received.	Days taught.	Enrollment.			Average attendance.	Days attendance.
								Males.	Females.	Aggregate.		
TAHLEQUAH DISTRICT.												
Mrs. W. R. Sartain	Eureka	Eureka	Cherokee		$35.00	$140.00	80	17	19	36	21	1,680
Mrs. H. M. Morgan	Swimmer	Gideon	do		36.00	138.25	70	9	11	20	11	869
Mary Davis	Ball Hill	Tahlequah	do	25	36.00	140.00	80	14	15	29	13	1,040
J. H. Covel	Union	do	do		36.00	140.00	80	17	19	26	18	1,440
Callie Leeser	Grand View	do	do		35.00	140.00	80	7	6	13	7	560
Joe L. Manns	Downing	Peggs	do		35.00	138.25	79	23	28	46	22	1,725
Mrs. Mollie Gourd	Bug Tucker	Moody	do		36.00	87.50	50	6	4	10	4	200
Mrs. Lizzie Triplett	Double Springs	Tahlequah	do		36.00	140.00	80	21	18	34	25	2,000
Mrs. Nannie Hatfield	Hart	Moody	do		36.00	140.00	90	9	7	16	13	1,040
Hart	Crittenden	Crittenden	do	20	35.00	131.25	75	11	28	42	15	1,200
Roseanna Harnage	Parkhill	Parkhill	do	21	35.00	129.50	74	11	13	24	17	1,960
Belle Cunningham	French	Melvin	do	24	36.00	140.00	80	11	12	25	19	1,405
Minnie L. Parker	Linder	Eureka	do		35.00	140.00	80	11	21	28	18	1,470
Trim Morris	North Tahlequah	Tahlequah	do		35.00	140.00	80	29	22	50	29	2,820
Mrs. Betsy Wyly	East Tahlequah	do	do		35.00	140.00	80	20	28	42	16	1,280
Mrs. H. C. Barnes	Four-mile Branch	do	Colored		35.00	140.00	80	38	38	74	46	3,680
Mrs. W. H. Fields	Tahlequah	do	do		35.00	140.00	80	28	38	66	38	2,640
Mrs. Fanny Lowery	Flint Ridge	Melvin	do		35.00	140.00	80	19	16	35	20	1,600
Avery E. Vann												

The Cherokee people have shown much kindness and appreciation in our mutual efforts to secure good educational advantages for their children. The public press of the nation has aided with vigor and intelligence. Subscription, mission, and church schools have materially aided in the general work, while the graded town and city schools have secured a permanent place of honor in educational affairs. I have left report of these schools for your office.

I especially thank you for suggestions, cooperation, and support in the sometimes difficult labor of the year.

Very respectfully,

BENJAMIN S. COPPOCK.

Hon. JOHN D. BENEDICT,
Superintendent of Schools in Indian Territory.

REPORT OF CHOCTAW SCHOOL SUPERVISOR.

SOUTH McALESTER, IND. T., *July 3, 1902.*

SIR: I have the honor and pleasure to submit my second annual report of the schools of the Choctaw Nation, Indian Territory.

THE SCHOOLS IN GENERAL.

The schools of the Choctaw Nation number 190 day schools and 5 academies.

There has been an enrollment in the day schools of 3,074 Indian children and 6,244 white children (the enrollment of white children includes the number enrolled in all of the town schools), and in the academies 509 Indian children.

The white children are permitted to attend the day schools by paying a small tuition to the teachers. There are only 30 schools in the nation in which white children have not been in attendance.

We think it is helpful to the Indian children to permit the white children to attend the schools, and we encourage their attendance.

Considering the uncomfortable school buildings, the absence of the necessary equipments, the inconveniences of the teachers from a social standpoint and in securing suitable boarding places, the general progress of the schools has been fairly satisfactory.

We have endeavored to bring about a friendly attitude among teachers, pupils, and parents, and from our observation in visiting the schools we find that this attitude exists in a large measure.

THE ACADEMIES.

In the general management of the academies the work has been better than in former years.

The schoolroom work has been good and the children have made rapid progress. Some of the employees, other than teachers, have not been satisfactory, and in the selection of these employees for another year great care will be taken to make the needed improvement.

The attendance has been very good, the limited number being present nearly the entire year.

Smallpox and pneumonia visited the academies, and there was quite a siege of sickness, especially in the orphan academies. A few deaths occurred.

SMALL BOARDING SCHOOLS.

Early in the year authority was granted to establish a few small boarding schools. We established nine such schools in locations suitable to accommodate children who live remote from established neighborhood schools.

This arrangement is a good one; it brings together a large number of children and better results are secured.

DAY OR NEIGHBORHOOD SCHOOLS.

The general success of the schools of the Choctaw Nation depends upon the efforts put forth on the neighborhood schools. We have exercised great care in the selection of teachers for these schools, and we feel that we have a class of teachers most of whom are progressive, enthusiastic, practical, and up to date.

More earnestness has been shown, a much better attendance ha
the feeling of indifference on the part of the parents has been c
degree.

SCHOOL VISITATION.

During the year all of the schools, except possibly six, have bee
a record of the visits made, showing the efficiency of the teacher,
children, the condition of the building and surroundings, the enr
ance, and the general tone of the school.

LOCAL TEACHERS' MEETINGS.

We have held eight teachers' meetings during the year at
thereby giving every teacher in the Choctaw Nation an opport
least one of these meetings.

While the attendance at these meetings was not compulsory, the
to the call very liberally and the meetings were very interesting.

The plan was as follows:

The teachers were notified that a meeting would be held on Fr
urday a. m.

On Friday p. m. the teacher in charge of the school at place of
his school as usual, the visiting teachers observing and making
done. On Saturday a. m. a general discussion of the Friday aft
entered into. The discussion at times became very spirited. "
visiting teachers an opportunity to see another teacher handle
instruction, and manage his school. It also stimulated the inc
have other teachers to inspect and criticise his work and commer

The Friday evening session was usually of much interest.
music, recitations, and short talks by the people of the town.

These local meetings have given us an excellent opportunit
quainted with the patrons of the schools, and we are sure th
resulted from them.

OUR SUMMER NORMAL.

During the month of June we held a very successful normal at
One hundred and sixty-five teachers were in attendance. (
was done throughout. We had five regular instructors during t
two special instructors for two weeks.

Much attention was given to the subject of "nature study," a
advantages the Territory affords for nature work, we may expec
by the teachers along this line during the coming year.

Two noticeable attractions at the normal were the class of fiv
orphan boys and the military work.

The orphans are from Armstrong Academy, and have been t
skillful primary teacher.

The primary instructor gave recitations every day with these b
recitations the teachers obtained many points that will be helpf
work.

Owing to the large attendance we were compelled to provide t
men. These tents were in charge of Superintendent Morley, of A
and the young men were put under military discipline.

The young men enjoyed this work and became quite proficient

Following are statements made by two of the instructors in our

DWIGHT,

In the normal here for the teachers of the Choctaw Nation I believe we have
of teachers. I have found them very willing to carry to completion all the li
and they have not only been willing to do the work, but have done it gladl
surprise to me to find just such a body of genial and enthusiastic teachers an
the work before them.

I am sure the work done here in normal fully equals that done in the insti
Kansas; and in many ways I have found the teachers here better prepared an
training. It is my opinion that Mr. Ballard and the Choctaw Nation are t
having such workers.

Very truly,

———

DEAR SIR: For Mrs. Carter and myself I desire to express the pleasure and
we experienced during our two weeks' work as instructors at your teachers' 1
emy. We were highly pleased with the superior scholarship and the deligh

the teachers in the Choctaw Nation. And we were especially pleased with the firm, courteous, and exact discipline which you, during recitation times, recess times, meal times, and all the time maintained. Your management of about 175 of us was one of the very pleasant surprises that has come to us in this Territory, in which pleasant surprises have been so plentiful.

The teachers were studious and very earnest in all their work. I believe I never saw any normal where more earnest endeavor was manifested. I think they learned much, and I also think there was no other line along which they learned that which will be of more value in conducting their schools than the object lesson which you gave them in school management.

Hoping you will continue in the work, and that all the time it will be as successful as was the normal institute of 1902, I am,

Yours, very truly,

JOSEPH CARTER.

Supervisor CALVIN BALLARD,
    South McAlester, Ind. T.

The following is a tabulated report of the Choctaw schools:

ARMSTRONG ACADEMY.

Employee.	Position.	Race.	Age.	Salary.	Amount received.	Months employed.
Sam. L. Morley	Superintendent	White	22		$10,111.39	
Gabe E. Parker	Principal teacher	Indian	25	$100	900.00	9
Jennie A. Clark	Assistant teacher	White	20	60	540.00	9
Arthur M. Rishel	do	do	21	60	540.00	9
Mrs. Gabe E. Parker	do	do	19	50	450.00	9
Dora Gardner	Matron	Indian	31	50	600.00	12
Mary Morley	Assistant matron	White	25	40	360.00	9
Ida Folsom	Seamstress	Indian	52	50	450.00	9
Mrs. M. Minehart	Assistant seamstress	White	38	40	320.00	8
George McBath	Cook	Negro	28	50	600.00	12
Sarah Young	do	do	32	35	315.00	9
James Phillips	Janitor	White		35	315.00	9

Number enrolled 111
Average attendance 97.85

Salaries paid $5,390.00
Other expenses 10,111.39

    Total annual cost 15,501.39
Annual cost per pupil 156.28
Cost per pupil, per month 15.62

WHEELOCK ACADEMY.

Employee.	Position.	Race.	Age.	Salary.	Amount received.	Months employed.	
						Mos.	*dys.*
W. W. Appleton	Superintendent	White	27		$7,924.10		
Nellie Diggs	Principal teacher	do	27	$60	520.65	8	21
Sue M. Oakes	Assistant teacher	Indian	23	60	520.65	8	21
Grace Powe	do	White	27	50	433.87	8	21
Mary E. Appleton	Matron	do	36	50	600.00	12	0
Sue Brown	Assistant matron	Indian	20	40	328.43	8	21
Margaret Mitchell	Seamstress	White	28	50	433.87	8	21
Katherine Hibberd	Assistant seamstress	do	19	40	347.10	8	21
Sina Perdy	Cook	Negro	50	35	315.00	9	0
John L. Elder	Janitor	White	28	35	269.50	7	21
Elizabeth Frazier	Laundress	Negro	40	35	315.00	9	0
Albert Byrd	Janitor	do	22	35	45.50	1	8

Number enrolled 94
Average attendance 79.44

Total salaries paid $4,129.54
Total other expenses 7,924.10

    Total annual cost 12,053.64
Annual cost per pupil 150.53
Cost per pupil, per month 15.06

TUSKAHOMA ACADEMY.

Employee.	Position.	Race.	Age.	Salary.	Amount received.	Months employed.
						Mos. dys.
Charles F. Trotter	Superintendent	White			$9,838.38	
Robert A. Bayne	Principal teacher	do	42	$100	174.19	1 23
Etta A. Bayne	Assistant teacher	do	41	60	104.52	1 23
Mary Kennon	do	do	21	50	185.71	3 24
Helen Severs	Music teacher	Indian	20	50	441.94	8 26
Julia Falconer	Matron	do	21	50	446.77	8 29
Mattie B. Mitchell	Assistant matron	do	23	40	357.42	8 29
Pauline Fewell	Seamstress	White	21	50	446.77	8 29
Mabel Ballard	Assistant seamstress	do	19	40	246.45	6 6
Mary Smith	Cook	Negro	48	50	450.00	9 0
W. J. Baldwin	Engineer	White	21	50	200.00	4 0
Mrs. J. H. Williams	Laundress	do	50	40	80.00	2 0
T. F. Skipwith	Laundryman	do	41	40	276.00	6 27
Andrew G. Gladney	Principal teacher	do	30	100	725.81	7 8
Francile Battenberg	Assistant teacher	do	21	50	362.90	7 8
Stella Blake	do	do		50	250.00	5 0
George Trotter	Janitor	do		50	105.00	3 0
Carrol R. Greenwood	do	do	25	35	161.45	4 19
Dora L. Lewis	Assistant seamstress	Indian	22	35	80.00	2 14
George Trotter	Engineer	White	24	40	250.00	5 0
				50		

Number enrolled 125
Average attendance 110

Total salaries paid $5,247.89
Total other expenses.. 9,838.38

Total annual cost... 15,086.27
Annual cost per pupil 138.08
Cost per pupil, per month... 15.33

JONES ACADEMY.

Employee.	Position.	Race.	Age.	Salary.	Amount received.	Months employed.
						Mos. dys.
Wallace B. Butz	Superintendent					
George Beck	Principal teacher	White	63	$100.00	$174.19	1 23
James N. Wilson	Assistant teacher	do	23	60.00	540.00	9 0
Cynthia Rainey	do	do	29	60.00	540.00	9 0
Francile Battenberg	do	do	21	50.00	87.10	1 23
Laura Collison	Matron	do	41	50.00	500.00	10 0
Nettie Coleman	Assistant matron	do	23	40.00	40.00	1 0
Sarah Hibbard	Seamstress	do	51	50.00	450.00	9 0
Gussie Hayes	Assistant seamstress	do	31	40.00	360.00	9 0
Warren Butz	Engineer	do	29	50.00	115.00	2 9
Mary F. Pamplin	Cook	Negro	28	50.00	500.00	10 0
Francis J. Pamplin	Laundress	do	54	40.00	280.00	7 0
John D. Plunkett	Janitor	White	33	35.00	350.00	10 0
Bess M. Severs	Assistant matron	Indian	19	40.00	312.26	7 24
William Caton	Engineer	White	45	50.00	335.00	6 21
Robert A. Bayne	Principal teacher	do	42	100.00	725.81	7 8
Etta A. Bayne	do	do	41	60.00	435.48	7 8
Katie Foster	Laundress	Negro	27	40.00	80.00	2 0

Number enrolled 123
Average attendance 103.11

Total salaries paid $5,864.84
Total other expenses... 9,269.25

Total annual cost... 15,154.09
Annual cost per pupil 146.00
Cost per pupil, per month... 16.22

ATOKA BAPTIST ACADEMY.

Superintendent, Edwin H. Rishel.

Number pupils enrolled 56
Number days attendance.. 14,970
Average daily attendance 49.4
Amount paid superintendent.. $6,125.45

The salaries of teachers and other employees are paid by the church board.

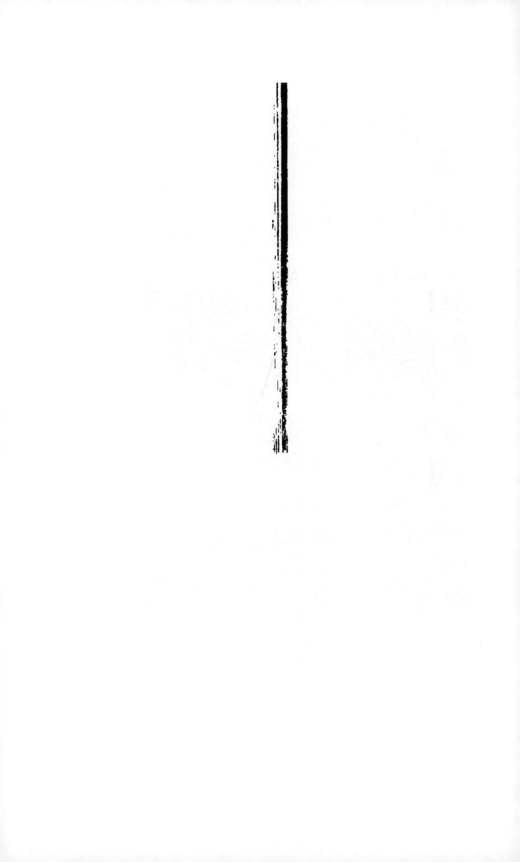

Report of Indian Inspector for the Indian Territory. 1902.

OFFICERS, JONES ACADEMY CADETS, CHOCTAW NATION

Day or neighborhood schools.

Teacher.	School.	Post-office address.	Race.	Age.	Salary.	Amount received.	Days attendance.	Indians M.	Indians F.	Whites M.	Whites F.	Days taught.
...tin, Elizabeth R	Cold Spring	Grant	White	54	$40	$272.80	1,724	16	6	6	12	177
Austin, D J	Allen	Allen	do	56	35	315.60	2,909	11	11	60	85	190
Alexander, H J	Good Spring	Tallihina	Indian	26	35	260.34	2,402	14	14			162
...kart, Charles P	Caddo	Caddo	White	40	2	456.40	4,455	19	21	110	94	179
Ater, Allen C	...sen	Canadian	do	26	45	272.20	2,474	10	19	38	42	169
Burgoyne, May	Big Lick	Tuskahoma	do	44	45	405.60	4,607	19	15			190
Bur...es, Rufus H	Big Hill	...lle	do	39	40	402.10	2,638	29	12	6	10	187
Bentley, Alva	...lo	...lo	do	30	40	280.00	1,569	18	4	41	23	145
Berry, Washington	Cowlington	Cowlington	do	49	40	149.60	1,531	18	8	6	4	188
Bales, J A	Pleasant Hill, No. 3	Caney	do	28	40	860.00	1,773	8	10			188
Brown, J J	Stock Bridge	...arn	do	41	40	360.00	3,455	19	14	1		189
Browning, ...ghes	Harkins	Donkaville	do	28	25	270.00	2,141	11	10	8	8	189
Baker, R S	...ad	Newberg	do	41	30	105.45	406	3	3	12	10	87
Baye, John A	Shadypoint	Shadypoint	do	67	2	113.23	439	4	8	5	4	79
Branson, ...rge L	Pine	Pine	do	29	30	22.70	203	8	9	1		20
...lah	Green Hill	...na	Indian	27	2	247.00	2,122	5	8	12	7	174
Ben, Frankie	Hills Chapel	Ludlow	White	23	30	80.00	791	6	5			101
Bohanan, L S	Spring Hill	Bokoshe	Indian	42	2	207.00	1,494	8	4	22	22	145
Burns, John L	Bokoshe	...bert	White	41	2	35.80	329	2	3	8	10	43
Baker, R S	Atwood	Scipio	do	28	2	40.00	348	8	4	19	7	58
Coleman, Richard S	Scipio	Shadypoint	Indian	21	2	14.90	144	2	7	7		58
Collins, Mattie	Shadypoint	Seth McAlester	White	18	30	144.19	711	8	2	9	8	30
Collins, Edmond	Zion	Hartshorne	do	44	2	90.00	397	6	5	7		105
Christian, ...wis E	Hartshorne	Grant	do	61	40	132.70	1,251	6	8	9	190	64
Collins, J Y	Grant	Tuskahoma	do	18	30	360.00	2,161	7	4	184	20	179
...y, Gertrude	...na	Heavener	do	36	2	86.00	502	2	7	20		189
Chaney, John A	...ian	Carterville	Indian	25	30	180.56	781	10	7	22	14	60
...mel, A H	Carterville	Reichert	do	30	30	254.82	1,597	5	6	32	24	115
Carney, W F	Reichert	Vireton	do	21	30	115.06	485	7	1	9	8	177
Collins, ...ssie	Vireton	Conser	Indian	25	40	70.65	386	7	9	8	2	78
...er, Ida	Yellow Spring	Scipio	Indian	20	25	262.10	1,910	8	4	2	1	52
...ings, T	Sittle...	Leflore	White	19	2	118.10	1,166	3	5	5	7	175
...y, Belle	Springfield	Hugo	Indian	39	30	17.15	72	8	4	1	8	159
Conover, Mrs. E D	Honey Spring	Milton	White	28	35	106.00	389	6	5	6	3	14
...t, Myrtie	Wolf Creek	Leflore	do	19	2	78.88	725	7	4	4	3	63
...y, Belle	Springfield	Braden	Indian	32	2	69.00	779	6	4	5	8	87
Carter, ...	Batteast	Goodland	Negro	17	2	40.00	371	8	6			100
...is, ...ison E	Rock Hill	Kiowa	Indian	31	40	147.10	466	5	9	5	2	40
...ll, ...le H	Kiowa	Cowlington	White	28	40	320.00	2,021	2	4	25	26	81
...ll, Frank	Short... Min	Antlers	do	25	25	218.88	1,494	9	6	8	11	145
Dickerson, J H	...rs No. 2	Durant	do	47	2	6.74	57	4		3	20	164
	Cox Chapel		do		30	7.74	38	2	5	15		11

Day or neighborhood schools—Continued.

Teacher.	School.	Post-office address.	Race.	Age.	Salary.	Amount received.	Days attendance.	Indians M.	Indians F.	Whites M.	Whites F.	Days taught.
Doyle, Nannie E	Pleasant Valley	Kiowa	White	19	32	$34.60	321	4	5	7	12	63
Dehazo, Alice	Pleasant Hill No. 2	Stringtown	do	28	30	289.26	1,135	6	5	5	4	169
Dehazo, Minnie	Sileena	Tushahoma	do	19	30	156.77	1,217	7	5			108
Eugenia, Sister M	Antlers No. 1	Antlers	do	31	2	269.70	2,559	14	17	38	32	179
Ervin, Ida	Bethel No. 1	Stigler	do	26	30	270.00	1,755	10	8			189
Ervin, Amanda	Enterprise	Enterprise	do	31	2	155.90	1,695	4	8	21	23	169
Essex, Daisy	Bolling Spring	Gowen	do	16	30	30.00	5	1		3	1	21
Edwards, Marie	Longtown	Eufaula	do	22	35	243.87	1,744	10	19	13	12	143
Essex, Daisy	Long Creek	Goodland	do	18	2	114.92	458	7	4		2	78
Evans, Zelma	Bokoshe	Bokoshe	do	18	40	22.70	219	5	5	12	19	40
Fisher, Elizabeth A	Featherston	Featherston	do	18	30	340.54	1,699	17	6	5	3	176
Fordyce, Lulu	Pryor	Stuart	do	28	30	24.19	145	6	9	3	2	19
Fronterhouse, Louvena	Impson Chapel	Antlers	do	28	30	87.68	634	5	6	7	4	65
Fordyce, Lulu	Choate	Choate	do	28	30	130.64	662	8	3	12	6	87
Ferguson, O. L.	James	Hartshorne	do	27	2	63.10	563	8	4	6	2	97
Fronterhouse, Louvena	Impson Chapel	Antlers	do	33	30	145.00	727	8	6	19	22	55
Fleming, Alice	Wilburton	Wilburton	do	31	2	34.90	831	8	2	6	1	195
Garland, J. G.	Ellis Chapel	Grant	do	57	2	270.00	1,589	9	14	2	7	173
Galyean, Lee	Albion	Albion	do	28	35	301.21	1,717	7	17	10	2	160
Gay, Wm	South McAlester	South McAlester	do	62	40	296.80	2,595	13	6	146	462	187
Hallman, Lena	Hochatown	Hochatown	do	28	40	356.00	2,681	19	15	1	2	180
Hankins, Mrs. C. M.	Kon Chito	Lukfata	do	21	40	298.06	2,522	13	8	2	2	187
Hotchkin, Mary P.	Lenox	Ironbridge	do	28	35	360.00	1,149	5	8	4	1	175
Hynson, Belle	Davenport	Antlers	do	27	30	285.16	1,911	12	8	2	3	174
Hatcher, Lizzie	Nunnih Takalo	Caddo	do	56	30	248.71	1,298	6	9	0	1	142
Hornidy, Emma	Rock Creek	Redoak	do	20	30	239.35	920	8	10	8	2	143
Hower, Jessie	Frazier	Doaksville	do	34	35	285.00	86	2	1	8	4	38
Hatcher, Lucy	High Hill	Durant	do	27	2	46.19	1,691	8	11	32	31	190
Hogg, Jay	Marysville	Ego	do	29	35	315.00	3,116	11	25	23	19	185
Holleman, John B	Stigler	Stigler	do	51	40	360.00	1,178	11	10			81
Hill, B. I	Beach Creek	Smithville	do	29	35	140.00	35	2	5	3	1	6
Holdsworth, Katie	Longtown	Eufaula	do	29	40	7.00	3,497	15	14	2	4	181
Hamilton, Mrs. Mae	Sulphur Springs	Bokchito	do	80	2	360.97	2,127	12	10	23	5	188
Hill, A. N.	Cedar	Lodi	do	24	30	262.00	1,299	7	6	4	4	186
Hewitt, J. C	Bald Mountain	Stringtown	do	32	30	126.00	1,126	1	1	8	5	22
Hollard, Anna	Choate	Choate	do	22	45	29.87	45	7	11	8	4	108
Holdsworth, Katie	Couser	Couser	do	19	30	382.50	2,828	11	8	12	5	49
Holdsworth, Lon	Celestine	Celestine	do	24	2	60.00	165	4	1	25	30	43
Hoffman, H. D	Redoak	Redoak	do	12	30	4.80	45	2	8	1	1	44
Hynson, Mrs. Rose	Sugar Loaf	Antlers	do	34	30	240.00	1,688	6	7	7	8	166
Hatcher, Lucy	Ushery	Hugo	do	54	30	167.84	602	7	8			115

Teacher	School	Post office	Race	Age	Salary
Holdsworth, Lou	Sardis	Dexter	do	19	180.23
Harrison, Almena	Calloway	Calloway	do	22	69.80
Holleman, Emma V.	Cedar Chapel	Panther	do	18	316.00
Irvine, Nettie	Pleasant Hill No. 1	Harris	do	89	245.00
Jones, D. F.	Tuloka	Garland	do	30	405.00
Johnson, A. M.	Gills	Coalgate	do	42	315.00
Jackson, Mrs. W. L.	Oaklodge	Oaklodge	do	31	405.00
Kirksey, J. A.	Bethel Hill	Bethel	do	56	356.13
Kennon, Mattie	Christian Hope	Atoka	do	19	270.00
Kennon, Grace	Stringtown	do	do	23	360.00
Locke, L. B.	Salem	Lenore	do	28	435.71
Larcey, W. E.	Sugar Creek	Nelson	do	25	296.98
Lacy, W. S.	Cameron	Cameron	do	36	221.00
Lott, J. H.	Frink	South McAlester	do	23	360.00
Lee, Robert E.	Summerfield	Summerfield	Indian	36	289.08
Loughinghouse, Martha	Bethlehem	Lehigh	White	23	815.00
Miller, Lizzie	Howe	Howe	do	81	105.84
Moore, Lizzie	Bokoshe	Bokoshe	Indian	20	66.91
Marshall, Hubert B.	Wilburton	Wilburton	White	18	405.00
Meraney, Lou J	Mt. Pleasant	Fowlerville	do	49	221.59
Moore, J. N.	Sanbois	Sanbois	Indian	24	120.81
Moore, Callie	Ward	Ward	do	18	47.42
Modisette, James O.	White Oak	Hartshorne	White	20	315.00
Morris, Florence B.	Savanna	Savanna	do	36	27.00
Morgan, John J	Vireton	Vireton	do	24	228.06
Minton, H. B	Utica	Utica	do	20	110.65
Marshall, J. H.	Bethel No. 1	Oak Lodge	do	27	185.00
Morrison, Margery	Old Goodland	Grant	do	88	161.10
Miller, Alice M.	Indianola	Indianola	do	47	200.00
Morris, S. P.	McAlester	McAlester	do	28	120.00
Murray, Mary	Guertie	Guertie	do	25	49.00
Marshall, Sinklie	Ward	Atoka	do	18	51.64
Marshall, Hubert B.	Langtown	Eufaula	do	27	24.10
Morrison, Margery	Old Goodland	Grant	do	30	62.50
Mabry, Edna	Hill	Spiro	do	50	44.80
Moore, W. L.	Brooken	Brooken	do	27	197.42
Morrison, Margery	Old Goodland	Grant	do	28	41.50
Marshall, Sinklie	Sockey	Panshawe	do	25	30.50
Merriman, Gus	Ward	Atoka	do	28	80.50
Merriman, Gus.	Hughes	Hughes	Indian	85	406.00
McClure, Mrs. C. L.	Kulli Chito	Bethel	White	25	182.58
McCurtain, Lou	Tushkahoma	Tushkahoma	do	23	120.81
McRaven, Elizabeth	Cedar Chapel	Panther	do	18	188.00
McMurtrey, Luelle	White Sand	Bennington	do	27	288.50
McBride, Howard	Mt. Zion	Bethel	do	58	166.10
McMinn, Samuel P.	Houston	Houston	Indian	25	77.14
McCurtain, Lou	Tushkahoma	Tushkahoma	White	19	45.80
McClelland, Ethel	Reichert	Reichert	do	31	174.00
Nash, Sallie	Doaksville	Doaksville	Indian	26	196.28
Noah, D. S.	Post Oak Grove	Albion	Indian	53	1,065.60
Neely, H. D	Calvin Institute	Durant	White		231.40
Neely, A	Durant	do	do		

Small boarding schools.

School.	Superintendent.	Enroll-ment.	Amount received.	Days at-tendance.
Durant	Ebenezer Hotchkin	70	$1,765.85	7,640
Gills	Emmett K. Gills	28	963.82	4,167
Big Lick	John W. Burgoyne	45	1,438.72	6,211
Old Goodland	Silas L. Bacon	13	409.66	2,300
Featherston	Lucius C. Featherston	17	380.17	1,639
Goodwater	Dixon J. McClure	30	1,103.24	4,746
Stigler	Joseph S. Stigler	18	282.14	1,277
Atoka	Edwin H. Rishel	18	295.76	1,664
Sardis	Mrs. Maye Sparks	18	385.77	1,662
Total		257	7,015.13	31,150

SUMMARY.

Academies:
Total enrollment 509
Average daily attendance 439.77
Total salaries paid $20,652.27
Total other expenses $38,264.57
Annual cost per pupil $133.29
Neighborhood schools:
Number Indian children enrolled 3,074
Number white children enrolled 6,244
Number days attendance 256,412
Total salaries paid $36,500.54
Amount paid for text-books $2,342.64
Small boarding schools:
Amount paid superintendents $7,015.13
  (Other statistics are in neighborhood schools.)
General:
Total enrollment in schools 9,827
Total salaries paid $57,152.81
Total other expenses $47,622.34
Total cost of schools $104,775.15

In the beginning of the year Mr. Eli E. Mitchell was appointed as Choctaw school representative, to work jointly with the United States school supervisor, and I am glad to report that our work has been very harmonious.

Mr. Mitchell is familiar with the customs of the Choctaw people and understands their wants and needs. He is an earnest worker and desires the advancement of his people.

My earnest endeavor shall be to administer the affairs of the schools of the Choctaw Nation with such judgment as shall tend to increase their efficiency. And in conclusion, I wish to express my appreciation of the courtesies you have shown me and of the intelligent support and cooperation you have given me.

Very respectfully,

CALVIN BALLARD,
School Supervisor Choctaw Nation.

Hon. JOHN D. BENEDICT,
Superintendent of Schools for Indian Territory.

REPORT OF SUPERVISOR OF CHICKASAW SCHOOLS.

TISHOMINGO, IND. T., *July 5, 1902.*

SIR: I have the honor, as school supervisor of the Chickasaw Nation, to submit the following report for the fiscal year ending June 30, 1902:

When I came upon this field, near the 1st of November last, the first quarter of the year was past and the second was well advanced. The work, as well as the field, was strange, and I was obliged to make acquaintance with both. My predecessor had left some months previous, and I found no record of his work.

Before the close of the year I had traveled over most of the ground, and visited a large proportion of the schools, some of them several times. I found among them quite a variety of character, as well as conditions.

There are five so-called academies or boarding schools, one of which—Rock Academy, near Wapanucka—more than a year ago, was condemned as unfit for use, and has not been occupied since.

Of the others, three are let by contract for a term of five years each, the contractor agreeing to furnish board, tuition, text-books, and medical attendance for a specified sum annually, based on an assumed number of pupils, and if more attended he is allowed pro rata for the increase.

The system is a vicious one, as it places the contractor under the constant temptation to furnish an inferior service to his own profit, and the fact that, in the main, the present contractors have not yielded to this pressure is evidence rather of their honorable conduct than of the absence of motive.

At the orphans' home the superintendent is engaged for five years at a specified salary, and the expenses of the school are provided by specific appropriations of the legislature. This is much more rational and businesslike than the other plan.

The term of the superintendent, as well as those of the contractors of two of the other academies, expires this year and new appointments are to be made the coming season.

These academies are not kept in proper repair, and two of them at least have a more or less dilapidated and distressing appearance externally, which is not relieved by internal inspection. This does not conduce to the comfort or the culture of the occupants nor inspire in them the knowledge of and desire for comfortable and pleasant homes so desirable among the people.

To this condition of things the Bloomfield Seminary is a marked and most agreeable exception, with its commodious, comfortable, and convenient buildings, its tidy, well-kept grounds, and its superior equipment. Its treatment by the legislature, though generous, is not extravagant, and could the others receive something of the same favor it would add greatly to their advantage and efficiency.

Besides the academies the Chickasaw Nation has this year sustained sixteen neighborhood or day schools. Several of these are kept in buildings which, originally very poor, are now in various stages of dilapidation, some of them containing neither table, desk, nor chair for pupil, teacher, or visitor. The seats are homemade, of plank, into which the idea of comfort has not entered in the slightest degree.

It is only just to say that several of the schools are different from these and are furnished with modern desks and seats.

In these schools the teachers are appointed by the Chickasaw superintendent and paid by the nation a uniform salary of $45 per month, except in two schools which have two teachers each, in which the salary is differently distributed.

The maximum limit of attendance at these schools, except the two last mentioned, is 35 pupils, and those who live near enough go back and forth daily, while those living farther away may be boarded near enough to the school to permit them to attend. In all cases an allowance of $10 per month for each child is paid from the National Treasury, so that many families having several children of their own in school depend upon this income for their entire living.

The more intimately I become acquainted with these schools the more strongly I become convinced that they are, as a whole, detrimental to the best interests of the Chickasaw children. In the full-blood neighborhoods, especially, they serve to separate the children from the influences which they must meet the very instant their environment changes, not only those against which they must contend, but those also whose contact would prove beneficial.

To some of these schools the children come daily, and passing through a routine of exercises not always very nutritious or stimulating they return to their homes, in many cases not hearing a word of spoken English between that which dismisses them in the evening and that which greets them the next morning on their return to school.

In a few cases Chickasaw children are attending schools with other children, and residing in the Chickasaw Nation are quite a number of Choctaw children who, if they attend school at all, must attend with white children, and to the unprejudiced observer it is clearly evident that these children make better progress than those in most of the national schools.

It should in fairness be stated that there are two or three of the national schools to which these strictures do not apply, and it so happens that they are those whose pupils themselves are members of mixed communities and whose associations outside of the school as well as within are of a general character. Some of the Chickasaws prefer sending their children to white schools, paying tuition and forfeiting a part or all of their board money, rather than send to the national schools.

If the money now paid for boarding the children could be put into improved buildings and up-to-date equipments, it would in my judgment be much more profitably invested and would produce far better educational results.

For instance, take one of these schools whose attendance is 30 pupils. At $10 per month for ten months the board would amount to $3,000. The teacher's salary together with fuel, repairs, and other expenses would at a very moderate estimate tax are in lawful possession of town property, and in enforcing the collection of these taxes the only penalty has been removal for nonpayment. The receipts from this source for the coming year will be extremely small.

COLLECTION OF REVENUE FROM CATTLEMEN AND OTHERS.

Rent to the amount of $5,082.25 has been received by the United States Indian agent during the past year from cattlemen and others, the same having been tendered as rent on the unselected part of their various inclosures, in accordance with the provisions of the regulations promulgated by the honorable Secretary of the Interior under date of July 23, 1901, which are in part as follows:

That parties desiring to introduce or graze cattle upon the public domain of the Creek Nation shall first make application to the United States Indian inspector for the Indian Territory, and shall pay to the United States Indian agent, Union Agency, the rate of $1 per head for cattle desired to be grazed thereon, which amount shall be paid prior to the time the cattle are so introduced; and that a description of such cattle, including the brands, together with any other desired information, shall be furnished; and that parties so introducing cattle shall agree to take such measures as may be necessary to prevent cattle so introduced from infringing upon the lands of adjoining allottees.

Where cattle are confined to fenced inclosures or pastures, part of which has been selected and leased by individual citizens, a grazing tax on the unselected portion of said pasture shall be based on a full, fair rental, provided such rental shall in no case be less than 15 cents per acre; and provided further, that in instances where any or all of the provisions herein enumerated are not complied with, such cattle shall be removed from the limits of the Creek Nation by the Indian agent, and the amount previously paid for grazing shall be forfeited.

The enforcement of these regulations has, in my judgment, been of great value to the Department, as well as the Creek Nation and the cattlemen. Many new pastures have been selected and many additional settlements have been outlined for the present grazing season, and the receipts under this head for the coming year should greatly exceed those shown above.

ROYALTY ON COAL.

The amount received for the benefit of the Creek Nation as royalty on coal mined during the past year is $2,761.20.

The principal mines are located at Howard, 3 miles east of Tulsa and in the vicinity of Henryetta, and have been operated under temporary permits. There are many valuable coal deposits within the limits of the Creek Nation, and oil has been discovered in several localities, notably in the vicinity of Red Fork, and much speculation is at present being indulged in with a view of controlling the future disposition of the mineral deposits.

In addition to the work outlined above, much has been done in preventing illegal coal mining, the cutting of hay, and the grazing of stock on the public domain, and a great variety of investigations and reports have been made, covering illegal land holdings, removal of Creek intruders, and such other matters as you have seen fit to assign me.

The total sum received by the United States Indian agent for the benefit of the Creek Nation is as follows:

Coal royalty	$2,761.20
Pasture and cattle tax	5,087.85
Merchandise and occupation tax	8,366.32
Total	16,215.37

The total expenses for the past year for salary and per diem, traveling expenses, clerical assistance, etc., amounted to $2,814.57, which shows a great reduction in the expenses for the current year as compared with the previous year.

I have been assisted in the work of the collection of the Creek revenues by a clerk and one district revenue inspector.

MERCHANDISE TAX IN THE CHEROKEE NATION.

The amount of revenue received from this source during the past year amounts to $3,375.68, practically all of which was received during the first three quarters of the year, and the same remarks apply to the future collection of this tax as made in connection with the trader and occupation tax in the Creek Nation.

HAY ROYALTY.

There is a royalty of 20 cents per ton due on all hay shipped from the Cherokee Nation. The amount of revenue received from this source during the past year amounts to $7,422.31.

As reported last year, this still continues to be one of the most hotly contested sources of revenue with which I have to contend, although I am pleased to report to you that the arrangements for its collection have not hitherto been so complete. The hay industry in the Cherokee Nation has already grown to great proportions, and, with the decline of the cattle business, large areas are devoted to this crop that were formerly used for grazing; at least 25 immense storage barns have been erected at points along the several railroads, nearly all of which are owned by noncitizens. Nearly all the railroads operating in the Cherokee Nation issued an order to their agents not to receive hay for shipment unless the royalty was paid, and it is my opinion that at the present time and during the past year very little hay has been exported from the Cherokee Nation without payment of tax imposed; some, however, has been hauled across the border in wagons and has avoided the payment of the tax.

FERRY LICENSE.

Section 739 of the laws of the Cherokee Nation is as follows:

Any person desirous of keeping a public ferry shall first be required to obtain a license for the purpose from the national treasurer, and for which he shall pay annually, in advance, the following tax, to wit: For a ferry on the Arkansas and Canadian rivers, the sum of $25 per annum; on the Illinois, Grand, Verdigris, and "Neosho" rivers, the sum of $10 per annum.

I have made diligent inquiry into this subject from time to time and have secured the payment of several license fees. Exact information concerning the owners of ferryboats is hard to obtain, for the reason that the boats frequently change ownership and some of the ferries are operated in season of high water only. My observation is that no list of ferry operators would be correct as to names for many months in succession. The receipts during the year from this source have been $225.

ROYALTY ON GRAVEL.

You will observe in the appropriate place herein that the sum of $236.52 has been collected as a royalty on gravel during the past year. This item of revenue arises from 2 cents per cubic yard for gravel taken from the banks of the Grand River near Fort Gibson by the Missouri Pacific Railway Company, to be used as ballast for the tracks of that road. While the amount from this source is not large up to the present time, I am informed by the officers of the railroad that it is the policy of the company to use a considerable quantity in the future. The gravel is easy of access and of excellent quality for the purpose, and the supply is almost unlimited.

CATTLE TAX.

The Cherokee act to prevent the introduction of cattle into the Cherokee Nation is as follows:

Whereas, the introduction of cattle into the Cherokee Nation from various States and Territories of the United States brings a disease known as Texas fever, for the prevention and cure of which no adequate remedy has been found; and

Whereas the introduction of cattle into the Cherokee Nation and the promiscuous grazing of same upon the public domain during certain seasons has practically destroyed the home industry of native cattle and placed the farmers at the mercy of the larger cattle dealers: Therefore,

Be it enacted by the national council, That it shall be unlawful for any person to introduce cattle of any kind whatever into the Cherokee Nation from any State or Territory of the United States or any other Indian territory for the purpose of holding or grazing them upon the public domain of the Cherokee Nation, whether the same be inclosed or otherwise: Provided, That citizens of the Cherokee Nation may introduce cattle between the 1st day of December and the 28th day of February of the following year, by paying 50 cents per head for each and every head of cattle so introduced.

Be it further enacted, That it shall be the duty of the principal chief of the Cherokee Nation to report all violations of the above section to the Indian agent at Muskogee, Ind. T., or other proper authority of the United States, with the request that said violators of said section be proceeded against as provided in section 2117 of the Revised Statutes of the United States, and that they and the cattle so introduced in violation of said section be removed from within the limits of the Cherokee Nation.

Be it further enacted, That all moneys collected under the provisions of this act, after paying the necessary expenses, shall be placed by the Indian agent to the credit of the school fund of the Cherokee Nation.

Approved by principal chief November 28, 1900.
Approved by President December 27, 1900.

And no payments have been received during the past year under such act, owing to the fact that there was a great scarcity of feed in the Cherokee Nation during the months when cattle could have been legally brought into the Cherokee Nation by Cherokee citizens, and such cattle as were introduced into the Cherokee Nation were introduced after the time prescribed under the act set forth above and in violation of law. Many investigations covering such cattle have been made and much time has been devoted to this work, and while it has not produced any revenue it has resulted in much benefit to the Cherokee Nation by preventing the introduction of a vast number of Southern cattle infected with fever.

Summary of receipts.

Coal royalty	$5,339.57
Hay royalty	7,422.31
Merchandise tax	3,375.66
Gravel tax	236.52
Ferry tax	225.00
Timber royalty	461.00
Total	17,060.06

The total expense incurred by me in connection with the collection of the Cherokee revenues and the performance of such other duties as you have seen fit to delegate to me has amounted to $2,598.84. I have been assisted in the work of the collection of the Cherokee revenues by a clerk and one district revenue inspector.

CHICKASAW CATTLE TAX.

Under the provisions of the regulations of the honorable Secretary of the Interior promulgated June 3, 1902, the work of collecting the Chickasaw cattle tax was organized, the plan followed being to personally serve on each noncitizen owner of cattle a written demand for payment within ten days from date of such demand, together with copy of such regulations and duplicate statements to assist cattlemen in making their remittances to the United States Indian agent's office. (See Appendix No. 18, Inspector Wright's report.)

The first formal services were had about June 21, 1902, and while the ten-day limit specified therein has not at this time expired in any one case, numerous remittances, amounting to $1,160.75, have been received by the United States Indian agent's office.

In some parts of the Chickasaw Nation payments will be readily made, but in other localities the feeling against this tax is extremely bitter.

Very respectfully,

GUY P. COBB, *Revenue Inspector.*

Hon. J. GEO. WRIGHT,
United States Indian Inspector for Indian Territory.

REPORT OF THE MINING TRUSTEES FOR THE CHOCTAW AND CHICKASAW NATIONS.

SOUTH McALESTER, IND. T., *August 29, 1902.*

SIR: We have the honor to respectfully submit herewith our report for the fiscal year ended June 30, 1902.

The following statements give the names of individuals and companies who are mining coal and asphalt in the Choctaw and Chickasaw nations:

Coal operators.

Name of operator.	Mines at—	Principal office.
Adkins, Charles G	Cameron, Ind. T	Cameron, Ind. T.
Arkansas-McAlester Coal Co	McAlester and Haileyville, Ind. T.	Kansas City, Mo.
Atoka Coal and Mining Co	Lehigh, Ind. T	St. Louis, Mo.
Bache & Denman	Red Oak, Ind. T	Alderson, Ind. T.
Busby, William	Baker and Alderson, Ind. T	Parsons, Kans.
Capital Coal and Mining Co	Savanna, Ind. T	Savanna, Ind. T.
Choctaw Coal and Mining Co	Sutter, Ind. T	Sutter, Ind. T.
Choctaw Mining and Mercantile Co	Savanna, Ind. T	Savanna, Ind. T.
Caston Coal Co.*a*	Wister, Ind. T	McAlester, Ind. T.
Choctaw, Oklahoma and Gulf R. R. Co	Alderson, Hartshorne, and Gowen, Ind. T.	Little Rock, Ark.
Degnan & McConnell	Wilburton, Ind. T	Wilburton, Ind. T.
Devlin-Wear Coal Co	Poteau, Ind. T	Topeka, Kans.

a Operations suspended in September, 1901.

Coal operators—Continued

Name of operator.	Mines at—	Principal office.
Edwards & Son, D	Kiowa, Ind. T	Kiowa, Ind. T.
Folsom-Morris Coal Mining Co	Lehigh, Ind. T	Ardmore, Ind. T.
Ford, M. A	Ardmore, Ind. T	Do.
Hailey Coal and Mining Co	Haileyville, Ind. T	Haileyville, Ind. T.
Kansas and Texas Coal Co	Carbon, Ind. T	St. Louis, Mo.
Kiowa Coal Co	Kiowa, Ind. T	Muskogee, Ind. T.
Mexican Gulf Coal and Transportation Co. a	Howe, Ind. T	St. Louis, Mo.
Milby & Dow Coal and Mining Co.a	Dow, Ind. T	Houston, Tex.
McAlester Coal Mining Co	Buck, Ind. T	Buck, Ind. T.
McMurray, John F	Baker, Ind. T	S. McAlester, Ind. T.
McAlester and Galveston Coal Mining Co	McAlester, Ind. T	McAlester, Ind. T.
McEvers, H. Newton	..do	Do.
McDougall, J. B	Coalgate, Ind. T	Coalgate, Ind. T.
McDougall Co	..do	Do.
Ola Coal and Mining Co.a	Ola, Ind. T	Ola, Ind. T.
Osage Coal and Mining Co	Krebs, Ind. T	St. Louis, Mo.
Ozark Coal and Rwy. Co	Panama, Ind. T	Panama, Ind. T.
Perona, Mike	Savanna, Ind. T	Savanna, Ind. T.
Perry Brothers	Coalgate, Ind. T	Coalgate, Ind. T.
Sans Bois Coal Co	McCurtain, Ind. T	Fort Smith, Ark.
Samples Coal and Mining Co	McAlester, Ind. T	McAlester, Ind. T.
St. Louis and Galveston Coal and Mining Co.	Lehigh, Ind. T	St. Louis, Mo.
Southwestern Coal and Improvement Co	Coalgate, Ind. T	Parsons, Kans.
Turkey Creek Coal Co	Hughes, Ind. T	Hughes, Ind. T.
Wilburton Coal and Mining Co.a	Wilburton, Ind. T	Parsons, Kans.

a Operations of these four companies carried on under contract on approved leases of Choctaw, Oklahoma and Gulf Railroad Company.

Asphalt operators.

Name of operator.	Mines at—	Principal office.
Brunswick Asphalt Co	Dougherty, Ind. T	New York City.
Caddo Asphalt Mining Co.a	Ardmore, Ind. T	Do.
Choctaw Asphalt Co	Antlers, Ind. T	St. Louis, Mo.
Downard Asphalt Co	Ardmore, Ind. T	Lima, Ohio.
Elk Asphalt Co	Elk, Ind. T	New York City.
Farmer Asphalt Co	Victor, Ind. T	Roff, Ind. T.
Gilsonite Roofing and Paving Co	Dougherty, Ind. T	St. Louis, Mo.
Mills, Geo. A. H	Ravia, Ind. T	Do.
Rock Creek National Asphalt Co	Dougherty, Ind. T	Topeka, Kans.
Schneider, M. & A	Woodward, Ind. T	Ardmore, Ind. T.
Tar Spring Asphalt Co	Comanche, Ind. T	Comanche, Ind. T.

a Lease canceled by Department April 3, 1902.

COAL ACREAGE LEASED.

The total number of acres of land covered by coal leases approved during the year is 23,640, as shown by the following statement:

Name of lessee.	Number of leases.	Land leased.
		Acres.
Arkansas-McAlester Coal Co	1	960
Atoka Coal and Mining Co	1	720
Bache & Denman	1	960
Chambers, Thomas H	1	960
Capital Coal and Mining Co	1	960
Essen Coal Co	1	960
Hailey Coal and Mining Co	2	1,920
Kansas and Texas Coal Co	4	3,840
Le Bosquet Coal and Mining Co	1	960
McDougall Co	1	960
Southwestern Coal and Improvement Co	10	9,480
Turkey Creek Coal Co	1	960
Total	25	23,640

RECAPITULATION.

Total number of acres of land covered by coal leases approved during fiscal year ended June 30, 1902 23,640

Total number of acres of land covered by coal leases approved previous to July 1, 1901 78,740

Total number of acres of land covered by approved coal leases June 30, 1902 97,380

ASPHALT ACREAGE LEASED.

During the year the only asphalt lease approved was that of the Choctaw Asphalt Company, of St. Louis, Mo., for 960 acres, and the following statement shows that the total number of acres of land covered by approved asphalt leases on June 30, 1902, was 4,320.

Total number of acres of land covered by asphalt leases approved during fiscal year ended June 30, 1902 960
Total number of acres of land covered by asphalt leases approved previous to July 1, 1901 4,320

Grand total 5,280
Less one lease of 960 acres canceled during fiscal year ended June 30, 1902 960

Total number of acres covered by asphalt leases on June 30, 1902 4,320

RECAPITULATION.

[Showing coal and asphalt acreage leased.]

Total number of acres of land covered by approved coal leases on June 30, 1902............... 97,380
Total number of acres of land covered by approved asphalt leases on June 30, 1902............ 4,320

Total number of acres of land covered by approved coal and asphalt leases on June 30, 1902. 101,700

ROYALTY ON COAL AND ASPHALT.

The royalty on coal and asphalt is the same as it was at the date of our last annual report, namely:
On coal, 8 cents a ton on all coal mined, including slack.
On asphalt, 60 cents a ton on refined and 10 cents a ton on crude asphalt.

COAL AND ASPHALT ROYALTY.

The following statements, on pages 126–128, show the total amounts of coal and asphalt mined and the total amounts of royalty paid by each coal and asphalt operator in the Choctaw and Chickasaw nations during the fiscal year ended June 30, 1902.

Statement showing total amount of coal mined and royalty paid by each operator in Choctaw and Chickasaw nations, Indian Territory, for fiscal year ended June 30, 1902, at 8 cents a ton.

Name of operator.	Coal mined.	Royalty paid.
	Tons	
Atoka Coal and Mining Co	313,431.6	$25,074.77
Adkins, Charles G......	1,320.15	105.61
Arkansas-McAlester Coal Co............................	17,874.2	1,429.93
Bache & Denman	1,955.15	156.41
Busby, William	15,584	1,246.72
Busby, William a...	12,628	1,010.24
Capital Coal and Mining Co	8,407	672.56
Choctaw Coal and Mining Co	40,837	3,266.96
Choctaw Mining and Mercantile Co.........................	18,926	1,514.08
Choctaw, Oklahoma and Gulf R. R Co......................	490,589	39,247.12
Caston Coal Co..	774	61.94
Degnan & McConnell	173,213	13,857.04
Devlin-Wear Coal Co.......................................	66,451	5,316.08
Edwards & Son, D	13,422	1,073.76
Folsom-Morris Coal Mining Co	22,709	1,816.72
Ford, M. A	778	62.24
Hailey Coal and Mining Co.................................	65,003	5,200.24
Kansas and Texas Coal Co..................................	104,454.975	8,356.40
Kiowa Coal Co..	81.13	6.49
Mexican Gulf Coal and Transportation Co.a	90,805	7,264.40
Missouri, Kansas and Texas Coal Co	581	46.48
Milby & Dow Coal and Mining Co.a	103,906	8,312.48
Moore, John G...	20	1.60
McMurray, John F..	15,315.5	1,225.24
McAlester Coal Mining Co....	100,240	8,019.20
McAlester and Galveston Coal Mining Co	5,615	449.20
McEvers, H. Newton	9,264	741.12
McDougall, J B	82,048	6,563.84
McDougall Company	3,604	288.32
Ola Coal and Mining Co.a	73,969.75	5,917.58
Osage Coal and Mining Co	264,407	21,152.58

a Operations of these companies carried on under contract on approved leases of Choctaw, Oklahoma, and Gulf R. R. Co.

Statement showing total amount of coal mined and royalty paid by each operator in Choctaw and Chickasaw nations, Indian Territory, etc.—Continued.

Name of operator.	Coal mined.	Royalty paid.
	Tons.	
Ozark Coal and Rwy. Co	25,489	$2,089.12
Perona, Mike	122	9.76
Perry Brothers	126,314	10,105.12
San Bois Coal Co	6,320.5	505.64
Southwestern Coal and Improvement Co	251,148	20,091.84
Samples Coal and Mining Co	50,884	4,070.72
St. Louis-Galveston Coal and Mining Co	5,778	462.24
Turkey Creek Coal Co	17,154	1,872.32
Watkins, Leslie	94.5	7.56
Wilburton Coal and Mining Co.a	133,845	10,707.60
Grand total	2,735,365.455	$218,829.27

a Operations of these companies carried on under contract on approved leases of Choctaw, Oklahoma, and Gulf R. R. Co.

Comparison.

	Tons.	Royalty.
Total amount of coal mined during fiscal year ended June 30, 1902	2,735,365.455	$218,829.27
Total amount of coal mined during fiscal year ended June 30, 1901	2,398,156.02	191,852.50
Increase	337,209.435	26,976.77

Statement showing total amount of asphalt mined and royalty paid by each operator in Choctaw and Chickasaw nations, Indian Territory, for fiscal year ended June 30, 1902, at 10 cents a ton.

Name of operator.	Asphalt mined.	Royalty paid.
	Tons.	
Brunswick Asphalt Co	931	$93.10
Busch, Baxter & Spencer	123	12.30
Caddo Asphalt Mining Co	0	0
Choctaw Asphalt Co	0	0
Downard Asphalt Co	1,048	104.80
Elk Asphalt Co	0	0
Farmer Asphalt Co	66	6.60
Gilsonite Roofing and Paving Co	2,158	215.80
Mills, George A. H	211.5	21.15
Moulton, George D	191	19.10
Rock Creek Natural Asphalt Co	375.7	37.57
Schneider, M. & A	0	0
Tar Spring Asphalt Co	0	0
Williams, Boone	0	0
Total	5,104.2	510.42

Comparison.

	Tons.	Royalty.
Total amount of asphalt mined during fiscal year ended June 30, 1902	5,104.2	$510.42
Total amount of asphalt mined during fiscal year ended June 30, 1901	3,492.97	349.30
Increase	1,611.23	161.12

RECAPITULATION OF COAL AND ASPHALT OUTPUT FOR 1902.

Mineral.	Amount mined.	Royalty paid.
	Tons.	
Coal	2,735,365.455	$218,829.27
Asphalt	5,104.2	510.42
Grand total	2,740,469.655	$219,339.69

Applications reported by mining trustees—Continued.

Name of applicant.	Mineral.	Applications.	
		Applied for.	Recommended
Chambers, Thomas H. a	Coal	1	1
Essen Coal Co	do	1	1
Elliott Coal Co	do	2	2
Fordyce, S. W.	do	1	0
Ferguson, J. B	do	1	0
Fahey & Ansley a	do	1	1
Farmer Asphalt Co	Asphalt	1	1
Folsom-Morris Coal Mining Co	Coal	1	1
Frisco Asphalt Co	Asphalt	1	0
Gilsonite Roofing and Paving Co	do	1	1
Gaines Creek Coal Co	Coal	1	0
Hailey Coal and Mining Co. b	do	2	2
Johnson Co.	do	1	1
Kiowa Coal Co	do	1	1
Kiowa-McAlester Coal Co	do	1	1
Le Bosquet Coal and Mining Co	do	1	1
Mills, Geo. A. H	Asphalt	1	1
Milby & Dow Coal and Mining Co	Coal	2	2
Mayo, Dave	do	1	0
Mazzard Coal and Mining Co	do	1	0
Oklahoma-Chickasaw Asphalt Co	Asphalt	1	0
Ohio Coal Co	Coal	1	1
Osage Coal and Mining Co	do	1	1
Perry Brothers	do	1	0
Parsons Coal and Mining Co	do	2	0
Pennsylvania Coal Co.	do	1	1
Pettis, Wm. Spencer	do	1	0
Southwestern Coal and Improvement Co. b	do	10	10
Southern Coal Co.	do	1	0
Spiro Coal and Mining Co.	do	1	0
Sebastian Asphalt Mining Co	Asphalt	1	0
Standard Coal Co	Coal	1	1
Torrence, L. C.	do	1	0
Tobucksy Coal Co	do	1	0
Trinidad Asphalt Manufacturing Co.	Asphalt	1	1
Tobucksy Mining Co.	Coal	1	1
Todd, James S.	do	1	1
Williams & Davies	do	1	0
Webster & Whitesell a	Asphalt	1	0
Williams, Boone	do	1	0
Watkins, Leslie	Coal	1	0
Total		73	8

a Mining permit.   b Heretofore operated under national contract.

Applications approved by Department.

Name of applicant.	Mineral.	Applications	
		Applied for.	Approved
Arkansas-McAlester Coal Co	Coal	1	1
Atoka Coal and Mining Co.	do	1	1
Adkins, Charles G	do	1	1
Ardmore Coal and Power Co	do	1	1
Bache & Denman	do	1	1
Chambers, Thomas H	do	1	1
Choctaw Asphalt Co.	Asphalt	1	1
Capital Coal and Mining Co	Coal	1	1
Essen Coal Co.	do	1	1
Folsom-Morris Coal Mining Co	do	1	1
Gilsonite Roofing and Paving Co	Asphalt	1	1
Hailey Coal and Mining Co. a	Coal	2	2
Johnson Co	do	1	1
Kansas and Texas Coal Co. a	do	3	3
Le Bosquet Coal and Mining Co	do	1	1
Mazzard Coal and Mining Co.	do	1	1
McDougall Co	do	1	1
Sans Bois Coal Co. b	do	1	1
Southwestern Coal and Improvement Co. a	do	10	9
Turkey Creek Coal Co	do	1	1
Trinidad Asphalt Manufacturing Co	Asphalt	1	1
Total		33	2

a Heretofore operated under national contract.   b New lease approved in exchange for one canceled

Applications disapproved by Department.

Name of applicant.	Mineral.	Applications.
Adkins, Charles G. a	Coal	1
Bonham, R. A	do	1
Brewer Mining Co. a	do	1
Black, William H	do	1
Cloakey, Josiah M	do	1
Chambers, Thomas H. b	do	1
Ferguson, J. B	do	1
Gilsonite Roofing and Paving Co. a	Asphalt	1
Kansas and Texas Coal Co	Coal	1
Kiowa Coal Co. a	do	1
Kansas and Indian Territory Coal Mining Co	do	1
Le Bosquet Coal and Mining Co. c	do	1
McAlester Coal Co	do	1
Mills, Geo. A. H. a	Asphalt	1
Oklahoma-Chickasaw Asp. Co	do	1
Rock Creek Natural Asphalt Co. a	do	1
Spiro Coal and Mining Co	Coal	1
Todd, James S	do	1
Torrence, L. C	do	1
Williams, Boone a	Asphalt	1
Weiser, C. H	Coal	1
Webster & Whitesell b	Asphalt	1
Watkins, Leslie	Coal	1
Total		23

a Mining permit granted.
b Application was for mining permit.
c Afterwards filed amended application, which was approved.

Leases executed by mining trustees and forwarded to Department.

Name of lessee.	Mineral.	Number leases.
Arkansas-McAlester Coal Co	Coal	1
Atoka Coal and Mining Co	do	1
Bache & Denman	do	1
Chambers, Thomas H	do	1
Capital Coal and Mining Co	do	1
Choctaw Asphalt Co	Asphalt	1
Essen Coal Co	Coal	1
Hailey Coal and Mining Co. a	do	2
Kansas and Texas Coal Co. a	do	4
LeBosquet Coal and Mining Co	do	1
McDougall Co	do	1
Southwestern Coal and Improvement Co. a	do	10
Turkey Creek Coal Co	do	1
Total		26

a Heretofore operated under a national contract.

Leases approved by Department.

Name of lessee.	Mineral.	Leases.	Date of approval.
Arkansas-McAlester Coal Co	Coal	1	Oct. 1, 1901
Atoka Coal and Mining Co	do	1	June 13, 1902
Bache & Denman	do	1	Apr. 22, 1902
Chambers, Thomas H	do	1	Dec. 9, 1901
Choctaw Asphalt Co	Asphalt	1	Apr. 22, 1902
Capital Coal and Mining Co	Coal	1	June 16, 1902
Essen Coal Co	do	1	Apr. 22, 1902
Hailey Coal and Mining Co. a	do	2	June 17, 1902
Kansas and Texas Coal Co. a	do	4	June 13, 1902
LeBosquet Coal and Mining Co	do	1	June 18, 1902
McDougall Co	do	1	do
Southwestern Coal and Improvement Co. a	do	10	Apr. 4, 1902
Turkey Creek Coal Co	do	1	Mar. 18, 1902
Total		26	

a Heretofore operated under national contract.

PROGRESS.

(a) Work at Durwood, Fort Gibson, Hartshorne, Hickory, Krebs, Lone Grove, Mannsville, Milburn, Oakland, and Sulphur was delayed by railroad, treaty, or other complications. Work is now under way, however, at most of these towns.

(b) The plats of Ada, Francis, Gray, Helen, Madill, Mill Creek, Ravia, Roff, and Scullin, which were made under the L. F. Parker contract, are held for the reason that the station grounds on these town plats were not shown in accordance with the plats previously approved by the Secretary of the Interior.

(c) The segregations for Bennington, Fort Towson, Garvin, Gilbert, Harrington, Hugo, Mead, New Bokchito, Purnell, Soper, Stringtown, and Valliant, made upon recommendation of the Dawes Commission, were not approved until June, 1902, too late to commence surveys prior to June 30. Surveying parties are now at work upon these towns.

(d) Plats of Adair, Afton, Bartlesville, Coalgate, Claremore, Fairland, Davis, Gans, Grove, Haileyville, Sapulpa, Pryor Creek, Stilwell, Tahlequah, Westville, Purcell, Tishomingo, Muldrow, Oolagah, Sallisaw, Vian, and Wapanucka were, on June 30, 1902, being checked in Muskogee, in transit, or being passed upon in Washington.

The status of the work June 30, 1902, is summarized as follows:

Towns delayed by complications (a) 10
Towns surveyed under Parker contract—plats held (b) 9
Town sites segregated in June, 1902, too late for work to commence during the year (c) 12
Towns surveyed and platted but plats not yet approved (d) 22
Towns surveyed and platted and plats approved. (See Table No. 2) 104

Total as above stated 157

It will be noted that while the last annual report showed 107 towns listed the work has been completed upon 126 towns.

RAILROAD COMPLICATIONS.

The completion of the plats has often been delayed by complications as to railroad grounds; for example:

Station grounds marked by permanent monuments incorrectly located (as at Canadian) and valuable improvements in the way of correcting station ground monuments to conform with approved plat, as at Pauls Valley.

Station grounds recognized as railroad property, but to which railroad company had no title and under previously existing laws could not acquire title (filing rights having been exhausted), as at Checotah, Muldrow, and Davis.

Right of way approved upon one location and track laid upon another, so that track is off the right of way, as at Coalgate.

Station grounds of two companies conflicting (as at Vinita), and data upon approved plats insufficient to determine the right of way or station grounds of either company, as at Purcell.

Station grounds along a line of railroad whose Congressional charter gave it the right to "all necessary grounds," no plats having ever been filed or required by law to be filed to show the location or extent of the necessary grounds (S. L. and S. F.).

Station grounds officially located by plusses from the mileposts of a series of miles which has long since been discarded for an entirely different chaining and with no record of the equation, as at Savanna, now in hand.

Misunderstanding between townspeople and railroad company during construction, the railroad company having filed upon and secured approval of a stated width of grounds, and the townspeople having erected store fronts 25 or 50 feet nearer to track and on railroad grounds, as at Spiro.

It has been necessary to eliminate all such discrepancies or ambiguities before submitting plats for approval, and the railroad companies have generally been glad to do their part toward straightening out these matters.

COST.

The cost of surveys under the supervision of the inspector has been as follows:

	Acres.	Cost.	Per acre.	Estimate.a
Exterior limits........................	37, 162. 395	$15,968. 47	$0. 42	$0. 38
Platting..............................	31, 843. 31	79, 260. 03	2. 42	2. 43
Total............................	34, 345. 455	99, 298. 42	2. 84	2. 81

a Page 156, Annual Report, June 30, 1901.

MISCELLANEOUS.

Changes have been ordered in the limits of most of the Cherokee towns, and the areas given for those towns in this report are greater than the areas which were first established and which were given in previous annual report.

There are appended hereto the following tables:

Table No. 1. Area segregated in each nation.

Table No. 2. Alphabetical list of towns in hand, with areas and dates of approval.

Table No. 3. Cost of surveys.

During the year Surveyors Frank Hackelman, Frank H. Boyd, Henry M. Tinker, and Sidney T. Emerson tendered their resignations, and Mortimer Z. Jones, a faithful and energetic surveyor, died of malarial fever.

Transitmen William E. McElree, J. Gus. Patton, Samuel P. Matthews, and Frank F. Sweet were commissioned as surveyors, and Surveyor John G. Joyce, jr., was commissioned assistant supervising engineer.

Respectfully,

H. V. HINCKLEY,
Supervising Engineer.

UNITED STATES INDIAN INSPECTOR FOR THE INDIAN TERRITORY.

TABLE No. 1.—*Indian Territory town-site segregations.*

[Areas in each nation June 30, 1902.]

Town.	Acres.	Town.	Acres.
CHICKASAW.		**CHICKASAW—continued.**	
Ada	559.90	Sulphur	948.14
Addington	145.40	Terral	280
Ardmore	2,262.14	Tishomingo	545
Berwyn	191.25	Woodville	165
Center	195	Wynnewood	767.50
Chickasha	1,246.19		
Colbert	134.77	Total of 57 towns	19,907.005
Comanche	437.04		
Connerville	180	**CHOCTAW.**	
Cornish	190.28		
Cumberland	173.98	Allen	120
Davis	531.46	Antlers	182.50
Dougherty	243.125	Atoka	277.18
Duncan	1,010.07	Bennington	140
Durwood	140	Caddo	400
Earl	125	Calvin	160
Elmore	145	Cameron	155
Emet	170	Canadian	197.50
Erin Springs	110	Coalgate	785
Francis	160	Cowlington	157.50
Gray	80	Durant	1,324
Helen	156.09	Enterprise	107.50
Hickory	170	Fort Towson	160
Johnson	90	Garvin	120
Kemp	120	Gilbert	100
Lebanon	164.92	Grant	131.22
Leon	165	Guertie	160
Lonegrove	195	Haileyville	681.05
Madill	160	Hartshorne	848.11
Mannsville	175	Heavener	175.64
Marietta	330	Harrington	45
Marlow	960	Howe	326.70
Mead	60	Hoyt	97.50
McGee	122.50	Hugo	160
Milburn	160	Krebs	330
Millcreek	155.45	Kiowa	360
Minco	285.35	Lehigh	1,050
Oakland	343.75	McAlester	759.07
Orr	185	New Bokchito	45
Paoli	85.48	Poteau	645
Pauls Valley	946.83	Purnell	89.39
Pontotoc	195	Redoak	132.50
Purcell	1,110.68	South McAlester	2,902.27
Purdy	116.25	Soper	90
Ravia	326.39	Spiro	225.78
Roff	595	Sterrett	485
Rush Springs	380	Stigler	102.33
Ryan	435.39	Stringtown	62.50
Scullin	120	Talihina	210.59
Silo	195	Tamaha	142.30
Stonewall	117.50	Valliant	120
Sugden	149.18	Wapanucka	425

TABLE No. 1.—*Indian Territory town-site segregations*—Continued.

Town.	Acres.	Town.	Acres.
CHOCTAW—continued.		**CHEROKEE.**	
Whitefield	100.57	Adair	150
Wilburton	275.58	Afton	532.50
Wister	149.78	Bartlesville	342.44
		Bluejacket	196.25
Total of 45 towns	15,714.06	Catoosa	165
		Centralia	177.50
CREEK.		Chelsea	452.59
Alabama	80	Choteau	130
Beggs	160	Claremore	657.50
Bixby	80	Collinsville	270
Bristow	385	Fairland	240
Checotah	503.75	Fort Gibson	412.65
Clarksville	147.50	Gans	115
Coweta	85	Grove	210
Eufaula	431.38	Hanson	95
Foster	120	Lenapah	118.12
Gibson	160	Muldrow	210.50
Henryetta	157.13	Nowata	375.63
Holdenville	429.79	Oolagah	170
Inola	165	Pryorcreek	365
Kellyville	85	Ramona	110
Lee	45	Sallisaw	257.78
Mounds	160	Stilwell	164.22
Muskogee	2,444.76	Tahlequah	682.50
Okmulgee	415	Talala	170
Sapulpa	501.25	Vian	220.62
Redfork	160	Vinita	946.23
Tulsa	654.58	Webbers Falls	80.50
Wagoner	2,700	Welch	160
Wetumka	160	Westville	179.99
Winchell	160		
Wildcat	158	Total of 30 towns	8,307.52
Total of 25 towns	10,548.14	Grand total of 157 towns	54,476.725

TABLE No. 2.—*Indian Territory town sites—areas and approvals, June 30, 1902.*

[In Remarks column R. R. signifies Railroad complications and D. C. signifies segregation on recommendation of Dawes Commission.]

Town.	Nation.	Exterior survey.		Interior survey, date of approval.	Remarks.
		Acres, including cemeteries.	Date of approval.		
Ada	Chickasaw	559.90	Feb. 6, 1901		D.C.; R.R.
Adair	Cherokee	150	Oct. 23, 1901		
Addington	Chickasaw	145.40	Mar. 4, 1902	May 9, 1902	
Afton	Cherokee	532.50	Apr. 17, 1902		
Alabama	Creek	80	Oct. 26, 1900	Nov. 13, 1901	D.C.
Allen	Choctaw	120	Sept. 5, 1901	Nov. 5, 1901	
Antlers	do	182.50	Feb. 8, 1901	June 7, 1901	
Ardmore	Chickasaw	2,262.14		Jan. 15, 1902	
Atoka	Choctaw	277.18		Feb. 23, 1900	Choc. T. C.
Bartlesville	Cherokee	342.44	Mar. 13, 1902		R.R.
Beggs	Creek	160	Oct. 26, 1900	Nov. 13, 1901	D.C.
Berwyn	Chickasaw	191.25	Aug. 23, 1901	Dec. 3, 1901	
Bluejacket	Cherokee	196.25	Mar. 22, 1902	July 10, 1902	
Bristow	Creek	385	Oct. 17, 1901	Dec. 23, 1901	
Bennington	Choctaw	140	June 24, 1902		D.C.; being platted.
Bixby	Creek	80	Mar. 11, 1902	Apr. 10, 1902	
Caddo	Choctaw	400	Feb. 9, 1901	June 7, 1901	
Calvin	do	160		Nov. 8, 1900	Choc. T. C.
Cameron	do	155	Feb. 21, 1901	July 8, 1901	
Canadian	do	197.50	Jan. 8, 1901	Dec. 18, 1901	
Catoosa	Cherokee	165	May 15, 1902	June 16, 1902	
Center	Chickasaw	195	Dec. 20, 1900	Mar. 4, 1902	
Centralia	Cherokee	177.50	Apr. 9, 1902	May 8, 1902	
Checotah	Creek	503.75	{Feb. 15, 1901 {Sept. 6, 1901	}Mar. 22, 1902	
Chelsea	Cherokee	452.59	Mar 10, 1902	June 16, 1902	
Chickasha	Chickasaw	1,246.19	Dec. 11, 1901	Dec. 11, 1901	
Choteau	Cherokee	130	Oct. 23, 1901	Apr. 12, 1902	
Claremore	do	657.50	June 13, 1902		R.R.
Clarksville	Creek	147.50	Feb. 15, 1901	Feb. 27, 1902	

TABLE No. 2.—*Indian Territory town sites—areas and approvals, June 30, 1902*—Cont'd.

Town.	Nation.	Exterior survey		Interior survey, date of approval.	Remarks.
		Acres, including cemeteries.	Date of approval.		
Coalgate	Choctaw	785	Oct. 1, 1901		R. R.
Colbert	Chickasaw	134.77	{Cemetery....} {Apr. 12, 1900}	Aug. 14, 1899	Chick. T. C.
Collinsville	Cherokee	270	May 15, 1902	June 16, 1902	
Comanche	Chickasaw	437.04	Oct. 1, 1901	Apr. 11, 1902	
Connerville	do	180	June 1, 1901	Nov. 7, 1901	
Cornish	do	190.28	Feb. 15, 1901	Jan. 8, 1902	
Coweta	Creek	85	Mar. 4, 1902	Apr. 16, 1902	
Cowlington	Choctaw	157.50	Feb. 7, 1901	Nov. 5, 1901	
Cumberland	Chickasaw	173.98	Nov. 27, 1901	Nov. 27, 1901	
Davis	do	581.46	May 29, 1902		Plat completed.
Dougherty	do	248.125	Jan. 31, 1901	June 2, 1902	
Duncan	do	1,010.07	Sept. 13, 1901	Mar. 4, 1902	
Durant	Choctaw	1,324	{Feb. 4, 1901} {Mar. 22, 1902}	May 15, 1902	
Durwood	Chickasaw	140	Dec. 15, 1900		Not yet completed.
Earl	do	125	Dec. 13, 1900	Dec. 3, 1901	
Emet	do	170	Dec. 15, 1900	Nov. 5, 1901	
Enterprise	Choctaw	107.50	Feb. 15, 1901	July 1, 1901	
Erin Springs	Chickasaw	110	Mar. 23, 1901	Dec. 3, 1901	
Eufaula	Creek	431.38	{June 25, 1901} {Oct. 28, 1901}	Mar. 17, 1902	
Elmore	Chickasaw	145	Apr. 7, 1902	May 8, 1902	
Fairland	Cherokee	240	June 16, 1902		R. R.
Foster	Creek	120	Oct. 26, 1900	Nov. 13, 1901	D. C.; "Yager."
Fort Gibson	Cherokee	412.65	July 7, 1902		Being platted; R. R.
Francis	Chickasaw	160	Oct. 26, 1900		D. C.; R. R.
Fort Towson	Choctaw	160	June 24, 1902		D. C.; being platted.
Garvin	do	120	do		Do.
Gibson	Creek	160	Oct. 24, 1901	Apr. 17, 1902	
Gilbert	Choctaw	100	June 24, 1902		Do.
Grant	do	131.22	Apr. 11, 1901	June 4, 1901	
Gray	Chickasaw	80	Oct. 26, 1900		D. C.; canceled.
Grove	Cherokee	210	June 16, 1902		R. R.; being completed.
Guertie	Choctaw	160		Nov. 2, 1900	Choc. T. C.
Gans	Cherokee	115	Apr. 15, 1902		Plat completed.
Hanson	do	95	Nov. 13, 1901	July 10, 1902	
Harrington	Choctaw	45	June 24, 1902		D. C.; being platted.
Hartshorne	do	848.11	June 25, 1902		Platting about done.
Haileyville	do	681.05	do		Not yet approved.
Heavener	do	175.64	Feb. 23, 1901	June 4, 1902	
Helen	Chickasaw	156.09	Oct. 26, 1900		D. C.; R. R.
Henryetta	Creek	157.13	do	Nov. 16, 1901	
Hickory	Chickasaw	170			R. R.
Holdenville	Creek	429.79	Feb. 7, 1901	Nov. 27, 1901	
Howe	Choctaw	326.70	{Feb. 6, 1901} {Apr. 8, 1901}	Sept. 10, 1901	
Hoyt	do	97.50	Feb. 15, 1901	July 3, 1901	
Hugo	do	160	June 24, 1902		D. C.; being platted.
Inola	Creek	165	Oct. 23, 1901	Mar. 4, 1902	
Johnson	Chickasaw	90	Feb. 7, 1901	Nov. 5, 1901	
Kellyville	Creek	85	Oct. 24, 1901	Mar. 20, 1902	
Kemp	Chickasaw	120	Dec. 15, 1900	Jan. 8, 1902	
Krebs	Choctaw	330			Coal town, held.
Kiowa	do	360		Nov. 2, 1900	Choc. T. C.
Lebanon	Chickasaw	164.92	Dec. 19, 1900	Nov. 5, 1901	
Lehigh	Choctaw	1,050	Sept. 5, 1901	May 8, 1902	
Lenapah	Cherokee	118.12	Mar. 5, 1902	Apr. 19, 1902	
Leon	Chickasaw	165	Dec. 20, 1900	Mar. 4, 1902	
Lonegrove	do	195	Sept 6, 1901		Not yet platted.
Lee	Creek	45	Mar. 26, 1902	May 8, 1902	
Madill	Chickasaw	160	Jan. 5, 1901		D. C.; R. R.
Mannsville	do	175	Dec. 15, 1900		Being platted; R. R.
Marietta	do	330	Jan. 12, 1901	Nov. 1, 1901	
Marlow	do	960	Oct. 26, 1900	Nov. 29, 1901	
McAlester	Choctaw	759.07	Sept. 5, 1901	Dec. 10, 1901	
McGee	Chickasaw	122.50	Dec. 17, 1900	Nov. 5, 1901	
Millcreek	do	155.45	Oct. 26, 1900		D. C.; "Bryant;" R. R.
Mineo	do	285.35	Nov. 27, 1901	Nov 27, 1901	
Milburn	do	160	Apr. 8, 1902		"Blue."
Mounds	Creek	160	Oct. 26, 1900	Jan. 3, 1901	
Muldrow	Cherokee	210.50	July 8, 1902		Plat completed.
Muskogee	Creek	2,444.76		June 4, 1900	Musk. T. C.
Mead	Chickasaw	60	June 24, 1902		D. C.
Nowata	Cherokee	375.63	Mar 6, 1902	Apr. 19, 1902	
New Bokchito	Choctaw	45	June 24, 1902		D. C.; being platted.
Oakland	Chickasaw	343.75	July 9, 1902		Being platted.
Okmulgee	Creek	415	Feb. 6, 1901	Nov. 6, 1901	
Oolagah	Cherokee	170	Apr. 17, 1902		Plat completed.

TABLE No. 2.—*Indian Territory town sites—areas and approvals, June 30, 1902*—Cont'd.

Town.	Nation.	Exterior survey.		Interior survey, date of approval.	Remarks.
		Acres, including cemeteries.	Date of approval.		
Orr	Chickasaw	185	Dec. 20, 1900	Mar. 4, 1902	
Paoli	do	85.48	Apr. 11, 1901	Nov. 30, 1901	
Pauls Valley	do	946.83	Dec. 17, 1900	Jan. 18, 1902	
Pontotoc	do	195	Dec. 15, 1900	Dec. 28, 1901	
Poteau	Choctaw	645		June 4, 1901	Choctaw T. C.
Pryorcreek	Cherokee	365	Nov. 23, 1901		Plat completed.
Purcell	Chickasaw	1,110.68			R. R.
Purdy	do	116.25	Sept. 11, 1901	Nov. 5, 1901	
Purnell	Choctaw	89.39	June 24, 1902		D. C.; being platted.
Ramona	Cherokee	110	Mar. 11, 1902	May 6, 1902	
Ravia	Chickasaw	326.89	Apr. 20, 1901		D. C.; R. R.
Redfork	Creek	160	Dec. 13, 1901	Feb. 20, 1902	
Redoak	Choctaw	132.50	Dec. 15, 1900	June 7, 1901	
Roff	Chickasaw	595	Feb. 6, 1901		Do.
Rush Springs	do	380	Oct. 26, 1900	Nov. 27, 1901	
Ryan	do	435.39	do	Mar. 7, 1902	
Sallisaw	Cherokee	257.78	May 15, 1902		Not yet approved.
Sapulpa	Creek	501.25	Feb. 15, 1901		Do.
Scullin	Chickasaw	120	Oct. 26, 1900		D. C.; R. R.
Silo	do	195	Dec. 15, 1900	Sept. 10, 1901	
South McAlester	Choctaw	2,902.27		Feb. 14, 1901	Choctaw T. C.
Spiro	do	225.78	Feb. 15, 1901 / Apr. 8, 1901 / Apr. 9, 1901 / Feb. 19, 1902	May 2, 1902	
Sterrett	do	485		Aug. 28, 1899	Do.
Stigler	do	102.33	Feb. 15, 1901	Nov. 5, 1901	
Stilwell	Cherokee	164.22	July 7, 1902		Not yet approved.
Stonewall	Chickasaw	117.50	Dec. 17, 1900	Jan. 9, 1902	
Sugden	do	149.18	Mar. 4, 1902	Apr. 11, 1902	
Sulphur	do	948.14			Held; suppl. treaty.
Soper	Choctaw	90	June 24, 1902		D. C.; being platted.
Stringtown	do	62.50	June 23, 1902		
Tahlequah	Cherokee	632.50	July 7, 1902		Plat completed.
Talala	do	170	May 22, 1902	July 11, 1902	
Talihina	Choctaw	210.59	June 4, 1901	June 4, 1901	
Tamaha	do	142.30	Feb. 5, 1901	July 11, 1901	
Terral	Chickasaw	280	Oct. 26, 1900	Mar. 7, 1902	
Tishomingo	do	545	May 24, 1902		Do.
Tulsa	Creek	654.58	Feb. 21, 1901	Apr. 11, 1902	
Vian	Cherokee	220.62	June 14, 1902		Do.
Vinita	do	946.23	Mar. 5, 1902	May 10, 1902	
Valliant	Choctaw	120	June 24, 1902		D. C.; being completed.
Wagoner	Creek	2,700		Oct. 10, 1900	Wagoner T. C.
Wapanucka	Choctaw	425	June 14, 1902		Plat completed.
Webbers Falls	Cherokee	80.50	Mar. 11, 1902	July 11, 1902	
Welch	do	160	Apr. 11, 1902	May 7, 1902	
Westville	do	179.99	May 31, 1902		Do.
Wetumka	Creek	160	Oct. 26, 1900	Nov. 13, 1901	
Whitefield	Choctaw	100.57	Feb. 12, 1901	July 3, 1901	
Wilburton	do	275.58	Oct. 16, 1901	Mar. 11, 1902	
Wildcat	Creek	158	Mar. 11, 1902	May 8, 1902	
Winchell	do	160	Oct. 26, 1900	Nov. 13, 1901	
Wister	Choctaw	149.78	Feb. 12, 1901 / June 22, 1901	Nov. 30, 1901	
Woodville	Chickasaw	165	Oct. 26, 1900	Jan. 31, 1901	
Wynnewood	do	767.50	Dec. 15, 1900	Mar. 4, 1902	
Total		54,481.725			

TABLE No. 3.—*Indian Territory town sites—Cost of surveys, June 30, 1902.*

Town.	Nation.	Acres, including cemeteries.	Cost. Exterior survey.	Per acre.	Interior survey.	Per acre.	Total. Cost.	Per acre.	Remarks.
Ada	Chickasaw	559.90	$207.73	$0.37	$90.00	$0.16	$297.73	$0.53	
Adair	Cherokee	150	87.38	.58	497.16	3.31	584.54	3.90	
Addington	Chickasaw	145.40	97.73	.67	484.14	3.33	581.87	4.00	
Afton	Cherokee	532.50	110.15	.21	931.75	1.75	1,041.90	1.96	
Alabama	Creek	80					85.00	1.06	
Allen	Choctaw	120	62.67	.52	240.00	2.00	302.67	2.52	
Antlers	do	182.50	112.95	.62	711.29	3.90	824.24	4.52	
Ardmore	Chickasaw	2,202.14					6,035.52	2.67	
Atoka	Choctaw	277.18							Choctaw T. C.
Bartlesville	Cherokee	342.44	87.25	.25	972.44	2.84	1,059.69	3.10	
Beggs	Creek	160					85.00	.53	
Berwyn	Chickasaw	191.25	135.50	.71	660.00	3.45	795.50	4.16	
Bluejacket	Cherokee	196.25	77.12	.39	524.50	2.67	601.62	3.06	
Bristow	Creek	385	93.94	.24	800.12	2.08	894.06	2.32	
Bennington	Choctaw	140							
Bixby	Creek	80					276.04	3.45	
Caddo	Choctaw	400	179.24	.45	1,192.07	2.98	1,371.31	3.43	
Calvin	do	160							Do.
Cameron	do	155	135.27	.87	494.35	3.19	629.62	4.06	
Canadian	do	197.50	121.15	.61	1,612.38	8.16	1,733.53	8.77	
Catoosa	Cherokee	165	96.40	.58	585.89	3.25	682.29	3.83	
Center	Chickasaw	195	90.68	.47	282.90	1.45	373.58	1.92	
Centralia	Cherokee	177.50	91.86	.52	562.00	3.17	653.86	3.68	
Checotah	Creek	503.75	141.22	.28	1,785.50	3.54	1,926.72	3.82	
Chelsea	Cherokee	452.59	91.38	.20	1,899.00	2.49	1,217.38	2.69	
Chickasha	Chickasaw	1,246.19	190.33	.15		1.30	810.38	1.45	
Choteau	Cherokee	130	57.48	.44		2.23	346.99	2.67	
Claremore	do	657.50	130.80	.20	2,	3.70	2,566.10	3.90	
Clarksville	Creek	147.50	47.65	.32	289.50	1.96	337.15	2.28	
Coalgate	Choctaw	785							
Colbert	Chickasaw	134.77							
Collinsville	Cherokee	270	104.80	.39	555.43	2.06	660.23	2.45	
Comanche	do	437.04	167.91	.38	1,476.89	3.38	1,644.80	3.76	
Connersville	do	180	77.04	.43	195.00	1.08	272.04	1.51	
Cornish	do	190.28	90.75	.48	480.00	2.52	570.75	3.00	
Coweta	Creek	85	46.75	.55	170.00	2.00	216.75	2.55	
Cowlington	Choctaw	157.50	61.15	.39	315.00	2.00	376.15	2.39	
Cumberland	Chickasaw	173.98	80.40	.46	405.00	2.33	485.40	2.79	
Davis	do	531.46	187.34	.35	1,669.15	3.14	1,856.49	3.49	
Dougherty	do	243.125	96.85	.40	753.59	3.10	850.44	3.50	
Duncan	do	1,010.07	187.74	.19	1,010.07	1.00	1,197.81	1.19	
Durant	Choctaw	1,324	310.34	.23	3,514.25	2.65	3,824.59	2.89	
Durwood	Chickasaw	140	91.00	.65					
Earl	do	125	60.00	.48	287.50	2.30	347.50	2.78	
Emet	do	170	136.00	.80	420.00	2.47	556.00	3.27	
Enterprise	Choctaw	107.50	95.75	.89	163.00	1.52	258.75	2.41	
Erin Springs	Chickasaw	110.10	42.85	.39	341.00	3.10	383.85	3.49	
Eufaula	Creek	431.38	174.76	.41	1,394.84	3.23	1,569.60	3.64	
Elmore	Chickasaw	145	105.21	.73	210.45	1.45	315.66	2.18	
Fairland	Cherokee	240	155.07	.65	560.66	2.34	715.73	2.98	
Foster	Creek	120					85.00	.71	" Yager."
Fort Gibson	Cherokee	412.65							
Francis	Chickasaw	160					85.00	.53	
Fort Towson	Choctaw	160							
Garvin	do	120							
Gibson	Creek	160	64.00	.40	377.69	2.36	441.69	2.76	
Gilbert	Choctaw	100							
Grant	do	131.22	81.80	.62	250.70	1.91	332.50	2.53	
Gray	Chickasaw	80					85.00	1.06	
Grove	Cherokee	210	76.58	.36	540.00	2.57	616.58	2.94	
Guertie	Choctaw	160							Choctaw T. C.
Gans	Cherokee	115	81.70	.71	355.00	3.09	436.70	3.80	
Hanson	do	95	88.56	.93	378.92	3.99	467.48	4.92	
Harrington	Choctaw	45							
Hartshorne	do	848.11	626.66	.74					
Haileyville	do	681.05	475.88	.70	1,481.00	2.17	1,956.88	2.87	
Heavener	do	175.64	88.65	.50	340.00	1.94	428.65	2.44	
Helen	Chickasaw	156.09					85.00	.54	
Henryetta	Creek	157.13					85.00	.54	
Hickory	Chickasaw	170	101.14	.59					
Holdenville	Creek	429.79	102.71	.24	85.00	.20	187.71	.44	
Howe	Choctaw	326.70	203.27	.62	1,427.95	4.37	1,631.22	4.99	
Hoyt	do	97.50	63.82	.65	165.00	1.69	228.82	2.35	
Hugo	do	160							
Inola	Creek	165	49.50	.30	259.28	1.57	308.78	1.87	
Johnson	Chickasaw	90	52.50	.58	144.00	1.60	196.50	2.18	
Kellyville	Creek	85	25.50	.30	228.92	2.69	254.42	2.99	
Kemp	Chickasaw	120	91.85	.77	310.00	2.58	401.85	3.35	
Krebs	Choctaw	330	142.20	.43					

TABLE No. 3.—*Indian Territory town sites—Cost of surveys, June 30, 1902*—Continued.

Town.	Nation.	Acres, including cemeteries.	Cost. Exterior survey.	Per acre.	Cost. Interior survey.	Per acre.	Total. Cost.	Total. Per acre.	Remarks.
Kiowa	Choctaw	360							Choctaw, T. C.
Lebanon	Chickasaw	164.92	$72.85	$0.44	$180.00	$1.09	$252.85	$1.53	
Lehigh	Choctaw	1,050	226.06	.22	4,734.43	4.51	4,960.49	4.72	
Lenapah	Cherokee	118.12	85.97	.73	220.44	1.87	306.41	2.59	
Leon	Chickasaw	165	93.10	.56	398.71	2.42	491.81	2.98	
Lonegrove	do	195	59.75	.31					
Lee	Creek	45	13.50	.30	90.00	2.00	103.50	2.30	
Madill	Chickasaw	160							
Mannsville	do	175	96.25	.54					
Marietta	do	330	91.30	.28	790.00	2.39	881.30	2.67	
Marlow	do	960	90.49	.09	1,680.00	1.75	1,770.49	1.84	
McAlester	Choctaw	759.07	145.00	.19	1,576.00	2.08	1,721.00	2.27	
McGee	Chickasaw	122.50	158.75	1.30	253.12	2.07	411.87	3.36	
Millcreek	do	155.45							"Bryant."
Minco	do	285.35	100.23	.35	521.46	1.83	621.69	2.18	
Milburn	do	160							"Blue."
Mounds	Creek	160					85.00	.53	
Muldrow	Cherokee	210.50	114.78	.54					
Muscogee	Creek	2,444.76							Muscogee T. C.
Mead	Chickasaw	60							
Nowata	Cherokee	375.63	112.25	.30	587.45	1.56	699.70	1.86	
New Bokchito	Choctaw	45							
Oakland	Chickasaw	343.75	152.80	.44					
Okmulgee	Creek	415	79.81	.19	85.00	.20	164.81	.40	
Oolagah	Cherokee	170	86.95	.51	317.56	1.87	404.51	2.38	
Orr	Chickasaw	185	92.00	.50	575.00	3.11	667.00	3.61	
Paoli	do	85.48	218.22	*a*2.55	247.93	2.90	466.15	*a*5.45	
Pauls Valley	do	946.83	211.12	.22	2,533.61	2.68	2,744.73	2.90	
Pontotoc	do	195	102.90	.53	288.00	1.48	390.90	2.00	
Poteau	Choctaw	645							Choctaw T. C.
Pryorcreek	Cherokee	365	87.31	.24	614.57	1.68	701.88	1.92	
Purcell	Chickasaw	1,110.68	836.62	.75	2,870.00	2.58	3,706.62	3.33	
Purdy	do	116.25	100.50	.86	372.00	3.20	472.50	4.06	
Purnell	Choctaw	89.39							
Ramona	Cherokee	110	69.22	.63	298.14	2.66	362.36	3.29	
Ravia	Chickasaw	326.39	110.20	.34					
Redfork	Creek	160					469.84	2.94	
Redoak	Choctaw	132.50	115.86	.87	361.71	2.73	477.57	3.60	
Roff	Chickasaw	595	188.90	.32					
Rush Springs	do	380	115.36	.30	577.60	1.52	692.96	1.82	
Ryan	do	435.39	166.82	.38	1,579.85	3.63	1,746.67	4.01	
Sallisaw	Cherokee	257.78	83.53	.32	660.03	2.56	743.56	2.88	
Sapulpa	Creek	501.25	152.55	.30	1,503.75	3.00	1,656.30	3.30	
Scullin	Chickasaw	120							
Silo	do	195	80.00	.41	220.00	1.13	300.00	1.54	
South McAlester	Choctaw	2,902.27							Do.
Spiro	do	225.78	114.92	.51	943.07	4.18	1,057.99	4.69	Do.
Sterrett	do	485							
Stigler	do	102.33	87.66	.66	199.00	1.95	266.66	2.61	
Stilwell	Cherokee	164.22	209.74	1.28	405.55	2.47	615.29	3.75	
Stonewall	Chickasaw	117.50	94.70	.81	229.55	1.96	324.25	2.76	
Sugden	do	149.18	59.67	.40	432.38	2.90	492.05	3.30	
Sulphur	do	948.14	213.23	.22					
Soper	Choctaw	90							
Tahlequah	Cherokee	632.50	466.87	.74					
Talala	do	170	102.81	.60	358.69	2.11	461.50	2.71	
Tallhina	Choctaw	210.59	187.17	.89	622.05	2.95	809.22	3.84	
Tamaha	do	142.30	70.50	.50	285.00	2.00	355.50	2.50	
Terral	Chickasaw	280	109.70	.39	1,167.90	4.17	1,277.60	4.56	
Tishomingo	do	545	310.44	.57	1,460.00	2.68	1,770.44	3.25	
Tulsa	Creek	654.58	152.00	.23	1,896.37	2.90	2,048.37	3.13	
Vian	Cherokee	220.62	85.70	.39	451.68	2.05	537.38	2.44	
Vinita	do	946.23	472.50	.50	2,591.47	2.74	3,063.97	3.24	
Valliant	Choctaw	120							
Wagoner	Creek	2,700							Wagoner T. C.
Wapanucka	Choctaw	425	89.10	.21	800.00	1.88	849.10	2.09	
Webbers Falls	Cherokee	80.50	66.37	.82	409.20	5.08	475.57	5.90	
Welch	do	160	47.42	.30	313.50	1.96	360.92	2.26	
Westville	do	179.99	159.35	.89	390.14	2.17	549.49	3.05	
Wetumka	Creek	160					85.00	.53	
Whitefield	Choctaw	100.57	86.50	.86	221.00	2.22	307.50	3.06	
Wilburton	do	275.58	129.44	.47	900.00	3.27	1,029.44	3.74	
Wildcat	Creek	158	90.85	.57	238.62	1.51	329.47	2·09	
Winchell	do	160					85.00	.53	
Wister	Choctaw	149.78	100.02	.67	599.11	4.00	699.13	4.67	
Woodville	Chickasaw	165					126.88	.77	
Wynnewood	do	767.50	208.50	.27	2,072.25	2.70	2,280.75	2.97	

a Includes $1.97 per acre extra subdivision.

APPENDIX NO. 1.

AGREEMENT BETWEEN THE COMMISSION TO THE FIVE CIVILIZED TRIBES AND THE SEMINOLE COMMISSION.

This agreement by and between the Government of the United States, of the first part, entered into in its behalf by the Commission to the Five Civilized Tribes, Henry L. Dawes, Tams Bixby, Frank C. Armstrong, Archibald S. McKennon, and Thomas B. Needles, duly appointed and authorized thereunto, and the government of the Seminole Nation in Indian Territory, of the second part, entered into on behalf of said government by its commission, duly appointed and authorized thereunto, viz, John F. Brown, Okchan Harjo, William Cully, K. N. Kinkehee, Thomas West, and Thomas Factor.

Witnesseth, that in consideration of the mutual undertakings herein contained, it is agreed as follows:

All lands belonging to the Seminole tribe of Indians shall be divided into three classes, designated as first, second, and third class, the first class to be appraised at five dollars, the second class at two dollars and fifty cents, and the third class at one dollar and twenty-five cents per acre, and the same shall be divided among the members of the tribe so that each shall have an equal share thereof in value, so far as may be, the location and fertility of the soil considered; giving to each the right to select his allotment so as to include any improvements thereon, owned by him at the time, and each allottee shall have the sole right of occupancy of the land so allotted to him, during the existence of the present tribal government, and until the members of said tribe shall have become citizens of the United States. Such allotments shall be made under the direction and supervision of the Commission to the Five Civilized Tribes in connection with a representative appointed by the tribal government; and the chairman of said Commission shall execute and deliver to each allottee a certificate describing therein the land allotted to him.

All contracts for sale, disposition, or encumbrance of any part of any allotment made prior to date of patent shall be void.

Any allottee may lease his allotment for any period not exceeding six years, the contract therefor to be executed in triplicate upon printed blanks provided by the tribal government, and before the same shall become effective it shall be approved by the principal chief and a copy filed in the office of the clerk of the United States court at Wewoka.

No lease of any coal, mineral, coal oil, or natural gas within said nation shall be valid unless made with the tribal government, by and with the consent of the allottee and approved by the Secretary of the Interior.

Should there be discovered on any allotment any coal, mineral, coal oil, or natural gas, and the same should be operated so as to produce royalty, one-half of such royalty shall be paid to such allottee and the remaining half into the tribal treasury until extinguishment of tribal government, and the latter shall be used for the purpose of equalizing the value of allotments; and, if the same be insufficient therefor, any other funds belonging to the tribe, upon extinguishment of tribal government, may be used for such purpose, so that each allotment may be made equal in value as aforesaid.

The town site of Wewoka shall be controlled and disposed of according to the provisions of an act of the general council of the Seminole Nation, approved April 23, 1897, relative thereto; and on extinguishment of the tribal government deeds of conveyance shall issue to owners of lots as herein provided for allottees; and all lots remaining unsold at that time may be sold in such manner as may be prescribed by the Secretary of the Interior.

Five hundred thousand dollars ($500,000) of the funds belonging to the Seminoles, now held by the United States, shall be set apart as a permanent school fund for the education of children of the members of said tribe, and shall be held by the United States at five per cent interest, or invested so as to produce such amount of interest, which shall be, after extinguishment of tribal government, applied by the Secretary of the Interior to the support of Mekasuky and Emahaka academies, and the district schools of the Seminole people; and there shall be selected and excepted from allotment three hundred and twenty acres of land for each of said academies and eighty acres each for eight district schools in the Seminole country.

There shall also be excepted from allotment one-half acre for the use and occupancy of each of twenty-four churches, including those already existing and such others as may hereafter be established in the Seminole country, by and with consent of the general council of the nation; but should any part of same at any time cease to be used for church purposes such part shall at once revert to the Seminole people and be added to the lands set apart for the use of said district schools.

One acre in each township shall be excepted from allotment, and the same may be purchased by the United States, upon which to establish schools for the education of children of noncitizens when deemed expedient.

When the tribal government shall cease to exist the principal chief last elected by said tribe shall execute, under his hand and the seal of the nation, and deliver to each allottee a deed conveying to him all the right, title, and interest of the said nation and the members thereof in and to the lands so allotted to him, and the Secretary of the Interior shall approve such deed, and the same shall thereupon operate as a relinquishment of the right, title, and interest of the United States in and to the land embraced in said conveyance and as a guaranty by the United States of the title of said lands to the allottee; and the acceptance of such deed by the allottee shall be a relinquishment of his title to and interest in all other lands belonging to the tribe, except such as may have been excepted from allotment and held in common for other purposes. Each allottee shall designate one tract of forty acres, which shall, by the terms of the deed, be made inalienable and nontaxable as a homestead in perpetuity.

All moneys belonging to the Seminoles remaining after equalizing the value of allotments as herein provided and reserving said sum of five hundred thousand dollars for school fund shall be paid per capita to the members of said tribe in three equal installments, the first to be made as soon as convenient after allotment and extinguishment of tribal government and the others at one and two years, respectively. Such payments shall be made by a person appointed by the Secretary of the Interior, who shall prescribe the amount of and approve the bond to be given by such person, and strict account shall be given to the Secretary of the Interior for such disbursements.

The "loyal Seminole claim" shall be submitted to the United States Senate, which shall make final determination of same, and, if sustained, shall provide for payment thereof within two years from date hereof.

There shall hereafter be held, at the town of Wewoka, the present capital of the Seminole Nation, regular terms of the United States court as at other points in the judicial district of which the Seminole Nation is a part.

The United States agrees to maintain strict laws in the Seminole country against the introduction, sale, barter, or giving away of intoxicants of any kind or quality.

This agreement shall in no wise affect the provisions of existing treaties between the Seminole Nation and the United States, except in so far as it is inconsistent therewith.

The United States courts now existing or that may hereafter be created in Indian Territory shall have exclusive jurisdiction of all controversies growing out of the title, ownership, occupation, or use of real estate owned by the Seminoles, and to try all persons charged with homicide, embezzlement, bribery, and embracery hereafter committed in the Seminole country, without reference to race or citizenship of the persons charged with such crime; and any citizen or officer of said nation charged with any such crime, if convicted, shall be punished as if he were a citizen or officer of the United States; and the courts of said nation shall retain all the jurisdiction which they now have, except as herein transferred to the courts of the United States.

When this agreement is ratified by the Seminole Nation and the United States the same shall serve to repeal all the provisions of the act of Congress approved June 7, 1897, in any manner affecting the proceedings of the general council of the Seminole Nation.

It being known that the Seminole Reservation is insufficient for allotments for the use of the Seminole people, upon which they, as citizens, holding in severalty, may reasonably and adequately maintain their families, the United States will make effort to purchase from the Creek Nation, at one dollar and twenty-five cents per acre, two hundred thousand acres of land, immediately adjoining the eastern boundary of the Seminole Reservation, and lying between the North Fork and South Fork of the Canadian River, in trust for, and to be conveyed by proper patent by the United States to, the Seminole Indians, upon said sum of one dollar and twenty-five cents per acre being reimbursed to the United States by said Seminole Indians; the same to be allotted as herein provided for lands now owned by the Seminoles.

This agreement shall be binding on the United States when ratified by Congress, and on the Seminole people when ratified by the general council of the Seminole Nation.

In witness whereof, the said commissioners have hereunto affixed their names at Muskogee, Indian Territory, this sixteenth day of December, A. D. 1897.

TAMS BIXBY,
FRANK C. ARMSTRONG,
ARCHIBALD S. McKENNON,
THOMAS B. NEEDLES.
   Commission to the Five Civilized Tribes.
ALLISON L. AYLESWORTH,
   Secretary.

JOHN F. BROWN,
OKCHAN HARJO,
WILLIAM CULLY,
K. N. KINKEHEE,
THOMAS WEST,
THOMAS FACTOR,
   Seminole Commission.
A. J. BROWN,
   Secretary.

APPENDIX NO. 2.

[PUBLIC—No. 162.]

AN ACT For the protection of the people of the Indian Territory, and for other purposes.

Be it enacted by the Senate and House of Representatives of the United States of America in Congress assembled, That in all criminal prosecutions in the Indian Territory against officials for embezzlement, bribery, and embracery the word "officer," when the same appears in the criminal laws heretofore extended over and put in force in said Territory, shall include all officers of the several tribes or nations of Indians in said Territory.

SEC. 2. That when in the progress of any civil suit, either in law or equity, pending in the United States court in any district in said Territory, it shall appear to the court that the property of any tribe is in any way affected by the issues being heard, said court is hereby authorized and required to make said tribe a party to said suit by service upon the chief or governor of the tribe, and the suit shall thereafter be conducted and determined as if said tribe had been an original party to said action.

SEC. 3. That said courts are hereby given jurisdiction in their respective districts to try cases against those who may claim to hold as members of a tribe and whose membership is denied by the tribe, but who continue to hold said lands and tenements notwithstanding the objection of the tribe; and if it be found upon trial that the same are held unlawfully against the tribe by those claiming to be members thereof, and the membership and right are disallowed by the Commission to the Five Tribes, or the United States court, and the judgment has become final, then said court shall cause the parties charged with unlawfully holding said possessions to be removed from the same and cause the lands and tenements to be restored to the person or persons or nation or tribe of Indians entitled to the possession of the same: *Provided always,* That any person being a noncitizen in possession of lands, holding the possession thereof under an agreement, lease, or improvement contract with either of said nations or tribes, or any citizen thereof, executed prior to January first, eighteen hundred and ninety-eight, may, as to lands not exceeding in amount one hundred and sixty acres, in defense of any action for the possession of said lands show that he is and has been in peaceable possession of such lands, and that he has while in such possession made lasting and valuable improvements thereon, and that he has not enjoyed the possession thereof a sufficient length of time to compensate him for such improvements. Thereupon the court or jury trying said cause shall determine the fair and reasonable value of such improvements and the fair and reasonable rental value of such lands for the time the same shall have been occupied by such person; and if the improvements exceed in value the amount of rents with which such persons should be charged, the court, in its judgment, shall specify such time as will, in the opinion of the court, compensate such person for the balance due, and award him possession for such time unless the amount be paid by claimant within such reasonable time as the court shall specify. If the finding be that the amount of rents exceed the value of the improvements, judgment shall be rendered against the defendant for such sum, for which execution may issue.

SEC. 4. That all persons who have heretofore made improvements on lands belonging to any one of the said tribes of Indians, claiming rights of citizenship, whose claims have been decided adversely under the act of Congress approved June tenth, eighteen hundred and ninety-six, shall have possession thereof until and including December thirty-first, eighteen hundred and ninety-eight; and may, prior to that time, sell or dispose of the same to any member of the tribe owning the land who desires to take the same in his allotment: *Provided,* That this section shall not apply to improvements which have been appraised and paid for or payment tendered by the Cherokee Nation under the agreement with the United States approved by Congress March third, eighteen hundred and ninety-three.

SEC. 5. That before any action by any tribe or person shall be commenced under section three of this Act it shall be the duty of the party bringing the same to notify the adverse party to leave the premises for the possession of which the action is about to be brought, which notice shall be served at least thirty days before commencing the action by leaving a written copy with the defendant, or, if he can not be found, by leaving the same at his last known place of residence or business with any person occupying the premises over the age of twelve years, or, if his residence or business address can not be ascertained, by leaving the same with any person over the age of twelve years upon the premises sought to be recovered and described in said notice; and if there be no person with whom said notice can be left, then by posting same on the premises.

SEC. 6. That the summons shall not issue in such action until the chief or governor of the tribe, or person or persons bringing suit in his own behalf, shall have filed a sworn complaint, on behalf of the tribe or himself, with the court, which shall, as near as practicable, describe the premises so detained, and shall set forth a detention without the consent of the person bringing said suit or the tribe, by one whose membership is denied by it: *Provided*, That if the chief or governor refuse or fail to bring suit in behalf of the tribe, then any member of the tribe may make complaint and bring said suit.

SEC. 7. That the court in granting a continuance of any case, particularly under section three, may, in its discretion, require the party applying therefor to give an undertaking to the adverse party, with good and sufficient securities, to be approved by the judge of the court, conditioned for the payment of all damages and costs and defraying the rent which may accrue if judgment be rendered against him.

SEC. 8. That when a judgment for restitution shall be entered by the court the clerk shall, at the request of the plaintiff or his attorney, issue a writ of execution thereon, which shall command the proper officer of the court to cause the defendant or defendants to be forthwith removed and ejected from the premises and the plaintiff given complete and undisturbed possession of the same. The writ shall also command the said officer to levy upon the property of the defendant or defendants subject to execution, and also collect therefrom the costs of the action and all accruing costs in the service of the writ. Said writ shall be executed within thirty days.

SEC. 9. That the jurisdiction of the court and municipal authority of the city of Fort Smith for police purposes in the State of Arkansas is hereby extended over all that strip of land in the Indian Territory lying and being situate between the corporate limits of the said city of Fort Smith and the Arkansas and Poteau rivers, and extending up the said Poteau River to the mouth of Mill Creek; and all the laws and ordinances for the preservation of the peace and health of said city, as far as the same are applicable, are hereby put in force therein: *Provided*, That no charge or tax shall ever be made or levied by said city against said land or the tribe or nation to whom it belongs.

SEC. 10. That all actions for restitution of possession of real property under this act must be commenced by the service of a summons within two years after the passage of this act, where the wrongful detention or possession began prior to the date of its passage; and all actions which shall be commenced hereafter based upon wrongful detention or possession committed since the passage of this act must be commenced within two years after the cause of action accrued. And nothing in this act shall take away the right to maintain an action for unlawful and forcible entry and detainer given by the act of Congress passed May second, eighteen hundred and ninety (Twenty-sixth United States Statutes, page ninety-five).

SEC. 11. That when the roll of citizenship of any one of said nations or tribes is fully completed as provided by law, and the survey of the lands of said nation or tribe is also completed, the Commission heretofore appointed under acts of Congress, and known as the "Dawes Commission," shall proceed to allot the exclusive use and occupancy of the surface of all the lands of said nation or tribe susceptible of allotment among the citizens thereof, as shown by said roll, giving to each, as far as possible, his fair and equal share thereof, considering the nature and fertility of the soil, location, and value of same; but all oil, coal, asphalt, and mineral deposits in the lands of any tribe are reserved to such tribe, and no allotment of such lands shall carry the title to such oil, coal, asphalt, or mineral deposits; and all town sites shall also be reserved to the several tribes, and shall be set apart by the Commission heretofore mentioned as incapable of allotment. There shall also be reserved from allotment a sufficient amount of lands now occupied by churches, schools, parsonages, charitable institutions, and other public buildings for their present actual and necessary use, and no more, not to exceed five acres for each school and one acre for each church and each parsonage, and for such new schools as may be needed; also sufficient land for burial grounds where necessary. When such allotment of the lands of any tribe has been by them completed, said Commission shall make full report thereof to the Secretary of the Interior for his approval: *Provided*, That nothing herein contained shall in any way affect any vested legal rights which may have been heretofore granted by act of Congress, nor be so construed as to confer any additional rights upon any parties claiming under any such act of Congress: *Provided further*, That whenever it shall appear that any member of a tribe is in possession of lands, his allotment may be made out of the lands in his possession, including his home if the holder so desires: *Provided further*, That if the person to whom an allotment shall have been made shall be declared, upon appeal as herein provided for, by any of the courts of the United States in or for the aforesaid Territory, to have been illegally accorded rights of citizenship, and for that or any other reason declared to be not entitled to any allotment, he shall be ousted and ejected from said lands; that all persons known as intruders who have been paid for their improvements under existing laws and have not surrendered possession thereof who may be found under the provisions of this act to be entitled to citizenship shall, within ninety days thereafter, refund the amount so paid them, with six per centum interest, to the tribe entitled thereto; and upon their failure so to do said amount shall become a lien upon all improvements owned by such person in such Territory, and may be enforced by such tribe; and unless such person makes such restitution no allotments shall be made to him: *Provided further*, That the lands allotted shall be nontransferable until after full title is acquired and shall be liable for no obligations contracted prior thereto by the allottee, and shall be nontaxable while so held: *Provided further*, That all towns and cities heretofore incorporated or incorporated under the provisions of this act are hereby authorized to secure, by condemnation or otherwise, all the lands actually necessary for public improvements, regardless of tribal lines; and when the same can not be secured otherwise than by condemnation, then the same may be acquired as provided in sections nine hundred and seven and nine hundred and twelve, inclusive, of Mansfield's Digest of the Statutes of Arkansas.

SEC. 12. That when report of allotments of lands of any tribe shall be made to the Secretary of the Interior, as hereinbefore provided, he shall make a record thereof, and when he shall confirm such allotments the allottees shall remain in peaceable and undisturbed possession thereof, subject to the provisions of this act.

SEC. 13. That the Secretary of the Interior is hereby authorized and directed from time to time to provide rules and regulations in regard to the leasing of oil, coal, asphalt, and other minerals in said Territory, and all such leases shall be made by the Secretary of the Interior; and any lease for any such minerals otherwise made shall be absolutely void. No lease shall be made or renewed for a longer period than fifteen years, nor cover the mineral in more than six hundred and forty acres of land, which shall conform as nearly as possible to the surveys. Lessees shall pay on each oil, coal, asphalt, or other mineral claim at the rate of one hundred dollars per annum, in advance, for the first and second years; two hundred dollars per annum, in advance, for the third and fourth years, and five hundred dollars, in advance, for each succeeding year thereafter, as advanced royalty on the mine or claim on which they are made. All such payments shall be a credit on royalty when each said mine is developed and operated and its production is in excess of such guaranteed annual advanced payments; and all lessees must pay said annual advanced payments on each claim, whether developed or undeveloped; and should any lessee neglect or refuse to pay such advanced annual royalty for the period of sixty days after the same becomes due and payable on any lease, the lease on which default is made shall become null and void, and the royalties paid in advance shall then become and be the money and property of the tribe. Where any oil, coal, asphalt, or other mineral is hereafter opened on land allotted, sold, or reserved, the value of the use of the necessary surface for prospecting or mining, and the damage done to the other land and improvements, shall be ascertained under the direction of the Secretary of the Interior and paid to the allottee or owner of the land by the lessee or party operating the same, before operations begin: *Provided*, That nothing herein contained shall impair the rights of any holder or owner of a leasehold interest in any oil, coal rights, asphalt, or mineral which have been assented to by act of Congress, but all such interest shall continue unimpaired hereby, and shall be assured to such holders or owners by leases from the Secretary of the Interior for the term not exceeding fifteen years, subject to the payment of advance royalties as herein provided, when such leases are not operated, to the rate of royalty on coal mined, and the rules and regulations to be prescribed by the Secretary of the Interior, and preference shall be given to such parties in renewals of such leases: *And provided further,* That when, under the customs and laws heretofore existing and prevailing in the Indian Territory, leases have been made of different groups or parcels of oil, coal, asphalt, or other mineral deposits, and possession has been taken thereunder and improvements made for the development of such oil, coal, asphalt, or other mineral deposits, by lessees or their assigns, which have resulted in the production of oil, coal, asphalt, or other mineral in commercial quantities by such lessees or their assigns, then such parties in possession shall be given preference in the making of new leases, in compliance with the directions of the Secretary of the Interior; and in making new leases due consideration shall be made for the improvements of such lessees, and in all cases of the leasing or renewal of leases of oil, coal, asphalt, and other mineral deposits preference shall be given to parties in possession who have made improvements. The rate of royalty to be paid by all lessees shall be fixed by the Secretary of the Interior.

SEC. 14. That the inhabitants of any city or town in said Territory having two hundred or more residents therein may proceed, by petition to the United States court in the district in which such city or town is located, to have the same incorporated as provided in chapter twenty-nine of Mansfield's Digest of the Statutes of Arkansas, if not already incorporated thereunder; and the clerk of said court shall record all papers and perform all the acts required of the recorder of the county, or the clerk of the county court, or the secretary of state. necessary for the incorporation of any city or town, as provided in Mansfield's Digest, and such city or town government, when so authorized and organized, shall possess all the powers and exercise all the rights of similar municipalities in said State of Arkansas. All male inhabitants of such cities and towns over the age of twenty-one years, who are citizens of the United States or of either of said tribes, who have resided therein more than six months next before any election held under this act, shall be qualified voters at such election. That mayors of such cities and towns, in addition to their other powers, shall have the same jurisdiction in all civil and criminal cases arising within the corporate limits of such cities and towns as, and coextensive with, United States commissioners in the Indian Territory, and may charge, collect, and retain the same fees as such commissioners now collect and account for to the United States; and the marshal or other executive officer of such city or town may execute all processes issued in the exercise of the jurisdiction hereby conferred, and charge and collect the same fees for similar services, as are allowed to constables under the laws now in force in said Territory.

All elections shall be conducted under the provisions of chapter fifty-six of said digest, entitled "Elections," so far as the same may be applicable; and all inhabitants of such cities and towns, without regard to race, shall be subject to all laws and ordinances of such city or town governments and shall have equal rights, privileges, and protection therein. Such city or town governments shall in no case have any authority to impose upon or levy any tax against any lands in said cities or towns until after title is secured from the tribe; but all other property, including all improvements on town lots, which for the purposes of this act shall be deemed and considered personal property, together with all occupations and privileges, shall be subject to taxation. And the councils of such cities and towns, for the support of the same and for school and other public purposes, may provide by ordinance for the assessment, levy, and collection annually of a tax upon such property, not to exceed in the aggregate two per centum of the assessed value thereof, in manner provided in chapter one hundred and twenty-nine of said digest, entitled "Revenue," and for such purposes may also impose a tax upon occupations and privileges.

Such councils may also establish and maintain free schools in such cities and towns, under the provisions of sections sixty-two hundred and fifty-eight to sixty-two hundred and seventy-six, inclusive, of said digest, and may exercise all the powers conferred upon special school districts in cities and towns in the State of Arkansas by the laws of said State when the same are not in conflict with the provisions of this act.

For the purposes of this section all the laws of said State of Arkansas herein referred to, so far as applicable, are hereby put in force in said Territory; and the United States court therein shall have jurisdiction to enforce the same, and to punish any violation thereof, and the city or town councils shall pass such ordinances as may be necessary for the purpose of making the laws extended over them applicable to them and for carrying the same into effect: *Provided,* That nothing in this act, or in the laws of the State of Arkansas, shall authorize or permit the sale, or exposure for sale, of any intoxicating liquor in said Territory, or the introduction thereof into said Territory; and it shall be the duty of the district attorneys in said Territory and the officers of such municipalities to prosecute all violators of the laws of the United States relating to the introduction of intoxicating liquors into said Territory, or to their sale, or exposure for sale, therein: *Provided further,* That owners and holders of leases or improvements in any city or town shall be privileged to transfer the same.

Sec. 15. That there shall be a commission in each town for each one of the Chickasaw, Choctaw, Creek, and Cherokee tribes, to consist of one member to be appointed by the executive of the tribe, who shall not be interested in town property, other than his home; one person to be appointed by the Secretary of the Interior, and one member to be selected by the town. And if the executive of the tribe or the town fail to select members as aforesaid, they may be selected and appointed by the Secretary of the Interior.

Said commissions shall cause to be surveyed and laid out town sites where towns with a present population of two hundred or more are located, conforming to the existing survey so far as may be, with proper and necessary streets, alleys, and public grounds, including parks and cemeteries, giving to each town such territory as may be required for its present needs and reasonable prospective growth; and shall prepare correct plats thereof, and file one with the Secretary of the Interior, one with the clerk of the United States court, one with the authorities of the tribe, and one with the town authorities. And all town lots shall be appraised by said commission at their true value, excluding improvements; and separate appraisements shall be made of all improvements thereon; and no such appraisement shall be effective until approved by the Secretary of the Interior, and in case of disagreement by the members of such commission as to the value of any lot, said Secretary may fix the value thereof.

The owner of the improvements upon any town lot, other than fencing, tillage, or temporary buildings, may deposit in the United States Treasury, Saint Louis, Missouri, one-half of such appraised value; ten per centum within two months and fifteen per centum more within six months after notice of appraisement, and the remainder in three equal annual installments thereafter, depositing with the Secretary of the Interior one receipt for each payment, and one with the authorities of the tribe, and such deposits shall be deemed a tender to the tribe of the purchase money for such lot.

If the owner of such improvements on any lot fails to make deposit of the purchase money as aforesaid, then such lot may be sold in the manner herein provided for the sale of unimproved lots; and when the purchaser thereof has complied with the requirements herein for the purchase of improved lots he may, by petition, apply to the United States court within whose jurisdiction the town is located for condemnation and appraisement of such improvements, and petitioner shall, after judgment, deposit the value so fixed with the clerk of the court; and thereupon the defendant shall be required to accept same in full payment for his improvements or remove same from the lot within such time as may be fixed by the court.

All town lots not improved as aforesaid shall belong to the tribe, and shall be in like manner appraised, and, after approval by the Secretary of the Interior, and due notice, sold to the highest bidder at public auction by said commission, but not for less than their appraised value, unless ordered by the Secretary of the Interior; and purchasers may in like manner make deposits of the purchase money with like effect, as in case of improved lots.

The inhabitants of any town may, within one year after the completion of the survey thereof, make such deposit of ten dollars per acre for parks, cemeteries, and other public grounds laid out by said commission with like effect as for improved lots; and such parks and public grounds shall not be used for any purpose until such deposits are made.

The person authorized by the tribe or tribes may execute or deliver to any such purchaser, without expense to him, a deed conveying to him the title to such lands or town lots; and thereafter the purchase money shall become the property of the tribe; and all such money shall, when titles to all the lots in the towns belonging to any tribe have been thus perfected, be paid per capita to the members of the tribe: *Provided, however,* That in those town sites designated and laid out under the provisions of this act where coal leases are now being operated and coal is being mined there shall be reserved from appraisement and sale all lots occupied by houses of miners actually engaged in mining, and only while they are so engaged, and in addition thereto a sufficient amount of land, to be determined by the appraisers, to furnish homes for the men actually engaged in working for the lessees operating said mines and a sufficient amount for all buildings and machinery for mining purposes: *And provided further,* That when the lessees shall cease to operate said mines, then, and in that event, the lots of land so reserved shall be disposed of as provided for in this act.

Sec. 16. That it shall be unlawful for any person, after the passage of this act, except as hereinafter provided, to claim, demand, or receive, for his own use or for

TABLE No. 2.—*Indian Territory town sites—areas and approvals, June 30, 1902*—Cont'c

Town.	Nation.	Exterior survey.		Interior survey, date of approval.	Remarks.
		Acres, including cemeteries.	Date of approval.		
Orr	Chickasaw	185	Dec. 20, 1900	Mar. 4, 1902	
Paoli	do	85.48	Apr. 11, 1901	Nov. 30, 1901	
Pauls Valley	do	946.83	Dec. 17, 1900	Jan. 18, 1902	
Pontotoc	do	195	Dec. 15, 1900	Dec. 28, 1901	
Poteau	Choctaw	645		June 4, 1901	Choctaw T. C.
Pryorcreek	Cherokee	365	Nov. 23, 1901		Plat completed.
Purcell	Chickasaw	1,110.68			R. R.
Purdy	do	116.25	Sept. 11, 1901	Nov. 5, 1901	
Purnell	Choctaw	89.39	June 24, 1902		D. C.; being platted.
Ramona	Cherokee	110	Mar. 11, 1902	May 6, 1902	
Ravia	Chickasaw	326.39	Apr. 20, 1901		D. C.; R. R.
Redfork	Creek	160	Dec. 13, 1901	Feb. 20, 1902	
Redoak	Choctaw	132.50	Dec. 15, 1900	June 7, 1901	
Roff	Chickasaw	595	Feb. 6, 1901		Do.
Rush Springs	do	380	Oct. 26, 1900	Nov. 27, 1901	
Ryan	do	435.39	....do	Mar. 7, 1902	
Sallisaw	Cherokee	257.78	May 15, 1902		Not yet approved.
Sapulpa	Creek	501.25	Feb. 15, 1901		Do.
Scullin	Chickasaw	120	Oct. 26, 1901		D. C.; R. R.
Silo	do	195	Dec. 15, 1900	Sept. 10, 1901	
South McAlester	Choctaw	2,902.27		Feb. 14, 1901	Choctaw T. C.
Spiro	do	225.78	Feb. 15, 1901 Apr. 8, 1901 Apr. 9, 1901 Feb. 19, 1902	May 2, 1902	
Sterrett	do	485		Aug. 28, 1899	Do.
Stigler	do	102.83	Feb. 15, 1901	Nov. 5, 1901	
Stilwell	Cherokee	164.22	July 7, 1902		Not yet approved.
Stonewall	Chickasaw	117.50	Dec. 17, 1900	Jan. 9, 1902	
Sugden	do	149.18	Mar. 4, 1902	Apr. 11, 1902	
Sulphur	do	948.14			Held; suppl. treaty.
Soper	Choctaw	90	June 24, 1902		D. C.; being platted.
Stringtown	do	62.50	June 23, 1902		
Tahlequah	Cherokee	632.50	July 7, 1902		Plat completed.
Talala	do	170	May 22, 1902	July 11, 1902	
Talihina	Choctaw	210.59	June 4, 1901	June 4, 1901	
Tamaha	do	142.30	Feb. 5, 1901	July 11, 1901	
Terral	Chickasaw	280	Oct. 26, 1900	Mar. 7, 1902	
Tishomingo	do	545	May 24, 1902		Do.
Tulsa	Creek	654.58	Feb. 21, 1901	Apr. 11, 1902	
Vian	Cherokee	220.62	June 14, 1902		Do.
Vinita	do	946.23	Mar. 5, 1902	May 10, 1902	
Valliant	Choctaw	120	June 24, 1902		D. C.; being completed
Wagoner	Creek	2,700		Oct. 10, 1900	Wagoner T. C.
Wapanucka	Choctaw	425	June 14, 1902		Plat completed.
Webbers Falls	Cherokee	80.50	Mar. 11, 1902	July 11, 1902	
Welch	do	160	Apr. 11, 1902	May 7, 1902	
Westville	do	179.99	May 31, 1902		Do.
Wetumka	Creek	160	Oct. 26, 1900	Nov. 13, 1901	
Whitefield	Choctaw	100.57	Feb. 12, 1901	July 3, 1901	
Wilburton	do	275.58	Oct. 16, 1901	Mar. 11, 1902	
Wildcat	Creek	158	Mar. 11, 1902	May 8, 1902	
Winchell	do	160	Oct. 26, 1900	Nov. 13, 1901	
Wister	Choctaw	149.78	Feb. 12, 1901 June 22, 1901	Nov. 30, 1901	
Woodville	Chickasaw	165	Oct. 26, 1900	Jan. 31, 1901	
Wynnewood	do	767.50	Dec. 15, 1900	Mar. 4, 1902	
Total		54,481.725			

TABLE No. 3.—*Indian Territory town sites—Cost of surveys, June 30, 1902.*

Town.	Nation.	Acres, including cemeteries.	Cost. Exterior survey.	Per acre.	Cost. Interior survey.	Per acre.	Total. Cost.	Per acre.	Remarks.
Ada	Chickasaw	559.90	$207.73	$0.37	$90.00	$0.16	$297.73	$0.53	
Adair	Cherokee..	150	87.38	.58	497.16	3.31	584.54	3.90	
Addington	Chickasaw	145.40	97.73	.67	484.14	3.33	581.87	4.00	
Afton	Cherokee..	532.50	110.15	.21	931.75	1.75	1,041.90	1.96	
Alabama	Creek	80					85.00	1.06	
Allen	Choctaw ..	120	62.67	.52	240.00	2.00	302.67	2.52	
Antlers	....do.....	182.50	112.95	.62	711.29	3.90	824.24	4.52	
Ardmore	Chickasaw	2,262.14					6,035.52	2.67	
Atoka	Choctaw ..	277.18							Choctaw T. C.
Bartlesville	Cherokee..	342.44	87.25	.25	972.44	2.84	1,059.69	3.10	
Beggs	Creek	160					85.00	.53	
Berwyn	Chickasaw	191.25	135.50	.71	660.00	3.45	795.50	4.16	
Bluejacket	Cherokee..	196.25	77.12	.39	524.50	2.67	601.62	3.06	
Bristow	Creek	385	93.94	.24	800.12	2.08	894.06	2.32	
Bennington	Choctaw ..	140							
Bixby	Creek	80					276.04	3.45	
Caddo	Choctaw ..	400	179.24	.45	1,192.07	2.98	1,371.31	3.43	
Calvin	....do.....	160							Do.
Cameron	....do.....	155	135.27	.87	494.35	3.19	629.62	4.06	
Canadian	....do.....	197.50	121.15	.61	1,612.38	8.16	1,733.53	8.77	
Catoosa	Cherokee..	165	96.40	.58	535.89	3.25	632.29	3.83	
Center	Chickasaw	195	90.68	.47	282.90	1.45	373.58	1.92	
Centralia	Cherokee..	177.50	91.86	.52	562.00	3.17	653.86	3.68	
Checotah	Creek	503.75	141.22	.28	1,785.50	3.54	1,926.72	3.82	
Chelsea	Cherokee..	452.50	91.38	.20	1,126.00	2.49	1,217.38	2.69	
Chickasha	Chickasaw	1,246.19	190.33	.15	1,620.05	1.30	1,810.38	1.45	
Choteau	Cherokee..	130	57.48	.44	289.51	2.23	346.99	2.67	
Claremore	....do.....	657.50	130.80	.20	2,435.30	3.70	2,566.10	3.90	
Clarksville	Creek	147.50	47.65	.32	289.50	1.96	337.15	2.28	
Coalgate	Choctaw ..	785							
Colbert	Chickasaw	134.77							
Collinsville	Cherokee..	270	104.80	.39	555.43	2.06	660.23	2.45	
Comanche	Chickasaw	437.04	167.91	.38	1,476.89	3.38	1,644.80	3.76	
Connersville	....do.....	180	77.04	.43	195.00	1.08	272.04	1.51	
Cornish	....do.....	190.28	90.75	.48	480.00	2.52	570.75	3.00	
Coweta	Creek	85	46.75	.55	170.00	2.00	216.75	2.55	
Cowlington	Choctaw ..	157.50	61.15	.39	315.00	2.00	376.15	2.39	
Cumberland	Chickasaw	173.98	80.40	.46	405.00	2.33	485.40	2.79	
Davis	....do.....	531.46	187.34	.35	1,669.15	3.14	1,856.49	3.49	
Dougherty	....do.....	243.125	96.85	.40	753.59	3.10	850.44	3.50	
Duncan	....do.....	1,010.07	187.74	.19	1,010.07	1.00	1,197.81	1.19	
Durant	Choctaw ..	1,324	310.34	.23	3,514.25	2.65	3,824.59	2.89	
Durwood	Chickasaw	140	91.00	.65					
Earl	....do.....	125	60.00	.48	287.50	2.30	347.50	2.78	
Emet	....do.....	170	136.00	.80	420.00	2.47	556.00	3.27	
Enterprise	Choctaw ..	107.50	95.75	.89	163.00	1.52	258.75	2.41	
Erin Springs	Chickasaw	110.10	42.85	.39	341.00	3.10	383.85	3.49	
Eufaula	Creek	431.38	174.76	.41	1,394.84	3.23	1,569.60	3.64	
Elmore	Chickasaw	145	105.21	.73	210.45	1.45	315.66	2.18	
Fairland	Cherokee..	240	155.07	.65	560.66	2.34	715.73	2.98	
Foster	Creek	120					85.00	.71	"Yager."
Fort Gibson	Cherokee..	412.65							
Francis	Chickasaw	160					85.00	.53	
Fort Towson	Choctaw ..	160							
Garvin	....do.....	120							
Gibson	Creek	160	64.00	.40	377.69	2.36	441.69	2.76	
Gilbert	Choctaw ..	100							
Grant	....do.....	131.32	81.80	.62	250.70	1.91	332.50	2.53	
Gray	Chickasaw	80					85.00	1.06	
Grove	Cherokee..	210	76.58	.36	540.00	2.57	616.58	2.94	
Guertie	Choctaw ..	160							Choctaw T. C.
Gans	Cherokee..	115	81.70	.71	355.00	3.09	436.70	3.80	
Hanson	....do.....	95	88.56	.93	378.92	3.99	467.48	4.92	
Harrington	Choctaw ..	45							
Hartshorne	....do.....	848.11	626.66	.74					
Haileyville	....do.....	681.05	475.88	.70	1,481.00	2.17	1,956.88	2.87	
Heavener	....do.....	175.64	88.65	.50	340.00	1.94	428.65	2.44	
Helen	Chickasaw	156.09					85.00	.54	
Henryetta	Creek	157.13					85.00	.54	
Hickory	Chickasaw	170	101.14	.59					
Holdenville	Creek	429.79	102.71	.24	85.00	.20	187.71	.44	
Howe	Choctaw ..	326.70	203.27	.62	1,427.95	4.37	1,631.22	4.99	
Hoyt	....do.....	97.50	63.82	.65	165.00	1.69	228.82	2.35	
Hugo	....do.....	160							
Inola	Creek	165	49.50	.30	259.28	1.57	308.78	1.87	
Johnson	Chickasaw	90	52.50	.58	144.00	1.60	196.50	2.18	
Kellyville	Creek	85	25.50	.30	228.92	2.69	254.42	2.99	
Kemp	Chickasaw	120	91.85	.77	310.00	2.56	401.85	3.35	
Krebs	Choctaw ..	330	142.20	.43					

the use of anyone else, any royalty on oil, coal, asphalt, or other mineral, or on any timber or lumber, or any other kind of property whatsoever, or any rents on any lands or property belonging to anyone of said tribes or nations in said Territory, or for anyone to pay to any individual any such royalty or rents or any consideration therefor whatsoever; and all royalties and rents hereafter payable to the tribe shall be paid, under such rules and regulations as may be prescribed by the Secretary of the Interior, into the Treasury of the United States to the credit of the tribe to which they belong: *Provided*, That where any citizen shall be in possession of only such amount of agricultural or grazing lands as would be his just and reasonable share of the lands of his nation or tribe and that to which his wife and minor children are entitled, he may continue to use the same or receive the rents thereon until allotment has been made to him: *Provided further*, That nothing herein contained shall impair the rights of any member of a tribe to dispose of any timber contained on his, her, or their allotment.

SEC. 17. That it shall be unlawful for any citizen of any one of said tribes to inclose or in any manner, by himself or through another, directly or indirectly, to hold possession of any greater amount of lands or other property belonging to any such nation or tribe than that which would be his approximate share of the lands belonging to such nation or tribe and that of his wife and his minor children as per allotment herein provided; and any person found in such possession of lands or other property in excess of his share and that of his family, as aforesaid, or having the same in any manner inclosed, at the expiration of nine months after the passage of this act, shall be deemed guilty of a misdemeanor.

SEC. 18. That any person convicted of violating any of the provisions of sections sixteen and seventeen of this act shall be deemed guilty of a misdemeanor and punished by a fine of not less than one hundred dollars, and shall stand committed until such fine and costs are paid (such commitment not to exceed one day for every two dollars of said fine and costs), and shall forfeit possession of any property in question, and each day on which such offense is committed or continues to exist shall be deemed a separate offense. And the United States district attorneys in said Territory are required to see that the provisions of said sections are strictly enforced and they shall at once proceed to dispossess all persons of such excessive holding of lands and to prosecute them for so unlawfully holding the same.

SEC. 19. That no payment of any moneys on any account whatever shall hereafter be made by the United States to any of the tribal governments or to any officer thereof for disbursement, but payments of all sums to members of said tribes shall be made under direction of the Secretary of the Interior by an officer appointed by him: and per capita payments shall be made direct to each individual in lawful money of the United States, and the same shall not be liable to the payment of any previously contracted obligation.

SEC. 20. That the commission hereinbefore named shall have authority to employ, with approval of the Secretary of the Interior, all assistance necessary for the prompt and efficient performance of all duties herein imposed, including competent surveyors to make allotments, and to do any other needed work, and the Secretary of the Interior may detail competent clerks to aid them in the performance of their duties.

SEC. 21. That in making rolls of citizenship of the several tribes, as required by law, the Commission to the Five Civilized Tribes is authorized and directed to take the roll of Cherokee citizens of eighteen hundred and eighty (not including freedmen) as the only roll intended to be confirmed by this and preceding acts of Congress, and to enroll all persons now living whose names are found on said roll, and all descendants born since the date of said roll to persons whose names are found thereon; and all persons who have been enrolled by the tribal authorities who have heretofore made permanent settlement in the Cherokee Nation whose parents, by reason of their Cherokee blood, have been lawfully admitted to citizenship by the tribal authorities, and who were minors when their parents were so admitted; and they shall investigate the right of all other persons whose names are found on any other rolls and omit all such as may have been placed thereon by fraud or without authority of law, enrolling only such as may have lawful right thereto, and their descendants born since such rolls were made, with such intermarried white persons as may be entitled to citizenship under Cherokee laws.

It shall make a roll of Cherokee freedmen in strict compliance with the decree of the Court of Claims rendered the third day of February, eighteen hundred and ninety-six.

Said commission is authorized and directed to make correct rolls of the citizens by blood of all the other tribes, eliminating from the tribal rolls such names as may have been placed thereon by fraud or without authority of law, enrolling such only as may have lawful right thereto, and their descendants born since such rolls were made, with such intermarried white persons as may be entitled io Choctaw and Chickasaw citizenship under the treaties and the laws of said tribes.

Said commission shall have authority to determine the identity of Choctaw Indians claiming rights in the Choctaw lands under article fourteen of the treaty between the United States and the Choctaw Nation concluded September twenty-seventh, eighteen hundred and thirty, and to that end they may administer oaths, examine witnesses, and perform all other acts necessary thereto and make report to the Secretary of the Interior.

The roll of Creek freedmen made by J. W. Dunn, under authority of the United States, prior to March fourteenth, eighteen hundred and sixty-seven, is hereby confirmed, and said commission is directed to enroll all persons now living whose names are found on said rolls, and all descendants born since the date of said roll to persons whose names are found thereon, with such other persons of African descent as may have been rightfully admitted by the lawful authorities of the Creek Nation.

It shall make a correct roll of all Choctaw freedmen entitled to citizenship under the treaties and laws of the Choctaw Nation, and all their descendants born to them since the date of the treaty.

It shall make a correct roll of Chickasaw freedmen entitled to any rights or benefits under the treaty made in eighteen hundred and sixty-six between the United States and the Choctaw and Chickasaw tribes and their descendants born to them since the date of said treaty, and forty acres of land, including their present residences and improvements, shall be allotted to each, to be selected, held, and used by them until their rights under said treaty shall be determined in such manner as shall be hereafter provided by Congress.

The several tribes may, by agreement, determine the right of persons who for any reason may claim citizenship in two or more tribes, and to allotment of lands and distribution of moneys belonging to each tribe; but if no such agreement be made, then such claimant shall be entitled to such rights in one tribe only, and may elect in which tribe he will take such right; but if he fail or refuse to make such selection in due time, he shall be enrolled in the tribe with whom he has resided, and there be given such allotment and distributions, and not elsewhere.

No person shall be enrolled who has not heretofore removed to and in good faith settled in the nation in which he claims citizenship: *Provided, however,* That nothing contained in this act shall be so construed as to militate against any rights or privileges which the Mississippi Choctaws may have under the laws of or the treaties with the United States.

Said commission shall make such rolls descriptive of the persons thereon, so that they may be thereby identified, and it is authorized to take a census of each of said tribes, or to adopt any other means by them deemed necessary to enable them to make such rolls. They shall have access to all rolls and records of the several tribes, and the United States court in Indian Territory shall have jurisdiction to compel the officers of the tribal governments and custodians of such rolls and records to deliver same to said commission, and on their refusal or failure to do so to punish them as for contempt; as also to require all citizens of said tribes, and persons who should be so enrolled, to appear before said commission for enrollment, at such times and places as may be fixed by said commission, and to enforce obedience of all others concerned, so far as the same may be necessary, to enable said commission to make rolls as herein required, and to punish anyone who may in any manner or by any means obstruct said work.

The rolls so made, when approved by the Secretary of the Interior, shall be final, and the persons whose names are found thereon, with their descendants thereafter born to them, with such persons as may intermarry according to tribal laws, shall alone constitute the several tribes which they represent.

The members of said commission shall, in performing all duties required of them by law, have authority to administer oaths, examine witnesses, and send for persons and papers; and any person who shall willfully and knowingly make any false affidavit or oath to any material fact or matter before any member of said commission, or before any other officer authorized to administer oaths, to any affidavit or other paper to be filed or oath taken before said commission, shall be deemed guilty of perjury, and on conviction thereof shall be punished as for such offense.

SEC. 22. That where members of one tribe, under intercourse laws, usages, or customs, have made homes within the limits and on the lands of another tribe, they may retain and take allotment, embracing same under such agreement as may be made within such tribes respecting such settlers; but if no such agreement be made the improvements so made shall be appraised, and the value thereof, including all damages incurred by such settler incident to enforced removal, shall be paid to him immediately upon removal, out of any funds belonging to the tribe, or such settler, if he so desire, may make private sale of his improvements to any citizen of the tribe owning the lands: *Provided*, That he shall not be paid for improvements made on lands in excess of that to which he, his wife, and minor children are entitled to under this act.

SEC. 23. That all leases of agricultural or grazing land belonging to any tribe made after the first day of January, eighteen hundred and ninety-eight, by the tribe or any member thereof, shall be absolutely void, and all such grazing leases made prior to said date shall terminate on the first day of April, eighteen hundred and ninety-nine, and all such agricultural leases shall terminate on January first, nineteen hundred; but this shall not prevent individuals from leasing their allotments when made to them as provided in this act, nor from occupying or renting their proportionate shares of the tribal lands until the allotments herein provided for are made.

SEC. 24. That all moneys paid into the United States Treasury at Saint Louis, Missouri, under provisions of this act shall be placed to the credit of the tribe to which they belong; and the assistant United States treasurer shall give triplicate receipts therefor to the depositor.

SEC. 25. That before any allotment shall be made of lands in the Cherokee Nation, there shall be segregated therefrom by the commission heretofore mentioned, in separate allotments or otherwise, the one hundred and fifty-seven thousand six hundred acres purchased by the Delaware tribe of Indians from the Cherokee Nation under agreement of April eighth, eighteen hundred and sixty-seven, subject to the judicial determination of the rights of said descendants and the Cherokee Nation under said agreement. That the Delaware Indians residing in the Cherokee Nation are hereby authorized and empowered to bring suit in the Court of Claims of the United States, within sixty days after the passage of this act, against the Cherokee Nation, for the purpose of determining the rights of said Delaware Indians in and to the lands and funds of said nation under their contract and agreement with the Cherokee Nation dated April eighth, eighteen hundred and sixty-seven; or the Cherokee Nation may bring a like suit against said Delaware Indians; and jurisdiction is conferred on said court to adjudicate and fully determine the same, with right of appeal to either party to the Supreme Court of the United States.

SEC. 26. That on and after the passage of this act the laws of the various tribes or nations of Indians shall not be enforced at law or in equity by the courts of the United States in the Indian Territory.

SEC. 27. That the Secretary of the Interior is authorized to locate one Indian inspector in Indian Territory, who may, under his authority and direction, perform any duties required of the Secretary of the Interior by law, relating to affairs therein.

SEC. 28. That on the first day of July, eighteen hundred and ninety-eight, all tribal courts in Indian Territory shall be abolished, and no officer of said courts shall thereafter have any authority whatever to do or perform any act theretofore authorized by any law in connection with said courts, or to receive any pay for same; and all civil and criminal causes then pending in any such court shall be transferred to the United States court in said Territory by filing with the clerk of the court the original papers in the suit: *Provided*, That this section shall not be in force as to the Chickasaw, Choctaw, and Creek tribes or nations until the first day of October, eighteen hundred and ninety-eight.

SEC. 29. That the agreement made by the Commission to the Five Civilized Tribes with commissions representing the Choctaw and Chickasaw tribes of Indians on the twenty-third day of April, eighteen hundred and ninety-seven, as herein amended, is hereby ratified and confirmed, and the same shall be of full force and effect if ratified before the first day of December, eighteen hundred and ninety-eight, by a majority of the whole number of votes cast by the members of said tribes at an election held for that purpose; and the executives of said tribes are hereby authorized and directed to make public proclamation that said agreement shall be voted on at the next general election, or at any special election to be called by such executives for the purpose of voting on said agreement; and at the election held for such purpose all male members of each of said tribes qualified to vote under his tribal laws shall have the right to vote at the election precinct most convenient to his residence, whether the same be within the bounds of his tribe or not: *Provided*, That no person whose right to citizenship in either of said tribes or nations is now contested in original or appellate proceedings before any United States court shall be permitted to vote at said election: *Provided further*, That the votes cast in both said tribes or nations shall be forthwith returned duly certified by the precinct officers to the national secretaries of said tribes or nations, and shall be presented by said national secretaries to a board of commissioners consisting of the principal chief and national secretary of the Choctaw Nation, the governor and national secretary of the Chickasaw Nation, and a member of the Commission to the Five Civilized Tribes, to be designated by the chairman of said commission; and said board shall meet without delay at Atoka, in the Indian Territory, and canvass and count said votes and make proclamation of the result; and if said agreement as amended be so ratified, the provisions of this act shall then only apply to said tribes where the same do not conflict with the provisions of said agreement; but the provisions of said agreement, if so ratified, shall not in any manner affect the provisions of section fourteen of this act, which said amended agreement is as follows:

This agreement, by and between the Government of the United States, of the first part, entered into in its behalf by the Commission to the Five Civilized Tribes, Henry L. Dawes, Frank C. Armstrong, Archibald S. McKennon, Thomas B. Cabaniss, and Alexander B. Montgomery, duly appointed and authorized thereunto, and the governments of the Choctaw and Chickasaw tribes or nations of Indians in the Indian Territory, respectively, of the second part, entered into in behalf of such Choctaw and Chickasaw governments, duly appointed and authorized thereunto, viz: Green McCurtain, J. S. Standley, N. B. Ainsworth, Ben Hampton, Wesley Anderson, Amos Henry, D. C. Garland, and A. S. Williams, in behalf of the Choctaw Tribe or Nation, and R. M. Harris, I. O. Lewis, Holmes Colbert, P. S. Mosely, M. V. Cheadle, R. L. Murray, William Perry, A. H. Colbert, and R. L. Boyd, in behalf of the Chickasaw Tribe or Nation.

ALLOTMENT OF LANDS.

Witnesseth, That in consideration of the mutual undertakings, herein contained, it is agreed as follows:

That all the lands within the Indian Territory belonging to the Choctaw and Chickasaw Indians shall be allotted to the members of said tribes so as to give to each member of these tribes so far as possible a fair and equal share thereof, considering the character and fertility of the soil and the location and value of the lands.

That all the lands set apart for town sites, and the strip of land lying between the city of Fort Smith, Arkansas, and the Arkansas and Poteau rivers, extending up said river to the mouth of Mill Creek; and six hundred and forty acres each, to include the buildings now occupied by the Jones Academy, Tushkahoma Female Seminary, Wheelock Orphan Seminary, and Armstrong Orphan Academy, and ten acres for the capitol building of the Choctaw Nation; one hundred and sixty acres each, immediately contiguous to and including the buildings known as Bloomfield Academy, Lebanon Orphan Home, Harley Institute, Rock Academy, and Collins Institute, and five acres for the capitol building in the Chickasaw Nation, and the use of one acre of land for each church house now erected outside of the towns, and eighty acres of land each for J. S. Murrow, H. R. Schermerhorn, and the widow of R. S. Bell, who have been laboring as missionaries in the Choctaw and Chickasaw nations since the year eighteen hundred and sixty-six, with the same conditions and limitations as apply to lands allotted to the members of the Choctaw and Chickasaw nations, and to be located on lands not occupied by a Choctaw or a Chickasaw, and a reasonable amount of land, to be determined by the town-site commission, to include all court-houses and jails, and other public buildings not hereinbefore provided for, shall be exempted from division. And all coal and asphalt in or under the lands allotted and reserved from allotment shall be reserved for the sole use of the members of the Choctaw and Chickasaw tribes, exclusive of freedmen: *Provided*, That where any coal or asphalt is hereafter opened on land allotted, sold, or reserved, the value of the use of the necessary surface for prospecting or mining, and the damage done to the other land and improvements, shall be ascertained under the direction of the Secretary of the Interior and paid to the allottee or owner of the land by the lessee or party operating the same before operations begin. That in order to such equal division the lands of the Choctaws and Chickasaws shall be graded and appraised so as to give to each member, so far as possible, an equal value of the land: *Provided further*, That the Commission to the Five Civilized Tribes shall make a correct roll of Chickasaw freedmen entitled to any rights or benefits under the treaty made in eighteen hundred and sixty-six between the United States and the Choctaw and Chickasaw tribes and their descendants born to them since the date of said treaty, and forty acres of land, including their present residences and improvements, shall be allotted to each, to be selected, held, and used by them until their rights under said treaty shall be determined in such manner as shall hereafter be provided by act of Congress.

That the lands allotted to the Choctaw and Chickasaw freedmen are to be deducted from the portion to be allotted under this agreement to the members of the Choctaw and Chickasaw tribes so as to reduce the allotment to the Choctaws and Chickasaws by the value of the same.

That the said Choctaw and Chickasaw freedmen who may be entitled to allotments of forty acres each shall be entitled each to land equal in value to forty acres of the average land of the two nations.

That in the appraisement of the lands to be allotted the Choctaw and Chickasaw tribes shall each have a representative, to be appointed by their respective executives, to cooperate with the Commission to the Five Civilized Tribes or anyone making appraisements under the direction of the Secretary of the Interior in grading and appraising the lands preparatory to allotment. And the land shall be valued in the appraisement as if in its original condition, excluding the improvements thereon.

That the appraisement and allotment shall be made under the direction of the Secretary of the Interior and shall begin as soon as the progress of the surveys, now being made by the United States Government, will admit.

That each member of the Choctaw and Chickasaw tribes, including Choctaw and Chickasaw freedmen, shall, where it is possible, have the right to take his allotment on land the improvements on which belong to him, and such improvements shall not be estimated in the value of his allotment. In the case of minor children allotments shall be selected for them by their father, mother, guardian, or the administrator having charge of their estate, preference being given in the order named, and shall not be sold during his minority. Allotments shall be selected for prisoners, convicts, and incompetents by some suitable person akin to them, and due care taken that all persons entitled thereto have allotments made to them.

All the lands allotted shall be nontaxable while the title remains in the original allottee, but not to exceed twenty-one years from date of patent, and each allottee shall select from his allotment a homestead of one hundred and sixty acres, for which he shall have a separate patent, and which shall be inalienable for twenty-one years from date of patent. This provision shall also apply to the Choctaw and Chickasaw freedman to the extent of his allotment. Selections for homesteads for minors to be made as provided herein in case of allotment, and the remainder of the lands allotted to said members shall be alienable for a price to be actually paid, and to include no former indebtedness or obligation—one-fourth of said remainder in one year, one-fourth in three years, and the balance of said alienable lands in five years from the date of the patent.

That all contracts looking to the sale or incumbrance in any way of the land of an allottee, except the sale hereinbefore provided, shall be null and void. No allottee shall lease his allotment, or any portion thereof, for a longer period than five years, and then without the privilege of renewal. Every lease which is not evidenced by writing, setting out specifically the terms thereof, or which is not recorded in the clerk's office of the United States court for the district in which the land is located, within three months after the date of its execution, shall be void, and the purchaser or lessee shall acquire no rights whatever by an entry or holding thereunder. And no such lease or any sale shall be valid as against the allottee unless providing to him a reasonable compensation for the lands sold or leased.

That all controversies arising between the members of said tribes as to their right to have certain lands allotted to them shall be settled by the commission making the allotments.

That the United States shall put each allottee in possession of his allotment and remove all persons therefrom objectionable to the allottee.

That the United States shall survey and definitely mark and locate the ninety-eighth (98th) meridian of west longitude between Red and Canadian rivers before allotment of the lands herein provided for shall begin.

MEMBERS' TITLES TO LANDS.

That as soon as practicable, after the completion of said allotments, the principal chief of the Choctaw Nation and the governor of the Chickasaw Nation shall jointly execute, under their hands and the seals of the respective nations, and deliver to each of the said allottees patents conveying to him all the right, title, and interest of the Choctaws and Chickasaws in and to the land which shall have been allotted to him in conformity with the requirements of this agreement, excepting all coal and asphalt in or under said land. Said patents shall be framed in accordance with the provisions of this agreement, and shall embrace the land allotted to such patentee and no other land, and the acceptance of his patents by such allottee shall be operative as an assent on his part to the allotment and conveyance of all the lands of the Choctaws and Chickasaws in accordance with the provisions of this agreement, and as a relinquishment of all his right, title, and interest in and to any and all parts thereof, except the land embraced in said patents, except also his interest in the proceeds of all lands, coal, and asphalt herein excepted from allotment.

That the United States shall provide by law for proper records of land titles in the territory occupied by the Choctaw and Chickasaw tribes.

RAILROADS.

The rights of way for railroads through the Choctaw and Chickasaw nations to be surveyed and set apart and platted to conform to the respective acts of Congress granting the same in cases where said rights of way are defined by such acts of Congress, but in cases where the acts of Congress do not define the same then Congress is memorialized to definitely fix the width of said rights of way for station grounds and between stations, so that railroads now constructed through said nations shall have, as near as possible, uniform rights of way; and Congress is also requested to fix uniform rates of fare and freight for all railroads through the Choctaw and Chickasaw nations; branch railroads now constructed and not built according to acts of Congress to pay the same rates for rights of way and station grounds as main lines.

TOWN SITES.

It is further agreed that there shall be appointed a commission for each of the two nations. Each commission shall consist of one member, to be appointed by the executive of the tribe for which said commission is to act, who shall not be interested in town property other than his home, and one to be appointed by the President of the United States. Each of said commissions shall lay out town sites, to be restricted as far as possible to their present limits, where towns are now located in the nation for which said commission is appointed. Said commission shall have prepared correct and proper plats of each town, and file one in the clerk's office of the United States district court for the district in which the town is located, and one with the principal chief or governor of the nation in which the town is located, and one with the Secretary of the Interior, to be approved by him before the same shall take effect. When said towns are so laid out, each lot on which permanent, substantial, and valuable improvements, other than fences, tillage, and temporary houses, have been made, shall be valued by the commission provided for the nation in which the town is located at the price a fee-simple title to the same would bring in the market at the time the valuation is made, but not to include in such value the improvements thereon. The owner of the improvements on each lot shall have the right to buy one residence and one business lot at fifty per centum of the appraised value of such improved property, and the remainder of such improved property at sixty-two and one-half per centum of the said market value within sixty days from date of notice served on him that such lot is for sale, and if he purchases the same he shall, within ten days from his purchase, pay into the Treasury of the United States one-fourth of the purchase price, and the balance in three equal annual installments, and when the entire sum is paid shall be entitled to a patent for the same. In case the two members of the commission fail to agree as to the market value of any lot, or the limit or extent of said town, either of said commissioners may report any such disagreement to the judge of the district in which such town is located, who shall appoint a third member to act with said commission, who is not interested in town lots, who shall act with them to determine said value.

If such owner of the improvements on any lot fails within sixty days to purchase and make the first payment on same, such lot, with the improvements thereon, shall be sold at public auction to the highest bidder, under the direction of the aforesaid commission, and the purchaser at such sale shall pay to the owner of the improvements the price for which said lot shall be sold, less sixty-two and one-half per cent of said appraised value of the lot, and shall pay the sixty-two and one-half per cent of said appraised value into the United States Treasury, under regulations to be established by the Secretary of the Interior, in four installments, as hereinbefore provided. The commission shall have the right to reject any bid on such lot which they consider below its value.

All lots not so appraised shall be sold from time to time at public auction (after proper advertisement) by the commission for the nation in which the town is located, as may seem for the best interest of the nations and the proper development of each town, the purchase price to be paid in four installments as hereinbefore provided for improved lots. The commission shall have the right to reject any bid for such lots which they consider below its value.

All the payments herein provided for shall be made under the direction of the Secretary of the Interior into the United States Treasury, a failure of sixty days to make any one payment to be a forfeiture of all payments made and all rights under the contract: *Provided,* That the purchaser of any lot shall have the option of paying the entire price of the lot before the same is due.

No tax shall be assessed by any town government against any town lot unsold by the commission, and no tax levied against a lot sold, as herein provided, shall constitute a lien on same till the purchase price thereof has been fully paid to the nation.

The money paid into the United States Treasury for the sale of all town lots shall be for the benefit of the members of the Choctaw and Chickasaw tribes (freedmen excepted), and at the end of one year from the ratification of this agreement, and at the end of each year thereafter, the funds so accumulated shall be divided and paid to the Choctaws and Chickasaws (freedmen excepted), each member of the two tribes to receive an equal portion thereof.

That no law or ordinance shall be passed by any town which interferes with the enforcement of or is in conflict with the laws of the United States in force in said Territory, and all persons in such towns shall be subject to said laws, and the United States agrees to maintain strict laws in the territory of the Choctaw and Chickasaw tribes against the introduction, sale, barter, or giving away of liquors and intoxicants of any kind or quality.

That said commission shall be authorized to locate, within a suitable distance from each town site, not to exceed five acres to be used as a cemetery, and when any town has paid into the United States Treasury, to be part of the fund arising from the sale of town lots, ten dollars per acre therefor, such town shall be entitled to a patent for the same as herein provided for titles to allottees, and shall dispose of same at reasonable prices in suitable lots for burial purposes, the proceeds derived from such sales to be applied by the town government to the proper improvement and care of said cemetery.

That no charge or claim shall be made against the Choctaw or Chickasaw tribes by the United States for the expenses of surveying and platting the lands and town sites, or for grading, appraising, and allotting the lands, or for appraising and disposing of the town lots as herein provided.

That the land adjacent to Fort Smith and lands for court-houses, jails, and other public purposes, excepted from allotment shall be disposed of in the same manner and for the same purposes as provided for town lots herein, but not till the Choctaw and Chickasaw councils shall direct such disposition to be made thereof, and said land adjacent thereto shall be placed under the jurisdiction of the city of Fort Smith, Arkansas, for police purposes.

There shall be set apart and exempted from appraisement and sale in the towns, lots upon which churches and parsonages are now built and occupied, not to exceed fifty feet front and one hundred feet deep for each church or parsonage; *Provided*. That such lots shall only be used for churches and parsonages, and when they ceased to be used shall revert to the members of the tribes to be disposed of as other town lots: *Provided, further*, That these lots may be sold by the churches for which they are set apart if the purchase money therefor is invested in other lot or lots in the same town, to be used for the same purpose and with the same conditions and limitations.

It is agreed that all the coal and asphalt within the limits of the Choctaw and Chickasaw nations shall remain and be the common property of the members of the Choctaw and Chickasaw tribes (freedmen excepted), so that each and every member shall have an equal and undivided interest in the whole; and no patent provided for in this agreement shall convey any title thereto. The revenues from coal and asphalt, or so much as shall be necessary, shall be used for the education of the children of Indian blood, of the members of said tribes. Such coal and asphalt mines as are now in operation, and all others which may hereafter be leased and operated, shall be under the supervision and control of two trustees, who shall be appointed by the President of the United States, one on the recommendation of the Principal Chief of the Choctaw Nation, who shall be a Choctaw by blood, whose term shall be for four years, and one on the recommendation of the Governor of the Chickasaw Nation, who shall be a Chickasaw by blood, whose term shall be for two years; after which the term of appointees shall be four years. Said trustees, or either of them, may, at any time, be removed by the President of the United States for good cause shown. They shall each give bond for the faithful performance of their duties, under such rules as may be prescribed by the Secretary of the Interior. Their salaries shall be fixed and paid by their respective nations, each of whom shall make full report of all his acts to the Secretary of the Interior quarterly. All such acts shall be subject to the approval of said Secretary.

All coal and asphalt mines in the two nations, whether now developed, or to be hereafter developed, shall be operated, and the royalties therefrom paid into the Treasury of the United States, and shall be drawn therefrom under such rules and regulations as shall be prescribed by the Secretary of the Interior.

All contracts made by the national agents of the Choctaw and Chickasaw nations for operating coal and asphalt, with any person or corporation, which were on April twenty-third, eighteen hundred and ninety-seven, being operated in good faith are hereby ratified and confirmed, and the lessee shall have the right to renew the same when they expire, subject to all the provisions of this act.

All agreements made by any person or corporation with any member or members of the Choctaw or Chickasaw nations, the object of which was to obtain such member or members' permission to operate coal or asphalt, are hereby declared void: *Provided*, That nothing herein contained shall impair the rights of any holder or owner of a leasehold interest in any oil, coal rights, asphalt, or mineral which have been assented to by act of Congress, but all such interests shall continue unimpaired hereby and shall be assured by new leases from such trustees of coal or asphalt claims described therein, by application to the trustees within six months after the ratification of this agreement, subject, however, to payment of advance royalties herein provided for.

All leases under this agreement shall include the coal or asphaltum, or other mineral, as the case may be, in or under nine hundred and sixty acres, which shall be in a square as nearly as possible and shall be for thirty years. The royalty on coal shall be fifteen cents per ton of two thousand pounds on all coal mined, payable on the 25th day of the month next succeeding that in which it is mined. Royalty on asphalt shall be sixty cents per ton, payable same as coal: *Provided*, That the Secretary of the Interior may reduce or advance royalties on coal and asphalt when he deems it for the best interests of the Choctaws and Chickasaws to do so. No royalties shall be paid except into the United States Treasury as herein provided.

All lessees shall pay on each coal or asphalt claim at the rate of one hundred dollars per annum, in advance, for the first and second years; two hundred dollars per annum, in advance, for the third and fourth years, and five hundred dollars for each succeeding year thereafter. All such payments shall be treated as advanced royalty on the mine or claim on which they are made, and shall be a credit as royalty when each said mine is developed and operated, and its production is in excess of such guaranteed annual advance payments, and all persons having coal leases must pay said annual advanced payments on each claim whether developed or undeveloped: *Provided, however*, That should any lessee neglect or refuse to pay such advanced annual royalty after the period of sixty days after the same becomes due and payable on any lease, the lease on which default is made shall become null and void, and the royalties paid in advance thereon shall then become and be the money and property of the Choctaw and Chickasaw nations.

In surface, the use of which is reserved to present coal operators, shall be included such lots in towns as are occupied by lessees' houses—either occupied by said lessees' employees or as offices or warehouses: *Provided, however*, That in those town sites designated and laid out under the provision of this agreement where coal leases are now being operated and coal is being mined, there shall be reserved from appraisement and sale all lots occupied by houses of miners actually engaged in mining, and only while they are so engaged, and in addition thereto a sufficient amount of land, to be determined by the town-site board of appraisers, to furnish homes for the men actually engaged in working for the lessees operating said mines, and a sufficient amount for all buildings and machinery for mining purposes: *And provided further*, That when the lessees shall cease to operate said mines then and in that event the lots of land so reserved shall be disposed of by the coal trustees for the benefit of the Choctaw and Chickasaw tribes.

That whenever the members of the Choctaw and Chickasaw tribes shall be required to pay taxes for the support of schools, then the fund arising from such royalties shall be disposed of for the equal benefit of their members (freedmen excepted) in such manner as the tribes may direct.

It is further agreed that the United States courts now existing, or that may hereafter be created, in the Indian Territory shall have exclusive jurisdiction of all controversies growing out of the titles, ownership, occupation, possession, or use of real estate, coal, and asphalt in the territory occupied by the Choctaw and Chickasaw tribes; and of all persons charged with homicide, embezzlement, bribery, and embracery, breaches, or disturbances of the peace, and carrying weapons, hereafter committed in the territory of said tribes, without reference to race or citizenship of the person or persons charged with such crime; and any citizen or officer of the Choctaw or Chickasaw nations charged with such crime shall be tried, and, if convicted, punished as though he were a citizen or officer of the United States.

And sections sixteen hundred and thirty-six to sixteen hundred and forty-four, inclusive, entitled "Embezzlement," and sections seventeen hundred and eleven to seventeen hundred and eighteen, inclusive, entitled "Bribery and embracery," of

Mansfield's Digest of the Laws of Arkansas, are hereby extended over and put in force in the Choctaw and Chickasaw nations; and the word "officer," where the same appears in said laws, shall include all officers of the Choctaw and Chickasaw governments; and the fifteenth section of the act of Congress entitled "An act to establish United States courts in the Indian Territory, and for other purposes," approved March first, eighteen hundred and eighty-nine, limiting jurors to citizens of the United States, shall be held not to apply to United States courts in the Indian Territory held within the limits of the Choctaw and Chickasaw nations; and all members of the Choctaw and Chickasaw tribes, otherwise qualified, shall be competent jurors in said courts: *Provided*, That whenever a member of the Choctaw and Chickasaw nations is indicted for homicide, he may, within thirty days after such indictment and his arrest thereon, and before the same is reached for trial, file with the clerk of the court in which he is indicted his affidavit that he can not get a fair trial in said court; and it thereupon shall be the duty of the judge of said court to order a change of venue in such case to the United States district court for the western district of Arkansas, at Fort Smith, Aakansas, or to the United States district court for the eastern district of Texas, at Paris, Texas, always selecting the court that in his judgment is nearest or most convenient to the place where the crime charged in the indictment is supposed to have been committed, which courts shall have jurisdiction to try the case; and in all said civil suits said courts shall have full equity powers; and whenever it shall appear to said court, at any stage in the hearing of any case, that the tribe is in any way interested in the subject-matter in controversy, it shall have power to summon in said tribe and make the same a party to the suit and proceed therein in all respects as if such tribe were an original party thereto; but in no case shall suit be instituted against the tribal government without its consent.

It is further agreed that no act, ordinance, or resolution of the council of either the Choctaw or Chickasaw tribes, in any manner affecting the land of the tribe, or of the individuals, after allotment, or the moneys or other property of the tribe or citizens thereof (except appropriations for the regular and necessary expenses of the government of the respective tribes), or the rights of any persons to employ any kind of labor, or the rights of any persons who have taken or may take the oath of allegiance to the United States, shall be of any validity until approved by the President of the United States. When such acts, ordinances, or resolutions passed by the council of either of said tribes shall be approved by the governor thereof, then it shall be the duty of the national secretary of said tribe to forward them to the President of the United States, duly certified and sealed, who shall, within thirty days after their reception, approve or disapprove the same. Said acts, ordinances, or resolutions, when so approved, shall be published in at least two newspapers having a bona fide circulation in the tribe to be affected thereby, and when disapproved shall be returned to the tribe enacting the same.

It is further agreed, in view of the modification of legislative authority and judicial jurisdiction herein provided, and the necessity of the continuance of the tribal governments so modified, in order to carry out the requirements of this agreement, that the same shall continue for the period of eight years from the fourth day of March, eighteen hundred and ninety-eight. This stipulation is made in the belief that the tribal governments so modified will prove so satisfactory that there will be no need or desire for further change till the lands now occupied by the Five Civilized Tribes shall, in the opinion of Congress, be prepared for admission as a State to the Union. But this provision shall not be construed to be in any respect an abdication by Congress of power at any time to make needful rules and regulations respecting said tribes.

That all per capita payments hereafter made to the members of the Choctaw or Chickasaw nations shall be paid directly to each individual member by a bonded officer of the United States, under the direction of the Secretary of the Interior, which officer shall be required to give strict account for such disbursements to said Secretary.

That the following sum be, and is hereby, appropriated, out of any money in the Treasury not otherwise appropriated, for fulfilling treaty stipulations with the Chickasaw Nation of Indians, namely:

For arrears of interest, at five per centum per annum, from December thirty-first, eighteen hundred and forty, to June thirtieth, eighteen hundred and eighty-nine, on one hundred and eighty-four thousand one hundred and forty-three dollars and nine cents of the trust fund of the Chickasaw Nation erroneously dropped from the books of the United States prior to December thirty-first, eighteen hundred and forty, and restored December twenty-seventh, eighteen hundred and eighty-seven by the award of the Secretary of the Interior, under the fourth article of the treaty of June twenty-second, eighteen hundred and fifty-two, and for arrears of interest.

at five per centum per annum, from March eleventh, eighteen hundred and fifty, to March third, eighteen hundred and ninety, on fifty-six thousand and twenty-one dollars and forty-nine cents of the trust fund of the Chickasaw Nation erroneously dropped from the books of the United States March eleventh, eighteen hundred and fifty, and restored December twenty-seventh, eighteen hundred and eighty-seven, by the award of the Secretary of the Interior, under the fourth article of the treaty of June twenty-second, eighteen hundred and fifty-two, five hundred and fifty-eight thousand five hundred and twenty dollars and fifty-four cents, to be placed to the credit of the Chickasaw Nation with the fund to which it properly belongs: *Provided*, That if there be any attorneys' fees to be paid out of same, on contract heretofore made and duly approved by the Secretary of the Interior, the same is authorized to be paid by him.

It is further agreed that the final decision of the courts of the United States in the case of the Choctaw Nation and the Chickasaw Nation against the United States and the Wichita and affiliated bands of Indians, now pending, when made, shall be conclusive as the basis of settlement as between the United States and said Choctaw and Chickasaw nations for the remaining lands in what is known as the "Leased District," namely, the land lying between the ninety-eighth and one hundredth degrees of west longitude and between the Red and Canadian rivers, leased to the United States by the treaty of eighteen hundred and fifty-five, except that portion called the Cheyenne and Arapahoe country, heretofore acquired by the United States, and all final judgments rendered against said nations in any of the courts of the United States in favor of the United States or any citizen thereof shall first be paid out of any sum hereafter found due said Indians for any interest they may have in the so-called leased district.

It is further agreed that all of the funds invested, in lieu of investment, treaty funds, or otherwise, now held by the United States in trust for the Choctaw and Chickasaw tribes, shall be capitalized within one year after the tribal governments shall cease, so far as the same may legally be done, and be appropriated and paid, by some officer of the United States appointed for the purpose, to the Choctaws and Chickasaws (freedmen excepted) per capita, to aid and assist them in improving their homes and lands.

It is further agreed that the Choctaws and Chickasaws, when their tribal governments cease, shall become possessed of all the rights and privileges of citizens of the United States.

ORPHAN LANDS.

It is further agreed that the Choctaw orphan lands in the State of Mississippi, yet unsold, shall be taken by the United States at one dollar and twenty-five cents ($1.25) per acre, and the proceeds placed to the credit of the Choctaw orphan fund in the Treasury of the United States, the number of acres to be determined by the General Land Office.

In witness whereof the said commissioners do hereunto affix their names at Atoka, Indian Territory, this the twenty-third day of April, eighteen hundred and ninety-seven.

<table>
<tr><td>GREEN McCURTAIN,
    Principal Chief.</td><td>R. M. HARRIS,
    Governor.</td></tr>
<tr><td>J. S. STANDLEY,
N. B. AINSWORTH,
BEN HAMPTON,
WESLEY ANDERSON,
AMOS HENRY,
D. C. GARLAND,
    Choctaw Commission.</td><td>ISAAC O. LEWIS,
HOLMES COLBERT,
ROBERT L. MURRAY,
WILLIAM PERRY,
R. L. BOYD,
    Chickasaw Commission.</td></tr>
</table>

FRANK C. ARMSTRONG,
    Acting Chairman.

ARCHIBALD S. McKENNON,
THOMAS B. CABANISS,
ALEXANDER B. MONTGOMERY,
Commission to the Five Civilized Tribes.

H. M. JACOWAY, Jr.,
    Secretary, Five Tribes Commission.

SEC. 30. * * *

Approved, June 28, 1898.

APPENDIX NO. 3.

[PUBLIC—No. 112.]

AN ACT To ratify and confirm an agreement with the Muskogee or Creek tribe of Indians, and for other purposes.

Be it enacted by the Senate and House of Representatives of the United States of America in Congress assembled, That the agreement negotiated between the Commission to the Five Civilized Tribes and the Muskogee or Creek tribe of Indians at the city of Washington on the eighth day of March, nineteen hundred, as herein amended, is hereby accepted, ratified, and confirmed, and the same shall be of full force and effect when ratified by the Creek national council. The principal chief, as soon as practicable after the ratification of this agreement by Congress, shall call an extra session of the Creek national council and lay before it this agreement and the act of Congress ratifying it, and if the agreement be ratified by said council, as provided in the constitution of said nation, he shall transmit to the President of the United States the act of council ratifying the agreement, and the President of the United States shall thereupon issue his proclamation declaring the same duly ratified, and that all the provisions of this agreement have become law according to the terms thereof: *Provided,* That such ratification by the Creek national council shall be made within ninety days from the approval of this act by the President of the United States.

This agreement by and between the United States, entered into in its behalf by the Commission to the Five Civilized Tribes, Henry L. Dawes, Tams Bixby, Archibald S. McKennon, and Thomas B. Needles, duly appointed and authorized thereunto, and the Muskogee (or Creek) tribe of Indians, in Indian Territory, entered into in behalf of said tribe by Pleasant Porter, principal chief, and George A. Alexander, David M. Hodge, Isparhecher, Albert P. McKellop, and Cub McIntosh, delegates, duly appointed and authorized thereunto,

Witnesseth that in consideration of the mutual undertakings herein contained it is agreed as follows:

DEFINITIONS.

1. The words "Creek" and "Muskogee," as used in this agreement, shall be deemed synonymous, and the words "Creek Nation" and "tribe" shall each be deemed to refer to the Muskogee Nation or Muskogee tribe of Indians in Indian Territory. The words "principal chief" shall be deemed to refer to the principal chief of the Muskogee Nation. The words "citizen or "citizens" shall le deemed to refer to a member or members of the Muskogee tribe or nation of Indians. The words "The Dawes Commission" or "commission" shall be deemed to refer to the United States Commission to the Five Civilized Tribes.

GENERAL ALLOTMENT OF LANDS.

2. All lands belonging to the Creek tribe of Indians in the Indian Territory. except town sites and lands herein reserved for Creek schools and public buildings. shall be appraised at their true value, excluding only lawful improvements on lands in actual cultivation. The appraisement shall be made under direction of the Dawes Commission by such number of committees, with necessary assistance, as may be deemed necessary to expedite the work, one member of each committee to be appointed by the principal chief; and if the members of any committee fail to agree as to the value of any tract of land, the value thereof shall be fixed by said commission. Each committee shall make report of its work to said commission, which shall from time to time prepare reports of same, in duplicate, and transmit them to the Secretary of the Interior for his approval, and when approved one copy thereof shall be returned to the office of said commission for its use in making allotments as herein provided.

3. All lands of said tribe, except as herein provided, shall be allotted among the citizens of the tribe by said commission so as to give each an equal share of the whole in value, as nearly as may be, in manner following: There shall be allotted to each citizen one hundred and sixty acres of land—boundaries to conform to the Government survey—which may be selected by him so as to include improvements which belong to him. One hundred and sixty acres of land, valued at six dollars and fifty cents per acre, shall constitute the standard value of an allotment, and shall be the measure for the equalization of values; and any allottee receiving lands of less than such standard value may, at any time, select other lands, which, at

their appraised value, are sufficient to make his allotment equal in value to the standard so fixed.

If any citizen select lands the appraised value of which, for any reason, is in excess of such standard value, the excess of value shall be charged against him in the future distribution of the funds of the tribe arising from all sources whatsoever, and he shall not receive any further distribution of property or funds of the tribe until all other citizens have received lands and money equal in value to his allotment. If any citizen select lands the appraised value of which is in excess of such standard value, he may pay the overplus in money, but if he fail to do so, the same shall be charged against him in the future distribution of the funds of the tribe arising from all sources whatsoever, and he shall not receive any further distribution of property or funds until all other citizens shall have received lands and funds equal in value to his allotment; and if there be not sufficient funds of the tribe to make the allotments of all other citizens of the tribe equal in value to his, then the surplus shall be a lien upon the rents and profits of his allotment until paid.

4. Allotment for any minor may be selected by his father, mother, or guardian, in the order named, and shall not be sold during his minority. All guardians or curators appointed for minors and incompetents shall be citizens.

Allotments may be selected for prisoners, convicts, and aged and infirm persons by their duly appointed agents, and for incompetents by guardians, curators, or suitable persons akin to them, but it shall be the duty of said commission to see that such selections are made for the best interests of such parties.

5. If any citizen have in his possession, in actual cultivation, lands in excess of what he and his wife and minor children are entitled to take, he shall, within ninety days after the ratification of this agreement, select therefrom allotments for himself and family aforesaid, and if he have lawful improvements upon such excess he may dispose of the same to any other citizen, who may thereupon select lands so as to include such improvements; but, after the expiration of ninety days from the ratification of this agreement, any citizen may take any lands not already selected by another; but if lands so taken be in actual cultivation, having thereon improvements belonging to another citizen, such improvements shall be valued by the appraisement committee, and the amount paid to the owner thereof by the allottee, and the same shall be a lien upon the rents and profits of the land until paid: *Provided*, That the owner of improvements may remove the same if he desires.

6. All allotments made to Creek citizens by said commission prior to the ratification of this agreement, as to which there is no contest, and which do not include public property, and are not herein otherwise affected, are confirmed, and the same shall, as to appraisement and all things else, be governed by the provisions of this agreement; and said commission shall continue the work of allotment of Creek lands to citizens of the tribe as heretofore, conforming to provisions herein; and all controversies arising between citizens as to their right to select certain tracts of land shall be determined by said commission.

7. Lands allotted to citizens hereunder shall not in any manner whatsoever, or at any time, be incumbered, taken, or sold to secure or satisfy any debt or obligation contracted or incurred prior to the date of the deed to the allottee therefor, and such lands shall not be alienable by the allottee or his heirs at any time before the expiration of five years from the ratification of this agreement, except with the approval of the Secretary of the Interior.

Each citizen shall select from his allotment forty acres of land as a homestead, which shall be nontaxable and inalienable and free from incumbrance whatever for twenty-one years, for which he shall have a separate deed, conditioned as above: *Provided*, That selections of homesteads for minors, prisoners, convicts, incompetents, and aged and infirm persons, who can not select for themselves, may be made in the manner herein provided for the selection of their allotments; and if, for any reason, such selection be not made for any citizen, it shall be the duty of said Commission to make selection for him.

The homestead of each citizen shall remain, after the death of the allottee, for the use and support of children born to him after the ratification of this agreement, but if he have no such issue, then he may dispose of his homestead by will, free from limitation herein imposed, and if this be not done, the land shall descend to his heirs according to the laws of descent and distribution of the Creek Nation, free from such limitation.

8. The Secretary of the Interior shall, through the United States Indian agent in said Territory, immediately after the ratification of this agreement, put each citizen who has made selection of his allotment in unrestricted possession of his land and remove therefrom all persons objectionable to him; and when any citizen shall thereafter make selection of his allotment as herein provided, and receive certificate therefor, he shall be immediately thereupon so placed in possession of his land.

9. When allotment of one hundred and sixty acres has been made to each citizen, the residue of lands, not herein reserved or otherwise disposed of, and all the funds arising under this agreement shall be used for the purpose of equalizing allotments, and if the same be insufficient therefor, the deficiency shall be supplied out of any other funds of the tribe, so that the allotments of all citizens may be made equal in value, as nearly as may be, in manner herein provided.

TOWN SITES.

10. All towns in the Creek Nation having a present population of two hundred or more shall, and all others may, be surveyed, laid out, and appraised under the provisions of an act of Congress entitled "An act making appropriations for the current and contingent expenses of the Indian Department and for fulfilling treaty stipulations with various Indian tribes for the fiscal year ending June thirtieth, nineteen hundred and one, and for other purposes," approved May thirty-first, nineteen hundred, which said provisions are as follows:

"That the Secretary of the Interior is hereby authorized, under rules and regulations to be prescribed by him, to survey, lay out, and plat into town lots, streets, alleys, and parks, the sites of such towns and villages in the Choctaw, Chickasaw, Creek, and Cherokee nations, as may at that time have a population of two hundred or more, in such manner as will best subserve the then present needs and the reasonable prospective growth of such town. The work of surveying, laying out, and platting such town sites shall be done by competent surveyors, who shall prepare five copies of the plat of each town site which, when the survey is approved by the Secretary of the Interior, shall be filed as follows: One in the office of the Commissioner of Indian Affairs, one with the principal chief of the nation, one with the clerk of the court within the territorial jurisdiction of which the town is located, one with the Commission to the Five Civilized Tribes, and one with the town authorities, if there be such. Where in his judgment the best interests of the public service require, the Secretary of the Interior may secure the surveying, laying out, and platting of town sites in any of said nations by contract.

"Hereafter the work of the respective town-site commissions provided for in the agreement with the Choctaw and Chickasaw tribes ratified in section twenty-nine of the act of June twenty-eighth, eighteen hundred and ninety-eight, entitled 'An act for the protection of the people of the Indian Territory, and for other purposes,' shall begin, as to any town site, immediately upon the approval of the survey by the Secretary of the Interior and not before.

"The Secretary of the Interior may, in his discretion, appoint a town-site commission consisting of three members for each of the Creek and Cherokee nations, at least one of whom shall be a citizen of the tribe and shall be appointed upon the nomination of the principal chief of the tribe. Each commission, under the supervision of the Secretary of the Interior, shall appraise and sell for the benefit of the tribe the town lots in the nation for which it is appointed, acting in conformity with the provisions of any then existing act of Congress or agreement with the tribe approved by Congress. The agreement of any two members of the commission as to the true value of any lot shall constitute a determination thereof, subject to the approval of the Secretary of the Interior, and if no two members are able to agree the matter shall be determined by such Secretary.

"Where in his judgment the public interests will be thereby subserved, the Secretary of the Interior may appoint in the Choctaw, Chickasaw, Creek, or Cherokee Nation a separate town-site commission for any town, in which event, as to that town, such local commission may exercise the same authority and perform the same duties which would otherwise devolve upon the commission for that nation. Every such local commission shall be appointed in the manner provided in the act approved June twenty-eighth, eighteen hundred and ninety-eight, entitled 'An act for the protection of the people of the Indian Territory.'

"The Secretary of the Interior, where in his judgment the public interests will be thereby subserved, may permit the authorities of any town in any of said nations, at the expense of the town, to survey, lay out, and plat the site thereof, subject to his supervision and approval, as in other instances.

"As soon as the plat of any town site is approved, the proper commission shall, with all reasonable dispatch and within a limited time, to be prescribed by the Secretary of the Interior, proceed to make the appraisement of the lots and improvements, if any, thereon, and after the approval thereof by the Secretary of the Interior, shall, under the supervision of such Secretary, proceed to the disposition and sale of the lots in conformity with any then existing act of Congress or agreement with the tribe approved by Congress, and if the proper commission shall not omplete such appraisement and sale within the time limited by the Secretary of he Interior, they shall receive no pay for such additional time as may be taken by hem, unless the Secretary of the Interior for good cause shown shall expressly direct therwise.

"The Secretary of the Interior may, for good cause, remove any member of any own-site commission, tribal or local, in any of said nations, and may fill the vacancy hereby made or any vacancy otherwise occurring in like manner as the place was originally filled.

"It shall not be required that the town-site limits established in the course of the platting and disposing of town lots and the corporate limits of the town, if incorporated, shall be identical or coextensive, but such town-site limits and corporate limits hall be so established as to best subserve the then present needs and the reasonable prospective growth of the town, as the same shall appear at the times when such limits are respectively established: *Provided further*, That the exterior limits of all own sites shall be designated and fixed at the earliest practicable time under rules nd regulations prescribed by the Secretary of the Interior.

"Upon the recommendation of the Commission to the Five Civilized Tribes the ecretary of the Interior is hereby authorized at any time before allotment to set side and reserve from allotment any lands in the Choctaw, Chickasaw, Creek, or 'herokee nations, not exceeding one hundred and sixty acres in any one tract, at uch stations as are or shall be established in conformity with law on the line of any ailroad which shall be constructed or be in process of construction in or through ither of said nations prior to the allotment of the lands therein, and this irrespective f the population of such town site at the time. Such town sites shall be surveyed, aid out, and platted, and the lands therein disposed of for the benefit of the tribe in he manner herein prescribed for other town sites: *Provided further*, That whenever ny tract of land shall be set aside as herein provided which is occupied by a member of the tribe, such occupant shall be fully compensated for his improvements hereon under such rules and regulations as may be prescribed by the Secretary of he Interior: *Provided*, That hereafter the Secretary of the Interior may, whenever he chief executive or principal chief of said nation fails or refuses to appoint a town-ite commissioner for any town or to fill any vacancy caused by the neglect or refusal f the town-site commissioner appointed by the chief executive or principal chief of aid nation to qualify or act, in his discretion appoint a commissioner to fill the acancy thus created."

11. Any person in rightful possession of any town lot having improvements thereon, ther then temporary buildings, fencing, and tillage, shall have the right to purchase uch lot by paying one-half of the appraised value thereof, but if he shall fail within ixty days to purchase such lot and make the first payment thereon, as herein pro-ided, the lot and improvements shall be sold at public auction to the highest bidder, nder direction of the appraisement commission, at a price not less than their ppraised value, and the purchaser shall pay the purchase price to the owner of the nprovements, less the appraised value of the lot.

12. Any person having the right of occupancy of a residence or business lot or both any town, whether improved or not, and owning no other lot or land therein, hall have the right to purchase such lot by paying one-half of the appraised value hereof.

13. Any person holding lands within a town occupied by him as a home, also any erson who had at the time of signing this agreement purchased any lot, tract, or arcel of land from any person in legal possession at the time, shall have the right purchase the lot embraced in same by paying one-half of the appraised value hereof, not, however, exceeding four acres.

14. All town lots not having thereon improvements, other than temporary build-igs, fencing, and tillage, the sale or disposition of which is not herein otherwise pecifically provided for, shall be sold within twelve months after their appraise-ient, under direction of the Secretary of the Interior, after due advertisement, at ublic auction to the highest bidder at not less than their appraised value.

Any person having the right of occupancy of lands in any town which has been r may be laid out into town lots, to be sold at public auction as above, shall have he right to purchase one-fourth of all the lots into which such lands may have been ivided at two-thirds of their appraised value.

15. When the appraisement of any town lot is made upon which any person has nprovements as aforesaid, said appraisement commission shall notify him of the mount of said appraisement, and he shall, within sixty days thereafter, make pay-ient of ten per centum of the amount due for the lot, as herein provided, and four iouths thereafter he shall pay fifteen per centum additional, and the remainder of he purchase money in three equal annual installments, without interest.

field's Digest of the Statutes of Arkansas now in force in Indian Territory: *Provided*, That only citizens of the Creek Nation, male and female, and their Creek descendants shall inherit lands of the Creek Nation: *And provided further*, That if there be no person of Creek citizenship to take the descent and distribution of said estate, then the inheritance shall go to noncitizen heirs in the order named in said chapter 49.

ROLLS OF CITIZENSHIP.

7. All children born to those citizens who are entitled to enrollment as provided by the act of Congress approved March 1, 1901 (31 Stat. L., 861), subsequent to July 1, 1900, and up to and including May 25, 1901, and living upon the latter date, shall be placed on the rolls made by said commission. And if any such child has died since May 25, 1901, or may hereafter die before receiving his allotment of lands and distributive share of the funds of the tribe, the lands and moneys to which he would be entitled if living shall descend to his heirs as herein provided and be allotted and distributed to them accordingly.

8. All children who have not heretofore been listed for enrollment living May 25, 1901, born to citizens whose names appear upon the authenticated rolls of 1890 or upon the authenticated rolls of 1895 and entitled to enrollment as provided by the act of Congress approved March 1, 1901 (31 Stat. L., 861), shall be placed on the rolls made by said Commission. And if any such child has died since May 25, 1901, or may hereafter die, before receiving his allotment of lands and distributive share of the funds of the tribe, the lands and moneys to which he would be entitled if living shall descend to his heirs as herein provided and be allotted and distributed to them accordingly.

9. If the rolls of citizenship provided for by the act of Congress approved March 1, 1901 (31 Stat. L., 861), shall have been completed by said Commission prior to the ratification of this agreement, the names of children entitled to enrollment under the provisions of sections 7 and 8 hereof shall be placed upon a supplemental roll of citizens of the Creek Nation, and said supplemental roll when approved by the Secretary of the Interior shall in all respects be held to be a part of the final rolls of citizenship of said tribe: *Provided*, That the Dawes Commission be, and is hereby, authorized to add the following persons to the Creek roll: Nar-wal-le-pe-se, Mary Washington, Walter Washington, and Willie Washington, who are Creek Indians but whose names were left off the roll through neglect on their part.

ROADS.

10. Public highways or roads 3 rods in width, being 1 and one-half rods on each side of the section line, may be established along all section lines without any compensation being paid therefor; and all allottees, purchasers, and others shall take the title to such lands subject to this provision. And public highways or roads may be established elsewhere whenever necessary for the public good, the actual value of the land taken elsewhere than along section lines to be determined under the direction of the Secretary of the Interior while the tribal government continues, and to be paid by the Creek Nation during that time; and if buildings or other improvements are damaged in consequence of the establishment of such public highways or roads, whether along section lines or elsewhere, such damages, during the continuance of the tribal government, shall be determined and paid in the same manner.

11. In all instances of the establishment of town sites in accordance with the provisions of the act of Congress approved May 31, 1900 (31 Stat. L., 231), or those of section 10 of the agreement ratified by act of Congress approved March 1, 1901 (31 Stat. L., 861), authorizing the Secretary of the Interior, upon the recommendation of the Commission to the Five Civilized Tribes, at any time before allotment, to set aside and reserve from allotment any lands in the Creek Nation not exceeding 160 acres in any one tract, at such stations as are or shall be established in conformity with law on the line of any railroad which shall be constructed, or be in process of construction, in or through said nation prior to the allotment of lands therein, any citizen who shall have previously selected such town site, or any portion thereof, for his allotment, or who shall have been by reason of improvements therein entitled to select the same for his allotment, shall be paid by the Creek Nation the full value of his improvements thereon at the time of the establishment of the town site, under rules and regulations to be prescribed by the Secretary of the Interior: *Provided, however*, That such citizens may purchase any of said lands in accordance with the provisions of the act of March 1, 1901 (31 Stat. L., 61): *And provided further*, That the lands which may hereafter be set aside and reserved for town sites upon recommendation of the Dawes Commission as herein provided shall embrace such acreage

31. All moneys to be paid to the tribe under any of the provisions of this agreement shall be paid, under direction of the Secretary of the Interior, into the Treasury of the United States to the credit of the tribe, and an itemized report thereof shall be made monthly to the Secretary of the Interior and to the principal chief.

32. All funds of the tribe and all moneys accruing under the provisions of this agreement, when needed for the purposes of equalizing allotments or for any other purposes herein prescribed, shall be paid out under the direction of the Secretary of the Interior, and when required for per capita payments, if any, shall be paid out directly to each individual by a bonded officer of the United States, under direction of the Secretary of the Interior, without unnecessary delay.

33. No funds belonging to said tribe shall hereafter be used or paid out for any purposes by any officer of the United States without consent of the tribe, expressly given through its national council, except as herein provided.

34. The United States shall pay all expenses incident to the survey, platting, and disposition of town lots, and of allotment of lands made under the provisions of this agreement, except where the town authorities have been or may be duly authorized to survey and plat their respective towns at the expense of such town.

35. Parents shall be the natural guardians of their children, and shall act for them as such unless a guardian shall have been appointed by a court having jurisdiction; and parents so acting shall not be required to give bond as guardians unless by order of such court, but they, and all other persons having charge of lands, moneys, and other property belonging to minors and incompetents, shall be required to make proper accounting therefor in the court having jurisdiction thereof in manner deemed necessary for the preservation of such estates.

36. All Seminole citizens who have heretofore settled and made homes upon lands belonging to the Creeks may there take, for themselves and their families, such allotments as they would be entitled to take of Seminole lands, and all Creek citizens who have heretofore settled and made homes upon lands belonging to Seminoles may there take, for themselves and their families, allotments of one hundred and sixty acres each, and if the citizens of one tribe thus receive a greater number of acres than the citizens of the other, the excess shall be paid for by such tribe, at a price to be agreed upon by the principal chiefs of the two tribes, and if they fail to agree, the price shall be fixed by the Indian agent, but the citizenship of persons so taking allotments shall in no wise be affected thereby.

Titles shall be conveyed to Seminoles selecting allotments of Creek lands in manner herein provided for conveyance of Creek allotments, and titles shall be conveyed to Creeks selecting allotments of Seminole lands in manner provided in the Seminole agreement, dated December sixteenth, eighteen hundred and ninety-seven, for conveyance of Seminole allotments: *Provided*, That deeds shall be executed to allottees immediately after selection of allotment is made.

This provision shall not take effect until after it shall have been separately and specifically approved by the Creek national council and by the Seminole general council; and if not approved by either, it shall fail altogether, and be elimated from this agreement without impairing any other of its provisions.

37. Creek citizens may rent their allotments, when selected, for a term not exceeding one year, and after receiving title thereto without restriction, if adjoining allottees are not injured thereby, and cattle grazed thereon shall not be liable to any tribal tax; but when cattle are introduced into the Creek Nation and grazed on lands not selected by citizens, the Secretary of the Interior is authorized to collect from the owners thereof a reasonable grazing tax for the benefit of the tribe; and section twenty-one hundred and seventeen, Revised Statutes of the United States, shall not hereafter apply to Creek lands.

38. After any citizen has selected his allotment he may dispose of any timber thereon, but if he dispose of such timber, or any part of same, he shall not thereafter select other lands in lieu thereof, and his allotment shall be appraised as if in condition when selected.

No timber shall be taken from lands not so selected, and disposed of, without payment of reasonable royalty thereon, under contract to be prescribed by the Secretary of the Interior.

39. No noncitizen renting lands from a citizen for agricultural purposes, as provided by law, whether such lands have been selected as an allotment or not, shall be required to pay any permit tax.

40. The Creek school fund shall be used, under direction of the Secretary of the Interior, for the education of Creek citizens, and the Creek schools shall be conducted under rules and regulations prescribed by him, under direct supervision of the Creek school superintendent and a supervisor appointed by the Secretary, and under Creek laws, subject to such modifications as the Secretary of the Interior may

deem necessary to make the schools most effective and to produce the best possible results.

All teachers shall be examined by or under direction of said superintendent and supervisor, and competent teachers and other persons to be engaged in and about the schools with good moral character only shall be employed, but where all qualifications are equal preference shall be given to citizens in such employment.

All moneys for running the schools shall be appropriated by the Creek national council, not exceeding the amount of the Creek school fund, seventy-six thousand four hundred and sixty-eight dollars and forty cents; but if it fail or refuse to make the necessary appropriations the Secretary of the Interior may direct the use of a sufficient amount of the school funds to pay all expenses necessary to the efficient conduct of the schools, strict account thereof to be rendered to him and to the principal chief.

All accounts for expenditures in running the schools shall be examined and approved by said superintendent and supervisor, and also by the general superintendent of Indian schools, in Indian Territory, before payment thereof is made.

If the superintendent and supervisor fail to agree upon any matter under their direction or control, it shall be decided by said general superintendent, subject to appeal to the Secretary of the Interior; but his decision shall govern until reversed by the Secretary.

41. The provisions of section thirteen of the Act of Congress approved June twenty-eighth, eighteen hundred and ninety-eight, entitled "An act for the protection of the people of the Indian Territory, and for other purposes," shall not apply to or in any manner affect the lands or other property of said tribe, or be in force in the Creek Nation, and no act of Congress or treaty provision inconsistent with this agreement shall be in force in said nation, except section fourteen of said last-mentioned act, which shall continue in force as if this agreement had not been made.

42. No act, ordinance, or resolution of the national council of the Creek Nation in any manner affecting the lands of the tribe, or of individuals after allotment, or the moneys or other property of the tribe, or of the citizens thereof, except appropriations for the necessary incidental and salaried expenses of the Creek government as herein limited, shall be of any validity until approved by the President of the United States. When any such act, ordinance, or resolution shall be passed by said council and approved by the principal chief, a true and correct copy thereof, duly certified, shall be immediately transmitted to the President, who shall, within thirty days after received by him, approve or disapprove the same. If disapproved, it shall be so indorsed and returned to the principal chief; if approved, the approval shall be indorsed thereon, and it shall be published in at least two newspapers having a bona fide circulation in the Creek Nation.

43. The United States agrees to maintain strict laws in said nation against the introduction, sale, barter, or giving away of liquors or intoxicants of any kind whatsoever.

44. This agreement shall in no wise affect the provisions of existing treaties between the United States and said tribe except so far as inconsistent therewith.

45. All things necessary to carrying into effect the provisions of this agreement, not otherwise herein specifically provided for, shall be done under authority and direction of the Secretary of the Interior.

46. The tribal government of the Creek Nation shall not continue longer than March fourth, nineteen hundred and six; subject to such further legislation as Congress may deem proper.

47. Nothing contained in this agreement shall be construed to revive or reestablish the Creek courts which have been abolished by former acts of Congress.

Approved, March 1, 1901.

APPENDIX NO. 4.

[PUBLIC—No. 200.]

AN ACT To ratify and confirm a supplemental agreement with the Creek tribe of Indians, and for other purposes.

Be it enacted by the Senate and House of Representatives of the United States of America in Congress assembled, That the following supplemental agreement, submitted by certain commissioners of the Creek tribe of Indians, as herein amended, is hereby ratified and confirmed on the part of the United States, and the same shall be of full force and effect if ratified by the Creek tribal council on or before the first day of

September, nineteen hundred and two, which said supplemental agreement is as, follows:

This agreement by and between the United States, entered into in its behalf by the Commission to the Five Civilized Tribes, Henry L. Dawes, Tams Bixby, Thomas B. Needles, and Clifton R. Breckenridge, duly appointed and authorized thereunto, and the Muskogee (or Creek) tribe of Indians, in Indian Territory, entered into in behalf of the said tribe by Pleasant Porter, principal chief, Roley McIntosh, Thomas W. Perryman, Amos McIntosh, and David M. Hodge, commissioners duly appointed and authorized thereunto, witnesseth, that in consideration of the mutual undertakings herein contained it is agreed as follows:

DEFINITIONS.

The words "Creek" and "Muskogee" as used in this agreement shall be deemed synonymous, and the words "Nation" and "tribe" shall each be deemed to refer to the Muskogee Nation or Muskogee tribe of Indians in Indian Territory. The words "principal chief" shall be deemed to refer to the principal chief of the Muskogee Nation. The words "citizen" or "citizens" shall be deemed to refer to a member or members of the Muskogee tribe or nation of Indians. The word "commissioner" shall be deemed to refer to the United States Commission to the Five Civilized Tribes.

ALLOTMENT OF LANDS.

2. Section 2 of the agreement ratified by act of Congress approved March, 1901 (31 Stat. L., 861), is amended and as so amended is reenacted to read as follows:

All lands belonging to the Creek tribe of Indians in Indian Territory, except town sites and lands reserved for Creek schools and churches, railroads, and town cemeteries, in accordance with the provisions of the act of Congress approved March 1, 1901 (31 Stat. L., 861), shall be appraised at not to exceed $6.50 per acre, excluding only lawful improvements on lands in actual cultivation.

Such appraisement shall be made, under the direction and supervision of the Commission to the Five Civilized Tribes, by such number of committees with necessary assistance as may be deemed necessary to expedite the work, one member of each committee to be appointed by the principal chief. Said Commission shall have authority to revise and adjust the work of said committees; and if the members of any committee fail to agree as to the value of any tract of land, the value thereof shall be fixed by said Commission. The appraisement so made shall be submitted to the Secretary of the Interior for approval.

3. Paragraph 2 of section 3 of the agreement ratified by said act of Congress approved March 1, 1901, is amended and as so amended is reenacted to read as follows:

If any citizen select lands the appraised value of which is $6.50 per acre, he shall not receive any further distribution of property or funds of the tribe until all other citizens have received lands and moneys equal in value to his allotment.

4. Exclusive jurisdiction is hereby conferred upon the Commission to the Five Civilized Tribes to determine, under the direction of the Secretary of the Interior, all controversies arising between citizens as to their right to select certain tracts of land.

5. Where it is shown to the satisfaction of said Commission that it was the intention of a citizen to select lands which include his home and improvements, but that through error and mistake he had selected land which did not include said home and improvements, said Commission is authorized to cancel said selection and the certificate of selection or allotment embracing said lands, and permit said citizen to make a new selection including said home and improvements; and should said land including said home and improvements have been selected by any other citizen of said nation, the citizen owning said home and improvements shall be permitted to file, within ninety days from the ratification of this agreement, a contest against the citizen having previously selected the same and shall not be prejudiced therein by reason of lapse of time or any provision of law or rules and regulations to the contrary.

DESCENT AND DISTRIBUTION.

6. The provisions of the act of Congress approved March 1, 1901 (31 Stat. L., 861), in so far as they provide for descent and distribution according to the laws of the Creek Nation, are hereby repealed, and the descent and distribution of land and money provided for by said act shall be in accordance with chapter 49 of Mans-

field's Digest of the Statutes of Arkansas now in force in Indian Territory: *Provided*, That only citizens of the Creek Nation, male and female, and their Creek descend- ants shall inherit lands of the Creek Nation: *And provided further*, That if there be no person of Creek citizenship to take the descent and distribution of said estate, then the inheritance shall go to noncitizen heirs in the order named in said chap- ter 49.

ROLLS OF CITIZENSHIP.

7. All children born to those citizens who are entitled to enrollment as provided by the act of Congress approved March 1, 1901 (31 Stat. L., 861), subsequent to July 1, 1900, and up to and including May 25, 1901, and living upon the latter date, shall be placed on the rolls made by said commission.   And if any such child has died since May 25, 1901, or may hereafter die before receiving his allotment of lands and distributive share of the funds of the tribe, the lands and moneys to which he would be entitled if living shall descend to his heirs as herein provided and be allotted and distributed to them accordingly.

8. All children who have not heretofore been listed for enrollment living May 25, 1901, born to citizens whose names appear upon the authenticated rolls of 1890 or upon the authenticated rolls of 1895 and entitled to enrollment as provided by the act of Congress approved March 1, 1901 (31 Stat. L., 861), shall be placed on the rolls made by said Commission.   And if any such child has died since May 25, 1901, or may hereafter die, before receiving his allotment of lands and distributive share of the funds of the tribe, the lands and moneys to which he would be entitled if living shall descend to his heirs as herein provided and be allotted and distributed to them accordingly.

9. If the rolls of citizenship provided for by the act of Congress approved March 1, 1901 (31 Stat. L., 861), shall have been completed by said Commission prior to the ratification of this agreement, the names of children entitled to enrollment under the provisions of sections 7 and 8 hereof shall be placed upon a supplemental roll of citi- zens of the Creek Nation, and said supplemental roll when approved by the Secretary of the Interior shall in all respects be held to be a part of the final rolls of citizenship of said tribe: *Provided*, That the Dawes Commission be, and is hereby, authorized to add the following persons to the Creek roll: Nar-wal-le-pe-se, Mary Washington, Walter Washington, and Willie Washington, who are Creek Indians but whose names were left off the roll through neglect on their part.

ROADS.

10. Public highways or roads 3 rods in width, being 1 and one-half rods on each side of the section line, may be established along all section lines without any com- pensation being paid therefor; and all allottees, purchasers, and others shall take the title to such lands subject to this provision.   And public highways or roads may be established elsewhere whenever necessary for the public good, the actual value of the land taken elsewhere than along section lines to be determined under the direc- tion of the Secretary of the Interior while the tribal government continues, and to be paid by the Creek Nation during that time; and if buildings or other improvements are damaged in consequence of the establishment of such public highways or roads, whether along section lines or elsewhere, such damages, during the continuance of the tribal government, shall be determined and paid in the same manner.

11. In all instances of the establishment of town sites in accordance with the pro- visions of the act of Congress approved May 31, 1900 (31 Stat. L., 231), or those of section 10 of the agreement ratified by act of Congress approved March 1, 1901 (31 Stat. L., 861), authorizing the Secretary of the Interior, upon the recommendation of the Commission to the Five Civilized Tribes, at any time before allotment, to set aside and reserve from allotment any lands in the Creek Nation not exceeding 160 acres in any one tract, at such stations as are or shall be established in conformity with law on the line of any railroad which shall be constructed, or be in process of construction, in or through said nation prior to the allotment of lands therein, any citizen who shall have previously selected such town site, or any portion thereof, for his allotment, or who shall have been by reason of improvements therein entitled to select the same for his allotment, shall be paid by the Creek Nation the full value of his improvements thereon at the time of the establishment of the town site, under rules and regulations to be prescribed by the Secretary of the Interior: *Provided, however*, That such citizens may purchase any of said lands in accordance with the provisions of the act of March 1, 1901 (31 Stat. L., 61): *And provided further*, That the lands which may hereafter be set aside and reserved for town sites upon recom- mendation of the Dawes Commission as herein provided shall embrace such acreage

as may be necessary for the present needs and reasonable prospective growth of such town sites, and not to exceed 640 acres for each town site, and 10 per cent of the net proceeds arising from the sale of that portion of the land within the town site so selected by him, or which he was so entitled to select; and this shall be in addition to his right to receive from other lands an allotment of 160 acres.

CEMETERIES.

12. A cemetery other than a town cemetery included within the boundaries of an allotment shall not be desecrated by tillage or otherwise, but no interment shall be made therein except with the consent of the allottee, and any person desecrating by tillage or otherwise a grave or graves in a cemetery included within the boundaries of an allotment shall be guilty of a misdemeanor, and upon conviction be punished as provided in section 567 of Mansfield's Digest of the Statutes of Arkansas.

13. Whenever the town-site surveyors of any town in the Creek Nation shall have selected and located a cemetery, as provided in section 18 of the act of Congress approved March 1, 1901 (31 Stat. L., 861), the town authorities shall not be authorized to dispose of lots in such cemetery until payment shall have been made to the Creek Nation for land used for said cemetery, as provided in said act of Congress, and if the town authorities fail or refuse to make payment as aforesaid within one year of the approval of the plat of said cemetery by the Secretary of the Interior, the land so reserved shall revert to the Creek Nation and be subject to allotment. And for lands heretofore or hereafter designated as parks upon any plat or any town site the town shall make payment into the Treasury of the United States to the credit of the Creek Nation within one year at the rate of $20 per acre, and if such payment be not made within that time the lands so designated as a park shall be platted into lots and sold as other town lots.

MISCELLANEOUS.

14. All funds of the Creek Nation not needed for equalization of allotments, including the Creek school fund, shall be paid out under direction of the Secretary of the Interior per capita to the citizens of the Creek Nation on the dissolution of the Creek tribal government.

15. The provisions of section 24 of the act of Congress approved March 1, 1901 (31 Stat. L., 861), for the reservation of land for the six established Creek court-houses, is hereby repealed.

16. Lands allotted to citizens shall not in any manner whatever or at any time be encumbered, taken, or sold to secure or satisfy any debt or obligation nor be alienated by the allottee or his heirs before the expiration of five years from the date of the approval of this supplemental agreement, except with the approval of the Secretary of the Interior. Each citizen shall select from his allotment forty acres of land, or a quarter of a quarter section, as a homestead, which shall be and remain nontaxable, inalienable, and free from any incumbrance whatever for twenty-one years from the date of the deed therefor, and a separate deed shall be issued to each allottee for his homestead, in which this condition shall appear.

Selections of homesteads for minors, prisoners, convicts, incompetents, and aged and infirm persons, who can not select for themselves, may be made in the manner provided for the selection of their allotments, and if for any reason such selection be not made for any citizen it shall be the duty of said commission to make selection for him. The homestead of each citizen shall remain, after the death of the allottee, for the use and support of children born to him after May 25, 1901; but if he have no such issue, then he may dispose of his homestead by will, free from the limitation herein imposed, and if this be not done the land embraced in his homestead shall descend to his heirs, free from such limitation, according to the laws of descent herein otherwise prescribed. Any agreement or conveyance of any kind or character violative of any of the provisions of this paragraph shall be absolutely void and not susceptible of ratification in any manner, and no rule of estoppel shall ever prevent the assertion of its invalidity.

17. Section 37 of the agreement ratified by said act of March 1, 1901, is amended, and as so amended is reenacted to read as follows:

"Creek citizens may rent their allotments, for strictly nonmineral purposes, for a term not to exceed one year for grazing purposes only and for a period not to exceed five years for agricultural purposes, but without any stipulation or obligation to renew the same. Such leases for a period longer than one year for grazing purposes and for a period longer than five years for agricultural purposes, and leases for mineral purposes may also be made with the approval of the Secretary of the Interior, and not otherwise. Any agreement or lease of any kind or character violative of this paragraph shall be absolutely void and not susceptible of ratification in any manner, and no rule of estoppel shall ever prevent the assertion of its invalidity. Cattle grazed upon leased allotments shall not be liable to any tribal tax, but when cattle are introduced into the Creek Nation and grazed on lands not selected for allotment by citizens, the Secretary of the Interior shall collect from the owners thereof a reasonable grazing tax for the benefit of the tribe, and section 2117 of the Revised Statutes of the United States shall not hereafter apply to Creek lands."

18. When cattle are introduced into the Creek Nation to be grazed upon either lands not selected for allotment or upon lands allotted or selected for allotment the owner thereof, or the party or parties so introducing the same, shall first obtain a permit from the United States Indian agent, Union Agency, authorizing the intro-duction of such cattle. The application for said permit shall state the number of cattle to be introduced, together with a description of the same, and shall specify the lands upon which said cattle are to be grazed, and whether or not said lands have been selected for allotment. Cattle so introduced, and all other live stock owned or controlled by noncitizens of the nation, shall be kept upon inclosed lands, and if any such cattle or other live stock trespass upon lands allotted to or selected for allotment by any citizen of said nation, the owner thereof shall for the first trespass, make reparation to the party injured for the true value of the damages he may have sustained, and for every trespass thereafter double damages to be recovered with costs, whether the land upon which trespass is made is inclosed or not.

Any person who shall introduce any cattle into the Creek Nation in violation of the provisions of this section shall be deemed guilty of a misdemeanor and punished by a fine of not less than $100, and shall stand committed until such fine and costs are paid, such commitment not to exceed one day for every $2 of said fine and costs; and every day said cattle are permitted to remain in said nation without a permit for their introduction having been obtained shall constitute a separate offense.

19. Section 8 of the agreement, ratified by said act of March 1, 1901, is amended. and as so amended be reenacted to read as follows:

"The Secretary of the Interior shall, through the United States Indian agent in said Territory, immediately after the ratification of this agreement, put each citizen who has made selection of his allotment in unrestricted possession of his land and remove therefrom all persons objectionable to him; and when any citizen shall thereafter make selection of his allotment as herein provided and receive certificate therefor, he shall be immediately thereupon so placed in possession of his land, and during the continuance of the tribal government the Secretary of the Interior, through such Indian agent, shall protect the allottee in his right to possession against any and all persons claiming under any lease, agreement, or conveyance not obtained in conformity to law."

20. This agreement is intended to modify and supplement the agreement ratified by said act of Congress approved March 1, 1901, and shall be held to repeal any provision in that agreement or in any prior agreement, treaty, or law in conflict herewith.

21. This agreement shall be binding upon the United States and the Creek Nation, and upon all persons affected thereby when it shall have been ratified by Congress and the Creek national council and the fact of such ratification shall have been proclaimed as hereinafter provided.

22. The principal chief, as soon as practicable after the ratification of this agree-ment by Congress, shall call an extra session of the Creek Nation council and submit this agreement, as ratified by Congress, to such council for its consideration; and if the agreement be ratified by the national council, as provided in the constitution of the tribe, the principal chief shall transmit to the President of the United States a certified copy of the act of the council ratifying the agreement, and thereupon the President shall issue his proclamation making public announcement of such ratifica-tion. Thenceforward all the provisions of this agreement shall have the force and effect of law.

Approved, June 30, 1902.

———

[Creek Agreement.]

PROCLAMATION.

Whereas the act of Congress entitled "An act to ratify and confirm a supplemental agreement with the Creek tribe of Indians, and for other purposes," approved on the thirtieth day of June, nineteen hundred and two, contains a provision as follows:

"That the following supplemental agreement, submitted by certain commissioners of the Creek tribe of Indians, as herein amended, is hereby ratified and confirmed on the part of the United States, and the same shall be of full force and effect if ratified by the Creek tribal council on or before the first day of September, nineteen hundred and two." * * *

And whereas the principal chief of the said tribe has transmitted to me an act of the Creek national council entitled "An act to ratify and confirm a supplemental agreement with the United States," approved the twenty-sixth day of July, nineteen hundred and two, which contains a provision as follows:

"That the following supplemental agreement by and between the United States and the Muskogee (or Creek) tribe of Indians, in Indian Territory, ratified and confirmed on the part of the United States by act of Congress approved June 30, 1902 (Public—No. 200), is hereby confirmed on the part of the Muskogee (or Creek) Nation." * * *

And whereas paragraph twenty-two provides as follows:

"The principal chief, as soon as practicable after the ratification of this agreement by Congress, shall call an extra session of the Creek Nation council and submit this agreement, as ratified by Congress, to such council for its consideration, and if the agreement be ratified by the national council, as provided in the constitution of the tribe, the principal chief shall transmit to the President of the United States a certified copy of the act of the council ratifying the agreement, and thereupon the President shall issue his proclamation making public announcement of such ratification; thenceforward all the provisions of this agreement shall have the force and effect of law."

Now, therefore, I, Theodore Roosevelt, President of the United States, do hereby declare said agreement duly ratified and that all the provisions thereof became law according to the terms thereof on the twenty-sixth day of July, nineteen hundred and two.

In witness whereof I have hereunto set my hand and caused the seal of the United States to be affixed.

Done at the city of Washington this 8th day of August, in the year of our Lord one thousand nine hundred and two and of the independence of the United States the one hundred and twenty-sixth.

[SEAL.]   THEODORE ROOSEVELT.

By the President:
    ALVEY A. ADEE, *Acting Secretary of State.*

APPENDIX NO. 5.

[PUBLIC—No. 241.]

AN ACT To provide for the allotment of the lands of the Cherokee Nation, for the disposition o town sites therein, and for other purposes.

Be it enacted by the Senate and House of Representatives of the United States of America in Congress assembled,

DEFINITION OF WORDS EMPLOYED HEREIN.

SECTION 1. The words "nation" and "tribe" shall each be held to refer to the Cherokee Nation or tribe of Indians in Indian Territory.

SEC. 2. The words "principal chief" or "chief executive" shall be held to mean the principal chief of said tribe.

SEC. 3. The words "Dawes Commission" or "Commission" shall be held to mean the United States Commission to the Five Civilized Tribes

SEC. 4. The word "minor" shall be held to mean males under the age of twenty-one years and females under the age of eighteen years.

SEC. 5. The terms "allottable lands" or "lands allottable" shall be held to mean all the lands of Cherokee tribe not herein reserved from allotment.

SEC. 6. The word "select" and its various modifications, as applied to allotments and homesteads, shall be held to mean the formal application at the land office, to be established by the Dawes Commission for the Cherokee Nation, for particular tracts of land.

SEC. 7. The words "member" or "members" and "citizen" or "citizens" shall be held to mean members or citizens of the Cherokee Nation, in the Indian Territory.

SEC. 8. Every word in this act importing the masculine gender may extend and be applied to females as well as males, and the use of the plural may include also the singular, and vice versa.

APPRAISEMENT OF LANDS.

SEC. 9. The lands belonging to the Cherokee tribe of Indians in Indian Territory, except such as are herein reserved from allotment, shall be appraised at their true value: *Provided*, That in the determination of the value of such land consideration shall not be given to the location thereof, to any timber thereon, or to any mineral deposits contained therein, and shall be made without reference to improvements which may be located thereon.

SEC. 10. The appraisement, as herein provided, shall be made by the Commission to the Five Civilized Tribes, under the direction of the Secretary of the Interior.

ALLOTMENT OF LANDS.

SEC. 11. There shall be allotted by the Commission to the Five Civilized Tribes and to each citizen of the Cherokee tribe, as soon as practicable after the approval by the Secretary of the Interior of his enrollment as herein provided, land equal in value to one hundred and ten acres of the average allottable lands of the Cherokee Nation, to conform as nearly as may be to the areas and boundaries established by the Government survey, which land may be selected by each allottee so as to include his improvements.

SEC. 12. For the purpose of making allotments and designating homesteads hereunder, the forty-acre, or quarter of a quarter section, subdivision established by the Government survey may be dealt with as if further subdivided into four equal parts in the usual manner, thus making the smallest legal subdivision ten acres, or a quarter of a quarter of a quarter of a section.

SEC. 13. Each member of said tribe shall, at the time of the selection of his allotment, designate as a homestead out of said allotment land equal in value to forty acres of the average allotable lands of the Cherokee Nation, as nearly as may be, which shall be inalienable during the lifetime of the allottee, not exceeding twenty-one years from the date of the certificate of allotment. Separate certificate shall issue for said homestead. During the time said homestead is held by the allottee the same shall be nontaxable and shall not be liable for any debt contracted by the owner thereof while so held by him.

SEC. 14. Lands allotted to citizens shall not in any manner whatever or at any time be encumbered, taken, or sold to secure or satisfy any debt or obligation, or be alienated by the allottee or his heirs, before the expiration of five years from the date of the ratification of this act.

SEC. 15. All lands allotted to the members of said tribe, except such land as is set aside to each for a homestead as herein provided, shall be alienable in five years after issuance of patent.

SEC. 16. If for any reason an allotment should not be selected or a homestead designated by or on behalf of any member of the tribe, it shall be the duty of said Commission to make said selection and designation.

SEC. 17. In the making of allotments and in the designation of homesteads for members of said tribe said Commission shall not be required to divide lands into tracts of less than the smallest legal subdivision provided for in section twelve hereof.

SEC. 18. It shall be unlawful after ninety days after the ratification of this act by the Cherokees for any member of the Cherokee tribe to inclose or hold possession of, in any manner, by himself or through another, directly or indirectly, more lands in value than that of one hundred and ten acres of average allottable lands of the Cherokee Nation, either for himself or for his wife, or for each of his minor children, if members of said tribe; and any member of said tribe found in such possession of lands, or having the same in any manner inclosed, after the expiration of ninety days after the date of the ratification of this act shall be deemed guilty of a misdemeanor.

SEC. 19. Any person convicted of violating any of the provisions of section eighteen of this act shall be punished by a fine of not less than one hundred dollars, shall stand committed until such fine and costs are paid (such commitment not to exceed one day for every two dollars of said fine and costs), and shall forfeit possession of any property in question, and each day on which such offense is committed or continues to exist shall be deemed a separate offense. The United States district attorney for the northern district is required to see that the provisions of said section eighteen are strictly enforced, and he shall immediately, after the expiration of the ninety days after the ratification of this act, proceed to dispossess all persons of such excessive holdings of lands and to prosecute them for so unlawfully holding the same, and the Commission to the Five Civilized Tribes shall have authority to make investigations of all violations of section eighteen and make report thereon to the United States district attorney.

SEC. 20. If any person whose name appears upon the roll prepared as herein provided shall have died subsequent to the first day of September, nineteen hundred and two, and before receiving his allotment, the lands to which such person would have been entitled if living shall be allotted in his name, and shall, with his proportionate share of other tribal property, descend to his heirs according to the laws of descent and distribution as provided in chapter forty-nine of Mansfield's Digest of the Statutes of Arkansas: *Provided*, That the allotment thus to be made shall be selected by a duly appointed administrator or executor. If, however, such administrator or executor be not duly and expeditiously appointed, or fails to act promptly when appointed, or for any other cause such selection be not so made within a reasonable and proper time, the Dawes Commission shall designate the lands thus to be allotted.

SEC. 21. Allotment certificates issued by the Dawes Commission shall be conclusive evidence of the right of an allottee to the tract of land described therein, and the United States Indian agent for the Union Agency shall, under the direction of the Secretary of the Interior, upon the application of the allottee, place him in possession of his allotment, and shall remove therefrom all persons objectionable to him, and the acts of the Indian agent hereunder shall not be controlled by the writ or process of any court.

SEC. 22. Exclusive jurisdiction is hereby conferred upon the Commission to the Five Civilized Tribes, under the direction of the Secretary of the Interior, to determine all matters relative to the appraisement and the allotment of lands.

SEC. 23. All Delaware Indians who are members of the Cherokee Nation shall take lands and share in the funds of the tribe, as their rights may be determined by the judgment of the Court of Claims, or by the Supreme Court if appealed, in the suit instituted therein by the Delawares against the Cherokee Nation, and now pending; but if said suit be not determined before said Commission is ready to begin the allotment of lands of the tribes as herein provided, the Commission shall cause to be segregated one hundred and fifty-seven thousand six hundred acres of land, including lands which have been selected and occupied by Delawares in conformity to the provisions of their agreement with the Cherokees dated April eighth, eighteen hundred and sixty-seven, such lands so to remain, subject to disposition according to such judgment as may be rendered in said cause; and said Commission shall thereupon proceed to the allotment of the remaining lands of the tribe as aforesaid. Said Commission shall, when final judgment is rendered, allot lands to such Delawares in conformity to the terms of the judgment and their individual rights thereunder. Nothing in this act shall in any manner impair the rights of either party to said contract as the same may be finally determined by the court, or shall interfere with the holdings of the Delawares under their contract with the Cherokees of April eighth, eighteen hundred and sixty-seven, until their rights under said contract are determined by the courts in their suit now pending against the Cherokees, and said suit shall be advanced on the dockets of said courts and determined at the earliest time practicable.

RESERVATIONS.

SEC. 24. The following lands shall be reserved from the allotment of lands herein provided for:

(a) All lands set apart for town sites by the provisions of the act of Congress of June twenty-eighth, eighteen hundred and ninety-eight (Thirtieth Statutes, page four hundred and ninety-five), the provisions of the act of Congress of May thirty-first, nineteen hundred (Thirty-first Statutes, page two hundred and twenty-one), and by the provisions of this act.

(b) All lands to which, upon the date of the ratification of this act, any railroad company may, under any treaty or act of Congress, have a vested right for right of way, depots, station grounds, water stations, stock yards, or similar uses only, connected with the maintenance and operation of the railroad.

(c) All lands selected for town cemeteries not to exceed twenty acres each.

(d) One acre of land for each Cherokee schoolhouse not included in town sites or herein otherwise provided for.

(e) Four acres for Willie Halsell College at Vinita.

(f) Four acres for Baptist Mission school at Tahlequah.

(g) Four acres for Presbyterian school at Tahlequah.

(h) Four acres for Park Hill Mission school south of Tahlequah.
(i) Four acres for Elm Springs Mission school at Barren Fork.
(j) Four acres for Dwight Mission school at Sallisaw.
(k) Four acres for Skiatook Mission near Skiatook.
(l) Four acres for Lutheran Mission school on Illinois River north of Tahlequah.
(m) Sufficient ground for burial purposes where neighborhood cemeteries are now located, not to exceed three acres each.
(n) One acre for each church house outside of towns.
(o) The square now occupied by the capitol building at Tahlequah.
(p) The grounds now occupied by the national jail at Tahlequah.
(q) The grounds now occupied by the Cherokee Advocate printing office at Tahlequah.
(r) Forty acres for the Cherokee Male Seminary near Tahlequah.
(s) Forty acres for the Cherokee Female Seminary at Tahlequah.
(t) One hundred and twenty acres for the Cherokee Orphan Asylum on Grand River.
(u) Forty acres for colored high school in Tahlequah district.
(v) Forty acres for Cherokee Insane Asylum.
(w) Four acres for the school for blind, deaf, and dumb children near Fort Gibson.

The acre so reserved for any church or schoolhouse in any quarter section of land shall be located where practicable in a corner of such quarter section adjacent to the section lines thereof.

Provided, That the Methodist Episcopal Church South may, within twelve months after the ratification of this act, pay ten dollars per acre for the one hundred and sixty acres of land adjacent to the town of Vinita, and heretofore set apart by act of the Cherokee national council for the use of said church for missionary and educational purposes, and now occupied by Willie Halsell College (formerly Galloway College), and shall thereupon receive title thereto; but if said church fail so to do it may continue to occupy said one hundred and sixty acres of land as long as it uses same for the purposes aforesaid.

Any other school or college in the Cherokee Nation which claims to be entitled under the law to a greater number of acres than is set apart for said school or college by section twenty-four of this act may have the number of acres to which it is entitled by law. The trustees of such school or college shall, within sixty days after the ratification of this act, make application to the Secretary of the Interior for the number of acres to which such school or college claims to be entitled, and if the Secretary of the Interior shall find that such school or college is, under the laws and treaties of the Cherokee Nation in force prior to the ratification of this act, entitled to a greater number of acres of land than is provided for in this act, he shall so determine and his decision shall be final. The amount so found by the Secretary of the Interior shall be set apart for the use of such college or school as long as the same may be used for missionary and educational purposes: *Provided,* That the trustees of such school or college shall pay ten dollars per acre for the number of acres so found by the Secretary of the Interior and which have been heretofore set apart by act of the Cherokee national council for use of such school or college for missionary or educational purposes, and upon the payment of such sum within sixty days after the decision of the Secretary of the Interior said college or school may receive a title to such land.

ROLL OF CITIZENSHIP.

SEC. 25. The roll of citizens of the Cherokee Nation shall be made as of September first, nineteen hundred and two, and the names of all persons then living and entitled to enrollment on that date shall be placed on said roll by the Commission to the Five Civilized Tribes.

SEC. 26. The names of all persons living on the first day of September, nineteen hundred and two, entitled to be enrolled as provided in section twenty-five hereof, shall be placed upon the roll made by said Commission, and no child born thereafter to a citizen, and no white person who has intermarried with a Cherokee citizen since the sixteenth day of December, eighteen hundred and ninety-five, shall be entitled to enrollment or to participate in the distribution of the tribal property of the Cherokee Nation.

SEC. 27. Such rolls shall in all other respects be made in strict compliance with the provisions of section twenty-one of the act of Congress approved June twenty-eighth, eighteen hundred and ninety-eight (Thirtieth Statutes, page four hundred and ninety-five), and the act of Congress approved May thirty-first, nineteen hundred (Thirty-first Statutes, page two hundred and twenty-one).

SEC. 28. No person whose name appears upon the roll made by the Dawes Commission as a citizen or freedman of any other tribe shall be enrolled as a citizen of the Cherokee Nation.

SEC. 29. For the purpose of expediting the enrollment of the Cherokee citizens and the allotment of lands as herein provided, the said Commission shall, from time to time, and as soon as practicable, forward to the Secretary of the Interior lists upon which shall be placed the names of those persons found by the Commission to be entitled to enrollment. The lists thus prepared, when approved by the Secretary of the Interior, shall constitute a part and parcel of the final roll of citizens of the Cherokee tribe, upon which allotment of land and distribution of other tribal property shall be made. When there shall have been submitted to and approved by the Secretary of the Interior lists embracing the names of all those lawfully entitled to enrollment, the roll shall be deemed complete. The roll so prepared shall be made in quadruplicate, one to be deposited with the Secretary of the Interior, one with the Commissioner of Indian Affairs, one with the principal chief of the Cherokee Nation, and one to remain with the Commission to the Five Civilized Tribes.

SEC. 30. During the months of September and October, in the year nineteen hundred and two, the Commission to the Five Civilized Tribes may receive applications for enrollment of such infant children as may have been born to recognized and enrolled citizens of the Cherokee Nation on or before the first day of September, nineteen hundred and two, but the application of no person whomsoever for enrollment shall be received after the thirty-first day of October, nineteen hundred and two.

SEC. 31. No person whose name does not appear upon the roll prepared as herein provided shall be entitled to in any manner participate in the distribution of the common property of the Cherokee tribe, and those whose names appear thereon shall participate in the manner set forth in this act: *Provided*, That no allotment of land or other tribal property shall be made to any person, or to the heirs of any person, whose name is on said roll and who died prior to the first day of September, nineteen hundred and two. The right of such person to any interest in the lands or other tribal property shall be deemed to have become extinguished and to have passed to the tribe in general upon his death before said date, and any person or persons who may conceal the death of anyone on said roll as aforesaid for the purpose of profiting by said concealment, and who shall knowingly receive any portion of any land or other tribal property or of the proceeds so arising from any allotment prohibited by this section, shall be deemed guilty of a felony, and shall be proceeded against as may be provided in other cases of felony, and the penalty for this offense shall be confinement at hard labor for a period of not less than one year nor more than five years, and in addition thereto a forfeiture to the Cherokee Nation of the lands, other tribal property, and proceeds so obtained.

SCHOOLS.

SEC. 32. The Cherokee school fund shall be used, under the direction of the Secretary of the Interior, for the education of children of Cherokee citizens, and the Cherokee schools shall be conducted under rules prescribed by him according to Cherokee laws, subject to such modifications as he may deem necessary to make the schools most effective and to produce the best possible results; said schools to be under the supervision of a supervisor appointed by the Secretary and a school board elected by the national council.

SEC. 33. All teachers shall be examined by said supervisor, and said school board and competent teachers and other persons to be engaged in and about the schools with good moral character only shall be employed; but where all qualifications are equal, preference shall be given to citizens of the Cherokee Nation in such employment.

SEC. 34. All moneys for carrying on the schools shall be appropriated by the Cherokee national council, not to exceed the amount of the Cherokee school fund; but if the council fail or refuse to make the necessary appropriations, the Secretary of the Interior may direct the use of a sufficient amount of the school fund to pay all necessary expenses for the efficient conduct of the schools, strict account therefor to be rendered to him and the principal chief.

SEC. 35. All accounts for expenditures in carrying on the schools shall be examined and approved by said supervisor, and also by the general superintendent of Indian schools in the Indian Territory, before payment thereof is made.

SEC. 36. The interest arising from the Cherokee orphan fund shall be used, under the direction of the Secretary of the Interior, for maintaining the Cherokee Orphan Asylum for the benefit of the Cherokee orphan children.

Sec. 37. Public highways or roads two rods in width, being one rod on each side of the section line, may be established along all section lines without any compensation being paid therefor, and all allottees, purchasers, and others shall take the title to such lands subject to this provision; and public highways or roads may be established elsewhere whenever necessary for the public good; the actual value of the land taken elsewhere than along section lines to be determined under the direction of the Secretary of the Interior while the tribal government continues and to be paid by the Cherokee Nation during that time; and if buildings or other improvements are damaged in consequence of the establishment of such public highways or roads, whether along section lines or elsewhere, such damages, during the continuance of the tribal government, shall be determined and paid for in the same manner.

TOWN SITES.

Sec. 38. The lands which may hereafter be set aside and reserved for town sites upon the recommendation of the Dawes Commission under the provisions of the act of Congress approved May thirty-first, nineteen hundred (Thirty-first Statutes, page two hundred and twenty-one), shall embrace such acreage as may be necessary for the present needs and reasonable prospective growth of such town sites, not to exceed six hundred and forty acres for each town site.

Sec. 39. Whenever any tract of land shall be set aside by the Secretary of the Interior for town-site purposes, as provided in said act of May thirty-first, nineteen hundred, or by the terms of this act, which is occupied at the time of such segregation by any member of the Cherokee Nation, such occupant shall be allowed to purchase any lot upon which he then has improvements other than fences, tillage, and temporary improvements, in accordance with the provisions of the act of June twenty-eighth, eighteen hundred and ninety-eight (Thirtieth Statutes, page four hundred and ninety-five), or, if he so elects, the lot will be sold under rules and regulations to be prescribed by the Secretary of the Interior, and he shall be fully compensated for his improvements thereon out of the funds of the tribe arising from the sale of the town sites, the value of such improvements to be determined by a board of appraisers, one member of which shall be appointed by the Secretary of the Interior, one by the chief executive of the tribe, and one by the occupant of the land, said board of appraisers to be paid such compensation for their services as may be determined by the Secretary of the Interior out of any appropriations for surveying, laying out, platting, and selling town sites.

Sec. 40. All town sites which may hereafter be set aside by the Secretary of the Interior on the recommendation of the Commission to the Five Civilized Tribes, under the provisions of the act of Congress approved May thirty-first, nineteen hundred (Thirty-first Statutes, page two hundred and twenty-one), with the additional acreage added thereto, as well as all town sites set aside under the provisions of this act having a population of less than two hundred, shall be surveyed, laid out, platted, appraised, and disposed of in like manner, and with like preference rights accorded to owners of improvements as other town sites in the Cherokee Nation are surveyed, laid out, platted, appraised, and disposed of under the act of Congress of June twenty-eighth, eighteen hundred and ninety-eight (Thirtieth Statutes, page four hundred and ninety-five), as modified or supplemented by the act of May thirty-first, nineteen hundred: *Provided*, That as to the town sites set aside as aforesaid the owner of the improvements shall be required to pay the full appraised value of the lot instead of the percentage named in said act of June twenty-eighth, eighteen hundred and ninety-eight (Thirtieth Statutes, page four hundred and ninety-five).

Sec. 41. Any person being in possession or having the right to the possession of any town lot or lots, as surveyed and platted under the direction of the Secretary of the Interior, in accordance with the act of Congress approved May thirty-first, nineteen hundred (Thirty-first Statutes, page two hundred and twenty-one), the occupancy of which lot or lots was originally acquired under any town-site act of the Cherokee Nation, and owning improvements thereon, other than temporary buildings, fencing, or tillage, shall have the right to purchase the same at one-fourth of the appraised value thereof.

Sec. 42. Any person being in possession of, or having the right to the possession of, any town lot or lots, as surveyed and platted under the direction of the Secretary of the Interior, in accordance with the act of Congress, approved May thirty-first, nineteen hundred (Thirty-first Statutes, page two hundred and twenty-one), the occupancy of which lot or lots was originally acquired under any town-site act of the Cherokee Nation, and not having any improvements thereon, shall have the right to purchase the same at one-half of the appraised value thereof.

Sec. 43. Any citizen in rightful possession of any town lot having improvements thereon other than temporary buildings, fencing, and tillage, the occupancy of which has not been acquired under tribal laws, shall have the right to purchase same by paying one-half the appraised value thereof: *Provided*, That any other person in undisputed possession of any town lot having improvements thereon other than temporary buildings, fencing, and tillage, the occupancy of which has not been acquired under tribal laws, shall have the right to purchase such lot by paying the appraised value thereof.

Sec. 44. All lots not having thereon improvements other than temporary buildings, fencing, and tillage, the sale or disposition of which is not herein otherwise specifically provided for, shall be sold within twelve months after appraisement, under the direction of the Secretary of the Interior, after due advertisement, at public auction, to the highest bidder, at not less than their appraised value.

Sec. 45. When the appraisement of any town lot is made and approved, the town-site commission shall notify the claimant thereof of the amount of appraisement, and he shall, within sixty days thereafter, make payment of ten per centum of the amount due for the lot, and four months thereafter he shall pay fifteen per centum additional, and the remainder of the purchase money he shall pay in three equal annual installments without interest; but if the claimant of any such lot fail to purchase same, or make the first and second payments aforesaid, or make any other payment within the time specified, the lot and improvements shall be sold at public auction to the highest bidder, under the direction of the Secretary of the Interior, at a price not less than its appraised value.

Sec. 46. When any improved lot shall be sold at public auction because of the failure of the person owning improvements thereon to purchase same within the time allowed in said act of Congress approved June twenty-eighth, eighteen hundred and ninety-eight (Thirtieth Statutes, page four hundred and ninety-five), said improvements shall be appraised by a committee, one member of which shall be selected by the owner of the improvements and one member by the purchaser of said lot; and in case the said committee is not able to agree upon the value of said improvements, the committtee may select a third member, and in that event the determination of the majority of the committee shall control. Said committee of appraisement shall be paid such compensation for their services by the two parties in interest, share and share alike, as may be agreed upon, and the amount of said appraisement shall be paid by the purchaser of the lot to the owner of the improvements in cash within thirty days after the decision of the committee of appraisement.

Sec. 47. The purchaser of any unimproved town lot sold at public auction shall pay twenty-five per centum of the purchase money at the time of the sale, and within four months thereafter he shall pay twenty-five per centum additional, and the remainder of the purchase money he shall pay in two equal annual installments without interest.

Sec. 48. Such towns in the Cherokee Nation as may have a population of less than two hundred people not otherwise provided for, and which, in the judgment of the Secretary of the Interior, should be set aside as town sites, shall have their limits defined as soon as practicable after the approval of this act in the same manner as provided for other town sites.

Sec. 49. The town authorities of any town site in said Cherokee Nation may select and locate, subject to the approval of the Secretary of the Interior, a cemetery within suitable distance from said town, to embrace such number of acres as may be deemed necessary for such purpose. The town-site commission shall appraise the same at its true value, and the town may purchase the same within one year from the approval of the survey by paying the appraised value. If any citizen have improvements thereon, said improvements shall be appraised by said town-site commission and paid for by the town: *Provided*, That lands already laid out by tribal authorities for cemeteries shall be included in the cemeteries herein provided for without cost to the towns, and the holdings of the burial lots therein now occupied for such purpose shall in no wise be disturbed: *And provided further*, That any park laid out and surveyed in any town shall be duly appraised at a fair valuation, and the inhabitants of said town shall, within one year after the approval of the survey and the appraisement of said park by the Secretary of the Interior, pay the appraised value to the proper officer for the benefit of the tribe.

Sec. 50. The United States shall pay all expenses incident to surveying, platting, and disposition of town lots, and all allotments of lands made under the provisions of this plan of allotment, except where the town authorities may have been or may be duly authorized to survey and plat their respective towns at the expense of such towns.

Sec. 51. No taxes shall be assessed by any town government against any town lot paid; and the timber and stone so procured under such contracts may be used for "domestic and industrial purposes, including the construction, maintenance, and repair of railroads and other highways" within the limits of the Indian Territory only.

Applications must be presented to the United States Indian inspector located in the Indian Territory and by him forwarded, with his recommendation, through the Commissioner of Indian Affairs, to the Department.

Applicants must state the quality and quantity of timber or stone proposed to be cut or quarried, the purpose or purposes for which and the place or places where said timber and stone are to be used, as the case may be, the amount considered just and reasonable to be paid by them, and their reasons for such conclusion. Each application must be accompanied by the affidavits of two disinterested persons corroborating specifically all the statements of the applicant, and the inspector is hereby authorized to require any other information as to the value of the timber or stone or to show the good faith of the applicant.

2. Before any timber shall be cut or any stone taken from any of the lands belonging to any of the Five Civilized Tribes, the person, persons, or corporation desiring to secure such timber or stone shall enter into a contract or contracts with said Indian agent, in accordance with the form hereto attached, which contract, however, shall not be of force until the Secretary of the Interior shall have indorsed his approval thereon: *Provided*, That each such person, persons, or corporation shall give bond (form attached hereto) in a sufficient sum, to be fixed by the Secretary of the Interior, with two good and sufficient sureties, or an approved surety company, as surety, conditioned for the faithful performance of the stipulations of the contract or contracts, and also conditioned for the faithful observance of all of the laws of the United States now in force or that may hereafter be enacted, and the regulations now prescribed or that may hereafter be prescribed by the Secretary of the Interior relative to any and all matters pertaining to the affairs of any of the Five Civilized Tribes.

3. The moneys so collected shall be placed to the credit of the tribe or tribes to which the land belongs from which such timber or stone was procured, as miscellaneous receipts, class three, "not the result of the labor of any member of such tribe;" but no timber or stone shall be taken from any land selected by any citizen of any of the Five Civilized Tribes as his prospective allotment without his consent, and only from such land being cleared, or to be cleared, for cultivation, and not until a contract shall have been entered into by the said United States Indian agent and the person, persons, or corporation desiring to procure such timber or stone, and the same shall have been approved.

The price to be paid under such contract shall be satisfactory to such prospective allottee: *Provided*, That the provisions of this section shall apply to all tracts now in possession of any citizens of any of the Five Civilized Tribes who intend to include such tracts in their prospective allotments, and the money derived from the sale of timber or stone taken from any such tracts shall be deposited in the United States Treasury, St. Louis, Mo., to the credit of the Secretary of the Interior and subject to his check in his official capacity only, and when the tract or tracts from which such timber or stone was taken shall have been allotted, the Secretary of the Interior shall pay the money so deposited to the citizen or citizens taking the said tract or tracts as his or their allotment, if found to be entitled to said money: *And provided further*, That the Indian agent shall be required to keep an accurate list, by legal subdivision, of the land from which such timber or stone was taken, and also an accurate list of the amount of money derived from the sale of timber or stone taken from each such legal subdivision. Value of timber and stone taken from unappraised selected lands must be added to the appraisement when made.

4. The contract or contracts entered into by said Indian agent with any person, persons, or corporation shall describe the land from which the timber or stone is to be taken by legal subdivisions, and if any contractor shall take timber or stone from any land other than that covered by his contract he shall be liable to forcible removal from the Indian Territory and suit on his bond, and such unlawful taking of timber and stone shall work also a forfeiture of his contract.

5. The act of Congress under which these rules are promulgated provides that "every person who unlawfully cuts, or aids, or is employed in unlawfully cutting, or wantonly destroys, or procures to be wantonly destroyed, any timber standing upon the land of either of said tribes, or sells or transports any of such timber or stone outside the Indian Territory, contrary to the regulations prescribed by the Secretary, shall pay a fine of not more than five hundred dollars, or be imprisoned not more than twelve months, or both, in the discretion of the court trying the same."

The Indian agent for the Union Agency shall see that any person, persons, or corporation who procures timber or stone from any of the lands belonging to any of the Five Civilized Tribes, under and in accordance with the provisions of the act of fully been contracted, and warrants therefor regularly issued upon the several funds of the tribe, as also warrants drawn by authority of law hereafter and prior to the dissolution of the tribal government, such payments to be made from any funds in the United States Treasury belonging to said tribe, and all such indebtedness of the tribe shall be paid in full before any pro rata distribution of the funds of the tribe shall be made.   The Secretary of the Interior shall make such payments at the earliest time practicable and he shall make all need' t: rules and regulations to carry this provision into effect.

SEC. 68. Jurisdiction is hereby conferred upon the Court of Claims to examine, consider, and adjudicate, with a right of appeal to the Supreme Court of the United States by any party in interest feeling aggrieved at the decision of the Court of Claims, any claim which the Cherokee tribe, or any band thereof, arising under treaty stipulations, may have against the United States, upon which suit shall be instituted within two years after the approval of this act; and also to examine, consider, and adjudicate any claim which the United States may have against said tribe, or any band thereof.   The institution, prosecution, or defense, as the case may be, on the part of the tribe or any band, of any such suit, shall be through attorneys employed and to be compensated in the manner prescribed in sections. twenty-one hundred and three to twenty-one hundred and six, both inclusive, of the Revised Statutes of the United States, the tribe acting through its principal chief in the employment of such attorneys, and the band acting through a committee recognized by the Secretary of the Interior.   The Court of Claims shall have full authority, by proper orders and process, to make parties to any such suit all persons whose presence in the litigation it may deem necessary or proper to the final determination of the matter in controversy, and any such suit shall, on motion of either party, be advanced on the docket of either of said courts and be determined at the earliest practicable time.

SEC. 69. After the expiration of nine months after the date of the original selection of an allotment by or for any citizen of the Cherokee tribe as provided in this act, no contest shall be instituted against such selection, and as early thereafter as practicable patent shall issue therefor.

SEC. 70. Allotments may be selected and homesteads designated for minors by the father or mother, if citizens, or by a guardian, or curator, or the administrator having charge of their estate, in the order named; and for prisoners, convicts, aged and infirm persons, and soldiers and sailors of the United States on duty outside of the Indian Territory, by duly appointed agents under power of attorney; and for incompetents by guardians, curators, or other suitable persons akin to them; but it shall be the duty of said Commission to see that said selections are made for the best interests of such parties.

SEC. 71. Any allottee taking as his allotment lands located around the Cherokee National Male Seminary. the Cherokee National Female Seminary, or Cherokee Orphan Asylum which have not been reserved from allotment as herein provided, and upon which buildings, fences, or other property of the Cherokee Nation are located, such buildings, fences, or other property shall be appraised at the true value thereof and be paid for by the allottee taking such lands as his allotment, and the money to be paid into the Treasury of the United States to the credit of the Cherokee Nation.

SEC. 72. Cherokee citizens may rent their allotments when selected for a term not to exceed one year for grazing purposes only, and for a period not to exceed five years for agricultural purposes, but without any stipulation or obligation to renew the same; but leases for a period longer than one year for grazing purposes and for a period longer than five years for agricultural purposes and for mineral purposes may also be made with the approval of the Secretary of the Interior and not otherwise. Any agreement or lease of any kind or character violative of this section shall be absolutely void and not susceptible of ratification in any manner, and no rule of estoppel shall ever prevent the assertion of its invalidity.   Cattle grazed upon leased allotments shall not be liable to any tribal tax, but when cattle are introduced into the Cherokee Nation and grazed on lands not selected as allotments by citizens, the Secretary of the Interior shall collect from the owners thereof a reasonable grazing tax for the benefit of the tribe, and section twenty-one hundred and seventeen of the Revised Statutes of the United States shall not hereafter apply to Cherokee lands.

SEC. 73. The provisions of section thirteen of the act of Congress approved June twenty-eighth, eighteen hundred and ninety-eight, entitled "An act for the protection of the people of the Indian Territory, and for other purposes," shall not apply to or in any manner affect the lands or other property of said tribe, and no act of Congress or treaty provision inconsistent with this agreement shall be in force in said nation except sections fourteen and twenty-seven of said last-mentioned act, which shall continue in force as if this agreement had not been made.

—— —— and —— ——, being by me first duly sworn, upon their oaths state, each for himself, that he is well acquainted with the land above described and with the quantity and quality of the timber and stone thereon, and with the place or places where it is proposed to use the above-mentioned material, and also with the values and prices of stone and timber in the vicinity of the place from which it is proposed to take and where it is proposed to use such material, and with the cost of removing and transporting timber and stone, and with all the facts stated by the applicant above named, and knows that the facts stated by him are true and correct in every particular.

—— ——.
—— ——.

Subscribed and sworn to before me, a —— for the ——, at my office in ——, this —— day of ——, ——.

—— ——,
—— ——.

FORM OF INDIAN TERRITORY TIMBER AND STONE CONTRACT.

—— Nation.

(Write all names and addresses in full.)

This agreement, made and entered into in quadruplicate at the Union Agency, Muskogee, Indian Territory, this —— day of ——, 19—, by and between ——
——, United States Indian agent for the Union Agency, party of the first part, and —— ——, of ——, part— of the second part, under and in pursuance of the provisions of the act of Congress approved June 6, 1900 (Public No. 174), and the rules and regulations prescribed by the Secretary of the Interior on February 14, 1901, relative to the procurement of timber and stone from any of the lands belonging to any of the Five Civilized Tribes, and the timber or stone procured under the provisions of this contract and the rules and regulations heretofore or that may hereafter be prescribed by the Secretary of the Interior:

Witnesseth, that the said party of the first part agrees to sell to said part— of the second part timber or stone of the kind or kinds hereinafter specified, standing, fallen, lying, or being on lands within the limits of the —— Nation, which said lands are described as follows, to wit: The —— of section ——, of township (*a*) ——, of range (*b*) ——, of the Indian meridian, and containing —— acres, more or less.

The part— of the second part agree— to cut and remove the timber or quarry and remove the stone hereinafter mentioned from within the above-described limits, and agree— to employ Indian labor in the cutting and removal of the timber and the quarrying and removal of the stone in preference to other labor on equal terms, whenever suitable Indian labor can be obtained.

For and in consideration of the foregoing, the said part— of the second part also agree— to pay to the United States Indian agent for the Union Agency, for the benefit of the —— tribe of Indians, for all such timber cut and stone quarried on said described lands, at the following rates, to wit:

MERCHANTABLE SAW TIMBER, I. E., TIMBER CAPABLE OF BEING MANUFACTURED INTO LUMBER, AS FOLLOWS:

For walnut timber, —— per thousand feet; for cypress timber, —— per thousand feet; for ash timber, —— per thousand feet; for oak timber, —— per thousand feet; for pine timber, —— per thousand feet; for cottonwood timber, —— per thousand feet, and for —— timber, —— per thousand feet.

TELEGRAPH POLES.

Cedar, four to five inch top, eight to ten inch bottom, —— feet long, —— cents each.

Cedar, six-inch top, twelve-inch bottom, —— feet long, —— cents each.

Cedar, —— inch top, —— inch bottom, —— feet long, —— cents each.

Oak, four to five inch top, eight to ten inch bottom, —— feet long, —— cents each.

Oak, six-inch top, twelve-inch bottom, —— feet long, —— cents each.

Oak, —— inch top, —— inch bottom, —— feet long, —— cents each.

---

a State whether north or south.   *b* State whether east or west.

which would otherwise devolve upon the commission for that nation. Every such local commission shall be appointed in the manner provided in the act approved June twenty-eighth, eighteen hundred and ninety-eight, entitled "An act for the protection of the people of the Indian Territory."

The Secretary of the Interior, where in his judgment the public interests will be thereby subserved, may permit the authorities of any town in any of said nations, at the expense of the town, to survey, lay out, and plat the site thereof, subject to his supervision and approval, as in other instances.

As soon as the plat of any town site is approved, the proper commission shall, with all reasonable dispatch and within a limited time, to be prescribed by the Secretary of the Interior, proceed to make the appraisement of the lots and improvements, if any, thereon, and after the approval thereof by the Secretary of the Interior, shall, under the supervision of such Secretary, proceed to the disposition and sale of the lots in conformity with any then existing act of Congress or agreement with the tribe approved by Congress, and if the proper commission shall not complete such appraisement and sale within the time limited by the Secretary of the Interior they shall receive no pay for such additional time as may be taken by them, unless the Secretary of the Interior for good cause shown shall expressly direct otherwise.

The Secretary of the Interior may, for good cause, remove any member of any town-site commission, tribal or local, in any of said nations, and may fill the vacancy thereby made or any vacancy otherwise occurring in like manner as the place was originally filled.

It shall not be required that the town-site limits established in the course of the platting and disposing of town lots and the corporate limits of the town, if incorporated, shall be identical or coextensive, but such town-site limits and corporate limits shall be so established as to best subserve the then present needs and the reasonable prospective growth of the town, as the same shall appear at the times when such limits are respectively established: *Provided further,* That the exterior limits of all town sites shall be designated and fixed at the earliest practicable time, under rules and regulations prescribed by the Secretary of the Interior.

Upon the recommendation of the Commission to the Five Civilized Tribes the Secretary of the Interior is hereby authorized, at any time before allotment, to set aside and reserve from allotment any lands in the Choctaw, Chickasaw, Creek, or Cherokee nations, not exceeding one hundred and sixty acres in any one tract, at such stations as are or shall be established in conformity with law on the line of any railroad which shall be constructed or be in process of construction in or through either of said nations prior to the allotment of the lands therein, and this irrespective of the population of such town site at the time. Such town sites shall be surveyed, laid out, and platted, and the lands therein disposed of for the benefit of the tribe in the manner herein prescribed for other town sites: *Provided further,* That whenever any tract of land shall be set aside as herein provided which is occupied by a member of the tribe, such occupant shall be fully compensated for his improvements thereon under such rules and regulations as may be prescribed by the Secretary of the Interior.

Nothing herein contained shall have the effect of avoiding any work heretofore done in pursuance of the said act of June twenty-eighth, eighteen ·hundred and ninety-eight, in the way of surveying, laying out, or platting of town sites, appraising or disposing of town lots in any of said nations, but the same, if not heretofore carried to a state of completion, may be completed according to the provisions hereof.

APPENDIX NO. 7.

REGULATIONS (FEBRUARY 14, 1901) GOVERNING THE PROCUREMENT OF TIMBER AND STONE, FOR DOMESTIC AND INDUSTRIAL PURPOSES, IN THE INDIAN TERRITORY, AS PROVIDED IN THE ACT OF JUNE 6, 1900. (31 STAT., 660.)

1. The United States Indian agent for the Union Agency is hereby authorized and directed to enter into a contract or contracts, upon applications, made in the form of affidavits, upon blanks prescribed, when approved by the Secretary of the Interior, with any responsible person, persons, or corporation for the purchase of timber or stone from any of the public lands belonging to any of the Five Civilized Tribes, and to collect, on or before the end of each month, the full value of such timber or stone as the Secretary of the Interior shall hereafter determine should be

[Indorsements on contract.]

No. ———.

DEPARTMENT OF THE INTERIOR,
WASHINGTON, D. C.

——— AGREEMENT.

——— ———, U. S. Indian Agent,
WITH
——— ———, of ———.

Sec. ———, Tp. ———, Range ———, in the ———
Nation, Indian Territory.
Dated ———, 19—.
Expires ———, 19—.

DEPARTMENT OF THE INTERIOR,
U. S. INDIAN SERVICE,
UNION AGENCY,
MUSKOGEE, I. T., ———, 19—.
Respectfully forwarded to the Commissioner
of Indian Affairs for consideration with my report
of even date.

——— ———,
U. S. Indian Agent.

DEPARTMENT OF THE INTERIOR,
OFFICE OF INDIAN AFFAIRS,
WASHINGTON, D. C., ———, 19—.
Respectfully submitted to the Secretary of the
Interior with favorable recommendation.

——— ———,
Commissioner.

DEPARTMENT OF THE INTERIOR,
WASHINGTON, D. C., ———, 19—.
Approved:

——— ———,
Secretary of the Interior.

FORM OF BOND.

Know all men by these presents, That we (a)——— ———, of ———, as principals,
and ——— ———, of ———, and ——— ———, of ———, as sureties, are held and
firmly bound unto the United States of America in the sum of ——— dollars, lawful
money of the United States, for the payment of which, well and truly to be made, we
bind ourselves and each of us, our heirs, successors, executors, and administrators,
jointly and severally, firmly by these presents.

Sealed with our seals and dated the ——— day of ———, 19—.

The condition of this obligation is such, That whereas the above-bounden ———
———, as principal—, ——— entered into a certain agreement dated ———, 19—,
with the United States Indian agent for the Union Agency, for the purchase of ———,
to be procured from (b) the ———, said ——— to be used in the Indian Territory
only for "domestic and industrial purposes, including the construction, maintenance.
and repair of railroads and other highways."

Now, if the above-bounden ——— ——— shall faithfully carry out and observe all
the obligations assumed in said agreement by ——— ———, and shall observe all the
laws of the United States and regulations made or which shall be made thereunder
for the government of trade and intercourse with the Indian tribes, and the rules
and regulations that have been or may be prescribed by the Secretary of the Interior
under the act of Congress approved June 6, 1900 (Public—No. 174), relative to the
procurement of timber and stone from lands belonging to any of the Five Civilized
Tribes in the Indian Territory, then this obligation shall be null and void, otherwise to remain it full force and effect.

Signed and sealed in the presence of (c)

——— ———.

——— ———.

——— ———.

——— ———.

——— ———. [L. S.] (d)
——— ———. [L. S.]
——— ———. [L. S.]
——— ———. [L. S.]

---

a The Christian names and residences of principals, and of the sureties, where personal sureties are given, of whom there must be two.

b Give description of land.

c There must be at least two witnesses to all signatures, though the same two persons may witness all.

d A seal must be attached by some adhesive substance to the signatures of principals and sureties.

PILING.

Cedar, —— cents per foot; oak, —— cents per foot, running measure.

RAILROAD CROSS-TIES (BRIDGE, HEWN, OR SAWED).

Oak (post, burr, white, red, and black), —— cents each.
Pine, —— cents each.
Cedar, bois d'arc, walnut, mulberry, sassafras, and red or slippery elm, ——
cents each.
Black locust and coffee bean, —— cents each.

RAILROAD SWITCH TIES.

Oak (post, white, burr, red, and black), —— cents each.
Pine, —— cents each.

FENCE POSTS.

—— cents each.

CORD WOOD.

—— dollar— per cord.

STONE.

—— dollar— per cubic yard.

It is agreed that full payment shall be made for said timber or stone before any of it is removed from the land hereinbefore described, and title to said timber or stone shall not vest in the part— of the second part until full payment shall have been made therefor.

It is further agreed that said timber shall be cut and removed and that said stone shall be quarried and removed from said land as soon as practicable after the date of this contract, so that no depreciation in value or waste may accrue to said party of the first part by reason of unnecessary delay in the removal of said timber or stone, provided that the terms of this contract shall not extend beyond the period of one year from the date hereof, and the timber or stone procured under this contract may be used within the limits of the Indian Territory only for "domestic and industrial purposes, including the construction, maintenance, and repair of railroads and other highways."

It is further understood and agreed by the part— of the second part that this agreement is void and of no effect unless approved by the Secretary of the Interior.

The part— of the second part further agree— that this agreement shall in all respects be subject to the rules and regulations heretofore or that may hereafter be prescribed under the said act of June 6, 1900, by the Secretary of the Interior relative to the procurement of timber and stone from any of the lands belonging to any of the Five Civilized Tribes, and to pay to the United States Indian agent for the Union Agency the full value of the timber or stone hereinbefore mentioned, in accordance with the provisions hereof.

The part— of the second part —— firmly bound for the faithful compliance with the stipulations of this agreement by and under the bond made and executed by the part— of the second part as principal— and —— ——, as sure—, entered into the —— day of ——, and which is on file in the office of the Commissioner of Indian Affairs.

In witness whereof the said parties of the first and second parts have hereunto set their hands and affixed their seals the day and year first above written.

Witnesses: (*a*)

—— ——} As to —— ——, [SEAL.](*b*)
                              U. S. *Indian Agent.*

—— ——} As to —— ——. [SEAL.]

—— ——} As to —— ——. [SEAL.]

—— ——} As to —— ——. [SEAL.]

a Two witnesses to each signature, including signature of agent.
b Stamps are required by the act of June 13, 1898. Party of second part must furnish stamps.

ment of any tax that may be lawfully assessed against them by either State, Territorial, or municipal authority; and Congress hereby expressly reserves the right to regulate the tolls or charges for the transmission of messages over any lines constructed under the provisions of this act: *Provided,* That incorporated cities and towns into or through which such telephone or telegraphic lines may be constructed shall have the power to regulate the manner of construction therein, and nothing herein contained shall be so construed as to deny the right of municipal taxation in such towns and cities.

APPENDIX NO. 9.

REGULATIONS OF THE DEPARTMENT OF THE INTERIOR UNDER SECTION 3 OF THE ACT OF MARCH 3, 1901, CONCERNING RIGHT OF WAY FOR A TELEPHONE AND TELEGRAPH LINE THROUGH ANY LANDS HELD BY AN INDIAN TRIBE OR NATION IN THE INDIAN TERRITORY, THROUGH ANY LANDS RESERVED FOR AN INDIAN AGENCY OR INDIAN SCHOOL OR FOR OTHER PURPOSE IN CONNECTION WITH THE INDIAN SERVICE, OR THROUGH ANY LANDS WHICH HAVE BEEN ALLOTTED IN SEVERALTY.

DEPARTMENT OF THE INTERIOR, OFFICE OF INDIAN AFFAIRS,
Washington, D. C., March 15, 1901.

The following regulations are prescribed under section 3 of the act of March 3, 1901 (Public—No. 137), granting right of way for a telephone and telegraph line through any Indian reservation, through any lands held by an Indian tribe or nation in the Indian Territory, lands reserved for an Indian agency or Indian school or for other purpose in connection with the Indian Service, or allotted lands:

1. Section 3 of the act of Congress approved March 3, 1901, entitled "An act making appropriations for the current and contingent expenses of the Indian Department and for fulfilling treaty stipulations with various Indian tribes for the fiscal year ending June thirtieth, nineteen hundred and two, and for other purposes," is as follows:

SEC. 3. That the Secretary of the Interior is hereby authorized and empowered to grant a right of way, in the nature of an easement, for the construction, operation, and maintenance of telephone and telegraph lines and offices for general telephone and telegraph business through any Indian reservation, through any lands held by an Indian tribe or nation in the Indian Territory, through any lands reserved for an Indian agency or Indian school or for other purpose in connection with the Indian Service, or through any lands which have been allotted in severalty to any individual Indian under any law or treaty, but which have not been conveyed to the allottee with full power of alienation, upon the terms and conditions herein expressed. No such lines shall be constructed across Indian lands, as above mentioned, until authority therefor has first been obtained from the Secretary of the Interior, and the maps of definite location of the lines shall be subject to his approval. The compensation to be paid the tribes in their tribal capacity and the individual allottees for such right of way through their lands shall be determined in such manner as the Secretary of the Interior may direct, and shall be subject to his final approval: and where such lines are not subject to State or Territorial taxation the company or owner of the line shall pay to the Secretary of the Interior, for the use and benefit of the Indians, such annual tax as he may designate, not exceeding five dollars for each ten miles of line so constructed and maintained; and all such lines shall be constructed and maintained under such rules and regulations as said Secretary may prescribe. But nothing herein contained shall be so construed as to exempt the owners of such lines from the payment of any tax that may be lawfully assessed against them by either State, Territorial, or municipal authority; and Congress hereby expressly reserves the right to regulate the tolls or charges for the transmission of messages over any lines constructed under the provisions of this act: *Provided,* That incorporated cities and towns into or through which such telephone or telegraphic lines may be constructed shall have the power to regulate the manner of construction therein, and nothing herein contained shall be so construed as to deny the right of municipal taxation in such towns and cities. * * *

2. No company or individual is authorized to construct a telephone or telegraph line across Indian lands as mentioned in the foregoing section of the act of March 3, 1901, until authority therefor has first been obtained from the Secretary of the Interior.

3. Any company or individual desiring to obtain such permission must file an application therefor in this office, for transmission to the Secretary of the Interior. Such application should, in as particular a manner as possible, describe the route of the proposed telephone or telegraph line within the lands named in the above section and must be accompanied, in the case of a company or corporation, by—

First. A copy of its articles of incorporation, duly certified to by the proper officer of the company under its corporate seal, or by the secretary of the State or Territory where organized.

Second. A copy of the State or Territorial law under which the company was organized, with the certificate of the governor or secretary of the State or Territory that the same is the existing law.

Third. When said law directs that the articles of association or other papers connected with the organization be filed with any State or Territorial officer, the certificate of such officer that the same have been filed according to law, with the date of the filing thereof.

Fourth. When a company is operating in a State or Territory other than that in which it is incorporated, the certificate of the proper officers of the State or Territory is required that it has complied with the laws of that State or Territory governing foreign corporations to the extent required to entitle the company to operate in such State or Territory.

Fifth. The official statement, under seal of the proper officer, that the organization has been completed; that the company is fully authorized to proceed with the construction of the line of telephone or telegraph according to the existing law. (Form 1.)

Sixth. An affidavit by the president, under the seal of the company, showing the names and designations of its officers at the date of the filing of the proofs. (Form 2.)

Seventh. Satisfactory evidence of the good faith of the company and its financial ability in the matter of the construction of the proposed line.

4. It is further provided in said section that maps of definite location of the lines shall be subject to the approval of the Secretary of the Interior.

5. All maps of location presented for approval under said section 3 should be filed with this office, and should be drawn on tracing linen and in duplicate.

6. Where the proposed line is greatly in excess of 20 miles, separate maps should be filed in 20-mile sections.

7. Where grounds are required for office purposes, the exact location of the same should be noted upon the maps of location, but separate plats of such grounds must be filed and approved.

8. The scale of maps showing the line of route should be 2,000 feet to an inch. The maps may, however, be drawn to a larger scale when necessary; but the scale must not be so greatly increased as to make the map inconveniently large for handling. Plats of grounds required for office purposes should be drawn on a scale of 50 feet to an inch, and must be filed separately from the line of route. Such plats should show enough of the line of route to indicate the position of the tract with reference thereto.

9. The termini of the line of route should be fixed by reference of course and distance to the nearest existing corner of the public survey. The map, engineer's affidavit, and president's certificate (Forms 3 and 4) should each show these conditions. A tract for grounds for office purposes must be similarly referenced and described on the plat.

10. In filing maps of location for approval under said section 3, the same should be accompanied by the affidavit of the president or other principal officer of the company, defining the purpose, intent, and financial ability of the company in the matter of the construction of the proposed line. Further, each map should be accompanied by evidence of the service of an exact copy thereof, and the date of such service upon (1) in case of allottees, or in case of a reservation, the agent in charge; (2) in case of the Five Civilized Tribes, upon the principal chief or secretary of such tribe or nation.

11. No action will be taken upon such map until the expiration of twenty days from the date of such service.

12. A company will not be permitted to proceed with the construction of any portion of its line until the map showing the location thereof has first been approved by the Secretary of the Interior.

13. When a line of telephone or telegraph is constructed, an affidavit of the presinent setting forth the fact must be filed in this office in duplicate. If a change from the route indicated upon the approved map of location is found to be necessary, on account of engineering difficulties or otherwise, new maps and field notes of the changed route must be filed and approved, and a right of way upon such changed lines must be acquired, damages ascertained, and compensation paid on account thereof, in all respects as in the case of the original location, before construction can be proceeded with upon such changed line.

14. Upon the approval of the map of definite location specific directions will be given in the matter of the acquirement of the right of way and determination of damages occasioned by the construction of the line.

15. The conditions on different reservations throughout the country are so varied that it is deemed inadvisable to prescribe definite rules in the matter of determining the tribal compensation and damages for right of way. As a rule, however, the United States Indian agent, or a special United States Indian agent, or Indian inspector will be designated to determine such compensation and damages, subject to the approval of the Secretary of the Interior.

16. Telephone and telegraph companies should not independently attempt to

negotiate with the individual occupants and allottees for right of way and damages. When the lands are not attached to an agency, some proper person will be designated to act with the allottee in determining the individual damages. Where such lands are attached to an Indian agency, the United States Indian agent or other proper person connected with the Indian service will be designated to act with and for the allottees or occupants in the matter of determining individual damages for right of way, subject to the approval of the Secretary of the Interior.

17. No company having secured a right of way under the provisions of this section will be permitted to lease or enter into any arrangements with any other company or individual for the use of any poles or fixtures erected and maintained by virtue of authority granted under this section without first obtaining the consent of the Secretary of the Interior.

18. The foregoing regulations shall be observed, so far as applicable, by any individual seeking to procure a right of way for the construction of telephone and telegraph lines under the provisions of this section, and particularly as to the purpose, intent, and financial ability of the applicant.

19. If in the administration of said section cases are found which are not covered by these regulations, such cases will be disposed of according to their respective merits under special instructions, or supplemental regulations embracing cases of that character will be adopted as may seem necessary.

Very respectfully,

W. A. JONES,
Commissioner.

DEPARTMENT OF THE INTERIOR, *March 26, 1901.*

Approved.

E. A. HITCHCOCK, *Secretary.*

Forms for proof of organization of company and verification of maps of location.

(1)

I, —— ——, secretary (or president) of the —— company, do herby certify that the organization of said company has been completed; that the company is fully authorized to proceed with the construction of the line according to the existing laws of the State (or Territory), and that the copy of the articles of association (or incorporation) of the company herewith (or heretofore filed in the Department of the Interior) is a true and correct copy.

In witness whereof I have hereunto set my name and the corporate seal of the company.

[SEAL.]

—— *of the* —— *Company,*

(2)

State of ——,
County of ——, *ss:*

—— ——, being duly sworn, says that he is the president of the —— company, and that the following is a true list of the officers of the said company, with the full name and official designation of each, to wit: (Here insert the full name and official designation of each officer.)

[SEAL OF COMPANY.]

President of the Company,

(3)

State of ——,
County of ——, *ss:*

—— ——, being duly sworn, says he is the chief engineer of (or is the person employed to locate) the line of telephone and telegraph of the —— company; that the location of the line of route of said lines from —— to ——, a distance of —— miles, was made by him or under his direction as surveyor employed by the company and under its authority, commencing on the —— day of ——, 19—, and ending on the —— day of ——, 19—; and that such survey is accurately represented on the accompanying map.

Sworn and subscribed to before me this —— day of ——, 19—.

[SEAL.]

Notary Public.

(4)

I, ――― ―――, do hereby certify that I am the president of the ――― company; that ――― ―――, who subscribed the foregoing affidavit, was employed to make the survey by the said company; that the survey of line of route of the company's lines, as accurately represented on the accompanying map, was made under authority of the company; that the said line of route so surveyed and as represented on the said map was adopted by the company by resolution of its board of directors on the ――― day of ―――, 19―, as the definite location of the telephone and telegraph line from ――― to ―――, a distance of ――― miles; and that the map has been prepared to be filed for the approval of the Secretary of the Interior, in order that the company may obtain the benefits of the third section of the act of Congress approved March 3, 1901 (Public—No. 137), entitled "An act making appropriations for the current and contingent expenses of the Indian Department and for fulfilling treaty stipulations with various Indian tribes for the fiscal year ending June thirtieth, nineteen hundred and two, and for other purposes."

――― ―――,
President of the ――― Company.

Attest:
――― ―――,
Secretary.
[SEAL OF THE COMPANY.]

―――

ADDENDA.

[Regulations, March 26, 1901.]

Regulations concerning the establishment or maintenance of local telephone exchanges in incorporated cities and towns in the Indian Territory, under section 3 of the act of March 3, 1901.

DEPARTMENT OF THE INTERIOR, OFFICE OF INDIAN AFFAIRS,
November 6, 1901.

No company or individual is authorized to establish or maintain a local telephone exchange in any incorporated city or town in the Indian Territory, under the provisions of the act of March 3, 1901, until authority therefor has first been obtained from the Secretary of the Interior.

Any company or individual desiring to obtain such permission must file an application therefor in this office, for transmission to the Secretary of the Interior. Such application should, in as particular a manner as possible, outline the general plan of the proposed system and must be accompanied, in the case of a company or corporation, by the showing required in subdivisions 1 to 7, both inclusive, of paragraph 3 of the regulations of March 26, 1901. If this showing has been made in connection with an application for a long-distance or other telephone line, a reference to the previous application will be sufficient.

This office, before transmitting such application to the Secretary of the Interior, will obtain an expression of the views of the city or town authorities upon the general plan of the proposed exchange.

The general outline of the plan should be submitted in duplicate.

The foregoing regulations shall be observed, so far as applicable, by any individual seeking to procure permission to establish or maintain a telephone exchange in any incorporated city or town in the Indian Territory, and particularly as to the purpose, intent, and financial ability of the applicant.

W. A. JONES,
Commissioner.

DEPARTMENT OF THE INTERIOR,
Washington, November 9, 1901.

Approved:

E. A. HITCHCOCK,
Secretary.

APPENDIX NO. 10.

[Extracts from Indian appropriation act for fiscal year 1903, approved May 27, 1902 (32 Stat , 245), showing legislation pertaining to the Indian Territory.]

INDIAN TERRITORY: For general incidental expenses of the Indian service . Indian Territory, including incidental expenses of the Indian inspector's office anu for pay of employees, eighteen thousand dollars.

* * * For salaries of four commissioners appointed under acts of Con approved March third, eighteen hundred and ninety-three, and March se eighteen hundred and ninety-five, to negotiate with the Five Civilized Tribes in Indian Territory, twenty thousand dollars: *Provided*, That said commission shall exercise all the powers heretofore conferred upon it by Congress: *Provided further*, That all children born to duly enrolled and recognized citizens of the Creek Nation up to and including the twenty-fifth day of May, nineteen hundred and one, and then living, shall be added to the rolls of citizenship of said nation made under the provisions of an act entitled "An act to ratify and confirm an agreement with the Muscogee or Creek tribe of Indians, and for other purposes," approved March first, nineteen hundred and one, and if any such child has died since the twenty-fifth day of May, nineteen hundred and one, or may hereafter die, before receiving his allotment of land and distributive share of the funds of the tribe, the lands and moneys to which he would be entitled if living shall descend to his heirs and be allotted and distributed to them accordingly: *And provided further*, That the act entitled "A to ratify and confirm an agreement with the Muscogee or Creek tribe of Indians, and for other purposes," approved March first, nineteen hundred and one, in so far as it provides for descent and distribution according to the laws of the Creek Nation, is hereby repealed and the descent and distribution of lands and moneys provided for in said act shall be in accordance with the provisions of chapter forty-nine of Mansfield's Digest of the Statutes of Arkansas in force in Indian Territory.

For expenses of commissioners and necessary expenses of employees, and three dollars per diem for expenses of a clerk detailed as special disbursing agent by the Interior Department while on duty with the Commission, shall be paid therefrom; for clerical help, including secretary of the Commission and interpreters (act of March third, nineteen hundred and one, volume thirty-one, page one thousand and seventy-four, section one), ninety-three thousand dollars; contingent expense the Commission (same act), two thousand dollars: *Provided further*, That this ap. priation may be used by said Commission in the prosecution of all work to be done by or under its direction as required by law; and said commissioners shall at once make an itemized statement to the Secretary of the Interior of all their expenditures up to January first, nineteen hundred and one, and annually thereafter: *And provided further*, That not to exceed ten thousand four hundred dollars of the above amount may be used in the temporary employment in the office of the Commissioner of Indian Affairs of three clerks, at the rate of one thousand six hundred dollars per annum; one clerk, at the rate of one thousand four hundred dollars, and one clerk at the rate of one thousand two hundred dollars, who shall be competent to examine records in disputed citizenship cases and law contests growing out of the work of said Commission, and in the temporary employment in said office of three competent stenographers, at the rate of one thousand dollars each per annum.

To pay all expenses incident to the survey, platting, and appraisement of town sites in the Choctaw, Chickasaw, Creek, and Cherokee nations, Indian Territory, as required by sections fifteen and twenty-nine of an act entitled "An act for the protection of the people of the Indian Territory, and for other purposes," approved June twenty-eighth, eighteen hundred and ninety-eight, and all acts amendatory thereof or supplemental thereto, fifty thousand dollars: *Provided*, That hereafter tl Secretary of the Interior may, whenever the chief executive of the Choctaw or Chickasaw nations fails or refuses to appoint a town-site commissioner for any town, or to fill any vacancy caused by the neglect or refusal of the town-site commissioner appointed by the chief executive of the Choctaw or Chickasaw nations to qualify or act, in his discretion, appoint a commissioner to fill the vacancy thus created: *Provided further*, That the limits of such towns in the Cherokee, Choctaw, and Chickasaw nations having a population of less than two hundred people, as in the judgment of the Secretary of the Interior should be established, shall be defined as early as practicable by the Secretary of the Interior in the same manner as provided for towns having over two hundred people under existing law, and the same shall not be subject to allotment.   That the land so segregated and reserved from allotment shall be disposed of in such manner as the Secretary of the Interior may direct by a town-site commission, one member to be appointed by the Secretary of the Interior and one by the executive of the nation in which such land is located; proceeds arising from the disposition of such lands to be applied in like manner as the proceeds of other lands in town sites.

For the purpose of removing intruders and placing allottees in unrestricted possession of their allotments, to be expended under the direction of the Secretary of ⁀ᵇ ₙₜerior and to be immediately available, fifteen thousand dollars; in all, one ₓₙdred and sixty thousand dollars: *Provided, however*, That it shall hereafter be unlawful to remove or deport any person from the Indian Territory who is in lawful ₚₛion of any lots or parcels of land in any town or city in the Indian Territory which has been designated as a town site under existing laws and treaties, ₙₒ part of this appropriation shall be used for the deportation or removal of any such person from the Indian Territory: *Provided*, That the just and reasonable share of each member of the Chickasaw, Choctaw, Creek, and Cherokee nations of Indians, in the lands belonging to the said tribes, which each member is entitled to hold in his possession until allotments are made, as provided in the act entitled "An act for the protection of the people of the Indian Territory, and for other purposes," approved June twenty-eighth, eighteen hundred and ninety-eight, be, and the same is hereby, declared to be three hundred and twenty acres for each member of the Chickasaw Nation, three hundred and twenty acres for each member of the Choctaw Nation, one hundred and sixty acres for each member of the Creek Nation, and one hundred acres for each member of the Cherokee Nation. * * *

SEC. 8. That the part of the northern district of the Indian Territory consisting of t' ₑₑk country, the Seminole country, and all that portion of the Cherokee and Choctaw nations included in the following-described boundaries, to wit: Commencing at the northeast corner of the Creek Nation and running east on the line between townships nineteen and twenty, to its intersection with the dividing line between ranges twenty and twenty-one east, thence south on said line to its intersection with the Arkansas River, thence down the Arkansas River to its intersection with the Canadian River, thence up the Canadian River to its intersection with the dividing line between ranges twenty and twenty-one east, thence south to the intersecting line between townships seven and eight, thence west on the intersecting line between townships seven and eight to the Creek Nation, be, and the same is hereby, made the western district in said Territory, and the places of holding courts in said western district shall be Muscogee, Wagoner, Sapulpa, Wewoka, Eufaula, and Okmulgee. ₜₕₑ ₓudge appointed under the act entitled "An act making appropriations for the ₚₙt and contingent expenses of the Indian Department, and for fulfilling treaty stipulations with various Indian tribes for the fiscal year ending June thirtieth, eighteen hundred and ninety-eight, and for other purposes," approved June seventh, eighteen hundred and ninety-seven, shall be the judge of said western district, and he is hereby authorized to appoint a clerk who shall reside and keep his office at one of the places of holding court in said western district. That each of the three commissioners with headquarters at Muscogee, Eufaula, and Wewoka, respectively, shall be United States commissioners for said western district for a period of four years from the date of their appointment and until their respective successors shall be appointed and qualified, and the two constables now in office whose headquarters are at Muscogee and Eufaula, respectively, shall be constables in said western district until their successors shall be appointed and qualified; and said judge may appoint a constable for the commissioner at Wewoka, and the said judge may appoint an additional commissioner to be located at Checotah, and an additional constable for said commissioner's court. Each of the United States commissioners and each of the four constables now located in the northern district as constituted by this act shall continue to be United States commissioners and constables, respectively, for said district until their successors shall be appointed and qualified. That the clerk's office at Vinita shall also be the recorder's office for the northern district, except that the clerk's office at Miami shall continue to be the recording office for the Quapaw Indian Agency, as now provided by law. The United States marshal of the present northern district shall be marshal of the western district, and there shall be appointed by the President, by and with the advice and consent of the Senate, a district attorney for said western district and a United States marshal for the northern district. The said officers shall be appointed and shall hold office for the period of four years, and shall receive the same salary and fees and discharge like duties as other similar officers in said Territory. The cases now pending in that part of the northern district which is hereby made the western district shall be tried the same as if brought in said western district. Terms of court shall continue to be held within the territory remaining in said northern district at the places now provided by law for the holding of courts therein, and in addition thereto at the towns of Sallisaw, Claremore, Nowata, and Pryor Creek, in the Cherokee country. All laws now applicable to the existing judicial districts in the Indian Territory, and to attorneys, marshals, clerks, and their assistants or deputies therein, not inconsistent herewith, are hereby made applicable to the western district.   In addition to the places now provided by law for holding courts in the southern and central districts, courts in the southern district shall also be held at Tishomingo and Ada, and in the central district at Durant.   The United States judge for the central district of the Indian Territory, after the approval of this act, may appoint a constable for the commissioner located at Durant.

To enable the Attorney-General to carry out the provisions of the act approved July seventh, eighteen hundred and ninety-eight, for the erection of three jails in the Indian Territory, and also to erect one additional United States jail in said Territory, forty thousand dollars is hereby appropriated, to be expended under the direction of the Attorney-General, to be immediately available, and to remain available until expended.   And the Attorney-General is hereby authorized and directed to cause to be erected a United States jail at each of the three places already formally designated by him, namely, at Muscogee in the western district, at South McAlester in the central district, and at Ardmore in the southern district, and one additional United States jail at Vinita in the northern district, at a total cost not exceeding one hundred thousand dollars.

That for the purpose of acquiring sites for United States jails as provided herein in the Indian Territory, there shall be appointed by the judge of the United States court in the district where such land is situated, on application of the United States by petition describing the land sought to be condemned, three disinterested referees, who shall determine the compensation and damage to be paid any owner, occupant, tribe, or nation by reason of the appropriation and condemnation of such land for the use and benefit of the United States for a jail at any of the places hereinbefore mentioned.   Such referees, before entering upon the duties of their appointment, shall each take and subscribe before the clerk of the said United States court an oath that he will faithfully and impartially discharge the duties of his appointment, which oaths, duly certified, shall be returned with the award of the referees to the clerk of the court by which they were appointed.   Before such referees shall proceed with the assessment of damages for any lands sought to be condemned under this act, ten days' personal notice of said hearing shall be given to all persons interested, and service may be had upon each tribe or nation in which said land may be located by service upon the principal chief thereof, and in case personal service can not be had upon any person interested, twenty days' notice of the time when the same shall be condemned shall be given, by publication in some newspaper in general circulation nearest said property in the district where said land is situated.

If the referees can not agree, then any two of them are authorized to and shall make the award.   Any party to the proceedings who is dissatisfied with the award of the referees shall have the right, within ten days after the filing of the award in the court by which said referees were appointed, to appeal by original petition to the United States court sitting at the place nearest and most convenient to the property sought to be taken, where the question of the damages occasioned by the taking of the land in controversy shall be tried de novo, and the judgment rendered by the court shall be final and conclusive.   And upon the payment into court of the amount or amounts awarded as damages fee simple title to said tract of land shall vest in the United States.   If such appeal is not taken as hereinbefore set forth, the award shall be conclusive and final, and shall have the same force and effect as a judgment of a court of competent jurisdiction, and upon the payment of the sum or sums so found due into the court a fee simple title to said land shall vest in the United States.

Each of said referees shall receive for his compensation the sum of five dollars per day while actually engaged in the appraisement of the property and the hearing of any matter submitted to them under this act.

That if any party or person other than the United States shall appeal from any award, and the judgment of the court does not award such appealing party or person more than the referees awarded, all costs occasioned by such appeal shall be paid by such appealing party or person.   It shall be the duty of the United States court in each district to promptly hear and determine the rights of all parties if any appeal shall be taken under this act.

Approved, May 27, 1902.

·APPENDIX NO. 11.

[PUBLIC—No. 26.]

AN ACT To grant the right of way through the Oklahoma Territory and the Indian Territory to the Enid and Anadarko Railway Company, and for other purposes.

Be it enacted by the Senate and House of Representatives of the United States of America in Congress assembled, That the Enid and Anadarko Railway Company, a corporation created under and by virtue of the laws of the Territory of Oklahoma, be, and the same is hereby, invested and empowered with the right of locating, constructing, owning, equipping, operating, using, and maintaining a railway and telegraph and telephone line through the Territory of Oklahoma and the Indian Territory, beginning at a point on its railway between Anadarko and Watonga, in the Territory of Oklahoma; thence in an easterly direction by the most practicable route to a point on the eastern boundary of the Indian Territory near Fort Smith, in the State of Arkansas, together with such branch lines to be built from any point on the line above described to any other point in the Indian Territory as said railway company may at any time hereafter decide to construct, with the right to construct, use, and maintain such tracks, turn-outs, sidings, and extensions as said company may deem it to its interest to construct along and upon the right of way and depot grounds hereby granted.

SEC. 2. That said corporation is authorized to take and use for all purposes of a railway, and for no other purpose, a right of way one hundred feet in width through said Oklahoma Territory and said Indian Territory, and to take and use a strip of land two hundred feet in width, with a length of two thousand feet, in addition to right of way, for stations, for every single miles of road, with the right to use such additional ground where there are heavy cuts or fills as may be necessary for the construction and maintenance of the roadbed, not exceeding one hundred feet in width on each side of said right of way, or as much thereof as may be included in said cut or fill: *Provided,* That no more than said addition of land shall be taken for any one station: *Provided further,* That no part of the lands herein authorized to be taken shall be leased or sold by the company, and they shall not be used except in such manner and for such purposes only as shall be necessary for the construction and convenient operation of said railway, telegraph, and telephone lines; and when any portion thereof shall cease to be so used such portion shall revert to the nation or tribe of Indians from which the same shall have been taken.

SEC. 3. That before said railway shall be constructed through any lands held by individual occupants according to the laws, customs, and usages of any of the Indian nations or tribes through which it may be constructed, full compensation shall be made to such occupants for all property to be taken or damage done by reason of the construction of such railway.   In case of failure to make amicable settlement with any occupant, such compensation shall be determined by the appraisement of three disinterested referees, to be appointed, one (who shall act as chairman) by the Secretary of the Interior, one by the chief of the nation to which said occupant belongs, and one by said railway company, who, before entering upon the duties of their appointment, shall take and subscribe, before a district judge, clerk of a district court, or United States commissioner, an oath that they will faithfully and impartially discharge the duties of their appointment, which oath, duly certified, shall be returned with their award to, and filed with, the Secretary of the Interior within sixty days from the completion thereof; and a majority of said referees shall be competent to act in case of the absence of a member after due notice.   And upon the failure of either party to make such appointment within thirty days after the appointment made by the Secretary of the Interior, the vacancy shall be filled by a judge of the United States court for the Indian Territory upon the application of the other party.   The chairman of said board shall appoint the time and place for all hearings within the nation to which such occupant belongs.   Each of said referees shall receive for his services the sum of four dollars per day for each day they are engaged in the trial of any case submitted to them under this act, with mileage at five cents per mile.   Witnesses shall receive the usual fees allowed by the courts of said nations.   Costs, including compensation of the referees, shall be made a part of the award, and be paid by such railway company.   In case the referees can not agree, then any two of them are authorized to make the award.   Either party being dissatisfied with the finding of the referees shall have the right, within ninety days after the making of the award and notice of the same, to appeal by original petition to the United States court for the Indian Territory, which court shall have jurisdiction to hear and determine the subject-matter of said petition, according to the laws of the Territory in which the same shall be heard provided for determining the damage when property is taken for railroad purposes. If upon the hearing of said appeal the judgment of the court shall be for a larger sum than the award of the referees, the cost of said appeal shall be adjudged against the railway company. If the judgment of the court shall be for the same sum as the award of the referees, then the costs shall be adjudged against the appellant. If the judgment of the court shall be for a smaller sum than the award of the referees, then the costs shall be adjudged against the party claiming damages. When proceedings have been commenced in court, the railway company shall pay double the amount of the award into court to abide the judgment thereof, and then have the right to enter upon the property sought to be condemned and proceed with the construction of the railway.

SEC. 4. That said railway company shall not charge the inhabitants of said Territory a greater rate of freight than the rate authorized by the laws of the Territory of Oklahoma for services or transportation of the same kind: *Provided*, That passenger rates on said railway shall not exceed three cents per mile. Congress hereby reserves the right to regulate the charges for freight and passengers on said railway and messages on said telegraph and telephone lines until a State government or governments shall exist in said Territory within the limits of which said railway, or a part thereof, shall be located; and then such State government or governments shall be authorized to fix and regulate the cost of transportation of persons and freights within their respective limits by said railway; but Congress expressly reserves the right to fix and regulate at all times the cost of such transportation by said railway or said company whenever such transportation shall extend from one State into another or shall extend into more than one State: *Provided, however*, That the rate of such transportation of passengers, local or interstate, shall not exceed the rate above expressed: *And provided further*, That said railway company shall carry the mail at such prices as Congress may by law provide; and until such rate is fixed by law the Postmaster-General may fix the rate of compensation.

SEC. 5. That said railway company shall pay to the Secretary of the Interior, for the benefit of the particular nations or tribes through whose lands said main line and branches may be located, the sum of fifty dollars, in addition to compensation provided for in this act for property taken and damages done to individual occupants by the construction of the railway, for each mile of railway that it may construct in said Territory, said payments to be made in installments of five hundred dollars as each ten miles of road is graded: *Provided*, That if the general council of said nations or tribes through whose lands said railway may be located or the principal executive officer of the tribe if the general council be not in session shall, within four months after the filing of maps of definite location, as set forth in section six of this act, dissent from the allowances provided for in this section, and shall certify the same to the Secretary of the Interior, then all compensation to be paid to such dissenting nation or tribe under the provisions of this act shall be determined as provided in section three for the determination of the compensation to be paid to the individual occupant of lands, with the right of appeal to the courts upon the same terms, conditions, and requirements as therein provided: *Provided further*, That the amount awarded or adjudged to be paid by said railway company for said dissenting nation or tribe shall be in lieu of the compensation that said nation or tribe would be entitled to receive under the foregoing provisions. Said company shall also pay, so long as said Territory is owned and occupied by the Indians in their tribal relations, to the Secretary of the Interior the sum of fifteen dollars per annum for each mile of railway it shall construct in said Territory. The money paid to the Secretary of the Interior under the provisions of this act shall be apportioned by him in accordance with the laws and treaties now in force between the United States and said nations or tribes, according to the number of miles of railway that may be constructed by said railway company through their lands: *Provided*, That Congress shall have the right, so long as said lands are occupied and possessed by said nation or tribe, to impose such additional taxes upon said railway as it may deem just and proper for their benefit; and any Territory or State hereafter formed through which said railway shall have been established may exercise the like power as to such part of said railway as may lie within its limits. Said railway company shall have the right to survey and locate its railway immediately after the passage of this act.

SEC. 6. That said company shall cause maps, showing the route of its located line through said Territory, to be filed in the office of the Secretary of the Interior, and also to be filed in the office of the principal chief of each of the nations or tribes through whose lands said railway may be located, and after the filing of said maps no claim for a subsequent settlement and improvement upon the right of way shown by said maps shall be valid as against said company: *Provided*, That when a map showing any portion of said railway company's located line is filed as herein provided for, said company shall commence grading said located line within six months thereafter, or such location shall be void; and said location shall be approved by the Secretary of the Interior in sections of twenty-five miles before construction of any such section shall be begun.

Sec. 7. That the officers, servants, and employees of said company necessary to the construction and management of said road shall be allowed to reside, while so engaged, upon such right of way, but subject to the provisions of the Indian intercourse laws and such rules and regulations as may be established by the Secretary of the Interior in accordance with said intercourse laws.

Sec. 8. That the United States court for the Indian Territory and such other courts as may be authorized by Congress shall have, without reference to the amount in controversy, concurrent jurisdiction over all controversies arising between the said Enid and Anadarko Railway Company and the nation and tribe through whose territory said railway shall be constructed. Said courts shall have like jurisdiction, without reference to the amount in controversy, over all controversies arising between the inhabitants of said nation or tribe and said railway company; and the civil jurisdiction of said courts is hereby extended within the limits of said Indian Territory, without distinction as to citizenship of the parties, so far as may be necessary to carry out the provisions of this act.

Sec. 9. That said railway company shall build at least one-tenth of its railway in said Territory within one year after the passage of this act, and complete its road within three years after the approval of its map of location by the Secretary of the Interior or the rights herein granted shall be forfeited as to that portion not built; that said railway company shall construct and maintain continually all road and highway crossings and necessary bridges over said railway wherever said roads and highways do now or may hereafter cross said railway's right of way, or may be by the proper authorities laid out across the same.

Sec. 10. That the said Enid and Anadarko Railway Company shall accept this right of way upon the express condition, binding upon itself, its successors and assigns, that they will neither aid, advise, nor assist in any effort looking toward the changing or extinguishing the present tenure of the Indians in their land, and will not attempt to secure from the Indian nation any further grant of land, or its occupancy, than is hereinbefore provided: *Provided*, That any violation of the condition mentioned in this section shall operate as a forfeiture of all the rights and privileges of said railway company under this act.

Sec. 11. That all mortgages executed by said railway company conveying any portion of its railway, with its franchises, that may be constructed in said Indian Territory, shall be recorded in the Department of the Interior, and the record thereof shall be evidence and notice of their execution, and shall convey all rights, franchises, and property of said company as therein expressed.

Sec. 12. That Congress may at any time amend, add to, alter, or repeal this act; and the right of way herein and hereby granted shall not be assigned or transferred in any form whatever prior to the construction and completion of the road, except as to mortgages or other liens that may be given or secured thereon to aid in the construction thereof.

Sec. 13. That the right to locate, construct, own, equip, operate, use, and maintain a railway and telegraph and telephone line or lines into, in, or through the Indian Territory, together with the right to take and condemn lands for right of way, depot grounds, terminals, and other railway purposes, in or through any lands held by any Indian tribe or nation, person, individual, or municipality in said Territory, or in or through any lands in said Territory which have been or may hereafter be allotted in severalty to any individual Indian or other person under any law or treaty, whether the same have or have not been conveyed to the allottee, with full power of alienation, is hereby granted to any railway company organized under the laws of the United States, or of any State or Territory, which shall comply with this act.

Sec. 14. That the right of way of any railway company shall not exceed one hundred feet in width except where there are heavy cuts and fills, when one hundred feet additional may be taken on each side of said right of way; but lands additional and adjacent to said right of way may be taken and condemned by any railway company for station grounds, buildings, depots, side tracks, turnouts, or other railroad purposes not exceeding two hundred feet in width by a length of two thousand feet. That additional lands not exceeding forty acres at any one place may be taken by any railway company when necessary for yards, roundhouses, turntables, machine shops, water stations, and other railroad purposes. And when necessary for a good and sufficient water supply in the operation of any railroad, any such railway company shall have the right to take and condemn additional lands for reservoirs for water stations, and for such purpose shall have the right to impound surface water or build dams across any creek, draw, canyon, or stream, and shall have the right to connect the same by pipe line with the railroad and take the necessary grounds for such purposes; and any railway company shall have the right to change or straighten its line, reduce its grades or curves, and locate new stations and to take the lands and right of way necessary therefor under the provisions of this act.

SEC. 15. That before any railroad shall be constructed or any lands taken or condemned for any of the purposes set forth in the preceding section, full compensation for such right of way and all land and all damage done or to be done by the construction of the railroad, or the taking of any lands for railroad purposes, shall be made to the individual owner, occupant, or allottee of such lands, and to the tribe or nation through or in which the same is situated: *Provided,* That correct maps of the said line of railroad in sections of twenty-five miles each, and of any lands taken under this act, shall be filed in the Department of the Interior, and shall also be filed with the United States Indian agent for Indian Territory, and with the principal chief or governor of any tribe or nation through which the lines of railroad may be located or in which said lines are situated.

In case of the failure of any railway company to make amicable settlement with any individual owner, occupant, allottee, tribe, or nation for any right of way or lands or improvements sought to be appropriated or condemned under this act, all compensation and damages to be paid to the dissenting individual owner, occupant, allottee, tribe, or nation by reason of the appropriation and condemnation of said right of way, lands, or improvements shall be determined by the appraisement of three disinterested referees, to be appointed by the judge of the United States court, or other court of jurisdiction in the district where such lands are situated, on application of the corporation or other person or party in interest. Such referees, before entering upon the duties of their appointment, shall each take and subscribe, before competent authority, an oath that he will faithfully and impartially discharge the duties of his appointment, which oaths, duly certified, shall be returned with the award of the referees to the clerk of the court by which they were appointed. The referees shall also find in their report the names of the person and persons, tribe, or nation to whom the damages are payable and the interest of each person, tribe, or nation in the award of damages. Before such referees shall proceed with the assessment of damages for any right of way or other lands condemned under this act, twenty days' notice of the time when the same shall be condemned shall be given to all persons interested, by publication in some newspaper in general circulation nearest said property in the district where said right of way or said lands are situated, or by ten days' personal notice to each person owning or having any interest in said lands or right of way: *Provided,* That such notice to any tribe or nation may be served on the principal chief or governor of the tribe. If the referees can not agree, then any two of them are authorized to and shall make the award. Any party to the proceedings who is dissatisfied with the award of the referees shall have the right, within ten days after the making of the award, to appeal, by original petition, to the United States court, or other court of competent jurisdiction, sitting at the place nearest and most convenient to the property sought to be taken, where the question of the damages occasioned by the taking of the lands in controversy shall be tried de novo, and the judgment rendered by the court shall be final and conclusive, subject, however, to appeal as in other cases.

When the award of damages is filed with the clerk of the court by the referees, the railway company shall deposit the amount of such award with the clerk of the court, to abide the judgment thereof, and shall then have the right to enter upon and take possession of the property sought to be condemned: *Provided,* That when the said railway company is not satisfied with the award, it shall have the right, before commencing construction, to abandon any portion of said right of way and adopt a new location, subject, however, as to such new location, to all the provisions of this act. Each of the referees shall receive for his compensation the sum of four dollars per day while actually engaged in the appraisement of the property and the hearing of any matter submitted to them under this act. Witnesses shall receive the fees and mileage allowed by law to witness in courts of record within the districts where such lands are located. Costs, including compensation of the referees, shall be made part of the award or judgment and be paid by the railway company: *Provided,* That if any party or person other than the railway company shall appeal from any award, and the judgment of the court does not award such appealing party or person more than the referees awarded, all costs occasioned by such appeal shall be paid by such appealing party or person.

SEC. 16. That where a railroad is constructed under the provisions of this act there shall be paid by the railway company to the Secretary of the Interior, for the benefit of the particular tribe or nation through whose lands any such railroad may be constructed, an annual charge of fifteen dollars per mile for each mile of road constructed, the same to be paid so long as said lands shall be owned and occupied by such nation or tribe, which payment shall be in addition to the compensation otherwise provided herein; and the grants herein are made upon the condition that Congress hereby reserves the right to regulate the charges for freight and passengers on said railways and messages on all telegraph and telephone lines until a State government or governments shall exist in said Territory within the limits of which any railway shall be located; and then such State government or governments shall be authorized to fix and regulate the cost of transportation of persons and freights within their respective limits by such railways; but Congress expressly reserves the right to fix and regulate at all times the cost of such transportation by said railways whenever such transportation shall extend from one State into another, or shall extend into more than one State; and that the railway companies shall carry the mail at such prices as Congress may by law provide; and until such rate is fixed by law the Postmaster-General may fix the rate of compensation.

Sec. 17. That any railway company authorized to construct, own, or operate a railroad in said Territory desiring to cross or unite its tracks with any other railroad upon the grounds of such other railway company shall, after fifteen days' notice in writing to such other railroad company, make application in writing to the judge of the United States court for the district in which it is proposed to make such crossing or connection for the appointment of three disinterested referees to determine the necessity, place, manner, and time of such crossing or connection. The provisions of section three of this act with respect to the condemnation of right of way through tribal or individual lands shall, except as in this section otherwise provided, apply to proceedings to acquire the right to cross or connect with another railroad. Upon the hearing of any such application to cross or connect with any other railroad, either party or the referees may call and examine witnesses in regard to the matter, and said referees shall have the same power to administer oaths to witnesses that is now possessed by United States commissioners in said Territory, and said referees shall, after such hearing and a personal examination of the locality where a crossing or connection is desired, determine whether there is a necessity for such crossing or not, and if so, the place thereof, whether it shall be over or under the existing railroad, or at grade, and in other respects the manner of such crossing and the terms upon which the same shall be made and maintained: *Provided*, That no crossing shall be made through the yards or over the switches or side tracks of any existing railroad if a crossing can be effected at any other place that is practicable. If either party shall be dissatisfied with the terms of the order made by said referees it may appeal to the United States court of the Indian Territory for the district wherein such crossing or connection is sought to be made in the same manner as appeals are allowed from a judgment of a United States commissioner to said court, and said appeal and all subsequent proceedings shall only affect the amount of compensation, if any, and other terms of crossing fixed by said referees, but shall not delay the making of said crossing or connection: *Provided*, That the corporation desiring such crossing or connection shall deposit with the clerk of the court the amount of compensation, if any is fixed by said referees, and shall execute and file with said clerk a bond of sufficient security, to be approved by the court or a judge thereof in vacation, to pay all damages and comply with all terms that may be adjudged by the court. Any railway company which shall violate or evade any of the provisions of this section shall forfeit for every such offense, to the person, company, or corporation injured thereby, three times the actual damages sustained by the party aggrieved.

Sec. 18. That when in any case two or more railroads crossing each other at a common grade shall, by a system of interlocking or automatic signals, or by any works or fixtures to be erected by them, render it safe for engines and trains to pass over such crossing without stopping, and such interlocking or automatic signals or works or fixtures shall be approved by the Interstate Commerce Commissioners. then, in that case, it is hereby made lawful for the engines and trains of such railroad or railroads to pass over such crossing without stopping, any law or the provisions of any law to the contrary notwithstanding; and when two or more railroads cross each other at a common grade, either of such roads may apply to the Interstate Commerce Commissioners for permission to introduce upon both of said railroads some system of interlocking or automatic signals or works or fixtures rendering it safe for engines and trains to pass over such crossings without stopping, and it shall be the duty of said Interstate Commerce Commissioners, if the system of works and fixtures which it is proposed to erect by said company are, in the opinion of the Commission, sufficient and proper to grant such permission.

SEC. 19. That any railroad company which has obtained permission to introduce a system of interlocking or automatic signals at its crossing at a common grade with any other railroad, as provided in the last section, may, after thirty days' notice, in writing, to such other railroad company, introduce and erect such interlocking or automatic signals or fixtures; and if such railroad company, after such notification, refuses to join with the railroad company giving such notice in the construction of such works or fixtures, it shall be lawful for said company to enter upon the right of way and tracks of such second company, in such manner as to not unnecessarily impede the operation of such road, and erect such works and fixtures, and may recover in any action at law from such second company one-half of the total cost of erecting and maintaining such interlocking or automatic signals or works or fixtures on both of said roads.

SEC. 20. That all mortgages executed by any railway company conveying any portion of its railway, with its franchises, that may be constructed in said Indian Territory, shall be recorded in the Department of the Interior, and the record thereof shall be evidence and notice of their execution, and shall convey all rights, franchises, and property of said company as therein expressed.

SEC. 21. That Congress hereby reserves the right at any time to alter, amend, or repeal this act, or any portion thereof.

SEC. 22. That any railway company which has heretofore acquired, or may hereafter acquire, under any other act of Congress, a railroad right of way in Indian Territory may, in the manner herein prescribed, obtain any or all of the benefits and advantages of this act, and in such event shall become subject to all the requirements and responsibilttfes imposed by this act upon railroad companies acquiring a right of way hereunder. And where the time for the completion of a railroad in Indian Territory under any act granting a right of way therefor has expired, or shall hereafter expire, in advance of the construction of such railroad, or of any part thereof, the Secretary of the Interior may, upon good cause shown, extend the time for the completion of such railroad, or of any part thereof, for a time not exceeding two years from the date of such extension.

SEC. 23. That an act entitled "An act to provide for the acquiring of rights of way by railroad companies through Indian reservations, Indian lands, and Indian allotments, and for other purposes," approved March second, eighteen hundred and ninety-nine, so far as it applies to the Indian Territory and Oklahoma Territory, and all other acts or parts of acts inconsistent with this act are hereby repealed: *Provided*, That such repeal shall not affect any railroad company whose railroad is now actually being constructed, or any rights which have already accrued; but such railroads may be completed and such rights enforced in the manner provided by the laws under which such construction was commenced or under which such rights accrued: *And provided further*, That the provisions of this act shall apply also to the Osages' Reservation and other Indian reservations and allotted Indian lands in the Territory of Olahoma, and all judicial proceedings herein authorized may be commenced and prosecuted in the courts of said Oklahoma Territory which may now or hereafter exercise jurisdiction within said reservations or allotted lands.

Approved, February 28, 1902.

APPENDIX NO. 12.

REGULATIONS PRESCRIBED BY THE SECRETARY OF THE INTERIOR TO GOVERN MINERAL LEASES IN THE CHOCTAW AND CHICKASAW NATIONS, INDIAN TERRITORY, UNDER THE PROVISIONS OF THE AGREEMENT OF APRIL 23, 1897, BETWEEN THE COMMISSION TO THE FIVE CIVILIZED TRIBES AND THE SAID CHOCTAW AND CHICKASAW NATIONS, AS RATIFIED BY ACT OF CONGRESS OF JUNE 28, 1898. (30 STAT., 495.)

MINERAL LEASES.

1. The agreement with the Choctaw and Chickasaw nations set out in section 29 of the act of Congress entitled "An act for the protection of the people of the Indian Territory, and for other purposes," approved June 28, 1898 (30 Stat., 495–510), which was duly ratified on August 24, 1898, provides that the leasing and operating of coal and asphalt lands in said nations shall be under the control of two trustees appointed by the President of the United States upon the recommendation of the executives of said nations, each of whom shall be an Indian by blood of the respective nation for which he may be appointed.

2. Each trustee to be appointed under the provisions of said agreement shall be required to file a bond, with two good and sufficient sureties or an approved trust or surety company; with the Secretary of the Interior in the penal sum of ten thousand dollars, conditioned for the faithful performance of his duties under said agreement as prescribed therein, and in accordance with these regulations. Said bonds shall be approved by the Secretary of the Interior before said trustees shall be permitted to enter upon their duties.

3. All applications must be made under oath, by parties desiring leases, to the United States Indian inspector located in the Indian Territory, upon blanks to be furnished by the inspector. Each party will be required to state that the application is not made for speculation, but in good faith for mining the mineral or minerals specified. A map must be filed with each application, showing the amount of land on each legal subdivision supposed to be underlaid with mineral and the quantity of mineral that can properly be mined. Applicants must furnish in detail any other information desired by the inspector regarding their prospective operations. All applications received by the inspector will, if satisfactory to him, be transmitted to said trustees for an immediate report to him of facts, and when they are returned he will transmit them to the department, through the Commissioner of Indian Affairs, with his recommendations. Applications by parties who do not themselves intend to operate mines upon the land applied for will be rejected by the inspector, subject to appeal, as provided hereafter in cases of controversies between applicants. Leases will not be transferable or negotiable, except with the consent of the Secretary, and any instrument with that purpose in view must be approved by him before it will become valid. No application will be received for any other mineral than coal and asphalt.

Should parties whose applications have been approved, and who have been so advised, fail to execute leases in accordance with these regulations within thirty days from notice, or to give good reason for such failure, the land applied for will be subject to lease by other parties. They should be so informed at time of notice of approval.

Said trustees shall at all times be under the direction and supervision of the inspector, and shall also make an examination from time to time, as often as it shall be deemed expedient, and at least once in every month, into the operations of all persons, corporations, or companies operating mines within said nations, with a view of ascertaining the quantity of mineral produced by each, the amount of royalty, if any, due and unpaid by each, and all other information necessary for the protection of the interests of the Choctaw and Chickasaw nations in the premises; and for this purpose all persons, corporations, or companies operating mines within the Choctaw and Chickasaw nations shall give said trustees access to any and all of their books and records necessary or required by them to be examined, and within fifteen days after the last day of each quarter said trustees shall make a joint report to the Secretary of the Interior, through the inspector, of all their acts under said agreement and these regulations.

4. All indentures of lease made by the trustees, as above provided, shall be in quadruplicate and shall contain a clear and full description by legal subdivisions of the tract or tracts of land covered thereby, not to exceed nine hundred and sixty acres, which legal subdivisions must be contiguous to each other. Said indentures of lease so executed shall be transmitted through the United States Indian inspector stationed in the Indian Territory to the Commissioner of Indian Affairs, for submission to the Secretary of the Interior, for his approval, and no lease shall be valid until the same shall have been approved by the Secretary of the Interior.

5. Royalties shall be required of all lessees as follows, viz:

On coal, 8 cents per ton of 2,000 pounds on mine run, or coal as it is taken from the mines, including that which is commonly called "slack," which rate went into force and effect on and after March 1, 1900.

On asphalt, 60 cents per ton for each and every ton produced weighing 2,000 pounds, of refined, and 10 cents per ton on crude asphalt.

The right is reserved, however, by the Secretary of the Interior in special cases to either reduce or advance the royalty on coal and asphalt on the presentation of facts which, in his opinion, make it to the interest of the Choctaw and Chickasaw nations, but the advancement or reduction of royalty on coal and asphalt in a particular case shall not operate in any way to modify the general provisions of this regulation fixing the minimum royalty as above set out.

Provided, That all lessees shall be required to pay advanced royalties, as provided in said agreement, on all mines or claims, whether developed or not, to be "a credit on royalty when each said mine is developed and operated and its production is in excess of such guaranteed annual advanced payments," as follows, viz: One hundred dollars per annum in advance for the first and second years, two hundred dollars per annum in advance for the third and fourth years, and five hundred dollars in advance for each succeeding year thereafter; and that, should any lessee neglect or refuse to pay such advanced royalty for the period of sixty days after the same becomes due and payable on any lease, the lease on which default is made shall become null and void, and all royalties paid in advance shall be forfeited and become the money and property of the Choctaw and Chickasaw nations.

All advanced royalties as above defined shall apply from date of approval of each lease, and when any mine on a tract leased is operated royalty due shall be paid monthly as required until the total amount paid equals the first annual advanced payment, after which royalty due shall be credited on such payments; and the lessee shall operate and produce coal from each and every lease in not less than the following quantities: Three thousand tons during the first year from date of approval of lease; four thousand tons the second year; seven thousand tons the third year; eight thousand tons the fourth year, and fifteen thousand tons the fifth and each succeeding year thereafter.

6. All lessees of coal and asphalt on land allotted, sold, or reserved shall be required, before the commencement of operations, to pay to the individual owner the value of the use of the necessary surface for prospecting and mining, including the right of way for necessary railways and the damage done to the lands and improvements; and in case of disagreement, for the purpose of the ascertainment of the fair value of the use of the land and the actual damage done, the owner of the land and the lessee shall each select an arbitrator, who, together with such person as shall be appointed or designated by the inspector located in the Indian Territory, shall constitute a board to consider and ascertain the amount that shall be paid by the lessee on account of use of the land and damage done, and the award of such board shall be final and conclusive, unless the award be impeached for fraud. All timber and other materials taken by the lessee from land allotted, sold, or reserved for use in the erection of buildings thereon, and in the mine or mines operated by him thereon, as for shoring levels in coal mines, and so forth, shall be paid for by the lessee at the usual rates.

7. Persons, corporations, and companies who, under the customs and laws of the Choctaw and Chickasaw nations, have made leases with the national agents of said nations of lands therein for the purpose of mining coal or asphalt, and who, prior to April 23, 1897, had taken possession of and were operating in good faith any mine of coal or asphalt in said nation, shall be protected in their right to continue the operation of such mines for the period and on the terms contained in the lease made to said persons, corporations, or companies by such national agents, and shall have the right, at the expiration of said term, to renew the lease of such mines, subject, however, to all the provisions of the said agreement and of these regulations: *Provided*, That such persons, corporations, or companies shall, within sixty days after the expiration of their leases with the national agents of the Choctaw and Chickasaw nations, apply to the said trustees for a renewal of their leases under said agreement.

8. All leases made prior to April 23, 1897, by any person or corporation with any member or members of the Choctaw or Chickasaw nations, the object of which was to obtain the permission of such member or members to operate coal or asphalt mines within the said nations, are declared void by said agreement, and no person, corporation, or company occupying any lands within either of said nations, under such individual leases, or operating coal or asphalt mines on such lands, under color of such leases, shall be deemed to have any right or preference in the making of any lease or leases for mining purposes embracing the lands covered by such personal leases, by reason thereof; but parties in possession of such land who have made improvements thereon for the purpose of mining coal or asphalt shall have a preference right to lease the land upon which said improvements have been made, under the provisions of said agreement and these regulations.

9. Where two or more persons, corporations, or companies shall make application for the leasing of the same tract of land for mining purposes, and a controversy arises between such persons, corporations, or companies as to the right of each to obtain the lease of such land, it shall be the duty of the United States Indian inspector stationed in the Indian Territory to investigate into the right of the parties and determine as to which shall be given the right to lease the lands in controversy, subject to appeal to the Commissioner of Indian Affairs, and from him to the Secretary of the Interior.

Twenty days from notice of any decision by the United States inspector, or the Commissioner of Indian Affairs, not interlocutory, will be allowed for appeal and service of the same upon the opposite party, whether notice of the decision is given by mail or personally. When notice is given by the inspector by mail it shall be by registered letter.

In cases pending on appeal before the Commissioner of Indian Affairs, or the Department, argument may be filed at any time before the same is reached in order for examination, and copy of the same shall be served upon the opposite party, and he shall be allowed ten days for reply and to serve the same.

Proof of personal service of appeal or agument shall be the written acknowledgment of the person served or the affidavit of the person who served the same attached thereto, stating the time, place, and manner of service. All notices shall be served upon the attorneys of record.

Proof of service by registered letter shall be the affidavit of the person mailing the letter, attached to a copy of the post-office receipt.

No leases will be executed where a conflict exists until the matter has been finally adjudicated by the Department, in case of appeal.

10. All lessees will be required to keep a full and correct account of all their operations under leases entered into under said agreement and these regulations, and their books shall be open at all times to the examination of said trustees, of the United States Indian inspector stationed in the Indian Territory, and such other officer or officers of the Indian department as shall be instructed by the Secretary of the Interior or the Commissioner of Indian Affairs to make such examination; but, except as to the said trustees and the United States Indian inspector located in the Indian Territory, no lessee will be held to have violated this regulation for refusing to permit an examination of his books by any person unless such person shall produce written instructions from the Secretary of the Interior or from the Commissioner of Indian Affairs requiring him to make such an examination, and said lessees shall make all their reports to said United States Indian inspector, and they shall be subject to any instructions given by him.

11. All royalties, including advanced royalties, as provided for in said agreement and in these regulations, shall be payable in lawful money of the United States, or exchange issued by a national bank in the United States, to the United States Indian agent at the Union Agency in the Indian Territory, who shall be at all times under the direction and supervision of the United States Indian inspector for the Indian Territory. The advanced royalties are payable one hundred dollars on the filing of the application, which may be made by a certified check on any national bank of the United States payable to the order of the United States Indian agent, which check shall be retained by the United States Indian inspector until the application is approved; one hundred dollars in one year thereafter; two hundred dollars in two years thereafter; two hundred dollars in three years thereafter, and five hundred dollars on the fourth and each succeeding year until the end of the term thereof. All monthly royalties shall be accompanied by a sworn statement, in duplicate, by the person, corporation, or company making the same as to the output of the mine of such person, corporation, or company for the month for which royalties may be tendered. One part of said sworn statement shall be filed with the United States Indian agent, to be transmitted to the Commissioner of Indian Affairs, and the other part thereof shall be filed with the United States Indian inspector located in the Indian Territory.

12. The said United States Indian agent shall receive and receipt for all royalties paid into his hands, when accompanied by a sworn statement as above provided, but not otherwise; and all royalties received by him shall be, as soon as practicable, deposited with the United States subtreasurer at St. Louis, in like manner as are deposited moneys known in the regulations of the Indian Office as miscellaneous receipts, Class III, with a statement showing the proportionate shares of each of the Choctaw and Chickasaw nations.

13. All royalties collected and deposited by the United States Indian agent, as above set forth, shall be held to the credit of the Choctaw and Chickasaw nations in their respective proportions, and shall be subject to disbursement by the Secretary of the Interior for the support of the schools of the Choctaw and Chickasaw nations in accordance with said agreement.

14. All lessees under said agreement and these regulations will be required to give bond, with two good and sufficient sureties or an approved surety company, for the faithful discharge of their obligations under their leases in such penalty as shall be prescribed in each case by the Secretary of the Interior, and until such bond is filed by the lessee and approved and accepted by the Secretary of the Interior no rights or interests under any lease shall accrue to such lessee.

15. The right to alter or amend these regulations is reserved.

E. A. HITCHCOCK,
Secretary of the Interior.

DEPARTMENT OF THE INTERIOR,
Washington, D. C., May 22, 1900.

FORMS.

APPLICATION FOR MINERAL LEASE.

(May 22, 1900.)

To THE UNITED STATES INDIAN INSPECTOR
   LOCATED IN THE INDIAN TERRITORY.

———— ————, desiring to avail ———— of the provisions of section twenty-nine of the act of Congress of June 28, 1898 (30 Stats., 495), entitled "An Act for the protection of the people of the Indian Territory, and for other purposes," hereby make—application to lease, for the purpose of mining ————, the following tract of land, viz: ———— ———— section ———— in township ———— of range ———— in the ———— Nation, containing ———— acres, more or less, the attached map showing the amount of land on each legal subdivision supposed to be underlaid with ———— and the quantity that can probably be mined; and ———— solemnly ———— that this application is made in good faith, and with no other object than that of mining the mineral specified.

Sworn to and subscribed before me this ———— day of ————, 190—.

Washington, D. C., ———— ————, 190—.
Approved:
———— ————,
  Secretary.

ADDITIONAL INFORMATION TO ACCOMPANY APPLICATION FOR MINING LEASE IN THE CHOCTAW AND CHICKASAW NATIONS, INDIAN TERRITORY.

———— ————, of ———— ————, makes the following statements, under oath, to accompany his application attached hereto, dated ————, for the purpose of mining ———— in the ———— Nation, covering the following described land: ———— ————.

1. The applicant has filed ———— other applications for leases to mine ———— in addition to the one herein asked, and is interested in ———— other ———— leases in the Indian Territory known as the ———— ————.

2. That he does not intend to sell or transfer this application or the lease arising therefrom; that there is no agreement, open or secret, whereby the applicant is to sell, assign, transfer to, or consolidate this application or the lease arising therefrom, with any other person or corporation whatsoever, but that the applicant proposes to operate the mines covered by his application for himself, or in case of a company or corporation, for said company or corporation.

3. Applicant has heretofore had ———— national contract with the Choctaw and Chickasaw Nations covering the land herein described. Under same, mines have been operated by the applicant on this tract for ———— years, such operations having been commenced on or about ———— by sinking a shaft or slope ———— feet, and has taken therefrom about ———— tons of ————, and has expended $———— in improvements on said tract, comprising ———— ————.

4. That the applicant will, within ———— months after formal lease is duly approved and delivered to him, commence active operations; that the applicant has ———— dollars now on hand for such operations, and that the applicant has good reasons to believe that he or it will produce from said mine ———— tons of ———— during the first year from the date of the approval of the lease; that he or it will produce ———— tons during the second year, and ———— tons during the third year, and that there is embraced within the tract applied for, from the best obtainable information, ———— tons of workable ————, and, in case of coal applications, there are ———— veins of coal on said tract, each vein ———— inches in thickness with a pitch of about ———— degrees; applicant further states that ———— acres of the tract applied for are underlaid with ———— as shown by the plat.

5. That the applicant will exercise no rights or privileges whatever under the application herein described nor commence operations until the lease shall have been duly approved and delivered to him.

6. That the applicant is a resident of ———— and engaged in the business of ————, and has had ———— years' experience in coal (or ————) business in company with ———— ————, at ————, and that there are ———— other persons interested in this application or lease, if granted; their names and post-office addresses are as follows:

—— ——. If the applicant is a corporation, the members interested in or composing the same are as follows: —— ——.

7. There is submitted herewith, in connection with said application, a certified check for $100, payable to the United States Indian agent, the same to be applied as advanced royalty on the lease applied for, as required by the regulations of the Secretary of the Interior.

(When the applicant is a corporation, the following should be filled out:)

8. Applicant is a corporation organized under the laws of the State of ——, with a capital stock of —— dollars; that there has been subscribed and paid into the treasury of the corporation, and now held subject to bona fide mining operations, the sum of —— dollars thereof.

The applicant's post-office is —— ——.

—— ——.
—— ——.
—— ——.

Subscribed and sworn to before me this —— day of ——, 190—.

—— ——.

NOTE.—When the applicant is a corporation the application and this affidavit must be signed by the proper officer thereof.

Plat accompanying should show land applied for, by legal subdivisions according to United States surveys, amount underlaid with mineral, veins of coal, etc., and any improvements, railroads, etc., that may be on the land.

If applicant has not heretofore operated under national contract, the word "No" should be inserted in the first line of section 3. and the latter clause of said section should be stricken out. If so operated, the word "shaft" or "slope" should be stricken out, as the case may be, unless mines have been operated by both, in which event the depth of each should be stated.

Each application should be confined to tracts underlaid with mineral so far as possible, and not exceed 960 acres in area. A less number of acres, however, will be considered.

[Transferable and negotiable only with the consent of the Secretary of the Interior.]

(Write all names and addresses in full.)

(May 22, 1900.)

INDIAN TERRITORY ASPHALT MINING LEASE (CHOCTAW AND CHICKASAW NATIONS).

Indenture of lease, made and entered into in quadruplicate, on this —— day of ——, A. D. 190—, by and between —— —— and —— ——, as mining trustees of the Choctaw and Chickasaw nations, parties of the first part, and —— —— of ——, county of ——, State of ——, part- of the second part, under and in pursuance of the provisions of the act of Congress approved June 28, 1898 (30 Stats., 495), the agreement set out in section twenty-nine thereof duly ratified on August 24, 1898, and the rules and regulations prescribed by the Secretary of the Interior on May 22, 1900, relative to mining leases in the Choctaw and Chickasaw nations.

Now, therefore, this indenture witnesseth: That the parties of the first part, for and in consideration of the royalties, covenants, stipulations, and conditions hereinafter contained and hereby agreed to be paid, observed, and performed by the part- of the second part, ——, executors, administrators, or assigns do hereby demise, grant, and let unto the part- of the second part, —— executors, administrators, or assigns, the following-described tract of land, lying and being within the —— Nation and within the Indian Territory, to wit: The —— —— of section ——, of township *a* ——, of range *b* ——, of the Indian meridian, and containing —— acres, more or less, for the full term of —— years from the date hereof for the sole purpose of prospecting for and mining asphalt —— ——.

In consideration of the premises, the part- of the second part hereby agree- and bind —— executors, administrators, or assigns to pay or cause to be paid to the United States Indian agent for the Union Agency, Indian Territory, as royalty, the sums of money as follows, to wit: —— cents per ton for each and every ton of asphalt produced weighing 2,000 pounds of refined and —— cents per ton on crude asphalt.

And all said royalties accruing for any month shall be due and payable on or before the twenty-fifth day of the month succeeding.

And the part- of the second part further agree- not to hold the land described for speculative purposes, but in good faith for mining the mineral specified.

---

a State whether north or south.   *b* State whether east or west.

And the part- of the second part further agree- and bind —— executors, administrators, or assigns to pay or cause to be paid to the United States Indian agent for the Union Agency, Indian Territory, as advanced royalty on each and every mine or claim within the tract of land covered by this lease, the sums of money as follows, to wit: One hundred dollars per annum, in advance, for the first and second years; two hundred dollars per annum, in advance, for the third and fourth years, and five hundred dollars per annum, in advance, for the fifth and each succeeding year thereafter of the term for which this lease is to run, it being understood and agreed that said sums of money to be paid as aforesaid shall be a credit on royalty should the part- of the second part develop and operate a mine or mines on the lands leased by this indenture and the production of such mine or mines exceed such sums paid as advanced royalty as above set forth; and further, that all advanced royalties as above defined shall apply from date of approval of each lease, and when any mine is operated royalty due shall be paid monthly as required until the total amount equals the first annual advanced payment, after which royalty due shall be credited on such payments; and further, that should the part- of the second part neglect or refuse to pay such advanced annual royalty for the period of sixty days after the same becomes due and payable under this lease, then this lease shall be null and void, and all royalties paid in advance shall become the money and property of the Choctaw and Chickasaw tribes of Indians, subject to the regulations of the Secretary of the Interior aforesaid.

The part- of the second part further covenant- and agree- to exercise diligence in the conduct of the prospecting and mining operations, and to open mines and operate the same in a workmanlike manner to the fullest possible extent on the above-described tract of land; to commit no waste upon said land or upon the mines that may be thereon, and to suffer no waste to be committed thereon; to take good care of the same, and to surrender and return the premises at the expiration of this lease to the parties of the first part in as good condition as when received, ordinary wear and tear in the proper use of the same for the purposes hereinbefore indicated and unavoidable accidents excepted, and not to remove therefrom any buildings or improvements erected thereon during said term by —— ——, the part- of the second part, but said buildings and improvements shall remain a part of said land and become the property of the owner of the land as a part of the consideration for this lease, in addition to the other considerations herein specified, except engines, tools, and machinery, which shall remain the property of the said part- of the second part; that —— will not permit any nuisance to be maintained on the premises, nor allow any intoxicating liquors to be sold or given away to be used for any purposes on the premises, and that —— will not use the premises for any other purpose than that authorized in this lease, nor allow them to be used for any other purpose; that —— will not at any time during the term hereby granted assign or transfer —— estate, interest, or term in said premises and land or the appurtenances thereto to any person or persons whomsoever without the written consent thereto of the parties of the first part being first obtained, subject to the approval of the Secretary of the Interior.

And the said part- of the second part further covenant- and agree- that —— will keep an accurate account of all mining operations, showing the whole amount of asphalt mined or removed, and that there shall be a lien on all implements, tools, movable machinery, and other personal chattels used in said prospecting and mining operations and upon all such asphalt obtained from the land herein leased as security for the monthly payment of said royalties.

And the part- of the second part agree- that this indenture of lease shall be subject in all respects to the rules and regulations heretofore or that may be hereafter prescribed under the said act of June 28, 1898, by the Secretary of the Interior relative to mineral leases in the Choctaw and Chickasaw nations; and further, that should the part- of the second part, —— executors, administrators, or assigns, violate any of the covenants, stipulations, or provisions of this lease, or fail for the period of thirty days to pay the stipulated monthly royalties provided for herein, then the Secretary of the Interior shall be at liberty, in his discretion, to avoid this indenture of lease and cause the same to be annulled, when all the rights, franchises, and privileges of the part- of the second part, —— executors, administrators, or assigns hereunder, shall cease and end without further proceedings.

That the part- of the second part —— firmly bound for the faithful compliance with the stipulations of this indenture by and under the bond made and executed by the part- of the second part as principal- and —— —— as suret- entered into the —— day of ——, ——, and which is on file in the Indian Office.

In witness whereof the said parties of the first and second parts have hereunto set their hands and affixed their seals the day and year first above mentioned.

a Witnesses:

———— ———— as to ———— ————,   [SEAL.]*b*
      Trustee for Choctaw Nation.

———— ———— as to ———— ————,   [SEAL.]
      Trustee for Chickasaw Nation.

———— ———— } as to ———— ————.   [SEAL.]

———— ———— } as to ———— ————.   [SEAL.]

———— ———— } as to ———— ————.   [SEAL.]

———— ———— } as to ———— ————.   [SEAL.]

———— ———— } as to ———— ————.   [SEAL.]

No. ————

DEPARTMENT OF THE INTERIOR,

WASHINGTON, D. C.

ASPHALT LEASE.

Mining Trustees.

TO

OF

Sec. ————, Tp. ————, R. ————, in the

———— Nation, Indian Territory.

Dated ———— ————, 190–.

Expires ———— ————, 19—.

DEPARTMENT OF THE INTERIOR,
U. S. INDIAN SERVICE,
UNION AGENCY,
Muscogee, I. T., ————, 190–.
Respectfully forwarded to the Commissioner of Indian Affairs for consideration with my report of even date.

———— ·————,
      Indian Inspector.

DEPARTMENT OF THE INTERIOR,
OFFICE OF INDIAN AFFAIRS,
Washington, D. C., ————, 190–.
Respectfully submitted to the Secretary of the Interior with favorable recommendation.

———— ————,
      Commissioner.

DEPARTMENT OF THE INTERIOR,
Washington, D. C., ————, 190–.
Approved:

———— ————,
      Secretary of the Interior.

[Transferable and negotiable only with the consent of the Secretary of the Interior.]

(Write all names and addresses in full.)

(May 22, 1900.)

INDIAN TERRITORY COAL MINING LEASE (CHOCTAW AND CHICKASAW NATIONS).

Indenture of lease, made and entered into in quadruplicate, on this ———— day of ————, A. D. 190–, by and between ———— ———— and ———— ————, as mining trustees of the Choctaw and Chickasaw nations, parties of the first part, and ———— ———— of ————, county of ————, State of ————, part– of the second part, under and in pursuance of the provisions of the act of Congress approved June 28, 1898

---

a Two witnesses to each signature, including signatures of trustees.
b Stamps are required by the act of June 13, 1898, to be placed on leases as follows, viz: Leases for one year, 25 cents; for more than one year and not exceeding three years, 50 cents; and for more than three years, $1. Lessees must furnish stamps for all leases.

(30 Stats., 495), the agreement set out in section twenty-nine thereof duly ratified on August 24, 1898, and the rules and regulations prescribed by the Secretary of the Interior on May 22, 1900, relative to mining leases in the Choctaw and Chickasaw nations.

Now, therefore, this indenture witnesseth, that the parties of the first part, for and in consideration of the royalties, covenants, stipulations, and conditions hereinafter contained and hereby agreed to be paid, observed, and performed by the part- of the second part, —— executors, administrators, or assigns, do hereby demise, grant, and let unto the part- of the second part, —— executors, administrators, or assigns, the following described tract of land, lying and being within the —— Nation, and within the Indian Territory, to wit: The —— —— of section ——, of township *a* ——, of range *b* —— of the Indian meridian, and containing —— acres, more or less, for the full term of —— years from the date hereof for the sole purpose of prospecting for and mining coal ——.

In consideration of the premises the part- of the second part hereby agree- and bind —— executors, administrators, or assigns, to pay or cause to be paid to the United States Indian agent for the Union Agency, Indian Territory, as royalty, the sums of money as follows, to wit:

On the production of all mines developed and operated under this lease the sum of —— cents per ton of 2,000 pounds on mine run, or coal as it is taken from the mines, including that which is commonly called "slack."

All of said royalties accruing for any month shall be due and payable on or before the twenty-fifth day of the month succeeding.

And the part- of the second part further agree- not to hold the land described for speculative purposes, but in good faith for mining the mineral specified.

And the part- of the second part further agree- and bind —— ——, executors, administrators, or assigns to pay or cause to be paid to the United States agent for the Union Agency, Indian Territory, as advanced royalty on each and every mine or claim within the tract of land covered by this lease the sums of money as follows, to wit: One hundred dollars per annum, in advance, for the first and second years; two hundred dollars per annum, in advance, for the third and fourth years; and five hundred dollars per annum, in advance, for the fifth and each succeeding year thereafter, of the term for which this lease is to run, it being understood and agreed that said sums of money to be paid as aforesaid shall be a credit on royalty should the part- of the second part develop and operate a mine or mines on the lands leased by this indenture, and the production of such mine or mines exceed such sums paid as advanced royalty as above set forth; and further, that all advanced royalties as above defined shall apply from date of approval of each lease, and when any mine is operated royalty due shall be paid monthly as required until the total amount paid equals the first annual advanced payment, after which royalty due shall be credited on such payments; and the part- of the second part agree- and bind —— ——, executors, administrators, or assigns to operate and produce coal from each and every lease of not less than the following quantities: Three thousand tons during the first year from date of approval of lease, four thousand tons the second year, seven thousand tons the third year, eight thousand tons the fourth year, and fifteen thousand tons the fifth and each succeeding year thereafter; and it is further agreed that should the part- of the second part neglect or refuse to pay such advanced annual royalty for the period of sixty days after the same becomes due and payable under this lease, then this lease shall be null and void, and all royalties paid in advance shall become the money and property of the Choctaw and Chickasaw tribes of the Indians, subject to the regulations of the Secretary of the Interior aforesaid.

The part- of the second part further covenant- and agree- to exercise diligence in the conduct of the prospecting and mining operations, and to open mines and operate the same in a workmanlike manner to the fullest possible extent on the above-described tract of land; to commit no waste upon said land or upon the mines that may be thereon, and to suffer no waste to be committed thereon; to take good care of the same, and to surrender and return the premises at the expiration of this lease to the parties of the first part in as good condition as when received, ordinary wear and tear in the proper use of the same for the purposes hereinbefore indicated and unavoidable accidents excepted, and not to remove therefrom any buildings or improvements erected thereon during said term by —— ——, the part- of the second part, but said buildings and improvements shall remain a part of said land and become the property of the owner of the land as a part of the consideration for this lease, in addition to the other considerations herein specified—except engines, tools, and machinery, which shall remain the property of the said part- of the sec-

---

a State whether north or south.   *b* State whether east or west.

ond part; that ———— will not permit any nuisance to be maintained on the premises, nor allow any intoxicating liquors to be sold or given away to be used for any purposes on the premises, and that———— will not use the premises for any other purpose than that authorized in this lease, nor allow them to be used for any other purpose; that ———— will not at any time during the term hereby granted, assign or transfer ———— estate, interest, or term in said premises and land or the appurtenances thereto to any person or persons whomsoever without the written consent thereto of the parties of the first part being first obtained, subject to the approval of the Secretary of the Interior.

And the said part- of the second part further covenant- and agree- that ———— will keep an accurate account of all mining operations, showing the whole amount of coal mined or removed, and that there shall be a lien on all implements, tools, movable machinery, and other personal chattels used in said prospecting and mining operations, and upon all such coal obtained from the land herein leased, as security for the monthly payment of said royalties.

And the part- of the second part agree- that this indenture of lease shall be subject in all respects to the rules and regulations heretofore or that may be hereafter prescribed under the said act of June 28, 1898, by the Secretary of the Interior relative to mineral leases in the Choctaw and Chickasaw nations; and further, that should the part- of the second part, ———— executors, administrators, or assigns, violate any of the covenants, stipulations, or provisions of this lease, or fail for the period of thirty days to pay the stipulated monthly royalties provided for herein, then the Secretary of the Interior shall be at liberty, in his discretion, to avoid this indenture or lease, and cause the same to be annulled, when all the rights, franchises, and privileges of the part- of the second part, ———— executors, administrator, or assigns, hereunder shall cease and end, without further proceedings.

The part- of the second part ———— firmly bound for the faithful compliance with the stipulations of this indenture by and under the bond made and executed by the part- of the second part as principal- and ———— ———— as suret-, entered into the ———— day of ————, ————, and which is on file in the Indian Office.

In witness whereof, the said parties of the first and second parts have hereunto set their hands and affixed their seals the day and year first above mentioned.

a Witnesses:

———— ———— as to ———— ————, [SEAL.]*b*
Trustee for Choctaw Nation.

———— ———— as to ———— ————, [SEAL.]
Trustee for Chickasaw Nation.

———— ————} as to ———— ————. [SEAL.]

———— ————} as to ———— ————. [SEAL.]

———— ————} as to ———— ————. [SEAL.]

———— ————} as to ———— ————. [SEAL.]

———— ————} as to ———— ————. [SEAL.]

a Two witnesses to each signature, including signatures of trustees.
b Stamps are required by the act of June 13, 1898, to be placed on leases as follows, viz: Leases for one year, 25 cents; for more than one year and not exceeding three years, 50 cents; and for more than three years, $1. Lessees must furnish stamps for all leases.

DEPARTMENT OF THE INTERIOR,
U. S. INDIAN SERVICE,
UNION AGENCY,

Muscogee, I. T., ————, 190—

Respectfully forwarded to the Commissioner of Indian Affairs for consideration with my report of even date.

————, Indian Inspector.

DEPARTMENT OF THE INTERIOR,
OFFICE OF INDIAN AFFAIRS,

Washington, D. C., ————, 190—.

Respectfully submitted to the Secretary of the Interior with favorable recommendation.

————, Commissioner.

DEPARTMENT OF THE INTERIOR,

Washington, D. C., ————, 190—.

Approved:

————, Secretary of the Interior.

No. ————

DEPARTMENT OF THE INTERIOR,
WASHINGTON D. C.

COAL LEASE.

———— Mining trustees,

TO

———— of ————

Sec. ————, Twp. ————, Range ————,
in the ———— Nation, Indian Territory.
Dated ————, 190-.
Expires ————, 19—.

BOND.

(May 22, 1900.)

Know all men by these presents, that [a]———— ————, of ———— ————, as principal-, and ———— ————, of ———— ————, as surety, are held and firmly bound unto the United States of America in the sum of ———— dollars, lawful money of the United States, for the payment of which, well and truly to be made, we bind ourselves, and each of us, our heirs, successors, executors, and administrators, jointly and severally, firmly by these presents.

Sealed with our seals, and dated ———— day of ————.

The condition of this obligation is such, that whereas the above-bounden ————
————, as principal-, entered into ———— certain indenture- of lease, dated ———— ————, with ———— and ———— ————, mining trustees of the Choctaw and Chickasaw nations, for the lease of a certain tract of land located in the ———— Nation, Indian Territory, for the purpose of prospecting for and mining ———— for the period of ———— years.

Now, if the above-bounden ———— ———— shall faithfully carry out and observe all the obligations assumed in said indenture- of lease by ———— ————, and shall observe

---

[a] The Christian names and residences of principals.

all the laws of the United States, and regulations made or which shall be made thereunder, for the government of trade and intercourse with Indian tribes, and all the rules and regulations that have been or may be prescribed by the Secretary of the Interior, under the act of June 28, 1898 (30 Stat., 495), relative to mining leases in the Choctaw and Chickasaw nations, in the Indian Territory, then this obligation shall be null and void, otherwise to remain in full force and effect.

Signed and sealed in the presence of—*b*

——— ———.   ——— ———.   [L. S.] *c*
——— ———.   ——— ———.   [L. S.]
——— ———.   ——— ———.   [L. S.]
——— ———.   ——— ———.   [L. S.]
——— ———.   ——— ———.   [L. S.]
——— ———.   ——— ———.   [L. S.]

DEPARTMENT OF THE INTERIOR, WASHINGTON, D. C.

BOND OF

——— Lessee of ——— in the ——— Nation, Indian Territory, for mining purposes.

WASHINGTON, D. C., ———, 190—.

Approved:

——— Secretary.

OATH.

We, the undersigned, mining trustees of the Choctaw and Chickasaw nations, Indian Territory, do solemnly swear that the leases hereunto annexed, numbered ———, to ———, were made by us personally with ——— ———, of ——— ———; that we have made the same fairly, without any benefit or advantage to ourselves, severally or jointly, or allowing any such benefit or advantage corruptly to the said ——— ——— (for mining purposes in the said nations), or any other person or persons.

———,
Trustee, Choctaw Nation.

———,
Trustee, Chickasaw Nation.

Subscribed and sworn to before me at ——— this ——— day of ———, 190—.

———,
Notary Public.

My commission expires ———, ———.

APPENDIX NO. 13.

[Copy of opinion of Judge William H. H. Clayton of the central district of the Indian Territory, in the matter of the application of the chairman of the Choctaw Townsite Commission for the appointment of the third commissioner to appraise certain lots in the town of South McAlester, Ind. T., opinion rendered about July 19, 1901.]

I find the facts to be: That these commissioners, appointed under the law, to lay out the town sites in the Choctaw Nation, found a pond or reservoir which had been

———

b There must be at least two witnesses to all signatures, though the same two persons may witness all.

c A seal must be attached by some adhesive substance to the signatures of principals and sureties.

Whereas said commission has appraised all of the town lots included in said plat at their true value, excluding improvements, which appraisal has been approved by the Secretary of the Interior; and

Whereas the said commission has awarded the real estate described hereinbelow to —— ——, who has paid —— dollars, the full amount of the purchase price, into the Treasury of the United States, to the credit of the Muskogee or Creek Nation of Indians, with the United States Indian agent, at ——, Indian Territory, and is, therefore, entitled to a patent;

Now, therefore, I, the undersigned, the principal chief of the Muskogee (Creek) Nation, do, by virtue of the power and authority vested in me by the aforesaid act of the Congress of the United States, hereby grant, sell, and convey unto the said —— ——, heirs and assigns forever, all the right, title, and interest of the Muskogee (Creek) Nation, aforesaid, in and to lot ——, numbered ——, in block ——, numbered ——, in the town of ——, Muskogee (Creek) Nation, Indian Territory, and according to the plat thereof on file as aforesaid.

In witness whereof I, the principal chief of the Muskogee (Creek) Nation, have hereunto set my hand and caused the great seal of said nation to be affixed, at the date hereinafter shown.

Date, —— ——, 190—.

[SEAL.]

————— —————,
Principal Chief of the Muskogee (Creek) Nation.

DEPARTMENT OF THE INTERIOR, ——— —, ——.

Approved ——— —, 190—.

——— ———, *Secretary.*

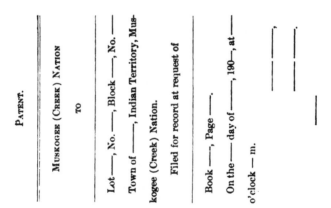

APPENDIX NO. 15.

THE CHOCTAW AND CHICKASAW NATIONS, INDIAN TERRITORY.

To all to whom these presents come, greeting:

Whereas a certain townsite commission, heretofore appointed, and acting in accordance with law, has appraised the lots in the town of ——, —— Nation, Indian Territory; and

Whereas the plat of said town was approved by the Secretary of the Interior on the —— day of ——, 1——, and was duly placed on file; and

Whereas the said commission has awarded the real estate described hereinbelow to —— ——, who has deposited —— dollars, the full amount of the purchase price, with the United States Indian agent at ——, Indian Territory, and is, therefore, entitled to a patent;

Now, therefore we, the undersigned, the principal chief of the Choctaw Nation and the governor of the Chickasaw Nation, do, by virtue of the power and authority vested in us by the twenty-ninth section of the act of Congress of the United States, approved June 28, 1898 (30 Stat., 495), hereby grant, sell, and convey unto the said ———— ————, heirs and assigns forever, all the right, title, and interest of the Choctaw and Chickasaw nations aforesaid in and to lot— numbered ————, in block— numbered ————, in the town of ————, ———— Nation, Indian Territory, and according to the plat thereof on file as aforesaid, saving and excepting from this conveyance, however, all coal and asphalt.

In witness whereof, we, the principal chief of the Choctaw Nation and the governor of the Chickasaw Nation, have hereunto set our hands and caused the great seal of our respective nations to be affixed at the dates hereinafter shown.

Date, ———— —, 190—.
[SEAL.]

————— —————,
Principal Chief of the Choctaw Nation.

Date, ———— —, 190—.
[SEAL.]

————— —————,
Governor of the Chickasaw Nation.

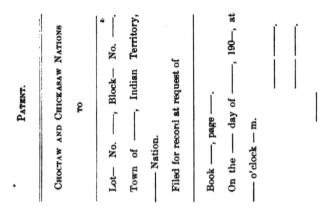

APPENDIX NO. 16.

REGULATIONS (JUNE 3, 1902) GOVERNING THE INTRODUCTION BY NONCITIZENS OF LIVE STOCK IN THE CHICKASAW NATION, INDIAN TERRITORY.

Section 29 of the act of Congress approved June 28, 1898 (30 Stat., 495), ratifying the agreement with the Choctaw and Chickasaw nations, Indian Territory, provides in part as follows:

It is further agreed that no act, ordinance, or resolution of the council of either the Choctaw or Chickasaw tribes, in any manner affecting the land of the tribe, or of the individuals, after allotment, or the moneys or other property of the tribe or citizens thereof (except appropriations for the regular and necessary expenses of the government of the respective tribes) or the rights of any persons who have taken or may take the oath of allegiance to the United States, shall be of any validity until approved by the President of the United States. When such acts, ordinances, or resolutions passed by the councils of either of said tribes shall be approved by the governor thereof, then it shall be the duty of the national secretary of said tribe to forward them to the President of the United States, duly certified and sealed, who shall, within thirty days after their reception, approve or disapprove the same. Said acts, ordinances, or resolutions, when so approved, shall be published in at least two newspapers having a bona fide circulation in the tribe to be affected thereby, and when disapproved shall be returned to the tribe enacting the same.

It is further agreed, in view of the modification of legislative authority and judicial jurisdiction herein provided, and the necessity of the continuance of the tribal governments so modified, in order to carry out the requirements of this agreement, that the same shall continue for a period of eight years from the fourth day of March, eighteen hundred and ninety-eight.

Under these provisions, the following act of the Chickasaw National Council, approved by the governor on May 3, 1902, was approved by the President of the United States on May 15, 1902, and entitled:

AN ACT To prescribe privilege or permit taxes and defining the manner of their collection.

Be it enacted by the legislature of the Chickasaw Nation:

SECTION 1. That there shall be paid upon live stock owned or held by noncitizens within the limits of the Chickasaw Nation an annual privilege or permit tax as follows: On cattle, horses, and mules, twenty-five cents per head; and on sheep and goats, five cents per head: *Provided*, That there shall be exempted from the provisions of this act, when owned and used by the head of a family, two cows and calves and one team, consisting of two horses or two mules, or one horse and one mule; and the provisions of this act shall also apply to all live stock introduced into the Chickasaw Nation since January 1, 1902, upon which the tribal taxes imposed by the laws of the Chickasaw Nation have not been paid, with like force and effect as if such cattle had been owned and held within the limits of Chickasaw Nation for one year prior to the passage and approval of this act.

SEC. 2. That such privilege or permit taxes shall hereafter be payable to such person or persons, and collected under such rules and regulations as may be prescribed by the Secretary of the Interior.

SEC. 3. That the expenses of collecting such privilege or permit taxes shall be deducted from the gross collections, and the balance paid quarterly into the treasury of the Chickasaw Nation.

SEC. 4. That such privilege or permit taxes shall be due and payable annually, upon demand, and if such taxes are not paid when demanded, the live stock upon which such taxes are due shall be held to be in the Chickasaw Nation without its consent, and unlawfully upon the lands of the Chickasaws, and the presence of such live stock, and owners or holders thereof, within the limits of said nation, shall be deemed detrimental to the peace and welfare of the Chickasaw Indians.

SEC. 5. That all acts or parts of acts in conflict herewith be, and the same are hereby, repealed; and this act shall take effect from and after its approval by the President of the United States.

In pursuance of the above and foregoing, the following regulations are promulgated:

Regulations prescribed by the Secretary of the Interior governing the introduction or holding of live stock in the Chickasaw Nation by noncitizens.

SECTION 1. Any person other than a recognized citizen of the Choctaw or Chickasaw nations desiring to introduce or hold stock of any description within the limits of the Chickasaw Nation, Indian Territory, shall first make application to the United States Indian inspector for the Indian Territory, Muskogee, Ind. T., and shall pay to the United States Indian agent, Union Agency, an annual tax of 25 cents per head on all cattle, horses, and mules, and on all sheep and goats 5 cents per head, provided that there shall be exempted from the provisions of these regulations, when owned and used by the head of a family, two cows and calves, and one team of horses, or two mules, or one horse and one mule.

SEC. 2. Such tax shall be paid January 1 of each year, or prior to the time of the introduction of such stock, and accompanying such remittance there shall be furnished, under oath, a full description of such stock, including the number and brands, together with any other desired information.

SEC. 3. Such taxes shall apply to all stock introduced within the limits of the Chickasaw Nation since January 1, 1902, upon which taxes have not already been paid to the Chickasaw Nation and for which the owners or holders can not produce receipts.

SEC. 4. The tax prescribed shall be paid annually in advance, whether such stock is held the entire succeeding twelve months or for a portion of such time.

SEC. 5. Where cattle are held by a citizen and mortgaged to a noncitizen, not in good faith, but for the purpose of evading the payment of taxes, said cattle shall be considered as owned or held by such noncitizen, and subject to these regulations and taxes.

SEC. 6. Parties who now hold stock within the limits of the Chickasaw Nation should remit the taxes prescribed promptly to the United States Indian agent at Muskogee, Ind. T., and such payments must be made within ten days from the date of receiving notice of these regulations. If such taxes are not paid within this time remittances made thereafter will not be accepted, but such stock and any other stock found within the limits of the Chickasaw Nation after July 1, 1902, upon which taxes have not been paid, will be considered as being within the limits of the Chickasaw Nation unlawfully, and measures will be adopted looking to the removal by the United States Indian agent of such stock, together with the owners or holders thereof, without further notice.

SEC. 7. Authorized agents of the Interior Department will make necessary investigations and reports and see that proper remittances are forwarded, acting under the direction of the United States Indian inspector for Indian Territory, but will not be authorized to receive or collect any taxes whatsoever, as all payments must be made direct to the United States Indian agent, who will furnish receipts for all payments made.

SEC. 8. These regulations and taxes will apply to all stock as indicated, held within the limits of the Chickasaw Nation by other than recognized citizens of the Choctaw or Chickasaw nations, whether held upon the public domain or upon lands leased from individual Indians.

THOS. RYAN, *Acting Secretary.*

DEPARTMENT OF THE INTERIOR,
Washington, D. C.

Approved, June 3, 1902.

APPENDIX NO. 17.

[PUBLIC—No. 228.]

AN ACT To ratify and confirm an agreement with the Choctaw and Chickasaw tribes of Indians, and for other purposes.

Be it enacted by the Senate and House of Representatives of the United States of America in Congress assembled, That the following agreement, made by the Commission to the Five Civilized Tribes with the commissions representing the Choctaw and Chickasaw tribes of Indians on the twenty-first day of March, nineteen hundred and two, be, and the same is hereby, ratified and confirmed, to wit:

AGREEMENT BETWEEN THE UNITED STATES AND THE CHOCTAWS AND CHICKASAWS.

This agreement, by and between the United States, entered into in its behalf by Henry L. Dawes, Tams Bixby, Thomas B. Needles, and Clifton R. Breckinridge, commissioners duly appointed and authorized thereunto, and the Choctaw and Chickasaw tribes of Indians in Indian Territory, respectively, entered into in behalf of such Choctaw and Chickasaw tribes, by Gilbert W. Dukes, Green McCurtain, Thomas E. Sanguin, and Simon E. Lewis in behalf of the Choctaw tribe of Indians; and Douglas H. Johnston, Calvin J. Grant, Holmes Willis, Edward B. Johnson, and Benjamin H. Colbert in behalf of the Chickasaw tribe of Indians, commissioners duly appointed and authorized thereunto—

Witnesseth that, in consideration of the mutual undertakings herein contained, it is agreed as follows:

DEFINITIONS.

1. Wherever used in this agreement the words "nations" and "tribes" shall each be held to mean the Choctaw and Chickasaw nations or tribes of Indians in Indian Territory.

2. The words "chief executives" shall be held to mean the principal chief of the Choctaw Nation and the governor of the Chickasaw Nation.

3. The words "member" or "members" and "citizen" or "citizens" shall be held to mean members or citizens of the Choctaw or Chickasaw tribe of Indians in Indian Territory, not including freedmen.

4. The term "Atoka agreement" shall be held to mean the agreement made by the Commission to the Five Civilized Tribes with the commissioners representing the Choctaw and Chickasaw tribes of Indians at Atoka, Indian Territory, and embodied in the act of Congress approved June twenty-eighth, eighteen hundred and ninety-eight. (30 Stats., 495.)

5. The word "minor" shall be held to mean males under the age of twenty-one years and females under the age of eighteen years.

6. The word "select" and its various modifications, as applied to allotments and homesteads, shall be held to mean the formal application at the land office, to be established by the Commission to the Five Civilized Tribes for the Choctaw and Chickasaw nations, for particular tracts of land.

7. Every word in this agreement importing the masculine gender may extend and be applied to females as well as males, and the use of the plural may include also the singular, and vice versa.

8. The terms "allottable lands" or "lands allottable" shall be deemed to mean all the lands of the Choctaw and Chickasaw tribes not herein reserved from allotment.

APPRAISEMENT OF LANDS.

9. All lands belonging to the Choctaw and Chickasaw tribes in the Indian Territory, except such as are herein reserved from allotment, shall be appraised at their true value: *Provided,* That in determining such value consideration shall not be given to the location thereof, to any mineral deposits, or to any timber except such pine timber as may have been heretofore estimated by the Commission to the Five Civilized Tribes, and without reference to improvements which may be located thereon.

10. The appraisement as herein provided shall be made by the Commission to the Five Civilized Tribes, and the Choctaw and Chickasaw tribes shall each have a representative to be appointed by the respective executives to cooperate with the said Commission.

11. There shall be allotted to each member of the Choctaw and Chickasaw tribes, as soon as practicable after the approval by the Secretary of the Interior of his enrollment as herein provided, land equal in value to three hundred and twenty acres of the average allottable land of the Choctaw and Chickasaw nations, and to each Choctaw and Chickasaw freedman, as soon as practicable after the approval by the Secretary of the Interior of his enrollment, land equal in value to forty acres of the average allottable land of the Choctaw and Chickasaw nations; to conform, as nearly as may be, to the areas and boundaries established by the Government survey, which land may be selected by each allottee so as to include his improvements. For the purpose of making allotments and designating homesteads hereunder, the forty-acre or quarter-quarter subdivisions established by the Government survey may be dealt with as if further subdivided into four equal parts in the usual manner, thus making the smallest legal subdivision ten acres, or a quarter of a quarter of a quarter of a section.

12. Each member of said tribes shall, at the time of the selection of his allotment, designate as a homestead out of said allotment land equal in value to one hundred and sixty acres of the average allottable land of the Choctaw and Chickasaw nations, as nearly as may be, which shall be inalienable during the lifetime of the allottee, not exceeding twenty-one years from the date of certificate of allotment, and separate certificate and patent shall issue for said homestead.

13. The allotment of each Choctaw and Chickasaw freedman shall be inalienable during the lifetime of the allottee, not exceeding twenty-one years from the date of certificate of allotment.

14. When allotments as herein provided have been made to all citizens and freedmen, the residue of lands not herein reserved or otherwise disposed of, if any there be, shall be sold at public auction under rules and regulations and on terms to be prescribed by the Secretary of the Interior, and so much of the proceeds as may be necessary for equalizing allotments shall be used for that purpose, and the balance shall be paid into the Treasury of the United States to the credit of the Choctaws and Chickasaws and distributed per capita as other funds of the tribes.

15. Lands allotted to members and freedmen shall not be affected or encumbered by any deed, debt, or obligation of any character contracted prior to the time at which said land may be alienated under this act, nor shall such lands be sold except as herein provided.

16. All lands allotted to the members of said tribes, except such land as is set aside to each for a homestead as herein provided, shall be alienable after issuance of patent as follows: One-fourth in acreage in one year, one-fourth in acreage in three years, and the balance in five years; in each case from date of patent: *Provided,* That such land shall not be alienable by the allottee or his heirs at any time before the expiration of the Choctaw and Chickasaw tribal governments for less than its appraised value.

17. If, for any reason, an allotment should not be selected, or a homestead designated by or on behalf of any member or freedman, it shall be the duty of said Commission to make said selection and designation.

18. In the making of allotments and in the designation of homesteads for members of said tribes, under the provisions of this agreement, said Commission shall not be required to divide lands into tracts of less than the smallest legal subdivision provided for in paragraph eleven hereof.

19. It shall be unlawful after ninety days after the date of the final ratification of this agreement for any member of the Choctaw or Chickasaw tribes to enclose, or hold possession of in any manner, by himself or through another, directly or indirectly, more lands in value than that of three hundred and twenty acres of average allottable lands of the Choctaw and Chickasaw nations, as provided by the terms of this agreement, either for himself or for his wife, or for each of his minor children, if members of said tribes; and any member of said tribes found in such possession of lands, or having the same in any manner enclosed, after the expiration of ninety days after the date of the final ratification of this agreement, shall be deemed guilty of a misdemeanor.

20. It shall be unlawful after ninety days after the date of the final ratification of this agreement for any Choctaw or Chickasaw freedman to enclose or hold possession of in any manner, by himself or through another, directly or indirectly, more than so much land as shall be equal in value to forty acres of the average allottable lands of the Choctaw and Chickasaw tribes as provided by the terms of this agreement, either for himself or for his wife, or for each of his minor children, if they be Choctaw or Chickasaw freedmen; and any freedman found in such possession of lands, or *having the same in any manner enclosed after the expiration of ninety days after*

the date of the final ratification of this agreement, shall be deemed guilty of a misdemeanor.

21. Any person convicted of violating any of the provisions of sections 19 and 20 of this agreement shall be punished by a fine not less than one hundred dollars, and shall stand committed until such fine and costs are paid (such commitment not to exceed one day for every two dollars of said fine and costs) and shall forfeit possession of any property in question, and each day on which such offense is committed or continues to exist shall be deemed a separate offense. And the United States district attorneys for the districts in which said nations are situated are required to see that the provisions of said sections are strictly enforced, and they shall immediately after the expiration of ninety days after the date of the final ratification of this agreement proceed to dispossess all persons of such excessive holdings of lands, and to prosecute them for so unlawfully holding the same. And the Commission to the Five Civilized Tribes shall have authority to make investigation of all violations of sections 19 and 20 of this agreement, and make report thereon to the United States district attorneys.

22. If any person whose name appears upon the rolls, prepared as herein provided, shall have died subsequent to the ratification of this agreement and before receiving his allotment of land the lands to which such person would have been entitled if living shall be allotted in his name, and shall, together with his proportionate share of other tribal property, descend to his heirs according to the laws of descent and distribution as provided in chapter forty-nine of Mansfield's Digest of the Statutes of Arkansas: *Provided*, That the allotment thus to be made shall be selected by a duly appointed administrator or executor. If, however, such administrator or executor be not duly and expeditiously appointed, or fails to act promptly when appointed, or for any other cause such selection be not so made within a reasonable and practicable time, the Commission to the Five Civilized Tribes shall designate the lands thus to be allotted.

23. Allotment certificates issued by the Commission to the Five Civilized Tribes shall be conclusive evidence of the right of any allottee to the tract of land described therein; and the United States Indian agent at the Union Agency shall, upon the application of the allottee, place him in possession of his allotment, and shall remove therefrom all persons objectionable to such allottee; and the acts of the Indian agent hereunder shall not be controlled by the writ or process of any court.

24. Exclusive jurisdiction is hereby conferred upon the Commission to the Five Civilized Tribes to determine, under the direction of the Secretary of the Interior, all matters relating to the allotment of land.

EXCESSIVE HOLDINGS.

25. After the opening of a land office for allotment purposes in both the Choctaw and the Chickasaw nations any citizen or freedman of either of said nations may appear before the Commission to the Five Civilized Tribes at the land office in the nation in which his land is located and make application for his allotment and for allotments for members of his family and for other persons for whom he is lawfully authorized to apply for allotments, including homesteads, and shall, after the expiration of ninety days following the opening of such land offices any such applicant may make allegation that the land or any part of the land that he desires to have allotted is held by another citizen or person in excess of the amount of land to which said citizen or person is lawfully entitled, and that he desires to have said land allotted to him or members of his family as herein provided; and thereupon said Commission shall serve notice upon the person so alleged to be holding land in excess of the lawful amount to which he may be entitled, said notice to set forth the facts alleged and the name and post-office address of the person alleging the same, and the rights and consequences herein provided, and the person so alleged to be holding land contrary to law shall be allowed thirty days from the date of the service of said notice in which to appear at one of said land offices and to select his allotment and the allotments he may be lawfully authorized to select, including homesteads; and if at the end of the thirty days last provided for the person upon whom said notice has been served has not selected his allotment and allotments as provided, then the Commission to the Five Civilized Tribes shall immediately make or reserve said allotments for the person or persons who have failed to act in accordance with the notice aforesaid, having due regard for the best interest of said allottees, and after such allotments have been made or reserved by said Commission, then all other lands held or claimed or previously held or claimed by said person or persons shall be deemed a part of the public domain of the Choctaw and Chickasaw nations and be subject to disposition as such: *Provided*, That any persons who have previously applied for any

part of said lands shall have a prior right of allotment of the same in the order of their applications and as their lawful rights may appear.

If any citizen or freedman of the Choctaw and Chickasaw nations shall not have selected his allotment within twelve months after the date of the opening of said land offices in said nations, if not herein otherwise provided, and provided that twelve months shall have elapsed from the date of the approval of his enrollment by the Secretary of the Interior, then the Commission to the Five Civilized Tribes may immediately proceed to select an allotment, including a homestead, for such person, said allotment and homestead to be selected as the Commission may deem for the best interest of said person, and the same shall be of the same force and effect as if such selection had been made by such citizen or freedman in person, and all lands held or claimed by persons for whom allotments have been selected by the Commission as provided, and in excess of the amount included in said allotments, shall be a part of the public domain of the Choctaw and Chickasaw nations and be subject to disposition as such.

RESERVATIONS.

26. The following lands shall be reserved from the allotment of lands herein provided for:

(a) All lands set apart for town sites either by the terms of the Atoka agreement, the act of Congress of May 31, 1900 (31 Stats., 221), as herein assented to, or by the terms of this agreement.

(b) All lands to which, at the date of the final ratification of this agreement, any railroad company may under any treaty or act of Congress have a vested right for right of way, depots, station grounds, water stations, stock yards, or similar uses connected with the maintenance and operation of the railroad.

(c) The strip of land lying between the city of Fort Smith, Arkansas, and the Arkansas and Poteau rivers, extending up the said Poteau River to the mouth of Mill Creek.

(d) All lands which shall be segregated and reserved by the Secretary of the Interior on account of their coal or asphalt deposits, as hereinafter provided. And the lands selected by the Secretary of the Interior at and in the vicinity of Sulphur in the Chickasaw Nation, under the cession to the United States hereunder made by said tribes.

(e) One hundred and sixty acres for Jones' Academy.
(f) One hundred and sixty acres for Tuskahoma Female Seminary.
(g) One hundred and sixty acres for Wheelock Orphan Seminary.
(h) One hundred and sixty acres for Armstrong Orphan Academy.
(i) Five acres for capitol building of the Choctaw Nation.
(j) One hundred and sixty acres for Bloomfield Academy.
(k) One hundred and sixty acres for Lebanon Orphan Home.
(l) One hundred and sixty acres for Harley Institute.
(m) One hundred and sixty acres for Rock Academy.
(n) One hundred and sixty acres for Collins Institute.
(o) Five acres for the capitol building of the Chickasaw Nation.
(p) Eighty acres for J. S. Murrow.
(q) Eighty acres for H. R. Schermerhorn.
(r) Eighty acres for the widow of R. S. Bell.
(s) A reasonable amount of land, to be determined by the town-site commissioners, to include all tribal court-houses and jails and other tribal public buildings.
(t) Five acres for any cemetery located by the town-site commissioners prior to the date of the final ratification of this agreement.
(u) One acre for any church under the control of and used exclusively by the Choctaw or Chickasaw citizens at the date of the final ratification of this agreement.
(v) One acre each for all Choctaw or Chickasaw schools under the supervision of the authorities of the Choctaw or Chickasaw nations and officials of the United States.

And the acre so reserved for any church or school in any quarter section of land shall be located when practicable in a corner of such quarter section lying adjacent to the section line thereof.

ROLLS OF CITIZENSHIP.

27. The rolls of the Choctaw and Chickasaw citizens and Choctaw and Chickasaw freedmen shall be made by the Commission to the Five Civilized Tribes, in strict compliance with the act of Congress approved June 28, 1898 (30 Stats., 495), and the act of Congress approved May 31, 1900 (31 Stats., 221), except as herein otherwise provided: *Provided*, That no person claiming right to enrollment and allotment and dis-

tribution of tribal property, by virtue of a judgment of the United States court in the Indian Territory under the act of June 10, 1896 (29 Stats., 321), and which right is contested by legal proceedings instituted under the provisions of this agreement, shall be enrolled or receive allotment of lands or distribution of tribal property until his right thereto has been finally determined.

28. The names of all persons living on the date of the final ratification of this agreement entitled to be enrolled, as provided in section 27 hereof, shall be placed upon the rolls made by said Commission; and no child born thereafter to a citizen or freedman and no person intermarried thereafter to a citizen shall be entitled to enrollment or to participate in the distribution of the tribal property of the Choctaws and Chickasaws.

29. No person whose name appears upon the rolls made by the Commission to the Five Civilized Tribes as a citizen or freedman of any other tribe shall be enrolled as a citizen or freedman of the Choctaw or Chickasaw nations.

30. For the purpose of expediting the enrollment of the Choctaw and Chickasaw citizens and Choctaw and Chickasaw freedmen, the said Commission shall, from time to time, and as early as practicable, forward to the Secretary of the Interior lists upon which shall be placed the names of those persons found by the Commission to be entitled to enrollment. The lists thus prepared, when approved by the Secretary of the Interior, shall constitute a part and parcel of the final rolls of citizens of the Choctaw and Chickasaw tribes and of Choctaw and Chickasaw freedmen, upon which allotment of land and distribution of other tribal property shall be made as herein provided. Lists shall be made up and forwarded when contests of whatever character shall have been determined, and when there shall have been submitted to and approved by the Secretary of the Interior lists embracing names of all those lawfully entitled to enrollment, the rolls shall be deemed complete. The rolls so prepared shall be made in quintuplicate, one to be deposited with the Secretary of the Interior, one with the Commissioner of Indian Affairs, one with the principal chief of the Choctaw Nation, one with the governor of the Chickasaw Nation, and one to remain with the Commission to the Five Civilized Tribes.

31. It being claimed and insisted by the Choctaw and Chickasaw nations that the United States courts in the Indian Territory, acting under the act of Congress approved June 10, 1896, have admitted persons to citizenship or to enrollment as such citizens in the Choctaw and Chickasaw nations, respectively, without notice of the proceedings in such courts being given to each of said nations; and it being insisted by said nations that, in such proceedings, notice to each of said nations was indispensable, and it being claimed and insisted by said nations that the proceedings in the United States courts in the Indian Territory, under the said act of June 10, 1896, should have been confined to a review of the action of the Commission to the Five Civilized Tribes, upon the papers and evidence submitted to such Commission, and should not have extended to a trial de novo of the question of citizenship; and it being desirable to finally determine these questions, the two nations, jointly, or either of said nations acting separately and making the other a party defendant, may, within 90 days after this agreement becomes effective, by a bill in equity filed in the Choctaw and Chickasaw citizenship court hereinafter named, seek the annulment and vacation of all such decisions by said courts. Ten persons so admitted to citizenship or enrollment by said courts, with notice to one but not to both of said nations, shall be made defendants to said suit as representatives of the entire class of persons similarly situated, the number of such persons being too numerous to require all of them to be made individual parties to the suit; but any person so situated may, upon his application, be made a party defendant to the suit. Notice of the institution of said suit shall be personally served upon the chief executive of the defendant nation, if either nation be made a party defendant as aforesaid, and upon each of said ten representative defendants, and shall also be published for a period of four weeks in at least two weekly newspapers having general circulation in the Choctaw and Chickasaw nations. Such notice shall set forth the nature and prayer of the bill, with the time for answering the same, which shall not be less than thirty days after the last publication. Said suit shall be determined at the earliest practicable time, shall be confined to a final determination of the questions of law here named, and shall be without prejudice to the determination of any charge or claim that the admission of such persons to citizenship or enrollment by said United States courts in the Indian Territory was wrongfully obtained, as provided in the next section. In the event said citizenship judgments or decisions are annulled or vacated in the test suit hereinbefore authorized, because of either or both of the irregularities claimed and insisted upon by said nations as aforesaid, then the files, papers, and proceedings in any citizenship case in which the judgment or decision is so annulled or vacated shall, upon written application therefor, made within ninety days thereafter by any

party thereto, who is thus deprived of a favorable judgment upon his claimed citizenship, be transferred and certified to said citizenship court by the court having custody and control of such files, papers, and proceedings, and, upon the filing in such citizenship court of the files, papers, and proceedings in any such citizenship case, accompanied by due proof that notice in writing of the transfer and certification thereof has been given to the chief executive officer of each of said nations, said citizenship case shall be docketed in said citizenship court, and such further proceedings shall be had therein in that court as ought to have been had in the court to which the same was taken on appeal from the Commission to the Five Civilized Tribes, and as if no judgment or decision had been rendered therein.

32. Said citizenship court shall also have appellate jurisdiction over all judgments of the courts in Indian Territory rendered under said act of Congress of June tenth, eighteen hundred and ninety-six, admitting persons to citizenship or to enrollment as citizens in either of said nations. The right of appeal may be exercised by the said nations jointly or by either of them acting separately at any time within six months after this agreement is finally ratified. In the exercise of such appellate jurisdiction said citizenship court shall be authorized to consider, review, and revise all such judgments, both as to findings of fact and conclusions of law, and may, wherever in its judgment substantial justice will thereby be subserved, permit either party to any such appeal to take and present such further evidence as may be necessary to enable said court to determine the very right of the controversy. And said court shall have power to make all needful rules and regulations prescribing the manner of taking and conducting said appeals and of taking additional evidence therein. Such citizenship court shall also have like appellate jurisdiction and authority over judgments rendered by such courts under the said act denying claims to citizenship or to enrollment as citizens in either of said nations. Such appeals shall be taken within the time hereinbefore specified and shall be taken, conducted, and disposed of in the same manner as appeals by the said nations, save that notice of appeals by citizenship claimants shall be served upon the chief executive officer of both nations: *Provided*, That paragraphs thirty-one, thirty-two, and thirty-three hereof shall go into effect immediately after the passage of this act by Congress.

33. A court is hereby created to be known as the Choctaw and Chickasaw citizenship court, the existence of which shall terminate upon the final determination of the suits and proceedings named in the last two preceding sections, but in no event later than the thirty-first day of December, nineteen hundred and three. Said court shall have all authority and power necessary to the hearing and determination of the suits and proceedings so committed to its jurisdiction, including the authority to issue and enforce all requisite writs, process and orders, and to prescribe rules and regulations for the transaction of its business. It shall also have all the powers of a circuit court of the United States in compelling the production of books, papers, and documents, the attendance of witnesses, and in punishing contempt. Except where herein otherwise expressly provided, the pleadings, practice, and proceedings in said court shall conform, as near as may be, to the pleadings, practice, and proceedings in equity causes in the circuit courts of the United States. The testimony shall be taken in court or before one of the judges, so far as practicable. Each judge shall be authorized to grant, in vacation or recess, interlocutory orders and to hear and dispose of interlocutory motions not affecting the substantial merits of the case. Said court shall have a chief judge and two associate judges, a clerk, a stenographer, who shall be deputy clerk, and a bailiff. The judges shall be appointed by the President, by and with the advice and consent of the Senate, and shall each receive a compensation of five thousand dollars per annum and his necessary and actual traveling and personal expenses while engaged in the performance of his duties. The clerk, stenographer, and bailiff shall be appointed by the judges, or a majority of them, and shall receive the following yearly compensation: Clerk, two thousand four hundred dollars; stenographer, twelve hundred dollars; bailiff, nine hundred dollars. The compensation of all these officers shall be paid by the United States in monthly installments. The moneys to pay said compensation are hereby appropriated, and there is also hereby appropriated the sum of five thousand dollars, or so much thereof as may be necessary, to be expended under the direction of the Secretary of the Interior, to pay such contingent expenses of said court and its officers as to such Secretary may seem proper. Said court shall have a seal, shall sit at such place or places in the Choctaw and Chickasaw nations as the judges may designate, and shall hold public sessions, beginning the first Monday in each month, so far as may be practicable or necessary. Each judge and the clerk and deputy clerk shall be authorized to administer oaths. All writs and process issued by said court shall be served by the United States marshal for the district in which the service is to be had. The fees for serving process and the fees of witnesses shall be paid by the

party at whose instance such process is issued or such witnesses are subpœnaed, and the rate or amount of such fees shall be the same as is allowed in civil causes in the circuit court of the United States for the western district of Arkansas. No fees shall be charged by the clerk or other officers of said court. The clerk of the United States court in Indian Territory, having custody and control of the files, papers, and proceedings in the original citizenship cases, shall receive a fee of two dollars and fifty cents for transferring and certifying to the citizenship court the files, papers, and proceedings in each case, without regard to the number of persons whose citizenship is involved therein, and said fee shall be paid by tne person applying for such transfer and certification. The judgment of the citizenship court in any or all of the suits or proceedings so committed to its jurisdiction shall be final. All expenses necessary to the proper conduct, on behalf of the nations, of the suits and proceedings provided for in this and the two preceding sections shall be incurred under the direction of the executives of the two nations, and the Secretary of the Interior is hereby authorized, upon certificate of said executives, to pay such expenses as in his judgment are reasonable and necessary out of any of the joint funds of said nations in the Treasury of the United States.

34. During the ninety days first following the date of the final ratification of this agreement, the Commission to the Five Civilized Tribes may receive applications for enrollment only of persons whose names are on the tribal rolls, but who have not heretofore been enrolled by said Commission, commonly known as "delinquents," and such intermarried white persons as may have married recognized citizens of the Choctaw and Chickasaw nations in accordance with the tribal laws, customs, and usages on or before the date of the passage of this act by Congress, and such infant children as may have been born to recognized and enrolled citizens on or before the date of the final ratification of this agreement; but the application of no person whomsoever for enrollment shall be received after the expiration of the said ninety days: *Provided*, That nothing in this section shall apply to any person or persons making application for enrollment as Mississippi Choctaws, for whom provision has herein otherwise been made.

35. No person whose name does not appear upon the rolls prepared as herein provided shall be entitled to in any manner participate in the distribution of the common property of the Choctaw and Chickasaw tribes, and those whose names appear thereon shall participate in the manner set forth in this agreement: *Provided*, That no allotment of land or other tribal property shall be made to any person, or to the heirs of any person whose name is on the said rolls and who died prior to the date of the final ratification of this agreement. The right of such person to any interest in the lands or other tribal property shall be deemed to have become extinguished and to have passed to the tribe in general upon his death before the date of the final ratification of this agreement, and any person or persons who may conceal the death of anyone on said rolls as aforesaid, for the purpose of profiting by the said concealment, and who shall knowingly receive any portion of any land or other tribal property, or of the proceeds so arising from any allotment prohibited by this section, shall be deemed guilty of a felony, and shall be proceeded against as may be provided in other cases of felony, and the penalty for this offense shall be confinement at hard labor for a period of not less than one year nor more than five years, and in addition thereto a forfeiture to the Choctaw and Chickasaw nations of the lands, other tribal property, and proceeds so obtained.

CHICKASAW FREEDMEN.

36. Authority is hereby conferred upon the Court of Claims to determine the existing controversy respecting the relations of the Chickasaw freedmen to the Chickasaw Nation and the rights of such freedmen in the lands of the Choctaw and Chickasaw nations under the third article of the treaty of eighteen hundred and sixty-six, between the United States and the Choctaw and Chickasaw nations, and under any and all laws subsequently enacted by the Chickasaw legislature or by Congress.

37. To that end the Attorney-General of the United States is hereby directed, on behalf of the United States, to file in said Court of Claims, within sixty days after this agreement becomes effective, a bill of interpleader against the Choctaw and Chickasaw nations and the Chickasaw freedmen, setting forth the existing controversy between the Chickasaw Nation and the Chickasaw freedmen and praying that the defendants thereto be required to interplead and settle their respective rights in such suit.

38. Service of process in the suit may be had on the Choctaw and Chickasaw nations, respectively, by serving upon the principal chief of the former and the governor of the latter a certified copy of the bill, with a notice of the time for answering

the same, which shall not be less than thirty nor more than sixty days after such service, and may be had upon the Chickasaw freedmen by serving upon each of three known and recognized Chickasaw freedmen a certified copy of the bill, with a like notice of the time for answering the same, and by publishing a notice of the commencement of the suit, setting forth the nature and prayer of the bill, with the time for answering the same, for a period of three weeks in at least two weekly newspapers having general circulation in the Chickasaw Nation.

39. The Choctaw and Chickasaw nations, respectively, may in the manner prescribed in sections twenty-one hundred and three to twenty-one hundred and six, both inclusive, of the Revised Statutes, employ counsel to represent them in such suit and protect their interests therein; and the Secretary of the Interior shall employ competent counsel to represent the Chickasaw freedmen in said suit and to protect their interest therein; and the compensation of counsel so employed for the Chickasaw freedmen, including all costs of printing their briefs and other incidental expenses on their part, not exceeding six thousand dollars, shall be paid out of the Treasury of the United States upon certificate of the Secretary of the Interior setting forth the employment and the terms thereof, and stating that the required services have been duly rendered; and any party feeling aggrieved at the decree of the Court of Claims, or any part thereof, may, within sixty days after the rendition thereof, appeal to the Supreme Court, and in each of said courts the suit shall be advanced for hearing and decision at the earliest practicable time.

40. In the meantime the Commission to the Five Civilized Tribes shall make a roll of the Chickasaw freedmen and their descendants, as provided in the Atoka agreement, and shall make allotments to them as provided in this agreement, which said allotments shall be held by the said Chickasaw freedmen, not as temporary allotments but as final allotments, and in the event that it shall be finally determined in said suit that the Chickasaw freedmen are not, independently of this agreement, entitled to allotments in the Choctaw and Chickasaw lands the Court of Claims shall render a decree in favor of the Choctaw and Chickasaw nations according to their respective interests and against the United States for the value of the lands so alloted to the Chickasaw freedmen as ascertained by the appraisal thereof made by the Commission to the Five Civilized Tribes for the purpose of allotment, which decree shall take the place of the said lands and shall be in full satisfaction of all claims by the Choctaw and Chickasaw nations against the United States or the said freedmen on account of the taking of the said lands for allotment to said freedmen: *Provided*, That nothing contained in this paragraph shall be construed to affect or change the existing status or rights of the two tribes as between themselves respecting the lands taken for allotment to freedmen or the money, if any, recovered as compensation therefor, as aforesaid.

MISSISSIPPI CHOCTAWS.

41. All persons duly identified by the Commission to the Five Civilized Tribes under the provisions of section 21 of the act of Congress approved June 28, 1898 (30 Stats., 495), as Mississippi Choctaws entitled to benefits under article 14 of the treaty between the United States and the Choctaw Nation concluded September 27, 1830, may, at any time within six months after the date of their identification as Mississippi Choctaws by the said Commission, make bona fide settlement within the Choctaw-Chickasaw country, and upon proof of such settlement to such Commission within one year after the date of their said identification as Mississippi Choctaws shall be enrolled by such Commission as Mississippi Choctaws entitled to allotment as herein provided for citizens of the tribes, subject to the special provisions herein provided as to Mississippi Choctaws, and said enrollment shall be final when approved by the Secretary of the Interior. The application of no person for identification as a Mississippi Choctaw shall be received by said Commission after six months subsequent to the date of the final ratification of this agreement, and in the disposition of such applications all full-blood Mississippi Choctaw Indians and the descendants of any Mississippi Choctaw Indians, whether of full or mixed blood, who received a patent to land under the said fourteenth article of the said treaty of eighteen hundred and thirty who had not moved to and made bona fide settlement in the Choctaw-Chickasaw country prior to June twenty-eighth, eighteen hundred and ninety-eight, shall be deemed to be Mississippi Choctaws, entitled to benefits under article fourteen of the said treaty of September twenty-seventh, eighteen hundred and thirty, and to identification as such by said Commission, but this direction or provision shall be deemed to be only a rule of evidence and shall not be invoked by or operate to the advantage of any applicant who is not a Mississippi Choctaw of the full blood, or who is not the descendant of a Mississippi Choctaw who received a patent to land under said treaty, or who is otherwise barred from the right of citizenship in the

Choctaw Nation.   All of said Mississippi Choctaws so enrolled by said Commission shall be upon a separate roll.

42. When any such Mississippi Choctaw shall have in good faith continuously resided upon the lands of the Choctaw and Chickasaw nations for a period of three years, including his residence thereon before and after such enrollment, he shall, upon due proof of such continuous bona fide residence, made in such manner and before such officer as may be designated by the Secretary of the Interior, receive a patent for his allotment, as provided in the Atoka agreement, and he shall hold the lands allotted to him as provided in this agreement for citizens of the Choctaw and Chickasaw nations.

43. Applications for enrollment as Mississippi Choctaws, and applications to have lands set apart to them as such, must be made personally before the Commission to the Five Civilized Tribes.   Fathers may apply for their minor children; and if the father be dead, the mother may apply; husbands may apply for wives.   Applications for orphans, insane persons, and persons of unsound mind may be made by duly appointed guardian or curator, and for aged and infirm persons and prisoners by agents duly authorized thereunto by power of attorney, in the discretion of said Commission.

44. If within four years after such enrollment any such Mississippi Choctaw, or his heirs or representatives if he be dead, fails to make proof of such continuous bona fide residence for the period so prescribed, or up to the time of the death of such Mississippi Choctaw, in case of his death after enrollment, he, and his heirs and representatives if he be dead, shall be deemed to have acquired no interest in the lands set apart to him, and the same shall be sold at public auction for cash, under rules and regulations prescribed by the Secretary of the Interior, and the proceeds paid into the Treasury of the United States to the credit of the Choctaw and Chickasaw tribes, and distributed per capita with other funds of the tribes.   Such lands shall not be sold for less than their appraised value.   Upon payment of the full purchase price patent shall issue to the purchaser.

TOWN SITES.

45. The Choctaw and Chickasaw tribes hereby assent to the act of Congress approved May 31, 1900 (31 Stats., 221), in so far as it pertains to town sites in the Choctaw and Chickasaw nations, ratifying and confirming all acts of the Government of the United States thereunder, and consent to a continuance of the provisions of said act not in conflict with the terms of this agreement.

46. As to those town sites heretofore set aside by the Secretary of the Interior on the recommendation of the Commission to the Five Civilized Tribes, as provided in said act of Congress of May 31, 1900, such additional acreage may be added thereto, in like manner as the original town site was set apart, as may be necessary for the present needs and reasonable prospective growth of said town sites, the total acreage not to exceed six hundred and forty acres for each town site.

47. The lands which may hereafter be set aside and reserved for town sites upon the recommendation of the Commission to the Five Civilized Tribes, under the provisions of said act of May 31, 1900, shall embrace such acreage as may be necessary for the present needs and reasonable prospective growth of such town sites, not to exceed six hundred and forty acres for each town site.

48. Whenever any tract of land shall be set aside for town-site purposes, as provided in said act of May 31, 1900, or by the terms of this agreement, which is occupied by any member of the Choctaw or Chickasaw nations, such occupant shall be fully compensated for his improvements thereon, out of the funds of the tribes arising from the sale of town sites, under rules and regulations to be prescribed by the Secretary of the Interior, the value of such improvements to be determined by a board of appraisers, one member of which shall be appointed by the Secretary of the Interior, one by the chief executive of the tribe in which the town site is located, and one by the occupant of the land, said board of appraisers to be paid such compensation for their services as may be determined by the Secretary of the Interior out of any appropriation for surveying, laying out, platting, and selling town sites.

49. Whenever the chief executive of the Choctaw or Chickasaw nation fails or refuses to appoint a town-site commissioner for any town, or to fill any vacancy caused by the neglect or refusal of the town-site commissioner appointed by the chief executive of the Choctaw or Chickasaw nation to qualify or act, or otherwise, the Secretary of the Interior, in his discretion, may appoint a commissioner to fill the vacancy thus created.

50. There shall be appointed, in the manner provided in the Atoka agreement, such additional town-site commissions as the Secretary of the Interior may deem

necessary, for the speedy disposal of all town sites in said nations: *Provided*, That the jurisdiction of said additional town-site commissions shall extend to such town sites only as shall be designated by the Secretary of the Interior.

51. Upon the payment of the full amount of the purchase price of any lot in any town site in the Choctaw and Chickasaw nations, appraised and sold as herein provided, or sold as herein provided, the chief executives of said nations shall jointly execute, under their hands and the seals of the respective nations and deliver to the purchaser of the said lot, a patent conveying to him all right, title, and interest of the Choctaw and Chickasaw tribes in and to said lot.

52. All town lots in any one town site to be conveyed to one person shall, as far as practicable, be included in one patent, and all patents shall be executed free of charge to the grantee.

53. Such towns in the Choctaw and Chickasaw nations as may have a population of less than two hundred people, not otherwise provided for, and which in the judgment of the Secretary of the Interior should be set aside as town sites, shall have their limits defined not later than ninety days after the final ratification of this agreement, in the same manner as herein provided for other town sites; but in no such case shall more than forty acres of land be set aside for any such town site.

54. All town sites heretofore set aside by the Secretary of the Interior on the recommendation of the Commission to the Five Civilized Tribes, under the provisions of the act of Congress approved May 31, 1900 (31 Stat., 221), with the additional acreage added thereto, and all town sites which may hereafter be set aside, as well as all town sites set aside under the provisions of this agreement having a population of less than two hundred, shall be surveyed, laid out, platted, appraised, and disposed of in a like manner, and with like preference rights accorded to owners of improvements as other town sites in the Choctaw and Chickasaw nations are surveyed, laid out, platted, appraised, and disposed of under the Atoka agreement, as modified or supplemented by the said act of May 31, 1900: *Provided*, That occupants or purchasers of lots in town sites in said Choctaw and Chickasaw nations upon which no improvements have been made prior to the passage of this Act by Congress shall pay the full appraised value of said lots instead of the percentage named in the Atoka agreement.

MUNICIPAL CORPORATIONS.

55. Authority is hereby conferred upon municipal corporations in the Choctaw and Chickasaw nations, with the approval of the Secretary of the Interior, to issue bonds and borrow money thereon for sanitary purposes and for the construction of sewers, lighting plants, waterworks, and schoolhouses, subject to all the provisions of laws of the United States in force in the organized Territories of the United States in reference to municipal indebtedness and issuance of bonds for public purposes; and said provisions of law are hereby put in force in said nations and made applicable to the cities and towns therein the same as if specially enacted in reference thereto; and said municipal corporations are hereby authorized to vacate streets and alleys, or parts thereof, and said streets and alleys, when so vacated, shall become the property of the adjacent property holders.

COAL AND ASPHALT.

56. At the expiration of two years after the final ratification of this agreement all deposits of coal and asphalt which are in lands within the limits of any town site established under the Atoka agreement, or the act of Congress of May 31, 1900, or this agreement, and which are within the exterior limits of any lands reserved from allotment on account of their coal or asphalt deposits, as herein provided, and which are not at the time of the final ratification of this agreement embraced in any then existing coal or asphalt lease, shall be sold at public auction for cash under the direction of the President as hereinafter provided, and the proceeds thereof disposed of as herein provided respecting the proceeds of the sale of coal and asphalt lands.

57. All coal and asphalt deposits which are within the limits of any town site so established, which are at the date of the final ratification of this agreement covered by any existing lease, shall, at the expiration of two years after the final ratification of this agreement, be sold at public auction under the direction of the President as hereinafter provided, and the proceeds thereof disposed of as provided in the last preceding section. The coal or asphalt covered by each lease shall be separately sold. The purchaser shall take such coal or asphalt deposits subject to the existing lease, and shall by the purchase succeed to all the rights of the two tribes of every kind and character, under the lease, but all advanced royalties received by the tribe shall be retained by them.

Choctaw Nation. All of said Mississippi Choctaws so enrolled by said Commission shall be upon a separate roll.

42. When any such Mississippi Choctaw shall have in good faith continuously resided upon the lands of the Choctaw and Chickasaw nations for a period of three years, including his residence thereon before and after such enrollment, he shall, upon due proof of such continuous bona fide residence, made in such manner and before such officer as may be designated by the Secretary of the Interior, receive a patent for his allotment, as provided in the Atoka agreement, and he shall hold the lands allotted to him as provided in this agreement for citizens of the Choctaw and Chickasaw nations.

43. Applications for enrollment as Mississippi Choctaws, and applications to have lands set apart to them as such, must be made personally before the Commission to the Five Civilized Tribes. Fathers may apply for their minor children; and if the father be dead, the mother may apply; husbands may apply for wives. Applications for orphans, insane persons, and persons of unsound mind may be made by duly appointed guardian or curator, and for aged and infirm persons and prisoners by agents duly authorized thereunto by power of attorney, in the discretion of said Commission.

44. If within four years after such enrollment any such Mississippi Choctaw, or his heirs or representatives if he be dead, fails to make proof of such continuous bona fide residence for the period so prescribed, or up to the time of the death of such Mississippi Choctaw, in case of his death after enrollment, he, and his heirs and representatives if he be dead, shall be deemed to have acquired no interest in the lands set apart to him, and the same shall be sold at public auction for cash, under rules and regulations prescribed by the Secretary of the Interior, and the proceeds paid into the Treasury of the United States to the credit of the Choctaw and Chickasaw tribes, and distributed per capita with other funds of the tribes. Such lands shall not be sold for less than their appraised value. Upon payment of the full purchase price patent shall issue to the purchaser.

TOWN SITES.

45. The Choctaw and Chickasaw tribes hereby assent to the act of Congress approved May 31, 1900 (31 Stats., 221), in so far as it pertains to town sites in the Choctaw and Chickasaw nations, ratifying and confirming all acts of the Government of the United States thereunder, and consent to a continuance of the provisions of said act not in conflict with the terms of this agreement.

46. As to those town sites heretofore set aside by the Secretary of the Interior on the recommendation of the Commission to the Five Civilized Tribes, as provided in said act of Congress of May 31, 1900, such additional acreage may be added thereto, in like manner as the original town site was set apart, as may be necessary for the present needs and reasonable prospective growth of said town sites, the total acreage not to exceed six hundred and forty acres for each town site.

47. The lands which may hereafter be set aside and reserved for town sites upon the recommendation of the Commission to the Five Civilized Tribes, under the provisions of said act of May 31, 1900, shall embrace such acreage as may be necessary for the present needs and reasonable prospective growth of such town sites, not to exceed six hundred and forty acres for each town site.

48. Whenever any tract of land shall be set aside for town-site purposes, as provided in said act of May 31, 1900, or by the terms of this agreement, which is occupied by any member of the Choctaw or Chickasaw nations, such occupant shall be fully compensated for his improvements thereon, out of the funds of the tribes arising from the sale of town sites, under rules and regulations to be prescribed by the Secretary of the Interior, the value of such improvements to be determined by a board of appraisers, one member of which shall be appointed by the Secretary of the Interior, one by the chief executive of the tribe in which the town site is located, and one by the occupant of the land, said board of appraisers to be paid such compensation for their services as may be determined by the Secretary of the Interior out of any appropriation for surveying, laying out, platting, and selling town sites.

49. Whenever the chief executive of the Choctaw or Chickasaw nation fails or refuses to appoint a town-site commissioner for any town, or to fill any vacancy caused by the neglect or refusal of the town-site commissioner appointed by the chief executive of the Choctaw or Chickasaw nation to qualify or act, or otherwise, the Secretary of the Interior, in his discretion, may appoint a commissioner to fill the vacancy thus created.

50. There shall be appointed, in the manner provided in the Atoka agreement, such additional town-site commissions as the Secretary of the Interior may deem

months after the final ratification of this agreement, and to embrace all the natural springs in and about said village, and so much of Sulphur Creek, Rock Creek, Buckhorn Creek, and the lands adjacent to said natural springs and creeks as may be deemed necessary by the Secretary of the Interior for the proper utilization and control of said springs and the waters of said creeks, which lands shall be so selected as to cause the least interference with the contemplated town site at that place consistent with the purposes for which said cession is made, and when selected the ceded lands shall be held, owned, and controlled by the United States absolutely and without any restriction, save that no part thereof shall be platted or disposed of for town-site purposes during the existence of the two tribal governments. Such other lands as may be embraced in a town site at that point shall be disposed of in the manner provided in the Atoka agreement for the disposition of town sites. Within ninety days after the selection of the lands so ceded there shall be deposited in the Treasury of the United States, to the credit of the two tribes, from the unappropriated public moneys of the United States, twenty dollars per acre for each acre so selected, which shall be in full compensation for the lands so ceded, and such moneys shall, upon the dissolution of the tribal governments, be divided per capita among the members of the tribes, freedmen excepted, as are other funds of the tribes. All improvements upon the lands so selected which were lawfully there at the time of the ratification of this agreement by Congress shall be appraised, under the direction of the Secretary of the Interior, at the true value thereof at the time of the selection of said lands, and shall be paid for by warrants drawn by the Secretary of the Interior upon the Treasurer of the United States. Until otherwise provided by law, the Secretary of the Interior may, under rules prescribed for that purpose, regulate and control the use of the water of said springs and creeks and the temporary use and occupation of the lands so ceded. No person shall occupy any portion of the lands so ceded, or carry on any business thereon, except as provided in said rules, and until otherwise provided by Congress the laws of the United States relating to the introduction, possession, sale, and giving away of liquors or intoxicants of any kind within the Indian country or Indian reservations shall be applicable to the lands so ceded, and said lands shall remain within the jurisdiction of the United States court for the southern district of Indian Territory: *Provided, however,* That nothing contained in this section shall be construed or held to commit the Government of the United States to any expenditure of money upon said lands or the improvements thereof, except as provided herein, it being the intention of this provision that in the future the lands and improvements herein mentioned shall be conveyed by the United States to such Territorial or State organization as may exist at the time when such conveyance is made.

MISCELLANEOUS.

65. The acceptance of patents for minors, prisoners, convicts, and incompetents by persons authorized to select their allotments for them shall be sufficient to bind such minors, prisoners, convicts, and incompetents as to the conveyance of all other lands of the tribes.

66. All patents to allotments of land, when executed, shall be recorded in the office of the Commission to the Five Civilized Tribes within said nations in books appropriate for the purpose, until such time as Congress shall make other suitable provision for record of land titles as provided in the Atoka agreement, without expense to the grantee; and such records shall have like effect as other public records.

67. The provisions of section three of the act of Congress approved June twenty-eighth, eighteen hundred and ninety-eight (30 Stats., 495), shall not apply to or in any manner affect the lands or other property of the Choctaws and Chickasaws or Choctaw and Chickasaw freedmen.

68. No act of Congress or treaty provision, nor any provision of the Atoka agreement, inconsistent with this agreement, shall be in force in said Choctaw and Chickasaw nations.

69. All controversies arising between members as to their right to select particular tracts of land shall be determined by the Commission of the Five Civilized Tribes.

70. Allotments may be selected and homesteads designated for minors by the father or mother, if members, or by a guardian or curator, or the administrator having charge of their estate, in the order named; and for prisoners, convicts, aged and infirm persons by duly appointed agents under power of attorney; and for incompetents by guardians, curators, or other suitable person akin to them; but it shall be the duty of said Commission to see that said selections are made for the best interests of such parties.

71. After the expiration of nine months after the date of the original selection of an allotment, by or for any citizen or freedmen of the Choctaw or Chickasaw tribes, as provided in this agreement, no contest shall be instituted against such selection.

58. Within six months after the final ratification of this agreement the Secretary of the Interior shall ascertain, so far as may be practicable, what lands are principally valuable because of their deposits of coal or asphalt, including therein all lands which at the time of the final ratification of this agreement shall be covered by then existing coal or asphalt leases, and within that time he shall, by a written order, segregate and reserve from allotment all of said lands. Such segregation and reservation shall conform to the subdivisions of the Government survey as nearly as may be, and the total segregation and reservation shall not exceed five hundred thousand acres. No lands so reserved shall be allotted to any member or freedman, and the improvements of any member or freedman existing upon any of the lands so segregated and reserved at the time of their segregation and reservation shall be appraised under the direction of the Secretary of the Interior, and shall be paid for out of any common funds of the two tribes in the Treasury of the United States, upon the order of the Secretary of the Interior. All coal and asphalt deposits, as well as other minerals which may be found in any lands not so segregated and reserved, shall be deemed a part of the land and shall pass to the allottee or other person who may lawfully acquire title to such lands.

59. All lands segregated and reserved under the last preceding section, excepting those embraced within the limits of a town site, established as hereinbefore provided, shall, within three years from the final ratification of this agreement and before the dissolution of the tribal governments, be sold at public auction for cash, under the direction of the President, by a commission composed of three persons, which shall be appointed by the President, one on the recommendation of the principal chief of the Choctaw Nation, who shall be a Choctaw by blood, and one on the recommendation of the governor of the Chickasaw Nation, who shall be a Chickasaw by blood. Either of said commissioners may, at any time, be removed by the President for good cause shown. Each of said commissioners shall be paid at the rate of four thousand dollars per annum, the Choctaw commissioner to be paid by the Choctaw Nation, the Chickasaw commissioner to be paid by the Chickasaw Nation, and the third commissioner to be paid by the United States. In the sale of coal and asphalt lands and coal and asphalt deposits hereunder, the commission shall have the right to reject any or all bids which it considers below the value of any such lands or deposits. The proceeds arising from the sale of coal and asphalt lands and coal and asphalt deposits shall be deposited in the Treasury of the United States to the credit of said tribes and paid out per capita to the members of said tribes (freedmen excepted) with the other moneys belonging to said tribes in the manner provided by law. The lands embraced within any coal or asphalt lease shall be separately sold, subject to such lease, and the purchaser shall succeed to all the rights of the two tribes of every kind and character, under the lease, but all advanced royalties received by the tribes shall be retained by them. The lands so segregated and reserved, and not included within any existing coal or asphalt lease, shall be sold in tracts not exceeding in area a section under the Government survey.

60. Upon the recommendation of the chief executive of each of the two tribes, and where in the judgment of the President it is advantageous to the tribes so to do, the sale of any coal or asphalt lands which are herein directed to be sold may be made at any time after the expiration of six months from the final ratification of this agreement, without awaiting the expiration of the period of two years, as hereinbefore provided.

61. No lease of any coal or asphalt lands shall be made after the final ratification of this agreement, the provisions of the Atoka agreement to the contrary notwithstanding.

62. Where any lands so as aforesaid segregated and reserved on account of their coal or asphalt deposits are in this agreement specifically reserved from allotment for any other reason, the sale to be made hereunder shall be only of the coal and asphalt deposits contained therein, and in all other respects the other specified reservation of such lands herein provided for shall be fully respected.

63. The chief executives of the two tribes shall execute and deliver, with the approval of the Secretary of the Interior, to each purchaser of any coal or asphalt lands so sold, and to each purchaser of any coal or asphalt deposits so sold, an appropriate patent or instrument of conveyance conveying to the purchaser the property so sold.

SULPHUR SPRINGS.

64. The two tribes hereby absolutely and unqualifiedly relinquish, cede, and convey unto the United States a tract or tracts of land at and in the vicinity of the village of Sulphur, in the Chickasaw Nation, of not exceeding six hundred and forty acres, to be selected, under the direction of the Secretary of the Interior, within four

72. There shall be paid to each citizen of the Chickasaw Nation, immediately after the approval of his enrollment and right to participate in distribution of tribal property, as herein provided, the sum of forty dollars. Such payment shall be made under the direction of the Secretary of the Interior, and out of the balance of the "arrears of interest" of five hundred and fifty-eight thousand five hundred and twenty dollars and fifty-four cents appropriated by the act of Congress approved June twenty-eighth. eighteen hundred and ninety-eight, entitled "An act for the protection of the people of the Indian Territory, and for other purposes," yet due to the Chickasaws and remaining to their credit in the Treasury of the United States; and so much of such moneys as may be necessary for such payment are hereby appropriated and made available for that purpose, and the balance, if any there be, shall remain in the Treasury of the United States, and be distributed per capita with the other funds of the tribes. And all acts of Congress or other treaty provisions in conflict with this provision are hereby repealed.

73. This agreement shall be binding upon the United States and upon the Choctaw and Chickasaw nations and all Choctaws and Chickasaws, when ratified by Congress and by a majority of the whole number of votes cast by the legal voters of the Choctaw and Chickasaw tribes in the manner following: The principal chief of the Choctaw Nation and the governor of the Chickasaw Nation shall, within one hundred and twenty days after the ratification of this agreement by Congress, make public proclamation that the same shall be voted upon at any special election to be held for that purpose within thirty days thereafter, on a certain day therein named; and all male citizens of each of the said tribes qualified to vote under the tribal laws shall have a right to vote at the election precinct most convenient to his residence, whether the same be within the bounds of his tribe or not. And if this agreement be ratified by said tribes as aforesaid, the date upon which said election is held shall be deemed to be the date of final ratification.

74. The votes cast in both the Choctaw and Chickasaw nations shall be forthwith returned and duly certified by the precinct officers to the national secretaries of said tribes, and shall be presented by said national secretaries to a board of commissioners consisting of the principal chief and the national secretary of the Choctaw Nation and the governor and national secretary of the Chickasaw Nation and two members of the Commission to the Five Civilized Tribes; and said board shall meet without delay at Atoka, Indian Territory, and canvass and count said votes, and make proclamation of the result.

In witness whereof the said commissioners do hereby affix their names at Washington, District of Columbia, this twenty-first day of March, 1902.

Approved, July 1, 1902.

Lightning Source UK Ltd.
Milton Keynes UK
UKHW021613051118
331792UK00010B/2135/P